T0176859

Soft Computing Evaluation Logic

Soft Computing Evaluation Logic
The LSP Decision Method and Its Applications

Jozo Dujmović

Department of Computer Science
San Francisco State University

This edition first published 2018
© 2018 John Wiley & Sons, Inc.

All rights reserved. No part of this publication may be reproduced, stored in a retrieval system, or transmitted, in any form or by any means, electronic, mechanical, photocopying, recording or otherwise, except as permitted by law. Advice on how to obtain permission to reuse material from this title is available at http://www.wiley.com/go/permissions.

The right of Jozo Dujmović to be identified as the author of this work has been asserted in accordance with law.

Registered Offices
John Wiley & Sons, Inc., 111 River Street, Hoboken, NJ 07030, USA

Editorial Office
111 River Street, Hoboken, NJ 07030, USA

For details of our global editorial offices, customer services, and more information about Wiley products visit us at www.wiley.com.

Wiley also publishes its books in a variety of electronic formats and by print-on-demand. Some content that appears in standard print versions of this book may not be available in other formats.

Limit of Liability/Disclaimer of Warranty
The publisher and the authors make no representations or warranties with respect to the accuracy or completeness of the contents of this work and specifically disclaim all warranties; including without limitation any implied warranties of fitness for a particular purpose. This work is sold with the understanding that the publisher is not engaged in rendering professional services. The advice and strategies contained herein may not be suitable for every situation. In view of on-going research, equipment modifications, changes in governmental regulations, and the constant flow of information relating to the use of experimental reagents, equipment, and devices, the reader is urged to review and evaluate the information provided in the package insert or instructions for each chemical, piece of equipment, reagent, or device for, among other things, any changes in the instructions or indication of usage and for added warnings and precautions. The fact that an organization or website is referred to in this work as a citation and/or potential source of further information does not mean that the author or the publisher endorses the information the organization or website may provide or recommendations it may make. Further, readers should be aware that websites listed in this work may have changed or disappeared between when this works was written and when it is read. No warranty may be created or extended by any promotional statements for this work. Neither the publisher nor the author shall be liable for any damages arising here from.

Library of Congress Cataloging-in-Publication Data

Names: Dujmović, Jozo- author.
Title: Soft computing evaluation logic : the LSP decision method and its
    applications / by Jozo Dujmović.
Description: Hoboken, NJ : John Wiley & Sons, 2018. | Includes
    bibliographical references and index. |
Identifiers: LCCN 2017039552 (print) | LCCN 2017046281 (ebook) |
    ISBN 9781119256465 (pdf) | ISBN 9781119256472 (epub) | ISBN 9781119256458 (cloth)
Subjects: LCSH: Soft computing. | Evaluation–Methodology. | Artificial intelligence.
Classification: LCC QA76.9.S63 (ebook) | LCC QA76.9.S63 D85 2018 (print) | DDC 006.3–dc23
LC record available at https://lccn.loc.gov/2017039552

Cover design by Wiley
Cover image: © g-stockstudio/Getty Images

Set in 10/12 pt Warnock by SPi Global, Pondicherry, India

Printed in the United States of America
V10004304_090518

To Kaća
Wife, computer scientist, and partner in everything

Contents

Preface

> *Seek simplicity and distrust it.*
> —Alfred North Whitehead

This book is a monograph on evaluation, an area of soft computing. It can also serve as a toolbox for solving practical evaluation problems. The goal of this book is to develop mathematical logic that can answer fundamental questions related to problems of evaluation, comparison, and selection of complex alternatives. These problems are common and present in business, engineering, and in everyday personal decision making. Our objective is to integrate results scattered in research papers published over many years and to present an evaluation methodology that is strong enough to be used in professional decision making. The methodology draws on work in soft computing, fuzzy systems, multi-criteria and multi-attribute decision making, or generally, on work in computational intelligence.

Evaluation is a common problem and is of interest to professionals in many disciplines. To serve readers with different backgrounds and a spectrum of interests, the book is organized using a stepwise refinement approach. All major topics appear multiple times at an increasing level of detail and precision. Readers are not expected to read sequentially cover to cover, but to directly access topics according to their specific priorities and their desired level of detail. Professional books are almost never read sequentially and this book is organized to make random access to material both natural and easy.

The reasons for writing this book are twofold: (1) to present evaluation as a scientific and engineering discipline in its totality, from theoretical origins to successful applications, and (2) to present a new approach to evaluation methodology that is different from those in the existing literature. The following are unique properties of this book:

1) It contains a detailed analysis and quantitative modeling of observable properties of human evaluation reasoning.
2) It demonstrates how soft computing logic aggregators can be developed as justifiable mathematical models of observable evaluation reasoning.

3) It shows how Graded Logic (GL) based on soft computing logic aggregators is a seamless generalization of classical Boolean logic and a model of both formal logic and semantic components of human reasoning.

4) It develops the Logic Scoring of Preference (LSP) evaluation method as a vital component of an industrial-strength decision engineering framework based on GL.

5) It verifies the LSP methodology using a diversified set of nontrivial applications.

Evaluation is an important area of decision making, devoted to designing and using complex criterion functions in various fields of application. It interacts with psychology, cognitive science, behavioral economics, fuzzy systems, business administration, management, industrial and systems engineering and even philosophy. However, this is not a book about psychology, cognitive science, behavioral economics, fuzzy systems, business administration, management, industrial and systems engineering, or philosophy. If our methodology is useful in these areas, that is certainly not accidental or unintentional. However, first and foremost, this is an engineering book about evaluation and justifiable and applicable logic aggregators, in the context of computational intelligence and professional multiattribute decision making.

Decision making frequently includes the process of evaluation, comparison, and selection of complex objects, systems, situations, and alternatives. Various forms of intuitive evaluation (e.g., the assessment of worth, suitability, quality, and convenience) are ubiquitous in human reasoning. The main objective of this book is to use observable properties of human evaluation reasoning to develop methodology for justifiable professional quantitative evaluation. The result is the LSP method for evaluation of complex objects and alternatives.

The LSP method is presented in this book in the whole range from theoretical foundations to a variety of applications in (both professional and personal) decision making. We approach decision making as an engineering discipline and provide methodology for decision engineers. The methodology must be justifiable from the standpoint of modeling human reasoning, structured in efficient procedures, supported by software tools, and above all, provably applicable in industrial settings.

Decision engineering is an emerging discipline stimulated by mathematical and computational background developed in soft computing, fuzzy logic, and related disciplines of computational intelligence, as well as by numerous applications that include complex systems and complex decisions. One could expect that decision engineering is a wide and heterogeneous area. However, the distribution of decision problems is very nonlinear and some problems are extremely frequent while others occur rarely. In particular, all evaluation decisions are based on human percepts of suitability and preference, and they are very frequent. Indeed, it is easy to see that humans are permanently exposed to evaluation and selection of alternatives. Creating percepts of suitability and preference from intuitive evaluation and comparison of currently available alternatives is an observable and extremely frequent mental activity. It is an indispensable component of many decisions and actions from simplest and insignificant, to those that are difficult and heavily consequential. Similarly, evaluation and comparison of alternatives is a fundamental component of important decisions in industry, business, government, medicine, and many other areas. Consequently, there is a clear interest in methodology for creating sophisticated and justifiable quantitative criteria for selecting the most suitable alternatives and making right decisions. This is one of central topics in decision engineering, and the central topic of this book.

To compute the overall suitability of a complex object or alternative, evaluation criteria must aggregate many component suitability attributes. Consequently, aggregation models and methods have an important role in decision engineering. In this book, our goal is to develop graded logic that is consistent with observable human evaluation reasoning, and apply it to develop a justifiable logic aggregation methodology. Our logic aggregators are centrally located between two extreme approaches to aggregation: the aggregation theory as an area of applied mathematics and aggregation practice used in the context of evaluation problems. On the mathematical side of the spectrum, aggregation theory offers an impressive body of mathematical results that have mathematical validity but are unrelated to human reasoning and have no applicability in real life decision problems. This is understandable, because the motivation for mathematical research does not have to be the solution of practical problems. On the other side of the spectrum, the aggregation practice in the context of evaluation problems in business, medicine, or geography usually favors simplicity instead of precision and frequently yields dangerous oversimplifications. Between these extremes, and equally dissatisfied with both of them, our goal is to develop methodology that has sufficient mathematical sophistication and high applicability, as well as seamless connectivity with classic logic and traditions of good engineering.

Following Whitehead's advice, in this book we seek simplicity and distrust it. We equally distrust the lack of applicability. The goal of decision engineering is to go beyond the "simplicity ceiling" providing decision models that have appropriate mathematical sophistication and expressive power to match the complexity of industrial decision problems that need high precision and reliability of decision results. This book is a step in that direction.

It might be useful to explain reasons for using terms *decision engineering* and *decision engineer*. Engineers make products and work in collaborative environments. Engineering products are based on clear goals and product specifications; they are produced using sophisticated tools and systematic, well documented, verified, and optimized procedures that can make products on time and within budget. Decision engineers are called engineers because they also make products. Their products are justifiable decision models built to accurately reflect stakeholder's goals and interests. Such products integrate many necessary components, need domain expertise, collaboration and interactions with social and industrial environment, and are primarily used in industrial settings to provide valid decisions about evaluation, comparison, and selection of complex objects, systems and alternatives. It is reasonable to identify such activities as decision engineering. Not surprisingly, some decision products can also be developed as Internet-based software for use by both professionals and general (nonprofessional) population.

Evaluated systems can be arbitrary collections of interrelated components and include both physical systems (e.g., industrial products, houses, medical conditions of patients, habitat of endangered species, etc.) and conceptual systems (e.g., software products, organizations, services, websites, suitability of locations for specific use, etc.). We assume that each evaluation project has stakeholders interested in ownership and/or use of evaluated systems and capable and authorized to specify requirements that the evaluated systems should satisfy. The stakeholders (supported by decision engineers and domain experts) become decision makers in all situations where they want to select the most suitable alternative, one that sufficiently satisfies justifiable requirements.

System evaluation is a process of determining the extent to which an evaluated system satisfies a set of requirements specified by decision maker. A perfect system completely satisfies all requirements. A completely unacceptable system does not satisfy justifiable requirements. All other systems partially satisfy requirements. The degree of satisfaction of requirements is an indicator of the overall suitability or quality of the evaluated system for a particular user. In many cases users must pay for the satisfaction of requirements, and the overall cost is an important component in the process of evaluation and decision making.

The degree of satisfaction of requirements can be expressed as the partial truth of the statement that the requirements are completely satisfied. The partial truth is a value between 0 (completely false) and 1 (completely true). The concepts of partial truth, partial conjunction, partial disjunction, partial absorption, andness, orness, graded importance, and others, belong to the area of *soft computing*, where everything is a matter of degree. Thus, we present *graded logic* as an infinite-valued propositional calculus and its applications. GL is a seamless soft computing generalization of the classic Boolean logic, defined in all points inside the unit hypercube $[0, 1]^n$. In the vertices $\{0, 1\}^n$ GL coincides with the classic bivalent Boolean logic. Of course, the field of soft computing also includes many other related concepts, such as fuzziness, computing with words, imprecision, and uncertainty.

The concept of partial truth is derived from observing human reasoning. Consequently, our main goal is to present human-centric mathematical models of observable properties of human reasoning in the area of evaluation and comparison of complex alternatives. Such models are used to expand human reasoning beyond the limits of intuitive decision making. So, this book is about reasoning models that are necessary in decision engineering and in design of computerized decision support systems. This topic is closely related to artificial intelligence, neural computing, knowledge engineering, and fuzzy logic.

The theory of fuzzy sets is essentially a theory of graded concepts, where the central concept is the grade of membership of an element in a fuzzy set. Since GL deals with partial truth and graded logic functions (continuous logic functions where conjunction, disjunction, and all other compound functions are a matter of degree), the methodology discussed in this book has direct applicability in fuzzy systems. However, our focus is in logic and not in the theory of fuzzy sets, since we present GL in the context of evaluation decision making, as a bridge between everyday intuitive evaluation and professional industrial evaluation projects.

Intuitive system evaluation, comparison, and selection are very frequent human mental activities and easily recognizable components of "everyday thinking." People instinctively and almost automatically evaluate all objects and situations they encounter. For example, all shopping experiences include intuitive evaluation and comparison of competitive products based on combining their estimated overall quality (suitability for the buyer) and their cost. Voting for political candidates, selecting a school for students, or a site for vacation, are also processes of evaluation and comparison. In almost all cases it is possible to observe the process of intuitive evaluation and to identify its logic properties.

Mathematical models that decision engineers use for complex professional system evaluation cannot have any credibility unless they are fully compatible with observable logic of intuitive human reasoning. Therefore, the process of intuitive evaluation cannot be ignored. Quite contrary, it is the main input for development of decision engineering models and the primary environment for their verification. All professional evaluation methods can only be a quantification, refinement, and consistent expansion of the intuitive evaluation process beyond its natural limits. That is the credo of this book.

The book includes four parts that cover introduction, a theory of graded logic and aggregation, the LSP method, and applications. *Part One* (*Evaluation Decision Problems*) is an introduction to evaluation. Its goal is to show why soft computing techniques are necessary for modeling evaluation decisions. This part also shows inconsistencies between properties of human reasoning and simple scoring techniques, and recommends the elimination of simple scoring from professional evaluation.

Part Two (*Graded Logic and Aggregation*) presents a detailed theoretical background for the logic aggregation of suitability and modeling of mental evaluation processes. We introduce a complete spectrum of logic aggregators from drastic conjunction to drastic disjunction, a soft computing generalization of Boolean logic, various forms of graded conjunction/disjunction, partial absorption, and other weighted compensative logic functions. We also introduce a model of perceptual computer that is later used for development of the LSP method.

Part Three (*LSP Method*) presents the area of professional evaluation, the design of complex evaluation logic criteria, and all other components of the LSP method. *Part Three* also includes advanced LSP techniques such as optimization and reliability analysis, auxiliary techniques of sensitivity and trade-off analyses, and a survey of appropriate software tools for professional evaluators.

Part Four (*Applications*) includes seven diverse applications of the LSP method. We included applications in personal decision making, space management, geography, medicine, ecology, and software engineering. Reduction to practice is a necessary test of any theory, and applications provide the moment of truth for all other parts of this book.

The book is written for a rather wide audience interested in decision making. That includes decision practitioners, managers, theoreticians, researchers, graduate students, and (above all) decision engineers. Each of these groups can benefit from reading a subset of sections presented in the book.

Decision practitioners are typically domain experts who from time to time have to solve a complex evaluation problem in their domain of expertise. Such readers can read *Part Three* and *Part Four*, focusing on engineering aspects of design and use of evaluation criteria.

Managers can get a fast and general overview of the whole area by reading *Part One* and selected applications from *Part Four*. This is sufficient for understanding evaluation problems and correct interpretation of evaluation results.

This book is also written for theoreticians (usually applied mathematicians) who work in the area of aggregation operators. Basic theoretical issues of evaluation models are investigated in *Part Two*, where we present all components of our graded logic. What might be more important, and much less frequent in the literature on aggregation, is our constant effort to interface the theory with observable properties of human reasoning and nontrivial applications.

Researchers and graduate students in the areas of decision methods, soft computing and fuzzy systems (in computer science, data engineering, industrial engineering, operational research and management) can find in this book many topics for additional research, thesis work, and development work. Modeling compound aggregators is currently an area of active research. In addition, it is possible to develop many new or improved evaluation models and expand existing application areas. Advanced software tools are another area where it is easy to find interesting projects.

Finally, decision engineers, practicing decision analysts, and domain experts are the main users of decision methods presented in this book. For them, the book can serve as a textbook, a toolbox, and a practical reference.

About the Companion Website

This book has a companion website hosted by Wiley:
www.wiley.com/go/Dujmovic/Soft_Computing_Evaluation_Logic

The website contains the following periodically updated information:

1) Educational materials (slides that can be used for classroom presentation of selected material from the book).
2) Access to LSP criteria and applications beyond those presented in the book.
3) Access points to LSP.NT and other software products that support the LSP method, and corresponding user manuals.
4) Selected papers related to the material presented in the book.
5) Errata: a list of errors discovered after printing and shown with corrections. Readers who discover errors are encouraged to report them directly to the author using email jozo@sfsu.edu.

LSP suitability maps

LSP suitability maps are transparent maps that display suitability degree on top of geographic maps. The use of Google maps, ESRI ArcGIS maps and Clark Labs TerrSet/Idrisi maps as the background of LSP suitability maps is gratefully acknowledged.

Previous Publications

This book includes parts of material that was previously published in some conference and journal papers (see References). Therefore, this book could not have its current form without generous permissions of publishers to reuse parts of copyrighted material.

Permissions of Springer to reuse parts of material originally published in papers [DUJ13, DUJ10a, DUJ04a, DUJ04b, DUJ07b, DUJ12a, HAT14, MON16a] are gratefully acknowledged. I am also indebted to Elsevier (for [BEL16a, DUJ07a, MON16b]), Institute "Mihajlo Pupin" (for [DUJ05a, DUJ05b, DUJ05c]), ComSIS (for [DUJ06c]), and University of Silesia (for [DUJ15c]).

Some material in this book comes from previous publications, which I prepared with co-authors. For their contributions to our previous joint work, which affected the contents of this book, I am very grateful to Will L. Allen III, Haishi Bai, Gleb Beliakov, Guy De Tré, Les Dorfman, Suzana Dragićević, Wen Yuan Fang, Kris Hatch, Meng-Kang Kao, Henrik Legind Larsen, Bryn Montgomery, Jeffrey W. Ralph, Margaret Schmidt, David Scheer, Navchetan Singh, Daniel Tomasevich, Nico Van de Weghe, Ryoichi Yokoohji, and Yufei Zhuang.

Acknowledgments

It is a great pleasure to express gratitude to people who directly or indirectly helped in my work on this book.

Over the years, many of my students contributed to results presented in this book through their thesis work, joint publications, or just through their creative participation in my courses that included the area of evaluation. These fine minds include Ivan Tomašević, Zeljko Milović, Aleksandar Erdeljan, Adnan Asar, Albeus Bayucan, Metin Kadaster, Mahesh Patsute, Luis Olsina, Ana Funes, Aristides Dasso, Hajime Nagashima, Wen Yuan Fang, Meng-Kang Kao, Jian Hui Zhen, Pyotr Kacherginsky, Tharawit Disyawongs, Greydon Buckley, Haishi Bai, Nicolas Roussis, Mahesh Patsute, Michalis Pittas, Harsh Shrivastava, Ryoichi Yokoohji, Yufei Zhuang, Navchetan Singh, Ketan Kapre and Sree Sastry.

My world-class professors from the University of Belgrade and the University of Zagreb who helped me go my way include Dragoslav Mitrinović, Petar Vasić, Vladimir Devidé, and Danilo Blanuša in mathematics and Tihomir Aleksić, Rajko Tomović, Branko Raković, Jovan Surutka, and Radoslav Horvat in electrical engineering. Their spirit is present in every page of this book.

I am very grateful to Petar Kokotović and Stanoje Bingulac who were generous advisors, teachers, coaches, collaborators, and role models during the delicate time of transition from student status to professional independence.

All my work in the United States, which started at the University of Florida, Gainesville, and the University of Texas at Dallas, would be impossible without the help of Roger Elliott, former chairman of the Computer Science Department at the University of Florida, and a trusted friend for more than 30 years. Support I received from Blake Cherrington, former Dean of the Eric Johnson School of Engineering and Computer Science at the University of Texas at Dallas, and Gerald Eisman, former chairman of Computer Science Department at San Francisco State University, are gratefully acknowledged.

Since 1997, the majority of developments of evaluation methodology presented in this book are related to the activities of the SEAS decision company (www.seas.com). In fact, the majority of ideas presented in this book were either generated or evaluated during many system evaluation projects performed for industry and governments (before 1992, mostly in Yugoslavia and then mostly in the United States). Special thanks go to all their representatives who created a friendly and productive environment and contributed to various aspects of system evaluation based on the LSP method. For example, the first LSP optimization algorithms were developed when working on evaluation of hybrid computers in the Mihajlo Pupin Institute, Belgrade, and the partial absorption function was developed to satisfy the requirements of the Yugoslav oil company Naftagas.

The LSP method particularly benefited from evaluation projects for Mihajlo Pupin Institute, Belgrade, Serbia; OECD, Paris, France; National Institute of Standards and Technology, Gaithersburg, MD, USA; Institute for Control Problems of the USSR Academy of Sciences, Moscow, Russia; The Conservation Fund, Arlington, VA, USA; the National Bank of Yugoslavia; Jugopetrol Oil Company, Belgrade, Serbia; Zenica Steel Industry, Bosnia; Statistical Institute of Slovenian Government, Ljubljana, Slovenia; Statistical Institute of the Government of Yugoslavia, Belgrade; Bosnian food industry UPI, Sarajevo, Bosnia; Yugoslav Airlines, Belgrade, Serbia; Jugohemija Chemical Industry, Belgrade, Serbia; Zagreb University Computing Center (SRCE), Zagreb, Croatia; Belgrade University Computing Center; City Government of Belgrade; Jugopetrol Oil Co., Belgrade; Naftagas Oil Co., Novi Sad, Serbia; Electra Power Co., Zagreb, Croatia; Industrial Consortium of the City of Pirot, Serbia; Kraljevo Power Utility Co., Serbia; Belgrade Bank, Belgrade, Serbia; Djerdap hydro power plant, Serbia; Copper Mill Sevojno, Serbia, and others. I am grateful to all my colleagues from SEAS Co. who contributed to evaluation software development and in particular to Mr. Daniel Tomasevich.

My colleagues and friends who offered stimulating discussions and collaboration include Professors Henrik Larsen, Guy de Tré, Vicenç Torra, Aïda Valls, Humberto Bustince, Radko Mesiar, Suzana Dragićević, Boris Kovalerchuk, Aleksandar Ignjatović, and Mr. Will L. Allen III.

Some of my friends supported the work on this book in various forms. I am particularly grateful for the support received from Mr. Vojislav Milojković, Dr. Goran Božović, Dr. Zlatomir Simić, Mr. and Mrs. Frederic M. Vickery, and Mr. and Mrs. Russell Henderson.

It was a great pleasure to have Wiley as a publisher of this book and to have Mr. Brett Kurzman as a knowledgeable, stimulating, and tolerant editor.

Last but not least, the largest support for all my work came from three computer scientists in my family: my wife, Kaća, and our children, Ivo and Ana. They helped at both the private and professional level, and provided frequent expert opinions that this book would never be completed. Well, even the biggest experts sometimes make mistakes.

Jozo Dujmović

List of Symbols and Abbreviations

Symbols

$\Diamond$	Graded conjunction/disjunction (combination of symbols $\wedge$ and $\vee$)
$\hat{\wedge}$	Drastic conjunction: $x \hat{\wedge} y = \lfloor xy \rfloor$
$\bar{\wedge}$	Hyperconjunction: $x \bar{\wedge} y \leq \min(x, y)$, $(\alpha > 1)$
$\wedge$	Conjunction: $x \wedge y = \min(x, y)$, $(\alpha = 1)$
$\bar{\bar{\Delta}}$	Extended hard partial conjunction: $\bar{\bar{\Delta}} \in \{\bar{\Delta}, \wedge\}$, $(\frac{1}{2} < \alpha \leq 1)$
$\bar{\Delta}$	Hard partial conjunction: $0\bar{\Delta}x = x\bar{\Delta}0 = 0$, $x \in [0,1]$, $(\frac{1}{2} < \alpha < 1)$
Δ	Partial conjunction: $\Delta \in \{\underline{\Delta}, \bar{\Delta}\}$, $(\frac{1}{2} < \alpha < 1)$
$\underline{\Delta}$	Soft partial conjunction: $0\underline{\Delta}x > 0$, $x\underline{\Delta}0 > 0$, $x > 0$, $(\frac{1}{2} < \alpha < 1)$
$\underline{\underline{\Delta}}$	Extended soft partial conjunction: $\underline{\underline{\Delta}} \in \{\underline{\Delta}, \ominus\}$, $(\frac{1}{2} \leq \alpha < 1)$
$\hat{\Delta}$	Total conjunction: $\hat{\Delta} \in \{\Delta, \wedge\}$, $(\frac{1}{2} < \alpha \leq 1)$
$\tilde{\Delta}$	Extended conjunction: $\tilde{\Delta} \in \{\hat{\Delta}, \ominus\}$, $(\frac{1}{2} \leq \alpha \leq 1)$
$\ominus$	Neutrality (arithmetic mean): $x \ominus y = (x + y)/2$, $(\alpha = \frac{1}{2})$
$\tilde{\nabla}$	Extended disjunction: $\tilde{\nabla} \in \{\breve{\nabla}, \ominus\}$, $(0 \leq \alpha \leq \frac{1}{2})$
$\breve{\nabla}$	Total disjunction: $\breve{\nabla} \in \{\nabla, \vee\}$, $(0 \leq \alpha < \frac{1}{2})$
$\underline{\underline{\nabla}}$	Extended soft partial disjunction: $\underline{\underline{\nabla}} \in \{\underline{\nabla}, \ominus\}$, $(0 < \alpha \leq \frac{1}{2})$
$\underline{\nabla}$	Soft partial disjunction: $1\underline{\nabla}x < 1$, $x\underline{\nabla}1 < 1$, $x < 1$, $(0 < \alpha < \frac{1}{2})$
∇	Partial disjunction: $\nabla \in \{\underline{\nabla}, \bar{\nabla}\}$, $(0 < \alpha < \frac{1}{2})$
$\bar{\nabla}$	Hard partial disjunction: $1\bar{\nabla}x = x\bar{\nabla}1 = 1$, $x \in [0,1]$, $(0 < \alpha < \frac{1}{2})$
$\bar{\bar{\nabla}}$	Extended hard partial disjunction: $\bar{\bar{\nabla}} \in \{\bar{\nabla}, \vee\}$, $(0 \leq \alpha < \frac{1}{2})$
$\vee$	Disjunction: $x \vee y = \max(x, y)$, $(\alpha = 0)$
$\bar{\vee}$	Hyperdisjunction: $x\bar{\vee}y \geq \max(x, y)$, $(\alpha < 0)$
$\hat{\vee}$	Drastic disjunction: $x\hat{\vee}y = 1 - \lfloor(1-x)(1-y)\rfloor$
$\unrhd$	Conjunctive partial absorption: usually $x\unrhd y = x\Delta(x \ominus y)$
$\bar{\rhd}$	Disjunctive partial absorption: usually $x\bar{\rhd}y = x\nabla(x \ominus y)$
α	Andness (default type of andness is global andness)

α_ℓ	Local andness
$\bar{\alpha}_\ell$	Mean local andness
α_g	Global andness
α_θ	Threshold andness (andness at the border of SPC and HPC)
ω	Orness (default type of orness is global orness)
ω_ℓ	Local orness
$\bar{\omega}_\ell$	Mean local orness
ω_g	Global orness
ω_θ	Threshold orness (orness at the border of SPD and HPD)
$\overline{(\ldots)}$	Negation or mean value, depending on context
$\bar{x}$	$1-x$ (standard negation)
$\overline{x \diamond y}$	$\overline{x \diamond y} = 1 - x \diamond y$ (negation, in the context of logic)
$\overline{x \diamond y}$	$\overline{x \diamond y} = \int_0^1 \int_0^1 (x \diamond y)\,dx\,dy$ (in the context of averaging)
$x \rightarrow y$ or $x \Rightarrow y$	Implication: if x then y; x implies y
$\mid$	Nand: $x \mid y = \overline{x \wedge y} = 1 - \min(x,y)$ or $x \mid y = \overline{x \Delta y} = 1 - x\Delta y$
$\downarrow$	Nor: $x \downarrow y = \overline{x \vee y} = 1 - \max(x,y)$ or $x \downarrow y = \overline{x \nabla y} = 1 - x\nabla y$
a_i	An attribute value $(a_i \in \mathbb{R})$
W, w	Sum-normalized weights ($\Sigma w_i = 1$)
V, v	Max-normalized weights ($\max v_i = 1$)
p	Count-normalized weights ($p_1 + \cdots + p_n = n, \ n > 1$)
X, x	Suitability/preference
$(\ )$	Tuple
$\mathbf{x} = (x_1, \ldots, x_n)$	Ordered n-tuple
$\mathbf{x} \leq \mathbf{y}$	$x_i \leq y_i, \ i = 1, \ldots, n$
ρ_i	Absolute influence range
ρ_{ri}	Relative influence range
δ_i^+	Preference increment
δ_i^-	Preference decrement
π_i	Relative position of output preference
γ_i	Conjunctive coefficient of impact
β_i	Coefficient of balance
Ψ	Degree of confidence
Ω	Optimum suitability
$\mathbb{R}$	$\mathbb{R} = \,]-\infty, +\infty[$, real numbers (improper elements $-\infty$ and $+\infty$ are not real numbers)
$\bar{\mathbb{R}}$	$\bar{\mathbb{R}} = [-\infty, +\infty] = \mathbb{R} \cup \{-\infty, +\infty\}$, extended real numbers

$]a,b[$ or (a, b)	$\{x \in \mathbb{R} \mid a < x < b\}$; ISO 31-11, ISO 80000-2
$[a, b]$	$\{x \in \mathbb{R} \mid a \leq x \leq b\}$
$[a,b[$ or $[a,b)$	$\{x \in \mathbb{R} \mid a \leq x < b\}$
$]a,b]$ or $(a,b]$	$\{x \in \mathbb{R} \mid a < x \leq b\}$
I	Unit interval $[0,1]$
$A \succ B$	A outperforms B (the ranking of object A is better than the ranking of object B)
$x := y$	x is by definition equal to y
$x \approx y$	x is approximately equal to y
C	Conjunction (full conjunction, AND)
C+	Strong partial conjunction
CA	Average partial conjunction
C-	Weak partial conjunction
A	Neutrality (arithmetic mean)
D-	Weak partial disjunction
DA	Average partial disjunction
D+	Strong partial disjunction
D	Disjunction (full disjunction, OR)
CC	Hyperconjunction
DD	Hyperdisjunction
HD	Hard Disjunction (annihilator 1)
SD	Soft Disjunction (no annihilator)
SC	Soft Conjunction (no annihilator)
HC	Hard Conjunction (annihilator 0)

Abbreviations

AD	Andness Directed (GCD)
AM or A	Arithmetic Mean
AGC	Interpolative GCD aggregator from A to G to C
AHP	Analytic Hierarchy Process
AHC	Interpolative GCD aggregator from A to H to C
AIWA	Andness-directed Importance Weighted Averaging
ANSY	Analysis and Synthesis of Aggregators
B2B	Business to Business
B2C	Business to Customer
Bn	Set of n basic GL functions

B7	{C, HPC, SPC, A, SPD, HPD, D}
B8	{C, HPC, SPC, A, SPD, HPD, D, NOT}
B9	{C, HPC, SPC, A, SPD, HPD, D, CPA, DPA}
B10	{C, HPC, SPC, A, SPD, HPD, D, CC, DD, NOT}
B12	{C, HPC, SPC, A, SPD, HPD, D, NOT, CPA, DPA, CC, DD}
BL	(Classic bivalent) Boolean Logic
BM	Bajraktarević Mean
BQR	Bounded Quality Range (internality)
CAS	Canonical Aggregation Structure
CCC	Command, Control, and Communications (also C3)
CDBS	Criterion Data Base System
CHM	Counter-Harmonic Mean
CI	Conjunctive Idempotent (aggregator)
CILA	Compensative Idempotent Logic Aggregator
CPA	Conjunctive Partial Absorption
CPA/A:H	CPA based on Arithmetic and Harmonic means
CWW	Computing With Words
DI	Disjunctive Idempotent (aggregator)
DM	Decision Maker
DPA	Disjunctive Partial Absorption
DPA/A:$\underline{H}$	DPA based on the Arithmetic mean and the dual of Harmonic mean
EC	Extended Conjunction
ED	Extended Disjunction
EGCD	Extended GCD (nonidempotent aggregator)
EHD	Extended Hard Disjunction
EL	Evaluation Logic (an alternative name for GL)
ELC	Elementary criterion
ESC	Extended Soft Conjunction
ESD	Extended Soft Disjunction
EUMV	Estimated Unique Monthly Visitors (search engines)
EXM	Exponential Mean
FL	Fuzzy Logic
FWS	US Fish and Wildlife Service
G or GM	Geometric Mean
GCD	Graded (or generalized) Conjunction/Disjunction
GCD.n	GCD with n levels of andness/orness
GCD/CHM	GCD implemented using CHM
GCD/EXM	GCD implemented using EXM

GCD/WLM	GCD implemented using WLM
GCD/WPM	GCD implemented using WPM
GGCD.n	General nonuniform GCD with n levels of andness/orness (n = 9,17,25)
GIS	Geographic Information System
GL	Graded logic
GM	Geometric Mean
GP	General Population (type of SE user)
GPA	Grade Point Average
GPS	Global Positioning System
GYM	Google, Yahoo, Microsoft (search engine trio)
H	Harmonic Mean
$\underline{H}$	De Morgan Dual of Harmonic Mean
HGCD	Strictly Hard GCD
HM	Harmonic Mean
HPC	Hard Partial Conjunction
HPD	Hard Partial Disjunction
HR	Human Resources
IDE	Integrated Software Development Environment
IEEE	Institute of Electrical and Electronics Engineers
ISEE	Integrated System Evaluation Environment
ILA	Idempotent Logic Aggregator
INS	Immigration and Naturalization Service
IR	Information Retrieval
IRS	Internal Revenue Service
ISO	International Organization for Standardization
LA	Logic Aggregator
LM	Logarithmic Mean
LSP	Logic Scoring of Preference
LSP DEF	LSP Decision Engineering Framework
MAG	Myelin-Associated Glycoprotein (anti-MAG peripheral neuropathy)
MAR	Missing At Random
MCAR	Missing Completely At Random
MNAR	Missing Not At Random
MSHCP	Multi-Species Habitat Conservation Plan
MSN	The Microsoft Network (including a web SE, which is now Bing)
NIST	National Institute of Standards and Technology
NSF	National Science Foundation
OD	Orness Directed (GCD)

ODD	Overall (medical) Disability Degree
ORE	Online Real Estate
OS	Operating System
OSD	Overall (disease) Severity Degree
OWA	Ordered Weighted Averaging
PA	Partial Absorption
PAS	Preference Aggregation Structure
PC	Partial Conjunction ($1/2 < \alpha < 1$)
PD	Partial Disjunction ($1/2 < \omega < 1$)
PDD	Patient Disability Degree
PM	Power Mean
POI	Point Of Interest
PST	Proprietary Search Technology
QAM	Quasi Arithmetic Mean
RFP	Request For Proposals
SAS	Simple Additive Scoring (also Suitability Aggregation Structure)
SAT	Suitability Attribute Tree
S/D	Severity/Disability
SE	Search Engine
SGCD	Strictly Soft GCD
SMER	Standard Model of Evaluation Reasoning
SMS	Simple Multiplicative Scoring
SPC	Soft Partial Conjunction
SPD	Soft Partial Disjunction
SU	Specialized User (type of SE user)
SWM	Simple Weighted Means (e.g., WPM, WEM, WLM)
TC	Total Conjunction
TCF	The Conservation Fund
TD	Total Disjunction
UGCD	Uniform GCD
UGCD.n	UGCD with n levels of andness/orness (n = 7, 15, 23)
URL	Uniform Resource Locator (a web address)
WCL	Weighted Compensative Logic
WEM	Weighted Exponential Mean
WLC	Weighted Linear Combination (name for SAS used in the GIS area)
WLM	Weighted Logarithmic Mean
WPM	Weighted Power Mean
WPM.n	Weighted Power Mean with n levels of andness/orness (typically n = 17)

PART ONE

EVALUATION DECISION PROBLEMS

> *If one does not know to which port one is sailing,*
> *no wind is favorable.*
> —Seneca

All engineering books explore the same topic: how to solve a complex problem. The point of departure is always the problem statement, and the destination points are various successful applications. The path that connects the problem statement and a specific application is meandering through two major areas: the theoretical background and the practical methods for problem solving. We intend to take this classic journey from the beginning to the end, and as the first step along our path, we have to understand the problem. Our problem is evaluation, which is a form of decision making, and in *Part One* of this book we present various aspects of the evaluation problem. According to Seneca, our first goal is to explain "to which port one is sailing." In other parts of the book we will look for "favorable winds."

We define evaluation as a process of determining the extent to which an object satisfies requirements specified by its users/stakeholders.[1] The evaluated object can be any physical or conceptual system having any degree of complexity. A *system* is defined as a set of interacting components forming an integrated whole. Evaluated objects frequently consist of many interacting components and qualify to be identified as complex systems. In the majority of evaluation studies, the terms *object* and *system* can be used interchangeably.

---

1 In the context of evaluation, the stakeholder denotes a person, or a group of people, or an organization interested in the ownership and/or use of an evaluated object/system. Each rational evaluation criterion must reflect justifiable goals and interests of a specific stakeholder.

Soft Computing Evaluation Logic: The LSP Decision Method and Its Applications,
First Edition. Jozo Dujmović.
© 2018 John Wiley & Sons, Inc. Published 2018 by John Wiley & Sons, Inc.
Companion website: www.wiley.com/go/Dujmovic/Soft_Computing_Evaluation_Logic

Intuitive evaluation is the process of assessment of worth, suitability, or preference. The goal of evaluation is to determine an overall degree of satisfaction of a set of requirements that an object is expected to satisfy. Of course, the requirements can only be defined by a decision maker. In addition, the degrees of suitability/preference/worth are strictly a matter of perception—they are not objectively measurable physical properties of evaluated objects, but concepts that exist only in the mind of decision maker.

The assessment of worth (the process of evaluation) is a logic reasoning process that is assumed to be conscious, rational, and justifiable. Indeed, the evaluation reasoning is an important component of human intelligence. Since logic is defined as a science of correct reasoning, it follows that evaluation reasoning is a logic process and its theoretical aspects naturally belong to the area of logic. Our main goals are to develop the evaluation logic that is provably consistent with formal logic and semantic aspects of human intuitive evaluation reasoning and then to use this logic to develop a professional evaluation methodology for solving industrial-grade evaluation problems. That is done in *Part Two* and *Part Three* of this book, followed by nontrivial applications presented in *Part Four*.

In *Part Two* we introduce *graded logic* (abbreviated as GL) as an area of soft computing. Computing is usually defined as information processing, i.e., the use of computers for transforming input information (represented by input data) into output information (data that represent the results of computing). In this context, it is useful to differentiate *hard information* and *soft information*: the hard information is based on *measurement* (and therefore is objective and precise), and the soft information is based on *perception*[2] (and therefore is subjective, i.e., based on human experience/expertise, expressed as a graded value, and to some extent imprecise). Consequently, we can differentiate hard computing, which is defined as the processing of hard information, and soft computing, which is defined as the processing of soft information.

The human assessment of worth is an observable process. It can be identified, recorded, analyzed, and modeled. Then, it can be used as a role model for developing reliable quantitative evaluation procedures in computational intelligence. The goal of such soft computing procedures is to refine, enhance, and expand human evaluation reasoning abilities beyond natural limitations of intuitive decision making. Using appropriate soft computing models, we can generate optimum decisions in cases of highly complex and costly alternatives. In other words, our goal is to take intuitive evaluation as a mandatory starting point for development of decision engineering methodology for professional solving of complex evaluation, optimization, comparison, and selection problems.

The simplest examples of evaluation can be found in everyday life, where people evaluate, compare, and select cars, homes, and various consumer products.

---

2 Perception denotes the act of apprehending by means of the mind. Percept denotes the mental result or product of perceiving. Percepts can be verbalized using rating scales.

We select the best alternative by simultaneously taking into account the overall level of satisfaction of our requirements and the total cost of the evaluated object. Evaluated systems are not always physical objects, like cars and homes. The selections of the most convenient health protection plan, the best job, or the most convenient school/university are equally frequent evaluation problems that deal with conceptual systems. Everyday evaluations are usually performed intuitively, without decision tools and calculations, using only logic reasoning and experience.

Evaluation problems are also frequent in public life, government, and industry. Examples of such problems are the optimum location of public objects (hospitals, schools, museums, airports, nuclear power plants, etc.), comparison and selection of information technology systems (architecture, organization, and performance of hardware and software), the evaluation of corporate social responsibility, development of suitability maps, evaluation problems in ecology, etc. Such problems need professional evaluation methods, domain expertise, and appropriate software tools.

All professional evaluation methods must be fully consistent with the observable process of intuitive evaluation. Indeed, nobody would trust a decision method for selecting and locating a nuclear power plant, if the same method fails to support known patterns of human reasoning, or fails to provide justifiable results in simple cases of selecting a job for a new graduate, or a car for a family.

It is important to clearly differentiate two related problems: *evaluation* and *comparison*. Evaluation is used to determine the overall value of a single object, based on the degree of satisfaction of justifiable requirements. Comparison needs at least two objects and tries to show that an object is better than another object, based on relative comparison, without determining the overall value of individual objects. Consequently, the comparison can be performed with or without evaluation.

To evaluate an object means to determine the degree of satisfaction of a clearly defined set of requirements that the object must satisfy. Once we know how good two or more separately evaluated objects are, their comparison is a trivial consequence of evaluation: we rank them according to decreasing degree of satisfaction and select the best object. The best object is one that has the highest degree of satisfaction. However, if the overall degree of satisfaction is not sufficient, we can decide to select none of the competitive objects. For example, graduate schools regularly reject candidates who have insufficient undergraduate GPAs, because they use an admission threshold value that all candidates must satisfy.

As opposed to evaluation, the problem of comparison is defined as the answer to question whether object A is better than object B, and nothing more. Obviously, both A and B can be worthless, but A can still be better than B. There are many decision methods that are based on pairwise comparisons and cannot be used for evaluation of given objects. Obviously, from a decision-making standpoint, the objective of comparison is much less significant than the objective of evaluation. If we know the overall values of competitive objects, we can easily compare them. If we know only the relative comparison of competitors, we know nothing about their overall value. Therefore, in this book we focus on evaluation methodology and perform comparison, ranking and selection of competitors using evaluation results.

1.1 Intuitive Evaluation as a Logic Decision Process

The whole of science is nothing more than a refinement of everyday thinking.
—Albert Einstein

Intuitive evaluation is a frequent mental activity performed in the background of many rational (and irrational) decisions in everyday life. A decision can be defined as a subjective selection of the most appropriate among several alternatives. The decision maker (DM) selects the most appropriate alternative according to an adequate evaluation and selection criterion. This is usually a criterion that evaluates the extent to which an alternative satisfies stakeholder's requirements and supports the achievement of a specific stakeholder's goals. At the end of an intuitive evaluation process, DM creates the perception of overall suitability of each evaluated alternative. The alternative that has the highest perception of suitability is the most preferred and proposed for realization.

In the context of evaluation decision making, we define *process* as a systematic procedural activity consisting of well-defined and observable steps. Both intuitive and formal decision processes include procedures that start by identifying a set of attributes that contribute to overall suitability and terminate when the overall suitability is obtained either as a subjective percept or as a quantitative score.

The main reason for our interest in the intuitive evaluation process is the fact that no quantitative evaluation method can be acceptable unless it is consistent with the intuitive evaluation activity. The consistency with the intuitive evaluation process is a necessary condition that each quantitative evaluation method must satisfy. Professional evaluation methods should support and expand the intuitive evaluation process. Consequently, it is first necessary to identify essential components of the intuitive evaluation (for more details, see Chapter 2.2).

Soft Computing Evaluation Logic: The LSP Decision Method and Its Applications,
First Edition. Jozo Dujmović.
© 2018 John Wiley & Sons, Inc. Published 2018 by John Wiley & Sons, Inc.
Companion website: www.wiley.com/go/Dujmovic/Soft_Computing_Evaluation_Logic

To attain this goal, let us analyze one typical example of intuitive evaluation. Convenient examples of intuitive evaluation can be easily found among consumer decisions performed during evaluation and selection of goods and services (e.g., a process of buying a car). A customer that buys the best among several competitive objects usually makes an intuitive decision by answering the following questions:

- What are the goals we want to attain using the evaluated object?
- Do the evaluated objects contribute to the goal attainment?
- What individual characteristics (attributes that affect suitability) should the evaluated objects have?
- What requirements (criteria) should each individual suitability attribute satisfy?
- For a specific analyzed object, what is the level of satisfaction of each individual attribute criterion?
- Combining the levels of satisfaction of individual attributes, how suitable/good is an evaluated object as a whole?
- For each of competitive objects, what is the total cost?
- Combining the overall suitability/quality and the total cost, what is the best among competitive objects?

In the case of simple and inexpensive objects, these questions can be simplified and the number of individual characteristics can be reduced to just a few. In such cases, the whole evaluation and selection process might take just a few minutes. In the case of objects that are more complex and expensive, the intuitive evaluation process becomes visible in all its components and details, and can easily take hours or days. In the next section, we exemplify the intuitive evaluation process in a typical case of the purchase of a car.

1.1.1 Main Observable Steps of the Intuitive Evaluation Process

When buying a car, the evaluation process typically follows eight observable action steps:

I) Specification of goals
II) Goal attainment feasibility analysis
III) Specification of elementary suitability attributes
IV) Specification of requirements that attributes must satisfy
V) Evaluation of elementary attributes
VI) Logic aggregation of attribute suitability/preference degrees
VII) Cost analysis
VIII) Cost-preference (suitability-affordability) analysis

These steps are summarized in Fig. 1.1.1 and can be described as follows.

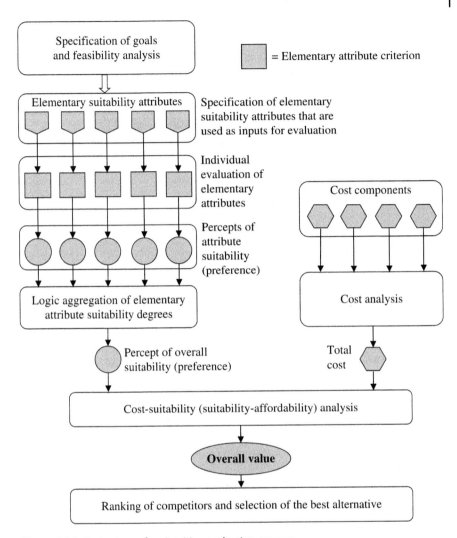

Figure 1.1.1 Basic steps of an intuitive evaluation process.

(I) Specification of Goals

Initially, the decision maker must be thoroughly aware of the car-dependent goals he or she wants to achieve. We generally assume one or more goals, and they can have various degrees of importance. If the goals are not sufficiently clear this will either prevent or make unclear and confusing all further evaluation steps. Examples of car-related goals might be to enable some professional activities, sports activities, commuting to work or to child care, to provide entertainment for family, etc. The purpose of the evaluation process is to predict the extent to which evaluated cars can support the achievement of goals.

Human goals can be everywhere between rational and irrational, and the purpose of system evaluation is not to question the validity of goals. While irrational and/or oversized goals are not surprising at the level of personal decision making, professional evaluators and expert teams are assumed to have knowledge needed to set appropriate (relevant, justifiable, and achievable) goals for professional evaluation of complex systems. In any case, the existences of goals, and a clear definition of the stakeholder (owner/user of evaluated object), are prerequisites for system evaluation and selection. For example, the stakeholder can be a family with three children, or a contrabass player who needs to transport his instrument, or a craftsman who needs space for transporting his tools and products. For each of them, it is necessary to develop a different evaluation criterion. Generally, each criterion must be attributed to a specific type of user and must reflect specific user needs.

(II) Goal Attainment Feasibility Analysis

The second question the decision maker (in our example, the car buyer) must answer is the following: "Is it possible to attain the goals by acquiring a car in a given price range?" Generally, the goals might not be sufficiently car-related: the career of a contrabass player might be better supported by buying a high-quality instrument than by buying a car that has ample space for the transport of contrabass. Therefore, the feasibility analysis can sometimes yield a negative answer, showing no need to consider the car procurement since it does not seem to sufficiently support the attainment of goals. The evaluation process may start if and only if the goal attainment feasibility analysis gives a positive answer.

In the case of car selection, the goal attainment feasibility analysis is rather simple, but in many cases of professional decision making this step can have substantial complexity. For example, to decide between two alternative locations for building an artificial lake, it can be necessary to develop and ana-lyze a list of complex ecological, energetic, social, and economic goals. Of course, this brings the feasibility analysis to levels beyond intuitive evaluation.

(III) Specification of Elementary Suitability Attributes

In order to initiate an evaluation process, the evaluator must identify a set of elementary attributes that affect the performance and suitability of evaluated system and can be used as inputs for evaluation. These elementary attributes are sometimes called the *performance variables*. Of course, there are also attributes that can be identified but do not affect the suitability. For example, urban drivers who do not use cruise control may decide not to include cruise control in the list of car suitability attributes. By definition, suitability attributes are only those features that contribute to the overall suitability.

We use the word *elementary* to denote that the attributes should be sufficiently simple to enable direct evaluation of their values. Of course, the attributes can be compound (e.g., *comfort* is a compound attribute that includes the available space, as well as the dimension, shape, material, and adjustability of seats, the quality of electronic equipment, air conditioning, etc.). For simplicity, it is convenient to assume that *attribute* means "elementary attribute that contributes to the overall suitability," while compound attributes are always explicitly denoted as compound. For the car selection problem, the possible elementary attributes include the number of passengers, the number of doors, the power of the engine, the maximum speed, the time to accelerate from 0 to specific speed, the ease of maintenance, previous experience with the car manufacturer, and so on. From 10 to 30 such indicators can be easily specified. Obviously, each DM can consider some attribute more important and some other less important, and the list of elementary attributes should be as complete as possible. It is reasonable to omit those attributes that are insufficiently important, since this can reduce the evaluation effort without reducing the quality of evaluation results. However, a frequent and serious mistake is to omit significant attributes because they are difficult for measurement and/or evaluation (e.g., car reliability records are not always readily available, but are certainly rather significant for car selection).

(IV) Specification of Requirements

For each elementary attribute, the evaluator should be able to specify requirements that competitors must satisfy in order to support the specified goals. For example, the car evaluator is frequently able to specify a desired range of the power of engine. The minimum power P_{min}, and all values that are less than P_{min}, are considered unacceptable (i.e., they satisfy none of user's requirements). The maximum power P_{max}, and all values greater than P_{max}, are considered perfect, in the sense that they completely satisfy user requirements. All values of power P that are greater than P_{max} cannot receive an extra credit. They make no significant contribution to user benefits, but increase the cost of purchasing and using the car. This intuitive criterion is not formally specified as a function (mapping the power of engine into the percept of satisfaction), but the results of intuitive evaluation should be similar to the percentage of satisfied requirements, $g(P) = 100\max(0, \min(1, (P - P_{min})/(P_{max} - P_{min})))$, illustrated in Fig. 1.1.2. Similar requirements should be specified for each of elementary attributes.

(V) Evaluation of Elementary Attributes

The individual intuitive evaluation consists now of comparing the value of an individual attribute (performance variable) with the previously specified user requirements. For example, the power of each evaluated engine is compared with the range of acceptable values. The result of this elementary evaluation is an intuitive feeling (i.e., a mental representation, or percept) of the degree to which the particular engine power meets the expectations of decision maker.

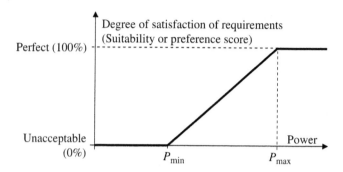

Figure 1.1.2 Typical criterion that specifies requirements for engine power.

This percept of the degree of satisfaction can be quantified and called the *elementary suitability score*, or the *elementary preference score*, or shortly *suitability* or *preference*.

Generally, percepts can be verbalized (expressed in words) and quantified. For example, a car buyer can investigate the comfort of a car and find that it is "very good" and satisfies 75% of expectations; in this example, "very good" is a verbalized percept of the degree of comfort, and 75% is a corresponding suitability score. We use the term *score* as a synonym for *quantified percept*. Thus, elementary suitability scores indicate how good (or bad) is the evaluated object depending on the value of the particular elementary attribute. For example, if the power of a given car engine is $(P_{min} + P_{max})/2$, the evaluator will most likely feel a medium preference for this component.

The percept of partial satisfaction of requirements should be considered in the context of the question "Are you completely satisfied with the power of engine?" The answer can be: "No, the statement that I am completely satisfied is only partially true." If the evaluator thinks that the power of engine satisfies one half of requirements, then the statement asserting complete satisfaction should be only 50% true. Therefore, *the partial satisfaction of requirements is equivalent to the partial truth of the statement that the satisfaction is complete.*

The percept of partial satisfaction or partial truth is not a physical, objectively measurable quantitative indicator. It is a percept (mental representation) created by the decision maker. Percepts of value are always a matter of degree (in the range from no satisfaction to complete satisfaction). Computing with such percepts (perceptual computing) belongs to the area of soft computing.

Reasoning with partial truth is one of the fundamental properties of human logic. In particular, partial truth is always present when we feel a partial satisfaction with an evaluated object/attribute. This is an observable property of human reasoning. Consequently, we can identify the ways people combine and manipulate partial truth, and then we can develop soft computing mathematical models that describe the observed phenomena. Partial truth is a limited value in the range from 0 (completely false) to 1 (completely true). It is frequently convenient to express partial truth in an equivalent range from 0% to 100%.

The intuitive evaluation process includes a separate analysis of each competitive system, sequentially, attribute by attribute. A car evaluator investigates each car by finding first the values of all elementary attributes for the analyzed car. That means to determine the exact power of engine, maximum speed, acceleration, comfort components, etc., for all competitive cars. Then, the intuitive evaluation of each of these values is done separately, by comparing a specific value and the range of acceptable/desired values for each attribute.

In some cases, evaluators may use relative comparison, by comparing a specific feature of all competitive cars, and assigning the highest satisfaction to the best competitor. For example, some people could be unable to set the requirement for car acceleration, but may still decide to be completely satisfied with the car that has the highest acceleration in a group of competitors. Of course, that form of reasoning is acceptable only if there are sufficient reasons to believe that all evaluated cars satisfy minimum requirements for acceleration. If that is not the case, the relative comparison is highly questionable and easily rejected by everybody who understands that the fact that object A is better than object B has no significance if both of them are unacceptable.

The described individual attribute evaluation process repeats for all elementary attributes. The main characteristic of the intuitive evaluation process is that humans in each step focus on a selected *single item* (attribute) and compare its value with their expectations (requirements). They sometimes perform this evaluation starting from the most important to the least important attribute, and immediately reject systems that insufficiently satisfy major attribute requirements. At the end, the evaluator generates a set of percepts of value (called attribute suitability/preference degrees), one precept for each elementary attribute. The attribute preference/suitability degrees denote the evaluator's degrees of satisfaction with individual characteristics of the analyzed system, and not the degree of satisfaction with the system as a whole. In order to differentiate between the individual attribute preferences and the preference of the whole system, the preferences that correspond to individual system attributes are frequently called *the elementary preferences (or suitability degrees)*, and the preference of the whole system is called *the overall (global) preference/suitability degree.*

(VI) Logic Aggregation of Preference/Suitability Degrees
The next step in intuitive evaluation is the aggregation of attribute suitability degrees and creating the overall suitability degree of evaluated object. Intuitive aggregation is a process based on systematic reviewing attribute suitability degrees and incrementally composing the percept of overall suitability. This process is logically more diverse, but otherwise similar to computing the

GPA of a student by averaging all individual course grades. For example, the preference for car performance can be obtained by aggregating preferences for the power of engine, acceleration, and the maximum speed. The preference for car comfort can be obtained by aggregating preferences for available space, comfortable seats, and the quality of internal equipment and organization. Then, we can aggregate percepts of suitability of performance and suitability of comfort. The human mind is an ultimate "aggregation engine" that naturally and automatically aggregates component suitability percepts and generates an aggregated suitability percept that is then used for decision making.

The fundamental property of the mental aggregation process is that it includes logic (i.e., most observed intuitive aggregation processes simultaneously include both formal logic and semantic components). Typical examples of "formal logic components" are requests for a specific degree of simultaneity or a specific degree of substitutability of input suitability degrees. On the other hand, each attribute always has a clear meaning, role, and significance for the evaluator. Based on desired goals, some suitability degrees are more important (more influential) and some suitability degrees are less important and less influential in the aggregation process. The adjustable degrees of importance are typical "semantic components" because they reflect the meaning and the role of aggregated suitability degrees. Surprisingly, the concept of importance, so clearly visible in human reasoning, is completely ignored in classic Aristotelian and Boolean logic.

The adjustment of importance is not the only semantic component in intuitive evaluation reasoning. For example, evaluators frequently consider some suitability degrees to be mandatory (i.e., they are very important and must be satisfied) and other are optional (their satisfaction is desired but not necessary). Obviously, this distinction is purely semantic, i.e., based on understanding the role of attributes and their groups.

Evaluators frequently request a highly simultaneous satisfaction of several requirements. For example, an evaluator of family sedan will regularly simultaneously require good performance *and* good comfort. In such cases the aggregated (output) preference degree for performance and comfort will be close to the minimum input preference degree, as shown in Fig. 1.1.3. Indeed, it is not acceptable if either performance or comfort is rather low, and evaluators penalize such cases with a lower aggregated preference degree. The proximity of aggregated preference and the minimum input preference can be expressed using a *degree of simultaneity*.

If the preference aggregation function that the evaluator intuitively uses is similar to conjunction, then it is called a *partial conjunction* (see details in *Part Two*). For this type of evaluation criterion, we say that it is *conjunctively polarized*. The evaluator intuitively selects a desired degree of simultaneity, and this degree determines the level of conjunctive polarization. In the case of partial conjunction, the evaluator wants to make sure that some important requirements are simultaneously sufficiently satisfied. In such cases, the simultaneity of fulfilling requirements gets credit, and an unbalanced fulfillment of requirements must be penalized. The degree of simultaneity (also called *andness*, and defined as $\alpha = s/t$ in Fig. 3.1.1) refers to the severity of penalizing cases where input requirements are not simultaneously satisfied. In the case of the maximum degree of simultaneity ($s = t$; $\alpha = 1$) the conjunctive aggregator becomes the pure conjunction, and the output becomes equal to the minimum input preference. In Fig. 1.1.3, the "performance and comfort" would have the same value as "performance."

The evaluator must also decide how to react to zero input preference degrees (i.e., whether to tolerate systems having some completely unsatisfactory components). If the zero input preferences cannot be tolerated, then such aggregator is a model of *mandatory requirements*: A single zero input causes zero output, and that may frequently mean the rejection of the whole system.

The difference between nonmandatory and mandatory requirements is illustrated in Fig. 1.1.4. If the preference score for car performance is 0 (completely

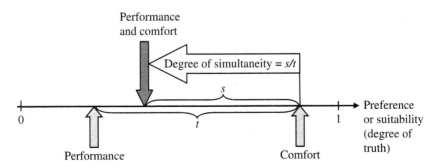

Figure 1.1.3 Degree of simultaneity during aggregation of performance and comfort.

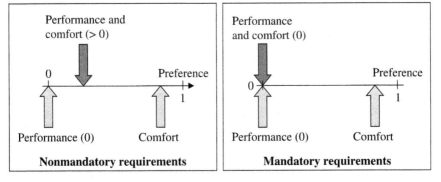

Figure 1.1.4 The difference between nonmandatory and mandatory requirements.

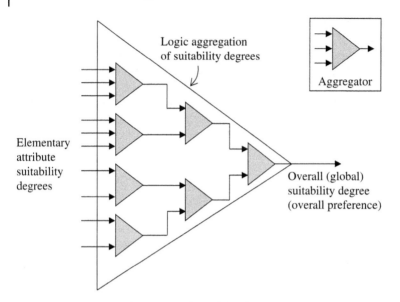

Figure 1.1.5 Hierarchical grouping of suitability degrees during the aggregation process.

unsatisfactory performance), and the preference score for comfort is positive (satisfactory comfort), the question is, what is the aggregated preference for performance and comfort of such a car? If the requirement for simultaneous performance and comfort is nonmandatory, the resulting performance and comfort score is positive. If the requirement is mandatory, then the aggregated performance and comfort score must be zero. Obviously, in this example, the majority of people would prefer to use the mandatory requirements.

The intuitive aggregation of preference degrees is usually done in a systematic stepwise hierarchical way illustrated in Fig. 1.1.5. Small groups of related suitability degrees are aggregated together, creating subsystem suitability degrees. Each input can have a different level of importance, and determining relationships between all inputs is easy only in small groups. For example, all components of car safety can be grouped in a single safety suitability degree. Then, all components of aesthetics and comfort can be grouped in an aggregated aesthetics and comfort suitability degree. Similarly, all components of speed, engine power, and acceleration can be grouped together in an aggregated performance suitability degree. By repeating this process, the evaluator finally combines a small group of aggregated suitability degrees to generate a single overall (global) suitability degree that is an indicator of the overall suitability of the analyzed car.

Intuitive evaluators regularly use this approach to deal with complexity and with different levels of importance of individual input suitability degrees. It is obvious, however, that the intuitive evaluation process is limited to cases with a modest number of input attributes. The maximum acceptable number of input attributes in an aggregation structure in intuitive evaluation depends on the type and complexity of evaluated systems. In cases where we need a reasonable accuracy and reliability of intuitive evaluation, the maximum number of simultaneously combined inputs should be between 5 and 9 [MIL56]. That is the ceiling of simple intuitive evaluation. For a larger number of inputs, we need quantitative models.

It is important to emphasize that each aggregation step implements a specific logic relationship that naturally reflects evaluator requirements. This is the reason why we call this phase of intuitive evaluation the *logic aggregation of preference/suitability degrees*. In the aggregation process shown in Fig. 1.1.5, the evaluator selects the hierarchical structure of aggregation, the desired logic properties of each aggregator, and the relative importance of each input. These adjustable components allow the precise intuitive modeling of stakeholder needs.

The conjunctive polarization of system requirements (the model of simultaneity) is the most frequent example of possible logic relationships evaluators intuitively use for aggregating suitability degrees, but it is certainly not the only one. Other frequently used relationships include the disjunctive polarization and more complex compound relations that can be expressed as a combination of basic conjunctive and disjunctive relationships.

The disjunctive polarization refers to cases of *substitutability* where there are several alternative ways of satisfying a requirement and each way is sufficient to secure the acceptability of the system and a good output suitability. For example, a car can have front-wheel drive, *or* rear-wheel drive, *or* (in the best case) all-wheel drive.

The disjunctive logic polarization is predominant in medical evaluations where the patient disability might depend on various motor problems (difficulties in movement) or sensory problems (e.g., pain), and any one of them is sufficient to cause serious problems resulting in patient disability.

The suitability aggregation process deals with partial truth. Each input suitability is a degree of partial truth of the statement that the corresponding input completely satisfies requirements. The aggregated (output) suitability degree in each aggregation node is a partial truth of the statement that the group of inputs (considered collectively) completely satisfies requirements. Eventually, the overall suitability degree that reflects the total system worth or suitability is the final overall percept expressed as a partial truth of the statement that the evaluated system as a whole completely satisfies requirements.

In almost all cases of intuitive evaluation, the overall level of satisfaction with a system cannot be higher than the level of satisfaction with the best component. Similarly, the overall level of satisfaction with a system cannot be lower than the level of satisfaction with the worst component. Consequently, the overall suitability is obtained as a mean value of input attribute suitability degrees, and the aggregation of suitability degrees is *idempotent* (if all inputs have equal values, the output must have the same value).

Aggregation methods that are intuitively used can include a variety of logic relations between inputs, and each input has its own degree of importance. In addition to simultaneity and substitutability, such relations can be asymmetric when we aggregate mandatory and optional inputs, or sufficient and optional inputs, or other more complex relations. A detailed study of these relations can be found in *Part Two*.

(VII) Cost Analysis

Many evaluated systems have cost associated with them. One of important steps in the evaluation process is to identify the type and components of cost. The most frequent options are:

- No cost
- Single fixed cost
- Compound cost
- Time-dependent cost

For example, a student can evaluate the quality of websites of several universities and compute and compare overall suitability degrees of the evaluated websites. No cost is associated with the evaluated systems (websites). The same student can evaluate, compare, and buy a computer, and there will be a single fixed cost associated with this acquisition.

A car buyer faces a more complex cost analysis because the cost of the car is a compound indicator. Rational evaluators combine the expected costs of fuel, maintenance, and insurance for all the years they expect to use the car, and then add these costs to the initial price of car and the cost of financing (if applicable) to compute the overall cost indicator for each competitive car. The evaluator may also decide to reduce the resulting cost by the anticipated car resale value after the expected utilization period. In addition to the intuitive process of evaluating the overall quality, most evaluators precisely compute and numerically express the total cost, and then try to intuitively compare the resulting cost-preference pairs.

In the case of professional system evaluation projects, the cost analysis can have complex time-dependent components. For example, there may be alternative and competitive financing plans that include several options: a purchase option, loan options, rent options, and various income-generating options. So, the dynamics of payments and earnings may differ for various options and must be compared using techniques that take time into account and compute aggregate (overall) cost indicators such as the present value [AA16a].

It is important to emphasize that the overall cost is the counterpart of the overall preference/suitability degree. It would be wrong to use cost as one of the attributes that is combined with various other attributes. The cost of the car should not be compared to the number of doors or the volume of the trunk, but to the utility of the car as a whole. When we buy a car, we don't pay for some specific parts of the car, but for its aggregated performance, comfort, and safety over years of service. Therefore, the overall cost and the overall suitability should be used as inputs for a cost-suitability (or cost-preference) analysis (Fig. 1.1.1).

(VIII) Cost-preference (Suitability-affordability) Analysis

The overall suitability degree of an object is the final result of an evaluation process only in those special cases where evaluated objects have no cost. In the case of car evaluation, as well as in all cases of objects that have a cost, the last step in the intuitive evaluation and selection process is a cost-preference (cost-suitability) analysis. The total cost of an object corresponds to the object as a whole, and the overall preference/suitability also corresponds to the object as a whole. Consequently, the evaluator compares the competitive objects by comparing the corresponding overall cost-suitability pairs. The intuitive evaluator feels that some cost-suitability combinations are more convenient than others. Each cost-suitability pair generates a percept of the overall value of an analyzed car (see Fig. 1.1.1). The highest overall value has a car that simultaneously combines a high overall suitability (preference) and a high affordability (moderate cost). Car evaluators usually characterize such a combination of the reasonable total cost and the high overall suitability simply as a "good deal."

Evaluators regularly require the simultaneity of high suitability and high affordability. The selected degree of simultaneity is an adjustable parameter. It determines the degree of penalizing systems that have low suitability or low affordability, and the degree of rewarding systems that simultaneously have high suitability and high affordability.

It is also easy to note that, in intuitive evaluation, the overall suitability and the overall affordability can have different degrees of importance. Indeed, if the evaluator is in modest financial conditions, then the high affordability (low cost) can be significantly more important than the high overall suitability. In such cases, the low cost will predominantly affect the overall value, and very expensive alternatives will be intuitively eliminated, regardless of the overall suitability.

Opposite situations are also possible. While no rational buyer is insensitive to cost, some evaluators in good financial standing might predominantly seek high quality and be more interested in high overall suitability and less in low cost. Therefore, intuitive evaluators aggregate the overall suitability and the overall affordability using a logic operator that takes into account their relative importance and an appropriate degree of simultaneity. The result of aggregation is a percept of the overall value of each analyzed object.

The overall suitability cannot be too low, and evaluators usually establish the suitability threshold value, so that all objects below the suitability threshold are rejected. Similarly, evaluators also have the total cost threshold, so that all affordable objects must not exceed the cost threshold. Among objects that are above the suitability threshold and below the cost threshold, the object that attains the highest value is selected as the final decision. If no object is in the region of acceptable solutions (i.e., above the suitability threshold and below the cost threshold), the final decision is that the evaluation and selection problem does not have an acceptable solution.

All eight steps of the intuitive evaluation process can be clearly identified and easily observed and analyzed in real-life situations. This process is a part of human intelligence, shaped by human experience, and we have good reasons to believe that it is sufficiently rational, appropriate, and efficient. Consequently, it is reasonable to develop quantitative models of this process and use them to build methods for professional evaluation, keeping always in mind the need for compatibility with the intuitive evaluation process. Next steps in this direction can be found in Chapters 2.2 and 3.1.

We have noticed that the intuitive evaluation process has a complexity ceiling and cannot be used for reliable evaluation of objects and alternatives of higher complexity. Therefore, it is necessary to clarify what is a "higher complexity." The intuitive evaluation works well for a few groups with a few attributes in each group. However, evaluation studies reported in [SU87, DUJ97a, DUJ06aa] show software systems characterized by the number of attributes in the range from more than 100 to more than 500. For such problems, we need quantitative methods.

1.1.2 Subjective and Objective Components in Evaluation

> *Any assessment of worth is by definition a subjective process.*
> —J.R. Miller III in Professional Decision-Making

In many evaluation projects, we can encounter people who initially react to evaluation problems by asking for "objective evaluation" and "objective values" because they assume that everything that is subjective is always arbitrary and has negative connotation. Such concerns primarily come from scientists and engineers when they face perceptual computing, evaluation problems, and evaluation methods for the first time. So, it is useful to investigate the problem of subjective and objective components in evaluation as early as possible.

The first terse and provocative sentence of the essay "The Subjectivity of Values" by Australian philosopher John Leslie Mackie (originally a chapter in [MAC77]) is, "There are no objective values." Of course, philosophers investigate the problems of the origin of values in general, and of moral values in particular.

Yet, the same general rule holds in the small world of evaluation decision making. Indeed, evaluation is not the search for fictional objective values, but for percept of high value in the mind of stakeholder who is the ultimate decision maker. Such a percept can be attributed to an individual, or a team, or an organization. Therefore, we cannot find objective values, but a perfectly acceptable substitute for them is the collective wisdom and experience of an appropriate group of experts, expressed in the form of a justifiable evaluation criterion.

In the case of a single evaluated system, the evaluation is a search for the overall degree of satisfaction of stakeholder requirements resulting from the stakeholder's goals and the properties of the evaluated system. In the case of multiple alternatives (two or more competitive systems), the evaluation process enables stakeholders to select an alternative that offers the highest satisfaction of their needs and requirements.

The reason for impossibility of objective evaluation is obvious. Only humans are able to specify goals and requirements for system evaluation. The overall values are not physical attributes of evaluated objects, but aggregated percepts of educated decision makers. Thus, the overall values cannot be objectively measured using any instrument. The value (in the sense of the degree of satisfaction of requirements at a reasonable cost) exists only in the human mind, and consequently, the evaluation process is essentially subjective [MIL66, MIL70].

Our goal is to model and predict human percepts of the overall value of complex systems. In this context, the meaning of word *subjective* is "based on human expertise." In the worst case, the evaluation process can be arbitrary, incomplete, or biased. In the best professional case, the evaluation process is well structured, impartial, systematic, quantified, and based on mathematical models that have a high expressive power to accurately reflect user needs, and provide a high level of justifiability and reliability of final results. The reliability of results is based on systematic use of quantitative models that precisely reflect observable properties of intuitive human evaluation reasoning.

For each evaluation problem, we can identify one or more stakeholders. Each stakeholder can provide a percept of the overall value of each of the evaluated systems or alternatives. For each evaluated system, the mean value of individual percepts of value of the stakeholder population is the indisputably accurate (or "the most objective") value of the system. Our quantitative evaluation criteria are built with intention to find the best estimate of the accurate overall value that corresponds to the complete population of stakeholders.

Each evaluation process includes indispensable subjective decision components, but that does not mean that there is no need for objectively measurable attributes. Quite the contrary, professional evaluation models are predominantly based on quantitative attributes that can be objectively measured. Quantification of evaluation models and their development using specialized software tools are effective means that control and reduce possible negative consequences of evaluator's imprecision, uncertainty, and/or subjectivity.

If an elementary criterion is defined in a quantitative form (as the case of the criterion for the power of car engine, Fig. 1.1.2), then the subjective components of such a function are reduced to the selection of the number and values of breakpoints (e.g., P_{min} and P_{max}) and the type of interpolation between them. The resulting function is then impartially applied to all competitive systems. If the evaluator can provide convincing justification for selecting the values of P_{min} and P_{max}, and the reasons for using linear interpolation, then the resulting criterion can be used with high confidence, providing results that can be considered "as objective as it gets."

Our goal is to organize evaluation as a process of structuring and quantifying the best of professional expertise, and the indispensable professional expertise is the only subjective component in the process. We consider evaluation subjective, not because it may have arbitrary components, but because it is inherently based on human perceptions and requires professional expertise to completely and accurately express stakeholder's interests and needs. Using scientific approach, quantitative models, and specialized tools, our goal is to make evaluation results as reliable as possible, fully consistent with stakeholder's goals and interests, impartial and justifiable, with a conscious effort to attain results that generate consensus of all participants in the evaluation process. We cannot reach objective values but we can go rather far in that direction.

1.2 Quantitative Evaluation—An Introductory Example

Example isn't another way to teach.
It is the only way to teach.
—A. Einstein

The process of determining the extent to which a given object (e.g., an industrial product or a complex software system) satisfies a set of stakeholder's requirements can be organized in a quantitative way. For example, if the evaluated object is a home (house or condo), then its users/stakeholders (members of homebuyer's family) may specify quantitative requirements for area, location, number of bedrooms, number of bathrooms, garage, backyard, kitchen and household appliances, neighborhood, availability of public transportation, and so on. Generally, the requirements are specified so that users can achieve desired goals; the achievement of goals depends on the availability and suitability of evaluated objects. We assume that the requirements are realistic and attainable. For example, in the case of home, it is not realistic to require features that are beyond the attainable price range. Generally, if the requirements are realistic, then evaluated objects should be able to satisfy the majority of requirements.

1.2.1 Stakeholders and Their Goals

All requirements reflect the needs of specific stakeholder/user, and evaluation criteria cannot be designed unless it is clear who the user is, and what are user's goals, interests and needs. Therefore, each evaluation starts by defining the stakeholder and the evaluated system. In this chapter we present a very simplified quantitative evaluation of a home, and a realistic home evaluation is presented in Chapter 4.2. We assume that the stakeholder is a family of five

Soft Computing Evaluation Logic: The LSP Decision Method and Its Applications,
First Edition. Jozo Dujmović.
© 2018 John Wiley & Sons, Inc. Published 2018 by John Wiley & Sons, Inc.
Companion website: www.wiley.com/go/Dujmovic/Soft_Computing_Evaluation_Logic

people: two parents, one child in elementary school, and two preschool children. This example will follow the steps of intuitive evaluation from Chapter 1.1.

If the stakeholder/homebuyer is defined as a family with children and the evaluated system is a home (house/condo), then the general goal is to provide an environment for healthy and prosperous life for all family members. In other words, we might think of a group of five stakeholders and each of them has a separate goal (e.g., the proximity to work, the proximity to school, etc.). In addition, a collective goal of the family is to simultaneously satisfy individual goals of all family members. To attain this collective goal, the family first specifies a list of home attributes that will be used for evaluation and the available home price range. In the next step, for each attribute it is necessary to specify a separate requirement that accurately reflects stakeholder's needs.

1.2.2   Attributes

The derivation of attributes is a process that is illustrated in Fig. 1.2.1. We create an attribute tree by decomposing each node into its components. In this simple example, the suitability of home is evaluated using only two components: the suitability of home location and the quality of home (reduced to the evaluation of available space). Each of these components can be further decomposed. The location is decomposed into the distance from work for parents and the distance from school for children. Similarly, the quality of the home is decomposed and the resulting attributes are the total area of home and the number of bedrooms. The decomposition process is completed when we generate components that cannot be further decomposed.

We will use the following terminology: All attributes that can be decomposed will be called *subsystem (compound) attributes*, and those that cannot be decomposed will be called *elementary (input) attributes*. For example, the number of bedrooms cannot be further decomposed, and consequently, that is one

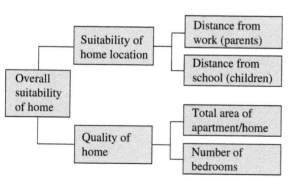

Figure 1.2.1 A simplified attribute tree for home evaluation.

of input attributes. In this simplified example, we will use only four input attributes (see Chapter 4.2 for a realistic list of 36 attributes and realistic criteria for home evaluation).

1.2.3 Attribute Criteria

The second step in the evaluation process is to specify requirements that each elementary attribute must satisfy. A sample requirement for the distance from work for parents is shown in Fig. 1.2.2. The degree of satisfaction of requirements is called the *preference or suitability score* (or, for short, the *preference or suitability*) and for simplicity it can be interpreted as the percentage of satisfied requirements. If the travel time to work (using any form of transportation) is less than or equal to 10 minutes, the working parent is completely satisfied. If the travel time is greater than 60 minutes, this is not acceptable and the degree of satisfaction is 0. For travel times between 10 minutes and 60 minutes we use for simplicity the linear interpolation. For example, if the travel time is 35 minutes, the corresponding degree of satisfaction is 50%. A soft computing interpretation of this value would be that the degree of truth is 0.5 for the statement that the working parent is completely satisfied with the travel time to work.

The criterion function shown in Fig. 1.2.2 is called the *elementary attribute criterion* or simply *elementary criterion,* to emphasize the fact that this is the simplest component requirement that the user can specify. Of course, every effort must be made that each elementary criterion reflects the stakeholder's needs in the most accurate way. For another stakeholder, the values of

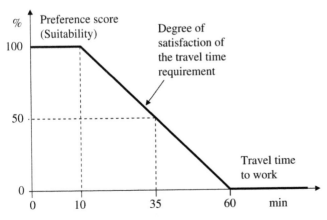

Figure 1.2.2 An elementary criterion function for evaluation of the travel time to work.

10 and 60 minutes might be different, and we assume that each stakeholder can provide strong arguments supporting the selected parameters of each elementary criterion.

Elementary criteria are frequently presented in the standardized rectangular form shown in Fig. 1.2.3. This rectangular form has three fields: title, preference scale, and description. The title field contains the full name of the evaluated attribute. The preference scale includes the values of breakpoints that correspond to specific degrees of satisfaction. It can have any number of breakpoints, and it assumes a linear interpolation between them. The description field contains comments that are necessary for correct interpretation of the criterion function, the definition of units of measurement, and (if necessary), the method for measurement or computation of the value of attribute.

The requirements for the travel time to school for small children must be stricter than the criterion for the travel to work for parents. A corresponding elementary criterion with four breakpoints is shown in Figs. 1.2.4 and 1.2.5. Let us note that the end values of all preference scales denote the beginning of the constant value of preference. In Fig. 1.2.5, if the time is greater than 25 minutes, the values of preference remain constant (zero). Similarly, if the time is less than or equal to 5 minutes, the preference is again constant (100%). Increasing the number of breakpoints increases the precision of the criterion function.

In this simplified case, the elementary criteria in Figs. 1.2.3 and 1.2.5 completely specify user requirements regarding the location of the home. Of course, in the case of intuitive evaluation, the requirements can be expressed in verbal and not in a quantitative way, but the homebuyer always knows what

Distance from work (parents)	
[%]　　[min] 100 ⊤ **10** 90 ┼ 15 80 ┼ 20 70 ┼ 25 60 ┼ 30 50 ┼ 35 40 ┼ 40 30 ┼ 45 20 ┼ 50 10 ┼ 55 0 ┴ **60**	The distance is evaluated as the travel time from home to work. If the travel time is 10 minutes or less, the user is completely satisfied, yielding an elementary preference score $X_w = 100\%$. If the travel time is 60 minutes or more, this is not acceptable, and yields a zero preference score. For values between 10 and 60 minutes we assume the use of linear interpolation (and in the preference scale it is enough to write only 10 and 60 min).

Figure 1.2.3 A rectangular form of an elementary criterion.

Figure 1.2.4 The elementary criterion function for evaluation of the travel time to school.

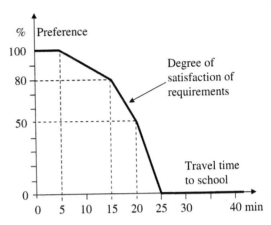

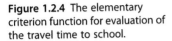

Distance from school (children)		
[%] [min]	The distance is evaluated as the travel time from home to school.	
100 ┬ 5		
90 ┼	If the time is less than or equal to 5 minutes, the user is completely satisfied. If the travel time is 25 minutes or more, this is not acceptable and yields a zero preference score.	
80 ┼ 15		
70 ┼		
60 ┼		
50 ┼ 20		
40 ┼	Interpolation is used to find the level of satisfaction for any time: e.g. if time =10 min, then the satisfaction = 90%; if time is 22 min then the satisfaction = 30%	
30 ┼		
20 ┼		
10 ┼		
0 ┴ 25		

Figure 1.2.5 Rectangular form of the elementary criterion for the travel time to school.

requirements must be satisfied and can use them in the process of evaluation and comparison of competitive homes.

In the case of the available space, the user must first specify a criterion for the total area of home. This criterion is shown in Fig. 1.2.6. The first property of this criterion is that the minimum acceptable area is specified to be 80 m^2. This area satisfies 50% of the stakeholder's requirements. However, the stakeholder is not ready to accept an area that would be less than 80 m^2. Consequently, the area of 79 m^2 yields a zero preference. The area of 120 m^2 completely satisfies the stakeholder's needs, and larger areas get no extra credit. The reason for this requirement is that the family feels that areas that are greater than 120 m^2 do

Area of home/appartment [m²]	
[%] [m²] 100 ┬ 120 90 ┼ 80 ┼ 100 70 ┼ 60 ┼ 50 ┼ 80 40 ┼ 30 ┼ 20 ┼ 10 ┼ 0 ┴ 79	The criterion for the area of home (or appartment) reflects these requirements: -Area less than 80 m² is not acceptable for the given family. -Area of 80 m² is acceptable but satisfies only 50% of requirements. -Area of 100 m² satisfies 80% of requirements. -Area of 120 m² or more satisfies all requirements.

Figure 1.2.6 Elementary criterion for the total area of home.

not yield significant benefit, but can cause significant increases of the cost of purchase and/or maintenance.

The requirements for the number of bedrooms are shown in Fig. 1.2.7. Because of three children, the ideal home should have four bedrooms. In extreme situations (financial difficulties, temporary solutions, etc.), two bedrooms might still be acceptable, even though such a home satisfies only one half of the family requirements. This is a discrete criterion because the number of bedrooms is a natural number, but the preference scale can be used as before.

With these four elementary criteria, the user systematically and precisely specified basic requirements, but this is not enough for evaluation. Any specific home can now be characterized by four input values: the travel time to work

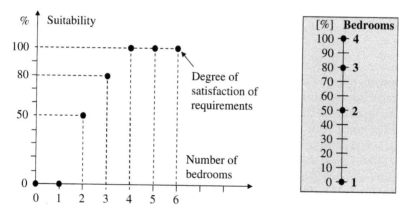

Figure 1.2.7 A discrete elementary criterion for the number of bedrooms.

Table 1.2.1 Attributes of four competitive homes.

Home	Location		Available space		Cost, C [k$]
	Travel time to work, T_w [min]	Travel time to school, T_s [min]	Total area A [m²]	Number of bedrooms, B	
Alpha	22	10	85	3	620
Beta	10	15	90	4	750
Gamma	15	8	110	4	699
Delta	45	5	88	3	505

Table 1.2.2 Preference scores generated by elementary criteria.

Home	Work X_w [%]	School X_s [%]	Area X_a [%]	Bedrooms X_b [%]
Alpha	76	90	57.5	80
Beta	100	80	65	100
Gamma	90	94	90	100
Delta	30	100	62	80

(T_w), the travel time to school (T_s), the total area (A) and the number of bedrooms (B). In addition, the cost of the home (C) will also play a critical role in deciding which home is the best alternative (i.e., the most suitable for the specific family).

Suppose that $ denotes an arbitrary monetary unit, not necessarily the US dollar. Let the available funding be limited to $750,000, and within that constraint we have four competitive homes called Alpha, Beta, Gamma, and Delta, shown in Table 1.2.1. Using the presented elementary criteria, the homebuyer can generate four suitability degrees (preference scores X_w, X_s, X_a, and X_b) shown in Table 1.2.2, that reflect homebuyer's degree of satisfaction with each of the four individual requirements. Of course, in both intuitive and quantitative evaluation, each individual requirement is separately investigated, but our goal is to determine how good is each home as a whole, not how good are individual components. Therefore, the next step is to find a method to combine (aggregate) the four elementary preference scores (suitability degrees) and the cost of each home to evaluate each of the competitors and to produce their final ranking.

1.2.4 Simple Direct Ranking

It is important to differentiate the evaluation and the relative ranking. The goal of evaluation is to determine the overall suitability of a home expressed as the degree of satisfying the homebuyer's requirements. The overall suitability can be determined for each home separately and independently of other homes. On the other hand, it is possible to perform simple ranking in a strictly relative way, without any evaluation. For example, we might directly take data from the Table 1.2.1 and perform ranking of each component, so that the best component gets the rank 1 and the worst gets the rank 4. Then we add ranks for each home, and the home with the lowest sum is the best alternative. This process, called *direct ranking* (a variation of the Borda count method [AA15]), is shown in Table 1.2.3. If some of the analyzed values are equal, then the resulting rank is the mean value of individual ranks; e.g., if two systems share the first place, their rank will be $(1+2)/2 = 1.5$. Using the sum of ranks, we generate the quality (suitability) rank that shows that Gamma is the best system.

The next step is to take into account the cost. We can introduce ranking for costs, where the rank of the cheapest system is 1. After adding the cost ranks and the quality ranks, we get Q + C sum, which is used in Table 1.2.3 to make final ranking that shows that Gamma and Delta share the first place. This is a typical example of trading accuracy for simplicity, and we do *not* suggest this approach (unfortunately, it is used in politics).

The presented direct ranking technique can sometimes be useful, because it is extremely simple, but it has many serious drawbacks. The first problem is that direct ranking indicates who the best system in a group is, but this does not mean that the best system is able to satisfy user needs. The winner of the competition can still be worthless according to the stakeholder's requirements. The second problem of direct ranking is that there is no information on how big is the difference between systems in the list; the same ranking applies to both negligible and substantial differences. The third problem is that all components have the same level of relative importance. For example, by adding ranks for home suitability and cost we implicitly consider that the home suitability and cost are always equally important; in many cases this is not true. The fourth problem is that ranking cannot express logic relationships between aggregated ranks. If one of components is so bad that the system becomes unacceptable, this can be ignored by the direct ranking method. For example, for system Delta $T_w = 45$ minutes and the corresponding rank in Table 1.2.3 is 4. However, all results in Table 1.2.3 would remain unchanged for any value $T_w > 45$ minutes. So, even if $T_w = 3$ hours the Delta house would not be rejected from the

Table 1.2.3 Direct ranking of homes.

Home	Work rank	School rank	Area rank	Bdrm rank	Sum of ranks	Quality rank	Cost rank	Q+C sum	Final rank
Alpha	3	3	4	3.5	13.5	4	2	6	3.5
Beta	1	4	2	1.5	8.5	2	4	6	3.5
Gamma	2	2	1	1.5	6.5	1	3	4	1.5
Delta	4	1	3	3.5	11.5	3	1	4	1.5

competition, but it remains one of the two winners. This is meaningless and unacceptable, and shows that in this case, the direct ranking is not a right approach. Indeed, the relative ranking and evaluation are two different things. We can evaluate to perform ranking, but we cannot perform ranking instead of evaluation.

1.2.5 Aggregation of Attribute Suitability Degrees

The process of evaluation can follow the usual pattern of intuitive reasoning that applies in such situations. The intuitive reasoning consists of two steps. First, the evaluator aggregates all elementary suitability degrees (preferences) to get an overall suitability score that indicates the suitability of the system as a whole. Second, the overall suitability score is combined with the total cost to find the most convenient combination (the highest value that combines both a good quality and a reasonable cost).

It is important to note that the cost of home is not an attribute that should be directly merged with other attributes. Indeed, the total cost corresponds to the overall suitability of home and consequently the cost should *not* be considered an individual attribute and mixed with other individual attributes of the evaluated home. So, our problem is now to find a method for aggregation of four elementary attribute suitability scores and computing the overall suitability scores for all competitive homes.

Following the pattern of intuitive reasoning, the process of aggregating attribute suitability scores is shown in Fig. 1.2.8. We first answer the question about the quality of location by aggregating attribute suitability scores for the travel time to work (X_w) and the travel time to school (X_s) to get the subsystem suitability score for the overall quality of home location (X_{loc}). Then, we evaluate the subsystem of space (which in this example represents the home quality) by aggregating preference scores of the area (X_a) and the number of bedrooms (X_b) to get the subsystem suitability score for the overall quality of available space (X_{space}).

Once we know the degree of satisfaction with the location and the space of home, we are ready for the final step: the aggregation of subsystem suitability scores for location and space to generate the resulting overall suitability for the home as a whole (X_0). The inputs for aggregation are X_w, X_s, X_a, and X_b. They are expressed as percentages of satisfied requirements. Consequently, the overall suitability X_0 is also interpreted as an overall percentage of satisfied requirements, taking properly into account all elementary attribute requirements. In other words, X_0 is an indicator of the overall suitability of the evaluated home. It is important to note that the computational structure shown in Fig. 1.2.8 represents a complete evaluation criterion: after selecting aggregators it will

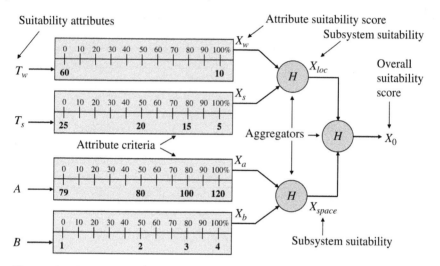

Figure 1.2.8 Aggregation of elementary preferences.

generate a meaningful value of X_0 for any combination of the input attribute values T_w, T_s, A, and B.

Since $X_{loc} = H(X_w, X_s)$, we must now find what kind of function should be the aggregator H. Let us immediately make clear that this is a hard question and one that is beyond this introductory section—its full answer is in *Part Two* and *Part Three* of this book. However, something can be done right now: we can easily see that we must *not* use the arithmetic mean $X_{loc} = (X_w + X_s)/2$. There are two questions that we must answer when selecting the aggregator H: (1) "Would you accept a home location if the travel time to work is greater than 60 minutes?" and (2) "Would you accept a home location if the travel time to school is greater than 25 minutes?" According to our elementary attribute criteria, the obvious answer to these questions is *no*. If any of the two travel times has a zero suitability score, that must yield $X_{loc} = 0$ to indicate a complete dissatisfaction with such home location. Thus, the conditions for the H function are: $H(0, X_s) = 0$, $X_s > 0$, and $H(X_w, 0) = 0$, $X_w > 0$. In Chapter 1.1 we called these conditions the mandatory requirements. Now we see that the arithmetic mean does not satisfy the mandatory requirement conditions and consequently, it must not be used as the aggregator of X_w and X_s.

The reason for rejecting the arithmetic mean is that the homebuyer essentially wants a home that *simultaneously* has a short distance to work and a short distance to school, but the arithmetic mean is an aggregator that cannot model this level of simultaneity. On the other hand, there are many functions that satisfy the mandatory requirement condition $H(0, X_s) = H(X_w, 0) = 0$, and one of those that have suitable properties is the harmonic mean illustrated in Fig. 1.2.9. For

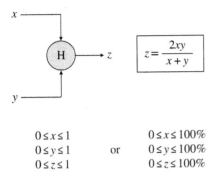

x [%]	y [%]	z [%]
0	100	0
100	0	0
100	10	18.2
100	20	33.3
100	30	46.2
100	40	57.1
100	50	66.7
100	60	75
100	70	82.4
100	80	88.9
100	90	94.7

$$z = \frac{2xy}{x+y}$$

$$0 \le x \le 1 \qquad 0 \le x \le 100\%$$
$$0 \le y \le 1 \quad \text{or} \quad 0 \le y \le 100\%$$
$$0 \le z \le 1 \qquad 0 \le z \le 100\%$$

Figure 1.2.9 Basic properties of the harmonic mean.

simplicity, we will assume equal importance of all inputs and use the harmonic mean to compute the subsystem suitability scores. For the location of home, we have: $X_{loc} = 2X_w X_s / (X_w + X_s)$.

In the case of aggregating the suitability scores for the area of home and the number of bedrooms, we have again two mandatory requirements. Homes with unacceptable area or unacceptable number of bedrooms should be rejected. Consequently, our second aggregator can also be the harmonic mean: $X_{space} = 2X_a X_b / (X_a + X_b)$. In the final step of aggregation, for simplicity we can again use the harmonic mean because homes with unacceptable location or unacceptable space should be rejected:

$$X_0 = \frac{2X_{loc}X_{space}}{X_{loc} + X_{space}} = \frac{4}{1/X_w + 1/X_s + 1/X_a + 1/X_b}.$$

We used equal weights for all inputs. Not surprisingly, some homebuyers may consider the home location more important than the available space (or vice versa). In quantitative models the level of relative importance is usually expressed using positive normalized weights that have the sum equal to 1. So, if the home location is considered two times more important than the available space, then the corresponding weights would be 0.67 and 0.33. In such a case, we might compute the overall preference as follows:

$$X_0 = 1 / (0.67 / X_{loc} + 0.33 / X_{space}).$$

Using the attribute criteria and three harmonic mean aggregators, we can now evaluate the four competitive homes and get the results shown in Table 1.2.4.

Table 1.2.4 Results of evaluation of competitive homes.

Home	Location X_{loc} [%]	Space X_{space} [%]	Overall suitability score X_0 [%]	Cost C [k$]	Overall value $V=X_0/C$	Normalized value $100V/V_{max}$
Alpha	82.4	66.9	73.9	620	0.1191	83.8%
Beta	88.9	78.8	83.5	750	0.1114	83.4%
Gamma	92	94.7	93.3	699	0.1335	100%
Delta	46.2	69.9	55.6	505	0.1101	82.5%

The location of home Delta is rather poor—it satisfies less than one half of sta-keholder's requirements. This is the reason why Delta is the least desirable from the standpoint of quality, but it is convincingly less expensive than other com-petitors. The best quality has the home Gamma, which satisfied 93.3% of home-buyer's requirements. So, now we know how good our best home is and we also know that the next competitor, Beta, satisfies approximately 10% less require-ments than the leading home Gamma. However, the selection of the best home cannot be based only on the overall preference/suitability scores because for most homebuyers the cost is also an important factor for making the final decision.

1.2.6 Using Cost and Suitability to Compute the Overall Value

Our last problem in this example is to combine the overall preference score X_0 and the total cost C to compute an overall indicator of the value of home, V. There are various models of the overall value function $V(X_0, C)$, and they are described in detail as part of the cost/preference (or suitability/affordability) analysis in Chapter 3.6. For simplicity, we use here the formula $V = X_0/C$ that shows the level of satisfaction of user requirements per monetary unit of cost. This model rewards high overall suitability and low cost, assuming that the total cost and the overall suitability have equal role and equal importance. Using this model, we computed the results in Table 1.2.4 and found that the home Gamma is the winner, having the highest overall value. The remaining three competitors have rather similar normalized overall values, more than 16% below the level of Gamma.

The resulting ranking of competitors is shown in Tables 1.2.5. These tables also show what would happen if instead of harmonic mean we made an over-simplification and used the arithmetic mean. The arithmetic mean is unable to sufficiently penalize the Delta home for its poor location. Consequently, even though it has the lowest overall suitability score (only 68%), in the case of arith-metic mean the Delta home would be the winner of this competition because of

Tables 1.2.5 Ranking as a function of aggregation operator.

Aggregation with the harmonic mean			Aggregation with the arithmetic mean			
Rank	Home	Value	Rank	Home	Score	Value
1	Gamma	0.1335	1	Delta	68.0	0.1347
2	Alpha	0.1191	2	Gama	93.5	0.1338
3	Beta	0.1114	3	Alpha	75.9	0.1224
4	Delta	0.1101	4	Beta	86.3	0.1150

its low price. This example shows the importance of using a correct logic of aggregation operators, and a significant part of this book is devoted to the development and use of flexible and justifiable aggregators. In particular, the problems of oversimplification of aggregation process caused by simple scoring techniques are analyzed in detail in the next chapter.

The presented simplified home selection example provides an outline of a typical evaluation process for any type of evaluated object. This process is the same for intuitive and for quantitative evaluation. In other words, the quantitative evaluation strictly follows the steps of the intuitive evaluation process. If we take into account that we only have four input attributes and their values summarized in Table 1.2.1, an interesting question is whether intuitive evaluators could generate the results from Tables 1.2.4 and 1.2.5. Regardless of the simplicity of this problem and the possibility to reach similar conclusion using the intuitive approach and the quantitative approach, it is easy to note that intuitive evaluation even with only four attributes and four systems needs substantial concentration and effort, and can yield uncertainty, low precision and justifiability problems.

It is easy to note that the intuitive evaluation process has a complexity ceiling and that ceiling is rather low, perhaps in the vicinity of the presented simple example problem. If the number of attributes and objects is larger, then the intuitive evaluation is not possible (professional evaluation problems can have up to several hundred inputs). On the other hand, the quantitative approach offers a sequence of easily justifiable simple steps and generates results with more accuracy and less effort.

Our goal in this section was to show the main steps and the basic properties of quantitative evaluation. However, the precision and usability of our model was obviously rather low: The number of inputs was too small, all inputs were equally important, and all aggregators were the same. The methodology for creating more complex, precise, realistic, and justifiable evaluation criteria is presented in *Part Two* and *Part Three* of this book.

1.3 Drawbacks of Simple Additive and Multiplicative Scoring and Utility Models

Everything should be made as simple as possible, but not simpler.
—A. Einstein

Simplicity is a good thing only for those who know and never cross the border line between simplicity and oversimplification. Unfortunately, it is in human nature to trade accuracy for simplicity. Simplicity at any cost is incompatible with professional problem solving. Simple scoring techniques are the area of decision making where accuracy is traded for simplicity. More often than not, the simple scoring models yield oversimplifications and questionable results. This is the reason why simple scoring and utility models are generally *not acceptable* in professional evaluation. In this chapter, our goal is to explain and prove this claim.

The simple scoring methods are used to score individual components of complex systems, and then to evaluate and compare competitive systems using a weighted mean of component scores [KLE78, KLE80]. The most important such approach is the *simple additive scoring* (SAS, also called simple additive weighting, SAW [TZE11], or weighted linear combination, WLC [MAL99]) that has been used for many years. SAS models for evaluation (e.g., [SCH69, SCH70, MIL66, MIL70, YOO95, TRI00, PAL02]) assume that the quality of an object is a weighted sum of the quality indicators of its components/attributes, as follows:

$$\text{Overall\_score} = \sum (\text{component\_weight} \times \text{component\_score})$$

In a similar way, *simple multiplicative scoring* (SMS) (e.g., [WHI63, CHE92, CHA01, YOO95, TRI00, VAN04]) uses a geometric mean model with a reasonable intention to more heavily penalize objects with poor component values:

$$\text{Overall\_score} = \prod (\text{component\_score})^{\text{component\_weight}}$$

Each component weight denotes the relative importance of the evaluated component, and the component score reflects the quality of evaluated

Soft Computing Evaluation Logic: The LSP Decision Method and Its Applications,
First Edition. Jozo Dujmović.
© 2018 John Wiley & Sons, Inc. Published 2018 by John Wiley & Sons, Inc.
Companion website: www.wiley.com/go/Dujmovic/Soft_Computing_Evaluation_Logic

component. The overall score is then used for decision making (evaluation, comparison, and selection of the best alternative).

It is self-evident that the next step toward stronger penalizing objects with poor components could be based on the harmonic mean:

$$\text{Overall\_score} = 1/\left[\sum(\text{component\_weight}/\text{component\_score})\right]$$

However, while the simple additive scoring is by far the most popular, and the multiplicative scoring is much less frequently discussed, it is interesting that the harmonic mean model seems to be completely neglected by the proponents of fixed (additive or multiplicative) scoring. Therefore, we will now focus on properties of additive and multiplicative scoring.

1.3.1 Simple Additive Scoring: The Irresistible Attractiveness of Simplicity

The SAS model can be mathematically written as follows:

$$S_0 = A(S_1,...,S_n) = \sum_{i=1}^{n} W_i S_i, \quad W_1 + \cdots + W_n = 1, \quad W_i > 0, \quad i = 1,...,n.$$

Here n denotes the number of inputs, $W_1, ..., W_n$ are normalized weights, $S_1, ..., S_n$ are attribute scores, and S_0 is the resulting overall (output) score. The scores can be in any range, and we will assume the unit interval $S_i \in I = [0, 1]$, $i = 0,...,n$. Since $W_1 + \cdots + W_n = 1$, the average weight is $\overline{W} = (W_1 + \cdots + W_n)/n = 1/n$. In other words, the fundamental property of additive scoring models is that the average relative importance of a component must decrease when the number of components increases.

Another view of this property can be obtained by computing the average impact of SAS inputs. The maximum impact of input S_i is the difference between output scores obtained for the extreme cases $S_i = 1$ and $S_i = 0$:

$$\delta_i = A(S_1,...,S_{i-1},1,S_{i+1},...,S_n) - A(S_1,...,S_{i-1},0,S_{i+1},...,S_n) = W_i.$$

Consequently, following is the average impact of an input of SAS:

$$\bar{\delta} = (\delta_1 + \cdots + \delta_n)/n = (W_1 + \cdots + W_n)/n = 1/n.$$

As n increases, the average impact decreases, and for larger values of n the impact becomes negligible. In other words, for large/complex systems[1] the

---

1 Complex systems with large number of attributes are easily found in the area of software. For example, evaluation models of operating systems and database systems typically include several hundred (typically 300–600) elementary attributes. Even a detailed car characterization model can have more than 200 attributes.

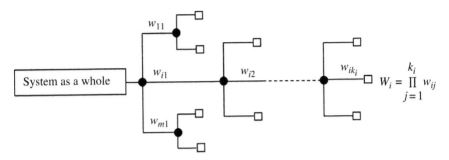

Figure 1.3.1 Hierarchical decomposition of weights.

number of attributes is also large, and each individual attribute automatically becomes insignificant. That is not a desirable property because of two main reasons: (1) it limits the number of inputs, and (2) there are critical attributes that must have significant impact regardless the number of inputs.[2] In addition, if a model is inappropriate for large n that does not implies that it is appropriate for small n.

The weights $W_1, ..., W_n$ are computed by decomposing the attribute tree as illustrated in Fig. 1.3.1. At the initial (root) level, the system as a whole is decomposed into m major components having individual weights (relative importance) $w_{11}, ..., w_{m1}$, $w_{11} + \cdots + w_{m1} = 1 (\forall i, j, \ w_{ij} > 0)$. This process systematically repeats for each component that can be further decomposed. The result is a tree structure where each branch has a weight and leaves denote elementary input attributes (performance variables). The resulting weights of attributes are obtained as products of weights along the path of k_i branches that connect a selected i^{th} leaf with the root of the weight decomposition tree:

$$W_i = \prod_{j=1}^{k_i} w_{ij}, \quad \sum_{i=1}^{n} W_i = \sum_{i=1}^{n} \prod_{j=1}^{k_i} w_{ij} = 1.$$

These weights are then used in the SAS formula, and if elementary scores are normalized so that $0 \le S_i \le 1$, $i = 1, ..., n$, then the overall score is also normalized: $0 \le S_0 \le 1$. The zero score denotes worthless (or nonexistent) component, and the score 1 (or 100%) denotes a perfect satisfaction of the evaluator's requirements. Additive models are particularly popular and carefully studied in utility theory [FIS64, FIS70], and its applications [EDW82].

---

2 In a simple example of a family car evaluation, if a family has six members, all cars with less than six seats should have zero score for the number of seats and should be rejected, regardless how many attributes are used for car evaluation and how good the other attributes are.

The main advantage of SAS is its simplicity, and this is the reason for its frequent use in a variety of evaluation problems. However, additive scoring has many disadvantages [DUJ72a, DUJ72b] that make this method unsuitable in a general case of professional evaluation of complex systems. Following is a summary of eight main SAS drawbacks.

(I) Limited Number of Components for Evaluation

If the evaluation model includes n input attributes, then the average weight (as well as the average impact) of each component is $1/n$. For example, in the case of 100 attributes, the average importance of each attribute is only 1%. In such a case, even the most important components change the final score for only a few percent, and many components affect the final score for only a negligible fraction of percent. This yields insufficient sensitivity to many relevant features and practically limits the number of components that can be evaluated.

A very convincing example of this drawback can be found in [GIL76] (MECCA method, same as Weighted Ranking by Levels [SCH69, SCH70]). In his model of IBM VM/CMS-TSO evaluation (actual MECCA evaluation of IBM VM/CMS and TSO software from a Danish user), Gilb suggests the following five-level decomposition path from the item called "Test Aids" to the leaf "Task Scheduling" (weights are expressed as percentages):

> 1. Test Aids [50%]
>> 11. Applications Development [50%]
>>> 115. OS Compatibility [15%]
>>>> 1152. Limitations of it [30%]
>>>>> 11523. Task Scheduling [10%]

Therefore, the weight of the leaf #11523 (Task Scheduling) is $0.5 \times 0.5 \times 0.15 \times 0.3 \times 0.1 = 0.001125$ (i.e., 0.1125%). This result should normally trigger several self-evident questions:

1) Why should we consider an insignificant component that causes an overall effect that is less than or equal to only 0.1125%?
2) How can we justify the cost of evaluating components that are insignificant and therefore easily negligible?
3) Mathematical models should have a concordant (balanced) level of accuracy of inputs and parameters. In [GIL76], the weights predominantly change in steps of 5% to 10%, suggesting that this is the highest level of accuracy that the evaluator can provide. From that standpoint, it is not reasonable to make efforts that support precision at the level of 0.1125%. How can this obvious discrepancy be justified?

Unfortunately, neither the author nor the reviewers of [SCH69, SCH70, GIL76] asked and answered these questions and similar obvious questions presented below.

(II) Evaluation Effort Wasted

Professional evaluation of complex systems can be a significant and expensive effort. The total evaluation effort (and cost) depends primarily on the number of attributes and the complexity of attribute evaluation. Evaluation of attributes that have negligible effect on the final result can be considered a waste of resources.

The attribute evaluation effort is distributed in a range from low-effort to high-effort attributes. A typical example of a low-effort attribute (in the case of car evaluation) is the power of engine. It is a well-known quantitative attribute, and its scoring can be based on a simple scoring function (Fig. 1.1.2). For more complex attributes, such as attributes related to a complex computer operating system (OS), the attribute evaluation may need significant effort, for both the development of an attribute evaluation criterion and the attribute evaluation process. Qualitative indicators, such as the above example of "OS compatibility," require a careful expert study of the OS implementation and properties. Such indicators cannot be reliably scored without a detailed and time-consuming expert investigation of all aspects of the evaluated attribute.

Similarly, there are quantitative attributes that are in the high-effort category. For example, early computer benchmarking studies [SHA69, BEN75, CUR84, FER78a, FER78b, NBS77] report examples of very high cost of mainframe computer performance measurements. At the present time, the cost of benchmarking is significantly reduced; nevertheless, any nonstandard evaluation of a response time of a computer system usually requires a time-consuming and expensive development of a test workload, as well as a subtle measurement procedure. Similarly, in the evaluation of ecological systems, measurements of attributes frequently require time consuming field trips of expert personnel. Therefore, it is only reasonable to invest the evaluation effort and resources in evaluation of attributes that sufficiently contribute to the overall evaluation result. SAS models with low-impact attributes cannot give good reason for expensive evaluation procedures. Unfortunately, some attributes become insignificant by the additive nature of the SAS model, and not because of evaluator's decision about negligible importance. If low-impact attributes are not eliminated then the effort needed for evaluation of low-impact attributes becomes unjustified and wasted. Generally, it is not reasonable to feed expensive and highly precise inputs into a very imprecise decision model based on simplistic additive scoring. The sophistication of decision models must match the sophistication of selecting attributes and their measurement and evaluation.

(III) Impossibility to Model Mandatory Requirements

SAS models do not support mandatory requirements since the absence of a necessary feature cannot decrease the overall score for more than the relative weight of that feature. Indeed, if a system has the score $S_0 = W_1S_1 + \cdots + W_iS_i + \cdots + W_nS_n$, then the difference between the cases where $S_i = 1$ and $S_i = 0$ is only W_i (and this is typically a small value, on the average $1/n$). Unfortunately, we frequently have situations where the total absence of a vital feature cannot be compensated by other inputs (i.e., it must generate the zero overall score). For example, a computer system with insufficient memory or insufficient processor speed cannot satisfy the requirements of a demanding user regardless the quality of other components. In such cases, the mathematical model must provide a possibility to properly penalize (to the level of rejecting) all competitors with insufficient satisfaction of vital requirements. Mathematically speaking, the corresponding aggregation function must support the annihilator $0.$[3] Additive scoring models lack this very important feature that is easily observable and frequently present in intuitive evaluation. In the majority of serious applications, this drawback is sufficient to eliminate SAS as an acceptable mathematical model. By definition, *all SAS inputs are always optional*.

(IV) Impossibility to Model the Simultaneity of Requirements

SAS models cannot express graded simultaneity (the need for simultaneous satisfaction of several requirements using adjustable degree of simultaneity). The additivity assumes independence of attributes where a limited decrement $\Delta S_i \leq \Delta S_{ij}$ of score S_i can always be compensated by an appropriate increment (ΔS_j) of *any* other score S_j, as long as $W_i(S_i - \Delta S_i) + W_j(S_j + \Delta S_j) = W_iS_i + W_jS_j$ or $W_i\Delta S_i = W_j\Delta S_j$. Since $S_j + \Delta S_j \leq 1$ and $W_i\Delta S_{ij} = W_j\Delta S_j$, it follows that the maximum decrement of score S_i that can be compensated by score S_j is $\Delta S_{ij} = W_j(1 - S_j)/W_i$. Consequently, the additive scoring is a model that has significant (nonadjustable) compensative properties. SAS does not sufficiently support penalizing systems that lack simultaneity in satisfaction of crucial components. So, the additive scoring is inappropriate in all cases where the mathematical model must be able to provide an adjustable level of penalizing systems with insufficient simultaneity in satisfaction of important requirements. For example, in the case of computer evaluation, we *simultaneously* need both quality hardware and quality software. However, if we use the SAS model, the lack of a software component can be compensated by an unrelated hardware property, such as large disk capacity, and vice versa. Additive scoring does not provide an appropriate way to require simultaneous presence of necessary software and hardware features because the constant overall andness of arithmetic mean is only 50%.

---

3 A logic function $F(x_1, ..., x_n)$ has an annihilator a if the condition $x_i = a$, $i \in \{1,...,n\}$ causes $F(x_1,...,x_n) = a$. The most important annihilators are $a = 0$ and $a = 1$.

(V) Impossibility to Model Sufficient Conditions and Substitutability

Simultaneity and substitutability are symmetric (dual) properties and all SAS problems with mandatory requirements and simultaneity are mirrored as problems with sufficient requirements and substitutability. Indeed, SAS models cannot properly express substitutability: the absence of a feature always decreases the overall score and cannot be *fully compensated* by the availability of some other equivalent feature. For example, if i and j are indices representing two fully substitutable alternative ways to satisfy a specific requirement, then only one of them should be sufficient for the complete satisfaction of user's needs. However, the additive scoring expression $W_i S_i + W_j S_j$ assumes that both S_i and S_j are needed to achieve the maximum overall score. The level of replaceability must be adjustable, and this is not supported by the additive scoring models. The relationship $(x + y)/2 = [(x \wedge y) + (x \vee y)]/2$ indicates that the arithmetic mean is located halfway between conjunction and disjunction, i.e., it is equally unsuitable to model simultaneity and substitutability. Both the global andness and the global orness of the arithmetic mean are only 50%. Consequently, both the sufficient conditions and the graded substitutability cannot be modeled using SAS models.

(VI) Impossibility to Model Asymmetric Logic Relationships

Human evaluation reasoning very frequently includes asymmetric criteria where some attributes are mandatory and some are optional. For example, in the evaluation of suitability of the house location a homebuyer may decide that the proximity to work and the proximity to school for children are *mandatory requirements* and the proximity to post office and public swimming pool are desired but not mandatory (i.e., these are *optional requirements*). In this example, the unacceptable proximity to work or school should yield the zero overall score, while the unacceptable proximity to post office or swimming pool should yield a controlled decrease of the overall score, but not the zero overall score and the rejection of the evaluated house. Generally, mandatory attributes must support the annihilator 0 and optional attributes must not support the annihilator 0; this property cannot be achieved using SAS. SAS models use weights as the *only means* for differentiating the role of inputs. This is not sufficient for expressing asymmetric logic relationships, such as a combination of mandatory, desired, and optional features, or a combination of sufficient and optional conditions. SAS attributes can be more or less important, but they cannot be necessary or sufficient.

(VII) Inappropriate Optimum Systems

In many cases, a component score S_i is a limited linear function of component cost C_i:

$$S_i(C_i) = \min(1, a_i C_i) = \begin{cases} a_i C_i, & 0 \le C_i \le 1/a_i \\ 1, & C_i \ge 1/a_i \end{cases}, \quad a_i = const., \ 0 \le S_i \le 1.$$

A typical example of such a function is the capacity of computer memory: memory blocks have a constant price, and by adding more blocks, we can linearly increase both the total cost and the user satisfaction. Users regularly have limited needs, and when the need for memory is completely satisfied, further addition of memory has no effect. The corresponding overall score and the overall cost are:

$$S_0 = \sum_{i=1}^{n} W_i S_i(C_i) = \sum_{i=1}^{n} A_i C_i, \quad A_i = a_i W_i,$$

$$C_0 = \sum_{i=1}^{n} C_i, \quad 0 \le C_i \le 1/a_i.$$

Let us now determine the optimum configuration in the case where the available resources are limited to C. So, we have to distribute the total amount C in a way that maximizes the overall score:

$$S_0^{max} = \max_{C_1 + \ldots + C_n \le C} \sum_{i=1}^{n} A_i C_i.$$

The additive components can come in any order, and let us assume that the cost weights are sorted so that $A_1 \ge A_2 \ge \ldots \ge A_n$. The *optimum configuration* is one that achieves the maximum overall score for a constrained overall cost. It is based on the following resource allocation procedure: Buy the maximum quantity of components according to the decreasing cost weight order, and stop when the available resources are exhausted. In other words, the resulting *optimum strategy* is:

$$C_i = C_i^{max} = 1/a_i, \quad i = 1, 2, \ldots, k-1$$

$$C_k = C - \sum_{i=1}^{k-1} C_i, \quad 0 < C_k \le 1/a_k = C_k^{max}$$

$$C_i = 0, \quad i = k+1, \ldots, n$$

$$S_0^{max} = \sum_{i=1}^{k-1} A_i C_i^{max} + A_k C_k = \sum_{i=1}^{k-1} W_i + A_k C_k.$$

For example, let $S_0 = 0.4S_1 + 0.3S_2 + 0.2S_3 + 0.1S_4$, and $S_1 = C_1$, $(0 \le C_1 \le 1)$, $S_2 = 2C_2$, $(0 \le C_2 \le 0.5)$, $S_3 = 4C_3$, $(0 \le C_3 \le 0.25)$, $S_4 = 5C_4$, $(0 \le C_4 \le 0.2)$. Consequently, $S_0 = 0.8C_3 + 0.6C_2 + 0.5C_4 + 0.4C_1$ and $0 \le C \le 1.95$. If the available resources are $C = 0.9$, then the optimum solution is $C_3 = 0.25, C_2 = 0.5$, $C_4 = 0.15$, $C_1 = 0$, $S_0^{max} = 0.575$. So, the first component (which is both the most important and the most expensive) will be missing (because its inclusion would decrease the value of S_0^{max}), regardless of the clear indication that this component might be vital for the proper functioning of the analyzed system.

The resulting policy is an extreme "first things first" approach: Allocate funding to achieve the maximum satisfaction of the highest cost weight requirement, then the maximum satisfaction of all requirements in the decreasing cost weight order. When the resources are exhausted, select zero satisfaction of all remaining requirements regardless of their importance. Obviously, such "optimum systems" can easily miss some vital system components (e.g., an optimum computer configuration might have the fastest processor, the largest monitor, and the maximum disk capacity, but no memory and no data communication units). Because of the linear character of the SAS model, the resulting optimum configuration is obviously wrong, and is sufficient to disqualify the SAS method.

(VIII) Preferential Independence is Rarely Present

The underlying assumption of SAS models is the preferential independence [KEE76, OLS96, YOO95]. There are various definitions of preferential independence [KEE76, BEL02]. The simplest informal definition is that the contribution of an individual input to the overall score is independent of other input values [YOO95]. In other words, in the case of preferential independence, $\partial S_0/\partial S_i$ is not a function of S_j, $j \neq i$, and for additive models $\partial S_0/\partial S_i = const$. Three simple examples where the preferential independence does not hold are shown in Table 1.3.1.

In the first case, the patient disability is a function of motor symptoms (e.g., inability to walk, or difficulties in using hands) and of sensory symptoms (e.g., pain). Obviously, a patient is disabled if either motor or sensory problems are present (disjunctive criterion). The effect of motor symptoms on disability is different when the pain is present and when the pain is absent. When the motor symptoms are present, the disability is already there and the pain contributes to the overall degree of disability less than in cases where the pain affects the disability alone.

In the second case, we have a conjunctive criterion where the evaluator wants simultaneously the powerful engine, good comfort, safety, and appearance. If the comfort, safety, and appearance are low, then the overall score will be low and the effect of the power of engine might be negligible. If the comfort, safety, and appearance are high, then the engine power is a bottleneck that

Table 1.3.1 Sample cases where preferential independence does not hold.

Evaluated system	Input 1	Input 2	Input 3	Input 4
Patient disability	Motor symptoms	Sensory symptoms		
Car	Power of engine	Comfort	Safety	Appearance
Home	Home location	Home quality		

has a decisive impact on the overall score. Similarly, if a home location is unacceptable, the home quality has a lower effect on the homebuyer's satisfaction than in cases of good locations. Therefore, in both conjunctive and disjunctive cases, there is no preferential independence that would warrant the use of additive scoring.

Another aspect of preferential independence is defined as the tradeoff (the substitution rate) of S_i and S_j, $j \neq i$ that is independent of all other scores S_k, $k \neq i$, $k \neq j$ [KEE76]. In the above car evaluation example, the high engine power of a sports car could partially compensate deficiencies in comfort, provided that safety and appearance are good. That might be impossible in cases of poor safety and appearance that already disqualify the car.

Human evaluation reasoning frequently includes conjunctive and disjunctive criteria that request simultaneity or substitutability of inputs. In all such cases, there is no preferential independence and the additive scoring in not appropriate. Consequently, SAS is a verification that everything should be as simple as possible, but not simpler. Simplicity (as the only reason and sufficient justification for SAS as a preferred method for solving delicate evaluation problems in social sciences) is clearly and explicitly visible in [EDW82, p. 74]: "Although the literature describes very complicated aggregation rules, we use only one because it is by far the simplest. The equation takes the following form: $U_j = \sum_{i=1}^{n} w_i u_{ij}$ ...." This method (called *multiattribute utility technology*) is introduced in [EDW82] by the series co-editor as "an appropriate way to go about a rigorous, quantitative assessment of social programs." Without apology, let us say that these statements are similar and equally unacceptable as the following one: "In mathematics, there are many different curves, but we use only the straight line because it is by far the simplest."

Oversimplified SAS models are frequent in GIS literature and justified by the fact that they are "easy-to-understand and intuitively appealing to decision-makers" [MAL06]. For example, urban development is not possible on excessive slopes of terrain. However, SAS models show positive suitability for building homes even on vertical slopes provided such locations satisfy some other requirements (e.g., the proximity to roads), what is meaningless. Chapter 4.6 and [DRA17] show examples of easily visible errors in SAS-generated suitability maps.

Our analysis convincingly disqualifies SAS in all applications where evaluation models must be compatible with human reasoning and decision making. Human mind is not a simple linear machine, and the unsuitability of SAS models is easily visible and provable. Consequently, it is necessary to explain where the high popularity of SAS comes from.

The grossly exaggerated popularity of SAS can be explained in three ways. First, it is in human nature to try to simplify problems, and oversimplification is just one little additional step in this attractive direction. Second, the majority of high-level corporate, public, military, social, and political decisions are done by people for whom, by the generalist nature of their job, everything beyond addition is simply "too mathematical." Third, there are cases where SAS is an appropriate evaluation technique (as in the case of using GPA for ranking of students), and such cases are then unjustifiably generalized.

1.3.2 Simple Multiplicative Scoring

The SMS model is a weighted geometric mean:

$$S_0 = \prod_{i=1}^{n} S_i^{W_i}, \quad W_1 + \cdots + W_n = 1, \quad W_i > 0, \quad i = 1,\ldots,n.$$

The multiplicative nature of this scoring model causes high importance of low input scores. Even one low input score can significantly reduce the value of the overall score S_0.

The following drawbacks of the multiplicative model are similar to the drawbacks of the additive model, and we are going to list them without detailed exemplifications.

(I) Impossibility to Model Requirements for Nonmandatory (Optional) Inputs

SAS models do not support mandatory inputs, and SMS models do not support optional inputs. If a system has the overall score $S_0 = S_1^{W_1} \cdots S_n^{W_n}$ then we have $S_0 = 0$ in all cases where $S_i = 0$, $i \in \{1,\ldots,n\}$. In other words, *all inputs are always mandatory*. Since there are no nonmandatory/optional inputs, if the most insignificant attribute of an evaluated system is not satisfied, such a system must be rejected. Obviously, this is an extreme requirement that is generally not acceptable.

(II) The Contradiction of Insignificant but Mandatory Inputs

Similar to additive models, if the number of inputs n increases then the weights must decrease, making some inputs completely insignificant. Unfortunately, due to the multiplicative nature of the model all inputs are mandatory. That creates inconsistent and contradictory conditions: The fact that each input is mandatory implies the significance of all inputs, while unavoidable low weights of some inputs imply their insignificance. Generally, there is no way to properly balance these inconsistent and contradictory standpoints. In Chapter 2.2, we show that the consequence of this contradiction is hypersensitivity, i.e., mathematical models where negligible increments of insignificant input attributes produce huge increments of the overall score (a property that is not observable in human evaluation reasoning).

(III) Incompleteness of Evaluation Models

The only way to use SMS models is to omit *all* nonmandatory requirements. Consequently, SMS models are incomplete because they include only the "tip of the iceberg," i.e., essential mandatory requirements—and omit all other contributing components that are classified as optional but not insignificant.

(IV) Impossibility to Adjust the Degree of Simultaneity of Requirements

SMS models significantly penalize systems that have any poor components. However, SMS models use a fixed level of hard simultaneity (as shown in *Part Two*, the global andness of geometric mean is relatively low, approximately 67%). SMS models cannot express frequently needed levels of simultaneity that are either greater than, or less than the simultaneity implemented by the geometric mean. In particular, the soft simultaneity that does not support annihilator 0 cannot be modeled using SMS.

(V) Impossibility to Model Adjustable Substitutability and Sufficient Conditions

Neither adjustable substitutability nor sufficient conditions can be expressed by the SMS models. The geometric mean is conjunctively polarized and cannot model any significant level of disjunctive polarization. It is important to note that this drawback is more exposed and critical for SMS then for SAS, because the SMS andness of 67% is further from the andness range for substitutability $[0, 50\%[$ than the fixed SAS andness of 50%. While SMS cannot directly model substitutability, the De Morgan dual of SMS can be used as a model of fixed hard substitutability (however, no soft substitutability and no adjustable orness).

(VI) Impossibility to Model Asymmetric Logic Relationships

SMS models are not able to express asymmetric logic relationships, such as a combination of mandatory, desired, and optional features, or a combination of sufficient and optional conditions.

(VII) Inappropriate Optimum Systems

The optimum systems in the case of SMS models require that for any available financial resources we must invest in each and every system component, including those that are the least significant. This is generally not realistic, particularly in cases where the resources are seriously limited.

(VIII) Inability to Model Preferential Independence

In all cases where the criterion is neither conjunctive nor disjunctive (like in the case of student GPA), we have justified cases of preferential independence and the need to use additive models. SMS cannot be used in such cases.

The SMS model can be valuable in the area of evaluation if it is used to define the average suitability ratio of two systems, A and B [BRI22, TRI00, YOO95]. If S_{Ai} and S_{Bi}, $i = 1,...,n$ denote attribute scores, or attribute values, and if both scores and values are defined so that higher value denotes better system, then the ratio S_{Ai}/S_{Bi} denotes how much system A outperforms system B in the case of input i. The average ratio of systems A and B is then defined as follows:

$$R_{AB} = \prod_{i=1}^{n} (S_{Ai}/S_{Bi})^{W_i}, \quad W_1 + \cdots + W_n = 1, \quad W_i > 0, \quad i = 1,\ldots,n.$$

If $R_{AB} > 1$, then R_{AB} denotes how much A is better than B. This model can be used in cases where there is no need for flexible adjustment of logic conditions.

1.3.3 Logic Unsuitability of Scoring and Utility Theory Models in Professional Evaluation

In professional evaluation, we use logic conditions to create quantitative evaluation criteria. These criteria are used to evaluate expected overall suitability of one or more competitive complex objects or alternatives and to select the best option. Evaluation and selection process is performed before the acquisition and use of the selected object. The goal of evaluation is to correctly predict satisfaction derived by stakeholder from using each of competitive objects.

The arithmetic mean is a frequent and useful component in almost all complex evaluation criteria. However, if it is used as the only component, then SAS takes the role of a general evaluation method [MIL66, MIL70, EDW82]. This is where SAS, SMS, and utility theory models fail the test of compatibility with properties of human reasoning and consequently fail to satisfy the requirements that we consider fundamental for professional evaluation.

Fixed andness decision models (SAS, SMS, and others) have very strong presence in the utility theory, which is primarily used in economics, management sciences, and related disciplines [FIS70, KEE76, KEE92, YOO95, OLS96, MOL97, KIR97, BOU00, TRI00, BEL02, KAH08, TZE11, ISH13, HEN15]. Some of listed references provide critical remarks about simple scoring but never move very far in that direction. Both additive aggregation and fixed multiplicative aggregation may occur in the context of certainty or uncertainty, crisp or fuzzy scoring, but in all cases, there is no support for flexible logic conditions. These references report many cases of the use of additive models in the area of sensitive professional evaluation. For example, those include the location or airports, selection of nuclear dump sites, and prioritizing factory automation investments [KEE76, OLS96]. According to [KOC14], the Ministry of Science and Higher Education of Poland currently uses SAS to combine four criteria (scientific and/or creative achievements, scientific potentiality, tangible benefits, and intangible benefits of the scientific activity) for evaluation of research entities in Poland.

The absence of logic conditions is particularly surprising in utility theory because utility is supposedly a psychological phenomenon where the goal is to determine the satisfying power of goods or services, and utility theory was developed "to explain human behavior in decision making" [OLS96]. This definition should yield interest in logic properties of human decision making and not in focusing on preferential independence and belief that the utility of a whole can be expressed as the sum of utilities of its parts. The use of simple additive or multiplicative models is typically justified in a scientific way by an axiomatic approach [FIS70], or in a naïve way by the attractiveness of simplicity [EDW82]. Some authors in the utility area noted that assumptions of axiomatic utility theory may not be acceptable in all cases, but the criticism of most authors rarely goes beyond that benevolent note.

To make this situation more delicate, the utility theory suffers from conflicting standpoints of cardinalists and ordinalists [OLS96, HEN15]. The classic cardinal utility theory is based on the assumption that the degree of satisfaction by goods and services is measurable and can be expressed numerically using the elusive units called *utils*. On the other hand, the ordinal utility theory believes that humans can do pairwise comparisons and produce rankings but cannot express degrees of satisfaction in absolute numerical terms [HEN15]. The strange conclusion of economists is that these two approaches are conflicting and mutually exclusive, while complex evaluation studies frequently show that cardinal and ordinal approach are complementary, cooperative, and can be simultaneously used. For example, whoever evaluates and compares mainframe computers or advanced servers knows that memory and disk storage can be easily evaluated in cardinal terms, while poorly predictable timing of some benchmark programs can be efficiently evaluated in ordinal terms; subsequently, cardinal and ordinal criteria are logically combined to yield the overall suitability of evaluated systems. In addition, practical evaluation studies show that whenever an expert provides ranking, i.e., expresses the percept that A is better or more preferred to B, the same expert is always capable of answering the natural subsequent question, to quantify to what extent is A better than B using any form of verbal or numerical rating scale.

We reject the strict ordinal approach where each pairwise comparison generates only 1 bit of information because we know that all domain experts have percepts that in pairwise comparisons can produce more than 1 bit of information. In most cases, if a decision maker cannot provide more than 1 bit in pairwise comparisons, such a decision maker does not qualify to be a domain expert and should not be given opportunities to provide pairwise comparisons.

Rigid strictly additive or equally rigid strictly multiplicative decision models, either crisp or fuzzy, either under certainty or under uncertainty, always automatically deny and reject the use of logic. This is not acceptable. Both strictly additive and strictly multiplicative models prevent the use of any form of adjustable simultaneity and substitutability in decision criteria, i.e., prevent the use of logic in decision models. Human evaluation reasoning provably requires a flexible adjustment of the degree of andness/orness in logic aggregation structures of complex criterion functions. Thus, all aggregators that use *fixed andness/orness* cannot be acceptable general models of human evaluation reasoning. These include all fixed means, SAS, SMS, additive and multiplicative utility models, and various fixed nonlinear preference and value models.

Generally, all mathematical models for professional evaluation of expected suitability of complex alternatives must be able to provide an adjustable level of penalizing systems with poor performance of any vital system component. Similarly, they must also be able to model alternative (substitutable) components and provide an adjustable level of rewarding systems that have a sufficiently high quality of any of alternative components. In addition, system evaluation models must be able to model asymmetric and compound logic relationships. SAS, SMS, cardinal, and ordinal utility models cannot satisfy these requirements. In a general case, simple scoring and utility methods are not able to model many observable and essential properties of human evaluation reasoning. In the majority of cases where SAS or SMS models are applied for solving professional evaluation and ranking problems, it is reasonable to suspect that the mathematical model is an oversimplification and that the results are questionable.

If SAS and SMS are applied for modeling the percepts of value resulting from human reasoning, then it is very naïve to expect that the subtleties of human reasoning and decision making could be reduced to simple weighted addition or equally simple weighted multiplication. This is an obvious case where we must distrust simplicity. For SAS all inputs are always optional, and for SMS all inputs are always mandatory. It is not that way in human reasoning. For both SAS, SMS, and utility models, the andness is not adjustable. Andness is definitely not constant in human reasoning. Indeed, SAS and SMS are models of only *two simple special cases* among many observable forms of human logic reasoning. Such special cases are useful as components of complex criteria, but they obviously cannot substitute a necessary general methodology that has expressive power to model a complete spectrum of observable forms of human evaluation reasoning. Elimination of drawbacks of fixed andness models is the primary motivation for development of graded evaluation logic and the LSP method presented in this book.

1.4 Introduction to Professional Quantitative Evaluation

This chapter contains an introductory survey of the area of professional quantitative evaluation based on the soft computing evaluation logic and the LSP decision method. Our motivation for development of the LSP method has three components: (1) the frequency and importance of complex evaluation problems in various application areas, (2) the disappointment with obvious shortcomings of simple scoring methods, and (3) the need to provide professional evaluation methodology that is consistent with observable logic properties of human intuitive evaluation reasoning. These objectives are the point of departure for the development of LSP method for modeling human evaluation reasoning and for building professional evaluation models.

At the point of departure, rational travelers first look at the road ahead and identify all activities that are necessary to reach the final destination. In our case, the final destination is the ability to solve evaluation decision problems with techniques and tools that have industrial strength and applicability. In this survey, we first define the fundamental types of evaluation problems. Then, we survey the areas of application of evaluation methods and itemize typical professional evaluation problems. Finally, we provide a short survey of main components of professional evaluation techniques. Our goal is to introduce the most important topics that we cover in subsequent parts of this book.

1.4.1 Five Fundamental Types of Professional Evaluation Problems

Evaluation problems are encountered in many areas including business, environmental and public decision making, computer hardware and software systems, Internet applications, engineering, military applications, medical applications, and personal decision making. However, all evaluation problems are not the same. We use *evaluation problems* as a generic name for the following

Soft Computing Evaluation Logic: The LSP Decision Method and Its Applications, First Edition. Jozo Dujmović.
© 2018 John Wiley & Sons, Inc. Published 2018 by John Wiley & Sons, Inc.
Companion website: www.wiley.com/go/Dujmovic/Soft_Computing_Evaluation_Logic

five characteristic types of professional decision problems: evaluation, comparison, reliability analysis, selection, and optimization of complex objects and systems. In most cases we assume one or more evaluated objects that have many interacting components and can be identified as complex systems. The corresponding evaluation problems can be summarized as follows:

1) *Evaluation*: This is the classic problem of determining the degree of satisfaction of specific stakeholder's requirements. We assume that evaluation is a process that can be done with a single system (a single evaluated object). For example, if stakeholders are software developers, then a software development company may decide to evaluate a selected integrated software development environment (IDE) with respect to a list of specific requirements that define the needs of software engineer in the case of software development using a specific programming language. In such a case, the evaluated IDE might be accepted only if it satisfies a specific degree (e.g., 80%) of user requirements, and has a satisfactory price. Of course, system evaluation can be applied to any number of systems in order to compare them and select the best alternative.

2) *Comparison*: In this case, we have two or more systems that must be compared and ranked according to the level of satisfying specific requirements. Generally, we assume that the comparison is based on the results of individual evaluation of competitive systems, where the best alternative is the system that provides the highest satisfaction of user requirements. The comparison sometimes includes the relative comparison of competitive systems based on the pairwise comparison of their attributes. In such cases, all systems in a group are compared relative to the system that has the best value of selected attribute (e.g., comparing the speed of several computers with the speed of the fastest computer in the group). Results of relative comparison of selected attributes can be aggregated with the results of absolute evaluation of other attributes to generate the overall ranking of competitive systems. It is important to emphasize that in the majority of cases stakeholders are primarily interested to know the overall degree of suitability of each competitive system. The relative ranking of competitors without knowledge of their individual (absolute) quality is not acceptable for the majority of stakeholders. For example, a pairwise comparison of 12,000-pound Class 3 city delivery trucks can show that truck T is significantly better than truck R, but both of them can be worthless if a company needs a 19,000-pound Class 5 city delivery truck. Similarly, a student who has GPA = 2.8 might be presented as "two times better" than a student who has GPA = 1.4, but neither of them qualifies for a graduate program that requires GPA ≥ 3.5. The relative comparison methods identify the best object in a specific group of objects, but such results are irrelevant in most evaluation studies. To be the best in a given group of competitors does not automatically mean to be good enough.

3) *Reliability analysis*: System comparison regularly needs a reliability analysis to determine the confidence level for the claim that system A outperforms system B. The difference between A and B may be caused by both the difference in performance and by errors in selecting parameters of evaluation models. The confidence level reflects the likelihood that errors in evaluator's selection of parameters do not affect the resulting system comparison and ranking of the given set of competitive systems. For example, in an extreme case where system A outperforms system B in all attributes, the ranking $A \succ B$ is 100% reliable and completely insensitive to parameters of the evaluation model. However, if in a part of attributes system A outperforms system B, and in the remaining attributes system B outperforms system A, it is possible to get the ranking $A \succ B$ or the reverse ranking $B \succ A$, depending on weights and other parameters that can be selected in an imprecise way. In such cases, we need a reliability analysis to find the likelihood that the ranking $A \succ B$ is correct and not sensitive to the degree of possible errors in the evaluation model.

4) *Selection*: This is the traditional problem of acquisition of a single, most convenient, system in a group of competitive systems. System selection is regularly based on the overall value obtained by the simultaneous analysis of the total cost and the overall level of satisfaction of requirements. The overall value of the selected best system is an indicator that predicts the expected overall capability of the selected system to attain the stakeholder's goals. Only one system will be selected, purchased, installed, and used. So, the evaluation is here an instrument of forecasting, because the other competitors will not have a chance to satisfy stakeholder's needs, and there will be no possibility to experimentally verify the validity of evaluation and selection results. This is the reason for differentiating system comparison and system selection. In the case of comparison, the result of evaluation is the ranking of all competitors; in the case of selection, the goal of evaluation is to predict the overall satisfaction with the final winner. System comparison needs two or more competitors, and system selection is possible even in the case of a single system.

5) *Optimization*: This is the problem of finding the best configuration of an evaluated system. For example, in a toy problem case of a personal computer that can have three different sizes of memory, two possible processor clock rates, four different disk sizes, two different graphic controllers, and three different screen sizes, we can create $3 \times 2 \times 4 \times 2 \times 3 = 144$ different computer configurations, where each of them has a different pair of the overall suitability and cost. Our problem is to find the best configuration for a specific stakeholder. There are three versions of this problem:

   a) ***Best performance:*** The input parameter of this problem is the maximum allowed/approved total cost of the evaluated system, C_{max}. The optimization problem is to find the best configuration of the analyzed system so that it attains the maximum satisfaction of requirements (the highest overall suitability score) for the total cost that is less than or equal to C_{max}.

b) ***Best cost:*** The input parameter of this problem is the minimum necessary (acceptable) level of satisfaction of stakeholder's requirements, X_{min} (typical minimum acceptable levels of satisfaction of justifiable requirements depend on stakeholder and usually are 75% or more). The optimization problem is to find the best configuration of the analyzed system so that it attains the satisfaction of requirements that is greater than or equal to X_{min} for the minimum value of the overall system cost.

c) ***Best value:*** The overall value V is defined as a combination of the overall suitability (preference) X and the total cost, C (e.g., in the simplest case, $V = X/C$). The optimization problem consists of analyzing all possible configurations of an analyzed system and finding the configuration that has the maximum value of V.

The described types of evaluation problems have three common properties. First, all of them use a sophisticated criterion function that computes the overall suitability from the values of n input suitability attributes, where n is frequently a large value. Second, most evaluation problems need a cost analysis to compute the total cost. Third, except in insignificant toy problem cases, evaluation problems cannot be solved intuitively, but require quantitative methodology suitable for industrial applications.

1.4.2 A Survey of Typical Professional Evaluation Problems

On the one hand, in some areas professional evaluation and selection methods have a long history. For example, computer evaluation, comparison, and selection problems are as old as the computer systems, and many early evaluation techniques were developed specifically for computer selection [JOS64, JOS68, DUJ69, SCH69, HIL69, SCH70, T1M73, DUJ73c, GIL76, DUJ77b, KLE78, MCQ78, and KLE80]. Problems of location of public objects, procurement of military systems, comparison of industrial products, selection of personnel, and so on also have a long history. On the other hand, new organizational forms and new forms of interaction between corporations, government, and public sector create new evaluation problems. Examples of such problems are the evaluation of corporate social responsibility, evaluation of corporate environmental performance, and general sustainability evaluation and reporting [GRI06].

Professional system evaluation problems can be found in a variety of areas. Following are some major application areas and itemized professional system evaluation, selection, and optimization problems.

Business

- B2B selection of manufacturing components (supply chain management)
- B2C product evaluation and comparison
- Full eRFP and eProcurement decision support
- Evaluation and ranking of objects in real estate
- Comparison and classification of professionals (HR)
- Employee/company matching problem (HR)
- Evaluation of news organization websites
- Evaluation of e-commerce websites
- Evaluation and comparison of corporate development plans
- Evaluation of corporate procurement and acquisition plans
- Standardization of corporate procurement and acquisition procedures
- Optimum location of development and manufacturing facilities
- Optimum location of sales facilities (e.g., pharmacies, food stores, malls)
- Optimum location of services (e.g., post offices, medical offices)
- Evaluation of corporate websites, web services, and intranets
- Comparison and selection of office software suites
- Comparison and selection of business software systems
- Comparison and selection of enterprise messaging and email systems
- Evaluation of corporate social responsibility
- Evaluation of corporate economic performance
- Evaluation of corporate environmental performance
- Sustainability evaluation and reporting
- Evaluation of safety of corporate computing environments

Computer Systems

- Computer system evaluation, comparison, and selection
- Evaluation and selection of corporate IT solutions
- Comparison and selection of complex application software
- Optimization of computer configurations
- Evaluation and comparison of network security
- Evaluation and comparison of cloud computing
- Global evaluation and comparison of computer networks
- Comparison of operating systems
- Comparison and selection of programming languages
- Comparison and selection of language processors (compilers, interpreters)
- Comparison and selection of database systems
- Comparison of windowed environments
- Comparison and selection of user interfaces
- Evaluation and comparison of integrated software development environments
- Modeling and evaluation of software quality based on ISO standards

Internet

- Evaluation and comparison of browsers
- Comparison of search engines
- Design of information retrieval criteria for flexible query answering systems
- Evaluation and comparison of security systems
- Evaluation and comparison of educational and university websites
- Evaluation and comparison of web sites of cultural, recreational, and sports organizations (museums, orchestras, theaters, sport clubs, parks, etc.)
- Evaluation of federal government websites (INS, IRS, NSF, NIST, national parks, etc.)
- Evaluation of state government websites
- Evaluation of city government websites
- Evaluation of medical websites
- Evaluation of news organization websites
- Comparison of Internet service providers
- Evaluation and comparison of social networks

Environmental and Public (Governmental) Decision Making

- Evaluation of quality of life in urban areas
- Evaluation problems in the context of smart cities
- Evaluation of walkability in urban areas
- Evaluation of suitability of urban areas for seniors
- Evaluation of suitability of urban areas for young families and children
- Evaluation of habitats for endangered species (including land, lakes, and sea)
- Ecologic evaluation of sea regions and fisheries
- Evaluation and comparison of tenders for governmental projects
- Ranking of countries according to the level of economic development
- Ranking of counties and municipalities according to the urbanistic and/or economic criteria
- Optimum location of public objects and services:
    - airports
    - pipelines, power plants, nuclear power plants, and nuclear dump sites
    - schools and universities
    - hospitals
    - theaters
    - museums
    - sport stadiums
    - recreation areas/facilities
    - shopping centers
    - post offices
    - pharmacies
    - restaurants

- city halls
- cemeteries
- churches
- Comparison of alternative urban/environmental development plans
- Evaluation of space management plans
- Evaluation and comparison of the quality of construction terrains for urbanization
- Evaluation of geographic locations from the standpoint of their intended use
- Evaluation of quality of life in urban areas
- Suitability evaluation based on suitability maps and/or equivalent online services
  - suitability maps for urban expansion and residential development
  - suitability maps for industrial development
  - suitability maps for commercial development
  - suitability for growing specific plants (agriculture)
  - suitability for sustainable farmland land use
  - suitability for sustainable forestland land use
  - suitability for natural areas land use
  - suitability for development of military objects
  - suitability maps for public safety and other law enforcement applications
- Risk and security evaluation for a wide spectrum of hazards
  - risk maps of risk from disease outbreak (e.g., malaria)
  - risk maps of risk from flooding
  - risk-related decision problems
  - security maps (antonym to hazard maps)
  - pollution analysis maps
- Comparison of alternative public policies (development, conservation, etc.)
- Evaluation and comparison of public agencies
- Quantitative assessment of social programs
- Distribution of public funds according to quantitative evaluation of needs

Engineering

- Product evaluation, comparison, and pricing
- Product optimization
- Technology evaluation, comparison, and selection
- Comparison and selection of manufacturing strategies
- System evaluation in mechanical, civil, and chemical engineering
- Evaluation and comparison of tenders for energetic objects
- Evaluation and selection of outsourcing policies
- Evaluation of locations for manufacturing products
- Suitability maps for wind farm locations
- Suitability maps for solar energy production

Military Applications

- Procurement of military software systems
- Procurement of weapons and CCC systems
- Procurement of military equipment (aircraft, vehicles, ships, computers, etc.)
- Comparison of alternative strategic and tactics plans
- Comparison of sites/areas for military use
- Military suitability maps

Personal Decision Making

- Job selection
- Home selection
- Car selection
- Comparison and selection of consumer products
- Comparison and selection of schools/universities
- Comparison and selection of health services and health maintenance organizations
- Evaluation and comparison of insurance plans and organizations
- Evaluation and comparison of retirement plans
- Self-evaluation of medical conditions
- Medical evaluation of disease severity
- Evaluation of patient disability
- Computation of optimum time for starting risky therapies
- Evaluation of the quality of living in various cities or geographic areas
- Evaluation of the quality of selected urban locations
- Comparison and selection of vacation locations and plans
- Evaluation and comparison of restaurants and entertainment amenities
- Evaluation and comparison of political candidates and organizations
- Social matching problems and marriage matching problems

The presented list of evaluation problems includes problems of various type, frequency, effort, importance, and complexity. Such problems can be solved using the LSP evaluation method that is presented in subsequent parts of this book. In particular, a group of representative evaluation problems is analyzed in *Part Four* of this book.

1.4.3 Components of Methodology for Professional Quantitative Evaluation

Evaluation is a mental process. It is a process of reasoning, and consequently, it belongs to logic. Suppose that we have a mathematical model of the mental process of evaluation. Would it be acceptable to use mathematical models of quantitative evaluation that are inconsistent with the model of the mental process of evaluation? Of course, this is unacceptable, because the human mind easily recognizes results that are inconsistent with the way the human mind operates. Unfortunately, there are plenty of such models, starting with simple additive and multiplicative scoring. Actually, wrong are all evaluation models that don't have as a primary goal the consistency with human intuitive evaluation reasoning. Mathematical correctness of many aggregation models is insufficient to compensate for or eliminate the inconsistency with observable properties of human reasoning.

The credibility of the whole area of perceptual computing depends on consistency with observable properties of human reasoning. It is very easy to show that human mind uses adjustable degrees of simultaneity and substitutability (continuous transition from conjunction to disjunction), hard partial conjunction (simultaneity that supports mandatory requirements), soft partial conjunction (simultaneity that does not support mandatory requirements), hard partial disjunction (substitutability that supports sufficient requirements), soft partial disjunction (substitutability that does not support sufficient requirements), noncommutativity (different degrees of importance of value statements), conjunctive partial absorption (asymmetric simultaneity that combines mandatory and optional requirements), and disjunctive partial absorption (asymmetric substitutability that combines sufficient and optional requirements). Therefore, all aggregators that do not support these properties should be automatically disqualified as both models of evaluation reasoning and models used in professional evaluation.

Based on the necessary consistency between intuitive and quantitative evaluation models, in the first step of development of a professional evaluation method we must provide an appropriate mathematical background consistent with intuitive evaluation. Such an approach is shown in Fig. 1.4.1. We start that process by developing the Graded Conjunction/Disjunction as a fundamental logic aggregator that supports the observable soft, hard, commutative, noncommutative, symmetric, and asymmetric properties of evaluation reasoning. This aggregator is then used as a fundamental component for development of the soft computing evaluation logic, which is a graded generalization of the classic Boolean logic, suitable for modeling logic aggregation process that is visible in human evaluation reasoning.

Soft computing evaluation logic is then used as a main component in the development of flexible models of complex criteria that we encounter in human logic. Such criteria are the backbone of the LSP decision method, and it is necessary to make efforts to secure their credibility. Two auxiliary techniques that are used in the process of quality assurance of LSP criteria are the sensitivity analysis and the tradeoff analysis (Fig. 1.4.1). The sensitivity analysis is a process of analysis of the variability of output values caused by changes of inputs or parameters of a criterion model. Evaluators and stakeholders have perceptions

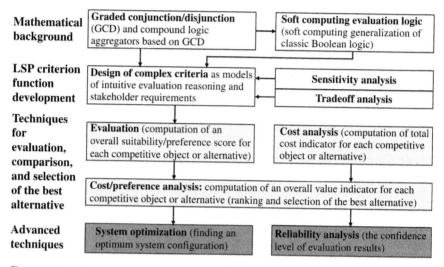

Figure 1.4.1 Main components of professional quantitative evaluation.

of expected variability of outputs. A good match between model behavior and evaluator's expectations contributes to the credibility of criterion.

Tradeoff analysis is another technique similar to the sensitivity analysis that is also used for quality assurance of LSP criteria. The goal of tradeoff analysis is to investigate compensative properties of criterion functions. In many cases, a deficiency of specific input can be compensated by a corresponding excess of another input, so that the output suitability remains unchanged. If the deficiency/excess ratio sufficiently matches evaluator's expectations, that can be used as an indicator of the validity of the criterion function and the credibility of evaluation results.

The central components of professional quantitative evaluation are techniques for evaluation, comparison and selection of the best alternative (i.e., selection of the most suitable among evaluated objects). All LSP criteria are based on a standard model of evaluation reasoning (introduced in Chapter 2.2). That model includes an attribute tree, a set of attribute criteria, and a logic aggregation structure based on the soft computing evaluation logic. In all cases where the evaluated objects have cost, we also perform a cost analysis and a cost/preference analysis to select the object that offers the best combination of suitability and affordability.

In some cases, the professional evaluation may include two advanced techniques: optimization, and the tradeoff analysis. Optimization methods can be used only in cases where evaluated objects have adjustable configuration with components that have individual cost. For example, web browsers or search engines are complex objects that can be evaluated, but they have no cost and no adjustable components; consequently, they cannot be optimized. As opposed to that, computer systems have hardware and software components that have adjustable individual cost and performance, and consequently can be optimized.

Reliability analysis is used in situations where we have a justified doubt that possible errors in selecting parameters of an LSP criterion could yield a reversed ranking of competitors. That analysis provides a quantitative degree of confidence in the final results of an evaluation study. Such analysis is useful because small differences between competitors are not automatically an indicator of low reliability and low confidence in such results. Similarly, larger differences are not sufficient to warrant high reliability and high confidence. As we show in *Part Three*, the degree of reliability depends on the internal structure of the LSP criteria and the distribution of attribute values of competitive objects. Thus, the reliability analysis is a quality assurance technique that can contribute to all professional evaluation projects.

Similar to other decision support methods, the professional LSP evaluation techniques require appropriate software support. We differentiate the *LSP core technology* (LSP evaluation engines and support for a database of current and previous evaluation projects), and *LSP tools* (criteria development tools, result presentation tools, sensitivity analyzers, and advanced optimization and reliability analysis tools). Some evaluation computations can be numerically sensitive, but in most cases the LSP decision support software needs relatively modest computing resources.

All techniques presented in Fig. 1.4.1 are extensively studied in separate chapters of this book. Readers who are interested only in applications might first browse applications presented in *Part Four*. *Part Two* includes the presentation of logic aggregators and soft computing evaluation logic. We focus on soft computing with partial truth and graded logic functions. This area is indispensable for all decision engineers, as well as for those who are particularly interested in theory. The LSP method is described in *Part Three* with visible intention to provide a rather self-contained presentation. Consequently, some readers may proceed to *Part Three* and then, when needed, refer to mathematical details presented in *Part Two*.

PART TWO

GRADED LOGIC AND AGGREGATION

> *How do human beings aggregate subjective categories, and which*
> *mathematical models describe this procedure adequately?*
> —H.-J. Zimmermann (question from the last chapter
> of his book Fuzzy Set Theory— and Its Applications)

In *Part Two* of the book, we study graded evaluation logic and develop logic aggregators using a strictly anthropocentric approach. We try to answer the fundamental question, "How do human beings aggregate subjective categories, and which mathematical models describe this procedure adequately?" [ZIM96]. We investigate this problem in the context of evaluation reasoning. We also believe that all books about logic and/or decision making should ask this fundamental question explicitly and as early as possible (well, not in the last chapter). In our case, the appropriate place for this question is right here. Then, in Section 2.1.8, we offer an explicit answer to this question.

In the area of aggregation, as the point of departure, it is necessary to differentiate two categories of aggregation problems:

1) Mathematical problems of aggregation of anonymous real numbers.
2) Decision engineering problems of aggregation of arguments that have specific semantic identity.

In the case of aggregation of anonymous real numbers, the goal is to study the widest possible class of aggregation functions. In the case of aggregation of arguments that have semantic identity (i.e. the role, meaning, units of measurement, and impact on attaining specific stakeholder's goals) it is necessary to create

Soft Computing Evaluation Logic: The LSP Decision Method and Its Applications,
First Edition. Jozo Dujmović.
© 2018 John Wiley & Sons, Inc. Published 2018 by John Wiley & Sons, Inc.
Companion website: www.wiley.com/go/Dujmovic/Soft_Computing_Evaluation_Logic

aggregators that provide appropriate support to the semantic identity of arguments. Following are three most important types of semantic identity:

- Degree of truth of a value statement (a statement that claims the complete satisfaction of justifiable requirements of a specific stakeholder).
- Degree of fuzzy membership (the membership in a fuzzy set of objects that have specific, precisely defined properties, relevant for a given stakeholder).
- Probability (the likelihood of occurrence of a precisely defined event, relevant for specific stakeholder).

Each type of semantic identity affects the necessary properties of basic aggregation operators, and the process of development of compound aggregation structures.

The evaluation methodology, its theoretical background, and all applications presented in this book are based on the following principles of anthropocentric logic aggregation:

1) Logic is a key component of human reasoning. Therefore, logic should be based on observable properties of human reasoning, and it should serve for quantitative modeling of human reasoning.
2) Decisions are the results of human mental activities. Consequently, trustworthy decision models cannot be developed without relating them explicitly to observable patterns of human reasoning.
3) The concepts of suitability, preference, value, importance, simultaneity and substitutability are human percepts. These percepts are primarily used in evaluation decision making.
4) Generally, all human percepts used in evaluation are graded: they have intensity (or degree) that varies in the range from the lowest (quantified as 0) to the highest (quantified as 1).
5) A stakeholder is defined as a decision maker (a single person, or a group, or an organization) who is interested in the ownership and/or use of a specific object. By definition, the stakeholder is capable and authorized to specify goals and requirements that are expected to be satisfied by *one or more* evaluated objects/alternatives.
6) The assertion that an object or alternative *completely satisfies* selected stakeholder's requirements is called the *value statement*. The degree of truth of a value statement is a human percept that reflects the degree of similarity between the statement and the objective reality. The degree of truth of a value statement can be quantified as a score that is used as an indicator of *suitability* or *preference*.
7) Evaluation is a process of creating the percept of overall suitability/preference of an evaluated object. Evaluation must take into account all relevant suitability attributes (i.e., only those attributes that provably affect the suitability of an evaluated object/alternative; various attributes that don't affect

the overall suitability, are irrelevant and should be neglected in the process of evaluation).

8) Evaluation can be intuitive (based on intuitive aggregation of attribute degrees of suitability) or quantitative (based on a mathematical model of the overall degree of satisfaction of stakeholder's requirements). The result of evaluation creates an intuitive percept (or a quantitative indicator) of the overall suitability, preference, or value of each alternative.

9) The partial truth is a human percept that has intensity from completely false (0) to completely true (1). By definition, the suitability, preference, and value are degrees of truth of corresponding value statements. They can also be interpreted as degrees of fuzzy membership.

10) The number of evaluated objects/alternatives can be *one or more*. Consequently, evaluation methods must be applicable for evaluation of a single object. Since the evaluation process can be applied to a single alternative, it follows that evaluation must be possible without pairwise comparison of competitive alternatives. Evaluation of complex objects/alternatives is primarily a cardinal process (and much less frequently an ordinal process). Stakeholders are always interested to know the overall cardinal value of each alternative (the degree of satisfaction of their justified requirements), even in cases where evaluation criteria include some pairwise comparisons. The ranking of alternatives can always be a natural consequence of the comparison of cardinal values of alternatives. The goal of evaluation is not to show that object A is better than the object B, but to show how good is each of them (obviously, A can be better than B while both of them are unacceptable).

11) Each evaluation process creates and aggregates degrees of truth. Consequently, evaluation is a logic process based on graded truth values. A graded evaluation logic is a propositional calculus used for processing degrees of partial truth (or fuzzy membership) defined on the interval $[0,1]$.

12) The propositional calculus inside the hypercube $[0,1]^n$, $n \geq 2$ must be consistent with the propositional calculus in vertices $\{0, 1\}^n$ (Boolean logic). Consequently, the graded evaluation logic must be a seamless generalization of classical Boolean logic.

These principles are easily defendable and clearly show in which direction we intend to move and what school of thought we want to promote. Our focal point is the observable human reasoning. It is important to note that the interest in human-centric approach to logic is clearly visible in the work of the founders of modern logic [DEM47, BOO47, BOO54].

Logic aggregation is the central component of our methodology, and consequently, this book complements other books on aggregation. At this time the most general books on aggregation are [BEL07] and [GRA09]. These books promote a purely mathematical approach to aggregation as a formal theory:

They define aggregation functions (aggregators) in an ultimately permissive way as nondecreasing (in each variable) functions $A : [0,1]^n \rightarrow [0,1]$, $n \geq 2$ that satisfy boundary conditions $A(0,...,0) = 0$ and $A(1,...,1) = 1$. The result of this definition is an extremely wide family of functions that are not focused on any particular application area. More significantly, this definition also eliminates the need for *semantics of aggregation*, i.e., it is neither necessary nor interesting to know what is being aggregated and for what reason. The general purpose of aggregation is to aggregate anonymous real numbers. Of course, this is a legitimate approach that perfectly fits in mathematics, but it does not fit in decision engineering. In decision engineering, we don't aggregate anonymous real numbers, but meaningful degrees of truth. Each degree of truth has precisely defined semantic identity and a justifiable degree of importance. In addition, such degrees of truth are used to make decisions that have both organizational and financial consequences. Therefore, in decision engineering, the purpose of aggregation is *insight*, not numbers. That yields the need for a modified definition of aggregators.

A more restrictive approach to aggregation is presented in [TOR07] and [BEL16], where the focus is mostly on averaging aggregators and applicability in the area of modeling decisions. This approach increases the practical value of the studied material and interacts with the mathematical literature devoted to means [GIN58, MIT69, MIT77, MIT89, BUL88, BUL03].

In the areas of averaging aggregators and means, the most fundamental properties are internality and idempotency. However, the internality $\min(\mathbf{x}) \leq A(\mathbf{x}) \leq \max(\mathbf{x})$ is most frequently interpreted *statistically* as averaging and not *logically* as a continuous transition from conjunction to disjunction. In this book, we interpret means as logic functions, and our approach to aggregators will be strictly human-centric and logic oriented. We will define and use logic aggregators as models of human aggregation of degrees of truth, or (what is equivalent) degrees of fuzzy membership.

Human evaluation reasoning can be investigated from many different standpoints. In particular, in this book we do not study evaluation reasoning from the standpoint of philosophy, psychology, sociology, and other social sciences. We are only interested in those aspects of intuitive evaluation processes that are observable and can be quantitatively modeled with intention to develop computerized decision-support systems used in decision engineering. Therefore, our primary area of interest is restricted to evaluation and its modeling; it is intentionally kept sufficiently narrow to secure the depth of our study and to avoid conflicting interference with other disciplines.

Observations and analyses of evaluation in the context of human intuitive and professional reasoning show that this logic process has both semantic and formal logic components (see Section 2.2.1). *Semantic components* reflect the goals, interests, and justified requirements of the stakeholder (decision maker) and affect the selection of relevant attributes of evaluated objects and specification of their overall importance. The *formal logic components* primarily define the aggregation of subjective categories, where "subjective categories" denote the percepts of value of selected components of evaluated objects. Thus, when we use the term *evaluation reasoning* in the context of logic, we primarily think about the process of aggregation of various percepts of value.

A natural way to answer the fundamental question about the aggregation of subjective categories is based on careful observation of human intuitive evaluation reasoning (primarily the evaluation reasoning in the context of complex professional decision problems, but also various frequently visible processes of intuitive evaluation in the context of personal decision making). The observations show that the human aggregation of subjective categories is most frequently characterized by the continuity, monotonicity, and grading of all variables and parameters (e.g., the degrees of truth, importance, simultaneity, and substitutability), as well as the internality (idempotency), noncommutativity, and compensativeness of aggregators. All these properties are clearly visible in the process of creating human evaluation decisions (i.e., in the intuitive assessment of worth). Their systematic and detailed analysis is presented in Chapter 2.2.

Mathematical models of logic aggregation of various percepts of value form an infinite-valued propositional calculus that can be identified as the evaluation logic. The main property of evaluation logic is that it operates with graded values. Such logic is based on degrees of truth, degrees of suitability, degrees of importance, degrees of conjunction, and degrees of disjunction: all values are graded. So, it is reasonable to call such logic a *graded logic* (GL).

GL is a necessary theoretical background for evaluation methodology presented in *Part Three* and *Part Four* of this book. As a propositional calculus, GL has the goal to determine the degree of truth of a compound statement from the degrees of truth of component statements and the logic connectives between them. All degrees of truth can also be interpreted as degrees of fuzzy membership, because fuzziness and partial truth are closely related interpretations of the same perceptual reality [DUJ17].

In extreme cases, the degrees of truth can be bivalent (0 or 1), and in such cases GL becomes the classical Boolean propositional logic. Thus, GL must be developed as a seamless generalization of the classical bivalent propositional calculus. That is the objective of *Part Two* of this book.

The search for the most appropriate name of GL produced multiple alternatives. Initially, in [DUJ73b] GL was interpreted as a "generalization of some functions in continuous mathematical logic." Then, in [DUJ07c], the use of GL aggregators for computing preferences resulted in the name "preference logic for system evaluation." Contrary to classical logic, GL uses weights to express importance of statements and has strong compensative properties that resulted in the name "weighted compensative logic" in [DUJ15a]. As a generalization of classical bivalent logic, GL might also be called "the generalized Boolean logic" and, because of its applicability in soft computing evaluation models, GL can also be called "the soft computing evaluation logic" or shortly "evaluation logic." The name "graded logic" that we use in this book has an obvious advantage: it is short and it is not limiting GL only to the area of evaluation. Indeed, GL models can be useful in many areas and in applications that are different from decision models.

The goal of *Part Two* of this book is to present the development of GL and its main properties. Initially, we study the necessary generalizations of Boolean logic, and the properties of fundamental functions used in GL models. Then, we present and compare various mathematical models of aggregators. Finally, we study aggregation structures used for modeling complex criteria and aggregation methods that are necessary in professional evaluation of complex alternatives.

2.1 Graded Logic as a Generalization of Classical Boolean Logic

This chapter introduces graded logic as a system of realistic models of observable properties of human aggregation reasoning. After an introduction to aggregation as the fundamental activity in evaluation logic, we discuss the relationships between graded evaluation logic and fuzzy logic. Then, we present a survey of classical bivalent Boolean logic and introduce evaluation logic as a weighted compensative generalization of the classical Boolean logic. At the end of this chapter, we present a brief history of graded logic.

Three of the most frequent words in this book are *means*, *logic*, and *aggregators*. If we have n real numbers $x_1,...,x_n$, $n > 1$, then according to common sense the mean value of these numbers is a value $M(x_1, ..., x_n)$, which is located somewhere between the smallest and the largest of the numbers:

$$\min(x_1,...,x_n) \leq M(x_1,...,x_n) \leq \max(x_1,...,x_n). \tag{2.1.1}$$

This property of function M is called *internality*. In our case, $x_1,...,x_n$ are degrees of truth, and they belong to the unit interval $I = [0,1]$. So, $x_i \in I$, $i = 1,...,n$ and $M : I^n \rightarrow I$. We can also rewrite relation (2.1.1) as follows:

$$AND = x_1 \wedge \cdots \wedge x_n \leq M(x_1,...,x_n) \leq x_1 \vee \cdots \vee x_n = OR, \tag{2.1.2}$$

Therefore, means are functions between conjunction and disjunction, and relation (2.1.2) obviously suggests that means can be interpreted as logic functions (and indeed, they are logic functions, assuming that *logic* means modeling observable properties of human reasoning). In particular, relation (2.1.2) indicates that the mean M (as a logic function) can be linearly interpolated between AND and OR as follows:

$$M(x_1,...,x_n) = (1-\omega)(x_1 \wedge \cdots \wedge x_n) + \omega(x_1 \vee \cdots \vee x_n), \quad 0 \leq \omega \leq 1, \tag{2.1.3}$$

The parameter $\omega \in I$ defines the location of M in the space between conjunction and disjunction. More precisely, ω denotes the proximity of M to

Soft Computing Evaluation Logic: The LSP Decision Method and Its Applications,
First Edition. Jozo Dujmović.
© 2018 John Wiley & Sons, Inc. Published 2018 by John Wiley & Sons, Inc.
Companion website: www.wiley.com/go/Dujmovic/Soft_Computing_Evaluation_Logic

disjunction, or the similarity between M and disjunction, and it can be called the *disjunction degree* or *similarity to OR*, or *orness*. According to (2.1.3), the disjunction degree of mean M is

$$\omega = \frac{M(x_1,...,x_n) - (x_1 \wedge \cdots \wedge x_n)}{(x_1 \vee \cdots \vee x_n) - (x_1 \wedge \cdots \wedge x_n)}. \tag{2.1.4}$$

Relations (2.1.3) and (2.1.4) indicate that each mean could be interpreted as a *mix of disjunctive and conjunctive properties*. From that standpoint, we are particularly interested in parameterized means. Such means have an adjustable parameter $r(\omega)$ that can be used to adjust the logic properties of mean and provide a *continuous transition from AND to OR*:

$$AND = x_1 \wedge \cdots \wedge x_n \leq M(x_1,...,x_n; r(\omega)) \leq x_1 \vee \cdots \vee x_n = OR,$$
$$f(x_1,...,x_n; r(0)) = x_1 \wedge \cdots \wedge x_n, \tag{2.1.5}$$
$$f(x_1,...,x_n; r(1)) = x_1 \vee \cdots \vee x_n.$$

The function $M(x_1, ..., x_n; r(\omega))$ can be interpreted as a logic function: it has an adjustable degree of similarity to disjunction (or to conjunction) and represents a fundamental component for building a graded logic. We call this function the *graded* (or *generalized* [DUJ07a]) *conjunction/disjunction* (in both cases, the abbreviation is GCD).

The above short story and relations (2.1.1 to 2.1.5) exactly describe my initial reasoning in 1972–1973, when I started developing a logic based on functions that provide continuous transition from AND to OR. My goals were to generalize the classic Boolean logic, to model observable properties of human reasoning, and to apply that methodology in the area of evaluation. These are also the main goals of this book.

2.1.1 Aggregators and Their Classification

Our first step is to introduce *logic aggregators*, i.e., functions that aggregate two or more degrees of truth and return a degree of truth in a way similar to observable patterns of human reasoning. The meaning and role of inputs and outputs of logic aggregators can be used as the necessary restrictive conditions that filter those functions and properties that have potential to serve in mathematical models of human evaluation reasoning. Not surprisingly, a general goal of mathematical definitions is the ultimate generality. In the area of aggregators, the mathematical generality means that highly applicable logic aggregators are mixed with lots of unnecessary mathematical ballast. Consequently, it is useful to first briefly investigate the families of functions that are closely related to logic aggregators. Such families are means, general aggregation functions, and triangular norms.

2.1.1.1 Means

Means are fundamental logic functions that we use in graded logic. Let us again note that our logic is continuous, all variables belong to unit interval $I = [0,1]$ and all logic phenomena and their models occur inside the unit hypercube I^n, $n > 1$. So, before we start using means as graded logic functions, it is necessary to have a definition of mean.

Mathematics provides various definitions of means. According to Oscar Chisini [CHI29], the mean $M(x_1, ..., x_n)$ (known as Chisini mean) generates a mean value x of n components of vector $(x_1, ..., x_n)$ if the following holds:

$$M(x,...,x) = M(x_1,...,x_n). \tag{2.1.6}$$

Both Chisini and Gini [GIN58] considered this definition too general and not implying internality (2.1.1). For purposes of applicability in logic, the internality (2.1.1) is the fundamental assumption, and consequently, we can consider that (2.1.1) is the most important component of any definition of means, and such means satisfy (2.1.6). By inserting $x_1 = \cdots = x_n = x$ in (2.1.1) we have $x \le M(x,...,x) \le x$ and we directly get idempotency:

$$M(x,...,x) = x, \quad x \in I.$$

All means are internal and idempotent. Similarly, all nondecreasing idempotent aggregation functions $I^n \to I$ are internal, i.e., they are means [GRA09].

Another fundamental property of means is monotonicity: Means should be nondecreasing in each variable. More precisely, Mitrinović, Vasić, and Bullen [MIT77, BUL03] specify that a function $f(x, y)$, in order to be considered a mean, should have the following fundamental properties:

- Continuity: $\lim_{\substack{\delta x \to 0 \\ \delta y \to 0}} f(x + \delta x, y + \delta y) = f(x,y).$
- Internality: $\min(x,y) \le f(x,y) \le \max(x,y).$
- Monotonicity: $x \le a, \ y \le b \Rightarrow f(x,y) \le f(a,b).$
- Idempotency (reflexivity): $f(x,x) = x.$
- Symmetry: $f(x,y) = f(y,x).$
- Homogeneity: $f(ax,ay) \le af(x,y).$

The above properties reflect the special case where all variables have the same weight. In a general case, we assume that symmetry is excluded because each argument may have a different degree of importance and commutativity is not desirable. More mathematical details about definitions and properties of means can be found in [CHI29, DEF31, GIN58, KOL30, NAG30, ACZ48, MIT77, MIT89, BUL88, BUL03, BEL16].

2.1.1.2 General Aggregation Functions

In addition to means, decision models also use the concept of aggregation functions on [0, 1] or *general aggregators* [FOD94, CAL02, GRA09, BEL07, MES15,

BEL16]. We call these aggregators "general" to differentiate them from the subclass of *logic aggregators* that will be defined and used later.

Definition 2.1.0. A general aggregator of n variables is defined as a function $A : I^n \to I$ that is nondecreasing in each argument (monotonicity) and idempotent in extreme points 0 and 1 (i.e., it must satisfy two boundary conditions) as follows:

$$\mathbf{x} = (x_1,...,x_n), \quad \mathbf{y} = (y_1,...,y_n), \quad x_i \in I, \quad y_i \in I, \quad i = 1,...,n$$

$$\mathbf{x} \le \mathbf{y} \implies A(\mathbf{x}) \le A(\mathbf{y}) \quad \text{(or } x_i \le y_i, \ i = 1,...,n \text{ implies}$$

$$A(x_1,...,x_n) \le A(y_1,...,y_n)) \tag{2.1.7}$$

$$A(0,0,...,0) = 0, \quad A(1,1,...,1) = 1.$$

According to (2.1.7), a general aggregator is defined less restrictively than a mean. Primarily, such aggregators do not need to support internality and idempotency. For example, $z = xy$ is an aggregator, but it is not idempotent and not a mean, while $z = \sqrt{xy}$ is both an aggregator and a mean. So, all means that we use are aggregators, but all aggregators are not means.

Graded logic decision models predominantly use idempotent aggregators (means) but sometimes may also use nonidempotent aggregators. As we already mentioned, all internal functions are idempotent, and all idempotent nondecreasing functions are internal. All means that we use in GL support internality and idempotency.

Aggregators have a *diagonal section function* $\delta_A(x) = A(x,...,x)$ that is defined as a value that an aggregator generates along the main diagonal of the unit hypercube. Obviously, all idempotent aggregators have the diagonal section function $\delta_A(x) = x$. For example, the idempotent aggregator $A(x,y) = \sqrt{xy}$ has the diagonal section function $\delta_A(x) = x$. The nonidempotent t-norm aggregator $P(x,y) = xy$ has the diagonal section function $\delta_P(x) = x^2$ and its De Morgan dual, the t-conorm $Q(x,y) = 1 - (1-x)(1-y)$ has the diagonal section function $\delta_Q(x) = 2x - x^2$. Since $[P(x,y) + Q(x,y)]/2 = (x+y)/2$, in this particular case we also have $[\delta_P(x) + \delta_Q(x)]/2 = x$.

Mathematical literature [FOD94, BEL07, GRA09, MES15, BEL16] uses the following classification of aggregators:

1) *Conjunctive aggregators:* $0 \le A(x_1,...,x_n) \le \min(x_1,...,x_n) = x_1 \wedge \cdots \wedge x_n$.
2) *Disjunctive aggregators:* $1 \ge A(x_1,...,x_n) \ge \max(x_1,...,x_n) = x_1 \vee \cdots \vee x_n$.
3) *Averaging aggregators:* $\min(x_1,...,x_n) \le A(x_1,...,x_n) \le \max(x_1,...,x_n)$.
4) *Mixed aggregators:* aggregators that do not belong to groups (1), (2), (3).

Unfortunately, this classification is not oriented toward the logic interpretation of aggregators. Primarily, the variables $x_1, ..., x_n$ are not assumed to be degrees of truth of corresponding statements, and aggregators are not assumed to be functions of propositional calculus. In addition, the averaging aggregation is not interpreted as a continuum of conjunctive or disjunctive logic operations, but mostly as a statistical computation of mean values. Simultaneity (conjunctive aggregation) is recognized only in the lowest region of the unit hypercube, and substitutability (disjunctive aggregation) is recognized only in the highest region of the unit hypercube. This is not consistent with the propositional logic interpretation of aggregation functions $[0,1]^n \rightarrow [0,1]$, $n > 1$. Therefore, we will *not* use the above definition and classification of *general aggregators*. We need a more restrictive definition of *logic aggregators*, as well as a different classification, outlined below and discussed in detail in subsequent sections.

2.1.1.3 Logic Aggregators

Our classification of logic aggregators will be based on the fact that basic logic aggregators are models of *simultaneity* or models of *substitutability*. In addition, the centroid of all logic aggregators is the logic *neutrality*, modeled as the arithmetic mean. Various degrees of predominant simultaneity can be modeled using aggregation functions that are located *below neutrality*. Various degrees of predominant substitutability can be modeled using aggregation functions that are located *above neutrality*. Therefore, assuming nonidentical arguments, we will use the following basic classification of logic aggregators:

1) *Neutral logic aggregator:* $A(x_1,...,x_n) = MID(x_1,...,x_n) = (x_1 + \cdots + x_n)/n$.
2) *Conjunctive aggregators:* $0 \le A(x_1,...,x_n) < MID(x_1,...,x_n)$.
3) *Disjunctive aggregators:* $MID(x_1,...,x_n) < A(x_1,...,x_n) \le 1$.

More specifically, conjunctive and disjunctive aggregators can be *regular* if they are means. On the other hand, all nonidempotent conjunctive logic aggregators that satisfy $0 \le A(x_1,...,x_n) < \min(x_1,...,x_n)$ will be denoted as *hyperconjunctive*. Similarly, all nonidempotent disjunctive aggregators that satisfy $\max(x_1,...,x_n) < A(x_1,...,x_n) \le 1$ will be denoted as *hyperdisjunctive*. A full justification of this classification, the definition of logic aggregators, and more details can be found in Sections 2.1.2 and 2.1.3.

2.1.1.4 Triangular Norms and Conorms

The areas of hyperconjunctive and hyperdisjunctive aggregators offer models of very high degrees of simultaneity and substitutability. These areas overlap with the areas of triangular norms (t-norms) and triangular conorms (t-conorms).

According to [FOD94] a t-norm is a function $T : I^2 \rightarrow I$ that satisfies the following conditions:

$$T(x,y) = T(y,x), \quad \forall x,y \in I \qquad \text{(commutativity)},$$
$$T(x,y) \le T(X,Y), \quad 0 \le x \le X \le 1, \quad 0 \le y \le Y \le 1 \qquad \text{(monotonicity)},$$
$$T(x,T(y,z)) = T(T(x,y),z), \quad \forall x,y,z \in I \qquad \text{(associativity)},$$
$$T(x,1) = x, \quad \forall x \in I \qquad \text{(neutral element)},$$
$$T(x,0) = 0, \quad \forall x \in I \qquad \text{(annihilator)}.$$

These properties indicate conjunctive behavior of t-norms [MES15], i.e., the possibility to use some of t-norms for modeling simultaneity. Particularly important in that direction are Archimedean t-norms that satisfy $T(x,x) < x, \quad \forall x \in]0,1[$. In other words, the diagonal section function of Archimedean t-norms satisfies $\delta_T(x) < x, \quad 0 < x < 1$, showing that the surface of such t-norm is located below the pure conjunction function: $T(x,y) < \min(x,y), \quad \forall x,y \in]0,1[$. For example, $T(x,y) = xy < \min(x,y), \quad \forall x,y \in]0,1[$. Therefore, Archimedean t-norms can be used as models of hyperconjunctive aggregators. The associativity of t-norms permits the use of t-norms in cases of more than two variables.

T-conorms are defined using *duality*: $S(x,y) = 1 - T(1-x,1-y)$. That yields the following properties of t-conorms that are symmetric to the properties of t-norms:

$$S(x,y) = S(y,x), \quad \forall x,y \in I \qquad \text{(commutativity)},$$

$$S(x,y) \le S(X,Y), \quad 0 \le x \le X \le 1, \quad 0 \le y \le Y \le 1 \qquad \text{(monotonicity)},$$

$$S(x,S(y,z)) = S(S(x,y),z), \quad \forall x,y,z \in I \qquad \text{(associativity)},$$

$$S(x,0) = x, \quad \forall x \in I \qquad \text{(neutral element)},$$

$$S(x,1) = 1, \quad \forall x \in I \qquad \text{(annihilator)}.$$

Among a variety of t-norms and t-conorms the most frequently used t-norms/conorms in literature are min/max (M), product (P), Łukasiewicz (L), and drastic (D), defined as follows:

$$T_M(x,y) = \min(x,y), \qquad\qquad S_M(x,y) = \max(x,y),$$

$$T_P(x,y) = xy, \qquad\qquad S_P(x,y) = x + y - xy,$$

$$T_L(x,y) = \max(x + y - 1, \ 0), \qquad\qquad S_L(x,y) = \min(x + y, \ 1),$$

$$T_D(x,y) = \begin{cases} \min(x,y) & \text{if } \max(x,y) = 1 \\ 0, & \text{otherwise} \end{cases} \qquad S_D(x,y) = \begin{cases} \max(x,y) & \text{if } \min(x,y) = 0 \\ 1, & \text{otherwise}. \end{cases}$$

Among these aggregators, M and P are sometimes used in logic aggregation for modeling very high levels of simultaneity and substitutability. Others have rather low applicability, as discussed in [DUJ07c]. The primary reasons are the incompatibility with observable properties of human reasoning: the absence of idempotency (except for M), the absence of weights, discontinuities (L, D), insensitivity to improvements (M, L, D), and insufficient support for modeling simultaneity or substitutability (L). For example, $T_L(0.5, 0.5) = T_L(0,0) = 0$, and there is absolutely no reward for the average satisfaction of inputs. This model might be called the "excess 50%" norm, because its main concern is to eliminate candidates who cannot make an average score of 50%. After that, $T_L(x, y)$ behaves similarly to the arithmetic mean, providing simple additive compensatory features. For example, $T_L(0.7, 0.7) = T_L(0.4, 1) = 0.4 = T_L(0.7 - \Delta x, 0.7 + \Delta x)$ and in this case the decrement Δx is insufficiently penalized because it can be compensated with the increment having the same size: $\Delta y = \Delta x$. So, $T_L(x, y)$ shows inability to properly penalize the lack of simultaneity, which is a fundamental issue in all models of simultaneity.

Such properties are not useful in graded evaluation logic and were among reasons for defining logic aggregators in Section 2.1.3 in a way that excludes $T_L(x, y)$ and $T_D(x, y)$ from the status of logic aggregators, in an attempt to reduce mathematical ballast generated by too permissive (insufficiently restrictive) definition of general aggregators (Definition 2.1.0). The main restrictive concept of our approach is that logic aggregators must be applicable as models of human reasoning, and we try to focus only on mathematical infrastructure that supports that fundamental goal.

Duals of Archimedean t-norms (Archimedean t-conorms) can be used as models of hyperdisjunctive aggregators. For example, $T_P(x,y) = xy$ is a t-norm and a hyperconjunctive aggregator and $S_P(x,y) = x + y - xy$ is a t-conorm and a hyperdisjunctive aggregator. On the other hand, $T_{P2}(x,y) = x^2 y^2$ can be used as a hyperconjunctive aggregator but it is not a t-norm. Its dual, $S_{P2}(x,y) = 1 - (1-x)^2 (1-y)^2$ can be used as a hyperdisjunctive aggregator, but is not a t-conorm.

Some of presented general aggregators are consistent and some are inconsistent with observable properties of human evaluation reasoning. Keeping in mind these basic types of aggregators and their properties, we can now focus on studying aggregation functions that are provably suitable for building models of evaluation reasoning.

2.1.2 How Do Human Beings Aggregate Subjective Categories?

The only way to answer this crucial question is to observe characteristic patterns of human aggregative reasoning and to identify necessary properties of aggregation. If we can identify a single case of an indisputably valid reasoning pattern, such a case is a sufficient proof of the existence of that reasoning pattern, as well as a proof that the mathematical models of logic reasoning must include and correctly quantitatively describe the properties of such reasoning.

Initial attempts to investigate human aggregation of subjective categories using empirical analysis based on experiments with human subjects can be found in [THO79, ZIM80, ZIM87, KOV92, ZIM96]. These valuable efforts were restricted to the study of nonidempotent gamma aggregator $y_g(\mathbf{x}, \gamma, n) = (x_1 \cdots x_n)^{1-\gamma} [1 - (1-x_1) \cdots (1-x_n)]^\gamma$, $0 \leq \gamma \leq 1$ and unfortunately remained isolated.

In this section, we identify basic characteristic patterns of aggregation of subjective categories. For each pattern, we first define the characteristic property and then provide the proof of existence. Our analysis is focused on aggregation in the context of evaluation reasoning. We assume that a decision maker has input percepts of the suitability degrees $x_1,...,x_n$, $x_i \in [0,1]$, $i = 1,...,n$ of a group of $n \geq 2$ components of an evaluated object. The decision maker then aggregates input suitability degrees to create a composite percept of the output (fused) suitability of the analyzed group of n components of the evaluated object, $y = A(x_1,...,x_n)$, $y \in [0,1]$. In most practical cases the evaluated objects are artifacts (products made by humans), but the evaluation can also include other forms of decision alternatives.

There are two clearly visible types of aggregation of subjective categories: *idempotent* and *nonidempotent*. Idempotent aggregation is based on assumption that any object is as suitable as its components in all cases where all components have the same suitability.

Nonidempotent aggregation is based on the assumption that if all components of an evaluated object have the same value, then the overall value of the object can be less then or greater than the value of components [ZIM96, DUJ07c]. One of such aggregators (originating in probability theory) is $z = xy$. So, if the values of two components x and y are 50%, then the value of the whole object is 25%. Proponents of nonidempotent aggregation rarely relate aggregation with human reasoning and decision making. An exception is the nonidempotent gamma aggregator of Zimmermann and Zysno [ZIM80], which was empirically validated.

In the context of evaluation, human beings aggregate subjective categories using observable reasoning patterns. This process is based on the following fundamental reasoning patterns that are further investigated in Section 2.1.8, as well as in Chapter 2.2.

Pattern 1. Idempotent Aggregation

This aggregation pattern is based on the assumption that the output (aggregated) suitability degree must be between the lowest and the highest input suitability degrees. This property is called *internality*. Consequently, if all input suitability degrees are equal, the output suitability must have the same value (typical idempotent operations include means, conjunction, disjunction, set union, and set intersection).

Proof of Existence

In all schools, the grade point average (GPA) reflects the overall satisfaction of educational requirements, and it is universally accepted as a valid percept of academic performance of students. Assuming a set of different individual grades, the GPA score is always higher than the lowest individual grade and lower than the highest individual grade. This reasoning is equally accepted by students, teachers, and schools as the most reasonable grade aggregation pattern.

Pattern 2. Nonidempotent Aggregation

This aggregation pattern is based on assumption that the aggregated suitability degree can be lower than the lowest or higher than the highest input suitability degree $(A(x,\ldots,x) < x$ or $A(x,\ldots,x) > x)$. This property is called *externality*.

Proof of Existence

In situations where suitability can be interpreted as probability (or likelihood), it is possible to find cases where input suitability degrees reflect independent events and the overall suitability is a product of input suitability degrees. For example, biathlon athletes combine cross-country skiing and rifle shooting. These two rather different skills can be considered almost completely independent. Consequently, if the performance of an athlete in cross-country skiing is x_1 and in rifle shooting is x_2, then the overall suitability of such an athlete for biathlon competitions might be $y = x_1 x_2 \leq \min(x_1, x_2)$. This model becomes obvious if x_1 and x_2 are interpreted as two independent probabilities: x_1 is the probability of winning in skiing and x_2 is the probability of winning is rifle shooting.

In a reversed case where x_1 denotes patient's motor impairment (disability) and x_2 denotes patient's visual impairment, it is not difficult to find unfortunate situations where the overall disability satisfies the condition $y = A(x_1, x_2) \geq \max(x_1, x_2)$.

In the area of evaluation the idempotent aggregation is significantly more frequent and more important than the nonidempotent aggregation. The reason for the high importance of idempotent aggregation is that objects of evaluation are most frequently human products (both physical and conceptual), human properties (like academic or professional performance), etc., where evaluation reasoning is similar as in the case of GPA: the overall suitability of an evaluated complex object cannot be higher than the suitability of its best component or less than the suitability of its worst component.

The industrial evaluation projects are predominantly focused on complex industrial products. Contrary to the assumption of fully independent components, all industrial products have components characterized by positively correlated suitability degrees. Indeed, all engineers develop products that have very balanced quality of components (positively correlated with the price of product). For example, if a typical car is driven 15,000 miles per year and typically lasts up to 200,000 miles, then it can be used approximately 14 years. It would be meaningless to install in such a car a windshield wiper mechanism that is designed to last 40 years. The design logic of engineering products is based on selected price range that is closely related to the expected overall quality degree. Consequently, the designers try to make all components as close as possible to the selected overall quality level. For example, an expensive car regularly has an expensive radio; a computer with a very fast processor usually has a very large main memory and large disk storage. Similarly, student grades on midterm exam are highly correlated with the grades on the final exam because both of them depend on student's ability and effort. Obviously, the evaluated components are not independent, and usually they have highly correlated suitability degrees. In such cases, the result of evaluation is an overall suitability degree, acting as a kind of centroid of suitability degrees of all relevant components and located inside the [min, max] range. Such evaluation models must be based on the idempotent aggregation. Therefore, we next focus on evaluation reasoning patterns that are necessary and sufficient for idempotent aggregation.

Pattern 3. Noncommutativity
In human reasoning, each truth has its degree of importance. Commutative (symmetric) aggregators are either special cases, or unacceptable oversimplifications.

Proof of Existence
In the GPA aggregation example, the grade G_4 of a course that has 4 hours of lectures per week cannot be equally important as the grade G_2 of a course that has 2 hours of lectures per week (G_4 should be two times more important than G_2). For most car buyers, the car safety features are much more important than the optional heating of the front seats. For most homebuyers, the quality of a living room is not as important as the quality of a laundry room.

Pattern 4. Adjustable Simultaneity (Partial Conjunction)
This is the most frequent aggregation pattern. It reflects the condition for simultaneous satisfaction of two or more requirements. The degree of simultaneity (or the percept of importance of simultaneity) can vary in a range from low to high and must be adjustable. In some cases, a moderate simultaneity is satisfactory, and in other cases only the high simultaneity is acceptable. The degree of simultaneity is called *andness*.

Proof of Existence
A homebuyer simultaneously requires a good quality of home, *and* a good quality of home location, *and* an affordable price of home. A biathlon athlete must simultaneously be a good skier *and* a good rifle shooter.

Pattern 5. Adjustable Substitutability (Partial Disjunction)
This aggregation pattern reflects the condition where the satisfaction of any of two or more requirements significantly satisfies an evaluation criterion. The degree of substitutability (or the percept of importance of substitutability) can vary in a range from low to high and must be adjustable. In some cases a low or moderate substitutability can be satisfactory, and in other cases decision makers may require a high substitutability. The degree of substitutability is called *orness*.

Proof of Existence

A patient has a medical condition that combines motor impairments (decreased ability to move) and sensory symptoms (pain). Patient disability degree is the consequence of either sufficient motor impairments *or* sufficiently developed sensory problems, yielding disjunctive aggregation.

Pattern 6. The Use of Annihilators

Human evaluation reasoning is frequently based on aggregators that support annihilators. The annihilator is an extreme value of suitability (either 0 or 1) that is sufficient to decide the result of aggregation regardless of the values of other inputs [BEL07a]. In the case of *necessary conditions* the annihilator is 0: If any of mandatory requirements is not satisfied, the evaluated object is rejected (in other words, $\forall i \in \{1,\ldots,n\}$, $x_i = 0 \Rightarrow A(x_1,\ldots,x_n) = 0$). In a dual case of *sufficient conditions* the annihilator is 1: If any of sufficient requirements is fully satisfied, the evaluation criterion is fully satisfied (in other words, $\forall i \in \{1,\ldots,n\}$, $x_i = 1 \Rightarrow A(x_1,\ldots,x_n) = 1$). The aggregators that support annihilators 0 and 1 are called *hard* and aggregators that do not support annihilators are called *soft*.

Proof of Existence

In many schools, a failure grade in a single course is sufficient to annihilate the effect of all other course grades and produce the overall failure, forcing the student to repeat the whole academic year. This annihilator has dual interpretation:

a) The overall failure is the failure in class #1 *or* the failure in class #2 *or* the failure in any other class (the annihilator is 1).

b) The overall passing grade assumes the passing grade in class #1 *and* the passing grade in class #2, *and* the passing grades in all other classes (the annihilator is 0).

Pattern 7. Partial and Full Hard Simultaneity (Hard Partial Conjunction)

This pattern is encountered in situations where it is highly desirable to simultaneously satisfy two or more inputs, and the satisfaction of all inputs is mandatory. The percept of aggregated satisfaction of hard simultaneous requirements will automatically be zero if any of inputs has zero satisfaction. It is going to be nonzero only if all inputs are partially satisfied. In the extreme case of full hard simultaneity, the aggregated suitability is equal to the lowest input suitability. In extreme cases, the lowest suitability cannot be compensated by increasing suitability of other inputs. In a more frequent case of partial hard simultaneity, nonzero low inputs can be partially compensated by higher values of other inputs.

Proof of Existence

In the process of selecting a home location, a senior citizen who cannot drive a car needs to be in the proximity of public transportation and food stores. If any of these mandatory requirements is not satisfied, the aggregated percept of satisfaction with a home location is zero, and the corresponding home location is rejected. Home locations are acceptable if and only if all inputs are positive (partially satisfied). In an extreme case of full hard simultaneity, the stakeholder does not want to accept any low input (neither remote food stores nor remote public transport). In such cases, the lowest input cannot be compensated by other higher inputs, and the aggregated percept of suitability is affected solely by the lowest of input suitability degrees. Much more frequently, however, the percept of aggregated suitability depends on all mandatory inputs and not only the lowest input. In other words, an adjustable partial compensation of the lowest (but always positive) suitability degree is usually possible.

Pattern 8. Soft Simultaneity (Soft Partial Conjunction)
This pattern is encountered in situations where it is desirable to simultaneously satisfy two or more inputs, but none of the inputs is mandatory. The percept of aggregated satisfaction of soft simultaneous requirements will not automatically be zero if one of the inputs has zero satisfaction. It is going to be nonzero as long as at least one of inputs is partially satisfied.

Proof of Existence
In the process of selecting a home location, a senior citizen would like to live in the proximity of park, restaurants, and public library. The percept of satisfaction with a given location depends on simultaneous proximity to park, restaurants, and libraries, but the stakeholder is usually ready to accept situations where some (but not all) of the desired amenities are missing.

Pattern 9. Partial and Full Hard Substitutability (Hard Partial Disjunction)
This pattern is encountered in situations where it is desirable to satisfy two or more inputs that can partially or completely replace each other. Each input is sufficient to alone completely satisfy all requirements. The percept of aggregated satisfaction of hard substitutability requirements will automatically be complete if any of inputs is completely satisfied. In the case of incomplete satisfaction of input requirements, each input has the capability to partially compensate the lack of other inputs. The percept of aggregated suitability is nonzero as long as at least one of inputs is partially satisfied. In the extreme case of full hard substitutability, the aggregated suitability is equal to the highest input suitability, and lower suitability degrees do not affect the aggregated suitability. In a more frequent case of partial hard substitutability and incomplete satisfaction of requirements, low inputs can affect (decrease) the aggregated percept of suitability.

Proof of Existence
A homebuyer in an area with very poor (or nonexistent) street parking needs a parking solution, and the options are: a private garage *or* a shared garage *or* a

reserved space in an outdoor parking lot. If any of these three options is completely satisfied, the homebuyer is fully satisfied. If the satisfaction with these options is incomplete (e.g., the homebuyer needs space for two cars but the available private garage has space for only one car), then the aggregated suitability of parking depends on all available options, or in an infrequent extreme case, it can depend only on the best option.

Pattern 10. Soft Substitutability (Soft Partial Disjunction)

This pattern is encountered in situations where it is desirable to satisfy two or more inputs that can partially replace each other, but none of them is sufficient to alone completely satisfy all requirements. The percept of aggregated satisfaction of soft substitutability requirements will not automatically be complete unless all inputs are completely satisfied. However, each input has the capability to partially compensate for the lack of other inputs. The percept of aggregated suitability is nonzero as long as at least one of inputs is partially satisfied.

Proof of Existence

A homebuyer with a very limited budget has a list of amenities (sport stadiums, restaurants, parks, etc.) that are desirable in the vicinity of home. None of the amenities is sufficient to completely satisfy the homebuyer, but a homebuyer who has a small number of choices is forced to be partially satisfied with any subset of them.

The patterns 6 to 10 are denoted in Fig. 2.1.1 as logically *symmetric*. In this context, the symmetry does not mean commutativity, but the fact that all inputs support (or do not support) annihilators in the same way. So, either all inputs are hard or all inputs are soft.

Pattern 11. Asymmetric Simultaneity (Conjunctive Partial Absorption)

This pattern is encountered in situations where it is desirable to simultaneously satisfy a *mandatory* input requirement and an *optional* input requirement. This form of aggregation is conjunctive but asymmetric. The mandatory input supports the annihilator 0 (if it is not satisfied the percept of aggregated suitability is zero regardless the level of satisfaction of the optional input). The optional input does not support the annihilator 0. If the mandatory requirement is partially satisfied, the zero optional input decreases the output suitability below the level of the mandatory input, but does not yield the zero result, showing the asymmetry of this form of simultaneity. Similarly, if the optional input is perfectly satisfied, it will, to some extent, increase the output suitability above the level of the mandatory input.

Proof of Existence

A homebuyer who needs parking in a moderately populated urban area would like to have a private garage in the home *and* good street parking in front of the home.

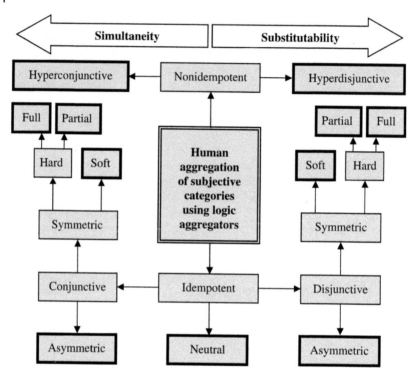

Figure 2.1.1 Types of aggregation and the classification of logic aggregators (bold frames).

However, the private parking garage is mandatory, while good street parking for the homeowner and occasional visitors is optional, i.e., it is desirable but not mandatory. The home without a private garage will be rejected regardless of the availability of good street parking, while a nice home with a private garage but poor street parking will be acceptable.

Pattern 12. Asymmetric Substitutability (Disjunctive Partial Absorption)
This pattern is encountered in situations where it is desirable to satisfy a *sufficient* input requirement and/or an alternative *optional* input requirement. This form of aggregation is disjunctive but asymmetric. The sufficient input supports the annihilator 1 (if it is fully satisfied the percept of aggregated suitability is the full satisfaction regardless the level of satisfaction of the optional input). The optional input does not support the annihilator 1. If the sufficient requirement is completely not satisfied, then a positive degree of satisfaction of the optional input can partially compensate for the lack of sufficient input, but it cannot yield the full satisfaction. That shows the asymmetry of this form of substitutability. Similarly to the case of asymmetric simultaneity, if the sufficient requirement is

partially satisfied, the zero optional input decreases the output suitability below the level of the sufficient input but does not yield the zero result. On the other hand, if the optional input is perfectly satisfied, it will to some extent increase the output suitability above the level of the sufficient input.

Proof of Existence

A homebuyer who needs parking in a highly populated urban area would like to have a private garage for two cars in the home *or* a good street parking in front of the home. A high-quality two-car private parking garage is sufficient to completely satisfy the parking requirements and in such a case the street parking becomes irrelevant. In the absence of private garage, a good street parking is acceptable as a nonideal (partial) solution of the parking problem. In addition, if a single-car (i.e., medium suitability) private garage is available, then a good street parking can increment (improve) the overall percept of parking suitability, and the corresponding parking suitability score will be higher than the private garage score. Similarly, in the case of single-car private garage, poor street parking can further decrement the overall percept of parking suitability and the parking suitability score, below the level of the medium suitability of the single-car private garage. These suitability increments and decrements are called *reward* and *penalty*. They can be used to adjust desired properties of all partial absorption aggregators.

Pattern 13. Neutrality (The Centroid of Logic Aggregators)

In its extreme version, *simultaneity* means that an aggregation criterion is completely satisfied only if all input components are simultaneously completely satisfied. In the extreme case of *substitutability,* any single input can completely satisfy an aggregation criterion and compensate the absence of all other inputs. Not surprisingly, human reasoning uses extreme versions of simultaneity and substitutability only in extreme situations. In normal situations, simultaneity and substitutability are used as complementary components in the process of aggregation. Humans can continuously adjust degrees of simultaneity and substitutability, making a smooth continuous transition from extreme simultaneity to extreme substitutability. Along that path, there is a central point where conjunctive and disjunctive properties are perfectly balanced. This point can be denoted as neutrality, and it represents a kind of *centroid of basic logic aggregators.* In the case of idempotent aggregators, the middle point between conjunction and disjunction is the arithmetic mean, as indicated in the simplest case of two inputs: $[(x \wedge y) + (x \vee y)]/2 = (x + y)/2$. It is most likely that neutrality is an initial default aggregator in human reasoning, which is subsequently adjusted (refined) moving in conjunctive or disjunctive direction, and using different weights of inputs. This is the reason why neutrality can be considered the centroid of all logic aggregators.

Proof of Existence

The logic behind using arithmetic mean as a school grade aggregator in computing the GPA score is the simultaneous presence and the perfect balance of two completely contradictory requirements: (1) excellent students must simultaneously have all excellent course grades (conjunctive property), and (2) any subset of good grades can partially compensate any subset of bad grades (disjunctive property). The logic neutrality reflects human ability to seamlessly combine and balance the effects of such diverse requirements.

Various patterns of human aggregation of subjective categories are summarized and classified in Fig. 2.1.1. There are nine idempotent and two nonidempotent aggregation patterns that are easily observable in human evaluation reasoning. These types of aggregation combined with negation are necessary and sufficient to model graded logic used in human reasoning, including evaluation and other applications of soft propositional logic. A detailed analysis supporting the concept of sufficiency is provided in subsequent sections.

In all presented reasoning patterns, exemplifying the characteristic property of reasoning is equivalent to proving that the property is necessary. Consequently, in the special case of idempotent logic aggregators, fundamental properties of aggregation can be specified as follows:

1) There are nine fundamental necessary and sufficient idempotent logic aggregation patterns used in evaluation logic: soft and (full or partial) hard symmetric conjunctive and disjunctive patterns, neutrality, and asymmetric conjunctive and disjunctive patterns.
2) If available aggregators do not explicitly support all the fundamental patterns of human aggregation of subjective categories, they cannot be used in logic aggregation models. Of course, there are many aggregators that can model only a subset of fundamental aggregation patterns, and such aggregators can be used if the aggregation problem does not need all aggregation patterns.

In the case of nonidempotent aggregators, we noticed their low applicability in the area of modeling human evaluation reasoning, but nevertheless, they are present in human reasoning. In the human mind, there is no switch for discrete transition from idempotent to nonidempotent aggregators. The transition from idempotent to nonidempotent aggregators and vice versa must be seamless, and logic aggregators must be developed to enable that form of transition. That is going to be one of our goals in the next chapters.

Let us again emphasize that in this book we are interested in *logic aggregation* (i.e., the aggregation of degrees of truth) and not in aggregation in the mathematical theoretical sense. Many aggregators that satisfy the extremely permissive aggregation function conditions (Definition 2.1.0) have properties that are obviously incompatible with properties of human reasoning (poor support for modeling simultaneity and substitutability, discontinuities of first derivatives, etc.). Therefore, the general study of aggregators is a much wider area than the study of logic aggregators. Logic aggregators satisfy the conditions (2.1.7), but they must satisfy a number of other restrictive conditions that reduce the number of possible aggregation function and restrictively specify their fundamental properties.

The basic logic reasoning patterns presented in this section are the point of departure for any study of evaluation logic reasoning. There are two "aggregation roads" diverging from this point of departure. One is to ignore the observable reasoning patterns and to build aggregation models as general (formal) mathematical structures; there are many travelers we can encounter along the aggregation theory road. The second option is to take "the road less traveled by" and to try to strictly follow, model, and further develop the observable reasoning patterns. If we want to reach the territory of professional evaluation applications, we must take the second road.

2.1.3 Definition and Classification of Logic Aggregators

Mathematical literature devoted to aggregators [GRA09, BEL07, BEL16] defines an aggregator $A(x_1, ..., x_n)$ as a function that is monotonically increasing in all arguments and satisfies two boundary conditions as shown in Definition 2.1.0. It is rather easy to note that the Definition 2.1.0 is extremely permissive, yielding various families of functions, which have properties not encountered in logic models, and not observable in human reasoning. Unfortunately, such functions are still called *conjunctive* or *disjunctive,* and these terms imply the proximity to logic and applicability in models of human reasoning. Therefore, it is useful to define the concept of logic aggregator in a more restrictive way, to exclude properties that are inconsistent with observable properties of human aggregative reasoning.

If aggregators are applied in evaluation logic, then we assume that input variables $x_1, ..., x_n$ have semantic identity as degrees of truth of value statements, and aggregators are functions of propositional calculus (also called sentential logic, sentential calculus, or propositional logic). Thus, undesirable properties of logic aggregators include the following:

- Discontinuities: *natura non facit saltum* (nature makes no leap) and logic aggregators should be continuous functions.
- If all arguments are to some extent true (i.e., positive), their aggregate cannot be false (0). To create aggregated falsity, at least one input argument must be false.
- If all arguments are not completely true, their aggregate cannot be completely true. To create a complete (perfect) aggregated truth, at least one input argument must be completely true.

- Discontinuities and/or oscillations of first derivatives are questionable properties, incompatible with human reasoning. They occur in special cases (e.g., as a consequence of using min and max functions), but not as a regular modus operandi in logic aggregation.

Taking into account these observations, we are going to use the following definition of logic aggregators.

Definition 2.1.1. A *logic aggregator* $A(x_1, ..., x_n)$ is a continuous function of two or more variables $A : I^n \rightarrow I$ that satisfies the following additional conditions:

$$\mathbf{x} = (x_1, ..., x_n), \quad \mathbf{y} = (y_1, ..., y_n), \quad x_i \in I, \quad y_i \in I, \quad i = 1, ..., n, \quad n > 1;$$

$\mathbf{x} \le \mathbf{y} \;\Rightarrow\; A(\mathbf{x}) \le A(\mathbf{y})$	(nondecreasing monotonicity);
$A(0, 0, ..., 0) = 0$	(boundary condition for falsity);
$A(1, 1, ..., 1) = 1$	(boundary condition for truth);
$A(x_1, ..., x_n) > 0$ if $x_i > 0, i = 1, ..., n$	(sensitivity to positive truth);
$A(x_1, ..., x_n) < 1$ if $x_i < 1, i = 1, ..., n$	(sensitivity to incomplete truth).

Therefore, we restricted the general Definition 2.1.0 by requesting the continuity of logic aggregation functions and two additional logic conditions. For example, according to this definition, both Łukasiewicz and drastic t-norms are not logic aggregators. Of course, in propositional logic we regularly use logic functions that are not classified as logic aggregators. In most cases, such functions use the standard negation ($x \mapsto 1 - x$), which can destroy nondecreasing monotonicity and result in logic functions that are not aggregators. On the other hand, it is easy to note that from Definition 2.1.1 it follows that compound functions created using superposition of logic aggregators are again logic aggregators. In this book, we are interested only in logic aggregators and in functions created using logic aggregators and standard negation. Therefore, wherever we use the term *aggregator* we assume logic aggregators based on Definition 2.1.1 and not general aggregators based on Definition 2.1.0.

The central position in propositional logic is reserved for logic aggregators that are models of simultaneity (conjunction), substitutability (disjunction), and negation. The most frequent logic models are based on combining various forms of conjunction, disjunction, and negation to create logic functions of higher complexity. Methods for building such models belong to propositional calculus. Consequently, our first step is to investigate models of simultaneity and substitutability.

According to [DUJ74a] and the analysis presented in Section 2.1.1, the area of *partial conjunction* is located between the arithmetic mean and the pure conjunction $x_1 \wedge \cdots \wedge x_n = \min(x_1, ..., x_n)$, and the area of *partial disjunction* is located between the arithmetic mean and the pure disjunction $x_1 \vee \cdots \vee x_n = \max(x_1,\ldots,x_n)$. Logic aggregators are characterized by their location in the space between the pure conjunction and the pure disjunction. The location of an aggregator can be quantified as the volume under the aggregator surface inside the unit hypercube. The intensity of partial conjunction is measured using the conjunction degree (or andness) α defined as follows[1] [DUJ73a, DUJ74a]:

$$\alpha = \frac{\int_0^1 \cdots \int_0^1 (x_1 \vee \cdots \vee x_n)dx_1\cdots dx_n - \int_0^1 \cdots \int_0^1 A(x_1,\ldots,x_n)dx_1\cdots dx_n}{\int_0^1 \cdots \int_0^1 (x_1 \vee \cdots \vee x_n)dx_1\cdots dx_n - \int_0^1 \cdots \int_0^1 (x_1 \wedge \cdots \wedge x_n)dx_1\cdots dx_n}$$

$$= \frac{\dfrac{n}{n+1} - \int_0^1 \cdots \int_0^1 A(x_1,\ldots,x_n)dx_1\cdots dx_n}{\dfrac{n}{n+1} - \dfrac{1}{n+1}}$$

$$= \frac{n-(n+1)\int_0^1 \cdots \int_0^1 A(x_1,\ldots,x_n)dx_1\cdots dx_n}{n-1}.$$

(2.1.8)

The intensity of partial disjunction is measured using the disjunction degree (or orness) ω defined as the complement of α:

$$\omega = 1 - \alpha = \frac{(n+1)\int_0^1 \cdots \int_0^1 A(x_1,\ldots,x_n)dx_1\cdots dx_n - 1}{n-1}.$$

(2.1.9)

Obviously, for idempotent aggregators, $\alpha \in I$, $\omega \in I$. In the case of pure conjunction, we have $\alpha = 1 - \omega = 1$, and in the case of pure disjunction we have $\omega = 1 - \alpha = 1$. In the case of arithmetic mean $A(x_1,\ldots,x_n) = (x_1 + \cdots + x_n)/n$ the andness and orness are equal:

$$\frac{1}{n}\int_0^1 \cdots \int_0^1 (x_1 + \cdots + x_n)dx_1\cdots dx_n = \frac{1}{n}\cdot\frac{1}{2}\cdot n = \frac{1}{2},$$

$$\omega = 1 - \alpha = \frac{(n+1)/2 - 1}{n-1} = \frac{1}{2} = \alpha.$$

---

1 In Chapter 2.3, the concepts and the models of conjunctive and disjunctive aggregation are presented in much more detailed way. There are several different definitions of andness and orness. The presented definitions of α and ω are known as "global andness" and "global orness." In this section we are going to call them simply "andness" and "orness" and use the definitions based on the volume of space under the surface of an aggregator $A(x_1, \ldots, x_n)$ inside the hypercube $[0, 1]^n$.

Therefore, the arithmetic mean is the central point (a centroid of logic aggregators) between the pure conjunction and the pure disjunction. Conjunctive aggregators are less than the arithmetic mean and therefore located in the area between the arithmetic mean and the pure conjunction where $\alpha > \omega$, $\frac{1}{2} < \alpha \leq 1$. Similarly, the disjunctive aggregators are greater than the arithmetic mean and therefore located in the area between the arithmetic mean and the pure disjunction where $\alpha < \omega$, $\frac{1}{2} < \omega \leq 1$.

Let us now investigate the basic means. The geometric mean $g = \sqrt{xy}$ is obviously a conjunctive logic function: It is less than the arithmetic mean[2] $a = (x+y)/2$, and for $x \in \{0,1\}$ and $y \in \{0,1\}$ it gives the same mapping as the pure conjunction: $\sqrt{xy} = x \wedge y$. Similar conjunctive logic function is the harmonic mean $h = 2xy/(x+y) = g^2/a$. Since $g = \sqrt{ah}$ and $g \leq a$, it follows $h \leq g \leq a$ (the geometric mean g is located between a and h). In other words, the harmonic mean is more conjunctive than the geometric mean. However, the quadratic mean $q = \sqrt{0.5x^2 + 0.5y^2}$ is disjunctive. From $q^2 = 0.5(x^2 + y^2) = 0.5\left[(x+y)^2 - 2xy\right]$ it follows that $q^2 = 0.5(4a^2 - 2g^2) = a^2 + (a^2 - g^2)$. Since $a^2 \geq g^2$ it follows $q^2 \geq a^2$ and $q \geq a$. Consequently, we have proved for two variables the inequality of basic conjunctive and disjunctive aggregators:

$$x \wedge y \leq \frac{2xy}{x+y} \leq \sqrt{xy} \leq \frac{x+y}{2} \leq \sqrt{0.5x^2 + 0.5y^2} \leq x \vee y.$$

In this expression, the equality holds only if $x = y$. Using more complex proving technique [BUL03], it is possible to show that the same inequality also holds for n variables, and in the general case of different normalized weights:

$$(x_1 \wedge \cdots \wedge x_n) \leq \left(\sum_{i=1}^{n} W_i/x_i\right)^{-1} \leq \prod_{i=1}^{n} x_i^{W_i} \leq \sum_{i=1}^{n} W_i x_i$$

$$\leq \sqrt{\sum_{i=1}^{n} W_i x_i^2} \leq (x_1 \vee \cdots \vee x_n),$$

$$0 < W_i < 1, \quad i = 1,...,n, \quad \sum_{i=1}^{n} W_i = 1, \quad n \geq 2.$$

This interpretation of *conjunctive* and *disjunctive* aggregation is different from the interpretation used in mathematical literature about general aggregators [BEL07, GRA09]. Indeed, in propositional logic which is consistent with classical Boolean logic, the extreme logic aggregators are the *pure conjunction* (the *min* function) and the *pure disjunction* (the *max* function).

---

2 For nonnegative x and y we have $\left(\sqrt{x} - \sqrt{y}\right)^2 \geq 0$. Then, $x - 2\sqrt{xy} + y \geq 0$ and $\sqrt{xy} \leq (x+y)/2$.

However, aggregation can sometimes go beyond the pure conjunction and the pure disjunction. For example, in the case of the nonidempotent t-norm aggregator $P(x,y) = xy$ from (2.1.8) and (2.1.9) we have

$$\int_0^1\int_0^1 xy\,dx\,dy = \frac{1}{4},$$

$$\omega = 1 - \alpha = 3\int_0^1\int_0^1 xy\,dx\,dy - 1 = -\frac{1}{4} < 0, \quad \alpha = \frac{5}{4} > 1.$$

Similarly, for the t-conorm $Q(x,y) = 1 - (1-x)(1-y) = x + y - xy$ we have

$$\int_0^1\int_0^1 (x + y - xy)\,dx\,dy = \frac{1}{2} + \frac{1}{2} - \frac{1}{4} = \frac{3}{4},$$

$$\omega = 1 - \alpha = 3\int_0^1\int_0^1 (x + y - xy)\,dx\,dy - 1 = \frac{9}{4} - 1 = \frac{5}{4} > 1, \quad \alpha = -\frac{1}{4} < 0.$$

Similar to drastic t-norm/conorm, GL models of simultaneity and substitutability inside the unit hypercube $[0, 1]^n$ have limit cases called the *drastic conjunction* and the *drastic disjunction*. The drastic conjunction is the most conjunctive GL function: $A(x_1,...,x_n) = 0$ with exception $A(1,...,1) = 1$. The drastic disjunction is the most disjunctive GL function: $A(x_1,...,x_n) = 1$ with exception $A(0,...,0) = 0$. These limit cases, which are graded logic functions, but not aggregators according to Definition 2.1.1, are discussed in Section 2.1.7.6. So, from formulas (2.1.8) and (2.1.9) we get the minimum and maximum possible values of andness and orness:

$$\omega_{max} = 1 - \alpha_{min} = \frac{(n+1)\int_0^1 \cdots \int_0^1 dx_1 \cdots dx_n - 1}{n-1} = \frac{n}{n-1} > 1,$$

$$\omega_{min} = 1 - \alpha_{max} = \frac{-1}{n-1} < 0.$$

Therefore, in a general case of n variables, the ranges of global andness and orness of graded conjunctive and disjunctive logic functions are

$$\alpha_{min} = \frac{-1}{n-1} \le \alpha \le \frac{n}{n-1} = \alpha_{max},$$

$$\omega_{min} = \frac{-1}{n-1} \le \omega \le \frac{n}{n-1} = \omega_{max}.$$

The values α_{min}, α_{max}, ω_{min}, ω_{max} correspond to the drastic conjunction and the drastic disjunction, which by Definition 2.1.1 are not logic aggregators. Thus, the range of andness/orness of logic aggregators is $]-1/(n-1), n/(n-1)[$, and the range of andness/orness of GL functions is $[-1/(n-1), n/(n-1)]$.

For the minimum number of variables $n = 2$ we have the largest range of andness and orness of GL functions:

$$\alpha_{min} = -1 \le \alpha \le 2 = \alpha_{max},$$

$$\omega_{min} = -1 \le \omega \le 2 = \omega_{max}.$$

However, the range of andness and orness decreases as the number of variables increases. According to [DUJ73a], we have:

$$\int_0^1 \cdots \int_0^1 (x_1 \wedge \cdots \wedge x_n) dx_1 \cdots dx_n = \frac{1}{n+1},$$

$$\int_0^1 \cdots \int_0^1 (x_1 \vee \cdots \vee x_n) dx_1 \cdots dx_n = \frac{n}{n+1}. \tag{2.1.10}$$

Let V_{int} denote the volume of the region inside the unit hypercube where internality and idempotency hold. Similarly, let V_{ext} denote the volume of the region where externality and nonidempotency hold. According to (2.1.10), these regions can be compared as follows:

$$\left. \begin{array}{l} \text{Internality and idempotency: } V_{int} = \dfrac{n-1}{n+1} \\[3mm] \text{Externality and nonidempotency: } V_{ext} = 1 - \dfrac{n-1}{n+1} = \dfrac{2}{n+1} \end{array} \right\} V_{int} = \dfrac{n-1}{2} V_{ext}. \tag{2.1.11}$$

If the number of variables increases, then the region of internality increases, and the region of externality decreases. For example, for $n = 5$, $V_{int} = 2/3$, $V_{ext} = 1/3$. Furthermore,

$$\lim_{n \to +\infty} \alpha_{min} = \lim_{n \to +\infty} \omega_{min} = 0,$$

$$\lim_{n \to +\infty} \alpha_{max} = \lim_{n \to +\infty} \omega_{max} = 1,$$

$$\lim_{n \to +\infty} V_{int} = 1; \lim_{n \to +\infty} V_{ext} = 0,$$

$$n \to +\infty \quad \Rightarrow \quad \begin{cases} 0 \le \alpha \le 1 \\ 0 \le \omega \le 1 \end{cases} \quad \text{(reduction to internality)}.$$

Taking into account these properties, the *graded logic aggregators* should be classified as follows:

- **Neutral aggregator:**
  The arithmetic mean:

  $$\alpha = \omega = \tfrac{1}{2}; \quad A(x_1,\ldots,x_n) = (x_1 + \cdots + x_n)/n.$$

- **Conjunctive aggregators:**
  - *Regular conjunctive aggregators:*

    $$\tfrac{1}{2} < \alpha \le 1; \quad x_1 \wedge \cdots \wedge x_n \le A(x_1,\ldots,x_n) \le (x_1 + \cdots + x_n)/n.$$

  - *Hyperconjunctive aggregators:*

    $$1 < \alpha < n/(n-1); \quad 0 \le A(x_1,\ldots,x_n) \le x_1 \wedge \cdots \wedge x_n.$$

- **Disjunctive aggregators:**
  - *Regular disjunctive aggregators:*

    $$\tfrac{1}{2} < \omega \le 1; \quad (x_1 + \cdots + x_n)/n \le A(x_1,\ldots,x_n) \le x_1 \vee \cdots \vee x_n.$$

  - *Hyperdisjunctive aggregators:*

    $$1 < \omega < n/(n-1); \quad x_1 \vee \cdots \vee x_n \le A(x_1,\ldots,x_n) \le 1.$$

We assume that regular conjunctive and regular disjunctive aggregators are implemented as idempotent means. Hyperconjunctive and hyperdisjunctive aggregators are not idempotent. They can be implemented as t-norms and t-conorms, or as various other hyperconjunctive and hyperdisjunctive functions. Conjunctive models of simultaneity and disjunctive models of substitutability cover the maximum possible range of andness/orness $[-1/(n-1),\ n/(n-1)]$ shown in Fig. 2.1.2. The centroid of all logic aggregation

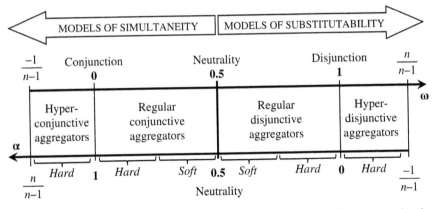

Figure 2.1.2 Andness/orness-based classification of logic aggregation functions used in the soft computing propositional logic.

models is the arithmetic mean, which is the model of conjunctive/disjunctive balance and neutrality.

In the area of evaluation logic, the idempotent regular conjunctive and regular disjunctive aggregators are much more frequent than the nonidempotent hyperconjunctive and hyperdisjunctive aggregators. For simplicity, in cases where only regular idempotent aggregators are used, we can omit the attribute *regular*, assuming that by default all conjunctive and disjunctive aggregators are regular.

2.1.4 Logic Bisection, Trisection, and Quadrisection of the Unit Hypercube

Let us now investigate the location of aggregators inside the unit hypercube $[0, 1]^n$. Logic aggregators are distributed in two main regions of the unit hypercube: conjunctive and disjunctive. The border between the conjunctive area and the disjunctive area is the neutrality plane (i.e., the arithmetic mean). The bisection of unit hypercube for $n = 2$ is shown in Fig. 2.1.3. All conjunctive aggregators, used as models of simultaneity, are located under the neutrality plane. All disjunctive aggregators, serving as models of substitutability, are located in the region above the neutrality plane. Not surprisingly, for any $n > 1$, the volumes of the conjunctive region (V_c) and the volume of the disjunctive region (V_d) are the same: $V_c = V_d = 1/2$.

Two important classic aggregators are the pure (or full) conjunction (C) and the pure (or full) disjunction (D), shown in Fig. 2.1.4. They provide a trisection of the unit hypercube: The resulting regions are *idempotent logic aggregators*

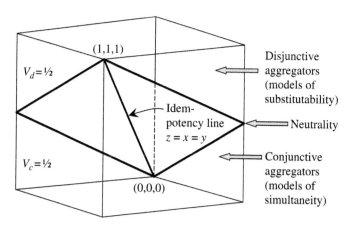

Figure 2.1.3 Bisection of unit cube using the neutrality plane $z = (x+y)/2$.

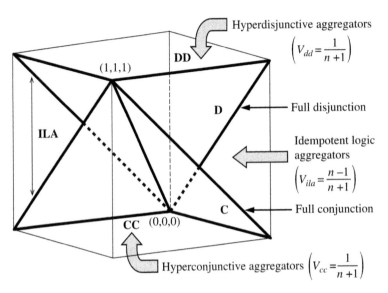

Figure 2.1.4 Trisection of the unit hypercube based on conjunction and disjunction.

(ILA), *hyperconjunctive aggregators* (CC), and *hyperdisjunctive aggregators* (DD). For example, nonidempotent t-norms are located in the CC area and nonidempotent t-conorms are located in the DD area. According to formulas (2.1.10) and (2.1.11), in the case $n = 2$, the resulting three regions have the same size $V_{cc} = V_{dd} = V_{ila} = 1/3$. However, already in the case of three variables, the situation changes: $V_{cc} = V_{dd} = ¼$, $V_{ila} = ½$. In other words, as the number of variables n grows, the region of ILA is growing, and the regions of CC and DD are shrinking.

If a logic aggregator $A(x_1, ..., x_n)$ has andness greater than 1 (or orness greater than one), it must be nonidempotent. Informal proof of this theorem for $n = 2$ directly follows from Definition 2.1.1 and geometric properties of conjunction and disjunction shown in Fig. 2.1.4. If the andness is greater than 1, then the volume under the surface of aggregator $A(x, y)$ must be less than the volume under the pure conjunction $z = \min(x,y)$. Obviously, there are only two ways to achieve such a property: either (1) the diagonal section function of such an aggregator must be below the idempotency line (i.e., $\delta_A(x) < x$), or (2) we keep the idempotency line $\delta_A(x) = x$ and bend the surface of $A(x, y)$ so that it is below the planar wings of the pure conjunction. So, if $y > x$ then $\min(x,y) = x$, but if we want to increase the andness of $A(x,y)$, then for $y > x$ we must have $A(x,y) < x = A(x,x)$. In other words, the aggregator $A(x, y)$ must be decreasing in y and it would no longer be nondecreasing. Since the cost of higher andness is the loss of nondecreasing monotonicity (and the loss of the status of

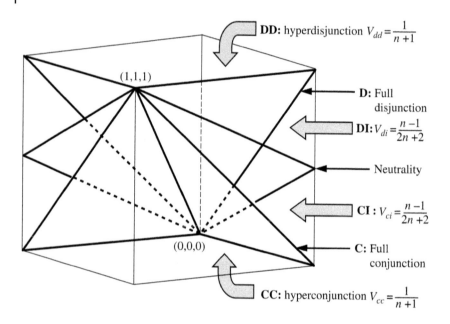

DD: hyperdisjunction $V_{dd} = \dfrac{1}{n+1}$

D: Full disjunction

DI: $V_{di} = \dfrac{n-1}{2n+2}$

Neutrality

CI : $V_{ci} = \dfrac{n-1}{2n+2}$

C: Full conjunction

CC: hyperconjunction $V_{cc} = \dfrac{1}{n+1}$

With increasing dimensionality, the range and importance of idempotent aggregators increase												
n	2	3	4	5	6	7	8	9	10	11	$n \gg 1$	Dimensionality
$V_{ci} + V_{di}$ [%]	33	50	60	67	71	75	78	80	82	83	100	Increasing volume
$V_{cc} + V_{dd}$ [%]	67	50	40	33	29	25	22	20	18	17	0	Decreasing volume

Figure 2.1.5 Quadrisection of the unit hypercube and four regions of logic aggregators.

aggregator), the option (2) must be rejected, and the only way to increase the andness is to use the option (1), i.e., to sacrifice the idempotency, and to get non-idempotent monotonic aggregators of higher andness such as $A(x,y) = xy$. Using duality, a similar reasoning can be applied in the case of orness greater than one, and in all cases where $n > 2$. Therefore, the full conjunction $\min(x_1, \ldots, x_n)$ is the most conjunctive idempotent aggregator, and the full disjunction $\max(x_1, \ldots, x_n)$ is the most disjunctive idempotent aggregator. All ILA are means, and all means can be used (more or less successfully) as ILA.

The most important logic decomposition of the unit hypercube is the quadrisection shown in Fig. 2.1.5. The four regions of the unit hypercube are denoted as follows:

- DD: nonidempotent hyperdisjunctive logic aggregators
- DI: regular disjunctive idempotent logic aggregators
- CI: regular conjunctive idempotent logic aggregators
- CC: nonidempotent hyperconjunctive logic aggregators

The volumes of these regions are:

$$V_{dd} = \frac{1}{n+1}, \quad V_{di} = \frac{n-1}{2n+2}, \quad V_{ci} = \frac{n-1}{2n+2}, \quad V_{cc} = \frac{1}{n+1},$$

$$V_{dd} + V_{di} + V_{ci} + V_{cc} = 1.$$

In the case of three variables, $V_{dd} = V_{di} = V_{ci} = V_{cc} = \frac{1}{4}$. For $n > 3$ the regions of DI and CI continue to grow and the regions of hyperconjunctive and hyperdisjunctive aggregators decrease, as shown in the table in Fig. 2.1.5. These facts have practical consequences in evaluation, because all hyperconjunctive and all hyperdisjunctive aggregators belong to the relatively small regions with volume $1/(n+1)$ and consequently, with increasing n, these aggregators must be rather similar. For example, if $A(x_1,...,x_n) = \Pi x_i$ then $\delta_A(x) = x^n$ and for $x \in [0,1]$ the values of Πx_i quickly come close to 0, reducing the diversity of hyperconjunctive and hyperdisjunctive aggregators for all values of arguments except those that are close to 1.

Further investigation of properties of aggregators located in four characteristic regions of the unit hypercube can be found in Sections 2.1.7 and 2.1.8.

2.1.5 Propositions, Value Statements, Graded Logic, and Fuzzy Logic

The meaning of *logic* permanently expands, including more and more human mental activities. A classic definition (e.g., one offered by the Webster's encyclopedic unabridged dictionary) is that *logic is the science that investigates the principles governing correct or reliable inference*. The central point of all classic definitions of logic is the valid human reasoning and its use.

We are interested in evaluation reasoning as a human mental activity, and in logic as a discipline focused on mathematical models of observable human reasoning. Of course, many authors go far beyond this basic approach. One direction is logic as an area for building abstract mathematical formalisms, and another area is logic as an engineering discipline interested in hardware and software solutions that use some basic logic components or deal with imprecision, uncertainty, and fuzziness.

Human communication is based on natural languages and consists of linguistic sentences. Some sentences are truth bearers, i.e., they can be *true* or *false* (or partially true and partially false). In logic, such sentences are called *propositions* or *statements*. In addition to propositions, human communication also includes sentences that are not truth bearers (e.g., questions, requests, commands, etc.). Many sentences (both truth bearers and not truth bearers) may include fuzzy expressions. For our purposes, the linguistic sentences and related logics can be classified as shown in Fig. 2.1.6.

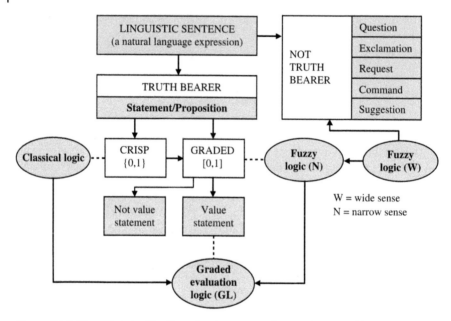

Figure 2.1.6 Simplified classification of various types of propositions and logics

In propositional logic, we study methods for correct use of propositions. Propositions can be *crisp* or *graded*, depending on the type of truth value they bear. Declarative sentences that express assertions that are either completely true (coded as 1) or completely false (coded as 0) are called *crisp propositions* or *crisp statements*. For example, the statement "a square has four sides" is a crisp proposition that is (completely) true. The classical logic (a propositional calculus from Aristotle to George Boole) deals with crisp propositions only. It is used to decide whether a statement is true or false.

The statement "Concorde is an ideal passenger jet airliner" is not crisp because it is neither completely true nor completely false. Of course, those who know history will agree that it is truer than the statement "Tu-144 is an ideal passenger jet airliner." These statements assert the value of evaluated object and their degree of truth is located between true and false. Such statements are called the *value statements*.

Truth comes in degrees. Graded propositions use degree of truth that can be continuously adjustable from false to true and coded in the interval [0,1]. Such a degree of truth can also be interpreted as the degree of membership in a fuzzy set where the full membership corresponds to the degree of truth 1, and no membership corresponds to the degree of truth 0. If a logic uses graded truth and process it using graded aggregators then we call it a *graded logic* (GL). Consequently, it is necessary to discuss relationships between GL and fuzzy logic.

That brings us to the definition of fuzzy logic. The originator of the concept of fuzzy logic is Lotfi Zadeh and it is natural to accept his explanation of this concept. On 1/25/2013, after receiving the BBVA Award, Zadeh addressed the BISC community with the message entitled "What is fuzzy logic?" that contains the following short but very precise definitions of fuzzy logic concepts in the way seen by the originator of these concepts:

> *The BBVA Award has rekindled discussions and debates regarding what fuzzy logic is and what it has to offer. The discussions and debates brought to the surface many misconceptions and misunderstandings. A major source of misunderstanding is rooted in the fact that fuzzy logic has two different meanings – fuzzy logic in a narrow sense, and fuzzy logic in a wide sense. Informally, narrow-sense fuzzy logic is a logical system which is a generalization of multivalued logic. An important example of narrow-sense fuzzy logic is fuzzy modal logic. In multivalued logic, truth is a matter of degree. A very important distinguishing feature of fuzzy logic is that in fuzzy logic everything is, or is allowed to be, a matter of degree. Furthermore, the degrees are allowed to be fuzzy. Wide-sense fuzzy logic, call it FL, is much more than a logical system. Informally, FL is a precise system of reasoning and computation in which the objects of reasoning and computation are classes with unsharp (fuzzy) boundaries. The centerpiece of fuzzy logic is the concept of a fuzzy set. More generally, FL may be a system of such systems. Today, the term fuzzy logic, FL, is used preponderantly in its wide sense. This is the sense in which the term fuzzy logic is used in the sequel. It is important to note that when we talk about the impact of fuzzy logic, we are talking about the impact of FL. Intellectually, narrow-sense fuzzy logic is an important part of FL, but volume-wise it is a very small part. In fact, most applications of fuzzy logic involve no logic in its traditional sense.*

According to Zadeh's dual (narrow/wide) classification, the wide-sense fuzzy logic includes all intellectual descendants of the concept of fuzzy set.[3] The narrow-sense fuzzy logic includes logic systems where truth is a matter of degree. Zadeh's classification is adopted in Fig. 2.1.6. According to this classification, GL is a generalization of classical bivalent and multivalued logic, as well as a fundamental component and refinement of the narrow-sense fuzzy logic.

---

3 From the time of Aristotle to the present time logic is considered a fundamental branch of philosophy. The fact that most FL applications "involve no logic in its traditional sense" but nevertheless persist in using the term "logic" may be a source of debates and controversies that are beyond the scope of this book.

The link between classical Boolean logic and GL in Fig. 2.1.6 shows that GL is a successor (and seamless generalization) of classical bivalent Boolean logic. All main properties of GL can be derived within the framework of classical logic, without explicitly using the concept of fuzzy set. On the other hand, *the partial truth of a value statement can also be interpreted as a degree of membership of the evaluated object in a fuzzy set of maximum-value objects*. Consequently, we can link FL/N and GL, and relationships between GL and FL are discussed in several sections of this book, particularly in Chapter 2.2.

Fuzzy logic has specific areas that deal with various forms of imprecision and uncertainty, and includes type 1 fuzzy logic [WIK11b, ZAD89, ZAD94, KLI95], interval type 2 fuzzy logic [WU11, MEN01, CAS08], and others.

In the area of evaluation we are primarily interested in *value statements* (propositions that affirm or deny value, based on decision maker goals and requirements). Typical examples of value statements are "the area of home H completely satisfies all our needs," "the location of airport A is perfectly suitable for city C," and "student S deserves the highest grade." All these statements can be partially true and partially false. The degree of truth of a value statement is a human percept, interpreted as the degree of satisfaction of stakeholder's requirements. Generally, we define GL as follows.

Definition 2.1.2. Graded logic (GL) is an infinite-valued propositional calculus based on continuous, monotonic, noncommutative (weighted) and compensative models of graded simultaneity (conjunction) and graded substitutability (disjunction), and used primarily to create aggregation structures for computing the degree of truth of compound value statements. By combining the graded conjunction, disjunction and standard negation, GL becomes a seamless generalization of the classic bivalent Boolean logic, extending it from $\{0, 1\}^n$ to $[0, 1]^n$.

According to this definition, GL is used for processing degrees of truth. The degree of truth of a value statement can be interpreted as the degree of suitability or the degree of preference. To have a compact notation we usually call these degrees simply "suitability" or "preference." Of course, the degrees of truth are human percepts and GL can also be interpreted as a mathematical infrastructure for perceptual computing. So, the term *suitability* means *the human percept of suitability*. One of our main objectives is to compute the overall suitability of a complex object as a logic function of the suitability degrees of its components (attributes).

The most distinctive GL properties (and the most frequently used) are internality and idempotency of graded simultaneity (partial conjunction) and substitutability (partial disjunction) models. In addition, using interpolative aggregators [DUJ05c, DUJ14], GL provides seamless connectivity between idempotent and nonidempotent logic aggregators [DUJ16a], covering all regions of the unit hypercube (see Section 2.1.7 and Chapter 2.4).

Internality holds in all cases where the overall suitability of a complex object cannot be greater than the suitability of its best component, or less than the suitability of its worst component. Internality yields the possibility to interpret means as logic functions, located between the pure conjunction (the minimum function) and the pure disjunction (the maximum function). Based on this interpretation, the first form of *graded (or generalized) conjunction/disjunction* (GCD) was proposed in [DUJ73b] as a general logic function that provides a continuous transition from conjunction to disjunction by selecting a desired conjunction degree (andness), or the desired disjunction degree (orness). By making conjunction a matter of degree and disjunction a matter of degree, and using weights as degrees of importance of inputs we made an explicit move toward a *graded logic*, where everything is a matter of degree.

Relationships between the classical bivalent Boolean logic (BL), the graded logic (GL), the fuzzy logic in the narrow sense (FL/N) and the fuzzy logic in the wide sense (FL/W) are subset-structured as follows: $BL \subset GL \subset FL/N \subset FL/W$. BL is primarily a crisp bivalent propositional calculus. GL includes BL plus graded truth, graded idempotent conjunction/disjunction, weight-based semantics, and (less frequently) nonidempotent hyperconjunction/hyperdisjunction (Section 2.1.7). GL also supports all nonidempotent basic logic functions (e.g., partial *implication*, partial *equivalence*, partial *nand*, partial *nor*, partial *exclusive or*, and others). All such functions are "partial" in the sense that they use adjustable degrees of similarity or proximity to their "crisp" equivalents in traditional bivalent logic. FL/N includes GL plus variety of forms of nonidempotent conjunction/disjunction, and other generalizations of multivalued logic. FL/W includes FL/N plus all a wide variety of models of reasoning and computation based on the concept of fuzzy set.

Because of its location between BL and FL/N, we can interpret GL as a descendant of both the classical bivalent logic, and the fuzzy logic. These two interpretations are complementary. In the case of logic interpretation, all variables represent suitability, i.e. the degrees of truth of value statements that assert the highest values of evaluated objects or their components. In the case of fuzzy interpretation, the variables represent the degrees of membership in corresponding fuzzy sets of highest-value objects. In the case of bivalent logic, GL is a direct and natural seamless generalization of BL (in points $\{0, 1\}^n$ of hypercube $[0, 1]^n$ we have GL=BL). In the case of fuzzy logic, GL is a special case, even if the fuzzy logic is defined in a narrow sense, because GL excludes various fuzzy concepts and techniques that are not related to logic. Since GL is primarily a propositional calculus, it is more convenient and more natural to interpret GL as a weighted compensative generalization of classical bivalent Boolean logic, than to interpret GL as a relatively narrow subarea in a heterogeneous set of models of reasoning and computation derived from the concept of fuzzy set. However, contacts of GL and the area of fuzzy sets are frequent and natural, in particular because GL provides logic infrastructure in all cases where fuzzy models need to include human percepts and human logic reasoning.

2.1.6 Classical Bivalent Boolean Logic

> *Omne enuntiatum aut verum aut falsum est.*
> *(Every statement is either true or false.)*
> —Marcus Tullius Cicero, *De Fato*, 44 BC

In this section we summarize a classical bivalent propositional calculus with crisp truth values formalized as a Boolean algebra. Let us assume that the only logic values are *true* (numerically coded as 1) and *false* (numerically coded as 0), and all logic variables, as well as andness and orness,[4] belong to the set $\{0,1\}$. The basic logic functions are the pure conjunction (*and* function) $z = x \wedge y = \min(x,y)$, the pure disjunction (*or* function) $z = x \vee y = \max(x,y)$, and negation $\bar{x} = 1 - x$. Obviously, $\bar{\bar{x}} = x$ (involution), $x \vee \bar{x} = 1$, $x \wedge \bar{x} = 0$, $x \wedge x = x \vee x = x$. Under these assumptions a Boolean function of n variables $z = f(x_1,...,x_n)$ is defined using 2^n combinations of input values (from 00...0 to 11...1). Consequently, there are 2^{2^n} different Boolean functions of n variables.

If $n=1$ there are four Boolean functions shown in Table 2.1.1 and if $n=2$ there are 16 Boolean functions shown in Table 2.1.2. We always assume that conjunction has higher precedence than disjunction. For example, we can write basic logic expressions without parentheses: $(x \wedge \bar{y}) \vee (\bar{x} \wedge y) = x \wedge \bar{y} \vee \bar{x} \wedge y$. Engineering literature frequently uses a simplified notation of logic expressions where the previous example is written as $x\bar{y} + \bar{x}y$ (conjunction is interpreted as *logic multiplication* and denoted using concatenation, and disjunction is interpreted

Table 2.1.1 Boolean Functions $y = f(x)$

x	0	1	Function	Name
y_0	0	0	$y_0 = 0$	Constant 0
y_1	0	1	$y_1 = x$	Variable x
y_2	1	0	$y_2 = \bar{x}$	Negation
y_3	1	1	$y_3 = 1$	Constant 1

---

4 Andness denotes an adjustable degree of simultaneity, and orness denotes an adjustable degree of substitutability; in the case of idempotent functions, the highest andness/orness is 1 and it corresponds to the pure conjunction/disjunction.

Table 2.1.2 Bivalent Boolean functions $z = f(x,y)$.

x	0	1	0	1	Function	Name
y	0	0	1	1		
z_0	0	0	0	0	$z_0 = 0$	Constant 0
z_1	1	0	0	0	$z_1 = x \downarrow y = \overline{x} \wedge \overline{y} = \overline{x \vee y}$	Nor
z_2	0	1	0	0	$z_2 = x \wedge \overline{y} = \overline{x \rightarrow y}$	Abjunction
z_3	1	1	0	0	$z_3 = \overline{y}$	Negation of y
z_4	0	0	1	0	$z_4 = \overline{x} \wedge y = \overline{y \rightarrow x}$	Abjunction
z_5	1	0	1	0	$z_5 = \overline{x}$	Negation of x
z_6	0	1	1	0	$z_6 = x \oplus y = (x \wedge \overline{y}) \vee (\overline{x} \wedge y) = \overline{x \sim y}$	Exclusive or
z_7	1	1	1	0	$z_7 = x \mid y = \overline{x} \vee \overline{y} = \overline{x \wedge y}$	Nand
z_8	0	0	0	1	$z_8 = x \wedge y$	Conjunction (*and*)
z_9	1	0	0	1	$z_9 = x \sim y = (\overline{x} \wedge \overline{y}) \vee (x \wedge y) = \overline{x \oplus y}$	Equivalence
z_{10}	0	1	0	1	$z_{10} = (x \wedge \overline{y}) \vee (x \wedge y) = x \wedge (\overline{y} \vee y) = x$	Absorption of y
z_{11}	1	1	0	1	$z_{11} = y \rightarrow x = \overline{y \wedge \overline{x}} = \overline{y} \vee x$	Implication
z_{12}	0	0	1	1	$z_{12} = (\overline{x} \wedge y) \vee (x \wedge y) = y \wedge (\overline{x} \vee x) = y$	Absorption of x
z_{13}	1	0	1	1	$z_{13} = x \rightarrow y = \overline{x \wedge \overline{y}} = \overline{x} \vee y$	Implication
z_{14}	0	1	1	1	$z_{14} = x \vee y$	Disjunction (*or*)
z_{15}	1	1	1	1	$z_{15} = 1$	Constant 1

as *logic addition* and denoted using the plus sign). To avoid ambiguity we will use different symbols for conjunction/disjunction and arithmetic operations.

Pure conjunction and disjunction are idempotent, commutative, associative, and distributive; there are also neutral elements, annihilators, and inverse elements:

$$x \wedge x = x, \qquad\qquad x \vee x = x,$$

$$x \wedge y = y \wedge x, \qquad\qquad x \vee y = y \vee x,$$

$$x \wedge y \wedge z = (x \wedge y) \wedge z = x \wedge (y \wedge z), \quad x \vee y \vee z = (x \vee y) \vee z = x \vee (y \vee z),$$

$$x \wedge (y \vee z) = (x \wedge y) \vee (x \wedge z), \qquad x \vee (y \wedge z) = (x \vee y) \wedge (x \vee z),$$

$$x \wedge 1 = x, \ x \wedge 0 = 0, \ x \wedge \overline{x} = 0, \qquad x \vee 0 = x, \ x \vee 1 = 1, \ x \vee \overline{x} = 1.$$

Since $\forall x \in \{0,1\}$, $x \wedge 0 = 0$, $x \vee 1 = 1$, it follows that 0 is the annihilator for conjunction and 1 is the annihilator for disjunction.

Using distributivity it is easy to show the following total absorption properties[5] that *completely* eliminate (absorb) the impact of variable y:

$$x \vee (x \wedge y) = (x \wedge 1) \vee (x \wedge y) = x \wedge (1 \vee y) = x \wedge 1 = x,$$
$$x \wedge (x \vee y) = (x \vee 0) \wedge (x \vee y) = x \vee (0 \wedge y) = x \vee 0 = x.$$

These relations are the reason for calling the corresponding functions in Table 2.1.2 the total absorption. In addition, we frequently use the following simplification properties:

$$(x \wedge y) \vee (x \wedge \bar{y}) = x \wedge (y \vee \bar{y}) = x \wedge 1 = x,$$
$$(x \vee y) \wedge (x \vee \bar{y}) = x \vee (y \wedge \bar{y}) = x \vee 0 = x,$$
$$x \vee (\bar{x} \wedge y) = (x \vee \bar{x}) \wedge (x \vee y) = 1 \wedge (x \vee y) = x \vee y,$$
$$x \wedge (\bar{x} \vee y) = (x \wedge \bar{x}) \vee (x \wedge y) = 0 \vee (x \wedge y) = x \wedge y.$$

Table 2.1.2 can be used to identify two important properties of Boolean functions that are subsequently inherited in GL: *monotonicity* and *idempotency*. Monotonicity is the fundamental property of conjunction and disjunction: it means that an increase (i.e., the change from 0 to 1) of any input variable either increases the output or keeps it unchanged, but can never cause a decrease (the change from 1 to 0). Similarly, a decrease (i.e., the change from 1 to 0) of any input variable either decreases the output or keeps it unchanged, but can never cause an increase (the change from 0 to 1). For monotonic functions, the output values either remain unchanged or change in the same direction as input variables. All compound functions that are obtained as superposition of monotonic functions are also monotonic. Nonmonotonicity can be realized by using negation.

Considering the important property of idempotency, in Table 2.1.2 idempotent are those functions $z = f(x, y)$ where $f(b, b) = b \in \{0, 1\}$, i.e., those functions that have 0 in the first column and 1 in the fourth column. So, the idempotency holds only for four functions: z_8, z_{10}, z_{12}, z_{14} (conjunction, disjunction, and two absorptions). No other Boolean function of two variables satisfies the boundary conditions $f(0, 0) = 0$ and $f(1, 1) = 1$. Since GL is a generalization of classical Boolean logic (obtained using the *graded conjunction*/disjunction instead of pure conjunction or pure disjunction), it follows that *the only idempotent GL functions are the graded conjunction/disjunction and compound aggregation functions (e.g., partial absorption) obtained as a superposition of special cases of the graded conjunction/disjunction.*

---

5 In Chapter 2.6 we present the partial absorption which is a generalization of these important properties.

Boolean functions that are listed in Table 2.1.2 sometimes appear in literature under different names. For example, the implication $x \rightarrow y = \overline{x} \wedge \overline{y}$ is also known as "material implication" and it means that if the antecedent x implies the consequent y, then it is not possible that x is satisfied and y is not satisfied. The negated implication $\overline{x \rightarrow y} = x \wedge \overline{y}$ is also known as material nonimplication, or abjunction. In the context of evaluation the abjunction is an elementary model of bipolarity because it aggregates a desired property x and an undesired property y. If $x \rightarrow y$ denotes implication, then $y \rightarrow x = \overline{y} \wedge \overline{\overline{x}}$ is a converse implication. The total absorption of x and y are sometimes called projection functions.

For $x_i \in \{0, 1\}$ and an arbitrary Boolean function of n variables, we can use the following decomposition (separation of x_i and other variables):

$$x_i \wedge f(x_1,\ldots,x_i,\ldots,x_n) = x_i \wedge f(x_1,\ldots,1,\ldots,x_n),$$

$$\overline{x}_i \wedge f(x_1,\ldots,x_i,\ldots,x_n) = \overline{x}_i \wedge f(x_1,\ldots,0,\ldots,x_n),$$

$$x_i \vee f(x_1,\ldots,x_i,\ldots,x_n) = x_i \vee f(x_1,\ldots,0,\ldots,x_n),$$

$$\overline{x}_i \vee f(x_1,\ldots,x_i,\ldots,x_n) = \overline{x}_i \vee f(x_1,\ldots,1,\ldots,x_n).$$

The above decomposition can be generalized. First, let us introduce a convenient notation $x^1 = x$, $x^0 = \overline{x}$. Then, we have the following decomposition theorem:

$$f(x_1,\ldots,x_k,x_{k+1},\ldots,x_n) = \bigvee_{\substack{a_i \in \{0,1\} \\ i=1,\ldots,k \leq n}} \left(x_1^{a_1} \wedge \ldots \wedge x_k^{a_k} \wedge f(a_1,\ldots,a_k,x_{k+1},\ldots,x_n)\right).$$

The above disjunction includes 2^k terms. For example, for $k = 2$, $n = 4$ we have

$$f(x,y,a,b) = (\overline{x} \wedge \overline{y} \wedge f(0,0,a,b)) \vee (\overline{x} \wedge y \wedge f(0,1,a,b)) \vee$$
$$(x \wedge \overline{y} \wedge f(1,0,a,b)) \vee (x \wedge y \wedge f(1,1,a,b)).$$

If $k = n = 2$ then we get a disjunctive normal form (disjunction of conjunctive clauses) of the function of two variables:

$$f(x,y) = (\overline{x} \wedge \overline{y} \wedge f(0,0)) \vee (\overline{x} \wedge y \wedge f(0,1)) \vee (x \wedge \overline{y} \wedge f(1,0))$$
$$\vee (x \wedge y \wedge f(1,1)).$$

Obviously, the disjunctive normal form includes only those terms where $f(x,y) = 1$ (e.g., $x \sim y = \overline{x} \wedge \overline{y} \vee x \wedge y$). Similar disjunctive normal forms can be easily written for any number of variables.

The negation of Boolean functions is based on De Morgan's laws $\overline{x \wedge y} = \overline{x} \vee \overline{y}$, $\overline{x \vee y} = \overline{x} \wedge \overline{y}$. These laws can be easily verified; if $x = 0$, then we have $\overline{0 \wedge y} = 1 \vee \overline{y} = 1$, $\overline{0 \vee y} = 1 \wedge \overline{y} = \overline{y}$ and if $x = 1$ then we have $\overline{1 \wedge y} = 0 \vee \overline{y} = \overline{y}$, $\overline{1 \vee y} = 0 \wedge \overline{y} = 0$. De Morgan's laws show the duality of conjunction and disjunction: if we have one of these operations, the other one can be obtained as a mirrored dual operation. To make conjunction from disjunction we use $x \wedge y = \overline{\bar{x} \vee \bar{y}}$ and to make disjunction from conjunction we use $x \vee y = \overline{\bar{x} \wedge \bar{y}}$. De Morgan's law can be written for general Boolean function $f: \{0,1\}^n \rightarrow \{0,1\}$ as follows:

$$\overline{f(x_1,...,x_n, \wedge, \vee, 0, 1)} = f(\bar{x}_1,...,\bar{x}_n, \vee, \wedge, 1, 0).$$

For example, if $f(x,y,z) = \overline{(\bar{x} \vee y)} \vee (x \wedge \bar{y} \wedge \bar{z})$ then $\overline{f(x,y,z)} = \overline{(x \wedge \bar{y})} \wedge (\bar{x} \vee y \vee z)$. This example illustrates that the generalized De Morgan's law assumes a parenthesized notation of Boolean expressions, and during the replacement of variables and operators all parentheses must remain unchanged. In simple cases that is not visible. For example, the implication $x \rightarrow y$ is interpreted as follows: if from x follows y then it is not possible that x is satisfied and y is not satisfied. Consequently, $x \rightarrow y = \overline{x \wedge \bar{y}} = \bar{x} \vee y$.

Frequently used functions of three variables are:

$$f_1(x,y,z) = (x \wedge y) \vee (x \wedge z) \vee (y \wedge z) = (x \vee y) \wedge (x \vee z) \wedge (y \vee z),$$
$$f_2(x,y,z) = (\bar{x} \wedge \bar{y} \wedge z) \vee (\bar{x} \wedge y \wedge \bar{z}) \vee (x \wedge \bar{y} \wedge \bar{z}) \vee (x \wedge y \wedge z),$$
$$f_3(x,y,z) = (\bar{x} \wedge \bar{y} \wedge \bar{z}) \vee (x \wedge y \wedge z).$$

Here $f_1(x,y,z) = 1$ if two or more inputs are equal to 1; $f_2(x,y,z) = 1$ if an odd number of inputs is equal to 1 (addition modulo 2); $f_3(x,y,z) = 1$ if all inputs are equivalent (either 0 or 1), i.e., $f_3(x, y, z)$ is the equivalence function.

Classical Boolean logic can be derived in a deductive axiomatic way as a Boolean algebra using a set with two elements $B = \{0,1\}$ and binary internal operations $\wedge$ and $\vee$ (i.e., $\forall x,y \in B \Rightarrow x \wedge y \in B$, $x \vee y \in B$), using the following three axioms:

A1. Binary operations $\wedge$ and $\vee$ are commutative and distributive:

$\forall x,y,z \in B:$

$$x \wedge y = y \wedge x, \qquad\qquad x \vee y = y \vee x,$$
$$x \wedge (y \vee z) = (x \wedge y) \vee (x \wedge z), \quad x \vee (y \wedge z) = (x \vee y) \wedge (x \vee z).$$

A2. On set B binary internal operations $\wedge$ and $\vee$ have two different neutral elements:

$$(\forall x \in B)\, (\exists 0 \in B) \Rightarrow x \vee 0 = x,$$
$$(\forall x \in B)\, (\exists 1 \in B) \Rightarrow x \wedge 1 = x.$$

A3. On set B each element x has a unique inverse element

$$(\forall x \in B)\, (\exists \bar{x} \in B) \Rightarrow x \vee \bar{x} = 1,$$
$$(\forall x \in B)\, (\exists \bar{x} \in B) \Rightarrow x \wedge \bar{x} = 0.$$

Using these axioms, it is possible to prove various properties presented in this section (idempotency, involution, absorption, associativity, Dr Morgan's laws, etc.). For example, the idempotency can be proved as follows:

$$x = x \wedge 1 \qquad \dots\dots \quad [A2]$$
$$= x \wedge (x \vee \bar{x}) \qquad \dots\dots \quad [A3]$$
$$= (x \wedge x) \vee (x \wedge \bar{x}) \qquad \dots\dots \quad [A1]$$
$$= (x \wedge x) \vee 0 \qquad \dots\dots \quad [A3]$$
$$= x \wedge x \qquad \dots\dots \quad [A2] \; .$$

$$x = x \vee 0 \qquad \dots\dots \quad [A2]$$
$$= x \vee (x \wedge \bar{x}) \qquad \dots\dots \quad [A3]$$
$$= (x \vee x) \wedge (x \vee \bar{x}) \qquad \dots\dots \quad [A1]$$
$$= (x \vee x) \wedge 1 \qquad \dots\dots \quad [A3]$$
$$= x \vee x \qquad \dots\dots \quad [A2] \; .$$

An important property of a Boolean algebra, clearly visible from A1, A2, A3, and the above examples, is the concept of *duality*: all axioms are given in pairs, separately for operation $\wedge$ and for operation $\vee$. In addition, these operations are symmetrical: if $\vee$ is replaced by $\wedge$, and 1 by 0, then using an axiom for $\vee$ we get the corresponding axiom for $\wedge$. According to duality, a dual of any Boolean expression can be derived by replacing $\vee$ by $\wedge$, $\wedge$ by $\vee$, 0 by 1, and 1 by 0. Then, any theorem that can be proved is thus also proved for its dual. This property is visible (and useful) in all other relations of classical Boolean logic. For example, consider the following simplification:

$$(x \wedge a) \vee (\bar{x} \wedge b) \vee (a \wedge b) = (x \wedge a) \vee (\bar{x} \wedge b).$$

The validity of this relation can be verified if we separately consider the cases $x = 0$ (when both sides of the relation reduce to b) and $x = 1$ (when both sides of the relation reduce to a). Now, we can use duality to claim that the following holds:

$$(x \vee a) \wedge (\bar{x} \vee b) \wedge (a \vee b) = (x \vee a) \wedge (\bar{x} \vee b).$$

Similarly, a conjunctive normal form can be derived as a dual of the corresponding disjunctive normal form.

All Boolean logic functions can be derived by superposing a set of basic functions. The most frequent sets of such functions are:

1) $z_8 = x \wedge y$, $z_{14} = x \vee y$, $z_5 = \bar{x}$.
2) $z_1 = x \downarrow y = \bar{x} \wedge \bar{y} = \overline{x \vee y}$.

3) $z_7 = x|y = \bar{x} \vee \bar{y} = \overline{x \wedge y}$.
4) $z_{14} = x \vee y,\ z_5 = \bar{x}$.
5) $z_8 = x \wedge y,\ z_5 = \bar{x}$.
6) $z_6 = x \oplus y,\ z_8 = x \wedge y,\ z_{15} = 1$.
7) $z_9 = x \sim y,\ z_8 = x \wedge y,\ z_0 = 0$.
8) $z_2 = x \wedge \bar{y} = \overline{x \rightarrow y},\ z_{15} = 1$.
9) $z_{13} = x \rightarrow y = \overline{x \wedge \bar{y}} = \bar{x} \vee y,\ z_0 = 0$.

For example, cases #2 and #3 show that negation, conjunction, and disjunction can be expressed using *nor* and *nand* functions as follows:

$$\bar{x} = x \downarrow x,$$

$$x \wedge y = \overline{\bar{x} \vee \bar{y}} = \bar{x} \downarrow \bar{y} = (x \downarrow x) \downarrow (y \downarrow y),$$

$$x \vee y = \overline{x \downarrow y} = (x \downarrow y) \downarrow (x \downarrow y),$$

$$\bar{x} = x|x,$$

$$x \wedge y = \overline{x|y} = (x|y)|(x|y),$$

$$x \vee y = \overline{\bar{x} \wedge \bar{y}} = \bar{x}|\bar{y} = (x|x)|(y|y).$$

In case #9, we can express negation, disjunction, and conjunction, as follows:

$$\bar{x} = x \rightarrow 0,$$

$$x \vee y = \bar{x} \rightarrow y = (x \rightarrow 0) \rightarrow y,$$

$$x \wedge y = \overline{\bar{x} \vee \bar{y}} = (x \rightarrow (y \rightarrow 0)) \rightarrow 0.$$

Note that $\forall x \in \{0,1\}$, $x \rightarrow x = \bar{x} \vee x = 1$, $x \rightarrow \bar{x} = \bar{x}$, $(x \rightarrow x) \rightarrow \overline{(x \rightarrow x)} = 1 \rightarrow 0 = 0$, and the implication can also be combined with negation. If $x \rightarrow y$ and $y \rightarrow x$, that means that x and y are equivalent: $(x \rightarrow y) \wedge (y \rightarrow x) = (\bar{x} \vee y) \wedge (\bar{y} \vee x) = (\bar{x} \wedge \bar{y}) \vee (x \wedge y) = x \sim y$.

In case #6 from $x \oplus y = (x \wedge \bar{y}) \vee (\bar{x} \wedge y)$, we have $x \oplus 1 = (x \wedge 0) \vee (\bar{x} \wedge 1) = \bar{x}$, $x \oplus 0 = x$ and consequently

$$\bar{x} = x \oplus 1,$$

$$x \vee y = \overline{\bar{x} \wedge \bar{y}} = 1 \oplus ((1 \oplus x) \wedge (1 \oplus y)).$$

If $x, y \in \{0,1\}$, then all basic binary Boolean functions can also be expressed using simple arithmetic operations of addition, subtraction, and multiplication, as follows:

$$\bar{x} = 1 - x,$$

$$x \wedge y = xy,$$

$$x \vee y = x + y - xy = x + \bar{x}y = y + x\bar{y},$$

$$x \oplus y = x + y - 2xy = x(1 - y) + y(1 - x) = x\bar{y} + y\bar{x},$$

$$x \sim y = 1 - x - y + 2xy,$$

$$x \rightarrow y = 1 - x + xy = 1 - x(1 - y).$$

In classical Boolean logic, simultaneity and substitutability are not graded. Conjunction is the only model of simultaneity and disjunction is the only model of substitutability (replaceability). Conjunction and disjunction are dual based on De Morgan's laws:

$$x \wedge y = \overline{(x \wedge y)} = \overline{(\bar{x} \vee \bar{y})} = 1 - (1-x) \vee (1-y),$$
$$x \vee y = \overline{(x \vee y)} = \overline{(\bar{x} \wedge \bar{y})} = 1 - (1-x) \wedge (1-y).$$

These laws are suitable for simplification of expressions, as in the following examples:

$$\overline{(\bar{x} \vee y)} \vee \overline{(\bar{x} \vee \bar{y})} = (x \wedge \bar{y}) \vee (x \wedge y) = x \wedge (\bar{y} \vee y) = x \wedge 1 = x \quad \text{(Huntington axiom)},$$

$$\overline{\overline{(x \vee y)} \vee \overline{(x \vee \bar{y})}} = (x \vee y) \wedge (x \vee \bar{y}) = x \vee (y \wedge \bar{y}) = x \vee 0 = x \quad \text{(Robbins axiom)}.$$

Axioms of Boolean algebra (A1, A2, A3) are not the only way to define Boolean algebra. They can be derived from, or replaced by, the Huntington axiom plus commutativity $x \vee y = y \vee x$ and associativity $x \vee (y \vee z) = (x \vee y) \vee z$, or by the Robbins axiom plus commutativity and associativity (i.e., the Huntington axiom is replaceable by the Robbins axiom).

A straightforward approach to propositional logic and propositional calculus consists of creating the models of simultaneity, substitutability, and negation, and then building all other compound functions by superposing these three fundamental components.

Tautologies are defined as formulas that are always true. Following are selected tautologies that are frequently used in bivalent logic reasoning.

The law of the excluded middle:

$$x \vee \bar{x} = 1.$$

Modus ponens (if x is satisfied and x implies y, then that implies that y is also satisfied):

$$(x \wedge (x \rightarrow y)) \rightarrow y = (x \wedge (\bar{x} \vee y)) \rightarrow y = (x \wedge y) \rightarrow y = \bar{x} \vee \bar{y} \vee y = \bar{x} \vee 1 = 1.$$

Syllogism (if x implies y and y implies z, then x implies z):

$$((x \rightarrow y) \wedge (y \rightarrow z)) \rightarrow (x \rightarrow z) = ((\bar{x} \vee y) \wedge (\bar{y} \vee z)) \rightarrow (\bar{x} \vee z)$$
$$= ((\bar{x} \wedge \bar{y}) \vee (\bar{x} \wedge z) \vee (y \wedge z)) \rightarrow (\bar{x} \vee z) = \overline{(\bar{x} \wedge \bar{y}) \vee (\bar{x} \wedge z) \vee (y \wedge z)} \vee \bar{x} \vee z$$
$$= (x \vee y) \wedge (x \vee \bar{z}) \wedge (\bar{y} \vee \bar{z}) \vee \bar{x} \vee z = \bar{x} \vee 1$$
$$= (x \vee y\bar{z}) \wedge (\bar{y} \vee \bar{z}) \vee \bar{x} \vee z = (x \wedge \bar{y}) \vee (x \wedge \bar{z}) \vee (y \wedge \bar{z}) \vee \bar{x} \vee z =$$
$$= ((x \wedge \bar{y}) \vee \bar{x}) \vee ((x \wedge \bar{z}) \vee z) \vee ((y \wedge \bar{z}) \vee z) \vee \bar{x} \vee z$$
$$= (\bar{y} \vee \bar{x}) \vee (x \vee z) \vee (y \vee z) \vee \bar{x} \vee z = (x \vee \bar{x}) \vee (y \vee \bar{y}) \vee z = 1 \vee 1 \vee z = 1.$$

Reductio ad absurdum (if x implies both y and its negation $\bar{y}$, then x must be false):

$$((x \rightarrow y) \wedge (x \rightarrow \bar{y})) \rightarrow \bar{x} = (\bar{x} \vee y) \wedge (\bar{x} \vee \bar{y}) \rightarrow \bar{x} = \bar{x} \rightarrow \bar{x} = x \vee \bar{x} = 1.$$

Classical Boolean functions of n variables are defined only in 2^n isolated vertices $\{0, 1\}^n$ of the unit hypercube $[0, 1]^n$. In the case of Boolean function $f : \{0,1\}^n \rightarrow \{0,1\}$ we have a binary value of function f defined in each vertex, yielding 2^{2^n} different Boolean functions of n variables. As opposed to that, in the case of GL function of n variables $F : [0,1]^n \rightarrow [0,1]$ the degrees of truth belong to the whole interval $[0,1]$, and the function F has a value from the unit interval in each and every point of the hypercube $[0, 1]^n$. Consequently, GL expands logic models in the whole unit hypercube using six important expansions presented in the next section.

2.1.7 Six Generalizations of Bivalent Boolean Logic

Graded logic is used for modeling human reasoning and decision making in the area of evaluation. The goal of this section is to introduce fundamental GL concepts and properties by systematically expanding and generalizing corresponding properties of the classical bivalent Boolean logic (BL). All presented generalizations are motivated by the applicability of GL in modeling human decision making.

Most concepts in human evaluation logic reasoning (such as truth, importance, suitability, simultaneity, etc.) are a matter of degree. Consequently, that area of human logic reasoning is not reducible to zeros and ones, and it cannot be modeled only in the vertices of the hypercube $\{0, 1\}^n$ as in the case of classical bivalent BL. Since the truth is a matter of degree, it belongs to interval $I = [0,1]$ and all humanized models of logic reasoning must be applicable everywhere inside the hypercube $[0, 1]^n$. Such models are observable in human evaluation reasoning and belong to GL.

Regardless of significant applicability of BL in the area of computing, the expressive power of bivalent BL as an infrastructure for modeling human reasoning and decision making, particularly in the area of evaluation, is extremely modest. Indeed, BL can be used only for modeling insignificant extreme cases of reasoning where conjunction is reduced to the minimum function and disjunction is reduced to the maximum function. On the other hand, these extreme cases must also be available in GL. Consequently, GL must be a seamless generalization of BL and in the vertices $\{0, 1\}^n$ of the hypercube $[0, 1]^n$ GL and BL must be identical.

Another important distinction is that BL ignores semantic aspects of logic, such as the percept of importance, and compensative logic properties where most deficiencies of some inputs can be compensated by excesses of other inputs, while GL takes semantic aspects explicitly into account. More precisely, GL is a weighted compensative generalization of classical BL, and can sometimes be denoted as a weighted compensative logic [DUJ15a].

Observations of human evaluation reasoning indicate that GL must provide six fundamental expansions (generalizations) of BL that can be summarized as follows:

1) *Expansion of function domain:* Boolean logic function domain is extended from $\{0,1\}^n$ to $[0,1]^n$, and crisp values are replaced by graded values.
2) *Expansion of logic domain:* The basic logic function, called *graded* (or generalized) *conjunction/disjunction* (GCD), must provide a parameterized continuous transition from conjunction to disjunction controlled by andness/orness.
3) *Expansion of annihilator adjustability:* GCD must provide adjustable support for annihilators 1 and 0.
4) *Expansion of semantic domain:* logic functions must provide the adjustability of degrees of importance of variables using weights.
5) *Expansion of compensative logic functions:* To keep compatibility with the observable properties of human intuitive logic reasoning (i.e., the applicability in decision models), GL must support compensative properties of aggregation operators.
6) *Expansion of the range of andness/orness from drastic conjunction to drastic disjunction:* GL provides a possibility to combine idempotent and nonidempotent logic aggregators, making a seamless transition from idempotent behavior to nonidempotent behavior inside the same aggregator and covering all regions of the unit hypercube from drastic conjunction ($\alpha = 2$) to drastic disjunction ($\omega = 2$).

Following is a detailed description and justification of these necessary expansions.

2.1.7.1 Expansion of Function Domain

The basic expansion of Boolean logic function domain from $\{0, 1\}^n$ to $[0, 1]^n$ is illustrated for $n = 3$ in Fig. 2.1.7. The GL must be a seamless generalization of BL, i.e., GL and BL must be identical in $\{0, 1\}^n$. In all points inside the hypercube $[0, 1]^n$ GL functions have values from the interval $[0,1]$.

From the standpoint of evaluation logic, the most important dichotomy of both BL and GL functions of two or more variables $f(x_1,...,x_n)$, $n > 1$ is the identification and separation of two fundamental categories of functions: idempotent functions ($\forall x \in [0,1]$, $f(x,...,x) = x$) and nonidempotent functions ($f(x,...,x) \neq x$, $x \in]0,1[$).

In the case of idempotent GL functions, the idempotency is present in all points of the idempotency line $x_1 = x_2 = \cdots = x_n \in [0,1]$. Fig. 2.1.7 shows the

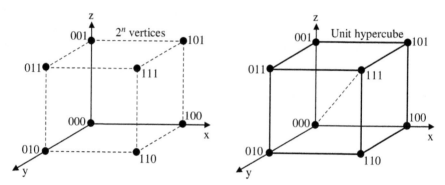

Figure 2.1.7 Expansion of logic function domain from vertices to the whole unit hypercube.

dashed idempotency line connecting for $n = 3$ the points $(x,y,z) = (0,0,0)$ and $(x, y, z)=(1, 1, 1)$. Thus, the idempotent partial conjunction, partial disjunction, and all compound functions obtained by superposition of idempotent partial conjunction and partial disjunction include (contain) the idempotency line, which connects the points $0, ..., 0$ and $1, ..., 1$.

Idempotent BL functions satisfy the conditions $f(0,...,0) = 0$ and $f(1,...,1) = 1$. For $n=2$, the only idempotent BL functions are conjunction $y = x_1 \wedge x_2$, disjunction $y = x_1 \vee x_2$, conjunctive (total) absorption $y = x_1 \wedge (x_1 \vee x_2) = x_1$ and disjunctive (total) absorption $y = x_1 \vee (x_1 \wedge x_2) = x_1$. Since GL and BL must be identical in 2^n vertices $\{0, 1\}^n$, for $n=2$ it follows that the only idempotent GL functions of two variables are conjunction, disjunction, and absorption. The terms *conjunction* and *disjunction* assume both the full and the partial versions of these functions, and the term *absorption* assumes both the total and the partial absorption (Chapter 2.6). These are the only functions that can be written without the use of negation. Both BL and GL functions of n variables are always a superposition of functions of two variables and negation ($\bar{x} = 1 - x$). It is easy to verify the following properties that hold in both BL and GL:

I) All functions made as a superposition of idempotent functions are idempotent.
II) If nonidempotent functions are based on idempotent forms of partial conjunction and disjunction, they must contain negation.
III) If a function $y = f(x_1,...,x_n)$ is idempotent, then its De Morgan dual $y_{dual} = g(x_1,...,x_n) = 1 - f(1 - x_1,..., 1 - x_n)$ is also idempotent.
IV) Logic functions that contain negation can be either idempotent or nonidempotent.

To verify the property (I) the functions of two or more variables should be written in form of a tree where each node represents an idempotent function.

If all leaves have the same value, then that value propagates through all nodes up to the root of the tree. To verify the property (II) we can consider the opposite case: if there is no negation involved, then the compound function must be a superposition of idempotent functions of conjunction, disjunction, and absorption, giving the idempotent function. Consequently, such nonidempotent functions must contain negation. To verify the property (III) let $x_1 = \ldots = x_n = x$. Then $y = f(x,\ldots,x) = x$, $y_{dual} = g(x,\ldots,x) = 1 - f(1-x,\ldots,1-x) = 1 - (1-x) = x$. The property (IV) follows directly form (II) and (III): The idempotent dual of an idempotent function is obtained by inserting negation in all input branches and in the output (root) branch of the function tree (each GL aggregation structure can be represented as a tree where the nodes are aggregators, the leaves are input degrees of truth, and the root is the output degree of truth).

2.1.7.2 Expansion of Logic Domain

Similarly to the percept of partial truth, human percepts of simultaneity and substitutability are also a matter of degree. Both simultaneity and substitutability are graded concepts: Decision makers sometimes require high degree of simultaneity an sometimes the degree of simultaneity can be low. The same holds for substitutability. Consequently, the basic GL function, GCD, must provide a continuous parameterized transition from the pure conjunction to the pure disjunction. The transition is controlled by two complementary parameters: the andness α and the orness ω ($\alpha \in [0,1]$, $\omega \in [0,1]$, $\alpha + \omega = 1$). For $n = 2$, that is illustrated in Fig. 2.1.8 where the pure conjunction ($\alpha = 1$, $\omega = 0$) is denoted C and the pure disjunction ($\alpha = 0$, $\omega = 1$) is denoted D. The presented sequence of functions C, C+, CA, C−, A, D−, DA, D+ and D corresponds to the values of orness ω = 0, ⅛, ¼, ⅜, ½, ⅝, ¾, ⅞, 1, or to the values of andness α = 1, ⅞, ¾, ⅝, ½, ⅜, ¼, ⅛, 0. All functions contain the idempotency line $z = x = y$ that connects the extreme points (0,0,0) and (1,1,1). In the middle of that sequence, as a *logic centroid*, is the arithmetic mean A ($z = 0.5x + 0.5y$) characterized by $\alpha = \omega = 1/2$.

The presented sequence of functions uses the andness/orness step 1/8. It can also use other steps, depending on the desired precision of andness/orness parameters. Fig. 2.1.8 shows that functions C+, CA and C− are similar to conjunction and respectively called strong, medium and weak partial conjunction. Similarly, functions D+, DA and D− are similar to disjunction and called strong, medium and weak partial disjunction. The partial conjunction and the full conjunction are models of simultaneity. Partial disjunction and the full disjunction are models of substitutability. Obviously, both the simultaneity and the substitutability are a matter of degree. All functions presented in Fig. 2.1.8 are idempotent, satisfy De Morgan's laws, and include the idempotency line.

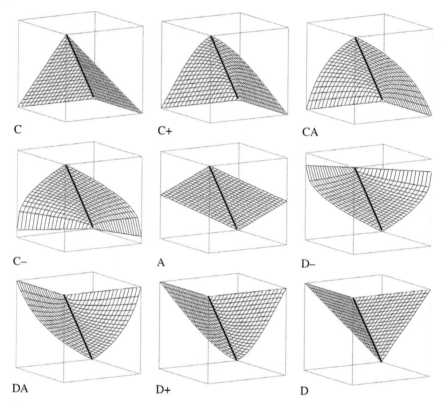

Figure 2.1.8 An example of continuous transition from *conjunction* (C) to *disjunction* (D) controlled by the adjustable parameters of andness or orness (the case of two variables).

2.1.7.3 Expansion of Annihilator Adjustability

Annihilators 0 and 1 are present and easily visible in human evaluation reasoning, and consequently, they are necessary in GL. A GL function $f : [0,1]^n \rightarrow [0,1]$ has the annihilator 0 if $\forall i \in \{1,\dots,n\}$, $x_i = 0 \;\Rightarrow f(x_1,\dots,x_n) = 0$. Similarly, f *has* the annihilator 1 if $\forall i \in \{1,\dots,n\}$, $x_i = 1 \;\Rightarrow f(x_1,\dots,x_n) = 1$. The annihilator 0 is visible in all cases where human reasoning includes mandatory requirements. For example, if a homebuyer rejects buying both an excellent house located in an unacceptable location and an unacceptable house located in a perfect location, then both the quality of house and the quality of location are simultaneously necessary and represent *mandatory requirements*. Modeling of such requirements is impossible without support of annihilator 0.

The use of annihilators in human reasoning can be more diversified, as illustrated in Table 2.1.3, where we compare three characteristic (annihilator-different)

Table 2.1.3 Three characteristic parking criteria.

Quality of a single car house garage (G)	Street parking in front of house (S)	Parking criterion $P(G,S)$		
		C1	C2	C3
0	0	0	0	0
0	1	0	0.1	0
1	0	0	0.45	0.7
0.5	1	0.65	0.65	0.65
1	1	1	1	1

C1: $P(G,S) = (0.5G^{-1.46} + 0.5S^{-1.46})^{-1/1.46}$.

C2: $P(G,S) = (0.674G^{0.492} + 0.326S^{0.492})^{1/0.492}$.

C3: $t = (0.463G^{1.367} + 0.537S^{1.367})^{1/1.367}$,

$P(g,s) = (0.394G^{-0.407} + 0.606t^{-0.407})^{-1/0.407}$.

criteria for quality of parking. The criterion C1 reflects the homebuyer who simultaneously needs both the garage in the house and the quality street parking in front of the house (e.g., for visitors/customers). So, both the house garage and the quality street parking are the mandatory requirements, and in such cases we need support for the annihilator 0. Such form of simultaneity is called a *hard partial conjunction*. The hard partial conjunction is a model of mandatory requirements.

The criterion C2 is different, and reflects a homebuyer who would like to have both the garage and street parking but can be partially satisfied if only one of them is available. The availability of garage is considered more important than the availability of street parking. Consequently, the criterion C2 reflects a visible simultaneity, but the annihilator 0 must not be supported. In other words, the criterion C2 specifies *optional requirements*. Such a form of simultaneity is called a *soft partial conjunction*. Generally, symmetric aggregators that support annihilators are called *hard* and those that do not support annihilators are called *soft*.

The criteria C1 and C2 are symmetric in the sense that all inputs either support or do not support the annihilator 0. This is not the case with the criterion C3, where we have the homebuyer for whom the garage is a *mandatory requirement* and the street parking in front of house is *optional* (i.e., not mandatory). This is obviously an asymmetric case where one input must support the annihilator 0 and the other must not support the annihilator. If a high-quality garage is available, then the absence of street parking is penalized 30% and the overall suitability of such parking is 0.7. On the other hand, if the quality of garage is only 50% and the high quality street parking is always available, then the street parking yields the reward of 30% and the overall suitability of such parking is 0.65. The selected penalty and reward reflect homebuyer's needs and can be different. Such an asymmetric aggregator is rather frequent. It is called the *conjunctive partial absorption* (an alternative name is the *asymmetric partial conjunction*). Note that from a formal standpoint, asymmetric aggregators do not support annihilators because the support is restricted to selected variable(s) and not available for optional variable(s). However, the use of asymmetric annihilators is frequent in human decision making, and consequently, it must be available in EL. Table 2.1.3 also shows sample idempotent analytic forms of criteria C1, C2, and C3, implemented using power means.

The use of annihilator 1 in models of substitutability is the De Morgan dual of the case of annihilator 0 in the area of simultaneity and all properties of annihilators 0 and 1 are symmetric. Fig. 2.1.8 shows a typical example of the presence and absence of annihilators in the case of GCD $z(x, y)$. For andness $3/4 \le \alpha \le 1$ GCD supports the annihilator 0, i.e., $z(0,y) = z(x,0) = 0$, and such support is not available for $1/2 \le \alpha < 3/4$. For orness $3/4 \le \omega \le 1$ GCD supports annihilator 1, i.e., $z(1,y) = z(x,1) = 1$, and such support is not available for $1/2 \le \omega < 3/4$. The lowest andness that supports the annihilator 0 is called the *threshold andness* and denoted α_θ. Similarly, the lowest orness that supports the annihilator 0 is called the *threshold orness* and denoted ω_θ. The values of α_θ and ω_θ are adjustable parameters of GL. In the special case where $\alpha_\theta = \omega_\theta = 3/4$, the hard and soft partial conjunction and partial disjunction have equal ranges and such a form of GCD is called the uniform GCD and denoted UGCD.

It is important to note that the diversified use of annihilators is a fundamental property of human evaluation reasoning and one of fundamental properties of *idempotent logic aggregators* (ILA) in GL; this property is not available in BL. The parameterized adjustability of the presence or the absence of support for the annihilator 0 in simultaneity models and the annihilator 1 in substitutability models (hard and soft partial conjunction and disjunction) for ILA can be summarized as follows:

a) **Simultaneity models**
    a) Symmetric simultaneity (symmetric annihilators characterized by $\alpha > \frac{1}{2}$)
        i) *Mandatory requirements* (annihilator 0 supported; high andness, hard partial conjunction)
        ii) *Nonmandatory or optional requirements* (annihilator 0 not supported; low andness, soft partial conjunction)
        iii) Adjustable location of threshold andness
    b) Asymmetric simultaneity (asymmetric annihilators)
        i) *Adjustable penalty* caused by low optional input
        ii) *Adjustable reward* caused by high optional input

c) **Substitutability models**
  a) Symmetric substitutability (symmetric annihilators characterized by $\alpha < \frac{1}{2}$)
    i) *Sufficient requirements* (annihilator 1 supported; high orness, hard partial disjunction)
    ii) *Nonsufficient or optional requirements* (annihilator 1 not supported; low orness, soft partial disjunction)
    iii) Adjustable location of threshold orness
  b) Asymmetric substitutability (asymmetric annihilators)
    i) *Adjustable penalty* caused by low optional input
    ii) *Adjustable reward* caused by high optional input

2.1.7.4 Expansion of Semantic Domain

Semantic components of human reasoning are those components that are related to the role and meaning of variables and statements, in the context of specific goals and interests of the decision maker (stakeholder). Generally, semantics is a branch of linguistics and logic concerned with meaning. In the context of GL, the most frequent semantic component is the percept of importance that is associated with the majority of variables in perceptual computing. In classical BL, semantic components are not present and the concept of importance is excluded from BL models. In GL, the semantic components are explicitly present in all decision models.

In the area of evaluation reasoning, decision makers select and use various attributes that contribute to the overall suitability of an evaluated object. Individual attributes and their groups regularly have different importance for the decision maker because they have different ability to contribute to the attainment of decision maker's goals. The percept of overall suitability is predominantly affected by those attributes and groups of attributes that have high overall importance.

The overall importance of an attribute or a group of attributes is a compound percept. Both the high andness and the high orness of a group of attributes contribute to the percept of their importance. Indeed, if all attributes in a group must simultaneously be sufficiently satisfied, that means all of them are important to the decision maker. Similarly, high orness indicates that each attribute in a group is so important that satisfying only one of them is sufficient to create the percept of group satisfaction. On the other hand, in each group of attributes there is also the percept of relative importance: some attributes can be more important than other attributes. Consequently, the compound percept of the overall importance of each attribute in this context consists of two principal components: the relative importance and the level of andness (or orness), as illustrated for a GCD aggregator in Fig. 2.1.9.

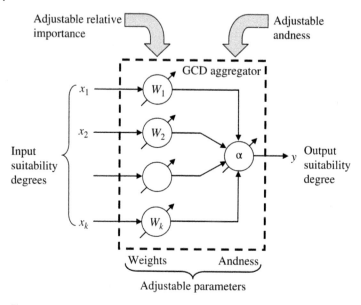

Figure 2.1.9 Adjustable semantic components of a GCD aggregator.

The relative importance is regularly expressed using adjustable normalized weights: $0 < W_i < 1$, $i = 1,...,k$, $W_1 + ... + W_k = 1$. The group importance of attributes $x_1, ..., x_k$ is adjusted by selecting the degree of andness/orness. Then, the percept of overall importance that the decision maker intuitively creates for each of k input attributes is obtained by combining the group importance and the individual relative importance of attributes.

The compound percept of the overall importance of individual inputs of GCD aggregators is the point of departure in creating the GCD aggregators. In other words, decision makers must decompose the percept of overall importance in order to adjust the weights and andness as illustrated in Fig. 2.1.9. This decomposition is a rather natural process, and decision makers can answer the questions about the desired degree of simultaneity/substitutability and the desired degrees of relative importance in any order. Rational and trained decision makers can specify the relative importance and the degree of simultaneity/substitutability in a way that is consistent with the percepts of overall importance of individual attributes. Not surprisingly, human reasoning can sometimes be inconsistent; an example is the request for high andness (i.e., high group importance) and simultaneously a very low weight (i.e., very low individual importance) of an attribute. For more detail, see Section 2.2.6.

2.1.7.5 Expansion of Compensative Logic Functions

The compatibility with observable properties of human intuitive logic reasoning requires the compensative properties of aggregators, where the deficiencies of specific inputs can be compensated by the excesses of other inputs. The pure conjunction and disjunction are not compensative, as illustrated in Fig. 2.1.10. Indeed, if $x < y$ and $z = \min(x,y)$, then a decrement of x cannot be compensated by an increment of y. More precisely, z is insensitive to both increments and decrements of y as long as $x < y$. Similarly, if $z = \max(x,y)$ and $x < y$, then decrement of y cannot be compensated by an increment of x. These are extreme properties, not frequently observable in human evaluation reasoning.

In human evaluation reasoning, we can easily observe the prevalence of compensative aggregation. For example, in all schools a bad grade in some class can be compensated by a good grade in another class. Similarly, most homebuyers are ready to compensate imperfections of house location by an increased house quality, and vice versa.

A soft computing aggregator $f(x_1, ..., x_n)$ is fully compensative if the deficiency of a selected input x_i can be fully compensated by the excesses of other inputs:

$$f(x_1 + \Delta x_1, ..., x_i - \Delta x_i, ..., x_n + \Delta x_n) = f(x_1, ..., x_n).$$

Of course, there are always deficiencies that cannot be compensated. If the deficiency Δx_i is larger than some threshold value it might be impossible to compensate it. Furthermore, if an input is mandatory, its absence can never be compensated. In addition, the compensation can sometimes be partial (incomplete). There are also cases where the deficiency Δx_i can be compensated by a selected other (sufficiently important) input, or by any other input. In the extreme case of sufficient inputs, each such input can fully compensate any deficiency of all other inputs. Consequently, compensative properties can vary in a wide range, but some form of compensation is frequently visible in human evaluation reasoning.

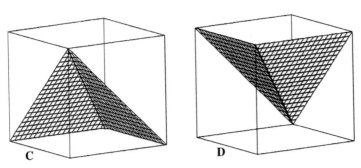

Figure 2.1.10 Pure conjunction C (the minimum function) and the pure disjunction D (the maximum function) in the case of two variables.

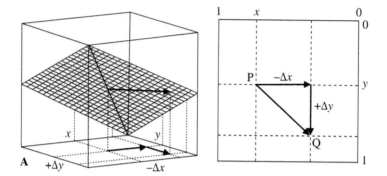

Figure 2.1.11 Conjunctive-disjunctive neutrality (the arithmetic mean) and its compensative properties.

Compensative properties of an aggregator are most visible in the case of the neutrality aggregator (the arithmetic mean) $z = (x+y)/2$ shown in Fig. 2.1.11. The obvious condition for compensation of deficiency Δx is $[(x-\Delta x)+(y+\Delta y)]/2 = (x+y)/2$, or $\Delta y = \Delta x$. So, the decrement $-\Delta x$ is compensated by the increment $+\Delta y$ and the suitability z in points P and Q is the same. Except for the full conjunction and the full disjunction, all other suitability aggregators in GL have some compensative properties and generally the compensation is achieved using $\Delta y \neq \Delta x$. There are seven categories of compensative GL aggregators shown in Table 2.1.4 and described in the next section.

2.1.7.6 Expansion of the Range of Andness/Orness from Drastic Conjunction to Drastic Disjunction

Idempotent aggregators restrict the range of andness and orness to interval $[0,1]$. However, human reasoning sometimes includes nonidempotent aggregation where we use the logic functions of hyperconjunction (stronger simultaneity than the pure conjunction) or hyperdisjunction (stronger substitutability than the pure disjunction). Therefore, general models of human reasoning should be capable to expand the range of andness and orness beyond the standard interval $[0,1]$, as shown in Fig. 2.1.2. For logic function $A(x_1, ..., x_n; \alpha)$ the global andness α is based on the volume V under $A(x_1, ..., x_n; \alpha)$:

$$\alpha = \frac{n-(n+1)V}{n-1}, \quad V = \int_0^1 \cdots \int_0^1 A(x_1,...,x_n;\alpha)dx_1\cdots dx_n,$$

$$0 \leq V \leq 1 \implies 1-\omega_{max} = \alpha_{min} = \frac{-1}{n-1} \leq \alpha \leq \frac{n}{n-1} = \alpha_{max} = 1-\omega_{min}.$$

Table 2.1.4 Nine most significant idempotent aggregators in graded logic.

Group	Logic model	Name of aggregator	Code	Role of input values		Annihilator	
				x	y	x	y
GCD	Complete (full) simultaneity	Pure conjunction	C	Mandatory	Mandatory	0	0
	Graded partial simultaneity (compensative)	Hard partial conjunction	HPC	Mandatory	Mandatory	0	0
		Soft partial conjunction	SPC	Optional	Optional	none	none
	Neutrality (compensative)	Neutrality (and/or)	A	Optional	Optional	none	none
	Graded partial substitutability (compensative)	Soft partial disjunction	SPD	Optional	Optional	none	none
		Hard partial disjunction	HPD	Sufficient	Sufficient	1	1
	Complete (full) substitutability	Pure disjunction	D	Sufficient	Sufficient	1	1
PA	Asymmetric simultaneity (compensative)	Conjunctive partial absorption	CPA	Mandatory	Optional	0	none
	Asymmetric substitutability (compensative)	Disjunctive partial absorption	DPA	Sufficient	Optional	1	none

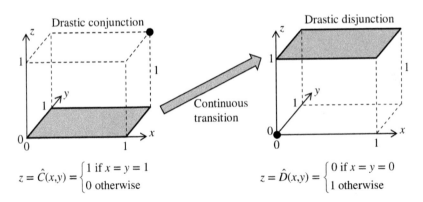

Drastic conjunction

Drastic disjunction

$$z = \hat{C}(x,y) = \begin{cases} 1 \text{ if } x = y = 1 \\ 0 \text{ otherwise} \end{cases}$$

$$z = \hat{D}(x,y) = \begin{cases} 0 \text{ if } x = y = 0 \\ 1 \text{ otherwise} \end{cases}$$

Figure 2.1.12 Drastic conjunction and drastic disjunction in the case of two variables.

Now is the time to introduce the extreme logic functions, those that have the lowest and the highest andness. The highest andness corresponds to the minimum volume $V = 0$. The corresponding most conjunctive logic function that yields the zero volume is the *drastic conjunction*, defined as follows:

$$A\left(x_1,\ldots,x_n;\frac{n}{n-1}\right) = \hat{C}(x_1,\ldots,x_n) = x_1 \wedge \cdots \wedge x_n = \lim_{p\to+\infty}(x_1\cdots x_n)^p$$

$$= \left\lfloor \prod_{i=1}^{n} x_i \right\rfloor = \begin{cases} 1 & \text{if } x_1 = \cdots = x_n = 1, \\ 0 & \text{otherwise.} \end{cases}$$

This is obviously the maximum possible degree of simultaneity. The drastic conjunction is satisfied only if all inputs are simultaneously perfectly satisfied. For example, in the case of student evaluation we accept only those candidates that have the GPA equal to the highest possible grade and all other candidates are rejected. Consequently, $V = 0$ and $\alpha = n/(n-1)$. It is impossible to imagine a higher degree of simultaneity.

The lowest andness corresponds to the maximum volume $V = 1$. The corresponding least conjunctive (and most disjunctive) logic function that yields the maximum volume is the *drastic disjunction,* defined as follows:

$$A\left(x_1,\ldots,x_n;\frac{-1}{n-1}\right) = \hat{D}(x_1,\ldots,x_n) = x_1 \vee \cdots \vee x_n = 1 - \lim_{p\to+\infty}[(1-x_1)\cdots(1-x_n)]^p$$

$$= 1 - \left\lfloor \prod_{i=1}^{n} (1-x_i) \right\rfloor = \begin{cases} 0 & \text{if } x_1 = \cdots = x_n = 0, \\ 1 & \text{otherwise.} \end{cases}$$

This is obviously the maximum possible degree of substitutability. The drastic disjunction is unsatisfied only if all inputs are simultaneously completely unsatisfied. For example, in the case of student evaluation, we reject only those student candidates that have the GPA equal to the lowest, failing grade. All other cases are fully acceptable, giving $V = 1$ and the minimum andness $\alpha = -1/(n-1)$. Even the slightest satisfaction of any input yields the maximum aggregated suitability. Obviously, it is not possible to imagine a higher degree of substitutability.

The drastic conjunction and the drastic disjunction belong to conjunctive or disjunctive graded logic functions. However, according to Definition 2.1.1, the drastic conjunction and the drastic disjunction do not have the formal status of logic aggregator. As conjunctive/disjunctive functions, they have andness and orness either $-1/(n-1)$ or $n/(n-1)$. Since andness and orness are properties of conjunctive/disjunctive functions, we always specify andness and orness in the range $[-1/(n-1), n/(n-1)]$ and not in the open range $]-1/(n-1), n/(n-1)[$ that formally corresponds to functions defined as logic aggregators. More precisely, basic conjunctive/disjunctive graded logic functions include logic aggregators, plus the drastic conjunction and the drastic disjunction as the closest flanking neighbors of logic aggregators.

The drastic conjunction and the drastic disjunction might look as abstract and unrealistic extreme cases. The reality can sometimes be different. Indeed, there are situations where only the best is acceptable and that is exactly the criterion expressed by the drastic conjunction (rejection of all suboptimal alternatives). Similarly, there are medical conditions where the patient is not sick only in cases where all serious symptoms are simultaneously absent. In all other cases the patient needs medical help. This type of criterion is expressed using a drastic disjunction.

In the case of two variables the drastic conjunction and the drastic disjunction are shown in Fig. 2.1.12. If we provide a continuous transition from the drastic conjunction to the drastic disjunction, so that all transitory functions along the path have acceptable logic properties, consistent with human reasoning, then we can traverse and cover all four regions defined by the logic quadrisection of the unit hypercube (Fig. 2.1.5). In other words, we can provide logic aggregators that are *necessary and sufficient* for modeling human logic criteria. That can be analytically achieved using the mean andness theorem [DUJ05c] and interpolative aggregators [DUJ14] presented in Sections 2.4.7 and 2.4.8.

To exemplify the process of expansion of the range of andness/orness, let us use two aggregators, $A_1(x_1, ..., x_n; \alpha_1)$ and $A_2(x_1, ..., x_n; \alpha_2)$, which have increasing andness:

$$V_1 = \int_0^1 \cdots \int_0^1 A_1(x_1, ..., x_n; \alpha_1) dx_1 \cdots dx_n; \quad \alpha_1 = \frac{n - (n+1)V_1}{n-1},$$

$$V_2 = \int_0^1 \cdots \int_0^1 A_2(x_1, ..., x_n; \alpha_2) dx_1 \cdots dx_n; \quad \alpha_2 = \frac{n - (n+1)V_2}{n-1}, \quad V_1 > V_2.$$

If $\alpha_2 > \alpha_1$ then according to [DUJ14, DUJ15a], we can create an aggregator $A(x_1, ..., x_n; \alpha)$ which linearly interpolates between $A_1(x_1, ..., x_n; \alpha_1)$ and $A_2(x_1, ..., x_n; \alpha_2)$ as follows:

$$A(x_1, ..., x_n; \alpha) = \frac{(\alpha_2 - \alpha)A_1(x_1, ..., x_n; \alpha_1) + (\alpha - \alpha_1)A_2(x_1, ..., x_n; \alpha_2)}{\alpha_2 - \alpha_1}, \quad \alpha_1 \le \alpha \le \alpha_2.$$

Using this method, we can seamlessly expand GL aggregators from idempotent to nonidempotent domain [DUJ16a]. A detailed presentation of this technique can be found in Chapter 2.4. To illustrate the idea of interpolative logic aggregators in the simple case of two variables, we can perform a continuous andness-directed transition from the drastic conjunction to the drastic disjunction using an interpolative aggregator $z = F(x, y; \alpha)$, $-1 \le \alpha \le 2$, as follows:

$$z = \begin{cases} F(x,y;\alpha) = \begin{cases} 1, \text{ if } x = y = 1, \text{ or } 0 \text{ otherwise} & \alpha = 2, \quad \text{Drastic conjunction} \\[2mm] (xy)^{\sqrt{3/(2-\alpha)}-1}, & 1.25 < \alpha < 2, \text{ High hyperconjunction} \\[2mm] xy, & \alpha = 1.25, \quad \text{Product } t-\text{norm (medium} \\[2mm] & \qquad\qquad\qquad \text{hyperconjunction)} \\[2mm] 4[(1.25-\alpha)\min(x,y) + (\alpha-1)xy], & 1 < \alpha < 1.25, \text{ Low hyperconjunction} \\[2mm] \min(x,y), & \alpha = 1, \quad \text{Full conjunction} \\[2mm] \left(0.5x^{r(\alpha)} + 0.5y^{r(\alpha)}\right)^{1/r(\alpha)}, & \tfrac{3}{4} \le \alpha < 1, \quad \text{Hard partial conjunction} \\[2mm] (3-4\alpha)(0.5x + 0.5y) + & \\[1mm] (4\alpha-2)(0.5x^R + 0.5y^R)^{1/R}, & \tfrac{1}{2} < \alpha < \tfrac{3}{4}, \quad \text{Soft partial conjunction} \\[2mm] 0.5x + 0.5y, & \alpha = \omega = \tfrac{1}{2}, \quad \text{Neutrality} \end{cases} \\[2mm] 1 - F(1-x, 1-y; 1-\alpha), & -1 \le \alpha < 0.5, \text{ Dual disjunctive} \\ & \qquad\qquad\qquad\qquad \text{aggregators.} \end{cases}$$

$$r(\alpha) = \frac{0.25 + 1.65811(\tfrac{1}{2}-\alpha) + 2.15388(\tfrac{1}{2}-\alpha)^2 + 8.2844(\tfrac{1}{2}-\alpha)^3 + 6.16764(\tfrac{1}{2}-\alpha)^4}{\alpha(1-\alpha)}.$$

$R = r(\tfrac{3}{4})$ = exponent of power mean which provides the fixed threshold andness $\alpha_\theta = \tfrac{3}{4}$ of uniform GCD aggregators).

The conjunctive aggregator $F(x_1, x_2; \alpha)$ is idempotent between the arithmetic mean and the pure conjunction and then seamlessly nonidempotent and hyperconjunctive between the pure conjunction and the drastic conjunction. This example illustrates the possibility to extend the domain of andness/ orness beyond the standard [0,1] range. So, basic GCD aggregators in GL can have any desired value of andness and orness in the maximum possible range $[-1/(n-1), \; n/(n-1)]$ (Fig. 2.1.2). In this way, GCD can cover all regions inside the unit hypercube. Examples of hyperconjunctive and hyperdisjunctive aggregators of two variables are shown in Fig. 2.1.13. Comparing Figs. 2.1.10 and 2.1.13, it is easy to see that the hyperconjunctive aggregators are located visibly under the pure conjunction and the idempotency line. Similarly, the hyperdisjunctive aggregators are located visibly over the pure disjunction and the idempotency line. Note also that hyperconjunctive and hyperdisjunctive aggregators satisfy all conditions of logic aggregators specified in Definition 2.1.1. Therefore, the use of hyperconjunctive and hyperdisjunctive aggregators is a way to expand the expressive power of GL, covering all regions of the unit hypercube.

Hyperconjunction ($\alpha = 1.85$) 　　　　Hyperdisjunction ($\omega = 1.85$)

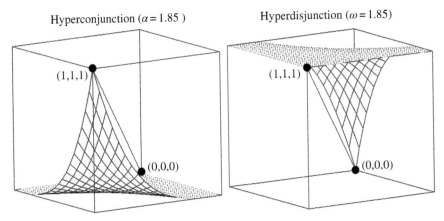

Figure 2.1.13 Sample highly hyperconjunctive and highly hyperdisjunctive aggregators of two variables close to the drastic conjunction and the drastic disjunction.

2.1.8　GL Conjecture: Ten Necessary and Sufficient GL Functions

Knowledge of components is a prerequisite for building systems. This holds for all kinds of systems. Hardware designers know (from the Charles Peirce theorem) that all digital logic circuitry can be built using either NOR or NAND gates. Software designers know (from Giuseppe Jacopini's structure theorem) that all software can be built using a loop with conditional exit, a sequence, and some auxiliary flag variables (e.g., theoretically, there is no need for branches such as if-then-else, because they can be made using flags and while loops). In the case of mathematical objects and systems, the fundamental question is to find necessary and sufficient basic components that must be available for building compound objects of any complexity. In this context, a component is *necessary* if we cannot build a compound object without that component. A set of components is *sufficient* if it contains *all* components that are necessary for building a compound object. A set of components is *necessary and sufficient* if it contains the minimum set of necessary components; i.e., if we omit any component from that set, we cannot build desired compound objects. For example, in the case of Boolean logic, one of sets of necessary and sufficient basic functions includes AND, OR, and NOT. So, we have to answer the same question for GL, and specify basic logic functions that are necessary and sufficient for building compound GL functions.

Before answering this question, we must answer the question about the acceptable way of demonstrating that an operator is necessary, and a group of operators is sufficient. Since these operators are used in the context of human decision making and not in the context of a formal mathematical proof, the only way to show that an operator is necessary is to show the situation where human decision makers provably use the analyzed operator. Sufficiency can be demonstrated using the geometric properties of the unit hypercube and relationships with classical logic. The following conjecture offers an answer to the question of necessary and sufficient aggregators:

> **The graded logic conjecture.** There are 10 necessary and sufficient graded logic functions: (1) *neutrality,* (2) *soft partial conjunction,* (3) *soft partial disjunction,* (4) *hard partial conjunction,* (5) *hard partial disjunction,* (6) *full conjunction,* (7) *full disjunction,* (8) *hyperconjunction,* (9) *hyperdisjunction,* and (10) *negation.* The functions (1) to (9) are graded logic aggregators that are special cases of the graded conjunction/disjunction (GCD). Except for negation, neutrality and full conjunction/disjunction, all other functions are *logic categories* with adjustable range of andness/orness.

Reasons that Support the Necessity

We assume that logic is derived from observing human intuitive decision making and logic aggregators provide quantitative models of human reasoning. Each of the 10 fundamental functions is provably present in human evaluation reasoning. For each of them we can present a proof of existence of a justifiable decision process which uses the selected operator (see Section 2.1.2 and Chapter 2.2). For example, a homebuyer *simultaneously* wants a high-quality home located in a sufficiently convenient location. So, this is a conjunctive aggregator. Most homebuyers would reject all homes having unacceptable quality or unacceptable location. In addition, if the degrees of satisfaction with the home quality and location are the same, that would be interpreted as the overall satisfaction with the home. Consequently, the aggregator is conjunctive, hard, and idempotent, and the type of such aggregator is obviously the hard partial conjunction. This type of aggregator has a range of continuously adjustable andness/orness. There is not a slightest doubt that the idempotent hard partial conjunction is necessary in human reasoning and, consequently, it is a necessary component in basic logic models. The empirical fact that the hard partial conjunction is used in most home selection processes (as well as in countless similar situations) should be a sufficient proof that this type of aggregator is necessary. We can provide similar proofs of necessity for each of the 10 fundamental functions. The set of 10 basic functions is denoted B10.

Reasons that Support the Sufficiency

Logic neutrality, full conjunction, and full disjunction are operators that logically partition the unit hypercube in four regions: (1) soft and hard partial conjunction; (2) soft and hard partial disjunction; (3) hyperconjunction; and (4) hyperdisjunction, as shown in Fig. 2.1.5. Inside the unit hypercube there are no other regions and no space for other types of logic aggregators. Consequently, the nine non-unary operators are sufficient to completely cover the unit hypercube. In addition, full conjunction, full disjunction, and negation are sufficient to secure the complete compatibility with classic Boolean logic, making graded logic a seamless generalization of Boolean logic. GCD and negation are necessary and sufficient graded logic functions in exactly the same way as conjunction, disjunction, and negation are necessary and sufficient for building the classic Boolean logic.

The presented reasoning about necessity and sufficiency of the 10 soft computing logic operators provides a strong empirical validation of the graded logic conjecture. In the context of perceptual computing, the empirical justification of the GCD conjecture seems to be equally appropriate as a formal proof based on a formal axiomatic theory.

The graded logic conjecture provides a convincing answer to Zimmermann's question from [ZIM96]:

> *"How do human beings aggregate subjective categories, and which mathematical models describe this procedure adequately?"*
>
> Our answer is: *"Human beings aggregate subjective categories using aggregation structures that are appropriate combinations of ten necessary and sufficient types of logic operators: nine aggregators that are special cases of the graded conjunction/disjunction and the standard negation. After selecting an appropriate type of aggregator humans regularly perform fine tuning of aggregator by additionally adjusting desired andness/orness."*

The fundamental 10 necessary and sufficient basic GL functions (called the basic group B10) and their symbolic notation are as follows:

1) **Full (or pure) conjunction (C):** $z = x \wedge y$.
2) **Hard partial conjunction (HPC):** $z = x \bar{\triangle} y$.
3) **Soft partial conjunction (SPC):** $z = x \underline{\triangle} y$.
4) **Neutrality (arithmetic mean) (A):** $z = x \ominus y = (x + y)/2$.
5) **Soft partial disjunction (SPD):** $z = x \underline{\nabla} y$.
6) **Hard partial disjunction (HPD):** $z = x \bar{\nabla} y$.
7) **Full (or pure) disjunction (D):** $z = x \vee y$.
8) **Hyperconjunction (CC):** $z = x \bar{\wedge} y$.
9) **Hyperdisjunction (DD):** $z = x \bar{\vee} y$.
10) **Standard negation (NOT):** $y = \bar{x} = 1 - x$.

The list of 10 necessary and sufficient GL functions yields the following obvious corollary: All aggregation functions that do not support the presented seven idempotent and two nonidempotent types of aggregation cannot be used as general models of human reasoning. GCD aggregator must be designed so as to support all nine necessary types of aggregation. Except for GCD, all currently used aggregators (some of them rather popular) support only a small subset of the necessary nine types of aggregation.

There are seven basic idempotent GL functions (idempotent aggregators) shown in Table 2.1.4: three forms of conjunction, neutrality, and three forms of disjunction. Those are our "magnificent seven," the most important and the most frequently used aggregators in evaluation: B7 = {C, HPC, SPC, A, SPD, HPD, D}. Then, B10 = B7 ∪ {NOT, CC, DD}.

Table 2.1.4 also contains two frequently used compound idempotent aggregators, denoted as partial absorption (PA): conjunctive partial absorption (CPA) and disjunctive partial absorption (DPA). CPA aggregates mandatory and optional inputs and DPA aggregates sufficient and optional inputs. These functions, introduced in [DUJ74a, DUJ75a, DUJ79a] are so frequent in applications that they must be included in the "inner circle" of the most important aggregators (the basic group B9). We study them in Chapter 2.2, and Chapter 2.6 is completely devoted to PA. PA functions are compound aggregators based on basic necessary and sufficient idempotent aggregators of partial conjunction, neutrality and partial disjunction. They are defined as follows:

Conjunctive partial absorption: $z = x \triangleright y = x \bar{\bar{\Delta}} \left(x \tilde{\triangledown} y \right)$, $\bar{\bar{\Delta}} \in \{\wedge, \bar{\Delta}\}$,
$$\tilde{\triangledown} \in \{\vee, \triangledown, \ominus\}, \quad \triangledown \in \{\bar{\triangledown}, \underline{\triangledown}\}.$$

Disjunctive partial absorption: $z = x \bar{\triangleright} y = x \bar{\bar{\triangledown}} \left(x \tilde{\Delta} y \right)$, $\bar{\bar{\triangledown}} \in \{\vee, \bar{\triangledown}\}$,
$$\tilde{\Delta} \in \{\wedge, \Delta, \ominus\}, \quad \Delta \in \{\underline{\Delta}, \bar{\Delta}\}.$$

These functions are a generalization of classical BL absorption theorems $x \wedge (x \vee y) = x$ and $x \vee (x \wedge y) = x$; here x plays the role of primary variable and y is a secondary variable. The BL version completely absorbs the variable y (making it insignificant). The above GL version absorbs the secondary variable y only partially (making it optional, but not negligible). Except for the extreme cases of full conjunction and disjunction (inherited from BL), all GL functions in Table 2.1.4 are compensative.

Inputs of idempotent GL aggregators can be *mandatory*, or *sufficient*, or *optional*. Mandatory inputs must be satisfied to avoid zero output values. Sufficient inputs denote important features that are completely sufficient to satisfy given requirements regardless of the satisfaction of other inputs in a group. Optional inputs contribute to satisfying the requirements of the criterion that uses them; they are certainly desired, but neither mandatory nor sufficient. Optional inputs are used in all conjunctive criteria that can tolerate some (but not all) zero input values without producing the zero output. In the case of disjunctive criteria, optional inputs are used to model desirable inputs that are not so important that they alone can completely satisfy a criterion function.

2.1.9   Basic Idempotent GL Aggregators

The adjustable simultaneity is modeled using either soft or hard partial conjunction. The characteristic forms of soft and hard partial conjunctions, in the case of two variables, are illustrated in Fig. 2.1.14. In the case of soft partial conjunction, we have that the aggregation function touches the plane $z = 0$ only in the point $(0, 0)$. As opposed to that, the hard partial conjunction function touches the plane $z = 0$ in all points where $x = 0$ or $y = 0$. That makes x and y mandatory inputs. However, contrary to the pure conjunction and the pure disjunction, for all positive x and y, the functions shown in Fig. 2.1.14 are compensative.

The degree of simultaneity (andness) is an indicator that reflects the similarity between the partial conjunction and the pure conjunction, as discussed in Section 2.1.3. GCD functions perform continuous transition from conjunction to disjunction inside the unit hypercube. Consequently, the simplest way to characterize the overall degree of simultaneity of GCD function can be based on computing the volume $Vol(GCD)$ under the function inside the unit hypercube, as shown in formula (2.1.8). For all aggregators in the GCD group, the andness α can be expressed as follows:

$$\alpha(GCD) = \frac{Vol(\max) - Vol(GCD)}{Vol(\max) - Vol(\min)}, \quad 0 \le \alpha(GCD) \le 1,$$

$$1/2 = \alpha(A) < \alpha(SPC) < \alpha(HPC) < \alpha(\min) = 1.$$

The andness $\alpha = \frac{1}{2}$ for the arithmetic mean (A) is an obvious consequence of the fact that $Vol(A) = \frac{1}{2}$ (see Fig. 2.1.3). The arithmetic mean is the "centroid of logic aggregators," because it is located exactly in the middle between the pure conjunction and the pure disjunction:

$$(x + y)/2 = [\min(x,y) + \max(x,y)]/2 = 0.5(x \wedge y) + 0.5(x \vee y).$$

The adjustable substitutability is modeled using either soft or hard partial disjunction. The characteristic forms of soft and hard partial conjunctions are

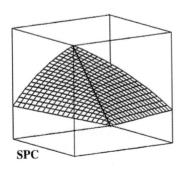
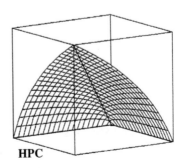

SPC HPC

Figure 2.1.14 Typical forms of the soft and hard partial conjunction.

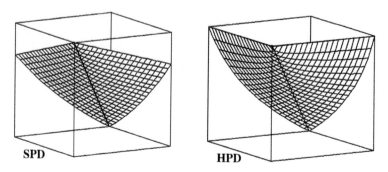

Figure 2.1.15 Typical forms of the soft and hard partial disjunction (compensative partial substitutability).

illustrated in Fig. 2.1.15. In the case of soft partial disjunction we have that the aggregation function touches the plane $z = 1$ only in the point $(1,1)$. As opposed to that, the hard partial disjunction function touches the plane $z = 1$ in all points, where either $x = 1$ or $y = 1$. That makes x and y sufficient inputs: if one of them is fully satisfied then $z = 1$ regardless the value of the other input.

Similar to the case of partial conjunction, the functions shown in Fig. 2.1.15 are compensative. The degree of substitutability (orness) is an indicator that reflects the similarity between the partial disjunction and the pure disjunction. Using the same approach we used for defining the global andness, the global orness ω of all GCD aggregators can be expressed as follows:

$$\omega(GCD) = \frac{Vol(GCD) - Vol(\min)}{Vol(\max) - Vol(\min)}, \quad 0 \le \omega(GCD) \le 1,$$

$$1/2 = \omega(A) < \omega(SPD) < \omega(HPD) < \omega(\max) = 1.$$

From Fig. 2.1.14 and Fig. 2.1.15, it is easy to see the symmetry between SPC and SPD, as well as the symmetry between HPC and HPD; most frequently these pairs are defined to be De Morgan duals: if one of them is $f(x, y)$, then the other is $g(x,y) = 1 - f(1-x, 1-y)$. If we compare the GCD functions HPC, SPC, A, SPD, and HPD (e.g., see Fig. 2.1.8), it is easy to see that all of them contain the idempotency line $x = y = z$ and consequently in the vicinity of the idempotency line all GCD aggregators behave similarly to the arithmetic mean.

Compensative functions can be asymmetric. Fig. 2.1.16 shows the partial absorption function (PA), which has two versions: conjunctive and disjunctive. The conjunctive partial absorption, CPA (also called the *asymmetric simultaneity*) has one mandatory input (x) and one optional input (y) and combines the properties of HPC and SPC. If $x>y$, then CPA behaves as SPC, and if $y>x$, then CPA is similar to HPC. If the optional input is not satisfied ($y=0$), then the output z is equal to the value of the mandatory input x reduced for a desired value of

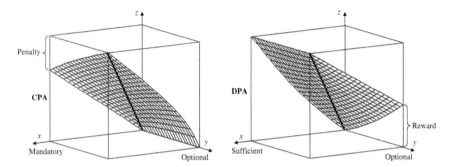

Figure 2.1.16 Typical forms of the conjunctive partial absorption (asymmetric simultaneity) and disjunctive partial absorption (asymmetric substitutability).

penalty. However, if the mandatory input is not satisfied ($x=0$) then the output is $z=0$. Thus, the mandatory input supports the annihilator 0, and the asymmetric optional input does not support annihilators.

The disjunctive partial absorption, DPA (also called the *asymmetric substitutability*) has one sufficient input (x) and one optional input (y) and combines the properties of HPD and SPD. If $x>y$, then DPA behaves as HPD, and if $y>x$, then DPA is similar to SPD. If the optional input is fully satisfied ($y=1$), then the value of output z is equal to the value of the sufficient input x increased for a desired value of reward. However, if the sufficient input is fully satisfied ($x=1$), then the output is $z=1$. Thus, the sufficient input supports the annihilator 1, and the asymmetric optional input does not support annihilators.

CPA and DPA functions presented in Fig. 2.1.16 are obtained as generalizations of BL absorption theorems ($x \vee (x \wedge y) = x$ and $x \wedge (x \vee y) = x$). However, taking into account that CPA is a mix of HPC and SPC, and DPA is a mix of HPD and SPD, it is also possible to interpret CPA as *asymmetric conjunction*, and DPA as *asymmetric disjunction*.

The classical bivalent Boolean logic provides models of the $\{0,1\}$-type of reasoning, while humans actually use the $[0,1]$-type of reasoning, as the theory of fuzzy systems clearly proves. GL extends the domain of logic functions from the vertices of the unit hypercube $\{0, 1\}^n$ to the complete volume of the unit hypercube $[0, 1]^n$, and, in addition, it offers other important extensions discussed in Section 2.1.7. Naturally, these extensions must be seamless, and in vertices $\{0, 1\}^n$ the BL and GL must be identical. A direct benefit that GL derives from the relationship with BL is that the bivalent ancestor provides a sound background for deciding about the necessary and sufficient material for building graded logic models.

In GL, we use specific notation of basic graded logic functions, and this notation is related to the notation used in classical Boolean logic. We assume that all variables belong to the unit interval $I = [0,1]$. Pure conjunction and pure disjunction are always realized as minimum and maximum: $x_1 \wedge x_2 = \min(x_1,x_2)$, $x_1 \vee x_2 = \max(x_1,x_2)$, $x_1 \in I$, $x_2 \in I$. The negation is defined as the standard negation $\bar{x} = 1 - x$, $x \in I$.

The *graded conjunction/disjunction* (GCD) is denoted using symbol $\diamond$, which combines the symbols of conjunction $\wedge$ and disjunction $\vee$. GCD is the most important GL function, and it can be realized in many different ways that have various desired features. The simplest possible implementation of GCD, in the case of two variables, is the following min-max function:

$$x_1 \diamond x_2 = \alpha(x_1 \wedge x_2) + \omega(x_1 \vee x_2), \quad x_1 \in I, \quad x_2 \in I, \quad \alpha \in I, \quad \omega \in I, \quad \alpha + \omega = 1.$$

The parameter α (introduced in Section 2.1.3) is called *andness* or *the conjunction degree*. The parameter ω is called *orness* or *the disjunction degree*. Andness and orness are complementary parameters. The high andness denotes that GCD is similar to conjunction, and the high orness denotes that GCD is similar to disjunction. We use $x_1 \diamond x_2$ as a symbolic notation of GCD, assuming that x_1 has the same degree of importance as x_2, and that aggregator $\diamond$ corresponds to a specific degree of andness/orness. By changing orness from 0 to 1, we can realize a continuous transition from conjunction to disjunction, as illustrated in Fig. 2.1.17.

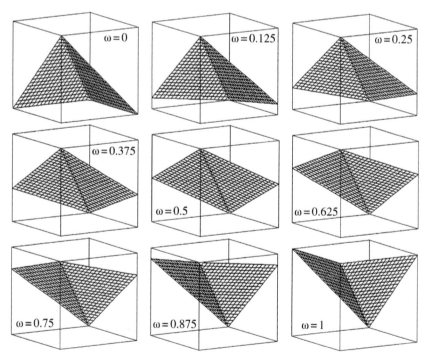

Figure 2.1.17 The simplest min-max implementation of the GCD of two variables.

If $0 < \omega < \frac{1}{2} < \alpha < 1$, then GCD becomes similar to conjunction, and in such cases $x_1 \diamond x_2$ is called *the partial conjunction* and symbolically denoted $x_1 \triangle x_2$. The aggregator $\triangle$ is called *andor*, and it is the symbol of partial conjunction. If $0 < \alpha < \frac{1}{2} < \omega < 1$, then GCD becomes similar to disjunction, and in such cases $x_1 \diamond x_2$ is called *the partial disjunction* and is denoted $x_1 \nabla x_2$. The aggregator ∇ is called *orand*, and it is the symbol of partial disjunction. In a special case where $\alpha = \omega = \frac{1}{2}$ we have that $x_1 \diamond x_2$ is called the *neutrality* function and is symbolically denoted $x_1 \ominus x_2$. Obviously, the neutrality function is located right in the middle between the pure conjunction and the pure disjunction, and it is implemented as the arithmetic mean:

$$x_1 \ominus x_2 = (x_1 \wedge x_2)/2 + (x_1 \vee x_2)/2 = (x_1 + x_2)/2.$$

We use $\ominus$ as a symbol of arithmetic mean or neutrality, indicating a perfectly balanced presence of conjunctive and disjunctive properties. Therefore, GCD has five major special cases and can be written as follows:

$$x_1 \diamond x_2 = \begin{cases} x_1 \wedge x_2, & \alpha = 1, \ \omega = 0 & \text{(Pure conjunction)} \\ x_1 \triangle x_2, & 0 < \omega < \frac{1}{2} < \alpha < 1 & \text{(Partial conjunction)} \\ x_1 \ominus x_2, & \alpha = \omega = \frac{1}{2} & \text{(Neutrality)} \\ x_1 \nabla x_2, & 0 < \alpha < \frac{1}{2} < \omega < 1 & \text{(Partial disjunction)} \\ x_1 \vee x_2, & \alpha = 0, \ \omega = 1 & \text{(Pure disjunction)}. \end{cases}$$

The presented GCD model assumes that all inputs (in this case, x_1 and x_2) are equally important. However, in human reasoning, that is an infrequent special case. In human evaluation logic, x_1 can be more or less important than x_2. The differences in importance are usually expressed as normalized weights, where W_1 denotes the relative importance of x_1 and W_2 denotes the relative importance of x_2, assuming $0 < W_1 < 1$, $\quad 0 < W_2 < 1$, and $W_1 + W_2 = 1$. In such cases, we have weighted GCD that can be symbolically written as follows:

$$W_1 x_1 \diamond W_2 x_2 = \begin{cases} x_1 \wedge x_2, & \alpha = 1, \ \omega = 0 \\ W_1 x_1 \triangle W_2 x_2, & 0 < \omega < \frac{1}{2} < \alpha < 1 \\ W_1 x_1 \ominus W_2 x_2, & \alpha = \omega = \frac{1}{2} \\ W_1 x_1 \nabla W_2 x_2, & 0 < \alpha < \frac{1}{2} < \omega < 1 \\ x_1 \vee x_2, & \alpha = 0, \ \omega = 1. \end{cases}$$

Again, this is a symbolic notation: $W_1 x_1$ and $W_2 x_2$ are *not* products, but symbols of the presence of different weights. Therefore, if the importance of inputs is the same, then the symbolic notation is $GCD(x_1, x_2) = x_1 \diamond x_2$. The notation without weights is a simplified notation that assumes equal importance of all inputs: $x_1 \diamond x_2 = \frac{1}{2}x_1 \diamond \frac{1}{2}x_2$, $x_1 \triangle x_2 = \frac{1}{2}x_1 \triangle \frac{1}{2}x_2$, $x_1 \ominus x_2 = \frac{1}{2}x_1 \ominus \frac{1}{2}x_2$, $x_1 \nabla x_2 = \frac{1}{2}x_1 \nabla \frac{1}{2}x_2$.

There are various functions that can be used as a model of weighted GCD. One of the frequently used functions is the weighted power mean (WPM) [GIN58, MIT69, BUL03]:

$$W_1 x_1 \diamond W_2 x_2 = \lim_{s \to r} \left(W_1 x_1^s + W_2 x_2^s \right)^{1/s} = \begin{cases} x_1 \wedge x_2, & r = -\infty, \ \alpha = 1, \ \omega = 0 \\ W_1 x_1 \triangle W_2 x_2, & -\infty < r < 1, \ 0 < \omega < \tfrac{1}{2} < \alpha < 1 \\ W_1 x_1 \ominus W_2 x_2, & r = 1, \ \alpha = \omega = \tfrac{1}{2} \\ W_1 x_1 \triangledown W_2 x_2, & 1 < r < +\infty, \ 0 < \alpha < \tfrac{1}{2} < \omega < 1 \\ x_1 \vee x_2, & r = +\infty, \ \alpha = 0, \ \omega = 1. \end{cases}$$

Consequently,

$$x_1 \wedge x_2 = \lim_{s \to -\infty} \left(W_1 x_1^s + W_2 x_2^s \right)^{1/s} = \min(x_1, x_2), \quad r = -\infty \ ;$$

$$W_1 x_1 \triangle W_2 x_2 = \lim_{s \to r} \left(W_1 x_1^s + W_2 x_2^s \right)^{1/s}, \quad -\infty < r < 1, \quad 0 < \omega < \tfrac{1}{2} < \alpha < 1;$$

$$W_1 x_1 \ominus W_2 x_2 = W_1 x_1 + W_2 x_2, \quad r = 1, \ \alpha = \omega = \tfrac{1}{2};$$

$$W_1 x_1 \triangledown W_2 x_2 = \left(W_1 x_1^r + W_2 x_2^r \right)^{1/r}, \quad 1 < r < +\infty, \quad 0 < \alpha < \tfrac{1}{2} < \omega < 1;$$

$$x_1 \vee x_2 = \lim_{s \to +\infty} \left(W_1 x_1^s + W_2 x_2^s \right)^{1/s} = \max(x_1, x_2), \quad r = +\infty .$$

For example, popular special cases of partial conjunction are the weighted geometric mean $W_1 x_1 \triangle W_2 x_2 = x_1^{W_1} x_2^{W_2}$ (the case $r = 0$) and the weighted harmonic mean $W_1 x_1 \triangle W_2 x_2 = 1/(W_1/x_1 + W_2/x_2)$ (the case $r = -1$). A popular special case of partial disjunction is the weighted quadratic mean $W_1 x_1 \triangledown W_2 x_2 = \sqrt{W_1 x_1^2 + W_2 x_2^2}$ (the case $r = 2$).

Presented WPM aggregators are special cases of a family of aggregators based on quasi-arithmetic means

$$W_1 x_1 \diamond \cdots \diamond W_n x_n = f^{-1}(W_1 f(x_1) + \cdots + W_n f(x_n)),$$

$$0 < W_i < 1, \quad i = 1, \dots, n, \quad W_1 + \cdots + W_n = 1.$$

Here $f : [0,1] \to \mathbb{R}$ is a continuous and strictly monotonic function. In the case of weighted power means, $f(x) = x^r$, $-\infty \leq r \leq +\infty$. In the case of equal weights, the symbolic notation can be simplified: $x_1 \diamond \cdots \diamond x_n = n^{-1} x_1 \diamond \cdots \diamond n^{-1} x_n = f^{-1}(n^{-1} f(x_1) + \cdots + n^{-1} f(x_n))$.

Generally, GL is the logic of partial truth and graded logic functions, used for modeling evaluation decisions. The graded logic functions are defined as logic functions where the andness α (the degree of simultaneity), the orness ω (the degree of substitutability), and the relative importance of inputs are *elastic*, i.e., graded and adjustable. Andness and orness, respectively, denote the conjunction degree and the disjunction degree. The term *conjunction* is mostly used for the full conjunction, $x_1 \wedge \dots \wedge x_n = \min(x_1, \dots, x_n)$, $n > 1$; it corresponds to the maximum andness of an idempotent aggregator, $\alpha=1$. The term *disjunction* is mostly used for the full disjunction, $x_1 \vee \ldots \vee x_n = \max(x_1,\ldots,x_n)$; it corresponds to the maximum orness of an idempotent aggregator, $\omega =1$.

The most frequently used GL functions are the partial conjunction and the partial disjunction. The partial conjunction is any function that is similar to conjunction, and its andness can be interpreted as the degree of similarity. The partial disjunction is any function that is similar to disjunction, and its orness can be interpreted as the degree of similarity. The inputs of partial conjunction and partial disjunction functions are assumed to have different and adjustable degrees of relative importance.

All idempotent logic aggregators are means. The most popular of all parameterized means is the weighted power mean $y = \left(W_1 x_1^r + \cdots + W_n x_n^r\right)^{1/r}$ because it is the parent of the most frequently used arithmetic, geometric, harmonic, and quadratic means. Looking at parameterized means from the GL perspective, we might ask the question, "What are means, and who needs them?" For example, is the weighted power mean a model of statistical averaging or a model of human logic aggregation?

The weighted power mean can obviously be used for both statistical averaging and for logic aggregation. However, only a few special cases of this model are widely used in averaging: The harmonic mean $(r = -1)$ is used for averaging speeds, the geometric mean $(r = 0)$ is used for averaging performance ratios, and the arithmetic mean $(r = 1)$ is used for averaging student grades and many other things (but not speeds and performance ratios!). The minimum $(r = -\infty)$ and the maximum $(r = +\infty)$ are legitimate extreme cases but not something that is useful as an average. In addition, in the area of averaging, equal weights are more frequent than unequal weights, and other exponents from the infinite range $-\infty \leq r \leq +\infty$ have little practical use, interpretation and significance.

As opposed to averaging, the weighted power mean can frequently be an appropriate model of idempotent human logic aggregation in the whole range from conjunction $(r = -\infty)$ to disjunction $(r = +\infty)$ and *all* exponents $r \in [-\infty, +\infty]$ have applicability in modeling simultaneity and substitutability, which are pillars of human propositional logic. For selected segments of parameters, weighted power means can be incorporated in various interpolative aggregators and conjunctive aggregators can be defined as a De Morgan's dual of disjunctive aggregators, and vice versa. In addition, unequal weights are suitable and necessary models of various degrees of importance, and the percept of importance is a cornerstone of semantics of human logic aggregation. So, as our contribution to highly controversial opinions, let us claim that means are more important as logic functions than as statistical averages. From the standpoint of GL, parameterized means are primarily logic functions used as models of idempotent human logic aggregation, and a few special cases of such means are also applicable in statistical averaging.

2.1.10 A Summary of Differences between Graded Logic and Bivalent Boolean Logic

The human mind should be a role model whenever we try to develop logic models. All trustworthy logic models (including GL models used in professional evaluation projects) must be compatible with observable properties of human reasoning; that requirement should be self-evident in all applications. Intention to model the laws of thought is visible in the seminal books of De Morgan and Boole [DEM47, BOO47, BOO54].

Generally, mathematical logic does not have to be applied, and does not have to relate to observable properties of human reasoning. Recent mathematical research in fuzzy logic, and theoretical aggregation models almost never claim intentions to model human reasoning, and do not include experiments with human subjects. A valuable exception is the work of H.-J. Zimmermann and his coauthors [ZIM79, THO79, ZIM87, ZIM96]. In most cases, including BL, mathematical logic is developed as a *formal theory*, where axioms are defined without any claim that they reflect some form of observable reality, and without any claim of usability. The goal of building such systems is to develop provably correct mathematical models consistent with their axiomatic roots.

In this section, we summarize the differences between GL and its ancestor BL. The classical logic is based on bivalence, which is the principle that no proposition is both true and false. In other words, every meaningful proposition is either true or false. The complete falsity and the complete truth are the only options for the degree of truth of any proposition; these are the only values that logic variables can take. In addition, the classical logic is based on the law of excluded middle that claims that every proposition is either true or not true. All propositions have the same importance, and the concept of relative importance does not exist in logic models. Logic functions have no adjustable parameters, and the absorption theorem provides a total absorption of the less significant input.

It is easy to note that basic classical logic concepts are a very simplified and incomplete model of clearly visible (both semantic and formal logic) properties of human logic reasoning. So, it is unbelievable that these concepts remained practically unchallenged from the time of Aristotle (i.e., for more than 23 centuries). The first significant challenges came in the twentieth century and culminated in Zadeh's concept of fuzziness.

GL is a human-centric generalization of BL. Following are the fundamental concepts of GL (as introduced in [DUJ73b, DUJ74a, DUJ75a, DUJ79a] and expanded in [DUJ05b, DUJ07a, DUJ07c, DUJ12, DUJ15a]) based on observable properties of human reasoning:

1) Each value statement is a verbal approximation/interpretation of perceived reality. However, human value statements rarely reflect reality with perfect precision. Much more frequently, human statements reflect the reality only

approximately, including imprecision, partial truth, fuzziness, inconsistencies, and errors. In general, value statements are only partially true, and not completely true or completely false.

2) The degree of truth is an indicator of similarity between a proposition and the reality. For example, if in reality S is an average student, then the similarity between the statement "S deserves the highest grade" and the reality is around 50%. Partial truth and partial falsity are positive values less than 1.

3) The maximum degree of truth is denoted by the numeric value 1 (or 100%), and it corresponds to value statements that are in perfect agreement with reality.

4) The minimum degree of truth is denoted by the numeric value 0, and it corresponds to value statements that are a perfect negation of reality (completely opposite to reality).

5) Let t be a degree of truth ($0 \le t \le 1$). The value statement "evaluated object completely satisfies all requirements" that has the degree of truth t is equivalent to the value statement "evaluated system satisfies the fraction t of the total requirements" that has the degree of truth 1.

6) In the context of evaluation reasoning the aggregation of value statements assumes that each input value statement has a specific degree of relative importance. The relative importance varies from low (close to 0) to high (close to 1).

7) Relative importance cannot be 0 (because irrelevant statements are excluded from evaluation) and cannot be 1 (because the ultimate relative importance of a value statement would exclude all other value statements). In other words, contrary to usual mathematical assumption, the relative importance always belongs to the interval $]0, 1[$.

8) Simultaneity and substitutability are the fundamental logic concepts. Both the simultaneity and the substitutability are partial (incomplete or graded), meaning that decision makers select adjustable degrees of penalizing incomplete simultaneity and incomplete substitutability. In evaluation reasoning, simultaneity and substitutability are opposite and complementary concepts (increasing the degree of simultaneity means decreasing the degree of substitutability and vice versa). Simultaneity and substitutability can be modeled using a single function called graded (or generalized) conjunction/disjunction (GCD).

9) Graded simultaneity is modeled using a partial conjunction. The conjunction degree (andness) belongs to the interval $[0,1]$ and the extreme value 1 denotes the full conjunction (the minimum function).

10) Graded substitutability is modeled using a partial disjunction. The disjunction degree (orness) belongs to the interval $[0,1]$ and the extreme value 1 denotes the full disjunction (the maximum function).

11) In exceptional cases, the simultaneity can be stronger than the full conjunction and the substitutability can be stronger than the full disjunction. Such

cases are called hyperconjunction and hyperdisjunction. The andness of hyperconjunction is greater than 1 and the orness of hyperconjunction is less than 0.

12) GCD and the standard negation ($\bar{x} = 1 - x$) are the basic evaluation logic functions.

Our presentation of GL in *Part Two* follows the above concepts. In that way we hope to keep both the process and the product of evaluation reasoning in agreement with reality. In addition, this approach contributes to the credibility of both the LSP evaluation models and the results of the LSP evaluation, comparison, and selection of complex systems. GL has both similarities and differences with BL. A summary of differences between BL and GL is shown in Table 2.1.5.

2.1.11 Relationships between Graded Logic, Perceptual Computing, and Fuzzy Logic

There is a significant difference between mathematical models of physical world and mathematical models of human logic reasoning. In the case of the physical world, all variables (e.g., speed, acceleration, length, voltage, current, force, temperature, etc.) have objective and measurable values. Mathematical models that predict the value of a variable under given conditions can always be justified by measuring the difference between the actual value and the value predicted by the mathematical model. In many cases (e.g., Ohm's law, Kirchhoff's circuit laws, and Maxwell's equations in electrical engineering), the models of physical phenomena can be so precise that any difference between the measured and predicted values are normally interpreted as errors of measurement equipment and not as errors of an imprecise model.

As opposed to models of physical world the models of human evaluation reasoning do not deal with objectively measurable values. Obviously, the concept of value does not exist in the physical word, but only in the human mind. All variables that participate in human logic processes are objectively nonmeasurable and inherently imprecise perceptions. Indeed, human perceptions of value, importance, truth, suitability, satisfaction, simultaneity, substitutability, goals, requirements, and so on cannot be measured. All quantifications of their values can only come from a human subject in the form of imprecise verbalization using primarily a natural language. Computational models that process human perceptions are called *perceptual computing* [MEN10]. Of course, human perceptions are subjective judgments, and according to Jerry M. Mendel, who is the primary contributor to this area, mathematical models for solving perceptual computing problems should be identified as *perceptual computers*. From that standpoint our goal in this book is to build a perceptual computer for solving

Table 2.1.5 Main differences between the classical bivalent Boolean logic and GL.

Classical bivalent Boolean logic	Graded logic
Bivalence: Every proposition is either completely true or completely false.	**Multivalence**: Every proposition is both partially true and partially false. Both truth and falsity are a matter of degree.
Law of excluded middle: Every proposition P is either true or not true. "Not true" can be false or something else. The degree of truth x satisfies $\forall x \in \{0,1\},\ x \vee \overline{x} = 1 = true,\ \overline{x} = 1 - x.$	**Law of included middle (law of incomplete truth)**: Every proposition P and its negation $\overline{P}$ have degrees of truth x and $\overline{x}$ that are inside the interval [false, true]: $\forall x \in [0,1],\quad x \vee \overline{x} = \max(x, \overline{x}) \in [\tfrac{1}{2},\ 1].$
Bivalent logic variables: Truth $\in \{0,1\} = \{$false, true$\}$ Logic variables $\in \{0,1\}$ Truth + Falsity = 1.	**Continuous logic variables**: false = $0 \le$ Partial truth $\le 1 =$ true Logic variables $\in [0,1]$ Partial truth + Partial falsity = 1.
Andness and orness are fixed and bivalent: andness $\in \{0, 1\}$ orness $\in \{0, 1\}$.	**Andness and orness are continuously adjustable** in the interval [0,1], enabling continuous transition from conjunction to disjunction: $0 \le$ andness $\le 1, 0 \le$ orness ≤ 1.
Full conjunction: x *and* y $x \wedge y = \min(x, y)$; *andness* = 1 = const. (no partial conjunction, and no hyperconjunction).	**Partial conjunction, full conjunction, and hyperconjunction**: $x \triangle y,\ x \wedge y, x \overline{\wedge} y$; *andness* $\gtreqless 1$; $\tfrac{1}{2} <$ *andness* < 1: $x \wedge y \le x \triangle y \le (x+y)/2$; *andness* = 1: $x \wedge y = \min(x, y)$ *andness* > 1: $x \overline{\wedge} y \le x \wedge y$.
Full disjunction: x *or* y $x \vee y = \max(x, y)$; *orness* = 1 = const. (no partial disjunction, and no hyperdisjunction).	**Partial disjunction, full disjunction, and hyperdisjunction**: $x \nabla y,\ x \vee y, x \overline{\nabla} y$; *orness* $\gtreqless 1$; $\tfrac{1}{2} <$ *orness* < 1: $(x+y)/2 \le x \nabla y \le x \vee y$; *orness* = 1: $x \vee y = \max(x, y)$ *orness* > 1: $x \overline{\nabla} y \ge x \vee y$.
Logic neutrality: not available andness $\in \{0, 1\}$, orness $\in \{0, 1\}$.	**Logic neutrality**: andness = orness = $\tfrac{1}{2}$ $x \ominus y = [(x \wedge y) + (x \vee y)]/2 = (x+y)/2$.
Conjunction and disjunction are two disjoint models of ultimate simultaneity and ultimate substitutability.	**Conjunction and disjunction are unified in GCD**: GCD provides a controllable mix of conjunctive and disjunctive properties.
Conjunction and disjunction are always commutative: $x \wedge y = y \wedge x$ $x \vee y = y \vee x$.	**Partial conjunction and disjunction are commutative only for equal weights**: $x \triangle y = y \triangle x;\ \ W_x \ne W_y \Rightarrow W_x x \triangle W_y y \ne W_x y \triangle W_y x$ $x \nabla y = y \nabla x;\ \ W_x \ne W_y \Rightarrow W_x x \nabla W_y y \ne W_x y \nabla W_y x$.
Conjunction and disjunction are always distributive: $x \wedge (y \vee z) = (x \wedge y) \vee (x \wedge z)$ $x \vee (y \wedge z) = (x \vee y) \wedge (x \vee z)$.	**Partial conjunction and disjunction are not distributive except in special cases. Generally, the errors are small**: $x \triangle (y \nabla z) \approx (x \triangle y) \nabla (x \triangle z)$ $x \nabla (y \triangle z) \approx (x \nabla y) \triangle (x \nabla z)$.

(Continued)

Table 2.1.5 (Continued)

Classical bivalent Boolean logic	Graded logic
Conjunction and disjunction have two different neutral elements: $x \vee 0 = x$ $x \wedge 1 = x$.	**Partial conjunction (PC) and partial disjunction (PD) do not have neutral elements:** $x \overline{\nabla} 0 < x, \quad x \Delta 1 > x, \quad 0 < x < 1$.
Conjunction and disjunction have annihilators 0 and 1: $x \wedge 0 = 0, \quad x \vee 1 = 1, \quad x \in [0,1]$.	**If partial conjunction and disjunction are hard (called HPC and HPD, denoted $\overline{\Delta}, \overline{\nabla}$) they have annihilators:** $x \overline{\Delta} 0 = 0, \quad x \overline{\nabla} 1 = 1$.
Conjunction and disjunction are always hard (they always support annihilators 0 and 1).	**Partial conjunction and disjunction can be soft, i.e. without annihilators** (called SPC and SPD and denoted $\underline{\Delta}, \underline{\nabla}$): $x \underline{\Delta} 0 > 0, \quad x \underline{\nabla} 1 < 1, \quad 0 < x < 1$.
Insensitivity to improvements: for idempotent functions $y = f(x_1, ..., x_n)$ let $x_i = 0$ and $y = 1$; then the improvement of ith input to $x_i = 1$ has no effect on y.	**Sensitivity to improvements:** all idempotent aggregation functions $y = f(x_1, ..., x_n)$ satisfy nondecreasing monotonicity: $\dfrac{\partial y}{\partial x_i} \geq 0, \; i = 1, ..., n$ (support for improvements).
Each element x has a unique inverse element $\overline{x} = 1 - x$ as follows: $x \vee \overline{x} = 1$ $x \wedge \overline{x} = 0$.	**For partial conjunction, partial disjunction and negation $\overline{x} = 1 - x$ we have:** $1/2 \leq x \overline{\nabla} \overline{x} \leq 1 \qquad 1/2 \leq x \underline{\nabla} \overline{x} < 1$ $0 \leq x \overline{\Delta} \overline{x} \leq 1/2 \qquad 0 < x \underline{\Delta} \overline{x} \leq 1/2$.
Total absorption of optional input: x = mandatory, y = optional $x \wedge (x \vee y) = x \neq f(x, y)$ $x \vee (x \wedge y) = x \neq f(x, y)$.	**Partial absorption of optional input:** x = mandatory, y = optional $x \Delta (x \nabla y) = f(x, y) = \begin{cases} x + reward, & 0 < x < y \leq 1 \\ x - penalty, & 0 \leq y < x \leq 1 \end{cases}$.
All logic variables have the same importance: Semantic aspects are excluded from logic models; no percept of importance.	**The percept of importance is fundamental in human reasoning and it can be different for each logic variable:** Semantic aspects are included in logic models.
Fixed logic functions: Everything is strictly bivalent; nothing is a matter of degree, and there are no adjustable parameters.	**Graded logic functions:** Everything is a matter of degree; adjustable parameters are andness/orness of aggregators and relative importance of variables.
Number of elementary idempotent logic functions: 2 (conjunction and disjunction). No nonidempotent models of simultaneity and substitutability.	**Number of elementary idempotent logic functions:** 7 (C, HPC, SPC, A, SPD, HPD, D). There are nonidempotent models of simultaneity and substitutability: hyperconjunction (CC) and hyperdisjunction (DD). Thus, the total number of basic types of simultaneity and substitutability is 9.

evaluation problems (Section 2.2.1), and GL is a mathematical infrastructure necessary for building such a computer.

In human evaluation reasoning, everything is a matter of degree. Human perception of value, and related cognition, reasoning, and communication regularly include imprecision, vagueness and partial truth. While various aspects of the concept of vagueness attract debates in philosophy [SMI08, WIL94, KEE97, DEE10], we are only interested in "quantifiable vagueness," i.e., in percepts that can be precisely defined and quantitatively modeled as fuzziness or partial truth. Outside mathematics and related theoretical disciplines, it is difficult to find statements that are perfectly crisp, having the bivalent degree of truth. Most of human reasoning, perception, and communication are fuzzy, and truth comes in degrees. A typical statement that is partially true is, "Person P is tall." This statement might be considered perfectly true for most professional basketball players and perfectly false for most professional jockeys, and for everybody else it would be partially true.

In the propositional calculus with crisp truth values (i.e., in the classical bivalent logic) the statement, "The glass is full," is true only if the glass is completely full, and it is false immediately when a drop is missing. A more natural (i.e., obviously closer to human reasoning) approach to logic is to consider that each statement has a truth value, or the degree of truth going continuously from the complete falsity (denoted 0) to the complete truth (denoted 1). In other words, "Truth comes in degrees." For example, the statement "the glass is full" can be perfectly false (if the glass is empty), perfectly true (if the glass is full), and partially true (in all other cases). So, if the reality is that the glass contains 75% of water, we can consider that the statement, "The glass is full," is 75% true. Consequently, humans use approximate reasoning based on partial truth.

The partial truth in the above example can be interpreted as a quantitative indicator of the difference between a value statement and the objective reality. In some cases, the *objective reality* is known and measurable, like in the cases of the fullness of the glass of water, or the capacity of computer memory. In such cases, the partial truth is related to the error of an imprecise statement. Much more frequently, however, the partial truth is related to human perception of value, in cases where the objective reality is not measurable. For example, a homebuyer usually creates a list of attributes that affect the perception of the suitability of home, then evaluates (intuitively or quantitatively) all attributes and aggregates the attribute suitability degrees to get an overall suitability degree/score. This procedure is then applied to each competitive home. The resulting overall suitability score is an approximation of the degree of truth of the value statement, "The evaluated home completely satisfies all homebuyer's requirements." The value statement is partially true because of those requirements that are incompletely satisfied or not satisfied.

The objective reality of the values of competitive homes might be established if the homebuyer could buy all competitive homes, live in all of them at the same time, and eventually find the real truth about their suitability. This is not possible, and the human percept of the overall suitability used to select and buy a home is just an estimate (or a prediction) of the inherently unknown reality.

Once we accept partial truth, it is less obvious but equally natural that we also accept the partial conjunction and partial disjunction to express various degrees of simultaneity and substitutability, and partial absorption to express elastic aggregation of mandatory and optional, or sufficient and optional inputs. In addition, each input has its role and adjustable degree of importance, which is proportional to the level of supporting attainment of stakeholder goals and requirements.

Reasoning with elastic concepts that are a matter of degree was always present in human logic. Computing with such graded values belongs to the area of *soft computing*, and it can be contrasted to traditional *hard computing* with crisp values. For our purposes, soft computing can be simply defined as computing with variables that are a matter of degree (see also [ZAD94]). A variable that is a matter of degree can regularly be interpreted as the degree of membership in an appropriate fuzzy set. Such variables can also be interpreted as degrees of truth of appropriate statements [DUJ17]. Consequently, GL provides soft computing results that have dual interpretation: as degrees of truth or as degrees of fuzzy membership. That creates a relationship between GL and fuzzy logic.

In soft computing, everything is graded and adjustable (i.e., a matter of degree: conjunction, disjunction, absorption, relative importance, etc.). A characteristic question, "Are you satisfied with the object X that you currently evaluate and intend to use?" does not have only two answers: *yes* or *no*. These are only rare extreme cases, or imprecise approximations, where "yes" (numerically coded as 1) denotes an absolutely complete satisfaction and "no" (numerically coded as 0) denotes an absolutely complete dissatisfaction. What is much more frequent in real life is the partial satisfaction, a value that is between yes and no, or numerically between 0 and 1. In fact, "true" and "false" are extreme special cases of partial truth. Similarly, black and white are extreme special cases of gray.

Soft computing properties of GL models for evaluation of complex systems can have a large number of inputs and parameters. Most of them are defined as a matter of degree, as illustrated in Fig. 2.1.18 where all graded variables and parameters are based on human percepts. All input suitability degrees and the overall suitability are soft computing variables, (i.e., a matter of degree). Parameters of evaluation models are also soft: the relative importance is graded, and so are degrees of simultaneity and substitutability. Compound functions, such as the partial absorption also have soft parameters (degrees of penalty and reward, described in Chapter 2.6) that are used to control the degrees of absorption of optional inputs in mandatory/optional and sufficient/optional aggregators. Using GCD as a fundamental function, GL is established in a way that is both consistent with classical (bivalent or continuous) logic and represents its natural extension/generalization.

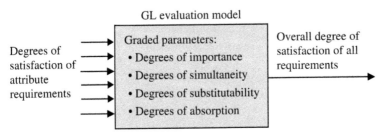

GL evaluation model

Degrees of satisfaction of attribute requirements →

Graded parameters:
• Degrees of importance
• Degrees of simultaneity
• Degrees of substitutability
• Degrees of absorption

Overall degree of satisfaction of all requirements →

Figure 2.1.18 In soft computing evaluation models, everything is a matter of degree.

In the majority of evaluation problems, the fuzzy interpretation and the logic interpretation of evaluation results are equivalent. Indeed, we can interpret elementary attribute criteria (Figs. 1.2.2 to 1.2.7) as membership functions of individual attributes, i.e., the degrees of membership in fuzzy sets of objects that completely satisfy given attribute requirements. Furthermore, we can interpret the overall suitability as the compound degree of membership in the fuzzy set of objects that completely satisfy all stakeholders' requirements.

On the other hand, the same concepts can be interpreted as logic concepts. Each attribute suitability score is a degree of truth of the statement claiming that a specific input completely satisfies user needs. The overall suitability is the degree of truth of the statement claiming that an evaluated system as a whole completely satisfies all stakeholders' requirements. So, in the area of evaluation, the fuzzy and logic interpretations are equally acceptable, and all GL results can also be interpreted in the context of fuzzy sets and fuzzy logic [DUJ17].

Fuzziness and partial truth belong to the same family of graded concepts, which are the central concepts of soft computing. However, the scope of fuzzy logic (FL) is much wider than the scope of GL, as we discussed in Section 2.1.5. FL penetrates areas such as linguistics and automatic control, while GL focuses on a narrow field of evaluation decision models. Both FL and GL are derived from observable properties of human reasoning, but in different areas. The narrow focus of GL (infinitely valued propositional calculus) permits us to identify and rather correctly model a spectrum of specific properties of evaluation reasoning. From the very beginning in the early 1970s, GL was a soft logic based on GCD and means, and used primarily for evaluation. As opposed to that, both the propositional and the predicate fuzzy logics mostly belong to t-norm fuzzy logics, where the emphasis is not on evaluation problems. FL evaluation models are not frequent and seem to be dominated by fuzzy weighted averages [KOS93, MEN10] without focus on specific needs of evaluation logic reasoning.

GL is a generalization of traditional Boolean logic based on concepts of graded conjunction, and graded disjunction. FL is based on the graded concept of fuzzy set, which is a generalization of the concept of traditional crisp set. GL provides aggregation models of finer granularity then FL, and it can be interpreted as a refinement of a specific segment of FL (Fig. 2.1.6). Readers interested in fuzzy sets, fuzzy logic (in a wide sense), and nonidempotent aggregation based of t-norms and conorms should consult the rich literature in fuzzy sets and fuzzy logic, primarily [ZAD65, ZAD73, ZAD74, ZAD76, ZAD89, ZAD94, ZAD96, ZIM84, ZIM87, ZIM96, KLI95, KOS93, FOD94, CAR02, LEE05, TOR07, MEN01, MEN10, BEL07, GRA09, ROS10].

2.1.12 A Brief History of Graded Logic

Graded logic, as it is presented in this book (as a model of human logic aggregation and criteria used in evaluation reasoning) was born in the early 1970s in the School of Electrical Engineering at the University of Belgrade (Fig. 2.1.19). This section shows the chronology of early developments of GL from author's personal point of view. In other words, I would like to present and comment on GL ideas not as an observer but as a developer. The goal is to show not only when GL ideas were introduced and initial results published, but also why and where that methodology for modeling the logic of evaluation reasoning became necessary.

The reason for developing GL was not theoretical. My motivation was to solve decision engineering problems related to the evaluation, comparison, selection, and optimization of mainframe computer systems, where decisions in the late 1960s and the early 1970s were based on approximately 80–120 input attributes.

Figure 2.1.19 School of Electrical Engineering at the University of Belgrade(reproduced by permission of PC Press, Belgrade, author Zoran Životić).

That number of inputs and logic relationships among them clearly showed the inadequacy of both discriminant analysis [DUJ69] and simple additive weighted scoring [MIL66, MIL70, SCH69, SCH70, DUJ72a, DUJ72b] (see details in Chapter 1.3). My first professional mainframe computer evaluation and selection project in 1968–1969 (for a major Belgrade bank) used discriminant analysis (I-distance, [IVA63, DUJ69]), and the second in 1970–1971 (for a utility company in Zagreb) used the additive weighted scoring. In both cases, there was a clear need for models of graded simultaneity and substitutability, and for making some requirements necessary and some optional, to use sufficient and desired inputs, and above all, to make mathematical models consistent with the intuitive reasoning of stakeholders. With existing (additive) methods, that was completely impossible, and I started to develop both the necessary mathematical infrastructure and the necessary software support, based on the theory of means [GIN58, MIT69]. Thus, my motivation for the development of GL, as well as the selection of necessary GL properties, came directly from the demands of decision engineering practice.

The interest in partial truth, multivalued logics, and reasoning with vague concepts emerged in logic in works of Bernard Russell, Jan Lukasiewicz, and Max Black in the early twentieth century [KOS93]. However, these ideas did not smoothly evolve in soft computing and engineering applications. The development of soft computing concepts originated in engineering as a response to practical needs for problem solving in decision engineering, computer science, and control engineering. The starting point of all engineering applications of soft computing concepts is 1965, when Lotfi Zadeh at the University of California Berkeley introduced fuzzy sets [ZAD65], the first successful step toward wide use of graded concepts in science, computing, and engineering. Important concepts of fuzzy logic (FL), namely linguistic variables and the calculus of fuzzy if-then-else rules, were introduced by Zadeh in 1973 [ZAD73] and 1974 [ZAD74].

GL was also introduced in 1973 [DUJ73b]. GL was developed independently from FL between 1970 and 1973 at the University of Belgrade and the Institute "M. Pupin," and initially used for the development of comprehensive models for evaluation of analog, hybrid, and digital computers developed by the Institute. Practical evaluation problems generated the need for graded logic aggregators that can be used to model simultaneity and substitutability. The "aha! moment" occurred when I realized that logic functions are not only conjunction and disjunction but also everything that is between them; so, parameterized means can be naturally interpreted as logic functions and the continuous transition from conjunction to disjunction must be controlled by appropriate parameters. To achieve that goal, in 1973 I introduced concepts of the conjunction degree (andness) and the complementary disjunction degree (orness) [DUJ73b] and started to use new graded logic functions: partial conjunction, partial disjunction, and partial absorption. I found that partial conjunction and partial disjunction are appropriate logic aggregators, good models of adjustable simultaneity and substitutability, and above all, consistent with observable human evaluation reasoning. Stakeholders (in mainframe computer selection projects) accepted GL as a model of their evaluation reasoning, and I was able to involve them into selecting andness/orness and weights in GL criteria, and to formally confirm that the developed criteria correctly reflect their goals and requirements. The ease of accepting GL models by practitioners participating in evaluation projects showed that they recognize these logic models from their intuitive evaluation reasoning experience more than from my mathematical explanation. That was a decisive signal that the development of GL moves in the right direction. Early developments of GL and papers published in 1973, 1974, and 1975 were strictly located in the framework of graded logic and interpreted GL as a generalization of the classical Boolean logic. Of course, the need for idempotency naturally connected GL models and the theory of means.

My work in early 1970s benefited very much from the research on means and their inequalities performed by my math professors, and later friendly colleagues, D. S. Mitrinović and P. M. Vasić [MIT69, MIT70], a few doors from my office in the School of Electrical Engineering at the University of Belgrade (some of the impressive work of D. S. Mitrinović and P. M. Vasić in the areas of means and related inequalities is presented after their death in [BUL03]). So, I was extremely lucky to be directly exposed to the work of that world-class group of mathematicians, and also to be stimulated (despite being an electronic engineer) to publish my work in their math journal and get valuable feedback. Following is a short survey of the initial GL publications.

The concepts of logic functions that provide a controlled continuous transition from conjunction to disjunction (graded conjunction/disjunction), as well as the adjustable andness/orness (both the local andness/orness and the mean local andness/orness), and corresponding logic aggregators, were introduced in [DUJ73b]. The LSP method, initially called Mixed Averaging by Levels (MAL) and renamed to LSP in 1987, is based on graded logic and soft computing aggregators controlled (initially) by the mean local andness. It was introduced in 1973 [DUJ73c] and was used for evaluation, comparison, and selection of analog, digital, and hybrid computer systems. The concept of global andness/orness, the sensitivity analysis of aggregation structures and sensitivity indicators, the system of 17 andness/orness levels of graded conjunction/disjunction, and the concept of asymmetric simultaneity and asymmetric substitutability aggregators (partial absorption function, with tables for computing parameters of the function) were introduced in 1974 [DUJ74b] and were applied to solving problems of computer evaluation [DUJ74d, DUJ75c] and optimization [DUJ74c].

All fundamental GL developments and corresponding applications in 1973 and 1974 were sponsored by the Laboratory for Computer Engineering of the Mihajlo Pupin Institute in Belgrade. The Institute was a manufacturer of analog, digital, and hybrid computers and evaluation models were used to verify the suitability of these products and for their comparison with other competitive products. The necessary software infrastructure for professional system evaluation consisted of a specialized System Evaluation Language SEL [DUJ76a] and a specialized criterion database support system [DUJ76b]. Most initial results were published in Serbo-Croatian, and therefore their use in decision engineering practice remained limited to former Yugoslavia.

Early papers written in English that introduced GL and the corresponding evaluation methodology include [DUJ73a, DUJ74a, SLA74, DUJ75a, DUJ75b, DUJ76d, DUJ77a, DUJ77b, DUJ79a]. The global andness/orness (initially called the conjunction degree and the disjunction degree) was first presented in English in [DUJ74a]. It is interesting to note that the global andness and orness in [DUJ74a] were defined for the following mean:

$$M_n(\mathbf{x};\Phi) = F^{-1}\left(\frac{\displaystyle\sum_{i=1}^{n}\Phi_i(x_i)F(x_i)}{\displaystyle\sum_{i=1}^{n}\Phi_i(x_i)}\right),$$

$$x_i \in I, \quad \Phi_i : I \to R^+ \cup \{0\}, \quad i = 1,\ldots,n,$$

$$F : I \to R \text{ (strictly monotone)}, \quad F^{-1} : R \to I,$$

$$\mathbf{x} = (x_1,\ldots,x_n), \quad \Phi = (\Phi_1,\ldots,\Phi_n).$$

Of course, this is the Bajraktarević mean, which includes as special cases the quasi-arithmetic means, exponential means, Gini means, counter-harmonic means, and weighted power means. So, the authors who claim that in [DUJ74a] the global andness and orness were introduced for the special case of power means are incorrect.

The term *partial absorption function* and the properties of asymmetric aggregators were first presented in English in [DUJ75a]; the first English paper fully devoted to mathematical details of the partial absorption function was [DUJ79a]. Except for [DUJ76d], all these papers were published in former Yugoslavia, and remained little known before [FOD94].

Starting in 1973, I was responsible for a sequence of more than 25 evaluation decision projects based on GL and the LSP method, for major governmental and corporate customers in former Yugoslavia. This industrial practice was the primary generator of theoretical advances. For example, the partial absorption function [DUJ74b] and asymmetric logic relationships (Chapter 2.6) were introduced in 1974 to satisfy the needs of the computer selection criterion for the Naftagas oil industry in Novi Sad. All logic models presented in this book originated in decision engineering practice, where the initial efforts were focused on evaluation and selection of mainframe digital computers [DUJ73c, DUJ74e, DUJ75c, DUJ76e, DUJ77b, DUJ78a, DUJ78b, DUJ79b, DUJ80], as well as analog computers [DUJ74d] and hybrid computers [DUJ76c, DUJ76d]. The first optimization method based on GL criteria was developed for optimizing computing units of analog and hybrid computers in [DUJ74c]. All theoretical GL results were first tested and used in industrial applications, and then published.

The first logic evaluation models of software systems, based on GL and the LSP method, were developed in 1979–1982, during my employment as a computer science faculty member at the University of Florida, Gainesville. The LSP method was used for a data management systems evaluation project for NIST in Washington, DC [DUJ82, SU82]. This work was later presented in a comprehensive paper [SU87].

Most fundamental concepts of GL and the LSP method were developed in the first half of the 1970s. In the 1980s, the LSP method was frequently used, and in 1987, it was presented as a rather complete and standardized industrial decision methodology in [DUJ87] and [SU87] under its current name, Logic Scoring of Preference. So, 1987 is the year that marks the end of early years (1973–1987) of GL and its applications.

Since 1987 there have been many new developments and publications related to GL and LSP (e.g., the first book chapter, [DUJ91]). These results are the basis of this book. In particular, in the 1990s and later, the GL applications expanded in a variety of new areas, such as advanced software systems, real estate, medical applications, ecology, geography, and others (see *Part Four*).

The logic concepts of andness, orness, and aggregators that realize a continuous transition from AND to OR, that the author introduced in 1973, are very natural and visible in human reasoning. So, it is not surprising that other people later independently created the same or similar ideas.

As a part of these early historic notes, let us mention that the graded logic functions, imprecision, partial truth, fuzziness, and similar soft computing concepts are easily visible in human reasoning, but their quantification and formalization found resistance in some academic circles, and the pioneers had to pay the price for taking "the road less traveled by." A plausible explanation for this is the difference between modeling physical processes that are objectively measurable and modeling human perceptions that are not objectively measurable. Traditional scientific education focuses on modeling measurable physical phenomena. People trained in modeling measurable phenomena expect that all models can always be verified only by analyzing the difference between the model results and the measured reality. In early years, when such people first encountered soft computing models of human perceptions (which are quantifiable but not precisely objectively measurable), they would discover the lack of traditional objective measurable justification, and interpret it as the undesirable "subjectivity." Consequently, they would sometimes aggressively distrust not only the quality of the models but also the very reason for their existence.

2.2 Observable Properties of Human Evaluation Logic

We understand human mental processes only slightly
better than a fish understands swimming.
—John McCarthy

The goal of logic is the study of valid reasoning. Consequently, the credibility of formal logic models depends on their compatibility with observable properties of human reasoning. The same holds for the whole area of perceptual computing. Consequently, before building evaluation logic models and perceptual computers we must first observe, identify, analyze and understand characteristic properties of human evaluation logic reasoning. After this first step we can try to develop mathematical models that describe those properties.

As a point of departure in this direction let us read an inspirational characterization of the study of mental processes written in 1847 by Augustus De Morgan in his seminal book *Formal Logic or the Calculus of Inference Necessary and Probable* [DEM47]:

With respect to the mind, considered as a complicated apparatus which is to be studied, we are not even so well off as those would be who had to examine and decide upon the mechanism of a watch, merely by observation of the functions of the hands, without being allowed to see the inside. A mechanician, to whom a watch was presented for the first time, would be able to give a good guess as to its structure, from his knowledge of other pieces of contrivance. As soon as he had examined the law of the motion of the hands, he might conceivably invent an instrument with similar properties, in fifty different ways. But in the case of the mind, we have manifestations only, without the smallest power of reference to other similar things, or the least knowledge of structure or process, other than what may be derived from those manifestations. It is the problem of the watch to those who have never seen any mechanism at all.

Soft Computing Evaluation Logic: The LSP Decision Method and Its Applications,
First Edition. Jozo Dujmović.
© 2018 John Wiley & Sons, Inc. Published 2018 by John Wiley & Sons, Inc.
Companion website: www.wiley.com/go/Dujmovic/Soft_Computing_Evaluation_Logic

Based on the fine compatibility of expert opinions of Augustus De Morgan and John McCarthy, it follows that the study of mental processes in the area of evaluation reasoning provides good opportunities to those who are looking for trouble. However, the only road toward justifiable evaluation models is going through this risky territory. We will try to move carefully and without rush, looking at all phenomena that might affect the way we should model logic reasoning. The result is one of the longest chapters in this book. The size of the chapter is proportional to our respect for the complexity of the mechanism we try to observe and then go on to model, reproduce, and utilize some of the observed properties.

De Morgan's analogy of studying the mechanism of a watch, merely by observation of the functions of the hands, is today called the *black-box approach:* we characterize a complex system by observing the relationships between its inputs and outputs, without knowing and analyzing details of its internal organization. In their influential books [DEM47, BOO47, BOO54], the founding fathers of formal logic, Augustus De Morgan and George Boole, very clearly indicated that their goal was the mathematical modeling of observable human mental activities. Their goal was not to build new formal mathematical theories—that was a consequence of their efforts to build justifiable models of human reasoning. We believe that the same goal must be adopted in the case of GL.

In this chapter we identify necessary GL properties derived from observing human perceptions and reasoning in the area of evaluation. This is not a trivial task. Indeed, in the case of perceptions that are processed by the human mind, the observer and the observed object are the same, the measurement tool and the measured object are the same, and the quality of mathematical models is evaluated by the modeled object (human mind) itself.

On the other hand, the evaluation reasoning is a rather narrow and easily observable area because the intuitive evaluation reasoning is a ubiquitous mental process offering opportunities to observe it and identify (with intention to quantify) its characteristic properties.[1] Indeed, every reading of a restaurant menu is an evaluation process that takes into account various characteristics of food as well as its cost and the aggregated degree of suitability is then used to select the best option and report it to the waiter. All visits to grocery stores are similar experiences of evaluation and selection based on attributes and costs of articles. All Internet purchasing experiences are in the same category. For example, any buyer of a laptop computer will take into account the cost, the size of screen, the speed of processor, the number of cores, the size of main memory, the size of external memory (disk or solid state drive), and various other attributes, in order to evaluate, select, and buy the most suitable machine. Of course, more expensive purchases need more precise evaluation. Most properties of human evaluation reasoning are visible during the careful comparison and

---

1 Well, according to Yogi Berra, *"You can observe a lot by just watching."*

selection of cars and homes. However, the most valuable insight into desired GL properties presented in this chapter comes from professional evaluation studies, where sophisticated corporate logic criteria are developed during the meticulous work within teams that include stakeholders, domain experts, managers, and professional evaluators. This is the environment where we identified the necessary properties of evaluation reasoning and the corresponding properties of their quantitative models.

Our list of observed properties of evaluation reasoning is rather long: we provide a detailed investigation of 33 properties that characterize evaluation reasoning and affect quantitative evaluation methods and the architecture of the corresponding perceptual computer. Our intention is to highlight the evaluation reasoning from all significant (and sometimes partially redundant) angles. For selected properties we investigate convenient mathematical models providing material that is necessary for the development of GL.

Realistic models of evaluation reasoning must satisfy many conditions. The number of satisfied conditions directly contributes to the credibility of corresponding mathematical models. Thus, the goals of GL models are different from the goals encountered in mathematics, philosophy, psychology, and behavioral economics. Contrary to formal axiomatic approaches to logic (that are encountered in mathematics and philosophy), the roots of GL approach are in applications and semantic interpretations of industrial evaluation processes. In addition, while in psychology and behavioral economics the primary goal is to investigate behavior of the population of rational choosers [SCH02], our goal is to build a machine (a perceptual computer for evaluation) that rational choosers can use in their decision making. Therefore, we see evaluation as an area of computational intelligence, i.e., we present evaluation as an applied engineering area and GL as its theoretical infrastructure. That said, we can now focus on building our machine the way system and software engineers build tools for their colleagues, decision engineers.

Human reasoning in the area of evaluation includes observable logic patterns that we call the *intuitive evaluation logic*. Formalized GL and evaluation criteria that are used in decision engineering should be based on mathematical models that are consistent with all properties of intuitive GL. The credibility of professional evaluation methods critically depends on their concordance with the intuitive evaluation logic. Any inconsistency between a mathematical model and observable properties of human reasoning should be sufficient to reject such a model and the corresponding evaluation method. Consequently, a detailed identification and characterization of observable properties of intuitive evaluation logic is a prerequisite for the development of trustworthy mathematical models. In this chapter, we define and investigate fundamental properties that are encountered in intuitive GL. For each of the necessary properties, the next step is to develop mathematical models that describe the identified property as precisely as possible.

In the case of intuitive GL, we cannot perform objective measurements of human perceptions and the processing performed by the human mind, but we can rely on careful observations and consensus of observers. Since the evaluation reasoning is a frequent activity of human mind, it is possible to find convincing examples of evaluation reasoning. Buying homes, cars, computers, comparing schools, universities, and websites, can serve as typical examples. We can also benefit from the fact that GL is a generalization of the well-known classic bivalent logic.

Both the intuitive GL and the formal GL are used by decision makers (DM). Generally, in industrial settings we assume that DM is a *team that consists of stakeholders, decision engineers (evaluators), and domain experts* (see Chapter 3.2). Their collective expertise is used for creating quantitative logic evaluation criteria based on rationality and thorough understanding of the environment in which the logic models are used to reach decisions that properly support the attainment of stakeholders' goals. In a special case, DM can also be an individual that (to some extent) integrates all properties of the DM team. Evaluation reasoning of such DMs can be characterized by the following list of observable significant properties:

Group 1. Perceptual computer and its basic properties

(P_1) Reasoning with graded values
(P_2) The role of rationality in evaluation reasoning
(P_3) Suitability attributes, requirements, and preference/suitability scores
(P_4) Standard model of evaluation reasoning and the architecture of perceptual computer for suitability evaluation
(P_5) Internality and idempotency
(P_6) Continuity, monotonicity, and compensativeness
(P_7) Granularity, uncertainty, linguistic labels, and rating scales

Group 2. Simultaneity and substitutability in evaluation reasoning

(P_8) Simultaneity
(P_9) Substitutability (replaceability)
(P_{10}) Combining simultaneity and substitutability
(P_{11}) Conjunctive/disjunctive neutrality
(P_{12}) Andness, orness, and continuous transition from *and* to *or*
(P_{13}) Sensitivity to orness and andness
(P_{14}) Standard negation and partial negation

Group 3. Basic semantic aspects of evaluation reasoning

(P_{15}) Environment and semantics of evaluation reasoning
(P_{16}) Noncommutativity, relative importance, and the use of weights
(P_{17}) Mandatory conjunctive requirements (hard partial conjunction)

(P_{18}) Nonmandatory conjunctive requirements (soft partial conjunction)
(P_{19}) Sufficient requirements (hard and soft partial disjunction)
(P_{20}) Nine special cases of graded conjunction/disjunction
(P_{21}) The compound percept of overall importance and its components
(P_{22}) The impact of relative importance for various degrees of andness/orness.
(P_{23}) Decomposition of overall importance
(P_{24}) Threshold andness and threshold orness

Group 4. Multipolarity: grouping and aggregation of semantically heterogeneous inputs

(P_{25}) Conjunctive bipolarity: Mandatory and desired/optional requirements
(P_{26}) Disjunctive bipolarity: Sufficient and desired/optional requirements
(P_{27}) Tripolarity: Mandatory, desired, and optional requirements
(P_{28}) Bipolarity of desirable (positive) and undesirable (negative) inputs

Group 5. Grouping and aggregation of semantically homogeneous inputs

(P_{29}) Grouping inputs using associativity
(P_{30}) Grouping inputs using distributivity

Group 6. Imprecision, incompleteness, logic inconsistency, and errors

(P_{31}) Limited accuracy of parameters and incompleteness of input attributes
(P_{32}) Inconsistent logic conditions and the problems of hypersensitivity
(P_{33}) Missing data, the concordance principle, and error compensation

This list includes logic properties that can be identified, exemplified, observed, and analyzed from the standpoint of quantitative modeling. Some of them we introduced and initially discussed in previous chapters. In subsequent sections, we present a detailed description of each of these properties.

Before we continue, let us explain the reasons for presenting and studying this long list of observable properties. Readers interested only in practically solving an evaluation problem might decide to skip this chapter (or read a few selected properties, starting with P_4). Nevertheless, we believe that this material is indispensable for the same reason as the knowledge of anatomy is necessary for successful surgery. First, the study of the anatomy of evaluation reasoning systematically identifies individual properties and investigates them under a magnifying glass in order to build justifiable models of logic decision making and provide necessary understanding and technical background for research in this area. Second, this study builds necessary confidence in the evaluation methodology we develop and use. Last but not least, we want to clearly show what is neglected when logic decision models are built only mathematically, without taking into account observable properties of human reasoning.

2.2.1 Perceptual Computer and Its Basic Properties

> *All existing things upon this earth, which have knowledge of their own*
> *existence, possess, some in one degree and some in another, the power of*
> *thought, accompanied by perception which is the awakening of thought by*
> *the effect of external objects upon the senses.*
> —Augustus De Morgan [DEM47]

> *What is a perception? A perception is what is perceived by the human*
> *brain in response to visual, aural, sensory or other stimuli.*
> —Lotfi Zadeh [ZAD15]

The central result of this section is the architecture of perceptual computer for suitability evaluation (P_4). Observations of intuitive evaluation show that intuitive evaluation is regularly based on a perceptual reasoning model called *standard model of evaluation reasoning* (SMER). That model is used as the architecture of the corresponding perceptual computer for suitability evaluation. GL must be developed as a mathematical infrastructure that supports SMER and the development of various specific versions of the perceptual computer.

The concepts of perceptual computing and perceptual computer were introduced by Jerry Mendel, and subsequently refined by Mendel and Wu [MEN01, MEN01a, MEN02, MEN08, MEN10] in the context of *computing with words* (CWW) [ZAD96, LIU08]. Mendel's perceptual computer implements CWW by accepting verbalized user input and generating verbalized output; both the verbalized input and the verbalized output represent human percepts. The perceptual computer is structured as an encoder that accepts verbal input and transforms it to numerically coded input for a CWW engine that produces numeric output; the output is then used by a decoder to produce verbalized and numeric results for the user. The perceptual computer described in [MEN08] operates with a rule-based CWW engine that processes interval type-2 fuzzy sets that represent words from a vocabulary [LIU08].

In the area of evaluation, the central concept of *value* is not an objectively measurable physical property: it is a subjective human percept. Therefore, mathematical models that are developed and used to process human percepts in the area of evaluation can be interpreted as perceptual computers and their activity can be denoted as perceptual computing. It is useful to note that perceptual computers and perceptual computing exist also in areas different from evaluation [MEN10].

Let us now clarify the concepts of perceptual computing and perceptual computer in the specific context of evaluation decision making. Evaluation decision making is conceptually compatible with the concepts of Mendel's perceptual computing and perceptual computer. The compatibility is not in the architecture of perceptual computer because our perceptual computers, which are based on LSP concepts (*Part Three*), use different organization of criteria and different logic aggregation structures. The compatibility is preserved in the fundamental idea that the perceptual computer is a model of processing human percepts. In our case, the inputs are either human percepts or attribute variables that can be directly mapped to human percepts using elementary attribute criteria, and the output generated by the perceptual computer is a compound human percept. Perceptual computers for evaluation can use verbalized inputs and outputs, but that is not the fundamental characteristic or the prerequisite for evaluation computing. Evaluation models use infinite-valued logic models and graded soft computing inputs, outputs, and parameters; thus, the primary interpretation of logic values is in terms of the degrees of truth, which can be easily verbalized using codebooks[2] and rating scales if users are not familiar with logic interpretations, but need interpretations based on words.

(P₁) Reasoning with Graded Values

In the area of evaluation, human reasoning is based on processing graded values. The graded values are either variables or parameters that are a matter of degree. Such values belong to a standardized range (from minimum to maximum, usually abstracted as $[0,1]$). Graded variables are interpreted as degrees of truth of value statements. In this context, *soft computing* can be defined as any processing of graded input variables in order to generate graded results using mathematical models that use graded parameters. The most important graded concepts used in evaluation reasoning include the following:

- *Satisfaction of an individual requirement* (e.g., an attribute requirement; a graded variable in the range from minimum to maximum satisfaction, e.g., from 0 to 100%).
- *Overall suitability or overall preference* (the average degree to which an evaluated object satisfies all nonfinancial requirements; we treat the cost separately).
- *Overall value* (a compound degree of satisfaction of all relevant requirements, including both nonfinancial requirements and financial requirements).
- *Simultaneity* (a degree to which we request simultaneous satisfaction of multiple requirements)
- *Substitutability or replaceability* (a degree to which the satisfaction of a single requirement in a group can replace the satisfaction of all other requirements in the group)
- *Relative importance* (the extent to which the satisfaction of a specific requirement in a group is more desirable than the satisfaction of another requirement in the same group)
- *Compound importance* (a combined percept of importance based on two (or a few) identifiable contributing components)

---

2 Very detailed 32-word codebooks are developed in [LIU08, MEN10, HAO16].

- *Overall importance* (the extent to which the satisfaction of a major group of requirements is significant for attainment of stakeholder's goals)
- *Penalty* (the extent to which DM wants to decrease an aggregated degree of satisfaction in the case where mandatory or sufficient inputs are partially satisfied, and an optional input component is not satisfied)
- *Reward* (the extent to which DM wants to increase an aggregated degree of satisfaction in the case where mandatory or sufficient inputs are partially satisfied, and an optional input component is perfectly satisfied)
- *Sensitivity* (the degree to which the overall suitability depends on satisfaction of a specific component requirement)
- *Tradeoff/compensativeness* (the degree to which the insufficient satisfaction of a specific requirement can be compensated by increasing the satisfaction of another requirement).

These graded concepts are regularly used by humans for perceptual processing in the context of intuitive evaluation reasoning. The degrees of these percepts can be expressed either numerically or verbally using rating scales (see P_7 and Chapter 2.9).

(P₂) The Role of Rationality in Evaluation Reasoning

The analysis of human perception of value is an important topic in psychology and behavioral economics where the focus is on the concept of rationality, individual human perception of value, and related economic behavior [VON44, SIM55, SIM56, SIM57, SIM79, KAH79, KAH84, KAH99]. The primary goal of such research is to understand human behavior (both rational and irrational) and reasons for various economic decisions. Since the analysis is focused on the behavior of individual DMs, conclusions are usually based on experiments designed to observe a selected DM population. The observations of population are then processed using statistical methods [SCH02].

Evaluation reasoning is a specific form of decision making where a rational mind decides about the *values* of competitive (physical or conceptual) objects and selects the best of multiple alternatives. The *value* is interpreted as a normalized overall degree to which a selected object satisfies justifiable requirements of the DM. If we use the statement "the evaluated object completely satisfies DM's requirements," then this statement is partially true because the truth is interpreted as a state of being in accord with facts or reality. Thus, the degree of satisfaction of requirements can be quantified as a degree of truth of the statement that claims a complete satisfaction of requirements. Since the result of evaluation is essentially a truth bearer (see Section 2.1.5), it follows that *evaluation reasoning is a logic process*. Consequently, let us first investigate how evaluation reasoning relates to the area of mathematical logic and what is the role of rationality in this relationship.

By a classic definition, logic is the science of correct reasoning. It is concerned with conscious judgments and inferences by which a rational mind interprets reality. In the context of professional/industrial evaluation we use the word *rational* to indicate reasoning that is seriously prepared, unbiased, exhaustive, based on facts, consistent with justifiable goals, reflecting and protecting a precisely defined stakeholder, sufficiently good (or the best possible) for a specific DM, acceptable for a convincing majority of similar (qualified and diversified) DMs, and usually based on collective wisdom of expert teams.[3] Of course, it is difficult to achieve a perfect consensus that an evaluation process is rational, but if there is a decision that is either optimum, or more frequently based on satisficing (satisfactory and sufficient behavior), then it can be confidently labeled as sufficiently rational. The concept of satisficing, introduced by Herbert Simon [SIM56, SIM79], refers to situations where decision makers accept choices or judgments that are "good enough" for their purposes (i.e., those that satisfy an acceptability threshold), but could be optimized. In evaluation, satisficing has many forms, including the use of overall suitability threshold in suitability-affordability analysis (see Chapter 3.6), as well as neglecting evaluation of those suitability attributes that have provably low significance, but cause excessive effort in evaluation (for details see section 1.3.1 and *Part Three*).

Professional/industrial evaluation used by companies (e.g., car manufacturers evaluating and selecting tires for their new car models) is assumed to be rational, if it provides an appropriate (optimum, or "good enough") support to the attainment of justifiable corporate goals. In such cases we assume that corporate DM teams properly interpret corporate goals and satisfy prerequisites for rational decisions. In addition, rationality is sometimes bounded by incomplete information, inappropriate DM preparation, and insufficient available time for the decision-making process.

In real life some decisions (particularly in the area of procurement) can also be intentionally irrational. For example, it is not difficult to detect decisions that primarily support the private goals of DM disguised as corporate goals (various forms of corruption, and unfair selection of job candidates are typical examples). So, many forms of irrationality are located in the gray area between legal and illegal decisions. For example, if a drug manufacturer offers rewards to medical institutions or practitioners who prescribe their drug instead of another superior drug, then the rationality of drug evaluation and selection is questionable because a rational goal is to prescribe therapy that is the best for a patient. In this example it is clear that the problem is in two conflicting stakeholders: the drug manufacturer and the patient. Another similar form of irrationality is the *inverse evaluation problem* where a DM has decided to select his favorite system F among competitive systems A, B, C, D, E, F and then tries to develop such a criterion that will produce ranking where the winner is F.

---

3 This list should be sufficient to exclude all biased political decisions where participants represent different stakeholders.

The simplest method to improve the rationality of decisions is the use of teams. This is particularly visible in legal evaluation problems (e.g., the use of jury consisting of 12 jurors), and medical evaluations where patients use multiple second opinions to decide whether to accept or reject a proposed therapy. In professional industrial evaluation DM is generally a team consisting of stakeholder(s), decision engineers, and domain experts (see Section 3.2.1). Such team organization regularly provides prerequisites for rationality of decisions.

Professional evaluation methods can also be used by individuals making consumer decisions (mostly in cases of buying expensive objects—homes, cars, and advanced electronic devices). In the case of general consumers, however, marketing studies show that common consumer decisions are frequently irrational, and irrational reasoning is a legitimate component of human reasoning practice in the area of intuitive evaluation of many consumer products. Irrational consumer criteria are typically context-sensitive, proxy-based, and significantly brand-sensitive (brand-sensitivity can be related to one or more of the brand personality dimensions, which according to [AAK97] include sincerity, excitement, competence, sophistication, and ruggedness). Consumers frequently accept higher price as a *proof* (or *proxy*) *of quality* of a product (e.g., people frequently buy an unknown wine thinking that it is good because it is expensive, or buy cars that are primarily a status symbol).

The comparison of products produced by known/famous brands is different from cases where consumers do not know the brand (e.g., consumers frequently compensate lower product quality with the recognizability of a product's brand, and the rationality of such evaluation is regularly questionable). In some consumer goods cases, brand value overshadows all other attributes in the consumer's choice (typical examples are products of large cola companies). From the seller's perspective, the brand might deliver a significant amount of value (see [INT10]) and brand is currently created and managed as a valuable business asset.

Decision making and irrational decision making are among significant research areas in psychology and subsequently in behavioral economics [KAH11, ARI10]. That research shows that irrationality is not only permanently present in human behavior and decision making but that in many decision situations humans are predictably irrational. Not surprisingly, imperfections of human reasoning and decision making regularly attract corporate attention intended to exploit these imperfections for economic gain. One of central conclusions of Dan Ariely's work in [ARI10] is that "we are pawns in a game whose forces we largely fail to comprehend." This conclusion is in fine concordance with John McCarthy's opinion about our understanding of human mental processes that we quoted at the very beginning of this chapter.

Fortunately, the evaluation reasoning belongs to Kahneman's "slow thinking," also called "System 2," and characterized as deliberate, effortful, and orderly mental activity, often combined with complex computations [KAH11].

This characterization certainly holds for professional evaluation teams working in industry.

Human perceptions are subjective representations of reality. We can define a population of qualified, diversified, and impartial decision makers to denote a hypothetical body that can provide the best collective representation of reality and provide an ideal specification of rational stakeholder's goals. Of course, each stakeholder is fully entitled to specify the goals that are more or less rational and different from the hypothetical ideal case. The process of evaluation is not supposed to question the specified goals but to find the alternative that provably offers the best support to goal attainment.

Irrationality sometimes affects the selection and formulation of goals, but it does not affect mathematical properties of the logic of evaluation reasoning. Indeed, *the irrational evaluation decisions formally follow the same patterns, rules, and models of logic as the rational decisions.* The simultaneity and substitutability of a group of components are modeled using partial conjunction and partial disjunction both in the case of components that reflect rational goals and in the case of components that reflect irrational goals. There is no evidence that humans use different formal logic aggregation models depending on the rationality of selected goals that are used to make an evaluation decision. The same holds for the use of weights to express relative importance of aggregated components. The same also holds when decision makers identify mandatory and optional attributes and aggregate them using partial absorption. All such decisions and decision models use the same logic concepts of simultaneity, substitutability, mandatory requirements, optional requirements, relative importance, etc., and are processed by the same aggregation engine (human mind). For example, it can be irrational to declare as optional an attribute that should be mandatory, but this decision does not affect the structure, properties, and the use of the corresponding partial absorption aggregator. The logic operators used in evaluation models remain unchanged regardless the rationality of inputs that DMs selected as appropriate expression of stakeholder's goals. Therefore, the issues of rationality/irrationality and satisficing do not affect properties of GL, but they can affect some aspects of the LSP method (primarily the selection of attributes) and will be investigated again in *Part Three*.

(P₃) Suitability Attributes, Requirements, and Preference/Suitability Scores

Evaluated objects can be characterized using a variety of attributes. Some of attributes affect the overall suitability of an object for specific use, and other attributes do not affect the suitability. A personal computer located under an office desk can be painted in gray or black and have a specific memory size. Both the color of the chassis and the memory capacity are attributes of the personal computer. The size of memory significantly affects the suitability of computer for performing efficient data processing, and the color of the chassis does not contribute to the computer performance and suitability. Consequently, only the memory capacity can be characterized as *suitability attribute*, i.e., as a contributor to the overall suitability of the personal computer. In the area of evaluation we are interested only in suitability attributes and not in other kinds of attributes that characterize evaluated objects. For simplicity, we sometimes denote suitability attributes shortly as attributes, but in all such cases we assume that the attributes contribute to the overall suitability of the evaluated object.

For each suitability attribute of an evaluated system, there are requirements that should be satisfied, and the degree of satisfaction is called the *suitability score* or the *preference score* (or simply the suitability or preference). The scores reflect DM's perception of suitability. To generate suitability scores DM can use a multilevel verbal rating scale (a codebook), or a value-score mapping (an attribute criterion function). The minimum value of the suitability/preference x is 0 (no satisfaction) and the maximum value is 1 (complete satisfaction). The values in the range $0 < x < 1$ denote a partial satisfaction. For example (Fig. 2.2.1), a computer buyer might specify a criterion for the available computer memory M that is unacceptable if $M \le M_{min}$ and perfect if $M \ge M_{max}$. Similarly, a criterion for the response time T of a benchmark program specifies that T is perfect if $T \le T_{min}$ and unacceptable if $T \ge T_{max}$. These criteria can be quantified as the following functions:

$$x(M) = \max\{0, \min[1, (M - M_{min})/(M_{max} - M_{min})]\},$$
$$x(T) = \max\{0, \min[1, (T_{max} - T)/(T_{max} - T_{min})]\},$$
$$M > 0, \quad T > 0, \quad x \in [0,1].$$

In the context of perceptual computing the memory size and the benchmark program run time are examples of suitability attributes, i.e., significant components used for computer evaluation. DM's requirements are expressed as attribute criteria, and the suitability scores reflect the perception of suitability. Using

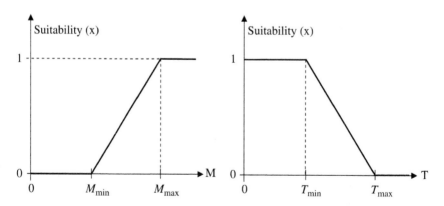

Figure 2.2.1 Sample memory and run time requirements.

an attribute criterion the DM specifies rules he or she intends to use to create the percept of quality that depends on the value of attribute. These examples indicate that from the perceptual standpoint it is useful to introduce the following definitions:

Definition 2.2.1. An *input suitability attribute* is any quantifiable input attribute of an evaluated object that in provable way contributes to the capability of evaluated object to satisfy stakeholder's goals (i.e., it contributes to the overall suitability of the evaluated object). We use the term *attribute* to denote an individual input suitability attribute, and the term *compound attribute* to denote an attribute obtained as an aggregate of other attributes.

Definition 2.2.2. The *value of an attribute* (e.g., the memory capacity) is a quantitative input used to create the percept of suitability.

Definition 2.2.3. The *attribute suitability score* (also called *suitability*, or *preference*, or *preference score*, or *elementary preference*) is a quantitative expression of the DM's percept of satisfaction with the value of specific attribute.

Definition 2.2.4. An *attribute criterion* (also called the *elementary criterion*) is a DM's specification of requirements as a value-suitability mapping, i.e., a functional transformation of a measurable input attribute value into perceptual output (suitability or preference score). The attribute criterion precisely specifies the method that DM uses to create the percept of suitability.

Definition 2.2.5. Attributes can be classified as *value attributes* or *perceptual attributes*. Value attributes assume the use of attribute criteria to transform attribute values into suitability scores. If that is inconvenient or impossible, we can use perceptual attributes, where DM creates the suitability score without formally defining an attribute criterion. Such a suitability score directly reflects DM's intuitive percept of suitability. This form of evaluation is called *direct preference (suitability) assessment*. It is usually based on rating scales (see Chapter 2.9).

The reason for using perceptual attributes is in the difficulty in defining the corresponding attribute value and the formal value-suitability mapping. A typical example is the quality of documentation of a complex software product. A criterion for evaluation of the quality of documentation can be rather complex. For example, it may include the volume, structure, and organization of documentation, readability, completeness, number of examples, and number and quality of illustrations. Instead of building a time-consuming formal criterion, a qualified DM can carefully inspect the documentation and create an intuitive percept of the quality of documentation. Then, the resulting percept can be directly expressed as a value between 0 and 1. Alternatively, the most appropriate level can be selected form a multilevel rating scale (e.g., *very poor, poor, average, good,* and *excellent,* representing suitability scores 0, 0.25, 0.5, 0.75, and 1).

Each preference score can be interpreted in various ways, depending on the application area. The following are the four most useful interpretations:

1) The degree of truth of the value statement "the evaluated object completely satisfies a specific requirement (or a group of requirements)"
2) The degree of membership of the evaluated object in a fuzzy set of objects that completely satisfy a specific requirement (or a group of requirements)
3) The anticipated likelihood (sometimes interpreted as estimated probability) that the evaluated object can completely satisfy requirement(s)
4) The percentage of satisfied requirement(s).

Each of these interpretations may yield differences in mathematical models. Models that we present in this book are suitable for both logic and fuzzy interpretation.

It is important to note that each degree of satisfaction of requirements is a bounded value. The selected numeric equivalents of the minimum and the maximum level of satisfaction should not affect the contents or the results of an evaluation process. The most suitable interval of satisfaction is $I = [0,1]$, because this interval is consistent with traditional range of values used in logic, in the fuzzy set theory, and in the probability theory. In practical cases it is also suitable to use the equivalent interval [0, 100%]. Consequently, we assume that all phenomena of GL occur in the hypercube $[0, 1]^n$, where n denotes the dimensionality of the evaluation problem. Generally, n is the number of analyzed attributes with the range from 2 to several hundred.

(P₄) Standard Model of Evaluation Reasoning and the Architecture of Perceptual Computer for Suitability Evaluation

Properties that are beyond any doubt observable in all cases of intuitive evaluation reasoning include the following (Fig. 2.2.2):

1) The suitability of an evaluated object is characterized using a set of suitability attributes.
2) Each attribute is separately evaluated using an attribute criterion.
3) The result of attribute evaluation is an attribute suitability degree.
4) Attribute suitability degrees are aggregated to get an overall suitability degree.
5) The DM selects the object with the highest overall suitability.

For example, in the case of car evaluation, the set of attributes includes the engine power, the number of doors, the number of passengers, the available internal space, and the size of the trunk, among others. Each attribute is separately evaluated. The DM can be completely satisfied, partially satisfied, or not

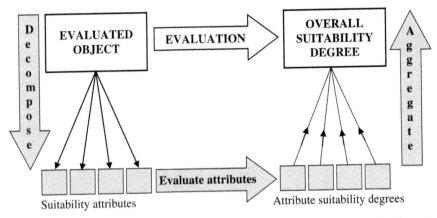

Figure 2.2.2 The process of intuitive evaluation (computing the overall suitability degree).

satisfied with the value of an attribute; e.g., if at least four doors are needed, the DM will not be satisfied with a car that has only two doors, and the power of engine of 180 HP will partially satisfy the requirement that the available power must be between 120 HP and 200 HP. The overall degree of satisfaction with a car will depend on the attribute degrees of satisfaction, based on some form of logic aggregation that might require simultaneous satisfaction of crucial requirements. Finally, the car with the highest overall suitability will be selected. This process is clearly visible in hundreds of examples of intuitive evaluation.

A more precise investigation of this process yields a *standard model of evaluation reasoning (SMER)* presented in Fig. 2.2.3. SMER consists of the following three fundamental steps:

1) *Definition of a set of suitability attributes $a_1, ..., a_n$.* The first step is a hierarchical decomposition of the overall suitability of the evaluated system into a set of suitability components. Similarly to the mathematical concept of *necessary and sufficient*, ideal components should be *nonredundant* (independent and nonoverlapping) and *complete* (containing all components that contribute to the overall suitability). At the beginning of the stepwise decomposition process, these components can be compound and too complex for direct evaluation. At the end, the decomposition process yields atomic components that cannot be further decomposed. These simplest components are *suitability attributes* (sometimes also called *elementary attributes* or *performance variables*), and they should be appropriate for both intuitive and quantitative evaluation (in quantitative models the attribute values are real numbers). It is important to note that suitability attributes exist because DM has requirements that the attributes must satisfy. The set of DM's justifiable requirements directs the process of hierarchical decomposition

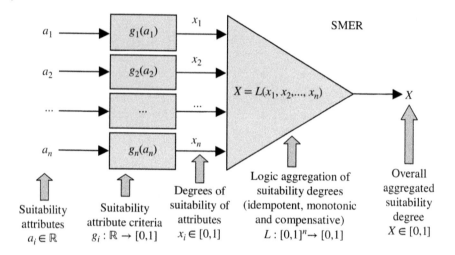

Figure 2.2.3 The basic form of a *standard model of evaluation reasoning* (SMER).

that yields suitability attributes as leaves of the suitability decomposition tree. For example, a homebuyer can decide to decompose the overall home suitability into the suitability of the home location, and the suitability of home features (excluding the home environment and location). Then, the suitability of a home location can be decomposed into distances from all points of interest that are relevant for family members. The distances from points of interest cannot be further decomposed, and they represent suitability attributes for the evaluation of location suitability.

2) *Independent intuitive evaluation of each attribute.* Intuitive evaluation is always based on a set of elementary components (attributes) that are individually evaluated. This step includes a careful specification of attribute requirements followed by the intuitive assessment of the degree of satisfaction of each elementary attribute requirement. The results are DM's perceptions denoted as the degrees of suitability of attributes (or "elementary attribute preferences"). According to Fig. 2.2.3, the degrees of suitability $x_1, ..., x_n$ are atomic components of the DM's satisfaction. Each such percept is a value in the range from no satisfaction to the complete (100%) satisfaction (this range is regularly normalized to [0,1]). At the end of this step, the DM has a set of n percepts of suitability, one per each input attribute. In intuitive evaluation, these percepts can be created in any order and can be revised and updated multiple times. They are used as inputs for the subsequent preference/suitability aggregation process.

3) *Intuitive logic aggregation of all attribute preference/suitability scores.* A single overall preference/suitability score for the whole evaluated system

is generated by intuitively aggregating attribute suitability scores $x_1, ..., x_n$. In the standard model of evaluation reasoning presented in Fig. 2.2.3 the overall suitability is denoted $X = L(x_1,...,x_n) = L(g_1(a_1),...,g_n(a_n)) \in [0,1]$. The resulting percept of overall satisfaction of DM's requirements (X) is a *logic aggregate* of the degrees of satisfaction with input suitability attributes. That intuitive evaluation regularly includes observable weighted compensative logic conditions: adjustable degrees of simultaneity, substitutability, and importance, as well as combinations of mandatory and optional inputs, and combinations of sufficient and optional inputs.

In the intuitive suitability aggregation process we can differentiate two fundamental aspects of human evaluation reasoning: (1) formal logic aspects of evaluation reasoning (a generalization of the classic bivalent logic models), and (2) semantic aspects of evaluation reasoning (the meaning of variables and decisions, and the degrees of their contribution to stakeholder's goals). It is important to emphasize that the result of intuitive evaluation is always a *single (scalar) indicator of the overall suitability* that reflects the corresponding aggregated percept of suitability created by DM.

The percept of overall suitability is sufficient to select the best alternative only in cases where evaluated objects or alternatives do not have cost. Examples of such objects are Internet browsers, search engines, and various websites; all of them do not have a price tag and are evaluated from the standpoint of functionality and usability. The winners of such competitions are selected according to the highest overall suitability. In such cases, the basic structure of perceptual computer is SMER, shown in Fig. 2.2.3.

The problem that is much more frequent and more important is the evaluation of objects that have price (e.g., cars, houses, computer servers, professional software tools and other industrial products always belong to this category). The satisfaction of the stakeholder's goals and suitability requirements regularly assumes expenses that are not negligible. Consequently, the cost of evaluated objects must be included in the evaluation process, and the SMER must be expanded to include cost.

The overall cost is usually not a single number, but a compound indicator that includes multiple cost components. Consequently, there are two alternative ways how to analyze cost components:

1) Cost components are interpreted as suitability attributes and scattered and mixed with other input attributes.
2) All cost components are grouped together using a cost analysis in order to generate a single overall aggregated cost (or affordability) indicator. That indicator is then aggregated with the overall suitability indicator.

The first approach is rather inconvenient because it yields unacceptable heterogeneity of inputs and difficulties in their comparison and aggregation.

For example, in the case of computer evaluation, a cost of printer cannot be naturally aggregated with the processor speed because these are heterogeneous attributes and it is not clear how to select relative importance that reflects the tradeoff between these inputs, and how to interpret the aggregated output. In addition, the total cost C is frequently limited by the available/approved funding ($C \leq C_{max}$) and C_{max} cannot be included in SMER if the cost components are arbitrarily scattered inside the list of attributes.

The second approach is much more natural, simpler for realization, and more frequent in intuitive evaluation. All cost components are aggregated together using an appropriate cost analysis. The final step is a cost/suitability analysis that aggregates the overall cost C and the overall suitability X. Here C must not exceed the threshold value C_{max}, and X must reach or exceed its acceptability threshold value X_{min}. Generally, we assume that the available funding is limited, and that stakeholder does not want to accept solutions where the overall degree of satisfaction of requirements is less than a specified minimum value (typically from 2/3 to 4/5). This approach yields the general form of SMER shown in Fig. 2.2.4. This general model is observable in human intuitive evaluation.

We use SMER shown in Fig. 2.2.4 as a *general architecture of perceptual computers for suitability evaluation*, as well as the structural model of the LSP method. Using this architecture we generate a single scalar indicator of the overall value (V) that is a function of all suitability attributes, all cost components, and acceptability thresholds X_{min} and C_{max}:

$$V = E(a_1,...,a_n;c_1,...,c_k;X_{min},C_{max}).$$

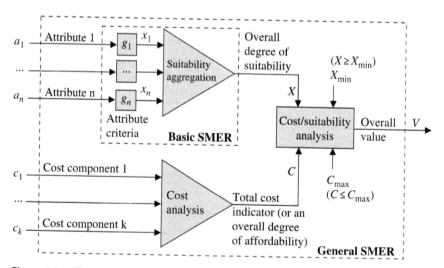

Figure 2.2.4 The general form of SMER and the general architecture of perceptual computers (and the LSP method) for suitability evaluation.

Assuming that stakeholders are not ready to buy objects that cannot satisfy at least X_{min} requirements, and/or are more expensive than the maximum available funding C_{max}, it follows that all acceptable competitive objects characterized by (X, C) must be inside the region of acceptable solutions R:

$$(X, C) \in R := [X_{min}, 1] \times [0, C_{max}].$$

All objects where $(X, C) \notin R$ are rejected in all cases of evaluation (both intuitive and formal).

The presented perceptual computer architecture is based on assumption that the overall suitability should be balanced with the overall cost. The overall cost indicator is the result of cost analysis that must take into account all positive and negative cost components. For example in the case of buying a car the cost components include the purchasing costs (the cost of car, the cost of financing, and the tax and registration expenses) plus the cost of usage for N years (the expected costs of fuel, maintenance, registration and insurance), minus an estimated resale value after N years. The total cost can be intuitively aggregated with the overall degree of suitability yielding an indicator of the overall value. The total cost can also be transformed in an overall indicator of affordability (e.g., $1/C$). In such a case the cost/suitability analysis can create the overall value indicator as an aggregated percept based on a desired level of simultaneity of the overall suitability and the overall affordability.

The general form of the presented perceptual computer includes four fundamental processing blocks: (1) elementary criteria, (2) logic aggregation of suitability, (3) cost analysis model, and (4) the cost/suitability analysis. These processing blocks are observable in intuitive evaluation: intuitive decision makers first select the attributes, then individually evaluate all attributes (identify good and bad components), aggregate the attribute suitability degrees and generate an overall perception of suitability, and perform simple forms of cost analysis (usually adding actual and expected expenses). In addition, intuitive evaluators also know the minimum level of suitability/satisfaction they want to achieve and the maximum expenses they can afford. Eventually, evaluators intuitively combine the overall suitability and the total cost of acceptable objects to get the resulting aggregated percepts of the overall value and the final ranking of competitors.

The overall value is the concluding aggregated perception that represents the final result of either intuitive or formal quantitative evaluation. The value that has sufficient intensity and dominates other evaluated alternatives is the motive for decision and subsequent actions that are needed to realize the decision. An accepted and realized decision is a proof that the intuitive evaluation process has been completed, yielding an aggregated scalar indicator of the overall value.

The general SMER presented in Fig. 2.2.4 is a perceptual computer that is indisputably observable in intuitive human reasoning, and building quantitative models of evaluation reasoning that differ from SMER would be unacceptable.

Consequently, Fig. 2.2.4 also represents the main components and the organization of the LSP method that we present in *Part Three* and use in *Part Four* of this book.

(P₅) Internality and Idempotency

For an evaluated system as a whole, the overall degree of satisfaction of all requirements is called the *overall (or global) preference (or suitability) score*, or shortly *the overall preference/suitability*. The overall preference is obtained using a perceptual computer that aggregates component preferences (Fig. 2.2.3). In the vast majority of evaluation problems the quality of a system cannot be better than the quality of its best component, or worse than the quality of its worst component. This property is called *internality*, or the *bounded quality range* (BQR). In cases where the BQR holds, an aggregator $A(x_1,...,x_n)$, $n > 1$ satisfies the condition

$$\min(x_1,...,x_n) \leq A(x_1,...,x_n) \leq \max(x_1,...,x_n).$$

Consequently, $A(x_1, ..., x_n)$ is an averaging operator and if $x_1 = ... = x_n = x$ then $x = \min(x,...,x) \leq A(x,...,x) \leq \max(x,...,x) = x$, and all aggregators that satisfy BQR (internality) also satisfy idempotency (reflexivity) $A(x,...,x) = x$.

For example, suppose that all component requirements of a homebuyer are satisfied at the level of 80%. So, if all component preference scores were 0.8, what would be the most reasonable overall preference score? The majority of people would agree that the overall preference score should also be 0.8. This is the same reasoning that is used to compute the GPA (overall average grade) of a student: GPA cannot be higher than the student's best course grade or worse than the student's worst course grade. A student whose all grades are B should have the GPA that is also B, and this reasoning is supported by all schools that use GPA or a similar overall indictor. These examples indicate that the corresponding preference aggregator should satisfy BQR and idempotency, and consequently it must be modeled as a mean.

In the case of two variables x and y and the aggregated value $z = A(x,y)$ the concept of internality is illustrated in Fig. 2.2.5 for cases where $x + y = c \leq 1$, $c = $ constant. The variables (in any order) are presented as two adjacent segments of abscissa, x and y, starting from 0. The shaded area bounded by conjunction $x \wedge y$ and disjunction $x \vee y$ represents the range of aggregated values $(x \wedge y \leq z \leq x \vee y)$. The point where the shaded triangles touch each other is the idempotency point $z = x = y$. The area in the close vicinity of the idempotency point is called the *idempotency region*. It is important to notice that the range of $A(x, y)$ decreases as we approach the idempotency point. In the idempotency region the differences between various types of aggregators are relatively small. That reduces the significance of careful selection of the aggregation operator, giving some credibility to simplistic models based on the arithmetic mean. Of course, this credibility disappears as we move outside the idempotency region.

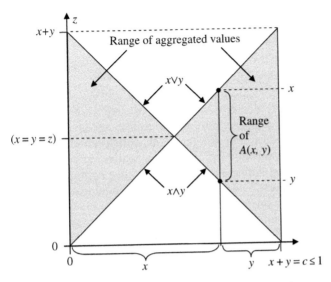

Figure 2.2.5 The concept of internality (BQR) in the case of two variables (x and y).

In a general case of n independent variables $x_1, ..., x_n$ the idempotency region is the region in the vicinity of line $x_1 = \cdots = x_n = x \in [0,1]$. The idempotency region is characterized by small values of the mean difference indicator:

$$\bar{D} = \frac{2}{n(n-1)} \sum_{i=1}^{n-1} \sum_{j=i+1}^{n} |x_i - x_j|, \quad \bar{D} \ll 1.$$

In that region the differences between aggregated values $A(x_1, ..., x_n)$ and the arithmetic mean are small. For example, if $x_1 = 0.4$, $x_2 = 0.45$, $x_3 = 0.5$, $x_4 = 0.55$, $x_5 = 0.6$ then $\bar{D} = (0.05 + 0.1 + 0.15 + 0.2 + 0.05 + 0.1 + 0.15 + 0.05 + 0.1 + 0.05)/10 = 0.1$. If the aggregation is based on the quadratic, arithmetic, geometric and harmonic means, then the results of aggregation only insignificantly differ from the arithmetic mean (either 1% or 2%) as follows:

$$\left(\frac{x_1^2 + x_2^2 + x_3^2 + x_4^2 + x_5^2}{5} \right)^{0.5} = 0.505, \quad \frac{x_1 + x_2 + x_3 + x_4 + x_5}{5} = 0.5$$

$$x_1^{0.2} \cdot x_2^{0.2} \cdot x_3^{0.2} \cdot x_4^{0.2} \cdot x_5^{0.2} = 0.495, \quad \left(\frac{x_1^{-1} + x_2^{-1} + x_3^{-1} + x_4^{-1} + x_5^{-1}}{5} \right)^{-1} = 0.490$$

In GL the only idempotent functions are (partial) conjunction, (partial) disjunction, (partial) absorption and all functions obtained by their superposition.[4]

---

4 Any superposition of idempotent functions yields an idempotent function.

The proof of this statement is based on the fact that GL is a generalization of Boolean logic and in the case of Boolean logic no functions other than conjunction, disjunction, and absorption are idempotent. In fact, we need only partial conjunction and partial disjunction, since the partial absorption is obtained as a superposition of the partial conjunction and the partial disjunction (for the idempotency in bivalent logic see Section 2.1.6).

In some rare cases, however, idempotency may be a questionable property in evaluation reasoning. For example, suppose that a leading university wants to hire a distinguished professor for the area of computational biology. A candidate was separately evaluated by computer scientists, and they found a moderate computer science competence expressed by the computer science suitability $c = 0.7$. The same result was obtained when the candidate was separately evaluated by biologists, yielding the biology suitability $b = 0.7$. What is now the overall suitability for this candidate, as a leading computational biologist? Most likely, it is less than 0.7, because the candidate should be able to simultaneously combine skills in two independent disciplines. If c is interpreted as a probability that the candidate can successfully solve a complex computer science problem, and b is interpreted in a similar probabilistic way, then in the worst case the probability of success in combining independent problems from computer science and biology would be $cb = 0.49$. Some evaluators might argue that this is the most appropriate overall suitability, but the majority would agree that the actual value is located somewhere in the interval [0.49, 0.7]. Of course, this is a trivial example that could be interpreted in various ways, but it is sufficient to indicate that the idempotency should not be specified as a necessary condition for *all* system evaluation models. We suggest the conclusion that the internality and idempotency are desirable properties in the vast majority of evaluation problems. In all such cases, the aggregation of suitability must be based on means. However, GL must also include models of hyperconjunction and hyperdisjunction.

(P$_6$) Continuity, Monotonicity, and Compensativeness

The only way to improve a compound system is to improve its components. In human intuitive evaluation it is regularly observable that if the percept of suitability of any component increases, the percept of the overall suitability cannot decrease. In most cases the percept of overall suitability increases. Exceptionally, if there is a limiting factor that prevents an increase of the overall suitability then the overall suitability remains unchanged (insensitive to the improvements of other components). Consequently, if $x_1, ..., x_n$ are degrees of satisfaction of n component requirements, and X denotes the overall satisfaction with the evaluated system, then the evaluation criterion must consist of aggregation operators that satisfy $\partial X/\partial x_i \geq 0$, $i = 1,...,n$. In frequent cases, where evaluation criteria don't use the pure conjunction and the pure disjunction, the sensitivity to improvements condition is a strict monotonicity $\partial X/\partial x_i > 0$, $0 < x_i < 1$, $i = 1,...,n$.

For example, the majority of homebuyers are rather sensitive to the area of the home being evaluated. If the satisfaction with the area of the home increases, so does the overall satisfaction with the home. It is easy to note that the overall satisfaction is a continuous function of the input degrees of satisfaction (if all inputs are partially satisfied, then an observable small increment of an input degree of satisfaction causes a corresponding small increment of the overall satisfaction). Two typical shapes of such sensitivity relationships are presented in Fig. 2.2.6.

In the first example, we assume that the homebuyer will reject the home that has completely unsatisfactory home area. Consequently, the curve starts from point (0,0). In the second example, we assume that the homebuyer can use a home garage, but a street parking next to home is still desirable. Such homebuyers might accept a home with unsatisfactory street parking. In this case the curve starts from the minimum value $X_{min} > 0$.

In both cases the sensitivity curves are strictly increasing concave functions that have the characteristic shape of soft saturation where $\partial^2 X / \partial x_i^2 < 0$ and $\partial^2 X / \partial x_j^2 < 0$ (more of a good is desirable but at a decreasing rate). Following is an intuitive explanation of this characteristic property. Suppose that the overall satisfaction with a home is $X = H$, and this value corresponds to the value of satisfaction with the home area $x_i = Q$, and the satisfaction with the available street parking $x_j = P$ as shown in Fig. 2.2.6. We distinguish two areas denoted by plus and minus arrows in Fig 2.2.6. In the plus arrow area we have $x_i > Q$ or $x_j > P$. Increasing x_i or x_j in that area causes only a modest effect because the growth of the overall satisfaction with home is limited by the fixed low values (less than H) of other necessary home components (different from x_i and x_j). So, for $H > 1/2$ most frequently $0 < \partial X / \partial x_i < 1$ and $0 < \partial X / \partial x_j < 1$, or even $0 < \partial X / \partial x_i \ll 1$ and/or $0 < \partial X / \partial x_j \ll 1$.

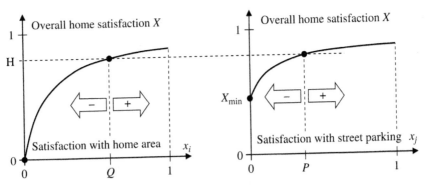

Figure 2.2.6 Two typical sensitivity relationships.

In the minus arrow area we have $x_i < Q$ and $x_j < P$. So, if the values of x_i and x_j are small, then these values act as the bottleneck values and their increase can significantly affect the growth of the overall satisfaction. For very significant (mandatory) inputs, the initial values of $\partial X / \partial x_i$ and $\partial X / \partial x_j$ can be rather large (i.e., significantly greater than 1).

Generally, if $A(\mathbf{x})$ is an aggregator of a real n-tuple $\mathbf{x} = (x_1,...,x_n)$, $n \geq 2$, then the observable sensitivity to improvements means that in GL $A(\mathbf{x})$ must have properties of continuity and monotonicity. If $\mathbf{a} \leq \mathbf{b}$ means componentwise $a_i \leq b_i$, $1 \leq i \leq n$ and $\mathbf{a} < \mathbf{b}$ means that at least one input value is strictly increasing ($a_i < b_i$, $i \in \{1,...,n\}$), then we have the following properties of logic aggregators:

$\lim_{\mathbf{h} \to 0} A(\mathbf{x} + \mathbf{h}) = A(\mathbf{x})$ (continuity);

$\mathbf{a} \leq \mathbf{b} \Rightarrow A(\mathbf{a}) \leq A(\mathbf{b})$ (*nondecreasing monotonicity*: a nonnegative response to any increase of inputs);

$\mathbf{a} < \mathbf{b} \Rightarrow A(\mathbf{a}) < A(\mathbf{b})$ (*strictly increasing monotonicity*: a positive response to the strict increase of at least one input);

$a_i < b_i$, $i = 1,...,n \Rightarrow A(\mathbf{a}) < A(\mathbf{b})$ (*unanimously increasing monotonicity*: a positive response to the strict increase of all inputs).

In other words, in the case of monotonicity any improvement of any input suitability degree improves (or, in an extreme case, leaves unchanged) the aggregated output. The nondecreasing monotonicity is a standard form of monotonicity observable in all cases of GL aggregators. The strictly increasing monotonicity is the most demanding form of monotonicity, which is not available if mandatory requirements are not satisfied. The unanimously increasing monotonicity is the least demanding form of monotonicity.

In all cases of strictly increasing monotonicity, there is a possibility to completely or partially compensate insufficient suitability of any input by increasing the suitability of one or more other inputs. This property is called *compensativeness*; e.g., a student who scores poorly in one class can usually compensate for its effect on GPA by getting better grades in one or more other courses. Similarly, a homebuyer can compensate the effect of a modest quality of a home by a very attractive location of the home. A quantitative analysis of compensation properties is called the *tradeoff analysis* and we study tradeoff problems in Chapter 3.7.

While the monotonicity is an indispensable property of GL aggregators, there are delicate questions related to the character of monotonicity because some forms of monotonicity do not occur in human reasoning and consequently cannot be acceptable. For example, the compatibility with human reasoning imposes limitations on the properties of derivatives $\partial A / \partial x_i$, $i = 1,...,n$. In human reasoning it is not observable that insignificant (imperceptible) increments of input suitability can cause significant (perceptible) increments of output suitability. Consequently, the values of the first derivatives should be limited: $|\partial A / \partial x_i| < d_{max}$, $i = 1,...,n$. Monotonicity beyond this limit is not acceptable.

In all asymmetric aggregators (mandatory/optional and sufficient/optional) the nature of monotonicity is not the same for all inputs: e.g., if x_m is a mandatory input and all other inputs are optional, then $x_m = 0$ implies $\forall i \neq m,\ \partial A/\partial x_i = 0$. However, if $x_m > 0$, then $\partial A/\partial x_i > 0,\ i = 1,...,n$. A similar property holds if x_m is a sufficient input and other inputs are optional. Then, for $x_m = 1$, we have $\forall i \neq m,\ \partial A/\partial x_i = 0$ and if $x_m < 1$, then $\partial A/\partial x_i > 0,\ i = 1,...,n$.

Therefore, the monotonicity is not a simple issue, because it quickly expands into the sensitivity analysis that investigates the acceptability of variations of A $(x_1, ..., x_n)$ caused by variations of $x_i,\ i = 1,...,n$. In P_{32} and in the Chapter 3.8 we investigate these issues in more detail.

(P₇) Granularity, Uncertainty, Linguistic Labels, and Rating Scales

Interpretation of graded variables (degrees of truth, degrees of importance, levels of simultaneity, etc.) can include *verbalization*, i.e., expressing graded variables in terms of a natural language. All graded variables are quantifications of human percepts and each natural language can be interpreted as "a system for describing perception(s)" [ZAD15]. Therefore, there is a strong connection between perceptions, graded variables, and verbalization (describing percepts using rating scales and semantics of natural languages). Rating scales are strictly ordered sets of linguistic descriptors used for unambiguous labeling of the intensity of percept, or the values of graded variables. A simple example of rating scale with three linguistic labels is *low* < *medium* < *high*.

Linguistic labels in rating scales frequently have a fuzzy interpretation. Verbal interpretation of variables that belong to the interval [0,1] is regularly based on several discrete levels identified by linguistic labels. According to Zadeh [ZAD08], "in fuzzy logic everything is or is allowed to be granulated, with a granule being a clump of elements drawn together by indistinguishability, similarity, proximity or functionality." Linguistic labels identify such granules (for detailed analysis of granular computing see [PED13]).

All humans know a limited number of words and use them to describe a limited number of semantic concepts. Words are frequently imprecise and reflect uncertainty. The modeling of uncertainty of verbal communication naturally yields the concept of fuzzy set. In all fuzzy models the central issue is to understand the degree of uncertainty. Related to uncertainty, it is useful to differentiate *professional evaluation* and all other forms of (nonprofessional) evaluation. To understand the concept of professional evaluation let us observe two characteristic cases of professional evaluators: instructors in schools and universities, and figure skating judges.

All instructors are expected to give grades with certainty, conviction, and justification. And they do. It is unthinkable that an instructor (even if she teaches fuzzy logic) would inform a student that his grade in a course is fuzzy and the membership function is somewhere between C+ and A-. Indeed, instructors are professional evaluators, and a significant part of their profession is to grade with confidence and precision (which is usually based on years of experience and on combining various numeric scores). In addition, the certainty and precision of instructors is trusted to the extent that the grading of courses in schools is regularly done by a single person, not by a team. Of course, the Zadeh's rule, "Everything is or is allowed to be granulated," equally applies to both professional and nonprofessional evaluators. However, the point is that for professional evaluators the granules are small and for nonprofessionals the granules are large. One of main goals of professional preparation of decision engineers is to reduce their "footprint of uncertainty" as much as possible.

There are similarities between most professional evaluation activities. For example, an Olympic figure skating competition is regularly done in front of millions of TV viewers, and such viewers will not hesitate to verbally evaluate each competitor using linguistic labels such as "very good" or "excellent" or "superb." However, the evaluation is not done by benevolent and superficial viewers. It is done by judges who have a very detailed professional training and knowledge for transforming the percept of quality into a very precise numeric value on the 0–6.0 scale, and the difference between the winner and other competitors in highly competitive events can be tiny.

These examples indicate that in professional evaluation, the main goal is precision, and the way to achieve precision is to switch from words to numbers. Indeed, many words are fuzzy and imprecise (e.g., large, poor, good, small, etc.), while numbers are always precise. So, professional evaluators define and process graded variables as numeric values or as verbalized scales with many levels (e.g., 12, as in the frequently used grading scale A, A-, B+, B, B-, C+, C, C-, D+, D, D-, F). The *professional evaluator* can be an individual or a team. In P_{15} and Chapter 3.2 we describe evaluation teams consisting of stakeholders, evaluators, and domain experts (one such team graces the front cover of this book).

The overall suitability can be interpreted as a logic concept, or as a degree of membership of evaluated object in a fuzzy set of ideal (perfect) objects. That kind of fuzzy interpretation is obviously based on type-1 fuzzy sets. In professional evaluation it is highly unlikely that evaluation teams are so poorly prepared that they must operate with so high degree of uncertainty that the computation of overall suitability as a single number (the degree of membership in a fuzzy set) becomes impossible and must be replaced by a membership function in another fuzzy set, forcing the evaluation team to use type-2 fuzzy sets. So, with possible exceptions, it is reasonable to assume that the professional evaluation occurs primarily within the scope of type-1 fuzzy logic. Exceptional cases occur if the evaluated systems are very complex, partially unknown, and/or interact with an environment that affects the evaluated system in random and unpredictable way, as in some cases of financial decision models, e.g., making investment choices [MEN10].

The inputs for evaluation criteria are not always easily measurable and straightforward numeric. In many cases the inputs are perceptual attributes based on verbalized rating scales. This approach can be used to evaluate non-numeric input attributes, such as the usability of software, the attractiveness of a website, the quality of output produced by a color laser printer, etc. In such cases an expert user can carefully investigate the evaluated attribute and report the resulting suitability percept using linguistic labels selected from a rating scale (see Table 2.9.2).

In evaluation models verbalization is used not only for defining input attributes but also for communicating evaluation results. While evaluation is assumed to be a numeric process, the final results of evaluation are usually delivered to stakeholders and other subjects in general population using communication with words. Consequently, verbalization, linguistic labels, and rating scales are important concepts in evaluation and deserve careful investigation.

Human percepts of graded variables such as satisfaction, truth, importance, quality, and simultaneity are by their nature continuous (infinitely valued, i.e., real numbers). However, the verbal expressions of such percepts must be granulated because we only use a finite vocabulary that expresses degrees using discrete linguistic labels. Even when we try to express the intuitive degrees numerically, we do that with limited precision and must use intervals of indistinguishable values, i.e., a granulation. Each granule is identified using a linguistic label and the ordered list of labels is called the *rating scale*.

Rating scales are most frequently prepared for general population and used in rating consumer products, evaluating customer experiences (e.g., rating hotels and restaurants), in political polls, etc. Customer satisfaction is sometimes evaluated as a percentage of the total/maximum satisfaction. For example, if a percent of total satisfaction is selected from the set {0, 10%, 20%, 30%, ..., 100%} then 20% usually means a granulated value in the interval [15%, 25%]. Of course, rating scales are also used in professional decision engineering and in such cases we regularly use various techniques for increasing precision (i.e., reducing the size of intervals of indistinguishable values).

Each linguistic label can be interpreted with various levels of precision and fuzziness. Suppose that a homebuyer evaluates the distance of home from an airport (measured as the driving time T) in the case where the goal is to live relatively close to the airport, but not in its immediate neighborhood. Four typical models are presented in Fig. 2.2.7. In the simplest case, let a single value $T = a$ be considered an "excellent location." If $T = a$ then the home belongs to a crisp set of excellent homes. In all other cases the home does not belong to that set. The same linguistic label "excellent location" can be interpreted using an interval $[a,b]$ and the membership function $\mu(T) = 1$, $T \in [a,b]$ and $\mu(T) = 0$, $T \notin [a,b]$. Using three real numbers $\{a,b,c\}$, the label "excellent location" can be interpreted using a triangular fuzzy set membership function $\mu(T)$ [ZAD65, KLI95]. For each value of T the function $\mu : \mathbb{R} \to [0,1]$ specifies

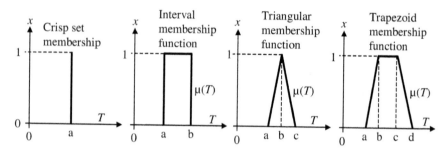

Figure 2.2.7 Interpretation of linguistic label with an increasing level of precision.

the degree of truth of the statement "*T* is excellent" or equivalently, the degree of membership of home in a fuzzy set of excellent locations. A more detailed interpretation uses four real numbers $\{a,b,c,d\}$ and the label "an excellent location" can be interpreted using a trapezoid fuzzy set membership function. So, if $T \in [b,c]$, that is considered ideal (full membership). If $T \notin \,]a,d[$, that is unacceptable (no membership) and if $T \in \,]a,b[\, \cup\,]c,d[$ then the membership is partial. The degree of membership denotes the degree of homebuyer's satisfaction, i.e., the suitability of location.

In the case of significant uncertainty linguistic labels can also be interpreted in terms of interval type-2 fuzzy sets [MEN01, MEN10]. Let us again use our homebuyer, but now we pick one of those who subscribe to the idea that the airport should be neither too close nor too far, but cannot specify the parameters a, b, c, d. At this point, it is completely legitimate to make a short break and ask, "Do such people exist at all?" There is no definitive answer to this question, but it is safe to say that if they exist, they must be a negligible minority, not because we believe that uncertainty is a very rare human property, but because real stakeholders regularly know their goals, and when there are doubts, skilled evaluators can discuss with them options that reduce doubts and uncertainty until it is possible to jointly select the parameters a, b, c, d with sufficient confidence. One way to stimulate the homebuyer's preparation is to quote Seneca (as we did in the first sentence of this book) who justly declared, "If one does not know to which port one is sailing, no wind is favorable." In other words, "If you don't have clear goals, no evaluation can help you to select the best way to achieve them." On the other hand, building an LSP evaluation criterion helps to crystallize goals and a detailed LSP criterion with sufficient number of input attributes can be considered a detailed quantitative specification of goals.

Generally, the uncertainty and vagueness of goals are directly against the stakeholder's interests, yielding the waste of money and/or substandard solutions. Consequently, evaluators should never accept, stimulate, or promote uncertainty as a modus operandi. Quite the contrary, the evaluator's role is to provide advices and reasoning that reduces uncertainty, clarifies goals, and builds confidence.

If all good intentions fail, then we have to serve a homebuyer who cannot specify a, b, c, and d. The simplest approach to this problem is to say, "If you are not sure what are appropriate crisp values of a, b, c, d, maybe you have enough confidence to safely specify intervals that must contain the values a, b, c, d." In other words, instead of a, b, c, d specify $a_1, a_2, b_1, b_2, c_1, c_2, d_1, d_2$, so that $a \in [a_1, a_2]$, $b \in [b_1, b_2]$, $c \in [c_1, c_2]$, $d \in [d_1, d_2]$. If that is possible, then the resulting model can be a type-2 fuzzy set, illustrated in Fig. 2.2.8. Now we don't have a single membership function $\mu(T)$ but a shaded region (called the footprint of uncertainty, FOU) that can contain a spectrum of membership functions (with uniform or general distribution), reflecting the uncertainty of decision maker.

All models presented in Figs. 2.2.7 and 2.2.8 specify only one granule or only one linguistic label, e.g., an "excellent location" or "an excellent value of T". Of course, we can use a set of matching labels and create a whole rating scale (e.g., using labels *very poor, poor, average, good* and *excellent*). Such scales are frequently used in evaluation.

A traditional five-level type-1 fuzzy verbalization (*very low, low, medium, high,* and *very high* satisfaction) is shown in Fig. 2.2.9. Each verbal level is based on traditional triangular or trapezoid fuzzy set membership, and covers a range of preferences (or suitability scores). For example, in the case of triangular membership functions, the *high preference/suitability* includes the range from 0.5 to 1. The values below 0.5 do not belong to the high preference fuzzy set. From 0.5 to 0.75 the membership linearly increases and at 0.75 we have the maximum level of membership, 1. Then the membership linearly decreases and reaches 0 for the preference that has the value 1. A specific preference is verbalized according to the maximum similarity level; e.g., the preference of 0.6 would be verbalized as "medium satisfaction" and the preference of 0.7 would be "high satisfaction." However, since all preferences in the range $3/4 \pm 1/8$ (from 0.625 to 0.875) are verbalized as "high satisfaction," in the case of reliable numerical results, the verbalization may cause a loss of valuable information.

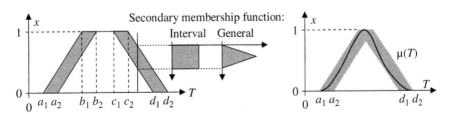

Figure 2.2.8 Interval and general type-2 fuzzy sets and a sample membership function.

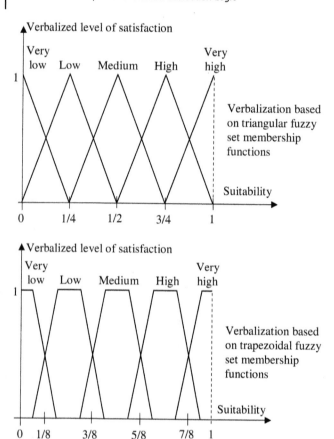

Figure 2.2.9 Verbalization of suitability/preference using fuzzy set membership functions.

In the case of triangular membership functions, if we use k levels of verbalization (from 0 to $k-1$), then the membership of preference x in the ith level fuzzy set is $\mu_i(x) = \max(0, \ 1-|(k-1)x-i|)$. For example, for $k = 5$ levels in Fig. 2.2.9 let us use symbols VL = *very low*, L = *low*, M = *medium*, H = *high*, and VH = *very high*. To verbalize the preference x we can use the symbol that corresponds to the maximum degree of membership. For example, if $x = 0.6$ and $x = 0.7$, then the degrees of membership can be computed using the following formulas:

$$\mu_{VL}(x) = \max(0, \ 1-|4x|), \qquad \mu_{VL}(0.6) = 0, \qquad \mu_{VL}(0.7) = 0;$$
$$\mu_{L}(x) = \max(0, \ 1-|4x-1|), \qquad \mu_{L}(0.6) = 0, \qquad \mu_{L}(0.7) = 0;$$
$$\mu_{M}(x) = \max(0, \ 1-|4x-2|), \qquad \mu_{M}(0.6) = 0.6, \qquad \mu_{M}(0.7) = 0.2;$$
$$\mu_{H}(x) = \max(0, \ 1-|4x-3|), \qquad \mu_{H}(0.6) = 0.4, \qquad \mu_{H}(0.7) = 0.8;$$
$$\mu_{VH}(x) = \max(0, \ 1-|4x-4|), \qquad \mu_{VH}(0.6) = 0, \qquad \mu_{VH}(0.7) = 0.$$

Consequently, the suitability score of 0.6 can be verbalized as the medium suitability and the suitability score of 0.7 can be verbalized as the high suitability.

Using k intervals and fuzzy quantization $(0,...,k-1)$, based on triangular-shaped membership functions, the corresponding level is

$$L = \lfloor 0.5 + (k-1)x \rfloor \in \{0,...,k-1\}.$$

For example, if $k = 5$ and $x = 0.7$ then $L = \lfloor 0.5 + (5-1)0.7 \rfloor = \lfloor 3.3 \rfloor = 3$, which is verbalized as "high suitability" because $0 = $ VL, $1 = $ L, $2 = $ M, $3 = $ H, and $4 = $ VH. Similarly, if $k = 9$ (abbreviated as $0 = $ LL, $1 = $ VL, $2 = $ L, $3 = $ ML, $4 = $ M, $5 = $ MH, $6 = $ H, $7 = $ VH, and $8 = $ HH), and $x = 0.7$, then $L = \lfloor 0.5 + (9-1)0.7 \rfloor = \lfloor 6.1 \rfloor = 6$, which is again a "high suitability." Such relationships use linear scales, where each interval (with possible exceptions of border intervals) covers the same range of values.

2.2.2 Simultaneity and Substitutability in Evaluation Models

Simultaneity and substitutability (replaceability) are fundamental logic properties. In classic bivalent logic they are modeled using conjunction $x_1 \wedge ... \wedge x_n = \min(x_1,...,x_n)$ and disjunction $x_1 \vee ... \vee x_n = \max(x_1,...,x_n)$. In observable human reasoning, the use of bivalent pure conjunction and pure disjunction is much less frequent than the use of their fuzzy equivalents. In GL, both simultaneity and substitutability are a matter of degree, and corresponding models are the partial conjunction and the partial disjunction.

(P₈) Simultaneity
Simultaneity of satisfying two or more criteria is the most frequent and the most easily observable requirement in the intuitive evaluation logic. For example, car buyers typically want a car that simultaneously satisfies criteria of performance, *and* safety, *and* comfort. If any component requirement is insufficiently satisfied, the overall satisfaction with such a car might be very low. If the requested level of simultaneity is sufficiently high, it may be very difficult or even impossible to compensate the insufficiency in any of vital attributes.

Simultaneity is a matter of degree. The traditional full conjunction $x \wedge y = \min(x,y)$ is a model of an extremely high level of simultaneity where a system is only as good as its weakest component. We frequently need a lower level of simultaneity. Such aggregators are called *partial conjunction* (PC), symbolically denoted $\triangle$, and satisfy the condition $x \wedge y \leq x \triangle y \leq (x+y)/2$. In the case of two variables x and y (assuming $x + y = const.$), Fig. 2.2.10 shows the range of partial conjunction (the shaded area below $(x+y)/2$) and a typical partial conjunction aggregator.

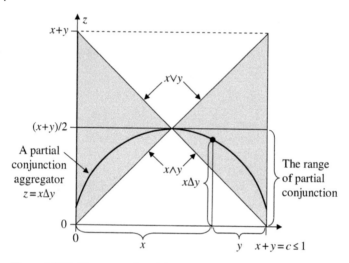

Figure 2.2.10 The range of partial conjunction and a typical partial conjunction aggregator.

Simultaneity in GL can also be expressed using linguistic labels. Sample linguistic simultaneity relationships equivalent to the harmonic mean $z_h = 2xy/(x+y)$ are shown in Tables 2.2.1 to 2.2.3. For example, at this level of simultaneity the aggregation of VH and L yields M in the case of five and seven levels, and ML in the case of nine levels.

(P₉) Substitutability (Replaceability)

If the insufficient satisfaction of any requirement in a group can be compensated by increased satisfaction of *any other* member of the group, then such an aggregator is a model of replaceability/substitutability. Substitutability is observable in human evaluation reasoning whenever the evaluator can be (partially, to a specified degree) satisfied with any input attribute in a group of attributes.

Table 2.2.1 Sample linguistic simultaneity and its numeric equivalent (5 levels).

5	VL	L	M	H	VH		%	0	25	50	75	100
VL	VL	VL	VL	VL	VL		0	0	0	0	0	0
L	VL	L	L	M	M		25	0	25	33.3	37.5	40
M	VL	L	M	M	H		50	0	33.3	50	60	66.7
H	VL	M	M	H	H		75	0	37.5	60	75	85.7
VH	VL	M	H	H	VH		100	0	40	66.7	85.7	100

Table 2.2.2 Sample linguistic simultaneity (7 levels).

7	LL	VL	L	M	H	VH	HH
LL	LL	LL	LL	LL	LL	LL	LL
VL	LL	VL	VL	L	L	L	L
L	LL	VL	L	L	M	M	M
M	LL	L	L	M	M	H	H
H	LL	L	M	M	H	H	VH
VH	LL	L	M	H	H	VH	VH
HH	LL	L	M	H	VH	VH	HH

Table 2.2.3 Sample linguistic simultaneity (9 levels).

9	LL	VL	L	ML	M	MH	H	VH	HH
LL	LL	LL	LL	LL	LL	LL	LL	LL	LL
VL	LL	VL	VL	L	L	L	L	L	L
L	LL	VL	L	L	ML	ML	ML	ML	ML
ML	LL	L	L	ML	ML	M	M	M	M
M	LL	L	ML	ML	M	M	MH	MH	MH
MH	LL	L	ML	M	M	MH	MH	H	H
H	LL	L	ML	M	MH	MH	H	H	VH
VH	LL	L	ML	M	MH	H	H	VH	VH
HH	LL	L	ML	M	MH	H	VH	VH	HH

Labels: LL = lowest, VL = very low, L = low, LM = low to medium, M = medium, MH = medium to high, H = high, VH = very high, HH = highest

For example, a homebuyer may evaluate the public transportation to the location of a new home, and be equally satisfied if the existing public transport is a bus, or a train. In this example, the bus transportation can replace the train transportation and vice versa. Generally, in evaluation models, substitutability is less frequently used than simultaneity. In medical applications, however, substitutability is a predominant aggregator in disability criteria: any strong sensory symptom or any strong motor symptom may be sufficient to cause a degree of patient disability.

Similarly to simultaneity, replaceability is also a matter of degree. The full disjunction $x \vee y = \max(x, y)$ is a model of an extremely high level of substitutability where a system is as good as its best component. Evaluators frequently need a lower level of substitutability. Such aggregators are called *partial disjunction* (PD), symbolically denoted ∇, and satisfy the condition $(x + y)/2 \leq x \nabla y \leq x \vee y$. In the case of two variables x and y (assuming $x + y = const.$), Fig. 2.2.11 shows

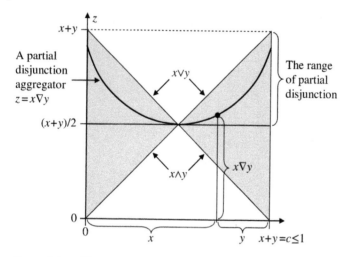

Figure 2.2.11 The range of partial disjunction and a typical partial disjunction aggregator.

the range of partial disjunction (the shaded area above the arithmetic mean $(x + y)/2$) and a typical partial disjunction aggregator.

(P_{10})   Combining Simultaneity and Substitutability

An essential feature of both intuitive and formal GL is an adjustable combination (or mix) of simultaneity and replaceability requirements. In the case of simplest logic aggregators, which model simultaneity and substitutability, the presence of simultaneity is a matter of degree, and the presence of substitutability is also a matter of degree. These two degrees are not independent. They are adjustable and complementary. More simultaneity means less substitutability and vice versa, resulting in the simultaneity/replaceability seesaw shown in Fig. 2.2.12.

To illustrate this feature of human reasoning, let us investigate logic properties of the arithmetic mean. For example, in the case of evaluating students using GPA (the average grade), the evaluation reasoning is based on simultaneous and perfectly balanced presence of two opposite requirements:

1) We prefer students who concurrently have high grades in all courses. This is a simultaneity requirement.
2) At the same time, we allow students to compensate for a low grade in any course with a high grade in any other course(s). This is a substitutability feature.

It is important to see that simultaneity and substitutability are opposite but complementary requirements. Indeed, if *all* grades must be high, then low grades cannot be tolerated and easily compensated by other high grades. On

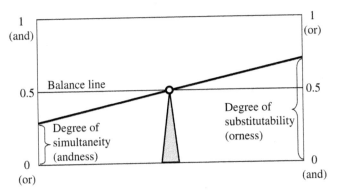

Figure 2.2.12 The simultaneity/substitutability seesaw.

the other hand, if any number of low grades could be completely compensated by a single high grade, then there will be no simultaneity of high grades. The presence of simultaneity reduces/eliminates substitutability, and the presence of substitutability reduces/eliminates simultaneity. Thus, the simultaneity and the replaceability are two *complementary* properties of GL and in the case of arithmetic mean they are equally present and perfectly balanced. Obviously, the arithmetic mean is located exactly in the middle between the pure conjunction and the pure disjunction aggregators. None of these properties dominates the other one. They are perceptually equally important and equally present. They hold simultaneously in a perfectly balanced way. This form of aggregation is clearly visible and frequently used in human evaluation reasoning.

In other cases, the simultaneity can be predominant (i.e., the evaluator considers that it is more important than substitutability), yielding a partial conjunction function, also called *andor*. For example, a homebuyer intuitive criterion is frequently the following:

< home suitability > = < quality of home > *andor* < quality of home location >

In this criterion, "and" is predominant, but not to the extent of pure conjunction, because the homebuyer regularly wants compensativeness, i.e., the possibility to compensate lack of one input with the high presence of the other input. Indeed, the homebuyer wants simultaneously a quality home located in a convenient location, but at the same time s/he is ready to substitute a minor lack of home quality with the attractiveness of home location (and vice versa). Note that the pure conjunction $z = x \wedge y = \min(x,y)$ does not support compensative properties: if $x < y$, then a low value of x cannot be compensated for by increasing the value of y.

Similarly, there are situations where substitutability is predominant, yielding a partial disjunction aggregator, also called *orand*. For example, in the case of peripheral neuropathy, a patient disability criterion is frequently perceived as follows:

< patient disability > = < sensory symptoms > *orand* < motor symptoms >

In this criterion "or" is predominant, but not to the extent of pure disjunction, because both the sensory symptoms (e.g., pain) and the motor symptoms (e.g., difficulties in walking) contribute to the patient disability and not only one of them (the greatest of these two inputs). Indeed, the pure disjunction $z = x \vee y = \max(x,y)$ does not support compensative properties: if $x > y$, then a high value of z cannot be decremented by decreasing the value of y. Complementary combining of simultaneity and substitutability is illustrated in Fig. 2.2.13.

The adjustable mixing of simultaneity and substitutability requirements is always present in human reasoning. It is a continuous process where the maximum level of simultaneity yields the traditional conjunction aggregator (*and*) and the maximum level of substitutability yields the traditional disjunction aggregator (*or*). We call these extreme cases the *full conjunction* and the *full*

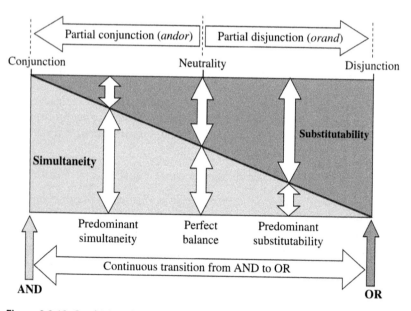

Figure 2.2.13 Combining degrees of simultaneity and substitutability yields a continuous transition from *and* to *or*.

disjunction to differentiate them from the less conjunctive *partial conjunction* (PC) and the less disjunctive *partial disjunction* (PD). The continuously adjustable combining of simultaneity and substitutability features yields the fundamental continuous logic aggregator called *Graded Conjunction/Disjunction* (GCD, symbolically denoted ◊) that enables a *continuous transition from and to or*. This concept was introduced in [DUJ73b, DUJ74a]. GCD is the fundamental GL aggregator.

(P_{11}) Conjunctive/Disjunctive Neutrality
In the case of perfect balance of simultaneity and substitutability, GCD becomes a logic function that is *conjunctively/disjunctively neutral* because it represents a middle point between conjunction and disjunction, as illustrated in Figs. 2.2.12 and 2.2.13. This function is the arithmetic mean. In the case of two variables, the arithmetic mean can be written as $(x + y)/2 = 0.5(x \wedge y) + 0.5(x \vee y)$, suggesting the equal presence of conjunctive and disjunctive properties. In the examples shown in Figs. 2.2.10 and 2.2.11, the conjunctive/disjunctive neutrality is represented as the horizontal line that separates the ranges of partial conjunction and partial disjunction.

The additive nature of the conjunctive/disjunctive neutrality gives balanced compensative properties: if x and y are equally important, then a decrement of input x can be easily compensated with an equal increment of the input y: from $(x + y)/2 = (x - \delta x + y + \delta y)/2$ it follows $\delta y = \delta x$. The conjunctive/disjunctive neutrality is usually abbreviated as *neutrality* and denoted using symbol ⊖ that indicates the central position of this aggregator: $x \ominus y = (x \wedge y + x \vee y)/2$. The neutrality aggregator plays the important role of centroid of all conjunctive and disjunctive aggregators. Because of its simplicity and central location among basic logic aggregators, it is the most frequently used (and abused) aggregator in all applications that exclude conjunctive and disjunctive properties of logic criteria. In addition, the neutrality seems to be the initial (default) aggregator in the mental process of stepwise refinement of logic polarization of GCD aggregators.

(P_{12}) Andness, Orness, and Continuous Transition from *and* to *or*
In intuitive evaluation reasoning humans continuously adjust the degree of simultaneity of partial conjunction and the degree of substitutability of partial disjunction, in order to achieve desired preference aggregation properties. The degree of simultaneity is called *andness* (α) or the *conjunction degree* [DUJ73b]. It is a degree of similarity between a GCD aggregator and the full (pure) conjunction (the minimum function). The degree of substitutability is called *orness* (ω) or the *disjunction degree*. It is a degree of similarity between a GCD aggregator and the pure disjunction (the maximum function). Andness and orness are fundamental graded parameters of GL functions.

Human evaluation logic is *continuous* (infinite-valued) and not finite multi-valued: similarly to all other human percepts, the intuitive adjustment of and-ness/orness is continuous—it is *not* going in discrete steps. Of course, discrete steps can be used for simplifying the selection of appropriate partial conjunction or partial disjunction models, as shown in P_7. Thus, human evaluation logic uses a *continuous transition from and to or*, as indicated in Figs. 2.2.12 and 2.2.13.

Andness/orness must be adjusted to get desired logic properties of the GCD aggregator. Therefore, in the process of building formal models, evaluators first select the most appropriate degree of simultaneity or substitutability, and then search for the aggregator that has the desired andness/orness. Andness or orness are fundamental human logic percepts and fundamental parameters necessary for creating both intuitive and formal evaluation criteria.

A simple two-variable example of continuous linear transition form *and* to *or* is presented in Fig. 2.2.14. We aggregate two variables, x and y, where $x < y$. The aggregated value $z = x \Diamond y$ satisfies $x = (x \wedge y) \leq x \Diamond y \leq (x \vee y) = y$. The andness $\alpha = a$ and the orness $\omega = b$ are parameters that determine the location of the aggregated value z in the interval $[(x \wedge y), (x \vee y)]$. The andness α can be defined as the proximity to conjunction or as a distance from disjunction (i.e., the distance from $x \Diamond y$ to $x \vee y$). Similarly, the orness ω can be defined as the proximity to disjunction or as a distance from conjunction (i.e., the distance from $x \Diamond y$ to $x \wedge y$). Assuming a linear transition from *and* to *or*, and vice versa, the equations of linear transition (straight lines connecting x and y in Fig. 2.2.14) are

$$z = x \Diamond y = \alpha(x \wedge y) + (1 - \alpha)(x \vee y),$$
$$z = x \Diamond y = \omega(x \vee y) + (1 - \omega)(x \wedge y).$$

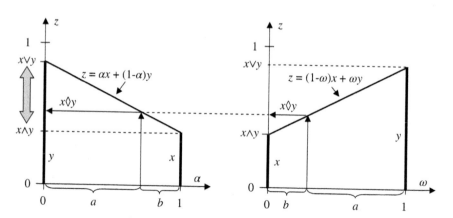

Figure 2.2.14 Continuous (linear) transition from *and* to *or*, and vice versa.

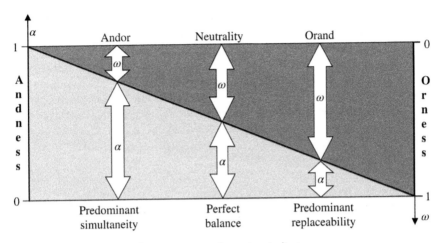

Figure 2.2.15 Andness and orness as complementary indicators.

From these equations, we can derive the following definitions of andness and orness:

$$\alpha = \frac{(x \vee y) - x \Diamond y}{(x \vee y) - (x \wedge y)}, \quad \omega = \frac{x \Diamond y - (x \wedge y)}{(x \vee y) - (x \wedge y)}, \quad x \neq y.$$

Thus, the andness α and the orness ω are complementary $(\alpha + \omega = 1)$, and they belong to the unit interval, $\alpha \in I, \omega \in I, I = [0,1]$, as shown in Fig. 2.2.15. In addition, both andness and orness are here defined as local features, i.e., they are functions of x and y. If $x \vee y = x \wedge y$ (i.e., $x = y$) or $x \vee y \approx x \wedge y$ then according to P$_5$ and Figs. 2.2.10 and 2.2.11 GCD becomes similar to the arithmetic mean. Using $x \Diamond y = 0.5(x \wedge y) + 0.5(x \vee y)$ it follows

$$\alpha = \frac{(x \vee y) - x \Diamond y}{(x \vee y) - (x \wedge y)} = \frac{(x \vee y) - 0.5(x \wedge y) - 0.5(x \vee y)}{(x \vee y) - (x \wedge y)} = \frac{1}{2}.$$

Therefore, if $x = y$ then α and ω are defined to be ½. If $x \approx y$ then $\alpha = 1 - \omega \approx \frac{1}{2}$.

(P$_{13}$) Sensitivity to Orness and Andness

In order to develop evaluation criteria, we must have the freedom to continuously adjust a desired degree of andness/orness. More orness means more opportunities to satisfy user requirements with one (or a small subset) of the component requirements.

Let $A(x_1, ..., x_n; \omega)$, $n > 1$ denote an aggregated suitability degree at the orness level ω. The aggregator $A : I^n \rightarrow I$ must satisfy the *orness monotonicity condition* $A(x_1,...;x_n;\omega_1) \leq A(x_1,...;x_n;\omega_2)$, $\omega_1 < \omega_2$. For a differentiable aggregation function A, this important feature can be denoted $\partial A / \partial \omega \geq 0$. In the majority of cases where $x_1 \wedge \cdots \wedge x_n \neq x_1 \vee \cdots \vee x_n$ (all inputs are not the same) and $0 < x_i < 1$, $i = 1, \ldots, n$ we have $\partial A / \partial \omega > 0$.

The andness can be interpreted as a metric of average distance between GCD and disjunction, and the orness can be interpreted as the metric of average distance between GCD and conjunction. Not surprisingly, there are multiple ways to define such metrics (Chapter 2.3). Since $\alpha = 1 - \omega$ the *andness monotonicity condition* and the sensitivity to andness for a differentiable aggregator A are: $A(x_1, \ldots, x_n; \alpha_1) \geq A(x_1, \ldots, x_n; \alpha_2)$, $\alpha_1 < \alpha_2$ and $\partial A / \partial \alpha \leq 0$. If $x_1 \wedge \cdots \wedge x_n \neq x_1 \vee \cdots \vee x_n$ and $0 < x_i < 1$, $i = 1, \ldots, n$, then $A(x_1, \ldots, x_n; \alpha_1) > A(x_1, \ldots, x_n; \alpha_2)$, $\alpha_1 < \alpha_2$, and $\partial A / \partial \alpha < 0$.

(P₁₄) Standard Negation and Partial Negation

An affirmative value statement is a claim that an evaluated object satisfies all stakeholder requirements. The degree of truth of such a statement, $x \in [0,1]$, can be interpreted as a fraction of satisfied requirements, and its complement $1 - x$ is the fraction of requirements that are not satisfied. This is observable in human reasoning: the fraction of candidates that fail a test is a complement of the fraction of candidates that pass the test; negative experiences with an evaluated object are the complement of positive experiences, etc. Based on this interpretation, and the need for negation in order to implement De Morgan duality, the involutive *standard negation* $N(x) = \bar{x} = 1 - x$, $N(N(x)) = x$ seems to satisfy most GL needs.

The standard negation can also be used to implement some other GL functions, such as the partial implication $x \rightarrow y = 1 - (x\Delta(1-y)) = (1-x)\nabla y$, the partial equivalence $x \sim y = (x\Delta y)\nabla[(1-x)\Delta(1-y)]$, etc.

The use of standard negation is frequently visible in bipolar criteria where aggregation includes desirable properties D and undesirable properties U; in such cases the suitability can be defined as the simultaneous presence of desirable properties and the absence of undesirable properties. It can be computed using the *partial abjunction* $S = D\Delta(1-U)$. In all such cases the suitability $1 - U$ is intuitively just a simple complement of unsuitability U. For example, if the unsuitability is 20%, then in 80% of cases (applications) the undesirable properties will not negatively affect the satisfaction of stakeholder's requirements.

Standard negation is regularly used in elementary attribute criteria. For example, let us consider the frequently used attribute criteria $L(a) =$ "preferred large values of the attribute a" and $S(a) =$ "preferred small values of the attribute a" (similar to Fig. 2.2.1). These criteria have the following form:

$$L(a) = \max\left\{0, \min\left[1, \frac{a - a_{min}}{a_{max} - a_{min}}\right]\right\} = \begin{cases} 0, & a \leq a_{min} \\ \dfrac{a - a_{min}}{a_{max} - a_{min}}, & a_{min} \leq a \leq a_{max}, \\ 1, & a_{max} \leq a \end{cases}$$

$$
S(a) = \max\left\{ 0, \min\left[1, \frac{a_{max} - a}{a_{max} - a_{min}} \right] \right\} = \begin{cases} 1, & a \le a_{min} \\[2mm] \dfrac{a_{max} - a}{a_{max} - a_{min}}, & a_{min} \le a \le a_{max}, \\[2mm] 0, & a_{max} \le a \end{cases}
$$

$0 \le a.$

In this case, based on sharing the same values of a_{min} and a_{max}, we have $L(a) + S(a) = 1$; so, $L(a)$ and $S(a)$ are defined as standard negations of each other. This approach is frequently used to avoid the use of abjunction: instead of $X = D \Delta (1 - L(a))$ we can use the complementary criterion $X = D \Delta S(a)$ (e.g., instead of distance we evaluate proximity).

In intuitive evaluation reasoning we can also encounter verbalized forms of negation that are different from the standard negation. The following quote from De Morgan's *Formal Logic* [DEM47] shows the presence of graded concepts and the non-involutive negation already in 1847:

> *The common proposition that two negatives make an affirmative, is true only upon the supposition that there are but two possible things, one of which is denied. Grant that a man must be either able or unable to do a particular thing, and then not unable and able are the same things. But if we suppose various degrees of performance, and therefore degrees of ability, it is false, in the common sense of the words, that two negatives make an affirmative. Thus, it would be erroneous to say,' John is able to translate Virgil, and Thomas is not unable; therefore, what John can do Thomas can do,' for it is evident that the premises mean that John is so near to the best sort of translation that an affirmation of his ability may be made, while Thomas is considerably lower than John, but not so near to absolute deficiency that his ability may be altogether denied. It will generally be found that two negatives imply an affirmative of a weaker degree than the positive affirmation.*

This interesting quote yields the following observations:

1) The primary goal of De Morgan's analysis is the understanding and modeling of actual human perceptions and actual human reasoning, as fuzzy and imperfect as they really are. So, the described form of negation is not involutive, i.e., it ignores the favorite property of axiomatic definitions of negation.
2) De Morgan clearly differentiated between bivalent logic and continuous logic, and explicitly showed the limitations of bivalent approach and the need for continuous logic if we want to model human perceptions and reasoning.

3) De Morgan spoke (170 years ago) about degrees of ability and degrees of performance in a way that is fully compatible with today's concepts of soft computing and fuzzy membership. This fact deserves a round of applause.

In the presented paragraph, De Morgan shows that from the standpoint of human verbalized perceptions, a glass that is "almost full" contains more liquid than the glass that is "not almost empty." Similarly, "an excellent computer" is perceived as better than "a computer that is not unacceptable." A man who is "not very old" is older than a man who is "very young." This form of reasoning is frequent in human verbal communication and deserves further investigation from the standpoint of rating scales that are used in soft computing.

The claim that an affirmative value statement is truer than its double negation seems to be an expression of intuitive perception mechanism in which the concept of value is related to linguistic variables and verbalized rating scales. Consider the following nine-level rating scale:

> **unacceptable** < **very poor** < **poor** < **below average** < **average** < **above average** < **good** < **very good** < **excellent**

The negation is frequently interpreted just as a moderate movement in either positive or negative direction along the rating scale. The perception of "not unacceptable" is regularly different from the perception of "excellent." Indeed, "not unacceptable" primarily means something "acceptable," which could be close to "average," but certainly is less than "excellent." Similarly, "not very good" does not mean the same as "very poor" but only a movement for one-two steps in a negative direction. If an object is characterized by a value statement claiming that it is "very good," then people somehow assume that the object is necessarily in the positive half of the rating scale (i.e., above the average), and easily accept that "not very good" can mean "good" or "above average." In addition, the same people might easily accept statements like "it is not good, it is excellent," or "this laptop is not very poor, it is completely unacceptable." If the evaluation reasoning is based on verbalized rating scales then the negation of a specific value can frequently be perceived *only as a difference*, and not as a complete negation (a complement) of a given value. This is the reason why "not very good" can be accepted as "good" or even as "excellent." In other words, we sometimes intuitively interpret "not x" simply as "different from x." That seems to be an intuitive descendant of the law of excluded middle, where we differentiate x and "something else," which is then simplified as "not x."

Looking at the above example of the nine-level rating scale, we see that negation could be graded using a *negation degree* $\nu \in [0,1]$, providing a continuous transition from x to its complement $1-x$. For example, if suitability is "very good," then the weakest form of "not very good" might be "good" and the strongest form might be "very poor." Verbalized value statements based on rating scales can give the following form of the graded (or partial) negation:

$$N(x,\nu) = \nu(1-x) + (1-\nu)x = \nu + x - 2\nu x = \begin{cases} x, & \nu = 0 \\ 0.5, & \nu = 0.5 \\ 1-x, & \nu = 1 \end{cases}$$

$$N(N(x,\nu),\nu) = x + 2\nu(1-\nu)(1-2x) = \begin{cases} x, & \nu = 0 \\ 0.5, & \nu = 0.5, \ 0 \le x \le 1, \ 0 \le \nu \le 1 \\ x, & \nu = 1 \end{cases}$$

For all $0 < \nu < 1$ this definition satisfies the condition *"two negatives imply an affirmative of a weaker degree than the positive affirmation."* Using the nine-level rating scale and this model we can get the following partial negation of "excellent":

$N(excellent, 1/4) = good$ (low negation)

$N(excellent, 1/2) = average$ (medium negation)

$N(excellent, 3/4) = poor$ (high negation)

$N(excellent, 1) = unacceptable$ (highest negation)

Thus, the involutive negation is a special case obtained for the highest (full or standard) negation using the maximum negation degree $\nu = 1$. The value $\nu = 0$ provides no negation at all (it is only used for the completeness of transition from x to $1-x$).

The above model of partial negation in the case of average suitability for each ν gives $N(0.5,\nu) = 0.5$, what is consistent with standard negation $N(0.5,1) = 1 - 0.5 = 0.5$. However, from the standpoint of rating scale logic, if we compare "average" and "not average" in the common sense of the words, then "not average" can be everything except average (i.e., either good or bad, but always "not average" $\neq$ "average"). Obviously, "not average" means only "different from average," and that is not a standard negation. It is not difficult to model that type of negation but such models would not be useful in GL.

De Morgan's claim that *"it will generally be found that two negatives imply an affirmative of a weaker degree than the positive affirmation"* for $x > \frac{1}{2}$ means $\bar{\bar{x}} < x$. This is consistent with the rating scale logic where negation can be perceived as decrementing of good values or incrementing of bad values. Unfortunately, the concept of duality $x \vee y = \overline{\bar{x} \wedge \bar{y}}$ does not hold for partial conjunction, partial disjunction and all versions of partial negation. Indeed, let us select a partial conjunction aggregator Δ and let us use duality based on partial negation to define a dual partial disjunction aggregator $x \nabla y = N((N(x,\nu) \Delta N(y,\nu)),\nu)$.

Using that form of partial disjunction the expression $N((N(x,\nu)\nabla N(y,\nu)),\nu)$ should return $x\Delta y$. However, $x\Delta y = N((N(x,\nu)\nabla N(y,\nu)),\nu)$ only for $\nu = 1$, i.e., for standard negation.

In GL we frequently need De Morgan duality, in order to provide symmetry between conjunctive and disjunctive aggregators. Therefore, there are good reasons to believe that the standard negation is the most appropriate model of negation in GL. However, when it comes to verbalization and the use of rating scales, we must keep in mind that human-verbalized perceptions yield the non-involutive partial negation.

Not surprisingly, mathematical literature offers various other forms of negation, e.g., $N(x) = (1-x)^{1/c}$, $c > 0$, or $N(x) = (1-x^c)^{1/c}$, $c > 0$, or $N(x) = (1-x)/(1-cx)$, $c > -1$, analyzed in [FOD94, TOR07, BEL07]. Further research is needed to find whether some forms of negation that are different from the standard negation might have significant applicability in the area of graded evaluation logic.

2.2.3 Basic Semantic Aspects of Evaluation Logic Reasoning

Evaluation problems are always solved in an environment where stakeholders want to purchase and/or use an object that contributes to attainment of their goals. The ability of an evaluated object to satisfy goals is expressed by using a set of attributes that must satisfy stakeholder's requirements. So, each evaluation problem has a specific *meaning* that affects the selection of attributes and their criteria, as well as the selection of aggregation operators and their parameters. Those aspects of evaluation reasoning that critically depend on understanding the meaning of an evaluation problem are called *semantic aspects of evaluation reasoning*. Of course, all components of a perceptual computer are to some extent related to the meaning of evaluation problem, but for some components that is particularly visible. The central semantic concept in all evaluation problems is the concept of importance. Indeed, it is always necessary to provide an explanation why something is more or less important and such explanations are always based on the expected contribution to attainment of stakeholder's goals.

In this section we investigate the dominant semantic aspect of evaluation reasoning, i.e., various properties of perceptual computer that are directly or indirectly derived from the concept of importance. The direct expression of importance is the concept of relative importance, implemented using weights, as well as the categorization of attributes as mandatory, sufficient, desired, or optional.

(P₁₅)   Environment and Semantics of Evaluation Reasoning

We assume that perceptual computers are developed for specific stakeholders, and they must reflect stakeholders' goals. The stakeholders are individuals or organizations interested in buying and/or using objects that contribute to attainment of their goals. The goals are defined after an analysis of potential benefits of having and/or using a specific physical or conceptual object. Typical physical objects are electronic equipment, aircraft, cars, homes, and so on, and typical conceptual objects are software, educational programs, websites, retirement plans, medical conditions, etc. In the case of intuitive evaluation reasoning, the evaluation is regularly related to individual goals of decision maker. For example, a homebuyer takes into account the needs of his or her family, financial constraints, etc. Thus, the specification of goals is a prerequisite for creating perceptional computers, and it assumes detailed understanding of the meaning and consequences of various goal attainment options.

Each evaluated object has some intrinsic properties and functionality. Understanding the intrinsic properties and the functionality of an evaluated object is called *domain expertise* and people (or teams) with such knowledge are *domain experts*. An evaluator who tries to evaluate an object for which he or she has no domain expertise cannot produce justifiable evaluation results. So, domain expertise is an indispensable prerequisite for creating perceptual computers and in professional evaluation processes domain experts are professionals who regularly use evaluated objects and know details of their internal organization and performance. For example, in the case of evaluating aircrafts, domain experts are experienced professional pilots.

In everyday intuitive evaluation, the domain expertise is very desirable but frequently insufficient. For example, people who don't understand the work of the car engine, transmission, and electronic equipment still evaluate, select, buy, and drive cars. Humans frequently make decisions based on incomplete information, and in the absence of any better knowledge, a car can be selected using only three attributes: color, price, and experience of a friend. However, the level of ignorance that can be tolerated in the case of car selection cannot be tolerated in the case of selecting the location of a nuclear power plant and its safety features.

It should be self-evident that good understanding of the environment in which an evaluation project is embedded, understanding of stakeholders and their goals and interests, and sufficient domain expertise are semantic components that crucially affect evaluation reasoning and evaluation logic. The most visible aspect of such expertise is the ability to properly select relevant attributes and the degrees of importance of components of suitability criteria. The percept of high importance is used to decide whether some attributes or groups of attributes are mandatory or sufficient to satisfy stakeholder's goals. In addition, a correct perception of importance is necessary for selecting the degrees of relative impact of inputs for each and every suitability aggregator.

Evaluation criteria are not mathematical objects created in semantic vacuum; they are primarily meaningful and useful decision models that reflect the understanding of the stakeholder's environment and goals, as well as the specificities of each evaluation problem from the standpoint of domain expertise. Consequently, the graded logic is not developed for manipulating anonymous real numbers (values without semantic identity). GL is processing degrees of truth, and each degree of truth is related to a specific statement, and each statement has semantic background, i.e., the meaning, role, and importance for a specific stakeholder. Therefore, GL is used in a well-defined environment of reasoning and decision making, and must support both the formal logic and semantic aspects of logic decision models.

(P_{16}) Noncommutativity, Relative Importance, and the use of Weights

Nothing in decision models has equal importance, and "first things first" is one of cornerstones of human reasoning. Any logic that ignores the need to model various aspect of importance has no chance to model human evaluation reasoning. Evaluation is always related to attaining specific goals, and those system components that more contribute to the goal attainment are automatically more important than those that yield smaller contribution. For example, a car buyer may have as a primary goal the safety of her family and have good reasons to believe that the car safety record is more important than the car performance, appearance, and comfort. Consequently, the corresponding evaluation criterion function must be able to clearly express the difference in relative importance between the safety, performance, appearance, and comfort. The relative importance of inputs is usually expressed using importance parameters that are called *weights*.

Weights are related to the *meaning and role of inputs* (with respect to the goal attainment) and consequently, they reflect *semantic aspects* of criterion functions while simultaneity and substitutability reflect *formal logic aspects*. Formal logic aspects of a decision model can sometimes be specified independently of semantic aspects. For example, an evaluator may claim: "We simultaneously need safety and performance (power, acceleration, speed) of a car." Independently, the same evaluator may claim: "We are convinced that safety is more important than performance." These claims can come in any order, illustrating their independence.

The independence does not mean that all combinations of simultaneity and relative importance are equally justifiable and acceptable. Indeed, in GL we cannot claim that semantic and formal logic components are *orthogonal*. A more careful observation of intuitive reasoning shows that in the case of compensative averaging aggregators, both semantic and formal logic components originate in the evaluator's compound percept of the overall importance of aggregated inputs. The supporting evidence of that claim is clearly visible in extreme and irregular cases of aggregators where the percept of high overall importance simultaneously necessitates the use of high andness/orness and prevents the use of low weights. That makes weights and andness/orness look dependent and consequently the combinations of a high andness/orness and very low weighs become contradictory and unacceptable.

A discussion of this problem can be found in Section 2.2.6 (P_{32}). In any case, evaluation criteria must be able to express both the simultaneity requirements and the importance requirements. It is desirable that the simultaneity and importance can be independently adjusted: the complexity decreases if a problem decomposes into relatively small and simple subproblems.

In the process of suitability aggregation, a decision maker aggregates inputs that have different degrees of importance. Consequently, such inputs cannot be swapped. Because of different levels of relative importance of inputs, *commutativity is not a desired property of suitability aggregators*, but it occurs as a special case.

Observations of the human perception of importance show that the importance of any elementary or compound attribute is regularly an integrated percept that combines two main components: the request for a specific degree of simultaneity/substitutability with other important components, and the relative importance with respect to other components. Therefore, the evaluators must be aware and trained to decompose the overall intuitive importance into desired level of andness/orness and desired relative importance.

If y denotes an output suitability degree, and input x_i is more important than input x_j, then generally $\partial y/\partial x_i \geq \partial y/\partial x_j$, and in the majority of cases we expect $\partial y/\partial x_i > \partial y/\partial x_j > 0$. The simplest model of aggregator with k inputs that uses multiplicative weights to express the relative importance is the conjunctive/disjunctive neutrality realized as a weighted arithmetic mean:

$$y = \sum_{i=1}^{k} W_i x_i, \quad \sum_{i=1}^{k} W_i = 1, \quad 0 < W_i < 1, \quad \frac{\partial y}{\partial x_i} = W_i, \quad i = 1,...,k, \quad k > 1.$$

The multiplicative weights are positive, limited, and normalized. If a weight were 0, then the corresponding input would be omitted, and if a weight were 1, then all other inputs would be eliminated. Therefore, the multiplicative weights always belong to $]0,1[$.

All weighted GCD aggregators have adjustable parameters shown in Fig. 2.1.9. Such aggregators are symbolically denoted $y = W_1 x_1 \Diamond ... \Diamond W_k x_k$ ($W_i x_i$ denotes that W_i is the weight of x_i; it does not denote multiplication). Weights W_1, ..., W_k determine the relative importance of inputs $x_1, ..., x_k$, and in the majority of cases they can be adjusted independently of the GCD operator $\Diamond$ (whose properties are adjusted by selecting the andness α).

The need for weighted aggregators is obvious in many applications. For example, the computation of the average grade of students (GPA) should be based on weighted aggregators. A course that has 4 credit hours should contribute to GPA two times more than a course that has only 2 credit hours.

In GL, weights express the relative importance of inputs and are directly related to compensatory properties of aggregators. Suppose that an input suitability is $x_i - \Delta x_i$ where x_i is a default value of the ith input, and Δx_i is an undesirable decrement of suitability. The question is whether a suitability increment of the jth input $(x_j + \Delta x_j)$ can compensate the decrement Δx_i, so that the output suitability y remains unchanged:

$$W_1 x_1 \lozenge ... \lozenge W_i(x_i - \Delta x_i) \lozenge ... \lozenge W_j(x_j + \Delta x_j) \lozenge ... \lozenge W_k x_k = W_1 x_1 \lozenge ... \lozenge W_i x_i ... \lozenge W_j x_j ... \lozenge W_k x_k.$$

In a general case, this should be possible for small decrements, and we can differentiate the following three possibilities:

$\Delta x_i \approx \Delta x_j$, if x_i is approximately equally important as x_j (i.e., $|\partial x_i / \partial x_j| \approx 1$),

$\Delta x_i > \Delta x_j$, if x_i is less important than x_j (i.e., $|\partial x_i / \partial x_j| > 1$),

$\Delta x_i < \Delta x_j$, if x_i is more important than x_j (i.e., $|\partial x_i / \partial x_j| < 1$).

The relationship between compensatory properties and weights is clearly visible in the case of weighted arithmetic mean where $\partial x_i / \partial x_j = - W_j / W_i$. For example, if $k = 2$ and an evaluator feels that $|\partial x_1 / \partial x_2| = 2$ (x_2 is two times more important than x_1), then from $W_2 / W_1 = 2$ and $W_1 + W_2 = 1$ it follows $W_1 = 1/3$ and $W_2 = 2/3$. In the case of aggregators that are different from the weighted arithmetic mean, the computation of weights becomes more complex but the concept of relationship between the relative importance and compensatory properties remains the same.

The role of multiplicative weights is visible in all quasi-arithmetic means:

$$y = F^{-1}\left(\sum_{i=1}^{k} W_i F(x_i)\right), \quad \sum_{i=1}^{k} W_i = 1, \quad x_i \in I = [0,1], \quad 0 < W_i < 1, \quad i = 1,...,k.$$

Here, F denotes a continuous strictly monotonic function that has the inverse function. The product $W_i F(x_i)$ indicates that the contribution of $F(x_i)$ is amplified W_i times so that more important inputs affect the output y more than less important inputs. In other words, it is not acceptable that an input is important and insufficiently satisfied.

Multiplicative weights are not the only model of relative importance. It is also possible to express the relative importance using maximum-normalized implicative weights $v_1, ..., v_k, \max(v_1,...,v_k) = 1$. The idea is based on the following verbal interpretation of the classic implication $x \to y = \overline{x \wedge \overline{y}} = \overline{x} \vee y$: if from x follows y, then it is not acceptable that x is satisfied and y is not satisfied. Thus, the implication $v_i \to x_i$ can be implemented as $(v_i \to x_i) = (1 - v_i) \nabla x_i$ where ∇ denotes a partial (or full) disjunction, and interpreted that it is not acceptable to have high importance v_i and low suitability x_i. In other words, if the importance is high, the suitability of such an input should also be high. So, the aggregation concepts $y = F^{-1}(W_1 F(x_1) + \cdots + W_k F(x_k))$ and $y = [(1 - v_1) \nabla x_1] \, \Delta \cdots \Delta \, [(1 - v_k) \nabla x_k]$ have a similar semantic interpretation. Their usability, however, is rather different (see Section 2.5.1).

(P₁₇) Mandatory Conjunctive Requirements (Hard Partial Conjunction)

Suppose that a car buyer evaluates cars using safety and comfort among other decision variables. Many car buyers would reject a car that does not satisfy minimum safety features. Similarly, a car that provides an insufficient comfort might also be rejected. In this example, both safety (x) and comfort (y) play the role of mandatory requirements. If a mandatory requirement input is rated zero, the aggregated suitability $(z = x \Diamond y)$ of such a car must also be zero. In other words, assuming equal relative importance, the aggregator must satisfy the condition $0 \Diamond y = x \Diamond 0 = 0$. This is a very frequent requirement in both intuitive and formal GL and holds also in the case of different weights. Consequently, we are interested in mathematical models that support this property.

The simplest way to satisfy these conditions would be to use the pure conjunction (i.e., the minimum function) $z = x \wedge y$. However, it is easy to see that this is not acceptable. If a car has mediocre safety and comfort $(x = y = 0.5)$, and another car has superb safety and average comfort $(x = 1, y = 0.5)$, then the conjunction model in both cases yields $z = x \wedge y = 0.5$. No car buyer would agree with such a model, because it is insensitive to improvements (see P₆). It would be much better to use a partial conjunction, $z = x \Delta y$, and to make a specific form of *andor* operator (denoted $\bar{\Delta}$), which satisfies the condition $0 \bar{\Delta} y = x \bar{\Delta} 0 = 0$ for selected value of andness, as well as $\partial(x \bar{\Delta} y)/\partial x > 0$, $\partial(x \bar{\Delta} y)/\partial y > 0$, $x > 0$, $y > 0$. For example, such properties can be provided by the geometric mean $x \bar{\Delta} y = \sqrt{xy}$, the harmonic mean $x \bar{\Delta} y = 2xy/(x + y)$, and many other aggregators. In other words, we need GCD aggregators that satisfy the condition $0 \Diamond y = x \Diamond 0 = 0$, while their andness is in the range $\frac{1}{2} < \alpha_\theta \leq \alpha \leq 1$.

The partial conjunction that supports mandatory requirements is called the *hard partial conjunction* (HPC, symbolically denoted $\bar{\Delta}$). Its parameter α_θ is called the *HPC threshold andness*. The constant 0 is called the *absorbing element (annihilator)* of HPC. The threshold andness is selected in the range $\frac{1}{2} < \alpha_\theta < 1$, so that in the range $\frac{1}{2} < \alpha < \alpha_\theta$ the partial conjunction is soft (see P₁₈) and in the range $\alpha_\theta \leq \alpha < 1$ the partial conjunction is hard.

Mandatory requirements are frequent and easily observable components of human evaluation reasoning. In fact, in all cases where we need simultaneous satisfaction of several requirements, and we use a partial conjunction aggregator, the first question is whether the selected aggregator should or should not support mandatory requirements. Therefore, a partial conjunction aggregators that cannot support mandatory requirements are not applicable in logic aggregation and in system evaluation models.

(P₁₈) Nonmandatory Conjunctive Requirements (Soft Partial Conjunction)

In addition to hard partial conjunction, intuitive evaluation regularly includes cases of mild simultaneity where partial conjunction must not support the mandatory requirements. For example, a homebuyer might like to buy a home that has installed washer *and* dryer *and* dishwasher. This is a simultaneity requirement that implies the use of partial conjunction. However, the majority of homebuyers agree that these are not mandatory requirements, and it would be wrong to reject an attractive home only because a dryer is not installed. Therefore, in GL we also need a *soft partial conjunction* (SPC, denoted using operator $\underline{A}$), which supports nonmandatory conjunctive requirements and must not have annihilator 0. The soft partial conjunction $x\underline{A}y$ satisfies the following conditions:

$$x \wedge y < x\underline{A}y < (x+y)/2, \quad x \neq y, \quad 0.5 < \alpha < \alpha_\theta,$$
$$0 < 0\underline{A}y < y/2, \quad x = 0, \quad y > 0.$$

In this case we use equal weights, but the same properties hold for the weighted soft partial conjunction. A simple example of SPC is

$$x\underline{A}y = 0.25x + 0.5\sqrt{xy} + 0.25y = \left[\sqrt{xy} + (x+y)/2\right]/2 < (x+y)/2, \quad x \neq y.$$

Since $0\underline{A}y = 0.25y$ the above aggregator does not support the annihilator 0. A similar example of weighted SPC can be obtained as an adjustable linear combination of the harmonic mean and the arithmetic mean:

$$x\underline{A}y = 2Wxy/(x+y) + (1-W)(x+y)/2, \quad 0 < W < 1.$$

In the above SPC examples we combine a HPC (geometric or harmonic mean) and the neutral arithmetic mean. The role of the arithmetic mean is to eliminate the annihilator 0 and to realize the SPC condition $0\underline{A}y > 0$, $y > 0$.

In the case of general partial conjunction, we use the operator Δ. In the special case of SPC, the corresponding operator is $\underline{\Delta}$ and in the special case of HPC the operator is $\bar{\Delta}$. Similar notation will also be used for partial disjunction.

(P_{19}) Sufficient Requirements (Hard and Soft Partial Disjunction)

There are situations in evaluation where a compound requirement is satisfied if any of inputs is sufficiently satisfied. For example, some medical conditions have multiple symptoms and one of them is sufficient to verify the existence of analyzed condition. Sufficient requirements are symmetrical (dual) to the mandatory requirements, and consequently we can differentiate a *hard partial disjunction* (HPD, denoted using operator $\bar{\nabla}$) and a *soft partial disjunction* (SPD, denoted using operator $\underline{\nabla}$). HPD satisfies the conditions $1\bar{\nabla}y = x\bar{\nabla}1 = 1$, $\partial(x\bar{\nabla}y)/\partial x > 0$, $\partial(x\bar{\nabla}y)/\partial y > 0$, $x < 1$, $y < 1$, $0.5 < \omega_\theta \leq \omega < 1$. The parameter ω_θ is the *HPD threshold orness*. Similarly, SPD satisfies the conditions $(x+1)/2 < (\bar{x}1) < 1$, $0 \leq x < 1$, $0.5 < \omega < \omega_\theta$.

An example of HPD is a dual of geometric mean $x\bar{\nabla}y = 1 - \sqrt{(1-x)(1-y)}$, and an example of SPD is $x\underline{\nabla}y = \sqrt{0.5(x^2+y^2)}$. The constant 1 is called the *absorbing element (annihilator)* of HPD. HPD is a model of sufficient requirements: similarly to the pure disjunction, if one of inputs is completely satisfied, that is enough for the complete satisfaction of the HPD aggregator. Contrary to HPD, the SPD aggregator must not have annihilator 1. Generally, in both intuitive and formal GL models for comparison and selection of complex objects, the sufficient requirements are used somewhat less frequently than mandatory requirements.

(P_{20}) Nine Special Cases of Graded Conjunction/Disjunction

Mandatory and sufficient requirements are easily observable in intuitive GL and we can empirically identify nine special cases of GCD: CC, C, HPC, SPC, A, SPD, HPD, D and DD, summarized in Table 2.2.4. Generally, the threshold values α_θ and ω_θ can be different, but in practice they are most frequently selected to be equal, $\frac{1}{2} < \alpha_\theta = \omega_\theta < 1$, and to define partial disjunction as De Morgan dual of partial conjunction and vice versa: $x\nabla y = 1 - (1-x)\Delta(1-y)$, $x\Delta y = 1 - (1-x)\nabla(1-y)$. The hard and soft aggregators CC, HPC, SPC, SPD, HPD and DD have adjustable degrees of andness/orness. According to GL conjecture (Section 2.1.8), it is safe to claim that they represent a complete set of basic logic properties, and no other special cases of GCD exist in intuitive human evaluation reasoning.

The frequency of use of these aggregators in GL is not uniform. The full conjunction and the full disjunction are rarely used alone, but they appear as components in some compound aggregators. Neutrality is frequently used both as a standalone aggregator and as a component in compound aggregators. SPC and HPC are the most frequent aggregators in all consumer evaluation problems (DMs usually want simultaneous satisfaction of the majority of their requirements). Nonidempotent CC and DD are very rarely used in evaluation.

Table 2.2.4 Nine observable special cases of GCD and their characteristic properties.

Andness	Orness	Aggregator	Characteristic property
$\alpha < 0$	$\omega > 1$	**DD** (hyperdisjunction)	$x\bar{\nabla}x > x, \quad 0 < x < 1$
$\alpha = 0$	$\omega = 1$	**D** (full disjunction)	$1 \vee x = x \vee 1 = 1, \quad 0 \leq x \leq 1$
$0 < \alpha \leq 1 - \omega_\theta$	$\omega_\theta \leq \omega < 1$	**HPD** (hard PD)	$1\bar{\nabla}x = x\bar{\nabla}1 = 1, \quad 0 \leq x \leq 1$
$1 - \omega_\theta < \alpha < 0.5$	$0.5 < \omega < \omega_\theta$	**SPD** (soft PD)	$(x+1)/2 < x\bar{\nabla}1 < 1, \quad 0 \leq x < 1$
$\alpha = 0.5$	$\omega = 0.5$	**A** (neutrality)	$x \ominus y = (x+y)/2$
$0.5 < \alpha < \alpha_\theta$	$1 - \alpha_\theta < \omega < 0.5$	**SPC** (soft PC)	$0 < x\Delta 0 < x/2, \quad 0 < x \leq 1$
$\alpha_\theta \leq \alpha < 1$	$0 < \omega \leq 1 - \alpha_\theta$	**HPC** (hard PC)	$0\bar{\Delta}x = x\bar{\Delta}0 = 0, \quad 0 \leq x \leq 1$
$\alpha = 1$	$\omega = 0$	**C** (full conjunction)	$0 \wedge x = x \wedge 0 = 0, \quad 0 \leq x \leq 1$
$\alpha > 1$	$\omega < 0$	**CC** (hyperconjunction)	$x\bar{\wedge}x < x, \quad 0 < x < 1$

HPD and SPD are less frequent components of consumer evaluation models. As standalone aggregators we encounter them in all situations where evaluated systems have several alternative options (e.g., an evaluated house/condo can have a private garage, or a shared garage, or a reserved uncovered parking space, or public parking, or some combination of previous options). On the other hand, HPD and SPD are predominant aggregators in models of impairments caused by medical conditions (patients feel difficulties if *any* of several possible symptoms is present; see Chapter 4.3). In addition, HPD and SPD are also encountered in some of compound aggregators (see Section 2.2.4).

The selection of GCD in the intuitive GL follows the decision pattern shown in Fig. 2.2.16. We select an appropriate GCD special case by answering the following questions:

1) What is the logic polarization (conjunctive, disjunctive, or neutral)?
2) Is the conjunction/disjunction partial or full or extreme (hyper)?
3) Is the partial conjunction/disjunction hard (with annihilator) or soft (without annihilator)? *In each special case of GCD, the annihilator is either necessary or unacceptable.*

The selection and adjustment of andness/orness and relative importance (weights) is a standard next step in this process. Intuitive evaluators may select HPC and SPC with any level of andness, and HPD and SPD with any level of orness (CC/DD usually reduce to t-norms or t-conorms). Of course, we assume that the andness of HPC is greater than the andness of SPC, and the orness of HPD is greater than the orness of SPD. We also expect that independent selection of hardness/softness and andness/orness is not arbitrary, but based on strong justification, and in each aggregation structure performed in a consistent way. The ranges of HPC andness and HPD orness used by intuitive evaluators are discussed in P_{24}.

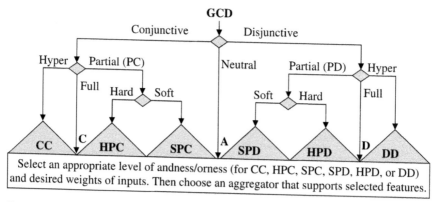

Figure 2.2.16 The process of selecting an appropriate special case of GCD.

In the majority of applications the threshold andness and the threshold orness are fixed properties of perceptual computers. Appropriate values of threshold andness and orness are selected before developing a criterion function and are not changed inside a given project. In the process of GCD modeling the adjustment of HPC and/or HPD thresholds at the level of individual aggregator is theoretically possible but it is significantly beyond the standard range of precision. Mathematical modeling of GCD is discussed in subsequent chapters.

If a DM aggregates two or more inputs using HPC, then all inputs are mandatory. If one of them is not satisfied the evaluated subsystem will be zero-rated and possibly cause rejection of the evaluated system. On the other hand, the use of SPC makes all inputs optional (i.e., DM can tolerate the cases where some of optional inputs are not satisfied). There are also many cases where evaluators combine two groups of inputs: mandatory and optional. This case cannot be modeled using GCD with different weights; it is necessary to have a specific form of asymmetric aggregator described in Section 2.2.4.

(P_{21}) The Compound Percept of Overall Importance and Its Components
Let us consider a simplified computer evaluation tree shown in Fig. 2.2.17. This tree follows the general SMER structure of perceptual computer shown in Fig. 2.2.4. For each component in the computer evaluation tree the decision maker creates the percept of importance. It is possible to ask questions "What is the importance of hardware?" or "What is the importance of central processor?" Such questions prompt the decision maker to create percepts of importance and then to express them in quantitative and/or verbal form.

However, it is easy to see that the above questions about importance are imprecise and incomplete. The problem is that the percept of importance requires context, and without context it is ill-defined. The question about

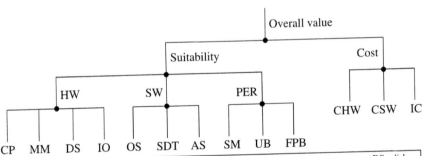

Figure 2.2.17 Simplified computer evaluation tree.

the importance of central processor can be asked in the context of hardware, or in the context of overall suitability, or in the context of the whole computer evaluation and selection problem. In the context of hardware, the question is how the central processor compares with other main hardware components: the size of main memory, the disk storage size, and the capability of input/output devices. Suppose that DM has the percept that the importance of central processor in that group is 35% (CP is very important because it is the only fixed component in its group that cannot be later upgraded, expanded, and improved). If the question is modified, asking for the importance of central processor in the context of the whole computer, then the percept of importance of central processor will decrease and maybe total only 18%, because now it must be compared with all hardware and software components and their performance. Finally, if the computer buyer has a very limited budget and the low cost is more important than the overall suitability of computer, then in the widest context of the whole evaluation problem the importance of processor might drop to only 8%. Thus, the percept of importance of selected component is the result of comparison with other competitive components in the selected group. If the group is a single aggregator, as in the case where $HW = f(CP,MM,DS,IO)$ then the importance of each component in the group can be called the *relative importance*, because the only problem is to compare the four components with each other and then to create the ranking of relative degrees of importance (e.g., 35%, 25%, 20%, 20%). On the other hand, we can also define the percept of *overall importance*, as the importance of selected component (e.g., the CP) in the widest context of the whole evaluation problem.

If a component has a high overall importance, it is interesting to analyze what is contributing to the percept of high importance. Of course, the percept of importance is regularly a compound percept. There are several principal components that can affect the percept of overall importance:

1) *Functional importance:* a part of the percept of overall importance based on the role of the analyzed component in the functioning of the evaluated system.
2) *Financial importance:* the percept of importance derived from a possible high cost of the analyzed component.
3) *Relative importance:* a part of the compound percept of overall importance derived from a dominant position with respect to other components in the analyzed group.
4) *Logic importance:* a part of the percept of overall importance derived from the high andness (α) or the high orness (ω) applied to components in the group.

The functional importance is a purely semantic aspect supported by domain expertise; it depends on the type of analyzed system. In the case of computer, the central processor has a very significant role; in the case of a car, the engine has a very significant role, etc. In an attribute decomposition tree, the functional importance of selected node also depends on the importance of all leaves that are descendants of that node. The financial importance is present only in cases where the analyzed component has a visible price tag and there are alternative components that can be selected by the decision maker (e.g., in the case of evaluating free web browsers the financial importance does not exist).

The remaining two components, logic and relative importance, do exist in each and every logic aggregator starting with the GCD. These components affect the structure of each aggregator and should be further analyzed. The relative importance is easy to investigate: in an isolated group of k inputs, it is necessary to perform $k(k-1)/2$ pairwise comparisons, then to make a ranking according to decreasing relative importance, and to assign the most appropriate weights. The logic importance is a more subtle issue, and the best way to analyze it is to select cases where all inputs have the same relative importance.

In the case of GCD aggregators the percept of logic importance of inputs is an increasing function of $\max(\alpha, \omega)$. This observation deserves a detailed explanation. To expose the main point let us use the case of a homebuyer who considers that the home location (L) and the home quality (Q) are *equally important*. In terms of weights and relative importance the homebuyer uses $W_L = W_Q = 0.5$ and the overall home suitability (H) is determined (either intuitively or quantitatively) using a GCD aggregator $H = 0.5L \lozenge 0.5Q$. If we ask such a homebuyer whether L and Q are important, the most likely answer would be that both L and Q are *very important*.

Let us now investigate the meaning of statements "L and Q are equally important" and "both L and Q are very important." Obviously, the first statement specifies the relative importance, i.e., it reflects a relative comparison of L and Q from the standpoint of deciding which input contributes more to the percept of overall suitability of evaluated homes. The fact that L contributes more/less than Q means only that one of them contributes more than the other one, and nothing more. In particular, such statement claims nothing about the significance of L and Q as the contributors to the percept of the overall suitability of a home.

Contrary to the first statement, the statement that both L and Q are very important represents an explicit claim that both L and Q simultaneously contribute to the percept of overall suitability of evaluated homes. Indeed, it is almost impossible to find a homebuyer who does not simultaneously care for the home location and the home quality. A natural next question is how to express, verbally and quantitatively, that both L and Q are simultaneously very important? Obviously, there is nothing we can do with weights since (by assumption) we know that L and Q are equally important and their weights are 0.5. A logical answer to this question is simple: in this case, a high importance means a high simultaneity, i.e., a high andness. Indeed, if both L and Q are very important that means we cannot accept homes where either L or Q are insufficiently satisfied. In other words, L and Q must be *simultaneously satisfied* and the fact that they are very important directly translates to the high level of andness of the corresponding simultaneity model.

If we look at this situation from the other side, it is obvious that high andness implies the high importance of aggregated inputs: if the andness is high, the partial conjunction is regularly strong, the inputs are mandatory, their absence is unacceptable, and all these facts directly yield the percept of high importance. It is easy to see that the same holds for the high orness. De Morgan duality is sufficient to prove this claim but it is not difficult to find real life situations where high orness implies the percept of importance of an attribute. For example, if the disability of a patient depends on either sensory symptoms (pain, itching, burning, tingling) or motor symptoms (inability to move), then either of these symptoms is sufficient to cause disability, and the degree of disability can be defined as a partial disjunction of sensory and motor symptoms. A high orness of this aggregator denotes a high overall importance of both inputs, and vice versa. If the inputs are very important, then only one of them will be enough to cause the disability effect. On the other hand, a high orness of sufficient inputs gives to each input the power to satisfy a disjunctive criterion and directly yields the percept of importance of inputs.

If the high overall importance causes the high andness/orness, then we can use that observation in evaluation practice. Instead of asking nonprofessional stakeholders what is the appropriate andness, we can ask what is their percept of the overall importance of simultaneous satisfaction of inputs. Then the appropriate values of andness/orness can be derived from the percept of overall importance of simultaneity or substitutability.

The percept of overall importance can be verbalized using a rating scale and quantified in the range $[0,1]$, where 1 denotes the maximum importance and 0 denotes no importance. Fig. 2.2.18 illustrates possible relationships between the verbalized overall importance V and the andness/orness. It is reasonable to expect that a medium importance causes a medium andness/orness and the maximum importance yields the maximum andness/orness. Acceptable $V(\alpha)$ functions can belong to the shaded area in Fig. 2.2.18. A simple piecewise linear (V-shaped) model of this function, shown in Fig. 2.2.18, is

$$V(\alpha) = \max(\alpha, \omega) = \max(\alpha, 1 - \alpha) = \max(\omega, 1 - \omega) = 0.5 + |\alpha - 0.5| = 0.5 + |\omega - 0.5|.$$

According to this example, if a homebuyer feels that the overall importance of having simultaneously excellent home location and high home quality is *high*, that could be interpreted as andness $\alpha = 0.75$. Similarly, *very high* would yield $\alpha = 0.875$.

(P$_{22}$) The Impact of Relative Importance for Various Degrees of Andness/Orness

In a general case input attributes of an aggregator have different relative importance, i.e., they produce a different impact on the output suitability. That is

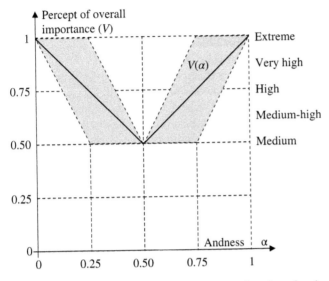

Figure 2.2.18 Percept of overall importance as a function of andness/orness.

easily visible in a simple case of a student who has two classes: one that has 4 credit hours per week and the other that has 2 credit hours per week. It is obvious that the grade obtained in the first class (x) should affect the GPA two times more than the grade obtained in the second class (y). In this example, the corresponding GCD aggregator is $z = (2/3)x \lozenge (1/3)y$. More precisely, in the case of GPA, all schools use the arithmetic mean and we have the following:

$$GPA = z = \frac{2}{3}x + \frac{1}{3}y, \quad \frac{\partial z}{\partial x} = \frac{2}{3}, \quad \frac{\partial z}{\partial y} = \frac{1}{3}, \quad \frac{\partial z}{\partial x} = 2\frac{\partial z}{\partial y}, \quad \frac{\partial y}{\partial x} = -2.$$

Therefore, the impact of x (defined as $\partial z/\partial x$) is two times greater than the impact of y. In the case of arbitrary weights, we have $z = Wx + (1 - W)y$ and $\partial z/\partial x = W$. So, a high weight of an input directly contributes to the percept of overall importance of the input. The impact of weight W, expressed as $\partial z/\partial W = W(x - y)$, decreases in the vicinity of the idempotency line $y = x$. So, if we want to analyze the general impact of weights and andness/orness on the percept of overall importance of an input, we must always assume $y \neq x$.

The percept of overall importance of any input is an increasing function of its weight, but at the same time, the percept of overall importance is also an increasing function of andness (or orness) of the aggregator, as shown in Fig. 2.2.18. These two impacts are not independent. The impact of weights is also affected by the degree of simultaneity/substitutability, i.e., by andness/orness. In the case of very high andness, the aggregator $z = Wx \lozenge \bar{W}y$ is a model of very high simultaneity where all inputs must be almost perfectly satisfied. Indeed, if $\alpha \rightarrow 1$ then $z = Wx \Diamond \bar{W}y \rightarrow x \wedge y$ and the impact of relative importance disappears, i.e., it becomes zero. Therefore, the impact of relative importance is attenuated by the high andness or high orness and has the maximum value in the point of minimum andness/orness: $\min(\alpha, \omega) = \min(\alpha, 1-\alpha) = \frac{1}{2}$, i.e., for $\alpha = \omega = 1-\alpha = \frac{1}{2}$. This is called *andness-domination* (or *orness-domination*) and investigated in Section 2.5.1.2. The expected impacts of andness/orness and relative weights are located in gray areas shown in Fig. 2.2.19.

The percept of overall importance of an input in a GCD aggregation block (either an attribute or an aggregated suitability degree) as a function of andness and weight can be modeled as shown in Fig. 2.2.20. The central point C of this function in the case of two variables corresponds to medium weight $W = 0.5$, medium andness $\alpha = 0.5$, and medium overall importance $V = 0.5$. As the relative importance increases, the V-shaped function of the percept of overall importance moves up from the central point. Similarly, as the relative importance decreases, the corresponding V-shaped function of the percept of overall importance moves down from the central point. This model is in qualitative agreement with observable compound percepts of overall importance. Such percepts are very important because they can be obtained from stakeholders, domain experts, and nonprofessional participants in evaluation process and

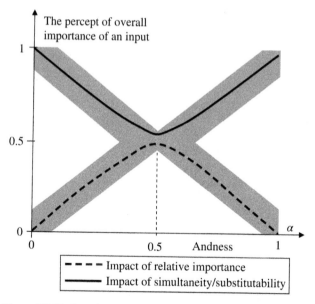

Figure 2.2.19 Complementary impact of simultaneity/substitutability and relative importance.

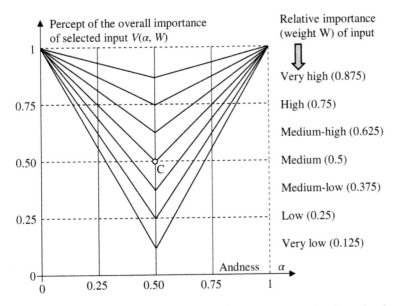

Figure 2.2.20 Model of the percept of overall importance as a function of andness and weight.

then used to model aggregators compatible with expectations and requirements of such DMs.

If we want to model properties shown in Fig. 2.2.19, it is necessary to investigate whether aggregators based on means support desired properties. In the case of weighted power mean the corresponding analysis is exemplified in Fig. 2.2.21 for equal weights and two different values of x and y. The function $r = \rho(\alpha)$ (Chapter 2.4) is used to compute the exponent r for a given value of andness α. Similarly to the previous example of GPA ($\alpha = 0.5$), the impact of relative importance $\partial z/\partial W$ depends on the difference between x and y; if $x \approx y$ we are in vicinity of idempotency area and the impact of weight is low. According to Fig. 2.2.21, weighted power means sufficiently support the concept of overall importance observable in human evaluation reasoning and presented in Fig. 2.2.19.

(P₂₃) Decomposition of Overall Importance

If several attributes are inputs of an aggregator, humans instinctively compare them and then rank them according to the percept of their overall importance. The percept of overall importance of an attribute is a compound concept that can be decomposed into its components. We introduced the logic importance and relative importance in (P₂₁). However, in addition to these basic

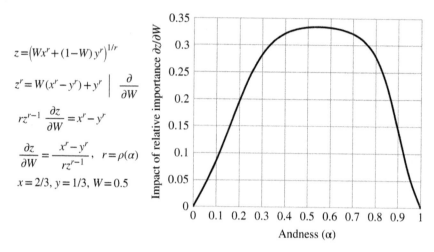

On the left side of the figure:

$$z = \left(Wx^r + (1-W) y^r \right)^{1/r}$$

$$z^r = W(x^r - y^r) + y^r \qquad \frac{\partial}{\partial W}$$

$$rz^{r-1} \frac{\partial z}{\partial W} = x^r - y^r$$

$$\frac{\partial z}{\partial W} = \frac{x^r - y^r}{rz^{r-1}}, \quad r = \rho(\alpha)$$

$$x = 2/3, \ y = 1/3, \ W = 0.5$$

Figure 2.2.21 The impact of relative importance in the case of weighted power mean.

components, we can also observe some derived components. Therefore, in the case of GCD aggregators we can identify the following four components:

1) *Logic importance:* High andness makes all input attributes important because their presence becomes highly desirable or even mandatory, yielding a high penalty for the insufficient presence/satisfaction of any input. High orness makes all input attributes important because their presence/satisfaction yields a high reward. The high satisfaction of a single input can be sufficient to satisfy a compound criterion. The high andness or the high orness significantly contribute to the percept of importance for all GCD inputs. Let us note that this is a percept of collective importance of all inputs of a GCD aggregator.

2) *Relative importance:* In a group of attributes, decision makers always know what is the most important and the least important component. High relative importance additionally contributes to the percept of the overall importance of a specific attribute.

3) *Sensitivity features:* An input attribute (x_i) becomes important if its variations significantly affect the aggregated (output) degree of satisfaction (y) of a compound criterion. In other words, a large value of $\partial y / \partial x_i$ significantly contributes to the perception of importance of x_i.

4) *Tradeoff (compensative) features:* An attribute can be important because its presence can significantly compensate for the absence of other attributes. In a complementary case, an attribute can be important because its absence cannot be compensated by other attributes. So, the compensative (tradeoff) features, either positive or negative, also contribute to the perception of overall importance.

In the case of GCD, the andness/orness, the relative importance of input variables, and the sensitivity and tradeoff features are components that contribute to the percept of overall importance. However, all these components are not independent. The ranking of attributes according to relative importance can frequently be done independently of andness/orness. Similarly, the degrees of simultaneity and replaceability for a group of attributes can regularly be selected without asking whether the attributes are equally or differently important. On the other hand, both the sensitivity and the tradeoff features are just predictable direct consequences of the selected andness/orness and the relative importance. Therefore, in the case of GCD, it is safe to assume that *the percept of overall importance is primarily derived from the desired level of andness/orness (of a group of attributes) and the percept of relative importance (of a specific attribute).*

There are multiple ways to decompose the percept of overall importance and derive the andness/orness and the relative importance of inputs [DUJ12, DUJ15a]. In the case of partial conjunction with andness $\alpha > 1/2$ and n inputs, let the overall importance of inputs be $V_i \in [0,1]$, $i = 1,...,n$. The relative importance $W_i \in [0,1]$, $i = 1,...,n$ is by definition normalized: $W_1 + ... + W_n = 1$. The fundamental assumption that the overall importance is proportional to andness/orness and the relative importance is the following:

$$V_i = c\alpha W_i, \quad c = const., \quad i = 1,...,n.$$

In the special case where all inputs have the same importance, the relative weights are $W_i = 1/n$, $i = 1,...,n$ and the overall importance is

$$V_i = c\alpha/n, \quad i = 1,...,n.$$

If we want the highest level of andness $\alpha = 1$ to correspond to the highest overall importance $V_i = 1$, $i = 1,...,n$, then the constant c must be equal to n. Consequently the percept of overall importance is

$$V_i = n\alpha W_i, \quad i = 1,...,n.$$

From this formula we get the following decomposition method:

$$\sum_{i=1}^{n} V_i = n\alpha \sum_{i=1}^{n} W_i = n\alpha,$$

$$\alpha = \frac{V_1 + ... + V_n}{n},$$

$$W_i = \frac{V_i}{n\alpha} = \frac{V_i}{V_1 + ... + V_n}, \quad i = 1,...,n.$$

The above derivation can be used as a proof of the following theorem:

Theorem 2.2.1. *If the overall importance is proportional to andness/orness and the relative importance, then the andness is the mean overall importance and the relative importance is the normalized overall importance.*

This theorem shows the relationship between the formal logic concept of simultaneity and the semantic concept of importance. The necessary degree of simultaneity (andness) is a direct consequence of the percept of overall importance.

(P₂₄) Threshold Andness and Threshold Orness

The use of hard and soft GCD is ubiquitous in human reasoning. The threshold andness is the border between SPC and HPC, and the threshold orness is the border between SPD and HPD. It is natural to expect that HPC has a higher level of andness than SPC. Similarly, we assume that HPD has a higher level of orness than SPD. The values of threshold andness α_θ and the threshold orness ω_θ determine the nature of GCD and obviously play a very important role in GL. Following are three characteristic cases of the threshold andness and orness values of GCD aggregators:

1) GCD is either strictly soft or strictly hard for all levels of andness/orness (there is no support for the hard behavior in one segment of andness/orness and the soft behavior in another segment of andness/orness).
2) Both hard and soft versions of PC and PD are available, and the threshold values α_θ and ω_θ are fixed (defined by the selected model of GCD).
3) Both hard and soft versions of PC and PD are available, and the threshold values α_θ and ω_θ are adjustable by the decision maker.

An example of an aggregator that does not support HPC and HPD is the exponential mean $x \Diamond y = r^{-1} \ln(0.5e^{rx} + 0.5e^{ry})$, $r \in \mathbb{R}$, that offers only soft partial conjunction and soft partial disjunction. It supports the conditions $1 \Diamond y = x \Diamond 1 = 1$ and $0 \Diamond y = x \Diamond 0 = 0$ only in the extreme cases of full disjunction and full conjunction, i.e., only for $r = \pm \infty$. An example of an aggregator that does not support SPC is a (nonmonotonic) counter-harmonic mean $x \Diamond y = (x^r + y^r)/(x^{r-1} + y^{r-1})$, which is nondecreasing monotonic (i.e., an aggregator) only for $0 \le r \le 1$ (and $r = \pm \infty$) and conjunctive for $0 \le r < 1$ and $r = -\infty$. Consequently, for each partial conjunction the exponents in the denominator are negative, yielding $0 \Diamond y = x \Diamond 0 = 0$, and therefore the partial conjunction is always hard. A typical example of fixed threshold values defined by the selected aggregator is the power mean $z = (0.5x^r + 0.5y^r)^{1/r}$ where $\alpha_\theta = 2/3$ (for $r = 0$) and $\omega_\theta = 1$, or its De Morgan's dual $z = 1 - [0.5(1-x)^r + 0.5(1-y)^r]^{1/r}$ where $\omega_\theta = 2/3$ and $\alpha_\theta = 1$.

Following are basic observations related to cases where the threshold and-ness/orness values of HPC and HPD are fixed:

- Evaluators can rather easily adapt to values of α_θ and ω_θ that are the property of a selected type of aggregator. In other words, α_θ and ω_θ are not adjustable, but can be indirectly selected as a consequence of selecting a specific form of GCD.
- The symmetric case $(\alpha_\theta = \omega_\theta)$ can be implemented using De Morgan's duals. Depending on application, the symmetric case can be more applicable or less applicable than the asymmetric case $(\alpha_\theta \neq \omega_\theta)$.
- Special symmetric case $\alpha_\theta = \omega_\theta = \frac{3}{4}$ provides the uniform distribution of HPC, SPC, SPD, and HPD. This special case is the default case. It should be used in all situations where DMs cannot provide convincing proof that some of four versions of GCD must be more present than other versions.
- In some applications, evaluators use aggregators that do not support HPC and/or HPD (the threshold values $\alpha_\theta < 1$ and $\omega_\theta < 1$ do not exist).

In the area of evaluation criteria, the intuitive percept of the overall impor-tance of an input suitability degree is related to the concepts of andness and orness, and that is an observable property of human reasoning. Let us again use the example of a homebuyer who feels that the location of home and the quality of home are rather important. The homebuyer can easily answer the fol-lowing question: "would you buy a quality home in a very bad location, or a very bad home in an excellent location?" If the answer is "no" (i.e., the requirements are mandatory and the aggregator must be a HPC) then the explanation for "no" is regularly "because both location and quality are very important to me." In other words, as the percept of importance increases, there is a level of impor-tance where the inputs become mandatory (the homebuyer/evaluator is not ready to accept alternatives that do not satisfy one of mandatory inputs). Obvi-ously, the percept of high importance at some point transforms into hard and-ness (or hard orness). Similarly, the mandatory or sufficient attributes create an overall percept of high importance (P$_{21}$).

It is not an observable property of human reasoning to claim that an attribute has no importance, but it must be mandatory (or, in a disjunctive case, suffi-cient). Of course, exceptions are possible, and there are always people who take a seat in the tails of normal distribution and enjoy generating extreme opinions, but generally we can observe the relationship shown in Fig. 2.2.18 and refined in Fig. 2.2.22. So, in this context it is legitimate to ask decision makers the question "at what level of the overall importance do the important simultaneous require-ments become mandatory (or, in a disjunctive case with replaceable require-ments, sufficient)?" This question is suitable for all respondents and it can be used as a simplified substitute for question "What is the level of andness where the soft partial conjunction becomes the hard partial conjunction (i.e., what is the threshold andness)?"

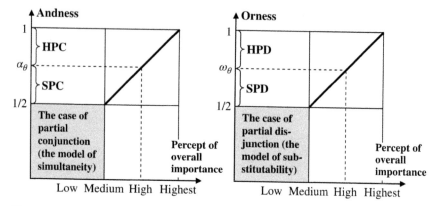

Figure 2.2.22 Relationships between the percepts of overall importance and the level of andness/orness in the cases of simultaneity and substitutability.

We designed an experiment to investigate the expert and nonexpert opinions about the location of threshold andness/orness. The experiment was based on 16 verbalized levels of importance presented in Table 2.2.5. We explained that if we aggregate important components then at some critical level of importance the components become mandatory (i.e., we confidently reject all objects that fail to satisfy the requirements related to any of mandatory components). In other words, we would like to ask, *"At what level of andness does a zero*

Table 2.2.5 The percept of overall importance in the case of 16 levels.

Percept of overall importance		Conjunction		Disjunction	
#	Level of importance	Andness	Symbol	Orness	Symbol
16	Highest	1	C	1	D
15	Slightly below highest	15/16	C++	15/16	D++
14	Very high	7/8	C+	7/8	D+
13	Slightly above high	13/16	C+−	13/16	D+−
12	High	3/4	CA	3/4	DA
11	Slightly below high	11/16	C−+	11/16	D−+
10	Medium-high	5/8	C−	5/8	D−
9	Slightly above medium	9/16	C−−	9/16	D−−
8	Medium	1/2	A	1/2	A
7	Slightly below medium				
...	....				
0	Lowest				

suitability score in any input result in zero aggregate score?" In this case it is convenient to replace andness with its proxy, the percept of overall importance. Then, two alternative versions of this question, suitable for general population, are: *"According to your feeling of importance, what is the most appropriate threshold level of importance (from 8 to 16) where components become mandatory?"* or simply, *"At what level of the overall importance do the important simultaneous requirements become mandatory?"*

The above question was given to 62 leading experts (all of them successful researchers in the area of fuzzy decision methods) and 83 nonexperts (low division undergraduate students). The distributions of expert and nonexpert opinions are presented in Fig. 2.2.23, and they show a remarkable agreement. The correlation between answers of experts and nonexperts is 97.1%.

According to Fig. 2.2.23, 82.2% of experts and 78.3% of nonexperts agree that the threshold andness should be in the range $0.75 \leq \alpha_\theta \leq 0.875$ (from CA to C+). The mean value of threshold andness $\bar{\alpha}_\theta$ and its coefficient of variation v_α are

$$\bar{\alpha}_\theta = \begin{cases} 0.805 & \text{(experts)} \\ 0.813 & \text{(non–experts)} \end{cases} ; \quad v_\alpha = \begin{cases} 11.6\% & \text{(experts)} \\ 12.2\% & \text{(non–experts)} \end{cases}$$

The distributions show two peaks, at CA and C+. The reason for this phenomenon is the imprecision of human perceptual assessment where major categories (e.g., medium, high, very high) attract more attention than intermediate categories. The same phenomenon was visible in the assessment of weights (see [DUJ04a] and Section 2.2.6) where the majority of participants select weights (w) that belong to major categories satisfying either $w \bmod 10 = 0$ or $w \bmod 5 = 0$ (Fig. 2.2.27).

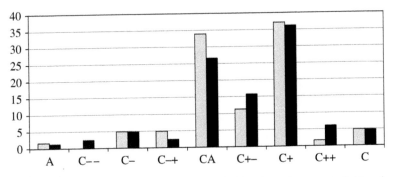

Figure 2.2.23 Distribution of estimated threshold andness for experts (left) and nonexperts (right).

Following are conclusions that can be derived from the presented experiment:

- Threshold andness and threshold orness are parameters that most people relate to a selected critical level of the perception of overall importance.
- Generally, the threshold andness and the threshold orness should be adjustable parameters of aggregation operators. Decision makers should be able to justify the selected values of threshold andness/orness or to use acceptable default values (e.g., 75%).
- For convincing majority of approximately 80% of people the threshold andness is in the range from CA to C+, i.e., the threshold andness is 75% or more. According to our experiments the area of soft conjunction (or disjunction) should be greater than or equal to the area of hard conjunction (or disjunction).
- The threshold andness of power means defined by the geometric mean is 2/3 (66.7%) and in most cases that seems to be too low. In the family of power means a more appropriate threshold aggregator would be the harmonic mean since its andness is 77.26%.
- The uniform distribution of HPC, SPC, SPD, and HPD based on $\alpha_\theta = \omega_\theta = 0.75$ is consistent with the expectations of the majority of people and can serve as a default case.

2.2.4 Multipolarity: Grouping and Aggregation of Semantically Heterogeneous Inputs

Compound models of evaluation reasoning include suitability aggregation structures based on superposition of basic logic functions: GCD, PA, and negation (set L10 introduced in Section 2.1.8). Many aggregation structures are *semantically homogeneous* in the sense that all inputs either do support or do not support annihilators. GCD is a semantically homogeneous type of function. This form of homogeneity means that all inputs have the same logical status: they can be all desirable/optional, or all mandatory, or all sufficient.

In the first case, if all inputs in a group are desirable/optional, then a partial satisfaction of only one of them is sufficient to produce nonzero satisfaction of the whole group. Of course, some inputs are more important and contribute more to the overall satisfaction, and some are less important, but logically all inputs have the same status.

In the second case, all inputs in a group are mandatory. In this case all of them must be partially satisfied in order to generate positive satisfaction of the whole group. Again, not all of them are equally important, but logically they all support the same annihilator 0.

In the third case, all inputs are sufficient. In this case any one of them is capable (i.e., sufficient) to produce full satisfaction for the whole group, provided it is fully satisfied. A partial satisfaction of inputs yields a partial satisfaction of the group requirements. A zero output is generated if and only if all inputs are zero.

The semantic homogeneity is frequently observable in human reasoning. However, we can also frequently observe *semantic heterogeneity*, where inputs can be grouped in groups that have different logical status and functionality. The most frequent such aggregators are used to aggregate mandatory and optional inputs. If any mandatory input is not satisfied, the output suitability is zero. This is not the case with optional inputs. They can have zero values and that will penalize (reduce) the output, but it will not annihilate.

In this section we investigate four characteristic observable forms of semantic heterogeneity that are usually called multipolarity [TRE14, TRE16]. The first is the most frequent form of bipolarity: the aggregation of heterogeneous mandatory and optional inputs. The second aggregation form is bipolarity where we aggregate heterogeneous sufficient and optional inputs. The third form is tripolarity—the aggregation of heterogeneous mandatory, desired, and optional inputs, or the aggregation of sufficient, desired, and optional inputs. The fourth form is the bipolarity of positive and negative inputs, i.e., the aggregation of desirable inputs (those that we want to satisfy as much as possible) and undesirable inputs (those that we want to satisfy as little as possible).

(P$_{25}$) Conjunctive Bipolarity: Mandatory and Desired/Optional Requirements

Very frequently, intuitive evaluators use asymmetric inputs that combine a *mandatory input* $m \in I$, $I = [0,1]$ and a *desired* (but nonmandatory, i.e., *optional*) input $d \in I$. The resulting suitability z is a function of two variables: $z = A_{m/d}(m,d)$. To support different roles of inputs the function $A_{m/d} : I^2 \to I$ must satisfy the following conditions:

$$A_{m/d}(0,d) = 0, \qquad 0 \le d \le 1,$$
$$0 < A_{m/d}(m,0) < m, \quad 0 < m \le 1,$$
$$m \le A_{m/d}(m,1) \le 1, \quad 0 \le m \le 1.$$

In other words, if the mandatory requirement is not satisfied, then the evaluated object is not acceptable. However, if the desired input is not satisfied, that reduces (penalizes) the output suitability z without rejecting such an object. The mean value of difference $m - A_{m/d}(m,0)$ is called the *average penalty*. If the desired input is perfectly satisfied, this yields an appropriate reward (a positive increment of output preference z above the value of m). The mean value of difference $A_{m/d}(m,1) - m$ is called the *average reward*.

For example, the evaluation of home location may include the distance from work (as a mandatory requirement) and the distance from entertainment locations (as a desired requirement). The evaluation of monetary compensation (in a job selection model) may include the monthly salary (as a mandatory requirement) and fringe benefits (as a desired requirement).

It is important to note that mandatory and desired requirements are asymmetric in a formal logic way, and their differences cannot be expressed only as differences in weights. The function $A_{m/d}(m, d)$ was introduced in [DUJ74b] and further investigated in [DUJ79a]. It is called the *conjunctive partial absorption (CPA)* because it is a soft computing generalization of the concept of conjunctive total absorption $m \wedge (m \vee d) = m$ (in this case, the input d is completely absorbed).

The conjunctive partial absorption function can be implemented in various ways. The simplest penalty-only example of this function that uses the full conjunction is $z = m \wedge (0.5m + 0.5d)$, shown in Fig. 2.2.24.

Conjunctive bipolarity is frequently encountered in human reasoning and expressed in verbalized form. Verbalization of criteria is important in the context of flexible database querying and was studied in many papers; a summary of various approaches was provided in [TRE16]. The verbalization of conjunctive bipolarity of two criteria C_m and C_d is based on so called *"and if possible"* connective [BOS12], which is used as an aggregator in the expression "C_m *and if possible* C_d." The meaning of this expression is that C_m is considered a criterion that must be satisfied, while C_d is less important but desirable. If possible, we would like to have both C_m and C_d, but if it is not possible to get C_d, that is a less desirable combination, but still acceptable. For example, a simplified job selection criterion could be "*a high salary and if possible good fringe benefits.*" This verbalization shows that C_m (high salary) is a mandatory requirement and C_d (fringe benefits) is desired for full satisfaction, but it is not indispensable. The criterion is the standard conjunctive partial absorption. Therefore, the conjunctive bipolarity is frequently encountered in a verbalized form.

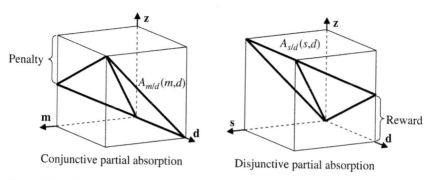

Conjunctive partial absorption   Disjunctive partial absorption

Figure 2.2.24 The concepts of conjunctive and disjunctive partial absorption.

CPA is a conjunctive aggregator. It combines HPC in mandatory input and SPC in optional input. Consequently, CPA can also be called the asymmetric conjunction.

(P$_{26}$) Disjunctive Bipolarity: Sufficient and Desired/Optional Requirements

The requirements that are symmetrical to the mandatory and desired case are the aggregation of a sufficient input (s) and a desired/optional input (d). Similarly to the mandatory/optional reasoning, the sufficient/optional reasoning is also easily observable. For example, a homebuyer might evaluate a parking space considering that a private garage is sufficient to completely solve the parking problem, while a good street parking is optional and to some (reduced) degree acceptable solution. If the output of this function of two variables is $z = A_{s/d}(s,d)$, then the function $A_{s/d} : I^2 \rightarrow I$ must satisfy the following conditions:

$$A_{s/d}(1,d) = 1, \quad 0 \le d \le 1,$$
$$0 < A_{s/d}(s,0) \le s, \quad 0 < s \le 1,$$
$$s < A_{s/d}(s,1) \le 1, \quad 0 \le s \le 1.$$

The average penalty and the average reward are respectively defined as mean values of differences $s - A_{s/d}(s,0)$ and $A_{s/d}(s,1) - s$. In system evaluation practice, this asymmetric criterion is slightly less frequent than the mandatory and desired/optional case. The function $A_{s/d}(s, d)$ is called the *disjunctive partial absorption (DPA)* because it is a soft computing generalization of the disjunctive total absorption $s \vee (s \wedge d) = s$. A reward-only sample of this function that uses full disjunction is $z = s \vee (0.5s + 0.5d)$, shown in Fig. 2.2.24. Conjunctive and disjunctive partial absorption are presented in Chapter 2.6.

DPA is a disjunctive aggregator. It combines HPD in sufficient input and SPD in optional input. Consequently, DPA can also be called the asymmetric disjunction.

Similarly to conjunctive bipolarity the verbalization of disjunctive bipolarity of two criteria C_s and C_d is based on so called "or else" connective [BOS12], which is used as an aggregator in the expression "C_s or else C_d." The meaning of this asymmetric disjunctive expression is that C_s is considered a significantly better alternative than C_d. In fact, we are completely satisfied if we can satisfy C_s, but if that is not possible, then C_d is still an acceptable (but less desirable) alternative. For example, a car buyer might be interested in buying "*a new car or else a good used car.*" This verbalization of the car age criterion shows that C_s (a new car) is sufficient to fully satisfy the car buyer and C_d (a good used car) is an acceptable alternative. There is a difference between this example and the example of criterion "*private garage or else a good street parking.*" In the first example, the disjunction is exclusive (we cannot have a car that is at the same time new and used); in the second example the disjunction is inclusive (we can have private garage and simultaneously a good street parking). Both cases can be modeled using a disjunctive partial absorption, but the simplicity of the first case provides the possibility to use a simple elementary criterion Crit(car age) = {(new, 100), (used, 67)} (we are 100% satisfied with a new car and 67% with a used car). Similarly to the conjunctive bipolarity, the disjunctive bipolarity is also frequently encountered in a verbalized form.

(P$_{27}$) Tripolarity: Mandatory, Desired, and Optional Requirements
In some cases, the mandatory/desired requirements can be nested to include three levels: mandatory (m), desired (d), and optional (t) [SU87]. The role of mandatory input is the same as in the $A_{m/d}(m, d)$ case: if the mandatory requirement is not satisfied, then the whole compound requirement is not satisfied regardless of the satisfaction of desired and optional inputs. Desired and optional inputs may be logically equivalent, but their effects have different intensity. The penalty and reward caused by the optional input are less than the penalty and reward caused by the desired input. The function $z = A_{m/d/o}(m, d, t)$ has similar properties as $z = A_{m/d}(m,d)$:

$$A_{m/d/o}(0,d,t) = 0, \qquad\qquad 0 \le d \le 1, \;\; 0 \le t \le 1,$$

$$0 < A_{m/d/o}(m,0,0) < m, \qquad\qquad 0 < m \le 1,$$

$$m \le A_{m/d/o}(m,1,1) \le 1, \qquad\qquad 0 \le m \le 1,$$

$$A_{m/d/o}(m,0,a) < A_{m/d/o}(m,a,0), \;\; 0 < a < 1,$$

$$A_{m/d/o}(m,1,a) > A_{m/d/o}(m,a,1), \;\; 0 < a < 1.$$

These conditions specify the difference between the desired and optional input only as a matter of degree. Sometimes, we can use a subtle addition to these conditions so that the desired input must be satisfied in order to enable the effects of the optional input:

$$A_{m/d/o}(m,0,a) = A_{m/d/o}(m,0,b), \quad \forall(a,b) \in I^2,$$
$$A_{m/d/o}(m,d,a) < A_{m/d/o}(m,d,b), \quad d > 0, \;\; a < b.$$

Tripolarity can be verbalized in a similar way as conjunctive and disjunctive bipolarity. In [TRE16] the general nesting of conjunctive partial absorption aggregators was verbalized as follows:

C_1 *and if possible* C_2 *and if possible* C_3 $\cdots$ *and if possible* C_k.

Similar verbalization for nested disjunctive partial absorption is the following:

C_1 *or else* C_2 *or else* C_3 $\cdots$ *or else* C_k.

Theoretically, k can be any value. However, so far we found no empirical evidence that DMs might need more than two levels of nesting of nonmandatory or nonsufficient inputs because the impact of C_k for $k > 3$ can easily become negligible.

(P$_{28}$) Bipolarity of Desirable (Positive) and Undesirable (Negative) Inputs
In many evaluation problems, it is possible to differentiate two opposed groups of inputs: desirable and undesirable. Of course, each elementary attribute criterion differentiates between desired and undesired values: those that are fully desirable are assigned the suitability score 1, and the opposite fully undesirable values are assigned the suitability score 0. Between these two extremes there are partially desirable and partially undesirable values. This is a standard way of structuring evaluation criteria.

Bipolarity of positive and negative inputs is defined as a method for structuring evaluation criteria where we define a group of "positive attributes" and a group of "negative attributes." This form of grouping is observable in human reasoning: decision makers easily identify the most desirable properties that form a "positive pole" of decision process and the most undesirable properties that form a "negative pole." For example, the positive pole for homebuyer can be the proximity to work for parents, the proximity to school for children, the proximity to public transportation, etc. Similarly, the negative pole can be the proximity to industrial pollution, the proximity to busy airport, the proximity to cemetery, etc. In such situations we assume that the set of n input attributes $\{x_1, ..., x_n\}$ can be decomposed into two disjoint subsets: k desirable attributes $\{d_1, ..., d_k\}$ and m undesirable attributes $\{u_1, ..., u_m\}$ as follows:

$$\{x_1,...,x_n\} = \{d_1,...,d_k\} \cup \{u_1,...,u_m\}, \quad \{d_1,...,d_k\} \cap \{u_1,...,u_m\} = \varnothing .$$

Now, we have to create the LSP criterion $X = A(x_1,...,x_n)$ that includes the desirable and undesirable attributes. A bipolar approach to computing the overall suitability X consists of creating an LSP criterion $d = D(d_1,...,d_k)$ for desired inputs and a separate LSP criterion for undesirable attributes $u = U(u_1,...,u_m)$. Here d denotes the degree of suitability of desirable inputs and u denotes the degree of unsuitability of undesirable inputs. Of course, the goal of decision maker is to simultaneously get the highest value of suitability d and the lowest value of unsuitability u. According to introduction provided in P$_{14}$, the corresponding mathematical model for this form of aggregation is the partial abjunction function (the partial conjunction of d and negated u):

$$S = A(x_1,...,x_n) = D(d_1,...,d_k) \; \Delta \; [1 - U(u_1,...,u_m)].$$

This approach is convenient in situation where there is a sharp contrast between positive and negative attributes and decision maker who has strong preferences about satisfying positive attributes and avoiding negative attributes. Of course, these conditions are not always satisfied. Frequently, we have attributes that are not dramatically positive or dramatically negative, but moderately desirable or moderately undesirable. In such cases, we can decide to work strictly with positive attributes. The idea is to invert the set of undesirable attributes transforming them to desirable attributes. For example, instead of proximity to the busy airport, we can use the distance from the busy airport. In this way, the set of undesirable attributes $\{u_1, ..., u_m\}$ can be converted to a set of desirable/suitable attributes $\{s_1, ..., s_m\}$. That can be done using the negation (inversion) of elementary criteria described in P_{14}, or if $u_1, ..., u_m$ denotes unsuitability degrees, then using standard negation $s_i = \bar{u}_i = 1 - u_i$, $i = 1,...,m$. Then we can compute the suitability of this group of inputs $s = S(s_1,...,s_m)$ and use the standard form of partial conjunction to compute the overall suitability:

$$X = A(x_1,...,x_n) = D(d_1,...,d_k) \; \Delta \; S(s_1,...,s_m).$$

We can conclude that multipolarity is observable in human reasoning as an organizational form of systematic thinking that is useful for structuring LSP criteria. Multipolarity is not an expression of logic functionality beyond the scope of GL. Multipolar logic relationships can be expressed within the set B10 = {CC, C, HPC, SPC, A, SPD, HPD, D, DD, NOT} of basic GL functions (see Section 2.1.8). Multipolarity affects the selection and grouping of attributes, the organization of elementary criteria, and the selection and use of canonic aggregation structures. However, evaluation criteria can always be based on desirable (positive) attributes and aggregation within the scope of GL.

2.2.5 Grouping and Aggregation of Semantically Homogeneous Inputs

Logic aggregation of suitability degrees is the essential component of evaluation reasoning. In each node of the suitability aggregation tree, the process of intuitive aggregation is limited to small number of inputs, typically two to five. Humans intuitively compare pairs of inputs to establish their relative importance and in the case of n inputs the number of pairs is $n(n-1)/2$, which is a fast growing quadratic function. For example, in the case of five inputs, the number of pairs is 10 and simultaneous intuitive investigation of 10 relationships may be too demanding and unreliable for most evaluators. Consequently, the process of intuitive aggregation is based on evaluation in small groups of related inputs. The same process is then repeated at higher hierarchical levels in a way defined by SMER in P_4. That process is based on algebraic properties of associativity and distributivity.

(P₂₉) Grouping Inputs Using Associativity

In intuitive system evaluation associativity means that DM can aggregate preferences (suitability degrees) in any order, or in any disjoint subgroups, yielding always the same (or very similar) final result. In the context of GL it is useful to know how frequent is the use of associativity and whether we need a strict satisfaction of this algebraic property in the process of evaluation.

The preference aggregation process regularly follows the structure of the attribute tree, and consequently, that tree defines the order of aggregation. A simple example of such a tree is shown in Fig. 2.2.25. In both the intuitive and formal aggregation process the number of inputs in a single aggregation step is limited by human inability to simultaneously handle large number of inputs (see P_{31} and [MIL56]). The most frequent number of inputs in aggregation nodes is from 2 to 5, as exemplified in Fig. 2.2.25 in the case where all inputs have the same weight (1/15). The relative importance of each input is determined as a product of weights along the path from the leaf to the root of the tree (e.g., the weights for attribute x_1 are 1/3, 1/2, and 2/5; their product is 1/15).

The preference aggregation structures are not arbitrary, but carefully designed following justifiable properties of the evaluation criterion, expressed as an attribute tree. Consequently, the aggregation process does not need associativity in the sense that it is possible to aggregate any input with any other input, in any order, and for any number of inputs. Both intuitive and formal aggregation processes strictly follow the structure of the attribute tree.

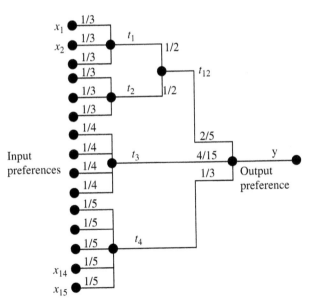

Figure 2.2.25 An example of preference aggregation tree (two to five inputs per node).

Consequently, the aggregation occurs at predefined aggregation nodes, and the associativity must be taken into account during the process of design of the attribute tree. To preserve the accuracy of evaluation models, and to control the weights and aggregation operators, evaluators create aggregation structures that have small number of inputs in each aggregation node. There are various techniques to achieve this goal, and the associativity of aggregators is one of them. If we have a node with more inputs, e.g., 6, then we can organize the aggregation in semantically justifiable groups, e.g., $3 + 3$, or $4 + 2$, or $5 + 1$, or $2 + 2 + 2$, or any other justifiable pattern. If the associativity holds (strictly or approximately), then in all cases the result of aggregation should be the same (or very similar).

Taking into account that the precision of input preferences, generated and used by DMs, is also limited, it follows that from the practical point of view the approximate associativity (studied in [DUJ75a] and in Chapter 2.5) can be sufficient. Of course, associativity has significance as a theoretical algebraic property. In practice, however, from the standpoint of both intuitive and formal GL, the significance of associativity is rather modest. More precisely, so far there is no empirical evidence that mathematical models that could accurately support associativity have any observable advantage over mathematical models that support associativity approximately but with sufficient accuracy.

Mathematical expression of associativity for aggregator $A_2 : I^2 \rightarrow I$ is the associativity functional equation

$$A_2(A_2(x_1,x_2),x_3) = A_2(x_1,A_2(x_2,x_3)).$$

For aggregator $\lozenge$ we can write $(x_1 \lozenge x_2) \lozenge x_3 = x_1 \lozenge (x_2 \lozenge x_3) = x_1 \lozenge x_2 \lozenge x_3$. This property enables an associative design of aggregators of n variables using aggregators of two variables:

$$A_3(x_1,x_2,x_3) = A_2(A_2(x_1,x_2),x_3), \quad A_3 : I^3 \rightarrow I,$$

$$A_4(x_1,x_2,x_3,x_4) = A_2(A_3(x_1,x_2,x_3),x_4) = A_2(A_2(A_2(x_1,x_2),x_3),x_4), \quad A_4 : I^4 \rightarrow I,$$

$$\ldots$$

$$A_n(x_1,\ldots,x_n) = A_2(A_{n-1}(x_1,\ldots,x_{n-1}),x_n)$$

$$= A_2(A_2(A_2(\ldots A_2(x_1,x_2),\ldots),x_{n-1}),x_n), \quad A_n : I^n \rightarrow I.$$

It is easy to note that these relations should be weighted to avoid reducing the impact of variables that are aggregated in the initial steps of the recursive process. Indeed, $A_n(x_1, \ldots, x_n)$ assumes that all inputs $x_1, \ldots, x_n$ have the same impact. In the case of an aggregator of two variables, $A_2(x_1, x_2)$, the variables x_1 and x_2 are assumed to have the same impact. However, in the aggregator $A_2(A_{n-1}(x_1,\ldots,x_{n-1}),x_n)$, the components $A_{n-1}(x_1,\ldots,x_{n-1})$ and x_n cannot have the same impact because that would make x_n equally important as all other inputs together. So, in the case of preference aggregators, the weight of x_n should be $1/n$, and the weight of $A_{n-1}(x_1,\ldots,x_{n-1})$ should be $(n-1)/n$. In other

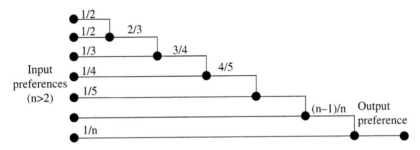

Figure 2.2.26 Aggregator of *n* inputs based on weighted aggregators of two inputs.

words, the presented classic recursive associativity relations should be modified to secure equal impact of all inputs.

If the inputs have different weights, it is necessary to make additional adjustments. The idea behind the weighting is that the product of weights along the path from the root to a specific leaf of the aggregation tree denotes the impact of the leaf. The example in Fig. 2.2.26 shows weights that must be used in the aggregation process in order to secure equal impact of all inputs.

Following this concept, weighted associativity (Chapter 2.5) has significance as a technique for creating aggregators of n variables using aggregators that are defined using only two variables, as shown in Fig. 2.2.26 for the case of equal impact of all input preferences. This is also a technique that some evaluators use in intuitive GL.

(P₃₀) Grouping Inputs Using Distributivity
Similarly to associativity, the distributivity is an algebraic property that in practical evaluation (i.e., in both intuitive and formal GL models) must be considered in the context of designing the preference aggregation tree. For example, suppose that an evaluator considers sports cars:

sports_car = small Δ high_speed Δ high_maneuverability Δ two_seats Δ two_doors.

Then, consider the following distributivity expression:

(red ∇ yellow) Δ sports_car = (red Δ sports_car) ∇ (yellow Δ sports_car)
= (red Δ small Δ high_speed Δ high_maneuverability Δ two_seats Δ two_doors)
∇ (yellow Δ small Δ high_speed Δ high_maneuverability Δ two_seats Δ two_doors).

To avoid redundancy in GL expressions, DM will most likely always use only the most compact form, i.e., (red ∇ yellow) Δ sports_car, which yields a simple, natural, and nonredundant aggregation tree, without expanding the expression according to distributivity law. Similarly to associativity, the significance of distributivity in GL is rather modest, and so far there is no empirical evidence that mathematical models that could accurately support distributivity have any observable advantage over mathematical models that support distributivity approximately but with sufficient accuracy [DUJ75a].

2.2.6 Imprecision, Incompleteness, Logic Inconsistency, and Errors

> *Humans have a remarkable capability to reason, compute and make rational decisions in an environment of imprecision, uncertainty and incompleteness of information.*
> —Lotfi Zadeh [ZAD16]

Human perceptions frequently include imprecision and uncertainty, resulting in inconsistencies and errors. In addition, many objects of reasoning are classes that have fuzzy borders. Examples of such classes are "high suitability," "low importance," "very high simultaneity" and many other similar concepts we use in evaluation reasoning, soft computing and decision engineering. Not surprisingly, limited accuracy is a natural property of perceptual computing.

(P$_{31}$) Limited Accuracy of Parameters and Incompleteness of Input Attributes
Evaluators select the logical structure of evaluation models and intuitively estimate the majority of their parameters. The accuracy of such estimations is limited, and minor errors are present in all system evaluation activities. This includes both intuitive and formal evaluation. In the case of formal evaluation models, possible errors can be classified in two groups:

1) Errors in assessment of continuous parameters.
2) Errors in selecting logic conditions that are used in evaluation models.

An error is defined as a difference between an estimated value and the corresponding accurate value. In the case of evaluation models there are no objectively measurable accurate values of parameters of evaluation models. Therefore, the accurate value can only be defined (and estimated) as a mean value of opinions of a large population of qualified evaluators. For example, it is reasonable to assume that the majority of evaluation requirements that reflect interests of a large company are better assessed by a team of sufficiently qualified experts than by a single equally qualified evaluator. Unfortunately, large teams of experts are almost never available, and the majority of evaluation criteria are defined by either a single evaluator or a small group of people with heterogeneous backgrounds. Consequently, the estimated parameters of evaluation models regularly differ from the optimum values that correspond to the large population of qualified evaluators.

Knowing the problem of limited accuracy in creating human percepts and then in converting percepts to real numbers, there are various techniques that are developed with intention to maximize the accuracy of data obtained from decision makers. Following are four techniques that can be frequently used:

- Verbalized ratings scales
- Tree search stepwise refinement techniques
- Pairwise comparison techniques for reduction of complexity
- Neural network training of aggregators

Verbalized rating scales use linguistic labels (words) that have familiar meaning and can help in the process of selection of the appropriate magnitude of various GL parameters and input variables. Examples of such labels are low, medium, high, weak, strong, poor, average, good and excellent. So, the familiar meaning of words helps decision makers to select appropriate numeric values of parameters (the design of andness/orness scales is discussed in [DUJ15b]).

The tree search stepwise refinement algorithms are exemplified in Fig. 2.2.16 and in Section 2.9.2. The idea is that the selection process is moving from node to node of a search tree, and in each node (similarly to binary search) it is necessary to make an easy decision of selecting among a very small number of options (typically 2 or 3). A trained evaluator can easily make such decisions, increasing the accuracy of selection in a systematic and justifiable way.

Typical representatives of techniques for reducing complexity are pairwise comparisons techniques [KOC16]. The idea is that pairwise comparisons are the simplest mental discriminations and a convenient way for ranking multiple objects and computing weights (Chapter 2.5). The best-known pairwise comparison method is the Analytic Hierarchy Process (AHP) proposed by Thomas Saaty [SAA77, SAA90, SAA01, SAA06, SAA10]. AHP is a simple technique and in [MOL97] it is qualified as "one of the most popular multicriteria decision-making methodologies available today." It is also used in modern decision-making literature [ISH13, TZE11], as well as a topic for study of inconsistencies in decision making [KOC14, FUL10, KOC16].

Neural network training of aggregators was proposed in [DUJ91] in conjunction with the ANSY software tool for training of preferential neurons (see Chapters 3.4 and 3.5). The method was further studied in [ERD96]. The idea is to consider each aggregator as a preferential neuron and to provide a training set of desired input/output mappings that reflect decision maker goals and requirements. The role of ANSY is to compute all parameters of the necessary aggregator (weights, andness, etc.) so that the aggregator provides the desired mapping specified by user's training set.

Techniques for reducing errors of perceptual computing are useful, but some errors cannot be avoided. The parameters of mathematical models of evaluation criteria include weights, andness, and other parameters that are continuously adjustable real values, most frequently selected from the interval $I = [0,1]$. In the case of continuously adjustable variables, evaluators can feel that two values, p and q, are different only if $|p - q| > \delta$, where δ denotes a corresponding insensitivity zone. For example, no evaluator can claim that the weight of 33% is more appropriate than the weight of 33.3%, but the majority of evaluators would easily select between 30% and 50%.

The problem of selection of real values is usually solved using discretization. In the case of interval $[0,1]$ the interval is replaced by $n + 1$ discrete points: 0, δ, 2δ,..., $n\delta$ where $n\delta = 1$. So, the number of discrete values depends on the evaluator's insensitivity zone: $n = 1/\delta$. Since the discrete values are spaced in increments that an evaluator can accurately differentiate, it follows that evaluators can select one of n values with reasonable confidence. Of course, an internal discrete value $j\delta$ $(0 < j < n)$ is the only representative of all real values from the interval $]j\delta - \delta/2, j\delta + \delta/2]$ and that is an obvious source of errors. The training of evaluators should develop skills of controlling and maximizing the value of n.

Based on Miller's analysis [MIL56], there are reasons to keep n close to the "magical number 7" and in the majority of cases we encounter values $5 \leq n \leq 20$. The value of δ can easily be identified if evaluators are freely selecting the values of continuous parameters, because the distribution of parameters has agglomeration points that are integer multiples of δ [DUJ04a]. For example, the majority of people select weights from the sequence 10%, 20%, ..., 90%; this indicates that $\delta = 0.1$ and $n = 10$. Those who have more experience and/or some training will use weights from the sequence 5%, 10%, ..., 95%; this indicates that $\delta = 0.05$ and $n = 20$.

An experiment with 3418 weights collected from 120 evaluators is presented in Fig. 2.2.27. This experiment shows that the most frequent weights are those that correspond to $\delta = 10\%$. Less frequent are weights from the sequence with

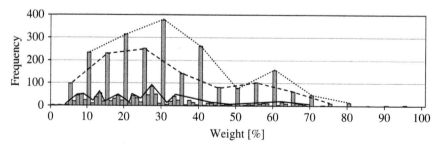

Figure 2.2.27 Distribution of 3418 weights collected from 120 evaluators.

increments $\delta = 5\%$. Finally, the least frequent are more precise estimates where $\delta = 1\%$.

An important special case of discretization is the use of dyadic intervals obtained using the structure of binary tree: $\delta = 1/2^k$, $k = 1,2,\ldots$ (each "child interval" is obtained by partitioning its "parent interval" into two equal halves). Since the number of intervals is now selected from the sequence 2,4,8,16,32, the most frequently used values are 8 and 16.

Basic errors in assessment of continuous parameters include the following:

1) *Errors in weight assessment.* Weights are usually rounded in steps of 5% or 10%. If weights are expressed as integers in the range (0, 100%) then usually $W \bmod 5 = 0$. This indicates an average error in weight selection that can be of the order of 5%.

2) *Andness/orness discretization errors.* Andness and orness are also frequently selected using discrete steps (regularly the dyadic intervals 1/8 or 1/16). This indicates average andness/orness errors that are similar to the weight errors.

3) *Errors caused by polygonal approximations of elementary criteria.* Elementary criteria that evaluate individual attributes are usually defined using piecewise linear approximations of continuous differentiable functions. Consequently, input preferences of aggregation operators are not perfectly accurate.

4) *Training set errors.* Aggregation operators can be interpreted as preferential neurons [DUJ91] and their parameters can be computed from a training set that consists of a table of desired input/output values. However, the training sets of preferential neurons may contain inappropriate and/or inconsistent requests and these inconsistencies are then transformed into errors of the resulting values of parameters.

Fig. 2.2.28 shows an example of the piecewise linear form of an elementary criterion for the response time of a website. The coordinates of breakpoints

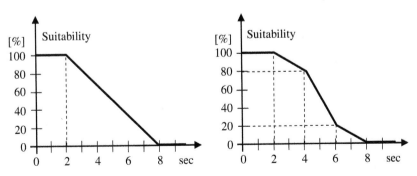

Figure 2.2.28 An example of refinement of an elementary criterion for response time.

are adjustable parameters. The criterion illustrates the case where evaluators believe that response times below 2 seconds are perfectly acceptable, and response times above 8 seconds are fully unacceptable. If evaluators have no additional requirements for the interval between 2 seconds and 8 seconds, then it is reasonable to use in this interval a simple linear interpolation. However, if this is considered imprecise, evaluators can put more effort in investigating expected effects of response time, and produce a multisegment refinement of the initial criterion. This example shows that more effort can yield more precision and reduction of possible errors. Of course, there is always a difference between the polygonal approximation and the unknown optimum curve. This generates unavoidable minor errors of the corresponding preference.

Generally, if for example we have three breakpoints (x_1, y_1), (x_2, y_2), (x_3, y_3) it is possible to use nonlinear Lagrange interpolation:

$$y = \frac{(x-x_2)(x-x_3)}{(x_1-x_2)(x_1-x_3)}y_1 + \frac{(x-x_1)(x-x_3)}{(x_2-x_1)(x_2-x_3)}y_2 + \frac{(x-x_1)(x-x_2)}{(x_3-x_1)(x_3-x_2)}y_3.$$

Using this approach some parts of elementary attribute criteria can look smooth, but that does not increase the available information, hides the location of breakpoints, and in some cases can cause undesirable overshoots and undershoots. Linear interpolation avoids these nonlinear phenomena, reveals the breakpoints, and maximizes simplicity.

Three basic types of elementary criteria are the criteria for preferred large values (L), preferred small values (S) and preferred a range of values (R), illustrated in Fig. 2.2.29. The footprint of uncertainty is presented as shaded areas and its size can vary depending on the capability of evaluator. In three upper examples in Fig. 2.2.29, we assume that the evaluator can select with certainty

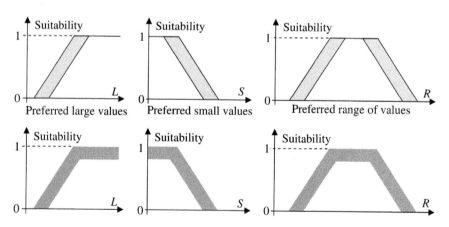

Figure 2.2.29 Typical forms of imprecision and uncertainty in three canonical shapes of attribute criteria.

some regions where the requirements are fully satisfied (suitability = 1). Lower examples illustrate situations where the uncertainty is larger and the criterion function can be anywhere inside the shaded area.

In development of LSP criteria the first step is to select a set of relevant attributes that are used as inputs of evaluation model. Obviously, the completeness of the set of attributes is the first source of possible errors. If we sort n input attributes according to the decreasing conjunctive coefficient of impact γ (an indicator of the overall importance of input attribute, defined in the range [0,100%], and described in Chapter 3.7) then we get a monotonically decreasing sequence $\gamma(k) \geq \gamma(k+1), k = 1,...,n-1$. On the other hand, each attribute should be defined, measured, documented, and evaluated in the same or similar way; consequently, the cost of evaluation is approximately a linear function of the number of attributes: $C(k) = ck, k = 1,...,n, c = const$. These functions are exemplified in Fig. 2.2.30 where the decreasing impact is taken from a real LSP criterion with 27 inputs (Table 4.4.3). This example clearly shows the evaluator's dilemma: as the number of attributes increases, the precision of evaluation increases, but at the same time both the evaluation effort and the cost of evaluation increase linearly. Sooner or later, included will inevitably be attributes with a very low impact on the final result. Therefore, the evaluator must at some point limit the number of inputs, in order to keep a reasonable balance between the cost of evaluation project and the precision of final results. For example, in Fig. 2.2.30 the impact of the most important attribute is 38.52% and the impact of the least important attribute is 1.28%. If we now decide to omit the least

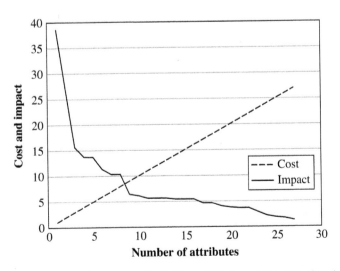

Figure 2.2.30 The impact of individual attribute and the cost of evaluation project as functions of the number of attributes (Section 4.4.4).

significant attribute (or a few of low impact attributes), the evaluation effort decreases linearly and the result of evaluation could change only insignificantly. Therefore, in all evaluation projects evaluators can select an impact threshold and omit attributes below the threshold. That causes controllable minor errors that characterize each evaluation project.

(P₃₂) Inconsistent Logic Conditions and the Problems of Hypersensitivity
Logic conditions that are used in evaluation models should be consistent with observable properties of intuitive GL. However, there are combinations of properties of aggregation operators that can be considered extreme, infrequent in human reasoning, or even counter-intuitive. Some extreme combinations of andness/orness and weights, and some combinations of andness/orness and mandatory/sufficient requirements may be questionable and interpreted as *inconsistent logic conditions*. They include the following:

1) High andness (in the region of hard partial conjunction) or a high orness (in the region of a hard partial disjunction) and a very low weight of an input.
2) Very high andness and nonmandatory inputs (or a dual high orness problem).
3) Low andness (slightly above the neutrality level $\alpha = 1/2$) and mandatory requirements.
4) Low orness (slightly above the neutrality level $\omega = 1/2$) and sufficient requirements.
5) Excessive truth amplification: indiscernible increment of input degree of truth causes significant increment of output degree of truth.

To illustrate these problems let us investigate consequences of the combination of contradictory requirements for high simultaneity (high andness) and low weight. The high simultaneity means that all inputs are very important because they all must be positive and uniformly high. The use of low weight of an input is contradictory to the high simultaneity requirement because it implies a low importance. Let us exemplify this problem using the simple case of harmonic mean of two variables $(\alpha = 77\%)$:

$$z = \frac{1}{W/x + (1-W)/y}.$$

Here W denotes the relative importance of x and $1 - W$ is the relative importance of y. For simplicity, let us assume that $y = 1$. Then the output preference and its first derivative are

$$z(x) = \frac{x}{(1-W)x + W}, \quad \frac{dz}{dx} = z'(x) = \frac{W}{[(1-W)x + W]^2}, \quad z'(0) = 1/W.$$

If the weight W is very small (e.g., less than 5%) then the first derivative $z'(0)$ becomes very large. For example, if $W = 0.02$, then $z'(0) = 50$ and if $x = 0.05$ then

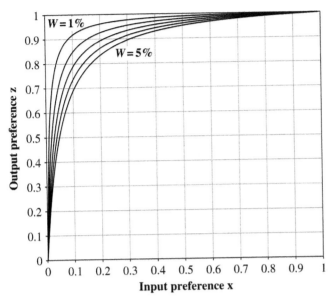

Figure 2.2.31 Function $z = 1/(W/x + 1 - W)$ for $W = 1\%$ (top), 2%, 3%, 4% and 5% (bottom).

$y = 0.725$. Therefore, according to Fig. 2.2.31, changing x in the small range from 0 to 5% causes the change of output from 0 to 72.5%, making the truth amplification of 14.5 times. However, such rapid changes of output preference in a very narrow range of x are *not* an observable property of human reasoning. Quite contrary, the observable property is that humans use truth amplification in moderation and the sensitivity to minute truth increments is never gigantic. The factor of 14.5 is undoubtedly in the area of excessive truth amplification. Consequently, a very small weight combined with a high andness is an example of inconsistent (contradictory) logic conditions that yield undesirable hypersensitivity (unrealistically high truth amplification). That is an example of logic errors typical for unqualified evaluators.

Unfortunately, the hypersensitivity is not restricted only to inconsistent combinations of large andness/orness and small weights. The excessive truth amplification is also a natural property of some aggregators. It is easily visible in the case of frequently used symmetric geometric mean $z = \sqrt{xy}$. Here the weights of x and y are equal (0.5) but nevertheless $\partial z/\partial x = 0.5\sqrt{y/x}$ and small values of x yield huge values of $\partial z/\partial x$. For example, if $x = 0.01$, then $z = 0.1\sqrt{y}$ and if $y = 1$ then $z = 0.1$ and the resulting truth amplification of x is 10. So, it is rather safe to claim that for most humans the truth increment of 1% is indiscernible and consequently, it cannot and should not cause significant impact on the output degree of truth.

The presented example of geometric mean shows a mathematical model inconsistent with human reasoning. That generates an obvious question: Should we use the geometric mean and similar aggregators in decision models? The simple answer is that every aggregator can be used if we can avoid the values of variables in critical regions where the aggregator behaves in unacceptable way. Fortunately, in practical problems it is highly unlikely that an input degree of truth can be 0.01. It can easily be 0 (if a mandatory condition is not satisfied), and most frequently it can take several easily discernible discrete values inside [0,1]. For example, the computer memory size is important in all evaluations of any of countless computerized devices, but the computer memory size is not continuously adjustable: it always comes in a few distinct sizes. Consequently, the corresponding degree of truth of the statement claiming a perfect satisfaction of memory requirements is also a variable that has a few distinct values, where extremely small positive values are highly unlikely. Fortunately, in the case of aggregation structures based on GCD aggregators, the problematic behavior can be encountered only for some specific aggregators (like the geometric mean) and only for extremely small positive values of variables.

Most aggregators do not have such problems. For example, in the case of equal weights the problems of geometric mean do not exist for the harmonic mean:

$$z = \frac{2xy}{x+y}, \quad \frac{\partial z}{\partial x} = 2\left(\frac{y}{x+y}\right)^2,$$

$$\forall y > 0, \quad x = 0 \quad \Rightarrow \quad \frac{\partial z}{\partial x} = 2.$$

Taking into account the frequent use of power means, let us investigate this problem in more detail. The analyzed aggregator is

$$z = [Wx^r + (1-W)y^r]^{1/r},$$

$$\frac{\partial z}{\partial x} = Wx^{r-1}[Wx^r + (1-W)y^r]^{(1-r)/r} = W\left[W + (1-W)\left(\frac{y}{x}\right)^r\right]^{(1-r)/r},$$

$$\forall y > 0, \quad r < 0, \quad x = 0 \quad \Rightarrow \quad \frac{\partial z}{\partial x} = W^{1/r}.$$

If $r < 0$ then the power mean is a model of hard partial conjunction and in Fig. 2.2.32 we present the corresponding sensitivity functions $\partial z/\partial x$ for $x = 0$ and $W = 0.1$ (top), 0.25, 0.5, 0.75 (bottom). We can notice that the harmonic mean and all other aggregators with higher andness in the usual range of weights do not cause the hypersensitivity problems. However, such problems occur in the vicinity of geometric mean, as well as in all questionable cases of high andness and very low weights. The same hypersensitivity problems occur for hard partial disjunction obtained as a De Morgan's dual of hard partial conjunction.

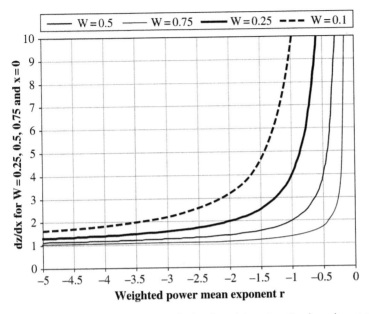

Figure 2.2.32 Sensitivity to inputs for hard partial conjunction based on power means.

Generally, the evaluation logic supports the principle *natura non facit saltum* (nature does nothing in jumps). A sequence of great thinkers who supported the idea that natural properties change gradually rather than suddenly (gradualism) include Aristotle, Gottfried Leibniz, Isaac Newton, and Charles Darwin. Observations of human evaluation reasoning, particularly the phenomena of monotonicity, compensativeness, and limited sensitivity also provide evidence that evaluation reasoning supports gradualism because it is based on human perceptions (of value, importance, etc.) that change gradually and in a limited range. Discontinuities in aggregators or their derivatives (except for min and max functions) are questionable properties. The same holds for convex/concave inconsistencies (oscillatory alternating concave and convex segments in partial conjunction or partial disjunction aggregators). Without convincing empirical validation such properties are unacceptable.

All observations of intuitive evaluation show that the reasoning with percepts of value is a continuous natural phenomenon. Nature makes no leap, nor does the aggregation used by intuitive evaluators. Consequently, many aggregators that are developed in recent mathematical research, that use aggregation functions A where either $A(x_1, ..., x_n)$ has discontinuities, or $\partial A(x_1,...,x_n)/\partial x_i$ has discontinuities (for any i) have little chance to be acceptable as appropriate models of human evaluation reasoning. Of course, the justifiability of mathematic research does not depend on its applicability. The aggregators that are consistent with observable properties of human reasoning are smooth, and are continuous in both values and their derivatives. Applicable aggregators must satisfy these conditions.

In building elementary criteria, we frequently use polygonal (piecewise linear) approximations of functions (e.g., see Fig. 2.2.28), and those approximations have points where the first derivative has discontinuity. Such models are necessary approximations based on incomplete information obtained from decision maker. Such information contains only the coordinates of vertices and for simplicity between vertices we use linear interpolation. Of course, it is possible to use models of elementary criteria that have continuous first derivatives, but in such cases the process of modeling would require unjustified efforts.

A general conclusion derived from observing properties of evaluation reasoning is that the corresponding logic models should support internality, idempotency, monotonicity, compensativeness, adjustable relative importance, and be continuous and smooth in values and their derivatives. Such logic models can be developed using means and denoted as a weighted compensative logic. Of course, GL belongs to this category of logic models.

The family of curves presented in Fig. 2.2.31 is an example of *sensitivity analysis*, applied to a single aggregator. Generally, the sensitivity analysis is used to analyze an arbitrary aggregation structure (one or more aggregators) in order to find variations of output suitability caused by variations of input suitability and/or variations of parameters (both the degrees of andness and the intensities of relative importance). The main goal of sensitivity analysis in GL is to validate that the attained variations of output suitability are consistent with expectations of decision maker. In human reasoning the observed sensitivity of output suitability with respect to input suitability or model parameters is always a limited value. It is highly unlikely that decision makers can perceive significant variations of output suitability caused by minute variations of inputs or parameters. This imposes conditions of *limited sensitivity* that aggregation operators must satisfy in order to be applicable in GL. A detailed presentation of sensitivity analysis can be found in Chapter 3.8.

Let δ be the insensitivity zone in the sense that if degrees of truth a and b are very close ($|a-b| < \delta$) decision makers may feel no difference and consider $a \approx b$. For example, if $a = 0.66$ and $b = 0.67$ the majority of evaluators might only feel $a = b = 2/3$. Suppose that we use a potentially hypersensitive aggregator $z = A(x,y)$ where, similarly to Fig. 2.2.31, for some excessive values of parameters, in the vicinity of coordinate axes, $\partial z / \partial x$ is so large that insignificant differences of an input degree of truth x can cause significant variations of the output degree of truth z (i.e., $0 < |a-b| < \delta$, and $|A(a,y) - A(b,y)| \gg \delta$). Such phenomena are beyond human control, and do not reflect human reasoning. However, that should not automatically disqualify such aggregators. For example, if $x \in \{0,1\}$ then $|a-b| = 1$ and consequently it is not possible to have

$|a - b| < \delta$ and $|A(a,y) - A(b,y)| \gg \delta$. In all such cases, even for inappropriate values of parameters, the hypersensitive aggregators cannot cause harmful effects, and need not to be blacklisted. Potentially hypersensitive aggregators can also be safely used in all cases with k discrete input values $x \in \{x_1,...,x_k\}$, $k \geq 2$ provided that discrete inputs are sufficiently apart $(\forall i \neq j,\ |x_i - x_j| > \delta)$ so that the possible values of inputs skip the areas where aggregators might have hypersensitivity.

Another logically inconsistent situation occurs if the requested andness is very high but the requirement is not mandatory. It does not seem logical to first firmly insist that all inputs must be strictly simultaneously satisfied, and then to fail to sufficiently punish alternatives that do not satisfy such requirements. For example, if $x_1 \Diamond x_2 = 0.9(x_1 \wedge x_2) + 0.1(x_1 \vee x_2)$ (Fig. 2.1.17), then it is necessary to provide a strong justification why a logic aggregator that is 90% conjunction does not support the annihilator 0 (what is the reason for $\forall x > 0,\ 0 \Diamond x = x \Diamond 0 > 0$?). Equally inconsistent might be the requirement for a low level of andness (α slightly above ½) combined with the ultimate level of punishment in the case of failing to satisfy even the least important input. These combinations of low andness and mandatory requirements are regularly not a part of human reasoning and the corresponding aggregators feature dramatic forms of hypersensitivity (an example is the counter-harmonic mean).

Errors in selecting parameters and/or logic properties of evaluation models can cause errors in evaluation results and incorrect ranking of competitive systems. The reliability of evaluation results can be analyzed using methodology presented in Chapter 3.8.

(P33) Missing Data, the Concordance Principle, and Error Compensation

In some evaluation studies we face the problem of missing data. Such cases can be easily found in databases of products offered for sale (homes, cars, etc.). For example, the Internet real estate databases of available homes include a standardized set of attributes [ZIL11], but for some homes only a subset of attributes is available. Such databases regularly include the total lot area, home area, the number of bedrooms, and various other attributes. However, if a legally correct area is not known, it might be more desirable to omit the area than to list a legally questionable approximate value. So, the evaluator who developed a criterion that includes the area (or any other missing input) cannot directly apply the criterion because of missing input data. That can be undesirable. If a home is located in an attractive location, has some attractive features, and has an attractive price, then the evaluation (either intuitive or formal) must be performed with existing incomplete data.

Let a preference aggregation function of n variables be $y = A_n(x_1,...,x_k,...,x_n)$, and let x_k be a potentially missing attribute. A typical sensitivity curve for x_k is shown in Fig. 2.2.33. If $x_k = C_k$, then $A_n(x_1,...,C_k,...,x_n) = C_k$. We call C_k the

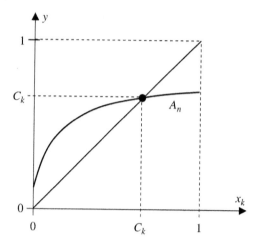

Figure 2.2.33 A typical sensitivity curve of an attribute and its concordance value.

concordance value[5] because for this value the kth input is in perfect concordance with remaining inputs $x_1, ..., x_{k-1}, x_{k+1}, ..., x_n$. This is easily visible in the case of quasi-arithmetic means where $C_k = A_{n-1}(x_1, ..., x_{k-1}, x_{k+1}, ..., x_n)$. In other words, if an input value is the same as an aggregated value, then it does not affect the aggegated value, because the aggregated value depends only on remaining inputs and the kth input is in concordance with them:

$$A_{n-1}(x_1, ..., x_{k-1}, x_{k+1}, ..., x_n)$$
$$= A_n(x_1, ..., x_{k-1}, A_{n-1}(x_1, ..., x_{k-1}, x_{k+1}, ..., x_n), x_{k+1}, ..., x_n).$$

A mathematical proof of this result for quasi-arithmetic means can be found in Section 2.8.3, and here we only offer the following simple example. Suppose that our aggregator is a simple arithmetic mean $y = 0.5x_1 + 0.3x_2 + 0.2x_3$. If x_1 is missing, then we should use the reduced aggregator $y = 0.6x_2 + 0.4x_3$, or the original aggregator where we insert the concordance value $x_1 = 0.6x_2 + 0.4x_3$. As shown in Fig. 2.2.33, in such a case we obtain the same result of aggregation: $y = 0.5(0.6x_2 + 0.4x_3) + 0.3x_2 + 0.2x_3 = 0.6x_2 + 0.4x_3$.

The concordance relationship has the following intuitive interpretation: if an input is missing then the most reasonable assumption is that its value (in the sense of preference or suitability) is in concordance with the values of remaining

---

5 In mathematics the fixed point of function $x \mapsto f(x)$ is a point x for which $f(x) = x$. There are various fixed-point theorems that specify the conditions under which $f(x)$ has a fixed point. Also, a related problem is the convergence of iteration $x_i = f(x_{i-1})$, $i > 0$. Our concordance value is a form of fixed point. However, instead of studying mathematical background of the fixed point property, we are here primarily interested in the evaluation-related semantic aspects of this property, i.e., in a cognitive interpretation of the concordance between the substitute of a missing value and the result computed using remaining arguments, obtained after excluding the missing/unknown value.

attributes in the group. This property can be called *the concordance principle*. In other words, if an attribute has a value that is in concordance with the aggregated value of remaining attributes in a group, then such an attribute is redundant, it does not affect the aggregated preference, and can be omitted without consequences.[6] If x_k is missing, then we can use the original aggregator $A_n(x_1, ..., x_k, ..., x_n)$ where the missing value is substituted by the concordance value $x_k = C_k = A_{n-1}(x_1,...,x_{k-1},x_{k+1},...,x_n)$ and the result of aggregation will again be $A_{n-1}(x_1,...,x_{k-1},x_{k+1},...,x_n)$, as shown in Fig. 2.2.33. Thus, we can omit the missing attribute and use directly the reduced aggregator $A_{n-1}(x_1,...,x_{k-1},x_{k+1},...,x_n)$.

It is important to note that the use of reduced aggregator A_{n-1} $(x_1,...,x_{k-1},x_{k+1},...,x_n)$ represents an essential observable property of human reasoning. Indeed, in the absence of some inputs, human evaluation reasoning adapts to reach the best solutions that can be derived from the aggregation of the remaining available data. The existence of "known unknowns" and "unknown unknowns" is a reason for cautious decision making, but not an obstacle capable of preventing rational reasoning with those inputs that are still available.

The concordance principle in the simplest case of two variables $A_2(x_1, x_2)$ means that if one variable is missing (e.g., x_2), then the preference is computed as $A_2(x_1,x_1) = x_1$, i.e., the resulting value is the value of the remaining variable. In the case of three variables, $A_3(x_1, x_2, x_3)$, the missing variable (e.g., x_3) should be substituted by the concordance value $A_2(x_1, x_2)$ yielding $A_3(x_1,x_2,A_2(x_1,x_2)) = A_2(x_1,x_2)$, and so forth. In some cases, the evaluator may want to penalize the missing data; the problem of penalty-controlled missingness-tolerant aggregation is analyzed in Chapter 2.8.

The study of imprecision, incompleteness, logic inconsistency, and perception errors is helpful to keep errors under control and to provide reliable results. Like in all cases of random errors, the distribution of errors is symmetric: some errors are positive (increasing the overall suitability) and some errors are negative (decreasing the overall suitability). There is no reason to believe that all errors will be strictly positive or strictly negative; consequently, in cases of complex LSP criteria with many parameters, the opposite errors partially compensate each other.

Industrial products usually have balanced quality of all components (all improvements and updates are primarily focused on the weakest components). As a trivial example, let us have only two attributes (x and y) and let the aggregated suitability be $\hat{S} = \hat{W}x + (1 - \hat{W})y$; here $\hat{W}$ denotes the correct value of

---

6 If the relation $A_{n-1}(x_1,...,x_{k-1},x_{k+1},...,x_n) = A_n(x_1,...,x_{k-1},e,x_{k+1},...,x_n)$ is satisfied by the unique *constant* value of e for any $k \in \{1,...,n\}$ and for any input values, then e is called the *extended neutral element* [GRA09]. Such element could substitute all missing data. Unfortunately, in GL the extended neutral element does not exist, but we can use the concordance value.

weight and $\hat{S}$ denotes the correct value of aggregated suitability. Suppose, now, that we made an error in weight assessment so that $W = \hat{W} + \delta$ and the suitability is now $S = (\hat{W} + \delta)x + (1 - \hat{W} - \delta)y = \hat{S} + \delta(x - y)$. So, the suitability error is $\Delta S = \delta(x - y)$ and if the quality of components is balanced, then we can frequently have $x \approx y$ and that to some extent automatically compensates the impact of the analyzed error.

Many input attributes are positively correlated. For example, the increase of price of a computer system simultaneously increases the size of memory, processor speed, the size of disk storage, and other attributes, making them positively correlated. If we have two competitors (denoted system 1 and system 2), then $S_1 = \hat{S}_1 + \delta(x_1 - y_1)$, $S_2 = \hat{S}_2 + \delta(x_2 - y_2)$ and the difference between competitors is $S_1 - S_2 = \hat{S}_1 - \hat{S}_2 + \delta[(x_1 - x_2) - (y_1 - y_2)]$. The fact that x and y are correlated reduces the impact of error $\delta[(x_1 - x_2) - (y_1 - y_2)]$ because the differences $x_1 - x_2$ and $y_1 - y_2$ are not independent but behave in a similar way and partially compensate each other (a more precise analysis of this form of error compensation can be found in [DUJ72a]).

In a special case where system 1 outperforms system 2 in all components we have in our trivial example $S_1 = Wx_1 + (1 - W)y_1$, $S_2 = Wx_2 + (1 - W)y_2$, $x_1 > x_2$ and $y_1 > y_2$. Consequently, $S_1 - S_2 = W(x_1 - x_2) + (1 - W)(y_1 - y_2) > 0$. That provides a reliable ranking $S_1 > S_2$ regardless of the value of weight and all other properties of the averaging aggregator. In other words, no error in criterion function can affect the correct ranking of competitors. Of course, this special case of total insensitivity to all errors is very unlikely, but it frequently occurs in subsystems of an LSP criterion and increases the robustness of LSP decision models.

If parameters of a criterion function contain random errors, then it is possible to simulate their effects and compute the degree of confidence that the ranking of competitive systems is correct. The results that provably have a high degree of confidence are fully acceptable in evaluation practice. The corresponding reliability and confidence analysis is presented in Chapter 3.8.

In this long chapter we provided a systematic survey of 33 observable properties of evaluation reasoning. These properties cannot be ignored. They directly or indirectly affect logic models of evaluation reasoning. Our analysis should be sufficient to promote the idea that all mathematical models of perceptual computing must be provably consistent with observable properties of human reasoning. Our goal was to describe a reasonably complete set of observable properties of intuitive GL. Now, we can use these properties as indispensable guidelines for development of mathematical models that are used in the rest of this book. Based on such mathematical models, we can develop a professional evaluation methodology that quantifies, refines, and expands the intuitive evaluation process.

2.3   Andness and Orness

A mathematical theory is not to be considered complete until you have made it so clear that you can explain it to the first man whom you meet on the street.
—David Hilbert

The goal of this chapter is to present the three most important forms of andness/orness: local andness, mean local andness, and global andness. We analyze and compare these indicators from the standpoint of their computational properties and usability in decision models.

The GCD aggregator (graded conjunction/disjunction, Section 2.1.7) is the most important GL aggregator. It is a model of simultaneity and substitutability, characterized by two complementary indicators: andness and orness. Andness (or conjunction degree) is a metric of similarity between GCD and the full conjunction. It is denoted α, $\alpha \in [0,1]$. Similarly, orness (or disjunction degree) is a metric of similarity between GCD and the full disjunction. It is denoted ω, $\omega \in [0,1]$, and it is a complement of andness: $\alpha + \omega = 1$. The basic concepts of andness and orness are introduced in section 2.2.2 (P_{12}). The history of development of these concepts is presented in section 2.1.12.

2.3.1   A General Definition of Andness/Orness

Fig. 2.3.1 is suitable to explain the concepts of andness and orness "to the first man whom you meet on the street." Generally, GCD is located somewhere between conjunction (the minimum function) and disjunction (the maximum function). The exact location of GCD can be specified using the *conjunction degree* (or *andness*) or its complement, the *disjunction degree* (or *orness*), shown in Fig. 2.3.1.

Soft Computing Evaluation Logic: The LSP Decision Method and Its Applications, First Edition. Jozo Dujmović.
© 2018 John Wiley & Sons, Inc. Published 2018 by John Wiley & Sons, Inc.
Companion website: www.wiley.com/go/Dujmovic/Soft_Computing_Evaluation_Logic

Let A denote a metric of distance (difference) between GCD and the pure disjunction, and let B denote the distance between GCD and the pure conjunction. The total distance between conjunction and disjunction is A + B. Then, the andness can be defined as a normalized distance between GCD and disjunction: *andness* = A/(A + B). This is also a degree of conjunction, (i.e., a metric of similarity/proximity between the GCD and conjunction). The maximum andness is 1 (or 100%). It corresponds to the pure conjunction (the maximum distance from disjunction). Similarly, the orness is a normalized distance between GCD and the pure conjunction: *orness* = B/(A + B). This is a metric of similarity/proximity between the GCD and the pure disjunction. The maximum orness is 1 (or 100%). In soft computing, where everything is a matter of degree, andness is the conjunction degree and orness is the disjunction degree. These concepts where introduced in [DUJ73b].

There are various ways for defining the metric of distance between GCD and conjunction or disjunction. A presentation and comparison of nine forms of andness/orness can be found in [DUJ06b] (see also [KOL09] for a general parametric characterization of aggregation functions). Each definition yields different form of andness/orness, but all definitions are consistent with the general principle shown in Fig. 2.3.1, and evaluators can easily learn how to use them. Indeed, the interest in different definitions of andness/orness is primarily theoretical. From a practical standpoint, all definitions are applicable and are used in a similar way. In this chapter, we focus on those definitions that are frequently used in practice.

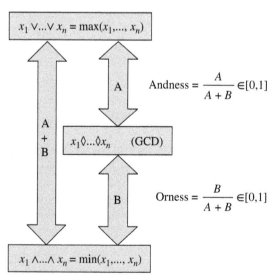

Figure 2.3.1 A general explanation of the concept of andness/orness.

$$x_1 \vee ... \vee x_n = \max(x_1,..., x_n)$$

$$\text{Andness} = \frac{A}{A + B} \in [0,1]$$

$$x_1 \Diamond ... \Diamond x_n \quad (GCD)$$

$$\text{Orness} = \frac{B}{A + B} \in [0,1]$$

$$x_1 \wedge ... \wedge x_n = \min(x_1,..., x_n)$$

It is important to emphasize that in evaluation studies the andness and orness are inputs, not outputs. Evaluators specify desired degrees of conjunction or disjunction using rating scales and then search for GCD function that has the desired andness/orness.

Andness and orness can be applied only to preference aggregators that model *simultaneity* and *substitutability*. It is meaningless to compute andness and orness for aggregators that model other types of GL functions, such as partial absorption, partial implication, and other GL functions. However, we also use andness and orness to characterize nonidempotent extensions of GCD (hyperconjunction and hyperdisjunction), because they are also models of simultaneity and substitutability.

2.3.2 Local Andness and Orness in the Simplest Case of Two Variables

Let us use the GCD aggregator $\Diamond$ to aggregate two preferences: $x \in I = [0,1]$ and $y \in I$, assuming $x < y$. The value $z = x \Diamond y$ is between x and y, i.e., $x \leq z \leq y$. The extreme cases of equality are obtained if the GCD becomes the pure (full) conjunction $z = x \wedge y = \min(x,y) = x$ or the pure (full) disjunction $z = x \vee y = \max(x,y) = y$. Fig. 2.3.2 illustrates a typical situation where the aggregated preference $x \Diamond y$ is between x and y, and the exact location is determined by either c or d.

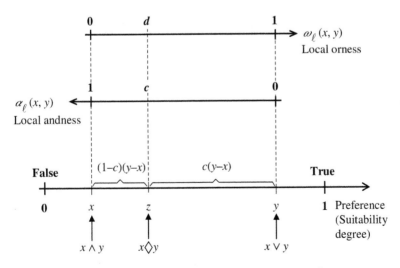

Figure 2.3.2 Local andness and orness of the GCD aggregator $x \Diamond y$.

The level of andness realized by the operation $z = x \Diamond y$ is visualized as the proximity of z and x: for high level of andness z is close to x. The evaluator who uses high andness GCD wants to penalize systems that have *one or more* weak components, and reward systems that simultaneously satisfy *all* input requirements. *Partial conjunction* (PC) is a generic name of such functions.

The level of orness realized by the operation $z = x \Diamond y$ is visualized as the proximity of z and y: for high level of orness z is close to y. The evaluator who uses high orness GCD wants to penalize systems that have *all* weak components and reward systems that satisfy *one or more* of input requirements. *Partial disjunction* (PD) is a generic name of such functions.

Since z can have any position between x and y it follows that andness and orness (as well as simultaneity and substitutability) are complementary: increasing andness (simultaneity) decreases orness (substitutability), and vice versa, increasing orness (substitutability) decreases andness (simultaneity). To model the intuitive evaluation process we need aggregation functions that generate any desired level of andness/orness. Of course, such functions must be capable to continuously move the aggregated value $z = x \Diamond y$ in the whole range between x and y.

Local andness and orness are not constant; they are defined in each point (x,y). The concepts of local andness $\alpha_\ell(x, y)$ and the local orness $\omega_\ell(x, y)$ were introduced in [DUJ73b] (see also [DUJ07b]) as follows:

$$\alpha_\ell(x,y) = \frac{(x \vee y) - (x \Diamond y)}{(x \vee y) - (x \wedge y)}, \quad \omega_\ell(x,y) = \frac{(x \Diamond y) - (x \wedge y)}{(x \vee y) - (x \wedge y)}, \quad (x \vee y) \neq (x \wedge y),$$

$$(x \wedge y) \le (x \Diamond y) \le (x \vee y),$$

$$0 \le \alpha_\ell(x,y) \le 1, \quad 0 \le \omega_\ell(x,y) \le 1, \quad \alpha_\ell(x,y) + \omega_\ell(x,y) = 1.$$

If $z = x \Diamond y = x \wedge y$, then $\alpha_\ell(x,y) = 1$, and this is the highest local andness that can be achieved. If $z = x \Diamond y = x \vee y$, then $\omega_\ell(x,y) = 1$, and this is the highest local orness that can be achieved. These forms of andness and orness are called *local* because their values are not constant: they vary depending on the values of input variables (input preferences).

By definition, the local andness and the local orness are complementary, indicating that GCD is a mix of conjunctive and disjunctive properties. If $\alpha_\ell(x,y) > \omega_\ell(x,y)$ then conjunctive properties are prevalent and $x \Diamond y$ is interpreted as a partial conjunction. Similarly, if $\alpha_\ell(x,y) < \omega_\ell(x,y)$ then disjunctive properties are prevalent and $x \Diamond y$ is interpreted as a partial disjunction. According to definition of local andness and orness, in the case $\alpha_\ell(x,y) = c$ and $\omega_\ell(x,y) = 1 - c = d$ (Fig. 2.3.2) we have

$$z = x \Diamond y = \alpha_\ell(x,y)(x \wedge y) + \omega_\ell(x,y)(x \vee y) = c(x \wedge y) + d(x \vee y).$$

Therefore, c determines the proximity of the resulting (aggregated) value z to the smaller of the two inputs, x. Since $x = \min(x,y) = x \wedge y$, the parameter c also determines the proximity of the aggregator $x \Diamond y$ to the operation that has the highest level of simultaneity, conjunction. Similarly, d determines the proximity of the aggregator $x \Diamond y$ to the operation that has the highest level of substitutability, disjunction.

In the case of two variables, the sum of two preferences is $x + y = (x \vee y) + (x \wedge y)$. Consequently, the local andness and the local orness of the arithmetic mean of two variables have an exceptional property—they are constant:

$$\alpha_\ell(x,y) = \frac{(x \vee y) - (x + y)/2}{(x \vee y) - (x \wedge y)} = \frac{(x \vee y) - ((x \vee y) + (x \wedge y))/2}{(x \vee y) - (x \wedge y)} = \frac{1}{2},$$

$$\omega_\ell(x,y) = 1 - \alpha_\ell(x,y) = 1/2 \; ; \quad x \neq y.$$

Not surprisingly, the arithmetic mean is a mix of 50% of conjunctive properties and 50% of disjunctive properties.

The region where $x \approx y$ is called the *idempotency region*. In the case of aggregation based on power means, the andness and orness satisfy the following idempotency region property:

Proposition 2.3.1. In the idempotency region, all idempotent aggregators behave as the arithmetic mean.

This property holds for all means, but we here restrict our interest to the andness and orness of power means. In the case of power means of two variables this property can be expressed as $\lim_{x \to y} \alpha_\ell(x,y) = \lim_{x \to y} \omega_\ell(x,y) = 1/2$. We can verify this claim for power means as follows:

$$\alpha_\ell(x,y) = \frac{(x \vee y) - (0.5x^r + 0.5y^r)^{1/r}}{(x \vee y) - (x \wedge y)} = \frac{(x \vee y) - (0.5(x \vee y)^r + 0.5(x \wedge y)^r)^{1/r}}{(x \vee y) - (x \wedge y)}$$

$$= \frac{1 - (0.5 + 0.5(x \wedge y)^r / (x \vee y)^r)^{1/r}}{(1 - (x \wedge y)/(x \vee y))} = \frac{1 - (0.5 + 0.5z^r)^{1/r}}{1 - z}, \quad z = \frac{x \wedge y}{x \vee y} \; ;$$

$$\lim_{x \to y} \alpha_\ell(x,y) = \lim_{z \to 1} \frac{1 - (0.5 + 0.5z^r)^{1/r}}{1 - z} = \lim_{z \to 1} \frac{\dfrac{d}{dz} \left[1 - (0.5 + 0.5z^r)^{1/r} \right]}{\dfrac{d}{dz}(1 - z)}$$

$$= \lim_{z \to 1} \frac{-(0.5 + 0.5z^r)^{1/r - 1} 0.5z^{r-1}}{-1} = \frac{1}{2} \; , \quad -\infty \leq r \leq +\infty.$$

Therefore, if $x \to y$ all power means have the local andness and orness that is equal to the local andness and orness of the arithmetic mean (½). This property (a consequence of the idempotency of means) shows that if $x \approx y$, then all power mean aggregators behave similarly to the arithmetic mean. Consequently, in cases where that might be useful, it is possible to expand the definitions of local andness and orness to include all values of x and y as follows:

$$\alpha_\ell(x,y) = \begin{cases} \dfrac{(x \vee y) - (x \Diamond y)}{(x \vee y) - (x \wedge y)} & , \quad x \neq y \\[2mm] 1/2 & , \quad x = y \end{cases}$$

$$\omega_\ell(x,y) = \begin{cases} \dfrac{(x \Diamond y) - (x \wedge y)}{(x \vee y) - (x \wedge y)} & , \quad x \neq y \\[2mm] 1/2 & , \quad x = y. \end{cases}$$

Characteristic properties of local andness are visible in the case of geometric mean $x \Diamond y = \sqrt{xy}$. The local andness and orness can be defined as follows:

$$\alpha_\ell(x,y) = \frac{(x \vee y) - \sqrt{xy}}{(x \vee y) - (x \wedge y)} = \frac{(x \vee y) - \sqrt{(x \vee y)(x \wedge y)}}{(x \vee y) - (x \wedge y)}$$

$$= \frac{\sqrt{x \vee y}}{\sqrt{(x \vee y)} + \sqrt{(x \wedge y)}} = \frac{\sqrt{x \vee y}}{\sqrt{x} + \sqrt{y}},$$

$$\omega_\ell(x,y) = \frac{\sqrt{xy} - (x \wedge y)}{(x \vee y) - (x \wedge y)} = \frac{\sqrt{(x \vee y)(x \wedge y)} - (x \wedge y)}{(x \vee y) - (x \wedge y)} = \frac{\sqrt{x \wedge y}}{\sqrt{x} + \sqrt{y}}.$$

If $x = 0.2$ and $y = 0.8$ then $z = \sqrt{xy} = 0.4$, $\alpha_\ell(x,y) = 2/3$, $\omega_\ell(x,y) = 1/3$, as shown in Fig. 2.3.3. The resulting preference z is below the mean value 0.5, and we can claim that the function $x \Diamond y = \sqrt{xy}$ is a model of simultaneity. In the point $(x,y) = (0.2, 0.8)$ the geometric mean can be used to realize a moderate level of simultaneity (67%). In other points, however, $\alpha_\ell(x, y)$ and $\omega_\ell(x, y)$ can take other different values. For all HPC aggregators the minimum value of $\alpha_\ell(x, y)$ is $\lim_{y \to x} \alpha_\ell(x,y) = 0.5$ and the maximum value is $\alpha_\ell(0,y) = \alpha_\ell(x,0) = 1$. The variations of local andness for the aggregator $x \Diamond y = \sqrt{xy}$ are shown in Fig. 2.3.3 and Fig. 2.3.4 ($r = 0$); they are consistent with HPC properties presented in Section 2.2.3 (P_{17}). A detailed analysis of the variability of local andness is presented in the next section.

2.3.3 Variability of Local Andness

In the case of power means of two variables, $z = (0.5x^r + 0.5y^r)^{1/r}$, Fig. 2.3.4 shows that the local andness has a distribution that can substantially vary inside the input space $[0, 1]^2$. For $x = y$ the local andness has the value ½, and that is a common property for all values of exponent r. In the case of HPC ($r \leq 0$) we have $\alpha_\ell(0,y) = \alpha_\ell(x,0) = 1$. For SPC the local andness is lower than in the case of HPC.

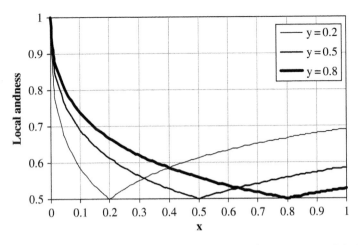

Figure 2.3.3 Local andness of the geometric mean for $0 \leq x \leq 1$, $y = 0.2$, 0.5, 0.8.

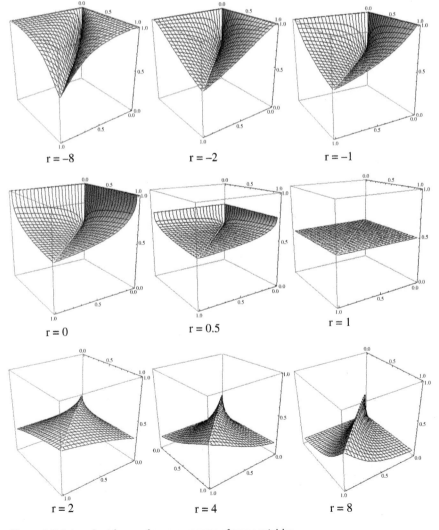

Figure 2.3.4 Local andness of power means of two variables.

For example, for $r > 0$ we have $\alpha_\ell(0,y) = \alpha_\ell(x,0) = 1 - 0.5^{1/r}$. So, for $r = 0.5$ we have $0.5 \leq \alpha_\ell(x,y) \leq 0.75$. In addition, it is easy to see that for $r \leq 0$ the andness of power means varies inside $[0,1]^2$ from 0.5 (along the line $x = y$) to 1 (along the sides $x = 0$, $0 \leq y \leq 1$ and $y = 0$, $0 \leq x \leq 1$).

The local andness of power means of two variables x and y can be analyzed using the following expressions (we use parentheses assuming that arithmetic operations have higher priority than logic operations):

$$x \Diamond y = (0.5x^r + 0.5y^r)^{1/r} = y[0.5(x/y)^r + 0.5]^{1/r} = y\left(\frac{x}{y}\Diamond 1\right),$$

$$\alpha_\ell(x,y) = \frac{(x \vee y) - (x \Diamond y)}{(x \vee y) - (x \wedge y)} = \frac{(x/y \vee 1) - (x/y \Diamond 1)}{(x/y \vee 1) - (x/y \wedge 1)} = \begin{cases} \dfrac{1 - (x/y \Diamond 1)}{1 - x/y}, & 0 \leq x < y \leq 1 \\[3mm] \dfrac{x/y - (x/y \Diamond 1)}{x/y - 1}, & 0 \leq y < x \leq 1. \end{cases}$$

Fig. 2.3.5 shows the resulting local andness as a function of the x/y ratio for power means and 17 values of the parameter r. The andness is constant (0.5) only for the arithmetic mean ($r = 1$). If the x/y ratio is close to 1 then, for any value of r, the local andness approaches 0.5. In other words, if input values are close, then all weighted power mean aggregators behave similarly to the arithmetic mean. If $x = 0$ then for all HPC cases the local andness becomes 1. This aggregator does not support HPD, and therefore the curves for partial

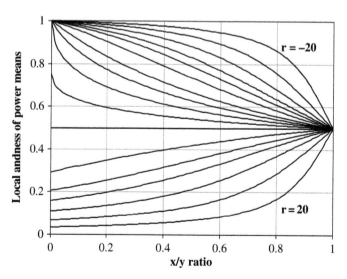

Figure 2.3.5 Local andness of the power mean for parameters $r = -20, -10, -6, -4, -3, -2, -1,$ $-0.5, 0, 0.5, 1, 2, 3, 4, 6, 10, 20.$

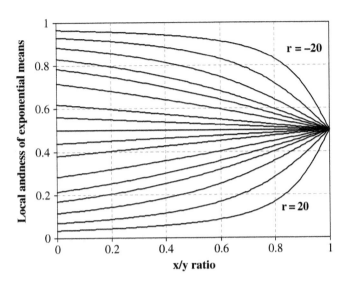

Figure 2.3.6 Local andness of the exponential mean for $r = -20, -10, -6, -4, -3, -2, -1, -0.5, 0,$ 0.5, 1, 2, 3, 4, 6, 10, 20 (bottom curve).

disjunction do not reach the orness 1 (andness 0). Of course, if we want to support HPD with power means, then partial disjunction must be defined as the De Morgan dual of the power mean implementation of partial conjunction.

The presented properties of power means can be contrasted with properties of the exponential mean, $E(x,y;r) = \lim_{s \to r} s^{-1} \ln(0.5e^{sx} + 0.5e^{sy})$, $-\infty \le r \le +\infty$, shown in Fig. 2.3.6. The local andness of the exponential mean is a symmetric function with respect to the arithmetic mean (the case $r = 0$):

$$\frac{E(x,y;r) + E(x,y;-r)}{2} = \frac{1}{2r}\ln\frac{e^{rx} + e^{ry}}{e^{-rx} + e^{-ry}} = \frac{1}{2r}\ln\left(\frac{e^{rx} + e^{ry}}{e^{-rx} + e^{-ry}} \cdot \frac{e^{rx}e^{ry}}{e^{rx}e^{ry}}\right) = \frac{x+y}{2};$$

$$\alpha_\ell(x,y;r) = \frac{(x \vee y) - E(x,y;r)}{(x \vee y) - (x \wedge y)}, \quad \alpha_\ell(x,y;-r) = \frac{(x \vee y) - E(x,y;-r)}{(x \vee y) - (x \wedge y)};$$

$$\alpha_\ell(x,y;r) + \alpha_\ell(x,y;-r) = \frac{2(x \vee y) - E(x,y;r) - E(x,y;-r)}{(x \vee y) - (x \wedge y)} = \frac{2(x \vee y) - (x + y)}{(x \vee y) - (x \wedge y)}$$

$$= \frac{2(x \vee y) - ((x \vee y) + (x \wedge y))}{(x \vee y) - (x \wedge y)} = 1 = \alpha_\ell(x,y;r) + \omega_\ell(x,y;r),$$

$$\therefore \quad \omega_\ell(x,y;r) = \alpha_\ell(x,y;-r).$$

According to Fig. 2.3.6, for finite values of r the exponential mean cannot reach the level of maximum andness/orness (i.e., $\alpha_\ell < 1$, $\omega_\ell < 1$). Consequently, the exponential mean cannot be used for modeling mandatory and sufficient requirements. This substantial drawback is also found in several other aggregators.

In the case of two variables the local andness has significant variability, but for more variables the situation is even worse. In the case of more than two variables the local andness can have rather complex properties, even in the case of simplest aggregators. To illustrate these problems let us investigate the local andness of the arithmetic mean of n variables:

$$\alpha_\ell(x_1,...,x_n) = \frac{(x_1 \vee \cdots \vee x_n) - (x_1 + \cdots + x_n)/n}{(x_1 \vee \cdots \vee x_n) - (x_1 \wedge \cdots \wedge x_n)}$$

$$x_1 \vee \cdots \vee x_n \neq x_1 \wedge \cdots \wedge x_n, \quad n \geq 2$$

In the case of two variables, the local andness has the constant value ½ (Section 2.3.2). In the case of three variables, we have

$$\alpha_\ell(x,y,z) = \frac{(x \vee y \vee z) - (x + y + z)/3}{(x \vee y \vee z) - (x \wedge y \wedge z)}$$

$$x \vee y \vee z \neq x \wedge y \wedge z$$

Inside the cube $[0,1]^3$ the local andness takes the following characteristic values:

1) Two variables are equal to 0 (along the coordinate axes, see Fig. 2.3.7):

$$\alpha_\ell(0,0,z) = \frac{z - z/3}{z} = \frac{2}{3} = \alpha_\ell(0,y,0) = \alpha_\ell(x,0,0).$$

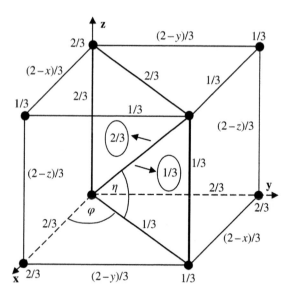

Figure 2.3.7 Characteristic values of the local andness of arithmetic mean for $n = 3$.

2) Two variables are equal to 1 (outer edges):

$$\alpha_\ell(1,1,z) = \frac{1-(2+z)/3}{1-z} = \frac{1}{3} = \alpha_\ell(1,y,1) = \alpha_\ell(x,1,1).$$

3) Two variables are equal ($x = y$, or $y = z$, or $x = z$):

$$\alpha_\ell(x,x,z) = \frac{(x \vee z) - (2x + z)/3}{(x \vee z) - (x \wedge z)} = \begin{cases} \dfrac{z-(2x+z)/3}{z-x} = \dfrac{2}{3}, & z > x \\[2ex] \dfrac{x-(2x+z)/3}{x-z} = \dfrac{1}{3}, & z < x. \end{cases}$$

Similarly,

$$\alpha_\ell(x,y,y) = \begin{cases} 2/3, & x > y \\ 1/3, & x < y \end{cases}$$

$$\alpha_\ell(z,y,z) = \begin{cases} 2/3, & y > z \\ 1/3, & y < z. \end{cases}$$

Therefore, along the idempotency line $x = y = z$ the local andness converges to different values at different directions, producing a discontinuity. Fig. 2.3.7 shows the local andness at the edges of the unit cube and the plane $x = y$ where we have the discontinuity of andness along the idempotency line $x = y = z$. Of course, such discontinuities also exist along the other two planes ($x = z$, and $y = z$, not shown in Fig. 2.3.7).

Other important special cases of local andness are obtained if one of variables is the mean value of remaining variables. There are three such cases: $z = (x + y)/2$, $y = (x + z)/2$, and $x = (y + z)/2$. In the plane $z = (x + y)/2$ we have $(x \wedge y) < z < (x \vee y)$, and the local andness is

$$\alpha_\ell\left(x,y,\frac{x+y}{2}\right) = \frac{(x \vee y) - [x + y + (x + y)/2]/3}{(x \vee y) - (x \wedge y)} = \frac{(x \vee y) - (x + y)/2}{(x \vee y) - (x \wedge y)} = \frac{1}{2}, \quad x \ne y.$$

Similarly,

$$\alpha_\ell\left(x,\frac{x+z}{2},z\right) = \frac{1}{2}, \quad x \ne z.$$

$$\alpha_\ell\left(\frac{y+z}{2},y,z\right) = \frac{1}{2}, \quad y \ne z.$$

Therefore, the local andness of the arithmetic mean is equal to ½ on three planes shown in Fig. 2.3.8.

In the vicinity of idempotency line $x = y = z$ the local andness has wild variations going from the minimum 1/3 through the mean 1/2, to the maximum 2/3. Variability of local andness is an important property of aggregators and the variations of local andness are rather large. This creates the need for finding more stable indicators of andness and orness, such as mean local andness/orness and global andness/orness.

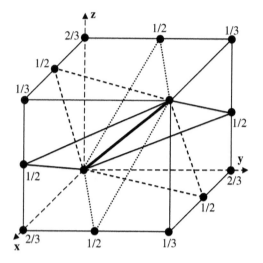

Figure 2.3.8 Three planes where local andness = ½.

2.3.4   Mean Local Andness and Orness in the Case of Two Variables

A desired level of andness and orness is one of inputs in the evaluation process. However, in applications we cannot specify desired level of andness in all points of $[0,1]^n$. The variability of local andness is inconvenient and we need a simpler way to specify andness and orness. More precisely, it would be useful to have an overall average indicator of simultaneity/substitutability that is not a function of input variables. A simple way to achieve this goal is to compute the *mean local andness and orness*. In the case of two variables, we have

$$\bar{\alpha}_\ell = \int_0^1 \int_0^1 \alpha_\ell(x_1,x_2)dx_1 dx_2 = \int_0^1 \int_0^1 \frac{(x_1 \vee x_2)-(x_1 \Diamond x_2)}{(x_1 \vee x_2)-(x_1 \wedge x_2)}dx_1 dx_2, \ 0 \le \bar{\alpha}_\ell \le 1,$$

$$\bar{\omega}_\ell = \int_0^1 \int_0^1 \omega_\ell(x_1,x_2)dx_1 dx_2 = \int_0^1 \int_0^1 \frac{(x_1 \Diamond x_2)-(x_1 \wedge x_2)}{(x_1 \vee x_2)-(x_1 \wedge x_2)}dx_1 dx_2, \ 0 \le \bar{\omega}_\ell \le 1, \ \ \bar{\alpha}_\ell + \bar{\omega}_\ell = 1.$$

In a general case, the computation of $\bar{\alpha}_\ell$ and $\bar{\omega}_\ell$ can be rather complex. However, in some special cases these indicators can be easily derived. Let's look at one such method. For simplicity, first consider the case of the harmonic mean of two variables: $y = x_1 \Diamond x_2 = 2x_1 x_2/(x_1 + x_2)$. At points where $x_1 < x_2$, the local andness is

$$\alpha_\ell(x_1,x_2) = \frac{x_2 - 2x_1 x_2/(x_1 + x_2)}{x_2 - x_1} = \frac{x_2}{x_1 + x_2}.$$

Along the line $x_2 = ax_1$, $a > 1$, the local andness is constant, $\alpha_\ell(x_1, x_2) = a/(a+1)$, as illustrated in Fig. 2.3.9. Similarly, if $x_1 > x_2$, then $\alpha_\ell(x_1, x_2) = x_1/(x_1 + x_2)$, and along the line $x_2 = x_1/a$, $a > 1$, the local andness is again $\alpha_\ell(x_1, x_2) = a/(a+1)$. Therefore, the minimum andness $\alpha_\ell = 1/2$ is along the line $x_1 = x_2$, and along coordinate axes we have the maximum andness $\alpha_\ell = 1$.

The region $a/(a+1) \le \alpha_\ell(x_1, x_2) \le 1$ consists of two right-angled triangles next to x_1 and x_2 axes with total area $1/a$. Hence, the probability that the local andness α_ℓ in a random point inside $[0, 1]^2$ is less than $a/(a+1)$ is $\Pr(\alpha_\ell < a/(a+1)) = 1 - 1/a$. After the substitution $z = a/(a+1)$ we have $a = z/(1-z)$, $1 - 1/a = (2z-1)/z$ and the probability distribution function $P_a(z)$ and its density $p_a(z)$ (according to Fig. 2.3.9) are:

$$P_a(z) = \Pr(\alpha_\ell < z) = \frac{2z-1}{z}, \quad p_a(z) = \frac{dP_a(z)}{dz} = \frac{1}{z^2}.$$

The triangular area above the line $x_2 = x_1$ in Fig. 2.3.9 is characterized by $1 \le a \le +\infty$ and $0.5 \le z \le 1$. Therefore, the corresponding mean local andness of the harmonic mean (H) of two variables is:

$$\bar{\alpha}_\ell[H;2] = \int_{0.5}^{1} z p_a(z)\,dz = \int_{0.5}^{1} \frac{dz}{z} = \ln(2) = 0.69314718,$$

$$\bar{\omega}_\ell[H;2] = 1 - \bar{\alpha}_\ell[H;2] = 0.30685282.$$

Figure 2.3.9 Local andness of the harmonic mean.

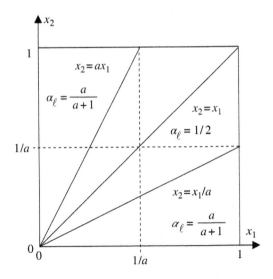

The presented technique can also be applied in the case of geometric mean:

$$x_1 \Diamond x_2 = \sqrt{xy}, \quad \alpha_\ell(x_1,x_2) = \begin{cases} \dfrac{\sqrt{x_2/x_1}}{1+\sqrt{x_2/x_1}}, & x_2 \geq x_1 \\[2ex] \dfrac{\sqrt{x_1/x_2}}{\sqrt{x_1/x_2}+1}, & x_2 \leq x_1 \end{cases}$$

$$\alpha_\ell(x_1,x_2) = \frac{\sqrt{a}}{\sqrt{a}+1}, \quad x_2 = \begin{cases} ax_1, & a \geq 1, \ x_2 \geq x_1 \\ x_1/a, & a \geq 1, \ x_2 \leq x_1 \end{cases}$$

$$z = \frac{\sqrt{a}}{\sqrt{a}+1}, \quad a = \left(\frac{z}{1-z}\right)^2.$$

$$\Pr\left(\alpha_\ell < \frac{\sqrt{a}}{\sqrt{a}+1}\right) = 1 - \frac{1}{a}, \quad 1 - \frac{1}{a} = 1 - \left(\frac{1-z}{z}\right)^2 = \frac{2z-1}{z^2},$$

$$P_a(z) = \Pr(\alpha_\ell < z) = \frac{2z-1}{z^2}, \quad p_a(z) = \frac{dP_a(z)}{dz} = \frac{2-2z}{z^3},$$

$$1 \leq a \leq +\infty, \quad 0.5 \leq z \leq 1,$$

$$\bar{\alpha}_\ell[G;2] = \int_{0.5}^{1} z p_a(z)\,dz = \int_{0.5}^{1} \frac{2-2z}{z^2}\,dz = 2 - \ln 4 = 0.61370564,$$

$$\bar{\omega}_\ell[G;2] = 1 - \bar{\alpha}_\ell[G;2] = 0.38629436.$$

In a general case of weighted power means, we have

$$x_1 \Diamond x_2 = \left(0.5 x_1^r + 0.5 x_2^r\right)^{1/r} = \begin{cases} x_1(0.5 + 0.5a^r)^{1/r} & x_2 = ax_1, \ a \geq 1, \ x_2 \geq x_1 \\[1ex] x_2(0.5 + 0.5a^r)^{1/r} & x_1 = ax_2, \ a \geq 1, \ x_2 \leq x_1, \end{cases}$$

$$\alpha_\ell(x_1,x_2) = \frac{a - (0.5 + 0.5a^r)^{1/r}}{a-1},$$

$$\Pr(\alpha_\ell < z) = 1 - \frac{1}{a}, \quad z = \frac{a - (0.5 + 0.5a^r)^{1/r}}{a-1}.$$

Unfortunately, the exact analytic computation of the value a from the equation $a - (0.5 + 0.5a^r)^{1/r} - z(a-1) = 0$ is possible only for a few values of r, and this reduces the applicability of the presented technique. Of course, numerical solutions are always possible and relatively simple. Correct values of three significant decimal digits can be obtained using simple Monte Carlo integration. A higher accuracy can be obtained using either analytic or numerical integration in Mathematica [WOL03].

2.3.5   Local and Mean Local Andness and Orness in the Case of *n* Variables

The oldest andness and orness indicators (initially called the conjunction degree and the disjunction degree), were introduced in 1973 as the following pointwise *local andness/orness* [DUJ73b] for logic aggregators of *n* variables:

$$\alpha_\ell(x_1,\ldots,x_n) = \frac{(x_1 \vee \cdots \vee x_n) - (x_1 \lozenge \cdots \lozenge x_n)}{(x_1 \vee \cdots \vee x_n) - (x_1 \wedge \cdots \wedge x_n)},$$

$$\omega_\ell(x_1,\ldots,x_n) = \frac{(x_1 \lozenge \cdots \lozenge x_n) - (x_1 \wedge \cdots \wedge x_n)}{(x_1 \vee \cdots \vee x_n) - (x_1 \wedge \cdots \wedge x_n)} = 1 - \alpha_\ell(x_1,\ldots,x_n),$$

$$0 \leq \alpha_\ell(x_1,\ldots,x_n) \leq 1, \quad 0 \leq \omega_\ell(x_1,\ldots,x_n) \leq 1, \quad x_1 \vee \cdots \vee x_n \neq x_1 \wedge \cdots \wedge x_n.$$

Consequently, the location of GCD with respect to conjunction and disjunction is defined as follows:

$$x_1 \lozenge \cdots \lozenge x_n = \omega_\ell(x_1,\ldots,x_n)(x_1 \vee \cdots \vee x_n) + \alpha_\ell(x_1,\ldots,x_n)(x_1 \wedge \cdots \wedge x_n)$$

The local andness and local orness are functions of *n* variables and can be interpreted as distributions of andness and orness in the hypercube $[0, 1]^n$. Those distributions can be rather complex (see Section 2.3.3). Taking into account that decision makers design decision models by creating aggregators based on a desired overall level of andness/orness, it follows that the pointwise local andness and orness have limited practical interest. This is the reason why we need overall andness/orness indicators that summarize the properties of GCD in all points of $[0, 1]^n$. Such an indicator is the *mean local andness/orness* that was introduced together with local andness and orness in [DUJ73b, DUJ73c]:

$$\bar{\alpha}_\ell = \int_0^1 dx_1 \ldots \int_0^1 \alpha_\ell(x_1,\ldots,x_n)dx_n, \quad 0 \leq \bar{\alpha}_\ell \leq 1,$$

$$\bar{\omega}_\ell = \int_0^1 dx_1 \ldots \int_0^1 \omega_\ell(x_1,\ldots,x_n)dx_n, \quad 0 \leq \bar{\omega}_\ell \leq 1,$$

$$\bar{\alpha}_\ell + \bar{\omega}_\ell = 1.$$

A general method for computing the mean local andness and orness was developed by Marichal [MAR08]. His method for computing $\bar{\alpha}_\ell$ and $\bar{\omega}_\ell$ is the following:

$$\bar{\omega}_\ell = \sum_{\substack{j,k=1 \\ j \neq k}}^{n} \int_0^1 dv \int_0^v du \int_{[0,1]^{n-2}} \frac{(x_1 \lozenge \cdots \lozenge x_n)|_{x_j = u, x_k = v} - u}{v - u} \prod_{\substack{1 \leq i \leq n \\ i \neq j, i \neq k}} dx_i.$$

$$\bar{\alpha}_\ell = 1 - \bar{\omega}_\ell$$

For example, if $x_1 \lozenge x_2 = (x_1 + x_2)/2$, then

$$\bar{\omega}_\ell[A;2] = 2 \int_0^1 dv \int_0^v \frac{(u+v)/2 - u}{v-u} du = \frac{1}{2}.$$

Using this method, Marichal computed the mean local orness for the geometric mean, as follows:

$$\bar{\omega}_\ell[G;n] = n(n-1)\left(\frac{n}{n+1}\right)^{n-2} \int_0^1 \frac{x^n(1-x^{n+1})^{n-2}}{1-x^n} dx - \frac{1}{n-2}$$

$$= \begin{cases} \ln 4 - 1 = 0.38629436, & n = 2 \\[2mm] \dfrac{\sqrt{3}\pi}{2} - \dfrac{47}{20} = 0.37069905, & n = 3 \\[2mm] \dfrac{96\ln 2}{25} - \dfrac{8837}{3850} = 0.36636050, & n = 4 \\[2mm] \dfrac{25\pi}{27}\sqrt{\left(125 - 55\sqrt{5}\right)/2} - \dfrac{2454487}{960336} = 0.36482091, & n = 5. \end{cases}$$

$\bar{\alpha}_\ell[G;2] = 1 - \bar{\omega}_\ell[G;2] = 0.61370564,$

$\bar{\alpha}_\ell[G;3] = 1 - \bar{\omega}_\ell[G;3] = 0.62930095,$

$\bar{\alpha}_\ell[G;4] = 1 - \bar{\omega}_\ell[G;4] = 0.63363950,$

$\bar{\alpha}_\ell[G;5] = 1 - \bar{\omega}_\ell[G;5] = 0.63517909.$

In a general case of arbitrary aggregators, the analytic computation is usually not possible, and we must use numerical methods. Of course, existing analytic results are then very useful for tuning of numerical procedures and checking their accuracy. In the case of power means of n variables, the mean local andness and orness can be numerically computed as functions of exponent r as follows:

$$\bar{\alpha}_\ell(r,n) = \int_0^1 dx_1 \cdots \int_0^1 \frac{(x_1 \vee \cdots \vee x_n) - \left(n^{-1}x_1^r + \cdots + n^{-1}x_n^r\right)^{1/r}}{(x_1 \vee \cdots \vee x_n) - (x_1 \wedge \cdots \wedge x_n)} dx_n, \quad 0 \le \bar{\alpha}_\ell \le 1,$$

$$\bar{\omega}_\ell(r,n) = \int_0^1 dx_1 \cdots \int_0^1 \frac{\left(n^{-1}x_1^r + \cdots + n^{-1}x_n^r\right)^{1/r} - (x_1 \wedge \cdots \wedge x_n)}{(x_1 \vee \cdots \vee x_n) - (x_1 \wedge \cdots \wedge x_n)} dx_n, \quad 0 \le \bar{\omega}_\ell \le 1.$$

The corresponding results for $n = 2,3,4,5$ are shown in Fig. 2.3.10 and in Table 2.3.1. We use 49 levels of andness/orness. The step $1/48$ is convenient for both the standard system of 17 GCD aggregators and the extended system of 25 GCD aggregators shown in Table 2.3.1. In the case of 17 aggregators, we use the andness/orness step $1/16 = 3/48$, and in the case of 25 aggregators the

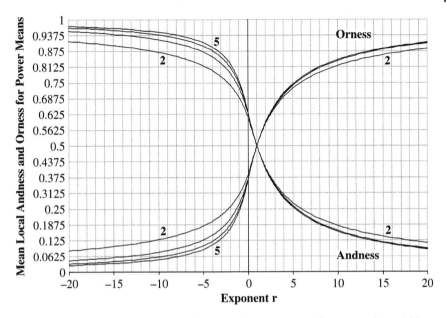

Figure 2.3.10 Mean local andness and orness of power means of 2, 3, 4, and 5 variables.

corresponding step is $1/24 = 2/48$. This granularity offers sufficient precision for evaluators to first select a desired mean local andness/orness and then to find the appropriate exponent of power mean.

2.3.6 Global Andness and Orness

The most convenient type of overall andness/orness indicators, introduced in [DUJ74a, DUJ74b], is called the *global andness/orness*. In the simplest case of two variables, it uses the mean value of the preference aggregation function $x \Diamond y$ in its complete domain (the volume of the fraction of unit cube under the surface $z = x \Diamond y$):

$$\overline{x \Diamond y} = \int_0^1 \int_0^1 (x \Diamond y)\, dx dy.$$

In this section, $\overline{x \Diamond y}$ denotes the mean value and not the negation of $x \Diamond y$. The global andness and orness (obtained by integrating the relation (2.1.3)) are now defined as follows:

$$\alpha_g = \frac{\overline{(x \vee y)} - \overline{(x \Diamond y)}}{\overline{(x \vee y)} - \overline{(x \wedge y)}}, \quad \omega_g = \frac{\overline{(x \Diamond y)} - \overline{(x \wedge y)}}{\overline{(x \vee y)} - \overline{(x \wedge y)}}, \quad x \neq y,$$

$$\overline{(x \wedge y)} \leq \overline{(x \Diamond y)} \leq \overline{(x \vee y)},$$

$$0 \leq \alpha_g \leq 1, \quad 0 \leq \omega_g \leq 1, \quad \alpha_g + \omega_g = 1.$$

Table 2.3.1 Selecting exponents of the power means of 2, 3, 4, and 5 variables for desired level of mean local andness/orness.

Mean local		Aggregators		WPM exponent			
Andness	**Orness**	**[17]**	**[25]**	r_2	r_3	r_4	r_5
0	1	D	D	$+\infty$	$+\infty$	$+\infty$	$+\infty$
0.02083	0.97917			172.920	100.467	96.765	99.895
0.04167	0.95833		DS++	78.093	48.177	46.836	48.379
0.06250	0.93750	D++		46.176	30.857	30.229	31.211
0.08333	0.91667		DS+	31.427	22.237	21.912	22.620
0.10417	0.89583			23.079	17.089	16.921	17.463
0.12500	0.87500	D+	DS	17.787	13.672	13.593	14.022
0.14583	0.85417			14.169	11.241	11.215	11.562
0.16667	0.83333		DS–	11.559	9.425	9.430	9.715
0.18750	0.81250	D+–		9.600	8.016	8.041	8.277
0.20833	0.79167		DS––	8.082	6.893	6.928	7.124
0.22917	0.77083			6.876	5.976	6.016	6.180
0.25000	0.75000	DA	DA	5.898	5.214	5.255	5.392
0.27083	0.72917			5.091	4.569	4.610	4.723
0.29167	0.70833		DW++	4.415	4.018	4.055	4.149
0.31250	0.68750	D–+		3.842	3.540	3.574	3.650
0.33333	0.66667		DW+	3.350	3.122	3.151	3.213
0.35417	0.64583			2.923	2.752	2.777	2.826
0.37500	0.62500	D–	DW	2.550	2.423	2.443	2.481
0.39583	0.60417			2.220	2.128	2.144	2.171
0.41667	0.58333		DW–	1.926	1.861	1.872	1.892
0.43750	0.56250	D––		1.662	1.618	1.625	1.638
0.45833	0.54167		DW––	1.422	1.396	1.400	1.407
0.47917	0.52083			1.203	1.190	1.192	1.195
0.50000	0.50000	A	A	1.000	1.000	1.000	1.000
0.52083	0.47917			0.810	0.822	0.821	0.819
0.54167	0.45833		CW––	0.629	0.654	0.654	0.651
0.56250	0.43750	C––		0.452	0.494	0.497	0.494
0.58333	0.41667		CW–	0.275	0.340	0.347	0.346
0.60417	0.39583			0.090	0.187	0.202	0.204
0.62500	0.37500	C–	CW	−0.112	0.033	0.060	0.066
0.64583	0.35417			−0.340	−0.130	−0.086	−0.071
0.66667	0.33333		CW+	−0.602	−0.305	−0.238	−0.211
0.68750	0.31250	C–+		−0.908	−0.500	−0.401	−0.359
0.70833	0.29167		CW++	−1.269	−0.721	−0.582	−0.520
0.72917	0.27083			−1.702	−0.973	−0.785	−0.699
0.75000	0.25000	CA	CA	−2.226	−1.268	−1.016	−0.899
0.77083	0.22917			−2.872	−1.617	−1.286	−1.129
0.79167	0.20833		CS––	−3.683	−2.037	−1.605	−1.399
0.81250	0.18750	C+–		−4.721	−2.554	−1.990	−1.721
0.83333	0.16667		CS–	−6.085	−3.204	−2.468	−2.116
0.85417	0.14583			−7.936	−4.048	−3.077	−2.615
0.87500	0.12500	C+	CS	−10.549	−5.184	−3.883	−3.269
0.89583	0.10417			−14.448	−6.793	−5.006	−4.170
0.91667	0.08333		CS+	−20.727	−9.235	−6.682	−5.504
0.93750	0.06250	C++		−32.090	−13.361	−9.465	−7.698
0.95833	0.04167		CS++	−57.267	−21.742	−15.016	−12.042
0.97917	0.02083			−144.399	−47.322	−31.647	−24.971
1	0	C	C	$-\infty$	$-\infty$	$-\infty$	$-\infty$

In this definition, the mean values of conjunction and disjunction are:

$$\overline{x \wedge y} = \int_0^1 dy \int_0^1 (x \wedge y)dx = \int_0^1 dy \left[\int_0^y (x \wedge y)dx + \int_y^1 (x \wedge y)dx \right] = \int_0^1 dy \left[\int_0^y x\,dx + \int_y^1 y\,dx \right]$$

$$= \int_0^1 \left(y - \frac{y^2}{2} \right) dy = \frac{1}{2} - \frac{1}{6} = \frac{1}{3}.$$

$$\overline{x \vee y} = \int_0^1 dy \int_0^1 (x \vee y)dx = \int_0^1 dy \left[\int_0^y (x \vee y)dx + \int_y^1 (x \vee y)dx \right] = \int_0^1 dy \left[\int_0^y y\,dx + \int_y^1 x\,dx \right]$$

$$= \int_0^1 \left(\frac{1 + y^2}{2} \right) dy = \frac{1}{2} + \frac{1}{6} = \frac{2}{3}.$$

These results yield the following global andness and global orness (or global conjunction and disjunction degrees) for GCD aggregators of two logic variables:

$$\alpha_g = \frac{2/3 - \overline{x \Diamond y}}{2/3 - 1/3} = 2 - 3\left(\overline{x \Diamond y} \right),$$

$$\omega_g = 1 - \alpha_g = 3\left(\overline{x \Diamond y} \right) - 1,$$

The primary reason for introducing global andness and orness was to reduce avoidable computational complexity related to both local and mean local andness/orness, and to reduce the variability caused by different numbers of variables. Indeed, in the case of global andness and orness there are more cases where we can use an analytic approach to compute the necessary indicators, and computations are simpler. In addition, logic aggregators are regularly smooth (with continuous partial derivatives with respect to all variables); so, their numerical integration is much simpler and more accurate than the numerical integration of wild and highly variable local andness and orness functions presented in previous sections.

For example, in the case of geometric mean $x \Diamond y = \sqrt{xy}$, the global andness and orness can be very easily computed:

$$\overline{\sqrt{xy}} = \int_0^1 \sqrt{xy}\,dxdy = \int_0^1 y^{1/2}dy \int_0^1 x^{1/2}dx = \left(\frac{2}{3} \right)^2 = \frac{4}{9},$$

$$\alpha_g[GEO] = 2 - 4/3 = 2/3 \quad (67\%),$$

$$\omega_g[GEO] = 1 - \alpha_g = 1/3 \quad (33\%).$$

This result shows that the geometric mean can be used to implement a partial conjunction with the global andness of 67%. This is different from the mean local andness of the geometric mean, which is 61.4%. The difference between these two metrics is not dramatic, and evaluators can be trained to use either one of them.

Similarly to the geometric mean, other basic means are also suitable for modeling simultaneity and substitutability. To demonstrate this possibility, let us compute the andness and orness of the traditional harmonic, arithmetic, and quadratic mean. In the case of harmonic mean $x \Diamond y = \frac{2xy}{x+y}$ we have:

$$\overline{\left(\frac{2xy}{x+y}\right)} = 2\int_0^1\int_0^1 \frac{xy}{x+y}dxdy = 2\int_0^1\int_0^1\left(y - \frac{y^2}{x+y}\right)dxdy = 2\left[\int_0^1 dx\int_0^1 ydy - \int_0^1 dy\int_0^1 \frac{y^2}{x+y}dx\right]$$

$$= 2\left[\frac{1}{2} - \int_0^1 y^2\ln(y+1)dy + \int_0^1 y^2\ln y\, dy\right] = 2\left[\frac{1}{2} - \left(\frac{\ln 2}{3} - \frac{1}{3}\int_0^1 \frac{y^3}{y+1}dy\right) - \frac{1}{3}\int_0^1 y^2 dy\right]$$

$$= 2\left[\frac{1}{2} - \left(\frac{\ln 2}{3} - \frac{1}{3}\left[\frac{y^3}{3} - \frac{y^2}{2} + y - \ln(y+1)\right]_0^1\right) - \frac{1}{9}\right]$$

$$= 2\left[\frac{1}{2} - \frac{\ln 2}{3} + \frac{1}{3}\left(\frac{1}{3} - \frac{1}{2} + 1 - \ln 2\right) - \frac{1}{9}\right]$$

$$= 2\left(\frac{2}{3} - \frac{2\ln 2}{3}\right) = \frac{4 - \ln 16}{3},$$

$$\alpha_g[HAR] = 2 - 3\overline{\left(\frac{2xy}{x+y}\right)} = \ln 16 - 2 = 0.7726 \qquad (77\%),$$

$$\omega_g[HAR] = 1 - \alpha_g = 3 - \ln 16 = 0.2274 \qquad (23\%).$$

The global andness is again greater than the mean local andness, which is 69.3%.

In the case of arithmetic mean $x \Diamond y = (x+y)/2$, we have:

$$\overline{\frac{(x+y)}{2}} = \frac{1}{2}\int_0^1\int_0^1 (x+y)dxdy = \frac{1}{2}\left[\int_0^1 xdx\int_0^1 dy + \int_0^1 ydy\int_0^1 dx\right] = \frac{1}{2},$$

$$\alpha_g[ARI] = 2 - 3/2 = 1/2 \qquad (50\%),$$

$$\omega_g[ARI] = 1 - \alpha_g = 1/2 \qquad (50\%).$$

The arithmetic mean has the expected property that the global andness is equal to the mean local andness.

In the case of quadratic mean $x \Diamond y = \sqrt{(x^2 + y^2)/2}$, we have:

$$\sqrt{\frac{x^2 + y^2}{2}} = \frac{1}{\sqrt{2}} \int_0^1 \int_0^1 \sqrt{x^2 + y^2} \, dx \, dy = \left| \begin{array}{l} x = \rho \cos\varphi \\ y = \rho \sin\varphi \end{array} \right| = \frac{2}{\sqrt{2}} \int_0^{\pi/4} d\varphi \int_0^{1/\cos\varphi} \rho^2 d\rho = \frac{\sqrt{2}}{3} \int_0^{\pi/4} \frac{d\varphi}{\cos^3\varphi}$$

$$= \frac{\sqrt{2}}{3} \left[\frac{\sin\varphi}{2\cos^2\varphi} + \frac{1}{2} \ln \left| \tan\left(\frac{\varphi}{2} + \frac{\pi}{4}\right) \right| \right]_0^{\pi/4} = \frac{\sqrt{2}}{3} \left[\frac{\sin(\pi/4)}{2\cos^2(\pi/4)} + \frac{1}{2} \ln \left| \tan\left(\frac{\pi}{8} + \frac{\pi}{4}\right) \right| \right]$$

$$= \frac{\sqrt{2}}{3} \left[\frac{1}{\sqrt{2}} + \frac{1}{2} \ln\tan\left(\frac{3\pi}{8}\right) \right] = \frac{1}{3} \left[1 + \frac{1}{\sqrt{2}} \ln\tan\left(\frac{3\pi}{8}\right) \right] = 0.5411,$$

$$\alpha_g[QUAD] = 1 - \frac{1}{\sqrt{2}} \ln\tan\left(\frac{3\pi}{8}\right) = 1 - \ln\left(1 + \sqrt{2}\right)^{1/\sqrt{2}} = 0.3768 \qquad (38\%),$$

$$\omega_g[QUAD] = \frac{1}{\sqrt{2}} \ln\tan\left(\frac{3\pi}{8}\right) = \ln\left(1 + \sqrt{2}\right)^{1/\sqrt{2}} = 0.6232 \qquad (62\%).$$

The geometric mean has a desirable annihilator property $0 \Diamond y = x \Diamond 0 = 0$, and represents HPC with the lowest andness of all power means. Therefore, in the case of two variables and aggregators based on weighted power means (WPM), the geometric mean determines the natural border between HPC and SPC. The corresponding threshold andness is $\alpha_\theta = 2/3$ and all aggregators that satisfy $\alpha_\theta \leq \alpha_g < 1$ represent models of HPC, and all aggregators in the range $1/2 < \alpha_g < \alpha_\theta$ are models of SPC.

It is useful to note that power means are a generalization of the harmonic, geometric, arithmetic, and quadratic means, as well as the minimum and the maximum functions. Power means are important because they provide a continuous transition from the pure conjunction to the pure disjunction, as follows:

$$M(x_1, \ldots, x_n; r) = \left(\frac{x_1^r + \cdots + x_n^r}{n} \right)^{1/r} = \begin{cases} x_1 \wedge \cdots \wedge x_n, & r = -\infty \\ \dfrac{n}{1/x_1 + \cdots + 1/x_n}, & r = -1 \\ (x_1 \cdots x_n)^{1/n}, & r = 0 \\ \dfrac{x_1 + \cdots + x_n}{n}, & r = 1 \\ \sqrt{\dfrac{x_1^2 + \cdots + x_n^2}{n}}, & r = 2 \\ x_1 \vee \cdots \vee x_n, & r = +\infty. \end{cases}$$

In the case $r = 0$, the power mean becomes the geometric mean. That can be shown using L'Hospital's rule as follows:

$$\lim_{r \to 0} \left(\frac{x_1^r + x_2^r + \cdots + x_n^r}{n} \right)^{1/r} = \lim_{r \to 0} \exp \left(\frac{\ln\left(x_1^r + x_2^r + \cdots + x_n^r \right) - \ln(n)}{r} \right)$$

$$= \exp \left(\lim_{r \to 0} \frac{\ln\left(x_1^r + x_2^r + \cdots + x_n^r \right) - \ln n}{r} \right)$$

$$= \exp \left(\lim_{r \to 0} \frac{\dfrac{\left(x_1^r \ln x_1 + x_2^r \ln x_2 + \cdots + x_n^r \ln x_n \right)}{x_1^r + x_2^r + \cdots + x_n^r}}{1} \right)$$

$$= \exp \left(\frac{\ln x_1 + \ln x_2 + \cdots + \ln x_n}{n} \right) = \exp \left(\ln(x_1 x_2 \ldots x_n)^{1/n} \right) = (x_1 x_2 \ldots x_n)^{1/n}.$$

In the extreme cases of power mean, we use the parameter $r = \pm\infty$. Without reducing the generality of analysis, let us assume that the input values are sorted:

$$x_{\min} = x_1 \leq x_2 \leq \ldots \leq x_n = x_{\max}.$$

Then we can analyze the extreme cases as follows:

$$\lim_{r \to +\infty} \left(\frac{x_1^r + x_2^r + \cdots + x_n^r}{n} \right)^{1/r} = \lim_{r \to +\infty} x_{\max} \left(\frac{x_1^r + x_2^r + \cdots + x_n^r}{n\, x_{\max}^r} \right)^{1/r}$$

$$= x_{\max} \lim_{r \to +\infty} \exp \ln \left(\frac{(x_1/x_{\max})^r + (x_2/x_{\max})^r + \ldots + 1}{n} \right)^{1/r}$$

$$= x_{\max} \exp \left(\lim_{r \to +\infty} \left(\frac{\ln\left((x_1/x_{\max})^r + (x_2/x_{\max})^r + \ldots + 1\right) - \ln n}{r} \right) \right)$$

$$= x_{\max} \exp(0) = x_{\max} = x_1 \vee x_2 \vee \cdots \vee x_n.$$

$$\lim_{r \to -\infty} \left(\frac{x_1^r + x_2^r + \cdots + x_n^r}{n} \right)^{1/r} = \lim_{r \to -\infty} x_{\min} \left(\frac{x_1^r + x_2^r + \cdots + x_n^r}{n\, x_{\min}^r} \right)^{1/r}$$

$$= x_{\min} \lim_{r \to -\infty} \exp \ln \left(\frac{1 + (x_2/x_{\min})^r + \ldots + (x_n/x_{\min})^r}{n} \right)^{1/r}$$

$$= x_{\min} \exp \left(\lim_{r \to -\infty} \left(\frac{\ln\left(1 + (x_2/x_{\min})^r + \ldots + (x_n/x_{\min})^r\right) - \ln n}{r} \right) \right)$$

$$= x_{\min} \exp(0) = x_{\min} = x_1 \wedge x_2 \wedge \cdots \wedge x_n.$$

The parameter r is adjustable in the range $-\infty \leq r \leq +\infty$. The power mean includes as special cases the maximum simultaneity function (full conjunction, for $r = -\infty$) and the maximum substitutability function (full disjunction, for $r = +\infty$). Therefore, the power mean enables a continuous adjustment of andness and orness in the full range from 0 to 1. For each value of andness/orness, there is a corresponding unique value of the parameter r.

Analytic computation of andness/orness indicators is not always simple. Selected accurate values of the global andness and orness for some of important aggregators are summarized in Table 2.3.2. These results show that basic means can be used to implement a spectrum of selected degrees of simultaneity and substitutability. In addition, these results are useful for testing and calibration of numerical programs for computation of andness/orness.

The harmonic and geometric mean are suitable as basic models of simultaneity, and the quadratic mean is a popular model of substitutability. The arithmetic mean is as a *neutrality function* since it provides a perfect balance of simultaneity and substitutability. All means in Table 2.3.2 having $1/2 < \alpha_g < 1$ can be used to implement partial conjunction, and means having $1/2 < \omega_g < 1$ can be used to implement partial disjunction.

Proposition 2.3.2. If aggregators ∇ and Δ satisfy De Morgan's duality (Section 2.4.1), then their global andness and orness are crosswise equal: $\alpha_g^{(x\nabla y)} = \omega_g^{(x\Delta y)}$ and $\omega_g^{(x\nabla y)} = \alpha_g^{(x\Delta y)}$.

Proof (for the case of two variables, presented in Table 2.3.2):

$$x\nabla y = \overline{\overline{x\nabla y}} = \overline{\bar{x}\Delta\bar{y}} = 1 - (1-x)\Delta(1-y),$$

$$x\Delta y = \overline{\overline{x\Delta y}} = \overline{\bar{x}\nabla\bar{y}} = 1 - (1-x)\nabla(1-y),$$

$$\alpha_g^{(x\nabla y)} = 2 - 3\int_0^1 dx \int_0^1 (x\nabla y)dy = 2 - 3\int_0^1 dx \int_0^1 [1-(1-x)\Delta(1-y)]dy$$

$$= -1 + 3\int_0^1 dx \int_0^1 [(1-x)\Delta(1-y)]dy = \begin{vmatrix} p = 1-x; & dp = -dx \\ q = 1-y; & dq = -dy \end{vmatrix}$$

$$= -1 + 3\int_1^0 dp \int_1^0 (p\Delta q)dq = 3\int_0^1 dx \int_0^1 (x\Delta y)dy - 1 = \omega_g^{(x\Delta y)},$$

$$\omega_g^{(x\nabla y)} = 1 - \alpha_g^{(x\nabla y)} = 1 - \omega_g^{(x\Delta y)} = \alpha_g^{(x\Delta y)}.$$

The results in Table 2.3.2 also show that if the global andness and orness are computed for t-norms and t-conorms, then the resulting values are outside the standard [0,1] range; they can be greater than 1 or negative. Obviously, t-norms and t-conorms provide stronger levels of simultaneity and substitutability than means, and we use them in GL as models of hyperconjunction and hyperdisjunction (see Section 2.1.3 and Fig. 2.1.2).

Let us now investigate the global andness/orness for the general case of n variables. The prerequisites for defining the global andness/orness are the mean values of conjunction and disjunction of n variables that are defined as follows:

Table 2.3.2 Accurate values of global andness and orness for selected popular aggregators.

Aggregator name	Function $x \Diamond y$	Global andness	Global orness
t-norm	xy	5/4	−1/4
Minimum	$\min(x, y) = x \wedge y$	1	0
Power mean $(r = -2)$	$\sqrt{2}xy \big/ \sqrt{x^2 + y^2}$	$2^{3/2} - 2 = 0.8284$	$3 - 2^{3/2} = 0.1716$
Harmonic mean $(r = -1)$	$\dfrac{2xy}{x + y}$	$\ln 16 - 2 = 0.7726$	$3 - \ln 16 = 0.2274$
Contraharmonic De Morgan's dual	$\dfrac{x(1 - x) + y(1 - y)}{(1 - x) + (1 - y)}$	$\ln 16 - 2 = 0.7726$	$3 - \ln 16 = 0.2274$
Power mean $(r = -1/2)$	$\dfrac{4xy}{\left(\sqrt{x} + \sqrt{y}\right)^2}$	$34 - 12\ln 16 = 0.7289$	$12\ln 16 - 33 = 0.2711$
Geometric mean	$\sqrt{xy}$	$2/3 = 0.6667$	$1/3 = 0.3333$
Square root power mean	$\left(\dfrac{\sqrt{x} + \sqrt{y}}{2}\right)^2$	$7/12 = 0.5833$	$5/12 = 0.4167$
Heronian mean	$(x + \sqrt{xy} + y)/3$	$5/9 = 0.5556$	$4/9 = 0.4444$
Generalized Heronian mean	$p\dfrac{x + y}{2} + (1 - p)\sqrt{xy},$ $0 \le p \le 1$	$\dfrac{4 - p}{6}$	$\dfrac{2 + p}{6}$
Arithmetic mean	$(x + y)/2$	0.5	0.5
OWA	$\alpha(x \wedge y) + \omega(x \vee y)$	α	ω
Centroidal mean	$\dfrac{2}{3}\left(\dfrac{x^2 + xy + y^2}{x + y}\right)$	$\dfrac{4 - \ln 16}{3} = 0.4091$	$\dfrac{\ln 16 - 1}{3} = 0.5909$
Quadratic mean	$\sqrt{\dfrac{x^2 + y^2}{2}}$	$1 - \left(1/\sqrt{2}\right)\ln\left(1 + \sqrt{2}\right)$ $= 0.37677$	$\left(1/\sqrt{2}\right)\ln\left(1 + \sqrt{2}\right)$ $= 0.62323$
Geometric mean De Morgan's dual	$1 - \sqrt{(1 - x)(1 - y)}$	$1/3 = 0.3333$	$2/3 = 0.6667$
Contraharmonic mean	$\dfrac{x^2 + y^2}{x + y}$	$3 - \ln 16 = 0.2274$	$\ln 16 - 2 = 0.7726$
Harmonic mean De Morgan's dual	$\dfrac{x(1 - y) + y(1 - x)}{(1 - x) + (1 - y)}$	$3 - \ln 16 = 0.2274$	$\ln 16 - 2 = 0.7726$
Maximum	$\max(x, y) = x \vee y$	0	1
t-conorm	$x + y - xy$	−1/4	5/4

Note: The contraharmonic mean and its De Morgan's dual are not monotonic and therefore are not considered aggregators; t-norms and conorms do not satisfy internality and idempotency.

$$\overline{x_1 \wedge \cdots \wedge x_n} := \int_0^1 dx_1 \int_0^1 dx_2 \cdots \int_0^1 (x_1 \wedge \cdots \wedge x_n) dx_n = \frac{1}{n+1}$$

$$\overline{x_1 \vee \cdots \vee x_n} := \int_0^1 dx_1 \int_0^1 dx_2 \cdots \int_0^1 (x_1 \vee \cdots \vee x_n) dx_n = \frac{n}{n+1}$$

This result was derived in [DUJ73a] recursively as follows:

$$m_{k,n} = (x_1 \wedge \cdots \wedge x_n)^k = \begin{cases} x_n^k, & 0 \le x_n \le m_{1,n-1} \\ m_{k,n-1}, & m_{1,n-1} \le x_n \le 1 \end{cases}$$

$$m_{k,n} = m_{1,n}^k, \quad m_{p,n} m_{q,n} = m_{p+q,n}$$

$$J_{k,n} = \overline{(x_1 \wedge \cdots \wedge x_n)^k} = \int_0^1 dx_1 \cdots \int_0^1 dx_{n-1} \int_0^1 m_{k,n} dx_n$$

$$= \int_0^1 dx_1 \cdots \int_0^1 dx_{n-1} \left(\int_0^{m_{1,n-1}} x_n^k dx_n + \int_{m_{1,n-1}}^1 m_{k,n-1} dx_n \right)$$

$$= \frac{1}{k+1} \int_0^1 dx_1 \cdots \int_0^1 m_{k+1,n-1} dx_{n-1} + \int_0^1 dx_1 \cdots \int_0^1 (1 - m_{1,n-1}) m_{k,n-1} dx_{n-1}$$

$$= \frac{1}{k+1} J_{k+1,n-1} + \int_0^1 dx_1 \cdots \int_0^1 m_{k,n-1} dx_{n-1} - \int_0^1 dx_1 \cdots \int_0^1 m_{k+1,n-1} dx_{n-1}$$

$$= J_{k,n-1} - \frac{k}{k+1} J_{k+1,n-1}.$$

The recurrent relation $J_{k,n} = J_{k,n-1} - \frac{k}{k+1} J_{k+1,n-1}$ is satisfied by $J_{k,n} = 1 / \binom{k+n}{n} = \frac{n!}{(k+1)\cdots(k+n)}$. If $k = 1$, then the mean value of conjunction is $J_{1,n} = \overline{x_1 \wedge \cdots \wedge x_n} = \frac{1}{n+1}$.

Similarly, in the case of disjunction, we have the following:

$$M_{k,n} = (x_1 \vee \cdots \vee x_n)^k = \begin{cases} M_{k,n-1}, & 0 \le x_n \le M_{1,n-1} \\ x_n^k, & M_{1,n-1} \le x_n \le 1 \end{cases}$$

$$M_{k,n} = M_{1,n}^k, \quad M_{p,n} M_{q,n} = M_{p+q,n}$$

$$I_{k,n} = \overline{(x_1 \vee \cdots \vee x_n)^k} = \int_0^1 dx_1 \cdots \int_0^1 dx_{n-1} \int_0^1 M_n dx_n$$

$$= \int_0^1 dx_1 \cdots \int_0^1 dx_{n-1} \left(\int_0^{M_{1,n-1}} M_{k,n-1} dx_n + \int_{M_{1,n-1}}^1 x_n^k dx_n \right)$$

$$= \int_0^1 dx_1 \cdots \int_0^1 M_{k+1,n-1} dx_{n-1} + \frac{1}{k+1} \int_0^1 dx_1 \cdots \int_0^1 (1 - M_{k+1,n-1}) dx_{n-1}$$

$$= I_{k+1,n-1} + \frac{1 - I_{k+1,n-1}}{k+1} = \frac{1 + k I_{k+1,n-1}}{k+1}$$

The recurrent relation $I_{k,n} = (1 + k I_{k+1,n-1})/(k+1)$ is satisfied by $I_{k,n} = n/(k+n)$. Consequently, if $k = 1$, then the mean value of disjunction is $I_{1,n} = \overline{x_1 \vee \cdots \vee x_n} = n/(n+1)$.

Based on the mean values of conjunction and disjunction, the global andness/orness in the case of n variables was introduced in [DUJ74a] as follows:

$$\alpha_g = \frac{\overline{x_1 \vee \cdots \vee x_n} - \overline{x_1 \lozenge \cdots \lozenge x_n}}{\overline{x_1 \vee \cdots \vee x_n} - \overline{x_1 \wedge \cdots \wedge x_n}} = \frac{n - (n+1)\left(\overline{x_1 \lozenge \cdots \lozenge x_n}\right)}{n-1},$$

$$\omega_g = \frac{\overline{x_1 \lozenge \cdots \lozenge x_n} - \overline{x_1 \wedge \cdots \wedge x_n}}{\overline{x_1 \vee \cdots \vee x_n} - \overline{x_1 \wedge \cdots \wedge x_n}} = \frac{(n+1)\left(\overline{x_1 \lozenge \cdots \lozenge x_n}\right) - 1}{n-1}.$$

$$\overline{x_1 \lozenge \cdots \lozenge x_n} = \int_0^1 dx_1 \int_0^1 dx_2 \cdots \int_0^1 (x_1 \lozenge \cdots \lozenge x_n) dx_n,$$

$$\alpha_g \in I, \quad \omega_g \in I, \quad \alpha_g + \omega_g = 1.$$

Not surprisingly, in the case of the arithmetic mean, we have

$$\overline{x_1 \lozenge \cdots \lozenge x_n} = \frac{1}{n} \int_0^1 dx_1 \int_0^1 dx_2 \cdots \int_0^1 (x_1 + \cdots + x_n) dx_n$$

$$= \frac{1}{n} \int_0^1 dx_1 \cdots \int_0^1 (x_1 + \cdots + x_{n-1} + \tfrac{1}{2}) dx_{n-1} = \tfrac{1}{2},$$

$$\alpha_g[A] = \tfrac{1}{2}, \quad \omega_g[A] = \tfrac{1}{2}.$$

The global andness and orness of the arithmetic mean are constant. They are constant also for conjunction and disjunction: $\alpha_g[C] = \omega_g[D] = 1$, $\omega_g[C] = \alpha_g[D] = 0$. However, for all other instances of power means, the global andness and orness are functions of n. According to [DUJ74a], in the case of the geometric mean we have

$$\overline{x_1 \Diamond \cdots \Diamond x_n} = \int_0^1 dx_1 \int_0^1 dx_2 \cdots \int_0^1 (x_1 \cdots x_n)^{1/n} dx_n = \int_0^1 x_1^{1/n} dx_1 \int_0^1 x_2^{1/n} dx_2 \cdots \int_0^1 x_n^{1/n} dx_n = \left(\frac{n}{n+1}\right)^n.$$

$$\alpha_g[G;n] = \frac{n}{n-1} - \frac{n+1}{n-1}\left(\frac{n}{n+1}\right)^n, \quad \frac{2}{3} = \alpha_g[G;2] > \alpha_g[G;3] > \cdots > \alpha_g[G;+\infty] = 1 - \frac{1}{e} = 0.632.$$

$$\omega_g[G;n] = \frac{n+1}{n-1}\left(\frac{n}{n+1}\right)^n - \frac{1}{n-1}, \quad \frac{1}{3} = \omega_g[G;2] < \omega_g[G;3] < \cdots < \omega_g[G;+\infty] = \frac{1}{e} = 0.368,$$

$$\alpha_g[G;2] = 0.66666667, \quad \omega_g[G;2] = 0.33333333,$$
$$\alpha_g[G;3] = 0.65625, \quad \omega_g[G;3] = 0.34375,$$
$$\alpha_g[G;4] = 0.65066667, \quad \omega_g[G;4] = 0.34933333,$$
$$\alpha_g[G;5] = 0.64718364, \quad \omega_g[G;5] = 0.35281636.$$

In the case of geometric mean the variations of andness and orness for various values of n can be illustrated using the relative global andness and orness indicators $\alpha_g[G;n]/\alpha_g[G;+\infty]$ and $\omega_g[G;n]/\omega_g[G;+\infty]$, shown in Fig. 2.3.11. In the most frequently used range $2 \le n \le 5$ the variations of global andness/orness of the geometric mean are less than 6%.

Computation of global andness requires the computation of the integral $\overline{x_1 \Diamond \cdots \Diamond x_n}$. Of course, the ideal situation is if we can compute the integral analytically because that yields the ultimate precision. Unfortunately, that is not frequently possible. In such cases, we must use sophisticated numerical methods because multiple integrals of functions that can have high values of derivatives cannot be easily computed with high precision. We have done that in all cases in

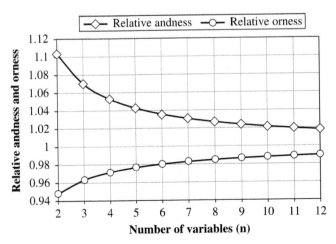

Figure 2.3.11 Relative andness and orness of the geometric mean as functions of *n*.

```cpp
#include <math.h>
#include <iostream>
using namespace std;

double urn(void) {return double(rand())/RAND_MAX;}

double ANDNESS(double (*F)(double, double))
{ int Total=10000000, Below, i;
  for(Below=i=0; i<Total; i++)
    if(urn() < F(urn(), urn())) Below++;
  return 2.- Below*3.0/Total;
}

double ANDNESS(double (*F)(double, double, double))
{ int Total=10000000, Below, i;
  for(Below=i=0; i<Total; i++)
    if(urn() < F(urn(), urn(), urn())) Below++;
  return 1.5- Below*2.0/Total;
}

double ANDNESS(double (*F)(double, double, double, double))
{ int Total=10000000, Below, i;
  for(Below=i=0; i<Total; i++)
    if(urn() < F(urn(), urn(), urn(), urn())) Below++;
  return (4.- Below*5./Total)/3.;
}

double ANDNESS(double (*F)(double, double, double, double, double))
{ int Total=10000000, Below, i;
  for(Below=i=0; i<Total; i++)
    if(urn() < F(urn(), urn(), urn(), urn(), urn())) Below++;
  return 1.25- Below*1.5/Total;
}

double A2(double a, double b) {return (a+b)/2.;}
double A3(double a, double b, double c) {return (a+b+c)/3.;}
double A4(double a, double b, double c, double d) {return (a+b+c+d)/4.;}
double A5(double a, double b, double c, double d, double e) {return (a+b+c+d+e)/5.;}
double G2(double a, double b) {return sqrt(a*b);}
double G3(double a, double b, double c) {return pow(a*b*c, 1./3.);}
double G4(double a, double b, double c, double d) {return pow(a*b*c*d, 0.25);}
double G5(double a, double b, double c, double d, double e) {return pow(a*b*c*d*e,
0.2);}

int main(void)
{
    cout << "A: " << ANDNESS(A2) << "  " << ANDNESS(A3) << "  "
         << ANDNESS(A4) << "  " << ANDNESS(A5) << "\n";
    cout << "A: " << ANDNESS(A2) << "  " << ANDNESS(A3) << "  "
         << ANDNESS(A4) << "  " << ANDNESS(A5) << "\n\n";
    cout << "G: " << ANDNESS(G2) << "  " << ANDNESS(G3) << "  "
         << ANDNESS(G4) << "  " << ANDNESS(G5) << "\n";
    cout << "G: " << ANDNESS(G2) << "  " << ANDNESS(G3) << "  "
         << ANDNESS(G4) << "  " << ANDNESS(G5) << "\n\n";
    return 0;
}

Results:
A: 0.499789  0.499981  0.500570  0.500522
A: 0.500360  0.499654  0.500043  0.500126

G: 0.666322  0.656563  0.650652  0.647356
G: 0.667183  0.656221  0.651042  0.647383
```

Figure 2.3.12 Monte Carlo computation of global andness in the case of 2, 3, 4, and 5 variables.

this chapter. However, there is also good news for those who are satisfied with the modest accuracy of three significant decimal digits. In such cases, the global andness can be computed in an extremely simple way using the Monte Carlo approach exemplified in Fig. 2.3.12 for functions of 2, 3, 4 and 5 variables. The test with the arithmetic and the geometric mean creates rather quickly

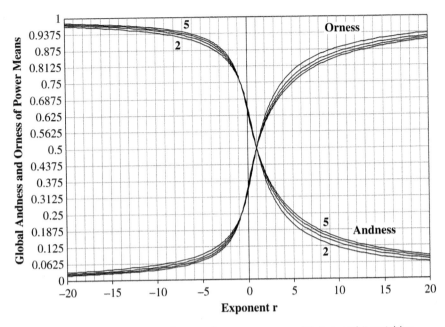

Figure 2.3.13 Global andness and orness for power means of 2, 3, 4, and 5 variables.

and reliably three correct decimal digits. This level of accuracy is frequently sufficient, and in such cases, this numeric method can be used for the analysis of many aggregation functions.

Global andness and orness of power means for various values of the exponent r and for 2, 3, 4, and 5 variables are presented in Fig. 2.3.13. Compared to the mean local andness/orness shown in Fig. 2.3.10, the global andness/orness has lower dependence on the number of variables. The variability in the range $2 \leq n \leq 5$ is rather low and in cases where precision is not critical, it is possible to replace individual curves with their average value, as shown in Fig. 2.3.14. That can eliminate the inconvenience caused by the fact that WPM exponents are functions of n, and provide associativity for GCD aggregators based on WPM (see Sections 2.2.3 and 2.4.4).

Let us note that the curves in Fig. 2.3.13 intersect not only at $r = 1$, but also at approximately $r \approx -0.7$ and $\alpha_g \approx 0.75$. This is a rather fortunate property, because in the most frequently used range of andness between 0.5 and 0.8 the differences between the four curves are negligible, justifying the use of the average values presented in Fig. 2.3.14.

In all applications where we use GCD for building preference aggregation structures, the first step is to select a desired andness/orness. Then, assuming that the GCD aggregator uses WPM, we can select the corresponding values of

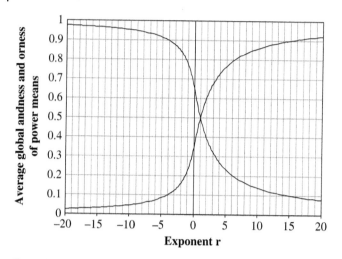

Figure 2.3.14 Average global andness and orness for power means in the range $2 \leq n \leq 5$.

exponents r_2, r_3, r_4, r_5 using Table 2.3.3. The same results for exponential means (EXM, Figs. 2.4.5, 2.4.11) are shown in Table 2.3.4.

The results shown in Tables 2.3.3 and 2.3.4 can be approximated using the following ratios of polynomials:

$$r_n^{(WPM)}(\omega_g) = \frac{0.25 + a_n^{(WPM)}(\omega_g - \frac{1}{2}) + b_n^{(WPM)}(\omega_g - \frac{1}{2})^2 + c_n^{(WPM)}(\omega_g - \frac{1}{2})^3 + d_n^{(WPM)}(\omega_g - \frac{1}{2})^4}{\omega_g(1 - \omega_g)},$$

$$r_n^{(EM)}(\omega_g) = \frac{a_n^{(EM)}(\omega_g - \frac{1}{2}) + c_n^{(EM)}(\omega_g - \frac{1}{2})^3 + e_n^{(EM)}(\omega_g - \frac{1}{2})^5}{\omega_g(1 - \omega_g)}, \quad n = 2,3,4,5.$$

The parameters of this approximation for WPM and EXM are shown in Tables 2.3.5 and 2.3.6. The accuracy of approximations can be evaluated by selecting a sequence $\omega_g(k) = k/K$, $k = 1...,(K-1)$ and computing the corresponding sequence of approximate $r_n(k)$ values. Then, for these $r_n(k)$ values we can compute corresponding correct values of orness $\Omega_g(k)$, $k = 1...,$ $(K-1)$ and compute the average value of error $|\Omega_g(k) - \omega_g(k)|$, $k = 1...,(K-1)$.

The orness of weighted power means and exponential means are defined as follows:

$$\Omega_n^{(WPM)}(r) = \frac{1}{n-1}\left[(n+1)\int_0^1 dx_1...\int_0^1 \left(\frac{x_1^r + ... + x_n^r}{n}\right)^{1/r} dx_n - 1\right],$$

$$\Omega_n^{(EM)}(r) = \frac{1}{n-1}\left[(n+1)\int_0^1 dx_1...\int_0^1 \ln\left(\frac{e^{rx_1} + ... + e^{rx_n}}{n}\right)^{1/r} dx_n - 1\right].$$

Table 2.3.3 Selecting WPM exponents for desired level of global andness/orness.

Global		Aggregators		WPM exponent				
Andness	**Orness**	**[17]**	**[25]**	r_2	r_3	r_4	r_5	r_{ave}
0	1	D	D	$+\infty$	$+\infty$	$+\infty$	$+\infty$	$+\infty$
0.02083	0.97917			65.0032	77.0544	86.2454	93.7053	80.4363
0.04167	0.95833		DS++	31.7259	37.4899	41.8126	45.3757	39.0660
0.06250	0.93750	D++		20.6305	24.2994	27.0795	29.3192	25.2736
0.08333	0.91667		DS+	15.0787	17.7005	19.6785	21.2647	18.3750
0.10417	0.89583			11.7455	13.7382	15.2348	16.4292	14.2339
0.12500	0.87500	D+	DS	9.5208	11.0937	12.2695	13.2031	11.4716
0.14583	0.85417			7.9295	9.2025	10.1490	10.8966	9.4971
0.16667	0.83333		DS–	6.7340	7.7819	8.5565	9.1647	8.0150
0.18750	0.81250	D+–		5.8024	6.6746	7.3159	7.8162	6.8610
0.20833	0.79167		DS––	5.0550	5.7870	6.3214	6.7357	5.9366
0.22917	0.77083			4.4421	5.0587	5.5060	5.8504	5.1791
0.25000	0.75000	DA	DA	3.9294	4.4502	4.8250	5.1113	4.5467
0.27083	0.72917			3.4937	3.9334	4.2469	4.4848	4.0107
0.29167	0.70833		DW++	3.1184	3.4884	3.7500	3.9468	3.5500
0.31250	0.68750	D–+		2.7918	3.1009	3.3180	3.4795	3.1496
0.33333	0.66667		DW+	2.5038	2.7604	2.9385	3.0695	2.7985
0.35417	0.64583			2.2479	2.4582	2.6018	2.7072	2.4872
0.37500	0.62500	D–	DW	2.0183	2.1872	2.3018	2.3846	2.2091
0.39583	0.60417			1.8113	1.9435	2.0315	2.0946	1.9594
0.41667	0.58333		DW–	1.6218	1.7216	1.7873	1.8337	1.7328
0.43750	0.56250	D––		1.4494	1.5190	1.5644	1.5962	1.5263
0.45833	0.54167		DW––	1.2892	1.3332	1.3612	1.3806	1.3375
0.47917	0.52083			1.1394	1.1602	1.1732	1.1821	1.1621
0.50000	0.50000	A	A	1.0000	1.0000	1.0000	1.0000	1.0000
0.52083	0.47917			0.8696	0.8507	0.8396	0.8322	0.8491
0.54167	0.45833		CW––	0.7428	0.7082	0.6881	0.6749	0.7053
0.56250	0.43750	C––		0.6196	0.5725	0.5455	0.5281	0.5686
0.58333	0.41667		CW–	0.5000	0.4449	0.4132	0.3928	0.4399
0.60417	0.39583			0.3841	0.3197	0.2841	0.2615	0.3134
0.62500	0.37500	C–	CW	0.2621	0.1930	0.1561	0.1333	0.1861
0.64583	0.35417			0.1341	0.0647	0.0293	0.0080	0.0579
0.66667	0.33333		CW+	0.0000	–0.0658	–0.0977	–0.1159	–0.0716
0.68750	0.31250	C–+		–0.1473	–0.2079	–0.2342	–0.2478	–0.2115
0.70833	0.29167		CW++	–0.3147	–0.3641	–0.3814	–0.3880	–0.3641
0.72917	0.27083			–0.5022	–0.5348	–0.5397	–0.5370	–0.5296
0.75000	0.25000	CA	CA	–0.7201	–0.7317	–0.7205	–0.7054	–0.7189
0.77083	0.22917			–0.9766	–0.9598	–0.9282	–0.8980	–0.9376
0.79167	0.20833		CS––	–1.2824	–1.2270	–1.1676	–1.1171	–1.1920
0.81250	0.18750	C+–		–1.6544	–1.5491	–1.4559	–1.3801	–1.4990
0.83333	0.16667		CS–	–2.1191	–1.9470	–1.8062	–1.6959	–1.8762
0.85417	0.14583			–2.7158	–2.4507	–2.2469	–2.0918	–2.3536
0.87500	0.12500	C+	CS	–3.5101	–3.1135	–2.8233	–2.6059	–2.9818
0.89583	0.10417			–4.6207	–4.0315	–3.6138	–3.3080	–3.8517
0.91667	0.08333		CS+	–6.2861	–5.3933	–4.7792	–4.3352	–5.1432
0.93750	0.06250	C++		–9.0600	–7.6392	–6.6886	–6.0098	–7.2781
0.95833	0.04167		CS++	–14.6067	–12.0898	–10.4522	–9.2892	–11.5210
0.97917	0.02083			–31.2447	–25.3397	–21.6154	–19.0257	–24.1910
1	0	C	C	$-\infty$	$-\infty$	$-\infty$	$-\infty$	$-\infty$

Table 2.3.4 Selecting EXM exponents for desired level of global andness/orness.

Global		Aggregators		Exponent of exponential means				
Andness	Orness	[17]	[25]	r_2	r_3	r_4	r_5	r_{ave}
0	1	D	D	$+\infty$	$+\infty$	$+\infty$	$+\infty$	$+\infty$
0.02083	0.97917			97.4110	103.1846	108.5019	113.2811	105.5957
0.04167	0.95833		DS++	47.4537	50.4076	52.9985	55.3238	51.5351
0.06250	0.93750	D++		30.7991	32.7956	34.4911	35.9737	33.5108
0.08333	0.91667		DS+	22.4438	23.9639	25.2087	26.2792	24.4696
0.10417	0.89583			17.4134	18.6447	19.6202	20.4443	19.0264
0.12500	0.87500	D+	DS	14.0437	15.0800	15.8765	16.5371	15.3799
0.14583	0.85417			11.6219	12.5164	13.1851	13.7295	12.7583
0.16667	0.83333		DS−	9.7912	10.5765	11.1491	11.6070	10.7755
0.18750	0.81250	D+−		8.3529	9.0509	9.5483	9.9391	9.2167
0.20833	0.79167		DS−−	7.1881	7.8135	8.2501	8.5872	7.9529
0.22917	0.77083			6.2211	6.7841	7.1699	7.4630	6.9019
0.25000	0.75000	DA	DA	5.4011	5.9092	6.2515	6.5074	6.0086
0.27083	0.72917			4.6930	5.1513	5.4555	5.6793	5.2352
0.29167	0.70833		DW++	4.0716	4.4839	4.7536	4.9494	4.5542
0.31250	0.68750	D−+		3.5185	3.8873	4.1252	4.2956	3.9456
0.33333	0.66667		DW+	3.0194	3.3463	3.5547	3.7020	3.3941
0.35417	0.64583			2.5633	2.8493	3.0296	3.1555	2.8879
0.37500	0.62500	D−	DW	2.1415	2.3872	2.5404	2.6462	2.4176
0.39583	0.60417			1.7470	1.9525	2.0793	2.1660	1.9757
0.41667	0.58333		DW−	1.3739	1.5389	1.6398	1.7082	1.5560
0.43750	0.56250	D−−		1.0169	1.1411	1.2165	1.2673	1.1531
0.45833	0.54167		DW−−	0.6716	0.7547	0.8049	0.8384	0.7622
0.47917	0.52083			0.3339	0.3756	0.4006	0.4173	0.3792
0.50000	0.50000	A	A	0.0000	0.0000	0.0000	0.0000	0.0000
0.52083	0.47917			−0.3339	−0.3756	−0.4006	−0.4173	−0.3792
0.54167	0.45833		CW−−	−0.6716	−0.7547	−0.8049	−0.8384	−0.7622
0.56250	0.43750	C−−		−1.0169	−1.1411	−1.2165	−1.2673	−1.1531
0.58333	0.41667		CW−	−1.3739	−1.5389	−1.6398	−1.7082	−1.5560
0.60417	0.39583			−1.7470	−1.9525	−2.0793	−2.1660	−1.9757
0.62500	0.37500	C−	CW	−2.1415	−2.3872	−2.5404	−2.6462	−2.4176
0.64583	0.35417			−2.5633	−2.8493	−3.0296	−3.1555	−2.8879
0.66667	0.33333		CW+	−3.0194	−3.3463	−3.5547	−3.7020	−3.3941
0.68750	0.31250	C−+		−3.5185	−3.8873	−4.1252	−4.2956	−3.9456
0.70833	0.29167		CW++	−4.0716	−4.4839	−4.7536	−4.9494	−4.5542
0.72917	0.27083			−4.6930	−5.1513	−5.4555	−5.6793	−5.2352
0.75000	0.25000	CA	CA	−5.4011	−5.9092	−6.2515	−6.5074	−6.0086
0.77083	0.22917			−6.2211	−6.7841	−7.1699	−7.4630	−6.9019
0.79167	0.20833		CS−−	−7.1881	−7.8135	−8.2501	−8.5872	−7.9529
0.81250	0.18750	C+−		−8.3529	−9.0509	−9.5483	−9.9391	−9.2167
0.83333	0.16667		CS−	−9.7912	−10.5765	−11.1491	−11.6070	−10.7755
0.85417	0.14583			−11.6219	−12.5164	−13.1851	−13.7295	−12.7583
0.87500	0.12500	C+	CS	−14.0437	−15.0800	−15.8765	−16.5371	−15.3799
0.89583	0.10417			−17.4134	−18.6447	−19.6202	−20.4443	−19.0264
0.91667	0.08333		CS+	−22.4438	−23.9639	−25.2087	−26.2792	−24.4696
0.93750	0.06250	C++		−30.7991	−32.7956	−34.4911	−35.9737	−33.5108
0.95833	0.04167		CS++	−47.4537	−50.4076	−52.9985	−55.3238	−51.5351
0.97917	0.02083			−97.4110	−103.1846	−108.5019	−113.2811	−105.5957
1	0	C	C	$-\infty$	$-\infty$	$-\infty$	$-\infty$	$-\infty$

Table 2.3.5 Parameters of numeric approximation for WPM and $K = 20$.

n	$a_n^{(WPM)}$	$b_n^{(WPM)}$	$c_n^{(WPM)}$	$d_n^{(WPM)}$	$\Delta_n^{(WPM)}$ [%]
2	1.64198	0.792841	1.80371	−1.83501	0.319
3	1.87086	1.51941	1.3928	−1.56091	0.334
4	1.96883	2.27386	1.68463	−2.82516	0.196
5	2.11599	2.54428	1.29513	−1.59209	0.363
Average r	1.89425	1.7044	1.47532	−1.42532	0.302

Table 2.3.6 Parameters of numeric approximation for EXM and $K = 20$.

n	$a_n^{(EM)}$	$c_n^{(EM)}$	$e_n^{(EM)}$	$\Delta_n^{(EM)}$ [%]
2	4.00946	0.657913	−0.282047	0.009
3	4.48248	−0.933978	2.39633	0.014241
4	4.77679	−1.62938	4.18994	0.019129
5	5.09628	−3.27263	9.41106	0.18422
Average r	4.5417	−0.699053	2.1609	0.056581

Using these functions, we can define the following average errors of approximations $r_n^{(WPM)}(\omega_g)$ and $r_n^{(EM)}(\omega_g)$:

$$\Delta_n^{(WPM)} = \frac{1}{\frac{1}{2}}\left[\frac{1}{K-1}\sum_{k=1}^{K-1}\left|\frac{k}{K} - \Omega_n^{(WPM)}\left(r_n^{(WPM)}\left(\frac{k}{K}\right)\right)\right|\right] \times 100 \ [\%]$$

$$\Delta_n^{(EM)} = \frac{1}{\frac{1}{2}}\left[\frac{1}{K-1}\sum_{k=1}^{K-1}\left|\frac{k}{K} - \Omega_n^{(EM)}\left(r_n^{(EM)}\left(\frac{k}{K}\right)\right)\right|\right] \times 100 \ [\%]$$

The resulting average errors are shown in Tables 2.3.5 and 2.3.6. The reason for better accuracy of numeric approximations of EXM is the fact that EXM functions are symmetrical with respect to point $\omega_g = \alpha_g = \frac{1}{2}$. Using this observation in the case of WPM, if we separate the cases of partial conjunction $(\omega_g \leq \alpha_g, \ 0 \leq \omega_g \leq \frac{1}{2})$ and partial disjunction $(\omega_g \geq \alpha_g, \ \frac{1}{2} \leq \omega_g \leq 1)$, we can get an order of magnitude better accuracy, shown in Table 2.3.7. For example, using the conditional expression notation, for $n = 2$ we have

$$r_2^{(WPM)}(\omega_g) = \frac{\left[\begin{array}{l}0.25 + (\omega_g \leq \frac{1}{2}?1.65811:1.62481)(\omega_g - \frac{1}{2}) + (\omega_g \leq \frac{1}{2}?2.15388:1.26214)(\omega_g - \frac{1}{2})^2 \\ + (\omega_g \leq \frac{1}{2}?8.2844:0.144343)(\omega_g - \frac{1}{2})^3 + (\omega_g \leq \frac{1}{2}?6.16764:-0.144343)(\omega_g - \frac{1}{2})^4\end{array}\right]}{\omega_g(1-\omega_g)}.$$

Table 2.3.7 Parameters of numeric approximation for WPM and $K = 20$.

n	Orness	$a_n^{(WPM)}$	$b_n^{(WPM)}$	$c_n^{(WPM)}$	$d_n^{(WPM)}$	$\Delta_n^{(WPM)}$ [%]
2	$0 \le \omega_g \le \frac{1}{2}$	1.65811	2.15388	8.2844	6.16764	0.02545
2	$\frac{1}{2} \le \omega_g \le 1$	1.62481	1.26214	0.144343	−0.144343	0.00302
3	$0 \le \omega_g \le \frac{1}{2}$	1.95419	3.69032	10.7073	9.46921	0.06132
3	$\frac{1}{2} \le \omega_g \le 1$	1.85971	1.9532	−0.17274	0.0213069	0.00038
4	$0 \le \omega_g \le \frac{1}{2}$	2.11034	4.4749	11.4962	10.5552	0.0803
4	$\frac{1}{2} \le \omega_g \le 1$	2.06781	1.83246	1.99365	−2.30786	0.0505
5	$0 \le \omega_g \le \frac{1}{2}$	2.21868	5.0574	12.0866	11.2383	0.08606
5	$\frac{1}{2} \le \omega_g \le 1$	2.09567	3.04673	−0.388745	0.0110307	0.00255

This model in the case of exact (analytically computed) values of orness of WPM for $r_2^{(WPM)} = -2, -1, 0, \frac{1}{2}, 1, 2$ yields the values $r_2^{(WPM)} = -1.9972, -100008, -0.00052, 0.5033, 1, 1.9997$. Similar level of accuracy is also obtained for $n = 3, 4, 5$.

The presented approximations are different for various values of n. In cases where we prefer simplicity, and the accuracy is not critical, an "average value of r" for $n = 2, 3, 4, 5$ can be computed using the following approximation:

$$r^{(WPM)}(\omega_g)$$
$$= \frac{0.25 + 1.89425(\omega_g - \frac{1}{2}) + 1.7044(\omega_g - \frac{1}{2})^2 + 1.47532(\omega_g - \frac{1}{2})^3 - 1.42532(\omega_g - \frac{1}{2})^4}{\omega_g(1 - \omega_g)}$$

Global andness is defined for GCD aggregators that have equal weights. However, the GCD aggregator also can be weighted: $z = \lim_{s \to -r}[Wx^s + (1 - W)y^s]^{1/s}$. In this case, the global andness becomes the function of weight, as shown in Fig. 2.3.15 for $r = -1, 0, 1, 2$ (i.e., top-down, for harmonic, geometric, arithmetic, and quadratic means).

According to Fig. 2.3.15, the global andness of the arithmetic mean is constant (0.5) and does not depend of weight. For all other cases, the global andness is stable in the vicinity of $W = 0.5$ and then approaches 0.5 as the weight approaches extreme points 0 and 1. The global andness (defined for $W = 0.5$) determines the vertical location of these curves.

The conclusion of our analysis of andness and orness is based on interpreting andness and orness as degrees of human percept of simultaneity and substitutability, used for building suitability aggregation structures. Evaluators select andness and orness as fundamental parameters of GCD (graded conjunction/disjunction), and GCD is the most important and the most frequently used

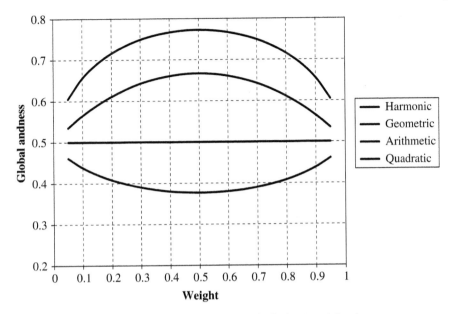

Figure 2.3.15 Global andness as a function of weight for basic weighted means.

GL function. Therefore, in practice we use only one type of andness/orness to express desired degrees of simultaneity and substitutability in logic criteria.

In soft computing literature there are multiple forms of andness/orness, and nine of them (more than enough!) are presented and compared in [DUJ05c, DUJ06b]. Obviously, multiple forms of andness/orness are the result of efforts to find the most convenient form. Since all forms of andness and orness have fixed values for conjunction $(\alpha = 1 - \omega = 1)$, disjunction $(\alpha = 1 - \omega = 0)$, and neutrality $(\alpha = \omega = \frac{1}{2})$, it follows that all forms of andness and orness generate similar results. Decision makers can be trained to use any kind of andness and orness indicators to successfully build complex criteria. Consequently, further work in this area has little practical impact. The only area that remains insufficiently explored is the experimental quantitative analysis of andness and orness indicators from the standpoint of the degree of their compatibility with human percepts of simultaneity and substitutability.

We have included in this chapter only three fundamental versions of andness/orness: local, mean local, and global. Local andness is useful for introducing and understanding the concept of andness, as well as for studying the range of variations of andness inside the unit hypercube. Unfortunately, the local andness and local orness are pointwise indicators that change in any point inside the unit hypercube. They have large variations and even discontinuities inside the unit hypercube. Therefore, the local andness cannot be used as a practical overall indicator of simultaneity or substitutability.

The mean local andness can be used as an overall indicator of andness, but for some aggregators (in particular for power means), it can be significantly less convenient than the global andness. Numerical computation of mean local andness/orness is significantly more complex than the computation of global andness/orness. In addition, the variations of mean local andness/orness for various numbers of variables are greater than the variations of global andness/orness.

The global andness is easily understandable because it is a simple concept based on the volume under the GCD surface inside the unit hypercube. It easily fits in the concept of decomposition of unit hypercube introduced in Section 2.1.4 and it conveniently describes hyperconjunction and hyperdisjunction. It is also very convenient for building interpolative aggregators, presented in the next section. The advantage of global andness over the mean local andness in the important case of power means is primarily in lower variability for various numbers of input variables. For global andness, the variability is mostly negligible for values of andness that are most frequently used, and in the case of mean local andness, that is not the case. In addition, problems of accurate numerical computation of global andness are lower than in the case of mean local andness. Therefore, the global andness can be considered the default form of andness and orness, and if we use symbols α and ω without indices (g or ℓ), we always assume that they denote the global andness and orness.

2.3.7 Mean Global Andness/Orness Theorems and Their Applications

Let us consider a general GCD aggregator of n variables used as a model of simultaneity or substitutability that has the global andness α:

$$y = A(\mathbf{x}; \mathbf{W}, \alpha)$$

$$\mathbf{x} = (x_1, \ldots, x_n), \quad 0 \le x_i \le 1, \quad i = 1, \ldots, n$$

$$\mathbf{W} = (W_1, \ldots, W_n), \quad 0 < W < 1, \quad i = 1, \ldots, n, \quad W_1 + \cdots + W_n = 1$$

$$\alpha = \frac{1}{n-1}\left(n - (n+1)\overline{A(\mathbf{x}; \underline{\mathbf{W}}, \alpha)}\right)$$

$$\overline{A(\mathbf{x}; \underline{\mathbf{W}}, \alpha)} = \int_{I^n} A(\mathbf{x}; \underline{\mathbf{W}}, \alpha)\, dx_1 \cdots dx_n, \quad \underline{\mathbf{W}} = (1/n, \ldots, 1/n), \quad I = [0,1].$$

Let us now create a compound aggregator that is a weighted arithmetic mean of k GCD aggregators:

$$A(\mathbf{x}; \mathbf{W}, \alpha) = \sum_{i=1}^{k} p_i A_i(\mathbf{x}; \mathbf{W}_i, \alpha_i), \quad 0 < p_i < 1, \quad i = 1, \ldots, n, \quad \sum_{i=1}^{k} p_i = 1.$$

For this compound aggregator and for global andness α we have the following theorem (introduced in [DUJ05c]):

Theorem 2.3.1.   Mean Andness Theorem (MAT)
The global andness of the weighted arithmetic mean of GCD aggregators can be computed as the weighted arithmetic mean of the global andness of component aggregators:

$$\alpha = p_1\alpha_1 + \dots + p_k\alpha_k.$$

Proof: The mean value of the compound aggregator is a weighted sum of mean values of component aggregators:

$$\overline{A(\mathbf{x};\underline{W},\alpha)} = \sum_{i=1}^{k} p_i \overline{A_i(\mathbf{x};\underline{W},\alpha_i)}, \tag{2.3.1}$$

$$\overline{A_i(\mathbf{x};\underline{W},\alpha_i)} = \int_{I^n} A_i(\mathbf{x};\underline{W},\alpha_i)\,dx_1\dots dx_n, \quad i=1,\dots,n.$$

According to the definition of global andness, we have

$$\overline{A(\mathbf{x};\underline{W},\alpha)} = \frac{n-(n-1)\alpha}{n+1}, \quad \overline{A_i(\mathbf{x};\underline{W},\alpha_i)} = \frac{n-(n-1)\alpha_i}{n+1}, \quad i=1,\dots,n.$$

After inserting these relations in (2.3.1) we can complete the proof:

$$\frac{n-(n-1)\alpha}{n+1} = \sum_{i=1}^{k} p_i \frac{n-(n-1)\alpha_i}{n+1} = \frac{n-(n-1)\sum_{i=1}^{k}p_i\alpha_i}{n+1}.$$

$$\therefore \quad \alpha = \sum_{i=1}^{k} p_i\alpha_i \quad \text{Q.E.D.}$$

Inserting $\alpha = 1-\omega$ and $\alpha_i = 1-\omega_i$ in the above formula, we get the following *mean orness theorem*:

$$\omega = \sum_{i=1}^{k} p_i\omega_i.$$

The mean andness and orness theorems have significant applicability. First, these theorems enable simple computation of global andness/orness of compound aggregators, and second, these theorems support the design of interpolative aggregators.

Using the above results, we can accurately compute the andness and orness of various linear combinations of the basic aggregators shown in Table 2.3.2. In the following examples, which expand the results from Table 2.3.2, we assume $0 \le p \le 1$, and $\omega = 1-\alpha$.

AG mean: $f_{ag}(x,y) = p\frac{x+y}{2} + (1-p)\sqrt{xy}$, ($p = 2/3$ for Heronian mean)

$$\alpha_{ag} = p\alpha_a + (1-p)\alpha_g = \frac{p}{2} + \frac{2(1-p)}{3} = \frac{4-p}{6} \in [1/2,\ 2/3].$$

AH mean: $f_{ah}(x,y) = p\frac{x+y}{2} + (1-p)\frac{2xy}{x+y}$,

$$\alpha_{ah} = p\alpha_a + (1-p)\alpha_h = \frac{p}{2} + (1-p)(\ln 16 - 2).$$

GH mean: $f_{gh}(x,y) = p\sqrt{xy} + (1-p)\frac{2xy}{x+y}$,

$$\alpha_{gh} = p\alpha_g + (1-p)\alpha_h = \frac{2p}{3} + (1-p)(\ln 16 - 2).$$

GHH mean: $f_{ghh}(x,y) = p\sqrt{xy} + (1-p)\frac{\sqrt{2}\cdot xy}{\sqrt{x^2 + y^2}}$,

$$\alpha_{ghh} = p\alpha_g + (1-p)\alpha_{hh} = \frac{2p}{3} + (1-p)\left(2^{3/2} - 2\right).$$

SQRT mean: $f_{sqrt}(x,y) = \left(\frac{\sqrt{x} + \sqrt{y}}{2}\right)^2 = \frac{1}{2}\frac{x+y}{2} + \frac{1}{2}\sqrt{xy}$,

$$\alpha_{sqrt} = \left(\alpha_a + \alpha_g\right)/2 = (1/2 + 2/3)/2 = 7/12.$$

GC mean: $f_{gc}(x,y) = (1-p)\sqrt{xy} + p\min(x,y)$,

$$\alpha_{gc} = (1-p)\alpha_g + p = \frac{2(1-p)}{3} + p = \frac{2+p}{3} \in [2/3, 1].$$

HC mean: $f_{hc}(x,y) = (1-p)\frac{2xy}{x+y} + p\min(x,y)$,

$$\alpha_{hc} = (1-p)\alpha_h + p = (1-p)(\ln 16 - 2) + p.$$

If we have aggregators $A_1(\mathbf{x};\mathbf{W}, \alpha_1)$ and $A_2(\mathbf{x};\mathbf{W}, \alpha_2)$, $\alpha_1 < \alpha_2$, then we can use MAT and create an *interpolative aggregator* $A(\mathbf{x};\mathbf{W}, \alpha)$ in the andness range $\alpha \in [\alpha_1, \alpha_2]$ as follows:

$$A(\mathbf{x};\mathbf{W}, \alpha) = pA_1(\mathbf{x};\mathbf{W}, \alpha_1) + (1-p)A_2(\mathbf{x};\mathbf{W}, \alpha_2)$$
$$\alpha = p\alpha_1 + (1-p)\alpha_2, \quad p \in I, \quad \alpha_1 \le \alpha \le \alpha_2. \tag{2.3.2}$$

The parameter p can be expressed as a function of andness: $p = (\alpha_2 - \alpha)/(\alpha_2 - \alpha_1)$ and inserted in (2.3.2) as follows:

$$A(\mathbf{x};\mathbf{W}, \alpha) = \frac{(\alpha_2 - \alpha)A_1(\mathbf{x};\mathbf{W}, \alpha_1) + (\alpha - \alpha_1)A_2(\mathbf{x};\mathbf{W}, \alpha_2)}{\alpha_2 - \alpha_1}, \quad \alpha_1 \le \alpha \le \alpha_2. \tag{2.3.3}$$

The interpolative aggregator $A(\mathbf{x}; \mathbf{W}, \alpha)$ has annihilator $a \in \{0,1\}$ if and only if both $A_1(\mathbf{x}; \mathbf{W}, \alpha_1)$ and $A_2(\mathbf{x}; \mathbf{W}, \alpha_2)$ support the annihilator a. If any of the border aggregators (either $A_1(\mathbf{x}; \mathbf{W}, \alpha_1)$ or $A_2(\mathbf{x}; \mathbf{W}, \alpha_2)$) does not support the annihilator a, then the interpolative aggregator $A(\mathbf{x}; \mathbf{W}, \alpha)$ also does not support the annihilator a.

Example

Suppose that we want to create an aggregator of two variables that has same andness as the geometric mean but does not have the annihilator 0 and is *not* a model of mandatory requirements. Such an aggregator can be interpolated between the arithmetic mean and the harmonic mean. So, there will be no annihilator 0 in the range from the arithmetic mean to the harmonic mean, i.e., we skip the annihilation that (in the case of weighted power means) would start at the level of geometric mean. From Table 2.3.2, the global andness of the harmonic mean for $n = 2$ is $\alpha_{har} = \ln 16 - 2$. According to (2.3.3), the resulting interpolative aggregator is

$$A(\mathbf{x}; \mathbf{W}, \alpha) = \frac{(\ln 16 - 2 - \alpha)(W_1 x_1 + W_2 x_2) + (\alpha - 1/2)(W_1/x_1 + W_2/x_2)^{-1}}{\ln 16 - 5/2},$$

$$1/2 \leq \alpha \leq \ln 16 - 2.$$

Inserting $\alpha = 2/3$ in the above formula, we get the "nonmandatory geometric mean"

$$A\left(\mathbf{x}; \mathbf{W}, \frac{2}{3}\right) = \frac{(\ln 16 - 8/3)(W_1 x_1 + W_2 x_2) + (1/6)(W_1/x_1 + W_2/x_2)^{-1}}{\ln 16 - 5/2}.$$

This aggregator is a partial conjunction: it has the same global andness as the geometric mean, but it is a model of nonmandatory requirements and has no annihilator 0. For example, if $W_1 = 0.5$, $x_1 = 1$, $x_2 = 0$, then $A(\mathbf{x}; \mathbf{W}, 2/3) = (\ln 16 - 8/3)/(\ln 256 - 5) = 0.1943 > 0$.

2.3.8 Geometric Interpretations of Andness and Orness

Andness, orness, and continuous transition from *and* to *or* are very important concepts. Geometric interpretations of these concepts in the simple case of aggregating two inputs can significantly contribute to understanding of the aggregation process. In this section, we present such geometric interpretations.

Fig. 2.3.16 illustrates the process of linear aggregation of two variables (x and y) using the aggregator $z = \lambda(x,y) = \alpha(x \wedge y) + \omega(x \vee y)$. We first create an auxiliary rectangle with base 1 and height $x + y$. Andness α and orness ω ($\alpha \in [0,1]$,

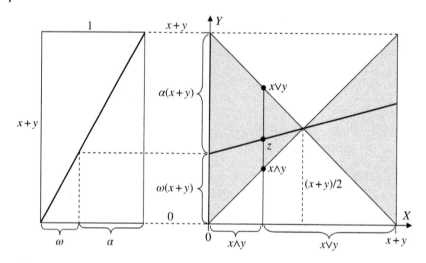

Figure 2.3.16 Geometric interpretation of a linear aggregator of two variables.

$\omega \in [0,1]$, $\alpha + \omega = 1$) are selected at the base of the rectangle. The diagonal line of the auxiliary rectangle is used to determine the values $\alpha(x+y)$ and $\omega(x+y)$. Then, we create in the coordinate system (X,Y) a square with sides $x+y$. The line connecting the points $(0,\omega(x+y))$ and $((x+y)/2, (x+y)/2)$ is

$$Y = \omega(x+y) + (\alpha-\omega)X = \omega[(x \wedge y) + (x \vee y)] + (\alpha-\omega)X.$$

Inserting $X = x \wedge y$ in this equation, we get

$$Y = \omega[(x \wedge y) + (x \vee y)] + (\alpha-\omega)(x \wedge y) = \alpha(x \wedge y) + \omega(x \vee y) = z.$$

Therefore, the aggregated values (z) for idempotent aggregators are always in the shaded triangle area. By increasing the orness ω from 0 to 1 the aggregated value z linearly moves from the conjunction $(x \wedge y)$ to the disjunction $(x \vee y)$.

Simultaneity and substitutability are usually modeled using nonlinear aggregators, such as the harmonic, geometric, and quadratic means. A circle-based geometric interpretation of the concept of simultaneity is shown in Fig. 2.3.17. Suppose that we have to aggregate two values: x and y. The aggregated value is $\lambda(0,y) = \lambda(x,0) = 0$. In a circle with diameter $x + y$, the distance between the point that connects segments x and y and the circle (perpendicular to diameter) is the geometric mean: from $\tan \varphi = x/z_g = z_g/y$ it follows $z_g = \sqrt{xy}$. The geometric mean aggregates x and y, assuming a moderate level of simultaneity, but one that still satisfies the mandatory requirement condition $\lambda(0,y) = \lambda(x,0) = 0$. For example, by reducing x we quickly reduce z_g, regardless the large size of y. So, both x and y must be simultaneously satisfied; otherwise the value of z_g may become very small. If we increase the level of simultaneity, we can reach the extreme case of conjunction shown in the lower half of circle in Fig. 2.3.17.

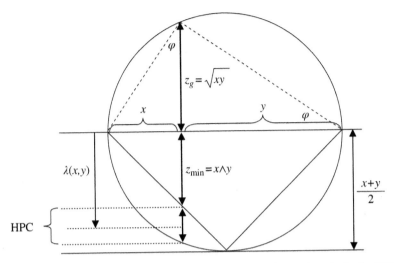

Figure 2.3.17 A geometric interpretation of low and high simultaneity in the HPC area.

The aggregated value is then $x \wedge y = z_{min} \le z_g$ where the equality holds only if $x = y$ or $x \wedge y = 0$. Fig. 2.3.17 also illustrates the idempotency: if $x = y$ then $z_{min} = z_g = x = y$. If $x > 0$, $y > 0$, $x \ne y$, then any increase in simultaneity yields a decrease of the aggregated value $\lambda(x, y)$. In the case of power means and simultaneity that is greater than the simultaneity of the geometric mean, we have $2/3 < \alpha < 1$, $x \wedge y < \lambda(x, y) < z_g$, as shown in the hard partial conjunction (HPC) area in Fig. 2.3.17. Let us also note that the semicircle that determines the value of geometric mean belongs to the shaded area shown in Fig. 2.3.16.

A geometric interpretation of a moderate degree of substitutability, in the case of quadratic mean $z = \sqrt{0.5x^2 + 0.5y^2}$, is shown in Fig. 2.3.18. A high value of z can be achieved using either a sufficiently large x or a sufficiently large y. One of inputs (either x or y) could even be 0. For example, if $x = 0$, then $z = y\sqrt{0.5}$, $0 \le z \le \sqrt{0.5} = 0.7071$. If we need $z > 0.7071$, then both inputs must be positive and contribute to z.

A trapezoid-based geometric interpretation of continuous transition from *and* to *or* is presented in Fig. 2.3.19. Suppose that we have to aggregate two preferences, x and y, assuming $x < y$. The aggregated preference is $z = x \Diamond y$, $x \le z \le y$. According to Fig. 2.3.19, the value of z is continuously adjustable between x and y. By adding more andness, z is monotonously decreasing, and by adding more orness, z is monotonously increasing. The height of the trapezoid is 1. The vertical axis represents global andness only in points 0 and 1, and $(y - z)/(y - x)$ denotes the local andness.

Fig. 2.3.19 also presents four important special cases denoted h, g, a, and q. The line denoted h is at the intersection of diagonals of trapezoid. Each diagonal

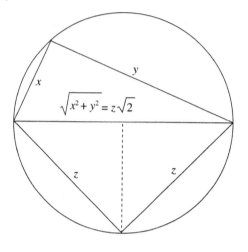

Figure 2.3.18 A geometric interpretation of moderate substitutability (quadratic mean).

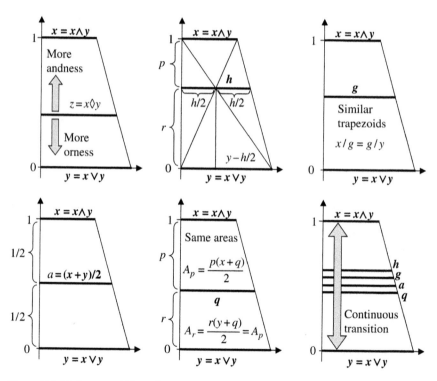

Figure 2.3.19 A trapezoid-based geometric interpretation of the continuous transition from *and* to *or*.

Figure 2.3.20 A semicircle interpretation of quadratic, arithmetic, geometric, and harmonic means of two variables x and y.

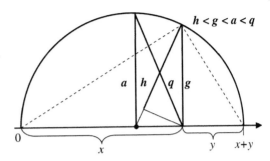

is the hypotenuse of a right triangle with cathetus equal 1. So, we have relationships $(y - h/2)/r = y$ and $(h/2)/r = x$. Then, $r = (y - h/2)/y = (h/2)/x$ and $h = 2xy/(x + y)$ (the harmonic mean of x and y).

The line denoted g divides the trapezoid into two similar trapezoids and from $x/g = g/y$ it follows $g = \sqrt{xy}$ (the geometric mean).

The line a is located in the middle and consequently $a = (x + y)/2$ (the arithmetic mean).

The line q divides the trapezoid into two equal areas yielding the equation $r(y + q) = (1 - r)(x + q)$. This equation and the equation $(y - q)/r = y - x$ after eliminating r yield the result $q = \sqrt{(x^2 + y^2)/2}$ (the quadratic mean). If $x \neq y$ then $h < g < a < q$.

Quadratic, arithmetic, geometric, and harmonic means of two variables can also be geometrically summarized using the semicircle with radius $(x + y)/2$ shown in Fig. 2.3.20, where $h = 2xy/(x + y)$, $g = \sqrt{xy}$, $a = (x + y)/2$, and $q = \sqrt{0.5(x^2 + y^2)}$. We have already shown the cases a and g. We can compute q using Pythagorean theorem for triangle $a, q, (x - y)/2$:

$$q^2 = a^2 + \left(\frac{x - y}{2}\right)^2 = \left(\frac{x + y}{2}\right)^2 + \left(\frac{x - y}{2}\right)^2 = \frac{x^2 + y^2}{2}.$$

Similarly, to compute h, we can use the smallest triangle in Fig. 2.3.20:

$$(a - h)^2 + (g^2 - h^2) = \left(\frac{x - y}{2}\right)^2,$$

$$a^2 - 2ah + g^2 = \left(\frac{x - y}{2}\right)^2,$$

$$h = \frac{1}{2a}\left(a^2 + g^2 - \left(\frac{x - y}{2}\right)^2\right) = \frac{g^2}{a} = \frac{2xy}{x + y} \; ; \; g = \sqrt{ah}.$$

The partial conjunction is frequently modeled using a power mean. In the case of two variables, we have

$$x \Delta y = (0.5x^r + 0.5y^r)^{1/r}, \; -\infty < r < 1.$$

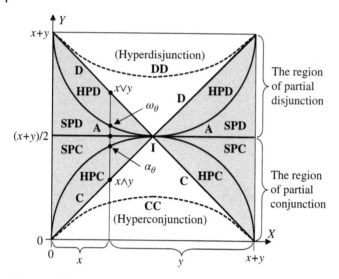

Figure 2.3.21 Geometric interpretation of the nine forms of GCD.

The HPC is obtained if $-\infty < r \leq 0$ and the SPC is obtained if $0 < r < 1$ (see P_{20} in Chapter 2.2). The geometric mean $x \Delta y = \sqrt{xy}$ corresponds to $r = 0$, and therefore, it represents the "softest aggregator in the HPC region," i.e., the border function between HPC and SPC, where the andness attains the threshold andness value α_θ. In Fig. 2.3.21, the geometric mean is represented using the lower semicircle. The border function that separates the regions of SPC and SPD is the arithmetic mean (denoted A in Fig. 2.3.21).

If the partial disjunction is organized as a De Morgan dual of the partial conjunction, then we have

$$x \nabla y = \overline{\overline{x} \nabla \overline{y}} = \overline{\overline{x} \Delta \overline{y}} = 1 - (1-x)\Delta(1-y) = 1 - \left[0.5(1-x)^r + 0.5(1-y)^r\right]^{1/r}, -\infty < r < 1.$$

This form of partial disjunction is symmetrical to the partial conjunction, as shown in Fig. 2.3.21. The border function between the SPD and HPD is the De Morgan dual of geometric mean $x \nabla y = 1 - \sqrt{(1-x)(1-y)}$. Its threshold orness ω_θ has the same value as the threshold andness of its dual (ω_θ[geometric mean dual] $= \alpha_\theta$[geometric mean]).

The shaded area in Fig 2.3.21 corresponds to seven fundamental forms of graded conjunction/disjunction (C, HPC, SPC, A, SPD, HPD, D). The border functions are the conjunction (C) at the bottom of the shaded area and the disjunction (D) at the top of the shaded area. All regular GCD functions include the central point I that corresponds to the idempotency of logic aggregators based on means.

Top and bottom white triangle areas in Fig. 2.3.21 correspond to nonidempotent logic aggregators, i.e., aggregators that do not include the central point I. The top triangle is the area for hyperdisjunctive aggregators (DD) and the bottom triangle is the area for hyperconjunctive aggregators (CC). One sample hyperconjunctive aggregator and its hyperdisjunctive dual are presented in Fig. 2.3.21 using dotted curves.

2.4 Graded Conjunction/Disjunction and Logic Modeling of Simultaneity and Substitutability

> *All models are wrong but some are useful.*
> —G.E.P. Box

Mathematical models of simultaneity (conjunctive logic aggregators) and substitutability (disjunctive logic aggregators) are the point of departure in all studies of logic. In GL simultaneity and substitutability are modeled using the graded (or generalized) conjunction/disjunction (GCD). According to GL conjecture (see Section 2.1.8 and P_{20} in Section 2.2.3) we need nine special cases of GCD. In this chapter we study mathematical properties and various implementations of GCD aggregators.

General aggregators of n variables are defined using Definition 2.1.0. This general definition includes functions that have no applicability in logic and we introduced a more restrictive Definition 2.1.1 to specify *logic aggregators* (LA) as functions of two or more variables that support nondecreasing monotonicity in all variables, boundary conditions for truth and falsity, and sensitivity to positive truth and incomplete truth. Aggregators based on that definition are suitable for GL applications. Logic aggregators can be either idempotent or nonidempotent and GCD supports both idempotent and nonidempotent aggregators that are models of simultaneity and substitutability, as shown in Fig. 2.4.1. In GL applications idempotent models of simultaneity and substitutability are more frequently used than nonidempotent models (hyperconjunction and hyperdisjunction) (see P_5 in Section 2.2.1).

Idempotent logic aggregators are implemented as means and used as a soft computing generalization of classic Boolean functions. The fundamental logic aggregator is GCD, which is then used for building the partial absorption (PA) and all other logic aggregation structures. We must primarily focus on idempotent logic aggregators (ILA) because that area consists of idempotent versions of GCD and PA. In addition, we will study GCD and interpolative techniques for GCD design in the whole unit hypercube, including both the ILA and the

Soft Computing Evaluation Logic: The LSP Decision Method and Its Applications,
First Edition. Jozo Dujmović.
© 2018 John Wiley & Sons, Inc. Published 2018 by John Wiley & Sons, Inc.
Companion website: www.wiley.com/go/Dujmovic/Soft_Computing_Evaluation_Logic

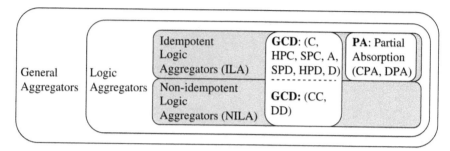

Figure 2.4.1 Classification of aggregators.

nonidempotent (NILA) areas. We will also define the basic mathematical properties of partial absorption (PA), but a detailed analysis of PA is presented in Chapter 2.6.

2.4.1 Definitions and Basic Mathematical Properties of Logic Aggregators

In GL we are not interested in aggregation functions that might have the following three properties inside the unit hypercube:

1) Discontinuities
2) Excessive values and discontinuities of first derivatives
3) Oscillatory properties (alternating concave and convex segments)

These three properties are not observable in common human evaluation reasoning. In intuitive human logic elementary aggregation functions are expected to have simple, smooth and consistent forms with second derivatives that are defined almost everywhere inside the unit hypercube. The only exceptions are the minimum and maximum functions (pure conjunction and pure disjunction) and interpolative aggregators that include the minimum and maximum functions. Interpolative aggregators are weighted arithmetic means of aggregators that may include minimum and maximum functions—for example, $A(\mathbf{x}) = a \cdot \min(\mathbf{x}) + b \cdot f(\mathbf{x}) + c \cdot \max(\mathbf{x})$, where $f(\mathbf{x})$ is an ILA (compensative and with continuous derivatives) and nonnegative weights a, b, c satisfy $a + b + c = 1$.

Aggregators $\min(\mathbf{x})$ and $\max(\mathbf{x})$ are extreme cases of ILA where first derivatives have discontinuities at the idempotency line $x_1 = \cdots = x_n$. These aggregators do not support compensative properties: if $\min(\mathbf{x}) = x_i$ then a further decrease of x_i cannot be compensated by an increase of any input $x_k, k \neq i$ because $x_k > x_i$. Since continuous derivatives and compensative arguments are desirable ILA properties, we will use the term "*compensative ILA*" (abbreviated CILA) for those ILAs that are different from $\min(\mathbf{x})$ and $\max(\mathbf{x})$. According to Fig. 2.1.5, ILA include all aggregators from **C** to **D**, and CILA are all aggregators between $\mathbf{C}$ and $\mathbf{D}$. Therefore, CILAs also include interpolative aggregators that are linear combinations of the type $A(\mathbf{x}) = a \cdot \min(\mathbf{x}) + b \cdot f(\mathbf{x}) + c \cdot \max(\mathbf{x})$, $a \geq 0, b > 0, c \geq 0$.

In the context of logic aggregation of degrees of suitability (or truth, or preference, or fuzzy membership), in GL we mostly use ILAs that generalize classic Boolean logic operations. GL aggregators have properties summarized in the following definitions.

Definition 2.4.1. An *idempotent logic aggregator* (ILA) $A : I^n \rightarrow I, n > 1, I = [0,1]$ is a logic aggregator implemented as an averaging function that satisfies (a) nondecreasing monotonicity, which is either concave or convex (but without alternating convexity and concavity), (b) continuity, and (c) internality, as follows:

(a) $\forall \mathbf{x} \in I^n, \forall \mathbf{y} \in I^n, \mathbf{x} \leq \mathbf{y} \Rightarrow A(\mathbf{x}) \leq A(\mathbf{y})$

$\forall i \in \{1,...,n\}, \ \forall a \in I, \forall b \in I, a \neq b, \ \forall t \in I, x_i = ta + (1-t)b \Rightarrow$

$$\Rightarrow \begin{cases} A(x_1,...,x_i,...,x_n) \geq tA(x_1,...,a,...,x_n) + (1-t)A(x_1,...,b,...,x_n) \text{ for conjunctive aggregators} \\ A(x_1,...,x_i,...,x_n) = tA(x_1,...,a,...,x_n) + (1-t)A(x_1,...,b,...,x_n) \text{ for neutral aggregators} \\ A(x_1,...,x_i,...,x_n) \leq tA(x_1,...,a,...,x_n) + (1-t)A(x_1,...,b,...,x_n) \text{ for disjunctive aggregators}; \end{cases}$$

(b) $\forall \mathbf{x} \in I^n, \mathbf{h} = (h_1,...,h_n) \Rightarrow \lim_{\mathbf{h} \to 0} A(\mathbf{x}+\mathbf{h}) = A(\mathbf{x})$;

(c) $\forall \mathbf{x} \in I^n \Rightarrow \min(\mathbf{x}) \leq A(\mathbf{x}) \leq \max(\mathbf{x})$.

Remark. Consequences of this definition are (d) idempotency, (e) boundary conditions, and (f) sensitivity to positive and incomplete truth:

(d) $\forall x \in I \Rightarrow A(x,x,...,x) = x$;

(e) $A(0,0,...,0) = 0, \quad A(1,1,...,1) = 1$;

(f) $A(x_1,...,x_n) > 0$, if $x_i > 0$, $i = 1,...,n$,

$\quad A(x_1,...,x_n) < 1$, if $x_i < 1$, $i = 1,...,n$.

Definition 2.4.2. ILAs that satisfy $\min(\mathbf{x}) < A(\mathbf{x}) < \max(\mathbf{x})$ are called compensative (CILA), if they satisfy the following condition:

$\forall x_i \in \,]0,1[\, , \quad \forall x_j \in \,]0,1[\, , \ i \neq j, \ \exists \delta_{ij} \in \,]0,1[\ \Rightarrow$

$\Rightarrow A(x_1,...,x_i - \varepsilon_i,...,x_j + \varepsilon_j,...,x_n) = A(x_1,...,x_i,...,x_j,...,x_n)$,

$0 < \varepsilon_i \leq \delta_{ij} \leq x_i, \ 0 < x_j + \varepsilon_j \leq 1$.

Remark. NILA can also be compensative (e.g. $z = xy$).

Definition 2.4.3. In a general case ILAs are *asymmetric* (noncommutative):

$\forall i \in \{1,...,n\}, \ \forall j \in \{1,...,n\}, \ i \neq j, \ x_i \neq x_j \Rightarrow$

$A(...,x_i,...,x_j,...) \neq A(...,x_j,...,x_i,...)$.

Remark. Asymmetry is indispensable for supporting semantic aspects of aggregation, primarily for modeling different degrees of importance or arguments. Asymmetry is usually realized using different weights of arguments and in such cases the symmetry is a special case that corresponds to equal weights. Weights are assumed to be positive and normalized: $0 < W_i < 1$, $i = 1,...,n$ and $\sum_{i=1}^{n} W_i = 1$. A normalized weight cannot be 0 because that would exclude a given input from aggregation, and it cannot be 1 because that would exclude all other inputs from aggregation.

Definition 2.4.4. For each input argument x_i of CILA A, an input truth increment ε causes an output truth increment $D_i^{(+)}(\varepsilon)$; similarly, an input truth decrement ε causes a corresponding output truth decrement $D_i^{(-)}(\varepsilon)$, as follows:

$$D_i^{(+)}(\varepsilon) = A(x_1,...,x_i + \varepsilon,...,x_n) - A(x_1,...,x_i,...,x_n),$$
$$D_i^{(-)}(\varepsilon) = A(x_1,...,x_i,...,x_n) - A(x_1,...,x_i - \varepsilon,...,x_n).$$

Since $x_i - \varepsilon \geq 0$ and $x_i + \varepsilon \leq 1$, we always assume $0 < \varepsilon \leq \varepsilon_{max} = \min(x_i, 1 - x_i)$.

Definition 2.4.5. A CILA A is *conjunctive* (a model of simultaneity) if it is concave in each argument: $D_i^{(-)}(\varepsilon) > D_i^{(+)}(\varepsilon)$, $\varepsilon > 0$, $i = 1,...,n$. Consequently,

$$\forall t \in I, \ \forall a \in I, \ \forall b \in I, \ a \neq b, \forall i \in \{1,...,n\}, \ x_i = ta + (1-t)b \Rightarrow$$
$$A(x_1,...,x_i,...,x_n) \geq tA(x_1,...,a,...,x_n) + (1-t)A(x_1,...,b,...,x_n).$$

Remark. The fundamental property of conjunctive ILA is that small variables have higher impact than large variables. In the simple case of two variables, for any $0 < \varepsilon \leq \varepsilon_{max}$, the decremental difference $A(x,y) - A(x - \varepsilon, y)$ cannot produce lower impact than the incremental difference $A(x + \varepsilon, y) - A(x,y)$. From $A(x,y) - A(x - \varepsilon, y) \geq A(x + \varepsilon, y) - A(x,y)$ it follows $A(x,y) \geq [A(x - \varepsilon, y) + A(x + \varepsilon, y)]/2$ and $A(x,y)$ is concave in x (and in y). If $A(x,y)$ is a conjunctive ILA, and $x \neq y$, then $A(x,y) < (x + y)/2$. If $\frac{1}{2} < \alpha < 1$ then increasing an argument is valuable, but at a decreasing rate, because the rate of increase is more and more disabled by small arguments. If $0 < x_i < 1$, $i = 1,...,n$, then all partial conjunction-based aggregators are strictly increasing and strictly concave; this property causes concave sensitivity curves $S_i(x_i) = A(x_1,...,x_i,...,x_n)$, $dS_i/dx_i > 0$, $d^2 S_i/dx_i^2 < 0$.

Definition 2.4.6. A CILA A is *disjunctive* (a model of substitutability) if it is convex in each argument: $D_i^{(-)}(\varepsilon) < D_i^{(+)}(\varepsilon)$, $\varepsilon > 0$, $i = 1,...,n$. Consequently,

$$\forall t \in I, \ \forall a \in I, \ \forall b \in I, \ a \neq b, \forall i \in \{1,...,n\}, \ x_i = ta + (1-t)b \Rightarrow$$
$$A(x_1,...,x_i,...,x_n) \leq tA(x_1,...,a,...,x_n) + (1-t)A(x_1,...,b,...,x_n).$$

Remark. The fundamental property of disjunctive ILA is that large variables have higher impact than small variables. For any $0 < \varepsilon \leq \varepsilon_{max}$ the decremental difference $A(x,y) - A(x - \varepsilon, y)$ cannot produce higher impact than the incremental difference $A(x + \varepsilon, y) - A(x,y)$. If $A(x,y) - A(x - \varepsilon, y) \leq A(x + \varepsilon, y) - A(x,y)$, then we have $A(x,y) \leq [A(x - \varepsilon, y) + A(x + \varepsilon, y)]/2$ and $A(x,y)$ is convex in x (and in y). If $A(x,y)$ is a disjunctive ILA, and $x \neq y$, then $A(x,y) > (x + y)/2$. If $\frac{1}{2} < \omega < 1$, then increasing an argument is valuable at an increasing rate; the rate of increase is more and more enabled by the size of the argument. If $0 < x_i < 1$, $i = 1,...,n$, then all partial disjunction-based aggregators are strictly increasing and strictly convex; this property causes convex sensitivity curves $S_i(x_i) = A(x_1,...,x_i,...,x_n)$, $0 \leq x_i \leq 1$, $x_j = const$, $j \neq i$, $i = 1,...,n$ where $dS_i/dx_i > 0$, $d^2 S_i/dx_i^2 > 0$.

Definition 2.4.7. A CILA A is *neutral* (and implemented as an arithmetic mean) if it is both concave and convex:

$$\forall t \in I, \ \forall a \in I, \ \forall b \in I, \ a \neq b, \ \forall i \in \{1,...,n\}, \ x_i = ta + (1-t)b \ \Rightarrow$$
$$A(x_1,...,x_i,...,x_n) = tA(x_1,...,a,...,x_n) + (1-t)A(x_1,...,b,...,x_n).$$

Definition 2.4.8. A *graded conjunction/disjunction* (GCD) aggregator is the most important GL function of two or more variables used to model simultaneity and substitutability of input arguments and realize a continuous transition through the whole spectrum of graded logic functions from the drastic conjunction (minimum orness) to the drastic disjunction (maximum orness). Our default assumption is that a GCD aggregator A is *parameterized*, denoted $A(\mathbf{x};p)$, $P_{min} \leq p \leq P_{max}$. The real parameter p enables a continuous nondecreasing transition from $A(\mathbf{x};P_{min}) = 0$ to $A(\mathbf{x};P_{max}) = 1$ inside the unit hypercube:

$$P_{min} < p_{min} < p_{max} < P_{max},$$
$$\forall p \in [P_{min}, P_{max}] \ \Rightarrow \ A(\mathbf{0};p) = 0, \ A(\mathbf{1};p) = 1,$$
$$\forall \mathbf{x} \neq \mathbf{1} \ \Rightarrow \ A(\mathbf{x};P_{min}) = 0, \ \forall \mathbf{x} \neq \mathbf{0} \ \Rightarrow \ A(\mathbf{x};P_{max}) = 1,$$
$$A(\mathbf{x};p_{min}) = x_1 \wedge \cdots \wedge x_n, \ A(\mathbf{x};p_{max}) = x_1 \vee \cdots \vee x_n,$$
$$\forall p, \forall q, \text{ such that } P_{min} \leq p < q \leq P_{max} \ \Rightarrow \ A(\mathbf{x};p) \leq A(\mathbf{x};q).$$

If GCD is weighted (what is a normal situation), then the notation is $A(\mathbf{x};\mathbf{W},p)$, $0 < \mathbf{W} < 1$. If $p \in [P_{min}, P_{max}] \backslash [p_{min}, p_{max}]$ then $A(\mathbf{x};\mathbf{W},p)$ is called an *extended* GCD aggregator (in Section 2.4.8 denoted EGCD). If $p \in [p_{min}, p_{max}]$ then $A(\mathbf{x};\mathbf{W},p)$ is called a *standard* (*idempotent*) GCD aggregator and that will be considered a default version of GCD. The nature of parameter p depends on the type of GCD aggregator; it is usually either a parameter of the mean used to model GCD (e.g., exponent of weighted power mean) or a global andness/orness.

Definition 2.4.9. GCD is *andness-directed (AD)* if it is parameterized directly with andness α: $A(\mathbf{x};\mathbf{W},\alpha)$; $A(\mathbf{x};W,1) = x_1 \wedge \cdots \wedge x_n$, $A(\mathbf{x};W,0) = x_1 \vee \cdots \vee x_n$, $-1/(n-1) = \alpha_{\min} \leq \alpha \leq \alpha_{\max} = n/(n-1)$. Andness-directed GCD must be a monotonically decreasing function of α: $\partial A(\mathbf{x};\mathbf{W},\alpha)/\partial\alpha \leq 0$. For $\alpha = \alpha_{\max}$ the AD-GCD becomes a *drastic conjunction*: $\forall \mathbf{x} \neq \mathbf{1}$, $A(\mathbf{x};\mathbf{W},\alpha_{\max}) = 0$, $A(\mathbf{1};\mathbf{W},\alpha_{\max}) = 1$.

Definition 2.4.10. GCD is *orness-directed (OD)* if it is parameterized directly with orness ω: $A(\mathbf{x};\mathbf{W},\omega)$; $A(\mathbf{x};W,1) = x_1 \vee \cdots \vee x_n$, $A(\mathbf{x};W,0) = x_1 \wedge \cdots \wedge x_n$, $-1/(n-1) = \omega_{\min} \leq \omega \leq \omega_{\max} = n/(n-1)$. Orness-directed GCD must be a monotonically increasing function of ω: $\partial A(\mathbf{x};\mathbf{W},\omega)/\partial\omega \geq 0$. If $\omega = \omega_{\max}$ the OD-GCD becomes a *drastic disjunction*: $\forall \mathbf{x} \neq \mathbf{0}$, $A(\mathbf{x};\mathbf{W},\omega_{\max}) = 1$, $A(\mathbf{0};\mathbf{W},\omega_{\max}) = 0$.

Definition 2.4.11. A logic aggregator A has annihilator $a \in I$ in a specific argument x_i, $i \in \{1,...,n\}$ if for $x_i = a$ and $\forall x_j \in I$, $j \neq i$ we have $A(x_1,...,x_i,...,x_n) = A(x_1,...,a,...,x_n) = a$. Otherwise, A is an aggregator without annihilator in argument x_i, $i \in \{1,...,n\}$. Annihilators can be either necessary or unacceptable.

Definition 2.4.12. A logic aggregator A has *homogeneous annihilators* if it is without annihilator in all arguments, or if it has an annihilator a in all arguments (e.g., $\forall i \in \{1,...,n\}$, $x_i = a \Rightarrow A(\mathbf{x}) = a$). GCD has homogeneous annihilators.

Definition 2.4.13. A logic aggregator A has *heterogeneous annihilators* if it has the annihilator a in a subset of arguments, and it is without annihilator in all other arguments. The partial absorption function (PA) has heterogeneous annihilators.

Definition 2.4.14. A conjunctive ILA A with homogeneous annihilators is *hard*, if it has the annihilator 0 in each argument:

$$\forall i \in \{1,...,n\}, \quad \forall j \neq i, \quad x_i = 0, \quad x_j > 0 \quad \Rightarrow \quad A(x_1,...,x_i,...,x_n) = 0.$$

Definition 2.4.15. A conjunctive ILA A with homogeneous annihilators is *soft*, if it is without the annihilator 0 in all arguments:

$$\forall i \in \{1,...,n\}, \quad \forall j \neq i, \quad x_i > 0, \quad x_j = 0 \quad \Rightarrow \quad A(x_1,...,x_i,...,x_n) > 0.$$

Definition 2.4.16. A parameterized conjunctive CILA A that has homogeneous annihilators, and can be either hard or soft (depending on parameters), is called a *partial (graded) conjunction (PC)*. PC satisfies the condition

$\min(\mathbf{x}) < A(\mathbf{x}) < \mathrm{mid}(\mathbf{x}) = (x_1 + \cdots + x_n)/n$, $\mathbf{x} \neq \underline{\mathbf{x}} = (x,\dots,x)$, $x \in I$. A symmetric PC is symbolically denoted $A(\mathbf{x};\alpha) = x_1 \Delta \cdots \Delta x_n$ and the asymmetric (weighted) version is $A(\mathbf{x};\mathbf{W},\alpha) = W_1 x_1 \Delta \cdots \Delta W_n x_n$. The andness of PC Δ is α ($\tfrac{1}{2} < \alpha < 1$).

Definition 2.4.17. A disjunctive ILA A with homogeneous annihilators is *hard*, if it has the annihilator 1 in each argument:

$$\forall i \in \{1,\dots,n\}, \quad \forall j \neq i, \quad x_i = 1, \quad x_j < 1 \quad \Rightarrow \quad A(x_1,\dots,x_i,\dots,x_n) = 1.$$

Definition 2.4.18. A disjunctive ILA A with homogeneous annihilators is *soft*, if it is without the annihilator 1 in all arguments:

$$\forall i \in \{1,\dots,n\}, \quad \forall j \neq i, \quad x_i < 1, \quad x_j = 1 \quad \Rightarrow \quad A(x_1,\dots,x_i,\dots,x_n) < 1.$$

Definition 2.4.19. A parameterized disjunctive CILA A that has homogeneous annihilators and can be either hard or soft (depending on parameters) is called a *partial (graded) disjunction (PD)*. PD satisfies the condition $\mathrm{mid}(\mathbf{x}) < A(\mathbf{x}) < \max(\mathbf{x})$, $\mathbf{x} \neq \underline{\mathbf{x}} = (x,\dots,x)$, $x \in I$. A symmetric PD is symbolically denoted $A(\mathbf{x};\alpha) = x_1 \nabla \cdots \nabla x_n$ and the asymmetric (weighted) version is $A(\mathbf{x};\mathbf{W},\alpha) = W_1 x_1 \nabla \cdots \nabla W_n x_n$. The ranges of andness α and orness ω of the PD aggregator ∇ are $0 < \alpha < \tfrac{1}{2}$, $\tfrac{1}{2} < \omega < 1$.

Definition 2.4.20. The threshold andness α_θ is the lowest andness of the hard partial conjunction. The partial conjunction has the andness in the range $\tfrac{1}{2} < \alpha < 1$. In the range $\tfrac{1}{2} < \alpha < \alpha_\theta$ the partial conjunction is soft and in the range $\alpha_\theta \leq \alpha < 1$ the partial conjunction is hard.

Definition 2.4.21. The threshold orness ω_θ is the lowest orness of the hard partial disjunction. The partial disjunction has the orness in the range $\tfrac{1}{2} < \omega < 1$. In the range $\tfrac{1}{2} < \omega < \omega_\theta$ the partial disjunction is soft and in the range $\omega_\theta \leq \omega < 1$ the partial disjunction is hard.

Definition 2.4.22. The GCD aggregator has homogeneous annihilators. In the case of andness-directed or orness-directed GCD and n arguments, the minimum andness and orness are $P_{\min} = \omega_{\min} = \alpha_{\min} = -1/(n-1)$. Similarly, the maximum andness and the maximum orness are $P_{\max} = \omega_{\max} = \alpha_{\max} = n/(n-1)$. Thus, $P_{\min} + P_{\max} = \omega_{\min} + \omega_{\max} = \alpha_{\min} + \alpha_{\max} = 1$. The GCD aggregator supports the drastic conjunction ($\alpha = \alpha_{\max}$), hyperconjunction (e.g., the product t-norm), full (pure) conjunction ($\min(\mathbf{x})$), PC, neutrality ($\mathrm{mid}(\mathbf{x})$), PD, full (pure) disjunction ($\max(\mathbf{x})$), hyperdisjunction (e.g., the product t-conorm) and the drastic disjunction ($\alpha = \alpha_{\min}$, $\omega = \omega_{\max}$). The continuous transition from conjunction to disjunction is realized by selecting appropriate values of andness/orness.

Remark. Generally, GCD supports the widest possible spectrum of idempotent and nonidempotent logic properties. In most applications only a fraction of the spectrum is used. The most frequent version of GCD is the idempotent version that covers the range from the pure conjunction to the pure disjunction, i.e., $\alpha \in [0,1]$, $\omega \in [0,1]$. Nonidempotent extended GCD aggregators have the range of andness/orness equal to $[-1/(n-1), \ n/(n-1)] \setminus [0,1]$.

Definition 2.4.23. GCD can be *symmetric* (commutative, equally weighted) or *asymmetric* (noncommutative, weighted). Andness and orness are defined for the symmetric version of GCD. The arguments of GCD have importance weights, and in the case of symmetric version of GCD all weights are equal: $W_1 = \cdots = W_n = 1/n$. Asymmetric versions of GCD are realized using two or more weights different from $1/n$. A symmetric version of GCD is symbolically denoted $y = x_1 \diamond \cdots \diamond x_n$ and the asymmetric version is $y = W_1 x_1 \diamond \cdots \diamond W_n x_n$. GCD can be expanded to nonidempotent domain in order to include hyperconjunction and hyperdisjunction.

Remark. In the case of GCD, the percept of overall importance of input arguments depends on both their relative importance and the value $\max(\alpha, \omega)$ (the proximity to high andness/orness), as studied in Section 2.2.3. The impact of relative importance of inputs is a decreasing function of $|\alpha - \frac{1}{2}|$. We believe that the impact of relative importance of inputs disappears at the level for pure conjunction and pure disjunction. At that level, either the simultaneity or the substitutability is already so strong that the aggregator is always hard and each and every input can cause the same annihilating effect on the output. Consequently, in GL we don't use weighted conjunction and weighted disjunction. We assume that in the range $\alpha, \omega \in [-1/(n-1), 0] \cup [1, n/(n-1)]$ all versions of the GCD aggregator must be symmetric (unweighted and commutative).

Definition 2.4.24. For all values of arguments GCD must be *nonincreasing in andness* and *nondecreasing in orness*. Indeed, if andness increases the impact of low arguments also increases and the output of aggregator must decrease or remain constant, but cannot increase. Similarly, if orness increases the impact of high arguments also increases and the output of aggregator must increase or remain constant, but cannot decrease. Generally, all andness-directed and orness-directed GCD aggregators with nonequal arguments satisfy:

$$0 < x_i < 1, \ \ i = 1,...,n \ \ \Rightarrow \ \ \frac{\partial A(\mathbf{x};\mathbf{W},\alpha)}{\partial \alpha} < 0 \ , \ \ \frac{\partial A(\mathbf{x};\mathbf{W},\omega)}{\partial \omega} > 0,$$

$$0 \leq x_i \leq 1, \ \ i = 1,...,n \ \ \Rightarrow \ \ \frac{\partial A(\mathbf{x};\mathbf{W},\alpha)}{\partial \alpha} \leq 0 \ , \ \ \frac{\partial A(\mathbf{x};\mathbf{W},\omega)}{\partial \omega} \geq 0.$$

Remark. This property has fundamental importance. The reason for using GCD aggregators in GL is to obtain desired logic properties of the aggregator by selecting the necessary level of andness/orness. This is possible only if the increase of orness has nondecreasing effect on the output degree of truth, and (what is equivalent) the increase of andness has nonincreasing effect on the output degree of truth.

Definition 2.4.25. Idempotent GCD is *uniform* (denoted UGCD) if each of its principal special cases (HPC, SPC, SPD, and HPD) partition the region of andness/orness in equal parts (1/4 for each of them). In other words, the uniform GCD is characterized by $\alpha_\theta = \omega_\theta = 3/4$. If HPC, SPC, SPD, and HPD partition the region of andness/orness in parts that are not equal, then such a version of GCD is *nonuniform*.

Definition 2.4.26. *Conjunctive partial absorption (CPA)* is a conjunctive ILA $A_{cpa} : I^2 \to I$ that has heterogeneous annihilators: one argument, called the mandatory input (x), has the annihilator 0, and the other argument, called the optional input (y), does not have the annihilator 0. So, $A_{cpa}(0,y) = 0$, $0 \le y \le 1$ and $0 < A_{cpa}(x,0) < x$, $0 < x \le 1$. Except for heterogeneous annihilators, CPA is similar to partial conjunction and can be called *asymmetric partial conjunction*.

Remark. CPA is usually implemented as $A_{cpa}(x,y) = W_2 x \Delta (1 - W_2)[W_1 x \nabla (1 - W_1)y]$ and in such a case it is a graded (soft computing) generalization of the classic Boolean total absorption theorem $x \wedge (x \vee y) = x$, $x \in I, y \in I$.

Definition 2.4.27. *Disjunctive partial absorption (DPA)* is a disjunctive ILA $A_{dpa} : I^2 \to I$ that has heterogeneous annihilators: one argument, called the sufficient input (x), has the annihilator 1, and the other argument, called the optional input (y), does not have the annihilator 1. So, $A_{dpa}(1,y) = 1$, $0 \le y \le 1$ and $x < A_{dpa}(x,1) < 1$, $0 \le x < 1$. Except for heterogeneous annihilators, DPA is similar to partial disjunction and can be called *asymmetric partial disjunction*.

Remark. DPA is usually implemented as $A_{dpa}(x,y) = W_2 x \nabla (1 - W_2) [W_1 x \Delta (1 - W_1)y]$ and in such a case it is a graded generalization of the classic Boolean total absorption theorem $x \vee (x \wedge y) = x$, $x \in I, y \in I$.

Definition 2.4.28. Default version of negation used in GL is the standard negation $not(x) = \bar{x} = 1 - x$.

Remark. The notation with bar has two interpretations that depend on context. For aggregator $A(\mathbf{x})$ we use the notation $\overline{A(\mathbf{x})} = 1 - A(\mathbf{x})$ to denote negation in logic expressions. We also use $\overline{A(\mathbf{x})} = \int_{[0,1]^n} A(\mathbf{x})dx_1 \cdots dx_n$ to denote the volume under the surface $A(\mathbf{x})$ inside the unit hypercube in calculations of andness and orness. The default interpretation is negation; e.g., $\bar{\mathbf{x}} = (\bar{x}_1,...,\bar{x}_n) = (1 - x_1,...,1 - x_n)$.

Definition 2.4.29. For any GCD aggregator $A(\mathbf{x}; \mathbf{W}, \alpha)$ De Morgan's laws are $1 - A(\mathbf{x}; \mathbf{W}, \alpha) = A(\bar{\mathbf{x}}; \mathbf{W}, \bar{\alpha})$ or $1 - A(\mathbf{x}; \mathbf{W}, \bar{\alpha}) = A(\bar{\mathbf{x}}; \mathbf{W}, \alpha)$. Aggregators $A(\mathbf{x}; \mathbf{W}, \alpha)$ and $A(\mathbf{x}; \mathbf{W}, \bar{\alpha}) = 1 - A(\bar{\mathbf{x}}; \mathbf{W}, \alpha)$ are dual. Thus, a GCD aggregator can be constructed by negating inputs and outputs of a dual aggregator. In the case $n = 2$, $\alpha = 1$, we have the following:

$$A(\mathbf{x}; \mathbf{W}, \alpha) = x_1 \wedge x_2, \quad A(\mathbf{x}; \mathbf{W}, \bar{\alpha}) = x_1 \vee x_2 \qquad \therefore A(\mathbf{x}; \mathbf{W}, \alpha) = \text{dual of } A(\mathbf{x}; \mathbf{W}, \bar{\alpha});$$

$$1 - A(\mathbf{x}; \mathbf{W}, \alpha) = \overline{x_1 \wedge x_2}, \quad A(\bar{\mathbf{x}}; \mathbf{W}, \bar{\alpha}) = \bar{x}_1 \vee \bar{x}_2 = \overline{x_1 \wedge x_2} \quad \therefore \overline{A(\mathbf{x}; \mathbf{W}, \alpha)} = A(\bar{\mathbf{x}}; \mathbf{W}, \bar{\alpha});$$

$$1 - A(\mathbf{x}; \mathbf{W}, \bar{\alpha}) = \overline{x_1 \vee x_2}, \quad A(\bar{\mathbf{x}}; \mathbf{W}, \alpha) = \bar{x}_1 \wedge \bar{x}_2 = \overline{x_1 \vee x_2} \quad \therefore \overline{A(\mathbf{x}; \mathbf{W}, \bar{\alpha})} = A(\bar{\mathbf{x}}; \mathbf{W}, \alpha);$$

$$1 - A(\bar{\mathbf{x}}; \mathbf{W}, \alpha) = \overline{\bar{x}_1 \wedge \bar{x}_2} = x_1 \vee x_2 = A(\mathbf{x}; \mathbf{W}, \bar{\alpha}), \qquad \therefore \overline{A(\bar{\mathbf{x}}; \mathbf{W}, \alpha)} = A(\mathbf{x}; \mathbf{W}, \bar{\alpha});$$

$$\overline{A(\bar{\mathbf{x}}; \mathbf{W}, \alpha)} = \text{dual of } A(\mathbf{x}; \mathbf{W}, \alpha) = \text{same aggregator with negated inputs and outputs}.$$

Remark. This concept is shown in Fig. 2.4.2. In the case of GCD, one of dual aggregators is conjunctive (having andness $\frac{1}{2} \le \alpha \le 1$) and the other is disjunctive (having andness $1 - \alpha$). The dual of conjunctive aggregator $A(\mathbf{x}; \mathbf{W}, \alpha)$ is a disjunctive aggregator $1 - A(\bar{\mathbf{x}}; \mathbf{W}, \alpha)$. The andness of a dual aggregator is equal to the orness of the original aggregator (see Proposition 2.3.2). Duality is also discussed in Sections 2.4.4, 2.4.7 and in Chapter 2.7.

Definition 2.4.30. The concept of duality applies to general GCD and its special cases. The andness-directed GCD aggregator $A(\mathbf{x}; \mathbf{W}, \alpha)$ can be classified according to duality as (1) *naturally dual*, (2) *not dual*, (3) *autodual (self-dual)*, (4) *conjunctive-dualized*, and (5) *disjunctive-dualized* as follows:

- $A(\mathbf{x}; \mathbf{W}, \alpha)$ is *naturally dual* if $A(\mathbf{x}; \mathbf{W}, 1 - \alpha) = 1 - A(\bar{\mathbf{x}}; \mathbf{W}, \alpha)$; the exponential mean is an example of naturally dual aggregator.

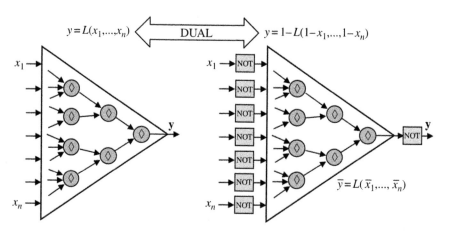

Figure 2.4.2 A general idempotent aggregation structure and its idempotent De Morgan's dual.

- $A(\mathbf{x}; \mathbf{W}, \alpha)$ is *not dual* if $A(\mathbf{x}; \mathbf{W}, 1-\alpha) \neq 1 - A(\bar{\mathbf{x}}; \mathbf{W}, \alpha)$; the weighted power mean is an example or aggregator that is not dual.
- $A(\mathbf{x}; \mathbf{W}, \alpha)$ is *autodual* if $A(\mathbf{x}; \mathbf{W}, \alpha) = 1 - A(\bar{\mathbf{x}}; \mathbf{W}, \alpha)$; the arithmetic mean is an example of aggregator that is autodual.
- $A(\mathbf{x}; \mathbf{W}, \alpha)$ is *conjunctive-dualized* if it is defined using an extended conjunction $C(\mathbf{x}; \mathbf{W}, \alpha)$, $\frac{1}{2} \leq \alpha$, to satisfy duality $A(\mathbf{x}; \mathbf{W}, \alpha) = \begin{cases} 1 - C(\bar{\mathbf{x}}; \mathbf{W}, 1-\alpha), & \alpha \leq \frac{1}{2}, \\ C(\mathbf{x}; \mathbf{W}, \alpha), & \frac{1}{2} \leq \alpha. \end{cases}$
- $A(\mathbf{x}; \mathbf{W}, \alpha)$ is *disjunctive-dualized* if it is defined using an extended disjunction $D(\mathbf{x}; \mathbf{W}, \alpha)$, $\alpha \leq \frac{1}{2}$, to satisfy duality $A(\mathbf{x}; \mathbf{W}, \alpha) = \begin{cases} D(\mathbf{x}; \mathbf{W}, \alpha), & \alpha \leq \frac{1}{2}, \\ 1 - D(\bar{\mathbf{x}}; \mathbf{W}, 1-\alpha), & \frac{1}{2} \leq \alpha. \end{cases}$

Remark. Naturally dual aggregators are rare, and the lack of duality is a drawback because in such cases there is no logic symmetry between the conjunctive and disjunctive part of GCD. Consequently, conjunctive-dualized and disjunctive-dualized GCD functions are an important way for supporting De Morgan's laws, designing aggregators with desired properties, and implementing GCD as a simple recursive function based on the following pseudocode:

$$\text{GCD}(\mathbf{x}, \mathbf{W}, \alpha) \{ \text{return } \alpha \geq 0.5 \ ? \ C(\mathbf{x}, \mathbf{W}, \alpha) : \text{GCD}(1 - \mathbf{x}, \mathbf{W}, 1 - \alpha) \}.$$

Some important properties of logic aggregators can be expressed using the following propositions.

Proposition 2.4.1. GCD (in the range $\alpha \in [0,1]$) and PA (CPA and DPA) are the only idempotent logic aggregators. To verify this statement it is sufficient to see that in the case of two variables and the special case of Boolean logic ($\alpha \in \{0,1\}$, $\omega \in \{0,1\}$) there are 16 functions of two variables (Table 2.1.2) and the boundary conditions $A(0,0) = 0$ and $A(1,1) = 1$ are satisfied only by four functions: conjunction $A_1(x,y) = x \wedge y$, disjunction $A_2(x,y) = x \vee y$ and two cases of total absorption: $A_3(x,y) = x \wedge (x \vee y) = x$ and $A_4(x,y) = y \wedge (x \vee y) = y$ (see Section 2.1.6). Therefore, other GL functions (e.g., implication, equivalence, etc.) do not have the status of aggregator.

Proposition 2.4.2. All compound logic aggregators obtained using superposition of idempotent aggregators are idempotent. If $\underline{x} = (x,...,x)$, $x \in I$, and $A(\underline{x}) = x$, then $A(A(\underline{x}),...,A(\underline{x})) = x$ and the same reasoning holds for different aggregators, for different number of variables in each aggregator, and for any depth of nesting. Since the basic GCD is idempotent and CPA and DPA are defined as a superposition of GCD aggregators, it follows that CPA and DPA must also be idempotent.

Proposition 2.4.3. The arithmetic mean is the only neutral logic aggregator. Since the neutral aggregator must simultaneously be concave and convex, it must be a hyperplane inside I^n that includes the points $(0, ..., 0)$ and $(1, ..., 1)$, i.e., the function $mid(\mathbf{x}) = W_1 x_1 + \cdots + W_n x_n$, $0 < W_i < 1$, $W_1 + \cdots + W_n = 1$. Due to its central location, the arithmetic mean can be considered the *logic centroid* of all logic aggregators.

Proposition 2.4.4. Using the standard negation $not(x) = \bar{x} = 1 - x$ De Morgan's duality is preserved in GL as shown in Fig. 2.4.2 ($n > 1$). De Morgan's dual of $y = L(x_1, ..., x_n)$ is $y = \overline{L(\bar{x}_1, ..., \bar{x}_n)}$ and vice versa. If $L(x_1, ..., x_n)$ is a conjunctive (or disjunctive) aggregator, then $1 - L(1 - x_1, ..., 1 - x_n)$ is a disjunctive (or conjunctive) aggregator. Thus, all conjunctions can be defined as De Morgan's duals of disjunctions, and vice versa:

$$W_1 x_1 \triangledown \cdots \triangledown W_n x_n = 1 - W_1(1 - x_1) \triangle \cdots \triangle W_n(1 - x_n)$$
$$W_1 x_1 \triangle \cdots \triangle W_n x_n = 1 - W_1(1 - x_1) \triangledown \cdots \triangledown W_n(1 - x_n)$$

This method is frequently used in the design of aggregators.

Proposition 2.4.5. De Morgan's dual of an idempotent aggregation structure is also idempotent. If $y = L(x_1, ..., x_n)$ is an idempotent function, then $y = L(x, ..., x) = x$. Using negation of all inputs and the negation of the output we get the De Morgan's dual of the idempotent structure $y = 1 - L(1 - x_1, ..., 1 - x_n)$. If $x_1 = \cdots = x_n = x$, then $y = 1 - L(1 - x, ..., 1 - x) = 1 - (1 - x) = x$.

Proposition 2.4.6. If a logic aggregator is more conjunctive than the pure conjunction, $min(x_1, ..., x_n)$, then it must be nonidempotent. This property was analyzed in Section 2.1.4. Basically, the diagonal section of such an aggregator must be *below the idempotency line*, because if that is not the case, the aggregator would no longer be nondecreasing in all arguments (and such a function would no longer be an aggregator). Therefore, the most conjunctive idempotent aggregator is the pure conjunction, and any hyperconjunction must be nonidempotent.

Proposition 2.4.7. If a logic aggregator is more disjunctive than the pure disjunction, $max(x_1, ..., x_n)$, then it must be nonidempotent. This property is dual to Proposition 2.4.6: the diagonal section of such an aggregator must be *above the idempotency line*, because if that is not the case, the aggregator would no longer be nondecreasing in all arguments (and would lose the status of aggregator). Therefore, the most disjunctive idempotent aggregator is the pure disjunction, and any hyperdisjunction must be nonidempotent.

2.4.2 Classification of Conjunctive and Disjunctive Logic Aggregators

The use of annihilators is so fundamental and ubiquitous in human evaluation reasoning that it represents a justifiable primary criterion for classification of logic aggregators. Annihilators of logic aggregators can be supported or not supported, arguments can be homogeneous or heterogeneous, and aggregators can be conjunctive or disjunctive. Based on these options, our primary classification of conjunctive and disjunctive logic aggregators is shown in Table 2.4.1. We used the case of two variables so that conjunctive and disjunctive aggregators can include the asymmetric aggregators (conjunctive and disjunctive partial absorption). A refined classification and characteristic properties of conjunctive and disjunctive aggregators are shown in Table 2.4.2. These tables include all aggregators that are necessary and sufficient for creating GL functions.

The LSP method for evaluation is primarily based on idempotent aggregators because the majority of human evaluation reasoning occurs in the central idempotent regions of the unit hypercube (see Section 2.1.8 and Chapter 2.2). Therefore, in cases where we investigate evaluation problems we regularly restrict our attention to the *default idempotent aggregation* based on seven necessary and sufficient types of idempotent aggregators: C, HPC, SPC, A, SPD, HPD, and D, introduced in Table 2.1.4. Hyperconjunctive and hyperdisjunctive aggregators will be used only in special cases where we have reasons to extend GCD to the whole unit hypercube from the drastic conjunction to the drastic disjunction.

In GL applications, logic aggregators from the GCD set are frequently combined (grouped) to create eight combined aggregators: extended conjunction and disjunction (EC, ED), extended hard conjunction (EHC) and disjunction (EHD), extended soft conjunction (ESC) and disjunction (ESD), and the total conjunction and disjunction (TC, TD). These functions are introduced and characterized in Table 2.4.2. Figs. 2.4.3 and 2.4.4 provide visual interpretation of structuring the combined aggregators and the development of their related symbols. Since HPC and C (or HPD and D) are adjacent aggregators and both are hard, then EHC (or EHD) are used as models of all hard idempotent properties. Similarly, SPC and A (or SPD and A) are adjacent aggregators and both are soft; so, ESC (or ESD) are used as model of all soft idempotent properties. All forms of conjunction can be grouped together in total conjunction, and all forms of disjunction can be grouped in total disjunction. So, TD = SPD +HPD+C, TC=SPC+HPC+C, GCD=TC+A+TD, EC∩ED=A. The total number of various conjunctive and disjunctive aggregators in GL is 20, and all of them are presented in Table 2.4.2.

Table 2.4.1 Classification of conjunctive and disjunctive logic aggregators (the case of two arguments that includes PA).

Type of logic aggregator	AH	Logic property modeled by the aggregator	Name of aggregator	Code and symbol	Location of aggregator F inside the unit hypercube	Idem	Range of andness (α) or orness (ω)	Role of input values x	Role of input values y	Supported annihilators x	Supported annihilators y	Group
Conjunctive	N	Asymmetric simultaneity (compensative)	Conjunctive partial absorption	CPA, $\underline{\triangle}\!\mid$	$MIN < F < A$	Y	N/A	Man	Opt	0	None	PA
	Y	Extreme simultaneity	Hyper-conjunction	CC, $\overline{\wedge}$	$0 < F < MIN$	N	$1 < \alpha \le 2$	Man	Man	0	0	GCD
		Complete (full) simultaneity	Full Conjunction	C, $\wedge$	$F = MIN$	Y	$\alpha = 1$	Man	Man	0	0	
		Graded partial simultaneity	Hard partial conjunction	HPC, $\overline{\triangle}$	$MIN < F \le CTA$	Y	$\alpha_\theta \le \alpha < 1$	Man	Man	0	0	
		Graded partial simultaneity (compensative)	Soft partial conjunction	SPC, $\underline{\triangle}$	$CTA < F < A$	Y	$1/2 < \alpha < \alpha_\theta$	Opt	Opt	None	None	
Neutral	Y	Neutrality (compensative)	Neutrality (arit. mean)	A, $\oplus$	$F = A$	Y	$\alpha = \omega = 1/2$	Opt	Opt	None	None	
Disjunctive	Y	Graded partial substitutability (compensative)	Soft partial disjunction	SPD, $\underline{\triangledown}$	$A < F < DTA$	Y	$1/2 < \omega < \omega_\theta$	Opt	Opt	None	None	
		Graded partial substitutability	Hard partial disjunction	HPD, $\overline{\triangledown}$	$DTA \le F < MAX$	Y	$\omega_\theta \le \omega < 1$	Suf	Suf	1	1	
		Complete (full) substitutability	Full disjunction	D, $\vee$	$F = MAX$	Y	$\omega = 1$	Suf	Suf	1	1	
		Extreme substitutability	Hyper-disjunction	DD, $\overline{\vee}$	$MAX < F \le 1$	N	$1 < \omega \le 2$	Suf	Suf	1	1	
	N	Asymmetric substitutability (compensative)	Disjunctive partial absorption	DPA, $\underline{\triangledown}\!\mid$	$A < F < MAX$	Y	N/A	Suf	Opt	1	None	PA

Abbreviations: AH = Annihilator homogeneity (all inputs support the same annihilator); Idem = idempotency; Y = yes; N = no; Man = mandatory; Suf = sufficient; Opt = optional ; GCD = graded conjunction/disjunction; PA = partial absorption; F = aggregation function of two variables $f(x,y)$; MIN = full conjunction $x \wedge y$; MAX = full disjunction $x \vee y$; CTA = conjunctive threshold aggregator with adjustable andness α_θ; DTA = disjunctive threshold aggregator with adjustable orness ω_θ; A = arithmetic mean; N/A = not applicable

Table 2.4.2 Characteristic properties of conjunctive and disjunctive logic aggregators.

Symbol	Aggregator	Ab.	Characteristic property
$\overline{\overline{\vee}}$	Hyperdisjunction	**DD**	$\max(x,y) \leq x\,\overline{\overline{\vee}}\,y \leq 1$, $x \in [0,1]$, $y \in [0,1]$, $\omega > 1$
$\vee$	Disjunction	**D**	$x \vee y = \max(x,y)$, $x \in [0,1]$, $y \in [0,1]$
$\overline{\nabla}$	Hard partial disjunction	**HPD**	$x\underline{\nabla}y < x\overline{\nabla}y \leq x \vee y$, $(\overline{\nabla}: \omega_\theta \leq \omega < 1)$ $1\overline{\nabla}y = x\overline{\nabla}1 = 1$, $x \in [0,1]$, $y \in [0,1]$, $x \neq y$
$\underline{\nabla}$	Soft partial disjunction	**SPD**	$x \ominus y < x\underline{\nabla}y < x\overline{\nabla}y$, $x \neq y$, $y < 1\underline{\nabla}y < 1$, $0 \leq y < 1$, $(\underline{\nabla}: \frac{1}{2} < \omega < \omega_\theta)$
$\ominus$	Neutrality	**A**	$x \ominus y = (x+y)/2$, $\alpha = \omega = \frac{1}{2}$, $x\triangle y < x \ominus y < x\overline{\nabla}y$, $x \neq y$
$\underline{\triangle}$	Soft partial conjunction	**SPC**	$x\overline{\triangle}y < x\underline{\triangle}y < x \ominus y$, $x \neq y$, $0 < 0\underline{\triangle}y < y$, $0 < y \leq 1$, $(\underline{\triangle}: \frac{1}{2} < \alpha < \alpha_\theta)$
$\overline{\triangle}$	Hard partial conjunction	**HPC**	$x \wedge y \leq x\overline{\triangle}y < x\underline{\triangle}y$, $(\overline{\triangle}: \alpha_\theta \leq \alpha < 1)$ $0\overline{\triangle}y = x\overline{\triangle}0 = 0$, $x \in [0,1]$, $y \in [0,1]$, $x \neq y$
$\wedge$	Conjunction	**C**	$x \wedge y = \min(x,y)$, $x \in [0,1]$, $y \in [0,1]$
$\overline{\overline{\wedge}}$	Hyperconjunction	**CC**	$0 \leq x\,\overline{\overline{\wedge}}\,y \leq \min(x,y)$, $x \in [0,1]$, $y \in [0,1]$, $\alpha > 1$
$\nabla \in \{\overline{\nabla},\underline{\nabla}\}$	Partial disjunction	**PD**	$x \ominus y < x\nabla y \leq x \vee y$, $x \neq y$, $\nabla: \quad 0 < \alpha < \frac{1}{2} < \omega < 1$
$\triangle \in \{\overline{\triangle},\underline{\triangle}\}$	Partial conjunction	**PC**	$x \wedge y \leq x\triangle y < x \ominus y$, $x \neq y$ $\triangle: \quad 0 < \omega < \frac{1}{2} < \alpha < 1$
$\overline{\overline{\nabla}} \in \{\overline{\nabla},\vee\}$	Extended hard disjunction	**EHD**	$x\underline{\nabla}y < x\overline{\overline{\nabla}}y \leq x \vee y$, $(\overline{\overline{\nabla}}: \omega_\theta \leq \omega \leq 1)$ $1\overline{\overline{\nabla}}y = x\overline{\overline{\nabla}}1 = 1$, $x \in [0,1]$, $y \in [0,1]$, $x \neq y$
$\underline{\underline{\nabla}} \in \{\underline{\nabla},\ominus\}$	Extended soft disjunction	**ESD**	$x \ominus y \leq x\underline{\underline{\nabla}}y < x\overline{\nabla}y$, $x \neq y$, $y < 1\underline{\underline{\nabla}}y < 1$, $0 \leq y < 1$, $(\underline{\underline{\nabla}}: \frac{1}{2} \leq \omega < \omega_\theta)$
$\underline{\underline{\triangle}} \in \{\underline{\triangle},\ominus\}$	Extended soft conjunction	**ESC**	$x\overline{\triangle}y < x\underline{\underline{\triangle}}y \leq x \ominus y$, $x \neq y$, $0 < 0\underline{\underline{\triangle}}y < y$, $0 < y \leq 1$, $(\underline{\underline{\triangle}}: \frac{1}{2} \leq \alpha < \alpha_\theta)$
$\overline{\overline{\triangle}} \in \{\overline{\triangle},\wedge\}$	Extended hard conjunction	**EHC**	$x \wedge y \leq x\overline{\overline{\triangle}}y < x\underline{\triangle}y$, $(\overline{\overline{\triangle}}: \alpha_\theta \leq \alpha \leq 1)$ $0\overline{\overline{\triangle}}y = x\overline{\overline{\triangle}}0 = 0$, $x \in [0,1]$, $y \in [0,1]$, $x \neq y$
$\check{\nabla} \in \{\nabla,\vee\}$	Total disjunction	**TD**	$(x+y)/2 < x\check{\nabla}y \leq x \vee y$, $\frac{1}{2} < \omega \leq 1$
$\hat{\triangle} \in \{\triangle,\wedge\}$	Total conjunction	**TC**	$x \wedge y \leq x\hat{\triangle}y < (x+y)/2$, $\frac{1}{2} < \alpha \leq 1$
$\check{\nabla} \in \{\underline{\nabla},\overline{\overline{\nabla}}\}$	Extended disjunction	**ED**	$(x+y)/2 \leq x\tilde{\nabla}y \leq x \vee y$, $\frac{1}{2} \leq \omega \leq 1$
$\tilde{\triangle} \in \{\underline{\triangle},\overline{\overline{\triangle}}\}$	Extended conjunction	**EC**	$x \wedge y \leq x\tilde{\triangle}y \leq (x+y)/2$, $\frac{1}{2} \leq \alpha \leq 1$
$\lozenge \in \{\tilde{\nabla},\tilde{\triangle}\}$	Idempotent graded conjunction/ disjunction	**GCD**	$x \wedge y \leq x\lozenge y \leq x \vee y$, $0 \leq \alpha \leq 1$, $0 \leq \omega \leq 1$, $\alpha + \omega = 1$

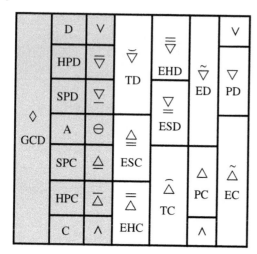

Figure 2.4.3 A tabular structure of idempotent conjunctive and disjunctive logic aggregators.

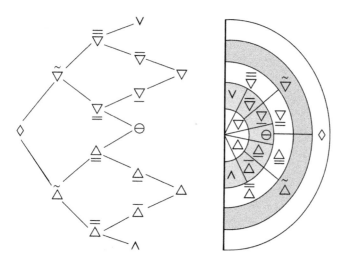

Figure 2.4.4 Visualizing decomposition of idempotent GCD, and relationships between symbols.

2.4.3   Properties of Means Used in Logic Aggregation

All means support internality and can be interpreted as idempotent logic aggregators. Most idempotent logic aggregators in GL are descendants of the Bajraktarević mean (BM). A chain of special cases of BM that terminates with the simple

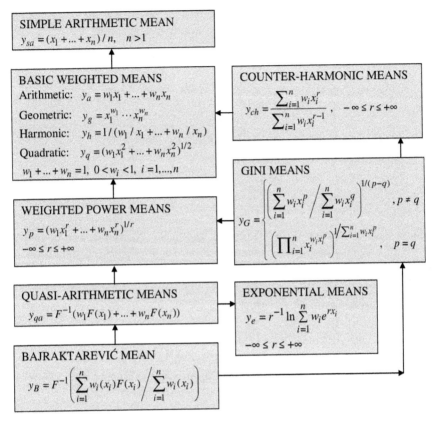

Figure 2.4.5 A chain of special cases of BM.

arithmetic mean is shown in Fig. 2.4.5. The importance of BM is based on their double parameterization: they offer the parameterization of andness/orness, as well as the parameterization of relative importance. Means that do not support these two forms of parameterization have no applicability in GL, but weights can be parameterized using the tree method presented in Section 2.5.5.

Means and their inequalities are a very wide area of mathematical interest and there are many different types of means [GIN58, MIT69, MIT77, BUL88, MIT89, BUL03]. A very detailed and carefully classified collection of mathematical properties of means can be found in [GIN58]. Various properties of idempotent and nonidempotent aggregators can be found in [FOD94, MAR99, DET00, GRA09, BEL07, BEL16, and TOR07].

Logic aggregators are most frequently implemented as means. Consequently, it is useful to know those mathematical properties of means that are relevant for design of aggregators. Following are the basic properties if $f(x_1, ..., x_n)$ is the arithmetic, geometric, harmonic, or quadratic mean [MIT89]:

$$f\left(x_1,...,x_i,x_{i+1},...,x_{j-1},x_j,...,x_n\right)$$
$$= f\left(x_1,...,x_j,x_{i+1},...,x_{j-1},x_i,...,x_n\right), \quad i \neq j; \quad i,j = 1,...,n. \qquad \text{(Commutativity)}$$

$$f\left(x_1,...,x_m,x_{m+1},...,x_n\right)$$
$$= f(M,...,M,x_{m+1},...,x_n), \quad M = f(x_1,...,x_m), \quad m < n. \qquad \text{(m-Associativity)}$$

$$f(cx_1,...,cx_n) = cf(x_1,...,x_n), \quad c > 0. \qquad \text{(Homogeneity)}$$

$$f(c,...,c) = c. \qquad \text{(Idempotency)}$$

$$f(x_1,...,x_n) > 0, \quad x_i > 0, \quad i = 1,...,n. \qquad \text{(Sensitivity)}$$

A direct generalization of the arithmetic, geometric, harmonic, and quadratic mean is the weighted power mean (WPM). In the following definition of WPM we use the limit to include the cases $r = 0, -\infty, +\infty$:

$$M_n^{[r]}(\mathbf{x}; \mathbf{W}) = \lim_{p \to r} \left(\sum_{i=1}^n W_i x_i^p \right)^{1/p}, \quad \mathbf{x} = (x_1,...,x_n), \quad \mathbf{W} = (W_1,...,W_n),$$

$$-\infty \leq r \leq +\infty, \quad 0 < W_i < 1, \quad i = 1,...,n, \quad \sum_{i=1}^n W_i = 1.$$

Basic mathematical properties of WPM are defined using the following theorem [MIT77]:

$$\min(x_1,...,x_n) \leq M_n^{[r]}(\mathbf{x}; \mathbf{W}) \leq \max(x_1,...,x_n); \qquad \text{(Internality)}$$

if $r < s$ then $M_n^{[r]}(\mathbf{x}; \mathbf{W}) \leq M_n^{[s]}(\mathbf{x}; \mathbf{W})$; (Transition from min to max)

$$M_n^{[rs]}(\mathbf{x}; \mathbf{W})^s = M_n^{[r]}(\mathbf{x}^s; \mathbf{W}); \qquad \text{(Power transform)}$$

if $\underline{\mathbf{x}} = (a,...,a)$ then $M_n^{[r]}(\underline{\mathbf{x}}; \mathbf{W}) = a$; (Idempotency)

$$M_n^{[r]}(c\mathbf{x}; \mathbf{W}) = cM_n^{[r]}(\mathbf{x}; \mathbf{W}), \quad c \geq 0; \qquad \text{(Homogeneity)}$$

$$\lim_{\mathbf{h} \to 0} M_n^{[r]}(\mathbf{x} + \mathbf{h}; \mathbf{W}) = M_n^{[r]}(\mathbf{x}; \mathbf{W}), \quad \mathbf{h} = (h_1,...,h_n); \quad \text{(Continuity)}$$

if $\mathbf{a} \leq \mathbf{b}$ then $M_n^{[r]}(\mathbf{a}; \mathbf{W}) \leq M_n^{[r]}(\mathbf{b}; \mathbf{W})$; (Monotonicity)

$$\begin{cases} M_n^{[r]}(\mathbf{x}; \mathbf{W}) = M_n^{[r]}((M,...,M,x_{m+1},...,x_n); \mathbf{W}), \\ \\ M = \lim_{p \to r} \left(\sum_{i=1}^m \frac{W_i}{\sum_{j=1}^m W_j} x_i^p \right)^{1/p}, \quad m < n; \end{cases} \qquad \text{(m-Associativity)}$$

$$
\begin{cases}
M_{k+m}^{[r]}\left((x_1,\ldots,x_k,M,\ldots,M);\mathbf{W}\right) = M = M_k^{[r]}(\mathbf{x}_k;\mathbf{W}_k), \quad \sum_{i=1}^{k+m} W_i = 1, \quad m > 0 \\[2em]
\mathbf{x}_k = (x_1,\ldots,x_k), \quad \mathbf{W}_k = \left(\dfrac{W_1}{\sum_{j=1}^{k} W_j},\ldots,\dfrac{W_k}{\sum_{j=1}^{k} W_j}\right), \quad M = \lim_{p \to r}\left(\sum_{i=1}^{k}\dfrac{W_i}{\sum_{j=1}^{k} W_j} x_i^p\right)^{1/p}.
\end{cases}
$$

(Reduced averaging)

The meaning of m-associativity is that the weighted power mean of n arguments remains unchanged if m arguments $(1 \le m \le n)$ are replaced by their normalized weighted mean. Similarly, the meaning of reduced averaging is that if m out of $n = k + m$ arguments are missing, then we can compute the reduced normalized weighted average M of k existing arguments and replace the missing arguments with this value. The resulting WPM will then have the same value M (i.e., we can use M as a neutral replacement of missing elements).

For our study of aggregators, we are here interested only in proving the m-associativity and the reduced averaging. In the case of m-associativity we have the following proof (for simplicity we use $0 < |r| < +\infty$):

$$
M = \left(\sum_{i=1}^{m}\frac{W_i}{\sum_{j=1}^{m} W_j} x_i^r\right)^{1/r}, \quad \mathbf{W} = (W_1,\ldots,W_n);
$$

$$
M_n^{[r]}\left((M,\ldots,M,x_{m+1},\ldots,x_n);\mathbf{W}\right) = \left(W_1 M^r + \ldots + W_m M^r + W_{m+1} x_{m+1}^r + \ldots + W_n x_n^r\right)^{1/r}
$$

$$
= \left(M^r \sum_{j=1}^{m} W_j + W_{m+1} x_{m+1}^r + \ldots + W_n x_n^r\right)^{1/r} = \left(W_1 x_1^r + \ldots + W_n x_n^r\right)^{1/r} = M_n^{[r]}(\mathbf{x};\mathbf{W}).
$$

Similarly, in the case of reduced averaging, assuming $0 < |r| < +\infty$ we have the following proof:

$$
M = \left(\sum_{i=1}^{k}\frac{W_i}{\sum_{j=1}^{k} W_j} x_i^r\right)^{1/r}, \quad \mathbf{W} = (W_1,\ldots,W_n), \quad W_1 + \cdots + W_n = 1, \quad n = k + m;
$$

$$
M_{k+m}^{[r]}\left((x_1,\ldots,x_k,M,\ldots,M);\mathbf{W}\right) = \left(W_1 x_1^r + \cdots + W_k x_k^r + W_{k+1} M^r + \cdots + W_{k+m} M^r\right)^{1/r}
$$

$$
= \left(\sum_{i=1}^{k} W_i x_i^r + (W_{k+1} + \cdots + W_{k+m}) M^r\right)^{1/r} = \left(\sum_{i=1}^{k} W_i x_i^r + \left(1 - \sum_{j=1}^{k} W_j\right)\sum_{i=1}^{k}\frac{W_i x_i^r}{\sum_{j=1}^{k} W_j}\right)^{1/r}
$$

$$
= \left(\sum_{i=1}^{k} W_i x_i^r + \sum_{i=1}^{k}\frac{W_i x_i^r}{\sum_{j=1}^{k} W_j} - \sum_{i=1}^{k} W_i x_i^r\right)^{1/r} = \left(\sum_{i=1}^{k}\frac{W_i x_i^r}{\sum_{j=1}^{k} W_j}\right)^{1/r} = M = M_k^{[r]}(\mathbf{x}_k;\mathbf{W}_k).
$$

Using a continuous and strictly monotonic function $F : [0,1] \to [-\infty, +\infty]$ (we are here interested only in the averaging of logic arguments from interval

[0,1]) the WPM can be generalized as the following quasi-arithmetic mean (QAM):

$$y = M_{qa}(\mathbf{x}; \mathbf{W}) = F^{-1}\left(\sum_{i=1}^{n} W_i F(x_i)\right), \quad 0 < W_i < 1, \quad i = 1,\dots,n, \quad \sum_{i=1}^{n} W_i = 1.$$

If $F(x) = x^r$, $r \neq 0$ and $F(x) = \ln(x)$, $r = 0$, then the QAM reduces to WPM. QAM can be applied to any segment of n-tuple $\mathbf{x}$, as follows:

$$M_{qa}\left(\mathbf{x}_{[k,m]}; \mathbf{W}_{[k,m]}\right) = F^{-1}\left(\frac{\sum_{i=k}^{m} W_i F(x_i)}{\sum_{i=k}^{m} W_i}\right), \quad 0 < W_i < 1, \quad i = k,\dots,m,$$

$$1 \le k < m \le n,$$

$$\mathbf{x}_{[k,m]} = (x_k,\dots,x_m), \quad \mathbf{W}_{[k,m]} = \left(\frac{W_k}{\sum_{j=k}^{m} W_j},\dots,\frac{W_m}{\sum_{j=k}^{m} W_j}\right).$$

Consequently,

$$\sum_{i=k}^{m} W_i F(x_i) = F\left(M_{qa}\left(\mathbf{x}_{[k,m]}; \mathbf{W}_{[k,m]}\right)\right)\sum_{i=k}^{m} W_i, \quad 1 \le k < m \le n.$$

Using the above relation, we can define the m-associativity in the case of quasi-arithmetic means as follows:

$$M_{qa}\left(\mathbf{x}_{[1,n]}; \mathbf{W}_{[1,n]}\right) = F^{-1}\left(\sum_{i=1}^{m} W_i F(x_i) + \sum_{i=m+1}^{n} W_i F(x_i)\right)$$

$$= F^{-1}\left((W_1 + \cdots + W_m)F\left(M_{qa}(\mathbf{x}_{[1,m]}; \mathbf{W}_{[1,m]}\right)\right.$$

$$+ (W_{m+1} + \cdots + W_n)F\left(M_{qa}(\mathbf{x}_{[m+1,n]}; \mathbf{W}_{[m+1,n]})\right))$$

$$= M_{qa}\left((M_{qa}\left(\mathbf{x}_{[1,m]}; \mathbf{W}_{[1,m]}\right), M_{qa}\left(\mathbf{x}_{[m+1,n]}; \mathbf{W}_{[m+1,n]}\right)\right);$$

$$(W_1 + \cdots + W_m, W_{m+1} + \cdots + W_n)),$$

$$1 < m < n.$$

The corresponding aggregation process is illustrated in Fig. 2.4.6.
Following is an example of the quasi-arithmetic mean associativity:

$$M_{qa}\left(\mathbf{x}_{[1,4]}; \mathbf{W}_{[1,4]}\right) = F^{-1}(0.1F(x_1) + 0.2F(x_2) + 0.3F(x_3) + 0.4F(x_4))$$

$$= F^{-1}\left(0.3\left(\frac{1}{3}F(x_1) + \frac{2}{3}F(x_2)\right) + 0.7\left(\frac{3}{7}F(x_3) + \frac{4}{7}F(x_4)\right)\right)$$

$$= F^{-1}\left(0.3F\left(F^{-1}\left(\frac{1}{3}F(x_1) + \frac{2}{3}F(x_2)\right)\right) + 0.7F\left(F^{-1}\left(\frac{3}{7}F(x_3) + \frac{4}{7}F(x_4)\right)\right)\right)$$

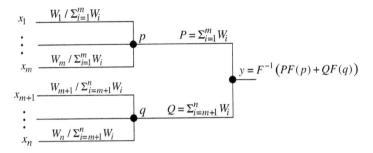

Figure 2.4.6 The concept of m-associativity of quasi-arithmetic means.

The corresponding associativity relations can also be written as follows:

$$M_{qa}\left(\mathbf{x}_{[1,4]};\mathbf{W}_{[1,4]}\right) = M_{qa}\left(\left(M_{qa}\left(\mathbf{x}_{[1,2]};\mathbf{W}_{[1,2]}\right),\right.$$
$$\left.M_{qa}\left(\mathbf{x}_{[3,4]};\mathbf{W}_{[3,4]}\right)\right);\left(W_1 + W_2, W_3 + W_4\right)\right)$$

$$M_{qa}(x_1,x_2,x_3,x_4;0.1,0.2,0.3,0.4)$$
$$= M_{qa}\left(\left(M_{qa}\left(\mathbf{x}_{[1,2]};\mathbf{W}_{[1,2]}\right),M_{qa}\left(\mathbf{x}_{[3,4]};\mathbf{W}_{[3,4]}\right)\right);(0.3,0.7)\right)$$
$$= M_{qa}\left(\left(M_{qa}(x_1,x_2;^1/_3,^2/_3),M_{qa}(x_3,x_4;^3/_7,^4/_7)\right);(0.3,0.7)\right)$$

The associativity of quasi-arithmetic means holds also for power means and all other special cases of quasi-arithmetic means. In addition, associativity relations can be expanded using multiple levels, as illustrated if Fig. 2.2.25, where, in the case of using geometric mean, we have

$$t_1 = (x_1,x_2,x_3)^{1/3}, \quad t_2 = (x_4,x_5,x_6)^{1/3},$$
$$t_3 = (x_7,x_8,x_9,x_{10})^{1/4}, \quad t_4 = (x_{11},x_{12},x_{13},x_{14},x_{15})^{1/5},$$
$$t_{12} = (t_1,t_2)^{1/2} = (x_1x_2x_3x_4x_5x_6)^{1/6},$$
$$y = t_{12}^{2/5}t_3^{4/15}t_4^{1/3} = (x_1x_2x_3x_4x_5x_6x_7x_8x_9x_{10}x_{11}x_{12}x_{13}x_{14}x_{15})^{1/15}.$$

QAM can be generalized in various ways [BUL03]. An important generalization of QAM is the Bajraktarević mean, obtained using generalized weights that can be functions of input arguments $W_i = w_i(x_i)/\sum_{i=1}^n w_i(x_i)$, $w_i : I \rightarrow]0, +\infty[$ (functions $F, w_1, ..., w_n$ are strictly monotonic):

$$y = F^{-1}\left(\sum_{i=1}^n w_i(x_i)F(x_i)/\sum_{i=1}^n w_i(x_i)\right).$$

The selection of a mean that is the most appropriate to serve as a logic aggregator is based on conditions that such a mean should satisfy. Let $M(x_1, ..., x_n; W_1, ..., W_n; r)$ denote a parameterized mean where r denotes the parameter affecting the andness/orness of the mean. Such means must satisfy the following basic mandatory and desired conditions:

Mandatory conditions that the mean $M(x_1, ..., x_n; W_1, ..., W_n; r)$ must satisfy:

1) Direct applicability for any number of input variables ($n \geq 2$).
2) The use of weights to express the relative importance of inputs ($W_1, ..., W_n$).
3) The use of an adjustable parameter (r) that enables a continuous transition from minimum (conjunction) to maximum (disjunction).
4) Ability to model hard and soft partial conjunction and disjunction as follows:
   a) HPC: M(one input is 0, all other inputs are positive) = 0.
   b) SPC: M(one input is positive, all other inputs are 0) > 0.
   c) SPD: M(one input is less than 1, all other inputs are 1) < 1.
   d) HPD: M(one input is 1, all other inputs are less than 1) = 1.

Desired conditions that the mean $M(x_1, ..., x_n; W_1, ..., W_n; r)$ should satisfy:

5) Capability to support the adjustability of threshold andness α_θ. The threshold andness is the andness at the border between SPC and HPC (the lowest andness of HPC).
6) Capability to support the adjustability of threshold orness. The threshold orness is the orness at the border between SPD and HPD (the lowest orness of HPD).

No mean can directly satisfy all these conditions. The mean that comes closest to these conditions is WPM. The conditions 1–3 are obviously satisfied by $y = \left(W_1 x_1^r + \cdots + W_n x_n^r \right)^{1/r}$, $n \geq 2$. HPC is naturally satisfied for $-\infty < r \leq 0$, and SPC for $0 < r < 1$. SPD is satisfied in the whole range $1 < r < +\infty$. HPD is satisfied by De Morgan's dual of HPC. Adjustability of threshold andness and threshold orness is achieved using interpolative aggregators. If $\alpha_\theta \geq 2/3$, then SPC is implemented using WPM interpolated between $\alpha = 1/2$ and $\alpha = \alpha_\theta$; WPM with andness α_θ is selected for $r = r_\theta \leq 0$. The threshold andness in the range $1/2 < \alpha_\theta < 2/3$ is unusual and frequently unjustifiable, but it can be achieved by combining WPM and a weighted counter-harmonic mean. The threshold orness ω_θ can be obtained using De Morgan's dual of conjunctive mean that has the threshold andness $\alpha_\theta = \omega_\theta$. Therefore, we are interested in development of logic aggregators based on WPM, and that is the topic of subsequent sections.

2.4.4 Algebraic Properties of Aggregators Based on Weighted Power Means

GL functions of n variables are defined inside the unit hypercube $[0, 1]^n$ using a superposition of GCD and negation, which are the fundamental GL functions. The idea of an algebra containing a single binary operation (denoted $\diamond$) and a single unary operation (denoted !) is known as Robbins algebra if the binary operation is commutative $(x \diamond y = y \diamond x)$, associative $(x \diamond (y \diamond z) = (x \diamond y) \diamond z)$ and satisfies Robbins axiom $(!(!(x \diamond y) \diamond !(x \diamond !y)) = x)$; Robbins algebra is proven to be Boolean algebra. GL follows that general idea of a single binary operation and a single unary operation: the binary operation is GCD and the unary operation is the standard negation. GCD is a model of simultaneity and substitutability having andness and orness that belong to the interval [0,1]. In vertices of the unit hypercube logic variables belong to the set {0,1} and if andness and orness also belong to the set {0,1} then GL functions have the same values as the corresponding classic Boolean logic functions, and only in that case GL has the properties of Boolean algebra. So, GL is a generalization of Boolean logic that extends Boolean logic beyond $\{0, 1\}^n$. GL functions are mappings $[0,1]^n \rightarrow [0,1]$ and use the values of andness and orness in the whole range [0,1].

For logic variables inside $[0, 1]^n$ GL is not a Boolean algebra. The main algebraic properties of GL based on WPM can be summarized as follows:

- Internality: satisfied
- Idempotency: satisfied
- Homogeneity: satisfied
- Continuity: satisfied
- Monotonicity: satisfied
- Additivity: satisfied only for the arithmetic mean
- Commutativity: satisfied in the case of equal weights
- Associativity: partially satisfied with sufficient accuracy
- Distributivity: partially satisfied with sufficient accuracy
- Absorption: partially satisfied with controllable level of absorption
- De Morgan's laws: satisfied for selected implementations of GCD
- No support for neutral, zero, and inverse elements

The meaning of *sufficient accuracy* is related to the fact that degrees of truth or fuzzy membership are known with limited accuracy pertinent to human perception capabilities. If the precision of expressing degrees of truth or fuzzy membership is based on "magical number 7" [MIL56], then errors of human perception up to 14% are not unusual. On the other hand, if algebraic properties such as associativity and distributivity hold with an average error of the order of 1–2% [DUJ75a], then this level of precision is sufficient for processing data that are much less precise. The average error is defined as the mean difference between the value obtained from an approximate formula and the expected (theoretical) value. This fact is insignificant from the mathematical point of view, because the associativity and distributivity are theoretically not satisfied. However, low average errors are very significant from the practical (decision engineering) point of view, because GCD/WPM provides mathematical models that are sufficiently precise for processing imprecise input data based on human perception.

Following is a short summary of algebraic properties of GL based on GCD/ WPM $W_1x_1 \diamond \cdots \diamond W_nx_n = \left(W_1x_1^r + \cdots + W_nx_n^r\right)^{1/r}$. We will explain in more detail only the properties of associativity, distributivity, and De Morgan's laws.

Internality
The internality relation $x_1 \wedge \cdots \wedge x_n \leq W_1x_1 \diamond \cdots \diamond W_nx_n \leq x_1 \vee \cdots \vee x_n$ is the fundamental property of GCD in GL. It is interpreted as the claim that the overall suitability of an object characterized by a group of inputs cannot be below the least suitable input or above the most suitable input.

Idempotency
As shown in Section 2.2.1 (property P_5), idempotency is the consequence of internality and it holds for all aggregators based on means.

Homogeneity
For GCD based on weighted power means we have $W_1(cx_1) \diamond \cdots \diamond W_n(cx_n) = c(W_1x_1 \diamond \cdots \diamond W_nx_n), c \geq 0$. If the suitability of components increases c times then the aggregated suitability also increases c times.

Continuity and Monotonicity
Continuity holds for WPM and therefore it also holds for GCD based on WPM. If $|r| < +\infty$ then $\partial(W_1x_1 \diamond \cdots \diamond W_nx_n)/\partial x_i \geq 0, i=1,\ldots,n$. More precisely, unless aggregation models use annihilators 0 or 1, GCD/WPM satisfies strict monotonicity.

Additivity
Additivity is an example of mathematical property that has no applicability in GL. Generally, $W_1(x_1 + y_1) \diamond \cdots \diamond W_n(x_n + y_n) \neq W_1x_1 \diamond \cdots \diamond W_nx_n + W_1y_1 \diamond \cdots \diamond W_ny_n$, except in case of the arithmetic mean.

Commutativity
Commutativity of GCD in the form $W_1x_1 \diamond W_2x_2 = W_1x_2 \diamond W_2x_1$ holds only if all weights are equal (i.e., $W_1 = W_2 = 1/2$). Unsurprisingly, commutativity is only exceptionally present in human reasoning. In all normal situations input attributes may have different levels of importance and the corresponding logic aggregators *must not* be commutative. Generally, GCD aggregators $(y = W_1x_1 \diamond \cdots \diamond W_nx_n)$ perform noncommutative operations.

Associativity
Associativity is an algebraic property that enables the aggregation of suitability in any grouping order. In Section 2.4.3 we proved the m-associativity of quasi-arithmetic means and therefore the m-associativity also holds for WPM. Of course, the underlying assumption is that all aggregators used in associativity

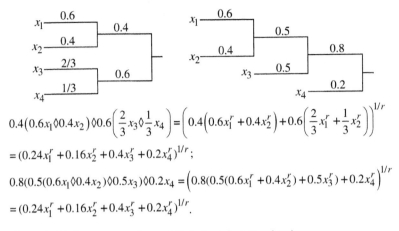

$$0.4\left(0.6x_1 \lozenge 0.4x_2\right)\lozenge 0.6\left(\frac{2}{3}x_3 \lozenge \frac{1}{3}x_4\right) = \left(0.4\left(0.6x_1^r + 0.4x_2^r\right) + 0.6\left(\frac{2}{3}x_1^r + \frac{1}{3}x_2^r\right)\right)^{1/r}$$

$$= (0.24x_1^r + 0.16x_2^r + 0.4x_3^r + 0.2x_4^r)^{1/r};$$

$$0.8(0.5(0.6x_1 \lozenge 0.4x_2)\lozenge 0.5x_3)\lozenge 0.2x_4 = \left(0.8(0.5(0.6x_1^r + 0.4x_2^r) + 0.5x_3^r) + 0.2x_4^r\right)^{1/r}$$

$$= (0.24x_1^r + 0.16x_2^r + 0.4x_3^r + 0.2x_4^r)^{1/r}.$$

Figure 2.4.7 An example of associativity based on weighted power means.

relations are identical. In the case of quasi-arithmetic means we must use the same generator function, and in the case of WPM we must use the same exponent r. The WPM exponent r determines the andness/orness of GCD. However, for a given level of global andness/orness, the exponent r is a function of the number of variables n. The variations of r for $n = 2,3,4,5$ are rather small, but sufficient to violate the assumption of the m-associativity. Consequently, the associativity for GL based on WPM holds strictly only for constant value of r. In all other cases the WPM associativity holds with minor errors discussed below.

An example of associativity, based on weighted power means is shown in Fig. 2.4.7. This example presents two aggregation structures that are equivalent because the products of weights from the root to the equivalent leaves are the same, and (assuming the use of weighted power means) the exponents of weighted power means are the same in all aggregation nodes. Using the same idea, for weights a_1, b_1, a_2, b_2 where $a_1 + b_1 = a_2 + b_2 = 1$ the GL associativity law can be defined as follows [DUJ75a]:

$$a_1x_1 \lozenge b_1(a_2x_2 \lozenge b_2x_3) = (a_1 + b_1a_2)\left(\frac{a_1}{a_1 + b_1a_2}x_1 \lozenge \frac{b_1a_2}{a_1 + b_1a_2}x_2\right)\lozenge b_1b_2x_3$$

However, the following associativity holds only approximately:

$$W_1x_1 \lozenge W_2x_2 \lozenge W_3x_3 \approx W_1x_1 \lozenge (W_2 + W_3)\left(\frac{W_2}{W_2 + W_3}x_2 \lozenge \frac{W_3}{W_2 + W_3}x_3\right) =$$

$$= (W_1 + W_2)\left(\frac{W_1}{W_1 + W_2}x_1 \lozenge \frac{W_2}{W_1 + W_2}x_2\right)\lozenge W_3x_3 \approx W_1x_1 \lozenge W_2x_2 \lozenge W_3x_3$$

The reason for this approximation is that in the case of weighted power means the exponent in the case of three inputs is slightly different from the exponent in the case of two inputs (see detailed analysis in Chapter 2.3). If the exponents were the same, then the above associativity would exactly hold (as shown in Section 2.4.3 for the quasi-arithmetic means) but the global andness/orness for two and three variables would be slightly different. Fortunately, the errors are rather small. According to [DUJ75a] selected average errors of associativity and distributivity for equal weights can be computed as follows:

$$E_{2+1}^{assoc}(\alpha) = \int_0^1 dx_1 \int_0^1 dx_2 \int_0^1 \left\{ \left(\frac{1}{3}x_1 \diamond \frac{1}{3}x_2 \diamond \frac{1}{3}x_3 \right) - \left[\frac{1}{3}x_1 \diamond \frac{2}{3} \left(\frac{1}{2}x_2 \diamond \frac{1}{2}x_3 \right) \right] \right\} dx_3,$$

$$E_{2+1}^{assoc}(0) = E_{2+1}^{assoc}(1/2) = E_{2+1}^{assoc}(1) = 0,$$

$$\bar{E}_{2+1}^{assoc} = \int_0^1 \left| E_{2+1}^{assoc}(\alpha) \right| d\alpha = 0.00516.$$

$$E_{3+1}^{assoc}(\alpha) = \int_0^1 dx_1 \int_0^1 dx_2 \int_0^1 dx_3 \int_0^1 \left\{ \left(\frac{1}{4}x_1 \diamond \frac{1}{4}x_2 \diamond \frac{1}{4}x_3 \diamond \frac{1}{4}x_4 \right) \right.$$
$$\left. - \left[\frac{3}{4} \left(\frac{1}{3}x_1 \diamond \frac{1}{3}x_2 \diamond \frac{1}{3}x_3 \right) \diamond \frac{1}{4}x_4 \right] \right\} dx_4,$$

$$E_{3+1}^{assoc}(0) = E_{3+1}^{assoc}(1/2) = E_{3+1}^{assoc}(1) = 0,$$

$$\bar{E}_{3+1}^{assoc} = \int_0^1 \left| E_{3+1}^{assoc}(\alpha) \right| d\alpha = 0.00612.$$

$$E_{2+2}^{assoc}(\alpha) = \int_0^1 dx_1 \int_0^1 dx_2 \int_0^1 dx_3 \int_0^1 \left\{ \left(\frac{1}{4}x_1 \diamond \frac{1}{4}x_2 \diamond \frac{1}{4}x_3 \diamond \frac{1}{4}x_4 \right) - \left[\frac{1}{2} \left(\frac{1}{2}x_1 \diamond \frac{1}{2}x_2 \right) \diamond \frac{1}{2} \left(\frac{1}{2}x_3 \diamond \frac{1}{2}x_4 \right) \right] \right\} dx_4,$$

$$E_{2+2}^{assoc}(0) = E_{2+2}^{assoc}(1/2) = E_{2+2}^{assoc}(1) = 0,$$

$$\bar{E}_{2+2}^{assoc} = \int_0^1 \left| E_{2+2}^{assoc}(\alpha) \right| d\alpha = 0.01006.$$

Of course, average errors that are mostly below 1% are acceptable from the practical point of view because the expected accuracy of inputs x_i, $i > 0$ in the majority of cases is significantly less than the accuracy of the associativity law.

Our symbolic notation of aggregators $y = W_1 x_1 \diamond ... \diamond W_n x_n$ can be used according to the following rule: in all parenthesized expressions with a given aggregator the parentheses can be left out, provided that the weights within each pair of parentheses are multiplied by the weights in front of them. For example, if $a_1 + b_1 = a_2 + b_2 = a_3 + b_3 = 1$, then we have:

$$a_1(a_2(a_3x_1 \Diamond b_3x_2) \Diamond b_2x_3) \Diamond b_1x_4 \approx a_1a_2a_3x_1 \Diamond a_1a_2b_3x_2 \Diamond a_1b_2x_3 \Diamond b_1x_4,$$

$$a_1a_2a_3 + a_1a_2b_3 + a_1b_2 + b_1 = a_1(a_2(a_3 + b_3) + b_2) + b_1 = a_1(a_2 + b_2) + b_1 = a_1 + b_1 = 1.$$

The condition for satisfying associativity in the case of WPM is to use a constant value of r for given andness/orness and for any number of aggregated variables. The consequence of such a decision would be to have for each r slightly different values of global andness/orness that depend on the number of variables. Since it is important to have fixed levels of andness/orness that reflect human percepts and define properties of aggregation operators, we decided to tolerate small and harmless errors in associativity laws.

Distributivity
Approximate distributivity laws in GL have the following form [DUJ75a]:

$$a_1x_1\Delta b_1(a_2x_2\nabla b_2x_3) \approx a_2(a_1x_1\Delta b_1x_2)\nabla b_2(a_1x_1\Delta b_1x_3);$$

$$a_1x_1\nabla b_1(a_2x_2\Delta b_2x_3) \approx a_2(a_1x_1\nabla b_1x_2)\Delta b_2(a_1x_1\nabla b_1x_3);$$

$$a_1 + b_1 = a_2 + b_2 = 1.$$

In the case of equal weights, the average error of the above distributivity law can be computed as follows:

$$E^{dis}(\alpha) = \int_0^1 dx_1 \int_0^1 dx_2 \int_0^1 \left\{ \left[\frac{1}{2}x_1\Delta\frac{1}{2}\left(\frac{1}{2}x_2\nabla\frac{1}{2}x_3\right)\right] - \left[\left(\frac{1}{2}\left(\frac{1}{2}x_1\Delta\frac{1}{2}x_2\right)\nabla\frac{1}{2}\left(\frac{1}{2}x_1\Delta\frac{1}{2}x_3\right)\right)\right]\right\} dx_3,$$

$$E^{dis}(0) = E^{dis}(1/2) = E^{dis}(1) = 0,$$

$$\bar{E}^{dis} = \int_0^1 |E^{dis}(\alpha)| d\alpha = 0.01439.$$

The GL distributivity law has a similar status as the GL associativity law: it holds with minor errors and it is applicable in practical computations.

Absorption
GL supports total absorption $(x \wedge (x \vee y) = x)$ only if andness and orness belong to $\{0,1\}$. In all other cases the absorption of optional variable is partial: $x\Delta(x\nabla y) = f(x,y) \neq x$ or $x\nabla(x\Delta y) = g(x,y) \neq x$. This is a desirable property used for modeling human reasoning in asymmetric cases where we aggregate mandatory (or sufficient) and optional variables.

De Morgan's Laws
If the andness α of a partial conjunction Δ^α is the same as the orness ω of a partial disjunction ∇^ω, and the operators Δ^α and ∇^ω are either naturally dual or

implemented using dualized functions (see also Sections 2.4.1, 2.7.2, and Proposition 2.3.2), then De Morgan's laws in GL can be defined (assuming $\alpha = \omega$) as follows:

$$\overline{W_1 x_1 \Delta \cdots \Delta W_n x_n} = 1 - W_1 x_1 \Delta \cdots \Delta W_n x_n = W_1(1-x_1)\nabla\cdots\nabla W_n(1-x_n) ;$$
$$\overline{W_1 x_1 \nabla \cdots \nabla W_n x_n} = 1 - W_1 x_1 \nabla \cdots \nabla W_n x_n = W_1(1-x_1)\Delta\cdots\Delta W_n(1-x_n).$$

Consequently, following are two equivalent definitions of dualized aggregators:

$$W_1 x_1 \Delta \cdots \Delta W_n x_n = 1 - W_1(1-x_1)\nabla\cdots\nabla W_n(1-x_n),$$
$$W_1 x_1 \nabla \cdots \nabla W_n x_n = 1 - W_1(1-x_1)\Delta\cdots\Delta W_n(1-x_n).$$

In these relations, $W_1 x_1 \nabla\cdots\nabla W_n x_n$ is called De Morgan's dual of $W_1 x_1 \Delta\cdots\Delta W_n x_n$ and vice versa. The complementary form of De Morgan's duality conditions for aggregators Δ and ∇ can be written as follows:

$$W_1 x_1 \Delta\cdots\Delta W_n x_n + W_1(1-x_1)\nabla\cdots\nabla W_n(1-x_n) = 1,$$
$$W_1 x_1 \nabla\cdots\nabla W_n x_n + W_1(1-x_1)\Delta\cdots\Delta W_n(1-x_n) = 1.$$

For example, in the case of the geometric mean we can use the following definitions:

$$wx\Delta(1-w)y = x^w y^{1-w},$$
$$wx\nabla(1-w)y = 1 - w(1-x)\Delta(1-w)(1-y) = 1 - (1-x)^w(1-y)^{1-w},$$
$$wx\Delta(1-w)y + w(1-x)\nabla(1-w)(1-y) = wx\nabla(1-w)y + w(1-x)\Delta(1-w)(1-y) = 1.$$

It is important to emphasize that Δ and ∇ cannot be arbitrary functions with identical andness and orness—these must be dual functions (functions that satisfy De Morgan's law). Unfortunately, naturally dual functions are very rare. As shown in the previous example of weighted geometric mean, the simplest way to provide the necessary duality and preserve and use De Morgan's laws is to dualize GCD by defining it as a combination of an aggregator and its dual. Such form of GCD always satisfies De Morgan's laws and the duality condition, according to the following definition:

$$W_1 x_1 \Diamond \cdots \Diamond W_n x_n = \begin{cases} W_1 x_1 \Delta^\alpha \cdots \Delta^\alpha W_n x_n, & 1-\omega = \alpha > 1/2, \\ W_1 x_1 + \cdots + W_n x_n, & \alpha = \omega = 1/2, \\ W_1 x_1 \nabla^\omega \cdots \nabla^\omega W_n x_n = 1 - W_1(1-x_1)\Delta^{1-\alpha}\cdots\Delta^{1-\alpha}W_n(1-x_n), & 1-\alpha = \omega > 1/2. \end{cases}$$

In the last line ∇^ω denotes partial disjunction with orness $\omega > 1/2$, and $\Delta^{1-\alpha}$ denotes partial conjunction with andness $1-\alpha$ (which is equal to orness). For example, to make partial disjunction with orness $\omega = 0.75$, the andness of such aggregator is $\alpha = 0.25$ and the aggregator is realized as

$1 - W_1(1-x_1)\Delta^{0.75}\cdots\Delta^{0.75}W_n(1-x_n)$. So, both the partial conjunction and the partial disjunction are realized using the same partial conjunction aggregator with andness greater than ½.

The frequently used WPM is not naturally dual and De Morgan's duality is *not* directly satisfied by WPM because disjunctive and conjunctive WPM aggregators are asymmetric (e.g., the partial conjunction is either hard or soft while the partial disjunction is only soft; numeric examples of De Morgan's asymmetry and symmetry are included in Section 2.7.2). In the case of WPM, however, De Morgan's duality can be defined using symmetry with respect to the central exponent $r = 1$. The exponent $r = 1 + p$ can be made dual to $r = 1 - p$, $p > 0$, as follows:

$$W_1x_1 \diamond \ldots \diamond W_nx_n = \begin{cases} W_1x_1\Delta\cdots\Delta W_nx_n = \lim_{q\to r}\left(\sum_{i=1}^n W_i x_i^q\right)^{1/q}, & a > 1/2, \ -\infty \leq r < 1; \\ W_1x_1 + \cdots + W_nx_n, & a = \omega = 1/2, \ r = 1; \\ W_1x_1\nabla\cdots\nabla W_nx_n = 1 - \lim_{q\to 2-r}\left(\sum_{i=1}^n W_i(1-x_i)^q\right)^{1/q}, & \omega > 1/2, \ 1 < r \leq +\infty. \end{cases}$$

This model supports the annihilator 0 and mandatory requirements, $W_1x_1\Delta\cdots\Delta W_nx_n = 0$, if $x_i = 0$, $i \in \{1,\ldots,n\}$, $r \leq 0$, and the annihilator 1 and sufficient requirements, $W_1x_1\nabla\cdots\nabla W_nx_n = 1$, if $x_i = 1$, $i \in \{1,\ldots,n\}$, $r \geq 2$. To provide the andness of partial conjunction that is the same as the orness of partial disjunction we can select a positive parameter p and for partial conjunction the WPM exponent $r = 1 - p$, $p > 0$; then, for partial disjunction we use the exponent $r = 1 + p$, $2 - r = 1 - p$, yielding the following GCD/WPM:

$$W_1x_1\Delta\cdots\Delta W_nx_n = \lim_{q\to 1-p}\left(\sum_{i=1}^n W_i x_i^q\right)^{1/q}, \qquad \alpha(p) > 1/2, \quad p > 0;$$

$$W_1x_1\nabla\cdots\nabla W_nx_n = 1 - \lim_{q\to 1-p}\left(\sum_{i=1}^n W_i(1-x_i)^q\right)^{1/q}, \qquad \omega(p) = \alpha(p) > 1/2.$$

Consequently, for selected p we get the andness of partial conjunction that is same as the orness of the dual partial disjunction. The same WPM is used both for partial conjunction and for partial disjunction, and De Morgan's duality condition is automatically satisfied:

$$W_1x_1\nabla\cdots\nabla W_nx_n + W_1(1-x_1)\Delta\cdots\Delta W_n(1-x_n)$$

$$= 1 - \lim_{q\to 1-p}\left(\sum_{i=1}^n W_i(1-x_i)^q\right)^{1/q} + \lim_{q\to 1-p}\left(\sum_{i=1}^n W_i(1-x_i)^q\right)^{1/q} = 1.$$

For $0 < p < 1$ this aggregator is soft. For $p \geq 1$ the aggregator is hard: it supports mandatory and sufficient requirements. The desired value of p can be easily selected using Table 2.3.3.

The presented model uses only the conjunctive part of WPM. Similarly, we can create an aggregator that uses only the disjunctive part of WPM, yielding strictly soft aggregation:

$$W_1x_1 \lozenge \ldots \lozenge W_nx_n = \begin{cases} W_1x_1\Delta\cdots\Delta W_nx_n = 1 - \lim\limits_{q\to 2-r}\left(\sum\limits_{i=1}^{n} W_i(1-x_i)^q\right)^{1/q}, & \alpha > 1/2, \ -\infty \le r < 1; \\ W_1x_1 + \cdots + W_nx_n, & \alpha = \omega = 1/2, \ r = 1; \\ W_1x_1\nabla\cdots\nabla W_nx_n = \lim\limits_{q\to r}\left(\sum\limits_{i=1}^{n} W_ix_i^q\right)^{1/q}, & \omega > 1/2, \ 1 < r \le +\infty. \end{cases}$$

Since the WPM exponents in this case are greater than 1, this aggregator is always soft: it does *not* support mandatory/sufficient requirements, but it satisfies De Morgan's laws. If the andness of partial conjunction must be the same as the orness of partial disjunction, then for partial conjunction $r = 1-p$, $2-r = 1+p$, $p > 0$ and for partial disjunction $r = 1+p$, $p > 0$, yielding the following De Morgan's duals:

$$W_1x_1\Delta\cdots\Delta W_nx_n = 1 - \lim_{q\to 1+p}\left(\sum_{i=1}^{n} W_i(1-x_i)^q\right)^{1/q}, \quad \alpha(p) > 1/2, \quad p > 0;$$

$$W_1x_1\nabla\cdots\nabla W_nx_n = \lim_{q\to 1+p}\left(\sum_{i=1}^{n} W_ix_i^q\right)^{1/q}, \quad \omega(p) = \alpha(p) > 1/2.$$

De Morgan's duality condition is again satisfied:

$$W_1x_1\nabla\cdots\nabla W_nx_n + W_1(1-x_1)\Delta\cdots\Delta W_n(1-x_n)$$

$$= \lim_{q\to 1+p}\left(\sum_{i=1}^{n} W_ix_i^q\right)^{1/q} + 1 - \lim_{q\to 1+p}\left(\sum_{i=1}^{n} W_ix_i^q\right)^{1/q} = 1.$$

For unmodified version of WPM where partial conjunction and partial disjunction are not dualized, De Morgan's laws are not satisfied, except for $\alpha, \omega \in \{0, 1/2, 1\}$. However, the average errors can be relatively small (typical average errors are less than 4% [DUJ75a]) and can be easily avoided using dualizing. Generally, WPM should not be used without dualizing.

Neutral, Zero, and Inverse Elements

Except in extreme cases ($\alpha, \omega \in \{0,1\}$), GL does not support neutral, zero, and inverse elements. Assuming $0 < x < 1$, corresponding properties of partial conjunction and partial disjunction are $x\Delta1 > x$, $x\Delta0 \ge 0$, $x\nabla0 < x$, $x\nabla1 \le 1$ (the equality holds only for hard versions of partial conjunction/disjunction). Furthermore, assuming $0 < x < 1$ and $x \ne 1/2$, we have $0 < \min(x,\bar{x}) < x\Delta\bar{x} < x\nabla\bar{x} < \max(x,\bar{x}) < 1$, $\bar{x} = 1-x$.

2.4.5 Logic Aggregators Based on Weighted Means with Adjustable Andness/Orness

Interpolative aggregators with adjustable threshold andness should be considered the primary form of GCD. However, in situations where the main goal is simplicity, we can use *simple weighted means* (SWM) which include the *weighted power mean* (WPM), and less frequently the *exponential mean* (EXM) and the *counter-harmonic mean* (CHM). In this section we discuss SWM and show their graphs in the case of two variables and equal weights (the impact of other weights is presented in Section 2.5.2).

The andness-directed native version of WPM uses exponent $r(\alpha)$ derived from the desired values of andness, as follows:

$$M_m(x_1, x_2; \alpha) = \left(0.5 x_1^{r_{wpm}(\alpha)} + 0.5 x_2^{r_{wpm}(\alpha)}\right)^{1/r_{wpm}(\alpha)}, \quad 0 \leq \alpha \leq 1.$$

The native version supports mandatory requirements (denoted using index m), but not sufficient requirements. So, it offers hard and soft partial conjunction and soft partial disjunction, illustrated in Fig. 2.4.8. This aggregator can be sufficient in many applications.

Native WPM can be conjunctive-dualized to offer hard and soft versions of partial conjunction and partial disjunction, as models of both mandatory and sufficinet requirements (index ms), as follows:

$$M_{ms}(x_1, x_2; \alpha) = \begin{cases} 1 - M_{ms}(1 - x_1, 1 - x_2; 1 - \alpha), & 0 \leq \alpha < \tfrac{1}{2}; \\ \left(0.5 x_1^{r_{wpm}(\alpha)} + 0.5 x_2^{r_{wpm}(\alpha)}\right)^{1/r_{wpm}(\alpha)}, & \tfrac{1}{2} \leq \alpha \leq 1. \end{cases}$$

The *ms* version of conjunctive-dualized WPM is presented in Fig. 2.4.9.

If we need aggregators that are soft and do not support mandatory and sufficient requirements, then we can use the following form of disjunctive dualization:

$$M(x_1, x_2; \alpha) = \begin{cases} \left(0.5 x_1^{r_{wpm}(\alpha)} + 0.5 x_2^{r_{wpm}(\alpha)}\right)^{1/r_{wpm}(\alpha)}, & 0 \leq \alpha < \tfrac{1}{2}; \\ 1 - M(1 - x_1, 1 - x_2; 1 - \alpha), & \tfrac{1}{2} \leq \alpha \leq 1. \end{cases}$$

The resulting disjunctive-dualized WPM aggregators are shown in Fig. 2.4.10.

Sometimes different aggregators can have similar behavior. Let us consider the weighted exponential mean (EXM):

$$E(\mathbf{x}; \mathbf{W}, r) = \begin{cases} \dfrac{1}{r} \ln\left(\displaystyle\sum_{i=1}^{n} W_i e^{r x_i}\right), & 0 < |r| < +\infty \\ \displaystyle\sum_{i=1}^{n} W_i x_i, & r = 0 \\ x_1 \wedge \ldots \wedge x_n, & r = -\infty \\ x_1 \vee \ldots \vee x_n, & r = +\infty \end{cases} = \ln M(e^{x_1}, \ldots, e^{x_n}; \mathbf{W}, r).$$

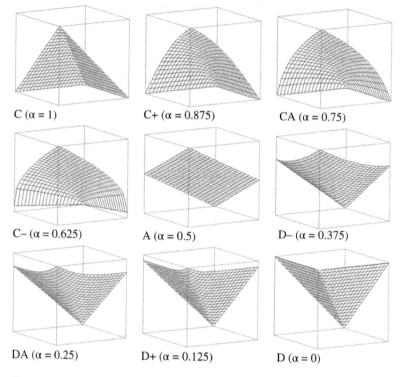

Figure 2.4.8 Native GCD/WPM aggregators (version WPM.9 with andness step 1/8).

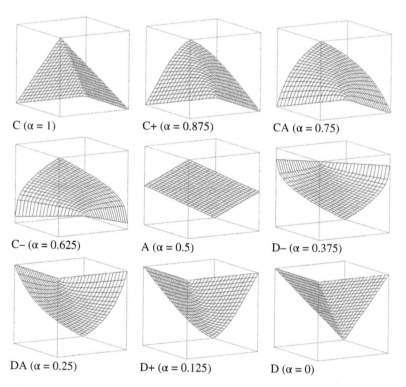

Figure 2.4.9 The mandatory/sufficient (*ms*) version of dualized GCD/WPM.9 aggregator.

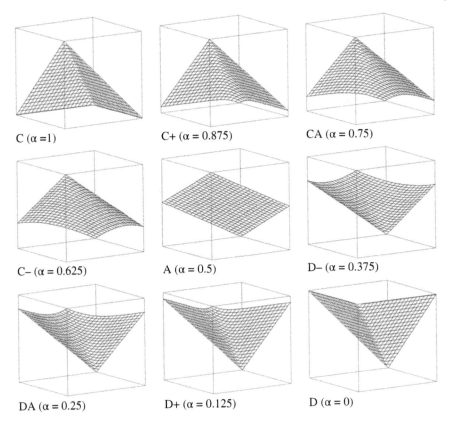

Figure 2.4.10 Soft GCD/WPM.9 aggregator that does not support mandatory and sufficient requirements.

For EXM we have $E(\mathbf{x};\mathbf{W},r) > 0$, $r > -\infty$, $x_i > 0$, $i \in \{1,...,n\}$, $x_j = 0$, $j \neq i$ and $E(\mathbf{x};\mathbf{W},\alpha) = E(\mathbf{x};\mathbf{W},r_{exm}(\alpha))$; here $E(\mathbf{x};\mathbf{W},\alpha)$ denotes the exponential mean with parameter r which yields the global andness α. The default EXM notation $E(\mathbf{x};\mathbf{W},r)$ uses the parameter r which can be derived from the desired value of α.

This aggregator is presented in Fig. 2.4.11, and function $r_{exm}(\alpha)$ is shown in Table 2.3.4. If we now compare Figs. 2.4.10 and 2.4.11 we can see a surprisingly high level of similarity (from practical standpoint, such aggregators could be interchangeable). Both aggregators are soft and do not support mandatory and sufficient requirements.

The exponential mean yields partial conjunction and partial disjunction that are symmetrical with respect to the central point $r = 0$. From the geometric mean of exponential functions $M(e^{x_1},...;e^{x_n},\mathbf{W},0) = e^{W_1 x_1}\cdots e^{W_n x_n} = \exp(W_1 x_1 + \cdots + W_n x_n)$ it follows $E(\mathbf{x};\mathbf{W},0) = M(\mathbf{x};\mathbf{W},1)$. In addition, the exponential mean is naturally dual:

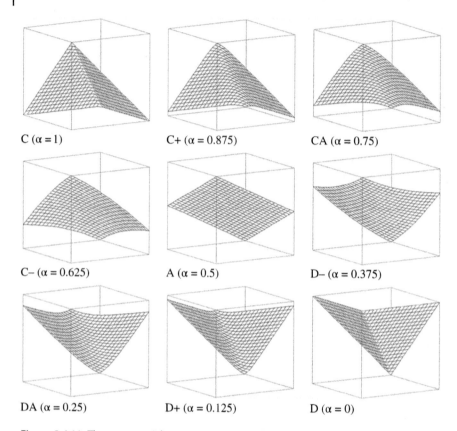

C ($\alpha = 1$)   C+ ($\alpha = 0.875$)   CA ($\alpha = 0.75$)

C– ($\alpha = 0.625$)   A ($\alpha = 0.5$)   D– ($\alpha = 0.375$)

DA ($\alpha = 0.25$)   D+ ($\alpha = 0.125$)   D ($\alpha = 0$)

Figure 2.4.11 The exponential mean aggregator GCD/EXM.9 with equal weights.

$$1 - E(1 - x_1, \ldots, 1 - x_n; W_1, \ldots, W_n, -r)$$

$$= 1 + \frac{1}{r} \ln \left(\sum_{i=1}^{n} W_i e^{-r(1-x_i)} \right) = 1 + \frac{1}{r} \ln \left(e^{-r} \sum_{i=1}^{n} W_i e^{rx_i} \right)$$

$$= 1 + \frac{1}{r} \left(-r + \ln \sum_{i=1}^{n} W_i e^{rx_i} \right) = \frac{1}{r} \ln \left(\sum_{i=1}^{n} W_i e^{rx_i} \right)$$

$$= E(x_1, \ldots, x_n; W_1, \ldots, W_n, r);$$

$$\therefore E(\mathbf{x}; \mathbf{W}, \alpha) = 1 - E(\mathbf{1} - \mathbf{x}; \mathbf{W}, 1 - \alpha), \quad E(\mathbf{x}; \mathbf{W}, 1 - \alpha) = 1 - E(\mathbf{1} - \mathbf{x}; \mathbf{W}, \alpha).$$

We can now compute the mean value and the andness as follows:

$$\overline{E(x_1,...,x_n;1/n,...,1/n,r)} = \int_0^1 dx_1 \cdots \int_0^1 E(x_1,...,x_n;1/n,...,1/n,r)dx_n$$

$$= \int_0^1 dx_1 \cdots \int_0^1 (1 - E(1-x_1,...,1-x_n;1/n,...,1/n,-r))dx_n$$

$$= 1 - \overline{E(x_1,...,x_n;1/n,...,1/n,-r)} ;$$

$$\alpha(r) = \frac{\overline{x_1 \vee ... \vee x_n} - \overline{E(x_1,...,x_n;1/n,...,1/n, r)}}{\overline{x_1 \vee ... \vee x_n} - \overline{x_1 \wedge ... \wedge x_n}}$$

$$= \frac{\overline{x_1 \vee ... \vee x_n} - 1 + \overline{E(x_1,...,x_n;1/n,...,1/n, -r)}}{\overline{x_1 \vee ... \vee x_n} - \overline{x_1 \wedge ... \wedge x_n}}$$

$$= \frac{\overline{E(x_1,...,x_n;1/n,...,1/n, -r)} - \overline{x_1 \wedge ... \wedge x_n}}{\overline{x_1 \vee ... \vee x_n} - \overline{x_1 \wedge ... \wedge x_n}} = \omega(-r) = 1 - \alpha(-r) .$$

Therefore, because of the natural duality of EXM, the andness of partial conjunction is a complement of the andness of partial disjunction and vice versa.

The last function in the SWM group is the counter-harmonic mean (CHM, studied also in Section 2.4.6). It is a permanently hard aggregator (it supports the annihilator 0), which in the case of two variables and equal weights has the following andness-directed form:

$$h_2(x_1,x_2;\alpha) = \left(x_1^{r_{chm}(\alpha)} + x_2^{r_{chm}(\alpha)} \right) / \left(x_1^{r_{chm}(\alpha)-1} + x_2^{r_{chm}(\alpha)-1} \right), \quad 0 \le \alpha \le 1.$$

The exponent r is a function of desired andness ($r_{chm}(\alpha)$ is different from the function $r_{wpm}(\alpha)$ used by WPM, as shown in Fig. 2.4.16). In the range from the arithmetic to the harmonic mean ($\alpha \in [0.5, 0.77]$, $r \in [0,1]$) CHM is nondecreasing monotonic and in Section 2.4.6 it is used as a hard low-andness segment of interpolative aggregators.

The conjunctive segment of CHM is shown in Fig. 2.4.12. Since CHM is strictly hard, it causes the hypersensitivity (extremely high slopes near coordinate axes) in the vicinity of the arithmetic mean; in Fig. 2.4.12 the hypersensitivity is visible for $\alpha = 0.6$. In the disjunctive area ($r_{chm} > 0$, $0 \le \alpha < \frac{1}{2}$), as shown in Section 2.4.6, CHM is not monotonic and consequently useless as an aggregator. The aggregators shown in Fig 2.4.12 look similar to other SWM and can be easily conjunctive-dualized as follows:

$$h(\mathbf{x};\mathbf{w},\alpha) = \begin{cases} 1 - h(1-\mathbf{x};\mathbf{w}, 1-\alpha), & 0 \le \alpha < \frac{1}{2} ; \\[2mm] \dfrac{w_1 x_1^{r_{chm}(\alpha)} + \cdots + w_n x_n^{r_{chm}(\alpha)}}{w_1 x_1^{r_{chm}(\alpha)-1} + \cdots + w_n x_n^{r_{chm}(\alpha)-1}}, & \frac{1}{2} \le \alpha \le 1. \end{cases}$$

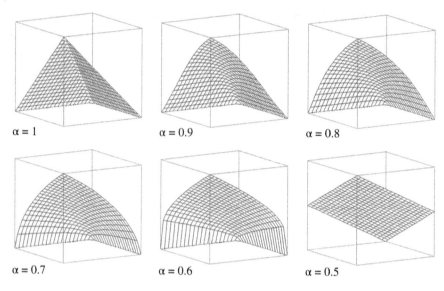

Figure 2.4.12 Hard conjunctive segment of GCD/CHM.

However, $h(\mathbf{x}; \mathbf{w}, \alpha)$ is monotonic for $0 \le r \le 1$, but not for $r < 0$. For example, in the simplest case of two variables and equal weights $C(x,y,r) = (x^r + y^r)/(x^{r-1} + y^{r-1})$ we have $C(0.1, 0.5, -1) = 0.115$ and $C(0.1, 1, -1) = 0.109 < C(0.1, 0.5, -1)$. That difference is small, and it is not visible in Fig. 2.4.12. Indeed, for andness higher than 0.77 (harmonic mean), the lines close to coordinate axes look parallel with the adjacent axes, but they are actually invisibly decreasing. Theoretically, for negative r CHM is not an aggregator. The CHM nonmonotonicity is primarily located close to coordinate axes (i.e., for small values of one of variables). So, if one of inputs is very small, then the other input(s) cannot compensate such small values. For larger values of arguments CHM is monotonic and similar to other members of the SWM group.

We can look at these properties from either a theoretical or a practical point of view. From a theoretical point of view, CHM is acceptable only for $0 \le r \le 1$ and we use it only in that range when it is incorporated in interpolative aggregators. From a practical perspective, it is possible to find applications where the described properties of conjunctive-dualized CHM might be desirable and useful. This is the reason for Fig. 2.4.12 and for the decision to keep CHM as a member of the SWM group.

2.4.6 Selection and Use of the Threshold Andness Aggregator

By definition, the threshold andness aggregator $A_\theta(x_1, ..., x_n; \alpha_\theta)$ is a hard conjunctive aggregator, which has the lowest value of andness. In this section, we analyze only the selection of threshold andness and the design of conjunctive aggregators because the disjunctive aggregators can be designed using De Morgan's duality (and vice versa).

Theoretically, the threshold andness α_θ can be selected in the whole interval $0.5 < \alpha_\theta < 1$. The most frequently used values are located in the middle section of that interval. In the case of interpolative aggregators, we assume that we use the mean andness theorem (Section 2.3.7, Theorem 2.3.1) to interpolate a soft aggregator $A(x_1, ..., x_n; \alpha)$ between the arithmetic mean and the threshold andness aggregator $A_\theta(x_1, ..., x_n; \alpha_\theta)$, as follows:

$$A(x_1,...,x_n;\alpha) = \frac{(\alpha_\theta - \alpha)(x_1 + \cdots + x_n)/n + (\alpha - 0.5)A_\theta(x_1,...,x_n;\alpha_\theta)}{\alpha_\theta - 0.5}, \quad 0.5 \le \alpha < \alpha_\theta.$$

If $\alpha < \alpha_\theta$, the corresponding interpolated aggregator is soft. The hard aggregator is obtained for $\alpha \ge \alpha_\theta$. Therefore, our problem is to select a convenient threshold andness aggregator.

The global andness is defined for equal weights, and consequently the search for $A_\theta(x_1, ..., x_n; \alpha_\theta)$ can be based on equal weights. Table 2.4.3 shows increasing andness of a sequence of aggregators located between the arithmetic and the harmonic mean (and beyond); those that are hard can serve as threshold aggregators. Not all of them support weights. So, if unweighted aggregators are used, we assume that the weights can be introduced using the method of idempotent binary aggregator trees (see [DUJ15c] and Chapter 2.5).

The selection of threshold andness aggregator is not arbitrary because the value of andness affects the percept of importance. Generally, high andness means a strong need to satisfy inputs, and consequently such inputs are very important. Similarly, low andness (close to 0.5) provides easier substitutability

Table 2.4.3 Aggregators located between the arithmetic and harmonic mean.

Aggregator	Andness	Type
$(x + y)/2$	0.5	Soft
$(x^{1-\varepsilon} + y^{1-\varepsilon})/(x^{-\varepsilon} + y^{-\varepsilon}), \quad \varepsilon \to 0^+$	0.5	Hard
$e^{-1}[(y^y)/(x^x)]^{1/(y-x)}$	0.554	Soft
$(y - x)/(\log y - \log x)$	0.614	Hard
$\sqrt{xy}$	0.666667	Hard
$(\log y - \log x)/(1/x - 1/y)$	0.710	Hard
$e[(x^y)/(y^x)]^{1/(y-x)}$	0.745	Hard
$2xy/(x + y)$	0.772589	Hard
$(0.5x^r + 0.5y^r)^{1/r}, \quad r \le -1$	≥ 0.772589	Hard

and indirectly reduces the importance of individual inputs. If the threshold andness is selected in the lower half of the interval [0.5, 1] (e.g., close to the arithmetic mean), then such a decision needs a very strong justification because it brings the risk of logic inconsistency and contradiction. By selecting a threshold andness we select a family of hard aggregators (bordered by the threshold aggregator) and claim that all of them have so important mandatory inputs that their dissatisfaction cannot be compensated. Simultaneously, by selecting a low value of threshold andness, we claim that the importance of equally weighted inputs is modest, and the compensation of low inputs is relatively easy. Such contradictory requirements usually yield hypersensitivity of inputs (extremely high first derivatives in the vicinity of zero inputs, i.e., a property that is not frequently observed in human reasoning).

In the case of power means, the natural threshold aggregator is the geometric mean $A_0(x_1,...,x_n;\alpha) = x_1^{1/n}\cdots x_n^{1/n_n}$. Its threshold andness is $\alpha_\theta = \dfrac{n}{n-1} - \dfrac{n+1}{n-1}\left(\dfrac{n}{n+1}\right)^n$, which is a decreasing function of n going from $2/3 = 0.667$ for $n = 2$ to 0.632 for $n \gg 1$. To some extent the geometric mean already shows problems that are characteristic for combinations of hard behavior and relatively low andness. Since $\partial\sqrt{xy}/\partial x = 0.5\sqrt{y/x}$, it follows that for small values of x, the slope of this function approaches infinity, and that is a questionable property from the standpoint of models of human reasoning. In the case of harmonic mean, the situation is different:

$$\frac{\partial}{\partial x}\left(\frac{2xy}{x+y}\right) = 2\left(\frac{y}{x+y}\right)^2 = 2 \text{ if } x = 0.$$

This slope is regularly acceptable. Generally, for power means we have the slope

$$\frac{\partial}{\partial x}(0.5x^r + 0.5y^r)^{1/r} = 0.5\left(0.5 + 0.5\left(\frac{y}{x}\right)^r\right)^{(1-r)/r} = 0.5^{1/r} \text{ if } r < 0, \ x = 0, \ y > 0.$$

This slope is presented in Fig. 2.4.13. The slope between 1 and 3 is fully acceptable (even for smallest y) and in that range power means can be conveniently used in as logic aggregators.

If, similarly to geometric mean, an aggregator has an infinite slope for small values of y near the coordinate axis $x = 0$, that is not the reason for not using such an aggregator. In evaluation practice the aggregator is never used for values $y \to 0$ but usually for values $y \in \{0, \delta, 2\delta, ...\}$ where δ denotes a small value that decision makers can clearly differentiate from 0 (or from 2δ). Such a typical value is in the vicinity of 5% and therefore regularly skips the critical region of excessive slope.

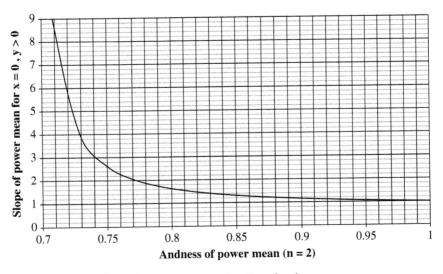

Figure 2.4.13 The slope of power mean as a function of andness.

In rare and exceptional cases where there is a strong justification for using hard aggregators with low andness (e.g., in the range of andness from 0.5 to 0.75), we need threshold aggregators different from power means. The most suitable candidate for that role is a weighted counter-harmonic mean (CHM). CHM has andness that can be adjusted by selecting the appropriate value of parameter r, as follows:

$$C_n^{[r]}(\mathbf{x};\mathbf{w}) = \frac{w_1 x_1^r + \cdots + w_n x_n^r}{w_1 x_1^{r-1} + \cdots + w_n x_n^{r-1}} = \begin{cases} \min(x_1,\ldots,x_n), & r = -\infty \\ \quad \updownarrow \text{Not monotonic} \\ (W_1/x_1 + \cdots + W_n/x_n)^{-1}, & r = 0 \\ \quad \updownarrow \text{Nondecreasing monotonicity} \\ W_1 x_1 + \cdots + W_n x_n, & r = 1 \\ \quad \updownarrow \text{Not monotonic} \\ \max(x_1,\ldots,x_n), & r = +\infty \end{cases}$$

$$W_i = w_i/(w_1 + \cdots + w_n), \quad i = 1,\ldots,n.$$

This aggregator has two convenient properties. First, for all $r < 1$ the CHM is hard: if any argument has the value 0, then $C_n^{[r]}(\mathbf{x};\mathbf{w}) = 0$. Second, the CHM is naturally weighted and includes the arithmetic mean and the harmonic mean, making easy interpolative connection with the WPM (see sections 2.4.7 and 2.4.8). CHM is nondecreasing monotonic for $0 \le r \le 1$ [BUL03], i.e., between the arithmetic and harmonic means, but for $r \notin [0,1]$ CHM can be monotonically decreasing and unacceptable as an aggregator. For example, for $r > 1$:

$$h_2(x,y;r) = \frac{x^r + y^r}{x^{r-1} + y^{r-1}} = x\frac{x^{r-1} + y^{r-1}(y/x)}{x^{r-1} + y^{r-1}}; \quad 0 < y < x \Rightarrow h_2(x,y;r) < h_2(x,0;r) = x.$$

The weights of counter-harmonic mean are used in both numerator and denominator. Thus, the weights can be multiplied by any positive constant without affecting the value of $C_n^{[r]}(\mathbf{x};\mathbf{w})$. In other words, the weights could be either not normalized or arbitrarily normalized (to have the sum equal to 1, or to have the sum equal to n, or to have the maximum weight equal to 1) without affecting the aggregation function. For compatibility with weighted power means we can assume that the sum of weights is equal to 1. If the weights are equal, then we have

$$h_n(x_1,\ldots,x_n;r) = \frac{x_1^r + \cdots + x_n^r}{x_1^{r-1} + \cdots + x_n^{r-1}}, \quad 0 \le r \le 1; \quad h_n(x_1,\ldots,x_n;1) = (x_1 + \cdots + x_n)/n.$$

For any small positive $\varepsilon \to 0$, if $r = 1 - \varepsilon$ CHM approaches the arithmetic mean, as follows:

$$h_n(x_1,\ldots,x_n;1-\varepsilon) = \frac{x_1^{1-\varepsilon} + \cdots + x_n^{1-\varepsilon}}{x_1^{-\varepsilon} + \cdots + x_n^{-\varepsilon}} = x_1^\varepsilon \cdots x_n^\varepsilon \frac{x_1^{1-\varepsilon} + \cdots + x_n^{1-\varepsilon}}{x_2^\varepsilon \cdots x_n^\varepsilon + \cdots + x_1^\varepsilon \cdots x_{n-1}^\varepsilon}$$

$$\approx x_1^\varepsilon \cdots x_n^\varepsilon \frac{x_1 + \cdots + x_n}{n}, \quad \varepsilon \to 0^+.$$

Therefore, if $x_i = 0$, $i \in \{1,\ldots,n\}$, then $h_n(x_1,\ldots,x_n;1-\varepsilon) = 0$, but for the smallest positive value $0 < x_i \ll 1$ it jumps to $h_n(x_1,\ldots,x_n;1-\varepsilon) \approx (x_1 + \cdots + x_n)/n$. So, for each i, in the vicinity of point $x_i = 0$ (i.e., next to all coordinate axes) $h_n(x_1, \ldots, x_n; r)$ has hypersensitivity (a huge derivative $\partial h_n/\partial x_i$), which is not a characteristic of human reasoning.

In the case of two variables and equal weights, in the middle of monotonic interval of exponents the CHM also includes the geometric mean:

$$h_2(x,y;r) = \frac{x^r + y^r}{x^{r-1} + y^{r-1}} = \begin{cases} 2xy/(x+y), & r = 0 \\ \sqrt{xy}, & r = 0.5 \\ (x+y)/2, & r = 1. \end{cases}$$

Consequently, the counter-harmonic mean has a unique property: along the whole traditional path connecting arithmetic, geometric, and harmonic means, it is nondecreasing monotonic and hard. It is useful to note that in the case $r = 2$, the corresponding nonmonotonic mean is called the *contraharmonic mean* $h_{ch}(x,y) = (x^2 + y^2)/(x+y)$ because it is located symmetrically to the harmonic mean with respect to the arithmetic mean:

$$\frac{1}{2}\left(\frac{2xy}{x+y} + \frac{x^2 + y^2}{x+y}\right) = \frac{x+y}{2}.$$

Since the arithmetic mean is in the middle between the harmonic mean and the contraharmonic mean, it follows from the mean andness theorem that the andness of arithmetic mean $\alpha_{ari} = 0.5$ is in the middle between the andness of harmonic mean $\alpha_{har} = \ln 16 - 2$ and the andness of contraharmonic mean α_{ch}:

$$\alpha_{har} + \alpha_{ch} = 2\alpha_{ari} = 1 \ \Rightarrow\ \alpha_{ch} = 1 - \alpha_{har} = 3 - \ln 16.$$

On the other hand, the andness of any mean and the andness of its De Morgan's dual are complementary (their sum is 1). So, if $M_h(x,y) = 2xy/(x+y)$, then its De Morgan's dual $M_{dh}(x,y) = 1 - M_h(1-x, 1-y) = 1 - 2(1-x)(1-y)/(2-x-y)$ has the same andness as the contraharmonic mean $\alpha_{dh} = \alpha_{ch} = 1 - \alpha_{har} = 3 - \ln 16$. Similarly, a dual of contraharmonic mean $h_{dch}(x,y) = 1 - h_{ch}(1-x, 1-y) = 1 - ((1-x)^2 + (1-y)^2)/(2-x-y)$ has the same andness as the harmonic mean $M_h(x, y)$. However, we have to be careful: $M_h(x, y)$ and $M_{dh}(x, y)$ are monotonic, but $h_{ch}(x, y)$ and $h_{dch}(x, y)$ are not monotonic.

The relationship between the global andness α and the exponent r of the counter-harmonic mean $h(x, y)$ is shown in Fig. 2.4.14. Numeric approximations of this relationship are the following:

$$\alpha = (-0.1216r - 0.1509)r + 0.7721, \quad 0 \le r \le 1,$$
$$r = ((-18.646\alpha + 29.866)\alpha - 18.678)\alpha + 5.2045, \quad 0.5 \le \alpha \le 0.772.$$

Exponent r	Andness of $\dfrac{x^r + y^r}{x^{r-1} + y^{r-1}}$
0	0.772589
0.1	0.755519
0.2	0.736613
0.3	0.715652
0.4	0.692408
0.5	0.666667
0.6	0.638235
0.7	0.607051
0.8	0.573233
0.9	0.537247
1	0.5

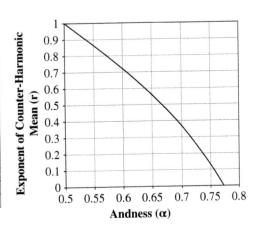

Figure 2.4.14 The global andness α and the exponent r of the counter-harmonic mean for $n = 2$.

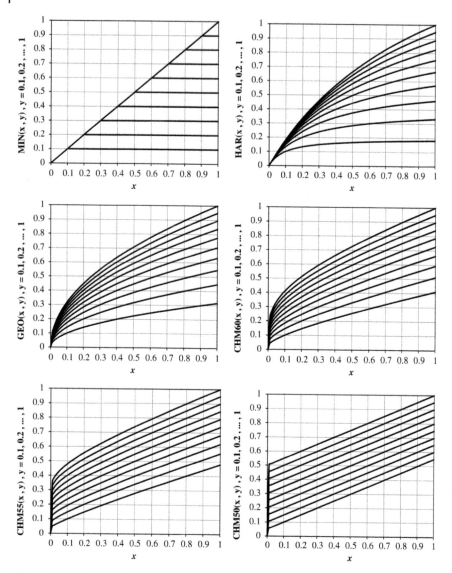

Figure 2.4.15 Counter-harmonic mean $h(x, y)$ for andness 1, 0.77, 0.66, 0.60, 0.55, and 0.5.

The properties of counter-harmonic mean $h(x, y)$ are illustrated in Fig. 2.4.15 where we present the characteristic cases, which satisfy the monotonicity requirement. For each aggregator $h(x, y)$ we fix the value of y ($y \in \{0.1, 0.2, ..., 1\}$) and then show $h(x, y)$ as a function of x. That yields a family of 10 functions, where the bottom curve corresponds to $y = 0.1$, and the top curve corresponds to $y = 1$.

It is easy to note the increase of hypersensitivity for small values of x as the andness decreases toward 0.5. If the selected andness is 1 and $r = -\infty$ the CHM becomes the pure conjunction (denoted MIN in Fig. 2.4.15) with the initial slope equal 1. Between the andness 1 and 0.77 the CHM is not monotonic. For $r = 0$ and andness 0.77 the CHM becomes the monotonic harmonic mean (denoted HAR) with the initial slope of 2. Then the initial slope increases, and for $r = 0.5$ and andness 0.667 the CHM becomes the monotonic geometric mean (denoted GEO) with the infinite initial slope. The initial slope remains infinite for the remaining three cases of CHM (CHM60, CHM55, and CHM50), where the andness is relatively low (0.60, 0.55, and 0.5).

If the desired threshold andness is selected above the geometric mean, then the most convenient threshold andness aggregator is the power mean $A_\theta(x_1,...,x_n;\alpha_\theta) = \left(n^{-1}x_1^{r_\theta} + \cdots + n^{-1}x_n^{r_\theta}\right)^{1/r_\theta}$ where the exponent r_θ is selected as a function of desired threshold andness: $r_\theta = r_{wpm}(\alpha_\theta)$. Numeric approximations of this function are presented in Chapter 2.3. In the most frequent case of uniform GCD we select $\alpha_\theta = 0.75$, yielding the following threshold andness aggregator and the corresponding interpolative soft partial conjunction:

$$A_\theta(x_1,...,x_n;0.75) = \left(n^{-1}x_1^r + \cdots + n^{-1}x_n^r\right)^{1/r}, \quad r = \begin{cases} -0.7201, & n = 2 \\ -0.7317, & n = 3 \\ -0.7205, & n = 4 \\ -0.7054, & n = 5 \end{cases}$$

$$A(x_1,...,x_n;\alpha) = (3 - 4\alpha)\left(\frac{x_1 + \cdots + x_n}{n}\right) + (4\alpha - 2)A_\theta(x_1,...,x_n;0.75), \quad 0.5 \le \alpha < 0.75.$$

The soft partial conjunction is interpolative. For andness above 0.75, we can directly use the power mean as the hard partial conjunction. Of course, all aggregators can be weighted.

In Fig. 2.4.14, we analyzed the counter-harmonic mean of two variables. For more variables (3,4,5) the differences between various cases are very small inside the interesting range between the arithmetic and harmonic means ($0 \le r \le 1$, $0.5 \le \alpha \le 0.773$). The precise numeric computation of exponents of the counter-harmonic mean can be done as follows:

$$r_{hn}(\alpha) = \begin{cases} ((-18.646\alpha + 29.866)\alpha - 18.678)\alpha + 5.2045, & n = 2, \\ ((-18.227\alpha + 30.481)\alpha - 19.946)\alpha + 5.6331, & n = 3, \\ ((-17.29\alpha + 29.599)\alpha - 19.918)\alpha + 5.7208, & n = 4, \\ ((-16.586\alpha + 28.974)\alpha - 19.932)\alpha + 5.7962, & n = 5, \quad (0.5 \le \alpha \le 0.773). \end{cases}$$

Counter-harmonic means are related to power means because they share the arithmetic mean, the harmonic mean, minimum, maximum, and (for two variables) the geometric mean. The reason for this relationship is that both the power means and the counter-harmonic mean are special cases of the following two-parameter Gini mean [BUL03]:

$$G_n^{[p,q]}(\mathbf{x};\mathbf{w}) = \begin{cases} \left(\dfrac{w_1 x_1^p + \cdots + w_n x_n^p}{w_1 x_1^q + \cdots + w_n x_n^q}\right)^{1/(p-q)}, & p \neq q, \\[2ex] \left(x_1^{w_1 x_1^p} \cdots x_n^{w_n x_n^p}\right)^{1/\left(w_1 x_1^p + \cdots + w_n x_n^p\right)}, & p = q, \end{cases}$$

$$\lim_{p \to +\infty} G_n^{[p,q]}(\mathbf{x};\mathbf{w}) = \max(\mathbf{x}), \quad \lim_{q \to -\infty} G_n^{[p,q]}(\mathbf{x};\mathbf{w}) = \min(\mathbf{x}).$$

So, $G_n^{[r,0]}(\mathbf{x};\mathbf{w}) = M_n^{[r]}(\mathbf{x};\mathbf{w}) = \left(W_1 x_1^r + \cdots + W_n x_n^r\right)^{1/r}$, $W_i = w_i/(w_1 + \cdots + w_n)$, $i = 1,\ldots,n$ and $G_n^{[r,r-1]}(\mathbf{x};\mathbf{w}) = C_n^{[r]}(\mathbf{x};\mathbf{w})$.

It is also possible to create hard aggregators with low andness by combining the basic power mean aggregators $H(x,y) = 2xy/(x+y)$, $G(x,y) = \sqrt{xy}$ and $Q(x,y) = \sqrt{(x^2+y^2)/2}$ which respectively have andness $\alpha_h = 0.773$, $\alpha_g = 0.667$ and $\alpha_q = 0.377$. For example, following are three hard aggregators and their andness:

$$F_{ggq}(x,y) = G(G(x,y), Q(x,y)), \alpha_{ggq} = 0.546,$$
$$F_{ghq}(x,y) = G(H(x,y), Q(x,y)), \alpha_{ghq} = 0.626,$$
$$F_{hgq}(x,y) = H(G(x,y), Q(x,y)), \alpha_{hgq} = 0.568.$$

Precise adjustment of desired andness can be achieved using weighted means. For example, if we use the weighted harmonic mean $H(x,y,w) = 1/(w/x + (1-w)/y)$, then the weighted version of the previous aggregator and its adjustable andness $\alpha_{hgq}(w)$ are as follows:

$$F_{whgq}(x,y,w) = H(G(x,y), Q(x,y), w),$$
$$\alpha_{hgq}(0.28) = 0.506, \quad \alpha_{hgq}(0.44) = 0.553,$$
$$\alpha_{hgq}(0.64) = 0.600, \quad \alpha_{hgq}(0.9) = 0.650.$$

Numerical computation of $\alpha_{hgq}(w)$ can be performed as follows:

$$\alpha_{hgq}(w) = 0.413 + w(0.3663 - 0.1155w), \quad 0.28 \le w \le 0.9,$$
$$w = \alpha_{hgq}\left(9.3077\alpha_{hgq} - 6.4853\right) + 1.1815, \quad 0.506 \le \alpha_{hgq} \le 0.65.$$

This range of andness covers the whole soft gap between the arithmetic mean and the geometric mean.

2.4.7 Andness-Directed Interpolative GCD Aggregators

The fundamental logic aggregator in GL is the andness-directed (or orness-directed) GCD aggregator of n variables (studied also in Section 2.4.10). In this section, we present interpolative forms of GCD aggregators based on distinctive features that were introduced and analyzed in Chapter 2.2. The necessary properties of general GCD aggregators include the following:

- The general GCD must be a graded aggregator, weighted and idempotent in the basic range of andness $0 \le \alpha \le 1$. The main parameter of GCD is the desired global andness/orness. For fixed input arguments, GCD must be a monotonically increasing function of global orness (or a monotonically decreasing function of global andness).
- GCD must be "andness-dominated": for $1-\omega = \alpha \in \{0,1\}$ the general weighted GCD should reduce to unweighted pure conjunction and pure disjunction. The impact of weights should fade out as andness or orness approach their maximum values.
- The GCD aggregator must support seamless unweighted extensibility beyond the idempotent range $1-\omega = \alpha \in [0,1]$. In order to cover the whole unit hypercube, the extended GCD in the case n variables must cover nonidempotent range of andness $1-\omega = \alpha \in [-1/(n-1), n/(n-1)] \setminus [0,1]$.
- The threshold andness and/or the threshold orness must be adjustable in the full range $0.5 < \alpha_\theta \le 1, 0.5 < \omega_\theta \le 1$.
- The GCD aggregator must be able to support De Morgan's duality between conjunctive and disjunctive functions. Consequently, in all such cases GCD must be dualized, providing symmetry of conjunctive and disjunctive aggregators.
- For all versions of partial conjunction ($\frac{1}{2} < \alpha < 1$) and partial disjunction ($\frac{1}{2} < \omega < 1$) and arguments in the range $]0,1[$ the GCD aggregator should be a strictly increasing function of input arguments and have continuous first partial derivatives.
- Since no single function satisfies all the above necessary properties, the general GCD aggregator must be interpolative.

We believe that these restrictive conditions properly reflect the observable properties of evaluation reasoning studied in Chapter 2.2. Of course, we could easily mathematically expand the GCD aggregators beyond these restrictive conditions, but we cannot prove any applicability of such extensions. Most of presented conditions should be self-evident, but a short summary of the rationale for these conditions, and an explanation of their consequences might still be useful.

First, the standard GCD logic aggregator must be monotonic and idempotent, and consequently it must be a mean. There is no mean that satisfies all the above conditions. In particular, means either have a fixed threshold andness (like the conjunctive version of power means) or have no threshold andness at all (like the exponential means or the disjunctive version of power means). There is no mean that has naturally adjustable threshold andness, but interpolative aggregators can solve this problem.

The use of variable threshold andness is a complex problem because it is based on experiments with human subjects. The only values of threshold andness that can be a priori selected are $\alpha_\theta = 0.75$ (in order to provide equal availability of all characteristic soft and hard properties of aggregators), or $\alpha_\theta \approx 2/3$ (in order to use natural threshold andness provided by the geometric mean in the context of power means), or $\alpha_\theta = 1$ (in order to work with only soft aggregators, such as the exponential mean, or OWA). In all other cases the threshold andness must be adjustable in the whole range $0.5 < \alpha_\theta < 1$ in order to offer sufficient generality and satisfy all possible requirements that decision makers might impose. However, each value of threshold andness and orness must be properly justified. In the absence of convincing proof that some specific values of threshold andness and orness are the most suitable and necessary, it is reasonable to use the following default approach:

- Threshold andness should be equal to threshold orness in order to provide symmetry of conjunctive and disjunctive aggregators as well as De Morgan's duality.
- In the area of idempotent aggregators it is reasonable to provide equal presence of soft and hard aggregators, i.e., equal opportunities for all forms of simultaneity and substitutability. This approach yields $\alpha_\theta = \omega_\theta = 0.75$.

De Morgan's duality is one of central logic properties inherited from the bivalent Boolean logic, where it is derived as a direct consequence of axiomatic origins of Boolean logic and involutive properties of negation. For simplicity of aggregation, as in the case of power means, useful LSP criteria can be developed without De Morgan's duality. We can also intentionally develop aggregators that are not dual, provided we can justify such a decision. However, if we want to make GL as a generalization of Boolean logic, then we must support De Morgan's duality. The simplest way to satisfy this condition is to define GCD as a dualized aggregator.

If the pure conjunction and disjunction are modeled as the minimum and maximum functions then the output suitability y of the aggregator grows when the smallest input suitability x is growing, and the growth rate has the maximum possible value $\partial y/\partial x = 1$. At the moment x is no longer the minimum input suitability the growth stops and $\partial y/\partial x = 0$. In other words, the first derivative has a break. We might ask whether this break is a natural expression of human reasoning, and the answer might be based on observation that human evaluation reasoning is primarily characterized by continuous incremental behavior and not by sharp jumps. So, if we accept such a break as an extreme model of human reasoning, then it should be acceptable only in the cases of pure conjunction and pure disjunction and not in cases of other logic aggregators. In all other cases, both y and $\partial y / \partial x$ should be continuous.

GCD must support semantic aspects of reasoning, differentiating various degrees of importance of input suitability degrees. Therefore, GCD aggregators should be noncommutative, and commutativity is acceptable only in situations where all inputs are equally important. It is easy to observe that the percept of importance of inputs reaches the extreme value when andness or orness approach their limit values, i.e., when $\max(\alpha, 1-\alpha) \to 1$. At the ultimate level of simultaneity (or substitutability) each input reaches the maximum degree of importance and has equal decisive power to fully satisfy of fully unsatisfy a criterion, regardless of the values of all other inputs. Consequently, at the highest levels of simultaneity or substitutability we see the reason for commutativity of aggregators and the use of unweighted conjunction and disjunction (see P_{22} in Section 2.2.3).

Infrequently, simultaneity and substitutability can reach levels of hyperconjunction and hyperdisjunction. In such cases the primary goal is a full satisfaction of all input requirements, in a way similar to probabilistic reasoning where the likelihood of satisfaction of independent conjunctive requirements is a product of likelihoods of satisfaction of individual input requirements. So, in such cases there is no idempotency and all inputs are usually equally important because the multiplicative nature of such aggregators gives to each input the power to reduce the degree of satisfaction achieved by all other inputs to a fraction specified by the value of the input. In such exceptional cases it is necessary to have a possibility of seamless extension of aggregators from idempotent to nonidempotent area.

In exceptional and infrequent cases it may be necessary to provide hard aggregators with low threshold andness. So, for completeness of general GCD aggregators we need hard aggregators that are weighted and can be located between the arithmetic and geometric mean. Counter-harmonic means are hard, weighted, idempotent, and monotonic in the region between the arithmetic mean and the harmonic mean. So, they are natural candidates for the role of low andness hard aggregators.

To satisfy all the above requirements we propose a combination of andness-directed weighted power means WPM(α) and counter-harmonic means CHM (α) as follows:

- If the threshold andness is in the range above the andness of the geometric mean (i.e. $\alpha_{geo} \le \alpha_\theta < 1$), then create the GCD aggregator as follows:
  a) Interpolate an aggregator between the arithmetic mean (ARI) and WPM(α_θ).
  b) Use directly WPM in the range $\alpha_\theta \le \alpha \le 1$, providing continuous properties.
  c) Create disjunctive aggregators as De Morgan's dual of conjunctive aggregators.

- If the threshold andness is in the range below the andness of the geometric mean (i.e. $0.5 < \alpha_\theta < \alpha_{geo}(n)$), then create the GCD aggregator as follows:
  a) Interpolate an aggregator between the arithmetic mean (ARI) and CHM(α_θ).
  b) Interpolate an aggregator from CHM(α_θ) to the geometric mean (GEO).
  c) Use unmodified WPM in the range $\alpha_{geo}(n) \le \alpha \le 1$.
  d) Create disjunctive aggregators as De Morgan's dual of conjunctive aggregators.
- If the threshold andness takes the highest value $\alpha_\theta = 1$, then create the GCD aggregator as follows:
  a) Use WPM(α) as a disjunctive aggregator in the range $0 \le \alpha \le 0.5$.
  b) Create conjunctive aggregators as De Morgan's dual of disjunctive aggregators.
- If there is a need for hyperconjunctive aggregators, interpolate them between the pure conjunction and the product t-norm $x_1 \cdots x_n$. Then, for higher andness, use product-power function $(x_1 \cdots x_n)^p$, $p > 1$, where p is selected according to the desired andness; if $p \to +\infty$ the product-power function becomes a drastic conjunction. Make hyperdisjunctive aggregators as De Morgan's duals of hyperconjunctive aggregators.

The described procedure is based on dualization of interpolative aggregators. In a general case, let us use an increasing sequence of $k>1$ andness values, $\alpha_1 < \alpha_2 < \cdots < \alpha_k$ for which we have desirable "base aggregators" $A_i(\mathbf{x}; \mathbf{W}, \alpha_i)$, $i = 1, \ldots, k$. According to Theorem 2.3.1 (the mean andness theorem, MAT) the global andness of expression $y = (\alpha_{i+1} - \alpha)A_i(\mathbf{x}; \mathbf{W}, \alpha_i) + (\alpha - \alpha_i)A_{i+1}(\mathbf{x}; \mathbf{W}, \alpha_{i+1})$ is $(\alpha_{i+1} - \alpha)\alpha_i + (\alpha - \alpha_i)\alpha_{i+1} = \alpha(\alpha_{i+1} - \alpha_i)$ and consequently $y/(\alpha_{i+1} - \alpha_i)$ is an aggregator that has the global andness α. We can now define the following *general interpolative form* of an andness-directed aggregator $A(\mathbf{x}; \mathbf{W}, \alpha)$ in the range $0 \le \alpha_1 \le \alpha \le \alpha_k \le 1$:

$$A(\mathbf{x}; \mathbf{W}, \alpha) = \frac{(\alpha_{i+1} - \alpha)A_i(\mathbf{x}; \mathbf{W}, \alpha_i) + (\alpha - \alpha_i)A_{i+1}(\mathbf{x}; \mathbf{W}, \alpha_{i+1})}{\alpha_{i+1} - \alpha_i},$$

$$\alpha_i \le \alpha \le \alpha_{i+1}, \quad i = 1, \ldots, k-1.$$

The general interpolative form can be applied to any range of andness. If we use the conjunctive sequence $\frac{1}{2} = \alpha_1 < \alpha_2 < \ldots < \alpha_k = 1$, then we can create a general andness-directed GCD aggregator using dualization of disjunctive part, as follows:

$$W_1 x_1 \diamond \cdots \diamond W_n x_n = \begin{cases} A(\mathbf{x}; \mathbf{W}, \alpha), & 0.5 \le \alpha \le 1 \\ 1 - A(1 - \mathbf{x}; \mathbf{W}, 1 - \alpha), & 0 \le \alpha < 0.5. \end{cases}$$

This aggregator satisfies De Morgan's laws and for each value of andness uses only the conjunctive properties of aggregation; such disjunctive and conjunctive aggregators are dual.

```
double r_wpm(double a, int n)        // a = andness, 2 <= n <= 5, r = WPM exponent
{                                    // If n>5 we use the same approximation as for n=5
  double eps = 0.00001;              // Avoiding the direct use of a=0 and a=1
  if(a < eps)     return  1.e20;     // Approximation of +infinity for disjunction
  if(a > 1.-eps)  return -1.e20;     // Approximation of -infinity for conjunction
  if(n<2){cout << "\nERROR in R_WPM function: n = " << n << "\n\n"; exit(1);}

  if(n == 2) return (0.25 + (a>=0.5 ? 1.65811 :  1.62481)*(0.5-a)
                          + (a>=0.5 ? 2.15388 :  1.26214)*pow(0.5-a,2)
                          + (a>=0.5 ? 8.2844  :  0.144343)*pow(0.5-a,3)
                          + (a>=0.5 ? 6.16764 : -0.144343)*pow(0.5-a,4))/(a-a*a);

  if(n == 3) return (0.25 + (a>=0.5 ? 1.95419 :  1.85971)*(0.5-a)
                          + (a>=0.5 ? 3.69032 :  1.9532)*pow(0.5-a,2)
                          + (a>=0.5 ? 10.7073 : -0.17274)*pow(0.5-a,3)
                          + (a>=0.5 ? 9.46921 :  0.0213069)*pow(0.5-a,4))/(a-a*a);

  if(n == 4) return (0.25 + (a>=0.5 ? 2.11034 :  2.06781)*(0.5-a)
                          + (a>=0.5 ? 4.4749  :  1.83246)*pow(0.5-a,2)
                          + (a>=0.5 ? 11.4962 :  1.99365)*pow(0.5-a,3)
                          + (a>=0.5 ? 10.5552 : -2.30786)*pow(0.5-a,4))/(a-a*a);

  return (0.25 + (a>=0.5 ? 2.21868 :  2.09567)*(0.5-a)
               + (a>=0.5 ? 5.0574  :  3.04673)*pow(0.5-a,2)
               + (a>=0.5 ? 12.0866 : -0.388745)*pow(0.5-a,3)
               + (a>=0.5 ? 11.2383 :  0.0110307)*pow(0.5-a,4))/(a-a*a);
}

double r_chm(double a, int n)        // a = andness, 2 <= n <= 5, r = CHM exponent
{                                    // If n>5 we use the same approximation as for n=5
  double r;
  if(n<2){cout << "\nERROR in R_WPM function: n = " << n << "\n\n"; exit(1);}

  if(n == 2)       r = ((-18.646*a + 29.866)*a - 18.678)*a + 5.2045;
  else if (n == 3) r = ((-18.227*a + 30.481)*a - 19.946)*a + 5.6331;
  else if (n == 4) r = ((-17.29*a  + 29.599)*a - 19.918)*a + 5.7208;
  else             r = ((-16.586*a + 28.974)*a - 19.932)*a + 5.7962;
  if( r > 1.) return 1.;
  if( r < 0.) return 0.;
  return r;  //  r is limited to range [0, 1] , i.e. [HAR, ARI]
}
```

Figure 2.4.16 Computation of the exponent of WPM and CHM from the desired value of andness.

In all versions of andness-directed GCD we need functions $r_{wpm}(\alpha)$ and $r_{chm}(\alpha)$ that convert a desired value of andness or orness to the exponents of WPM and CHM. Numeric implementations of these functions are presented in Fig. 2.4.16.

In the case where $\alpha_{geo}(n) \le \alpha_\theta < 1$ (like in the case of uniform GCD where $\alpha_\theta = 0.75$) we use only WPM and create a soft conjunctive aggregator by interpolating between the andness 0.5 and α_θ. Then, we use WPM to provide a hard conjunctive aggregator for $\alpha \ge \alpha_\theta$. All disjunctive GCD aggregators are then defined as duals of conjunctive aggregators. We use recursive notation of dualization: we define the aggregator $A(\mathbf{x}, \mathbf{W}; \alpha)$ in terms of $1 - A(\mathbf{1}-\mathbf{x}; \mathbf{W}, 1-\alpha)$ because such notation is the most compact and directly applicable for writing simple recursive computer programs, as follows:

$$W_1 x_1 \diamond \cdots \diamond W_n x_n$$

$$= A(\mathbf{x}; \mathbf{W}, \alpha) = \begin{cases} M(\mathbf{x}; \mathbf{W}, \alpha), & \alpha_\theta \le \alpha \le 1 \\[2mm] \dfrac{(\alpha_\theta - \alpha)M(\mathbf{x}; \mathbf{W}, 0.5) + (\alpha - 0.5)M(\mathbf{x}; \mathbf{W}, \alpha_\theta)}{\alpha_\theta - 0.5}, & 0.5 \le \alpha < \alpha_\theta \\[2mm] 1 - A(1 - \mathbf{x}; \mathbf{W}, 1 - \alpha), & 0 \le \alpha < 0.5, \end{cases}$$

$$M(\mathbf{x}; \mathbf{W}, \alpha) = \begin{cases} \min(x_1, \dots, x_n), & \alpha = 1 \\[2mm] \left(W_1 x_1^{r_{wpm}(\alpha)} + \cdots + W_n x_n^{r_{wpm}(\alpha)} \right)^{1/r_{wpm}(\alpha)}, & 0 < \alpha < 1 \\[2mm] \max(x_1, \dots, x_n), & \alpha = 0, \end{cases}$$

$$\alpha_{geo}(n) = \frac{n}{n-1} - \frac{n+1}{n-1}\left(\frac{n}{n+1}\right)^n \le \alpha_\theta < 1,$$

$$\mathbf{x} = (x_1, \dots, x_n), \quad x_i \in [0,1],$$

$$\mathbf{W} = (W_1, \dots, W_n), \quad W_1 + \cdots + W_n = 1.$$

Along the idempotency line the pure conjunction $M(\mathbf{x}; \mathbf{W}, 1) = x_1 \wedge \cdots \wedge x_n$ has a discontinuity of the first derivative. This discontinuity remains in all interpolative aggregators that interpolate between an arbitrary aggregator $F(\mathbf{x}; \mathbf{W}, \alpha_1)$ and $M(\mathbf{x}; \mathbf{W}, 1)$. So, if possible, it is advisable to avoid linear forms $qF(\mathbf{x}; \mathbf{W}, \alpha_1) + (1-q)M(\mathbf{x}; \mathbf{W}, 1), \ 0 \le q \le 1$. If $\alpha_1 < 1$ then we can interpolate between $F(\mathbf{x}; \mathbf{W}, \alpha_1)$ and $M(\mathbf{x}; \mathbf{W}, \alpha_2)$, $\alpha_1 < \alpha_2 < 1$, and then use natural properties of $M(\mathbf{x}; \mathbf{W}, \alpha)$ in the range $\alpha_2 \le \alpha \le 1$. In the case of hyperconjunction, however, we have $\alpha_1 > 1$ and we are forced to interpolate from $x_1 \wedge \cdots \wedge x_n$ to $x_1 \cdots x_n$ and then use $(x_1 \cdots x_n)^p, p \ge 1$; in such a case the properties of $x_1 \wedge \cdots \wedge x_n$ remain visible in the interpolative part of the hyperconjunctive aggregator.

The discontinuity of the first derivative is a natural property of the pure conjunction. For other aggregators, discontinuities of first derivatives are not observable natural properties of human reasoning. So, we generally try to avoid or to minimize such discontinuities. However, all interpolative aggregators that interpolate toward the pure conjunction inherit the discontinuity of the pure conjunction. Fortunately, there is no evidence that the minor visibility of the discontinuity of the first derivative reduces the applicability of such aggregators. Logic aggregators are used for aggregating imprecise degrees of truth, and under such circumstances minor imprecisions of aggregators are harmless. Thus, there is no reason to automatically blacklist all aggregators that interpolate to the pure conjunction or to the pure disjunction if that yields some visible benefits (including the computational simplicity).

If $0.5 < \alpha_\theta < \alpha_{geo}(n)$ then we interpolate a soft PC between the arithmetic mean and the CHM. A hard PC is then interpolated between the CHM and the geometric mean. For andness above $\alpha_{geo}(n)$ we use WPM. Following is the resulting standard GCD aggregator:

$$W_1 x_1 \diamond \cdots \diamond W_n x_n = A(\mathbf{x}; \mathbf{W}, \alpha)$$

$$= \begin{cases} M(\mathbf{x}; \mathbf{W}, \alpha), & \alpha_{geo}(n) \leq \alpha \leq 1 \\[2mm] \dfrac{\left(\alpha_{geo}(n) - \alpha\right) h(\mathbf{x}; \mathbf{W}, \alpha_\theta) + (\alpha - \alpha_\theta) M\left(\mathbf{x}; \mathbf{W}, \alpha_{geo}(n)\right)}{\alpha_{geo}(n) - \alpha_\theta}, & \alpha_\theta \leq \alpha < \alpha_{geo}(n) \\[4mm] \dfrac{(\alpha_\theta - \alpha) M(\mathbf{x}; \mathbf{W}, 0.5) + (\alpha - 0.5) h(\mathbf{x}; \mathbf{W}, \alpha_\theta)}{\alpha_\theta - 0.5}, & 0.5 \leq \alpha < \alpha_\theta < \alpha_{geo}(n) \\[4mm] 1 - A(1 - \mathbf{x}; \mathbf{W}, 1 - \alpha), & 0 \leq \alpha < 0.5 \end{cases}$$

$$h(\mathbf{x}; \mathbf{W}, \alpha) = \dfrac{W_1 x_1^{r_{chm}(\alpha)} + \cdots + W_n x_n^{r_{chm}(\alpha)}}{W_1 x_1^{r_{chm}(\alpha) - 1} + \cdots + W_n x_n^{r_{chm}(\alpha) - 1}}, \quad 0.5 \leq \alpha \leq \alpha_{har}(n) \text{ (monotonicity range)}$$

$$\alpha_{har}(n) = r_{chm}^{-1}(0) = \begin{cases} 0.773, & n = 2 \\ 0.774, & n = 3 \\ 0.777, & n = 4 \\ 0.781, & n = 5 \end{cases}$$

In presented interpolative aggregators we linearly interpolate between functions that are continuous and have continuous first derivatives. Consequently, these properties are preserved for the interpolative aggregator. However, if we linearly interpolate between an aggregator with continuous first derivatives and another aggregator that has discontinuity in the first derivatives, then the interpolative aggregator also has the discontinuity in the first derivatives. In the above general GCD models we avoided that problem by using directly WPM for higher values of andness. In addition, in the second step of aggregation between the CHM(α_θ) and the geometric mean WPM(α_{geo}), it is clear that we could go with CHM aggregation up to the harmonic mean, which is the highest andness where CHM is still monotonic. Then we can use the convenient property WPM(α_{har}) = CHM (α_{har}) for any number of variables. Similar relation for geometric mean holds in the case of two variables and it is convenient to transfer to WPM as early as possible and the earliest opportunity is for the geometric mean.

In the extreme case $\alpha_\theta = 1$ we can define GCD as the following aggregator that is soft everywhere except for $\alpha \in \{0,1\}$:

$$W_1 x_1 \diamond \cdots \diamond W_n x_n = A(\mathbf{x}; \mathbf{W}, \alpha) = \begin{cases} 1 - M(1 - \mathbf{x}; \mathbf{W}, 1 - \alpha), & 0.5 \leq \alpha \leq 1 \\ M(\mathbf{x}; \mathbf{W}, \alpha), & 0 \leq \alpha < 0.5. \end{cases}$$

The presented three types of standard idempotent GCD aggregator satisfy all possible requests for location of threshold andness and orness. In subsequent sections, we will analyze selected special cases of the standard GCD aggregator as well as its extension in the areas of hyperconjunction and hyperdisjunction.

2.4.8 Uniform and Nonuniform Interpolative GCD Aggregators

In this section we present three characteristic interpolative aggregators: (1) the uniform GCD aggregator (UGCD), (2) an example of extremely soft interpolative aggregator, and (3) an example of extremely hard interpolative aggregator. All examples are andness-directed and include weights.

2.4.8.1 The Uniform Interpolative GCD Aggregator (UGCD)

In the case of two variables and the threshold andness $\alpha_\theta \geq 2/3$, the interpolative aggregator can be based on the use of power means. The most important of such aggregators is the andness-directed uniform interpolative GCD aggregator $U(x_1, x_2; \mathbf{W}, \alpha)$ based on $\alpha_\theta = 3/4$:

$$r_2(\alpha) = \frac{0.25 + \beta(1.65811 + \beta(2.15388 + \beta(8.2844 + 6.16764\beta)))}{\alpha(1-\alpha)},$$

$$\beta = \tfrac{1}{2} - \alpha, \quad \tfrac{1}{2} \leq \alpha < 1,$$

$$M_\theta(x_1, x_2; \mathbf{W}) = \left(W_1 x_1^{-0.7201} + W_2 x_2^{-0.7201}\right)^{-1/0.7201}, \quad (W_1 + W_2 = 1);$$

$$U(x_1, x_2; \mathbf{W}, \alpha) = \begin{cases} \min(x_1, x_2), & \alpha = 1 \\[2mm] \left(W_1 x_1^{r_2(\alpha)} + W_2 x_2^{r_2(\alpha)}\right)^{1/r_2(\alpha)}, & 0.75 < \alpha < 1 \\[2mm] (3-4\alpha)(W_1 x_1 + W_2 x_2) + (4\alpha-2)M_\theta(x_1, x_2; \mathbf{W}), & 0.5 \leq \alpha \leq 0.75 \\[2mm] 1 - U(1-x_1, 1-x_2; \mathbf{W}, 1-\alpha), & 0 \leq \alpha < 0.5 \end{cases}$$

$$U(x_1, x_2; \alpha) = U(x_1, x_2; (\tfrac{1}{2}, \tfrac{1}{2}), \alpha).$$

The resulting interpolative aggregator $U(x_1, x_2; \mathbf{W}, \alpha)$ is the symmetric uniform GCD (called UGCD) for two variables, which is continuous, and satisfies $\partial U(x_1, x_2; \mathbf{W}, \alpha)/\partial x_1 \geq 0$ and $\partial U(x_1, x_2; \mathbf{W}, \alpha)/\partial x_2 \geq 0$ in all points inside $[0, 1]^2$ in the whole interval $0 < \alpha < 1$. In addition, $\partial U(x_1, x_2; \mathbf{W}, \alpha)/\partial \alpha \leq 0$.

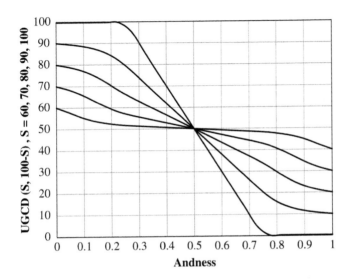

Figure 2.4.17 Sample results of UGCD aggregation for different degrees of andness.

The properties of equally weighted andness-directed UGCD are illustrated in Fig 2.4.12. We aggregate five pairs of suitability degrees (expressed as percentages): (40,60), (30,70), (20,80), (10,90), (0,100). Fig. 2.4.17 shows the aggregated suitability $\text{UGCD}(S,100-S) = U(S,100-S;\alpha)$ as a function of desired degree of andness. In the case of the pair (0, 100) we see the effect of mandatory requirements: for $\alpha \geq 0.75 = \alpha_\theta$ we have $\text{UGCD}(0,100) = 0$. A symmetric behavior we have in the case of sufficient requirements: for $\alpha \leq 0.25$, $\omega \geq 0.75 = \omega_\theta$ we have $\text{UGCD}(0,100) = 100$. These curves go from the maximum value to the minimum value of each aggregated pair.

In the case of two variables x and y and equal weights, the simplest commutative continuous, differentiable and dual UGCD aggregator that interpolates in the range $\frac{1}{2} \leq \alpha < \frac{3}{4}$ and uses the natural WPM in the range $\frac{3}{4} \leq \alpha < 1$, can be presented as follows:

$$U(x,y;\alpha) = \begin{cases} \min(x,y), & \alpha = 1 \\ \left(0.5x^{r_2(\alpha)} + 0.5y^{r_2(\alpha)}\right)^{1/r_2(\alpha)}, & \frac{3}{4} < \alpha < 1 \\ (3-4\alpha)(0.5x + 0.5y) + (4\alpha-2)\left(0.5x^R + 0.5y^R\right)^{1/R}, & \frac{1}{2} \leq \alpha \leq \frac{3}{4} \\ 1 - U(1-x,1-y;1-\alpha), & 0 \leq \alpha < \frac{1}{2} \end{cases}$$

$$R = -0.7201.$$

This aggregator is presented in Fig. 2.4.18 using the step of andness 1/14. The resulting aggregator is denoted UGCD.15 because it provides 15 degrees of

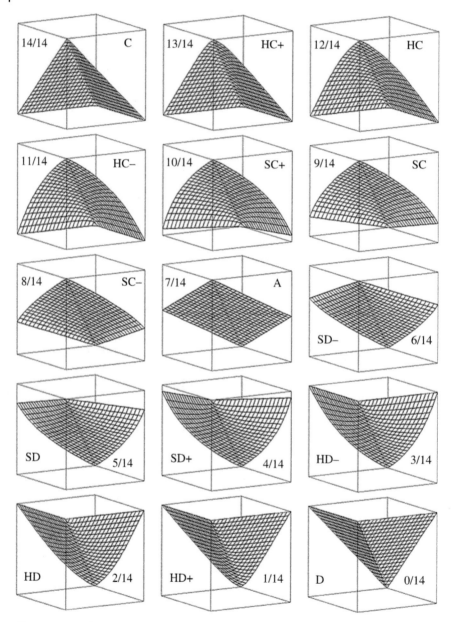

Figure 2.4.18 The uniform interpolative GCD aggegator with andness step 1/14 (UGCD.15).

andness that are convenient in applications: $\alpha = 0,\ 1/14\ ,...,1$. The symbols and names of individual aggregators are the following:

- C: Pure (full) conjunction ($\alpha = 1$);
- HC+: High (strong) hard partial conjunction ($\alpha = 13/14$);
- HC: Medium hard partial conjunction ($\alpha = 12/14 = 6/7$);
- HC-: Low (weak) hard partial conjunction ($\alpha = 11/14$);
- SC+: High (strong) soft partial conjunction ($\alpha = 10/14 = 5/7$);
- SC: Medium soft partial conjunction ($\alpha = 9/14$);
- SC-: Low (weak) soft partial conjunction ($\alpha = 8/14 = 4/7$);
- A: Neutrality (arithmetic mean) ($\alpha = 7/14 = \frac{1}{2}$);
- SD-: Low (weak) soft partial disjunction ($\alpha = 6/14 = 3/7$);
- SD: Medium soft partial disjunction ($\alpha = 5/14$);
- SD+: High (strong) soft partial disjunction ($\alpha = 4/14 = 2/7$).
- HD-: Low (weak) hard partial disjunction ($\alpha = 3/14$);
- HD: Medium hard partial disjunction ($\alpha = 2/14 = 1/7$);
- HD+: High (strong) hard partial disjunction ($\alpha = 1/14$);
- D: Pure (full) disjunction ($\alpha = 0$).

Each of the four soft and hard groups has three levels: low (weak), medium, and high (strong). That simplifies the selection of aggregators: we first select conjunctive or disjunctive type of polarization, then hard or soft mode, and finally low, medium, or high level. Fig. 2.4.18 shows the fundamental properties of hard and soft aggregators: hard partial conjunction reaches the plane $z = U(x,y;\alpha) = 0$ along x and y axes, while soft partial conjunction touches the plane $z = 0$ only in one point ($x = y = 0$). A dual behavior is visible in the case of partial disjunction where hard disjunctive aggregators reach the plane $z = 1$ along lines $x = 1$ and $y = 1$, and soft aggregators only in one point ($x = y = 1$).

In the case of uniform GCD aggregator, the threshold andness is $\alpha_\theta = 0.75$. That value is very close to the andness of the harmonic mean $\alpha_h = 0.7726$. So, in cases where the precision is not critical, the UGCD aggregator can use the harmonic mean as the threshold andness aggregator, as follows:

$$U_h(x,y;\alpha) = \begin{cases} \min(x,y), & \alpha = 1, \\[2mm] \left(0.5x^{r_2(\alpha)} + 0.5y^{r_2(\alpha)}\right)^{1/r_2(\alpha)}, & \alpha_h \le \alpha < 1, \\[2mm] \dfrac{\alpha_h - \alpha}{\alpha_h - 0.5}\left(\dfrac{x+y}{2}\right) + \dfrac{\alpha - 0.5}{\alpha_h - 0.5}\left(\dfrac{2xy}{x+y}\right), & \frac{1}{2} \le \alpha \le \alpha_h, \\[2mm] 1 - U_h(1-x, 1-y; 1-\alpha), & 0 \le \alpha < \frac{1}{2}; \end{cases}$$

$\alpha_h = \ln 16 - 2 = 0.7726$ (andness of the harmonic mean of two variables).

The aggregator HC- has andness $11/14 = 0.7857 > \alpha_h$ and the aggregator SC+ has andness $10/14 = 0.7143 < \alpha_h$. Consequently, the use of harmonic mean as threshold aggregator yields the result very similar to Fig. 2.4.18. If the preservation of continuous first derivatives is not necessary, it is possible to define the simplest UGCD aggregator (called AHC) based on interpolation between the arithmetic mean, the harmonic mean, and the full conjunction:

$$U_{ahc}(x,y;\alpha) = \begin{cases} \dfrac{1-\alpha}{1-\alpha_h}\left(\dfrac{2xy}{x+y}\right) + \dfrac{\alpha-\alpha_h}{1-\alpha_h}\min(x,y), & \alpha_h \le \alpha \le 1, \\[3ex] \dfrac{\alpha_h-\alpha}{\alpha_h-0.5}\left(\dfrac{x+y}{2}\right) + \dfrac{\alpha-0.5}{\alpha_h-0.5}\left(\dfrac{2xy}{x+y}\right), & \tfrac{1}{2} \le \alpha < \alpha_h, \\[3ex] 1 - U_{ahc}(1-x, 1-y; 1-\alpha), & 0 \le \alpha < \tfrac{1}{2}. \end{cases}$$

2.4.8.2 An Extremely Soft Interpolative Aggregator

In some applications it is possible to use only soft aggregators. In such cases, both the threshold andness and the threshold orness are equal to 1. Examples of soft aggregators include the disjunctive part of WPM, exponential means, OWA [YAG88] and AIWA [LAR03]. Following is the interpolative version of a soft aggregator of two variables based on WPM:

$$S(x,y;\alpha) = \begin{cases} \max(x,y), & \alpha = 0, \\[2ex] \left(0.5x^{r_2(\alpha)} + 0.5y^{r_2(\alpha)}\right)^{1/r_2(\alpha)}, & 0 < \alpha \le 0.5, \\[2ex] 1 - S(1-x, 1-y; 1-\alpha), & 0.5 < \alpha \le 1, \end{cases}$$

$$r_2(\alpha) = \dfrac{0.25 + 1.62481(\tfrac{1}{2}-\alpha) + 1.26214(\tfrac{1}{2}-\alpha)^2 + 0.144343(\tfrac{1}{2}-\alpha)^3 - 0.144343(\tfrac{1}{2}-\alpha)^4}{\alpha(1-\alpha)}.$$

This aggregator is presented in Fig. 2.4.19 as a nonuniform soft GCD with 15 levels of andness (SGCD.15).

2.4.8.3 An Extremely Hard Interpolative Aggregator

In the case of 15-level aggregators, an extremely hard aggregator can be based on requirement that all 15 levels are hard, as shown (for equal weights) in Fig 2.4.20. The lowest andness above the arithmetic mean is 8/14=0.57. That value can be selected as the threshold andness. Suppose that in the case $n = 2$ we have justification for extremely low threshold andness $\alpha_\theta = 0.57$ and the corresponding counter-harmonic mean exponent $r_\theta = 0.8066$. In this example the range of soft partial conjunction is very narrow, as follows:

$$H(x_1,x_2;\mathbf{W},\alpha) = \dfrac{(\alpha_\theta - \alpha)(W_1x_1 + W_2x_2) + (\alpha-0.5)h(x_1,x_2;\mathbf{W},\alpha_\theta)}{\alpha_\theta - 0.5}, \quad 0.5 \le \alpha < \alpha_\theta = \dfrac{8}{14};$$

$$h(x_1,x_2;\mathbf{W},\alpha_\theta) = \dfrac{W_1 x_1^{r_\theta} + W_2 x_2^{r_\theta}}{W_1 x_1^{r_\theta-1} + W_2 x_2^{r_\theta-1}}, \quad r_\theta = r_{chm}(\alpha_\theta) = r_{chm}(8/14) = 0.8044.$$

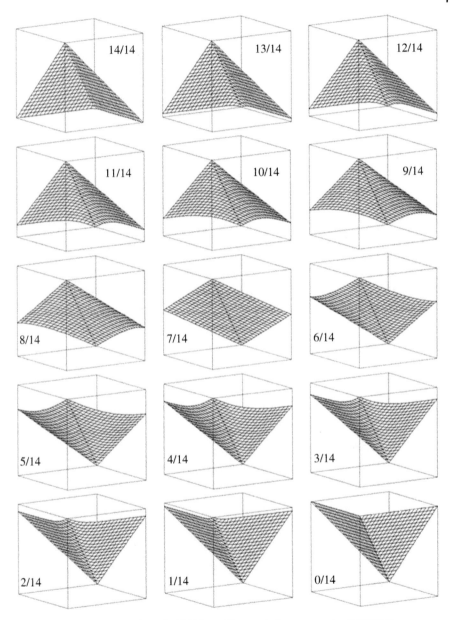

Figure 2.4.19 An extremely soft WPM-based interpolative aggregator (SGCD.15).

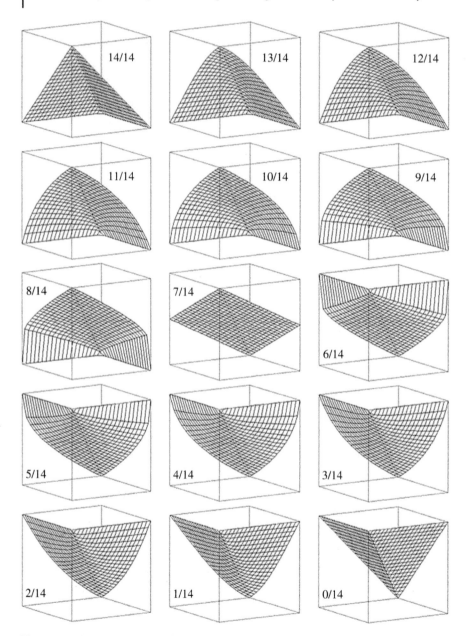

Figure 2.4.20 An extremely hard HGCD.15 aggregator (threshold andness = 0.57).

Then, we might use the counter-harmonic mean between $\alpha = 0.57$ and $\alpha = 0.772589$ (harmonic mean), followed by the weighted power mean between $\alpha = 0.772589$ and $\alpha = 1$. The resulting symmetric andness-directed GCD aggregator $H(x_1, x_2; \mathbf{W}, \alpha)$ includes the partial disjunction as De Morgan's dual of the partial conjunction, as follows:

$$r_2(\alpha) = \frac{0.25 + 1.65811(\frac{1}{2}-\alpha) + 2.15388(\frac{1}{2}-\alpha)^2 + 8.2844(\frac{1}{2}-\alpha)^3 + 6.16764(\frac{1}{2}-\alpha)^4}{\alpha(1-\alpha)};$$

$$r_{h2}(\alpha) = -18.646\alpha^3 + 29.866\alpha^2 - 18.678\alpha + 5.2045.$$

$$h(x_1, x_2; \mathbf{W}, \alpha) = \frac{W_1 x_1^{r_{h2}(\alpha)} + W_2 x_2^{r_{h2}(\alpha)}}{W_1 x_1^{r_{h2}(\alpha)-1} + W_2 x_2^{r_{h2}(\alpha)-1}},$$

(applicability range : $0.5 \le \alpha < 0.772589$);

$$H(x_1, x_2; \mathbf{W}, \alpha) = \begin{cases} \min(x_1, x_2), & \alpha = 1, \\[2mm] \left(W_1 x_1^{r_2(\alpha)} + W_2 x_2^{r_2(\alpha)} \right)^{1/r_2(\alpha)}, & 0.772589 \le \alpha < 1, \\[2mm] h(x_1, x_2; \mathbf{W}, \alpha), & 8/14 \le \alpha < \ln 16 - 2 = 0.772589, \\[2mm] \begin{pmatrix} (8-14\alpha)(W_1 x_1 + W_2 x_2) \\ + (14\alpha - 7)h(x_1, x_2; \mathbf{W}, \alpha_\theta) \end{pmatrix}, & 0.5 \le \alpha < 8/14 = \alpha_\theta, \\[2mm] 1 - H(1-x_1, 1-x_2; \mathbf{W}, 1-\alpha), & 0 \le \alpha < 0.5 \, ; \end{cases}$$

$W_1 > 0, \quad W_2 > 0, \quad W_1 + W_2 = 1.$

All individual aggregators in Fig. 2.4.20 are hard, and we denote this aggregator HGCD.15. The only soft regions are the soft partial conjunction between the andness of 0.5 and 8/14, as well as the soft partial disjunction between the andness of 6/14 and 0.5. These soft aggregators are not visible in Fig. 2.4.20. Unsurprisingly, the aggregators in the vicinity of the arithmetic mean with the andness 6/10 and 8/14 show clear hypersensitivity. Obviously, these are hard aggregators with the andness close to 0.5, and the volume under their surfaces must be close to 0.5. Consequently, if such aggregators must be hard, the only way is to have huge first derivatives in the vicinity of coordinate axes. The result is the hypersensitivity.

The interpolative aggregation sequence arithmetic mean → counter-harmonic mean → harmonic mean → WPM → conjunction is not the only way to implement the requested hard aggregators. An alternative way is the interpolative sequence arithmetic mean → counter-harmonic mean → geometric mean → WPM → conjunction. Following is a simple implementation of such an interpolative aggregator in the case of equal weights:

$$h(x_1,x_2;\alpha) = \frac{x_1^{r_{h2}(\alpha)} + x_2^{r_{h2}(\alpha)}}{x_1^{r_{h2}(\alpha)-1} + x_2^{r_{h2}(\alpha)-1}},$$

$$r_{h2}(\alpha) = ((-18.646\alpha + 29.866)\alpha - 18.678)\alpha + 5.2045,$$

$$H(x_1,x_2;\alpha) = \begin{cases} \min(x_1,x_2), & \alpha = 1, \\ \left(0.5x_1^{r_2(\alpha)} + 0.5x_2^{r_2(\alpha)}\right)^{1/r_2(\alpha)}, & 2/3 < \alpha < 1, \\ \dfrac{(2/3-\alpha)h(x_1,x_2;8/14) + (\alpha-8/14)\sqrt{x_1 x_2}}{2/3 - 8/14}, & 8/14 \le \alpha \le 2/3, \\ ((8-14\alpha)(0.5x_1 + 0.5x_2) + (14\alpha-7)h(x_1,x_2;\alpha_\theta)), & 0.5 \le \alpha < 8/14 = \alpha_\theta, \\ 1 - H(1-x_1, 1-x_2; 1-\alpha), & 0 \le \alpha < 0.5. \end{cases}$$

The presented interpolative method for design of GCD aggregators shows that any desired aggregator, with any desired value of threshold andness, can be designed with precision, flexibility, and modest computational requirements. Unsurprisingly, all GCD aggregators are not equally applicable. In GL applications, the most appropriate are aggregators that have the threshold andness in the vicinity of $\alpha = 3/4$. Thus, UGCD can be considered the default version of GCD.

2.4.9 Extending GCD to Include Hyperconjunction and Hyperdisjunction

The extreme case of GCD is the extension of GCD in the area of hyperconjunction and hyperdisjunction. Such aggregators can be called the extended GCD and denoted EGCD. We assume that EGCD includes a hyperconjunction (denoted CC, for andness $1 < \alpha \le n/(n-1)$) and hyperdisjunction (denoted DD, for orness $1 < \omega \le n/(n-1)$). DD is regularly selected as a dual of CC. The simplest method for designing EGCD aggregators consists of the following three steps:

1) Select an idempotent standard GCD aggregator that provides continuous transition from minimum to maximum (pure conjunction, $\alpha = 1$, to pure disjunction, $\omega = 1$).
2) Interpolate CC in two or more steps between the pure conjunction and the drastic conjunction (from $\alpha = 1$ to $\alpha = n/(n-1)$).
3) Define DD as a dual of CC. Assuming that the minimum (conjunction) and the maximum (disjunction) are not weighted, it follows that the hyperconjunction and the hyperdisjunction need not be weighted.

The resulting EGCD logic aggregators provide a continuous transition from drastic conjunction to drastic disjunction. A convenient form of hyperconjunction can be based on the product-power function $y = (x_1 \cdots x_n)^p$, $p \geq 1$. There are four reasons for using the product-power function:

1) For $p = 1$ EGCD becomes the product t-norm $y = \prod_{i=1}^{n} x_i$ building a bridge between logic and probabilistic reasoning.
2) The product-power function can be used for all values of parameter $p \geq 1$, and its andness is a strictly increasing function of p. For $p \to +\infty$ (or, in practice, for any $p \gg 1$) EGCD becomes the drastic conjunction:

$$y = \hat{C}(x_1,\ldots,x_n) = \lim_{p \to +\infty} (x_1 \cdots x_n)^p = \left\lfloor \prod_{i=1}^{n} x_i \right\rfloor = \begin{cases} 1, & \text{if } x_1 = \cdots = x_n = 1 \\ 0, & \text{otherwise (inside } I^n) \end{cases}$$

3) The area between $y = x_1 \wedge \cdots \wedge x_n$ and $y = x_1 \cdots x_n$ can be properly covered using interpolative aggregators.
4) Hyperdisjunction is easily obtained as De Morgan's dual of hyperconjunction: $y = 1 - [(1-x_1) \cdots (1-x_n)]^p$, $p \geq 1$, and generally $\hat{D}(x_1,\ldots,x_n) = 1 - \hat{C}(1-x_1,\ldots,1-x_n)$.

We use unweighted forms of these functions as the consequence of accepting unweighted pure conjunction and pure disjunction, where the percept of overall importance of all inputs is considered sufficiently high to annihilate the impact of relative differences expressed by weights. Since the product-power function extends andness and orness beyond the [0,1] range, CC is a stronger simultaneity than the pure conjunction and DD is a stronger substitutability than the pure disjunction. Thus, for the product-power function we apply the same reasoning about weights elimination as for the pure conjunction and the pure disjunction. The andness and orness of the product-power function are computed as follows:

$$\bar{y} = \int_0^1 \cdots \int_0^1 (x_1 \cdots x_n)^p dx_1 \cdots dx_n = \frac{1}{(p+1)^n},$$

$$\alpha_{cc}(n,p) = \frac{n - (n+1)\bar{y}}{n-1} = \frac{n - (n+1)/(p+1)^n}{n-1} > 1,$$

$$\omega_{cc}(n,p) = 1 - \alpha_{cc}(n,p) = \frac{(n+1)/(p+1)^n - 1}{n-1} < 0,$$

$$\alpha_{cc}(n,p) = \omega_{dd}(n,p), \qquad \alpha_{dd}(n,p) = \omega_{cc}(n,p),$$

$$\alpha_{cc}(n,p) + \alpha_{dd}(n,p) = 1, \qquad \omega_{cc}(n,p) + \omega_{dd}(n,p) = 1.$$

If we want to use the product t-norm, then $p = 1$ and we have the following values of andness and orness:

$$\alpha_{cc}(n,1) = \frac{n-(n+1)/2^n}{n-1}; \qquad \alpha_{cc}(2,1) = \omega_{dd}(2,1) = \frac{5}{4};$$

$$\alpha_{dd}(n,1) = \frac{(n+1)/2^n - 1}{n-1}; \qquad \alpha_{dd}(2,1) = \omega_{cc}(2,1) = -\frac{1}{4}.$$

Generally, we can select a desired value α_{cc} and then compute the resulting value of p:

$$p(n,\alpha_{cc}) = \left(\frac{n+1}{n-(n-1)\alpha_{cc}}\right)^{1/n} - 1.$$

The andness $\alpha_{cc}(n, p)$ of the product-power function is shown in Fig. 2.4.21. In the case of two variables, the range of andness for various values of p is shown in Table 2.4.4. In the interesting particular case $p = \sqrt{3} - 1$ the product-power function has andness 1 and its dual has orness 1, yielding the nonidempotent pseudoconjunction and pseudodisjunction functions shown in Fig 2.4.22.

The pseudoconjunction and the pseudodisjunction have obvious similarities with the pure conjunction and the pure disjunction. However, these functions intersect the pure conjunction and the pure disjunction. For example, if $x < y = 1$ then $\min(x,y) = x$; however, the pseudoconjunction is $z = (xy)^p = x^p$. So, as long

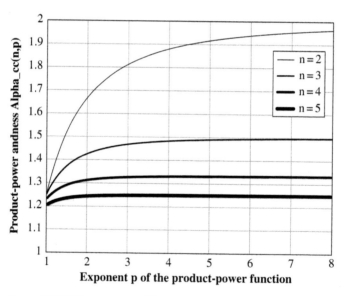

Figure 2.4.21 The andness of the product-power function.

Table 2.4.4 Range of andness for the product-power function of two variables.

$p(2,\alpha_{cc})$	α_{cc}	$\omega_{cc} = \alpha_{dd}$
$\sqrt{12/5}-1=0.5492$	¾ =0.75	0.25
$\sqrt{3}-1=0.73205$	1	0
1	5/4 =1.25	−0.25
$\sqrt{6}-1=1.449$	3/2 =1.5	−0.5
2	5/3=1.667	−0.667
3	29/16 =1.8125	−0.8125
4	47/25 =1.88	−0.88
$p \gg 1$	2	−1

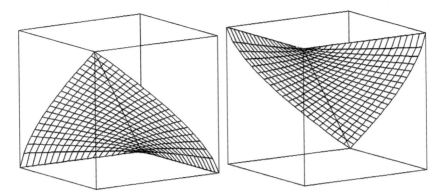

Figure 2.4.22 Pseudoconjunction ($\alpha = 1$) and pseudodisjunction ($\omega = 1$) for the product-power function of two variables.

as $p < 1$, the pseudoconjunction is above the pure conjunction, as illustrated in Fig. 2.4.22. If $p > \frac{1}{2}$ and $x = y$ then the pseudoconjunction is below the pure conjunction and consequently, for $\frac{1}{2} < p < 1$ the two surfaces intersect. Therefore, pseudoconjunction and pseudodisjunction do not offer a path toward the idempotent segment of GCD and do not seem to have features that would compete with the pure conjunction and disjunction. If we want to extend GCD, we need the product-power function that satisfies $(x_1 \cdots x_n)^p \le \min(x_1 \cdots x_n)$ for all values of variables. In the extreme case where $x_2 = \cdots = x_n = 1$, we have the condition $x_1^p \le x_1$ and consequently the power must satisfy the condition $p \ge 1$. In such a case, the EGCD can be interpolated between $\min(x_1 \cdots x_n)$ and $(x_1 \cdots x_n)^p$ using any of previous andness-directed idempotent GCD aggregators $A(\mathbf{x}; \mathbf{W}, \alpha)$ as follows:

$$W_1 x_1 \diamond \cdots \diamond W_n x_n$$

$$= \begin{cases} \dfrac{(\alpha_{cc}(n,p) - \alpha)\min(x_1,\ldots,x_n) + (\alpha-1)(x_1 \cdots x_n)^p}{\alpha_{cc}(n,p) - 1}, & 1 < \alpha \le \alpha_{cc}(n,p), \\[2ex] A(\mathbf{x}; \mathbf{W}, \alpha), & 0 \le \alpha \le 1, \\[2ex] \dfrac{\alpha(1 - [(1-x_1)\cdots(1-x_n)]^p) + (\alpha_{dd}(n,p) - \alpha)\max(x_1,\ldots,x_n)}{\alpha_{dd}(n,p)}, & \alpha_{dd}(n,p) \le \alpha < 0 \, ; \end{cases}$$

$$A(\mathbf{x}; \mathbf{W}, 1) = \min(x_1,\ldots,x_n) \le A(\mathbf{x}; \mathbf{W}, \alpha) \le \max(x_1,\ldots,x_n) = A(\mathbf{x}; \mathbf{W}, 0) \, ;$$

$$\alpha_{cc}(n,p) = \frac{n - (n+1)/(p+1)^n}{n-1} > 1, \qquad \alpha_{dd}(n,p) = \frac{(n+1)/(p+1)^n - 1}{n-1} < 0,$$

$$(x_1 \cdots x_n)^p \le W_1 x_1 \diamond \cdots \diamond W_n x_n \le 1 - [(1-x_1)\cdots(1-x_n)]^p.$$

The EGCD aggregator $W_1 x_1 \diamond \cdots \diamond W_n x_n$ is now a general andness-directed aggregator providing continuous transition from hyperconjunction to hyperdisjunction in the extended andness range $\alpha_{dd}(n,p) \le \alpha \le \alpha_{cc}(n,p)$.

In the special case $n = 2$, $p = 1$ we have $\alpha_{cc}(2,1) = 1.25$, $\alpha_{dd}(2,1) = -0.25$ and the resulting aggregators (product t-norm and its dual t-conorm, the probabilistic sum) are shown in Fig. 2.4.23. These aggregators are the border aggregators because they have the lowest value of the power p. Therefore, the presented interpolative aggregator is necessary to support an interpolative bridge between the pure conjunction/disjunction and the hyperconjunctive/hyperdisjunctive aggregators. The remaining area of hyperconjunctive and hyperdisjunctive aggregators can be covered using directly the product-power aggregator as shown in Section 2.4.10.

The product t-norm (the special case $p = 1$) can also be interpreted as the probability of an event that consists of simultaneous (conjunctive) occurrence of n independent events. That can be a useful aggregation property in cases where the component events are provably independent (or close to independence). Such situations (discussed as pattern 2 in Section 2.1.2 and property $\mathbf{P_5}$ in Section 2.2.1) are not frequent but show an intersection point of logic and probabilistic reasoning, and an area of overlap of concepts developed in fuzzy logic and in probability theory.

Idempotent aggregators that are located between hyperconjunction and hyperdisjunction can be organized in many different ways. Generally, we assume that the threshold andness remains adjustable inside the idempotent

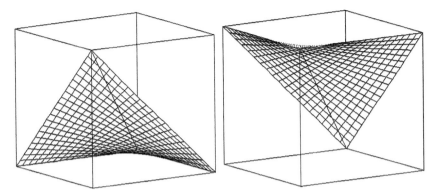

Figure 2.4.23 Medium hyperconjunctive and hyperdisjunctive EGCD aggregators for $p = 1$.

segment of the EGCD aggregator. For example, if we want to extend a weighted UGCD aggregator in the case $n = 2$ and $\alpha_\theta = 0.75$, then according to Table 2.3.3, we have $r_{wpm}(0.75) = -0.7201$ and the resulting aggregator is the following:

$$W_1 x_1 \diamond W_2 x_2 = F(x_1, x_2; \mathbf{W}, \alpha)$$

$$= \begin{cases} \dfrac{(\alpha_{max} - \alpha)\min(x_1, x_2) + (\alpha - 1)(x_1 x_2)^p}{\alpha_{max} - 1}, & 1 < \alpha \leq \alpha_{cc}(2, p), \\[2mm] \min(x_1, x_2), & \alpha = 1, \\[2mm] \left(W_1 x_1^{r_{wpm}(\alpha)} + W_2 x_2^{r_{wpm}(\alpha)} \right)^{1/r_{wpm}(\alpha)}, & \tfrac{3}{4} \leq \alpha < 1, \\[2mm] (3 - 4\alpha)(W_1 x_1 + W_2 x_2) + (4\alpha - 2)\left(W_1 x_1^R + W_2 x_2^R \right)^{1/R}, & \tfrac{1}{2} \leq \alpha < \tfrac{3}{4}, \\[2mm] 1 - F(1 - x_1, 1 - x_2; \mathbf{W}, 1 - \alpha), & 1 - \alpha_{cc}(2, p) \leq \alpha < \tfrac{1}{2}\,; \end{cases}$$

$$R = r_{wpm}(\tfrac{3}{4}) = -0.7201.$$

2.4.10 From Drastic Conjunction to Drastic Disjunction: A General GCD Aggregator

The interpolative method for building aggregation functions can be used to precisely realize desired properties of aggregators. In this section, we present the most general version of a GCD aggregator for applications in graded logic. The general GCD aggregator must satisfy seven essential conditions:

1) It must be applicable for any number of variables $n > 1$.
2) It must provide a graded continuous transition in the full range from the drastic conjunction to the drastic disjunction.

3) It must be andness-directed in the full range $-1/(n-1) \le \alpha \le n/(n-1)$.
4) It must have adjustable threshold andness α_θ.
5) It must be weighted in the idempotent range $0 < \alpha < 1$ and unweighted outside the idempotent range.
6) It must satisfy De Morgan's duality.
7) It must maximize the use of models that have continuous first derivatives.

This general aggregator in all its glory is presented as Fig. 2.4.24, and the recursive concept of implementing its duality is shown in Fig. 2.4.25. In Fig 2.4.24 we assume that the threshold andness is not less than the andness of the geometric mean. This assumption is regularly satisfied; in rare exceptional cases, if the threshold andness is below the andness of the geometric mean, we can use interpolative techniques introduced in Section 2.4.7.

The design of general GCD aggregator is based on combining the weighted power mean and the product-power function. We use adjustable threshold andness and interpolate between the neutrality and the threshold andness aggregator. Between the threshold andness aggregator and the full conjunction we use natural hard properties of the weighted power mean. In the nonidempotent hyperconjunctive area, we select the product t-norm as a medium point and interpolate between it and the full conjunction. This short interpolative segment is the only area where the first derivative has a discontinuity inherited from the full conjunction. All other segments provide continuous first derivatives. For andness beyond the product t-norm, we use natural properties of the product-power function that ultimately yields the drastic conjunction. The process of continuous transition from the drastic conjunction to the full conjunction is presented in Fig 2.4.26. In the case $\alpha = 1.125$, we see consequences of linear interpolation between the case $\alpha = 1$ and $\alpha = 1.25$ (both $\partial z/\partial x$ and $\partial z/\partial y$ have discontinuity for $x = y$). From $\alpha = 1.25$ to $\alpha = 2$ we directly use the product-power function.

Figs. 2.4.26 and 2.4.27 show hyperconjunctive and hyperdisjunctive aggregators of two variables, where the corresponding range of andness and orness is $[-1,2]\setminus[0,1]$. Generally, for hyperconjunctive and hyperdisjunctive aggregators the range of andness/orness is $[-1/(n-1),n/(n-1)]\setminus[0,1]$. Obviously, as n increases, this range shrinks. According to the quadrisection of the unit hypercube (Fig. 2.1.5), the regions of hyperconjunction and hyperdisjunction have decreasing volumes $V = 1/(n+1)$ while the region of idempotent logic aggregators increases: $V_{ILA} = 1 - 2V = (n-1)/(n+1)$.

2.4.11   Gamma Aggregators versus Extended GCD Aggregators

In this section we study *gamma aggregators* and compare them to GCD aggregators. Gamma aggregators were introduced in 1980 (seven years after GCD), independently of GCD, and with the same goal as GCD: to model simultaneity

$$z = \begin{cases} F(\mathbf{x};\mathbf{W},\alpha) = \begin{cases} \textbf{Drastic conjunction:} \\[4pt] \left\lfloor \Pi_{i=1}^{n} x_i \right\rfloor, \qquad\qquad\qquad \alpha = \alpha_{max} = n/(n-1). \\[6pt] \textbf{High hyperconjunction:} \\[4pt] \left(\prod_{i=1}^{n} x_i \right)^{\{(n+1)/[n-(n-1)\alpha]\}^{1/n}-1}, \qquad \alpha_{cc}(n,1) < \alpha < \alpha_{max}. \\[6pt] \textbf{Medium hyperconjunction (product t-norm):} \\[4pt] \prod_{i=1}^{n} x_i, \qquad\qquad \alpha = \alpha_{cc}(n,1) = \dfrac{n2^n - n - 1}{(n-1)2^n} \\[6pt] \textbf{Low hyperconjunction:} \\[4pt] 4[(\alpha_{cc}(n,1)-\alpha)\min(\mathbf{x}) + (\alpha-1)\prod_{i=1}^{n} x_i], \qquad 1 < \alpha < \alpha_{cc}(n,1). \\[6pt] \textbf{Full conjunction:} \\[4pt] \min(x_1,\ldots,x_n), \qquad\qquad \alpha = 1. \\[6pt] \textbf{Hard partial conjunction:} \\[4pt] \left(\sum_{i=1}^{n} W_i x_i^{r_{wpm}(\alpha)} \right)^{1/r_{wpm}(\alpha)}, \qquad \alpha_\theta \le \alpha < 1. \\[6pt] \textbf{Soft partial conjunction:} \\[4pt] \dfrac{\alpha_\theta - \alpha}{\alpha_\theta - \frac12}\left(\sum_{i=1}^{n} W_i x_i \right) + \dfrac{\alpha - \frac12}{\alpha_\theta - \frac12}\left(\sum_{i=1}^{n} W_i x_i^R \right)^{1/R}, \qquad \frac12 < \alpha < \alpha_\theta. \\[6pt] \textbf{Neutrality:} \\[4pt] \sum_{i=1}^{n} W_i x_i, \qquad\qquad \alpha = \omega = \frac12. \end{cases} \\[6pt] \textbf{Dual disjunctive aggregators:} \\[4pt] 1 - F(\mathbf{1}-\mathbf{x};\mathbf{W},1-\alpha), \qquad \alpha_{min} = -1/(n-1) \le \alpha < 0.5 \end{cases}$$

$$n > 1, \quad \mathbf{x} = (x_1,\ldots,x_n), \quad \mathbf{1}-\mathbf{x} = (1-x_1,\ldots,1-x_n),$$

$$\mathbf{W} = (W_1,\ldots,W_n), \quad 0 < W_i < 1, \quad i = 1,\ldots,n, \quad \sum_{i=1}^{n} W_i = 1$$

$$r_{wpm}(\alpha) = \frac{0.25 + a_n(\frac12 - \alpha) + b_n(\frac12-\alpha)^2 + c_n(\frac12-\alpha)^3 + d_n(\frac12-\alpha)^4}{\alpha(1-\alpha)}.$$

For models of $r_{wpm}(\alpha)$ and the values of a_n, b_n, c_n, d_n see Fig. 2.4.16 and Table 2.3.7

$R = r_{wpm}(\alpha_\theta)$ = exponent of power mean for the threshold andness α_θ in the following range:

$$\frac{2}{3} \le \frac{n}{n-1} - \frac{n+1}{n-1}\left(\frac{n}{n-1} \right)^n \le \alpha_\theta < 1; \quad \text{for UGCD we use } \alpha_\theta = \tfrac34.$$

Figure 2.4.24 A general form of the GCD aggregator for applications in graded logic.

and substitutability as logic relationships that are observable and measurable in human reasoning. Gamma aggregators and GCD can be first compared from the standpoint of their supported logic functionality. In addition, an important property of gamma aggregators is that they were experimentally verified as

```
double GCD( double x[],        // Input degrees of truth (suitability)
            double W[],        // Weights (relative importance) of inputs
            double alpha,      // Desired andness ∈ [-1/(n-1), n/(n-1)]
            double alpha_t,    // Desired threshold andness ∈ ]1/2, 1[
            int n              // Number of inputs ( size of x[] and W[])
          )
{ double not_x[n];
  if(alpha >= 0.5)     // Conjunctive aggregator realized as an
  {                    // interpolative aggregation function
    return F(x, W, alpha, alpha_t, n);
  }
  else                 // Disjunctive aggregator realized as a dual
  {                    // of conjunctive interpolative aggregator
    for(int i=0; i<n; i++) not_x[i] = 1. -x[i];
    return 1. - GCD(not_x, W, 1.-alpha, alpha_t, n);
  }
}
```

Figure 2.4.25 The concept of recursive implementation of duality of GCD aggregators.

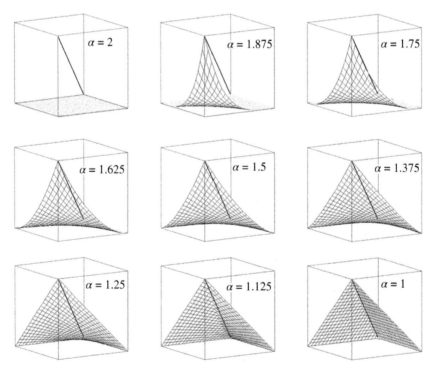

Figure 2.4.26 Hyperconjunction: continuous transition between the drastic conjunction and the full conjunction.

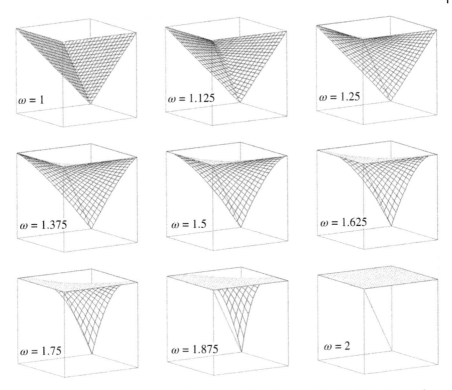

Figure 2.4.27 Hyperdisjunction: continuous transition between the full disjunction and the drastic disjunction.

models of logic reasoning results collected from 60 human subjects [ZIM80]. Obviously, experimental validation significantly contributes to the credibility of aggregators. Thus, we can also compare the performance of gamma aggregators and GCD if both types of aggregators are adjusted to be models of the same set of experimental data.

2.4.11.1 Multiplicative and Additive Gamma Aggregators

Gamma aggregators [ZYS79, ZIM80, DOM82] are an attempt to create aggregators similar to GCD (i.e., compensative aggregators that can realize a continuous transition from intersection of fuzzy sets to the union of fuzzy sets). The idea of gamma aggregators is that conjunctive aggregation is performed by the simple product $\Pi_{i=1}^{n} x_i$ (one of basic t-norms) and disjunctive aggregation by its De Morgan's dual $1 - \Pi_{i=1}^{n}(1 - x_i)$. The gamma aggregators are then defined as multiplicative or additive combinations of the conjunctive and disjunctive aggregators:

$$y_g(\mathbf{x},\gamma,n) = \left(\prod_{i=1}^{n} x_i\right)^{(1-\gamma)} \left(1-\prod_{i=1}^{n}(1-x_i)\right)^{\gamma}$$

$$y_a(\mathbf{x},\gamma,n) = (1-\gamma)\left(\prod_{i=1}^{n} x_i\right) + \gamma\left(1-\prod_{i=1}^{n}(1-x_i)\right), \quad 0 \le \gamma \le 1$$

Obviously, the parameter γ plays a role similar to orness. It is easy to see that gamma aggregators are not idempotent, except in the case $y_a(\mathbf{x}, 0.5, 2)$. For example, if $\gamma = 0$ then $y_g(\mathbf{x},0,n) = y_a(\mathbf{x},0,n) = x_1 x_2 \cdots x_n$ and the product is not an idempotent function. If $x_1 = \ldots = x_n = x$ then the gamma aggregators yield the following nonlinear functions:

$$y_g(x,\gamma,n) = x^{n(1-\gamma)}(1-(1-x)^n)^{\gamma}$$
$$y_a(x,\gamma,n) = (1-\gamma)x^n + \gamma(1-(1-x)^n), \quad 0 \le \gamma \le 1$$

The following weighted variants of gamma aggregators were also discussed in [ZYS79, ZIM80, DOM82, ZIM87]:

$$y_g(\mathbf{x},\mathbf{p},\gamma,n) = \left(\prod_{i=1}^{n} x_i^{p_i}\right)^{(1-\gamma)} \left(1-\prod_{i=1}^{n}(1-x_i)^{p_i}\right)^{\gamma}$$

$$y_a(\mathbf{x},\mathbf{p},\gamma,n) = (1-\gamma)\left(\prod_{i=1}^{n} x_i^{p_i}\right) + \gamma\left(1-\prod_{i=1}^{n}(1-x_i)^{p_i}\right),$$

$$\mathbf{p} = (p_1,\ldots,p_n), \quad \sum_{i=1}^{n} p_i = n.$$

Some of weights $p_1, \ldots, p_n$ can be greater than 1 and some can be less than 1.

According to [ZIM96], the parameters of gamma aggregators are adjusted only by fitting empirical data provided by domain experts. This process is essentially the same as training of neural networks, where the domain experts provide a training set, and then the parameters of the gamma aggregator are adjusted to minimize the error of the model. Gamma aggregators do not have mechanism for selecting the parameter γ and/or weights directly by decision makers using desired logic and semantic properties of the aggregator. The gamma aggregator parameters do not represent or explain specific properties of the mental aggregation process. Consequently, the use of gamma aggregators in the area of evaluation models [ZIM79, ZIM87, ZIM96] is restricted to the cases with very small number of inputs.

In this section, we investigate the properties of gamma aggregators from the standpoint of their applicability in logic models. We first analyze the andness and orness of gamma aggregators and then we compare the gamma aggregators and EGCD.

The andness $\alpha(\gamma, n)$ of additive and multiplicative gamma aggregator in extreme cases $\gamma = 0$ and $\gamma = 1$ is the following:

$$\alpha(0,n) = \frac{n - (n+1)\int_0^1 x_1 dx_1 \cdots \int_0^1 x_n dx_n}{n-1} = \frac{n - (n+1)/2^n}{n-1} \; ;$$

$$\alpha(0,2) = \frac{5}{4} = 1.25, \quad \lim_{n \to +\infty} \alpha(0,n) = 1 \; ; \quad \text{(maximum andness)}$$

$$\alpha(1,n) = \frac{n - (n+1)\left[1 - \int_0^1 (1-x_1)dx_1 \cdots \int_0^1 (1-x_n)dx_n\right]}{n-1} = \frac{n - (n+1)(1 - 1/2^n)}{n-1} \; ;$$

$$\alpha(1,2) = -\frac{1}{4} = -0.25, \quad \lim_{n \to +\infty} \alpha(1,n) = 0, \quad \text{(minimum andness)} .$$

Therefore, the maximum range of andness of gamma aggregators is $\alpha(\gamma,2) \in [-0.25, 1.25]$. For $\gamma = 0$ the andness of gamma aggregators is up to 25% stronger than the andness of pure conjunction. Similarly, for $\gamma = 1$, the orness of gamma aggregators is up to 25% stronger than the orness of pure disjunction. In the case of multiplicative gamma aggregator, its numerically computed andness is a nonlinear function of γ as shown in Fig. 2.4.28. The table attached to Fig. 2.4.28 shows that $\gamma = 0.5$ is not a middle point between the intersection (conjunction) and the union (disjunction). So, the multiplicative gamma aggregator is predominantly conjunctive and for any given value of andness

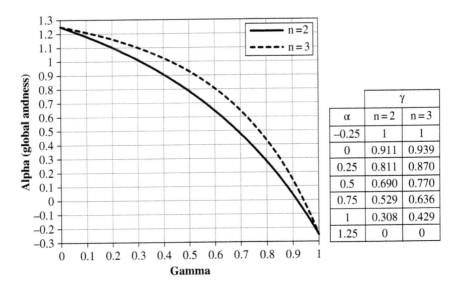

α	γ	
	$n=2$	$n=3$
−0.25	1	1
0	0.911	0.939
0.25	0.811	0.870
0.5	0.690	0.770
0.75	0.529	0.636
1	0.308	0.429
1.25	0	0

Figure 2.4.28 Andness of multiplicative gamma aggregators.

$\alpha \in [-0.25, 1.25]$, it is possible to numerically compute the corresponding value of gamma using simple polynomial approximations as follows:

$$\gamma_g(\alpha, n) = 0.9115 - 0.3828\alpha - 0.0181\alpha^2 - 0.203\alpha^3, \quad n = 2;$$

$$\gamma_g(\alpha, n) = 0.9394 - 0.2344\alpha - 0.0807\alpha^2 - 0.5889\alpha^3 + 0.9244\alpha^4 - 0.5311\alpha^5, \quad n = 3.$$

Therefore, a symmetric version of the gamma aggregator, controlled by and-ness, can be organized as the following *alpha aggregator,* where the middle point is $\alpha = 0.5$:

$$y_g(\mathbf{x}, \alpha, n) = \left(\prod_{i=1}^{n} x_i \right)^{(1-\gamma_g(\alpha, n))} \left(1 - \prod_{i=1}^{n} (1-x_i) \right)^{\gamma_g(\alpha, n)}, \alpha \in [-0.25, 1.25].$$

In the case of additive gamma aggregator the andness is a linear function of γ, as follows:

$$\alpha_a(n, \gamma) = \frac{n - (n+1)\left[(1-\gamma)\left(\int_0^1 x_1 dx_1 \cdots \int_0^1 x_n dx_n \right) + \gamma \left(1 - \int_0^1 (1-x_1) dx_1 \cdots \int_0^1 (1-x_n) dx_n \right) \right]}{n-1}$$

$$= \frac{n - (n+1)[(1-\gamma)/2^n + \gamma(1-1/2^n)]}{n-1} = \frac{n - (n+1)[1/2^n + \gamma(1-1/2^{n-1})]}{n-1}.$$

Therefore, in the additive case, for a given value of andness, it is possible to compute the corresponding value of gamma using the above expression as follows:

$$\gamma_a(\alpha, n) = \frac{n - (n+1)/2^n - (n-1)\alpha}{(n+1)(1-1/2^{n-1})},$$

$$\gamma_a(1/2, n) = \frac{n - (n+1)/2^n - (n-1)/2}{(n+1)(1-1/2^{n-1})} = \frac{n/2 - n/2^n - 1/2^n + 1/2}{n - n/2^{n-1} - 1/2^{n-1} + 1} = \frac{1}{2}.$$

Unfortunately, if $\gamma_a = 0.5$, $\alpha = 0.5$, $n > 2$, additive gamma aggregators do not yield the arithmetic mean. In the case of $y_a(\mathbf{x}, \gamma, n)$, following are some characteristic values of andness:

$$\alpha_a(\gamma, 2) = \alpha_a(\gamma, 3) = 1.25 - 1.5\gamma, \quad \alpha_a(0, 2) = \alpha_a(0, 3) = 1.25, \quad \alpha_a(1, 2) = \alpha_a(1, 3) = -0.25;$$

$$\alpha_a(\gamma, 4) = \frac{59 - 70\gamma}{48}, \quad \alpha_a(0, 4) = 1 + 11/48 = 1.229, \quad \alpha_a(1, 4) = -11/48 = -0.229;$$

$$\lim_{n \to +\infty} \alpha_a(\gamma, n) = 1 - \gamma \quad (\gamma \text{ plays the role of orness for large values of } n).$$

Asymmetric behavior of gamma aggregators is easily visible in simple numeric examples. For $\gamma_a = 0.5$, the aggregation of $x_1 = 0.5$ and $x_2 = 1$ yields the expected mean value $y_a = 0.5x_1x_2 + 0.5[1 - (1-x_1)(1-x_2)] = 0.75$, indicating the arithmetic mean. The same example for three variables $x_1 = 0.5$, $x_2 = 1$,

$x_3 = 0.75$ and $\gamma_a = 0.5$ is also expected to generate the same result $y_a = 0.75$. However, the result is less than the expected value:

$$y_a = 0.5x_1x_2x_3 + 0.5[1 - (1-x_1)(1-x_2)(1-x_3)] = 11/16 = 0.6875 < 0.75.$$

So, this aggregator behaves as a partial conjunction regardless the global andness $\alpha_a(0.5,3) = 0.5$. The consequence of inconsistent logic properties of the additive (or multiplicative) gamma aggregator is that users cannot select desired logic properties by simply selecting the appropriate value of gamma. Such aggregators can be adjusted only by fitting an empirical training set. That is a serious restriction.

An obvious advantage of gamma aggregators is that according to their definitions, we can compute the optimum values of parameter γ directly from the training set:

$$\gamma_g = \frac{\log y_g(\mathbf{x},\gamma,n) - \log \prod_{i=1}^{n} x_i}{\log\left(1 - \prod_{i=1}^{n}(1-x_i)\right) - \log \prod_{i=1}^{n} x_i} \quad , \quad \gamma_a = \frac{y_a(\mathbf{x},\gamma,n) - \prod_{i=1}^{n} x_i}{1 - \prod_{i=1}^{n}(1-x_i) - \prod_{i=1}^{n} x_i}.$$

$$(2.4.1)$$

In the case of m observations obtained from domain experts, each observation generates a different value of parameter γ. In [ZIM80] the final value of γ is computed as the arithmetic mean of m values generated from m observations.

An important contribution of research reported in [THO79, ZIM80, ZIM87, KOV92, ZIM96)] is that the authors provided empirical analysis based on human subjects to select the most appropriate value of γ in the case of conjunctive aggregation (intersection of fuzzy sets). Most results of the empirical research on the aggregators of the fuzzy membership functions can be found in [ZIM96].

2.4.11.2 Comparison of Gamma Aggregators and GCD

The experiments with fuzzy conjunction include a set of objects that belong to two fuzzy sets A and B, as well as to their intersection C = A *and* B. In [ZIM80] the objects were tiles and the sets were A = precision of shape, B = material quality, C = tile quality. For each tile the respondents were asked to determine the degree of fuzzy membership in sets A, B, and C. That reveals a latent connective that is used in human reasoning, and the gamma aggregator was selected using the method (2.4.1). Similarly, in [ZIM87] the experiment was based on A = metallic object, B = container, C = metallic container, and in [KOV92] on A = heavy objects, B = balls, C = heavy balls.

The experiment with tiles reported in [ZIM80] included $m = 24$ observations used to find the optimum aggregator

$$y_g = (x_1 x_2)^{(1-0.562)} [1 - (1 - x_1)(1 - x_2)]^{0.562}; \quad r(y_{observed}, y_g) = 0.971.$$

The quality of this approximation is evaluated using the coefficient of correlation r between the 24 observed (measured) values and the values predicted by the gamma aggregator. We performed the same experiment using the simple weighted power mean (WPM) of two variables and the preferential neuron training tool ANSY [DUJ91]. The resulting WPM aggregator is the following:

$$y_{wpm} = (0.448229 x_1^t + 0.551771 x_2^t)^{1/t}, \quad t = 0.376647 \, ; \, r(y_{observed}, y_{wpm}) = 0.978.$$

So, the WPM aggregator generates little better results and offers multiplicative normalized weights and idempotent soft partial conjunction with known andness, i.e., clear formal logic and semantic properties of the aggregation process.

The experiment with metallic containers reported in [ZIM87] (p. 216) included $m = 20$ observations. The gamma aggregator based on formula (2.4.1) and the GCD aggregator obtained using ANSY are the following:

$$y_g = (x_1 x_2)^{(1-0.474)} [1 - (1 - x_1)(1 - x_2)]^{0.474}; \quad r(y_{observed}, y_g) = 0.956;$$

$$y_{wpm} = (0.502009 x_1^t + 0.497991 x_2^t)^{1/t}; \, t = -2.314741, \, r(y_{observed}, y_{wpm}) = 0.987.$$

Again, the WPM aggregator provides slightly better results than the gamma aggregator. The WPM results are illustrated in Fig. 2.4.29.

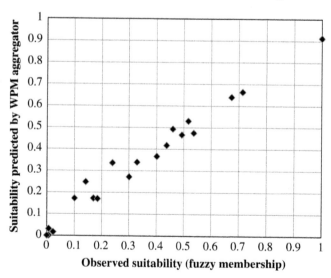

Figure 2.4.29 Observed results and their modeling using WPM aggregator.

Gamma aggregators have the property that they can extend the andness and orness outside the standard interval [0,1]. They also provide continuous transition between various degrees of andness by adjusting the parameter γ. For extreme values $\gamma \in \{0,1\}$ the gamma aggregator is hard (supports annihilators 0 and 1). Unfortunately, from the standpoint of evaluation logic, in the range $0 < \gamma < 1$ the aggregators $y_g(\mathbf{x}, \gamma, n)$ and $y_a(\mathbf{x}, \gamma, n)$ have the following logic drawbacks:

- Gamma aggregators are nonidempotent and the arithmetic mean (which is the centroid of logic aggregators) is not one of their special cases (the only exception is $y_a(\mathbf{x}, 0.5, 2)$).
- Two necessary aggregators, the pure conjunction $x_1 \wedge ... \wedge x_n = \min(x_1,...,x_n)$ and the pure disjunction $x_1 \vee ... \vee x_n = \max(x_1,...,x_n)$, are not special cases of the gamma aggregators.
- Transition between hard and soft conjunctive/disjunctive aggregators cannot be performed using the parameter γ.
- Neither $y_g(\mathbf{x}, \gamma, n)$ nor $y_a(\mathbf{x}, \gamma, n)$ can model the indispensable hard partial disjunction, restricting the use of gamma aggregators.
- Aggregator $y_a(\mathbf{x}, \gamma, n)$ is strictly soft.
- Aggregator $y_g(\mathbf{x}, \gamma, n)$ provides a hard partial conjunction. The indispensable soft partial conjunction is not available.
- Neither the parameter γ nor the weights have a simple logic interpretation so that decision makers could intuitively select their most appropriate values.
- Selection of parameters of aggregators needs unacceptably large number of domain experts (18 in the creditworthiness problem in [ZIM87]). That reduces the affordable number of inputs in evaluation models.

The listed logic drawbacks make gamma aggregators unacceptable in many cases: e.g., most medical evaluations (Chapter 4.3) that depend on predominantly disjunctive aggregators cannot be modeled using $y_g(\mathbf{x}, \gamma, n)$, all criteria that depend on asymmetric aggregators (partial absorptions) cannot be modeled, and most significantly, in all cases where idempotency is a necessary property the inadequacy of gamma aggregators becomes obvious.

Gamma aggregators were used as components in evaluation models. The largest gamma aggregator-based evaluation model in [ZIM87, ZIM96] is an 8-input binary tree model of creditworthiness. The development of the model engaged 18 banking domain experts for 15 hours to develop 21 parameters of the creditworthiness model. However, industrial evaluation problems include much bigger number of inputs, as well as trees that are not only binary but have more branches in each node. For example, a GCD-based LSP model for evaluating data management systems for the National Bureau of Standards (currently NIST), developed in 1981 and presented in detail in [SU87], uses 147 inputs. Such number of inputs requires a different role of domain experts and much easier design of evaluation criteria. Below we use gamma aggregators to exemplify this general problem.

Most mathematical models of observable natural phenomena use some input values and produce some output values (results). For example, in the case of GL, inputs of basic logic aggregator (GCD) are two or more input degrees of truth and the output is an aggregated degree of truth. Such models also include parameters that are used to adjust the properties of the model. In the GCD example, the parameters of the aggregation model are the degree of conjunction (andness) and the degrees of importance (weights) of inputs. Mathematical models of natural phenomena can frequently be classified in two large groups: (1) *models that reflect intrinsic nature of the analyzed process and can explain, predict and extrapolate observed phenomena*, and (2) *models that only fit and interpolate observed or measured data*. The primary difference between these groups is in the role and the use of parameters.

In the case of GL models, the first group usually has parameters that have clear interpretation as human percepts and can be directly selected by decision makers in order to adjust desired properties and behavior of the model. Weights and andness/orness are such parameters. An adjusted model can then be used to explain and predict the behavior of a modeled natural phenomenon, such as logic aggregation of degrees of truth. In the case of evaluation models, the parameters can be selected *a priori* by a trained user in order to secure a desired logic behavior of the model. If the natural phenomenon is observable and measurable, then the parameters can also be determined *a posteriori* by selecting the parameters that produce the best fit of the measured input/output relation. Such parameters are then used for explaining/understanding the properties of the analyzed phenomenon. In the GCD example, evaluators select the desired andness and the desired relative importance (weights) of inputs and then use the obtained model for any combination of input degrees of truth. In the case illustrated in Fig 2.4.29, the derived parameters are the andness of approximately 84% (corresponding to the WPM exponent of -2.31) and approximately equal weights of inputs.

The second group of mathematical models can adjust parameters only *a posteriori*. We first have to have measurements, and then we adjust parameters of a selected model so to optimally fit the measurements. However, the adjusted parameters do not have any particular interpretation. Traditional neural networks can serve as a typical example. The back propagation algorithm [LAW94] adjusts many parameters in layers of neurons, and the values of these parameters taken individually have neither interpretation nor other meaning related to the analyzed process. They explain nothing about the process. Similarly, coefficients of interpolation polynomials defined in Tables 2.3.5 to 2.3.7 do not have any particular meaning except that collectively they best fit and interpolate the available data.

When faced with a complex process, such as modeling human perceptions, the first step is to perform measurements and to fit data with an initial mathematical model. The second step is to refine models to the extent where their parameters can be selected without measurements. The gamma aggregator is a typical initial model. It can fit the data, it shows the need for weights and continuous transition from AND to OR, but it cannot be used without fitting measurements.

To exemplify this problem let us use a simple aggregator of two variables y (x_1, x_2), $x_1, x_2 \in [0,1]$. Let us now compare a GCD aggregator and gamma aggregators with two inputs:

$$y_{\text{gcd}}(x_1, x_2) = W_1 x_1 \Diamond W_2 x_2, \quad 0 \leq \alpha \leq 1, \quad W_1 + W_2 = 1,$$

$$y_g(x_1, x_2) = (x_1^{p_1} x_2^{p_2})^{(1-\gamma)} [1 - (1-x_1)^{p_1}(1-x_2)^{p_2}]^{\gamma},$$

$$y_a(x_1, x_2) = (1-\gamma)(x_1^{p_1} x_2^{p_2}) + \gamma[1 - (1-x_1)^{p_1}(1-x_2)^{p_2}], \quad p_1 + p_2 = 2, \quad 0 \leq \gamma \leq 1.$$

All models have three parameters: GCD uses two weights and andness, and the gamma aggregator uses two weights and the gamma parameter. Now, let us satisfy these conditions:

- We want to model equal intensity of simultaneity and substitutability (equal presence of conjunctive and disjunctive properties, i.e., logic neutrality).
- The first input is three times more important than the second input (e.g., $y(1,0) = 3y(0,1)$ or $\partial y/\partial x_1 = 3\partial y/\partial x_2$).

In the case of GCD, we want to have andness equal orness and that means we have to use the arithmetic mean. Since the GCD weights are normalized and $W_1 = 3W_2$ the desired aggregator is

$$y_{\text{gcd}}(x_1, x_2) = 0.75x_1 + 0.25x_2, \quad y_{\text{gcd}}(1,0) = 3y_{\text{gcd}}(0,1), \partial y_{\text{gcd}}/\partial x_1 = 3\partial y_{\text{gcd}}/\partial x_2.$$

In the case of multiplicative gamma aggregator, we cannot answer the question in a simple and direct way. First, the middle value $\gamma = 0.5$ is not providing equal presence of conjunctive and disjunctive properties (to get $\alpha = 0.5$ we need $\gamma = 0.69$). Second, there is no rule for selecting the gamma aggregator weights based on relative importance. If we can have a set of desired triplets $(x_1[i], x_2[i], y_g[i], \quad i = 1,...,m)$ provided by domain experts, then we could select one of classic function minimization algorithms [NEL64, PAU78, POW64] to find the best values of parameters w_1, w_2, γ, which minimize the following error function:

$$E(w_1, w_2, \gamma) = \sum_{i=1}^{m} \left| y_g[i] - (x_1^{w_1}[i]x_2^{w_2}[i])^{(1-\gamma)} [1 - (1-x_1^{w_1}[i])(1-x_2^{w_2}[i])]^{\gamma} \right|.$$

Therefore, regardless the facts that γ determines the position between the conjunctive product and its disjunctive dual, and the weights are related to the concept of importance, we cannot directly select these parameters even in the simplest case of logic neutrality. In addition, the necessary training set of triplets generally comes from a large group of domain experts [ZIM80, ZIM87, ZIM96, KOV92] and that makes the process inconvenient and expensive. We also have the problem that $y_g(1,0) = y_g(0,1) = 0$, which shows that the gamma aggregator is predominantly conjunctively polarized: it has the annihilator 0 (but not the symmetric annihilator 1), causing difficulties in modeling of disjunctive criteria.

In the case of additive version of gamma aggregator, which is less conjunctive than the multiplicative version, we can try $\gamma = 0.5$ and appropriate weights $w_1 = 1.5$, $w_2 = 0.5$, but we again face the same problem of incorrect importance ratio:

$$y_a(x_1, x_2) = 0.5\left(x_1^{1.5} x_2^{0.5}\right) + 0.5\left[1 - (1 - x_1)^{1.5}(1 - x_2)^{0.5}\right],$$

$$y_a(0,1) = 0.5, \quad y_a(1,0) = 0.5 = y_a(0,1).$$

It is easy to see that if $\gamma = 0.5$ than $y_a(1,0) = y_a(0,1)$ for any combination of weights and the impact of weights is eliminated in some points of the unit hypercube. The same problem is present for any number of variables.

Gamma aggregators are useful to understand the importance of direct versus indirect representation of human percepts: the parameter γ is related to the percept of andness, but *indirectly and nonlinearly*, and the exponential weights $p_1, ..., p_n$, $p_1 + ... + p_n = n$ are related to the percepts of importance, but also *indirectly and nonlinearly*. As opposed to that, interpolative GCD aggregators use the percepts of andness and importance *directly*, as parameters of all logic models. That is a fundamental difference that enables efficient development of large LSP logic aggregation structures.

There are four fundamental advantages of EGCD with respect to similar aggregators of Zimmerman and Zysno [ZIM80] and Krishnapuram and Lee [KRI92]:

1) Linear transition from intersection to union controlled directly by the andness and orness and not by parameters that nonlinearly map to andness/orness.
2) Symmetry with respect to the central neutrality aggregator.
3) Independent parameterized adjustability of the regions of hard and soft partial conjunction and hard and soft partial disjunction.
4) A balanced mix of conjunctive and disjunctive properties with flexible selection of weights that directly reflect the percept of importance (as opposed to using parameters that indirectly and nonlinearly affect the resulting importance effects).

Therefore, GCD aggregators belong to the group of models that support perceptual computing by explaining and predicting the process of aggregation of subjective categories, while gamma aggregators belong to the group of models that are primarily used to fit data provided by domain experts.

2.4.12 Four Main Families of GCD Aggregators and Sixteen Conditions They Must Satisfy

Graded conjunction/disjunction aggregators $W_1x_1 \diamond \cdots \diamond W_nx_n = A(\mathbf{x}; \mathbf{W}, \alpha)$ are logic models of simultaneity and substitutability. They are used in GL to create compound aggregators, from the simplest cases with two inputs to complex aggregation structures with several hundred inputs. In evaluation decision problems the necessary logic properties of GL aggregators include 16 requirements specified in the following proposition.

Proposition 2.4.8.   Necessary properties of GCD logic aggregators.
In GL the GCD logic aggregators must satisfy the following necessary conditions:

1) Nondecreasing monotonicity in all arguments.
2) Boundary conditions in extreme points $(0,...,0)$ and $(1,...,1)$.
3) Validity in the whole unit hypercube divided in four basic regions of idempotent and nonidempotent conjunctive, disjunctive, hyperconjunctive, and hyperdisjunctive aggregators.
4) Internality, idempotency, and compatibility with Boolean logic in the central regions of the unit hypercube.
5) Continuous transition from idempotent to nonidempotent types of aggregators in the full range of andness (or orness) from $-1/(n-1)$ to $n/(n-1)$ (integration of all logic aggregators, including means, t-norms and beyond).
6) Continuity in all arguments.
7) Compensativeness for arguments in $]0, 1[^n$ and for andness in the whole range except four critical values: $\alpha \in]-1/(n-1), n/(n-1)[\setminus \{0,1\}$.
8) Sensitivity to positive and incomplete truth.
9) Support for semantics of aggregation: all variables have meaning, interpretation, and relative importance, yielding noncommutativity based on importance weights.
10) Support for annihilators 0 and 1 in the regions of hard properties.
11) No support for annihilators 0 and 1 in the regions of soft properties.
12) Mixed hard/soft support of annihilators in inputs of asymmetric aggregators.
13) Adjustability (or a convenient fixed/default location) of the threshold andness and the threshold orness.
14) Andness/orness parameterization: the availability of andness-directed or orness-directed aggregation.

15) Nonincreasing monotonicity in andness and nondecreasing monotonicity in orness.
16) De Morgan's duality of conjunctive and disjunctive aggregators.

These properties summarize the necessary logic conditions introduced in Chapter 2.2 and studied in previous sections of this chapter. For each of these requirements it is possible to find convincing examples where the nonsatisfaction of requirement creates unacceptable aggregation results. The natural way to satisfy all these requirements is to use interpolative aggregators presented in Sections 2.4.7 and 2.4.8. It is important to emphasize that the above list of 16 fundamental properties includes conditions that are fully justifiable and necessary in a general case; without their satisfaction we could not develop and use GL. It is also obvious that these conditions are restrictive and eliminate many general aggregators that satisfy the Definition 2.1.0. However, if any of the above 16 requirements is not satisfied, the resulting aggregators (and decision models that use them) would be inconsistent with observable properties of human logic reasoning in the area of evaluation. In a general case, such aggregators should not be used.

Unsurprisingly, there are many applications where only a subset of the listed 16 conditions is necessary, and the literature on aggregation includes many aggregators that satisfy only a subset of the above restrictive conditions. As we reduce the number of conditions, the number of candidate aggregators quickly increases. Eventually, in order to maximize the number of aggregation functions, the mathematical literature [GRA09, BEL07, MES15, BEL16], uses the absolute minimum of only the first two conditions from our list of 16, as specified in Definition 2.1.0. The natural result of such approach is that the number of possible aggregators is huge and the fraction of applicable aggregators is negligible. That is easily understandable because all restrictive conditions come from needs of specific application areas. Our 16 restrictive conditions come from the applicability in GL, or more precisely, in logic modeling of human evaluation reasoning.

We introduced GL as a complete logic system in all regions of the unit hypercube, from the drastic conjunction to the drastic disjunction. That is necessary in order to provide a sound theoretical background for logic evaluation models. However, in practical evaluation criteria we almost exclusively use idempotent GCD aggregators located in central regions of the unit hypercube. This is the reason why we now summarize this chapter by presenting a classification of four families of GCD aggregators with focus on idempotent members of the families, which we will use in the LSP method and its applications.

All applications in logic assume the adjustability of andness and the only practical way is to create and use andness rating scales that include L levels of andness (for details, see Chapters 2.9 and 3.4). The individual degrees of andness are then uniformly distributed and the difference between adjacent levels is $1/(L-1)$. Practical GL values of L are 7, 15, 23, or 9, 17, 25.

The granularity $L \in \{7,15,23\}$ is used for modeling UGCD where we have four groups of soft/hard conjunctive/disjunctive aggregators. Depending on desired precision we use $k \in \{1,3,5\}$ aggregators in each group, plus three fixed aggregators (conjunction, neutrality, and disjunction), giving the number of levels $L = 3 + 4k \in \{7,15,23\}$. The levels are numbered from 0 (for full disjunction) to $L-1$ (for full conjunction). The resulting sets of aggregators are denoted UGCD.7, UGCD.15, and UGCD.23. The threshold andness is always assumed to be at the level $\alpha = \frac{3}{4}$ and the level of the first hard conjunctive aggregator is $L_h = (3L-1)/4$ (i.e., 5 or 11 or 17).

The granularity $L \in \{9,17,25\}$ is based on modeling core aggregators with andness $\alpha_k = k/8$, $k = 0,\ldots,8$ and then (if we need higher precision) inserting equidistantly between them one or two additional aggregators. The result is a *general GCD aggregator* (denoted GGCD), where the threshold andness can be located in any of $(L-1)/2$ degrees above the middle neutral aggregator. The lowest precision system denoted GGCD.9 provides nine equidistant levels of andness. If we insert one aggregator between each pair of nine basic aggregators, the resulting system will have 9+8=17 levels of andness. It is denoted GGCD.17 and provides a medium precision. If we insert two aggregators between each pair of nine basic aggregators, the resulting high precision system will have 9+16=25 equidistant degrees of andness; it is denoted GGCD.25. The four main families of GCD aggregators and their members are presented in Fig. 2.4.30.

The four main groups of aggregators give a large number of options; naturally, the applicability of all of them is not the same. The basic ideas for selecting the most appropriate aggregators are outlined below.

SWM are rigid models characterized by insufficient flexibility: their threshold andness is fixed, and the location of threshold andness can sometimes be inconvenient. Nevertheless, SWM are the simplest of all GCD aggregators and consequently they are popular and useful in many applications. The most appropriate of them is the WPM, which is the only SWM that offers both soft and hard aggregation. WPM can be used either with continuously adjustable andness or with granulated andness (for low precision WPM.9 and for medium precision WPM.17). A disadvantage of WPM is that the range of soft conjunctive aggregation is narrow (between the arithmetic mean and the geometric mean, in the narrow andness range from ½ to approximately ⅔) and the range of hard aggregation is too wide. Disjunctive aggregation is only soft, unless it is replaced by De Morgan's dual of conjunctive WPM. We generally assume that WPM and CHM aggregators are always dualized to reflect user's needs.

The use of EXM is limited to cases where the aggregator is extremely soft, i.e., soft in the whole interval $0 < \alpha < 1$. Such cases are not frequent. For $0 < \alpha \le 0.5$, EXM behaves very similarly as WPM. EXM is naturally dual, but it does not offer other attractive properties.

(1) Simple parameterized weighted means with adjustable andness/orness (**SWM**)
    a. Weighted power means (**WPM**), most frequently **WPM.17**
    b. Exponential means (**EXM**)
    c. Counter-harmonic means (**CHM**)
(2) Idempotent uniform GCD aggregators (**UGCD**)
    a. **UGCD.7** – low precision (7 levels of andness)
    b. **UGCD.15** – medium precision (15 levels of andness)
    c. **UGCD.23** – high precision (23 levels of andness)
(3) Idempotent general GCD aggregators with adjustable threshold andness (**GGCD**)
    a. **GGCD.9** – low precision ($L=9$, $\alpha_\theta \in \{5/8,\ 6/8,...,1\}$)
    b. **GGCD.17** – medium precision ($L=17$, $\alpha_\theta \in \{9/16,\ 10/16,...,1\}$)
    c. **GGCD.25** – high precision ($L=25$, $\alpha_\theta \in \{13/24,\ 14/24,...,1\}$)
(4) Extended GCD aggregators (**EGCD**)from drastic conjunction to drastic disjunction
    a. Interpolative nonidempotent extended SWM
    b. Interpolative nonidempotent extended UGCD
    c. Interpolative nonidempotent extended GGCD

Figure 2.4.30 Twelve major members of the four main families of GCD aggregators.

The use of CHM is limited to cases where the aggregator must be conjunctive and hard in the relatively narrow range of its monotonicity, between the arithmetic mean and the harmonic mean. These properties are unique, and very restrictive. So, the standalone applicability of CHM is rather low. The most useful role of CHM is to fill the low andness and low orness hard aggregation gaps in general interpolative aggregators.

The group of uniform GCD aggregators is the most attractive from the standpoint of logic aggregation models. This claim is justified by the fact that humans provably use hard and soft conjunctive and disjunctive aggregators. Since at this time we have no evidence that any of these four groups is more frequent/important/useful than other groups, it follows that default versions of aggregators must support uniform distribution of hard and soft properties. The result is the UGCD family of aggregators and three levels of precision. The low precision is acceptable in cases where simplicity is the main goal, and such cases are frequent in the context of introductory education in this area. Medium precision is the most convenient in applications because it offers sufficient granularity and low complexity of use (see details in Chapter 3.4). Indeed, UGCD.15 provides a good compromise between the simplicity and precision. In the area of professional evaluation, the use of software tools for designing aggregators can create the need for higher granularity, and that is where high precision groups of aggregators become necessary.

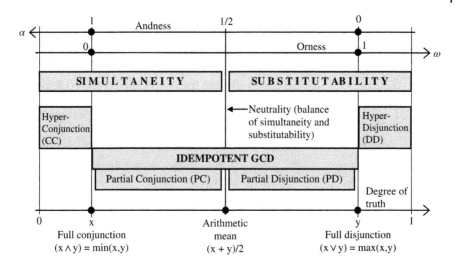

Figure 2.4.31 Summary of simultaneity and substitutability models for aggregating x and y.

The GGCD and EGCD groups of aggregators are primarily generalizations of the UGCD group. In all cases where there are reasons to request threshold andness different from 0.75, we should use GGCD. Experiments with decision makers show the distribution of threshold andness that includes aggregators below and above the 0.75 level (i.e., below and above the medium conjunctive aggregator CA). We use GGCD aggregators that cover the whole spectrum of threshold andness, from extremely soft to extremely hard, and offer adjustable precision.

The EGCD aggregators are a nonidempotent extension of basic idempotent GCD aggregators and connection with t-norms/conorms and similar functions. In some decision situations, we need hyperconjunction and hyperdisjunction, and in such cases EGCD offers parameterized adjustable aggregators that include the popular product t-norm. The summary of main logic models of simultaneity and substitutability is presented in Fig. 2.4.31.

Since this is a chapter about GCD aggregators, it is useful to provide a ranking of aggregators from the standpoint of their applicability in GL evaluation models. From the standpoint of utility, applicability, frequency, and importance of aggregators in logic aggregation models used in GL our general ranking is the following:

1) UGCD.15 (in educational environment preceded by UGCD.7)
2) WPM.17 (either natural or dualized)
3) GGCD.17 with the threshold andness close to 0.75
4) All other aggregators

Of course, while our interest in SWM, UGCD, GGCD, and EGCD is primary focused on GL and logic aggregation, there is nothing that restricts the use of these aggregators in other areas. More details about selection and use of UGCD and GGCD aggregators can be found in Chapter 3.4.

GCD aggregators are the core components of graded logic. It is essential that these aggregators satisfy the fundamental 16 conditions presented in Proposition 2.4.8. More precisely, *the graded logic is a formal system built on three fundamental components:*

1) *Thirty-three observable properties of human evaluation reasoning* (Chapter 2.2).
2) *The graded logic conjecture specifying 10 necessary and sufficient GL functions* (Section 2.1.8).
3) *Sixteen necessary properties of GCD logic aggregators* (Proposition 2.4.8).

These properties and conditions are necessary to provide models of human reasoning used in intuitive aggregation of degrees of truth of value statements. Such models are also used in professional evaluation based on the LSP method. In all cases, arguments of GL functions have clear semantic identity: they are degrees of truth of value statements that reflect the satisfaction of stakeholder's goals and requirements. The conclusion of this chapter is that it is possible to develop GL that has all desired properties and uses interpolative aggregators that satisfy all 16 necessary conditions. One such aggregator is presented in Fig. 2.4.24.

There are many aggregators that are popular in literature but do not satisfy our list of 16 necessary requirements. Such aggregators are not suitable as models of simultaneity and substitutability in graded evaluation logic. Examples are OWA [YAG88, YAG97], gamma [ZIM80], t-norms and t-conorms [FOD94], unweighted fixed-andness means [GIN58, BUL03], and many other complex aggregators presented in mathematical aggregation literature [GRA09, BEL07, BEL16]. Some of the listed aggregators are only soft (e.g., the classic OWA), some of them are only hard (e.g., the multiplicative gamma), some of them are predominantly nonidempotent (only hyperconjunctive or hyperdisjunctive) and/or have discontinuities (e.g., some t-norms and t-conorms), and many of them are strictly unweighted and have fixed andness (e.g., various specific means). Consequently, such aggregators are insufficiently compatible with observable properties of human evaluation reasoning, and their applicability is outside the area of graded logic aggregation.

2.5 The Percept of Importance and the Use of Weights

> *The purpose of computing is insight, not numbers.*
> Richard Hamming

The percept of importance is the fundamental component in evaluation reasoning and in intuitive aggregation of degrees of truth. This is a semantic component—it is based on understanding the definition, origin, and the role of each input degree of truth, as well as its impact on attaining stakeholder's goals. Therefore, modeling importance is indispensable for development of evaluation criteria.

The presence of the percept of importance in many areas of human reasoning shows that this fundamental percept should regularly be present in mathematical logic. Unfortunately, that is not the case. From the time of Aristotle to the time of Augustus De Morgan and George Boole, all degrees of truth were considered equally important. It is difficult to explain why for many centuries logic was studied primarily as a theoretical mathematical discipline, and not as a discipline of practical modeling of human mental activity. Unsurprisingly, modeling the percept of importance is a fundamental topic in graded logic, and we study it in this chapter.

Human evaluation reasoning evidently combines formal logic and semantic components. If the inputs of an aggregator have any meaningful role and interpretation, they will immediately and automatically have perceptible degrees of importance. We can safely claim that degrees of importance are indispensable whenever arguments are degrees of truth. Indeed, degrees of truth are not anonymous real numbers (numbers without interpretation), because they quantify the truth of semantically rich value statements. In evaluation, each such statement is interpreted as a contributor to the overall suitability, and consequently, the individual contributions are generally different. Of course, if there is no clear and acceptable interpretation of the role and meaning of inputs, then there is no

Soft Computing Evaluation Logic: The LSP Decision Method and Its Applications,
First Edition. Jozo Dujmović.
© 2018 John Wiley & Sons, Inc. Published 2018 by John Wiley & Sons, Inc.
Companion website: www.wiley.com/go/Dujmovic/Soft_Computing_Evaluation_Logic

need for degrees of importance and all inputs can be unweighted and commutative. However, in decision engineering, we then unavoidably face another question: what is the reason for aggregating something that has no meaning and interpretation? Indeed, *the purpose of logic aggregation is insight, not numbers.*[1]

If mathematical logic models do not explicitly include degrees of importance, such models are far from the reality of human evaluation reasoning. Consequently, defining aggregators as commutative structures is equivalent to making them useless in the context of evaluation decision models. Human decision making is never performed in semantic vacuum.

Generally, whenever we have multiple desirable criteria, we try to satisfy all of them. The importance of satisfying a criterion depends on the role of that criterion in attaining stakeholder's goals. Criteria that contribute more to goal attainment are obviously more important than criteria with a lower contribution. It is difficult to find multicriteria decision problems where all individual criteria have exactly the same importance. Naturally, decision makers put the most effort into satisfying the most important criteria. As the overall importance of individual attributes decreases, we can reach the level where some insufficiently significant attribute criteria can be omitted without affecting the quality of decision.

Evaluation reasoning regularly includes aggregation of degrees of truth that have rather different degrees of importance. For example, for some homebuyers, the importance of home location can be significantly higher (or lower) than the importance of home quality, and the importance of affordable price can be higher (or lower) than the joint importance of the home location and quality. Of course, there are special cases where inputs of aggregation models have equal degrees of importance, but such special cases are not frequent in the context of evaluation and they primarily reflect the size of indiscernible differences of degrees of importance caused by insufficient expertise and/or perceptual imperfection of decision makers. For example, importance degrees are frequently selected in increments of 5%, and all inputs where importance degrees differ for less than 5% can be considered equally important. So, equal weights are frequently an expression of imprecision of criterion developer. Typical situations that clearly justify equal degrees of importance are various forms of voting, where all voters are assumed to have the same impact on the result of voting (e.g., equal degrees of importance are appropriate for averaging the votes of judges in various dance or figure skating competitions).

Each percept of importance can be expressed using a quantitative degree of importance, which is usually called *weight*. Degrees of importance are regularly verbalized and expressed using linguistic labels from rating scales in the range from very low to very high (see Chapter 2.9). In this chapter, we study the role

---

1 We might say the same for any kind of aggregation, provided that aggregation models have any applicability. In decision engineering, "why" must come before "how." In the theory of aggregation, "why" does not exist, and the whole interest is regularly focused on "how."

and use of weights as quantifiers of importance in models of human evaluation reasoning.

2.5.1 Multiplicative, Implicative, and Exponential Weights as Importance Quantifiers

A natural way to quantify weights is to use real numbers from a fixed interval. In the context of evaluation, we assume that weights in direct proportion express the degree of importance, which is always positive. Indeed, in the area of evaluation, weights cannot be zero. A zero weight obviously denotes the total insignificance of an input (elementary or compound attribute), and such inputs are justifiably excluded from consideration. Rational thinkers ignore insignificant inputs and focus on reasoning based on the "first things first" concept. So, in evaluation logic, weights are always positive, regardless of what theoreticians might think about it.

Inherently, importance is a concept based on comparison of alternatives. Nothing can be important in complete isolation from alternatives. The percept of importance is created in comparison with one or more alternatives that could be more or less important. For example, a homebuyer can have a percept of importance of the home location that is either higher or lower than the percept of importance of the quality of home. The percept of importance is also created in the process of comparison of various suitability degrees; e.g., the percept of importance of home location is created and adjusted in the process of comparing good and bad locations. In other words, weights are adjusted by selecting desired degrees of penalizing poor solutions and rewarding good solutions.

In the context of evaluation reasoning, the percept of importance must be limited. The lowest percept of importance is the first positive level of an importance rating scale, just above the insignificant and negligible. The highest percept of importance is the highest positive level of an importance rating scale.

Similarly to zero-sum games, increasing the relative importance (impact) of an input in a group of inputs automatically means decreasing the relative importance (impact) of all other inputs in the group. Therefore, the weights must be normalized. The most important normalization methods are the following:

1) **Sum-normalized weights** (constant sum of weights equal 1):

$$\mathbf{W} = (W_1,..., W_n), \quad W_1 + \cdots + W_n = 1, \quad 0 < W_i < 1, \quad i = 1,...,n, \ n > 1.$$

2) **Max-normalized weights** (constant maximum weight equal 1):

$$\mathbf{v} = (v_1,...,v_n), \quad \max(v_1,...,v_n) = 1, \quad 0 < v_i \le 1, \quad i = 1,...,n, \ n > 1.$$

3) **Count-normalized weights** (sum of weights equals the number of inputs n):

$$\mathbf{p} = (p_1,...,p_n), \quad p_1 + \cdots + p_n = n, \quad 0 < p_i < n, \quad i = 1,...,n, \ n > 1.$$

These weights are used in different contexts. Assuming that they express the same importance degrees, it is easy to transform one of them into another by keeping them proportional as follows:

$$W_i = v_i/(v_1 + \cdots + v_n) = p_i/n, \quad i = 1,...,n \ ;$$

$$v_i = W_i/\max(W_1,...,W_n) = p_i/\max(p_1,...,p_n), \quad i = 1,...,n \ ;$$

$$p_i = nW_i = nv_i/(v_1 + \cdots + v_n), \quad i = 1,...,n \ .$$

In the special case of equal importance and equal weights, the values of weights become $W_i = 1/n$, $v_i = 1$, $p_i = 1$, $i = 1,...,n$.

All forms of weights support the same "implication concept:" *it is not acceptable that an important input (requirement) is insufficiently satisfied.* If x denotes an input argument and w denotes its importance (weight), then the implication concept emerges in three characteristic forms:

- Multiplicative: $w \cdot x$
- Implicative: $w \to x = \overline{w \wedge \bar{x}} = 1 - [w \wedge (1-x)]$
- Exponential: x^w

All these forms support the same idea: if w is large, then x should also be large in order to provide a high contribution to the overall score. Multiplicative weights are used in additive aggregation forms and exponential weights are used in multiplicative aggregation forms. In the case of implicative weights, the situation is more complex because there are various algebraic ways to implement the necessary negation and conjunction. The simplest way to implement conjunction is to use a product, yielding the Reichenbach implication $w \to x = 1 - w(1-x)$.

If the sum of weights is selected to be constant (1 or n) then all weights must be positive and less than the sum of weights. The reasons why weights cannot be 0 or the maximum value are similar: zero weights mean that we consider totally irrelevant and justifiably negligible inputs, and if a weight takes the maximum value (which is the sum of weights), then the selected input is so significant that it excludes the existence of all other inputs in a group of n inputs. Hence, $0 < W_i < 1$ and $0 < p_i < n$, $i = 1,...,n$, $n > 1$.

2.5.1.1 Multiplicative Weights

The idea of multiplicative weights is that the impact of an input suitability on the output suitability is directly proportional to the weight of input, as in the simple case of arithmetic mean $y = W_1 x_1 + \cdots + W_n x_n$. By multiplying weight and suitability (or a function of suitability, like $y = F^{-1}[W_1 F(x_1) + \cdots + W_n F(x_n)]$), those inputs that are more important are more rewarded for having high suitability (and more penalized for having low suitability) than less important inputs. In other words, the product $W_i x_i$ means that it is not acceptable that W_i is high (very important) and the suitability x_i is low. Note that this is the same interpretation as one used by implication $W_i \rightarrow x_i = \overline{W_i \wedge \bar{x}_i} = \overline{W}_i \vee x_i$.

Weights are usually selected with intention to affect the sensitivity of output w.r.t. an input or a parameter of the analyzed model. A sensitivity coefficient is defined as a derivative of output value (y) w.r.t. selected variable (e.g., the input x_i): $\partial y / \partial x_i$. A dimensionless logarithmic sensitivity $\partial(\log y)/\partial(\log x_i) = (\partial y / \partial x_i)(x_i / y)$ is also frequently used to express the importance of selected input x_i. The logarithmic sensitivity denotes how a small relative increment/decrement of an input variable $\Delta x_i / x_i$ affects the corresponding small relative increment/decrement of the output value $\Delta y / y$:

$$\frac{\partial(\log y)}{\partial(\log x_i)} \approx \frac{\Delta y / y}{\Delta x_i / x_i}.$$

For the arithmetic mean and the geometric mean, we have:

$$y = \sum_{i=1}^{n} W_i x_i \quad \Rightarrow \quad \frac{\partial y}{\partial x_i} = W_i \; ;$$

$$y = \prod_{i=1}^{n} x_i^{W_i} \quad \Rightarrow \quad \frac{\partial(\log y)}{\partial(\log x_i)} = W_i \; .$$

Multiplicative weights are positive and normalized: $0 < W_i < 1$, $W_1 + \cdots + W_n = 1$. In a general case, multiplicative weights multiply strictly increasing or strictly decreasing functions of input suitability degrees, as in the case of andness-directed weighted power means:

$$y = M(\mathbf{x}; \mathbf{W}, \alpha) = \left(W_1 x_1^{r_n(\alpha)} + \cdots + W_n x_n^{r_n(\alpha)} \right)^{1/r_n(\alpha)}, \quad 0 \le \alpha \le 1,$$

$$y^{r_n(\alpha)} = W_1 x_1^{r_n(\alpha)} + \cdots + W_n x_n^{r_n(\alpha)} \; ;$$

$$\frac{\partial}{\partial x_i} y^{r_n(\alpha)} = r_n(\alpha) y^{r_n(\alpha)-1} \frac{\partial y}{\partial x_i} = r_n(\alpha) W_i x_i^{r_n(\alpha)-1},$$

$$\frac{\partial y}{\partial x_i} = W_i \left(\frac{x_i}{y} \right)^{r_n(\alpha)-1} , \qquad \frac{\partial y}{\partial x_i} \cdot \frac{x_i}{y} = \frac{\partial \log y}{\partial \log x_i} = W_i \left(\frac{x_i}{y} \right)^{r_n(\alpha)}.$$

If $x_i = y$ (or if $\alpha = 1/2$, $r_n(\alpha) = 1$), then $\partial y / \partial x_i = W_i$, and in these cases, W_i is directly a sensitivity coefficient of output suitability w.r.t. selected input suitability. In all other cases, both the sensitivity of output suitability to changes of input suitability and the corresponding logarithmic sensitivity are proportional to the degree of importance W_i.

In a more general case of quasi-arithmetic means, we have a similar situation:

$$y = F^{-1}(W_1 F(x_1) + \cdots + W_n F(x_n)) , \quad F(y) = W_1 F(x_1) + \cdots + W_n F(x_n) ;$$

$$\frac{\partial F(y)}{\partial x_i} = \frac{\partial F(y)}{\partial y} \frac{\partial y}{\partial x_i} = W_i \frac{\partial F(x_i)}{\partial x_i} , \quad \frac{\partial y}{\partial x_i} = W_i \left(\frac{\partial F(x_i)}{\partial x_i} \bigg/ \frac{\partial F(y)}{\partial y} \right) ,$$

$$x_i = y \quad \Rightarrow \quad \frac{\partial y}{\partial x_i} = W_i .$$

Thus, multiplicative weights directly affect the input-output sensitivity of aggregators.

The output suitability of graded conjunction/disjunction must be a nonincreasing function of andness. This is a fundamental logic requirement: if we increase the degree of simultaneity, we increase the degree of penalizing low inputs, resulting in the decrease of the output of GCD aggregators. In most cases, GCD is a strictly decreasing function of andness for any combination of weights. This is exemplified in Fig. 2.5.1 for the dualized WPM aggregator $M(\mathbf{x}; \mathbf{W}, \alpha)$ and for the interpolative UGCD aggregator $U(\mathbf{x}; \mathbf{W}, \alpha)$. In the case of two variables, these aggregators are defined as follows:

$$M(\mathbf{x}; \mathbf{W}, \alpha) = \begin{cases} \min(x_1, x_2), & \alpha = 1, \\ \left(W_1 x_1^{r_2(\alpha)} + W_2 x_2^{r_2(\alpha)} \right)^{1/r_2(\alpha)}, & \tfrac{1}{2} \le \alpha < 1, \\ 1 - M(1 - \mathbf{x}; \mathbf{W}, 1 - \alpha), & 0 \le \alpha < \tfrac{1}{2}; \end{cases}$$

$$U(\mathbf{x}; \mathbf{W}, \alpha) = \begin{cases} \min(x_1, x_2), & \alpha = 1, \\ \left(W_1 x_1^{r_2(\alpha)} + W_2 x_2^{r_2(\alpha)} \right)^{1/r_2(\alpha)}, & \tfrac{3}{4} \le \alpha < 1, \\ (3 - 4\alpha)(W_1 x_1 + W_2 x_2) \\ \quad + (4\alpha - 2) \left(W_1 x_1^{r_2(3/4)} + W_2 x_2^{r_2(3/4)} \right)^{1/r_2(3/4)}, & \tfrac{1}{2} \le \alpha < \tfrac{3}{4}, \\ 1 - U(1 - \mathbf{x}; \mathbf{W}, 1 - \alpha), & 0 \le \alpha < \tfrac{1}{2}; \end{cases}$$

$$W_1 + W_2 = 1 .$$

For various values of W_1, W_2, x_1, x_2, Fig. 2.5.1 shows that (for both WPM and the interpolative UGCD) the impact of multiplicative weights disappears at the extreme values of andness $\alpha \in \{0, 1\}$. Consequently, multiplicative weights yield andness-dominated aggregators. In the case of implicative weights, the situation is different (implicative weights yield weight-dominated aggregators).

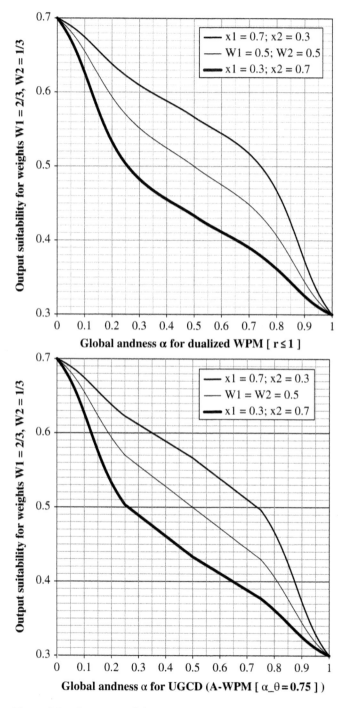

Figure 2.5.1 Output suitability as a monotonically decreasing function of andness.

2.5.1.2 Implicative Weights and the Weighted Conjunction/Disjunction

Traditional implication is a Boolean function of two variables $z = x \rightarrow y = \bar{x} \vee y$ where x is called the antecedent and y is called the consequent. It is true that antecedent implies consequent if the consequent is at least as true as the antecedent. Consequently, $z = 1$ in all cases except in the case $1 \rightarrow 0 = 0$. Another interpretation of implication is that it is not possible that the antecedent is satisfied and the consequent is not satisfied. In other words, the consequent should be interpreted as the consequence of the antecedent yielding the modus ponens tautology (formula that is always true): $(x \wedge (x \rightarrow y)) \rightarrow y = 1$.

In bivalent Boolean logic, the logic operations of conjunction, disjunction and negation can be modeled using arithmetic operations of addition, subtraction, and multiplication: $x \wedge y = xy$, $x \vee y = x + y - xy$, $\bar{x} = 1 - x$. Using these relations, it is easy to derive a similar formula for implication:

$$x \rightarrow y = \bar{x} \vee y = \bar{x} + y - \bar{x}y = 1 - x + y - (1-x)y = 1 - x + xy = 1 - x(1-y) = \overline{x\bar{y}}.$$

Applied on the unit interval, this form of implication is called the Reichenbach implication [REI34]. Obviously, the Dienes implication $x \rightarrow y = \max(1-x, y)$ and the Reichenbach implication $x \rightarrow y = 1 - x(1-y)$ are two different functions and they produce different effects if used in the context of GCD aggregators. Various forms of implication can be found in [FOD94, BAC08, ZIM96, BAC07, YAG80, YAG04a], as well as in Table 2.5.1.

Table 2.5.1 A dozen popular implications.

Name	$v \rightarrow x$	Name	$v \rightarrow x$
Dienes	$\max(1-v, x)$	Einstein	$1 - \dfrac{v(1-x)}{1+(1-v)x}$
Reichenbach	$1 - v(1-x)$	Hamacher	$1 - \dfrac{v(1-x)}{1-(1-v)x}$
Gödel	$\begin{cases} 1 & \text{if } v \le x \\ x & \text{otherwise} \end{cases}$	Goguen	$\begin{cases} 1 & \text{if } v \le x \\ x/v & \text{otherwise} \end{cases}$
Yager	x^v	Rescher	$\begin{cases} 1 & \text{if } v \le x \\ 0 & \text{if } v > x \end{cases}$
Lukasiewicz	$\min(1 - v + x, 1)$	Zadeh	$\max(1 - v, \min(v, x))$
Drastic	$\begin{cases} 1-v & \text{if } x = 0 \\ x & \text{if } v = 1 \\ 1 & \text{otherwise} \end{cases}$	Fodor	$\begin{cases} 1 & \text{if } v \le x \\ \max(1-v, x) & \text{if } v > x \end{cases}$

Implicative weights are based on the concept that "it is not acceptable that an input is important and insufficiently satisfied," yielding the following Dienes implication:

$$\overline{v_i \wedge \bar{x}_i} = (v_i \rightarrow x_i) = \bar{v}_i \vee x_i = \max(1 - v_i, x_i) = \begin{cases} 1 - v_i, & x_i \leq 1 - v_i, \\ x_i, & x_i \geq 1 - v_i, \end{cases}$$

$$\lim_{v_i \rightarrow 0} \bar{v}_i \vee x_i = 1, \qquad \lim_{v_i \rightarrow 1} \bar{v}_i \vee x_i = x_i, \qquad \bar{v}_i \vee x_i \geq x_i.$$

Implicative weights are maximum-normalized to give a constant maximum weight: $\max(v_1, ..., v_n) = 1$.

Since $v_i, x_i \in [0,1]$, $i = 1, ..., n$, both v_i and x_i can be interpreted as degrees of truth. The suitability x_i is the degree of truth of a *value statement*, such as, "The area of house completely satisfies our family requirements." Similarly, the weight v_i is the degree of truth of the *importance statement*, such as, "The area of house has the highest importance for our decision." The value statement and the importance statement are combined in human reasoning. They are orthogonal (independent) and can come in any order.

This truth-value logic interpretation is a unique feature of implicative weights. Multiplicative means and exponential means do not have the interesting property that semantic aspects of evaluation (degrees of importance) can be interpreted in the same way as the degrees of satisfaction. In this way, using implicative weights, evaluation models can be developed strictly inside the domain of logic, by combining the partial truth of value statements and the partial truth of importance statements. So, that is the primary reason for our interest in implicative weights.

The implication $v_i \rightarrow x_i$ can be called the "i^{th} contributor" to the result of an aggregator [DUJ07a]. The logic of this contributor is acceptable, but it is far from perfect. A high contribution is obtained either for insignificant inputs or for highly satisfied inputs. We would certainly like for the impact of x_i to be less significant for low degrees of importance and more significant for high degrees of importance. Unfortunately, for implicative contributors a low weight is acting as a shield (mask) for poor performance: if $x_i \leq 1 - v_i$ the poor performance of x_i is *not* becoming "less significant" but it is becoming *completely invisible* (i.e., it is excluded from evaluation). There is no difference between $x_i = 0$ and $x_i = 1 - v_i$. So, the impact of x_i is invisible in the whole range $x_i \in [0, 1 - v_i]$. Thus, the implication $\bar{v}_i \vee x_i$ is a *shielded contributor*, which, depending on weight v_i, protects the visibility of poor performance. That is certainly not what we need in evaluation criteria. On the other hand, it is easy to logically accept the criterion "we want simultaneous contributions from all inputs" expressed as the following weighted conjunction model:

$$y(\mathbf{x}, \mathbf{v}) = (v_1 \rightarrow x_1) \Delta \cdots \Delta (v_n \rightarrow x_n).$$

The basic drawback of this model is that in the default case, it means the following:

- Excellent performance $(x_i \geq 1 - v_i)$ is visible for all contributors.
- Poor performance is visible only for sufficiently important contributors.

The key idea of selectively including/excluding inputs based on degrees of their importance is generally questionable. Such an idea is frequently unacceptable in evaluation criteria where our main goal is to provide equal visibility and equal opportunities for all contributions, big and small. However, implicative weights are very present in the literature, and it is necessary to evaluate their usability in GL and in the area of evaluation.

The weighted conjunction and the weighted disjunction were first proposed by Ronald R. Yager in the context of information retrieval [YAG87] (see also [YAG04] for weighted t-norms). Unsurprisingly, information retrieval queries are predominantly conjunctive starting from the pure conjunctive query $q(d) = x_1(d) \wedge \cdots \wedge x_n(d)$, which determines the suitability $q(d)$ of document d based of simultaneous satisfying n individual criteria $x_1(d), \ldots, x_n(d)$. Yager generalized this criterion by introducing the weighted conjunction based on weights $v_i \in [0,1]$, yielding a *general conjunctive query*:

$$q(d) = [(1 - v_1) \vee x_1(d)] \wedge \cdots \wedge [(1 - v_n) \vee x_n(d)].$$

Yager also suggested a further generalization where conjunction and disjunction are replaced by a t-norm (T) and t-conorm (S) respectively, as follows (for $n = 2$):

$$q(d) = T(S(1 - v_1, x_1(d)), \ S(1 - v_2, x_2(d))).$$

Of course, there are many t-norms and t-conorms and one of them is a product $q(d) = x_1(d)x_2(d)$ which can be then generalized using exponential weights as follows:

$$q(d) = (x_1(d)^{v_1} x_2(d)^{v_2})^{2/(v_1 + v_2)}$$

$$= x_1(d)^{p_1} x_2(d)^{p_2}, \quad p_1 + p_2 = 2 \ (\text{or } n \text{ in the case of } n \text{ variables}).$$

In the case of equal weights, this form of weighted conjunction reduces to product.

If we use the criterion $(v_1 \rightarrow x_1) \Delta \cdots \Delta (v_n \rightarrow x_n)$, then the point of departure is to note that "$\rightarrow$" denotes "some kind of implication" and "Δ" denotes "some kind of simultaneity," which is very different from "any implication" and "any simultaneity." This situation opens a can of worms, because there are many implications and many models of simultaneity. Table 2.5.1 shows a dozen popular implications, and Chapter 2.4 (and literature such as [FOD94, GRA09, BEL07, BEL16, LAR09, LAR12]) presents a spectrum of various simultaneity models. So, we have a matching problem: for any application we have to find the optimum combination of implication and simultaneity models.

All implications shown in Table 2.5.1 satisfy the conditions of implication in Boolean logic: $0 \rightarrow 0 = 1$, $0 \rightarrow 1 = 1$, $1 \rightarrow 0 = 0$, $1 \rightarrow 1 = 1$. Using Dienes implication (a form of implication defined in binary Boolean logic, and extended to interval $[0, 1]$) and the pure conjunction, it is possible to define weighted conjunction and weighted disjunction [YAG87], applicable as evaluation statements (and used in information retrieval), as follows:

$$y_\wedge(\mathbf{x},\mathbf{v}) = (v_1 \rightarrow x_1) \wedge \cdots \wedge (v_n \rightarrow x_n) = (\bar{v}_1 \vee x_1) \wedge \cdots \wedge (\bar{v}_n \vee x_n),$$
$$y_\vee(\mathbf{x},\mathbf{v}) = \overline{y_\wedge(\bar{\mathbf{x}},\mathbf{v})} = \overline{(\bar{v}_1 \vee \bar{x}_1) \wedge \cdots \wedge (\bar{v}_n \vee \bar{x}_n)} = (v_1 \wedge x_1) \vee \cdots \vee (v_n \wedge x_n).$$

A verbal interpretation of weighted conjunction is "all important inputs should be simultaneously satisfied." Similarly, for weighted disjunction, "at least one important input should be completely satisfied." Both the weighted conjunction and the weighted disjunction are idempotent:

$$(\bar{v}_1 \vee x) \wedge \cdots \wedge (\bar{v}_n \vee x) = x,$$
$$(v_1 \wedge x) \vee \cdots \vee (v_n \wedge x) = x.$$

The idempotency of weighted conjunction and weighted disjunction can be proved as follows:

$$v_m = \max(v_1,\dots,v_n) = 1, \quad m \in \{1,\dots,n\} \quad \Rightarrow \quad \bar{v}_m \vee x = v_m \wedge x = x,$$
$$(\bar{v}_i \vee x) \geq x, \quad i = 1,\dots,n,$$
$$(\bar{v}_1 \vee x) \wedge \cdots \wedge (\bar{v}_m \vee x) \wedge \cdots \wedge (\bar{v}_n \vee x) = (\bar{v}_1 \vee x) \wedge \cdots \wedge x \wedge \cdots \wedge (\bar{v}_n \vee x) = x,$$
$$(v_i \wedge x) \leq x, \quad i = 1,\dots,n,$$
$$(v_1 \wedge x) \vee \cdots \vee (v_m \wedge x) \vee \cdots \vee (v_n \wedge x) = (v_1 \wedge x) \vee \cdots \vee x \vee \cdots \vee (v_n \wedge x) = x.$$

Since $(\bar{v}_i \vee x_i) \geq x_i$ and $(v_i \wedge x_i) \leq x_i$, it follows that the weighted conjunction is greater than or equal to the pure conjunction and the weighted disjunction is less than or equal to the pure disjunction:

$$(\bar{v}_1 \vee x_1) \wedge \cdots \wedge (\bar{v}_n \vee x_n) \geq x_1 \wedge \cdots \wedge x_n,$$
$$(v_1 \wedge x_1) \vee \cdots \vee (v_n \wedge x_n) \leq x_1 \vee \cdots \vee x_n.$$

The weighted conjunction equals conjunction and weighted disjunction equals disjunction only if all weights are equal (i.e., if $v_1 = \cdots = v_n = 1$). In all other cases, there are indices $j \in \{1,\dots,n\}$ and $k \in \{1,\dots,n\}$, so that we have the following:

$$(\bar{v}_1 \vee x_1) \wedge \cdots \wedge (\bar{v}_n \vee x_n) = \min((\bar{v}_1 \vee x_1),\dots,(\bar{v}_n \vee x_n))$$
$$= \bar{v}_j \vee x_j = \begin{cases} \bar{v}_j & \text{if } \bar{v}_j \geq x_j, \\ x_j & \text{if } \bar{v}_j \leq x_j. \end{cases}$$

$$(v_1 \wedge x_1) \vee \cdots \vee (v_n \wedge x_n) = \max((v_1 \wedge x_1),...,(v_n \wedge x_n))$$

$$= v_k \wedge x_k = \begin{cases} v_k \text{ if } v_k \leq x_k, \\ x_k \text{ if } v_k \geq x_k. \end{cases}$$

Thus, the result of weighted conjunction and weighted disjunction in many cases can be a weight, and therefore independent (or very indirectly dependent) of the input degrees of truth. Regardless the formal correctness, these results deserve careful investigation because their logic validity and applicability in GL is highly questionable. Essentially, these results claim that in logic decision-making semantic components (relative weights) can dominate the formal logic components (degrees of simultaneity or substitutability). That is exactly the opposite of what we claimed in property P_{22} in Section 2.2.3. Our standpoint was that observations of intuitive reasoning indicate that, in the area of evaluation, formal logic aspects dominate semantic aspects and at the highest levels of simultaneity (or substitutability), the human percepts of overall importance are affected predominantly by formal logic aspects, causing the impact of weights (which denote relative importance) to fade out. Indeed, as the andness increases, the satisfaction of inputs becomes more and more important, increasing the importance of inputs so that at high levels of andness all inputs become extremely (i.e., equally) important. The same reasoning holds for the percept of importance as a function of orness. If that is not the case, then the resulting logic must be incompatible with the classical Boolean logic. For example, in the classical Boolean logic, if $x_1 = 1$ and $x_2 = 0$, then the pure conjunction gives $x_1 \wedge x_2 = 1 \wedge 0 = 0$. However, in the case of weighted conjunction, that is not the case if x_1 is four times more important than x_2 (i.e., $v_1 = 1$, $v_2 = \frac{1}{2}$): $(0 \vee x_1) \wedge (\frac{3}{4} \vee x_2) = (0 \vee 1) \wedge (\frac{3}{4} \vee 0) = \frac{3}{4}$. Consequently, if in the graded logic we decided to use the weighted conjunction and the weighted disjunction, we would lose the compatibility with classical Boolean logic, i.e., GL would no longer be a graded generalization of classical Boolean logic. It would reduce to Boolean logic only for equal weights (i.e., in cases when it is no longer semantically graded).

By definition, aggregators should aggregate inputs to create an aggregated output. How can weighted conjunction claim the status of aggregator if the result of aggregation is a weight that does not explicitly and directly depend on all inputs? Of course, one can claim that the output always depends on inputs, but indirectly and having insensitivity zones. In the previous example, we get the same result $\frac{3}{4}$ for all values $0 \leq x_2 \leq \frac{3}{4}$. Consequently, the weighted conjunction claims that if x_1 is four times more important than x_2, then that necessarily means that there is no difference between the cases $x_2 = 0$ and $x_2 = \frac{3}{4}$, regardless of the fact that the weighted conjunction is a model of simultaneity. How can we logically justify this bizarre claim? We should find a convincing example where human reasoning manipulates percepts in this way, and if we cannot find it, then we must conclude that the weighted conjunction is not a logic aggregator, or at least not a model of human logic.

The concepts of *weight-domination* and *andness-domination* are conflicting concepts. The weight-domination is a consequence of weighted conjunction and of the properties of implicative weights. A simple way to show problems caused by the use of weighted conjunction in evaluation problems is to provide a convincing *reductio ad absurdum* example.

Suppose that a homebuyer reduced the decision about the home suitability (H) to two fundamental final components: the suitability of home location (L) and the quality of home (Q). Therefore, $H = f(L,Q)$ and there is no doubt that the function f is conjunctive because everybody simultaneously likes a good home and a nice location. Let us follow the usual mantra of real estate agents, "Location, location, location," and let the location be two times more important than the home quality (the owner can improve the quality of home, while the quality of location usually remains unchanged). If we use the weighted conjunction, then we have the following:

$$H_{wc}(L,Q) = (\bar{v}_L \vee L) \wedge (\bar{v}_Q \vee Q),$$
$$v_L = 1, \quad v_Q = 0.5 \quad \Rightarrow \quad H_{wc}(L,Q) = L \wedge (0.5 \vee Q).$$

This criterion yields the following completely meaningless results:

$H_{wc}(0.5,0) = 0.5$: An unacceptable home in an average location makes the homebuyer 50% satisfied.

$\forall Q \in [0,1] \Rightarrow H_{wc}(0.5,Q) = 0.5$: In an average location, homebuyer's satisfaction is always 50% and does not depend on home quality.

$H_{wc}(0.5,0.5) = H_{wc}(1,0.5) = 0.5$: An average home in an average location and an average home in an ideal location are equally desirable.

The problem we face with the weighted conjunction is clearly visible in the general case of weights $v_L = 1, 0 < v_Q < 1$, as follows:

$$\forall L \geq \bar{v}_Q, \quad \forall Q \leq \bar{v}_Q \quad \Rightarrow \quad H_{wc}(L,Q) = L \wedge (\bar{v}_Q \vee Q) = \bar{v}_Q = const.$$

Thus, this criterion absurdly claims that in the large range of values of input arguments L and Q the resulting suitability does not depend on arguments at all, but it is equal to the weight complement $\bar{v}_Q$. However, $\bar{v}_Q$ is a parameter that reflects the interests of homebuyer and has nothing in common with the specific properties of the evaluated object, while the properties of evaluated object (L and Q) are made irrelevant and completely neglected in a wide range of their values. Obviously, in the case of weighted conjunction, weights unjustifiably play the dominant role, and that property we call the *weight-domination*. In GL, this is not acceptable: we need the andness-domination and not the weight-domination.

The fundamental property of both weighted conjunction and weighted disjunction is that in the case of different weights these aggregators are *hard only for the largest input(s) and soft for all other arguments*. In the case of different weights, let us assume $1 = v_1 > v_2 > \cdots > v_n > 0$. Then, it is easy to verify the following hard and soft properties:

$$y_\wedge(x_1,\ldots,x_n;\mathbf{v}) = x_1 \wedge (\bar{v}_2 \vee x_2) \wedge \cdots \wedge (\bar{v}_n \vee x_n),$$

$$y_\wedge(0,1;\ldots,1;\mathbf{v}) = 0,$$

$$y_\wedge(1,0;\ldots,0;\mathbf{v}) = \bar{v}_2 > 0;$$

$$y_\vee(x_1,\ldots,x_n;\mathbf{v}) = x_1 \vee (v_2 \wedge x_2) \vee \cdots \vee (v_n \wedge x_n),$$

$$y_\vee(1,0;\ldots,0;\mathbf{v}) = 1,$$

$$y_\vee(0,1;\ldots,1;\mathbf{v}) = v_2 < 1.$$

In the case $n = 2$, $1 = v_1 > v_2 > 0$ and $x_1 = \frac{1}{2}$ we have:

$$y_\wedge(x_1,x_2;1,v_2) = x_1 \wedge (\bar{v}_2 \vee x_2), \qquad y_\vee(x_1,x_2;1,v_2) = x_1 \vee (v_2 \wedge x_2),$$

$$y_\wedge(\tfrac{1}{2},1;1,v_2) = x_1 = \tfrac{1}{2}, \qquad\qquad y_\vee(\tfrac{1}{2},0;1,v_2) = x_1 = \tfrac{1}{2},$$

$$y_\wedge(\tfrac{1}{2},0;1,v_2) = \tfrac{1}{2} \wedge \bar{v}_2 \le x_1, \qquad y_\vee(\tfrac{1}{2},1;1,v_2) = \tfrac{1}{2} \vee v_2 \ge x_1.$$

Consequently, for large importance of x_2 (in this example for $v_2 > \frac{1}{2}$) small or zero values of x_2 (i.e., $x_2 < x_1 < \bar{v}_2$) can penalize (reduce) the weighted conjunction. Large or maximum values of x_2 (i.e., $x_1 < x_2 < v_2$) can reward (increase) the weighted disjunction. However, the large values of x_2 (i.e., $x_2 > x_1$) cannot increase/compensate the weighted conjunction and small or zero values of x_2 (i.e., $x_2 < x_1$) cannot decrease the weighted disjunction. This form of insensitivity is questionable as a model of evaluation reasoning; e.g., in the case of weight $v_2 = \frac{1}{2}$ (x_1 is two times more important than x_2), we have the complete absorption of argument x_2:

$$y_\wedge(\tfrac{1}{2},x_2;1,\tfrac{1}{2}) = \tfrac{1}{2} \wedge (\tfrac{1}{2} \vee x_2) = \tfrac{1}{2} = \text{const.} \ne f(x_2),$$

$$y_\vee(\tfrac{1}{2},x_2;1,\tfrac{1}{2}) = \tfrac{1}{2} \vee (\tfrac{1}{2} \wedge x_2) = \tfrac{1}{2} = \text{const.} \ne f(x_2).$$

Generally, if $x_1 \le \bar{v}_2$, then $y_\wedge(x_1,x_2;1,v_2) = x_1$ and similarly, if $x_1 \ge v_2$, then $y_\vee(x_1,x_2;1,v_2) = x_1$. So, we can rightfully ask what logic reason can justify the complete elimination of the impact of argument x_2 in these cases. These asymmetric absorbent properties have more similarity with partial absorption then with conjunction or disjunction.

The implication-based conjunctive criterion $(v_1 \rightarrow x_1) \wedge \cdots \wedge (v_n \rightarrow x_n)$ is intuitively acceptable but in the case of Dienes implication $v \rightarrow x = 1 - [v \wedge (1-x)] = (1-v) \vee x$ it creates unacceptable results. Consequently, we might try another form of implication. The Reichenbach implication

$v \to x = 1 - v(1-x)$ differs from the Dienes implication only in using the arithmetic product instead of conjunction. Our conjunctive criterion could be modified in two characteristic ways (conjunction and product), as follows:

$$(v_1 \to x_1) \wedge \cdots \wedge (v_n \to x_n) = [1 - v_1(1-x_1)] \wedge \cdots \wedge [1 - v_n(1-x_n)] \quad \text{(conjunction)},$$
$$(v_1 \to x_1) \wedge \cdots \wedge (v_n \to x_n) = [1 - v_1(1-x_1)] \cdots [1 - v_n(1-x_n)] \quad \text{(product)}.$$

For the conjunction-based criterion $H_{rc}(L, Q)$ and for the product-based criterion $H_{rp}(L, Q)$ the homebuyer example now generates the following results:

$$H_{rc}(L,Q) = L \wedge [1 - 0.5(1-Q)]; \qquad H_{rp}(L,Q) = L[1 - 0.5(1-Q)];$$
$$H_{rc}(0.5,0) = 0.5, \quad (?) \qquad\qquad H_{rp}(0.5,0) = 0.25, \qquad\qquad (?)$$
$$H_{rc}(0.5,0.5) = 0.5, \qquad\qquad\quad H_{rp}(0.5,0.5) = 0.375, \qquad\quad (?)$$
$$H_{rc}(0.5,1) = 0.5, \quad (?) \qquad\qquad H_{rp}(0.5,1) = 0.5, \qquad\qquad\quad (?)$$
$$H_{rc}(1,0.5) = 0.75, \qquad\qquad\quad H_{rp}(1,0.5) = 0.75 .$$

The question marks denote cases where the Reichenbach implication yields obviously questionable (unacceptable) results.

The Reichenbach implication satisfies the same inequalities as the Dienes implication. For each $i \in \{1,\ldots,n\}$ we have

$$x_i \le 1 \mid \times (1-v_i),$$
$$x_i - x_i v_i \le 1 - v_i,$$
$$x_i \le 1 - v_i + x_i v_i = 1 - v_i(1-x_i) = v_i \to x_i,$$
$$x_1 \cdots x_n \le [1 - v_1(1-x_1)] \cdots [1 - v_n(1-x_n)] .$$

So, we generally have $x_1 \wedge \cdots \wedge x_n \le (v_1 \to x_1) \wedge \cdots \wedge (v_n \to x_n)$.

Aggregators related to weighted conjunctions and weighted disjunctions are reported to have applicability in the area of information retrieval. However, in GL, that is not the case: the presented meaningless results convincingly disqualify the analyzed forms of weighted conjunction (and we believe that they can be equally harmful in information retrieval). However, we have to be careful before we declare that all implicative weights and all weighted conjunctions/disjunctions are always inappropriate for aggregation in the context of evaluation criteria. The problem is that there are many forms of implication and many models of simultaneity. Obviously, some combinations are more suitable and some combinations are less suitable. In GL, the proper solution of the homebuyer criterion problem is any idempotent *hard partial conjunction*. For example, let us take a simple weighted harmonic mean:

$$H_{har}(L,Q) = \frac{1}{W_L/L + W_Q/Q} = \frac{LQ}{QW_L + LW_Q},$$
$$W_L = 2/3, \quad W_Q = 1/3 \quad \Rightarrow \quad H_{har}(L,Q) = (0.667L^{-1} + 0.333Q^{-1})^{-1}$$
$$= \frac{LQ}{2Q/3 + L/3} = \frac{3LQ}{L + 2Q} .$$

Here we again assume that the quality of home location is two times more important than the quality of the home. Following are four characteristic examples of results generated by this aggregator:

$H_{har}(0.5,0) = 0$ (an unacceptable home is rejected in any location),

$H_{har}(0.5,0.5) = 0.5$ (an average home in an average location gives average satisfaction),

$H_{har}(0.5,1) = 0.6$ (in an average location an ideal home satisfies 60% of requirements),

$H_{har}(1,0.5) = 0.75$ (in an ideal location an average home satisfies 75% of requirements).

These results are intuitively acceptable, and we can ask the obvious question: Is it possible to achieve such results using weighted conjunction based on an appropriate implication function? So, let us compare the implicative criterion $H_{imp}(L,Q) = (v_L \rightarrow L) \wedge (v_Q \rightarrow Q)$ and the GCD criterion $H_{gcd}(L,Q) = [w_L/(w_L + w_Q)]L \Diamond [w_Q/(w_L + w_Q)]Q$ in the case $v_L = 1$, $v_Q = 0.5$. For the implicative criterion we use all 12 implications defined in Table 2.5.1. For GCD we use the harmonic mean, which is a hard partial conjunction with andness 0.77, assumed to be an intuitively acceptable model of homebuyer's reasoning. The weighted absolute error of the implicative criterion depends on weights, and can be computed as follows:

$$\text{Error}(v_L, v_Q) = 100 \frac{\sum_{k=1}^{K} W(L_k, Q_k)\left|H_{\text{imp}}(L_k, Q_k) - H_{\text{gcd}}(L_k, Q_k)\right|}{\sum_{k=1}^{K} W(L_k, Q_k)} [\%]$$

The results of this analysis are shown in Table 2.5.2. We computed the value of harmonic mean (column Har) and all implications for nine combinations of arguments L and Q belonging to set $\{0, 0.5, 1\}$. For comparison of implicative weighted conjunction and the harmonic mean, we used weights $W(L_k, Q_k)$, also presented in Table 2.5.2. The idea of these weights is that some errors can be easier tolerated than other errors. Following are the reasons for weights 4,3,2,1 used for computing errors in the bottom rows of Table 2.5.2:

4 = Idempotency errors
3 = Boolean implication compatibility errors
2 = Annihilation errors
1 = Other errors

The results show three (highlighted) implications (Yager, Gödel, and Goguen) that offer the best results. Following is a summary of this analysis: (1) capabilities

Table 2.5.2 Comparison of 12 implication functions as models of implicative weights.

L	Q	W	Har	Die	Rei	Göd	Yag	Luk	Dra	Ein	Ham	Gog	Res	Zad	Fod
0	0	4	0	0	0	0	0	0	0	0	0	0	0	0	0
0	0.5	2	0	0	0	0	0	0	0	0	0	0	0	0	0
0	1	3	0	0	0	0	0	0	0	0	0	0	0	0	0
0.5	0	2	0	0.5	0.5	0	0	0.5	0.5	0.5	0.5	0	0	0.5	0.5
0.5	0.5	4	0.5	0.5	0.5	0.5	0.5	0.5	0.5	0.5	0.5	0.5	0	0.5	0.5
0.5	1	1	0.6	0.5	0.5	0.5	0.5	0.5	0.5	0.5	0.5	0.5	0	0.5	0.5
1	0	3	0	0.5	0.5	0	0	0.5	0.5	0.5	0.5	0	0	0.5	0.5
1	0.5	1	0.75	0.5	0.75	1	0.707	1	1	0.8	0.667	1	1	0.5	1
1	1	4	1	1	1	1	1	1	1	1	1	1	1	0.5	1
Error (1,1)			**0**	1.39	1.39	1.39	1.39	1.39	1.39	1.39	1.39	1.39	13.9	1.39	1.39
Error (1,0.5)			**0**	11.9	10.8	1.46	0.595	11.9	11.9	11	11.2	1.46	11.9	20.2	11.9

of various implications to serve as implicative weights vary in wide range; (2) in the case of equal weights all implications except one show the same (good) accuracy, and errors change with increasing difference between weights; (3) 3 out of 12 implications showed acceptable results and can serve in the context of weighted conjunction expressions; (4) the winner of this competition is the Yager implication [YAG80, YAG87] and the implicative aggregator

$$\left(v_L \rightarrow L\right) \wedge \left(v_Q \rightarrow Q\right) = L^{v_L} \wedge Q^{v_Q} = L \wedge Q^{v_Q}.$$

The root of some weighted implication problems is visible in the extreme case of classic bivalent Boolean implication, where $v \rightarrow x = 1$ in all cases except for $v = 1$, $x = 0$. Two cases yield correct interpretation: $1 \rightarrow 0 = 0$ means that it is not acceptable if an important input is not satisfied, and similarly, $0 \rightarrow 0 = 1$ means that it is acceptable if an insignificant input is not satisfied. However, since $1 \rightarrow 1 = 0 \rightarrow 1 = 1$, it follows that Boolean implication makes no difference if the satisfied argument is important or not important. Of course, this insensitivity is unacceptable in evaluation reasoning, and this problem then propagates from {0, 1} to [0, 1].

The $H_{har}(L, Q)$ results can be additionally precisiated by adjusting andness and weights. For example, a homebuyer can decide to use WPM (weighted power mean) as a GCD aggregator and adjust its parameters according to desired evaluation results using the preferential neuron training tool ANSY [DUJ91]. Following are results for three training sets:

$$H_{wpm}(1,0) = H_{wpm}(0,1) = 0 \ ;$$

$$H_{wpm}(0.5,0.5) = 0.5 \ \ (\text{common condition in all examples});$$

$$\left.\begin{array}{l} H_{wpm}(0.5,1) = 0.6 \\ H_{wpm}(1,0.5) = 0.7 \end{array}\right\} \Rightarrow H_{wpm}(L,Q)$$

$$= \left(0.62185 L^{-1.607793} + 0.37815 Q^{-1.607793}\right)^{-1/1.607793};$$

$$\left. \begin{array}{l} H_{wpm}(0.5,1) = 0.65 \\ H_{wpm}(1,0.5) = 0.75 \end{array} \right\} \Rightarrow H_{wpm}(L,Q)$$

$$= (0.603418L^{-0.22039} + 0.396582Q^{-0.22039})^{-1/0.22039};$$

$$\left. \begin{array}{l} H_{wpm}(0.5,1) = 2/3 \\ H_{wpm}(1,0.5) = 3/4 \end{array} \right\} \Rightarrow H_{wpm}(L,Q) = L^{0.584963}Q^{0.415037}.$$

Obviously, GCD/WPM aggregators can be easily adjusted to precisely reflect decision maker's needs, and create fully acceptable evaluation models. A similar analysis and similar conclusions hold in the dual case of weighted disjunction.

Weighted conjunctions can be organized with various models of conjunction. In addition, weighted conjunction and weighted disjunction can be natural limit cases of aggregators that perform continuous andness-directed transition from the weighted conjunction to the weighted disjunction. Such an aggregator was proposed by Henrik Legind Larsen. Larsen developed a graded conjunction/disjunction aggregator based on Reichenbach implication, called AIWA [LAR03, LAR09], and the remainder of this section is devoted to interesting properties of this aggregator. AIWA can be interpreted as a form of GCD where the weighted conjunction $y_\wedge$ and the weighted disjunction $y_\vee$ (based on Reichenbach implication) are special cases of AIWA for andness 1 and 0, respectively. The AIWA aggregator uses the maximum-normalized weights $\mathbf{v} = (v_1,...,v_n)$, $\max(v_1,...,v_n) = 1$ and the following implementation concepts:

1) The logic properties of AIWA are adjusted using the AIWA andness $a \in [0,1]$. The AIWA andness is similar, but not identical to the global andness α.
2) For $a \in [0,\frac{1}{2}]$ (extended disjunction) AIWA is implemented as a weighted power mean with exponent $r = 1/a - 1$ and weights $W_i = v_i^r/(v_1^r + \cdots + v_n^r)$, $i = 1,...,n$.
3) For $a \in [\frac{1}{2},1]$ (extended conjunction) AIWA is implemented as a De Morgan dual of extended disjunction.
4) Implicative weights are based on the Reichenbach implication [REI34] $v_i \rightarrow x_i = 1 - v_i(1 - x_i)$.
5) Taking into account that $v_i \rightarrow x_i = \bar{v}_i \vee x_i$, Reichenbach implication can also be interpreted as a model of disjunction: $\bar{v}_i \vee x_i = 1 - v_i(1 - x_i)$. Using De Morgan duality, the conjunction $w_i \wedge x_i$ can now be implemented as the t-norm algebraic product, $v_i \wedge x_i = \overline{\bar{v}_i \vee \bar{x}_i} = 1 - \bar{v}_i \vee \bar{x}_i = 1 - (1 - v_i(1 - \bar{x}_i)) = v_i x_i$.

Using the Reichenbach implication, it is possible to define weighted conjunction and weighted disjunction as follows:

$$y_\wedge(\mathbf{x};\mathbf{v}) = (v_1 \rightarrow x_1) \wedge \cdots \wedge (v_n \rightarrow x_n) = \min[1 - v_1(1 - x_1),...,1 - v_n(1 - x_n)];$$

$$y_\vee(\mathbf{x};\mathbf{v}) = 1 - y_\wedge(\mathbf{1}-\mathbf{x};\mathbf{v}) = 1 - \min[1 - v_1 x_1, \ldots, 1 - v_n x_n] = \max(v_1 x_1, \ldots, v_n x_n).$$

The AIWA aggregator includes the weighted conjunction and the weighted disjunction as extreme cases, as follows:

$$h(\mathbf{x};\mathbf{v},a) = \begin{cases} \max(v_1 x_1, \ldots, v_n x_n), & a = 0, \\[2mm] \left(\dfrac{\sum_{i=1}^{n} (v_i x_i)^r}{\sum_{i=1}^{n} v_i^r} \right)^{1/r}, & 0 < a \le \tfrac{1}{2}, \\[4mm] \left(1 - \dfrac{\sum_{i=1}^{n} (v_i(1-x_i))^{1/r}}{\sum_{i=1}^{n} v_i^{1/r}} \right)^{r}, & \tfrac{1}{2} \le a < 1, \\[4mm] \min[1 - v_1(1-x_1), \ldots, 1 - v_n(1-x_n)], & a = 1. \end{cases}$$

$$r = \frac{1}{a} - 1 = \frac{1-a}{a} = \frac{\bar{a}}{a}, \quad \max(v_1, \ldots, v_n) = 1,$$

$$\min[1 - v_1(1-x_1), \ldots, 1 - v_n(1-x_n)] = 1 - \max[v_1(1-x_1), \ldots, v_n(1-x_n)].$$

The parameter a is called the AIWA andness and it is similar to the global andness. At andness 1 and 0, AIWA becomes the implicative weighted conjunction and weighted disjunction respectively, based on Reichenbach implication. At andness ½, the AIWA aggregator becomes the weighted arithmetic mean. In the case of equal weights $v_1 = \cdots = v_n = 1$ the AIWA aggregator becomes the power mean:

$$h(\mathbf{x};1,a) = \begin{cases} \left(\dfrac{1}{n} \sum_{i=1}^{n} x_i^r \right)^{1/r}, & a \le \dfrac{1}{2}, \ r = \dfrac{1}{a} - 1 \ge 1, \\[2mm] & \text{(partial disjunction)} \\[2mm] \left(1 - \dfrac{1}{n} \sum_{i=1}^{n} (1-x_i)^{1/r} \right)^{r}, & a \ge \dfrac{1}{2}. \end{cases}$$

In the case of partial disjunction, the AIWA andness a is $a = 0.5 - c$, $0 < c \le 0.5$ and the exponent is $r = (1-a)/a = (0.5+c)/(0.5-c)$. In the symmetric case of partial conjunction, $a = 0.5 + c$, $0 < c \le 0.5$ and the corresponding exponent is again $1/r = a/(1-a) = (0.5+c)/(0.5-c)$. This shows De Morgan duality: the partial conjunction is De Morgan's dual of the partial disjunction and vice versa. Consequently, the AIWA aggregator can also be defined as follows:

$$h(\mathbf{x};\mathbf{v},a) = \begin{cases} \lim_{r \to (1-a)/a} \left(\dfrac{\sum_{i=1}^{n} (v_i x_i)^r}{\sum_{i=1}^{n} v_i^r} \right)^{1/r}, & 0 \le a \le \dfrac{1}{2}, \\[4mm] 1 - h(\mathbf{1}-\mathbf{x};\mathbf{v}, 1-a), & \dfrac{1}{2} \le a \le 1. \end{cases}$$

The consequence of using De Morgan duality is that numeric computations are always performed for partial disjunction and $r \geq 1$. In the case of $n = 2$ variables and equal weights, exponent r of the power mean is the following function of the global orness ω:

$$r = \frac{0.25 + 1.6016(\omega - \tfrac{1}{2}) + 1.0509(\omega - \tfrac{1}{2})^2 + 2.1631(\omega - \tfrac{1}{2})^3 - 3.3896(\omega - \tfrac{1}{2})^4}{\omega(1 - \omega)}.$$

Consequently, the AIWA andness and the global andness are related as follows:

$$a = \frac{\alpha(1 - \alpha)}{\alpha(1 - \alpha) + 0.25 + 1.6016(\tfrac{1}{2} - \alpha) + 1.0509(\tfrac{1}{2} - \alpha)^2 + 2.1631(\tfrac{1}{2} - \alpha)^3 - 3.3896(\tfrac{1}{2} - \alpha)^4},$$

$$0 \leq \alpha \leq 0.5, \quad 0 \leq a \leq 0.5.$$

Fig. 2.5.2 shows that $a < \alpha$, $0 < \alpha < 0.5$. Similarly, in this range AIWA orness is greater than the global orness.

Similarly to the exponential mean, the AIWA partial disjunction is a *soft aggregator*, and because of De Morgan's duality the corresponding partial conjunction is also soft. Therefore, AIWA cannot be used in cases where we need hard partial conjunction or disjunction aggregators. In addition, the implicative weighted conjunction and weighted disjunction based on Reichenbach implication are also soft. More precisely, they are hard in the case of the most important input and soft in the case of all less important inputs. In that sense they seem to be more related to partial absorption than to conjunction or disjunction. It is not

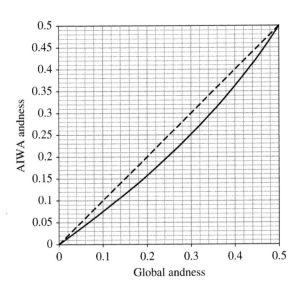

Figure 2.5.2 AIWA andness a as a function of the global andness α.

an observable human property that at the highest level of simultaneity or substitutability the slightest inequality of weights deprives an input of the right to be mandatory or sufficient. This AIWA property is inconsistent with the fact that the hard partial conjunction/disjunction can be observed in human reasoning already at the level of andness/orness below 75% (see Fig. 2.2.23 and [DUJ15a]).

In the case of logic aggregators, the output of GCD must be a monotonically decreasing function of andness. Indeed, any increase of andness increases the penalty for insufficient simultaneity, and the output suitability should monotonically decrease toward the minimum input value, as illustrated in Fig. 2.5.1 (property #15 in Proposition 2.4.8). Similar examples for AIWA aggregators yield results shown in Fig. 2.5.3. For some combinations of inputs and weights, AIWA output monotonically decreases when we increase andness, but for other combinations, that is not the case. Consequently, in a general case, AIWA does not have the status of logic aggregator.

All weighted aggregators $A(\mathbf{x}; \mathbf{v}, \alpha)$ that for extreme values of andness/orness reduce to Dienes version of weighted conjunction and weighted disjunction satisfy the following inequality:

$$x_1 \wedge \cdots \wedge x_n \le (\bar{v}_1 \vee x_1) \wedge \cdots \wedge (\bar{v}_n \vee x_n) = A(\mathbf{x}; \mathbf{v}, 1) \le A(\mathbf{x}; \mathbf{v}, \alpha) \le A(\mathbf{x}; \mathbf{v}, 0) =$$
$$= (v_1 \wedge x_1) \vee \cdots \vee (v_n \wedge x_n) \le x_1 \vee \cdots \vee x_n.$$

Therefore, for extreme values of andness/orness, such aggregators inherit all previously analyzed problems of weighted conjunction/disjunction.

This analysis of implicative weights and weighted conjunction shows that implicative weights currently provide a limited applicability in graded evaluation logic. We found six main problems with implicative weights in graded logic applications:

1) Implicative weights cause weight-dominated aggregation where, at the extreme levels of andness, instead of fading out, the weights can become a dominant contributor to the result of aggregation. This property prevents compatibility with classic Boolean logic.
2) There are significant differences of properties of aggregators in the case of equal weights, and the same aggregators in the case of different weights. There is also a weight insensitivity problem for highly satisfied arguments.
3) There are significant regions of insensitivity to variations of input values. That reduces both the compensativeness of aggregators and the desirable monotonicity.
4) Because of the absence of homogeneous annihilators, regardless of andness, the power of annihilation is reserved only for the most important input.
5) Implicative weights cause insufficient monotonicity of aggregation results with respect to andness/orness.

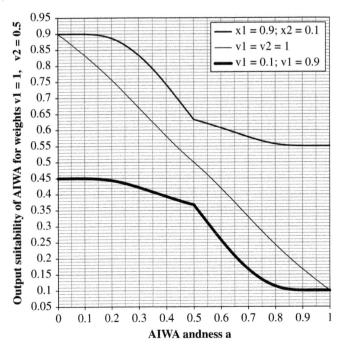

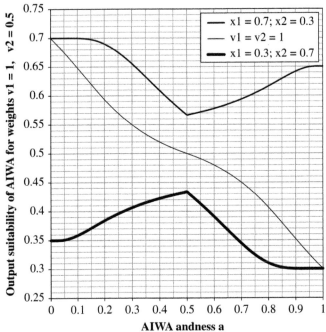

Figure 2.5.3 AIWA suitability as a function of AIWA andness.

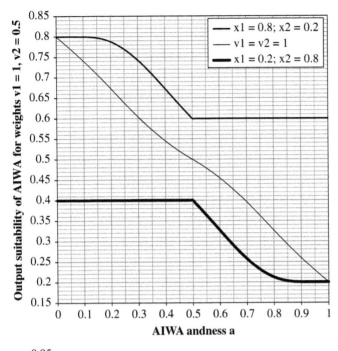

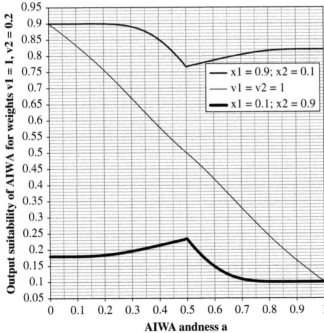

Figure 2.5.3 (Continued)

6) Predominantly soft aggregation is insufficient for modeling all observable properties of human evaluation reasoning.

Implicative weights and most of related aggregators seem to have a modest potential for applicability in modeling evaluation criteria. Taking into account the variety of existing implication functions, and the variety of simultaneity models, it is always necessary to match these two components to find the most convenient combination for each particular application area (in addition, it is necessary to show that the winning combination is better than GCD). Unfortunately, that can be a significant effort.

The conclusion (and the purpose) of this long section about implicative weights and the weighted conjunction/disjunction is that all logic models need verification and validation in intuitive human reasoning. Seemingly attractive correct mathematical models need additional justification to be acceptable as logic evaluation models. Mathematical correctness is a necessary condition in this area, but it is not sufficient.

2.5.1.3 Exponential Weights

Exponential weights are used in the context of multiplicative aggregators, such as gamma aggregators [ZYS79, ZIM80] and t-norms [YAG04]. In the case of modeling the intersection and union of fuzzy sets, the exponential weights have the fixed sum (n) as follows:

$$y_\cap(\mathbf{x};\mathbf{p},n) = \prod_{i=1}^{n} x_i^{p_i}, \quad y_\cap(\mathbf{x};\mathbf{p},n) = 1 - y_\cup(1-\mathbf{x};\mathbf{p},n),$$

$$y_\cup(\mathbf{x};\mathbf{p},n) = 1 - \prod_{i=1}^{n}(1-x_i)^{p_i}, \quad y_\cup(\mathbf{x};\mathbf{p},n) = 1 - y_\cap(1-\mathbf{x};\mathbf{p},n),$$

$$0 < p_i < n, \quad i = 1,...,n, \quad \sum_{i=1}^{n} p_i = n.$$

In multiplicative forms of criterion functions the low importance factors $x_i^{p_i}$ have a low impact if they are close to 1. Such factors must use small values of weight p_i. Similarly, high importance factors have high impact if they are close to 0. Such factors use large values of weight p_i. Exponential weights cause highly nonlinear amplification/attenuation of suitability illustrated in Fig. 2.5.4. Obviously, the product of n factors that are less than 1 causes in conjunctive cases low resulting values typical for hyperconjunction, or in dual disjunctive cases it causes high resulting high values typical for hyperdisjunction.

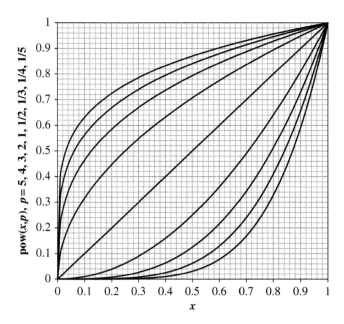

Figure 2.5.4 Exponential weights causing amplification or attenuation of suitability x.

In the special case of equal weights, all weights are equal to 1 and the models of intersection and union become the product t-norm and a dual t-conorm:

$$y_\cap(\mathbf{x};n) = \prod_{i=1}^{n} x_i \leq \min(x_1,...,x_n), \quad y_\cup(\mathbf{x};n) = 1 - \prod_{i=1}^{n}(1-x_i) \geq \max(x_1,...,x_n).$$

These aggregators are obviously nonidempotent, and therefore applicable in GL only in rare cases where evaluation models need nonidempotent hyperconjunctive or hyperdisjunctive aggregation. In such cases, they are used as interpolative extensions of idempotent GCD aggregators.

Unfortunately, it is not possible to intuitively select exponential weights because the product form of aggregators can produce large variations of the output value above and below the minimum input argument. For example, in the case of aggregator $z = y^p x^{2-p}$ if $y^p x^{2-p} = y$ then $x = y^{(p-1)/(p-2)}$. So, if $x > y^{(p-1)/(p-2)}$, then $z > y$ and if $x < y^{(p-1)/(p-2)}$ then $z < y$. This is illustrated for $y = 0.5$ in Fig. 2.5.5, where for $p = 0.5$ the condition for $z > y$ is $x > \sqrt[3]{0.5} = 0.7937$.

This example shows that it is difficult to intuitively select exponential weights that are consistent with specific form of human reasoning. Since the adjustment of exponential weights cannot be done intuitively, it must be based on software tools that fit a training set generated by domain experts [ZIM96]. Rare

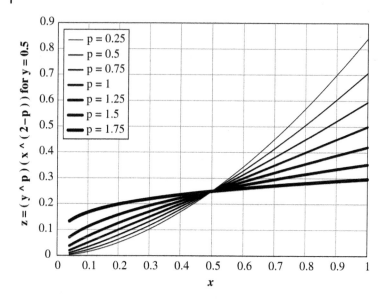

Figure 2.5.5 Sample output of a multiplicative aggregator with exponential weights.

applicability of hyperconjunction and hyperdisjunction, as well as difficulties in adjustment of exponential weights, reduce the significance of exponential weights in GL.

So far, we have studied two weighted generalizations of a simple product aggregator: the exponentially weighted product and the weighted geometric mean:

$$y(\mathbf{x}; \mathbf{p}, n) = \prod_{i=1}^{n} x_i^{p_i}, \quad \sum_{i=1}^{n} p_i = n$$

$$g(\mathbf{x}; \mathbf{W}, n) = \prod_{i=1}^{n} x_i^{W_i}, \quad \sum_{i=1}^{n} W_i = 1$$

These aggregators have two similar properties: (1) based on their product form, they are hard and conjunctive; and (2) both the weighted product and the geometric mean have fixed andness. However, there are also two significant differences between these aggregators: (1) the geometric mean is idempotent and conjunctive while the weighted product is nonidempotent and hyperconjunctive; and (2) the geometric mean can use intuitively selected weights, while the weighted product must select parameters using numerical procedures.

In the area of aggregation, multiplicative, implicative, and exponential weights are used as importance quantifiers. In the area of evaluation logic, these three methods do not have the same applicability. Multiplicative weights have by far the highest applicability. Their primary advantage is that it is easy to intuitively select their values based on desired relative importance of individual inputs. In addition, multiplicative weights are used in andness-dominated averaging operators, where their significance decreases as andness or orness approach their maximum values. This is consistent with human reasoning, where all inputs of hard aggregators are mandatory, regardless of differences in their relative importance.

2.5.2 Impact of Weights on Aggregation Results

Evaluation criteria must provide adjustable weights that represent the level of relative importance of inputs in a suitability aggregation process. Weights significantly affect the aggregation results. In this section we first analyze the impact of weights in the case of GDC/WPM aggregators $W_1 x_1 \diamond \cdots \diamond W_n x_n = \left(W_1 x_1^r + \cdots + W_n x_n^r \right)^{1/r}$. In the case of two variables, the impact of weights $W_1 = 0.75$, $W_2 = 0.25$ for various degrees of andness is shown in Fig. 2.5.6. The impact of weights is the highest for andness in the vicinity of 0.5 and then decreases as the andness approaches 0 or 1. In the case of arithmetic mean, we have $z(x,y) = 0.75x + 0.25y$ and $z(1,0) = 0.75$; that can be used to identify the more important variable (x). The less important variable (y) is identified by large value of slope $\partial z(x,y)/\partial y$ for CA and small values of y, as well as $z(0,1) = 0.005$ for C–. A more detailed presentation of the impact of GCD/WPM weights for fixed andness is shown in Fig. 2.5.7.

The first three versions of the CA aggregator presented in Fig. 2.5.7 show clear signs of hypersensitivity for small weights $W = 0.05$, 0.1, 0.15. The hypersensitivity (visible also in Fig. 2.2.31) shows the consequences of inconsistent importance requests: e.g., $W = 0.05$ specifies an input of very low (almost negligible) significance, while the medium andness hard conjunctive aggregator CA claims relatively high significance of all inputs. This inconsistency yields unrealistically high first derivative $\partial z/\partial x$ for the low significance input x. In the area of hypersensitivity, minor differences in x cause big differences in z what is not an observable property of human reasoning. However, if the variable x is binary, or incremented is steps that skip the hypersensitivity area, such aggregators are acceptable and applicable in evaluation models.

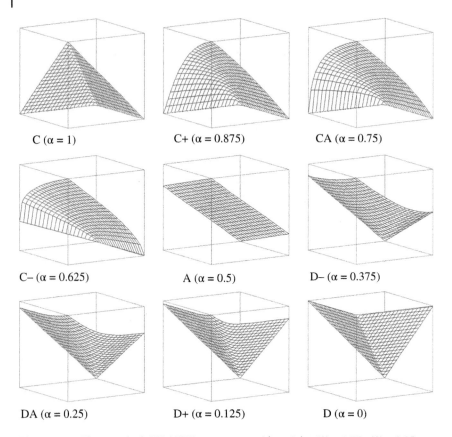

C (α = 1)   C+ (α = 0.875)   CA (α = 0.75)

C− (α = 0.625)   A (α = 0.5)   D− (α = 0.375)

DA (α = 0.25)   D+ (α = 0.125)   D (α = 0)

Figure 2.5.6 The non-dual GCD/WPM aggregator with weights $W_1 = 0.75$, $W_2 = 0.25$.

Let us now study the impact of weights on andness-directed UDCD, where the threshold andness is 0.5. Following is a dualized andness-directed UGCD aggregator in the case of two variables:

$$U_2(x,y;W,\alpha) = \begin{cases} \min(x,y), & \alpha = 1, \\ \left(Wx^{r_{wpm}(\alpha,2)} + (1-W)y^{r_{wpm}(\alpha,2)}\right)^{1/r_{wpm}(\alpha,2)}, & \tfrac{3}{4} < \alpha < 1, \\ (3-4\alpha)(Wx + (1-W)y) + (4\alpha-2)(Wx^R + (1-W)y^R)^{1/R}, & \tfrac{1}{2} \le \alpha \le \tfrac{3}{4}, \\ 1 - U_2(1-x,1-y;W,1-\alpha), & 0 \le \alpha < \tfrac{1}{2}, \end{cases}$$

$$R = r_{wpm}(\tfrac{3}{4}, 2) = -0.7201, \quad 0 < W < 1.$$

In this model, the weight W denotes the relative importance of input x, and $1 - W$ denotes the relative importance of input y. The presented form of UGCD

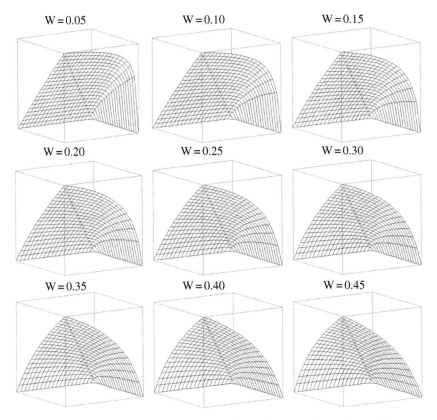

W = 0.05 W = 0.10 W = 0.15

W = 0.20 W = 0.25 W = 0.30

W = 0.35 W = 0.40 W = 0.45

Figure 2.5.7 CA aggregator ($\alpha = 0.75$) for weights in the range from 5% to 45%.

```
double UGCD2(double x, double y, double W, double alpha)
{
    if(alpha < 0.5) return 1.- UGCD2(1.-x, 1.-y, W, 1.-alpha);
    if(alpha > 0.995) return min(x,y);
    double   r   = r_wpm(max(alpha, 0.75) , 2);
    double   WPM = pow(W*pw(x,r) + (1.-W)*pow(y,r), 1./r);
    if(alpha > 0.75) return WPM;
    return   (3.-4.*alpha)*(W*x+(1.-W)*y) + (4.*alpha-2.)*WPM;
}
```

Figure 2.5.8 UGCD aggregator in the case of two variables.

aggregator is suitable for programming and the corresponding UGCD2 function is presented in Fig. 2.5.8; the auxiliary function r_wpm is shown in Fig. 2.4.16.

Fig. 2.5.9 shows the results of aggregation of two complementary variables (x and $y = 1 - x$) in the case of UGCD.15 aggregator (UGCD for a sequence of

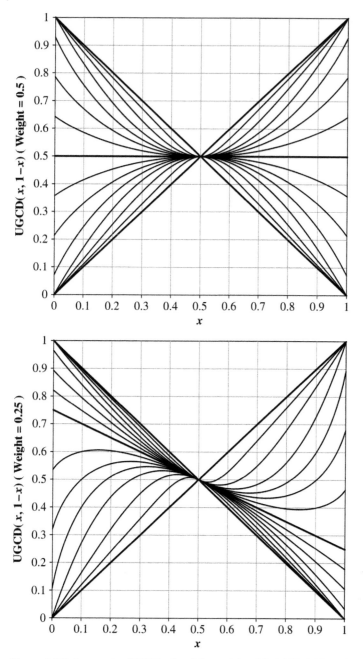

Figure 2.5.9 Aggregator UGCD(x, 1 − x) for weights 0.5, 0.375, 0.25, and 0.125.

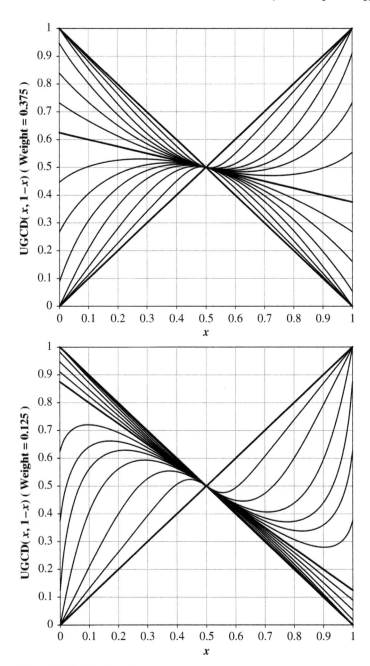

Figure 2.5.9 (Continued)

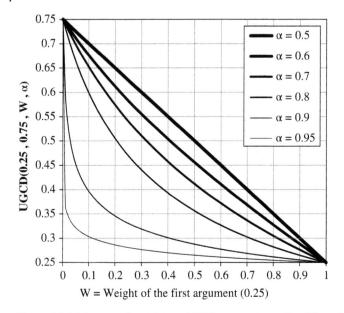

Figure 2.5.10 Impact of weights on UGCD aggregators with different value of andness.

15 values of andness $\alpha = 0, 1/14, ..., 1$). If the weight of the variable x is small the slope of conjunctive aggregators for small values of x is large. Because of duality, we also have a large slope of disjunctive aggregators for large values of x.

In the case of UGCD aggregators, we can analyze the impact of weights by keeping the constant value of andness and changing the value of selected weight in the whole range from 0 to 1. In the case of two variables, let us use a conjunctive andness-directed UGCD aggregator $UGCD(x, y; W, \alpha) = Wx\Delta(1 - W)y$ and values $x = 0.25$ and $y = 0.75$. The aggregated value $UGCD(0.25, 0.75; W, \alpha)$ is shown in Fig. 2.5.10. Predictably, if the weight of x is small then the aggregated value is close to the maximum value $y = 0.75$ and if the weight is large then the aggregated value is close to the minimum value $x = 0.25$. For large values of andness (0.9 and above), the impact of different weights is relatively low, except in the initial part of the quickly decreasing curve where we can see the phenomenon of hypersensitivity.

2.5.3 Semantic Components in Logic Aggregation Models

All logic aggregators (both GCD and more complex aggregators) include two fundamental components: (1) formal logic components (determined by selecting appropriate levels of andness/orness between GCD inputs) and (2) semantic components (determined by selecting appropriate degrees of relative importance of inputs using weights). A detailed background analysis of decomposition and aggregation of formal logic and semantic components in evaluation reasoning is presented in Section 2.2.3. In this section we explore the semantic nature of weights selection.

The origins of percepts of importance are visible in any practical evaluation problem. The percepts of importance always reflect the goals and interests of a particular stakeholder. Let us illustrate different semantic backgrounds using an example of three drivers evaluating the comfort and performance of their vehicles. Fig. 2.5.11 shows different levels of importance that three different drivers might assign to the comfort and performance of a vehicle. A professional racecar driver might consider that the car performance is extremely important (90%), and the comfort has to satisfy only minimum standards necessary to provide efficient control of the car during training and races. A professional truck driver needs performance of his vehicle but equally needs comfort to safely control the vehicle during many long hours of professional driving. Our third driver has a sedan. She transports two kids and a dog, as well as miscellaneous soccer pads, hockey sticks, and ballet shoes. Although she expects the car to have sufficient engine power, she is primarily concerned with the comfort and safety of her children. She considers the importance of comfort to be 80%, while the importance of performance is only 20%.

If the suitability of car performance is $P = 60\%$ and the suitability of comfort is $C = 90\%$, these values will cause three different interpretations in the minds of the three drivers. Assuming that all three drivers use the same criterion of weighted arithmetic mean, their overall satisfaction (E) will be as follows:

Racecar driver:	$E = 0.9P + 0.1C = 63\%$;
Truck driver:	$E = 0.5P + 0.5C = 75\%$;
Family sedan driver:	$E = 0.2P + 0.8C = 84\%$.

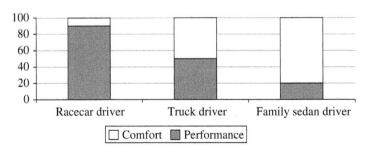

Figure 2.5.11 The importance of car performance and comfort for three different drivers.

Therefore, the meaning of the same pair of values $(P,C) = (60\%,90\%)$ is not the same for all drivers: the family sedan driver is rather happy, the truck driver might still be ready to accept this combination, and the racecar driver would certainly try to reject the offered car. Whenever the same inputs cause different suitability percepts associated with them in the minds of their interpreters (stakeholders/evaluators), such effects can be classified as semantic components of the decision process.

If the three drivers decide to increase the level of simultaneity of performance and comfort, e.g., if they increase the andness from 50% (the arithmetic mean) to 77% (the harmonic mean), then the aggregated suitability decreases as follows:

Racecar driver:	$E = 1/(0.9/P + 0.1/C) = 62.1\%,$
Truck driver:	$E = 1/(0.5/P + 0.5/C) = 72\%,$
Family sedan driver:	$E = 1/(0.2/P + 0.8/C) = 81.8\%.$

By increasing the level of simultaneity in the given range, we cause changes in final results. However, these are minor differences (less than 4%), and they will not change the final decisions of the three decision makers. On the other hand, the differences of weights in this example yield significant differences in the aggregated suitability degrees. This illustrates the significance of semantic components in evaluation models.

The vehicle example shows that mathematical models for logic evaluation must be able to quantitatively express various levels of importance of input arguments. Logic models that do not offer explicit means for expressing the levels of importance of degrees of truth cannot be used in GL and in practical evaluation.

The formal logic components of aggregation models are primarily used to adjust a desired behavior of a criterion function for all possible combinations of input suitability degrees, deciding about logic combining simultaneity and substitutability of inputs. On the other hand, semantic components primarily answer the question about the relative importance of individual inputs. Other important questions about conditions for accepting, rejecting, rewarding, penalizing, as well as deciding about what should be mandatory, sufficient, desired, or optional might be interpreted as a combination of formal logic and semantic aspects of human reasoning.

The independence in adjusting the level of simultaneity and the level of relative importance is a significant factor in simplifying the selection of parameters of the GCD function and other logic aggregators. In this way, the problem of adjusting aggregation parameters is decomposed into two simpler problems.

One of remarkable capabilities of human mind is that the percept of overall importance of inputs can be intuitively decomposed in a way that generates a desired degree of simultaneity/substitutability (andness/orness), and degrees of relative importance (weights) of inputs, as shown in Fig. 2.5.12 [DUJ12, DUJ15a]. We can first specify the desired level of simultaneity α for an andness-directed GCD aggregator. An independent next step is to adjust all weights using various techniques presented in the next section. These steps are sufficiently independent, and they can also come in the reversed order. Consequently, Fig. 2.5.12 suggests that both semantic components (degrees of relative importance) and formal logic components (degrees of simultaneity/substitutability) originate in the common aggregated percept of overall importance which is naturally generated in the mind of decision maker for each of n inputs of an aggregator, and for the aggregator as a whole, as introduced in Section 2.2.3 and refined in the next section.

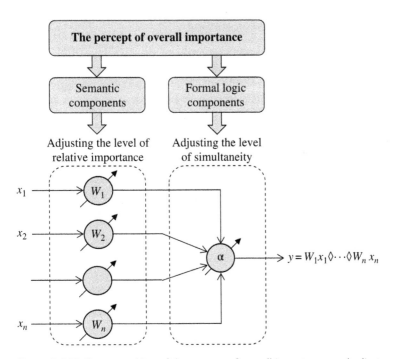

Figure 2.5.12 Decomposition of the percept of overall importance and adjustment of GCD parameters.

2.5.4 Seven Techniques for Weight Adjustment

The process of selecting weights can be organized is several ways. This section examines the following seven techniques:

1) Importance decomposition method
2) Direct weight assessment
3) Weights based on ranking
4) Weights based on menu
5) Collective weight determination
6) Weights obtained from pairwise comparisons
7) Weights based on preferential neuron training.

These techniques can be used separately, or combined, depending on the complexity, cost, desired precision, and the size of the decision making team. All these techniques, except the collective one, can be used by a single evaluator.

2.5.4.1 Importance Decomposition Method

The process of adjusting parameters of an andness-directed GCD function is illustrated in Fig. 2.5.12. This figure suggests that the intuitive adjustment of logic properties (the degree of simultaneity/substitutability) can be done independently of semantic properties (the importance quantifiers such as weights), and vice versa. In other words, the andness of the GCD aggregator and the weights of arguments are orthogonal components in evaluation reasoning.

Each input of an aggregator is associated with an overall percept of importance. The high andness and the high orness, as well as the percept of relative importance contribute to the percept of overall importance. According to Fig. 2.5.12 and the analysis presented in Section 2.2.3, the compound percept of overall importance can be decomposed in order to derive relative weights and the degree of simultaneity/substitutability (andness or orness).

The importance decomposition method is based on property P_{23} and Theorem 2.2.1. It is exemplified in Table 2.5.3 in the case of conjunctive GCD aggregator with four inputs. The overall degree of importance is verbalized in the range from medium to the highest and quantified with degrees (S) in the range from 8 to 16.

In the case of n inputs, the evaluator selects for each input the most appropriate degree of overall importance S_i, $i = 1, ..., n$. In the case of example shown in Table 2.5.3 we have $n = 4$ and $S_1 = 14$, $S_2 = 12$, $S_3 = 15$, $S_4 = 13$. The maximum degree of importance is $S_{max} = 16$.

Table 2.5.3 Selecting overall importance in the case of simultaneity.

α	S	Overall importance	Input 1	Input 2	Input 3	Input 4	Input 5
1	16	**Highest**					
0.9375	15	Slightly below highest			✓		
0.875	14	**Very high**	✓				
0.8125	13	Slightly above high				✓	
0.75	12	**High**		✓			
0.6875	11	Slightly below high					
0.625	10	**Medium-high**					
0.5625	9	Slightly above medium					
0.5	8	**Medium**					

According to Theorem 2.2.1, the andness can be determined as a mean overall importance:

$$\alpha = \frac{S_1 + \cdots + S_n}{n S_{\max}} = \frac{14 + 12 + 15 + 13}{4 \times 16} = \frac{54}{64} = 0.84375.$$

The relative weights of inputs reflect the relative importance, and they can be computed using the *proportional scaling* (PS) method [DUJ15a] as follows:

$$W_i = \frac{S_i}{S_1 + \cdots + S_n}, \quad 0 \le S_i \le S_{\max}.$$

Therefore,

$$W_1 = \frac{14}{54} = 0.26, \quad W_2 = \frac{12}{54} = 0.22, \quad W_3 = \frac{15}{54} = 0.28, \quad W_4 = \frac{13}{54} = 0.24.$$

If we use the weighted power means aggregator, then we first compute the value of exponent r and then the aggregator. According to Table 2.3.3, the andness $\alpha = 0.84375$ falls between andness $\alpha_1 = 0.83333$ $(r_1 = -1.8062)$ and $\alpha_2 = 0.85417$ $(r_2 = -2.2469)$. Consequently, the exponent r can be interpolated between these values as follows:

$$r = r_1 + \frac{(r_2 - r_1)(\alpha - \alpha_1)}{\alpha_2 - \alpha_1}$$

$$= -1.8062 + \frac{(-2.2469 + 1.8062)(0.84375 - 0.83333)}{0.85417 - 0.83333} = -2.02655 .$$

The corresponding GCD aggregator is

$$y = \left(0.26x_1^{-2.02655} + 0.22x_2^{-2.02655} + 0.28x_3^{-2.02655} + 0.24x_4^{-2.02655}\right)^{-0.49345}.$$

The presented PS method is not the only way to determine the weights of inputs of this aggregator. Two more methods (the linear shift model and the general linear model) can be found in [DUJ15a]. The idea behind these methods is that the obtained weights (in our example 0.26, 0.22, 0.28, 0.24) can be modified, keeping the same andness if the evaluator can provide some additional information about the importance ratios of inputs. In such a case, the weight range (the difference between the largest and the smallest weight) can be increased or decreased. From the PS method, we see that $W_i = S_i/(S_{max}n\alpha)$. Therefore, all weights are located on the line L going through the origin and the point P with coordinates $S_i/S_{max} = \alpha$ and $W_i = 1/n$ as shown in Fig. 2.5.13. The weights are located on line L in the initial PS range between the minimum weight W_{min} (point c) and the maximum weight W_{min} (point e). If we want to extend the range of weights, we can increase the slope of line that maps S_i/S_{max} to weight W_i going through the point P (e.g., as in the case of line K). Similarly, the slope and the range of weights can be reduced, as in the case of line M. Of course, lines K and M are no longer the PS method, but the linear transformations preserve some of original relationships of weights.

Similarly to the case of high andness, the percept of overall importance increases in the case of high orness. For high orness, each input becomes capable of fully satisfying the aggregated criterion, regardless of its relative importance. That increases the percept of overall importance in the same way as the high andness. Therefore, the importance decomposition method can be used in equivalent way for finding appropriate orness and weights in models of substitutability.

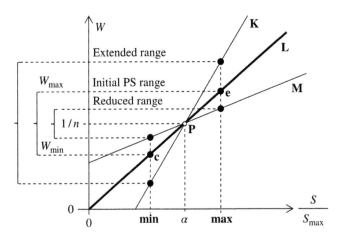

Figure 2.5.13 Linear adjustment of the range of weights.

2.5.4.2 Direct Weight Assessment

The direct weight assessment is the simplest and most frequent approach used by experienced evaluators who directly assign weights according to desired levels of importance. The only condition is to have the sum of weights equal to 1 (or 100%). The most frequent intuitive process is based on successive refinements starting from a trivial initial condition, such as equal weights. For example, let a criterion for an advanced computer system be based on four fundamental components: $H =$ hardware, $S =$ software, $P =$ performance, and $V =$ vendor support. In this case, the initial weights are $W_H = W_S = W_P = W_V = 0.25$. In the next step the evaluator might decide that the most important components are hardware and performance, while system software and offered vendor support are less significant yielding, $W_H = W_P = 0.3$, $W_S = W_V = 0.2$. In the final corrective adjustment step, weights could be redistributed as follows: $W_H = 0.35$, $W_P = 0.3$, $W_S = 0.2$, $W_V = 0.15$.

Direct weight assessment is frequently combined with ranking. For example, if importance ranking is $H \succ P \succ S \succ V$, then we can start from $W_H > W_P > W_S > W_V$ where in the first step we assign $W_H = 0.4$, $W_P = 0.3$, $W_S = 0.2$, $W_V = 0.1$. Subsequently we can perform successive refinements of this initial estimate. Verbalized rating scales presented in Chapter 2.9 are very useful in this process.

2.5.4.3 Weights Based on Ranking

In some cases, the evaluator has incomplete information and can only provide simple ranking of inputs according to decreasing level of importance, as follows:

1.	Most important input	(Weight $= w_1 = n$),
2.	Second most important input	(Weight $= w_2 = n-1$),
3.	....	
n.	Least important input	(Weight $= w_n = 1$); $w_1 + \cdots + w_n = n(n+1)/2$.

The sum-normalized weights are $W_i = 2(n+1-i)/n(n+1)$. The resulting weights are:

$$n = 2, \quad W_i = (3-i)/3 : \quad W_1 = 2/3, \quad W_2 = 1/3 \ ;$$
$$n = 3, \quad W_i = (4-i)/6 : \quad W_1 = 1/2, \quad W_2 = 1/3, \quad W_3 = 1/6 \ ;$$
$$n = 4, \quad W_i = (5-i)/10 : \quad W_1 = 2/5, \quad W_2 = 3/10, \quad W_3 = 1/5, \quad W_4 = 1/10 \ ;$$
$$n = 5, \quad W_i = (6-i)/15 : \quad W_1 = 1/3, \quad W_2 = 4/15, \quad W_3 = 1/5, \quad W_4 = 2/15,$$
$$W_5 = 1/15 \ .$$

These fixed values can be further refined by selecting the range of weights from desired minimum to maximum. Following is a general ranking of equidistant weights:

1.	Most important input	(Weight $= W_1$)
2.	Second most important input	(Weight $= W_2$)
3.	....	
n.	Least important input	(Weight $= W_n$)

We assume that W_1 is the maximum weight and that all weights have a constant difference $d = W_i - W_{i+1}$. Consequently,

$$W_1 = W_{\max},$$
$$W_2 = W_1 - d,$$
$$W_3 = W_2 - d = W_1 - 2d,$$
$$\cdots$$
$$W_n = W_1 - (n-1)d = W_{\min};$$
$$W_1 + W_2 + \cdots + W_n = nW_1 - (1 + 2 + \cdots + n-1)d = nW_1 - \frac{n(n-1)}{2}d = 1,$$
$$W_1 = \frac{1}{n} + \frac{n-1}{2}d.$$

$$(2.5.1)$$

From $W_n = W_{\min} > 0$ we have $W_1 > (n-1)d$ and the range of d is: $0 < d < W_1/(n-1) = d_{\max}$. From the last formula in (2.5.1) and conditions $d > 0$ and $d < d_{\max}$ it follows $W_1 > 1/n$, and $W_1 < 1/n + (n-1)d_{\max}/2 = 1/n + W_1/2$, $W_1 < 2/n$. Therefore, the most important weight W_1 and the weight difference d satisfy the relations:

$$\frac{1}{n} < W_1 < \frac{2}{n},$$
$$0 < d < \frac{W_1}{n-1} < \frac{2}{n(n-1)}.$$

$$(2.5.2)$$

If the value of W_1 is selected from its range, then

$$d = \frac{2(nW_1 - 1)}{n(n-1)}, \quad \frac{W_{\max} + W_{\min}}{2} = \frac{W_1 + W_n}{2} = W_1 - \frac{n-1}{2}d = \frac{1}{n}. \quad (2.5.3)$$

Formulas (2.5.2) and (2.5.3) can be used for computing weights: we first select the desired value of W_1 from (2.5.2) and then compute the corresponding difference from (2.5.3) and all weights from (2.5.1). For example, if $n = 4$ then $0.25 < W_1 < 0.5$. If we select $W_1 = 0.4$ then $d = 0.1$ and consequently $W_2 = 0.3$,

$W_3 = 0.2$, $W_4 = 0.1$ (of course, $W_1 + W_2 + W_3 + W_4 = 1$). Using this approach we can facilitate the selection of weights by computing tables with all relevant combinations of equidistant weights. Tables 2.5.4 show 19 values from the range of W_1 for $n = 2,3,4,5$. The weight of the most important input (W_1) is denoted FIRST, the second most important is denoted SECOND, etc. In cases where such an approach is appropriate, practitioners can select weights from the most suitable row in Tables 2.5.4.

The combinations of weights in Tables 2.5.4 are restricted by strictly decreasing values of weights and equal differences in the sequence of weights. In a case where that is not appropriate we can use other techniques for determining weights.

2.5.4.4 Weights Based on Menu

In many cases, it is useful to select weights using verbalized rating scales. This technique is similar to weights based on ranking, but it is more understandable and more precise. The levels of importance are verbally specified using a menu. Examples of importance rating scales with 5, 7, and 9 levels of importance are presented in Fig. 2.5.14. In all cases, the middle point is labeled "medium." Other labels are semantically acceptable inside each individual scale but are not consistently interpreted in all scales. More detail about the design and labeling of rating scales can be found in Chapter 2.9.

In all rating scales, the ranks can be interpreted as weights. For an aggregator with n input values, the user specifies n appropriate ranks taken from the selected rating scale: $r_1, r_2, ..., r_n$. The weights are then computed as normalized ranks:

$$W_i = 100 r_i \bigg/ \sum_{j=1}^{n} r_j \ [\%] , \quad i = 1,...,n.$$

For example, let us use the seven-level rating scale and aggregate three inputs that respectively have low, medium, and high importance. So, the weights are computed as follows:

$$r_1 = 2, \quad r_2 = 4, \quad r_3 = 6,$$
$$w_1 = 200/12 = 16.7\%, \quad w_2 = 400/12 = 33.3\%, \quad w_3 = 600/12 = 50\%.$$

Some weights can be equal. For example,

$$r_1 = 2, \quad r_2 = r_3 = 4, \quad r_4 = 6,$$
$$w_1 = 200/16 = 12.5\%, \quad w_2 = w_3 = 400/16 = 25\%, \quad w_4 = 600/16 = 37.5\%.$$

The initial weight of the medium importance, 33.3%, is now reduced to 25%. Other weights are also changed. Therefore, using this technique the weight that corresponds to a specific item from the menu is not constant. It depends on the context. Fig. 2.5.15 shows several examples of a dialog with the program AGOPcalc [SEA11a] that computes weights according to the menu technique (the case of a seven-level menu).

Tables 2.5.4 Weight combinations for $n = 2, 3, 4, 5$.

FIRST	SECOND
52.5%	47.5%
55.0%	45.0%
57.5%	42.5%
60.0%	40.0%
62.5%	37.5%
65.0%	35.0%
67.5%	32.5%
70.0%	30.0%
72.5%	27.5%
75.0%	25.0%
77.5%	22.5%
80.0%	20.0%
82.5%	17.5%
85.0%	15.0%
87.5%	12.5%
90.0%	10.0%
92.5%	7.5%
95.0%	5.0%
97.5%	2.5%

FIRST	SECOND	THIRD
35.0%	33.3%	31.7%
36.7%	33.3%	30.0%
38.3%	33.3%	28.3%
40.0%	33.3%	26.7%
41.7%	33.3%	25.0%
43.3%	33.3%	23.3%
45.0%	33.3%	21.7%
46.7%	33.3%	20.0%
48.3%	33.3%	18.3%
50.0%	33.3%	16.7%
51.7%	33.3%	15.0%
53.3%	33.3%	13.3%
55.0%	33.3%	11.7%
56.7%	33.3%	10.0%
58.3%	33.3%	8.3%
60.0%	33.3%	6.7%
61.7%	33.3%	5.0%
63.3%	33.3%	3.3%
65.0%	33.3%	1.7%

FIRST	SECOND	THIRD	FOURTH
26.3%	25.4%	24.6%	23.8%
27.5%	25.8%	24.2%	22.5%
28.7%	26.3%	23.8%	21.3%
30.0%	26.7%	23.3%	20.0%
31.3%	27.1%	22.9%	18.8%
32.5%	27.5%	22.5%	17.5%
33.8%	27.9%	22.1%	16.2%
35.0%	28.3%	21.7%	15.0%
36.3%	28.7%	21.3%	13.8%
37.5%	29.2%	20.8%	12.5%
38.8%	29.6%	20.4%	11.2%
40.0%	30.0%	20.0%	10.0%
41.3%	30.4%	19.6%	8.8%
42.5%	30.8%	19.2%	7.5%
43.8%	31.3%	18.8%	6.3%
45.0%	31.7%	18.3%	5.0%
46.3%	32.1%	17.9%	3.7%
47.5%	32.5%	17.5%	2.5%
48.8%	32.9%	17.1%	1.2%

FIRST	SECOND	THIRD	FOURTH	FIFTH
21.0%	20.5%	20.0%	19.5%	19.0%
22.0%	21.0%	20.0%	19.0%	18.0%
23.0%	21.5%	20.0%	18.5%	17.0%
24.0%	22.0%	20.0%	18.0%	16.0%
25.0%	22.5%	20.0%	17.5%	15.0%
26.0%	23.0%	20.0%	17.0%	14.0%
27.0%	23.5%	20.0%	16.5%	13.0%
28.0%	24.0%	20.0%	16.0%	12.0%
29.0%	24.5%	20.0%	15.5%	11.0%
30.0%	25.0%	20.0%	15.0%	10.0%
31.0%	25.5%	20.0%	14.5%	9.0%
32.0%	26.0%	20.0%	14.0%	8.0%
33.0%	26.5%	20.0%	13.5%	7.0%
34.0%	27.0%	20.0%	13.0%	6.0%
35.0%	27.5%	20.0%	12.5%	5.0%
36.0%	28.0%	20.0%	12.0%	4.0%
37.0%	28.5%	20.0%	11.5%	3.0%
38.0%	29.0%	20.0%	11.0%	2.0%
39.0%	29.5%	20.0%	10.5%	1.0%

5 = very high	7 = very high	9 = highest
4 = high	6 = high	8 = very high
3 = medium	5 = medium to high	7 = high
2 = low	4 = medium	6 = medium to high
1 = very low	3 = low to medium	5 = medium
	2 = low	4 = low to medium
	1 = very low	3 = low
		2 = very low
		1 = lowest

Figure 2.5.14 Importance rating scales with 5, 7, and 9 levels of importance.

```
The importance level can be:
1.  Very low
2.  LOW
3.  Low to medium
4.  MEDIUM
5.  Medium to high
6.  HIGH
7.  Very high

How many inputs do you want to aggregate? 4
Enter 4 importance levels from the above menu: 1 2 3 4
The resulting weights are: 10.0% 20.0% 30.0% 40.0%

More experiments (y/n)? y
Enter 4 importance levels from the above menu: 2 3 4 5
The resulting weights are: 14.3% 22.5% 28.6% 35.7%

More experiments (y/n)? y
Enter 4 importance levels from the above menu: 3 4 5 6
The resulting weights are: 16.7% 22.2% 27.8% 33.3%

More experiments (y/n)? y
Enter 4 importance levels from the above menu: 4 5 6 7
The resulting weights are: 18.2% 22.7% 27.3% 31.8%

More experiments (y/n)? y
Enter 4 importance levels from the above menu: 1 2 6 7
The resulting weights are: 6.3% 12.5% 37.5% 43.8%

More experiments (y/n)? y
Enter 4 importance levels from the above menu: 2 3 5 6
The resulting weights are: 12.5% 18.8% 31.3% 37.5%
```

Figure 2.5.15 Computing weights using a seven-level menu.

2.5.4.5 Collective Weight Determination

This technique assumes a team of K evaluators $(K \geq 2)$. The evaluators average their individual opinions to improve the accuracy of their estimates. The simplest way to average individual opinions is to use the weights based on menu technique. The weights can be computed using the sum of individual ranks that are assigned by individual evaluators. Consequently, this approach is a version of the Borda count method [AA15]. For inputs i the evaluator k provides the rank $r_i^{(k)}$ (the highest rank denotes the most important input). In the case of K evaluators in the team, the corresponding weights are computed as follows:

$$w_i = 100 \frac{\sum_{k=1}^{K} r_i^{(k)}}{\sum_{j=1}^{n} \sum_{k=1}^{K} r_j^{(k)}} \ [\%], \quad i = 1,\dots,n.$$

In this formula, r can be a rank taken from a rating scale (i.e., an integer value), but it can also be any other real or integer value estimated by evaluators (e.g., a weight, a suitability score, a performance indicator, a quality indicator, or anything else).

The following example illustrates the case of $K = 3$ evaluators and the seven-level rating scale (1 = very low, 2 = low, 3 = low to medium, 4 = medium, 5 = medium to high, 6 = high, 7 = very high):

$$r_1^{(1)} = 2, \quad r_2^{(1)} = 4, \quad r_3^{(1)} = 6;$$
$$r_1^{(2)} = 2, \quad r_2^{(2)} = 5, \quad r_3^{(2)} = 7;$$
$$r_1^{(3)} = 4, \quad r_2^{(3)} = 5, \quad r_3^{(3)} = 5;$$
$$w_1 = 800/40 = 20\%, \quad w_2 = 1400/40 = 35\%, \quad w_3 = 1800/40 = 45\%.$$

This approach assumes that all evaluators have the same weight ($1/K$), i.e., they affect the decision in the same way, as independent voters.

The accuracy of collective decisions can be improved if the more competent team members have higher impact than the less competent team members. In other words, individual evaluators can have their weights $W_1, \dots, W_K$. This problem is studied in Section 3.2.7, where we describe a technique where evaluators have different competence degrees and the example of three experts having individual weights $W_1 = 47/72$, $W_2 = 13/72$, and $W_3 = 12/72$. The best collective estimate X is then based on the weighted linear combination of the individual member estimates X_1, X_2, X_3: $X = (47X_1 + 13X_2 + 12X_3)/72$. Applying this formula to ranks, we get the following collective rank estimates:

$$r_1 = \left(47r_1^{(1)} + 13r_1^{(2)} + 12r_1^{(3)}\right)\Big/72 = (47 \times 2 + 13 \times 2 + 12 \times 4)/72 = 168/72,$$
$$r_2 = \left(47r_2^{(1)} + 13r_2^{(2)} + 12r_2^{(3)}\right)\Big/72 = (47 \times 4 + 13 \times 5 + 12 \times 5)/72 = 313/72,$$
$$r_3 = \left(47r_3^{(1)} + 13r_3^{(2)} + 12r_3^{(3)}\right)\Big/72 = (47 \times 6 + 13 \times 7 + 12 \times 5)/72 = 433/72.$$

The resulting percent weights are obtained by normalizing the above ranks as follows:

$$w_1 = 100r_1/(r_1 + r_2 + r_3) = 100 \times 168/(168 + 313 + 433) = 16800/914 = 18.4\% \ ,$$

$$w_2 = 100r_2/(r_1 + r_2 + r_3) = 31300/914 = 34.2\% \ ,$$

$$w_3 = 100r_3/(r_1 + r_2 + r_3) = 43300/914 = 47.4\% \ .$$

These weights are slightly corrected with respect to the initial results, based on higher impact of estimates, given by more qualified evaluators.

2.5.4.6 Weights Obtained from Pairwise Comparisons

If we have to determine the most appropriate distribution of n weights $W_1, ..., W_n$ and at the same time satisfy the condition $W_1 + \cdots + W_n = 1$, then this problem generates $n(n-1)/2$ pairwise comparisons of each weight with each other weight. So, that is an $O(n^2)$ problem; i.e., a problem of quadratic complexity that even for small n can become inconvenient for intuitive solving. On the other hand, a comparison of two isolated properties is the simplest form of comparison, and humans should be capable to perform such comparisons with the highest accuracy. The most popular method based on pairwise comparisons is the *analytic hierarchy process* (AHP) introduced by Thomas L. Saaty in [SAA77, SAA80] and then expanded and applied in many publications (e.g., [SAA90, SAA01, SAA06, SAA10, SAA16]). AHP reduces complex decisions to a sequence of pairwise comparisons. Similarly to LSP, AHP is a method inspired by observing human mental activities and according to [SAA80] the participants find that AHP is compatible with "their intuitive understanding of a problem." Pairwise comparisons are a controversial area and mathematical background of such controversies can be found in [KOC16]. We use AHP as one of techniques for determining the values of weights and will exemplify it to the extent it is implemented in the AHP calculator, which is a part of AGOPcalc [SEA11a].

Suppose that we have an aggregator with five inputs denoted A, B, C, D, E. These inputs have different (e.g., decreasing) degrees of importance, and the process of determining the individual degrees of importance can be based on 10 pairwise comparisons: AB, AC, AD, AE, BC, BD, BE, CD, CE, DE. The result of pairwise comparison of two inputs X and Y can be that they have equal or different importance. If X is more important than Y, then the dominance can be verbalized as moderate, strong, very strong, and extreme. The AHP method inserts intermediate levels between this basic five-level scale, and then codes the degrees of dominance with integers 1,2,...,9 as shown in Fig. 2.5.16. The meaning of reciprocals in the AHP scale is the inverse domination: e.g., if X moderately dominates Y, that is denoted as level 3, and in such a case the domination of Y over X is considered to be 1/3. The AHP calculator of weights then accepts all 10 pairwise comparisons as exemplified in Fig. 2.5.17.

```
1. EQUAL                          1.000 = 1/1
2.    Equal to moderate           0.500 = 1/2
3. MODERATE                       0.333 = 1/3
4.    Moderate to strong          0.250 = 1/4
5. STRONG                         0.200 = 1/5
6.    Strong to very strong       0.167 = 1/6
7. VERY STRONG                    0.143 = 1/7
8.    Very strong to extreme      0.125 = 1/8
9. EXTREME                        0.111 = 1/9
```

Figure 2.5.16 A nine-level importance rating scale used by AHP.

```
Inputs denote how much the item in a row dominates
the item in a column. Enter only 1 value in the first
row, 2 values in the second row, and so forth.

      E    D    C    B
D     7
C     8    2
B     9    4    2
A     9    5    3    2
```

Figure 2.5.17 Pairwise importance comparison (inputs for the AHP weight calculator).

Let us note that human inputs regularly contain some inconsistencies. For example, the domination of A over E is specified as AE = 9, same as the domination of B over E, which is also BE = 9. That might mean that A and B are equally important. However, in the last row we find AB = 2, i.e. A is slightly dominating B. Consequently, inputs of the AHP process cannot avoid typical human imprecisions and inconsistencies, and obviously the reliability of final results depends on the reliability of inputs. However, it is reasonable to expect that the accuracy of pairwise comparisons is better than the accuracy of simultaneous intuitive comparison of more than two inputs. The resulting matrix of pairwise comparisons is then completed by the AHP calculator, as follows:

$$P = \begin{pmatrix} 1 & 1/7 & 1/8 & 1/9 & 1/9 \\ 7 & 1 & 1/2 & 1/4 & 1/5 \\ 8 & 2 & 1 & 1/2 & 1/3 \\ 9 & 4 & 2 & 1 & 1/2 \\ 9 & 5 & 3 & 2 & 1 \end{pmatrix}.$$

Since each row shows the domination of selected input over all other inputs we might be tempted to apply a version of "Borda style reasoning" and add all numbers in each row, and normalize them to generate sum-normalized weights $W[1], ..., W[n]$ as follows:

$$R[i] = \sum_{j=1}^{n} P[i][j], \quad i = 1,...n ;$$

$$W[j] = R[j] \Big/ \sum_{i=1}^{n} R[i], \quad j = 1,...n .$$

The weights $W[1], ..., W[n]$ would not be useless, because they are the first approximation of the desired result. AHP uses the eigenvector, and the computation is based on the normalized sum of rows of the sequence of matrices $M_0 = P$, $M_k = M_{k-1}^2$, $k = 1,2,3,....$ The process is terminated when the normalized sums of rows of matrices M_k and M_{k-1} differ for a selected very small value ε (AGOPcalc uses $\varepsilon = 10^{-6}$).

The algorithm used by AGOPcalc is shown in Fig. 2.5.18. The resulting arrays $E \cong W$ are the resulting weights of inputs. The results generated by this algorithm are shown in Fig. 2.5.19. The difference between the final weights and the initial normalized sum of rows is visible but not dramatic. So, in cases where imprecision of inputs justifies the moderate accuracy of evaluation models, the AHP approach can be replaced with the simple normalized sum of rows.

The presented AHP example shows that the use of 9 levels of dominance can create big differences between the most important and the least important input. Very small weights (e.g., 2.686%) indicate insignificant inputs that could

$A = P$;
repeat
$\quad B = A^2$;
$\quad R[i] = \sum_{j=1}^{n} B[i][j], \quad i = 1,...,n; \quad W[j] = R[j] \Big/ \sum_{i=1}^{n} R[i], \quad j = 1,...,n;$
$\quad A = B^2$;
$\quad R[i] = \sum_{j=1}^{n} A[i][j], \quad i = 1,...,n; \quad E[j] = R[j] \Big/ \sum_{i=1}^{n} R[i], \quad j = 1,...,n;$
until $\max_{1 \le i \le n} \big| E[i] - W[i] \big| < \varepsilon;$

Figure 2.5.18 The AHP weight calculation algorithm used by AGOPcalc.

```
The resulting vector of weights [and the initial normalized sum of rows]

E weight =    2.686 %      [  2.535 % ]
D weight =   10.074 %      [ 15.228 % ]
C weight =   16.523 %      [ 20.134 % ]
B weight =   28.092 %      [ 28.074 % ]
A weight =   42.625 %      [ 34.029 % ]
```

Figure 2.5.19 Sample weight computation results.

be omitted; if retained, such inputs usually create hypersensitivity effects. The AHP verbal dominance scale is obviously highly nonlinear because it achieves a "strong dominance" right in the middle of the scale, which is inconsistent with linear methods of designing verbalized rating scales (see Chapter 2.9). So, for weight calculation, it is frequently sufficient to use the first half of the AHP scale. Instead of changing the verbalization of the AHP scale many authors suggested an equivalent change of numeric coding, replacing the AHP linear coding 1,2,...,9 with various nonlinear coding scales. Rather complete surveys of various problems related to pairwise comparisons and the AHP technique can be found in [FUL10, ISH13].

2.5.4.7 Weights Based on Preferential Neuron Training

All aggregators can be interpreted as preferential neurons [DUJ91]. So, we can use a learning process to simultaneously determine the optimum level of simultaneity/substitutability (or other logic relationships) and the relative importance of inputs. The basic steps of this technique, as implemented in the software tool ANSY [SEA10], include the following:

1) The user selects a desired aggregator (in this case, GCD) and selects the number of inputs. The parameters of the function include both weights and the parameters that define the logic properties of the selected function.
2) The user specifies a training set consisting of any number of desired input-output values. That specifies the desired input-output mapping.
3) An error function of all adjustable parameters is created for computing the difference between desired outputs and achieved outputs.
4) The optimum values of parameters are computed as values that yield the minimum of the error function. These optimum parameters also include the optimum weights.

To exemplify this approach, let us use the basic weighted power mean model of GCD:

$$y = W_1 x_1 \diamond \cdots \diamond W_n x_n = \left(W_1 x_1^r + \cdots + W_n x_n^r \right)^{1/r}.$$

The evaluator is expected to define a training set, which is a table containing k desired input-output combinations, shown in Table 2.5.5.

The next step is to find the optimum values of parameters $W_1, W_2, \cdots, W_n, r$ that yield the minimum value of the error function:

$$E(W_1, \ldots, W_n, r) = \sum_{i=1}^{k} \left| y_i - \left(W_1 x_{1i}^r + \cdots + W_n x_{ni}^r \right)^{1/r} \right|.$$

To find the minimum of this function of $n + 1$ variables, we use the Nelder-Mead algorithm [NEL64]. The Nelder-Mead algorithm is convenient because it uses

Table 2.5.5 Desired inputs and output of selected aggregator.

Inputs				Output
x_1	x_2	...	x_n	y
x_{11}	x_{21}	...	x_{n1}	y_1
x_{12}	x_{22}	...	x_{n2}	y_2
...	...	...	...	...
x_{1k}	x_{2k}	...	x_{nk}	y_k

the error function $E(W_1, ..., W_n, r)$ but it does not need its derivatives. Details of this process can be found in [DUJ91].

The optimum values of parameters $W_1, ..., W_n, r$ include solutions of two problems: (1) the optimum level of simultaneity/substitutability is adjusted by the resulting parameter r, and (2) the degrees of importance of inputs are adjusted by the resulting weights $W_1, ..., W_n$. Let us exemplify the training process using a software tool ANSY to find parameters of the following GCD function:

$$y = W_1 x_1 \diamond W_2 x_2 \diamond W_3 x_3 \diamond W_4 x_4 = \left(W_1 x_1^r + W_2 x_2^r + W_3 x_3^r + W_4 x_4^r \right)^{1/r}.$$

Initially, ANSY prompts the user to enter a training set, as shown in Fig. 2.5.20. This sample of training set consists of four input/output requirements (the last line contains sentinel values, outside the [0,1] interval). The intention of these requirements is to specify the desired output (y) if all inputs are perfectly satisfied, except one input that is satisfied only 50%. This specification should be easy for the user because it isolates the desired effect of a single input. The training set can have any number of input/output requirements and they can be to some extent inconsistent.

After the minimization of the error function, ANSY returns results presented in Fig. 2.5.21. In this example, we had four conditions (plus the condition

```
Enter a training set containing any number of desired I/O values
(a value outside the [0,1] interval denotes the end of input data)

x1   x2   x3   x4      y
--------------------------
.5    1    1    1     .80
 1   .5    1    1     .85
 1    1   .5    1     .70
 1    1    1   .5     .90
 9    9    9    9      9
```

Figure 2.5.20 A typical ANSY specification of a GCD training set.

```
THE RESULTING OPTIMUM VALUES OF PARAMETERS
W1 =      .259443
W2 =      .183951
W3 =      .440307
W4 =      .116299
r  =     -.861743
The minimum value of criterion function =   .584E-07
The number of function computations     =   335
W1+...+Wn =  .1000E+01,  Max error of result =  .941E-06
=================================================
   Training set           | Trained GCD neuron
------------------------------+-------------------
  x1    x2   x3    x4      y   |   y         Error
------------------------------+-------------------
 .50 1.00 1.00 1.00    .8000   | .8000   -.21E-07
1.00  .50 1.00 1.00    .8500   | .8500    .13E-07
1.00 1.00  .50 1.00    .7000   | .7000   -.71E-08
1.00 1.00 1.00  .50    .9000   | .9000   -.95E-07
=================================================
```

Figure 2.5.21 The results of GCD training returned by ANSY.

that the sum of weights must be 1) and determined four weights and the exponent r. Since $r < 1$ the resulting function is the following partial conjunction:

$$y = W_1 x_1 \Delta W_2 x_2 \Delta W_3 x_3 \Delta W_4 x_4$$

$$= \left(0.26 x_1^{-0.86} + 0.18 x_2^{-0.86} + 0.44 x_3^{-0.86} + 0.12 x_4^{-0.86}\right)^{-1.16}.$$

In this example, the differences between the desired values (in the training set) and the achieved values are almost zero. If the training set is expanded, and includes inconsistent requests, then the errors would become more visible (and could be used as a measure of inconsistency). The training set can frequently contain explicit request that one of zero inputs causes zero output; the result of such a request is a hard partial conjunction.

The presented seven techniques for weight adjustment are suitable for applications in GL and for development of aggregators used in evaluation criteria. Obviously, the most convenient techniques are the importance decomposition and the preferential neuron training because these are the only techniques that simultaneously derive both the importance weights and the necessary andness of aggregator. These parameters are derived either from the percept of overall importance or directly from desired suitability mappings. Other techniques focus on percepts of relative importance and use them to derive weight estimates.

2.5.5 Multivariate Weighted Aggregation Based on Binary Aggregation Trees

In GL, we need weighted and parameterized logic aggregators of n variables. The number of idempotent logic aggregators (means) that naturally have such properties is very limited. Fortunately, in the case of means, it is possible to create general multivariate idempotent weighted aggregators by expanding symmetric idempotent aggregators of two variables. A sample of symmetric means of two variables is shown in Table 2.5.6. For example, if we select the logarithmic mean, then our problem is to transform a simple logarithmic mean of two variables into an equivalent weighted mean of n variables. In this section we describe a computational method for creating such general aggregators. This method, together with interpolative aggregation, can be used for the development of general idempotent logic aggregators that satisfy a variety of conditions necessary for building decision models in the graded logic and its applications.

Methods for expanding symmetric means of two variables to n variables are studied in mathematical literature [PIT85, SIM08, GRA09, BEL16a]. However, creating multivariate weighted forms of idempotent logic aggregators is primarily a computational problem, and it needs a computational solution. The basic idea that importance can be interpreted as cardinality originates in the work of Calvo and Mesiar [CAL03, CAL04]. Based on that idea, in this section we present a computational method introduced in [DUJ15c] and subsequently refined in [BEL16a] and [DUJ17a].

Suppose that F is an idempotent symmetric *bivariate logic aggregator*: $F : I^2 \rightarrow I$, $I = [0,1]$, similar to aggregators shown in Table 2.5.6. A general multivariate weighted aggregation of n input variables $y = A(x_1,...;x_n, W_1,..., W_n)$, $x_i \in I$, $0 < W_i < 1$, $W_1 + \cdots + W_n = 1, i = 1,...,n$ can be organized as a binary tree

Table 2.5.6 Sample means of two variables.

Name	Mean	Andness
Heronian mean	$\dfrac{x+\sqrt{xy}+y}{3}$	0.556
Centroidal mean	$\dfrac{2(x^2+xy+y^2)}{3(x+y)}$	0.409
Logarithmic mean	$\dfrac{x-y}{\log x - \log y}$	0.614
Identric mean	$\dfrac{1}{e}\left(\dfrac{x^x}{y^y}\right)^{1/(x-y)}$	0.553
Counter-harmonic mean for $r=0.75$	$\dfrac{x\sqrt[4]{y}+y\sqrt[4]{x}}{\sqrt[4]{x}+\sqrt[4]{y}}$	0.590

of idempotent "base aggregators" F, as shown in Fig. 2.5.22. In order to adjust the weight (importance and impact) of ith input, we use K_i replicas of the variable x_i, $i = 1,...,n$. So, the total number of inputs in the binary tree is $K_1 + ... + K_n = N = 2^L$, where L denotes the number of levels of the binary tree. The multiplicity K_i reflects the degree of importance of the variable x_i, $i = 1,...,n$ (i.e., $W_i \approx K_i/N$).

This method has six benefits:

1) The tree consists of base aggregators F and therefore the compound aggregator A preserves all intrinsic properties of the base aggregator F. Thus, if F is hard then A is hard, and if F is soft then A is also soft. Since F is idempotent, A is also idempotent.

2) The method can be applied to any idempotent bivariate aggregator. Therefore, it is a general way for expanding symmetric idempotent bivariate aggregators to weighted aggregators of $n > 2$ variables.

3) Precision of the proposed method (in terms of matching the desired weights W_i) depends on the size of the tree. By increasing the number of levels L and the number of inputs N we can achieve any desired level of precision.

4) Due to idempotency of F it is not necessary to compute the outputs of all F aggregators but only those that have different inputs. In other words, the tree can be pruned. This significantly reduces the computational complexity and can be done in run time $O[(n-1)L]$.

5) If the multiplicities are (approximately) the same $(K_1 \approx K_2 \approx \cdots \approx K_n \approx K \approx N/n)$, then the resulting aggregator A is numerically very close to symmetric multivariate aggregation. Otherwise it is asymmetric (weighted).

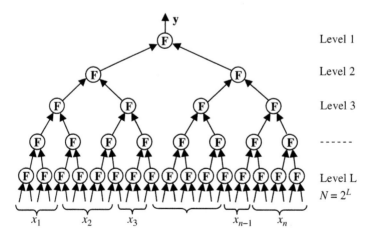

Figure 2.5.22 A general weighted aggregator A structured as a binary tree.

6) For associative aggregators (in the sense of Kolmogorov-Nagumo [KOL30. NAG30]), like various quasi-arithmetic means, the binary tree aggregation method generates exactly the same results as analytic models based on associativity. If the base aggregator is not associative the binary tree method is providing properties that are equivalent to associativity.

Let us now focus on solving the computational problem of creating general weighted aggregators using repetition of arguments and binary trees of suitable basic bivariate aggregators. Associativity offers a way for transforming bivariate aggregators that use equal weights to aggregators that use multiple inputs and different weights. Let us use associative logic aggregators based on quasi-arithmetic means (QAM):

$$a_1x_1 \Diamond \cdots \Diamond a_nx_n = f^{-1}(a_1f(x_1) + \cdots + a_nf(x_n)),$$
$$0 < a_i < 1, \ i = 1, \ldots, n, \ a_1 + \ldots + a_n = 1.$$

Here $f : [0,1] \rightarrow \mathbb{R}$ denotes a continuous and strictly monotonic function. Using QAM we can easily verify the following basic properties of the symbolic notation $y = a_1x_1 \Diamond \ldots \Diamond a_nx_n$ (note: as discussed in Section 2.1.9, a_ix_i is not multiplication, but a symbolic notation specifying that for each i the weight $a_i \in]0,1[$ corresponds to the argument $x_i \in [0,1]$ in the aggregation process based on the GCD operator $\Diamond$):

$$a_1x \Diamond \ldots \Diamond a_nx = x,$$
$$a_1x_1 \Diamond a_2x_2 \Diamond a_3x_1 = (a_1 + a_3)x_1 \Diamond a_2x_2,$$
$$a_1x_1 \Diamond a_2(b_1x_2 \Diamond b_2x_3) = a_1x_1 \Diamond a_2b_1x_2 \Diamond a_2b_2x_3,$$
$$a_1x_1 \Diamond a_2(b_1x_1 \Diamond b_2x_2) = (a_1 + a_2b_1)x_1 \Diamond a_2b_2x_2,$$
$$a_1x_1 \Diamond a_2x_2 \Diamond a_3x_3 = a_1x_1 \Diamond (a_2 + a_3)((a_2/(a_2 + a_3))x_2 \Diamond (a_3/(a_2 + a_3))x_3).$$

Suppose that we want to transform a symmetric (unweighted) bivalent aggregator $F(x_1,x_2) = 0.5x_1 \Diamond 0.5x_2$ that does not have adjustable weights, to its adjustable weighted form $y = Wx_1 \Diamond (1 - W)x_2$. That can be achieved by using a binary tree of symmetric aggregators $F(x_1, x_2)$ that has L levels and $N = 2^L$ input arguments as exemplified in Fig. 2.5.23 for $L = 4$, $N = 16$, and $W = 11/16$. To achieve the effect of weight W, the argument x_1 should be repeated $K_1 = WN = 11$ times, and the argument x_2 should be repeated $K_2 = (1 - W)N = 5$ times. If we use idempotency to simplify the tree as shown in Fig. 2.5.23 then the resulting aggregator is the following:

$$y = \frac{1}{2}x_1 \Diamond \frac{1}{2}\left(\frac{1}{2}x_2 \Diamond \frac{1}{2}\left(\frac{1}{2}x_1 \Diamond \frac{1}{2}\left(\frac{1}{2}x_1 \Diamond \frac{1}{2}x_2\right)\right)\right)$$
$$= \frac{1}{2}x_1 \Diamond \frac{1}{4}x_2 \Diamond \frac{1}{8}x_1 \Diamond \frac{1}{16}x_1 \Diamond \frac{1}{16}x_2 = \frac{11}{16}x_1 \Diamond \frac{5}{16}x_2.$$

This example illustrates that instead of computing 15 aggregators in the binary tree, we reduced the problem to computing a sequence of 4 aggregators which

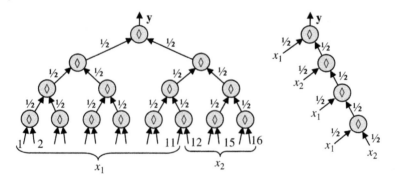

Figure 2.5.23 Creating a weighted aggregator from aggregators that use equal weights.

alternate in a suitable way the arguments x_1 and x_2. Now, we need an algorithm that creates that "suitable way."

A general algorithm for creating the weighted aggregator $y = A(x_1, x_2; W_1, W_2)$ from a symmetric unweighted aggregator $F(x_1, x_2)$ can be developed using an L-level binary tree with N leaves and the technique of repetition of arguments in a way exemplified in Fig. 2.5.24 for $W_1 \in \{1/16, \ldots, 15/16\}$. We want to aggregate two input suitability degrees (x_1 and x_2) using weights $W_1 = W$ and $W_2 = 1 - W$ respectively. The desired weighted aggregator of two variables is $y = Wx_1 \Diamond (1 - W)x_2$. We assume $0 < W < 1$. The weighted aggregation is achieved by using K_1 inputs with value x_1 followed by $N - K_1$ inputs with value x_2. The value of K_1 is proportional to W and can be computed using the rounding $\lfloor WN + 1/2 \rfloor$. The approximate value of W and the corresponding relative error are

$$K_1 = \lfloor WN + 1/2 \rfloor, \quad K_1 \in \{1, \ldots, N - 1\},$$
$$W \approx K_1/N = \lfloor WN + 1/2 \rfloor / N,$$
$$E = 100(\lfloor WN + 1/2 \rfloor / N - W)/W \ [\%].$$

We assume that weights are not 0 or 1 (otherwise, F just returns the argument with weight 1). Using L levels of a binary tree we get $N - 1$ discrete weights from the sequence $1/N, 2/N, \ldots, (N-1)/N$. The distance between two adjacent weights is $1/N$, and after rounding the maximum absolute error is $0.5/N$ yielding the maximum relative error $E_{max} = (50/N)/W \ [\%]$. For example, if $W = 0.73$ and $L = 4$, $N = 16$ (as in Fig. 2.5.24), then $K_1 = \lfloor 0.73 \times 16 + 1/2 \rfloor = 12$. The obtained weight approximation is $W \approx 12/16 = 0.75$, the achieved error is $100(0.75 - 0.73)/0.73 = 2.74\%$ and the maximum possible error is $E_{max} = 50/(0.73 \times 16) = 4.28 \ \%$. The precision can be increased by using larger values of L. If $L = 10$, then $K_1 = \lfloor 0.73 \times 1024 + 1/2 \rfloor = 748$, the obtained weight is $W \approx 748/1024 = 0.7305$, and the errors are $E = 0.064\%$, $E_{max} = 0.067\%$. If we

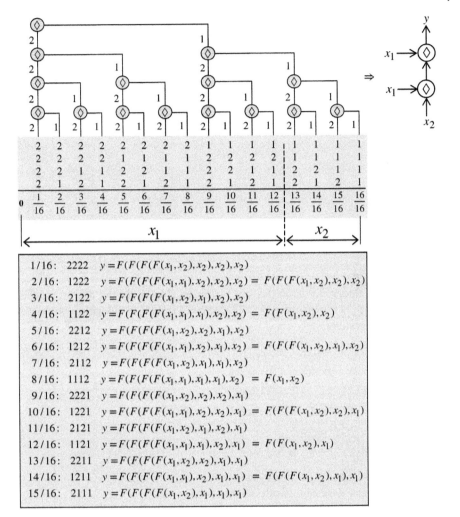

Figure 2.5.24 A binary tree with 16 inputs and weighted aggregation formulas for weights 1/16,…,15/16.

increase the value of L (typically $24 \le L \le 56$), then the inaccuracies become negligible.

An efficient algorithm for computation of weighted means can be derived by observing Fig. 2.5.24. In the case of example $W = 0.73$, the first 12 inputs should be x_1 and the remaining 4 inputs should be x_2. Of course, due to idempotency, it is not necessary to compute function in all nodes but only in nodes with different inputs. The computation can be done according to the algorithm WA2 shown in Fig. 2.5.25.

WEIGHTED AGGREGATION ALGORITHM WA2 FOR COMPUTING THE
WEIGHTED AGGREGATOR $y = Wx_1 \Diamond (1-W)x_2$ FROM $y = F(x_1, x_2) = 0.5x_1 \Diamond 0.5x_2$

(1) Compute the path index value: $B = K - 1 = \lfloor WN + 1/2 \rfloor - 1$.

(2) Convert B to n-bit binary number (binary sequence) $b_n b_{n-1}...b_1$, $b_i \in \{0,1\}$:

$\left[b_i = B \bmod 2 \in \{0,1\}; \quad B := \lfloor B/2 \rfloor \right], i = 1,...,n.$

(3) Transform the binary sequence $b_1 b_2...b_n$ to the path sequence $p = p_1 p_2...p_n$, where

$p_i = 2 - b_i, \quad p_i \in \{1,2\}, \quad i = 1,...,n.$

(4) Simplification based on idempotency: delete leading 1's from the sequence p
so that it starts with 2 and rename the truncated sequence $t = t_1 t_2 ...t_m$, $t_1 = 2$, $m \le n$.

(5) The resulting weighted aggregation function is $y = F(...F(F(x_1, x_{t_1}), x_{t_2}),..., x_{t_m})$.

Figure 2.5.25 The weighted aggregation algorithm WA2 for aggregating two variables.

The WA2 algorithm is based on formulas shown in the lower part of Fig. 2.5.24. In the case where $W = 0.73$ and $L = 4$ the WA2 algorithm generates the following results:

1) Path index: $B = \lfloor 0.73 \times 2^4 + 1/2 \rfloor - 1 = 11$.
2) Conversion to the binary sequence

$$B = 11, \qquad b_1 = 11 \bmod 2 = 1;$$
$$B : = \lfloor B/2 \rfloor = 5, \quad b_2 = 5 \bmod 2 = 1;$$
$$B : = \lfloor B/2 \rfloor = 2, \quad b_3 = 2 \bmod 2 = 0;$$
$$B : = \lfloor B/2 \rfloor = 1, \quad b_4 = 1 \bmod 2 = 1; \qquad \therefore \ 11_{10} = 1011_2 = b_4 b_3 b_2 b_1.$$

3) The path sequence: $p = p_1 p_2 p_3 p_4 = 1121$.
4) Simplification based on idempotency: $t = t_1 t_2 = 21$.
5) The resulting weighted aggregator (also shown in Fig. 2.5.24):

$$y = F(F(x_1, x_2), x_1) = \tfrac{1}{2}(\tfrac{1}{2}x_1 \Diamond \tfrac{1}{2}x_2) \Diamond \tfrac{1}{2}x_1 = \tfrac{1}{4}x_1 \Diamond \tfrac{1}{4}x_2 \Diamond \tfrac{1}{2}x_1 = \tfrac{3}{4}x_1 \Diamond \tfrac{1}{4}x_2.$$

If we need a better accuracy, then the same procedure can be performed with larger value of L. For example, the same algorithm for $W = 0.73$, $L = 10$ yields the following:

1) Path index: $B = \lfloor 0.73 \times 2^{10} + 1/2 \rfloor - 1 = 747$.
2) Conversion to the binary sequence: $747_{10} = 1011101011_2 = b_{10} b_9 b_8 b_7 b_6 b_5 b_4 b_3 b_2 b_1$.
3) The path sequence: $p_1 p_2 p_3 p_4 p_5 p_6 p_7 p_8 p_9 p_{10} = 1121211121$.

4) Simplification based on idempotency: $t = t_1 t_2 t_3 t_4 t_5 t_6 t_7 t_8 = 21211121$.
5) The resulting weighted aggregator:

$$y = F(F(F(F(F(F(F(F(x_1,x_2),x_1),x_2),x_1),x_1),x_1),x_2),x_1).$$

The manual computation of weighted aggregators can be tedious. Fortunately, an elegant and efficient version of the WA2 algorithm can be implemented as shown in Fig. 2.5.26. Note that the time complexity of this algorithm is $O(L)$.

The binary tree expansion method presented in Fig. 2.5.24 can be generalized to include n variables $x_1, ..., x_n$ and different weights $W_1, ..., W_n$. Similarly to the case of two variables, a general weighted aggregator of n variables $y = W_1 x_1 \Diamond ... \Diamond W_n x_n$ can be derived using a related symmetric bivariate base aggregator $F(x_1,x_2) = 0.5x_1 \Diamond 0.5x_2$, as shown in Fig. 2.5.27. The idempotency of F is the only prerequisite for this method. The idea is that each node preserves the intrinsic characteristics of the base symmetric logic aggregator $\Diamond$ and weights are represented by the numbers of repeated inputs. So, in this case the weights are represented and adjusted as follows:

$$K_i = \lfloor W_i N + \tfrac{1}{2} \rfloor, \quad i = 1, ..., n-1, \quad K_n = N - K_1 - \cdots - K_{n-1}.$$

Suppose that we want to create the aggregator $y = 0.5x_1 \Diamond 0.3x_2 \Diamond 0.2x_3$. If we use four levels, then $N = 16$, $K_1 = \lfloor 0.5 \cdot 16 + \tfrac{1}{2} \rfloor = 8$, $K_2 = \lfloor 0.3 \cdot 16 + \tfrac{1}{2} \rfloor = 5$,

```
// WEIGHTED AGGREGATION ALGORITHM WA2 (the iterative case of 2 variables)
// Function F is the symmetric idempotent base aggregator.
// Input x1 has the weight W
// Input x2 has the weight 1-W
// L = number of binary tree levels
// Run time = O(L)

double WA2(double x1, double x2, double W, double(*F)(double,double),int L)
{
    int B = int(W*pow(2.,L)+0.5) - 1;
    double y = x1;
    while(L--)
    {
        y = F(y, B%2 ?  x1 : x2);
        B/=2;
    }
    return y;
}
```

Figure 2.5.26 A C++ function that implements the WA2 algorithm.

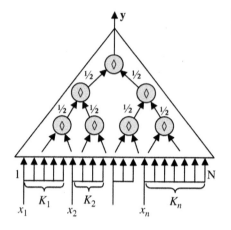

Figure 2.5.27 A general weighted aggregation structure.

and $K_3 = N - K_1 - K_2 = 3$. The resulting binary tree and its simplification based on idempotency are shown in Fig. 2.5.28. The desired approximation is:

$$0.5x_1 \Diamond 0.5(0.5x_2 \Diamond 0.5(0.5x_3 \Diamond 0.5(0.5x_2 0.5x_3)))$$
$$= 0.5x_1 \Diamond 0.5^2x_2 \Diamond 0.5^3x_3 \Diamond 0.5^4x_2 \Diamond 0.5^4x_3$$
$$= 0.5x_1 \Diamond \left(0.5^2 + 0.5^4\right)x_2 \Diamond \left(0.5^3 + 0.5^4\right)x_3$$
$$= 0.5x_1 \Diamond 0.3125x_2 \Diamond 0.1875x_3 \approx 0.5x_1 \Diamond 0.3x_2 \Diamond 0.2x_3 \ .$$

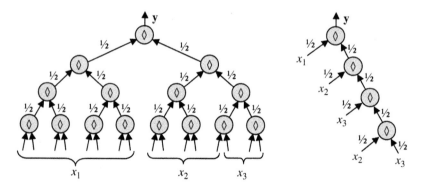

Figure 2.5.28 Creating a weighted aggregator with multiple inputs from a bivariate aggregator with equal weights.

In the case of quasi-arithmetic means we can develop a general weighted aggregation algorithm for n variables based on the following quasi-arithmetic means associativity:

$$y = f^{-1}[W_1 f(x_1) + W_2 f(x_2) + \ldots + W_{n-1} f(x_{n-1}) + W_n f(x_n)]$$

$$= f^{-1}\left[W_1 f(x_1) + W_2 f(x_2) + (W_{n-1} + W_n) \frac{W_{n-1} f(x_{n-1}) + W_n f(x_n)}{W_{n-1} + W_n} \right]$$

$$= f^{-1}\left\{ W_1 f(x_1) + W_2 f(x_2) + (W_{n-1} + W_n) f\left[f^{-1}\left(\frac{W_{n-1} f(x_{n-1}) + W_n f(x_n)}{W_{n-1} + W_n} \right) \right] \right\}.$$

Consequently, a general WAn algorithm for $n > 2$ variables can be organized by repeating $n-1$ times the WA2 algorithm as follows:

$$y \leftarrow WA2 \leftarrow WA2 \leftarrow WA2 \leftarrow WA2 \leftarrow WA2 \leftarrow x_n$$
$$\uparrow \qquad \uparrow \qquad \uparrow \qquad \uparrow \qquad \uparrow$$
$$x_1 \qquad x_2 \qquad \ldots \qquad x_{n-2} \qquad x_{n-1}$$

Using this form of QAM associativity, a fast iterative IWAn algorithm with time complexity $O[(n-1)L]$ can be written as shown in Fig. 2.5.29.

Two basic performance components of the WA algorithms are the accuracy and the speed of computation. The performance can be analyzed using as a base aggregator the simple symmetric power mean of two variables $F(x_1, x_2) = \left(0.5 x_1^r + 0.5 x_2^r\right)^{1/r}$ to implement the target weighted power mean (WPM) of n variables $M^{[r]}(\mathbf{x}; \mathbf{W}) = \left(W_1 x_1^r + \ldots + W_n x_n^r\right)^{1/r}$. For the analysis of accuracy of

```
// WEIGHTED AGGREGATION ALGORITHM IWAn (the iterative case of n>=2 variables)
// Function F is the symmetric idempotent base aggregator.
// W[ ] = array of weights of inputs x[ ]
// L = number of binary tree levels
// Run time = O[(n-1)L]

double IWAn(double x[], double W[], int n, double(*F)(double,double),int L)
{
    --n;
    double Wsum = W[n], y = x[n];
    while(n)
    { --n;
      y = WA2(x[n], y, W[n]/(W[n]+Wsum), F, L);
      Wsum += W[n];
    }
    return y;
}
```

Figure 2.5.29 Iterative version of the WAn algorithm.

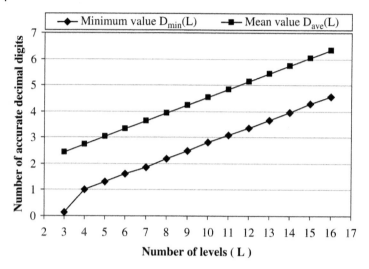

Figure 2.5.30 The number of accurate decimal digits *D(L)* generated by WA2.

WA2, we can compute the number of accurate significant decimal digits delivered by the WA2: $D(L) = |\log|WA2(x_1,x_2,W,F,L) - M^{[r]}(\mathbf{x};\mathbf{W})|/\log 10|$. If we use uniformly distributed random values of x_1, x_2, W and r, then a simulation model with 10^7 samples creates results shown in Fig. 2.5.30.

The results of simulation show that the mean number of accurate significant decimal digits generated by WA2 is a linear function of the number of levels: $D_{ave}(L) = 0.301L + 1.5233$. This result is obviously related to the binary coding of real numbers using mantissa and exponent. Indeed, if a *b*-bit binary number and a *d*-digit decimal number are equivalent, then $2^b = 10^d$ and $d = b\log_{10}(2) = 0.301b$, i.e., each bit contributes 0.301 significant decimal digit and 3.322 bits of mantissa are needed to provide one significant decimal digit. Thus, $D_{ave}(L)$ shows that each level in the WA tree contributes one correct bit of mantissa. So, a convenient value of *L* is *L* = 24 because that is the number of mantissa bits provided in the case of 32-bit standard precision real numbers.

A more detailed mathematical analysis of the presented procedure can be found in [BEL16a] and more examples showing accurate creation of multivariate aggregators can be found in [DUJ17a]. These papers also include very efficient recursive implementations of the WA algorithms. Binary trees of idempotent symmetric two variable aggregators are proved to be a general computational method for development and implementation of weighted idempotent aggregators of *n* variables. The run time of WA programs is $T = O(n)$, and the accuracy of results is a linear function of the number of levels *L* in the binary aggregation tree. This computational method has applicability that is equivalent to various analytical methods for expansion of specific two variable means proposed in the literature. However, the methods proposed in mathematical literature regularly apply to only a single specific mean and produce only symmetric aggregators of n variables. In contrast, the binary tree method applies to all idempotent aggregators (means) and generates both symmetric and asymmetric (weighted) aggregators of n variables.

2.6 Partial Absorption: A Fundamental Asymmetric Aggregator

Growing old is mandatory, growing wise is optional.

The most important simple aggregator in GL is GCD, and the most important compound aggregator is the partial absorption (PA). Introductory presentations of PA can be found in many places in this book: PA was introduced as Pattern 11 and Pattern 12 in section 2.1.2, then as a basic idempotent GL aggregator in Section 2.1.9, as the origin of the concept of multipolarity in Section 2.2.4, and as a model of heterogeneous annihilators in definitions 2.4.26 and 2.4.27 of Section 2.4.1. In this chapter we study PA in more detail, focusing on its analytic forms and implementation options.

Mixing mandatory and optional requirements is the most frequent type of asymmetric logic aggregation based on heterogeneous annihilators. It is present in almost all evaluation problems. For example, when people select the location of their home they usually aggregate components such as distance from work (for parents), distance from school (for children), distance from entertainment, shopping, hospitals, post office, etc. These individual criteria are usually partitioned into two groups: mandatory and optional. The low distances from work and school are frequently interpreted as mandatory requirements, while the low distances from the post office or entertainment facilities may be optional (desired, but not mandatory). This asymmetry means that a home that is too far from school will be rejected, while a suitably located home that is too far from a post office will be moderately penalized in scoring but not rejected. The aggregator that is used for aggregating mandatory and optional/desired inputs is called the *conjunctive partial absorption* (CPA). According to Definition 2.4.26, CPA can be interpreted as an asymmetric partial conjunction.

Another similar asymmetric aggregation with heterogeneous annihilators is the mix of sufficient and desired requirements. For example, buyers of an apartment in an urban area might prefer to have a private garage for their car, but in the absence of garage they would also accept a suitable public parking. If a private garage is available, buyer's requirements are completely satisfied regardless

Soft Computing Evaluation Logic: The LSP Decision Method and Its Applications,
First Edition. Jozo Dujmović.
© 2018 John Wiley & Sons, Inc. Published 2018 by John Wiley & Sons, Inc.
Companion website: www.wiley.com/go/Dujmovic/Soft_Computing_Evaluation_Logic

of the availability of public parking. Therefore, the garage plays the role of sufficient requirement, while the public parking is desired, but not sufficient to fulfill all buyer's expectations. The aggregator that is used for aggregating sufficient and desired inputs is called the *disjunctive partial absorption* (DPA). According to Definition 2.4.27, DPA can be interpreted as an asymmetric partial disjunction.

Heterogeneous annihilators of CPA and DPA should be contrasted to homogeneous annihilators of GCD. GCD combines logically symmetric inputs and uses homogeneous annihilators. The only asymmetry of GCD inputs comes from unequal weights, but from the formal logic standpoint all inputs express the same type of requirements (conjunctive or disjunctive) that sometimes can be mandatory, or sufficient. All GCD inputs reflect the same mix of conjunctive and disjunctive properties. All GCD inputs are either hard or soft. As opposed to that, in the cases of CPA and DPA, one input is hard and the other one is soft.

CPA and DPA are special cases of the PA function. The CPA was first introduced in [DUJ74b]; then, CPA and DPA were presented in [DUJ75a] and a detailed analysis of PA is provided in [DUJ79a] and later expanded in [DUJ14a].

2.6.1 Conjunctive Partial Absorption

Partial conjunction (PC) and partial disjunction (PD) are functions that model simultaneity and substitutability with adjustable andness and orness. The hard partial conjunction (HPC) supports the annihilator 0 in all input variables and the soft partial conjunction (SPC) is a model of low-andness simultaneity and does not support the annihilator 0. Similarly, the hard partial disjunction (HPD) supports the annihilator 1 in all input variables and the soft partial disjunction (SPD) is a model of low-orness substitutability and does not support the annihilator 0.

All inputs of PC or PD must satisfy the same type of requirements. In the case of PC, all inputs are expected to be simultaneously satisfied and failure of any one of them to satisfy its corresponding requirement has the same consequence: low output preference for SPC or zero output preference for HPC. Of course, the weights are used to differentiate the importance of individual inputs, but they do not change the essential logic features of the GCD function. Similarly, in the case of substitutability each of inputs is sufficient to partially (for SPD) or completely (for HPD) satisfy user's requirements. For both PC and PD weights determine the relative level of satisfaction without affecting the annihilator homogeneity of inputs.

In many evaluation problems, however, we need more sophisticated logic relationships, where inputs have different roles that require annihilator heterogeneity. The annihilator heterogeneity is most frequently modeled using the CPA (also called the *mandatory/desired function*). CPA is symbolically

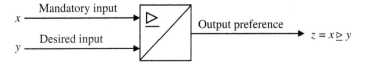

Figure 2.6.1 Inputs and output of the CPA aggregator.

presented in Fig. 2.6.1. This function is an asymmetric combination of a mandatory component x that must be satisfied (i.e., it supports the annihilator 0) and an optional component y that is desired, but not mandatory (i.e., it does not support the annihilator 0). The desired input can contribute to the value of the output preference, but it cannot replace the mandatory component. The CPA operator $\unrhd$ uses two arguments *mandatory* $\unrhd$ *desired* (the mandatory input is always on the left of the operator $\unrhd$ and the desired input is on the right).

The role of the mandatory input x is different from the role of the desired input y. If the mandatory input is not satisfied ($x = 0$) then the output preference is 0 regardless the value of the desired/optional input y. On the other hand, if the mandatory input is partially satisfied ($x > 0$) and the desired/optional input is not satisfied ($y = 0$), then the output preference would still be positive, according to the following conditions:

$$0 \unrhd y = 0, \quad 0 \leq y \leq 1,$$

$$x \unrhd 0 > 0, \quad 0 < x \leq 1,$$

$$x \unrhd 0 < x, \quad x \unrhd 0 = x - P_{CPA}, \quad 0 < x \leq 1, \quad 0 < P_{CPA} < 1,$$

$$x \unrhd 1 > x, \quad x \unrhd 1 = x + R_{CPA}, \quad 0 < x < 1, \quad 0 < R_{CPA} < 1. \tag{2.6.1}$$

The positive values P_{CPA} and R_{CPA} are, respectively, called *penalty* and *reward*. Both the penalty and the reward can be multiplied by 100 and expressed as percentages. In the majority of applications $P_{CPA} > R_{CPA}$. A typical penalty range is from 10% to 30% and a typical reward is from 5% to 20%. The parameters P_{CPA} and R_{CPA} can be adjusted according to specific user needs, and this process is presented in Chapter 3.5. The relations (2.6.1) can be summarized as shown in Table 2.6.1.

Examples of the mandatory/desired function can be found in many areas. In the case of traditional job selection problem the evaluator can establish the following asymmetric criterion:

Monetary compensation (as a part of job evaluation problems):

- Mandatory
  - Monthly salary (regular pay)
- Desired (but not mandatory)
  - Fringe benefits (free life and/or health insurance, a pension, paid holidays, free parking, etc.)

Table 2.6.1 Fundamental properties of the mandatory/desired function.

Mandatory input x	Desired input y	Output
0% (worthless)	100% (perfect)	0%
100%	0%	100% – Penalty
0<X<100%	0%	X – Penalty
0<X<100%	100%	X + Reward

Obviously, a sufficiently high monthly salary can always compensate poor or nonexistent fringe benefits. On the other hand, the best fringe benefits cannot compensate the absence of salary. So, this is an obvious asymmetric relationship.

Homebuyers always consider the location of home as one of the most important criteria. For example:

Location of home:
- Mandatory
  - Distance from work
- Desired
  - Distance from theater

Assuming that the homebuyer has to go to work every working day, it is mandatory that the distance from work is sufficiently low. The frequency of going to theater is supposed to be substantially less than the frequency of going to work. Therefore, the homebuyer will reject a home that is located next to theater, but very far from work. On the other hand, if the home is located very close to work, the homebuyer may be ready to accept it even if the theater is located rather far from home. A numerical example that illustrates such evaluation is presented in Table 2.6.2. In this example, the evaluator applies the penalty of 20% if the desired input (distance from theater) is not satisfied. If the home is very close to the theater, this rewards the location of home by 10% above the preference obtained for the distance from work. However, the distance from work is the mandatory requirement, and it is the distance from work that primarily affects the output preference.

Table 2.6.2 Sample suitability scores for evaluation of the location of home.

Distance from work	Distance from theater	Location of home
0%	100%	0%
100%	0%	80%
70%	0%	56%
70%	100%	77%

The number of mandatory and desired criteria can be greater than one. For example, a family with a child can establish the following criterion:

Location of home:

- Mandatory:
  - Distance from work for husband
  - Distance from work for wife
  - Distance from school for child
- Desired:
  - Distance from theater
  - Distance from shopping area
  - Distance from swimming pool

Since the mandatory/desired function has only two inputs, this criterion can be organized as shown in Fig. 2.6.2. The mandatory items are aggregated using a hard simultaneity operator (e.g., a geometric mean or stronger), and desired items are aggregated using the neutrality operator (arithmetic mean). The weights define the level of importance: this family considers the distance from school for their child two times more important than the work distance for one of parents. Similarly, shopping distance is considered the most important among desired items, and the theater distance is the least important.

Possible implementations and the adjustment of parameters of the mandatory/desired function are presented in detail in Chapter 3.5. As an introduction to this area, let us note that the aggregation of a mandatory input x and a desired input y is similar to the classic logic absorption theorem:

$$x \trianglerighteq y = x \wedge (x \vee y) = (x \wedge x) \vee (x \wedge y) = x \vee (x \wedge y) = x \wedge (1 \vee y) = x \wedge 1 = x,$$

$$0 \leq x \leq 1, \quad 0 \leq y \leq 1.$$

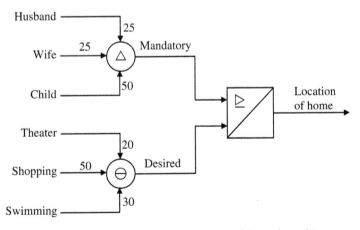

Figure 2.6.2 A criterion with three mandatory and three desired inputs.

This theorem can also be written as follows:

$$x \trianglerighteq y = \min(x, \max(x,y)) = \begin{cases} \min(x,x) = x, & x \geq y, \\ \min(x,y) = x, & x \leq y. \end{cases}$$

Here, the mandatory input *completely absorbs* the desired input: $x \trianglerighteq y = x$. The output does not depend on y, and this is *not* what we need for the mandatory/desired function. However, if the conjunction is substituted by the partial conjunction, and the disjunction is substituted by the partial disjunction, then we get the following *conjunctive partial absorption* function:

$$z = x \trianglerighteq y = x\Delta(x \nabla y). \tag{2.6.2}$$

The CPA function implements the mandatory/desired functionality. This function has exactly the properties that we need: x is a mandatory input, y is a desired input, and x partially absorbs y. It can be implemented using weighted power means as follows:

$$z = x \trianglerighteq y = x\Delta(x \nabla y) = \left\{ (1-W_2)[W_1 x^q + (1-W_1)y^q]^{r/q} + W_2 x^r \right\}^{1/r},$$

$$0 < W_1 < 1, \quad 0 < W_2 < 1, \quad 0 \leq x \leq 1, \quad 0 \leq y \leq 1,$$

$$1 \leq q \leq +\infty, \quad -\infty \leq r < 1, \quad 0 \leq z \leq 1.$$

$$\tag{2.6.3}$$

The parameters of this function are W_1, W_2, q, and r. They can be adjusted to achieve desired properties of the function (e.g., desired penalty and reward levels). A simpler special case of this function can be obtained if the partial disjunction ∇ is replaced by the arithmetic mean $\ominus$:

$$z = x \trianglerighteq y = x\Delta(x \ominus y). \tag{2.6.4}$$

By inserting $q = 1$ in (2.6.3), we have

$$z = x \trianglerighteq y = x\Delta(x \ominus y) = \left\{ (1-W_2)[W_1 x + (1-W_1)y]^r + W_2 x^r \right\}^{1/r}.$$

The implementations of functions (2.6.2) and (2.6.4) are shown in Fig. 2.6.3.

Mandatory and desired inputs are two logical levels in decreasing level of influence. Sometimes, it can be necessary to have three levels: *mandatory*, *desired*, and *optional*. Fundamental properties of the mandatory/desired/optional (MDO) function are shown in Table 2.6.3. The function implements two levels of penalty and can also be tuned to have two levels of reward.

To implement this compound function, we can use two levels of the partial absorption, as shown in Fig. 2.6.4. Adjustment of parameters is now more

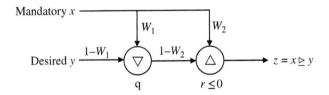

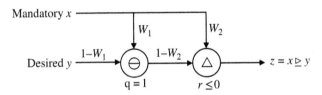

Figure 2.6.3 Two implementations of the conjunctive partial absorption function.

Table 2.6.3 Fundamental properties of the mandatory/desired/optional function.

Mandatory input x	Desired input y	Optional input t	Output preference z
0% (worthless)	100% (perfect)	100% (perfect)	0%
100%	0%	100%	100% – MajorPenalty
100%	100%	0%	100% – MinorPenalty
0<X<100%	0%	100%	X – MajorPenalty
0<X<100%	100%	100%	X + Reward

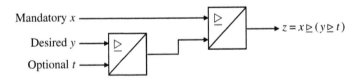

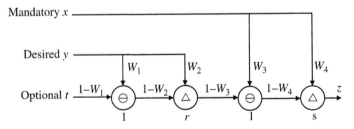

Figure 2.6.4 The mandatory/desired/optional function.

difficult because there are six adjustable parameters (W_1, W_2, W_3, W_4, r, s). The function $z = x \trianglerighteq (y \trianglerighteq t)$ is not the only way to implement the MDO aggregator. Alternative implementations, discussed in Section 3.5.6 and shown in Fig. 3.5.10, are the following:

$$z = (x \trianglerighteq y) \trianglerighteq t),$$

$$z = x \trianglerighteq (y \ominus t) = x\bar{\Delta}(x \ominus y \ominus t).$$

2.6.2 Disjunctive Partial Absorption

The *sufficient/desired function* (or the disjunctive partial absorption, DPA) is an asymmetric combination of a component y that is desired and a component x that is sufficient to completely satisfy the user's requirements. The sufficient/desired operator is $\bar{\triangleright}$. It is used as follows: *sufficient$\bar{\triangleright}$desired* (the sufficient input is always on the left of the operator and the desired input is on the right). A typical behavior of this function is presented in Table 2.6.4. In practice, the value of penalty is regularly very small (e.g., less than 10%), and the rewards are rather large (typically from 20% to 75%). A symbolic presentation of the sufficient/desired function is shown in Fig. 2.6.5.

There is symmetry between the mandatory/desired function (conjunctive partial absorption, CPA) and the sufficient/desired function. The mandatory/desired function was based on the traditional absorption theorem $x \wedge (x \vee y) = x \wedge (1 \vee y) = x$. A dual absorption theorem is $x \vee (x \wedge y) = (x \vee x) \wedge (x \vee y) = x \wedge (x \vee y) = x$, or

Table 2.6.4 Fundamental properties of the sufficient/desired function (DPA).

Sufficient input x	Desired input y	Output
100% (perfect)	X (any value)	100%
0<X<100%	0% (worthless)	X – Penalty
0≤X<100%	100%	X + Reward

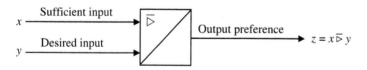

Figure 2.6.5 Inputs and output of the sufficient/desired function.

$$\max(x, \min(x,y)) = \begin{cases} \max(x,y) = x, & x \geq y, \\ \max(x,x) = x, & x \leq y, \end{cases}$$

$$0 \leq x \leq 1, \quad 0 \leq y \leq 1.$$

This theorem can be used to organize the sufficient/desired function using partial conjunction and partial disjunction, as follows:

$$z = x \bar{\triangleright} y = x \nabla (x \Delta y). \tag{2.6.5}$$

Other versions of this function are:

$$z = x \bar{\triangleright} y = x \nabla (x \ominus y), \tag{2.6.6}$$

and

$$z = x \bar{\triangleright} y = x \vee (x \ominus y). \tag{2.6.7}$$

Therefore, similarly to CPA, DPA can also be implemented using the weighted power mean:

$$z = x \bar{\triangleright} y = \left\{ (1 - W_2)[W_1 x^q + (1 - W_1)y^q]^{r/q} + W_2 x^r \right\}^{1/r},$$
$$0 < W_1 < 1, \quad 0 < W_2 < 1, \quad 0 \leq x \leq 1, \quad 0 \leq y \leq 1, \tag{2.6.8}$$
$$-\infty \leq q \leq 1, \quad 1 < r \leq +\infty, \quad 0 \leq z \leq 1.$$

The implementations of DPA based on definitions (2.6.5) and (2.6.6) are shown in Fig. 2.6.6. The difference between CPA and DPA is only in the range of parameters. Consequently, CPA and DPA are two different interpretations

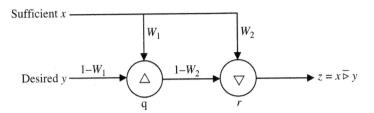

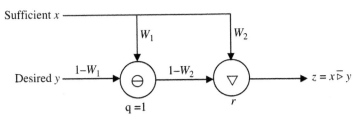

Figure 2.6.6 Two implementations of the disjunctive partial absorption function.

of the same partial absorption function, which can be implemented using formula (2.6.8).

As an example of the sufficient/desired criterion, let us again consider the buyer of an apartment in an urban area that has parking problems. The buyer has a car and would prefer that the apartment includes a private garage. However, if this is not available, the buyer might accept the apartment in an area where s/he can use acceptable public parking. The quality of public parking is evaluated using three elementary criteria: distance from home, safety, and permanent (24/7) availability. If the garage is available, then this is the preferred solution that is sufficient to fully satisfy the buyer. However, if the garage is not available, then it is desired to have a good public parking. Therefore, the structure of the parking criterion is as follows:

Parking:
- Sufficient
  - Garage in home
- Desired
  - Distance from home to public parking
  - Safety of public parking
  - Availability of public parking at any time of day

If the buyer believes that the public parking solution can satisfy only 65% of his/her needs, and all desired public parking components are equally important and must be simultaneously satisfied, then the corresponding sufficient/desired function can be organized as shown in Fig. 2.6.7. This function has zero penalty and the maximum reward of 60%, realized by an ideal public parking, but no garage. This function uses the pure disjunction as in definition (2.6.7) and, consequently, the output aggregator does not use weights. The quality of this parking is $Q = \max(G, 0.6P + 0.4G)$. So, if the home garage is better than the public parking $(G > P)$, then $Q = G$ and the output is not affected by the suitability of public parking. However, if the public parking is better than the private garage $(G \le P)$, then $Q = 0.6P + 0.4G$ and both the private garage and the public

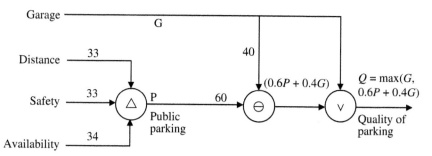

Figure 2.6.7 A sufficient/desired criterion for the evaluation of private/public parking.

parking contribute to the overall suitability of parking. Regardless the ultimate simplicity, this aggregator can be useful. If the evaluator wants the quality of public parking to affect the output suitability in a more flexible way, either model (2.6.5) or (2.6.6) must be used, substituting the pure disjunction in Fig. 2.6.7 with an appropriate hard partial disjunction.

2.6.3 Visualizing the Partial Absorption Function, Penalty, and Reward

The introductory presentation of CPA and DPA in Sections 2.6.1 and 2.6.2 can be summarized shown in Fig. 2.6.8. According to Table 2.4.2, the functions used to make CPA and DPA include the following: Δ (partial conjunction, either hard or soft), $\bar{\Delta}$ (hard partial conjunction or HPC), $\bar{\bar{\Delta}}$ (extended hard partial conjunction or EHPC, $\bar{\bar{\Delta}} \in \{\bar{\Delta}, \wedge\}$), ∇ (partial disjunction, either hard or soft), $\bar{\nabla}$ (hard partial disjunction or HPD), $\bar{\bar{\nabla}}$ (extended hard partial disjunction or EHPD,

Figure 2.6.8 Three characteristic implementations of the CPA and DPA aggregators.

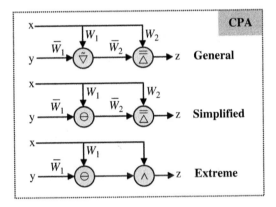

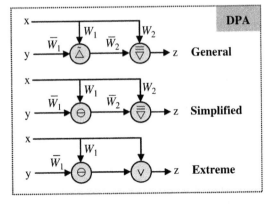

$\bar{\bar{\nabla}} \in \{\bar{\nabla}, \vee\}$), $\ominus$ (neutrality or arithmetic mean), $\tilde{\Delta}$ (extended conjunction $\tilde{\Delta} \in \{\ominus, \bar{\bar{\Delta}}\}$), and $\tilde{\nabla}$ (extended disjunction $\tilde{\nabla} \in \{\ominus, \bar{\bar{\nabla}}\}$).

Fig. 2.6.8 shows three types of CPA and DPA: *general* (covering the whole spectrum PC and PD combinations), *simplified* (combinations that always use the neutrality for aggregating the optional input), and *extreme* (the simplest combination of arithmetic mean and full conjunction/disjunction). Using the simplified CPA where the GCD is based on WPM.17 aggregators C, C+, CA, C−, A, D−, DA, D+, and D, we can perform a continuous transition from the extreme CPA to the extreme DPA, as shown in Fig. 2.6.9.

The first of the presented graphs shows an extreme case of CPA. The mandatory axis (going left from the origin) shows the penalty of 50%. The optional axis (going right from the origin) shows a strict zero value, corresponding to the zero mandatory input. A typical conjunctive partial absorption is illustrated by the graphs denoted C+ and CA.

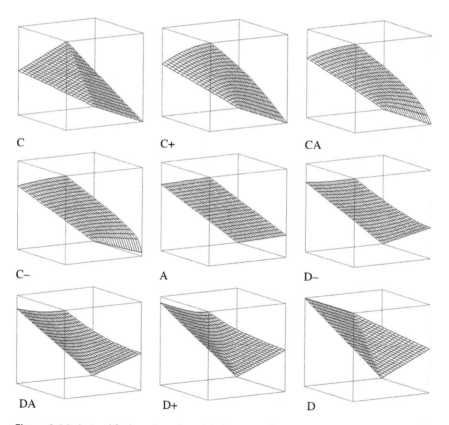

Figure 2.6.9 A simplified version of partial absorption function for $W_1 = W_2 = 0.5$ and aggregator GCD/WPM.17.

The last of the presented graphs shows an extreme case of DPA. The sufficient axis (going left from the origin) shows the strict value $z = 1$ if the sufficient input has the value 1. The optional axis (going right from the origin) shows a reward of 50%, corresponding to the maximum values 1 of the optional input, even if the sufficient input is zero. A typical disjunctive partial absorption is illustrated by the graphs denoted DA and D+.

The extreme cases of CPA and DPA, the values of penalty and reward, and the regions of penalty and reward are shown in Fig. 2.6.10. The models of extreme CPA and DPA aggregators are the following:

$$CPA: \quad z = x \unrhd y = \min(x, W_1 x + \bar{W}_1 y) = \begin{cases} W_1 x, & y = 0, \\ W_1 x + \bar{W}_1 y, & y < x, \\ x, & y \geq x; \end{cases}$$

$$DPA: \quad z = x \bar{\rhd} y = \max(x, W_1 x + \bar{W}_1 y) = \begin{cases} \bar{W}_1 y, & x = 0, \\ W_1 x + \bar{W}_1 y, & x < y, \\ x, & x \geq y. \end{cases}$$

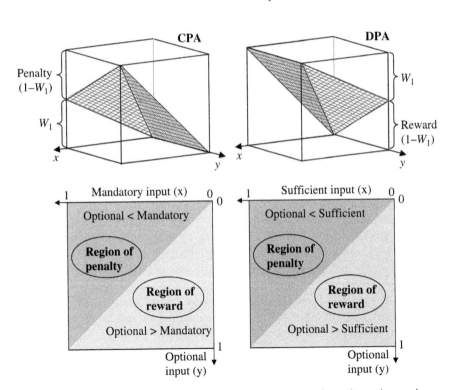

Figure 2.6.10 Extreme cases of CPA and DPA and the regions of penalty and reward.

In the case of CPA, if $y = 0$ the output value is

$$z = x - penalty = W_1 x \;\Rightarrow\; penalty = (1 - W_1)x \;\Rightarrow\; \max(penalty) = 1 - W_1.$$

Similarly, in the case of DPA, if $x = 0$ the output value is

$$z = reward = \bar{W}_1 y \;\Rightarrow\; \max(reward) = 1 - W_1.$$

Therefore, the weight of the optional input $(1 - W_1)$ determines both the maximum penalty and the maximum reward of the partial absorption function. However, in the case of PA aggregators that are not extreme and have nonlinear properties shown in Fig. 2.6.9 the computation of penalty and reward is more complex. We study these problems in the next section.

2.6.4　Mathematical Models of Penalty and Reward

The reason for our interest in penalty and reward indicators of the partial absorption aggregator is practical. According to formulas (2.6.3) and (2.6.8), general PA aggregators have four parameters: the weights W_1, W_2 and the power mean exponents q and r. Thus, users of PA aggregators must adjust four independent parameters and that cannot be done in a simple intuitive way. We either need software tools or a simpler method for adjustment of parameters. That is where we need penalty and reward.

The primary input of the PA aggregator has a fixed role: it is either mandatory or sufficient. On the other hand, the role of the optional input is to penalize cases where the optional input is less than the main mandatory/sufficient input and to reward cases where the optional input is greater than the main/sufficient input. Fortunately, it is very easy to choose between CPA and DPA and it is not difficult to select desired values of penalty and reward. So, our practical goal is to use penalty and reward as inputs for computing appropriate parameters of the partial absorption aggregator. In [DUJ79a] that was achieved using tables and in [DUJ91], using a software tool.

The fundamental property of CPA is $0 \trianglerighteq y = 0$ making x a mandatory input. Similarly, for DPA from $1 \triangleright y = 1$ it follows that x is a sufficient input. For both CPA and DPA y is an optional input: it is desirable that y has a high value but this is not necessary because the output is mostly affected by the primary input x.

Suppose that $0 < x < 1$ and let us now investigate two characteristic cases: $y < x$ and $y > x$. If $y < x$ then both $x \trianglerighteq y < x$ and $x \triangleright y < x$. Consequently, we can say that the provided value of x is penalized by the insufficient satisfaction of y. That yields the following definitions of the *local penalty*:

$$P_{CPA}(x,y) = x - x \trianglerighteq y,$$
$$P_{DPA}(x,y) = x - x \triangleright y, \quad y < x.$$

If $y > x$ then both $x \trianglerighteq y > x$ and $x \bar{\triangleright} y > x$. So, we can say that the provided value of x is rewarded by the abundant satisfaction of y. That yields the following definitions of the *local reward*:

$$R_{CPA}(x,y) = x \trianglerighteq y - x,$$

$$R_{DPA}(x,y) = x \bar{\triangleright} y - x, \quad y > x.$$

The regions of penalty and reward for CPA and DPA are shown in Fig. 2.6.10 and, in more detail, in Fig. 2.6.11.

Similarly to local andness/orness, the local penalty and the local reward are inconvenient indicators because they are different in each point. More convenient indicators are the mean relative penalty and the mean relative reward that should be integrated over the whole triangular region of penalty or the whole triangular region of reward. According to Fig. 2.6.10, we can note that for CPA, a high penalty can be achieved using a low value of W_1 (i.e., a high value of $\bar{W}_1 = 1 - W_1$) and a high andness of the output aggregator to maximize the impact of changes of y. So, a high CPA penalty corresponds to the pure conjunction shown in Fig. 2.6.10. Similarly, for DPA, a high reward can be achieved in the case of using a low value of W_1 and a high orness of the output aggregator. Thus, a high DPA reward corresponds to the pure disjunction (Fig. 2.6.10).

In a general case of partial absorption (either conjunctive or disjunctive, $\trianglerighteq \in \{ \trianglerighteq , \bar{\triangleright} \}$), we can define the *mean relative penalty* $\bar{P}$ and the *mean relative reward* $\bar{R}$ as follows:

$$\bar{P} = \frac{\text{mean penalty}}{\max(\text{mean penalty})} = \frac{\int_0^1 dx \int_0^x [x - (x \trianglerighteq y)] dy}{\int_0^1 dx \int_0^x [x - (x \wedge y)] dy} = \frac{\int_0^1 dx \int_0^x (x - x \trianglerighteq y) dy}{\int_0^1 dx \int_0^x (x - y) dy}$$

$$= 2 - 6 \int_0^1 dx \int_0^x (x \trianglerighteq y) dy;$$

$$\bar{R} = \frac{\text{mean reward}}{\max(\text{mean reward})} = \frac{\int_0^1 dx \int_x^1 [(x \trianglerighteq y) - x] dy}{\int_0^1 dx \int_x^1 [(x \vee y) - x] dy} = \frac{\int_0^1 dx \int_x^1 [(x \trianglerighteq y) - x] dy}{\int_0^1 dx \int_x^1 (y - x) dy}$$

$$= 6 \int_0^1 dx \int_x^1 (x \trianglerighteq y) dy - 1.$$

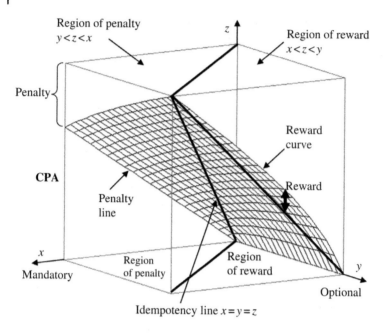

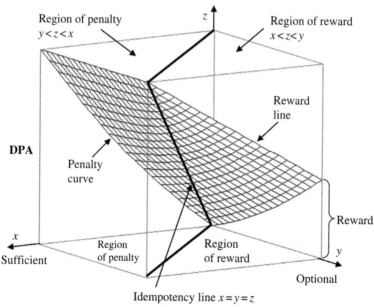

Figure 2.6.11 General forms of CPA and DPA aggregators with penalty and reward curves.

To test the penalty and reward indicators, let us consider extreme cases of CPA and DPA shown in Figs. 2.6.8 and 2.6.10. For CPA, the resulting $\bar{P}$ and $\bar{R}$ are

$$\bar{P} = 2 - 6 \int_0^1 dx \int_0^x [W_1 x + (1 - W_1)y] \, dy = 1 - W_1,$$

$$\bar{R} = 6 \int_0^1 dx \int_x^1 x \, dy - 1 = 0.$$

For DPA, the resulting $\bar{P}$ and $\bar{R}$ are

$$\bar{P} = 2 - 6 \int_0^1 dx \int_0^x x \, dy = 0,$$

$$\bar{R} = 6 \int_0^1 dx \int_x^1 [W_1 x + (1 - W_1)y] \, dy - 1 = 1 - W_1.$$

Therefore, the extreme cases of CPA and DPA aggregators are a zero-reward CPA and a zero-penalty DPA. In a general case, CPA and DPA provide both a penalty and a reward, as shown in Fig. 2.6.11. The role of the optional input y is to provide penalty in cases where $y < x$ and reward in cases where $y > x$. The mean relative penalty $\bar{P}$ and the mean relative reward $\bar{R}$ are suitable indicators, but not the only possible indicators of penalty and reward.

Designers of evaluation criteria are particularly interested in the boundary values of penalty and reward, i.e., the values $x \trianglerighteq 0$ and $x \trianglerighteq 1$. The function $x \mapsto x \trianglerighteq 0$ shows the boundary (maximum) penalty caused by the absence of optional input ($y = 0$). Similarly, the function $x \mapsto x \trianglerighteq 1$ shows the boundary (maximum) value of reward caused by the complete satisfaction of the optional input ($y = 1$). According to Fig. 2.6.11, the *boundary penalty* for CPA is $\widetilde{P}_{CPA} = 1 - (1 \trianglerighteq 0)$, and the *boundary reward* for DPA is $\widetilde{R}_{DPA} = 0 \trianglelefteq 1$.

The boundary penalty and reward functions are shown in Fig. 2.6.12. These functions can be used to derive specific penalty and reward indicators.

In the case of CPA, the *equivalent reward indicator* $\left(\widetilde{R}\right)$ is computed from the condition that the area under the straight line $z = \widetilde{R} + \left(1 - \widetilde{R}\right)x$ equals the area under the curve $z_m(x) = x \trianglerighteq 1$:

$$1 - \frac{1 - \widetilde{R}_{CPA}}{2} = \int_0^1 (x \trianglerighteq 1) \, dx,$$

$$\widetilde{R}_{CPA} = 2 \int_0^1 (x \trianglerighteq 1) \, dx - 1.$$

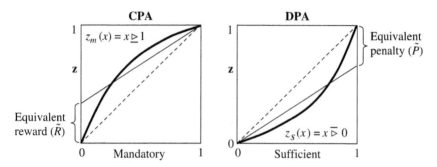

Figure 2.6.12 Boundary forms of penalty and reward functions.

In the extreme CPA case, we have $x \trianglerighteq y = x \wedge (W_1 x + \bar{W}_1 y)$ and $x \trianglerighteq 1 = x \wedge (W_1 x + \bar{W}_1) = x$. As expected, the equivalent reward is $\tilde{R}_{CPA} = 2 \int_0^1 x dx - 1 = 0$.

Similar condition can be used for the equivalent penalty in the case of DPA. The *equivalent penalty indicator* $(\tilde{P})$ can be computed from the condition that the area under the straight line $z = (1 - \tilde{P})x$ equals the area under the curve $z_s(x) = x \bar{\triangleright} 0$:

$$\frac{1 - \tilde{P}_{DPA}}{2} = \int_0^1 (x \bar{\triangleright} 0) dx,$$

$$\tilde{P}_{DPA} = 1 - 2 \int_0^1 (x \bar{\triangleright} 0) dx.$$

Let us now investigate PA aggregators implemented using the weighted power means (Figs. 2.6.9 and 2.6.11). In the case of CPA, we use the following model:

$$z = CPA(x, y; W_1, \omega, W_2, \alpha) = \left[\bar{W}_2 (W_1 x^q + \bar{W}_1 y^q)^{r/q} + W_2 x^r \right]^{1/r},$$

$$0 < W_1 < 1, \quad 0 < W_2 < 1, \quad 0 \leq x \leq 1, \quad 0 \leq y \leq 1, \quad 0 \leq z \leq 1,$$

$$1 \leq q(\omega) \leq +\infty, \quad q(\frac{1}{2}) = 1, \quad q(1) = +\infty,$$

$$-\infty \leq r(\alpha) \leq 0, \quad r(2/3) = 0, \quad r(1) = -\infty.$$

If $y = 0$, we get the penalty line shown in Fig. 2.6.11:

$$z = CPA(x,0; W_1, \omega, W_2, \alpha) = \left[\bar{W}_2 (W_1 x^q)^{r/q} + W_2 x^r \right]^{1/r} = x \left(\bar{W}_2 W_1^{r/q} + W_2 \right)^{1/r},$$

$$P_{CPA}(x,0) = x - x \trianglerighteq 0 = x \left[1 - \left(\bar{W}_2 W_1^{r/q} + W_2 \right)^{1/r} \right],$$

$$\tilde{P}_{CPA} = P_{CPA}(1,0) = 1 - \left(\bar{W}_2 W_1^{r/q} + W_2 \right)^{1/r}.$$

Similarly, the equivalent reward is

$$\tilde{R}_{CPA} = 2 \int_0^1 \left[\bar{W}_2 (W_1 x^q + \bar{W}_1)^{r/q} + W_2 x^r \right]^{1/r} dx - 1.$$

Let us now introduce two characteristic special cases of PA, denoted AG and AH in Fig. 2.6.13 and in Table 2.6.5. These are cases of CPA, where the output HPC aggregator is implemented as the geometric mean (G) or the harmonic mean (H).

Using the WPM penalty and reward indicators, we have the following maximum penalty and reward for AG:

$$\tilde{P}_{AG} = 1 - \lim_{r \to 0} \left(\bar{W}_2 W_1^r + W_2 \right)^{1/r} = 1 - W_1^{\bar{W}_2},$$

$$\tilde{R}_{AG} = 2 \lim_{r \to 0} \int_0^1 \left[\bar{W}_2 (W_1 x + \bar{W}_1)^r + W_2 x^r \right]^{1/r} dx - 1 = 2 \int_0^1 (W_1 x + \bar{W}_1)^{\bar{W}_2} x^{W_2} dx - 1.$$

$$(2.6.9)$$

Similarly, for AH we have

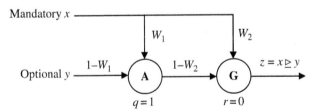

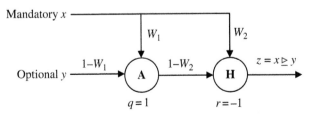

Figure 2.6.13 Special cases of CPA based on the arithmetic and geometric mean (AG) and based on the arithmetic and harmonic mean (AH).

Table 2.6.5 Characteristic special cases of CPA and DPA.

Type	Symbol	Description
CPA	DC	Disjunction and conjunction (extreme general case) $x \unrhd y = x \wedge (x \vee y) = x$
	A:PC	Arithmetic mean and partial conjunction $x \unrhd y = W_2 x \Delta \bar{W}_2 (W_1 x + \bar{W}_1 y)$
	AG	Arithmetic mean and geometric mean $x \unrhd y = x^{W_2}(W_1 x + \bar{W}_1 y)^{\bar{W}_2}$
	AH	Arithmetic mean and harmonic mean $x \unrhd y = 1/[W_2/x + \bar{W}_2/(W_1 x + \bar{W}_1 y)]$
	AC	Arithmetic mean and pure conjunction $x \unrhd y = x \wedge (W_1 x + \bar{W}_1 y)$
DPA	CD	Conjunction and disjunction (extreme general case) $x \, \bar{\rhd} \, y = x \vee (x \wedge y) = x$
	A:PD	Arithmetic mean and partial disjunction $x \, \bar{\rhd} \, y = W_2 x \nabla \bar{W}_2 (W_1 x + \bar{W}_1 y)$
	A$\underline{G}$	Ari. mean and a dual of geometric mean $x \, \bar{\rhd} \, y = 1 - \bar{x}^{W_2}(1 - W_1 x - \bar{W}_1 y)^{\bar{W}_2}$
	A$\underline{H}$	Ari. mean and a dual of harmonic mean $x \, \bar{\rhd} \, y = 1 - 1/[W_2/\bar{x} + \bar{W}_2/(1 - W_1 x - \bar{W}_1 y)]$
	AD	Arithmetic mean and pure disjunction $x \, \bar{\rhd} \, y = x \vee (W_1 x + \bar{W}_1 y)$

$$\tilde{P}_{AH} = 1 - (\bar{W}_2/W_1 + W_2)^{-1},$$

$$\tilde{R}_{AH} = 2\int_0^1 [\bar{W}_2/(W_1 x + \bar{W}_1) + W_2/x]^{-1} dx - 1. \tag{2.6.10}$$

AG and AH aggregators are rather similar. For example, for $W_1 = W_2 = \frac{1}{2}$, we have $\tilde{P}_{AG} = 0.293$, $\tilde{P}_{AH} = 0.333$. If we select desired values of penalty and reward then from (2.6.9) and (2.6.10) we can develop numerical procedures for computing the necessary values of the parameters W_1 and W_2.

In the case of DPA we need a hard partial disjunction (HPD) (i.e., an aggregator that supports the annihilator 1). Since WPM provides good models of HPC but does not support HPD, it follows that the necessary HPD must be created as a De Morgan dual of HPC: $x \bar{\nabla} y = 1 - \bar{x} \bar{\Delta} \bar{y}$. De Morgan duals of geometric and harmonic means are denoted $\underline{G}$ and $\underline{H}$ and used in Table 2.6.5 to create DPA aggregators A$\underline{G}$ and A$\underline{H}$. In a general case of WPM the GCD aggregator of two variables (symbolically denoted $W_1 x_1 \lozenge W_2 x_2$) that supports both HPC and HPD can be defined as follows:

$$W_1 x_1 \lozenge W_2 x_2 = \begin{cases} \lim_{p \to r} (W_1 x_1^p + W_2 x_2^p)^{1/p}, & -\infty \leq r \leq 1, \\ 1 - \lim_{p \to 2-r} (W_1 \bar{x}_1^p + W_2 \bar{x}_2^p)^{1/p}, & 1 \leq r \leq +\infty. \end{cases}$$

$$HPC(x_1,x_2;W_1,W_2,r) = \left(W_1 x_1^r + W_2 x_2^r\right)^{1/r}, \quad r \le 0,$$

$$HPD(x_1,x_2;W_1,W_2,r) = 1 - \left(W_1 \bar{x}_1^{2-r} + W_2 \bar{x}_2^{2-r}\right)^{1/(2-r)}, \quad r \ge 2.$$

$$\underline{G}(x_1,x_2;W_1,W_2) = HPD(x_1,x_2;W_1,W_2,2) = 1 - \bar{x}_1^{W_1} \bar{x}_2^{W_2},$$

$$\underline{H}(x_1,x_2;W_1,W_2) = HPD(x_1,x_2;W_1,W_2,3) = 1 - 1/(W_1/\bar{x}_1 + W_2/\bar{x}_2),$$

$$0 < W_1 < 1, \quad W_2 = \bar{W}_1 = 1 - W_1.$$

Penalty and reward indicators can also be defined in specific points of the unit cube. A suitable point for such a definition is the central point $x = y = z = \frac{1}{2}$. The *central point model* of penalty and reward can be defined as follows:

$$\hat{P} = \frac{(\frac{1}{2} \trianglerighteq \frac{1}{2}) - (\frac{1}{2} \trianglerighteq 0)}{(\frac{1}{2} \trianglerighteq \frac{1}{2})} = 1 - 2(\frac{1}{2} \trianglerighteq 0),$$

$$\hat{R} = \frac{(\frac{1}{2} \trianglerighteq 1) - (\frac{1}{2} \trianglerighteq \frac{1}{2})}{(\frac{1}{2} \trianglerighteq \frac{1}{2})} = 2(\frac{1}{2} \trianglerighteq 1) - 1,$$

$$\trianglerighteq \in \{\trianglerighteq, \bar{\triangleright}\}.$$

For example, for the AG aggregator and $W_1 = W_2 = \frac{1}{2}$ we have $x \trianglerighteq y = \sqrt{x(x+y)/2}$, $\hat{P} = 1 - 1/\sqrt{2} = 0.293$ and $\hat{R} = 0.225$.

2.6.5 Selecting Parameters of Partial Absorption

The indicators of penalty and reward are overall logic indicators that can be easily related to semantic aspects of the PA aggregator. For example, let us consider a homebuyer who evaluates a potential home location according to two input attributes: the mandatory vicinity to his/her job location and the desired but optional vicinity to restaurants. The majority of homebuyers have a clear perception of the overall importance of the optional PA input. Based on that perception, the homebuyer can select an appropriate overall degree of penalty if the restaurants are not available and an overall degree of reward if the restaurants are available. For example, if the presence of restaurants has relatively high importance, the homebuyer might select penalty and reward $P = 30\%$, $R = 20\%$, and in the case of low importance, the appropriate values might be $P = 15\%$, $R = 10\%$. In evaluation practice (see Chapter 3.5), decision makers are regularly capable of selecting desired values of penalty and reward. However, the same decision makers cannot easily determine all parameters of the PA function. Consequently, it is very desirable to have a technique for determining the values of PA parameters from the desired values of penalty and reward.

Generally, the PA aggregator has four parameters: the andness and weight of the input GCD aggregator (α_1, W_1) and the andness and weight of the output GCD aggregator (α_2, W_2). In the most frequent case of GCD based on WPM, the andness α_1 depends on the exponent q (Fig. 2.6.13) and the andness α_2 depends on the exponent r (and vice versa). So, the parameters can also be specified as q, W_1, r, W_2. All our penalty and reward parameters are functions of these parameters:

$$\bar{P} = \bar{\pi}(q, W_1, r, W_2), \quad \bar{R} = \bar{\rho}(q, W_1, r, W_2),$$
$$\widetilde{P} = \tilde{\pi}(q, W_1, r, W_2), \quad \widetilde{R} = \tilde{\rho}(q, W_1, r, W_2), \tag{2.6.11}$$
$$\hat{P} = \hat{\pi}(q, W_1, r, W_2), \quad \hat{R} = \hat{\rho}(q, W_1, r, W_2).$$

Analytic solution of any of the three systems of equations (2.6.11) in a general case is not possible. There are four unknown values (q, W_1, r, W_2), but we only have two equations specifying the desired values of P and R. To avoid problems with multiple solutions, we can select constant values for two of PA parameters. The simplest way is to use constant values of α_1 and α_2 (i.e., the fixed values of q and r), and then to use the desired penalty and reward conditions for computing the weights W_1 and W_2. In the majority of cases, it is convenient to select $\alpha_1 = \frac{1}{2}$, $q = 1$ because the PA aggregators that use the arithmetic mean as the input GCD aggregator behave similarly to the PA aggregators that use partial conjunction/disjunction as the input aggregator. Now we have a three parameter problem where W_1 and W_2 can be computed for a sequence of different values of α_2 and the desired values of P and R (cf. [DUJ79a]). In Fig. 2.6.8 such aggregators are denoted as "simplified."

Another general technique for computing q, W_1, r, W_2 is to specify a training set consisting of n desired x,y,z triples and to use it for training the PA preferential neuron using a software tool ANSY [DUJ91, SEA10]. This is realized as a function minimization problem, using the following criterion function:

$$f(q, W_1, r, W_2) = \sum_{i=1}^{n} |z_i - (x_i \trianglerighteq y_i)|^p,$$
$$p \in \{1,2\}, \quad \trianglerighteq \in \{\trianglerighteq, \triangleright\}.$$

The procedure is similar to the procedure we used in Section 2.5.4 for computing parameters of GCD. A detailed presentation can be found in Chapter 3.4.

Table 2.6.6 summarizes a numerical comparison of the mean relative penalty/reward ($\bar{P}, \bar{R}$), the boundary penalty/reward ($\widetilde{P}, \widetilde{R}$), and the central point penalty/reward ($\hat{P}, \hat{R}$) for the AH and AG aggregators with weights $W_1 = W_2 = \frac{1}{2}$. From this table we see that all three types of penalty/reward indicators generate consistent results. Differences between indicators are smaller for penalty than for reward. Because of the linear nature of boundary penalty, in the case of WPM aggregators we have $\widetilde{P} = \hat{P}$. Similarly, $\widetilde{R} = \bar{R}$. So, there is an overlap between the boundary penalty/reward and other two methods. The computational complexity is the lowest for the central point penalty/reward method and the highest for the mean relative penalty/reward. The boundary penalty/reward has a medium computational complexity and overlaps with the other two

Table 2.6.6 Numerical comparison of penalty and reward indicators.

Aggregator	Penalty			Reward		
	$\bar{P}$	$\tilde{P}$	$\hat{P}$	$\bar{R}$	$\tilde{R}$	$\hat{R}$
AH	0.301	0.333	0.333	0.145	0.145	0.2
AG	0.276	0.293	0.293	0.188	0.188	0.225

methods. Therefore, in this group of three methods, the boundary penalty/reward method takes the central position and seems to be the most convenient in applications. In cases where the primary goal is to reduce the computational complexity, the most suitable method is the central point penalty/reward.

Table 2.6.6 also shows that in the case of CPA, increasing the output andness (going from G to H) increases the value of penalty and decreases the value of reward, which is what should be expected since any increase of andness amplifies the impact of low input values. De Morgan versions of DPA aggregators are symmetric with the original CPA, and the properties of DPA and CPA are also symmetric.

To conclude this chapter, let us emphasize that the partial absorption aggregators play an important role in logic aggregation structures. Asymmetric properties of PA allow the aggregation of optional inputs and those that are mandatory or sufficient. Those are the most frequent forms of bipolarity. Semantic aspects of aggregation regularly make possible a rather easy specification of two overall indicators of PA: the overall penalty caused by no satisfaction of the optional input and the overall reward caused by the perfect satisfaction of the optional input. We assume that the overall penalty and the overall reward can always be provided by decision makers, derived from the semantic background of decision problems. Consequently, the use of partial absorption depends on the efficiency of deriving its parameters from given values of the overall penalty and the overall reward. This problem has several effective numerical solutions, demonstrated in Chapter 3.4.

2.7 Logic Functions That Use Negation

All GL functions obtained as superposition of idempotent functions are also idempotent. Non-idempotent functions can be developed using the GCD and negation. In this chapter, we investigate the use of negation as a component in both idempotent and nonidempotent GL functions. In particular, we study the properties and practical use of De Morgan's duality, complementing and expanding the introduction presented in Sections 2.4.1 and 2.4.4.

2.7.1 Negation and De Morgan's Duality

Negation is a unary operation, $y = not(x)$, $x \in [0,1]$, $y \in [0,1]$. It determines the truth value of negated proposition and satisfies the boundary conditions $not(0) = 1$ and $not(1) = 0$. According to [FOD94], we can differentiate three types of negation:

1) *Strict negation*: $not(x)$ is continuous and strictly decreasing.
2) *Strong negation*: $not(x)$ is strict and also involutive, $not(not(x)) = x$, $x \in [0,1]$.
3) *Standard negation*: $not(x) = 1 - x$.

Typical examples of strict negation (but not strong) are $not(x) = (1-x)^p$ and $not(x) = 1 - x^p$, $p > 0$, $p \neq 1$. An example of strong negation is $not(x) = (1-x)/(1+px)$, $p > -1$. For $p = 0$, this negation becomes standard, which is also strong. In GL, we strictly use standard negation.

In the case of any involutive strong negation, a serial connection of two *not* gates (invertors) creates the unchanged input signal, as shown in Fig. 2.7.1. So, such a sequence can be inserted in any branch that connects two aggregators. That is shown in Fig. 2.7.2, where we create De Morgan's dual of partial conjunction.

Soft Computing Evaluation Logic: The LSP Decision Method and Its Applications,
First Edition. Jozo Dujmović.
© 2018 John Wiley & Sons, Inc. Published 2018 by John Wiley & Sons, Inc.
Companion website: www.wiley.com/go/Dujmovic/Soft_Computing_Evaluation_Logic

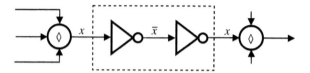

Figure 2.7.1 A sequence of two involutive invertors returns the unchanged input signal.

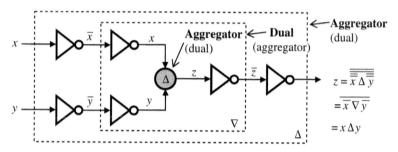

Figure 2.7.2 Using involutive invertors for creating dual aggregation functions.

In Boolean logic De Morgan's laws $\overline{x \wedge y} = \bar{x} \vee \bar{y}$ and $\overline{x \vee y} = \bar{x} \wedge \bar{y}$ define conjunction as a dual of disjunction, and vice versa: $x \wedge y = \overline{\bar{x} \vee \bar{y}}$ and $x \vee y = \overline{\bar{x} \wedge \bar{y}}$. In the case of partial conjunction (Δ) and partial disjunction (∇), the aggregators Δ and ∇ are dual if $x \Delta y = \overline{\bar{x} \nabla \bar{y}}$ and $x \nabla y = \overline{\bar{x} \Delta \bar{y}}$. Duality of aggregators is a reciprocal relationship based on involution of negation, as shown in Fig. 2.7.2. A necessary condition for duality is that the andness of Δ must be equal to the orness of ∇. Therefore, the volumes under dual functions are complementary:

$$Vol(x_1 \Delta \cdots \Delta x_n) = \int_{I^n} (x_1 \Delta \cdots \Delta x_n) dx_1 \cdots dx_n;$$

$$\alpha = \frac{n - (n+1) Vol(x_1 \Delta \cdots \Delta x_n)}{n-1}, \quad 0.5 < \alpha < 1,$$

$$Vol(x_1 \nabla \cdots \nabla x_n) = \int_{I^n} (x_1 \nabla \cdots \nabla x_n) dx_1 \cdots dx_n;$$

$$\omega = \frac{(n+1) Vol(x_1 \nabla \cdots \nabla x_n) - 1}{n-1}, \quad 0.5 < \omega < 1.$$

$$Vol(x_1 \Delta \cdots \Delta x_n) = \frac{n - (n-1)\alpha}{n+1}; \quad Vol(x_1 \nabla \cdots \nabla x_n) = \frac{(n-1)\omega + 1}{n+1};$$

$$Vol(x_1 \Delta \cdots \Delta x_n) + Vol(x_1 \nabla \cdots \nabla x_n) = \frac{n + 1 + (n-1)(\omega - \alpha)}{n+1}.$$

$$\therefore \ \omega = \alpha \ \Rightarrow \ Vol(x_1 \Delta \cdots \Delta x_n) + Vol(x_1 \nabla \cdots \nabla x_n) = 1,$$

$$\frac{Vol(x_1 \Delta \cdots \Delta x_n) + Vol(x_1 \nabla \cdots \nabla x_n)}{2} = \frac{1}{2} = Vol(x_1 \ominus \cdots \ominus x_n),$$

$$x_1 \Delta \cdots \Delta x_n \le x_1 \ominus \cdots \ominus x_n \le x_1 \nabla \cdots \nabla x_n.$$

Volumes under the partial conjunction and partial disjunction are complementary and symmetrically located with respect to the volume under the neutrality surface (the arithmetic mean). However, the global andness is not a pointwise indicator, and in a general case, individual points on the neutrality plane are *not* located in the middle between the partial conjunction surface and its dual partial disjunction surface:

$$\frac{(x_1\Delta\cdots\Delta x_n) + (x_1\nabla\cdots\nabla x_n)}{2} \lesseqgtr \frac{x_1 + \cdots + x_n}{n} = x_1 \ominus \cdots \ominus x_n$$

The equality holds only in special cases. For example, in the case of commutative partial conjunction aggregator $z = x\Delta y$, the corresponding De Morgan's dual is defined as $x\nabla y: = \overline{\bar{x}\Delta\bar{y}} = 1-(1-x)\Delta(1-y)$. Along the line $x + y = 1$, we have that x and y are complementary. Consequently, $x\Delta y = x\Delta(1-x)$, $x\nabla y = 1-x\Delta(1-x)$, and $x\nabla y + (1-x)\Delta(1-y) = 1 = (x+y)$. In this special case along the line $x + y = 1$ we have the pointwise symmetry with respect to the arithmetic mean: $[x\nabla y + (1-x)\Delta(1-y)]/2 = (x+y)/2 = \frac{1}{2}$.

However, this is not the case for other x,y points (for $y \neq 1-x$). For example, for the geometric mean we have $x\Delta y = \sqrt{xy}$ and the dual is $x\nabla y = 1 - \sqrt{(1-x)(1-y)}$. Both aggregators are hard: $x\Delta y$ supports the annihilator 0 and $x\nabla y$ supports the annihilator 1. Dual GCD operators share the same value of threshold andness and threshold orness. Along the line $x + y = 1$ we have $x\Delta y = \sqrt{x(1-x)}$, $x\nabla y = 1 - \sqrt{(1-x)x}$. So, $(x\Delta y + x\nabla y) = 1 = x + y$ and $(x\Delta y + x\nabla y)/2 = x \ominus y$. For example, $x = 0.2$, $y = 0.8$, $x\Delta y = \sqrt{0.16} = 0.4$, and $x\nabla y = 0.6$, yielding $x \ominus y = 0.5 = (x\Delta y + x\nabla y)/2$. However, if $x = 0.1$, $y = 0.8$, $x\Delta y = \sqrt{0.08} = 0.283$, and $x\nabla y = 0.576$, then $x \ominus y = 0.45 \neq (x\Delta y + x\nabla y)/2 = 0.429$.

2.7.2 De Morgan's Laws for Weighted Aggregators and Dualized Weighted Aggregators

For weighted aggregators, De Morgan's laws hold in extreme cases of the unweighted pure conjunction $(x_1 \wedge \cdots \wedge x_n)$, pure disjunction $(x_1 \vee \cdots \vee x_n)$, and the neutrality (the arithmetic mean), which is autodual:

$$\overline{W_1\bar{x}_1 + \cdots + W_n\bar{x}_n} = 1 - [W_1(1-x_1) + \cdots + W_n(1-x_n)]$$
$$= 1 - (W_1 + \cdots + W_n) + (W_1x_1 + \cdots + W_nx_n) = W_1x_1 + \cdots + W_nx_n .$$

If we have a weighted partial conjunction $W_1x_1\Delta\cdots\Delta W_nx_n$, then we can dualize this aggregator by defining the dual partial disjunction using De Morgan's law, as follows:

$$W_1x_1\nabla\cdots\nabla W_nx_n : = \overline{W_1\bar{x}_1\Delta\cdots\Delta W_n\bar{x}_n}.$$

Obviously, if the partial conjunction Δ has the andness α, then the dual partial disjunction ∇ has the orness $\omega = \alpha$. From this definition, it is easy to derive the following useful relationships:

$$\overline{W_1x_1\nabla \cdots \nabla W_nx_n} = W_1\bar{x}_1\Delta \cdots \Delta W_n\bar{x}_n$$

$$\Rightarrow \quad W_1x_1\nabla\cdots\nabla W_nx_n = 1 - W_1(1-x_1)\Delta\cdots\Delta W_n(1-x_n)$$

$$\overline{W_1x_1\Delta \cdots \Delta W_nx_n} = W_1\bar{x}_1\nabla \cdots \nabla W_n\bar{x}_n$$

$$\Rightarrow \quad W_1x_1\Delta\cdots\Delta W_nx_n = 1 - W_1(1-x_1)\nabla\cdots\nabla W_n(1-x_n) \ .$$

It is useful to note that WPM has asymmetric conjunctive and disjunctive properties, and no natural duality. Consequently, these relationships do not hold for unmodified WPM. For example, in the case $\omega = \alpha = 0.75$ (aggregators CA and DA), according to Table 2.3.3, we have

$$W_1x_1 \ \Delta \ W_2x_2 = \left(W_1x_1^{-0.7201} + W_2x_2^{-0.7201}\right)^{-1/0.7201},$$

$$W_1x_1 \ \nabla \ W_2x_2 = \left(W_1x_1^{3.9294} + W_2x_2^{3.9294}\right)^{1/3.9294}.$$

However, in this case $W_1x_1 \ \Delta \ ... \ \Delta \ W_nx_n \neq \overline{W_1\bar{x}_1 \ \nabla\cdots\nabla \ W_n\bar{x}_n}$, because this version of partial conjunction is hard $(r < 0)$ and the partial disjunction is soft $(r > 0)$. To show a numeric example, for $W_1 = 0.7$, $W_2 = 0.3$, $x_1 = 0.5$, $x_2 = 0.9$, we have

$$\left(W_1x_1^{-0.7201} + W_2x_2^{-0.7201}\right)^{-1/0.7201} = 0.58,$$

$$1 - \left[W_1(1-x_1)^{3.9294} + W_2(1-x_2)^{3.9294}\right]^{1/3.9294} = 0.54 \ .$$

For selected values, the difference is relatively small but sufficient to see that De Morgan's laws do not hold for WPM. This problem is easily solved if we dualized all aggregators by defining partial disjunction as the dual (the "mirror function") of partial conjunction, or vice versa:

$$W_1x_1 \ \nabla \ \cdots \ \nabla \ W_nx_n : \ = 1 - W_1(1-x_1) \ \Delta \ \cdots \ \Delta \ W_n(1-x_n),$$

$$W_1x_1 \ \Delta \ \cdots \ \Delta \ W_nx_n : \ = 1 - W_1(1-x_1) \ \nabla \ \cdots \ \nabla \ W_n(1-x_n).$$

Obviously, a dual of soft aggregator is soft and a dual of hard aggregator is hard. Each of the above relations can be obtained from the other one (e.g., by replacing $x_1, ..., x_n$ in the first relation with $1-x_1,..., 1-x_n$, we get the second relation). In other words, we define either the partial conjunction or the partial disjunction and then use their duals to secure the validity of De Morgan's laws, as in the following example of weighted geometric mean:

$$0.7x\Delta0.3y = x^{0.7}y^{0.3},$$

$$0.7x\nabla0.3y = 1 - 0.7(1-x)\Delta0.3(1-y) = 1 - (1-x)^{0.7}(1-y)^{0.3},$$

$$0.7x\Delta0.3y + 0.7(1-x)\nabla0.3(1-y) = 1 \ .$$

Aggregation operators that naturally satisfy De Morgan's laws must satisfy the condition:

$$W_1 x_1 \; \nabla \; \dots \; \nabla \; W_n x_n \; + \; W_1(1-x_1) \; \Delta \; \dots \; \Delta \; W_n(1-x_n) = 1.$$

For example, in the case of exponential mean, we have a rare example of natural duality:

$$W_1 x_1 \; \nabla \; \dots \; \nabla \; W_n x_n \; = \; \frac{1}{r}\ln(W_1 e^{rx_1} + \dots + W_n e^{rx_n}), \quad r > 0;$$

$$W_1 x_1 \; \Delta \; \dots \; \Delta \; W_n x_n \; = \; \frac{-1}{r}\ln(W_1 e^{-rx_1} + \dots + W_n e^{-rx_n}), \quad r > 0;$$

$$W_1 x_1 \; \nabla \; \dots \; \nabla \; W_n x_n \; + \; W_1(1-x_1) \; \Delta \; \dots \; \Delta \; W_n(1-x_n)$$

$$= \frac{1}{r}\ln(W_1 e^{rx_1} + \dots + W_n e^{rx_n}) \; - \; \frac{1}{r}\ln\left(W_1 e^{-r(1-x_1)} + \dots + W_n e^{-r(1-x_n)}\right)$$

$$= \frac{1}{r}\ln(W_1 e^{rx_1} + \dots + W_n e^{rx_n}) \; - \; \frac{1}{r}\ln[e^{-r}(W_1 e^{rx_1} + \dots + W_n e^{rx_n})]$$

$$= \frac{1}{r}\ln(W_1 e^{rx_1} + \dots + W_n e^{rx_n}) \; - \; \frac{1}{r}[-r + \ln(W_1 e^{rx_1} + \dots + W_n e^{rx_n})] = 1.$$

The exponential mean is naturally dual, i.e., it has the rare property that it naturally satisfies De Morgan's laws. Unfortunately this mean is also naturally soft and cannot be used for modeling of hard aggregators.

Weighted power means $y = \left(W_1 x_1^r + \dots + W_n x_n^r\right)^{1/r}$ are not naturally dual. Thus, De Morgan's laws are not naturally satisfied. For $-\infty < r \le 0$ this aggregator is a hard partial conjunction, for $0 < r < 1$, the aggregator is a soft partial conjunction, and for $1 < r < +\infty$ the aggregator is a soft partial disjunction. The hard partial disjunction is not naturally available and consequently the aggregator does not satisfy De Morgan's laws. Unless we need (or can tolerate) the asymmetric properties of WPM, it is necessary to redefine this aggregator using De Morgan's duals. If we need soft and hard aggregators, then the dualized GCD aggregator can be defined as follows:

$$W_1 x_1 \; \Delta \; \dots \; \Delta \; W_n x_n \; = \; \left(W_1 x_1^r + \dots + W_n x_n^r\right)^{1/r}, \qquad r = 1-p, \;\; 0 \le p \le +\infty;$$

$$W_1 x_1 \; \nabla \; \dots \; \nabla \; W_n x_n \; = 1 - W_1(1-x_1) \; \Delta \; \dots \; \Delta \; W_n(1-x_n)$$

$$= 1 - \left(W_1(1-x_1)^{2-r} + \dots + W_n(1-x_n)^{2-r}\right)^{1/(2-r)}, \qquad r = 1+p, \;\; 0 \le p \le +\infty.$$

If $p = 0$, the resulting aggregator is the arithmetic mean. For $0 < p < 1$ this aggregator is a soft partial conjunction or the soft partial disjunction. For $1 \le p < +\infty$, the result is a hard partial conjunction or the hard partial disjunction. The pure conjunction/disjunction are obtained for $p = +\infty$.

Similarly to the previous case, following is the strictly soft dualized WPM aggregator similar to the exponential mean:

$$W_1x_1 \, \nabla \cdots \nabla \, W_nx_n \, = \, \left(W_1x_1^r + \cdots + W_nx_n^r\right)^{1/r}, \qquad r = 1+p, \;\; 0 \le p \le +\infty;$$

$$W_1x_1 \, \Delta \cdots \Delta \, W_nx_n \, = 1 - W_1(1-x_1) \, \nabla \cdots \nabla \, W_n(1-x_n)$$

$$= 1 - \left(W_1(1-x_1)^{2-r} + \cdots + W_n(1-x_n)^{2-r}\right)^{1/(2-r)}, \qquad r = 1-p, \;\; 0 \le p \le +\infty \, .$$

The presented dualized WPM aggregators that use exponents $r = 1 + p$, $0 < p < +\infty$ are dual to aggregators that use exponents $r = 1 - p$. The parameter p is used to adjust the desired values of andness and orness: the andness that corresponds to exponent $r = 1 - p$ is the same as the orness that corresponds to the exponent $r = 1 + p$, $0 \le p \le +\infty$.

2.7.3 De Morgan's Duals of Compound Functions

Compound functions can also have their De Morgan's duals. This process is illustrated in Fig. 2.7.3 where we show three versions of the same nonidempotent function. For simplicity, we use equal weights but the aggregators could also have different weights. The original nonidempotent sample function $z = \left(a \, \Delta \, b \, \Delta \, c\right) \Delta \, (d \nabla e)$ is shown at the top of Fig. 2.7.3. In the next step, we insert pairs of involutive invertors in each branch. That opens the possibility to replace all idempotent aggregators with their De Morgan's duals, yielding the final version of the function shown at the bottom of Fig. 2.7.3.

If $W_1x_1 \, \nabla \cdots \nabla \, W_nx_n = \overline{W_1\bar{x}_1 \, \Delta \cdots \Delta \, W_n\bar{x}_n}$ and $W_1x_1 \, \Delta \cdots \Delta \, W_nx_n = \overline{W_1\bar{x}_1 \, \nabla \cdots \nabla \, W_n\bar{x}_n}$ then the disjunctive aggregator ∇ is De Morgan's dual of the conjunctive aggregator Δ and vice versa. Generally, for an arbitrary GL function $f(x_1 \ldots x_n; \nabla, \Delta)$ based on dual aggregators, a generalized De Morgan's law is: $f(x_1, \ldots, x_n; \nabla, \Delta) = \overline{f(\bar{x}_1, \ldots, \bar{x}_n; \Delta, \nabla)}$. In other words, De Morgan's dual of function $f(x_1, \ldots, x_n; \Delta, \nabla)$ is the function $f(x_1, \ldots, x_n; \nabla, \Delta)$, which is obtained by replacing each conjunctive aggregator Δ with its dual disjunctive aggregator ∇, and each disjunctive aggregator ∇ with its dual conjunctive aggregator Δ, and keeping all invertors inside the analyzed function $f(x_1, \ldots, x_n; \Delta, \nabla)$ unchanged:

$$F(x_1, \ldots, x_n) = f(x_1, \ldots, x_n; \nabla, \Delta),$$

$$F_{dual}(x_1, \ldots, x_n) = f(x_1, \ldots, x_n; \Delta, \nabla),$$

$$F(x_1, \ldots, x_n) = 1 - F_{dual}(1-x_1, \ldots, 1-x_n) = 1 - f(1-x_1, \ldots, 1-x_n; \Delta, \nabla),$$

$$F_{dual}(x_1, \ldots, x_n) = 1 - F(1-x_1, \ldots, 1-x_n) = 1 - f(1-x_1, \ldots, 1-x_n; \nabla, \Delta).$$

Therefore, De Morgan's dual of function $F(x_1 \ldots x_n)$ can be obtained by inserting invertors in all input branches and in the output branch, as shown in Fig. 2.7.4.

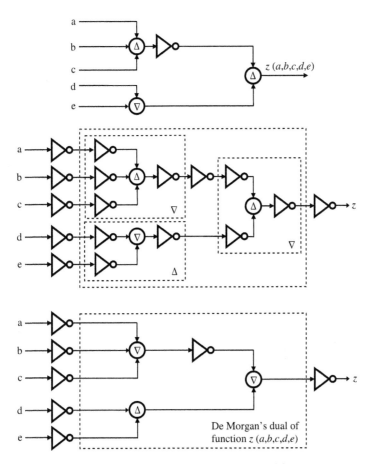

Figure 2.7.3 A stepwise transformation of a compound function to its De Morgan's dual.

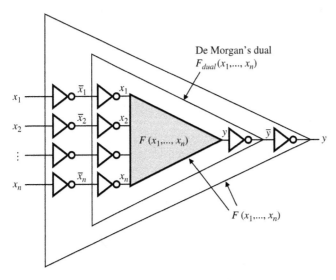

Figure 2.7.4 Function *F* and its De Morgan's dual.

2.7.4   Nonidempotent Logic Functions

In classic Boolean logic, all functions can be grouped in two fundamental groups idempotent and nonidempotent. In the case of two variables x and y, the basic idempotent functions are:

- Conjunction: $z(x,y) = x \wedge y$.
- Disjunction: $z(x,y) = x \vee y$.
- Absorption: $z(x,y) = x \wedge (x \vee y) = x \vee (x \wedge y) = x$.

Any superposition of idempotent functions generates a compound idempotent function. This rule applies to absorption, which is a superposition of idempotent conjunction and disjunction that totally absorbs the impact of one of input variables.

The basic nonidempotent logic functions of two variables are:

- Nand (negated conjunction): $z(x,y) = \overline{x \wedge y} = \bar{x} \vee \bar{y}$.
- Nor (negated disjunction): $z(x,y) = \overline{x \vee y} = \bar{x} \wedge \bar{y}$.
- Implication: $z(x,y) = \overline{x \wedge \bar{y}} = \bar{x} \vee y$.
- Abjunction (nonimplication): $z(x,y) = x \wedge \bar{y}$.
- Exclusive or: $z(x,y) = (x \wedge \bar{y}) \vee (\bar{x} \wedge y)$.
- Equivalence: $z(x,y) = (x \wedge y) \vee (\bar{x} \wedge \bar{y})$.

In these functions, conjunction, disjunction, nand, nor, exclusive or, and equivalence are commutative: $z(x,y) = z(y,x)$. As opposed to that, absorption, implication, and abjunction are asymmetric and noncommutative: $z(x,y) \neq z(y,x)$. A general property visible from these functions is that all functions that do not include negation are idempotent. Nonidempotent Boolean functions of two or more variables include negation. Of course, if $x \in \{0,1\}$, then negation is useful for simplifying logic functions: $\bar{\bar{x}} = x$, $x \wedge \bar{x} = 0$ and $x \vee \bar{x} = 1$. Assuming that all such simplifications are performed and taking into account the example in Fig. 2.7.3, it follows that De Morgan's duals of idempotent functions can have either even or odd number of negations and still remain idempotent: the expressions $x \vee y = \overline{\bar{x} \wedge \bar{y}}$ and $x \vee y \vee z = \overline{\bar{x} \wedge \bar{y} \wedge \bar{z}}$ are examples of idempotent functions with three and four negations.

In the area of evaluation logic, the idempotent functions are much more frequently used than the nonidempotent functions. Compound idempotent functions are obtained as superposition of two fundamental idempotent functions: partial conjunction and partial disjunction. Nonidempotent GL functions can be derived directly from their bivalent counterparts (see [DUJ91]):

- Partial (graded) nand (negated partial conjunction): $z(x,y) = 1 - (x \Delta y)$.
- Partial (graded) nor (negated partial disjunction): $z(x,y) = 1 - (x \nabla y)$.
- Partial (graded) implication: $z(x,y) = (1-x) \nabla y$.
- Partial (graded) abjunction (nonimplication): $z(x,y) = x \Delta (1-y)$.

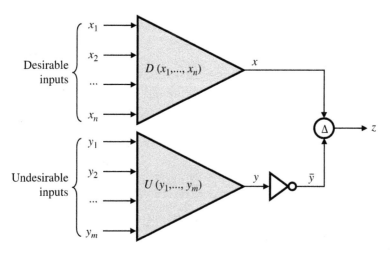

Figure 2.7.5 Using abjunction to aggregate desirable and undesirable features.

- Partial (graded) exclusive or: $z(x,y) = [x\Delta(1-y)] \triangledown [(1-x)\Delta y]$.
- Partial (graded) equivalence: $z(x,y) = (x\Delta y) \triangledown [1-(x\triangledown y)]$.

A characteristic GL usage of nonidempotent function is encountered in the case of bipolar criteria that aggregate desirable and undesirable features, illustrated in Fig. 2.7.5. The criterion is verbally defined as "we want desirable features but not undesirable features," which is logically expressed as the *material nonimplication* or *abjunction*:

$$z = x\Delta\bar{y} = D(x_1,...,x_n) \; \Delta \; [1-U(y_1,...,y_m)].$$

Here, $x = D(x_1,...,x_n)$ denotes the degree of suitability x of desirable features $x_1, ..., x_n$ and $y = U(y_1,...,y_m)$ denotes the degree of unsuitability y of undesirable features $y_1, ..., y_m$. The functions $D : [0,1]^n \rightarrow [0,1]$ and $U : [0,1]^m \rightarrow [0,1]$ can have any complexity and usually combine mandatory and optional components.

2.8 Penalty-Controlled Missingness-Tolerant Aggregation

Aggregation of degrees of truth or degrees of fuzzy membership using GL aggregation structures assumes the availability of all input data. Unfortunately, in many applications some inputs are missing. In this chapter, we present an aggregation process that controllably tolerates missing data [DUJ12a]. The aggregation process is implemented in the context of LSP evaluation criteria. Using the presented method, the aggregators automatically reconfigure themselves so that only the available data are aggregated. Consequently, evaluation decisions can be based on incomplete data. A typical example of missing data in online real estate and missingness-tolerant aggregation can be found in Section 4.2.4, where we use an evaluation engine based on methodology presented in subsequent sections.

2.8.1 Missing Data in Evaluation Problems

The problem of missing data is ubiquitous in statistical analysis [ALL01, LIT87, HOW07, HOW09]. Statisticians usually differentiate three types of "missingness." If the attributes $a_1, ..., a_n$ are used to compute an indicator $x = G(a_1, ..., a_n)$, then the probability p_i that an attribute a_i is missing can be constant and independent of the values of $a_1, ..., a_n$. Such an attribute is *missing completely at random* (denoted MCAR). If p_i does not depend on a_i but it can depend on $a_k, k \neq i$, then this form of missingness is *missing at random* (denoted MAR). If p_i is a function of a_i, then this case is classified as *missing not at random* (MNAR). The MNAR cases usually occur when data are intentionally omitted (in self-administered surveys these are regularly inconvenient values that respondents refuse to disclose). For example, instead of disclosing that a home does not have a breakfast room/area, or a laundry, a home seller may decide to leave those attributes unknown (to leave corresponding fields without a value).

Soft Computing Evaluation Logic: The LSP Decision Method and Its Applications,
First Edition. Jozo Dujmović.
© 2018 John Wiley & Sons, Inc. Published 2018 by John Wiley & Sons, Inc.
Companion website: www.wiley.com/go/Dujmovic/Soft_Computing_Evaluation_Logic

An example of MAR is the case where the probability of missing data about the type of floor is value-independent, i.e., the same for all types of floor, but it depends on the type of home, and can be different for a condo, townhouse, duplex, or a single family house.

In statistical analysis the treatments of missing data include the deletion of all incomplete data sets, or substitution of missing data with some appropriate substitutes (e.g., mean substitution, regression substitution, and other techniques [ALL01, LIT87]). The goal of statistical techniques is to provide best estimates of statistical parameters of the population based on incomplete sample data.

The problem of missing data is also present in database systems [COD86, REI86] and in related fuzzy decision models [LIA99, TRE08]. In database systems, missing (or unknown) data are classified as missing and applicable (A) and missing and inapplicable (I) [COD86, TRE08]. So, each atomic relation of a tuple can have four distinct values obtained by combining known (true or false) and unknown (A or I). Then, a four-valued logic can be used to manipulate missing information in a way that enables search and processing of incomplete tuples. If the cases A and I are not differentiated, then they are considered a null value, and a three-valued logic is used to deal with incomplete tuples.

There is a significant difference between the missing data in evaluation problems and missing data in statistical analysis or database systems. In the case of statistical analysis and database systems, the available sets of data are regularly large, and the results of analysis are most frequently indicators that hold for the whole population. In contrast, in the case of evaluation problems, the population is very small (usually less than 10, and possibly only one). The goal of suitability aggregation consists of evaluating an incompletely specified object of MNAR type generating a realistic estimate of its overall suitability. Evaluated objects can be complex and expensive, and the analysis is focused on individual objects, with intention to select the most suitable competitor. In such situations, it is rarely acceptable to eliminate objects having incomplete data because existing data can be attractive, and it is usually undesirable to reduce an already small group of available objects.

In the area of evaluation, we can identify the following three characteristic reasons for missing data:

- *Intentionally undisclosed data.* In most cases, these are data that are inconvenient for the data provider (e.g., a home seller). So, for some evaluated objects data are available, and for other objects data are unknown.
- *Temporary unavailable data.* In many evaluation projects, we encounter data that must be obtained through expensive activities or complex experiments. Typical examples are ecological problems where collection of input data requires field activities and delicate measurements. Such data remain unknown during initial phases of an evaluation project, and are provided in the final stage and/or only for selected systems.

- *Permanently unavailable data.* These are data that were considered relevant and were initially included in an LSP criterion, but for some objects such data cannot be collected. For example, some special computer systems performance measurements can be too expensive to perform and the corresponding data remain unknown.

In the case of the LSP evaluation method, there are four approaches to missing data management:

1) *Eliminate attributes from the LSP criterion function.* In this case, the evaluation criterion can be restructured, omitting the attributes that do not have complete data. This is an appropriate approach in the case of low-impact attributes that are not easily obtainable.
2) *Replace with neutral data without penalty.* Missing data are replaced by concordance values that produce the same results as the reduced aggregator (i.e., the aggregator obtained by omitting the missing inputs).
3) *Replace with penalized data.* Missing data are replaced by values that are lower than concordance values and produce lower results than the reduced aggregator (the penalty with respect to the neutral case must be adjustable).
4) *Eliminate objects with incomplete data.* This is a drastic approach that can be applicable only in infrequent cases where evaluation includes a large number of competitive objects.

The idea of neutral data can be explained using the following simple example. Suppose that we use sum-normalized weights a, b, c for computing suitability as a function of three attributes x, y, z, as follows:

$$S(x,y,z) = ax + by + cz, \quad a + b + c = 1.$$

Without input z, the suitability would be $S(x,y) = (ax + by)/(a + b)$, and this value (also called the concordance value, see P_{33} in Section 2.2.6) should be used as the neutral value for variable z:

$$S\left(x,y,\frac{ax + by}{a + b}\right) = ax + by + (1 - a - b)\frac{ax + by}{a + b} = \frac{ax + by}{a + b}.$$

Thus, if the missing variable z is replaced by the neutral concordance value $S(x, y)$, then the result of aggregation remains unaffected by z and depends only on available variables x and y.

2.8.2 Penalty-Controlled Numerical Coding of Missing Data

LSP criterion functions strictly follow the standard model of evaluation reasoning shown in Fig. 2.2.3. Input attributes $a_1, ..., a_n$ are either numerical values (e.g., the area of home) or numerically coded discrete values of attributes (e.g., numerical codes for various types of roof or floor). Each attribute is separately evaluated using an elementary attribute criterion function that maps the values of attribute to the degree of truth (or, alternatively, the degree of fuzzy membership) $g_i : R \to I$, $i = 1,...,n$. Attribute criteria reflect user needs regarding each individual attribute. The degrees of truth $x_i = g_i(x_i)$, $i = 1,...,n$ are called elementary attribute preferences or attribute suitability scores. They denote the degrees of suitability of attributes $a_1, ..., a_n$ from the standpoint of satisfying user requirements.

The final phase of the LSP method is a logic aggregation of the degrees of truth $x_1, ..., x_n$ that generates the overall suitability score $x = L(x_1,...,x_n)$ of an evaluated object. The logic aggregation function $L : I^n \to I$ is organized as a tree-like structure based on superposition of basic GL aggregators specified in the graded logic conjecture (Section 2.1.8) and specified in Table 2.1.4. Therefore, the LSP criterion $G : R^n \to I$ determines the overall suitability $x = L(x_1(a_1),...,x_n(a_n)) = G(a_1,...,a_n)$ and for this calculation it is necessary to know the values of n attributes. If some of the attributes are missing, then there are only two options: either we exclude the incomplete object, or (as shown below) we substitute null values with appropriate substitutes.

Let us first note that in almost all cases, the values of attributes are nonnegative. In very rare cases (e.g., if evaluation includes temperatures or elevation with respect to the see level), the values of attributes can be negative. However, we can claim with certainty that the values of attributes are never less than some large negative threshold value T (e.g., $T = -10^{30}$). Therefore, in all regular cases $a_i > T$, $i = 1,...,n$. Consequently, for incomplete sets of attributes, the values $a_i \le T$, $i \in \{1,...,n\}$ can be used for numerical coding of missing input data.

If a_i, $i \in \{1,...,n\}$ is missing, we can differentiate two cases: the case where there is no reason for penalty, and the case where there is a reason for penalty. The cases where it is justifiable to apply a penalty for missing data are those where we have reasons to believe that if a_i were known, the overall suitability would be less than the suitability computed using reduced criterion that excludes a_i replacing it by a concordance value. In other words, these are cases where a_i is intentionally missing because it has an inconvenient value. Let $P_i \in I$ denote a desired penalty for this specific attribute (most frequently, it is possible to use the same penalty for all attributes). Cases without penalty are characterized using $P_i = 0$. The effect of maximum penalty $P_i = 1$ should be the same as the effect of $g_i(a_i) = 0$. Consequently, the elementary criteria can express missing data as follows:

$$x_i = \widetilde{g}_i(a_i) = \begin{cases} -1 + P_i, & a_i \le T \text{ (missing data)} \\ g_i(a_i), & a_i > T \text{ (regular data)} \end{cases} \quad ; \quad \text{now, } \widetilde{g}_i : R \to [-1,1].$$

This definition generates the following characteristic values of preference/suitability:

$x_i = -1$ Missing data without penalty $(P_i = 0)$.

$-1 < x_i < 0$ Missing data with a degree of penalty $P_i = 1 + x_i$; $(0 < P_i < 1)$.

$x_i = 0$ Missing data with maximum penalty $(P_i = 1)$, or no satisfaction.

$0 < x_i < 1$ Partial satisfaction of user requirements.

$x_i = 1$ Total (perfect) satisfaction of user requirements.

Therefore, elementary attribute criteria transmit information about missing data as negative or zero values of preference/suitability. The next step is to organize the aggregation process so that it tolerates negative data (data in the range $[-1,1]$).

2.8.3 A Penalty-Controlled Missingness-Tolerant Aggregation Algorithm

Aggregation of preference can be based on a variety or aggregators. In this chapter we assume that the essential GCD aggregator is based on quasi-arithmetic means. Let a preference aggregation function of m variables be $z = A_m(x_1,...,x_k,...,x_m)$, and let x_k be an attribute whose value is $x_k = e$, $e \in I$, yielding the aggregated preference $z_e = A_m(x_1,...,e,...,x_m)$. If x_k is missing, then we must use the reduced criterion $A_{m-1}(x_1,...,x_{k-1},x_{k+1},...,x_m)$, and for some values of e we can get the unchanged result:

$$A_{m-1}(x_1,...,x_{k-1},x_{k+1},...,x_m) = A_m(x_1,...,e,...,x_m) = z_e.$$

If a unique constant value of e satisfies the above relation for any $k \in \{1,...,n\}$ and for any input values, then it is called the *extended neutral element* [GRA09]. Such element should substitute all missing data.

Unfortunately, in evaluation logic the extended neutral element does not exist. However, for all aggregators based on quasi-arithmetic means, we can select $e = A_{m-1}(x_1,...,x_{k-1},x_{k+1},...,x_m)$ and the following holds:

$$A_{m-1}(x_1,...,x_{k-1},x_{k+1},...,x_n) =$$
$$A_m(x_1,...,x_{k-1},A_{m-1}(x_1,...,x_{k-1},x_{k+1},...,x_m),x_{k+1},...,x_m).$$

This relationship has the following intuitive interpretation: if an input is missing, then the most reasonable assumption is that its value (in the sense of preference or suitability) is in concordance with the values of remaining attributes in the group. This property can be called *the concordance principle*. In other words, if an attribute has a value that is in concordance with the aggregated value of remaining attributes in a group, then such an attribute is redundant, it does not affect the aggregated preference, and it can be omitted without consequences.

The concordance principle shows that if x_k is missing, then there are two options. The first option is to use the original aggregator $A_m(x_1, ..., x_k, ..., x_m)$ where the missing value is substituted by the concordance value $x_k = C_k = A_{m-1}(x_1,...,x_{k-1},x_{k+1},...,x_m)$ and the result of aggregation will again be $A_{m-1}(x_1,...,x_{k-1},x_{k+1},...,x_m)$. Clearly, the second option, which is simpler and more natural, is the "use what you have" option, which omits the missing attribute and directly uses the reduced aggregator $A_{m-1}(x_1,...,x_{k-1},x_{k+1},...,x_m)$.

The concordance principle is related to the m-associativity property studied in Section 2.4.3. In the case of aggregation based on quasi-arithmetic means with a strictly monotonic generator function $F : I \rightarrow R \cup \{\pm\infty\}$, a simple proof of the concordance principle can be organized as follows:

$$A_m(x_1,...,x_k,...,x_m) = F^{-1}\left(\sum_{i=1}^{m} W_i F(x_i)\right), \quad 0 < W_i < 1, \quad i = 1,...,m, \quad \sum_{i=1}^{m} W_i = 1.$$

Then, we insert in this aggregator the following concordance value of x_k:

$$x_k = A_{m-1}(x_1,...,x_{k-1},x_{k+1},...,x_m) = F^{-1}\left(\frac{1}{1-W_k}\sum_{\substack{i=1 \\ i\neq k}}^{m} W_i F(x_i)\right), \quad 1 - W_k = \sum_{\substack{i=1 \\ i\neq k}}^{m} W_i.$$

The proof can be now completed as follows:

$$A_m(x_1,...,x_{k-1},A_{m-1}(x_1,...,x_{k-1},x_{k+1},...,x_m),x_{k+1},...,x_m) = F^{-1}\left(\sum_{i=1}^{m} W_i F(x_i)\right)$$

$$= F^{-1}\left(\sum_{i=1}^{k-1} W_i F(x_i) + \frac{W_k}{1-W_k}\sum_{\substack{i=1 \\ i\neq k}}^{m} W_i F(x_i) + \sum_{i=k+1}^{m} W_i F(x_i)\right)$$

$$= F^{-1}\left(\left(1 + \frac{W_k}{1-W_k}\right)\sum_{\substack{i=1 \\ i\neq k}}^{m} W_i F(x_i)\right) = F^{-1}\left(\frac{1}{1-W_k}\sum_{\substack{i=1 \\ i\neq k}}^{m} W_i F(x_i)\right)$$

$$= A_{m-1}(x_1,...,x_{k-1},x_{k+1},...,x_m).$$

For example, if we have a simple geometric mean $z = x_1^{0.5}x_2^{0.3}x_3^{0.2}$, and if x_1 is missing, then we should use the reduced aggregator $z = x_2^{0.6}x_3^{0.4}$, or the original aggregator where we insert the concordance value $x_1 = x_2^{0.6}x_3^{0.4}$ to obtain the same result of aggregation: $z = \left(x_2^{0.6}x_3^{0.4}\right)^{0.5}x_2^{0.3}x_3^{0.2} = x_2^{0.6}x_3^{0.4}$.

The concordance principle in the simplest case of two variables $A_2(x_1, x_2)$ means that if one variable is missing (e.g., x_2) then the preference is computed as $A_2(x_1, x_1) = x_1$, that is, the resulting value is the value of the remaining variable. In the case of three variables, $A_3(x_1, x_2, x_3)$, the missing variable (e.g., x_3) should be substituted by the concordance value $A_2(x_1, x_2)$ yielding $A_3(x_1, x_2, A_2(x_1, x_2)) = A_2(x_1, x_2)$, and so forth.

In the case where two variables (x_j and x_k) are missing, the presented technique can be expanded in an analogous way, as follows:

$$x_j = x_k = A_{m-2}\left(x_1, \ldots, x_{j-1}, x_{j+1}, \ldots, x_{k-1}, x_{k+1}, \ldots, x_m\right)$$

$$= F^{-1}\left(\frac{1}{1 - W_j - W_k} \sum_{\substack{i=1 \\ i \notin \{j,k\}}}^{m} W_i F(x_i)\right), \quad 1 - W_j - W_k = \sum_{\substack{i=1 \\ i \notin \{j,k\}}}^{m} W_i \;.$$

Then,

$$A_m\left(x_1, \ldots, x_{j-1}, A_{m-2}\left(x_1, \ldots, x_{j-1}, x_{j+1}, \ldots, x_{k-1}, x_{k+1}, \ldots, x_m\right), x_{j+1}, \ldots \right.$$

$$\left. \ldots, x_{k-1}, A_{m-2}\left(x_1, \ldots, x_{j-1}, x_{j+1}, \ldots, x_{k-1}, x_{k+1}, \ldots, x_m\right), x_{k+1}, \ldots, x_m\right)$$

$$= F^{-1}\left(\sum_{i=1}^{m} W_i F(x_i)\right)$$

$$= F^{-1}\left(\sum_{\substack{i=1 \\ i \notin \{j,k\}}}^{m} W_i F(x_i) + \frac{W_j}{1 - W_j - W_k} \sum_{\substack{i=1 \\ i \notin \{j,k\}}}^{m} W_i F(x_i) + \frac{W_k}{1 - W_j - W_k} \sum_{\substack{i=1 \\ i \notin \{j,k\}}}^{m} W_i F(x_i)\right)$$

$$= F^{-1}\left(\left(1 + \frac{W_j + W_k}{1 - W_j - W_k}\right) \sum_{\substack{i=1 \\ i \notin \{j,k\}}}^{m} W_i F(x_i)\right) = F^{-1}\left(\frac{1}{1 - W_j - W_k} \sum_{\substack{i=1 \\ i \notin \{j,k\}}}^{m} W_i F(x_i)\right)$$

$$= A_{m-2}\left(x_1, \ldots, x_{j-1}, x_{j+1}, \ldots, x_{k-1}, x_{k+1}, \ldots, x_m\right).$$

In a general case, we can have a set of μ missing inputs $\{x_i\}$, $i \in \theta \subset \{1, \ldots, m\}$, $\mu = |\theta| \in \{1, \ldots, m-1\}$. In such a case, we first compute the aggregate of existing (known) inputs (this is a direct generalization of the previous cases, $\mu = 1$ and $\mu = 2$):

$$x_k|_{k \in \theta} = A_{m-\mu}\left(\ldots x_i|_{i \notin \theta} \ldots\right) = F^{-1}\left(\frac{1}{1 - \sum_{i \in \theta} W_i} \sum_{i \notin \theta}^{m} W_i F(x_i)\right), \quad 1 - \sum_{i \in \theta} W_i = \sum_{i \notin \theta}^{m} W_i.$$

Then, this value can be inserted as a concordance substitute for all missing inputs using a general substitution relation for $0 < \mu < m$, as follows:

$$A_m\left(\ldots x_i|_{i \notin \theta} \ldots x_k|_{k \in \theta} \ldots\right) = A_m\left(\ldots x_i|_{i \notin \theta} \ldots A_{m-\mu}\left(\ldots x_i|_{i \notin \theta} \ldots\right) \ldots\right) = A_{m-\mu}\left(\ldots x_i|_{i \notin \theta} \ldots\right).$$

The presented technique as applicable in all cases, where we use the zero penalty. In cases where we want to have nonzero penalty, we have

$$A_m\left(\ldots x_i|_{i \notin \theta} \ldots x_k|_{k \in \theta} \ldots\right)$$

$$= A_m\left(\ldots x_i|_{i \notin \theta} \ldots \left[(1 - P_k)A_{m-\mu}\left(\ldots x_i|_{i \notin \theta} \ldots\right)\right]\Big|_{k \in \theta} \ldots\right) \le A_{m-\mu}\left(\ldots x_i|_{i \notin \theta} \ldots\right),$$

$$0 \le P_k \le 1, \quad k \in \theta, \quad 0 < \mu < m.$$

In the case of partial conjunction, partial disjunction, and neutrality, if $0 < \mu < m$, then we have $x_i = P_i - 1 \le 0$, $i \in \theta \ne \emptyset$ and $x_i \ge 0$, $i \notin \theta$; note that the cases of maximum penalty $(P_i = 1)$ and no value $(x_i = 0)$ are equivalent. Thus, the penalty-controlled missingness-tolerant aggregator is defined as follows:

$$z = \begin{cases} A_m(x_1, \ldots, x_m), \quad 0 \le x_i \le 1, \quad i = 1, \ldots, m, & \mu = 0, \quad \theta = \emptyset; \\ A_m\left(\ldots x_i|_{i \notin \theta} \ldots \left[|x_k|A_{m-\mu}\left(\ldots x_i|_{i \notin \theta} \ldots\right)\right]\Big|_{k \in \theta} \ldots\right), & 0 < \mu < m; \\ -A_m(|x_1|, \ldots, |x_m|), \quad -1 \le x_i < 0, \quad i = 1, \ldots, m, & \mu = m. \end{cases}$$

Using the quasi-arithmetic mean $z = F^{-1}(W_1 F(x_1) + \ldots + W_m F(x_m))$ we can now perform missingness-tolerant aggregation based on the following algorithm:

1) Using preferences $x_1, \ldots, x_m$, $x_i \in [-1,1]$, $i = 1, \ldots, m$ generated by penalty-controlled elementary criteria, compute the sum of weights of known attributes:

$$W_{sum} = \sum_{x_i \ge 0} W_i, \quad 0 \le W_{sum} \le 1.$$

2) If $W_{sum} = 1$, then return $z = F^{-1}(W_1 F(x_1) + \ldots + W_m F(x_m))$ (no missing data).

3) If $W_{sum} = 0$, then return $z = -F^{-1}\left(\sum_{i=1}^{m} W_i F(|x_i|)\right)$, i.e., a negative average negated penalty ($|x_i| = 1 - P_x = \neg P_x$), which is a nonpositive value that will propagate in the subsequent stage of aggregation.

4) Compute the reduced aggregated preference $\bar{x} = F^{-1}\left(W_{sum}^{-1} \sum_{x_i \ge 0} W_i F(x_i)\right)$.

5) If all penalties of missing data are zero, then return the aggregated preference $z = \bar{x}$. Otherwise return $z = F^{-1}\left(\sum_{x_i \ge 0} W_i F(x_i) + \sum_{x_i < 0} W_i F(|x_i|\bar{x})\right)$.

Generally, the value of penalty can be different for each input attribute. More often than not, it is convenient to use a fixed penalty $\forall i,\ P_i = P$. Penalties propagate (coded as negative preferences) through the aggregation structure and disappear after they are combined with regular positive preference scores.

Let us now investigate the missingness-tolerant aggregation in the case of conjunctive ($\trianglerighteq$) and disjunctive ($\vartriangleright$) partial absorption functions (Chapter 2.6). The conjunctive partial absorption (CPA) is a combination of a mandatory input x and a desired/optional input y. The mandatory input x must be (at least partially) satisfied. Assuming $x > 0$, the optional input (y) can partially compensate an insufficient level of x: $x \trianglerighteq y = x \bar{\bar{\triangle}} \left(x \tilde{\triangledown} y \right)$ ($\bar{\bar{\triangle}}$ denotes a full conjunction or a hard partial conjunction and $\tilde{\triangledown}$ denotes the total disjunction, i.e., any form of disjunction or the arithmetic mean; we assume that $\bar{\bar{\triangle}}$ and $\tilde{\triangledown}$ are modeled using quasi-arithmetic means). Applying strictly the missingness-tolerant algorithm to the CPA aggregator, we have:

$$x \trianglerighteq y = \begin{cases} x \ \bar{\bar{\triangle}} \ \left(x \tilde{\triangledown} y \right), & x \geq 0,\ y \geq 0; \\[2mm] x \ \bar{\bar{\triangle}} \ \left[x \tilde{\triangledown} |y| x \right], & x \geq 0,\ y < 0; \\[2mm] \left[|x| \left(|x| y \tilde{\triangledown} y \right) \right] \bar{\bar{\triangle}} \ \left(|x| y \tilde{\triangledown} y \right), & x < 0,\ y \geq 0; \\[2mm] -|x| \ \bar{\bar{\triangle}} \left(|x| \ \tilde{\triangledown} \ |y| \right), & x < 0,\ y < 0. \end{cases}$$

If the optional input y is missing ($x \geq 0,\ y < 0$), the nonexistent value is substituted by $|y| x = (1 - P_y)x$, where P_y denotes the desired y-penalty. In the case of maximum penalty ($P_y = 1$), the aggregation is equivalent to zero optional input, and in the case without penalty, we have $x \trianglerighteq y = x$. If the mandatory input x is missing ($x < 0,\ y \geq 0$), then in the case of maximum penalty we have $x \trianglerighteq y = 0$. In the case of zero penalty, however, we have $x \trianglerighteq y = y$, which may sometimes be a questionable result. If we use penalty $P_x > 0$, then $x \trianglerighteq y < y$. If both inputs are missing, the output is a partial absorption of negated input penalties. For example, for partial absorption based on the arithmetic and harmonic means, if $P_x = 1 - |x| = P_y = 1 - |y| = 1/2$, $x \tilde{\triangledown} y = (x + y)/2$ and $x \tilde{\triangle} y = 2xy/(x + y)$, then we have the following CPA:

$$x \trianglerighteq y = \begin{cases} 2x(x + y)/(3x + y), & x \geq 0,\ y \geq 0; \\[1mm] 2x(1 + |y|)/(3 + |y|) = 6x/7, & x \geq 0,\ y = -\tfrac{1}{2}; \\[1mm] |x| y = 0.5y, & x = -\tfrac{1}{2},\ y \geq 0; \\[1mm] 2x(x + y)/(3x + y) = -0.5, & x = -\tfrac{1}{2},\ y = -\tfrac{1}{2}. \end{cases}$$

The disjunctive partial absorption is a combination of a sufficient input x and a desired/optional input y. The sufficient input x can fully compensate for the lack of optional input y. The desired input can partially (and frequently significantly) compensate the lack of sufficient input: $x \triangleright y = x \bar{\bar{\nabla}} \left(x \tilde{\Delta} y \right)$ ($\bar{\nabla}$ denotes a full disjunction or a hard partial disjunction and $\tilde{\Delta}$ denotes the total conjunction, i.e., any form of conjunction or the arithmetic mean). The missingness-tolerant disjunctive partial absorption aggregator can be organized in the same way as in the case of conjunctive partial absorption.

2.8.4 The Impact of Penalty on Missingness-Tolerant Aggregation

In many LSP evaluation problems, input data can be missing, and it is necessary to perform evaluation with incomplete input data. In such cases, we must perform evaluation using the reduced set containing only the available input attributes. However, if incomplete input data reflect an intention to hide inconvenient inputs, it is appropriate to use penalties to discourage the practice of hiding disadvantages and to compute overall suitability that is more realistic than the result obtained without penalty.

In order to deal with missing data, evaluators must decide about the most suitable value of the missingness penalty parameter. Typical effects of missingness penalty, taken from an online real estate evaluation study with incomplete input data, are shown in Fig. 2.8.1. In all cases, increasing the missingness penalty causes a decrease of the overall suitability. For the maximum penalty, the overall suitability for missing nonmandatory attributes is positive, and for missing mandatory attributes, it is zero.

Selecting the missingness penalty is based on the decision maker's missingness tolerance level. Indeed, the missing data can be intentionally hidden

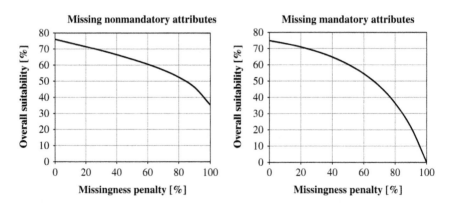

Figure 2.8.1 An example of overall suitability as a function of missingness penalty.

because they are inconvenient, or they can be unknown to all data providers. In the case of convincingly suspected inconvenient data, it is justifiable to apply the highest penalty. In the case where we have reasons to believe that the unknown attributes are satisfied (e.g., the house with missing parking data is in a residential district that is known to have free public parking space), we may select a lower penalty value. To decide about the most appropriate missingness penalty, it is suitable first to plot and analyze the overall suitability curves similar to those shown in Fig. 2.8.1. The suitability functions in Fig. 2.8.1 are strictly concave and the penalty of 80% should be applied if we want to get the overall suitability that is approximately halfway between the extreme values.

2.9 Rating Scales and Verbalization

*Graduation and granulation play key roles in the ways in which humans
deal with complexity and imprecision*
—Lotfi A. Zadeh

In human reasoning, everything is a matter of degree, and that holds for human percepts of truth, suitability, importance, simultaneity, value, and so on. The most natural way we use to express our percepts are words (i.e., verbalization). To express the intensity of our percepts, we naturally use verbalized rating scales. Therefore, rating scales provide necessary units of measurement for all percepts that are a matter of degree, and graded logic is directly related to the design and use of rating scales.

In the area of evaluation, we are primarily interested in granular verbalization of three fundamental soft computing variables: (1) *suitability*, (2) *andness/orness* (the degree of simultaneity or substitutability), and (3) *importance*. For each of them, we can create an appropriate rating scale. Both the suitability and the andness/orness belong to interval $[0,1]$, and the endpoints of their scales (*scale anchors*) correspond to the extreme values 0 and 1. The corresponding anchor labels can be "lowest"/"highest" or "minimum"/"maximum," or "unacceptable"/"excellent." If the size of granule is $1/(G-1)$ then the percepts of suitability and andness/orness can be numerically labeled with G labels (from 0 to $G-1$), as illustrated in Fig. 2.9.1 for the granularity $G = 9$.

The case of verbalizing importance is different because we assume the sum-normalized importance weights that use the interval $]0,1[$. Indeed, the importance cannot be 0 (since irrelevant attributes are not included in evaluation) and it cannot be 1 (because that would exclude all other attributes in a given group). Consequently, if the size of importance granule is $1/(G-1)$, then the percepts of importance can be numerically labeled using $G-2$ labels (from 1 to $G-2$ or in the range from "least important" to "most important" or from "very low" to "very high"), as illustrated in Fig. 2.9.1. The verbal expression of strength of the importance scale anchors must be less than the verbal expression of strength of the

Soft Computing Evaluation Logic: The LSP Decision Method and Its Applications,
First Edition. Jozo Dujmović.
© 2018 John Wiley & Sons, Inc. Published 2018 by John Wiley & Sons, Inc.
Companion website: www.wiley.com/go/Dujmovic/Soft_Computing_Evaluation_Logic

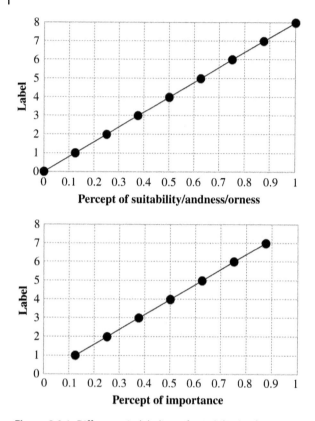

Figure 2.9.1 Difference in labeling of suitability/andness/orness and importance.

suitability/andness/orness scale anchors. In other words, the label "very high" should not be replaced with "maximum" or "highest" of "extreme."

In this chapter, we investigate methods for design of rating scales for suitability, andness/orness, and importance. In addition, we analyze some of popular rating scales from the standpoint of their conformity with general principles of rating scale design.

2.9.1 Design of Rating Scales

Let us now focus on design and use of rating scales, first for a general population (i.e., professionally unprepared respondents) and then for professional evaluators (professionally prepared decision analysts/engineers).

Rating scales for general population (voters, consumers, customers, medical patients, etc.) are extensively studied in business (marketing), economics, psychometrics, politics, and medicine [FRI99, PRE00, NUN67, COX80, SMI13,

KRO10, ROH07, HER06]. A recent survey [SMI13] identified significantly more than 100 publications devoted to the rating scales for polling general population.

Properties of rating scales primarily depend on their specific application areas, and, in this chapter, we are interested only in the *magnitude scaling of the intensity of percept* and not in other forms of scaling. More precisely, we are primarily interested in scaling the intensity of *andness/ orness, suitability*, and *importance*. The term *magnitude scaling* is used here to denote a verbalized scaling of the percept of intensity of a selected attribute in a range from a given minimum to a given maximum value. The magnitude scaling can be applied to attributes such as intensity, frequency, probability and others. Of course, the type of attribute determines appropriate linguistic labels. For example, the frequency scaling includes labels such as [never < sometimes < often], the probability scaling includes labels such as [unlikely < possibly < likely], and intensity scaling includes labels such as [low < medium < high], or, in the case of quality, [poor < average < excellent]. We use symbol "<" to denote increasing ordering of scales. So, in the case of suitability, we can use both the [low < medium < high] and the [poor < average < excellent] style of labels. For andness, orness, and importance, however, the appropriate labeling is in the style of [low < medium < high], or [weak < average < strong].

In evaluation logic the verbalization with rating scales should have the following five fundamental properties: (1) *strict monotonicity of linguistic labeling*, (2) *linearity*, (3) *balance*, (4) *sufficient cardinality*, and (5) *hybrid (numeric and linguistic) labeling*.

2.9.1.1 Strict Monotonicity of Linguistic Labeling

In the area of evaluation, the linguistic labels such as "large," "small," "low," "high," "good," "poor," and others are primarily used to verbally express the percept of the degree of suitability, which is a value in the interval [0,1] or [0,100%]. Suppose that we experiment with human subjects, and that each respondent is given a numeric scale with n equidistant points (usually 11, numerically denoted as 0,1,2,...,10 or 0%, 10%, 20%,...,100%). These points are interpreted as numeric expressions of magnitude, from the lowest to the highest. Then, the respondents are given a specific linguistic label (e.g., "large"). Of course, everybody has a perception of magnitude specified by the given label and everybody (thinking of T-shirts) agrees that [*small < medium < large < extra-large*]. This is a strictly monotonic scale. We define *strict monotonicity* as labeling where there is no ambiguity in label ordering. For example, a respondent can perceive the label "large" as a verbal expression of the magnitude of 80%. Other respondents may perceive that "large" corresponds to 90% or 70%, or to other values. However, for strictly monotonic scales, the *ordering of labels* should never be questionable (all respondents should perceive the same ordering of labels).

If we collect perceptions from sufficiently large number of respondents ($m \gg 1$), we will have a large array of numeric values $x_1, x_2, \ldots, x_m$ distributed between the minimum value $x_{min} = \min(x_1, \ldots, x_m)$ and the maximum value $x_{max} = \max(x_1, \ldots, x_m)$. In such a case we can create a continuous probabilistic model based on the cumulative probability distribution function $P(t) = \mathrm{Prob}[x \leq t]$. Then, the most reasonable numeric equivalent of the given linguistic label would be the mean value of this distribution $\bar{x} = \int_0^\infty [1 - P(t)]dt = (x_1, \ldots, x_m)/m$.

In the case of linguistic labels that denote magnitude (such as "large," "high," "strong," etc.) the mean value $\bar{x}$ can also have a straightforward logic interpretation as the degree of truth of the assertion that the analyzed label denotes the highest magnitude. For example, if for the label "high quality" we compute $\bar{x} = 0.8$, then 0.8 denotes the degree of truth that "high quality" is the best possible (i.e., equivalent to "maximum quality").

Linguistic labels of magnitude always come with a degree of uncertainty. They are fuzzy and can naturally by interpreted as generators of type-1 fuzzy sets. Consequently, for a given label (e.g., "high"), we need the membership function $\mu : [x_{min}, x_{max}] \rightarrow [0,1]$ of the "high fuzzy set" (we obviously assume $\forall x \notin [x_{min}, x_{max}] \Rightarrow \mu(x) = 0$). The maximum value of $\mu(x)$ corresponds to the value of x where the density of respondents' answers reaches the maximum value. For the analyzed linguistic label the membership of x in the fuzzy set identified with that label must be directly proportional to the fraction of respondents who voted for the numeric equivalent x. A high degree of membership of any value x can only be achieved by the high fraction of respondents who supported that value. The simplest way to satisfy these conditions is to use $\mu(x) = dP(x)/dx$ (i.e., the membership function coincides with the probability density function).

The next approach to modeling uncertainty of respondents would be to assume that (due to high uncertainty) the respondents cannot select the most appropriate numeric value that corresponds to the linguistic label but can select an interval that they believe contains the desired numeric equivalent. Of course, we might ask what kind of reasoning is behind the selection of the interval. A rather natural interpretation of this process would be that people select their favorite value— say, 80%—and then start investigating the degree of uncertainty they feel is associated with their estimate of 80%. Then they select the width of "uncertainty zone" around their central estimate—say, 10%—and then report that the interval is [70%, 90%]. Less uncertain respondents might take the uncertainty zone of 5% and select the interval [75%, 85%], while more uncertain respondents with the uncertainty zone of 15% could select the interval [65%, 95%].

It is possible to argue that if in most cases people indeed apply the method

interval = [*favorite value* − *uncertainty zone, favorite value* + *uncertainty zone*], then in most cases we don't need intervals because respondents who are asked to declare intervals also know the favorite value because it is centrally located inside the interval (as a midrange or centroid). In such cases, the use of intervals for assessment of numeric equivalents of linguistic labels can be considered a deliberate specification of uncertainty rather than a provable need. The *singleton approach* (selection of a single favorite value) yields type-1 fuzzy models of uncertainty (Figs. 2.2.7, 2.2.9) and the alternative (but not necessarily superior) *interval approach* yields the type-2 fuzzy models of uncertainty (Fig. 2.2.8).

The singleton approach to magnitude scaling is experimentally investigated in the research of Rohrmann [ROH07], and the interval approach to magnitude scaling is experimentally investigated in the research of Mendel and his collaborators [MEN01, LIU08, MEN10, WU12]. In both cases, the respondents were given the 11-point scale (0–10) and a set of linguistic labels. In the singleton case, they were asked to select a single most appropriate value from the scale, and in the interval approach they were asked to select two values that define an interval associated with the label. Rohrmann's research appears in the context of linguistics and social sciences. Mendel's 16-words and 32-words codebooks are applied in the context of computing with words.

Professional evaluation is primarily done with numbers, not with words, but the results of Rohrmann and Mendel are applicable in the area of evaluation in all cases that need linguistic labels, and that includes the following: (1) rating scales for andness/orness, (2) rating scales for importance, (3) rating scales for suitability/preference, (4) rating scales for direct suitability assessment in elementary criteria, and (5) verbalizing evaluation results for stakeholders and for general population of LSP users. So, our study of verbalized rating scales is limited to those five areas of application.

Generally, the points on a rating scale can be labeled in three ways: (1) strictly with linguistic labels (*worded scale*), (2) strictly with numeric values/labels (*numbered scale*), and (3) combining linguistic and numeric labels (*hybrid, or labeled numeric scale*). For example, the scale [*low < medium < high*] is strictly linguistic; we have not assigned numeric interpretation of labels "low," "medium" and "high." Strictly numeric scales are usually based on the following question: On a scale of 1 to G, with 1 being "poor" and G being "excellent," how would you rate a selected object of evaluation? A main advantage of simple numbered scales is in their simplicity and cultural independence, but in some cases, for general population, numeric scales can be less reliable than worded scales.

The combination of numbered and worded scale can be exemplified using medical scales for pain sensation (whoever had a serious surgery knows them very well). Medical pain scales used in clinical practice have 11 levels. Patients are asked to identify the level of pain using a number from 0 to 10 associated with one of three verbal interpretations shown in Table 2.9.1. Selected numeric values are described (or "anchored") with linguistic labels. The first two

Table 2.9.1 Three labeled numeric scales of pain sensation.

Level	Verbal Interpretations		
0	No pain	No hurt	No pain
1			
2		Hurts a little bit	Mild pain
3			
4		Hurts a little more	
5	Distressing pain		Moderate pain
6		Hurts even more	
7			
8		Hurts a whole lot	Severe pain
9			
10	Unbearable pain	Hurts worst	Unbearable

columns show verbal interpretations of some selected pain levels and are used to help patients understand the meaning of numeric values. The third column shows an interpretation that covers all levels using three intensities in each of the three main pain categories (mild, moderate, and severe). This is a labeled numeric scale, and the patient must eventually provide a numeric value of the level of pain sensation.

Table 2.9.2 shows examples of various linguistic labels for strictly monotonic magnitude scaling. The labels used as descriptors of points on a scale should be selected so that (a) ordering of labels is strictly monotonic and (b) the perceived psychological distance between adjacent labels is always the same (linearity). The condition (a) is rather easy to satisfy, particularly for magnitude scales with smaller number of points. On the other hand, satisfying the linearity condition (b) is a difficult problem and requires experimental proofs.

To prove strict monotonicity, it is necessary to pass the following *strict monotonicity test*: take all adjacent pairs of labels and for each pair, taken out of context, ask respondents to verify the ordering. If and only if all respondents verify the same ordering, the scale is strictly monotonic. For example, for the scale [low < medium < high] there is no doubt that low < medium, and medium < high. When the cardinality of a scale increases, it is difficult to pass the strict monotonicity test. For cardinality up to 7 the scales in Table 2.9.2 are strictly monotonic. The scales with cardinality 9 and 11 in Table 2.9.2 look reasonably ordered, but out of context, some adjacent pairs (e.g., *poor < significantly below average*) might have difficulties in passing the strict monotonicity test.

The fuzziness of linguistic labels is clearly visible in each thesaurus. For example, the word processor suggests that synonyms for "good" are: "high-quality," "good quality," "first-class," "first-rate," "superior," "fine," and "excellent." Obviously, there are significant differences between some of these labels (e.g., instead of *good ≈ excellent*, it is rather clear that *good < excellent*).

The rating scales literature includes variety of examples of human imprecision and inconsistent use of linguistic labels and rating scales. It is important to emphasize that all results reported in the literature describe the behavior of general population of respondents and not the way how the rating scales should be

Table 2.9.2 Numeric and linguistic labels for magnitude scaling with cardinality $3 \le G \le 11$.

G	0	1	2	3	4	5	6	7	8	9	10
3	Least important	Average importance	Most important								
	Poor	Fair	Good								
	Low	Medium	High								
4	Least important	Somewhat important	Important	Very important							
	Very poor	Poor	Good	Very good							
	None	Slight	Considerable	Great							
	None	A little	Quite a bit	Completely							
5	Least important	Somewhat important	Important	Very Important	Extremely Important						
	Unimportant	Of little importance	Moderately important	Important	Very important						
	Not very important	Somewhat important	Moderately important	Important	Very important						
	Not at all	Slightly	Moderately	Considerably	Completely						
	Not at all	Somewhat	Moderately	Very	Extremely						
	Very low	Low	Medium	High	Very high						
	Unacceptable	Poor	Average	Good	Perfect						
	Very bad	Bad	Average	Good	Very good						
	Very poor	Poor	Fair	Good	Very good						
	Bad	Weak	Fair	Good	Excellent						
	Very poor	Below average	Average	Above average	Excellent						
	Very poor	Poor	Average	Good	Excellent						
	Lowest	Low	Medium	High	Highest						
6	Worst	Bad	Not bad	Good	Very good	Excellent					
7	Unacceptable	Very poor	Poor	Average (Fair)	Good	Very good	Excellent				
	Extremely small	Very small	Small	Moderate	Large	Very large	Extremely large				
	Lowest	Very low	Low	Medium	High	Very high	Highest				
9	Lowest	Very low	Low	Mid-low	Medium	Mid-high	High	Very high	Highest		
	Lowest	Very low	Low	Below average	Average	Above average	High	Very high	Highest		
	Unacceptable	Very poor	Poor	Below average	Average	Above average	Good	Very good	Excellent		
	Extremely dislike	Very much dislike	Moderately dislike	Slightly dislike	Neutral (bipolar)	Slightly like	Moderately like	Very much like	Extremely like		
11	Worst	Very poor	Poor	Significantly below average	Below average	Average	Above average	Significantly above average	Good	Very good	Best

designed and used by trained professionals (e.g., decision analysts). Sample problems reported in the case of general population include the following [FRI99]:

1) The interpretation of linguistic labels is not the same for all professions of respondents.
2) The inverted scales [most negative < ... < most positive] and [most positive > ... > most negative] do not generate the same results. Respondents prefer scales that start with the most positive label.
3) Respondents are more willing to select positive labels than negative labels. So, to get a uniform coverage, the negative extreme of scale should use labels with lesser strength.
4) In some cases, linguistic labels are preferred to numeric labels, but there are also cases where the opposite is true.
5) Grammatically balanced scales can generate unbalanced results (e.g., "dissatisfied" and "satisfied" in Table 2.9.3 are not symmetric with respect to "medium" in the middle of the scale).
6) The results of numeric scales depend on the range of numbers used as labels, and a general suggestion is to avoid negative numbers.

Table 2.9.3 Rohrmann's verbalization measurements [ROH07] compared to [MEN10].

Intensity					Quality		
Linear G=5	Label	% [ROH07]	% [MEN10]		Linear G=5	Label	% [ROH07]
I	Not at all	0				Very dissatisfied	5
	Not	4				Bad	10
	Hardly	15				Poor	15
II	Slightly	25				Unsatisfactory	18
II	A little	25	23			Dissatisfied	19
	Partly	35				Mostly dissatisfied	19
	Somewhat	45	45			Inadequate	19
III	In between	48				So-so	45
III	Average	48				Not too bad	46
III	Medium	49	51		III	Average	49
III	Moderately	50	49		III	Medium	50
III	Fairly	53	52		III	Fair	52
	Rather	58				Adequate	56
	Quite	59				Satisfactory	59
	Quite a bit	65	71			Satisfied	70
	Mainly	68				Mostly satisfied	72
IV	Considerably	76	76		IV	Good	72
	Very	79	83			Very good	85
	Highly	86	85			Very satisfied	89
	Very much	87			V	Excellent	97
	Fully	94			V	Outstanding	99
	Extremely	96	95				
V	Completely	98					

7) Weaker and stronger "anchor values" (labels used for two extremes of each scale) produce different results because respondents are reluctant to use extremely strong labels (e.g., the anchor "very bad" is used more often than the anchor "terrible").

2.9.1.2 Linearity of Rating Scales

Rating scales can be linear or nonlinear. The predominant forms of scales are linear scales, i.e., interval scales where respondents perceive intervals/granules of equal size. That yields the equal difference between adjacent labeled points on the scale. The nonlinear scales have different sizes of intervals and their applicability in the area of evaluation is less significant. For example, consider the following scale:

frequency of an event = [*never* < *rarely* < *occasionally* < *sometimes* < *usually* < *always*]

The scale seems to be strictly monotonic, but that is not a proof that distances between adjacent labels are the same. In linear scales, we would like to have equidistant labels and additional experiments are necessary to verify the desired linearity.

The linearity of magnitude rating scales means equal perceived psychological distance between all pairs of adjacent labels. Linearity must be experimentally proved using a representative population of respondents. The first step in experiments with linearity is to establish the relationship between linguistic labels and the corresponding numeric interpretation of such labels. A simple method to investigate this relationship for magnitude scaling consists of taking a numbered 0–10 scale, and a randomly selected label (e.g., "medium" or "poor") and ask respondents to indicate what intensity on the scale best corresponds to the selected label [ROH07] (a singleton approach), or what interval on the scale best corresponds to the selected label [MEN01] (an interval approach). The corresponding distributions can be used to develop type-1 or type-2 fuzzy set membership functions. In addition, the mean value of the distribution represents an estimate of the numeric equivalent of the linguistic label.

Rohrmann's study [ROH07] includes (among other quantifiers) empirical results for the "intensity" and "quality" indicators, which can be interpreted in evaluation problems as importance and suitability. The respondents were asked to locate the appropriate position of a randomized linguistic label on a 0–10 scale. Table 2.9.3 shows the sorted mean values of numeric equivalents of selected labels normalized using the interval [0,100%]. The values in one column are computed (for identical or almost identical labels) as normalized mean points of intervals (midrange) reported by Mendel [MEN10] in his 32-word codebook/vocabulary. Taking into account completely different populations used independently by Rohrmann and Mendel, the agreement of Rohrmann's and Mendel's results is excellent, and indicates that some linguistic labels might have rather stable interpretation in a given language (in this case, English). On the other hand, it is rather easy to find labels that mean different things to different people and have significant standard deviation when analyzed on the 0–10 scale.

The labels "average," "medium," "moderate," and "fair" represent the middle region of most magnitude scales [ROH07, MEN01]. All scales are assumed to be "anchored," i.e., their endpoints represent opposite extreme cases (e.g., lowest vs. highest, worst vs. best, very poor vs. very good, least important vs. most important, etc.). According to [FRI99], the labels most frequently used for the negative extreme include "extremely poor" and "exceptionally poor," as well as "horrible," "terrible," and "awful." Similarly, the labels used for the positive extreme include "excellent" and "superb," as well as "superior," "fantastic," and "tremendous."

If we want to create a linear five-point rating scale, then we need labels located at 0%, 25%, 50%, 75%, and 100%, or convincingly close to these values. The corresponding candidate labels are shown in Table 2.9.3 denoted with Roman numerals I, II, III, IV, and V (note that Rohrmann's quality labels are selected so that they cannot represent granules I and II of the five-point rating scale).

The label "moderately," located in the middle of the scale, is two times stronger than the label "slightly," and the label "considerably" is three times stronger than the label "slightly." In other words, the distance between the labels "slightly" and "moderately" is practically the same as the distance between the labels "moderately" and "considerably." Consequently, Rohrmann's measurements indicate (or practically prove) that the rating scale [*not at all < slightly < moderately < considerably < completely*] is almost perfectly linear, because it is based on almost perfectly equidistant labels (0, 25%, 50%, 76%, 98%).

Measurements reported in [ROH07, MEN01, LIU08, MEN10, WU12, HAO16] show that linguistic labels are fuzzy and nonuniformly distributed. Except in very rare cases and for very low cardinality, it is not possible to create strictly monotonic and linear worded rating scales. This conclusion is graphically illustrated in Figs. 2.9.2 and 2.9.3.

The sorted magnitudes of Mendel's 32-point scale (centers of centroids of labels reported in [MEN10]) and Rohrmann's 23-point scale are shown in Fig. 2.9.2; it is easy to see nonuniform distances between adjacent labels. That is even more obvious in Fig. 2.9.3, where both scales have nonuniform distribution of points, multiple points with the same magnitude, and visible gaps (e.g., the biggest gap is shown in the upper scale between 27.6% and 45%). It should be noted that the presented magnitude scales are the two most carefully designed and most carefully studied scales with the highest cardinality. So, these scales show the best linearity that can be achieved with worded scales. For example, if we want to create a strictly monotone linear 11-point scale, then, for each

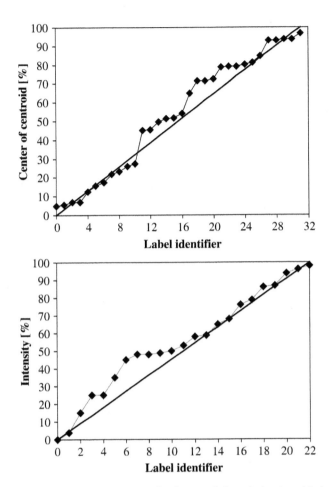

Figure 2.9.2 Sorted magnitudes for Mendel's scale (top) and Rohrmann's scale (bottom).

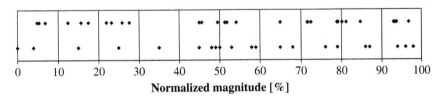

Figure 2.9.3 Mendel's scale (top, 32 points) and Rohrmann's scale (bottom, 23 points).

of 11 vertical lines shown in Fig. 2.9.3, we must find a point that is located either strictly on the line or in its immediate vicinity. This is obviously not possible. The conclusion is that if we want strict monotonicity and linearity (and we do), the scale must be hybrid.

2.9.1.3   Balance of Rating Scales

One of the fundamental requirements that rating scales must satisfy is the balance, which is defined as the symmetry between favorable (superior) options and unfavorable (inferior) options. For normalized intervals between 0 and 100% the rating scale is balanced if the number of options below 50% is equal to the number of options above 50% (the middle point of 50% can be included in the scale, or not included).

The scale [*low* < *medium* < *high*] is obviously balanced because medium is defined as a central point and low and high are antonyms (semantically symmetric concepts). However, the frequently used five-point scale [*poor* < *fair* < *good* < *very good* < *excellent*] is positively unbalanced because "fair" is the central label and there are three favorable and only one unfavorable option. Such unbalanced scales are used in cases where the analyst wants to provoke an apparently positive response; of course, such scales are considered unethical in all cases where favorable and unfavorable answers naturally occur with equal probability. The rating scales can also be negatively unbalanced, e.g., [*good* > *fair* > *poor* > *very poor* > *awful*].

Some authors claim that unbalanced scales are justified if the probability of specific (e.g., favorable) responses is much higher than the probability of other responses, and consequently there is no reason to offer many options in the area where there will be no responses [FRI99]. The sample scales shown in Table 2.9.2 are all balanced.

Both Rohrmann's and Mendels's measurements can be used to prove the balance of a general magnitude rating scale. Following are two typically worded and numbered magnitude rating scales based on Rohrmann's measurements:

[*poor* < *average* < *good* < *very good* < *outstanding*] = [15 < 49 < 72 < 85 < 99]
[*not at all* < *slightly* < *moderately* < *considerably* < *completely*] = [0 < 25 < 50 < 76 < 98]

The mean value of the first scale is 64% (which is significantly above 50%) and the mean value of the second scale is 49.8% (which is an almost perfect result). Therefore, the first scale is positively unbalanced while the second one is balanced.

Unbalanced scales with nonlinear verbalization where granules have different (usually strictly decreasing) sizes, are frequently used for evaluation of candidates for admission in various graduate schools. A good example of reasonable nonlinear verbalization is the graduate admission evaluation scale used by UC San Diego:

Below average	= Below 40%
Average	= 40%–60%
Above average	= Top 40%
Very good	= Top 20%
Outstanding	= Top 10%
Superior	= Top 5%
Extraordinary	= Top 1%

A good example of extremely nonlinear verbalization, following is a nonlinear scale with labels that reflect excessive elitism, used at UC Berkeley:

Below average	= Lower 50%
Average	= 51%–70%
Somewhat above average	= 71%–80%
Good	= 81%–90%
Superior	= 91%–95%
Outstanding	= 96%–99%
Truly exceptional	= Top 1%

The definition of label "average" seems bizarre, since its range is completely above the mathematical average expressed as the median of 50% (which means "located in the middle of a sorted list of candidates"). Then, the actual median of 50% is considered "below average."[1] Most likely, candidates who outperform 80% of other candidates would not agree to be classified as "somewhat above average," and candidates who outperform 90% of other candidates certainly feel that they are something more than "good."

These examples show that in many cases, there is no consensus in interpreting even the most common labels, such as "average," "good," and "outstanding," even in cases where that is done by similar officials working inside a similar system. For example, in the case of UCSD *outstanding < superior* and in the case of UCB *superior < outstanding*. It is rather clear that words mean different things to different people [MEN01].

The example of inconsistent labeling at USCD and UCB illustrates an important property that is useful in the area of evaluation: *for hybrid scales*

---

1 A possible justification of positively unbalanced rating scales is that numerical classification reflects general population and linguistic labels reflect local population based on fact that superior schools attract superior candidates, creating population that is very different from the general population. Among other things, the Berkeley scale claims that an average Berkeley candidate is typically 10 points above candidates that are average in the general population.

(combination of numeric and linguistic labels), numeric labels are automatically accepted as primary specifiers of granule identity, while fuzzy linguistic labels are used only as auxiliary (supplemental) verbal descriptors of the selected numeric values. This is useful for creating perfectly linear hybrid rating scales (Section 2.9.1.5).

2.9.1.4 Cardinality of Rating Scales

Each scale contains a finite set of labels and cardinality (or granularity, G) is the number of elements in the set. The researchers of rating scales intended for use by the general population are mostly focused on the study of imperfection of human perceptions. So, they are primarily interested in simple rating scales with no more than 11 points. A more precise professional labeling system with 16 levels was developed by Mendel in [MEN01], followed by a 32-level system proposed in [LIU08, MEN10, WU12]. In the case of andness/orness, the initially proposed 9-level scale [DUJ74a] was expanded to 17 levels [DUJ75a] and this is the most frequently used andness/orness scale (in Part Three we also use high precision scales with cardinality 23 and 25).

The fundamental questions related to cardinality are: (1) what is the justifiable (maximum acceptable) cardinality, and (2) should the cardinality be even or odd. The cardinality is constrained by human limitation to reliably distinguish and categorize magnitudes of unidimensional stimuli. The most influential paper in this area is [MIL56] where G. A. Miller suggests the cardinality $G = 7 \pm 2$ (a.k.a., "the magical number seven plus or minus two") (i.e., from 5 to 9). This result is verified and confirmed many times [COX80], and sometimes extended to the range from 3 to 11 [FRI99, PRE00, KRO10]. Reliability of correct selection of a point in a scale decreases when the cardinality increases above some threshold value, and this value is frequently between 5 and 9.

Regarding the even/odd cardinality, the most frequently used scales in research papers and in practice are based on cardinality $G = 3, 5, 7, 9, 11$. The reason for odd cardinality is simple: If the number of points is odd, then the scale includes the middle point at the level of 50%. This point is usually labeled "medium," "fair," or "average." Such labels are very clear and precise and serve as anchors that help respondents better understand the meaning of other labels below and above of the middle point. Of course, there are situations where an even number of points in a scale can be convenient, but such cases are less frequent (some of them are included in Table 2.9.2).

It is important to note that all scales studied in business, psychology, and medical literature are *flat*—just a sequence of points where each respondent must select one among available ordered (sorted) options. The general population is never given a search algorithm (i.e., a method how to process a scale in multiple steps, segment by segment). Not surprisingly, flat scales restrict cardinality to modest values and limit the accuracy that can be provided by a single respondent or a small team. In addition, the rating scales for general population are only used as an input instrument (i.e., for collecting data from respondents).

In soft computing, the rating scales can be used as either input or output. The worded magnitude scales with high cardinality (like the 32-word flat codebook in [MEN10]) are not linear, and are very difficult as an input instrument since they are not strictly monotonic (different people would interpret ordering of numerous linguistic labels in different ways). So, the expected reliability of correct selection of one among 32 linguistic labels is certainly low. However, if the same 32-word flat codebook is used as an output instrument, for converting numeric results to verbalized form and delivering results of decision models to stakeholders, management, and general population, then the precision of such a high granularity instrument can be fully utilized.

The cardinality of andness/orness rating scales can be increased if we have an efficient selection method that can select the most appropriate label with good accuracy. In Section 2.9.2, we present a rating scale stepwise refinement method that combines good cardinality and good precision for andness/orness rating scales.

2.9.1.5 Hybrid Rating Scales

Hybrid scales are defined as rating scales that identify granules using simultaneously numbers and words. Hybrid scales are predominant in professional applications. Their use with general population is less frequent. The basic property of hybrid scales is that whenever we have a labeled numeric value (e.g., in Table 2.9.3, *good* = 72%, *very good* = 85%), then the crisp numeric value is automatically accepted as the primary and precise descriptor of specific granule, and the linguistic label, which is fuzzy, plays the role of supplemental fuzzy descriptor. The descriptor is just a symbolic name, and there is plenty of freedom in selecting the name. Therefore, the basic advantage of hybrid scales is that they can be imprecisely verbalized, but at the same time *strictly monotonic, balanced,* and *perfectly linear.*

As an example of harmless inconsistencies in labeling, suppose that we use a seven-point scale [*unacceptable < very poor < poor < average < good < very good < excellent*]. Now, *good* = 66.7% (level = 4/6) and *very good* = 83.3% (level = 5/6). Similarly, if we use a nine-point scale [*unacceptable < very poor < poor < below average < average < above average < good < very good < excellent*] then *good* = 75% (level = 6/8), and *very good* = 87.5% (level = 7/8). These numeric values are different from the natural (respondent-generated) values *good* = 72%, *very good* = 85%, but both the seven-point and the nine-point hybrid scales, numerically labeled $1, ..., G$, or $0, ..., G-1$, or

$i/(G-1)$, $i=0,...,G-1$, $G \in \{7,9\}$ will be easily accepted by decision makers with the redefined interpretation of labels "good" and "very good."

An interesting hybrid unbalanced rating scale, developed for scoring NIH grant proposals [NIH13], is presented in Table 2.9.4. In the light of Rohrmann's and Mendel's interpretation of linguistic labels, this example provides five observations:

1) Based on descriptors, the NIH rating scale is highly unbalanced because the descriptor "fair" is proved to have the same meaning as "medium" and "average." Consequently, score 7 is the middle point of the scale and there are six favorable and only two unfavorable scores.

2) The guidelines for users [NIH13] claim "5 is considered an average score" and "a score of 5 is a good, medium-impact application." In other words, "good" and "average" are considered equivalent and located at 50% of the overall impact. Unfortunately, this is not correct because both Rohrmann and Mendel proved that "good" > "average." In [ROH07], "good" is located at 72% and in [MEN10] "good amount" has center of centroid range located at 65%.

3) According to [ROH07], descriptors "exceptional," "outstanding," and "excellent" are all located in the top 3%. It seems strange that NIH expects that "high overall impact" means *only* top 3%.

4) According to the rating scales theory, NIH descriptors are wrong. However, the NIH scoring system is essentially a hybrid scale. Descriptors are just a "supporting component" because the evaluators are focused on numeric scores and not on their verbal descriptors. Thus, in hybrid (numbered and worded) scales, the primary carriers of information are numbers and not words. Numbers are precise and not subject to interpretation. Words are imprecise, and various linguistic labels can be attached to a given number without serious negative consequences. Indeed, labels are only auxiliary descriptors and not the primary information carriers. Since each linguistic label is just a name of a numeric object, it does not affect the object itself.

Table 2.9.4 NIH scoring system.

Overall impact	Score	Descriptor	Rohrmann %
High	1	Exceptional	-
	2	Outstanding	99
	3	Excellent	97
	4	Very good	85
Medium	5	Good	72
	6	Satisfactory	59
	7	Fair	52
Low	8	Marginal	-
	9	Poor	15

It is desirable but not necessary to have the best possible naming of objects. If each descriptor is interpreted as a fuzzy set, then a value from that fuzzy set can be associated with the descriptor even in cases of non-maximum membership. Humans are flexible and easily adjust the interpretation of a linguistic label as a descriptor of a given numeric score in the context of a specific evaluation process.

5) In the case of NIH scale, the scale is positively unbalanced, and a possible justification for that can be based on the fact that most proposals have significant merits and belong in the region above the average value. So, more points are needed above the average than below the average.

The only method for creating rating scales that are strictly monotonic, strictly linear, and balanced consists of using the hybrid scales. In hybrid scales, numeric labeling provides monotonicity, linearity, and balance, while the linguistic labeling is used for symbolic identification of numeric values. Since all magnitude scale labels have their "natural values" that are assigned by a carefully selected population of human respondents, it is desirable that linguistic labels in hybrid scales are selected close to their natural values.

2.9.2 Stepwise Refinement of Rating Scales for Andness and Orness

High cardinality is a necessary (but not sufficient) condition for precision in the use of magnitude rating scales. The accurate selection of the most appropriate among many options remains a problem that needs an algorithmic solution. Strict monotonicity, linearity, and balance are provided by numerical labeling of hybrid scales for magnitude rating. To achieve precision, we would like to have high cardinality, but without problems caused by going beyond the "magical number seven." This can be achieved using a stepwise refinement method presented in this section.

The idea of stepwise refinement of magnitude rating scale for andness/orness is based on a ternary selection algorithm presented in Figs. 2.9.4 and 2.9.5. In each refinement step we select one of the three offered options. Of course, such selection is easy, and it can be done with accuracy and confidence. We repeat the ternary selection steps four times until we select the most appropriate among 17 levels of andness/orness, used by WPM.17 and GGCD.17 versions of the GCD aggregator (see Fig. 3.4.1). We start with the question Q1 about the type of aggregator: pure conjunction or pure disjunction of partial conjunction/disjunction. After selecting the partial conjunction/disjunction as the type of GCD aggregator, we continue with the second ternary choice: in question Q2 we select among three characteristic forms of GCD: neutrality, partial conjunction, or partial disjunction. In question Q3 we select the range of

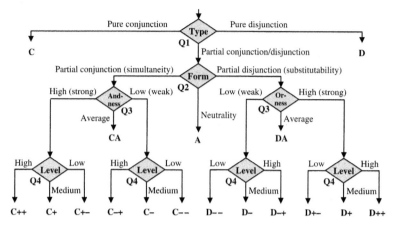

Figure 2.9.4 Flowchart of the ternary search in the case of a 17-point andness/orness scale.

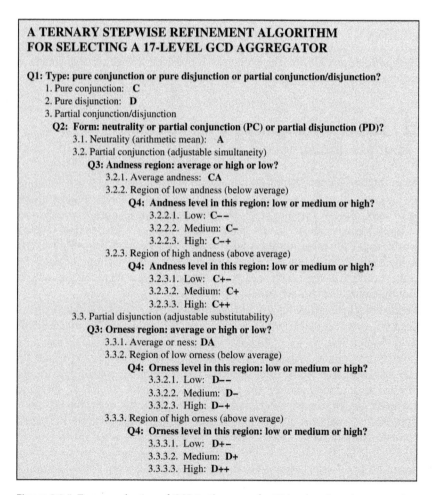

A TERNARY STEPWISE REFINEMENT ALGORITHM FOR SELECTING A 17-LEVEL GCD AGGREGATOR

Q1: Type: pure conjunction or pure disjunction or partial conjunction/disjunction?
    1. Pure conjunction: **C**
    2. Pure disjunction: **D**
    3. Partial conjunction/disjunction
        Q2: Form: neutrality or partial conjunction (PC) or partial disjunction (PD)?
            3.1. Neutrality (arithmetic mean): **A**
            3.2. Partial conjunction (adjustable simultaneity)
                Q3: Andness region: average or high or low?
                    3.2.1. Average andness: **CA**
                    3.2.2. Region of low andness (below average)
                        Q4: Andness level in this region: low or medium or high?
                            3.2.2.1. Low: **C‒‒**
                            3.2.2.2. Medium: **C‒**
                            3.2.2.3. High: **C‒+**
                    3.2.3. Region of high andness (above average)
                        Q4: Andness level in this region: low or medium or high?
                            3.2.3.1. Low: **C+‒**
                            3.2.3.2. Medium: **C+**
                            3.2.3.3. High: **C++**
            3.3. Partial disjunction (adjustable substitutability)
                Q3: Orness region: average or high or low?
                    3.3.1. Average or ness: **DA**
                  3.3.2. Region of low orness (below average)
                        Q4: Orness level in this region: low or medium or high?
                            3.3.2.1. Low: **D‒‒**
                            3.3.2.2. Medium: **D‒**
                            3.3.2.3. High: **D‒+**
                  3.3.3. Region of high orness (above average)
                        Q4: Orness level in this region: low or medium or high?
                            3.3.3.1. Low: **D+‒**
                            3.3.3.2. Medium: **D+**
                            3.3.3.3. High: **D++**

Figure 2.9.5 Ternary selection of GCD in the case of a 17-level andness/orness scale.

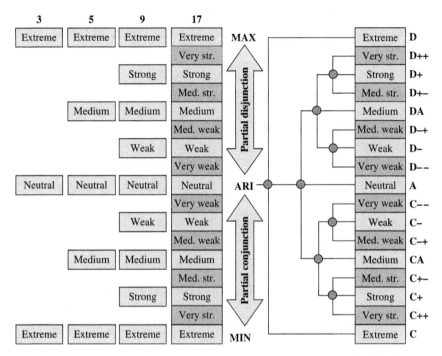

Figure 2.9.6 A ternary stepwise refinement of GCD and selection of symbolic labels.

andness or orness that can be below average, or above the average, or average. Finally, question Q4 determines the level of andness/orness inside the selected group: low, medium, or high. The ternary stepwise refinement process can also be visualized and verbalized as shown in Fig. 2.9.6.

The systematic sequence of simple ternary decision steps provides a way to select the most appropriate level of andness/orness by a top-down stepwise refinement process. The basic benefit is that each step is simple and it is easy to justify each of ternary decisions. The result of this process is a justifiable selection of the most appropriate aggregator in Table 2.9.5 without problems related to the accuracy of verbal labeling of 17 levels of the resulting linear and balanced andness/orness rating scale.

The ternary selection algorithm described in Figs. 2.9.4 to 2.9.6 primarily shows the background reasoning that justifies the process of andness/orness adjustment. Of course, after some training and practice evaluators quickly connect and aggregate individual steps and easily and directly select the version of GCD (WPM.17 or GGCD.17) that best reflects their percept of simultaneity or substitutability.

Table 2.9.5 Alternative ways of verbalizing andness and orness for granularity $G = 17$.

S	Andness (Degree of simultaneity)		Op	α	Orness (Degree of replaceability)		R
16	Highest	Highest	C	1.0000	Lowest	Lowest	0
15	Slightly below highest	Very high+	C++	0.9375	Very low–	Slightly above lowest	1
14	Very high	Very high	C+	0.8750	Very low	Very low	2
13	Slightly above high	Very high–	C+–	0.8125	Very low+	Slightly below low	3
12	High	High	CA	0.7500	Low	Low	4
11	Slightly below high	Medium-high+	C–+	0.6875	Medium-low–	Slightly above low	5
10	Medium-high	Medium-high	C–	0.6250	Medium-low	Medium-low	6
9	Slightly above medium	Medium-high–	C––	0.5625	Medium-low+	Slightly below medium	7
8	Medium	Medium	A	0.5000	Medium	Medium	8
7	Slightly below medium	Medium-low+	D––	0.4375	Medium-high–	Slightly above medium	9
6	Medium-low	Medium-low	D–	0.3750	Medium-high	Medium-high	10
5	Slightly above low	Medium-low–	D–+	0.3125	Medium-high+	Slightly below high	11
4	Low	Low	DA	0.2500	High	High	12
3	Slightly below low	Very low+	D+–	0.1875	Very high–	Slightly above high	13
2	Very low	Very low	D+	0.1250	Very high	Very high	14
1	Slightly above lowest	Very low–	D++	0.0625	Very high+	Slightly below highest	15
0	Lowest	Lowest	D	0.0000	Highest	Highest	16

The presented 17-level rating scale is based on bisection of intervals between adjacent points in the rating scale. That is clearly visible in Fig. 2.9.6, where we create a sequence of rating scales with granularity $G = 3,5,9,17$. It is easy to see that these scales provide symmetry between week (below average) and strong (above average) aggregators, but cannot provide symmetry of hard and soft aggregators: the number of hard aggregators is always different from the number of soft aggregators, and it is not possible to have a symmetric uniform GCD (denoted UGCD.G in the case of granularity G).

The stepwise refinement method for generating UGCD aggregators can be developed as shown in Fig. 2.9.7. We again use four decision steps. The first step is the selection of the type of GCD aggregator: conjunctive, disjunctive, or neutral. The second step is the binary choice of form, which can be full or partial. In most cases, the selected form is partial. The third step is the binary choice of mode, which can be hard or soft. These three steps are extremely simple and can be easily justified and performed without errors. The final fourth step is also simple and consists of selecting the intensity/strength of aggregator within the selected mode. In Fig. 2.9.7 we offer $n = 1,...,7$ degrees of precision. That yields granularity in the wide range from 7 to 31.

In the simplest possible case ($n = 1$, suitable for initial educational experiences), there is nothing to select in the fourth step. The aggregator is automatically located inside the corresponding interval, in a way that provides the strict linearity of rating scale, i.e., the uniform distribution of points inside [0,1] with step 1/6. This approach yields 7 degrees of andness: $\alpha = 0, 1/6, 1/3, 1/2, 2/3, 5/6, 1$. Note that an alternative approach would be to locate aggregators in the middle of each of four characteristic intervals and the resulting sequence of andness

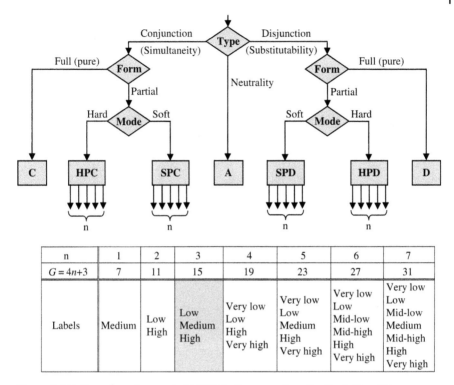

Figure 2.9.7 Stepwise refinement of UGCD in the case of cardinality 7, 11,...,31.

would be α = 0, 1/8, 3/8, ½, 5/8, 7/8, 1. However, this scale is not linear and consequently not desirable.

The granularity (and precision) can be increased by using $n > 1$. For example, if $n = 3$, in the fourth step of the selection process the user decides between three degrees of intensity denoted *low*, *medium*, and *high*. The corresponding scale has the cardinality $G = 15$ and the andness is incremented with the step 1/14. Figs. 2.9.8 and 2.9.9 summarize the results of the stepwise refinement algorithm for GCD ($G = 17$) and UGCD ($G = 15$). Note that in the case of GCD, we can select any of the PC aggregators to serve as the threshold andness aggregator. Similarly, any PD aggregator can be used as the threshold orness aggregator. The border between soft and hard aggregators is adjustable, and aggregators are identified as either weak or strong. In the case of UGCD, the border between soft and hard aggregators is fixed (both the threshold andness and the threshold orness are 75%). Consequently, all UGCD aggregators are identified as either soft or hard. The selection of GCD aggregators for LSP criteria is discussed in Sections 3.1.4 and 3.4.1.

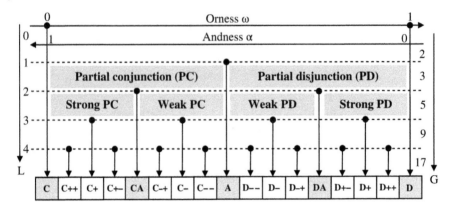

Figure 2.9.8 The medium precision GCD andness/orness rating scale ($G = 17$).

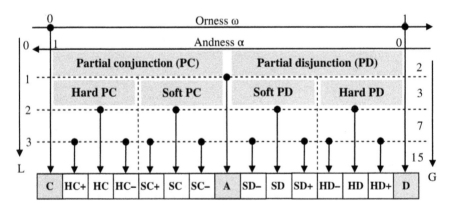

Figure 2.9.9 The medium precision UGCD andness/orness rating scale ($G = 15$).

2.9.3 Scaling and Verbalizing Degrees of Importance

In the case of verbalizing degrees of importance, we assume N discrete levels denoted $1, 2, ..., N$. The extreme values 0 and 1 are excluded from importance rating scales, as shown in Fig. 2.9.1 and Table 2.9.6. The importance at level L is expressed using weights $W = L/(N + 1)$, $L = 1, ..., N$. Importance rating scales are hybrid and the importance is primarily expressed using the numeric weight. This is the reason why a given linguistic label can be assigned to multiple numeric values (e.g., in Table 2.9.6 VL describes 1/6, 1/8, and 0.2). The binary approach to verbalization (inserting new values in the middle of existing intervals) can be used in the case of importance, as shown in Table 2.9.7 for $N = 17$.

Table 2.9.6 Assigning linguistic labels to various degrees of importance.

Number of levels (N)	Numeric and verbalized degree of importance								
3	0		1/4		1/2		3/4		1
			L		M		H		
5	0	1/6		1/3	1/2	2/3		5/6	1
		VL		L	M	H		VH	
7	0	1/8	1/4	3/8	1/2	5/8	3/4	7/8	1
		VL	L	LM	M	MH	H	VH	
9	0	0.1	0.2	0.3	0.4	1/2	0.6	0.7	0.8	0.9	1
		EL	VL	L	LM	M	MH	H	VH	EH	

Labels: EL=extremely low, VL=very low, L=low, LM=low to medium, M=medium, MH=medium to high, H=high, VH=very high, EH=extremely high

2.9.4 Scaling and Verbalizing Degrees of Suitability/Preference

Verbalization of suitability is exemplified in Table 2.9.8. For a 17-point scale, the levels of suitability are denoted $L = 0,...,16$. Each level corresponds to a range of suitability. If the maximum level is N (in Table 2.9.8, $N = 16$), then the level that corresponds to suitability X can be computed as follows:

$$L_N = \lfloor NX + 1/2 \rfloor.$$

For example, let us verbalize the suitability $X = 0.84$. In the case of a 17-point scale, $N = 16$ and we have $L_{16} = \lfloor 16 \times 0.84 + 1/2 \rfloor = 13$, what can be verbalized as

Table 2.9.7 Verbalizing 17 levels of importance.

Level	Weight	Importance descriptors	
17	17/18 = 0.944	Highest	Highest
16	8/9 = 0.889	Slightly above very high	+Very high
15	5/6 = 0.833	Very high	Very high
14	7/9 = 0.778	Slightly below very high	−Very high
13	13/18 = 0.722	High	High
12	2/3 = 0.667	Slightly above medium-high	+Medium-high
11	11/18 = 0.611	Medium-high	Medium-high
10	5/9 = 0.556	Slightly below medium-high	−Medium-high
9	½ = 0.500	Medium	Medium
8	4/9 = 0.444	Slightly above medium-low	+Medium-low
7	7/18 = 0.389	Medium-low	Medium-low
6	1/3 = 0.333	Slightly below medium-low	−Medium-low
5	5/18 = 0.278	Low	Low
4	2/9 = 0.222	Slightly above very low	+Very low
3	1/6 = 0.167	Very low	Very low
2	1/9 = 0.111	Slightly below very low	−Very low
1	1/18 = 0.056	Lowest	Lowest

Table 2.9.8 Verbalizing 17 levels of suitability/preference.

Level	Suitability range	Alternative suitability descriptors			Symbol
16	[31/32, 1]	Highest	Highest	Excellent/perfect	HH
15	[29/32, 31/32 [	Slightly below highest	Highest–	Slightly below perfect	HH–
14	[27/32, 29/32 [	Very high	Very high	Very good	VH
13	[25/32, 27/32 [	Slightly above high	High+	Slightly above good	H+
12	[23/32, 25/32 [	High	High	Good	H
11	[21/32, 23/32 [	Slightly below high	High–	Slightly below good	H–
10	[19/32, 21/32 [	Medium-high	Medium-high	Above average	MH
9	[17/32, 19/32 [	Slightly above medium	Medium+	Slightly above average	M+
8	[15/32, 17/32 [	Medium	Medium	Average	M
7	[13/32, 15/32 [	Slightly below medium	Medium–	Slightly below average	M–
6	[11/32, 13/32 [	Medium-low	Medium-low	Below average	ML
5	[9/32, 11/32 [	Slightly above low	Low+	Slightly above poor	L+
4	[7/32, 9/32 [	Low	Low	Poor	L
3	[5/32, 7/32 [	Slightly below low	Low–	Slightly below poor	L–
2	[3/32, 5/32 [	Very low	Very low	Very poor	VL
1	[1/32, 3/32 [	Slightly above lowest	Lowest+	Slightly above inadequate	LL+
0	[0,1/32 [	Lowest	Lowest	Inadequate	LL

"slightly above good" (or "slightly below very good"). However, if we decide to use a less precise nine-point scale [(0) *inadequate* < (1) *very poor* < (2) *poor* < (3) *below average* < (4) *average* < (5) *above average* < (6) *good* < (7) *very good* < (8) *excellent*], then $N = 8$ and $L_8 = \lfloor 8 \times 0.84 + 1/2 \rfloor = 7$, what is verbalized as "very good." However, if $X = 0.85$, then $L_{16} = 14$, $L_8 = 7$, and in both cases the suitability of 85% is verbalized as "very good" or "very high satisfaction of requirements." The level for verbalization $L_8 = \lfloor 8X + 1/2 \rfloor$ is presented in Fig. 2.9.10. This form of verbalization can be compared with a similar fuzzy verbalization shown in Fig. 2.2.9.

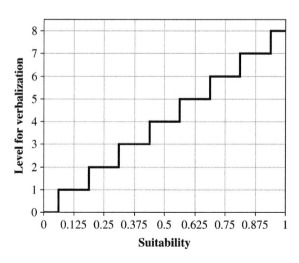

Figure 2.9.10 Level for verbalization L_8 as a function of suitability.

PART THREE

LSP METHOD

> *In the beginner's mind there are many possibilities.*
> *In the expert's mind there are few.*
> —Shunryu Suzuki

In *Part Three* we present the Logic Scoring of Preference (LSP) method for evaluation, comparison, and optimization of complex systems. The point of departure is an overview of the LSP method presented in Chapter 3.1. The presentation in Chapter 3.1 is simple and suitable for all readers. All other chapters in *Part Three* provide refinements and extensions of the material presented in Chapter 3.1.

The goal of *Part Three* is to introduce the LSP Decision Engineering Framework (LSP DEF) as a set of professional evaluation techniques and evaluation tools developed from the theoretical basis of graded logic and aggregation introduced in *Part Two*.

The LSP DEF is developed for solving professional evaluation problems (i.e., problems that need a significant level of domain expertise). For example, the evaluation of computer systems, medical conditions, military equipment, complex software systems, urban plans, and ecologic solutions would not be possible without appropriate domain expertise. So, in many cases domain experts are interested in evaluation methodology and evaluation problem solving using the LSP method. *Part Three* of this book is written having in mind the needs of all kinds of professional evaluators, including both decision analysts and a wide variety of domain experts.

Evaluation problems that are less dependent on professional expertise in a specific domain are usually personal decision problems, such as evaluating

Soft Computing Evaluation Logic: The LSP Decision Method and Its Applications,
First Edition. Jozo Dujmović.
© 2018 John Wiley & Sons, Inc. Published 2018 by John Wiley & Sons, Inc.
Companion website: www.wiley.com/go/Dujmovic/Soft_Computing_Evaluation_Logic

and selecting jobs, cars, homes, and schools for students. Such problems are extremely frequent, but are rarely solved using any quantitative methodology. The main reason for our interest in such evaluation problems is their educational value, and they will be presented both in *Part Three* and in *Part Four* of this book. Indeed, such problems are accessible to all categories of readers and enable readers to focus on fully exposed decision aspects of the problem. On the other hand, the need for domain expertise as a prerequisite for building and using evaluation models significantly reduces the number of those who can follow the logic of evaluation. Let us note that the low frequency of quantitative methods in personal decision making also reflects the lack of appropriate decision support tools, specifically designed to be suitable for use by the general population.

3.1   An Overview of the LSP Method

LSP is a decision method, and decisions are human mental processes performed by human perceptual computers. Consequently, the main credo of the LSP method is that the only right way to develop a decision method is by strictly following those logic patterns that are observable in intuitive human reasoning. To satisfy those goals, the LSP method follows the structure of SMER (Standard Model of Evaluation Reasoning), introduced in Section 2.2.1. The corresponding outline of the LSP method is shown in Fig. 3.1.1.

The first step in the LSP method is to define the stakeholder and to specify the evaluation project based on stakeholder's goals and interests. The second step is to develop a set of elementary suitability attributes, which contains all quantifiable inputs that affect the overall suitability of the evaluated object. The third step is to create for each elementary attribute an elementary criterion that specifies the suitability score as a degree of satisfaction of stakeholder's requirements. Suitability scores are indicators between 0 (interpreted as no satisfaction) and 1, or 100% (interpreted as a complete satisfaction). Once we have n attribute suitability scores, it is necessary to aggregate them and generate an overall suitability score. So, in the fourth step of the LSP method we must develop a stepwise suitability aggregation structure. That structure includes various logic conditions that reflect the stakeholder's goals and interests. At the end of the suitability aggregation process, the resulting suitability score represents the overall degree of satisfaction of *all* the stakeholder's requirements. In a general case, the final steps of the LSP method include financial aspects of evaluation.

In some cases evaluated objects don't have a price. For example, some evaluated software products like browsers, search engines, and most language processors are free and can simply be downloaded from the Internet. Similarly, suitability analyses of public websites do not include financial components. In such cases the overall suitability score is the final result of evaluation.

Soft Computing Evaluation Logic: The LSP Decision Method and Its Applications,
First Edition. Jozo Dujmović.
© 2018 John Wiley & Sons, Inc. Published 2018 by John Wiley & Sons, Inc.
Companion website: www.wiley.com/go/Dujmovic/Soft_Computing_Evaluation_Logic

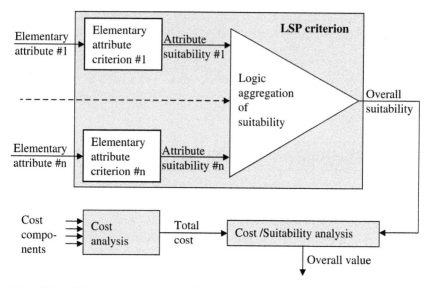

Figure 3.1.1 Main components of the LSP method.

However, more often than not (including all industrial evaluation projects), stakeholders have to buy the evaluated object. In such cases, the price of evaluated objects can substantially affect the final decision. The final step of the LSP method consists of a cost analysis that aggregates all direct and indirect cost components and generates a total cost indicator. Then, the overall suitability (that should be as high as possible, and regularly has a significant degree of importance for the stakeholder) and the total cost (that should be as low as possible, and has another degree of importance for the stakeholder) are combined together using a *cost/suitability analysis*, and the final result is the *overall value* (or the *overall worth*) of each evaluated object. The overall value is a single scalar indicator that reflects *all* relevant nonfinancial and financial suitability attributes and can be used for comparison and ranking of a group of competitive objects and selecting the best alternative. Of course, the most suitable object is one that has the highest overall value, and ranking of competitors is based on decreasing overall values.

The overall value generated by the LSP method can also be interpreted as a justifiable quantitative model of the overall aggregated human percept of suitability.

In addition to providing a justified final result of an evaluation project, the process of computing the overall value also offers possibilities for verbalized justification of the final result, explaining the reasons why the best object outperforms the second best and all other competitors. In many projects the verbalization is an important and sometimes necessary decision support component that builds confidence that the final result (the decision based on the total value) is correctly serving the best interests of the stakeholder and should be accepted and realized.

In addition to the presented main steps of the LSP method, the evaluation process also includes various supporting activities and can be generally structured as follows:

1) Definition of the stakeholder and the evaluation project
2) Development of the suitability attribute tree
3) Development of elementary attribute criteria
4) Logic aggregation of suitability
5) Verification of properties of the decision criterion:
   - Sensitivity analysis
   - Tradeoff analysis
6) Evaluation and comparison of competitive objects
   - Cost analysis
   - Cost/suitability analysis
   - Analysis of the reliability of evaluation results
   - Optimization
7) Documentation that presents evaluation results
   - Evaluation reports
   - Executive summary

3.1.1 Characterization of Stakeholder and Organization of an Evaluation Project

All engineering projects start with the clear statement of the problem. That holds also for evaluation projects. The statement of the evaluation problem is usually organized as answers to the following questions:

1) Who is the stakeholder?
2) Stakeholder characterization: What are the stakeholder's goals and interests?
3) In what way do evaluated objects contribute to the stakeholder goal attainment?
4) What is the available/approved price range for the evaluated object acquisition?
5) Who are the potential vendors of evaluated object?
6) What objects will be included (or not included) in the evaluation project?
7) What is the schedule of evaluation activities?

The first step is a clear identification of the stakeholder of evaluated object. By definition, the stakeholder is a party interested in ownership and/or use of a selected object of evaluation. Typical stakeholders include: (1) individuals,

(2) families, (3) groups of people, (4) organizations, (5) governments (city, state, etc.), (6) companies, (7) armed forces, and (8) educational institutions. Each stakeholder is characterized by goals and interests that are used to specify requirements that evaluated objects must satisfy.

For example, the stakeholder can be a family of two parents and three children and the object of evaluation can be a home. The homebuyer can easily specify a number of goals that potential homes must satisfy: for example, the location should be in the proximity of the day care and schools for children, it must be in acceptable distance from jobs of parents, maybe close to grandparents, the neighborhood must have a good safety record, and the house must have specific number of bedrooms and specific minimum area, etc. Of course, there will be an available price range, and only houses inside the available price range will be considered.

The stakeholder can also be a company that is buying computer equipment. In this case, the approved budget will define the type of equipment that can be purchased as well as the potential vendors who can deliver the desired equipment. In some cases, multiple vendors can be invited to submit proposals, and in other cases the compatibility with existing equipment can limit the vendors to a small group or to only one.

In the case of a family car selection, the family should have a list of precisely specified goals that the car should support: the car should be able to transport the whole family, it should be new (or used), it should be within an affordable price range, it should not be manufactured by selected unreliable manufacturers, it should have easily accessible maintenance, it should have specific type (e.g., SUV), and satisfy a list of technical requirements.

By definition, the stakeholder is the originator and initiator of each evaluation project and in many cases is also the investor and employer of other participants in the evaluation project. The stakeholder is the only party affected (in the whole range from beneficially to detrimentally) by the results of evaluation and by implementing the proposed (good or bad) decision. Therefore, no evaluation can be successful without some form of presence and active participation of stakeholder. The development of all evaluation criteria is based on inputs from stakeholder. Those inputs (derived from the *stakeholder characterization*) can come in two forms: *implicit* and *explicit*.

Implicit stakeholder characterization is the most frequent case where the stakeholder actively participates in all phases of the development of an evaluation criterion and directly affects the selection of attributes and the structure and parameters of the evaluation model. This is the case wherever a stakeholder is a company that hires an evaluator (decision consultant) and selects representatives providing management and domain expertise. The stakeholder representatives directly participate in the evaluation, negotiations, selection, and contracting process. In such cases, the resulting LSP criterion can be considered a formal expression of stakeholder's goals and requirements.

Explicit stakeholder characterization is a process of formal identification of the stakeholder's plans, goals, and interests, expressed using a *stakeholder characterization questionnaire* [DUJ97a, DUJ97b]. This process specifies the expected forms of use of evaluated object and provides information that is necessary for development of an LSP criterion that realistically reflects stakeholder needs and interests. Explicit stakeholder characterization is needed in cases where we develop criteria for users who do not participate in the criterion development team.

Each evaluation project must specify a schedule of necessary activities, and for some evaluation projects it is necessary to reserve significant time and prepare the evaluation team. Typical industrial evaluation projects include the following sequence of activities:

1) Organization of evaluation team (the stakeholder selects its representatives, and then selects the evaluator, and domain experts).
2) Stakeholder characterization.
3) Development of the LSP criterion function to be used in the evaluation project.
4) Stakeholder's inspection and formal acceptance of the LSP criterion function.
5) Preparation of the *request for proposals* (and other tender documentation).
6) Distribution of tender documentation to potential vendors.
7) Preparation of proposals.
8) Proposals adjustments/improvements through contacts with selected vendors.
9) Evaluation process (evaluation, optimization, and comparison of proposals).
10) Financial negotiations.
11) Cost/suitability analysis and the final ranking of competitive objects.
12) Preparation of the executive summary and the evaluation report(s).
13) Stakeholder's formal acceptance of evaluation documentation.
14) Preparation and signing of contract with selected vendor.
15) Delivery of contracted equipment.
16) Installation of equipment and acceptance test.
17) Test operation followed by regular operation using the purchased equipment.

In the context of industrial evaluation projects, the term *decision maker* (DM) assumes an evaluation team that consists of one or more *stakeholders, evaluators*, and *domain experts*. The stakeholder representatives are responsible for interpreting the goals and interests of the organization they represent. Domain experts are selected among those who have detailed knowledge and user experience with evaluated objects (e.g., in the case of evaluating and selecting aircraft, the domain experts should include experienced pilots, and/or aeronautical/aerospace engineers). The evaluator should be a person familiar with the LSP method and the use of software tools that support the evaluation process. In most cases, DM is a small professional team that consists of one or few stakeholder representatives, a single evaluator, and one or few domain experts that participate in the work only in those activities where their expertise becomes necessary. Sometimes a single person can play multiple roles. For example, the evaluator can also be a domain expert for a specific area, or a domain expert can master the evaluation methodology to the extent that s/he can perform the role of both evaluator and the domain expert. Similarly, the stakeholder representatives are frequently also domain experts in a selected area. A more detailed analysis can be found in Chapter 3.2.

The decision-making team should carefully follow the activities planned in the accepted evaluation project schedule. To control this process, one of stakeholder representatives has the role of the decision-making team leader/manager. The team leader/manager responsibilities are to interpret and protect stakeholder interests, to synchronize the decision-making team, to secure the adherence to project plan and schedule, to provide conflict resolution, and to oversee financial aspects of the evaluation project.

In the subsequent sections of this chapter, we focus on the activities of evaluator, i.e., the development and use of an LSP criterion that specifies all requirements that contribute to the attainment of stakeholder's goals. At the end of each section (including this one) we will present an introductory short location suitability example, step by step. To avoid the need for domain expertise, our example will consider an everyday situation in which a senior citizen compares alternative home locations.

Location Suitability Example, Step 1: Stakeholder Identification and Project Definition
The stakeholder is a senior citizen who is looking for a suitable location in a city where s/he could rent or buy an apartment or a house. S/he uses public transportation, and must have food stores located close to the home. So, proximity to public transportation and proximity to food stores are mandatory. Desired (but nonmandatory) amenities include the availability of parks, restaurants, and public libraries. The evaluation should be based on proximity of the analyzed location to the selected points of interest, and on the cost of renting or buying home at the analyzed location.

3.1.2 Development of the Suitability Attribute Tree

The next step of the LSP method is a systematic development of a list that contains all necessary and sufficient suitability attributes that are needed for evaluation. Fig. 3.1.3 illustrates this process for our introductory senior citizen example. On the surface this process looks very simple. In reality, however, an incorrect selection of suitability attributes can easily ruin every evaluation project. Consequently, we must spend necessary space to study how to avoid various errors is selecting suitability attributes.

Generally, the selection of suitability attributes must reflect the stakeholder's goals and interests. In other words, we are not interested in all attributes. We are interested only in suitability attributes, i.e., in those attributes that affect the overall suitability of evaluated object, support stakeholder's interests, and contribute to the attainment of stakeholder's goals. For example, the color of car can be a significant suitability attribute for many car buyers (particularly those who would never buy a black car, as well as for those who always buy black cars). In contrast, the chassis color of a mainframe computer is largely irrelevant for corporate buyers and it cannot be used as a suitability attribute.

The suitability attributes are organized as a tree structure. For example, in the case of evaluating mainframe computer systems, the first level of decomposition usually yields four composite attributes: (1) hardware, (2) software, (3) performance, and (4) vendor support. Obviously, the composite attributes cannot be directly evaluated, and the next step is to further decompose each of them, yielding simpler attributes (Fig. 2.2.17). At the end of the systematic decomposition process, we reach the leaves of the attribute tree and generate elementary attributes that cannot be further decomposed and can be directly evaluated (see Section 2.2.1, P_3, and Definitions 2.2.1 to 2.2.5).

The identification of individual attributes and their aggregated groups is based on numbering all nodes and all leaves of the aggregation tree. Following is a standard node numbering and tree structuring policy (Fig. 3.1.3):

1) The root of the attribute tree represents (and is labeled as) the overall suitability of evaluated object. The root node is regularly identified as node #1.
2) Starting at the root, each node attribute is decomposed into child attributes. Child attribute nodes of the root are numbered #11, #12, etc. (as in Fig. 3.1.3). The child attributes can be node attributes (that can be further decomposed) or leaf attributes (that are simple enough and need not or cannot be further decomposed). The leaf attributes are also called the elementary suitability attributes, or simply elementary attributes.
3) The number of child nodes in each node of an attribute tree should be limited because the human ability to accurately select relative weights and simultaneously evaluate multiple components significantly decreases if the number of items is large [MIL56]. Practical evaluation experiences show that it is advisable to limit the number of children in each node to 5. If the number of child nodes is greater than 5, then it is reasonable to create multiple groups of up to 5 members and then separately aggregate such groups (e.g., instead of aggregating 6 attributes, it is better and easier to use 3+3 or 2+4 or 2+2+2; see P_{29} in Section 2.2.5).

The selection of suitability attributes is a semantic component of evaluation process because it is based on understanding the stakeholder's goals and requirements derived from selected goals. Evaluated objects can have a variety of attributes, and the understanding of their role in supporting stakeholder's goals is a prerequisite for including relevant and excluding irrelevant attributes. For example, the color of a house is certainly one of the house attributes, but it can easily be excluded from suitability attributes by a rational homebuyer who is strictly focused on the suitability of the internal organization of house and the quality of house location.

As a consequence of semantic aspects of selecting suitability attributes, various stakeholders can have different views of rationality, inclusion, and exclusion of attributes. Since the stakeholder is by definition the ultimate authority for goal specification, external observers could qualify some goals and suitability attributes as rational and some as irrational. Both rational and irrational goals are equally legitimate in personal evaluation reasoning, and it is in human nature to select suitability attributes on the basis of both rational and irrational goals (See P_2 in Section 2.2.1).

In the case of professional evaluation projects, we assume that the selected goals are first specified and verified by expert teams of the corporate stakeholder. Suitability attributes are then selected after a careful analysis performed by the decision-making team, which includes stakeholder representatives, evaluators, and domain experts (Section 3.2.1). In the majority of such situations, the goals and suitability attributes are selected in a rational and professionally justifiable way, supporting the best interests of the stakeholder.

The above discussion shows that suitability attributes always reflect stakeholder's goals and the selection of suitability attributes is based on understanding the way selected attributes contribute to the stakeholder's goal attainment. The professional selection of suitability attributes is a semantic process that combines the domain expertise and the expertise in evaluation methodology. Consequently, it must follow strict rules because the correctness and usability of evaluation results depends on the correctness of the attribute tree. Generally, the attributes should be *relevant, necessary, sufficient, independent,* and *correctly grouped.* More precisely, during the attribute tree development process, it is necessary to apply the following four fundamental rules:

1) *No missing attributes*: The selected set of suitability attributes must be complete, i.e., sufficient to perform an accurate and justifiable evaluation. If an attribute significantly (or just nonnegligibly) affects the overall suitability of an evaluated object, such an attribute is necessary and must be used as an input of the LSP evaluation criterion. Incomplete lists of attributes (unintentional or intentional) are a rather frequent error that should be avoided.
2) *No irrelevant attributes*: Lists of attributes sometimes include insignificant attributes, i.e., attributes that have negligible impact on the overall suitability

(see section 1.3.1). Such attributes should be excluded because they increase the complexity, the effort, and the cost of evaluation without contributing to the accuracy and the usability of results.

3) *No highly redundant attributes*: Ideally, all attributes should be independent. In the real world, there is always some degree of redundancy and correlation between attributes. If the degree of redundancy is provably too high, then the highly redundant (duplicate) attributes are not necessary and should be omitted to avoid the unjustified increase of importance and impact of the redundant properties.

4) *Correct grouping of attributes*: Correlated and moderately redundant attributes that reflect the same property should be grouped together. If multiple attributes reflect the same property of evaluated object, and they are scattered in various parts of the criterion function, then their aggregated effect cannot be properly controlled, and it can be inappropriate (either too high or too low). Grouping of related attributes in the same group (an attribute subtree) is necessary to subsequently assign both the importance weights and the logic aggregator that properly reflect the role of the group.

The suitability attributes can be graphically illustrated as rectangles presented in Fig. 3.1.2. The similar attributes are presented as adjacent rectangles that in the case of redundancy have overlapping areas shown as shaded rectangles.

In practical evaluation projects of any nontrivial complexity, it is almost impossible to make attributes mutually exclusive and collectively exhaustive as in the ideal case of nonredundant attributes shown in Fig. 3.1.2. In this example, $A_1 \cup A_2 \cup \ldots \cup A_n$ represents all necessary attributes where nothing is missing and nothing can be omitted because $A_i \cap A_j = \emptyset$, $1 \le i \le n$, $1 \le j \le n$, $i \ne j$. On the other hand, in all realistic cases we assume partial redundancy and

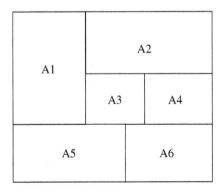
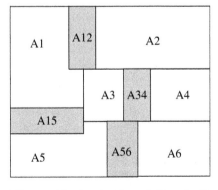

Figure 3.1.2 A graphic interpretation of *n*=6 attributes without redundancy (left) and with redundancy (right).

$A_i \cap A_j = A_{ij} \neq \emptyset$, which can be illustrated as redundant overlap of selected attributes (shaded rectangles) in Fig. 3.1.2.

The attribute redundancy and grouping problems are visible in many applications, and it is useful to identify them in a realistic evaluation environment. Let us exemplify these problems in the case of evaluation of computer performance. We will first show an example of redundancy of suitability attributes. Then, we will use the same environment to discuss the problems associated with grouping of attributes. At the end of this section, we present the suitability tree for our standard short example.

Computer workloads are frequently classified as floating point operation intensive (e.g., computation of integrals, matrix operations, solutions of differential equations, operations with polynomials, etc.) and combinatorial (or integer) workloads (sorting, searching, compiling, text processing, combinatorial games, etc.). Suppose that we measure computer performance using a matrix inversion, which is a typical floating-point intensive benchmark, and a recursive sort, which is a typical combinatorial/integer intensive benchmark. Let V_{fp} be the speed attribute based on floating operations and let V_{int} be the speed attribute based on integer operations performed by the sort program. Similar indicators are SPECint and SPECfp developed by Standard Performance Evaluation Corporation [SPE06, HEN06, DUJ98a]. The questions that need answers are:

(Q1) Are V_{fp} and V_{int} independent nonredundant attributes?
(Q2) Are V_{fp} and V_{int} correlated?
(Q3) If V_{fp} and V_{int} are redundant and correlated, should we use them as performance indicators and suitability attributes in an LSP criterion?
(Q4) How should we deal with correlation between attributes?

Following are the answers:

(A1) V_{fp} and V_{int} are not independent because there are common operations performed by both the matrix inversion and the sort program. Such operations are data transfer, array access and processing, as well as various control structures. So, our benchmarks include some operations that are shared and some that are different.
(A2) As the result of sharing the same operations, V_{fp} and V_{int} are correlated. The coefficient of linear correlation $r \in [-1, +1]$ is positive (computed using a set of measurements on different computers) and can be used as an indicator of redundancy between the attributes V_{fp} and V_{int}. Similarly, $1-r$ can be used as an indicator of individual independent characteristics of these two benchmarks.
(A3) As long as the correlation is not too high, it is reasonable to use both attributes. We use them to provide an opportunity to see effects of those properties that are unique in each benchmark. In addition, the magnified effect of the redundant part is justified because it reflects performance of the most

frequently used operations. Naturally, these redundant attributes must belong to the same group, so that the summary degree of importance is permanently under control and cannot unintentionally become too high or too low.

(A4) A moderate correlation between attributes is perfectly normal. Of course, correlation does not imply causation. In majority of cases the correlated attributes simultaneously depend on another common cause and most frequently that is the price. A basic concept of engineering design is elimination of bottlenecks and weak spots in various products. For example, as the cost of a computer increases, the designer will simultaneously increase the performance of the processor and the size and performance of both memory and disk units. That will cause correlation between the speed of processor and the size and speed of disk regardless of the physical independence of these units.

The computer performance evaluation is a suitable environment for exposing and discussing suitability attributes grouping problems. If a computer evaluation criterion follows the architecture or hardware and software, then performance indicators can be scattered in various parts of the evaluation criterion. For example, the evaluation of processor can include processor speed (clock rate, instructions per second, floating-point operations per second, etc.). The evaluation of memory can include the memory speed (read and write times, transfer rate, etc.). The evaluation of disk memory can include disk speed (seek time, latency time, data transfer time, etc.). The evaluation of compilers frequently includes the speed of compilation (compiled logical lines of code per second, performance effects of code optimization, etc.). The evaluation of an operating system usually includes the boot time. Finally, the overall performance of a computer system regularly includes benchmarking, i.e., measuring run times of various benchmark programs and using the measured values as suitability attributes.

According to the described structuring of the computer evaluation criterion, the performance attributes are not grouped together—they are distributed in various subtrees of the suitability attribute tree. There are three attribute selection problems that are clearly visible in this example. First, it is not possible to control and adjust the overall impact of computer performance on an evaluation decision since the performance indicators are scattered in various parts of a nonlinear evaluation criterion. Second, the performance attributes are redundant (e.g., all benchmark program run times directly depend on the performance of processor, memory, disks, and other hardware and software components). Third, there is obvious correlation between all performance indicators (by the elementary logic of engineering design a fast processor will be connected to a fast memory and will also use a fast disk, while inexpensive computers will have lower performance of all components making these attributes positively correlated).

The result of presented attribute tree organization would be a reduced quality of the evaluation criterion and the reduced validity of decisions based on such criteria. However, if we can identify those problems, it is possible to eliminate or alleviate them. Thus, the attribute tree should be reorganized so that all related attributes (e.g., various performance attributes) are grouped together and their suitability aggregated within the group before it is merged with other parts of the criterion function. For example, if the main subtrees of a mainframe computer evaluation tree are (1) hardware, (2) software, (3) performance, and (4) vendor support, then performance indicators should not appear in the hardware, software, and vendor support subtrees. Indeed, if the hardware subtree includes processor speed, memory bus speed, and disk seek, latency and transfer times, while the performance subtree includes performance indicators based on SPEC benchmarks and user benchmarks, then the evaluator cannot clearly control the overall impact of performance in the decision process, because performance indicators are scattered in various parts of the criterion function and their aggregated effect is not visible in any node of the suitability aggregation tree. Furthermore, it is always necessary and possible to reduce the unnecessary complexity of criterion and the cost of evaluation by keeping track of redundancy and avoiding the use of exceedingly redundant suitability attributes (e.g., it is unjustified to use both a disk mean access time provided by disk manufacturer and the time measured using a disk random access benchmark program, because both of them reflect the same performance feature). However, if moderately correlated attributes remain in the group, then a beneficial effect of correlation is that it compensates errors in correct selection of attribute weights that define the relative importance of attributes [DUJ72b].

Location Suitability Example, Step 2: Suitability Attribute Tree
The quality of location can be decomposed into various components, and a very simple decomposition is presented in Figs. 3.1.3 and 3.1.4.

```
1  Quality of location
   11 Basic needs
      111 Public transportation
          1111 Distance from train stations
          1112 Distance from bus stations
      112 Distance from local food stores
   12 Desired amenities
      121 Distance from parks
      122 Distance from restaurants
      123 Distance from public libraries
```

Figure 3.1.3 Standard notation of the location attribute tree.

Quality of location	M	O	S
Basic needs	*		
Public transportation	*		
Distance from train stations		*	
Distance from bus stations		*	
Distance from local food stores	*		
Desired amenities		*	
Distance from parks		*	
Distance from restaurants		*	
Distance from public libraries		*	

Figure 3.1.4 Tabular notation of the location attribute tree.

A standard notation of the attribute tree in Fig. 3.1.3 uses a decimal numeration of nodes. The nodes that are further decomposed (1, 11, 111, 12) are composite nodes and can be interpreted as composite attributes. The terminal nodes that are leaves of the aggregation tree (1111, 1112, 112, 121, 122, 123) are elementary attributes (sometimes called performance variables or input attributes). Those attributes that cannot be further decomposed (as well as those who might be decomposed but can be evaluated without further decomposition, as, e.g., the quality of documentation of engineering products) are used as inputs of the LSP criterion function.

The suitability attribute tree can also be presented in a tabular form shown in Fig. 3.1.4. This form can be used with or without decimal numeration. In most cases, it is useful to classify all attributes in three basic categories:

M = mandatory attributes (very important attributes that must be satisfied; if a mandatory requirement in a group of attributes is not satisfied, then the whole group is rejected, or the whole evaluated object is rejected).

S = sufficient attributes (any sufficient attribute in a group of attributes has the capability to completely satisfy the requirements of the group regardless to the degrees of satisfaction of other attributes).

O = optional attributes (they are desired, but neither mandatory nor sufficient).

In Fig. 3.1.4, all attributes (both elementary and composite) are classified using the M/O/S columns appended to the suitability attribute table.

The attribute tree precisely defines the structure of the evaluation process, both the elementary attributes and an outline of their aggregation structure. In our location evaluation example we have six elementary input attributes:

1111 Distance from train stations
1112 Distance from bus stations
112 Distance from local food stores
121 Distance from parks

122 Distance from restaurants
123 Distance from public libraries

For each elementary attribute, we must create an appropriate attribute criterion.

3.1.3 Elementary Attribute Criteria

Generally, the value of each elementary attribute is a real number: $a_i \in \mathbb{R}$, $i = 1,...,n$. A specific value a_i generates a percept of satisfaction of the stakeholder's requirements, x_i, in the range from no satisfaction (0) to complete satisfaction (1). The elementary input attribute criterion (or simply the elementary criterion or the attribute criterion) is the mapping $g_i : \mathbb{R} \to [0,1]$, $i = 1,...,n$. The elementary criterion is used to determine the suitability that corresponds to the given value of attribute: $x_i = g_i(a_i)$, $i = 1,...,n$. The elementary suitability degrees $x_1, ..., x_n$ are then logically aggregated to compute the overall suitability of the evaluated object.

Each elementary attribute belongs to a specific set of values: $a_i \in A_i \subset \mathbb{R}$. Depending on the type and meaning of the set A_i, there are various types of elementary criteria. A detailed study presented in Chapter 3.3 includes 12 different types of elementary criteria. The three most frequent forms of elementary criteria are the following:

Type S: Preferred small values (e.g., a small distance between a home and a park).
Type L: Preferred large values (e.g., large distance from a source of air pollution).
Type R: Preferred range of values (e.g., a home located neither too close nor too far from a major international airport).

The L, S, R forms of attribute criteria are exemplified in Fig. 3.1.5 where the suitability attributes have continuous nonnegative value and the piecewise linear criterion function is approximated using straight lines interpolated between vertices located at a=A, B, C, D. The vertices have a verbal interpretation that is also shown in Fig. 3.1.5.

The graphical user interface shown in Fig. 3.1.5 is used for evaluating the distance from points of interest and can be used to specify three typical forms: preferred large values, preferred small values and preferred range of values. In the case of distance, the preferred large values are used in cases where the stakeholder wants to be far from undesirable points of interest, such as sources of industrial air pollution, unsafe city areas, cemeteries, prisons, areas that are frequently flooded by rivers, etc. An example of such criterion is shown in Fig. 3.1.6 where the stakeholder prefers to be 2.5 km far from cemetery and

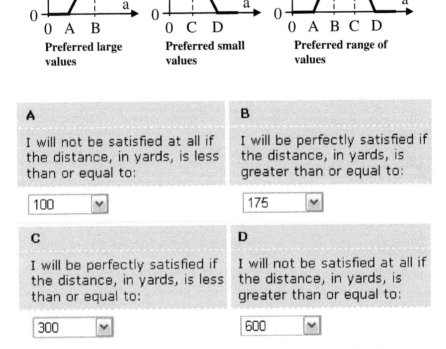

Figure 3.1.5 Three characteristic forms of elementary criteria and their verbal interpretation.

refuses to be closer than 1.5 km. For example, in the case of computer evaluation criteria, the preferred large values are used for the size of main memory, cache memories and disk memory, the number of parallel units (like processor cores, disks units, and workstations) speed of computing units, and screen size.

In the case of evaluating distances, the preferred small values are used in cases where the stakeholder wants to be close to desirable points of interest, such as school or day care for children, work location for parents, homes of relatives, theaters, sport facilities, parks, lakes, beaches, medical offices, and shopping areas. In the case of computer evaluation, the preferred small values are used for run times of benchmark programs, memory access time, instruction mix times, disk access times, etc. Fig. 3.1.6 shows an example where up to 20 minutes of driving to work is considered completely satisfactory, and 80 minutes or more is unacceptable.

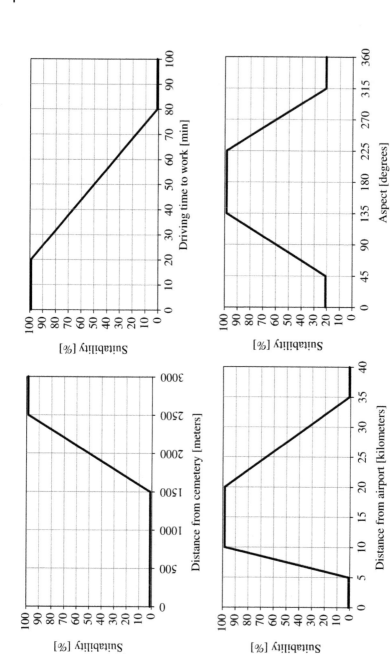

Figure 3.1.6 Characteristic examples of elementary criteria.

In many cases, it is desirable that attributes belong to a range of values. For example, experienced buyers of new and unverified models of machines (computers, cars, software products, aircraft, etc.) regularly hesitate to be among the first to buy a new product, but also do not want to buy a product that is too long on market and will be soon replaced by a new model. Homebuyers don't like to live next to the airport to avoid noise, pollution, traffic density, and safety problems, but also do not want to be too far and need a long drive to reach the airport. Fig. 3.1.6 shows an example of a stakeholder who considers that the distance from 10 to 20 km is ideal, and distances less than 5 km or greater than 35 km are unacceptable.

Elementary criteria frequently cover the whole range of suitability, from 0 to 100%. However, that is not necessary, as shown in the example of aspect (the direction that a slope faces, or the positioning of building in a specific direction) shown in Fig. 3.1.6. In this example we assume that 180 degrees denotes that the front of a house faces the south and receives more solar radiation. The most desirable southern exposure is in the range from 135 to 225 degrees. However, the presented criterion for aspect is penalizing but not rejecting the northern exposure; in the absence of better exposure, the stakeholder is ready to position the house facing the north.

A continuous elementary criterion $x = g(a)$ is approximated using a piecewise linear function that connects the sequence of points $(a_0, s_0), ..., (a_k, s_k)$ where $a_0, ..., a_k$ denotes a strictly increasing sequence of values of input attribute a and $s_0, ..., s_k$ is a corresponding sequence of suitability scores. The points (a_i, s_i), $i = 0, ..., k$ are called vertices, or breakpoints, because the first derivative dx/da has breaks in these points. Between vertices we always assume simple linear interpolation. So, the general analytic form of a piecewise linear elementary criterion is the following:

$$x = g(a) = \begin{cases} s_0 & , \ a \leq a_0 \\ \dfrac{s_{i-1}(a_i - a) + s_i(a - a_{i-1})}{a_i - a_{i-1}} & , \ a_{i-1} \leq a \leq a_i, \ i = 1, ..., k \\ s_k & , \ a \geq a_k \ ; \end{cases}$$

$$a_0 < a_1 < ... < a_k \ ,$$

$$a_j \in \mathbb{R}, \ s_j \in [0, 100\%], \ j = 0, ..., k, \ k > 0 \ .$$

The sequence of vertices/breakpoints is suitable as a condensed "vertex notation" of elementary criteria: $Crit(a) = \{(a_0, s_0), ..., (a_k, s_k)\}$. In the case of the three basic types of elementary criteria shown in Fig. 3.1.5 for $A < B < C < D$ this notation yields the following:

Preferred large values : $Crit(a) = \{(A,0), (B,100)\}$.

Preferred small values : $Crit(a) = \{(C,100), (D,0)\}$.

Preferred range of values $Crit(a) = \{(A,0), (B,100), (C,100), (D,0)\}$.

It is important to notice that the extreme values s_0 and s_k define the suitability for the values of attribute outside the range $[a_0, a_k]$. Keeping that in mind, the vertex notation of criteria in Fig. 3.1.6 yields the following:

$$Crit(cemetery[\mathrm{m}]) = \{(1500, 0), (2500, 100)\}.$$

$$Crit(work[\min]) = \{(20, 100), (80, 0)\}.$$

$$Crit(airport[\mathrm{km}]) = \{(5, 0), (10, 100), (20, 100), (35, 0)\}.$$

$$Crit(aspect[°]) = \{(45, 20), (135, 100), (225, 100), (315, 20)\}.$$

For each criterion, we use the following syntax:

$$Crit(<\text{attribute name}>[<\text{unit}>]) = \{<\text{sequence of two or more vertices}>\}.$$

Location Suitability Example, Step 3: Elementary Attribute Criteria
In the case of the senior citizen home location evaluation, we have to propose six elementary criteria. The criteria are shown in the piecewise linear notation in Fig. 3.1.7. The vertex notation equivalent is the following:

$$Crit(train[\mathrm{m}]) = \{(400, 100), (1000, 0)\}.$$

$$Crit(bus[\mathrm{m}]) = \{(50, 100), (700, 0)\}.$$

$$Crit(food[\mathrm{m}]) = \{(100, 100), (400, 50), (600, 0)\}.$$

$$Crit(park[\mathrm{m}]) = \{(0, 100), (3500, 0)\}.$$

$$Crit(restaurant[\mathrm{m}]) = \{(0, 40), (150, 100), (300, 100), (900, 0)\}.$$

$$Crit(library[\mathrm{m}]) = \{(1000, 100), (3000, 0)\}.$$

Another important notation of elementary criteria is the tabular notation exemplified in Table 3.1.1 (produced by the software tool LSP.NT [SEA17]). The advantage of this notation is that it includes all components of attribute criteria: (1) the unique numerical identifier, (2) the title, (3) the criterion function presented as a table of breakpoints, and (4) the verbal explanation of the purpose and rationale for using the criterion, justification of selected function, the description of measurement units, possibilities for modification, and any other relevant information.

The elementary criteria for home location would be rather different if we assumed that the stakeholder uses a car. In such a case, the proximity to public transportation would be less critical, and the access to food store and the amenities could be expressed in minutes of driving instead of meters. However, the

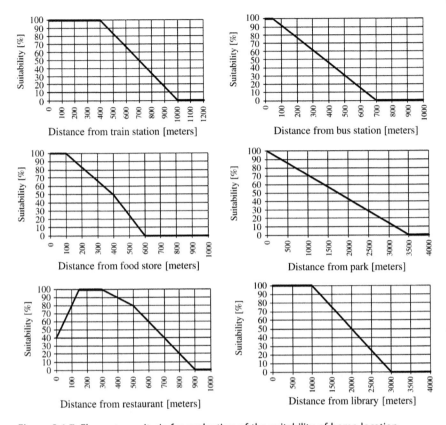

Figure 3.1.7 Elementary criteria for evaluation of the suitability of home location.

criterion for proximity to park could remain unchanged if walking to the park is considered an important and very frequent activity.

Using the set of six elementary criteria we can create six suitability scores for each analyzed location. The next step is to perform logic aggregation of attribute suitability degrees and to create a single overall suitability degree.

3.1.4 Logic Aggregation of Suitability

Logic aggregation of suitability is the decisive step that distinguishes the LSP method from all other evaluation methods. The process of logic aggregation is the motive for development of the graded logic (GL); the name of the LSP method is naturally derived from this essential activity. The material presented

Table 3.1.1 Tabular form of elementary criteria for the suitability of home location (generated using LSP.NT).

1111	Distance from train stations

Value	%	The distance from train stations is measured in meters. If there are more stations, only the distance to the closest station is taken into account. (Other approaches are also possible: e.g., scores given to each station, etc.). All distances below 400 meters are considered excellent and equally acceptable. Similarly, all distances of 1000 meters or more are considered unacceptable.
400	100	
1000	0	

1112	Distance from bus stations

Value	%	The distance from bus stations is measured in meters. If there are more stations only the distance to the closest station is taken into account. (Other approaches are also possible: e.g., scores given to each station, etc.). Bus stations are expected to be closer than train stations.
50	100	
700	0	

112	Distance from local food stores

Value	%	The distance is measured in meters. We assume the closest (walking distance) food store. The criterion assumes that only walking distances are acceptable because the stakeholder (senior citizen) does not use car and must make frequent visits to the local food store.
100	100	
400	50	
600	0	

121	Distance from parks

Value	%	The distance is measured in meters. Parks are very desirable for this kind of stakeholder. The ideal location would be immediately next to a park.
0	100	
3500	0	

122	Distance from restaurants

Value	%	The average (or minimum) distance from local restaurants (measured in meters). The criterion for the distance from restaurant reflects the standpoint that living in the immediate neighborhood of a restaurant brings some inconveniences (high traffic of unknown people, parking and security problems, air pollution, etc.). However, the proximity of restaurants is highly desirable and they are expected to be within a short walking distance.
0	40	
150	100	
300	100	
500	80	
900	0	

123	Distance from public library

Value	%	The distance is measured in meters. The relatively large distance to public library reflects infrequent visits, possibly using public transportation.
1000	100	
3000	0	

in *Part Two* of this book provides the groundwork supporting the logic aggregation of suitability. In this section, we overview the logic aggregation of suitability as a phase in the development of LSP criteria. Additional necessary details are presented in Chapters 3.4 and 3.5.

Elementary criteria create a set of n attribute suitability degrees $x_1, ..., x_n$, one for each input attribute. The attribute suitability degrees affect the percept of the overall suitability of evaluated object $x = L(x_1,...,x_n)$. The function $L : [0,1]^n \rightarrow [0,1]$ must provide all logic conditions that are visible in human reasoning: some inputs must be simultaneously satisfied, some can substitute each other, some must be mandatory, or optional, or sufficient to satisfy stakeholder requirements, and the importance of individual attributes can differ in a wide range. However, we must be careful, because some combinations of logic properties can be inconsistent (e.g., the low importance and the high andness/orness) as shown in Section 2.2.6.

We assume that the aggregation function L is idempotent: $\forall s \in [0,1] \Rightarrow L(s,...,s) = s$. If the suitability of all input attributes is s then the suitability of the whole evaluated object must also be s. Thus, L must be based on superposition of basic idempotent aggregators.[1] As shown in Chapter 2.1, there are nine categories of idempotent GL aggregation operators: three categories of simultaneity, three categories of substitutability, the neutrality, and two categories of asymmetric partial absorption aggregators. The appropriate category is selected according to desired logic properties.

For readers who decided to skip *Part Two* of this book, a precise summary of nine characteristic logic properties is presented in Table 3.1.2. These logic properties are distinct, and the selection of the appropriate category can be performed in an unmistakable way. It is important to emphasize that the listed categories are *necessary and sufficient*—we need all of them, and they fully cover the whole spectrum of basic logic aggregation patterns that are observable in intuitive evaluation reasoning. A clear understanding and the use of nine presented types of aggregators is the prerequisite for correct modeling of human percepts of worth and suitability.

The aggregation function L has the form of a tree where each node contains one of nine aggregators shown in Table 3.1.2. The aggregation tree is regularly structured in the same way as the suitability attribute tree. In the case of our location suitability example, the suitability aggregation structure is outlined in Fig. 3.1.8 and an equivalent tabular notation of the aggregation tree with basic logic relationships between inputs are shown in Fig. 3.1.9. The next step of the LSP criterion development is to specify each individual aggregator (either a GCD or a partial absorption) in the aggregation structure.

---

1 In rare and exceptional cases where this assumption is not acceptable, it is possible to use extended (hyperconjunctive and hyperdisjunctive) GCD aggregators introduced in Section 2.4.9.

Table 3.1.2 Logic properties of the basic group of nine idempotent logic aggregators B9 = {C, HPC, SPC, A, SPD, HPD, D, CPA, DPA}

#	Symbol: Category	Logic properties of aggregators in the category
1	D: Pure disjunction $x_1 \vee \cdots \vee x_n$	Model of the highest/extreme degree of substitutability. The output is defined by the largest input value (all other inputs do not affect the output). Any input is sufficient to completely satisfy this criterion. Pure OR operator.
2	HPD: Hard partial disjunction (High substitutability) $W_1 x_1 \bar{\triangledown} \cdots \bar{\triangledown} W_n x_n$	Modeling the requirement for an adjustable high degree of substitutability that supports sufficient requirements. All inputs represent sufficient requirements, and a single completely satisfied input is sufficient to completely satisfy this criterion. If no input is completely satisfied, then all inputs affect the output. High input values have a significantly stronger impact on the output than low input values. The criterion is not satisfied only if all inputs are not satisfied. This is a strong partial OR operator.
3	SPD: Soft partial disjunction (Low substitutability) $W_1 x_1 \underline{\triangledown} \cdots \underline{\triangledown} W_n x_n$	Modeling the requirement for an adjustable low to medium degree of substitutability that does not support sufficient requirements. All inputs affect the output. High input values affect the output more strongly than the low input values. To completely satisfy this criterion all inputs must be completely satisfied. The criterion is not satisfied only if all inputs are not satisfied. This is a weak to medium partial OR operator.
4	A: Neutrality (Same simultaneity & substitutability) $W_1 x_1 + \cdots + W_n x_n$	The weighted arithmetic mean of inputs. Fixed and balanced simultaneity and substitutability requirements. Low and high inputs have an equal opportunity to affect output. This criterion is not satisfied only if all inputs are not satisfied. The criterion is completely satisfied only if all inputs are completely satisfied. Neither the mandatory/sufficient requirements nor the adjustable degree of simultaneity/substitutability can be modeled using this aggregator.
5	SPC: Soft partial conjunction (Low simultaneity) $W_1 x_1 \underline{\triangle} \cdots \underline{\triangle} W_n x_n$	Modeling the requirement for an adjustable low-to-medium degree of simultaneity that does not support mandatory requirements. All inputs affect output. Low input values affect the output stronger than the high input values. To completely satisfy this criterion, all inputs must be completely satisfied. The criterion is not satisfied only if all inputs are not satisfied. This is a weak to medium partial AND operator.
6	HPC: Hard partial conjunction (High simultaneity) $W_1 x_1 \bar{\triangle} \cdots \bar{\triangle} W_n x_n$	Modeling the requirement for an adjustable high degree of simultaneity that supports mandatory requirements. Only one completely unsatisfied input is sufficient to completely not satisfy the entire criterion; so, it is mandatory to at least partially satisfy all inputs. If no input is completely unsatisfied, then all inputs affect the output. Low input values affect the output significantly stronger than the high input values. To completely satisfy this criterion, all inputs must be completely satisfied. Strong partial AND operator.
7	C: Pure conjunction $x_1 \wedge \cdots \wedge x_n$	Model of the highest/extreme degree of simultaneity. The output is defined by the smallest input value (all other inputs do not affect the output). All input requirements must be simultaneously fully satisfied. Pure AND operator.
8	CPA: Conjunctive partial absorption (Asymmetric simultaneity) $x \trianglerighteq y$	Output depends on two asymmetric inputs: the mandatory input x and the optional input y. If the mandatory input is completely unsatisfied and has a zero value, then the output also is zero, regardless of the value of the optional input. If the mandatory input is positive, and the optional input is zero, then the output is positive. For a partially satisfied mandatory input, a higher/lower optional input can increase/decrease the output value with respect to the mandatory input for an adjustable degree of reward/penalty.
9	DPA: Disjunctive partial absorption (Asymmetric substitutability) $x \trianglerighteq y$	Output depends on two asymmetric inputs: the sufficient input x and the optional input y. If the sufficient input is fully satisfied, then the entire criterion is fully satisfied, regardless of the optional input. If the sufficient input is partially (incompletely) satisfied, and the optional input is completely satisfied, then the output is incompletely satisfied. For a partially satisfied sufficient input, a higher/lower optional input can increase/decrease the output value with respect to the sufficient input for an adjustable degree of reward/penalty.

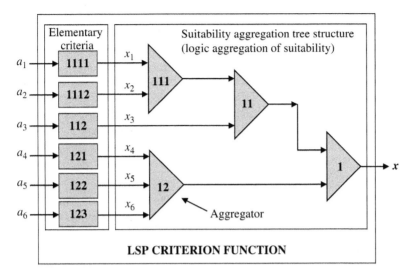

Figure 3.1.8 The LSP criterion function: elementary criteria and the suitability aggregation structure ($a_1, \ldots, a_6$ = input attributes, $x_1, \ldots, x_6$ = attribute suitability degrees, x= overall suitability degree).

1111 Train	Sub.	111 Public				
1112 Bus	Sub.	transportation	Man.	11 Basic		
121 Food store			Man.	needs	Man.	1 Overall
121 Park	Opt.					suitability
122 Restaurant	Opt.	12 Desired amenities			Opt.	of home
123 Library	Opt.					location

(Abbreviations: Man = mandatory, Sub = substitutable, Opt = optional)

Figure 3.1.9 Basic logic relationships of inputs in aggregation blocks.

3.1.4.1 Logic Aggregation Using Graded Conjunction/Disjunction

According to *Part Two* (Section 2.4.12 and Fig. 2.4.30), the LSP method offers seven groups of GCD aggregators: UGCD.7, UGCD.15, UGCS.23, WPM.17, GGCD.9, GGCD.17, and GGCD.25. Following are criteria for selection of the most appropriate group:

- UGCD.7: low precision uniform aggregators suitable for introductory educational experiences.
- UGCD.15: medium precision uniform aggregators suitable for most applications (good combination of simplicity and precision).

- UGCD.23: high precision uniform aggregators suitable for sensitive professional applications.
- WPM.17: direct use of medium precision weighted power means. Suitable in cases where there is no need for hard partial disjunction.
- GGCD9: low precision general aggregators suitable for introductory training in the use of adjustable threshold andness/orness.
- GGCD17: medium precision general aggregators suitable for most applications (good combination of flexibility, precision and simplicity).
- GGCD.25: general aggregators offering highest flexibility and precision and suitable for very sensitive professional applications.

All seven groups are implemented in the LSP.NT tool [SEA17],[2] and the first step in the logic aggregation process is to select the most appropriate among the above groups. In the majority of LSP applications we use medium precision aggregators, because they offer the best combination of simplicity and precision. Three basic groups of medium precision GCD aggregators are summarized in Tables 3.1.3 to 3.1.5.

Table 3.1.3 UGCD.15 aggregators (fixed threshold andness 0.75).

Type of logic model	Form	Mode	Level	Symbol	Andness	Orness
Substitutability	Pure dis.	Hard	Extreme	D	0	1
	Partial disjunction	Hard	High	HD+	0.0714	0.9286
			Medium	HD	0.1429	0.8571
			Low	HD−	0.2143	0.7857
		Soft	High	SD+	0.2857	0.7143
			Medium	SD	0.3571	0.6429
			Low	SD−	0.4286	0.5714
Neutrality				A	0.5	0.5
Simultaneity	Partial conjunction	Soft	Low	SC−	0.5714	0.4286
			Medium	SC	0.6429	0.3571
			High	SC+	0.7143	0.2857
		Hard	Low	HC−	0.7857	0.2143
			Medium	HC	0.8571	0.1429
			High	HC+	0.9286	0.0714
	Pure con.	Hard	Extreme	C	1	0

---

2 LSP.NT is available on the Internet and we assume that all readers can use it in free demo mode. The LSP.NT access point is posted on the book companion web site hosted by Wiley.

The UGCD.15 group is presented in Table 3.1.3. UGCD aggregators are studied in Sections 2.4.8 and 2.5.2, and shown in Figs. 2.4.18, 2.5.9, and 2.5.10. The selection of specific aggregator depends on desired andness/orness and can be based on stepwise refinement algorithm presented in Figs. 2.9.7 and 2.9.9. According to Table 3.1.3, users first select the type of aggregator: simultaneity or substitutability. The next step is to decide whether the mode should be hard or soft. The final step of this simple procedure is to select one of three levels (low, medium, high). The threshold andness of all UGCD aggregators is 0.75; however, in the case of granularity 15, the lowest hard andness is 0.7857 and the highest soft andness is 0.7143.

The WPM.17 group is presented in Table 3.1.4. Native WPM aggregators are studied in Sections 2.4.4 and 2.4.5, and shown in Figs. 2.4.8, 2.5.6, and 2.5.7. The selection of specific aggregator depends on desired andness/orness and can be based on the ternary search algorithm presented in Figs. 2.9.4 and 2.9.5. According to Table 3.1.4, users first select the type of aggregator: simultaneity of substitutability. Substitutability aggregators are always soft. Two simultaneity aggregators (C-- and C-) are soft and remaining simultaneity aggregators are hard because the threshold andness is approximately 0.67. According to Fig. 2.9.6, WPM.17 (and GGCD.17) aggregators can be verbalized as weak (below medium) and strong (above medium). Note that "weak" does not mean soft, and "strong" does not mean hard.

Table 3.1.4 WPM.17 aggregators.

Type of logic model	Form	Mode	Level	Symbol	Andness	Orness
	Pure dis.	Hard	Extreme	D	0	1
Substitutability	Partial disjunction	Soft	Very high	D++	0.0625	0.9375
			High	D+	0.125	0.875
			Mid-high	D+−	0.1875	0.8125
			Medium	DA	0.25	0.75
			Mid-low	D−+	0.3125	0.6875
			Low	D−	0.375	0.625
			Very low	D−−	0.4375	0.5625
Neutrality				A	0.5	0.5
Simultaneity	Partial conjunction	Soft	Very low	C−−	0.5625	0.4375
			Low	C−	0.625	0.375
		Hard	Mid-low	C−+	0.6875	0.3125
			Medium	CA	0.75	0.25
			Mid-high	C+−	0.8125	0.1875
			High	C+	0.875	0.125
			Very high	C++	0.9375	0.0625
	Pure con.	Hard	Extreme	C	1	0

Table 3.1.5 GGCD.17 aggregators with adjustable threshold andness.

Type of logic model	Form	Mode	Level	Symbol	Andness	Orness
	Pure dis.	Hard	Extreme	D	0	1
Substitutability	Partial disjunction	Hard	Very high	D++	0.0625	0.9375
			High	D+	0.125	0.875
			Mid-high	D+−	0.1875	0.8125
			Medium	DA	0.25	0.75
		Soft	Mid-low	D−+	0.3125	0.6875
			Low	D−	0.375	0.625
			Very low	D−−	0.4375	0.5625
Neutrality				A	0.5	0.5
Simultaneity	Partial conjunction	Soft	Very low	C−−	0.5625	0.4375
			Low	C−	0.625	0.375
			Mid-low	C−+	0.6875	0.3125
		Hard	Medium	CA	0.75	0.25
			Mid-high	C+−	0.8125	0.1875
			High	C+	0.875	0.125
			Very high	C++	0.9375	0.0625
	Pure con.	Hard	Extreme	C	1	0

The most general of all GCD aggregators are the GGCD aggregators. The GGCD.17 group is shown in Table 3.1.5, where the threshold andness and the dual threshold orness are set to 0.75. LSP.NT accepts the location of threshold andness anywhere from C-- to C, and Table 3.1.5 shows the case where the threshold andness aggregator is CA and the symmetric threshold orness aggregator is DA. The location of threshold andness is selected according to Fig. 2.2.23 and the most frequent location is in the vicinity of CA.

3.1.4.2 Logic Aggregation Using Partial Absorption

Two fundamental asymmetric aggregators are the Conjunctive Partial Absorption (CPA) and the Disjunctive Partial Absorption (DPA). The simplest implementations of these aggregators are the "AH" aggregators shown in Fig. 3.1.10. The implementations shown in Fig. 3.1.10 use the combination of the neutral arithmetic mean A, the conjunctive harmonic mean H, and the disjunctive De Morgan dual of harmonic mean $\underline{H}$. In the simplest case of equal weights these aggregators are $A(a,b) = (a+b)/2$, and $H(a,b) = 2ab/(a+b)$, and $\underline{H}(a,b) = 1 - H(1-a,1-b) = 1 - 2(1-a)(1-b)/(2-a-b)$. Using fixed aggregators A, H and $\underline{H}$, the AH forms of CPA and DPA have only two adjustable parameters: the weights W_1 and W_2.

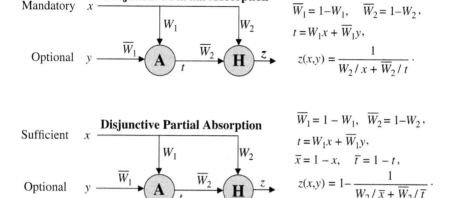

Figure 3.1.10 Asymmetric aggregators: CPA/AH and DPA/A$\underline{H}$.

The parameters of the CPA and DPA aggregators depend on the desired penalty and reward. The penalty and reward determine the impact of the optional input of the CPA aggregator. The condition is that the CPA reward must be less than the penalty. This condition is justified by the conjunctive nature of CPA aggregator: we want simultaneous satisfaction of inputs and (similarly to partial conjunction) the effect of low input suitability must be stronger than the effect of high input suitability. Similarly, the DPA reward must be greater than the penalty. This condition is justified by the disjunctive nature of DPA aggregator: we want substitutability of inputs and (similarly to partial disjunction) the effect of high input suitability must be stronger than the effect of low input suitability.

For simple AH versions of CPA and DPA and the central point penalty (Sections 2.6.4 and 3.5.1) we can determine desired weights W_1 and W_2 using Table 3.1.6 as follows:

1) Select the desired central point penalty: $P = 100[\frac{1}{2} - z(\frac{1}{2}, 0)]/0.5$ [%].
2) Select the desired central point reward: $R = 100[z(\frac{1}{2}, 1) - \frac{1}{2}]/0.5$ [%].
3) Select weights W_1 (top value) and W_2 (bottom value) from Table 3.1.6.

For example, in the case of CPA, if $P = 50\%$ and $R = 25\%$, then $W_1 = 0.333$ and $W_2 = 0.5$ (the same result is obtained for DPA if $R = 50\%$ and $P = 25\%$).

The presented logic aggregation techniques are now reduced to the simple selection of GCD aggregators from Tables 3.1.3 to 3.1.5 and the equally simple selection of CPA and DPA aggregators from Table 3.1.6. Of course, this is a rudimentary version of LSP aggregation, but it offers the possibility to quickly develop justifiable logic aggregation structures without using sophisticated software tools.

Table 3.1.6 CPA and DPA weights as functions of the central point penalty and reward.

W_1 / W_2 [%]		Desired CPA penalty [%] OR DPA reward [%]													
		75	70	65	60	55	50	45	40	35	30	25	20	15	10
C P A	5	3.13	4	5	6.15	7.5	9.09	11	13.3	16.3	20	25	32	42.5	60
		90.3	90.3	90.2	90.2	90.1	90	89.9	89.7	89.6	89.3	88.9	88.2	87	83.3
	10	5.88	7.5	9.33	11.4	13.8	16.7	20	24	28.9	35	42.9	53.3	68	
		81.3	81.1	80.9	80.6	80.4	80	79.5	78.9	78.1	76.9	75	71.4	62.5	
r	15	8.33	10.6	13.1	16	19.3	23.1	27.5	32.7	39	46.7	56.3	68.6		
		72.7	72.4	71.9	71.4	70.8	70	69	67.6	65.6	62.5	57.1	45.5		
e w	20	10.5	13.3	16.5	20	24	28.6	33.8	40	47.3	56	66.7			
		64.7	64.1	63.4	62.5	61.4	60	58.1	55.6	51.7	45.5	33.3			
a r	25	12.5	15.8	19.4	23.5	28.1	33.3	39.3	46.2	54.2	63.6				
		57.1	56.3	55.2	53.8	52.2	50	47.1	42.9	36.4	25				
d	30	14.3	18	22.1	26.7	31.8	37.5	44	51.4	60					
		50	48.8	47.3	45.5	43.1	40	35.7	29.4	19.2					
	35	15.9	20	24.5	29.5	35	41.2	48.1	56						
OR		43.2	41.7	39.7	37.3	34.2	30	24.1	15.2						
	40	17.4	21.8	26.7	32	37.9	44.4	51.8							
D		36.8	34.9	32.5	29.4	25.4	20	12.2							
P A	45	18.8	23.5	28.6	34.3	40.5	47.4								
		30.8	28.4	25.5	21.7	16.8	10								
	50	20	25	30.4	36.4	42.9									
		25	22.2	18.8	14.3	8.33									
p e	55	21.2	26.4	32.1	38.3										
		19.5	16.3	12.3	7.04										
n a	60	22.2	27.7	33.6											
		14.3	10.6	6.02											
l	65	23.2	28.9												
		9.3	5.21												
t y	70	24.1													
		4.55													

Location Suitability Example, Step 4.1: Suitability Aggregation Structure

In this example, we are going to build the aggregation structure based on UGCD.15 aggregators (Table 3.1.3). Using GCD aggregators from UGCD.15 and AH version of PA, the aggregation structure outlined in Figs. 3.1.8 and 3.1.9 can be transformed in the final result shown in Fig. 3.1.11. The process of selecting aggregators should be justified by the stakeholder's precise specification of the role and the relative importance of inputs. Following is the reasoning used in the process of selecting four aggregators shown in Fig. 3.1.8 and 3.1.11.

Aggregator 111

We assume that in the case of a senior citizen without a private car, it is mandatory to have good public transportation. In addition, we assume that train and bus can effectively substitute for each other, but not to the extent that the excellent value of one component makes the other component irrelevant. The

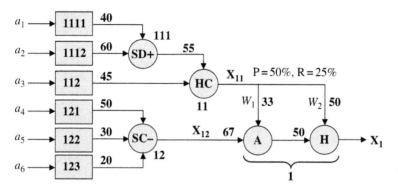

Figure 3.1.11 The UGCD version of the suitability aggregation structure for location evaluation.

stakeholder would like to have access to both busses and trains. The model that has requested properties is a soft partial disjunction. The selection between SD-, SD, and SD+ is based on the assumption that in the given urban environment, the substitutability of trains and busses is high, but none of them is completely sufficient. That yields SD+ as the most appropriate aggregator. The assumption that for short distances the bus transport is somewhat more flexible than the train transport is reflected in selecting weights 60% vs. 40%.

Aggregator 11
Both food stores and some form of public transportation in the proximity of home are mandatory (simultaneously necessary), yielding the obvious selection of the hard partial conjunction. While local food stores are indispensable, good public transportation is considered slightly more important than the proximity to food stores (55% vs. 45%) simply because it provides access to all shopping experiences, including buying fresh food. The selection between HC-, HC, and HC+ is based on assumption that the stakeholder has no reasons for extreme values of the aggregator and in such a case HC is the most appropriate.

Aggregator 12
Parks, restaurants and public libraries are desired amenities but in the worst case the stakeholder is ready to accept locations where some (or all) of them are missing. The stakeholder would prefer to simultaneously have all of them but these expectations in a given urban environment cannot be high. That yields the soft partial conjunction, and its lowest level, which is SC-. Parks are considered to have the same importance as local restaurants and public libraries together. In addition, restaurants are assumed to be more

frequently visited than public libraries. This reasoning yields the weights 50:30:20.

The conjunctive polarization of this aggregator shows the situation where the stakeholder can simultaneously require the desired amenities. If the conditions of our stakeholder are more modest s/he might be forced to be satisfied if any of amenities is available. In such as case, the logic of aggregation would be disjunctive, i.e., between SD- and SD+.

Aggregator 1

The overall suitability of home location is a percept based on asymmetric simultaneity of the mandatory public transportation and food stores (input 11), and the optional amenities (input 12). Consequently, this aggregator must be a CPA, which can be interpreted as an asymmetric conjunction, where the stakeholder would like to have simultaneously good transportation and food stores, as well as the attractive amenities. The asymmetry stems from different approaches to annihilators: if the input X_{11} is zero, then the output X_1 must also be zero. However, if the optional input X_{12} is zero (but X_{11} is positive), then the output X_1 remains positive. More precisely, if the mandatory input X_{11} is positive and the optional input X_{12} is zero, then the output X_1 must be decremented (penalized), but it should not be zero: $0 < X_1 < X_{11}$. On the other hand, if the optional input X_{12} is greater than the mandatory input X_{11} then we expect a reward: $0 < X_{11} < X_1 < X_{12}$.

In the case of a senior citizen, the amenities are assumed to be optional, but nevertheless they can be very desirable. At least some amenities are expected to be available. So, the complete absence of amenities should significantly penalize the analyzed location. The selected penalty shown in Fig. 3.1.11 is 50%. On the other hand, the amenities cannot significantly compensate for the absence of mandatory features. So, the corresponding reward should be modest (but not negligible), and in this case it is selected to be a half of the penalty, i.e., 25%. Using the maximum penalty of 50% and the maximum reward of 25%, we can now use Table 3.1.6 to select the weights 33% and 50% for the CPA aggregator shown in Fig. 3.1.11. This completes the development of the suitability aggregation structure and we can now perform evaluation of competitive locations.

In the presented example, we have not used the DPA aggregator (Fig. 3.1.10). However, we might use it in block 111 to make a criterion where the good bus transport is sufficient to satisfy the stakeholder, and the train transport is desirable but optional. In situations where this aggregator is appropriate, the procedure for selecting parameters is similar to the case of CPA. In the case of DPA/AH aggregator shown in Fig. 3.1.12, we can again use the Table 3.1.6. However, this is a disjunctive aggregator, and now the reward must be greater than the penalty. One of the inputs (1112) is sufficient to completely satisfy requirements, and the other input (1111) contributes to partial

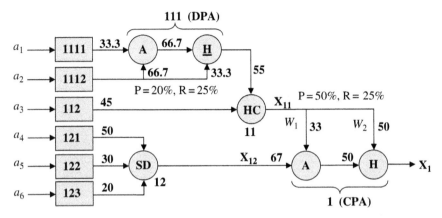

Figure 3.1.12 The UGCD version of the suitability aggregation structure for location evaluation illustrating the use of all types of idempotent aggregators.

satisfaction, but alone it cannot completely satisfy the requirements. If we select the reward of 25% and the penalty of 20%, then the resulting weights are $W_1 = 0.667$, $W_2 = 0.333$ yielding the aggregation structure shown in Fig. 3.1.12. We also assumed the modest conditions of the stakeholder, which yield a soft disjunctive aggregator 12.

The example in Fig. 3.1.12 illustrates an important point. This small example with only six inputs justifiably needs all different types of logic aggregators: hard and soft, conjunctive and disjunctive, CPA and DPA. It clearly shows what kind of errors are made in decision analysis and utility theory if logic aggregators are not available but the aggregation is based on any kind of operators that use fixed andness. In professional problems with hundreds of inputs, there are abundant opportunities to make serious errors if the criterion functions are based on over-simplified fixed-andness aggregators.

Let us now solve the senior citizen demo problem using the WPM.17 group of aggregators shown in Table 3.1.4. WPM.17 offers seven soft partial disjunction aggregators but no hard partial disjunction. The pure disjunction is the only hard disjunctive aggregator. In addition, the number of soft partial conjunction aggregators is only two, and there are five hard partial conjunction operators. However, these properties are not a significant obstacle for using GCD/WPM. Indeed, in many LSP criteria soft partial disjunction is sufficient to express the disjunctive properties, because at the high orness WPM behaves similarly as a hard partial disjunction. The spectrum of available partial conjunction functions is sufficient in many applications. Let us assume that we use the same reasoning as in the case of aggregation structure shown in Fig. 3.1.11. Then, the equivalencing of UGCD.15 and WPM.17 aggregators can be based on Fig. 3.1.13. The resulting WPM.17 aggregation structure is

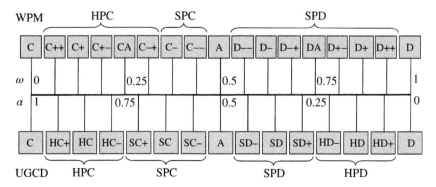

Figure 3.1.13 Comparison and equivalencing of UGCD.15 and WPM.17.

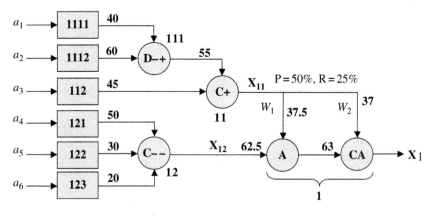

Figure 3.1.14 The GCD/WPM version of the suitability aggregation structure for location evaluation.

shown in Fig. 3.1.14, where the partial absorption structure is developed using Table 3.1.7. Tables 3.1.6 and 3.1.7 are used in a similar way. The only difference is that Table 3.1.6 defines the penalty and reward as the maximum value in the middle point ½, while Table 3.1.6 uses slightly different indicators, the mean boundary penalty and the mean boundary reward computed as defined in Chapter 2.6.

Location Suitability Example, Step 4.2: Sensitivity Analysis
Functional properties of any LSP aggregation structure can be investigated and verified using sensitivity analysis. This step is frequently optional and can be omitted without negative consequences. For purposes of our short example it

Table 3.1.7 Approximate values of W_1/W_2 pairs for the CPA/A:CA aggregator.

W_1 / W_2	Mean penalty												
	70	65	60	55	50	45	40	35	30	25	20	15	10
5	5 / 82	5 / 85.5	7 / 84	7 / 86.5	8 / 87.5	16.5 / 79.5	13 / 86.5	17.5 / 85.5	19.5 / 87	30.5 / 83	36 / 84	49 / 81.5	*7.5 / 87
10	7.5 / 74.5	9.5 / 74.5	12 / 74	14.5 / 74	18 / 73.5	22.5 / 72	27 / 71.5	32.5 / 70.5	40 / 68.5	49.5 / 65	61.5 / 58.5	75.5 / 44.5	*23.5 / 74
15	11 / 64.5	14 / 63.5	17.5 / 63	21.5 / 61.5	26 / 60.5	31.5 / 58.5	37 / 57.5	44.5 / 54	53 / 49.5	63 / 41.5	74.5 / 26.5	*20 / 64	*35.5 / 62
20	14.5 / 54	18 / 53.5	22.5 / 51.5	27 / 50.5	32.5 / 48	38.5 / 45.4	44.5 / 42	53 / 37	62 / 29	71.5 / 16	*16.5 / 55.5	*27 / 54	*44.5 / 50.5
25	17.5 / 45	21.5 / 44	26.5 / 42	31.5 / 40	37.5 / 37	44 / 33	51 / 28.5	59 / 21.5	67.5 / 10.5	*13.5 / 48	*21 / 47	*33.5 / 44.5	*51 / 40
30	20 / 37	24.5 / 35	30 / 32.5	35.5 / 30	41.5 / 26.5	48.5 / 21.5	55.5 / 16	*7 / 42	*11 / 41.5	*17 / 40.5			
35	22 / 29.5	27 / 27.5	32.5 / 25	38.5 / 21.5	45 / 17	51.5 / 12	58.5 / 5.5	*8.5 / 36	*13 / 35	*19.5 / 34			
40	24 / 23	29.5 / 20.5	35 / 17.5	41 / 14	47.5 / 9	53.5 / 5	*6.5 / 31	*10 / 30	*15 / 29.5	*22 / 28			
45	25.5 / 17.5	31 / 14.5	37 / 11	43 / 7.5	48.5 / 5	*5 / 26	*8 / 25.5	*11.5 / 25	*17 / 24	*24 / 23			
50	27 / 12	32.5 / 9.5	38.5 / 6	43.5 / 5	*5 / 21.5	*6 / 21.5							
55	28 / 8	33.5 / 5	38.5 / 5	*5 / 18	*5 / 18	*6.5 / 17.5							
60	28.5 / 5				*5 / 14.5	*7 / 14.5							

LEGEND
W_1 : upper value [%]
W_2 : lower value [%]
* : instead of **A** use the **DA** aggregator

Mandatory x
Desired or
Optional

is useful to briefly review the basic nonlinear features of selected UGCD.15 aggregators.

There are many different aspects of sensitivity analysis (see Chapter 3.7). In the simplest case we are interested in the value of output suitability as a function of selected input suitability. For example, let us first analyze the CPA and DPA aggregators shown in Fig. 3.1.10. In the case of conjunctive partial absorption, the analyzed function is $z = CPA(x, y, W_1, W_2)$. In the case of disjunctive partial absorption, the analyzed function is $z = DPA(x, y, W_1, W_2)$. The sensitivity analysis typically keeps fixed all inputs except one and then investigates the effects of the selected input on the output. For example, the impact of inputs x and y on CPA and DPA functions can be analyzed using functions

$$z_{CPA}(x) = CPA(x, 1, \tfrac{1}{3}, \tfrac{1}{2}), \quad z_{CPA}(x) = CPA(1, y, \tfrac{1}{3}, \tfrac{1}{2}),$$
$$z_{DPA}(x) = DPA(x, 0, \tfrac{1}{3}, \tfrac{1}{2}), \quad z_{DPA}(y) = DPA(0, y, \tfrac{1}{3}, \tfrac{1}{2}).$$

The results are shown in Fig. 3.1.15.

Another form of sensitivity analysis is the analysis of the whole aggregation structure. That can be done either for the same constant value of all inputs

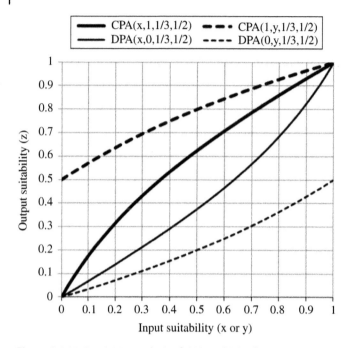

Figure 3.1.15 Sensitivity analysis of CPA and DPA functions.

(typically 0.5, 0.75, or 1) or for specific input values that correspond to an analyzed object. A frequent case of fixed inputs is to use the maximum value 1 for all inputs, in which case the output is also 1. Then we select one of inputs and analyze the reduction of the output value if the input is changing from 1 to 0. In the case of the UGCD.15 aggregation structure shown in Fig. 3.1.11, the sensitivity curves for all inputs are shown in Fig. 3.1.16. The curves at the top correspond to less significant inputs, and the lower curves correspond to more significant inputs. Those curves that correspond to mandatory inputs reach point (0,0), as the bottom curve for input 112 (mandatory food stores) shown in Fig. 3.1.16. Note that if one of inputs 1111 and 1112 were 0, the other one would automatically become mandatory.

The aggregation example presented in Figs. 3.1.11, 3.1.12, and 3.1.14 is extremely simple and has only four aggregators. However, let us once again note that even in the case of such simplicity, there is the undeniable need for conjunctive, disjunctive, hard, soft, symmetric, and asymmetric aggregators. This shows that even in simplest everyday reasoning, humans need and use logic properties of including/excluding annihilators, and symmetric/asymmetric aggregation. Therefore, the hard and soft partial conjunction and partial disjunction, as well as the conjunctive and disjunctive partial absorption, are

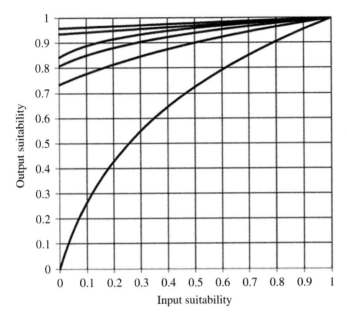

Figure 3.1.16 Sensitivity analysis for inputs 1111, 1112, 123, 122, 121, 112 (top-down).

indispensable components of all aggregation structures that have the goal to model human reasoning. The fundamental goal of the LSP method is to provide the logic infrastructure for building human-like aggregation structures in the context of quantitative decision models.

Location Suitability Example, Step 4.3: Logic Aggregation in the Case of Missing Data

In regular cases, all input data are assumed to be available. In many situations, however, some input data can be missing. Input values of attributes can be temporary or permanently not available, and in such cases, we can either postpone/ cancel evaluation, or to perform penalty-controlled missingness-tolerant evaluation, following the algorithm presented in Chapter 2.8. The idea of missingness-tolerant aggregation is that it is necessary to discourage situations where missing data actually exist but are intentionally kept not available because they are inconvenient. To discourage such behavior, we use the missingness penalty indicator, P where $P \in [0\%, 100\%]$.

In the case of evaluation with missing data, the evaluator must select the value of P that is most appropriate in a given situation. The value $P = 0$ is used to eliminate the penalty and replace missing data with neutral values, which are selected so that they yield the results of aggregation affected only by those inputs that are actually available. The value $P = 100\%$ is used to maximize the effect of

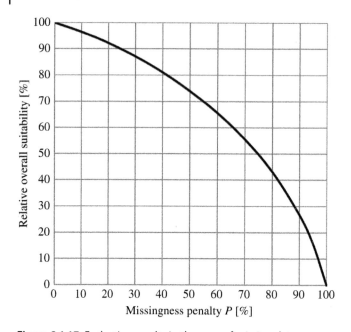

Figure 3.1.17 Evaluation results in the case of missing data.

penalty by evaluating missing attributes as attributes that are not satisfied and yield zero suitability. In all other cases we select $0 < P < 100\%$.

The effects of the missingness penalty are exemplified in Fig. 3.1.17 for the home location evaluation in the case where attributes a_1 and a_2 are missing. In such a case the aggregated value #111 is also missing. Therefore, the overall suitability depends only on $a_3, ..., a_6$. Fig. 3.1.17 shows the normalized relative overall suitability that decreases as a function of P. For $P = 0$ we get the unreduced output suitability (normalized as 100%). Since the output of aggregator #111 is a mandatory requirement (public transportation), in the case $P = 100\%$ the overall suitability is zero, as it should be for locations that offer no public transportation at all (i.e., do not satisfy a mandatory requirement). If we decide to use the penalty of 50%, the overall suitability is reduced to 73.9% of its initial value, penalizing to some extent the competitor that has incomplete data.

3.1.5 Cost/Suitability Analysis and Comparison of Evaluated Objects Using Their Overall Value

If we have the LSP criterion function and the values of attributes, we can compute the overall suitability of each evaluated object. The total cost of evaluated object should not be used as an attribute because it is an overall indicator that reflects an important property of the object as a whole. Similarly, the overall suitability is an overall indicator that reflects the perception of quality of the object as a whole. Consequently, the overall suitability should be compared to the total cost (see Fig. 2.2.4).

We use the term *total cost* to emphasize that in a general case the cost is a compound indicator that consists of combining various positive and negative cost components. For example, if the evaluated object is a car, then the usual cost components are the costs of car, registration, financing, fuel, insurance, and maintenance, possibly reduced by the resale value after N years of use. In this case, the total cost indicator includes all the above components, including positive (expenses) and negative (income obtained from the used car sale). So, we use the total cost of car ownership for N years. Note that all costs do not occur at the same time and some decision makers can use discounting of future costs in a way analyzed in [WRI73, SEI69] and Chapter 3.7.

By combining the overall suitability X and the overall cost C, decision makers create a percept of the overall value V of the evaluated object. Obviously, the most desirable object is the object that combines high suitability and low cost. In other words, we are interested in simultaneity of suitability and affordability, and the overall value $V = f(X, C)$ reflects the simultaneous presence of high suitability and high affordability.

Unsurprisingly, there are many ways for organizing the $V = f(X, C)$ model. The simplest case is illustrated in Fig. 3.1.18. The presented cost/suitability analysis is based on the following concepts:

1) The funding is assumed to be limited. The maximum available funding is C_{max} and objects having the overall cost $C > C_{max}$ are rejected as too expensive.
2) The overall suitability has the minimum threshold value X_{min} and objects below this threshold $(X < X_{min})$ are rejected as unsuitable. The most frequently used threshold values satisfy $67\% \leq X_{min} \leq 75\%$. In other words, from ⅔ to ¾ of reasonable requirements specified by an LSP criterion must be satisfied to create an acceptable solution for decision maker.
3) The region of acceptable solutions is defined as a rectangle $X_{min} \leq X \leq 100\%$, $0 < C \leq C_{max}$. The objects outside this rectangle are rejected, and the objects inside the rectangle are compared using various overall value models.
4) The simplest overall value model is $V = X/C$. This model reflects the suitability per monetary unit. A geometric interpretation of the overall value is $X/C = \tan\varphi$, where φ denotes the angle of line connecting the origin $(0,0)$ and the point (C, X) inside the region of acceptable solutions.
5) The ranking of competitive objects is based on decreasing values of angle φ. The object having the maximum slope of the line $(0,0)$-(C, X) has the highest percept of value.

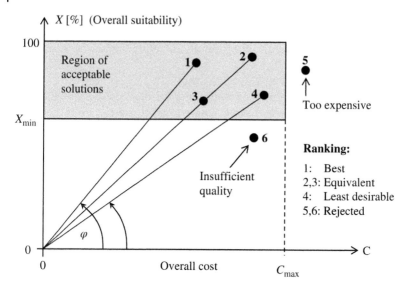

Figure 3.1.18 The simplest concept of cost/suitability analysis.

Location Suitability Example, Step 5: Evaluation and Cost/suitability Analysis
Using the UGCD.15 criterion presented in Fig. 3.1.11, we can now evaluate four competitive locations denoted Alpha, Beta, Gamma, and Delta. The summary of evaluation result is presented in Table 3.1.8. We assume that evaluation is based on the suitability of location. The total costs of purchasing or renting at each location (C) are normalized (the highest value is 1). We assume that all total costs are within the range of acceptable values.

Using six distances from given points of interest, we can compute all intermediate results (suitability in all points of the aggregation structure) and the overall suitability X. The first step is to use elementary attribute criteria to compute elementary attribute scores (presented in the column "Score" in Table 3.1.8). All suitability scores are degrees of truth of statements that the available values completely satisfy stakeholder's requirements. In the next step, we aggregate the attribute suitability scores to compute the subsystem suitability scores and the final result, the overall suitability. All suitability scores in Table 3.1.8 are expressed as percentages. Assuming that the threshold suitability is $X_{min} = 67\%$, it follows that the location Beta should be rejected because of insufficient overall suitability.

The ranking of competitive locations is based on the overall value that is computed simply as the ratio $V = X/C$. The resulting ranking is (1) Gamma, (2) Delta, and (3) Alpha. Therefore, the result of evaluation is that the best location is Gamma and that it satisfies 81.4% of stakeholder's requirements. This

Table 3.1.8 Comparison of four competitive locations.

Evaluation summary	Locations							
	Alpha		Beta		Gamma		Delta	
	Input	Score	Input	Score	Input	Score	Input	Score
Train	600	66.7	800	33.3	300	100	750	41.7
Bus station	120	89.2	200	76.9	100	92.3	250	69.2
Food store	350	58.3	410	47.5	200	83.3	80	100
Park	1100	68.6	900	74.3	250	92.9	200	94.3
Restaurant	250	100	300	100	220	100	460	84
Library	500	100	1500	75	2750	12.5	1900	55
Public transport		84.2		66.8		99		61.2
Basic needs		65.8		53.1		88.3		69.4
Amenities		83.5		81.8		69		82.5
Overall suitability [%]		**71.2**		**61.2**		**81.4**		**73.5**
Total cost	1		0.92		0.95		0.9	
Overall value		**0.712**		**0.665**		**0.857**		**0.816**

result can also be interpreted as the degree of truth (0.814) of the statement "location Gamma satisfies all stakeholder's requirements." Similarly, another interpretation is that the location Gamma belongs to the fuzzy set of ideal locations and the degree of membership is 0.814.

This example offers an opportunity to compare the locations Gamma and Delta in more detail and show an example of reasoning behind financial negotiations. The overall suitability degrees of Gamma and Delta (81.4% and 73.5%) are final results and cannot be changed. However, the costs can be modified: the seller can change the asking price and the buyer can change the offered amount. Using the results presented in Table 3.1.8, it is easy to see that the seller at the location Gamma could increase the asking price and still be the leading competitor. More precisely, the possible increase of price is limited by the competition with Delta. So, the maximum price of Gamma can be obtained from the relation $0.814/C_{max}(Gamma) \geq 0.816$, yielding $C_{max}(Gamma) \leq 0.9975$. Therefore, using this analysis the seller of Gamma might increase the asking price from 0.95 to 0.9975 without losing the leading position. On the other hand, the buyer might offer the asking price 0.95 with confidence that the obtained value is above what competition is offering. Alternatively, the buyer might decide to make an offer above the asking price in order to secure the deal.

If the buyer is primarily interested in savings, s/he might focus on Delta and ask for reduction of price. Indeed, in this competition the maximum price of Delta should satisfy the relation $0.735/C_{max}(Delta) \geq 0.857$ yielding $C_{max}(Delta) \leq 0.84$. So, the buyer has justification to ask for reduction of Delta price from 0.9 to 0.84. Similarly, the seller of Delta might use this analysis as a justification for offering a discount.

3.1.6 Summary of Properties of the LSP Method

At the end of this chapter, it is useful to summarize the presented main properties of the LSP method. The basic idea of LSP methodology is that the quantitative evaluation must be consistent with intuitive evaluation process that is easily observable in human reasoning (Chapter 2.2). That yields the LSP evaluation model based on systematic derivation of an attribute tree, the development of elementary attribute criteria for all attributes used in evaluation, and the aggregation of attribute suitability degrees based on nine fundamental logic functions presented in Table 3.1.2.

The set of nine basic aggregators is necessary and sufficient to develop any form of idempotent logic aggregation structure, consistent with intuitive evaluation. The selection of basic GCD aggregators is andness-directed and importance-weighted. Both the andness (orness) and the weights are the quantifiers of well-defined human percepts. Consequently, the routine choice of appropriate andness/orness and weights that reflect relative importance can be done intuitively based on modest training. On the other hand, the selection of more complex partial absorption aggregators is based on percepts of desired penalty and reward and simplified using appropriate tables and/or software tools. Therefore, LSP criteria can be interpreted as quantitative models of human perceptual computer for evaluation decisions.

The complexity of evaluated objects does not create problems and limitations for the applicability of the LSP method. The development of LSP criteria is a linear process that is performed attribute by attribute and aggregator by aggregator. The complexity of each individual operation and the corresponding effort (creating an attribute criterion or creating an aggregator) is approximately the same. In the case of n attributes, there are n elementary criteria and up to $n-1$ aggregators (this maximum value corresponds to the structure of a binary tree with $n = 2^k$ leaves where the number of aggregators is $n/2 + n/4 + \cdots + 2 + 1 = 2^{k-1} + 2^{k-2} + \cdots + 2 + 1 = 2^k - 1 = n - 1$). Therefore, the total number of operations is at most $2n-1$, and the LSP method effort complexity is linear: $O(n)$. In other words, complex criteria can be easily developed as a sequence of small and simple steps, and if the effort to develop a specific LSP criterion is E, then the effort for creating two times bigger a criterion is simply $2E$.

Using LSP criterion functions, we can compute the overall suitability of evaluated complex objects as quantitative indicators consistent with human intuitive percepts. The final result of LSP evaluation is sometimes the overall suitability, but more frequently the evaluated objects have cost, in which case the LSP criteria seamlessly combine the suitability analysis and a cost analysis providing indicators of the total value that can be used for financial negotiations, yielding optimum decisions.

In this chapter we used a simple home location decision problem to exemplify all major steps in the development and use of LSP criteria. The most important conclusion that we can derive from this example is that even in the simplest everyday intuitive evaluation reasoning humans use sophisticated logic aggregators of hard and soft partial conjunction and disjunction, as well as conjunctive and disjunctive partial absorption. Consequently, all methods that do not provide these properties of aggregators cannot model human evaluation reasoning, and most frequently represent oversimplifications.

In subsequent chapters, we expand and refine all major activities used in the LSP evaluation process outlined in this chapter. In addition, we present LSP evaluation as a professional activity that needs teamwork, software tools, and domain expertise, which was not necessary in our simple home location suitability example. In this way, we prepare for solving more complex problems presented in *Part Four* of this book.

3.2 LSP Decision Engineering Framework for Professional Evaluation Projects

> *An expert is a person who has made all the mistakes*
> *that can be made in a very narrow field.*
> —Niels Bohr

The evaluation process can be denoted as *professional* if the evaluated systems have substantial complexity and require professional domain expertise to specify the structure and parameters of LSP evaluation criteria. Examples of professional evaluation can be found in the area of complex systems such as aircrafts, computer systems, database systems, medical conditions, environmental and agricultural systems, military equipment, and system software (see Section 1.4). Such problems are characterized by the need to have substantial expertise in the areas of organization, role, functionality, and features of evaluated systems. That expertise is then used for development of an LSP criterion for evaluation and comparison of competitive alternatives, and selection of the alternative that is most suitable for a given stakeholder.

In this chapter we are interested in professional evaluation based on the LSP Decision Engineering Framework (DEF). The LSP DEF is defined as a set of evaluation techniques supported by a set of software tools and based on theoretical background that includes graded logic and the methodology for designing evaluation criteria based on logic aggregation structures.

Professional evaluation usually takes place in corporate environments (typically in industry, banks, governmental and military organizations, utility companies, etc.) and it can be contrasted to personal evaluation problems (everyday comparison and selection of goods and services). Personal evaluation problems are frequent but they rarely use advanced quantitative methodology. In addition, personal evaluation problems usually involve a single decision maker while in professional evaluation the decision maker is always a team. Personal decisions are usually based on intuitive aggregation of imprecise perceptions, while

Soft Computing Evaluation Logic: The LSP Decision Method and Its Applications,
First Edition. Jozo Dujmović.
© 2018 John Wiley & Sons, Inc. Published 2018 by John Wiley & Sons, Inc.
Companion website: www.wiley.com/go/Dujmovic/Soft_Computing_Evaluation_Logic

professional evaluation assumes quantitative aggregation of quantitative suitability degrees derived using justifiable expertise. Thus, the LSP DEF is primarily aimed at professional evaluation of complex systems and assumes the presence of experts that are qualified to help in selecting the type, structure, and parameters of evaluation criteria.

3.2.1 Participants in a Professional Evaluation Process Based on LSP DEF

We assume that the evaluated system can be almost any physical or conceptual object, from simple to extremely complex. In a typical situation, let us assume that an organization is buying an expensive system that is indispensable for normal operation of the organization. For example, an organization is buying equipment that includes many hardware and software components. Assuming that the evaluation is based on the LSP method, the decision maker is defined as a team with participants shown in Fig. 3.2.1.

The four principal participants in the system evaluation process are the *stakeholder* (buyer/user), the *vendor* (manufacturer or provider), the *evaluator* (decision engineer), and the *domain expert*. Generally, each participant can be an individual, a team, or an organization. Following are the main roles of all participants:

- *Stakeholder (buyer/user):* An organization interested in ownership and/or use of a new system (e.g., a company buying IT systems). The stakeholder must be authorized and able to set the evaluation project goals, to control the

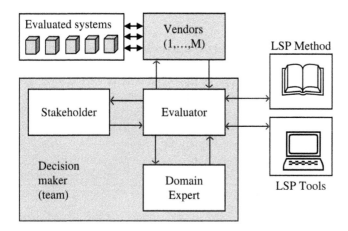

Figure 3.2.1 Participants in a professional evaluation process.

evaluation process and at some point to formally approve all requirements that the evaluator inserts in the criterion for evaluation. At the end of the evaluation process, the stakeholder is the final decision maker that may accept or (in exceptional cases) reject the results of evaluation, and sign or not sign a contract with the vendor.

- *Vendor:* The provider and/or manufacturer of the new system. The vendor is usually represented by salespeople and supporting technical personnel. For example, in the case of IT acquisitions, salespeople prepare the business components of proposal, and technical personnel perform required performance measurements (benchmarking) of evaluated computers.
- *Evaluator:* A decision engineer (sometimes a team) that uses quantitative evaluation methods and tools to prepare a decision model for system evaluation and selection. The model must have a high expressive power and flexibility to precisely reflect user's needs, goals, and requirements. It is also necessary that the evaluator has some domain expertise (knowledge about the role and functions of the evaluated system). The evaluator is the central initiator of communication with the vendor and represents and interprets the stakeholder's interests. This usually also includes the participation in final financial negotiations.
- *Domain expert:* A specialist for functions and operation of the evaluated system in user's environment. In cases where the evaluator lacks the specific domain knowledge, the domain expert assists the evaluator contributing to the specification of system attributes and related requirements. For example, if the object of evaluation is an aircraft, then an experienced pilot would be suitable as a domain expert.

The domain expert usually belongs to the stakeholder organization, and the evaluator is an external consultant. In the case of organizations that have frequent procurements, the evaluator can also belong to the buyer/user organization. Less frequent are situations where the stakeholder organization cannot provide domain expertise.

Readers who have reached this point deserve an "official explanation" regarding the magnificent decision-making trio shown on the front cover of this book. Unsurprisingly, the focused lady in the middle represents the stakeholder. Standing on the right-hand side is the evaluator, providing an inspired justification of the proposed LSP criterion. Siting alertly on the left-hand side is the domain expert.[1] On their desk, hiding behind the cup, is this very book. They are watching on their screen the results of evaluation obtained from a server that runs LSP.NT.

---

1 The publisher seems to strongly believe that moustache and beard are indispensable for successful application of the LSP method. However, practical evaluation experiences show that beardless evaluators and domain experts can be equally successful and should not be discouraged.

3.2.2   Relationships between Evaluators and Domain Experts

System evaluation process is usually a cooperative effort between the evaluator (who is specialized in system evaluation methods and tools) and the domain expert (an expert who knows the user's interests and is specialized in the domain of the evaluated system). In the case of IT procurements, the domain expert is usually a member of the user's IT management team. The success of the system evaluation effort depends on the effective relationship between these two experts.

Three characteristic types of the relationship between evaluators and domain experts are illustrated in Fig. 3.2.2. The first relationship is characterized by the lack of overlap between the evaluator and the domain expert. That occurs if the evaluator has insufficient understanding of the evaluated object and/or insufficient knowledge about the needs of the specific stakeholder. Alternatively, it is possible that the designated domain expert lacks the minimum knowledge about evaluation methodology, and/or has no confidence (or no interest to participate) in this form of decision making. This scenario has all the prerequisites for failure of the evaluation process. Therefore, it is important to detect and correct such a situation as early as possible.

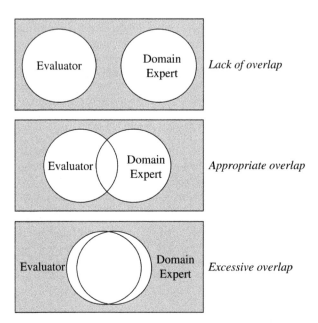

Figure 3.2.2 Characteristic relationships between the evaluator and the domain expert.

Excessive overlap between the evaluator and the domain expert is also not desirable. If the evaluator and the domain expert are too redundant, then using both of them can be a waste of resources. With a little extra effort, each of them could be qualified to manage the whole evaluation process. In such cases, the evaluation and selection process can be organized as an internal (in-house) stakeholder's project directed by the domain expert.

If an external evaluator is also a domain expert, then it is possible to organize the evaluation process without a designated domain expert. In such cases the stakeholder employs the evaluator as both a domain consultant and a decision engineer. This situation is common for acquisition of systems where the stakeholder starts working with a new kind of systems for which in-house expertise is not yet available and the evaluator is sufficiently familiar with the evaluated system.

The highest productivity is achieved when there is an appropriate level of overlap between the evaluator and the domain expert. This means that the evaluator knows basic user interests and understands the basics of operation of the evaluated system. The domain expert knows basics of evaluation methodology and can effectively complement evaluator's efforts. This combination yields synergistic effects and usually yields a successful evaluation process. Such a process yields provable satisfaction of user's needs with minimum resources.

3.2.3 The Structure of LSP DEF and the Corresponding Professional Evaluation Process

The LSP Decision Engineering Framework and the corresponding typical professional evaluation process are presented in Fig. 3.2.3. It starts with a stakeholder organization that identifies an evaluation and selection problem and decides to solve it using a quantitative approach. In a general case, let us assume that the organization intends to buy and use a complex and expensive piece of equipment (e.g., a computer/communication system). Initially, the problem is discussed between the stakeholder (buyer/user) and evaluator, as illustrated in Fig. 3.2.3. We assume that the domain expert assists in this process.

As suggested in Figs. 3.2.1 and 3.2.3, the prerequisite for application of the LSP method is the LSP DEF: we assume that the evaluator knows evaluation techniques, has access to software tools, and knows the background graded logic theory. All evaluation projects create project documentation, and previous projects remain in the project database. So, in most cases, it is possible to reuse parts of previous projects, and that simplifies development of new criteria. The necessary software tools for project development (ANSY, LSPcalc, LSP.NT, ISEE, and others) are described in Chapter 3.10. The current project creates evolving project documentation that is used in criterion design, evaluation, sensitivity analysis, and other LSP evaluation activities.

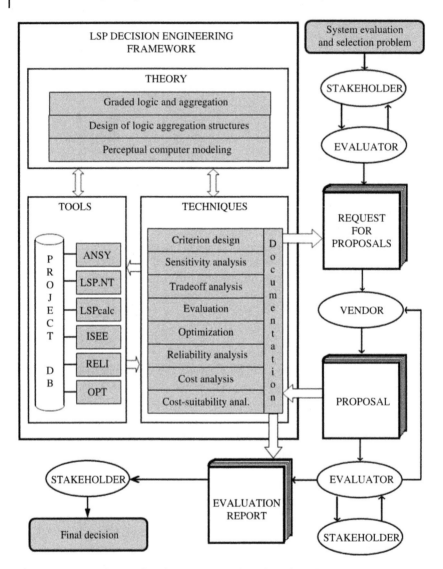

Figure 3.2.3 A professional evaluation process based on the LSP DEF.

The initial interaction between the stakeholder and the evaluator identifies the stakeholder's goals, system attributes, and all requirements expressed as an LSP criterion. The product of the initial interaction of evaluator and stakeholder is the development of the LSP criterion that correctly reflects the stakeholder's needs. Consequently, this process usually has a point where the stakeholder formally approves the criterion for evaluation of competitive systems. The criterion is the main component of the request for proposals (RFP), prepared by the evaluator with assistance from the stakeholder. In the context of the LSP DEF, the RFP typically contains the following components:

- An introductory description of the stakeholder organization
- Specification of the user's goals and needs
- The complete LSP criterion for system evaluation and selection
- Guidelines on how to prepare an LSP-based proposal
- Description (if required) of system tests/benchmarks
- Description of financial conditions
- Evaluation schedule and description of deliverables.
- An appendix containing a short presentation of the LSP DEF

This list sometimes includes system tests/benchmarks (e.g., performance measurement of computer hardware using specific benchmark programs). Of course, the nature of such tests and their role in the evaluation process depend on the type of evaluated systems, and there are systems where such tests do not apply.

The LSP criterion function in RFP plays the role of explicit request for satisfaction of user requirements. Let us offer two examples. If the capacity of disk memory of a computer system is evaluated using criterion $Cr(D) = \{(D_{min},0),(D_{max},100)\}$, then this is an explicit request and the vendors know exactly what degree of satisfaction they will achieve for any disk memory they offer. Another typical example is binary criterion $Cr(C) = \{("No",0),("Yes",100)\}$, where C is a contract request, such as "Do you accept a contract article that all delivered equipment will be new and unused?" Here again, the vendors clearly see the consequences of answering the question in a specific way. The major part of the proposal consists of the explicit list of values of the specific LSP criterion attributes. This facilitates the preparation of proposals, communication between the parties, evaluation of proposals, and contracting.

The RFP should be distributed to all potential vendors. The next step is the preparation of proposals by competitive vendors. This is an iterative process in which the evaluator (after consulting with the stakeholder) may require improvements and modifications to the proposal. In Fig. 3.2.3, this is represented by the feedback loop going from evaluator to vendor; we call this loop the *proposal improvement loop*. In this phase, the main goal of the evaluator is to help all vendors to produce the best possible proposals, which is in the mutual interest of both parties. There are multiple reasons for suboptimal proposals: for example, the vendor might apply a wrong strategy (e.g., offering systems that are insufficiently powerful or too powerful), inappropriate benchmarking may result in suboptimal performance results, or salespeople can be insufficiently prepared/motivated to correctly satisfy the LSP requirements. In any case, it is the evaluator's responsibility to verify that collected proposals include systems that can be considered the best that vendors can offer.

The cost of evaluated systems and related financial conditions are equally important as the overall performance and suitability. Once the configurations of proposed systems are fixed and the LSP suitability evaluation is completed, it is time for financial negotiations. These negotiations are based on cost-suitability analysis (see Chapter 3.7) and include the evaluator and stakeholder on one side and selected vendors on the other side. The basic idea of this process is that vendors are offered opportunities to reduce the cost to the point that brings an offer to the leading position in competition. This is a cyclic process and it terminates when all vendors declare that they are no longer able to improve their proposals. At that time, the proposal improvement loop terminates and the evaluator is ready to prepare the evaluation report.

The evaluation report is the final part of the LSP project documentation. It contains all results of the evaluation process and the final ranking of competitive systems. The recommendation for buying the system that is proved to be the best alternative for the stakeholder must be clear and fully justified. In normal situations, the role of the evaluator terminates after the stakeholder accepts a satisfactory evaluation report. The next step for the stakeholder is to make the final decision, and typically this is the decision to accept the best proposal and work with the selected vendor on contract details.

After the contract has been signed and payments have been made, there will typically be a delivery of the selected system, followed by the installation of equipment, an acceptance test, and a period of test work. In the case of equipment that has tests and benchmarks, after the installation the equipment must pass the acceptance test, which must verify the results of benchmarks reported during evaluation. The acceptance test procedure should be specified in the evaluation report and sometimes includes the evaluator and/or domain expert.

In order to help in the process of final decision making, contracting, and post-contract activities, the evaluation report typically includes the following components:

- Description of evaluation process
- Review of all vendors and their proposals
- LSP criterion used for evaluation
- Complete results of system evaluation
- Final ranking of competitors
- Final recommendation and its detailed justification
- Suggested conditions of system acceptance test
- Executive summary

The typical scenario of evaluation projects based of the LSP DEF corresponds to situations where various organizations buy equipment. Not surprisingly, there are many professional LSP evaluation projects that are different from equipment acquisition and that follow different scenario (see medical evaluation criteria, or suitability maps presented in *Part Four*). In all such projects evaluators are supposed to be familiar with the LSP DEF, and this book provides the necessary professional preparation.

3.2.4 Predictive Nature of Evaluation Models

> *Prediction is very difficult, especially about the future.*
> —Niels Bohr

Evaluation and selection of complex systems is a process that starts by specifying a set of requirements that competitive systems are expected to satisfy, and terminates by ranking the competitive systems according to an overall value indicator that reflects the overall level of satisfying the requirements combined with the total system cost. The user is then expected to select, acquire, and use the best system. For example, a homebuyer can evaluate four possible homes in a desired area, select the best home, buy it, and live in it for a period of time.

We sometimes face the question of whether it is possible to practically verify the validity of evaluation results. Obviously, the homebuyer cannot buy all four homes and live in them in parallel, in order to establish the actual levels of satisfaction and compare them with the final results of home evaluation. Similarly, a company that is buying computer equipment will select and install only the equipment of the winning competitor, and will never be able to practically compare the effectiveness of the selected equipment and the effectiveness of other competitors that were not selected.

The results of system evaluation must be considered a *prediction* of expected level of satisfaction if the user selects one of the evaluated options. In a general case, a practical verification of the accuracy of the final results is not possible, because the goal of the process is to select one (the best) and not all alternatives. The predictive nature of system evaluation is an inherent property of the evaluation process, and not its drawback. In addition, this is not a unique property of evaluation decisions. The nature of all decisions that select one among several alternatives is the same: the selected alternative is used and the rejected alternatives do not become operational.

There are exceptional cases where the prediction of the global system value can be verified. For example, this is possible in cases where we are not interested in system comparison and selection, but in evaluation of a single system to determine to what extent the system satisfies user's requirements. Other exceptional cases include experimental parallel use of some (free) software systems (such as search engines and web browsers) in order to establish their practical utility and verify the predictive power of evaluation models. All described cases are either exceptional or theoretical, and they do not change the general predictive nature of the system evaluation process.

3.2.5   Interpretation of Evaluation Results

Final results of an evaluation process are overall suitability scores of evaluated systems. So, the meaning of high/low suitability scores should be interpreted in the context of requirements specified by the LSP criterion. Evaluators first analyze the evaluated system, and then select system attributes that will be used for evaluation, define system requirements, and build a criterion function. The values of system attributes are transformed by the criterion function to a single overall level of satisfaction of requirements, the overall (global) suitability/preference, as illustrated in Fig. 3.2.4.

Evaluators should specify requirements and evaluation criteria so that the resulting global preferences are in a reasonable range (neither too low nor too high), where "reasonable" means consistent with realistic stakeholder expectations. The most frequent error made by inexperienced evaluators is to define too demanding criteria, such as criteria that require too much simultaneity even for components that are only moderately significant. The results of such criteria are low suitability scores of all competitive systems. For example, if all competitive systems satisfy less than 50% of user requirements, this most

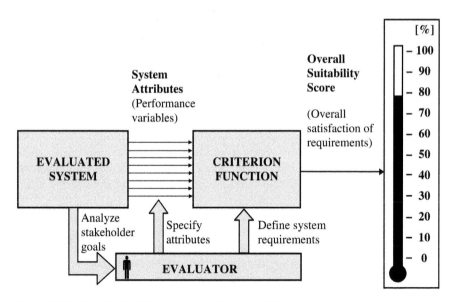

Figure 3.2.4 Overall suitability as a percentage of satisfied requirements.

likely identifies too harsh requirements that no system can satisfy. The other (less likely) possibility is that the requirements are correct but all competitive systems are too weak. In such a case, it is again the evaluator's responsibility to stimulate competitors to change their offers on time to achieve better final results.

The overall suitability reflects the overall degree of satisfaction of requirements. It is not a simple numerical score without interpretation. Therefore, the resulting value must be in the range that realistically reflects the degree of user satisfaction. In the majority of practical system evaluation and selection projects users are not ready to accept systems that satisfy less than $^2/_3$ (67%) of properly defined requirements. Such users include computer users, home-buyers, car buyers, and many others.

A typical distribution of overall suitability scores should generally have a very small number of systems that must be rejected because they satisfy less than 67% of requirements. To achieve such results it is necessary to properly adjust both the evaluation criterion and the system parameters. It is unacceptable to use "grading on a curve" approach to shift and shape the final distribution, because this would destroy the proper interpretation of final results. One assignment given to professional evaluators is to avoid mistakes of inappropriate level of requirements. Of course, too low global preferences reflect excessive and unrealistic requirements, but if all competitors attain extremely high overall scores, this is an equally questionable result. Too high overall suitability scores are a signal of low expectations and insufficient requirements, as well as a signal that the criterion for evaluation is incomplete and focused only on basic standard requirements that all competitors regularly satisfy. In the case or professional evaluators, such mistakes should not be expected. In all successful evaluation projects based on LSP DEF the final results must be close to intuitive expectations of a realistic stakeholder.

3.2.6 Complexity, Completeness, and Accuracy of Evaluation Models

In the case of intuitive evaluation, the complexity of the problem primarily depends on the number of attributes, the intricacy of attribute criteria and logic conditions, and the number of evaluated objects. The intuitive complexity increases rather fast because in the case of problem size n (e.g., n attributes or n objects) the intuitive evaluator must usually consider $n(n-1)/2$ pairwise comparisons, and this indicates a quadratic order of complexity ($O(n^2)$). Consequently, the accuracy of intuitive qualitative evaluation is a quickly decreasing function of problem size, as shown in Fig. 3.2.5. As opposed to that, the professional quantitative methodology solves evaluation problems as a linear

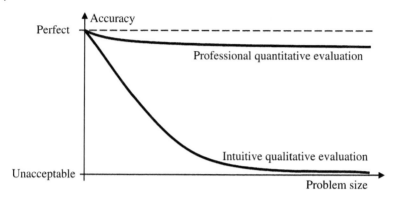

Figure 3.2.5 Accuracy and size of evaluation projects.

sequence of small steps, where each step is performed in a single node of the attribute tree where the number of inputs can be kept conveniently small (e.g., less than or equal to five). If n denotes the number of attributes, then there are n attribute criteria. The maximum number of aggregators (for a binary tree) is $n - 1 = n/2 + n/4 + \cdots + 2 + 1$. Thus, for each major step of the LSP method the effort is proportional to n, and each evaluation project is an $O(n)$ effort. Complex criteria can be developed as a sequence of small and simple steps. That yields a good control of complexity and provides a high and almost constant accuracy even for very large problems (Fig. 3.2.5).

In order to generate reliable results, the professional evaluation models must be as complete and accurate as possible. Completeness means two things: extracting from the stakeholder and domain experts as much useful information as possible, and generating a list of attributes and their requirements that includes as many components as reasonable, including components that have a wide range of importance levels.

It is easy to realize that the completeness and accuracy are directly related to the effort and the cost of evaluation. As the completeness and accuracy of an evaluation model increase, so do the effort and the cost of evaluation. The accuracy of evaluation increases asymptotically, as illustrated in Fig. 3.2.6 (see also Section 2.2.6, $\mathbf{P_{31}}$, and Fig. 2.2.30). In all cases there is an appropriate affordability limit that reflects either the maximum available funding or the sufficient level of accuracy, or the maximum time that is available for the evaluation process. So, it is either impossible or not reasonable to invest in the evaluation effort beyond that limit. There is also a minimum necessary degree of completeness and accuracy that determines the minimum necessary cost and effort. Such limits exist in all evaluation studies regardless of the cost of evaluated objects. For complex and expensive objects the desired accuracy should be higher than for simpler and inexpensive objects.

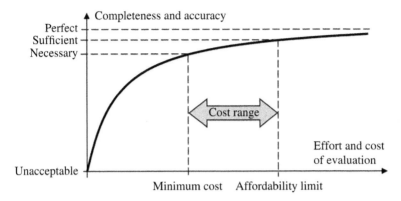

Figure 3.2.6 Completeness and accuracy of evaluation project as a function of cost.

3.2.7 Combining Opinions of *n* Experts

Professional evaluation projects base on LSP DEF regularly yield various forms of teamwork. Suppose that we have *n* experts working together on an evaluation problem. The experts provide perceptions of all parameters of LSP criteria (suitability scores, vertices of elementary criteria, weights, andness, orness, penalty, reward, etc.). Their estimates of a given parameter *X* are not identical and we want to combine their opinions in an optimum way. Let us assume that experts provide estimates $X_1, ..., X_n$ and we want to compute their collective estimate $X = F(X_1,...,X_n)$.

In this situation there is no objectively measurable accurate value X^* (as in physical measurements, e.g., the measurements of temperature using a set of thermometers). In the case of human perceptions, a reasonable approach would be to consider that X^* is defined as an unknown collective opinion of *all N existing world experts*. In practical evaluation studies, however, we only have a group of $n < N$ experts. Below, we consider two methods that are suitable for combining opinions of *n* experts: the maximum likelihood estimate, and the expert competence estimate.

3.2.7.1 The Maximum Likelihood Estimate

Let us first consider an idealized case where, for all experts, individual estimates of a given parameter are normally distributed as follows: $\mathcal{N}(\mu, \sigma_i)$, $\mu = E(X_i) = X^*$, $i = 1,...,n$ (*E* denotes the mathematical expectation). Therefore, we assume that the experts are capable of generating the correct mean value (after an infinite number of estimates), but their precision is different: high-quality experts have small standard deviation and low-quality experts have large standard deviation. The "best expert" can be defined as the kth expert that has the lowest standard deviation: $\sigma_k = \min(\sigma_1,...,\sigma_n)$. Under these idealized conditions, the question is to find the best form of function F. In particular, we are interested in the following two questions:

- Should the best expert k be given the right to impose his/her opinion (X_k) as the best estimate of X^*?
- Is it reasonable to use the mean value $\bar{X} = (X_1 + ... + X_n)/n$ of the opinions of n experts as the best estimate of X^*?

To answer this question let us first define the *maximum likelihood estimate* (MLE) as follows:

$$F_{MLE}(X_1,...,X_n) = \frac{\displaystyle\sum_{i=1}^{n} X_i / \sigma_i^2}{\displaystyle\sum_{i=1}^{n} 1 / \sigma_i^2}.$$

Under the above assumptions (normal distributions with the same mathematical expectations but different standard deviations), it is possible to prove that mathematical expectations satisfy the following inequalities:

$$E(F_{MLE}(X_1,...,X_n) - \mu)^2 \le E(F(X_1,...,X_n) - \mu)^2,$$
$$E(F_{MLE}(X_1,...,X_n) - \mu)^2 < E(X_k - \mu)^2, \quad \sigma_k = \min(\sigma_1,...,\sigma_n).$$

From these inequalities it follows that in an ideal case, $F_{MLE}(X_1, ..., X_n)$ is the best estimate, i.e., it is generally more convenient than *any* other estimate function F. That yields the following answers to the above specific questions:

- The best expert k should not be given the right to impose his/her opinion (X_k) as the best estimate of X^*. The opinions of better experts should have higher weights, but (in order to maximize the accuracy of the collective estimate) all experts should have the right to participate in a decision.
- The mean value $\bar{X} = (X_1 + ... + X_n)/n$ of the opinion of n experts is appropriate only if all experts have equal quality (same standard deviations of their estimates).

These results are obtained under rather restrictive assumptions, and for all mathematical models it is usual to ask what happens if the assumptions used to derive a mathematical model are not satisfied. That is usually called the *robustness* of a mathematical model: a mathematical model is robust if it is practically applicable in cases where the conditions used to derive the model are not perfectly satisfied. In the case of expert teams, the experts could be biased and the mathematical expectations of their estimates can differ. Furthermore, the distributions of estimates are regularly not normal (e.g., we never have extremely large or infinite values), and the opinions of experts in a team can be correlated.

Generally, correct answers to questions of robustness require complex mathematical investigations that are inconsistent with the scope and goals of this book. However, it is important to emphasize that many mathematical models show a remarkable degree of robustness, in the sense that the results obtained under idealized conditions approximately hold in situations where the idealized conditions are not satisfied.[2] Therefore, while the MLE model strictly holds only in cases of unbiased normal distributions, it provides a very good hint of how to behave in cases of heterogeneous experts working in the same team. In particular, expert teams can use various techniques to select the weights of individual experts and then use such weights to average independent heterogeneous opinions of team members in a way similar to MLE.

3.2.7.2 The Expert Competence Estimate

In the case of the maximum likelihood estimate, we use a weighted linear model $F_{MLE}(X_1,...,X_n) = \sum_{i=1}^{n} W_i X_i$. The weights $W_i = \sigma_i^{-2} / \sum_{i=1}^{n} \sigma_i^{-2}$, $i = 1,...,n$ reflect the degree of competence of experts, and in the case of MLE they are computed assuming unbiased normal distributions. This model clearly exposes two general principles: (1) better experts should have higher weights, and (2) all experts should have the right to participate.

Let us now address the question of what happens in cases where we cannot prove the existence of unbiased normal distributions and cannot compute the weights based on standard deviations. The degrees of competence of experts can be determined using the hypothesis introduced in [CHE72]: *if an expert has the degree of competence W_i to participate in solving an evaluation problem, s/he has the same degree of competence to estimate the degrees of competence of other (or all) members of the expert team.* If we accept this reasonable hypothesis, then we can define c_{ij} as a normalized coefficient of competence of the i-th expert according to the assessment of the j-th expert. For example, if the first expert in a group of three means that the other two experts are two times more experienced than him, this gives competences 1,2,2 and the normalized values $c_{11} = 1/5 = 0.2$, $c_{21} = 2/5 = 0.4$, $c_{31} = 2/5 = 0.4$. Thus, we have the following equations:

$$W_i = \sum_{j=1}^{n} W_j c_{ij}, \quad i = 1,...,n;$$

$$\sum_{i=1}^{n} c_{ij} = 1, \quad j = 1,...,n.$$

---

2 Readers familiar with queuing theory are particularly aware of this property because queuing models derived assuming exponentially distributed interarrival and service times show significant robustness and can be useful in many practical cases where the distributions are not exponential.

In this way, we formed a competence matrix $C = (c_{ij})_{n,n}$, which is singular because of the normalization condition. Consequently, we cannot directly solve the following system of equations:

$$\begin{pmatrix} c_{11}-1 & \cdots & c_{1n} \\ \vdots & \ddots & \vdots \\ c_{n1} & \cdots & c_{nn}-1 \end{pmatrix} \begin{pmatrix} W_1 \\ \vdots \\ W_n \end{pmatrix} = \begin{pmatrix} 0 \\ \vdots \\ 0 \end{pmatrix}.$$

However, if one of the equations (e.g., the first one) is substituted by the normalizing condition $W_1 + \ldots + W_n = 1$, then we get equations that can be easily solved:

$$\begin{pmatrix} 1 & 1 & \cdots & 1 \\ c_{21} & c_{22}-1 & \cdots & c_{2n} \\ \vdots & \vdots & \ddots & \vdots \\ c_{n1} & c_{n2} & \cdots & c_{nn}-1 \end{pmatrix} \begin{pmatrix} W_1 \\ W_2 \\ \vdots \\ W_n \end{pmatrix} = \begin{pmatrix} 1 \\ 0 \\ \vdots \\ 0 \end{pmatrix}.$$

We assume that no expert considers another expert in the group fully incompetent, because such a group would be dysfunctional. Consequently, $c_{ij} > 0$, $i \neq j$. However, in many cases it is reasonable to assume that experts cannot properly assess the degree of their own competence. In such cases, it is appropriate to define $c_{ii} = 0$, $i = 1,\ldots,n$, yielding the following equations:

$$\begin{pmatrix} 1 & 1 & \cdots & 1 \\ c_{21} & -1 & \cdots & c_{2n} \\ \vdots & \vdots & \ddots & \vdots \\ c_{n1} & c_{n2} & \cdots & -1 \end{pmatrix} \begin{pmatrix} W_1 \\ W_2 \\ \vdots \\ W_n \end{pmatrix} = \begin{pmatrix} 1 \\ 0 \\ \vdots \\ 0 \end{pmatrix}.$$

Example

Let us investigate a group of three experts who propose the following competence matrix:

$$C = \begin{pmatrix} c_{11} & c_{12} & c_{13} \\ c_{21} & c_{22} & c_{23} \\ c_{31} & c_{32} & c_{33} \end{pmatrix} = \begin{pmatrix} 0.6 & 0.5 & 0.4 \\ 0.2 & 0.3 & 0.3 \\ 0.2 & 0.2 & 0.3 \end{pmatrix}.$$

The corresponding system of equations is

$$\begin{pmatrix} 1 & 1 & 1 \\ 0.2 & -1 & 0.3 \\ 0.2 & 0.2 & -1 \end{pmatrix} \begin{pmatrix} W_1 \\ W_2 \\ W_3 \end{pmatrix} = \begin{pmatrix} 1 \\ 0 \\ 0 \end{pmatrix}.$$

The resulting weights are $W_1 = 47/72$, $W_2 = 13/72$, $W_3 = 12/72$. Therefore, the best collective estimate based on a linear model is

$$X = F(X_1, X_2, X_3) = \frac{47X_1 + 13X_2 + 12X_3}{72} = 0.65X_1 + 0.18X_2 + 0.17X_3.$$

Some expert teams can use *consensus weights* where a group of cooperative experts examines the experience of individual members in selected areas and permits members to modify their weight if they feel that they have insufficient or abundant experience in a particular area. That is similar to the MLE approach except that the weights are now determined using subjective estimates.

3.3 Elementary Attribute Criteria

> *Nothing is particularly hard*
> *if you divide it into small jobs.*
> —Henry Ford

Elementary attribute criteria (or simplified, *elementary criteria* or ELC, or *attribute criteria*) are functions that generate attribute suitability scores for all attributes of an evaluated object. In most cases, attributes are single variables, and in such cases elementary criteria are functions of a single variable. Less frequently, attributes can be compound and in such cases elementary criteria can be functions of more than one variable. We introduced attribute criteria in Sections 1.2.1 and 3.1.3.

A justifiable elementary criterion must be developed for each elementary input attribute. Let the elementary attributes be $a_i \in \mathbb{R}$, $i = 1, ..., n$. The process of evaluation of elementary attributes consists of specifying requirements that elementary attributes must satisfy and then computing normalized degrees of satisfaction (preference or suitability scores) $X_i \in I = [0,1]$ (or $X_i \in [0,100\%]$), $i = 1, ..., n$. The requirements are specified in the form of elementary criteria, which are mappings $g_i : \mathbb{R} \rightarrow I$, $i = 1, ..., n$. Not surprisingly, there are various forms and types of elementary criteria. They are presented in subsequent sections.

3.3.1 Notation of Elementary Criteria

Elementary criteria can have six basic forms of notation:

1) Verbal notation
2) Analytic notation
3) Graphic notation

Soft Computing Evaluation Logic: The LSP Decision Method and Its Applications,
First Edition. Jozo Dujmović.
© 2018 John Wiley & Sons, Inc. Published 2018 by John Wiley & Sons, Inc.
Companion website: www.wiley.com/go/Dujmovic/Soft_Computing_Evaluation_Logic

4) Preference scale notation
5) Vertex notation
6) Full description notation

The following example illustrates all six notation forms.

Example
Users of search engines are always interested in a fast response time. Let the user requirements be *verbally specified* as follows:

1) It is not acceptable if a search engine average response time t is greater than t_{max} seconds.
2) The average response time, which is less than t_{min} seconds, satisfies completely user expectations.
3) For average response times between t_{min} and t_{max}, use linear interpolation.

The *analytic notation* for computing the corresponding preference score X is the following:

$$X = 100 \min \left[1, \ \max\left(0, \ \frac{t_{max} - t}{t_{max} - t_{min}} \right) \right], \quad 0 \le X \le 100\%.$$

The corresponding *graphic notation* of this piecewise linear function (the polygonal curve) in the case where $t_{min} = 2$ sec, $t_{max} = 8$ sec is presented in Fig. 3.3.1.

This mapping can also be expressed using the *preference scale* shown in Fig. 3.3.2. The preference scale is a convenient combination of compactness and readability.

The *vertex notation* for the response time criterion is the most compact:

$$Crit(t) = \{(t_{min}, 100), \ldots, (t_{max}, 0)\}.$$

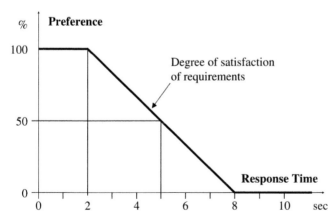

Figure 3.3.1 Elementary criterion for the web page response (retrieve) time.

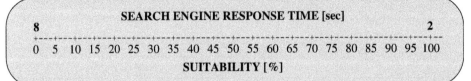

Figure 3.3.2 An example of the preference scale notation.

Response time for fetching a Web page	
[%] [sec] 100 ⊤ 2 90 ┼ 80 ┼ 70 ┼ 60 ┼ 50 ┼ 40 ┼ 30 ┼ 20 ┼ 10 ┼ 0 ┴ 8	If the response time is less than of equal to 2 seconds, the user is perfectly satisfied (the corresponding preference score is 100%). If the response time is greater than or equal to 8 seconds, this is not acceptable and yields the zero preference score. For values between 2 and 8 seconds we can use linear interpolation: for example, if the response time is 5 seconds, then the corresponding preference score is 50% (this value satisfies 50% of user's requirements).

Figure 3.3.3 An example of preference scale notation.

This notation assumes that the vertex values of attribute always form a strictly increasing sequence (in this case $t_{min} < t_{max}$). We use the vertex notation very frequently (see Section 3.1.3 and the school location criterion in Section 4.5.1). The vertex notation is also suitable for exceptional cases where the suitability never reaches 0 or 100% (see the aspect criterion in Fig. 3.1.6). For example, in the criterion $Crit(x) = \{(a,A),(b,B),(c,C)\}$ the values of A and C can be different from each other, and different from the extreme values 0 or 100%. The precise meaning of this criterion is the following:

$$Crit(x) = \begin{cases} A, & x \leq a, \\ \{(a,A),(b,B),(c,C)\}, & a \leq x \leq c, \quad a < b < c, \\ C, & x \geq c. \end{cases}$$

Many attribute criteria have a more complex structure or a specific measurement method and units that need description. In such cases we use the *full description notation* that combines the name of attribute, the preference scale and the description field, as shown in Fig. 3.3.3. We use the full description

LSP Method	Project:		Page
	Date:		
Elementary Criteria	Author:		

%		%	
100 -		100 -	
90 -		90 -	
80 -		80 -	
70 -		70 -	
60 -		60 -	
50 -		50 -	
40 -		40 -	
30 -		30 -	
20 -		20 -	
10 -		10 -	
0 -		0 -	

Figure 3.3.4 A fragment of standard LSP form for documenting elementary criteria.

notation as a standard form of elementary criteria in almost all criteria presented in *Part Four.*

An example of a form that can be used for creating LSP documentation is shown in Fig. 3.3.4. The form has a standard header specifying the project name, date, author, and the page number in a multipage documentation. All elementary criteria are supposed to have identification numbers written in small boxes in the title field of elementary criterion. The form shown in Fig. 3.3.4 is suitable for hand-made initial drafts of elementary criteria. More detailed professional documentation of elementary criteria is obtained using software tools (see Table 3.1.1 for elementary criteria made using LSP.NT and Fig. 4.2.14 for elementary criteria made using CDBS).

The compactness of vertex notation enables sometimes to merge the attribute tree and the elementary criteria giving extremely compact notation exemplified in Fig. 4.6.16. For example, the attribute tree can contain the following line:

Distance to parks [meters] $\{(200,100), (2000,0)\}$

Obviously, the given location is evaluated with respect to the distance to the closest park. The distance is measured in meters. If the distance is less than or equal to 200 m we are perfectly satisfied, and if the distance is greater than or equal to 2000 m we are completely unsatisfied. For points between 200 m and 2000 m we use linear interpolation. This notation is possible if the attribute is simple and understandable, as a distance from parks, but cannot be used for more complex attributes that need the full descriptor notation.

It is sometimes necessary to use analytical forms of elementary criteria. Canonical forms of elementary criteria can be analytically expressed as follows:

- *Preferred large values:* $Crit(a) = \{(A,0),(B,100)\}$ (unacceptable if $a \leq A$, and perfect if $A < B \leq a$):

$$\lambda(a) = 100 \max\left[0,\ \min\left(1,\ \frac{a-A}{B-A}\right)\right] = 100 \min\left[1,\ \max\left(0,\ \frac{a-A}{B-A}\right)\right].$$

- *Preferred small values:* $Crit(a) = \{(C,100),(D,0)\}$ (perfect if $a \leq C$, and unacceptable if $C < D \leq a$):

$$\sigma(a) = 100 \max\left[0,\ \min\left(1,\ \frac{D-a}{D-C}\right)\right] = 100 \min\left[1,\ \max\left(0,\ \frac{D-a}{D-C}\right)\right].$$

- *Preferred range of values:* $Crit(a) = \{(A,0),(B,100),(C,100),(D,0)\}$ (assuming $A < B < C < D$, perfect if $a \in [B,C]$, and unacceptable if $a \leq A$ or $a \geq D$):

$$\rho(a) = \lambda(a) + \sigma(a) - 100 = 100 \max\left[0,\ \min\left(1,\ \frac{a-A}{B-A},\ \frac{D-a}{D-C}\right)\right]$$

$$= 100 \min\left[1,\ \max\left(0,\ \frac{a-A}{B-A},\ \frac{D-a}{D-C}\right)\right].$$

In a general case of vertex notation of elementary criteria with $k + 1$ vertices, the suitability x for any value of a can be computed as follows:

$$x = g(a) = \begin{cases} x_0 & ,\ a \leq a_0; \\[2mm] \left\{\begin{array}{l} x_{i-1} + \dfrac{(a-a_{i-1})}{(a_i-a_{i-1})}(x_i - x_{i-1}) \\[3mm] = \dfrac{x_{i-1}(a_i-a) + x_i(a-a_{i-1})}{a_i - a_{i-1}} \end{array}\right\} & ,\ a_{i-1} \leq a \leq a_i,\ 0 < i \leq k; \\[2mm] x_k & ,\ a \geq a_k; \end{cases}$$

$$a_0 < a_1 < \ldots < a_k,\quad a_i \in \mathbb{R},\quad x_i \in [0,100\%],\quad i = 0,\ldots,k,\quad k > 0.$$

3.3.2 Verbalization of Elementary Criteria

Elementary criteria are frequently elicited from nonprofessional decision makers and in such cases it is necessary to describe criteria using only words. The cases of verbalization of elementary criteria are particularly visible on the Internet where criteria must be designed for the use of general public. In such situations, we cannot use any mathematical concept to define the shape of an elementary criterion function. Fortunately, in many cases elementary criteria can be expressed in a simple verbalized form.

The verbalization of elementary criteria is exemplified in Fig. 3.1.5, where three basic canonical forms of elementary criteria are verbally specified using description of vertices A, B, C, D. A more refined verbalization of canonical forms with additional vertices is also presented in Fig. 3.3.5. In all cases the maximum preference score is denoted by the statement "I am perfectly satisfied if..." and the zero preference score is denoted by the statement "It is unacceptable if..." In addition, we increase the precision of elementary criteria by adding more vertices specified by sentences "If attribute has the value x, my satisfaction is y%." The presented forms of verbalization are implemented in the graphical user interface of LSPmap, presented in Fig. 4.6.13.

3.3.3 Continuous Nonlinear Elementary Criteria

Mathematical properties of continuous elementary criteria can be characterized using the first and the second derivatives of these functions. The first derivatives of polygonal approximations are piecewise constant and the second derivatives are always zero (except in vertices, where derivatives are not defined). In most cases the precision of polygonal forms of elementary criteria depends on the number of vertices: small number of vertices indicates modest precision. Since the precision can be increased by increasing the number of vertices, it follows that ultimately all continuous elementary criteria can be designed as continuous nonlinear functions with continuous nonzero derivatives. Of course, that is done very infrequently because it significantly increases the cost of creating elementary criteria, and it must be based on an organized effort to closely investigate all details of the mental process of attribute evaluation. However, that mental process is based on human perceptions that are neither sufficiently precise nor deterministic. In fact, this process is considered to be fuzzy, and in the area of perceptual computing [MEN10] it is considered to be so imprecise that it is modeled using type 2 fuzzy sets (i.e., fuzzy models where even the membership functions are fuzzy).

While precise continuous elementary criteria are rare, their characterization based on signs of first and second derivatives is reasonable and it was first used as a part of professional decision making by James R. Miller III in [MIL66, MIL70]. The classification of characteristic shapes is shown in Fig. 3.3.6. In the case of increasing elementary criteria the increase of suitability can be constant $(d^2g/da^2 = 0)$, accelerated $(d^2g/da^2 > 0)$, or decelerated $(d^2g/da^2 < 0)$. Similarly, for decreasing elementary criteria, the decrease of suitability can be constant $(d^2g/da^2 = 0)$, accelerated $(d^2g/da^2 < 0)$, or decelerated $(d^2g/da^2 > 0)$.

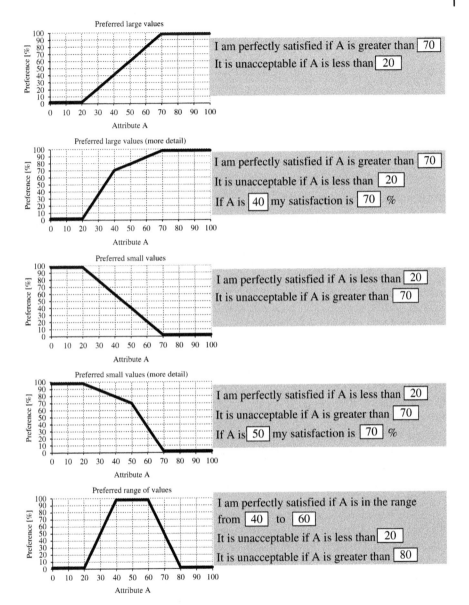

Figure 3.3.5 Verbal equivalents of basic shapes of attribute criteria suitable for general users.

The simplest nonlinear criteria are modeling either acceleration or deceleration. In more complex cases, a segment of acceleration is followed by a segment of deceleration, or a segment of deceleration is followed by a segment of acceleration. Precise deterministic modeling of nonlinear shapes in Fig. 3.3.6 requires

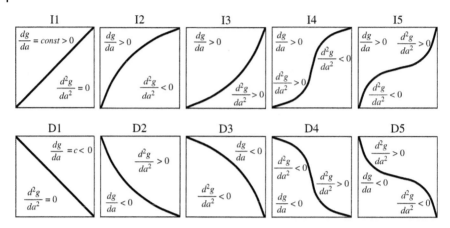

Figure 3.3.6 Characteristic shapes of increasing (upper row, I1-I5) and decreasing (lower row, D1-D5) elementary criteria.

a proof that the nonlinear model exactly reflects the perception of decision maker, which is generally quite difficult. However, the selection of the most appropriate among the 10 characteristic shapes is relatively simple and easily verbally justifiable.

To illustrate the process of selecting an appropriate shape and designing a continuous criterion let us consider a criterion for evaluation of home location. In the process of specifying requirements for home evaluation, homebuyers usually select a desired ideal location and the maximum distance (D) from the ideal location where they want to consider homes. Therefore, the acceptable homes are inside a circle that is centered at the ideal location, and has the radius D. Let d denote the distance of an evaluated home from the ideal central point. In the ideal location we have $d = 0$ and the corresponding suitability score is $S = 100\%$. The elementary criterion function $d \mapsto S(d)$ is monotonously decreasing, and if $d \geq D$ then $S(d) = 0$.

If the homebuyer has strong reasons to consider homes only in the close proximity of the specific ideal location, then the simplest appropriate shape would be D2. As opposed to that, if the homebuyer wants to be in a given area but without strong preferences for the immediate vicinity of the ideal location, then the appropriate shape of the elementary criterion would be D3.

There are many functions that can be used for creating the elementary criteria shaped as D2 or D3. A family of such functions, shown in Fig. 3.3.7, can be derived from the following model: $S(d) = 100(1 - d/D)^p$.

The property of such an elementary criterion can be determined by selecting the value of parameter p. If we introduce the normalized relative distance $x = 100d/D$, then we can use the family of criteria $S(x) = 100(1 - x/100)^p$, $0 \leq x \leq 100$.

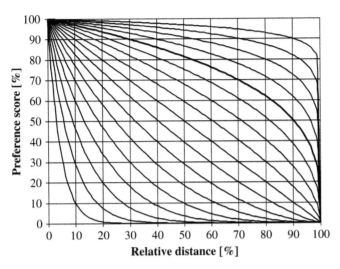

Figure 3.3.7 A family of elementary criteria for the relative distance from an ideal location.

For example, if we want the value $x = 70\%$ to cause $S(x) = 70\%$, then we have $0.7 = 0.3^p$ and $p = \log 0.7 / \log 0.3 = 0.2962$. Fig. 3.3.7 shows a family of normalized curves $S(x) = 100(1 - x/100)^p$ in the case where p is selected so that $S(q) = q$, $q = 10, 15, \ldots, 85, 90$, and consequently $p = \log (q/100) / \log(1 - q/100)$.

The line $S(x) = 100(1 - x/100)$ obtained for parameter $p = 1$ is the border case between strictly convex criteria that rigorously require proximity to ideal location $(p > 1)$ and strictly concave criteria that tolerate a wider range of distances $(p < 1)$. Assuming that homebuyers usually tolerate a range of distances from the ideal location, we select as the most appropriate the concave function where $S(70\%) = 70\%$ (shown as a bold curve in Fig. 3.3.7). A sufficiently precise polygonal approximation of the selected criterion function $S(x) = 100(1 - x/100)^{0.2962}$ (in the vertex notation) is Crit(x) = {(0,100), (40,86), (70,70), (90,50.6), (100,0)}, and it is shown in Fig. 3.3.8.

3.3.4 Classification of Twelve Characteristic Types of Elementary Criteria

In previous sections, we studied the simplest forms of elementary criteria—continuous functions of a single continuous variable. In many practical cases, we use different types of elementary criteria. We differentiate 12 characteristic types of elementary criteria according to classification presented in

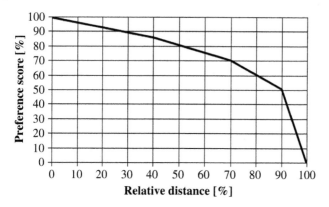

Figure 3.3.8 Polygonal form of the elementary criterion for the relative distance from an ideal location.

Table 3.3.1 Classification of twelve basic types of LSP elementary criteria.

ELEMENTARY ATTRIBUTE CRITERIA	ABSOLUTE CRITERIA	CONTINUOUS VARIABLE CRITERIA	1	Single-variable criteria
			2	Normalized-variable criteria
			3	Multivariable criteria
			4	Direct preference assessment
		DISCRETE VARIABLE CRITERIA	5	Binary criteria
			6	Multilevel criteria
			7	Subset-structured criteria
			8	Multivariable criteria
			9	Point-additive criteria
	RELATIVE CRITERIA		10	Single-variable criteria
			11	Normalized-variable criteria
			12	Statistical criteria

Table 3.3.1. A summary of their characteristic properties is shown in Table 3.3.2.

Two basic groups of elementary criteria are absolute and relative criteria. Absolute criteria are criteria that can be used to evaluate a single system without taking into account the presence or absence of other competitive systems and the values of their attributes. If it is possible to use only absolute criteria, then the overall suitability of each evaluated system is independent from the suitability of other systems. In other words, each system is individually evaluated, and if there are two or more systems, then their comparison is based on their independently computed overall suitability scores. Consequently, absolute criteria can be applied even when evaluating only one system.

Table 3.3.2 Characteristic properties of twelve basic types of LSP elementary criteria.

TYPE OF CRITERION	CHARACTERISTIC PROPERTY
1. Single-variable continuous absolute criterion	$X_i = g_i(a_i)$, $a_i \in [a_{i\min}, a_{i\max}] \subset \mathbb{R}$, $i \in \{1,...,n\}$
2. Normalized-variable continuous absolute criterion	$X_i = g_i(a_i^{norm})$, $a_i^{norm} = a_i / a_i^{ref}$, $i \in \{1,...,n\}$ a_i^{ref} = referent value used for normalization
3. Multivariable continuous absolute criterion	$X_i = g_i(a_i)$, $a_i = \Sigma_{j=1}^m w_j a_{ij}$, $m > 1$, $i \in \{1,...,n\}$, $a_{ij} \in \mathbb{R}$, $w_j \in \mathbb{R}$
4. Direct preference assessment	$X_i = a_i$, $i \in \{1,...,n\}$
5. Binary discrete absolute crit.	$X_i = g_i(a_i)$, $i \in \{1,...,n\}$, $a_i \in \{Y,N\}$, $X_i \in \{0,1\}$
6. Multilevel discrete absolute criterion	$X_i = g_i(a_i)$, $a_i \in \{0,1,...,k\}$, $k > 1$, $i \in \{1,...,n\}$
7. Subset-structured discrete absolute criterion	$X_i = g_i(a_i)$, $a_i \in \{S_1,...,S_k\}$, S_j = set of properties, $j = 1,...,k$, $S_1 \subset S_2 \subset ... \subset S_k$, $i \in \{1,...,n\}$
8. Multivariable discrete absolute criterion	$X_i = g_i(a_{i1},...,a_{im})$, $i \in \{1,...,n\}$, $m > 1$, $a_{ij} \in \{0,...,M_j\}$, $M_j \geq 1$
9. Point-additive discrete absolute criterion	$X_i = g_i(\Sigma_{j=1}^m p_j(a_{ij}))$, $i \in \{1,...,n\}$, $m > 1$, $a_{ij} \in \mathbb{R}$, $p_j(a_{ij}) \in \mathbb{R}$
10. Single-variable relative criterion	$X_i = g_i(a_i^{(k)} / \max(a_i^{(1)},...,a_i^{(K)}))$, or $X_i = g_i(a_i^{(k)} / \min(a_i^{(1)},...,a_i^{(K)}))$, $i \in \{1,...,n\}$ k = index of competitive system, $1 \leq k \leq K$ K = number of competitive systems
11. Normalized-variable relative criterion	$X_i = g_i(a_i^{(k)norm} / \max(a_i^{(1)norm},...,a_i^{(K)norm}))$, or $X_i = g_i(a_i^{(k)norm} / \min(a_i^{(1)norm},...,a_i^{(K)norm}))$ $a_i^{(k)norm} = a_i^{(k)} / a_i^{(k)ref}$, $i \in \{1,...,n\}$ k = index of competitive system, $1 \leq k \leq K$ $a_i^{(k)ref}$ = referent value used for normalization K = number of competitive systems
12. Statistical relative criterion	$X_i = g_i(a_i^{norm})$, $i \in \{1,...,n\}$ $a_i^{norm} = (a_i - \bar{a}_i)/\sigma_i$, or $a_i^{norm} = (a_i - \bar{a}_i)/\bar{a}_i$, or $a_i^{norm} = (a_i - a_{i\min})/(a_{i\max} - a_{i\min})$, where the mean value $(\bar{a}_i)$, standard deviation (σ_i), min and max values are computed for K competitive systems

Relative criteria evaluate the performance ratio between an attribute of evaluated system and the same attribute of another system (typically the best, or the worst, or the average) among competitive systems. Relative criteria can only be used in cases where the number of evaluated systems is greater than one and it is difficult to specify absolute criteria. For example, the comparison of speed of computer systems is usually performed using a mix of benchmark programs. If a benchmark program is standardized and its run time is well known, it might be possible to specify an absolute criterion based on run time T_{min} that is considered an excellent result and run time T_{max} that is considered unacceptable. However, if benchmarks are complex and competitors are not known, it is usually not possible to predict run times. In such cases, we can develop a relative criterion based on ratio t/t_{min} where t_{min} denotes the run time of the fastest among competitive computers and t is the run time of a selected competitive computer. In such cases the best competitor will get the relative run time 1 (which might perfectly satisfy the decision maker) and other scores will be determined relative to the best result.

Relative criteria have two major drawbacks: (1) they cannot be applied for evaluation of a single system, and (2) the fact that one system outperforms others is not a proof that the quality of the best competitor sufficiently satisfies user needs. Therefore, relative criteria are used in cases where it is not possible to create acceptable absolute criteria.[1]

All attributes can be divided into two big groups: continuous and discrete, yielding another method for classification of elementary criteria. For example, the benchmark program run time is obviously a continuous variable, but the number of disk units is a discrete value (a cardinal number). Frequently used discrete attributes are binary attributes that usually provide information about the presence or absence of a specific feature.

By combining continuous and discrete attributes and absolute and relative approaches to the evaluation, we can generate 12 useful types of elementary criteria, identified in Table 3.3.1. We will now shortly describe and exemplify all 12 types of elementary criteria, according to classification shown in Tables 3.3.1 and 3.3.2 and sample criteria shown in Figs. 3.3.9 and 3.3.10.

1) *Single-variable continuous absolute criterion:* This form of elementary criterion is the most frequently used. The first step is to define the range of values of attribute, i.e., the values that cause the minimum and maximum values of suitability. Very frequently, such criteria use the canonical forms

---

1 The drawbacks of relative criteria are also the drawbacks of all decision methods based on relative criteria, and/or pairwise comparison of attributes.

1. Single-variable continuous absolute criterion

Memory capacity (any kind of memory)		
[%]	[GB]	If the memory capacity C is greater than or equal to $Cmax$, the user is perfectly satisfied ($E = 100\%$). If the memory capacity is less than or equal to $Cmin$, this is not acceptable and yields the zero preference score. For values between $Cmin$ and $Cmax$ we assume the use of linear interpolation: $$E(C) = 100\ \frac{C - Cmin}{Cmax - Cmin}\ [\%]$$
100	$Cmax$	
90		
80		
70		
60		
50		
40		
30		
20		
10		
0	$Cmin$	

2. Normalized-variable continuous abs.crit.

Normalized sort time (S)	
[%]	This criterion compares the efficiency of system sort programs that run on different computers. $$S = Tsort/Tref$$ $Tref$ = run time of a referent standard benchmark program (this time reflects the hardware performance of the analyzed computer) $Tsort$ = run time of the evaluated sort program S eliminates the effects of different hardware performance of various computers and exposes the algorithmic performance of the sort program.
100 — $Smin$	
90	
80	
70	
60	
50	
40	
30	
20	
10	
0 — 2.5$Smin$	

3. Multivariable continuous absolute criterion

Total available training time (T)	
[%] [month]	This criterion compares the total training time offered by competitive training centers. The performance variable is a function (sum) of individual training times $T1,...,Tn$ offered in n different areas: $$T = T1 + T2 + ... + Tn$$ T reflects the total training capacity of a training center, in all existing areas. An alternative approach would be to aggregate n separate criteria, one for each of n areas.
100 — 30	
90	
80	
70 — 20	
60	
50	
40	
30	
20	
10	
0 — 10	

4. Direct suitability/preference assessment

Quality of documentation	
[%] [%]	Quality of documentation is directly assessed after a careful investigation of completeness, readability, size, accuracy, compactness, and visual attractiveness of documentation. Direct preference assessment should be avoided as much as possible. It is used only in cases where the evaluated attribute is relevant and cannot be omitted, but it is too complex and the effort needed for precise evaluation based on decomposition and assessment of components is excessive and cannot be justified.
100 — 100	
90	
80	
70	
60	
50	
40	
30	
20	
10	
0 — 0	

5. Binary criterion

Availability of 24/7 maintenance service	
[%]	The service is evaluated as follows: 1 = available, 0 = not available. Binary criteria evaluate the presence or the absence of a relevant feature. The usual meaning of 0 and 1 is as follows: 1 = yes / available / accepted, 0 = no / not available / rejected.
100 — 1	
90	
80	
70	
60	
50	
40	
30	
20	
10	
0 — 0	

6. Multilevel discrete absolute criterion

Transport options	
[%]	Existing transport options for a group of people are: 0 = not available 1 = car 2 = bus 3 = train 4 = air (Multi-level criteria are a generalization of binary criteria).
100 — 4	
90	
80 — 3	
70	
60	
50	
40 — 2	
30 — 1	
20	
10	
0 — 0	

Figure 3.3.9 Characteristic forms of absolute elementary attribute criteria.

or refined (precisiated) canonical forms with additional vertices. We use such criteria in Section 3.1.3 and in Fig. 3.3.5, and in classification of criteria shown in Fig. 3.3.9.

2) *Normalized-variable continuous absolute criterion:* In performance measurements, we frequently have situations where it is necessary to use normalized attributes. In such cases, we evaluate relations between two characteristics of the same system. If two measurable variables (X and Y) depend on a third (unknown) variable v, then the effect of the unknown variable can be completely or partially eliminated if we use a normalized attribute $a = X(v)/Y(v)$.

7. Subset-structured discrete absolute criterion

Software monitor (SM)

[%] 100 (4), 90, 80, 70, 60, 50, 40 (1), 30, 20, 10, 0 (0)

Existing incremental options are:

0 = SM is not available.

1 = SM is available and only displays selected performance indicators.

2 = 1 + SM creates log files for off-line analysis of computer performance.

3 = 2 + the availability of software for off-line statistical analysis of created log files.

4 = 3 + on-line performance tuning.

8. Multivariable discrete absolute criterion

Redundant hardware units (E)

[%] 100, 90, 80, 70, 60, 50, 40, 30, 20, 10, 0   [%] 100

$P/D/R$ = number of processors/disks/printers.

Evaluation table:

P	D	R	E[%]
1	1	1	0
1	1	2	50
1	2	1	40
1	2	2	80
2	1	1	30
2	1	2	70
2	2	1	60
2	2	2	100

Evaluation formula:

$E = 50(P - 2)(D - 2)(R - 1)$
$+40(P - 2)(D - 1)(R - 2)$
$-80(P - 2)(D - 1)(R - 1)$
$+30(P - 1)(D - 2)(R - 2)$
$-70(P - 1)(D - 2)(R - 1)$
$-60(P - 1)(D - 1)(R - 2)$
$+100(P - 1)(D - 1)(R - 1)$.

9. Point-additive discrete absolute criterion

Ink - jet color printer

[%] 100, 90, 80, 70, 60, 50, 40, 30, 20, 10, 0   [points] 130

Assign points up to the following values:

Resolution (dots per inch) 10
Separate color and B&W cartridge 5
Consumption of ink 15
Quality if used with inexpensive copier paper 15
Paper formats and paper tray capacity 10
B&W printing speed (pages per minute)................25
Photo quality printing speed (pages per minute)....10
Photo printing: paper type, sizes and quality 20
Printer size and design..............................10
Software support (user interface and options) 10

Evaluation is based on the sum of assigned points.

10. Single-variable relative criterion

Relative multiprogramming run time (Q)

[%] 100 (1), 90, 80, 70, 60, 50, 40, 30, 20, 10, 0 (2.5)

This criterion compares measured performance of competitive computers, as followes:

$$Q = Tmulti/Tmin.$$

$Tmulti$ = run time of a comprehensive multiprogramming benchmark workload (this time reflects the global performance of the analyzed computer).

$Tmin$ = minimum $Tmulti$ ($Tmulti$ of the fastest competitive computer).

This criterion reflects the fact that computers having $Q = 1$ and $Q = 3$ cannot belong to the same category.

11. Normalized-variable relative criterion

Relative efficiency of a sort system (ES)

[%] 100 (1), 90, 80, 70, 60, 50, 40, 30, 20, 10, 0 (3)

This criterion compares the efficiency of sort programs that run on different computers.

$$ES = S / Smin, \qquad S = Tsort / Tref.$$

$Tref$ = run time of a referent standard benchmark program (this time reflects the hardware performance of the analyzed computer).

$Tsort$ = run time of the evaluated sort program.

$Smin$ = S of the best competitive computer.

ES eliminates the effects of different hardware performance of various computers. It works without adjustment for any $Tsort/Tref$ ratio.

12. Statistical relative criterion

Relative performance of a computer system (E)

[%] 100 (-0.5), 90, 80, 70, 60, 50, 40, 30, 20, 10, 0 (1); 0 at 60–50

This criterion is based on a deviation from the mean performance measured for a set of competitive computers:

$$E = (T - Tave) / Tave.$$

T = run time of a representative benchmark workload.

$Tave$ = the average value of T for all competitive computers.

The average performance satisfies 60% of user requirements and excellence is defined as performance that is two times above the average.

Figure 3.3.10 Characteristic forms of absolute and relative elementary attribute criteria.

An example of normalization is presented in Fig. 3.3.9 where we want to evaluate the algorithmic performance of a system sort program for various computer systems. Unfortunately, the sort program run time T_{sort} depends on two variables: (1) the quality of sort algorithm, and (2) the speed of computer hardware. Consequently, if we measure T_{sort} for two or more computers, we cannot know whether a good performance is the consequence of a good sort program or the consequence of a mediocre program executed using a very fast hardware.

To eliminate the effect of hardware speed v we can select a fixed referent standard benchmark that on analyzed machine has the run time T_{ref}. If we define the normalized sort time $S = T_{sort}/T_{ref}$ that eliminates the effects of the hardware speed v and exposes the algorithmic quality of the sort program. Now, we can compare different sort programs using the normalized attribute S. If desirable value of S is S_{min}, then we can use the elementary criterion $Crit(S) = \{(S_{min},100),(pS_{min},0)\}$ where parameter p reflects the acceptable performance range (typically $p \in [2,3]$), as exemplified in Fig. 3.3.9.

3) *Multivariable continuous absolute criterion:* Evaluation attributes can sometimes be defined as functions of two or more variables. In the simplest but still rather general case such a compound attribute can be expressed as a weighted linear form $a_i = \Sigma_{j=1}^{m} w_j a_{ij}$, $m > 1$, $a_{ij} \in \mathbb{R}$, $w_j \in \mathbb{R}$, $a_i \in \mathbb{R}$, where weights $w_1, ..., w_m$ reflect the degree of importance or a scaling factor for m sub-attributes $a_{i1}, ..., a_{im}$. The corresponding elementary criterion is $X_i = g_i(a_i) \in [0,1]$, $i \in \{1,...,n\}$. In some cases X_i could be computed using a complete LSP criterion with input attributes $a_{i1}, ..., a_{im}$. Of course, that would increase the evaluation effort, and multivariable continuous criteria are primarily a way to simplify the evaluation process. One such criterion for evaluation of a training center is shown in Fig. 3.3.9.

4) *Direct suitability/preference assessment:* If a quantitative elementary criterion function cannot be established using an acceptable effort, and the criterion is important so that it cannot be omitted, then the evaluator and domain expert may directly estimate the elementary suitability score based on experience. An example of such a criterion, shown in Fig. 3.3.9, is the quality of documentation that comes with computer software or with other complex products. It is usually too expensive to decompose the quality of documentation into many simpler components (e.g., readability, understandability, size, usability, correctness, completeness, compactness, number of illustrations, language, style, etc.) and develop corresponding quantitative elementary criteria. However, it is also not acceptable to neglect the quality of documentation and avoid its evaluation. So, the evaluator may decide to use a "direct preference assessment," which is the subjective assignment of suitability score based on expert investigation of the evaluated attribute (the quality of documentation). That generates a percept of quality that can be verbalized using a rating scale and then quantified in the form of suitability score. If the available expertise is insufficient, then this process can contribute a considerable level of uncontrolled subjectivity. Therefore, it should be avoided whenever possible. In LSP evaluation projects, the overuse of direct preference assessment is an indicator of the low quality of criterion function, and it is typical for beginners in this area. Evaluators who don't know how to design elementary attribute criteria tend to overuse the direct suitability assessment. This practice should be discouraged.

If the direct suitability assessment cannot be avoided, then it should be based on hybrid verbalized rating scales presented in Chapter 2.9

(Table 2.9.2). For example, the degree of satisfaction with the quality of documentation, reported by an expert evaluator as an overall percept created after a careful investigation of the available documentation, can be rated as (0) not at all, (1) slightly, (2) moderately, (3) considerably, and (4) completely. More precisely, the quality can be (0) unacceptable, (1) very poor, (2) poor (3), average, (4) good, (5) very good, and (6) excellent. Then, we can use a linear criterion, for example, $Crit(Doc) = \{(0,0),(6,100)\}$. However, we can also request a high quality of documentation and express such a requirement using a nonlinear criterion $Crit(Doc) = \{(0,0),(4,50),(6,100)\}$.

In many cases, the presented technique can generate useful and accurate results. However, it is obvious that direct suitability assessment generally has the following three drawbacks. First, the quality of results critically depends on the quality of the domain expert/evaluator. Second, the evaluation process can require significant effort and is more expensive than evaluation based on other types of elementary attribute criteria; so, the quality of results also depends on available resources (time and money). Third, if the evaluation process does not generate a convincing report that justifies the assigned suitability score, the process can be interpreted as excessively subjective and unreliable.

5) *Binary criterion:* Binary criteria are the simplest discrete criteria. They provide only one bit of information: whether a condition is (completely) satisfied or (completely) not satisfied, present or absent, accepted or rejected. For example, in Fig. 3.3.9 we evaluate whether a 24/7 maintenance service is available or not available. Binary criteria are frequently used to evaluate whether some legal contractual obligations are accepted or rejected, and the stakeholder can force their acceptance by making the corresponding attribute mandatory.

6) *Multilevel discrete absolute criterion:* This is the most frequent form of discrete criteria, used to evaluate multiple discrete options of satisfaction of a given requirement. It is used in Fig. 3.3.9 to evaluate four transport options.

7) *Subset-structured discrete absolute criterion:* A special case of the multilevel discrete absolute criterion is the criterion that is structured as a sequence of subsets, where each new discrete level adds one feature on top of previous features. That is exemplified in Fig. 3.3.10 using four levels of evaluations of software monitors.

8) *Multivariable discrete absolute criterion:* Fig. 3.3.10 exemplifies this form of criterion using a table where suitability is defined as a discrete function of three variables. In such case, analytic forms can be created using an approach similar to Lagrange interpolation. For example, if we need a function that computes suitability scores $S = S_0, S_1, S_2, S_3$ if input variables x and y respectively have values $xy = 00, 01, 10, 11$, then the corresponding formula is obviously

$$S = S_0(1-x)(1-y) + S_1(1-x)y + S_2x(1-y) + S_3xy.$$

Similarly, if instead of 00,01,10,11 we have arbitrary values aa, ab, ba, and bb, then the interpolative formula is

$$S = S_0\frac{(x-b)(y-b)}{(a-b)^2} + S_1\frac{(x-b)(y-a)}{(a-b)(b-a)} + S_2\frac{(x-a)(y-b)}{(b-a)(a-b)} + S_3\frac{(x-a)(y-a)}{(b-a)^2}.$$

9) *Point-additive discrete absolute criterion:* This is a criterion organized as a simple scoring, where each feature gets specific number of points and the sum of points (which denotes the availability of all features is assigned the maximum suitability (100%).

10) *Single-variable relative criterion:* This type of elementary criterion is based on comparison of specific competitor with the best in its group. The example in Fig. 3.3.10 compares the speed of computers using the ratio of run time and the best run time. This ratio shows how many times a given computer is slower than the fastest competitive computer. The best computer has the ratio 1, and the typical unacceptable values are between 2 and 3. The winning competitor is better than others, but that cannot be used as a proof of perfect satisfaction or stakeholder's needs.

11) *Normalized-variable relative criterion:* This criterion is shown in Fig. 3.3.10 as a generalization of the normalized-variable criterion (combination of type 2 and 10). It uses the normalized performance and compares the normalized value with the best achieved normalized value.

12) *Statistical relative criterion:* Relative criteria can be based on statistical indicators. The sample statistical relative criterion shown in Fig. 3.3.10 is based on deviation from the mean value computed for all competitors. The mean value is assigned an average suitability score, and competitors with deviations above and below the mean value are assigned appropriate higher or lower scores than the mean value.

3.4 Aggregation Techniques and Tools

> *E pluribus unum (From many, one).*
> —The Seal of the United States

Theoretical aspects of aggregation operators are presented in detail in *Part Two,* and the use of LSP aggregators to build LSP criteria is introduced in Section 3.1.4. In this chapter, we assume that readers are familiar with the basic knowledge about idempotent aggregators and their use in the LSP method. So, we will now focus on strategic decision, techniques, and tools that are necessary in the process of professional development of complex LSP criteria and their aggregation structures.

3.4.1 Selecting GCD Aggregators for an LSP Project

The first strategic decision that must be made at the beginning of each LSP project is the selection of the type of GCD aggregators. The seven main types (discussed in Sections 2.4.12, 2.9.2, and 3.1.4) are presented in the decision tree shown in Fig. 3.4.1. UGCD aggregators are a default choice based on a constant number of soft and hard aggregators. GGCD is a more general group selected when evaluators know to select a suitable location of threshold andness. Low-precision aggregators are suitable for introductory educational experiences. High-precision aggregators are used in most delicate professional projects. Medium-precision aggregators (including WPM.17) are used in all other situations, and consequently, they are most frequently used in practice, as a balanced combination of simplicity and precision.

A more detailed approach to selecting GCD aggregators is to offer a crisp granulation of andness and orness and let the user select the level of andness that seems to be the most appropriate. Such granulation must always include the central neutrality aggregator (the arithmetic mean, A) and the extreme cases

Soft Computing Evaluation Logic: The LSP Decision Method and Its Applications, First Edition. Jozo Dujmović.
© 2018 John Wiley & Sons, Inc. Published 2018 by John Wiley & Sons, Inc.
Companion website: www.wiley.com/go/Dujmovic/Soft_Computing_Evaluation_Logic

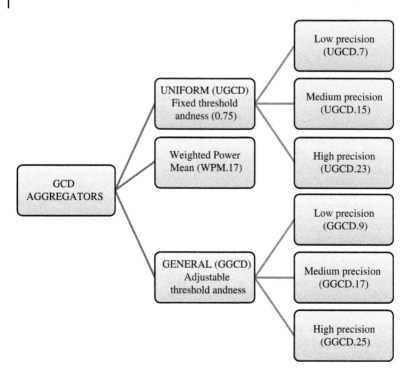

Figure 3.4.1 Selection of the type of GCD aggregators.

of pure conjunction (C) and pure disjunction (D). Between these three fixed aggregators we can insert any number (K) of partial conjunction and the same number of partial disjunction aggregators, giving the total granularity (or cardinality) of $G = 2K + 3$ aggregators. Therefore, the granularity G is always an odd number.

Ten characteristic cases of granularity, and a general notation of aggregators, in the range $7 \le G \le 25$ are presented in Fig. 3.4.2, where the number of inserted PC (partial conjunction) aggregators and PD (partial disjunction) aggregators is $K = 2, 3, 4, 5, 6, 7, 8, 9, 10, 11$. In practice, there is no need for all presented 10 groups of aggregators, but only for aggregators having precision denoted as low, medium, or high, shown in Fig. 3.4.3.

Fig. 3.4.3 shows mnemonic notation of individual aggregators, which is based on the following: C = conjunctive aggregator, D = disjunctive aggregator. For UGCD, we use H = hard aggregator, S = soft aggregator, and for GGCD we use S = strong, W = weak, and A = medium aggregator. The hierarchical processes for selecting the most appropriate individual UGCD and GGCD aggregators are presented in Fig. 3.4.4. Verbalizing of all presented aggregators can be done according to Tables 2.9.5 to 2.9.7, 3.1.3 to 3.1.5, and Figs. 2.9.4 to 2.9.7.

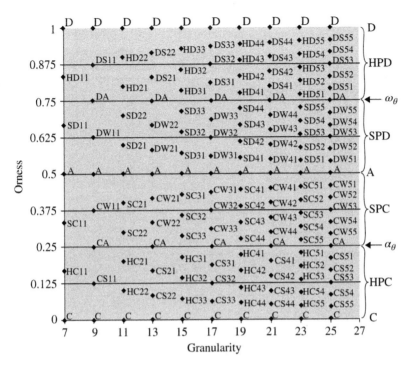

Figure 3.4.2 A general notation for 10 groups of GCD aggregators.

3.4.2 Selecting GCD Aggregators by Training Preferential Neurons

Aggregation structures consisting of LSP aggregators can be interpreted as preferential neural networks where individual aggregators are interpreted as preferential neurons [DUJ91]. A characteristic property of such networks is that each neuron has inputs and an output that have a clear meaning for decision makers. Instead of aggregating anonymous x and y to produce an anonymous z, LSP aggregation structures aggregate interpretable suitability degrees, e.g., the quality of location and the quality of home to produce the overall home suitability, or motor symptoms and sensory symptoms of a patient to produce patient disability.

Based on the role and meaning of inputs and output, a decision maker can specify a table containing desired input-output mapping of an aggregator, and then use the mapping table as a training set for optimum adjustment of the aggregator parameters. Therefore, the characteristic property of preferential neural networks is that each neuron/aggregator has semantic identity and can be separately trained. This is different from traditional multilayered

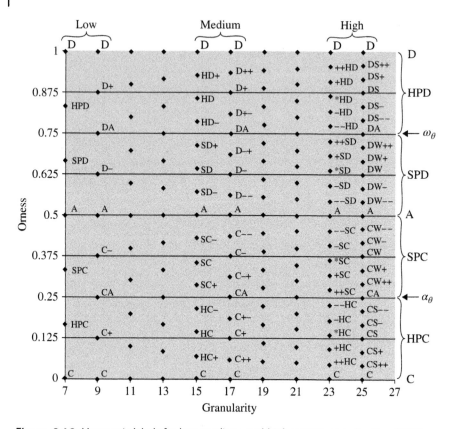

Figure 3.4.3 Mnemonic labels for low, medium, and high precision/cardinality of GCD.

feed-forward neural networks [LAW94, KAC15] where neurons don't have semantic identity and cannot be individually trained.

Generally, each aggregator has an array of inputs **X** and an array of parameters **P**: $y = A(\mathbf{X}; \mathbf{P})$, $\mathbf{X} = (x_1,...,x_k)$, $\mathbf{P} = (p_1,...,p_m)$. The training set, exemplified in Table 3.4.1, consists of M rows, and each row specifies one condition that the aggregator should satisfy. The criterion for tuning of m adjustable parameters is

$$E(\mathbf{P}) = E(p_1,...,p_m) = \sum_{i=1}^{M} |y_i - A(x_{1i},...,x_{ki}; p_1,...,p_m)|,$$

So, the problem is to find the minimum of $E(p_1, ..., p_m)$, i.e., the optimum parameters $\mathbf{P}^* = (p_1^*,...,p_m^*)$ so that $E(\mathbf{P}) \geq E(\mathbf{P}^*)$, $\forall \mathbf{P} \neq \mathbf{P}^*$. In this section we are going to show the solution of this problem based on a tool called AnSy (<u>An</u>alysis and <u>Sy</u>nthesis of preferential neurons) [DUJ91, SEA10] that implements

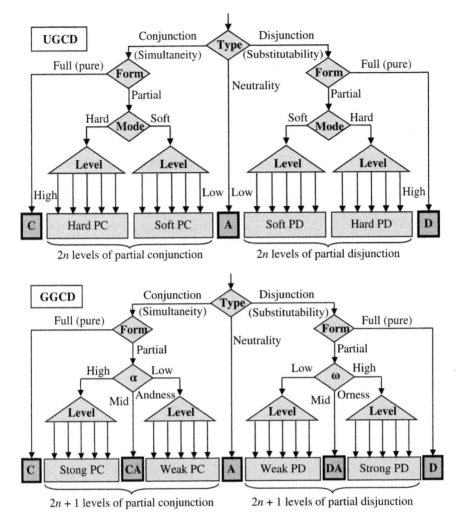

Figure 3.4.4 The selection process for UGCD and GGCD aggregators.

Table 3.4.1 Training set for aggregator
$A(x_1, \ldots, x_k; p_1, \ldots, p_m)$.

Inputs			Desired output
x_1	...	x_k	y
x_{11}	...	x_{k1}	y_1
x_{12}	...	x_{k2}	y_2
...	...	...	...
x_{1M}	...	x_{kM}	y_M

aggregators using weighted power means. In this case, the continuously adjustable parameters are the WPM weights and exponent.

Let us first discuss the relation between M and m. Obviously, there are three possibilities: $M < m$, $M = m$, and $M > m$. The AnSy algorithm that minimizes E ($\mathbf{P}$) generates solutions in all cases. However, we cannot find unique set of m parameters unless we have at least $M = m$ conditions. If $M < m$ the minimization algorithm will find one of multiple solutions, and that is generally not acceptable because in addition to specified conditions such aggregators can also generate some values $y = A(\mathbf{X}; \mathbf{P}^*)$ that are inconsistent with the decision maker's expectations. So, we should use $M \geq m$.

If $M = m$ then we expect the unique solution (provided that such a solution exists). It is easy to see that (theoretically) training sets can contain inconsistent or contradictory conditions in which case no acceptable solution can be generated. Of course, such cases do not happen to qualified decision makers but they are possible. In cases where $M > m$, we have more conditions than unknown variables, and that is acceptable if it helps decision makers to quantify knowledge about desired properties of the aggregator. The problem is whether all conditions are consistent, because some input-output combinations may be in some implicit way partially inconsistent. Fortunately, by finding the minimum error $E(\mathbf{P}^*)$ we obtain the parameters that satisfy the given conditions as much as possible.

In the case of WPM $y = \left(W_1 x_1^r + \cdots + W_k x_k^r \right)^{1/r}$ the necessary number of parameters is $m = k$ because we have $m - 1$ independent weights (one of m weights comes from the normalization condition $W_1 + \ldots + W_k = 1$) and the exponent (or andness/orness). So, in such cases, it is advisable to use $M \geq k$ conditions in the training set.

Let us now present the training of GCD neurons/aggregators. In the case of partial conjunction with three inputs a typical example of conditions is shown in Table 3.4.2. The first condition specifies the existence of the annihilator 0 and consequently it is the requirement for a hard partial conjunction. All other conditions specify the desired individual impact of selected inputs. We keep the maximum value 1 for all inputs except one that is separated and given a lower value (e.g., 0.5). If an input is very important, then its reduction to the half of the maximum value will significantly reduce the output value. According to inputs shown in Table 3.4.2, we expect $W_1 > W_2 > W_3$.

A complete dialog with AnSy is shown in Fig. 3.4.5. The training set contains values from Table 3.4.14 followed by a terminator row containing the values outside [0,1]. The optimum parameters and the resulting WPM function are

$$y = \left(0.546 x_1^{-2.625} + 0.3 x_2^{-2.625} + 0.154 x_3^{-2.625} \right)^{-1/2.625}.$$

With this aggregator we get the output of the trained neuron practically identical to the desired values from Table 3.4.2.

Table 3.4.2 Typical training set for a partial conjunction aggregator.

Inputs			Desired output	Comment
x_1	x_2	x_3	y	
0	1	1	0	Request for hard partial conjunction
0.5	1	1	0.6	Individual impact of the first input
1	0.5	1	0.7	Individual impact of the second input
1	1	0.5	0.8	Individual impact of the third input

The training of preferential neurons can include the search for any subset of parameters. The most frequent situation is illustrated in Fig. 3.4.6, where we want to realize the mapping shown in Table 3.4.2 using the C+ aggregator (andness $\alpha = 0.875$). This aggregator in the case of three variables requires the fixed exponent $r = -3.1135$ (Table 2.3.3). Therefore, the training is now restricted to weights only. The resulting aggregator is

$$y = \left(0.58x_1^{-3.1135} + 0.283x_2^{-3.1135} + 0.137x_3^{-3.1135}\right)^{-1/3.1135}.$$

According to Fig. 3.4.6, this aggregator cannot fit the requested mapping perfectly, but the differences between desired and achieved values shown in Fig. 3.4.6 are rather small (less than 3.4%).

Some GCD aggregators do not support annihilators. Such an example is shown in Fig. 3.4.7 for the case of soft partial disjunction. The training set consists of specifying desired degrees of individual positive effects caused by each input. We set all inputs except one to the mean value 0.5 and then specify the desired output caused by the maximum value 1 of the selected input. Of course, those inputs that produce higher positive effects must have higher weights, and the WPM exponent must be greater than 1. The resulting aggregator is

$$y = \left(0.053x_1^{8.078} + 0.094x_2^{8.078} + 0.162x_3^{8.078} + 0.266x_4^{8.078} + 0.425x_5^{8.078}\right)^{1/8.078}.$$

AnSy trains WPM aggregators, but WPM does not support the hard partial disjunction. Consequently, if we want to create a HPD aggregator based on WPM, then we must use De Morgan's dual of a corresponding HPC aggregator. This technique is exemplified in Fig. 3.4.8. Suppose that we want to create a HPD aggregator so that x_1, x_2, and x_3 affect the output y as shown in Table 3.4.3.

In the first step we must create the training set of the De Morgan dual of HPD, as shown in Table 3.4.3. Then, we perform the training of the De Morgan dual as shown in Fig. 3.4.9. This training produces perfect accuracy with the HPD aggregator:

$$y = 1 - \left[0.1988(1-x_1)^{-0.7536} + 0.3041(1-x_1)^{-0.7536} + 0.4971(1-x_1)^{-0.7536}\right]^{-1/0.7536}.$$

```
.-------------------------------------------------.
| AnSy      -      ANALYSIS  AND  SYNTHESIS        |
| V3.2             OF AGGREGATION FUNCTIONS        |
'-------------------------------------------------'

The following options are available:

1. Fundamental preference aggregation functions
2. Analysis  of Graded Conjunction/Disjunction (GCD)
3. Analysis  of Partial Absorption (CPA & DPA)
4. Synthesis of Graded Conjunction/Disjunction (GCD)
5. Synthesis of Partial Absorption (CPA & DPA)
H. Help
Q. Quit (CR or any input different from 1..5,H causes exit)


Enter the identifier of selected option (1..5, H, Q): 4

THE SYNTHESIS OF GRADED CONJUNCTION/DISJUNCTION

                  W1
    x1 ------>----------.
                  W2    |       GCD Neuron
    x2 ------>--------. |
     .                | |
     .               .---.
     . ------>------>| r |------> y
     .               '---'
     .            Wn  |
    xn ------>--------'

Enter the number of input variables:   n = 3

This function has the following parameters:

Identifier:    1    2    3    4
-------------------------------
Parameter :    W1   W2   W3   r

How many parameters do you want to determine? 4

Enter a training set containing any number of desired I/O values
(a value outside the [0,1] interval denotes the end of input data)

x1  x2  x3     y
------------------
 0   1   1     0
.5   1   1    .6
 1  .5   1    .7
 1   1  .5    .8
 9   9   9     9

THE RESULTING OPTIMUM VALUES OF PARAMETERS

W1 =    0.546033
W2 =    0.299926
W3 =    0.154041
r  =   -2.625496


The minimum value of criterion function = 0.439E-07
The number of function computations    = 241
W1+...+Wn = 0.1000E+01,  Max error of result = 0.961E-06


================================================
  Training set        | Trained GCD neuron
----------------------+-------------------------
  x1    x2    x3    y |    y         Error
----------------------+-------------------------
0.00 1.00 1.00  0.0000 | 0.0000     0.00E+00
0.50 1.00 1.00  0.6000 | 0.6000    -0.62E-07
1.00 0.50 1.00  0.7000 | 0.7000    -0.39E-07
1.00 1.00 0.50  0.8000 | 0.8000    -0.29E-07
================================================
```

Figure 3.4.5 Training of a hard conjunctive GCD/WPM neuron (search for all parameters).

```
Enter the number of input variables:    n =  3

This function has the following parameters:

Identifier:    1    2    3    4
--------------------------------
Parameter :   W1   W2   W3    r

How many parameters do you want to determine? 3
Enter the identifier(s) of selected parameter(s): 1 2 3

Enter fixed values of remaining parameters:
r   = -3.1135

Enter a training set containing any number of desired I/O values
(a value outside the [0,1] interval denotes the end of input data)

x1   x2   x3      y
------------------------
 0    1    1      0
.5    1    1     .6
 1   .5    1     .7
 1    1   .5     .8
 9    9    9      9

THE RESULTING OPTIMUM VALUES OF PARAMETERS

W1 =    0.580017
W2 =    0.283370
W3 =    0.136613

The minimum value of criterion function = 0.112E-01
The number of function computations    =  232  155
W1+...+Wn = 0.1000E+01,   Max error of result = 0.870E-06

===============================================
  Training set           | Trained GCD neuron
-------------------------+---------------------
  x1    x2    x3     y   |    y        Error
-------------------------+---------------------
0.00 1.00 1.00  0.0000   | 0.0000    0.00E+00
0.50 1.00 1.00  0.6000   | 0.5804   -0.20E-01
1.00 0.50 1.00  0.7000   | 0.6904   -0.96E-02
1.00 1.00 0.50  0.8000   | 0.7946   -0.54E-02
===============================================
```

Figure 3.4.6 Training of a hard conjunctive GCD/WPM neuron (search for weights only).

If we want to use aggregators from the WPM.17 set, then the ideal exponent $r = -0.753613$ is closest to the exponent $r = -0.7317$ that corresponds to the CA aggregator with three inputs (see Table 2.3.3). Therefore, we repeat the training with the fixed value of the CA exponent, as shown in Fig. 3.4.10. This gives the following final result (a hard DA aggregator):

$$y = 1 - \left[0.20192(1-x_1)^{-0.7317} + 0.30644(1-x_1)^{-0.7317} + 0.49164(1-x_1)^{-0.7317}\right]^{-1/0.7317}.$$

Previous examples illustrated the benefits of designing GCD aggregators by training preferential neurons. Of course, the efficiency of training depends on the logic correctness of training set. Consequently, it is useful to see examples of wrong or useless training sets. A number of such examples are presented in Table 3.4.4 (individual examples are separated by double line).

```
    THE SYNTHESIS OF GRADED CONJUNCTION/DISJUNCTION

                  W1
    x1 ------>----------.
                  W2    |        GCD Neuron
    x2 ------>--------.  |
     .                |  |
     .                .---.
     .    ------>----->| r |------>  y
     .                `---'
     .                Wn   |
    xn ------>---------'


    Enter the number of input variables:   n =  5

    This function has the following parameters:

    Identifier:    1    2    3    4    5    6
    -------------------------------------------
    Parameter :    W1   W2   W3   W4   W5   r

    How many parameters do you want to determine? 6

    Enter a training set containing any number of desired I/O values
    (a value outside the [0,1] interval denotes the end of input data)

    x1   x2   x3   x4   x5      y
    ------------------------------------
     1   .5   .5   .5   .5     .7
    .5    1   .5   .5   .5     .75
    .5   .5    1   .5   .5     .8
    .5   .5   .5    1   .5     .85
    .5   .5   .5   .5    1     .9
     9    9    9    9    9      9

    THE RESULTING OPTIMUM VALUES OF PARAMETERS

    W1 =    0.052556
    W2 =    0.094535
    W3 =    0.161768
    W4 =    0.266334
    W5 =    0.424806
    r  =    8.078189


    The minimum value of criterion function = 0.124E-06
    The number of function computations      =   819
    W1+...+Wn = 0.1000E+01,  Max error of result = 0.760E-06

    ======================================================
     Training set                    | Trained GCD neuron
    ---------------------------------+--------------------
     x1    x2    x3    x4    x5     y |   y       Error
    ---------------------------------+--------------------
    1.00 0.50 0.50 0.50 0.50  0.7000 | 0.7000    0.15E-07
    0.50 1.00 0.50 0.50 0.50  0.7500 | 0.7500    0.73E-08
    0.50 0.50 1.00 0.50 0.50  0.8000 | 0.8000    0.43E-07
    0.50 0.50 0.50 1.00 0.50  0.8500 | 0.8500   -0.13E-07
    0.50 0.50 0.50 0.50 1.00  0.9000 | 0.9000   -0.67E-07
```

Figure 3.4.7 Training of a soft disjunctive GCD/WPM neuron.

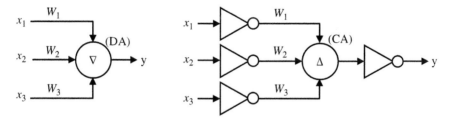

Figure 3.4.8 Creating a hard partial disjunction using De Morgan's dual of WPM.

Table 3.4.3 Training sets in the case of using the De Morgan's dual of HPD.

HPD aggregator				De Morgan Dual of HPD			
Inputs			Desired output	Inputs			Desired output
x_1	x_2	x_3	y	$\bar{x}_1$	$\bar{x}_2$	$\bar{x}_3$	$\bar{y}$
0	0	1	1	1	1	0	0
0.9	0.1	0.1	0.6	0.1	0.9	0.9	0.4
0.1	0.9	0.1	0.7	0.9	0.1	0.9	0.3
0.1	0.1	0.9	0.8	0.9	0.9	0.1	0.2

3.4.3 Analytic Techniques for Selecting Partial Absorption Aggregators

Partial absorption (PA) aggregators are selected by specifying desired penalty and reward (Section 2.6.4). Obviously, the selection of PA parameters is different from the selection of GCD parameters. The GCD parameters (andness and relative importance of inputs) are human percepts, and the parameters can be selected either intuitively, or using tools, such as AnSy. As opposed to that, four parameters of PA aggregators (two weights and two degrees of andness) are not human percepts. They must be derived from human percepts of penalty and reward using appropriate analytic, or tabular, or software tools. The purpose of this section is to present such tools.

3.4.3.1 AH Version of the Conjunctive Partial Absorption Aggregator

The general form of the PA aggregator is the combination of partial conjunction and partial disjunction shown in Figs. 2.6.3 and 2.6.6. Essential properties of PA aggregator are preserved if we use simplified versions shown in Fig, 2.6.8. A particularly interesting simplified version of CPA and DPA are the AH versions shown in Fig. 3.1.10. Those forms of CPA and DPA use fixed aggregators, the arithmetic and harmonic means. Then the adjustment of penalty and reward in a rather wide range can be achieved by selecting weights W_1 and W_2.

```
x1   x2   x3      y
- - - - - - - - - - - - - - - - - -
 1    1    0       0
.1   .9   .9      .4
.9   .1   .9      .3
.9   .9   .1      .2
 9    9    9       9


THE RESULTING OPTIMUM VALUES OF PARAMETERS

W1 =    0.198819
W2 =    0.304083
W3 =    0.497098
r  =   -0.753613


The minimum value of criterion function = 0.156E-06
The number of function computations      =   290   411
W1+...+Wn = 0.1000E+01,   Max error of result = 0.827E-06


=================================================
  Training set                 | Trained GCD neuron
- - - - - - - - - - - - - - - - - - -+- - - - - - - - - - - - - - - - - -
  x1    x2    x3      y        |   y         Error
- - - - - - - - - - - - - - - - - - -+- - - - - - - - - - - - - - - - - -
 1.00 1.00 0.00   0.0000  |  0.0000     0.00E+00
 0.10 0.90 0.90   0.4000  |  0.4000     0.26E-06
 0.90 0.10 0.90   0.3000  |  0.3000     0.15E-06
 0.90 0.90 0.10   0.2000  |  0.2000    -0.22E-07
=================================================
```

Figure 3.4.9 Training of a De Morgan's dual of HPD.

In addition, for these simple forms of CPA and DPA (denoted CPA/AH and DPA/AH)[1] the values of weights can be computed analytically from the desired values of penalty and reward.

The conjunctive partial absorption (CPA) function $z = x \trianglerighteq y$ aggregates the mandatory input x and the optional input y. Generally, the CPA function is used to create the effects of controlled penalty and reward, as follows:

$$z(x,y) = x \trianglerighteq y = \begin{cases} x - P(x,y), & y < x, \\ x & y = x, \\ x + R(x,y), & y > x. \end{cases}$$

---

1 In some cases it is convenient to use notation < type of aggregator>/<input aggregator>:<output aggregator>. For example, it is equivalent and understandable to use the notation CPA/AH or CPA/A:H. However, if the symbol of aggregator uses multiple characters, then it is necessary to use the colon delimiter between input and output aggregators, as in the following examples: CPA/DA:CA, DPA/A:D+, CPA/C- -:C++, and CPA/A:HC-.

```
Enter the number of input variables:    n =   3

This function has the following parameters:

Identifier:     1    2    3    4
--------------------------------
Parameter :    W1   W2   W3    r

How many parameters do you want to determine? 3
Enter the identifier(s) of selected parameter(s) : 1 2 3

Enter fixed values of remaining parameters:
r   = -0.7317

Enter a training set containing any number of desired I/O values
(a value outside the [0,1] interval denotes the end of input data)

x1   x2   x3     y
-----------------
 1    1   0      0
.1   .9   .9    .4
.9   .1   .9    .3
.9   .9   .1    .2
 9    9   9     9

THE RESULTING OPTIMUM VALUES OF PARAMETERS

W1 =    0.201921
W2 =    0.306436
W3 =    0.491643

The minimum value of criterion function = 0.234E-02
The number of function computations      =  195   149
W1+...+Wn = 0.1000E+01,  Max error of result = 0.832E-06

=============================================
 Training set            | Trained GCD neuron
------------------------+--------------------
 x1    x2    x3     y    |    y        Error
------------------------+--------------------
1.00 1.00 0.00  0.0000  | 0.0000    0.00E+00
0.10 0.90 0.90  0.4000  | 0.4012    0.12E-02
0.90 0.10 0.90  0.3000  | 0.3020    0.20E-02
0.90 0.90 0.10  0.2000  | 0.2040    0.40E-02
=============================================
```

Figure 3.4.10 Training of a De Morgan's dual of a hard WPM/DA aggregator.

The penalty $P(x, y)$ and the reward $R(x, y)$ depend on both x, y and the parameters of the CPA aggregator. In extreme cases, $y = 0$ and $y = 1$ the output value of the CPA function is the following:

$$z = x \trianglerighteq 0 = x - P_{\max}(x), \quad 0 \le P_{\max}(x) \le x,$$

$$z = x \trianglerighteq 1 = x + R_{\max}(x), \quad 0 \le R_{\max}(x) \le 1 - x.$$

Table 3.4.4 Examples of errors in the GCD training set.

Inputs			Desired output	Description of error
x_1	x_2	x_3	y	
0	1	1	0	Request for hard partial conjunction
1	0	1	0	Useless, redundant with the first line
1	1	0	0	Useless, redundant with the first line
0	0	1	0	Useless, redundant with the first line
0	1	0	0	Useless, redundant with the first line
1	0	0	0	Useless, redundant with the first line
0	0	0	0	Useless, always holds for all aggregators
1	1	1	1	Useless, always holds for all aggregators
0.5	0.5	0.5	0.7	Violation of idempotency
0.5	0.7	0.9	0.6	Request for partial conjunction
0.5	0.7	0.9	0.6	Useless repetition of the previous line
0.5	0.7	0.9	0.6	Contradiction with the next line
0.5	0.7	0.9	0.8	Contradiction with the previous line
0.5	0.6	0.8	0.7	Request for partial disjunction
0.5	0.6	0.9	0.6	Violation of monotonicity; y should increase
0.3	0.4	0.5	0.4	Request for the arithmetic mean
0.5	0.7	0.9	0.6	Inconsistent request for partial conjunction
0.6	0.8	1	0.9	Inconsistent request for partial disjunction
0	1	1	0	According to Table 3.4.2 and Fig. 3.4.5 these
0.5	1	1	0.6	conditions yield $r = -2.625496$. If we use the
1	0.5	1	0.7	same conditions but require $r=0$ or $r > 0$, the
1	1	0.5	0.8	inconsistency of requests will yield large errors

The value $P_{max}(x)$ is the maximum penalty and the value $R_{max}(x)$ is the maximum reward and they depend on x. For various measures of penalty and reward see Sections 2.6.4 and 2.6.5.

The AH version of CPA (CPA/AH, Fig. 3.1.10) has only two adjustable parameters: the weights W_1 and W_2. In this case, it is possible to compute the value of weights from the desired values of the maximum penalty and the maximum reward. Using the notation $\bar{W}_1 = 1 - W_1$ and $\bar{W}_2 = 1 - W_2$ we have

$$z(x,y) = \frac{(W_1 x + \bar{W}_1 y)x}{\bar{W}_2 x + (W_1 x + \bar{W}_1 y)W_2} = \frac{W_1 x^2 + \bar{W}_1 xy}{W_1 W_2 x + \bar{W}_1 W_2 y + \bar{W}_2 x};$$

$$z(x,0) = \frac{W_1 x}{W_1 W_2 + \bar{W}_2}; \quad z(x,1) = \frac{W_1 x^2 + \bar{W}_1 x}{W_1 W_2 x + \bar{W}_1 W_2 + \bar{W}_2 x}.$$

For the central point $x = \frac{1}{2}$ the maximum penalty P_{max} and the maximum reward R_{max} are

$$P_{max} = \tfrac{1}{2} - z(\tfrac{1}{2},0) = \frac{1}{2} - \frac{1}{2}\frac{W_1}{W_1 W_2 + \bar{W}_2} = \frac{1}{2}\frac{\bar{W}_1 \bar{W}_2}{W_1 W_2 + \bar{W}_2}, \quad P_{max} < \tfrac{1}{2},$$

$$R_{max} = z(\tfrac{1}{2},1) - \tfrac{1}{2} = \frac{1}{2}\frac{\bar{W}_1 \bar{W}_2}{\bar{W}_1 W_2 + 1}, \quad R_{max} < \tfrac{1}{2}.$$

The maximum normalized penalty and reward (with respect to the central point $\tfrac{1}{2}$) are:

$$p_{max} = \frac{P_{max}}{\tfrac{1}{2}} = \frac{\bar{W}_1 \bar{W}_2}{W_1 W_2 + \bar{W}_2},$$

$$r_{max} = \frac{R_{max}}{\tfrac{1}{2}} = \frac{\bar{W}_1 \bar{W}_2}{\bar{W}_1 W_2 + 1}.$$

The normalized penalty p_{max} denotes the relative decrease of z caused $y = 0$ in the case where $x = \tfrac{1}{2}$. Generally, $p_{max}(x) = [x - z(x,0)]/x$ and $z(x,0) = x$ $[1 - p_{max}(x)]$. Similarly, for reward, $r_{max}(x) = [z(x,1) - x]/x$ and $z(x,1) = x[1 + r_{max}(x)]$. To eliminate the dependence on x, we used the central point $x = \tfrac{1}{2}$. So, if $p_{max} = 0.2$ then $z(\tfrac{1}{2},0) = \tfrac{1}{2}(1 - 0.2) = 0.4$. Similarly, if $r_{max} = 0.2$ then $z(\tfrac{1}{2},1) = \tfrac{1}{2}(1 + 0.2) = 0.6$.

Typically, p_{max} and r_{max} are small values and $p_{max} > r_{max}$. The reason for using $p_{max} > r_{max}$ is in the conjunctive nature of CPA: we expect a simultaneous satisfaction of the mandatory input x and the optional input y. Since low values of y damage the desired simultaneity, such negative effects should be stronger than the positive compensatory effects of high values of y. Of course, the situation is different in the case of disjunctive partial absorption (DPA) where we want to give higher compensatory power to large values of the optional input.

If we select desired values of p_{max} and r_{max}, then we can compute W_1 and W_2 from the following equations:

$$\bar{W}_1 \bar{W}_2 - p_{max} W_1 W_2 - p_{max} \bar{W}_2 = 0,$$

$$\bar{W}_1 \bar{W}_2 - r_{max} \bar{W}_1 W_2 - r_{max} = 0.$$

After substituting $\bar{W}_1 = r_{max}/(\bar{W}_2 - r_{max} W_2)$ from the second equation into the first equation, we get the following results:

$$W_1 = \frac{2 r_{max}(1 - p_{max})}{p_{max} + r_{max}},$$

$$W_2 = \frac{p_{max} - r_{max}}{p_{max} - r_{max} + 2 p_{max} r_{max}}, \quad p_{max} > r_{max}.$$

For this aggregator the maximum penalty must be greater than the maximum reward. For example, if we select $p_{max} = 1/3$ and $r_{max} = 1/5$, then the resulting weights are $W_1 = W_2 = 0.5$. The values of W_1 and W_2 can also be graphically presented as functions of p_{max} and r_{max}, as shown in [DUJ14a]. Similarly, we can use tables such as Table 3.1.6.

3.4.3.2 AH Version of the Disjunctive Partial Absorption Aggregator

Disjunctive aggregators can be organized as De Morgan's duals of corresponding conjunctive aggregators: $W_1 x_1 \nabla W_2 x_2 = 1 - W_1(1-x_1) \Delta W_2(1-x_2)$ (Figs. 3.1.10 and 3.4.8). So, a disjunctive aggregator $\underline{H}$, which is a De Morgan's dual of the harmonic mean H, is the following:

$$H = W_1 x_1 \Delta W_2 x_2 = \frac{x_1 x_2}{W_1 x_2 + x_1 W_2},$$

$$\underline{H} = W_1 x_1 \nabla W_2 x_2 = \overline{W_1 x_1 \nabla W_2 x_2} = \overline{W_1 \bar{x}_1 \Delta W_2 \bar{x}_2}$$

$$= 1 - W_1(1-x_1) \Delta W_2(1-x_2) = 1 - \frac{\bar{x}_1 \bar{x}_2}{W_1 \bar{x}_2 + \bar{x}_1 W_2} = \frac{x_1 W_1 \bar{x}_2 + \bar{x}_1 W_2 x_2}{W_1 \bar{x}_2 + \bar{x}_1 W_2},$$

$$\bar{x}_1 = (1-x_1), \quad \bar{x}_2 = (1-x_2).$$

Using the harmonic mean H or its De Morgan's dual $\underline{H}$ we can create the DPA/A$\underline{H}$ aggregator shown in Fig. 3.1.10. Its analytic form is:

$$z(x,y) = x \overline{\rhd} y = 1 - \frac{[1 - (W_1 x + \bar{W}_1 y)] \bar{x}}{\bar{W}_2 \bar{x} + [1 - (W_1 x + \bar{W}_1 y)] W_2},$$

$$z(x,0) = 1 - \frac{(1 - W_1 x) \bar{x}}{\bar{W}_2 \bar{x} + (1 - W_1 x) W_2}; \quad z(x,1) = 1 - \frac{[1 - (W_1 x + \bar{W}_1)] \bar{x}}{\bar{W}_2 \bar{x} + [1 - (W_1 x + \bar{W}_1)] W_2}.$$

In the central point $x = \frac{1}{2}$ we have:

$$z(\tfrac{1}{2},0) = 1 - \frac{(1 - W_1 \tfrac{1}{2}) \tfrac{1}{2}}{\bar{W}_2 \tfrac{1}{2} + (1 - W_1 \tfrac{1}{2}) W_2} = \frac{2 W_2 - 2 W_1 W_2 + W_1}{2 + 2 W_2 - 2 W_1 W_2};$$

$$p_{max} = \frac{\tfrac{1}{2} - z(\tfrac{1}{2},0)}{\tfrac{1}{2}} = 1 - 2z(\tfrac{1}{2},0) = \frac{1 - W_1 - W_2 + W_1 W_2}{1 + W_2 - W_1 W_2} = \frac{\bar{W}_1 \bar{W}_2}{1 + \bar{W}_1 W_2};$$

$$z(x,1) = 1 - \frac{[1 - (W_1 \tfrac{1}{2} + \bar{W}_1)] \tfrac{1}{2}}{\bar{W}_2 \tfrac{1}{2} + [1 - (W_1 \tfrac{1}{2} + \bar{W}_1)] W_2} = \frac{2 - 2 W_2 + 2 W_1 W_2 - W_1}{2 - 2 W_2 + 2 W_1 W_2};$$

$$r_{max} = \frac{z(\tfrac{1}{2},1) - \tfrac{1}{2}}{\tfrac{1}{2}} = 2z(\tfrac{1}{2},1) - 1 = \frac{1 - W_1 - W_2 + W_1 W_2}{1 - W_2 + W_1 W_2} = \frac{\bar{W}_1 \bar{W}_2}{1 - \bar{W}_1 W_2};$$

$$\frac{r_{max}}{p_{max}} = \frac{1 + \bar{W}_1 W_2}{1 - \bar{W}_1 W_2} > 1, \quad \therefore r_{max} > p_{max}.$$

These results are symmetrical to the CPA/A$\underline{H}$ results. For example, if $W_1 = W_2 = \frac{1}{2}$ then $r_{max} = 1/3$, $p_{max} = 1/5$ (in the case of CPA/A$\underline{H}$, we had $p_{max} = 1/3$, $r_{max} = 1/5$). The equations for computing W_1 and W_2 from r_{max} and p_{max} are the following:

$$p_{max} + p_{max} \bar{W}_1 W_2 - \bar{W}_1 \bar{W}_2 = 0;$$

$$r_{max} - r_{max} \bar{W}_1 W_2 - \bar{W}_1 \bar{W}_2 = 0.$$

The solutions are:

$$W_1 = \frac{2p_{max}(1 - r_{max})}{r_{max} + p_{max}};$$

$$W_2 = \frac{r_{max} - p_{max}}{r_{max} - p_{max} + 2r_{max}p_{max}}, \quad r_{max} > p_{max}.$$

If we compare these solutions and the solutions in the case of the CPA/AH aggregator, we find exactly the same expressions except that the penalty p_{max} and the reward r_{max} swap their places. This symmetry is caused by De Morgan's duality.

The harmonic mean ($\alpha = 0.77$) and the WPM.17 aggregator CA ($\alpha = 0.75$) are very close, and so are CPA/AH and CPA/A:CA. Similarly to the case of CPA/AH aggregator, De Morgan's dual of the harmonic mean is very close to De Morgan's dual of the CA aggregator (the hard DA aggregator, $\alpha = 0.25$). Therefore, the formulas for computing W_1 and W_2 as functions of p_{max} and r_{max} can be used as an approximation for computing the parameters of the CPA/A:CA and DPA/A:DA aggregators that are frequently used in LSP evaluation models. Of course, that assumes the use of central point models of penalty and reward, but not other models presented in Section 2.6.4.

3.4.4 Boundary Penalty/Reward Tables for Selecting Partial Absorption Aggregators

In the case of CPA aggregator that combines an arithmetic mean and a hard partial conjunction function (Fig. 2.6.3) the adjustable parameters are the weights W_1, W_2, and the andness of the hard partial conjunction. If the hard partial conjunction is implemented as a weighted power mean, then it is easy to see that $x \trianglerighteq 0$ is a linear function of x and $x \trianglerighteq 1$ is a nonlinear function of x. According to Section 2.6.4 a convenient method for defining penalty and reward are the boundary forms introduced in [DUJ79a]. The mean boundary penalty and reward can be computed for various combinations of weights and andness of the hard partial conjunction. If $\bar{\Delta} = CA$, then the corresponding mean boundary penalty and reward pairs for CPA/A:CA are shown in Table 3.4.5, and for $\bar{\Delta} = C+$ the corresponding results for CPA/A:C+ are shown in Table 3.4.6. Similar tables for all hard conjunctive aggregators can be found in [DUJ79a].

The method of using these tables is simple. After specifying a desired penalty/reward pair, we try to find the closest similar pair in Tables 3.4.5 and 3.4.6. The closest pair is then used to determine W_1, W_2, and the best HPC aggregator. This process is illustrated in four examples presented in Table 3.4.7 where we select between the best pairs of CPA/A:CA and CPA/A:C+. If we use more tables, the likelihood of finding a good match increases. Not surprisingly, it is

Table 3.4.5 Penalty (negative %) and the mean boundary reward (positive %) for the CPA/A:CA.

CPA/A:CA		W_1 0.1	0.2	0.3	0.4	0.5	0.6	0.7	0.8	0.9
W_2	0.1	−88.8 / 64.0	−77.9 / 57.8	−67.4 / 51.5	−57.2 / 45.0	−47.1 / 38.2	−37.3 / 31.3	−27.7 / 24.0	−18.3 / 16.5	−9.1 / 8.5
	0.2	−87.2 / 49.4	−75.5 / 45.0	−64.4 / 40.4	−53.9 / 35.7	−44.0 / 30.6	−34.5 / 25.4	−25.3 / 19.8	−16.6 / 13.8	−8.1 / 7.3
	0.3	−85.3 / 38.7	−72.5 / 35.5	−60.9 / 32.1	−50.3 / 28.5	−40.5 / 24.7	−31.4 / 20.6	−22.8 / 16.3	−14.8 / 11.5	−7.2 / 6.2
	0.4	−82.8 / 30.3	−68.8 / 27.9	−56.7 / 25.4	−46.1 / 22.6	−36.6 / 19.7	−28.0 / 16.6	−20.1 / 13.2	−12.9 / 9.4	−6.2 / 5.1
	0.5	−79.4 / 23.3	−64.2 / 21.6	−51.7 / 19.7	−41.3 / 17.7	−32.3 / 15.5	−24.3 / 13.1	−17.3 / 10.5	−11.0 / 7.6	−5.2 / 4.2
	0.6	−74.8 / 17.4	−58.2 / 16.1	−45.7 / 14.8	−35.7 / 13.3	−27.4 / 11.7	−20.3 / 10.0	−14.3 / 8.0	−8.9 / 5.8	−4.2 / 3.3
	0.7	−68.1 / 12.2	−50.4 / 11.4	−38.2 / 10.5	−29.0 / 9.5	−21.8 / 8.4	−16.0 / 7.1	−11.0 / 5.8	−6.8 / 4.2	−3.2 / 2.4
	0.8	−57.4 / 7.7	−39.6 / 7.2	−28.7 / 6.6	−21.2 / 6.0	−15.6 / 5.3	−11.2 / 4.6	−7.6 / 3.7	−4.6 / 2.7	−2.1 / 1.6
	0.9	−38.9 / 3.6	−24.0 / 3.4	−16.4 / 3.1	−11.7 / 2.9	−8.3 / 2.5	−5.9 / 2.2	−3.9 / 1.8	−2.4 / 1.3	−1.1 / 0.8

Table 3.4.6 Penalty (negative %) and the mean boundary reward (positive %) for the CPA/A:C+.

CPA/A:C+		W_1 0.1	0.2	0.3	0.4	0.5	0.6	0.7	0.8	0.9
W_2	0.1	−89.7 / 37.0	−79.4 / 34.7	−69.1 / 32.1	−58.8 / 29.3	−48.6 / 26.1	−38.5 / 22.5	−28.5 / 18.3	−18.7 / 13.4	−9.2 / 7.5
	0.2	−89.3 / 26.9	−78.7 / 25.4	−68.1 / 23.7	−57.5 / 21.9	−47.0 / 19.7	−36.8 / 17.2	−26.9 / 14.3	−17.3 / 10.7	−8.3 / 6.2
	0.3	−88.9 / 20.5	−77.9 / 19.5	−66.9 / 18.3	−55.9 / 16.9	−45.2 / 15.4	−34.9 / 13.6	−25.0 / 11.4	−15.8 / 8.7	−7.5 / 5.2
	0.4	−88.4 / 15.8	−76.9 / 15.0	−65.4 / 14.2	−54.1 / 13.2	−43.1 / 12.0	−32.7 / 10.7	−23.0 / 9.0	−14.2 / 7.0	−6.6 / 4.2
	0.5	−87.8 / 12.0	−75.7 / 11.5	−63.6 / 10.8	−51.8 / 10.1	−40.5 / 9.3	−30.0 / 8.3	−20.6 / 7.0	−12.4 / 5.5	−5.6 / 3.4
	0.6	−87.0 / 8.9	−74.1 / 8.5	−61.3 / 8.1	−48.9 / 7.5	−37.3 / 6.9	−26.9 / 6.2	−17.9 / 5.3	−10.5 / 4.2	−4.6 / 2.6
	0.7	−85.9 / 6.2	−71.9 / 6.0	−58.1 / 5.7	−45.1 / 5.3	−33.2 / 4.9	−23.0 / 4.4	−14.7 / 3.8	−8.3 / 3.0	−3.5 / 1.9
	0.8	−84.2 / 3.9	−68.5 / 3.7	−53.3 / 3.6	−39.4 / 3.4	−27.4 / 3.1	−17.9 / 2.8	−10.9 / 2.4	−5.9 / 1.9	−2.4 / 1.2
	0.9	−80.7 / 1.8	−61.8 / 1.8	−44.2 / 1.7	−29.4 / 1.6	−18.4 / 1.5	−10.9 / 1.3	−6.2 / 1.2	−3.1 / 0.9	−1.2 / 0.6

Table 3.4.7 Examples of the use of penalty/reward tables for selecting the CPA aggregator.

Desired mean penalty/reward	Operator	Closest pair	Weights		Select
			W_1	W_2	
−20/10	A:CA	−20.3/10.0	0.6	0.6	yes
	A:C+	−20.6/7.0	0.7	0.5	no
−25/15	A:CA	−24.3/13.1	0.6	0.5	yes
	A:C+	−26.9/14.3	0.7	0.2	no
−35/15	A:CA	−35.7/13.3	0.4	0.6	no
	A:C+	−34.9/13.6	0.6	0.3	yes
−45/15	A:CA	−45.7/14.8	0.3	0.6	no
	A:C+	−45.2/15.4	0.5	0.3	yes

possible to develop software tools that provide high accuracy and simplicity of use. One such tool that supports both numeric and verbal communication is AGOPcalc [SEA11a].

Penalty/reward tables can also use the desired penalty and reward as inputs. Table 3.1.7 is an example of this approach. For example, if we want the penalty of 35% and the mean reward of 20%, then it is necessary to use aggregators A and CA and weights $W_1 = 53\%$ and $W_2 = 37\%$. The CPA/A:CA can model only aggregators where penalty is greater than reward. However, if the arithmetic mean is replaced by a soft DA aggregator, then we can create CPA/DA:CA aggregators where the reward is greater than penalty. For example, if we want the penalty of 35% and the mean reward of 40%, then it is necessary to use CPA/DA:CA with weights $W_1 = 10\%$ and $W_2 = 30\%$.

3.4.5 Selecting Partial Absorption Aggregators by Training Preferential Neurons

Conjunctive and disjunctive partial absorption aggregators $z = x \trianglerighteq y$ and $z = x \overline{\triangleright} y$ can also be interpreted as preferential neurons. In such cases, we assume the combination of two general independent WPM aggregators shown in Fig. 3.4.11. The main input x is either mandatory or sufficient and the input y is optional. This model of CPA and DPA has four adjustable parameters: two weights (W_1 and W_2) and two exponents (q and r). Both CPA and DPA are represented by the following general model:

$$z = \left[W_2 x^r + (1 - W_2)(W_1 x^q + (1 - W_1)y^q)^{r/q} \right]^{1/r}.$$

The synthesis of CPA and DPA aggregators follows similar procedure as the synthesis of GCD. A technique that is useful for defining parameters of CPA is summarized in Table 3.4.8, and a similar technique for specifying properties of

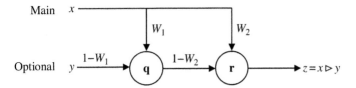

Figure 3.4.11 CPA and DPA aggregators based on two WPM aggregators.

Table 3.4.8 Typical training set for conjunctive partial absorption.

Inputs		Desired output	Comment
x	y	$z = x \trianglerighteq y$	
0	1	0	Defining x as a mandatory input
1	0	1 – penalty	Specification of desired penalty
0.5	0	0.5 – penalty	Alternative specification of desired penalty
0.5	1	0.5 + reward	Specification of desired reward
a	b	c	Additional conditions: $\min(a,b) < c < \max(a,b)$

Table 3.4.9 Typical training set for disjunctive partial absorption.

Inputs		Desired output	Comment
x	y	$z = x \overline{\triangleright} y$	
1	0	1	Defining x as a sufficient input
1	0	1 – penalty	Specification of desired penalty
0	1	reward	Specification of desired reward
0.5	1	0.5 + reward	Alternative specification of desired reward
a	b	c	Additional conditions: $\min(a,b) < c < \max(a,b)$

DPA is shown in Table 3.4.9. The need for avoiding inconsistent and useless conditions is similar as in the case of GCD.

If we use only three main conditions (selection of CPA/DPA type, the definition of penalty, and the definition of reward), then we can comfortably determine two (or more) parameters. Typically, we can approximately select the exponents q and r that correspond to some desired WPM-based type and then ask AnSy to compute the optimum values of weights W_1 and W_2. In cases where we have sufficient information to provide more than three conditions in the training set tables, we can determine more parameters, including, if necessary, all four parameters. An example of synthesis of the CPA aggregator is shown in Fig. 3.4.12. We decided to use the arithmetic mean and the harmonic mean ($q = 1, r = -1$) and we want to determine the optimum weights W_1 and W_2 for penalty of 20% and approximate reward of 10% in selected points (note that this is different from mean boundary penalty/reward in Table 3.4.7. The errors of the resulting model are negligible.

```
THE SYNTHESIS OF PARTIAL ABSORPTION FUNCTION

   x  ------>--------.-------->----------.
                     |                   |              PA Neuron
                     |W1                 |W2
                     |                   |
        1-W1    .---.           1-W2    .---.
   y ---------->| q |------------->| r |------>  z
                `---'                   `---'

   This function has the following parameters:

   Identifier:    1    2    3    4
   ------------------------------
   Parameter :    W1   W2   q    r

   How many parameters do you want to determine? 2
   Enter the identifier(s) of selected parameter(s): 1 2

   Enter fixed values of remaining parameters:
   q  = 1
   r  = -1

   Enter a training set containing any number of desired x,y,z values
   (a value outside the [0,1] interval denotes the end of data)

   x    y    z
   -----------
   0    1    0
   1    0    .8
   .5   1    .55
   9    9    9
```

THE RESULTING OPTIMUM VALUES OF PARAMETERS

```
W1 =    0.533334
W2 =    0.714286

The minimum value of criterion function = 0.669E-07
The number of function computations      =   82
The achieved maximum error of result     = 0.000001
```

```
==========================================================
  T r a i n i n g    s e t   |    Trained PA neuron
-----------------------------+----------------------------
      x       y       z      |     z          Error
-----------------------------+----------------------------
   0.000   1.000   0.0000    |   0.0000     0.0000000
   1.000   0.000   0.8000    |   0.8000     0.0000001
   0.500   1.000   0.5500    |   0.5500     0.0000000
==========================================================
```

Figure 3.4.12 A typical example of AnSy dialog for the synthesis of a CPA aggregator.

In the next example (Fig. 3.4.13), we determine three parameters (all except the arithmetic mean, $q = 1$) in the case where the desired penalty is 40% and the desired reward is 20%. Again, we have the maximum accuracy of results. The output aggregator is close to the geometric mean (the exponent r is close to 0). If we want to analyze the resulting aggregator, AnSy provides a sensitivity analysis and its draft graphs. The sensitivity curves are shown in Fig. 3.4.14 for the referent point $x = y = z = 0.5$. If the mandatory input takes the value $x = 0$ then $z = 0$. However, if the optional input takes the value $y = 0$ then $z = 0.3$ (the referent output 0.5 penalized 40%). If the optional input takes the value $y = 1$ then $z = 0.6$ (the referent output 0.5 rewarded 20%). So, the penalty and reward are explicitly visible at the edges of the $z = 0.5 \unrhd y$ curve (see also Fig. 3.7.5).

The simultaneous adjustability of q and r permits the creation of CPA aggregators in which the reward is greater than the penalty. An example where the penalty is 20% and the reward is 40% is presented in Fig. 3.4.15, where AnSy is requested to compute all the four CPA parameters. That is done with perfect accuracy. However, there is a significant difference between the sensitivity curve $z = x \unrhd 0.5$ in Figs. 3.4.14 and 3.4.15. Can you see and explain the difference?

In Section 2.2.6 ($\mathbf{P_{32}}$), we discussed logic inconsistencies, and one of them is visible in Fig. 3.4.15. The CPA aggregator is, by definition, aggregating the mandatory (i.e., very significant) input x and the optional (rather insignificant) input y. This natural property of this aggregator is artificially modified by requesting a high reward (40%) caused by the optional input. If the optional input can cause a reward of 40%, while its penalty is only 20%, it follows that y is optional but certainly not insignificant. The significance of y affects the values of parameters, and the resulting problem is very visible for $x < 0.1$. Indeed, on one hand we ask x to be mandatory (i.e., $0 \unrhd 0.5 = 0$) and on the other hand we give y such a compensative power that $0.1 \unrhd 0.5 = 0.27$, forcing the curve $z(x) = x \unrhd 0.5$ to make a sharp turn in the interval $0 < x < 0.1$. Now, $0.01 \unrhd 0.5 = 0.12$ amplifying 12 times a tiny (and indiscernible) increment of x suitability, as well as a huge first derivative $\partial z / \partial x$ in the vicinity of $x = 0$. Of course, huge first derivatives are not an observable property of human evaluation reasoning. So, by detecting hypersensitivity, we have proved the presence of a logic inconsistency. Indeed, in human evaluation reasoning, where we deal with percepts of suitability, an imperceptible increment of input cannot cause a significant increment of output.

The question that naturally follows from the above analysis is whether the CPA model in Fig. 3.4.15 is now fully disqualified. From a practical standpoint, it is not. There is no problem in the point $x = 0$. The problems are certainly visible in the range $0 < x < 0.1$. However, if $x > 0.1$ the results seem to be reasonable and can be acceptable. Therefore, if we are solving an evaluation problem where mandatory requirements are regularly satisfied (e.g., usually $x > 0.5$), then it is highly unlikely to encounter disqualifying results. This example is primarily a

```
THE SYNTHESIS OF PARTIAL ABSORPTION FUNCTION

    x ------>-------.-------->---------.
                    |                  |            PA Neuron
                    |W1                |W2
                    |                  |
         1-W1    .---.      1-W2    .---.
    y ---------->| q |------------->| r |------->  z
                 `---'              `---'

    This function has the following parameters:

    Identifier:    1    2    3    4
    ------------------------------------
    Parameter :    W1   W2   q    r

    How many parameters do you want to determine? 3
    Enter the identifier(s) of selected parameter(s): 1 2 4

    Enter fixed values of remaining parameters:
    q = 1

    Enter a training set containing any number of desired x,y,z values
    (a value outside the [0,1] interval denotes the end of data)

    x    y    z
    -----------
    0    1    0
    1    0    .6
    .5   1    .6
    9    9    9

    THE RESULTING OPTIMUM VALUES OF PARAMETERS

    W1 =    0.205040
    W2 =    0.685468
    r  =   -0.045538

    The minimum value of criterion function = 0.319E-09
    The number of function computations     = 172
    The achieved maximum error of result    = 0.000000

    ========================================================
    T r a i n i n g    s e t   |   Trained PA neuron
    ---------------------------+----------------------------
       x       y       z       |      z           Error
    ---------------------------+----------------------------
      0.000   1.000   0.0000   |    0.0000      0.0000000
      1.000   0.000   0.6000   |    0.6000      0.0000000
      0.500   1.000   0.6000   |    0.6000      0.0000000
    ========================================================
    Do you want to analyze this function (yes/NO) ? y

    Enter    x, y :  0.5   0.5

    Parameters: W1 = 0.21    W2 = 0.69    q =    1.000000   r =    -0.045538
    Inputs:     x  = 0.50    y  = 0.50
    Result:     z  = 0.500000
                                             SENSITIVITY ANALYSIS
    ==================================================================
    x = 0.000 0.100 0.200 0.300 0.400 0.500 0.600 0.700 0.800 0.900 1.000
    z = 0.000 0.155 0.255 0.343 0.423 0.500 0.574 0.645 0.715 0.784 0.852
    ------------------------------------------------------------------
    y = 0.000 0.100 0.200 0.300 0.400 0.500 0.600 0.700 0.800 0.900 1.000
    z = 0.300 0.362 0.407 0.443 0.473 0.500 0.524 0.545 0.565 0.583 0.600
    ==================================================================

    Do you want draft graphs of the sensitivity functions (yes/NO)? y
```

Figure 3.4.13 The synthesis of a CPA aggregator and its sensitivity analysis.

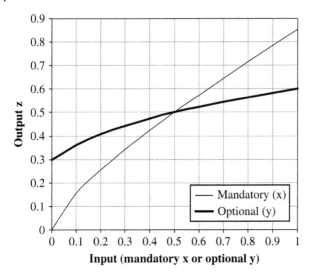

Figure 3.4.14 Sensitivity curves $z = x \unrhd 0.5$ and $z = 0.5 \unrhd y$.

gentle warning. It is important that evaluators can notice, identify, and minimize or avoid inconsistent logic conditions and requirements. Perfect precision is not the main characteristic of human evaluation reasoning. Evaluation reasoning can frequently include coarse granularity, and the precision of aggregation models should be commensurate with the precision of human-generated inputs.

3.4.6 Nonstationary LSP Criteria

All LSP criteria have parameters. The most important parameters are andness/orness and weights. In addition, parameters also include vertex coordinates of elementary criteria. The majority of LSP criteria have constant values of parameters. We call such criteria *stationary* (or *static*). Less frequently, LSP criteria can be *nonstationary* (or *dynamic*), and that means that the parameters are not constant but functions of input attributes. Generally, if we use nonstationary WPM aggregation, both weights $W_1(\mathbf{x})$, ..., $W_n(\mathbf{x})$ and andness $\alpha(\mathbf{x})$ can be functions of attributes $\mathbf{x} = (x_1,...,x_n)$:

$$M(\mathbf{x}) = \left(\sum_{i=1}^{n} W_i(\mathbf{x}) x_i^{r(\alpha(\mathbf{x}))} \right)^{1/r(\alpha(\mathbf{x}))},$$

$$\sum_{i=1}^{n} W_i(\mathbf{x}) = 1, \quad 0 \le \alpha(\mathbf{x}) \le 1, \quad -\infty \le r(\alpha(\mathbf{x})) \le +\infty.$$

```
x     y     z
- - - - - - - - - - -
0     1     0
.5    0     .4
.5    1     .7
9     9     9

THE RESULTING OPTIMUM VALUES OF PARAMETERS

W1 =     0.622960
W2 =     0.091150
q  =     1.941974
r  =    -0.702554

The minimum value of criterion function = 0.125E-07
The number of function computations      = 217
The achieved maximum error of result     = 0.000001


=============================================================
  T r a i n i n g   s e t    |    Trained PA neuron
- - - - - - - - - - - - - - - - - - +- - - - - - - - - - - - - - - - - - - -
       x       y       z     |       z        Error
- - - - - - - - - - - - - - - - - - +- - - - - - - - - - - - - - - - - - - -
     0.000   1.000   0.0000  |     0.0000   0.0000000
     0.500   0.000   0.4000  |     0.4000   0.0000000
     0.500   1.000   0.7000  |     0.7000   0.0000000
=============================================================
```

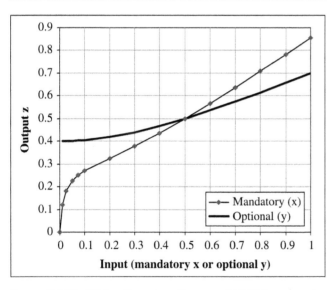

Figure 3.4.15 CPA function where the reward (40%) is greater than the penalty (20%).

In this case, attributes also affect the andness, and the selected andness determines the exponent of WPM. While this approach is theoretically possible, the complexity of such solutions in practice is regularly too high. To illustrate nonstationary criteria, let us use a simple parking problem.

A homebuyer has two cars and can keep them in a home garage and/or on the street in front of the home. The overall quality of parking P is a function of the quality of garage G and the quality of street parking S. Following are the possible values of G and S:

$$G = \begin{cases} 0, & \text{(the home garage is not available)} \\ \frac{1}{2}, & \text{(the home garage for one car is available)} \\ 1, & \text{(the home garage for two cars is available).} \end{cases}$$

$$S = \begin{cases} 0, & \text{(the street parking is not available)} \\ \frac{1}{2}, & \text{(the street parking is frequently available)} \\ 1, & \text{(the street parking is always available).} \end{cases}$$

Ideally, the home should have a garage for two cars, and in such a case the street parking is not important. Let us first evaluate the quality of parking using the simple arithmetic mean:

$$P = (1 - W(G))G + W(G)S, \quad 0 \le W(G) \le 1.$$

The parameter W is the importance of good street parking, and in this case it is not constant, but a function of the availability of garage. If the home garage for two cars is available, then the quality of street parking is fully negligible, i.e., $W(1) = 0$. On the other hand, if the garage is not available, then the only parking is on the street, i.e., $W(0) = 1$. If the garage holds only one car, then the garage and the street parking are equally important, i.e., $W(\frac{1}{2}) = \frac{1}{2}$. In other words, the weight of street parking can be expressed as $W(G) = 1 - G$ yielding the following criterion:

$$P(G,S) = G^2 + (1 - G)S = G(G - S) + S.$$

This function is presented in Fig. 3.4.16 (a). Of course, this nonstationary arithmetic mean criterion can be easily criticized from the standpoint that for $G = 0$ we have $P = S$ and this might be questionable because it is not penalizing the complete absence of garage. In addition, if there is garage for a single car and no street parking ($G = \frac{1}{2}$, $S = 0$), then there is no place for the second car, but our criterion still returns $P = \frac{1}{4} > 0$ what is not acceptable. So, we might modify the criterion by requesting good street parking whenever we don't have the home garage for two cars. In this case, we can use the conditional expression $W(G) = (G < 1 \ ? \ 1 : 0)$, or equivalently

$$P(G,S) = (G < 1 \ ? \ S : G).$$

Unfortunately, this criterion, shown in Fig. 3.4.16 (b), offers no credit for the single car garage.

(a) $\quad W(G) = 1-G$

P(G,S)		S		
		0	½	1
	0	0	½	1
G	½	¼	½	¾
	1	1	1	1

(b) $\quad W(G) = (G < 1 \,?\, 1 : 0)$

P(G,S)		S		
		0	½	1
	0	0	½	1
G	½	0	½	1
	1	1	1	1

(c) $\quad$ General case

z(x,y)		y		
		y_1	y_2	y_3
	x_1	z_{11}	z_{12}	z_{13}
x	x_2	z_{21}	z_{22}	z_{23}
	x_3	z_{31}	z_{32}	z_{33}

(d) $\quad$ Compound attribute P(G,S)

P(G,S)		S		
		0	½	1
	0	0	¼	½
G	½	0	½	¾
	1	1	1	1

Figure 3.4.16 Three versions of the parking criterion.

To improve this criterion, we might define the weight as a function of both G and S, and create a table of desired weights $W(G, S)$ and then use $P = (1 - W(G,S))G + W(G,S)S$. A general form of such 3×3 case is shown in Fig. 3.4.16 (c) and can be modeled using Lagrange interpolation:

$$z = \frac{(x-x_2)(x-x_3)}{(x_1-x_2)(x_1-x_3)}\left[z_{11}\frac{(y-y_2)(y-y_3)}{(y_1-y_2)(y_1-y_3)} + z_{12}\frac{(y-y_1)(y-y_3)}{(y_2-y_1)(y_2-y_3)} + z_{13}\frac{(y-y_1)(y-y_2)}{(y_3-y_1)(y_3-y_2)}\right]$$
$$+ \frac{(x-x_1)(x-x_3)}{(x_2-x_1)(x_2-x_3)}\left[z_{21}\frac{(y-y_2)(y-y_3)}{(y_1-y_2)(y_1-y_3)} + z_{22}\frac{(y-y_1)(y-y_3)}{(y_2-y_1)(y_2-y_3)} + z_{23}\frac{(y-y_1)(y-y_2)}{(y_3-y_1)(y_3-y_2)}\right]$$
$$+ \frac{(x-x_1)(x-x_2)}{(x_3-x_1)(x_3-x_2)}\left[z_{31}\frac{(y-y_2)(y-y_3)}{(y_1-y_2)(y_1-y_3)} + z_{32}\frac{(y-y_1)(y-y_3)}{(y_2-y_1)(y_2-y_3)} + z_{33}\frac{(y-y_1)(y-y_2)}{(y_3-y_1)(y_3-y_2)}\right].$$

Fortunately, instead of using the nonstationary arithmetic mean aggregator, we can define $P(G, S)$ simply as a compound attribute in the range $0 \le P(G,S) \le 1$ and then use the criterion $Crit(P(G,S)) = \{(0,0),(1,1)\}$. For example, the criterion can be modified as shown in Fig. 3.4.16 (d). This criterion properly specifies all requirements: in all acceptable cases we can park two cars and full satisfaction is not possible unless we have a garage. After inserting the values from Fig. 3.4.16 (d) in the Lagrange interpolation formula, we get the following improved criterion for the suitability of parking:

$$P(G,S) = S(1-G)(½ + 4G - 2GS) + G(2G-1), \quad Crit(P(G,S)) = \{(0,0),(1,1)\}.$$

So, instead of making complex nonstationary aggregators, this problem is easier solved as an interpolative elementary attribute criterion. Of course, this example is not a proof that nonstationary criteria are useless. However, it shows that the complexities of highly nonlinear nonstationary criteria are acceptable only after we prove that a standard simple LSP criterion cannot be designed.

3.4.7 Graphic Notation of Aggregation Structures

Analytic notation of logic operators is not appropriate for aggregation structures that contain more than two aggregators. On the other hand, the graphic notation of aggregation operators is understandable and convenient, regardless the size of the aggregation structure. We use two types of graphic notation of logic operators: standard diagrams and rectangular diagrams, shown in Table 3.4.10. The standard diagrams are general and can be used to describe any kind of aggregation structure, including those that are not idempotent. The rectangular diagrams have advantage that all their components are

Table 3.4.10 Typical standard and rectangular diagrams of basic logic operators.

Operator	Standard diagram	Rectangular diagram
Partial conjunction (PC)	Input 1 W_1, Input 2 W_2 — CA — Output, Input 3 W_3	Input 1 W_1 / Input 2 W_2 CA Output / Input 3 W_3
Partial disjunction (PD)	Input 1 W_1, Input 2 W_2 — DA — Output, Input 3 W_3	Input 1 W_1 / Input 2 W_2 DA Output / Input 3 W_3
Conjunctive partial absorption (CPA/A:CA)	Mandatory — $(-P, +R)$; W_1 W_2; Optional $\frac{1-W_1}{}$ (A) $\frac{1-W_2}{}$ (CA) Output; $-P$ = mean penalty [%]; $+R$ = mean reward [%]	Mandatory $-P$ $+R$ / W_1 W_2 Output / Optional A CA ; Optional A CA / W_1 W_2 Output / Mandatory $-P$ $+R$
Disjunctive partial absorption (DPA/A:DA)	Sufficient — $(-P, +R)$; W_1 W_2; Optional $\frac{1-W_1}{}$ (A) $\frac{1-W_2}{}$ (DA) Output; $-P$ = mean penalty [%]; $+R$ = mean reward [%]	Sufficient $-P$ $+R$ / W_1 W_2 Output / Optional A DA ; Optional A DA / W_1 W_2 Output / Sufficient $-P$ $+R$
Negation	Input — ▷o— Output	Input NOT Output

rectangular. Consequently, in a rectangle that represents an input we can insert a complete rectangular diagram that denotes some previous aggregation node in the aggregation tree. A rectangular diagram is created by making a table with many rows and columns and then merging selected cells. Fig. 3.4.17 shows a rectangular diagram equivalent to the home location aggregation structure presented in Fig. 3.1.14.

If we compare the aggregation structure from Fig. 3.1.14 and the equivalent rectangular aggregation structure shown in Fig. 3.4.17, we can conclude that the standard diagrams are more readable than the rectangular diagrams. In particular, if the aggregation tree has many levels, then the rightmost fields in rectangular diagrams become big, but their content is regularly very modest. This is the reason why we frequently cut large diagrams into independent rectangular subsystems, which are named according to their output suitability. Then, we use

1111 Train	40	D−+	111 Public	55	C+	11 Basic	−50% 25%	1
1112 Bus	60		Transport.			needs	37.5 · · · 37	Overall
112 Food [m]{(100,100),(400,50),(600,0)		45		(mandatory)		suita-
121 Park	50	C−−	12 Desired amenities (optional)				bility of
122 Restaurant	30				A	CA	home
123 Library	20						location

Figure 3.4.17 A rectangular diagram equivalent to the aggregation structure from Fig. 3.1.14.

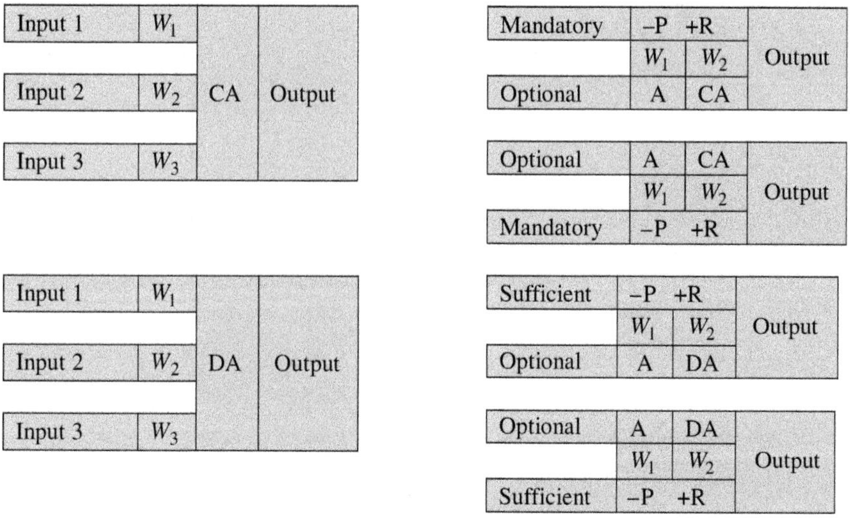

Figure 3.4.18 Sample shade diagrams.

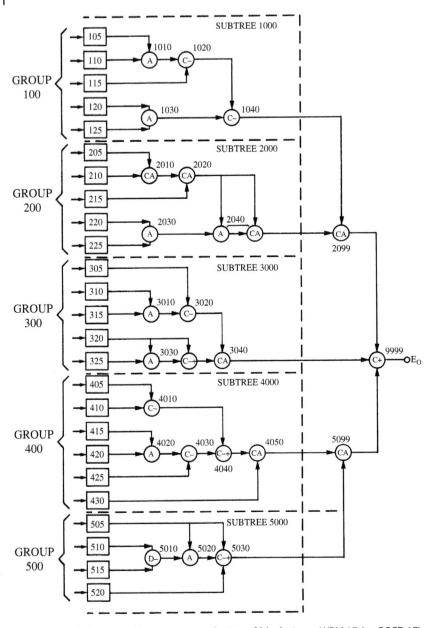

Figure 3.4.19 A grouped bottom-up numbering of blocks in an WPM.17 (or GGCD.17) aggregation structure.

these named suitability degrees as inputs in the next aggregation steps. Similarly, in the case of standard diagrams we can cut them in subsystems, and each subsystem is terminated with a labeled connector, which is then used as input in other aggregation structures (Fig. 4.7.5). At the end, we always generate the overall suitability of the evaluated object.

In the case of the food attribute in Fig. 3.4.17 we inserted the vertex form of elementary criterion in the attribute field (and ruined the readability of the aggregation structure). This shows that theoretically the whole LSP criterion of any complexity can be presented in the form of a single rectangular diagram. The result is a compact notation at the cost of reduced readability. A good opportunity for comparison of standard and rectangular diagrams with separate notation of elementary criteria is visible in Figs. 4.5.6 to 4.5.8.

A special case of rectangular diagrams is called *shade diagrams*, shown in Fig. 3.4.18. Shade diagrams are interpreted in the same way as rectangular diagrams. In many cases, shade diagrams are more useful than plain rectangular diagrams because they better visualize the structure of aggregation. The practical use of shade diagrams is presented in Fig. 4.2.7.

Each aggregation block must have an identification number. In most cases we use the top-down numbering method that strictly follows the structure of the attribute tree. In this numbering the overall suitability (the root of the attribute tree) is always denoted as the node number 1. At the next level we have nodes 11, 12, ..., etc. The number of digits denotes the level of the aggregation tree; e.g., in Fig. 4.2.7, the attribute "private garage" uses the ID number 1213111 and occurs at the seventh level of aggregation.

Long ID numbers can be inconvenient. To simplify the numbering of aggregation nodes, we can use a bottom-up numbering scheme that is introduced in Fig. 3.4.19. The idea of the bottom-up numbering is to use only three-digit or four-digit identifiers. The input attributes are denoted by three-digit identifiers where the first digit denotes a group of similar attributes and the next two digits denote the attribute ID inside the group. Up to nine groups with up to 100 attributes per group are sufficient for almost all evaluation projects. Aggregation operators are denoted using four digits where the first digit denotes the group and the next three digits denote the node inside the group. The final aggregation node (the root of the tree) denotes the overall suitability, and it is always denoted using the largest four-digit number 9999. This form of notation is implemented in CDBS [DUJ76b] and shown in Figs. 4.2.14 and 4.2.15.

3.5 Canonical Aggregation Structures

All aggregation structures must have logic justification. In other words, some aggregation structures are logically correct and some can be logically incorrect. Consequently, the design of aggregation structures is not an arbitrary procedure—it must follow justifiable patterns and design rules. In this chapter, we present basic design rules for logic aggregation structures used in LSP criteria.

Logic aggregation structures usually consist of combining the GCD, standard negation $(x \mapsto 1 - x)$, CPA and DPA. Theoretically, aggregation structures can have arbitrary configuration and parameters. However, some aggregation structures have regular and recognizable forms and are frequently encountered in evaluation models. These structures can be called *canonical aggregation structures* (CAS) and include the following:

- Conjunctive CAS with increasing andness
- Disjunctive CAS with increasing orness
- Aggregated mandatory/optional and sufficient/optional CAS
- Distributed mandatory/optional and sufficient/optional CAS
- Mandatory/desired/optional and sufficient/desired/optional CAS

3.5.1 Conjunctive CAS with Increasing Andness

For each aggregator, we can define its *shadow* as the set of input attributes that affect the output of the aggregator. This concept is illustrated in Fig. 3.5.1 and can also be used for aggregation structures that are not regular trees, because some suitability scores can be used as inputs to more than one aggregator (e.g., as in the case of partial absorption aggregators). If the total number if input attributes is n, then the shadow of an aggregator can have the size from 2 (for the

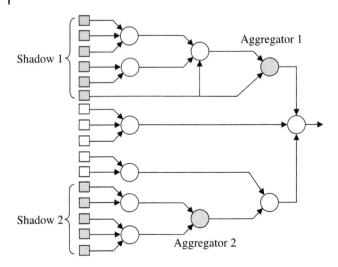

Figure 3.5.1 The concept of the shadow of an aggregator.

simplest aggregator in the initial aggregation layer) to n (for the root aggregator, which generates the overall suitability).

The main property of all tree-like aggregation structures is that by increasing the level of aggregation and approaching the root of tree, the shadow of an aggregator increases, including more and more of input attributes. In other words, the importance of an aggregator is generally an increasing function of the size of its shadow. As an aggregator approaches the root of aggregation tree, its overall importance increases, and the overall importance of an aggregator regularly affects its logical properties (see Section 2.2.3 and Theorem 2.2.1).

The first aggregation structure based on selecting the logic properties of aggregators as functions of the size of their shadow is the conjunctive CAS with increasing andness shown in Fig. 3.5.2. The main idea of this CAS is that with increasing degree of aggregation both the shadow and the importance of an aggregator increase, and the andness of each conjunctive aggregator is proportional to its overall importance. Both the shadow and the andness attain the maximum value (not necessarily the pure conjunction) for the root aggregator.

In Fig. 3.5.2, we assume that the initial leaf layer of aggregation includes neutral aggregators. Of course, we frequently use other aggregators in initial layers, but the general logic of aggregation applied by this CAS remains unchanged. Regardless of the type of leaf layer, in the process of conjunctive aggregation, at some point the size of the shadow reaches the level where the aggregators must become HPC because it is not acceptable that a significant segment of inputs has zero suitability. Therefore, the CAS with strictly increasing andness makes mandatory all terminal results of the soft partial conjunction layer.

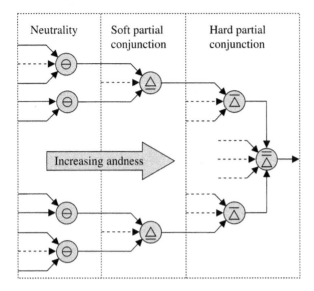

Figure 3.5.2 Conjunctive CAS with increasing andness and nonmandatory inputs.

In this CAS there is a possibility that no individual input attribute is mandatory, and the input aggregation layer may start with aggregators that have a medium andness (either neutrality or SPC), as shown in Fig. 3.5.2. However, at the beginning of the HPC layer we do not accept that the whole shade of any input of a HPC aggregator (that can contain a relatively large group of input attributes) has zero suitability. That is a frequent and reasonable requirement.

In many cases, it is necessary to provide mandatory and nonmandatory (desired or optional) inputs. An input attribute becomes mandatory if the path through the aggregation tree that connects the attribute and the root of the tree is going only through HPC aggregators. Such a version of conjunctive CAS is shown in Fig. 3.5.3. The mandatory input attributes are separated in a group that forms a HPC subtree, and the nonmandatory inputs are separated in a group that forms an SPC subtree. This happens mostly in cases where we aggregate heterogeneous requirements that can be grouped into mandatory requirements and desired (but not mandatory) requirements. It should be noted, however, that the CAS shown in Fig. 3.5.3 requires that at least one nonmandatory input must be properly satisfied because the terminal node of the nonmandatory subtree is an input in a HPC aggregator. In other words, for the CAS in Fig. 3.5.3, the group of nonmandatory inputs is collectively mandatory, and this sometimes may be unacceptable. For complex aggregation structures, that property is not a problem because there are always satisfied nonmandatory requirements. If that is not the case (as in the case of criteria with a small number of inputs), it is advisable to use one of mandatory/optional (conjunctive partial absorption) aggregation structures.

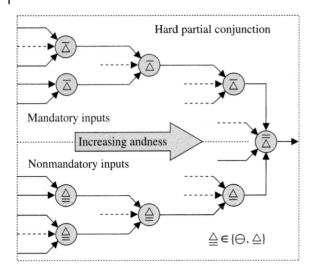

Figure 3.5.3 Conjunctive CAS with increasing andness and separated mandatory and nonmandatory inputs.

The conjunctive structure with increasing andness is the most frequent CAS. It is used in all conjunctive applications shown in *Part Four* where the aggregation structures reflect graded simultaneity (ideal systems must satisfy all component requirements).

3.5.2 Disjunctive CAS with Increasing Orness

The disjunctive CAS with increasing orness is a structure symmetric to the conjunctive CAS with increasing andness. The version shown in Fig. 3.5.4 is based on the concept that the orness of an aggregator should be proportional to the size of its shadow. No individual input attribute is considered sufficient to replace all other attributes. At some level of the size of shadow the aggregators become HPD. If we want to have sufficient input aggregators, then we can use the CAS shown in Fig. 3.5.5. Similarly to the conjunctive case shown in Fig. 3.5.3, the CAS shown in Fig. 3.5.5 has the property that the group of non-sufficient[1] inputs is collectively sufficient because the terminal aggregator of

---

1 A nonsufficient (or optional) input of a disjunctive aggregator is an input that can be completely satisfied, but the complete satisfaction of such an input is not sufficient to automatically cause the complete satisfaction of the analyzed aggregator. As opposed to that, a complete satisfaction of a sufficient input causes the complete satisfaction of such an aggregator, regardless of the values of other inputs.

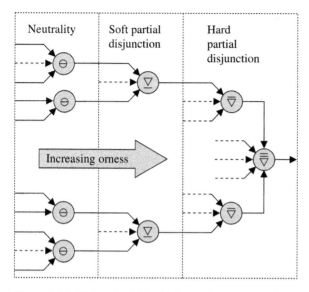

Figure 3.5.4 Disjunctive CAS with increasing orness and nonsufficient inputs.

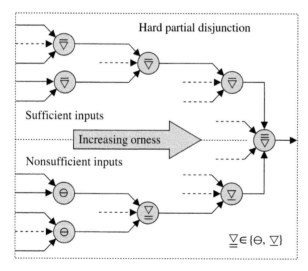

Figure 3.5.5 Disjunctive CAS with increasing orness and separated sufficient and nonsufficient inputs.

the nonsufficient subtree is an input in a HPD aggregator. This property is sometimes desirable. In all other cases, this problem can be solved by feeding the output of the nonsufficient subtree into an optional/desired input of DPA aggregators. Disjunctive CAS with increasing orness is used in medical criteria (Fig. 4.3.6).

3.5.3 Aggregated Mandatory/Optional and Sufficient/Optional CAS

Separation of mandatory and nonmandatory inputs can be realized if we use the CAS shown in Fig. 3.5.6. This CAS is particularly suitable for a relatively small number of inputs where all mandatory inputs can be grouped and all optional inputs can be grouped based on their mandatory/nonmandatory status. The mandatory inputs are aggregated using an HPC aggregation tree and the optional inputs are aggregated using a tree based on SPC and neutrality. In particularly simple special cases where the number of inputs is small (exemplified in Fig. 3.5.7), the aggregation can be done directly on an expanded CPA aggregator.

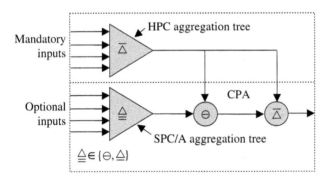

Figure 3.5.6 Aggregated mandatory/optional CAS.

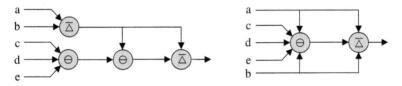

Figure 3.5.7 An example of transfiguration of a simple aggregated mandatory/optional CAS.

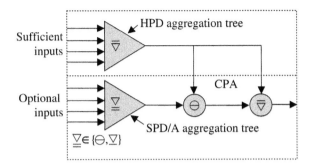

Figure 3.5.8 Aggregated sufficient/optional CAS.

Aggregated mandatory/optional CAS is not suitable in cases where grouping of all mandatory and all optional inputs may be inappropriate because of heterogeneity of members in each group. In such cases, we can use distributed mandatory/optional CAS.

If the HPC aggregators ($\bar{\Delta}$) in Fig. 3.5.6 are replaced by the HPD aggregators ($\bar{\nabla}$), we get the aggregated sufficient/optional CAS that combines a group of sufficient inputs and a group of optional inputs, as shown in Fig. 3.5.8. The main property of this CAS is that the optional inputs can significantly compensate deficiencies of sufficient inputs.

3.5.4   Design of a Simple LSP Evaluator Tool

Suppose that we have to design the simplest LSP evaluator tool for general nonprofessional users. The tool is based on the mandatory/optional CAS (Fig. 3.5.6). The evaluator will enable users to specify any number of input attributes according to specifications in Table 3.5.1. Each input attribute can be either mandatory or optional and has the degree of importance from the lowest (1) to the highest (9). Attribute criteria are specified using the tabular vertex specification. The evaluation can be based on relaxed requirements, standard requirements, and strict requirements. Obviously, the use of this tool is extremely simple and requires no training. Two tools in this category are LSPeval [KAP17] and the LSPmap evaluator [SEA11], described in Section 4.6.4.

The evaluator tool, which is based on the canonical mandatory/optional structure, can be implemented using WPM. According to Fig. 3.5.6, we have to first determine weights and andness of two input aggregators (for mandatory and optional inputs). This can be based on Theorem 2.2.1. Suppose that the user specifies m mandatory inputs with importance levels $V_1, ..., V_m, \ V_i \in \{1,...,9\}, \ i = 1,...,m$ and k optional inputs with importance levels $P_1, ..., P_k, \ P_i \in \{1,...,9\}, \ i = 1,...,k$.

Table 3.5.1 Adjustable parameters of the simple evaluator tool.

Input attributes			CPA aggregator		
Level	Importance		Relaxed	Standard	Strict
1	Lowest	Penalty [%]	15	30	45
2	Very Low	Reward [%]	30	25	20
3	Low				
4	Medium-low				
5	Medium	Type of input attribute			
6	Medium-high	Mandatory (a requirement that must be satisfied;			
7	High	if not satisfied the overall score will be zero)			
8	Very high	Optional (if this requirement is not satisfied the			
9	Highest	overall score will be penalized but not zero)			

Obviously, the relative weights of mandatory and optional inputs are the normalized importance levels:

$$W_i = V_i/(V_1 + \cdots + V_m), \quad i = 1, \ldots, m,$$
$$w_j = P_j/(P_1 + \cdots + P_k), \quad j = 1, \ldots, k.$$

The andness of the mandatory HPC input aggregator must not be below the geometric mean because this aggregator must be hard. So, we can select the andness of HPC approximately in the interval $\alpha \in [\alpha_{min}, \alpha_{max}] = [2/3, 1]$. Now we can compute the mean weight $\bar{V} = (V_1 + \cdots + V_m)/m$. The minimum mean weight $\bar{V}_{min} = 1$ should correspond to α_{min}, and the maximum mean weight $\bar{V}_{max} = 9$ should correspond to α_{max} as follows:

$$\alpha_{min} = 2/3, \quad \alpha_{max} = 1,$$
$$\alpha_{HPC} = \alpha_{min} + \frac{\bar{V} - \bar{V}_{min}}{\bar{V}_{max} - \bar{V}_{min}}(\alpha_{max} - \alpha_{min}) = \frac{2}{3} + \frac{\bar{V} - 1}{8} \cdot \frac{1}{3} = \frac{\bar{V} + 15}{24} \in \left[\frac{2}{3}, 1\right].$$

If we keep the optional aggregator to be the arithmetic mean, then we can use only the normalized means w_j, $j = 1, \ldots, k$, and in such a case this aggregator does not depend on the mean $\bar{P} = (P_1 + \cdots + P_k)/k$. In other words, if the user specifies that the importance of all optional inputs is 9, the result will be the same as in the case where the user specifies that the importance of all inputs is 1. So, valuable information provided by the user would be lost. On the other hand, we might use the same logic as for the mandatory HPC aggregator but now locate the optional aggregator andness α_{OPT} in the SPC range between the arithmetic and the geometric mean:

$$\alpha_{min} = 1/2, \quad \alpha_{max} = 2/3,$$

$$\alpha_{OPT} = \alpha_{min} + \frac{\bar{P} - \bar{P}_{min}}{\bar{P}_{max} - \bar{P}_{min}}(\alpha_{max} - \alpha_{min}) = \frac{1}{2} + \frac{\bar{P} - 1}{8} \cdot \frac{1}{6} = \frac{\bar{P} + 23}{48} \in \left[\frac{1}{2}, \frac{2}{3}\right].$$

In this case, the minimum average importance would map to the arithmetic mean and the maximum average importance to the geometric mean. In this case, the optional aggregator is conjunctive, requesting more simultaneity for the satisfaction of optional requirements. This is convenient for the strict evaluation mode. Of course, we assume that no user would enter the maximum possible importance for all optional inputs. Thus, in regular use, there should be no practical possibility to reach the geometric mean.

We can also decide to map the mean value $\bar{P}_{mid} = 5$ to the arithmetic mean, and in such a case we have

$$\alpha_{mid} = 1/2, \quad \alpha_{max} = 2/3 ,$$

$$\alpha_{OPT} = \alpha_{mid} + \frac{\bar{P} - \bar{P}_{mid}}{\bar{P}_{max} - \bar{P}_{mid}}(\alpha_{max} - \alpha_{mid}) = \frac{1}{2} + \frac{\bar{P} - 5}{4} \cdot \frac{1}{6} = \frac{\bar{P} + 7}{24} \in \left[\frac{1}{3}, \frac{2}{3}\right] .$$

In the extreme case $\bar{P} = 1$ the resulting aggregator has andness $\alpha_{OPT} = 1/3$, which is a disjunctive aggregator (approximately D−+). Assuming that most users will select the importance of optional attributes in the vicinity of medium level, the optional aggregator will be rather close to the arithmetic mean, but if the user thinks that the optional inputs are more important, then the optional aggregator would be mildly conjunctive, putting more pressure to provide satisfaction of optional inputs. Similarly, for low importance inputs the optional aggregator is mildly disjunctive, giving relaxed requirements.

Relaxed, standard, and strict evaluations are selectable by the user and are realized using three penalty/reward pairs defined in Table 3.5.1. They can also be combined with selecting a desired range of optional andness. In special cases where $m = 0$ or $k = 0$, we reduce the LSP evaluator to the input aggregator that has inputs, as shown in Fig. 4.6.14.

3.5.5 Distributed Mandatory/Optional and Sufficient/Optional CAS

Distributed mandatory/optional CAS is presented in Fig. 3.5.9. This CAS can have any number of mandatory and nonmandatory inputs that are grouped according to similarity or connectivity of attributes in N groups/subsystems.

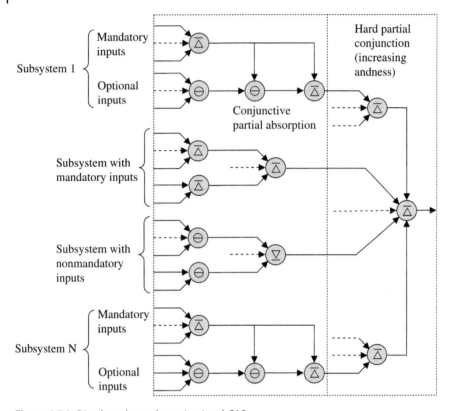

Figure 3.5.9 Distributed mandatory/optional CAS.

This CAS is frequent in simple moderate size criteria with 20 to 40 inputs, but it can be used as a building block of criteria with higher complexity. The process typically includes the following seven steps:

1) Identify subsystems (groups of related attributes).
2) In each subsystem, select attributes that are mandatory and those that are nonmandatory (desired but optional.)
3) Aggregate all mandatory attributes using an HPC and all optional attributes using soft aggregators (SPC, SPD, or the arithmetic mean).
4) Compute the subsystem suitability using a CPA aggregator.
5) If a subsystem contains only mandatory attributes, aggregate inputs using HPC structures with increasing andness.
6) If a subsystem contains only nonmandatory attributes, aggregate inputs using soft aggregators (in most cases also with increasing andness).
7) Aggregate all subsystems using conjunctive structures with increasing andness. In most cases, such structures are hard (if all subsystems are mandatory).

If the HPC aggregators ($\bar{\Delta}$) in Fig. 3.5.9 are replaced by the HPD aggregators ($\bar{\triangledown}$), we get the distributed sufficient/optional CAS that combines any number of sufficient/optional subsystems, strictly sufficient subsystems, and any number of strictly optional subsystems. In addition to DPA aggregators such CAS usually includes SPD and HPD aggregators that support the increasing orness. As in all sufficient/optional structures, the optional inputs can significantly compensate for deficiencies of sufficient inputs.

3.5.6 Nested Mandatory/Desired/Optional and Sufficient/Desired/Optional CAS

Mandatory/optional and sufficient/optional structures can be nested as shown in Fig. 3.5.10 (see also applications in [SU87]). The common form of such CAS is based on nesting $t = (x \unrhd y) \unrhd z$. The inputs x, y, and z can be interpreted as mandatory, desired, and optional inputs, respectively. Both desired and optional inputs are nonmandatory, and the penalty/reward effects of desired input are assumed to be greater than the effects of the optional input. Similar effects (with a stronger impact of y and a weaker impact of z) can be achieved with nesting of the form $t = x \unrhd (y \unrhd z)$, as well as with the approximation $t = x \unrhd (y \ominus z)$ that uses a single CPA without nesting. In all cases, x is the mandatory input. The effects of desired and optional inputs y and z can be additionally adjusted by selecting appropriate weights.

It is important to note that the impact of the desired and optional inputs can be low, but it must not be negligible because there is no reason for using negligible attributes. Generally, it is important to check the impact of the optional input z, in particular for the aggregator $t = x \unrhd (y \unrhd z)$, which uses two stages of

Figure 3.5.10 Nested CPA aggregators and their CPA approximation.

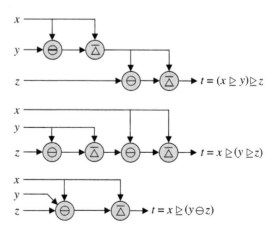

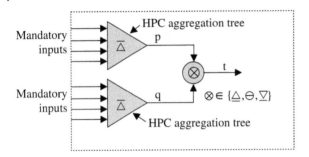

Figure 3.5.11 Andness as a decreasing function of the shadow of an aggregator.

attenuation of the impact of z. The examples in Fig. 3.5.10 show PA nesting with two levels of PA. Nesting deeper than two levels of PA is theoretically possible but has no practical significance because it generates negligible inputs.

Similarly to other canonical structures that use CPA, we can replace the HPC aggregators by the HPD aggregators to get nested sufficient/desired/optional CAS. All nested CPA and DPA structures can be expanded by using appropriate input aggregation trees to generate the inputs x, y, and z, similarly as in the case of aggregated mandatory/optional and sufficient/optional CAS (Figs. 3.5.6 and 3.5.8).

3.5.7 Decreasing Andness and Decreasing Orness CAS

Decreasing andness and decreasing orness forms are symmetric to increasing andness and increasing orness forms, but their applicability is rather low. They deserve to be discussed mostly to help avoiding their inappropriate use.

The simplest example of CAS where the andness of the partial conjunction aggregator is a decreasing function of the size of its shadow is shown in Fig. 3.5.11. Both p and q are functions of mandatory inputs. So, all inputs must be satisfied in order to have $p > 0$ and $q > 0$. That implies that both p and q are rather significant. However, the aggregation of p and q is based on an aggregator that is close to neutrality (andness close to 1/2). That indicates a modest importance of both p and q because only one of them is sufficient to produce the output $t > 0$. Of course, this inconsistence in the interpretation of significance of p and q is unacceptable unless there is a strong and detailed justification. Similar request for detailed justification also holds in the case of decreasing orness that can be obtained if HPC aggregators in Fig. 3.5.11 are replaced by HPD aggregators.

Generally, in human reasoning the percept of overall importance is an increasing function of the size of the shade of aggregator. Consequently, aggregation structures with decreasing andness or decreasing orness are possible, but they are exceptions that always require a careful justification.

3.6 Cost/Suitability Analysis as a Graded Logic Problem

> *Price is what you pay. Value is what you get.*
> —Warren E. Buffett / Benjamin Graham

At the end of an evaluation process, the decision maker knows the overall suitability degrees of all evaluated objects. We assume that the overall suitability is expressed as a score that determines the degree of satisfaction of justifiable stakeholder's requirements. In addition, the overall suitability has to be in balance with the total cost the stakeholder must pay to attain the given degree of satisfaction of requirements. Finding the degree of such a balance is the subject of the cost/suitability analysis. More precisely, we are interested in the relationship of the overall suitability and its counterpart, the total cost.

We call this analysis the cost/suitability analysis, but other terms are equally convenient and sometimes used: instead of *suitability* we sometimes use *preference*, and instead of *cost* it is sometimes convenient to use its reciprocal, and call it *affordability*. This problem is closely related to traditional cost-effectiveness analysis [SEI69] and cost-value techniques [JOS64, JOS68]. However, our approach to cost/suitability analysis is from the soft computing point of view, and our solution is based on graded logic.

3.6.1 Cost Analysis

In this section our goal is to compute a total cost indicator that reflects aggregated cost components of an evaluated object. The total cost can be decomposed into individual components, creating a cost tree, similarly as the overall suitability is decomposed into components creating the attribute tree.

Soft Computing Evaluation Logic: The LSP Decision Method and Its Applications,
First Edition. Jozo Dujmović.
© 2018 John Wiley & Sons, Inc. Published 2018 by John Wiley & Sons, Inc.
Companion website: www.wiley.com/go/Dujmovic/Soft_Computing_Evaluation_Logic

For example, in a typical case of car purchase, the cost tree includes the following components:

1) Purchasing (+)
   1.1 Car price (new or used)
   1.2 Cost of financing (total loan interest)
   1.3 Tax
   1.4 Registration
2) Ownership and usage for N years (+)
   2.1 Cost of fuel
   2.2 Cost of tires
   2.3 Cost of maintenance
   2.4 Cost of repairs
   2.5 Cost of insurance
   2.6 Cost of inspection and registration renewal
   2.7 Costs of parking, tolls, washing, and traffic tickets
3) Resale value at the end of ownership (after N years) (−)

Some of these components are increasing the total cost (denoted +) and some are reducing the total cost (denoted −). Some of them are paid only once, and some of them are paid periodically, over the lifespan of the car (the buyer expects that to be N years). Some of them are fixed, and some of them depend of the intensity of use. The majority of common car buyers would decide to estimate the expected use, and then add all positive and negative components and generate the total cost indicator that will be used as a counterpart of the overall suitability. Rational buyers would then analyze these two fundamental components and try to find a solution that simultaneously maximizes the overall suitability and minimizes the total cost.

In decision-making literature, it is not difficult to find models that mix components of suitability and components of cost on an equal footing as attributes of a criterion function. We reject that approach because it is too difficult to control the impact of individual cost components and related tradeoff properties. We discussed this problem in the context of SMER (Fig. 2.2.4) and suggested that suitability analysis and cost analysis should always be separated. Following are the basic reasons why we suggest keeping cost analysis as a separate subproblem in LSP evaluation projects:

- Elementary criteria for various cost components should transform a cost component into suitability score, and substantial efforts are needed to establish acceptable individual cost criteria for each cost component of a specific evaluated object.
- Cost components regularly create additive compensation patterns (i.e., we usually add all costs and can compensate higher costs of some components by lower costs of other components). However, the logic aggregation of

suitability is usually based on complex and nonlinear logic aggregation functions with many adjustable parameters, causing cost compensation patterns that are not easily justifiable.

- The overall suitability for attaining stakeholder's goals is paid with the total cost of attaining such goals. Therefore, by the very nature of this problem, the overall suitability relates to the total cost, and the overall value should be obtained by aggregating the total cost and the overall suitability.
- Balancing the overall suitability and the total cost is not difficult and represents an activity that all humans learn very early, and permanently practice, whenever they buy goods and services.

It is important to emphasize that the total cost is a compound indicator that includes all cost components of an evaluation project. Some costs are direct and some are indirect, but they are equally important. For example, if the evaluated object is electronic equipment, which cannot work without raised floors for cable connections and special air conditioning system, then the total cost should include the cost of equipment (as a direct cost) and the cost of raised floors and air conditioning (as indirect costs). Similarly to the suitability analysis, which needs to identify all relevant attributes, the goal of cost analysis is to identify all cost components (direct and indirect) related to each competitive object in an evaluation project.

In simple problems, as in the case of car selection, the user might identify individual cost components $c_1, ..., c_k$ computed over the expected ownership period, and then simply define the total cost as the sum $C = c_1 + \cdots + c_k$. This includes both positive and negative cost components.

In the case of expensive industrial projects, which last for a longer period, it is usually necessary to take into account the time value of money and use the discounted cash flow [WRI73] to compute the total cost as the net present value of cash flow. Suppose that r denotes the interest rate at which an amount A compounds each period (typically a year). Then the present value of amount A after k such periods transforms into the future value $F_k = A(1 + r)^k$. Conversely, the present value of the future payment F_k is $A = F_k/(1 + r)^k$. Therefore, if the cost analysis identifies a sequence of (positive or negative) amounts $C_0, ..., C_N$ over N such periods, then the total cost defined as a net present value of cash flow can be computed as the sum of discounted future amounts:

$$C = \sum_{k=0}^{N} \frac{C_k}{(1 + r)^k}.$$

The rate r is called the discount rate. The discount rate is not the simple interest rate, because it is also increased by a risk premium that reflects stakeholder's estimate of risk related with future behavior of sequence $C_0, ..., C_N$.

3.6.2 Cost/Suitability Analysis Based on Linear Equi-Value Model

The essential components of the cost/suitability analysis are shown in Fig. 3.6.1. The overall suitability X is computed from strictly nonfinancial suitability attributes $(a_1, ..., a_n)$. The total cost indicator C is computed using a total cost model that aggregates all individual cost components and related financial conditions $(c_1, ..., c_k)$. In a trivial case, the cost model can be the simple sum of all cost components, and in more complex cases C can take into account the dynamics of cash flow expressed by the net present value.

Cost/suitability analysis models for computing the overall value V as a function of the overall suitability X and the total cost C can be designed in a variety of ways. Generally, we would like to simultaneously have a high suitability and a low cost. In the simplest case, this requirement could be expressed as $V = f(X, C) = X/C$. This simplistic model assumes that the cost and the suitability are equally important and the value is defined as the overall suitability per unit of total cost. We used this model in Section 3.1.5.

In all cost/suitability models, we assume that stakeholders cannot accept solutions that are below the minimum suitability threshold X_{min}. Typically, $2/3 \le X_{min} \le 3/4$. Similarly, we assume that the available funding is limited and stakeholders cannot accept the total cost, which is above the approved cost threshold C_{max}. Therefore, the cost-suitability plane can be partitioned in three regions shown in Fig. 3.6.2:

- Region of insufficient suitability: $X < X_{min}$
- Region of unacceptable cost: $C > C_{max}$
- Region of acceptable solutions: $X_{min} \le X \le 1, \quad 0 < C \le C_{max}$

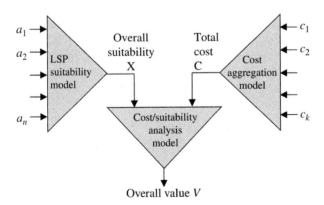

Figure 3.6.1 Computation of the overall value using a cost/suitability model.

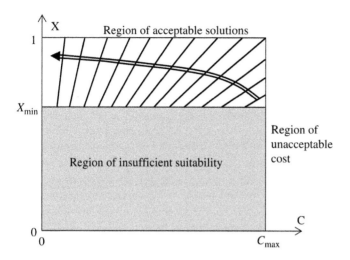

Figure 3.6.2 Region of acceptable solutions with equi-value lines.

Competitive systems that are outside the region of acceptable solutions are automatically rejected and cost/suitability analysis is performed with systems located inside the region of acceptable solutions. The comparison is based on equi-value (or iso-value) curves, which are functions connecting points of equal stakeholder perceived value. The comparison based on the value model $V = X/C$ gives the model where equi-value curves are straight lines shown inside the region of acceptable solutions in Fig. 3.6.2. The double-line arrow shows the direction of increasing perceived value. Competitive systems located on the same line are considered equivalent. They have the same perceived value because the decision maker considers that on each line any increment of suitability fully justifies the corresponding increment of cost. Consequently, the system with the highest value is the most suitable according to stakeholder's requirements built in the whole process of suitability and cost analysis.

Regardless of the limitation of equal importance of cost and suitability and the ultimate simplicity of the presented linear model, it can be successfully used in the process of financial negotiations with vendors of evaluated systems. This is exemplified in the next section.

3.6.3 Using Cost/Suitability Analysis in Competitive Bidding

The main advantage of the LSP method in system procurement is that the overall suitability scores reflect very precisely the quality of each competitive system and can be used in the process of competitive bidding. The following example is taken from a real project of procurement of complex computer networks. Suppose that we compare three finalists (located in the region of acceptable solutions), denoted A, B, and C. Their proposals are reduced to the overall suitability X [%] and the total cost indicator C [$]. Suppose that the total value indicator is defined as $V = X/C$ (other more elaborate models are also used in the cost-suitability analysis). The situation at the beginning of financial negotiations is presented in Table 3.6.1. According to this table, the best offer is B because it attains the highest overall value $V = 20$. At the end of evaluation the overall suitability is fixed. However, if the competitors reduce their cost, the ranking can change. The suitability results prepared for the first meeting with vendors are shown in Table 3.6.2.

At the end of the evaluation process the vendors A, B, and C are invited to financial negotiations. Table 3.6.2 is used during the negotiations. At the first meeting with the vendor A, here is what the buyer would say:

> "Thank you for your offer. It is a good system and it is among our finalists. We have completed our evaluation, and your proposal satisfied 86% of our requirements. You are the best system in our ranking. However, your cost is too high. Other competitors have offered similar systems at lower cost. If you want to reach the level of the best offer that we currently have, you have to reduce your cost by **$301,150**. Additional discount would make your offer the best, assuming that other competitors do not change their offers. You have 3 days to give us your decision concerning the possible discount. Thanks!"

Table 3.6.1 Initial results of the cost/suitability analysis.

Competitive systems	Suitability X [%]	Total cost C [$]	Overall value V = X / C [%/M$]
A	86	4,600,000	18.70
B	82	4,100,000	20.00
C	75	4,000,000	18.75

Table 3.6.2 Modified results prepared for meeting with vendors.

Competitive system	Suitability X [%]	Initial cost C [$]	Reduced cost [$]	Discount [$]	Overall value V = X / C [%/M$]
A	86	4,601,150	4,300,000	301,150	20.00
B	82	4,100,000	-	-	20.00
C	75	4,007,750	3,750,000	257,750	20.00

In the case of vendor B, the buyer's statement would be the following:

"Thank you for your offer. It is a good system, and it is among our finalists. We have completed our evaluation and your proposal satisfied 82% of our requirements. You are the second best system in our ranking. At this time we expect the other finalists to offer significant discounts. By giving a discount, you can improve your position in our final ranking. You have 3 days to give us your decision concerning the possible discount. Thanks!"

In the case of vendor C, the buyer's statement would be the following:

"Thank you for your offer. It is a good system and it is among our finalists. We have completed our evaluation and your proposal satisfied 75% of our requirements. You are the third best system in our ranking. However, your cost is too high. Other competitors have offered better systems at lower cost. If you want to reach the level of the best offer that we currently have, you have to reduce your cost by **$257,750**. *Additional discount would make your offer the best, assuming that other competitors do not change their offers. You have 3 days to give us your decision concerning the possible discount. Thanks!"*

After three days, all vendors will come with reduced prices. Then the whole process repeats in exactly the same way (but with different numbers). After a few iterations, the vendors reach their lowest prices, and then the buyer can confidently select the optimum (highest value) system. Then, it is possible to contract the best system or to buy more equipment at the reduced cost, if there is surplus funding achieved through the obtained discounts.

The cost/suitability bidding process is extremely effective if the buyer comes with the exact value of the requested discount (e.g., $301,150), because this proves that the decision process is based on a reliable quantitative method and not on arbitrary interpretations of costs and benefits. This puts a heavy weight on the buyer's requests.

This example clearly shows that it is not possible to organize the presented competitive bidding process unless there is a constant value of the overall suitability that is obtained by a detailed and reliable LSP analysis. If the buyer accepts with confidence the final result of suitability evaluation, this result can be used as a powerful input for financial negotiations even in cases where the total value is determined using the simplistic $V = X/C$ model.[1]

---

1 Just in case you are curious to learn what the buyer (a food industry) paid at the end of the described bidding process: it was slightly above $3.5 million. So, the result of cost/suitability analysis was the buyer's savings greater than 15%.

3.6.4 Conjunctive Suitability-Affordability Method

As long as there are rich and poor, the cost and suitability cannot have equal weights. For rich buyers, suitability and quality are more important than low cost. For poor buyers, low cost is more important than high suitability. Therefore, we need a cost/suitability model that has adjustable relative importance of cost and suitability. It will be used by both rich and poor.

The suitability-affordability logic is very simple: the ideal (highest value) system should simultaneously offer high suitability and high affordability. Therefore, in order to compare a set of M competitors, we have to define a logic indicator of relative suitability, then a logic indicator of relative affordability, and then to aggregate them using a partial conjunction. This process is summarized in Fig. 3.6.3.

The relative suitability of system m is $S_m = X_m/\max(X_1,...,X_M)$. So, S_m is the degree of truth of the statement, "System m is the most suitable in this competition." Similarly, the relative affordability of system m is $A_m = \min(C_1,...,C_M)/C_m$. It is the degree of truth of the statement, "System m is the most affordable in this competition." Then we can compute the overall value as the weighted simultaneous suitability and affordability: $V_m = W_s S_m \Delta W_a A_m$. The overall value V_m is the degree of truth of the statement, "System m is the best value in this competition because it offers the best combination of suitability and affordability." Therefore, this method solves the system comparison and selection problem as a logic problem in graded logic.

Number of competitive systems:	$M > 1.$
Overall suitability:	$X_m,\ m = 1,...,M.$
Relative overall suitability:	$S_m = X_m\ /\max(X_1,...,X_M),$
	$0 < S_m \le 1,\ m = 1,...,M.$
Total cost (result of cost analysis):	$C_m,\ m = 1,...,M.$
Relative affordability:	$A_m = \min(C_1,...,C_M)/C_m,$
	$0 < A_m \le 1,\ m = 1,...,M.$
Relative importance of high suitability:	$W_s \in]0,1[.$
Relative importance of high affordability:	$W_a \in]0,1[,\ W_s + W_a = 1.$
Overall value (simultaneous S_m and A_m):	$V_m = W_s S_m \Delta W_a A_m =$
	$\left(W_s S_m^r + W_a A_m^r \right)^{1/r},\ r < 1,\ m = 1,...,M.$
Typical case:	$\alpha = 67\%,\ V_m = S_m^{W_s} A_m^{W_a},\ m = 1,...,M.$

Figure 3.6.3 Weighted suitability/affordability analysis.

Example

All LSP software tools implement the presented conjunctive suitability-affordability method. In the case of the senior citizen home location problem defined in Chapter 3.1, we can use the elementary criteria defined in Table 3.1.1 and the *LSPeval* tool discussed in Section 3.5.4. In this case, the aggregation structure is the canonical mandatory/optional structure shown in Fig. 4.6.14 where the mandatory inputs are distances from bus station, food store, and train station, and the optional inputs are distances from public library, parks, and restaurants. The criterion function is shown in Fig. 3.6.4, together with attributes of four competitive locations (Alpha, Beta, Gamma, Delta). The prices of these locations are normalized so that the most expensive location has the normalized cost 1 and all other locations have proportionally lower prices.

The results of evaluation, generated by *LSPeval*, are shown in Fig. 3.6.5 and the overall values generated by the cost/suitability analysis are presented in Fig. 3.6.6. LSPeval, as well as other LSP evaluation software systems, require that each evaluation and comparison problem is identified using a unique project name. The name of this project is "Location." This name appears in the title of all results generated by LSPeval.

All results are generated for standard requirements (the results for relaxed and strict requirements are slightly different). The aggregator of suitability and affordability is the weighted geometric mean, a hard aggregator with andness 67%. The relative importance of high suitability is denoted w and the relative importance of high affordability is $1-w$. The presented overall value is computed for eleven different importance parameters: $w = 0, 10, \ldots, 100\%$. If $w = 0$, then the overall value is equal to the relative cost. On the other side of this scale, if $w = 100\%$, then the overall value is equal to the relative suitability. Between these extreme values we have a continuous transition, which provides insight into effects of various forms of balancing degrees of importance of suitability and cost.

Attributes	Importance	Systems and their prices				Attribute criterion
		Alpha	Beta	Delta	Gamma	
		1.000	0.920	0.850	0.950	
Mandatory						
Distance from bus station [m]	Medium	120	200	250	100	{ (50, 100), (700, 0) }
Distance from food store [m]	Very high	350	410	80	200	{ (100, 100), (400, 50), (600,0) }
Distance from train station [m]	Medium-low	600	800	750	300	{ (400, 100), (1000, 0) }
Optional						
Distance from library [m]	Low	500	1500	1900	2750	{ (1000, 100), (3000, 0) }
Distance from park [m]	High	1100	900	200	250	{ (0, 100), (3500, 0) }
Distance from restaurant [m]	Medium	250	300	460	220	{ (0, 40), (150, 100), (300, 100), (900, 0) }

Figure 3.6.4 The criterion and the attribute values of four competitive locations.

Standard suitability scores for project location

Attributes	Importance	Systems and their prices			
		Alpha	Beta	Delta	Gamma
		1.000	0.920	0.850	0.950
Total mandatory attributes score [%]		67.15	48.10	68.49	89.40
Distance from bus station [m]	Medium	89.23	76.92	69.23	92.31
Distance from food store [m]	Very high	58.33	47.50	100.00	83.33
Distance from train station [m]	Medium-low	66.67	33.33	41.67	100.00
Total optional attributes score [%]		85.33	83.00	79.44	79.17
Distance from library [m]	Low	100.00	75.00	55.00	12.50
Distance from park [m]	High	68.57	74.29	94.29	92.86
Distance from restaurant [m]	Medium	100.00	100.00	73.33	100.00
Final results					
Overall suitability score [%]		72.4	58.04	71.66	86.41

Figure 3.6.5 The results of evaluation of four competitive locations.

Standard evaluation report for project location

Overall value of system k: 100* $(Score_k/ Score_{max})^W (Cost_{min}/ Cost_k)^{1-W}$ [%]

System	Cost	Relative importance of high scores (w)											Overall score [%]
		0%	10%	20%	30%	40%	50%	60%	70%	80%	90%	100%	
Alpha	1.000	85.00	84.88	84.76	84.63	84.51	84.39	84.27	84.15	84.03	83.91	83.79	72.4
Beta	0.920	92.39	89.49	86.68	83.96	81.33	78.78	76.30	73.91	71.59	69.34	67.17	58.04
Delta	0.850	100.00	98.15	96.33	94.54	92.79	91.07	89.38	87.72	86.09	84.50	82.93	71.66
Gamma	0.950	89.47	90.47	91.49	92.51	93.54	94.59	95.65	96.72	97.80	98.89	100.00	86.41

Normalized report

System	Cost	Relative importance of high scores (w)											Overall score [%]
		0%	10%	20%	30%	40%	50%	60%	70%	80%	90%	100%	
Alpha	1.000	85.00	84.48	87.99	89.52	90.34	89.22	88.10	87.00	85.92	84.85	83.79	72.4
Beta	0.920	92.39	91.18	89.99	88.81	86.94	83.28	79.78	76.42	73.20	70.12	67.17	58.04
Delta	0.850	100.00	100.00	100.00	100.00	99.19	96.27	93.44	90.70	88.03	85.44	82.93	71.66
Gamma	0.950	89.47	92.18	94.98	97.85	100.00	100.00	100.00	100.00	100.00	100.00	100.00	86.41

Figure 3.6.6 Overall values generated by the LSP cost/suitability analysis.

The normalized values reported in Fig. 3.6.6 are obtained by interpreting the largest value in each column as 100%. For $40\% \le w \le 100\%$, the winner is the location Gamma; this location combines the highest suitability (86.41%) with a moderate cost (0.95). However, for $0\% \le w \le 30\%$, we have that location Delta is the best solution; it is convenient for seniors on a modest budget because it combines a reasonable suitability (71.66%) with the lowest cost (0.85). Locations Alpha and Beta are rejected; Alpha has the highest cost, and Beta has the lowest suitability. The normalized value report shows the range of dominance of winning competitors. This contributes to the confidence of stakeholder; e.g., if a specific senior considers that his/her appropriate high suitability weight is $w \approx 70\%$, then it is rather endorsing to know that the optimum location Gamma would be dominant in the whole range $40\% \le w \le 100\%$.

The presented conjunctive suitability-affordability method works effectively for other hard aggregators $(\alpha \ge 2/3)$ and can be used for solving different cost/suitability problems. In section 4.2.5, we present the optimum pricing problem where the cost/suitability analysis is performed from both the buyer's and seller's standpoint. The winning competitor who has access to results of cost/suitability analysis knows to what extent s/he can increase the price without losing the dominant position. On the other hand, the buyer of the best alternative knows that s/he got a good deal because the price could be higher, and that would still be the best alternative. In all cases, the cost/suitability analysis generates very useful information for decision makers.

3.7 Sensitivity Analysis and Tradeoff Analysis

The process of building complex criteria includes activities of verification and validation. It is important to verify that the properties of complex criteria are consistent both with general properties of human reasoning and with goals and expectations of a specific evaluator. Two basic processes that are used for tuning and justification of complex criteria are sensitivity analysis and trade-off analysis.

3.7.1 Sensitivity Analysis

The goal of sensitivity analysis is to investigate how various inputs and para-meters affect the results of evaluation. The goal of tradeoff analysis is to inves-tigate compensatory features of inputs of complex criteria. These analyses are auxiliary processes that contribute to the quality of decision models and the reli-ability of evaluation.

In a general case, let us consider a criterion function where the output y depends on n inputs and k independent parameters:

$$y = F(\mathbf{x}\,;\mathbf{p}), \quad \mathbf{x} = (x_1,\dots,x_n), \quad \mathbf{p} = (p_1,\dots,p_k).$$

A typical structure of a general LSP criterion function is shown in Fig. 3.7.1. Inputs $x_1, \dots, x_n$ can be either input attributes $(a_1, \dots, a_n)$ or the corresponding attribute suitability scores $(s_1, \dots, s_n)$, or subsystem suitability scores (e.g. S_{im}), or parameters (weights, or andness/orness). The output y can be any value affected by a selected input value. For example, the attribute a_i in Fig. 3.7.1 affects the value of subsystem suitability scores S_{im}, S_{1m}, as well as the overall suitability S. However, we might also be interested in investigating how the attribute suita-bility score s_1 affects the subsystem suitability S_{1m} or how the subsystem

Soft Computing Evaluation Logic: The LSP Decision Method and Its Applications,
First Edition. Jozo Dujmović.
© 2018 John Wiley & Sons, Inc. Published 2018 by John Wiley & Sons, Inc.
Companion website: www.wiley.com/go/Dujmovic/Soft_Computing_Evaluation_Logic

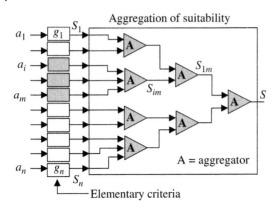

Figure 3.7.1 The structure of an LSP criterion and its subsystems S_{im} and S_{1m}.

suitability S_{im} affects the overall suitability S. The subsystem S_{im} includes input attributes in the range from i to m. Therefore, in sensitivity analysis we can investigate effects of any input (or any parameter) on any output in a complex criterion function. In a general case, we will denote selected inputs using vector **x** and the selected output as y.

Using the traditional sensitivity analysis of dynamic systems [TOM63], we might characterize the sensitivity of y with respect to x_i and p_j using the following three types of sensitivity coefficients:

$$u_{xi} = \frac{\partial y}{\partial x_i} \approx \frac{\Delta y}{\Delta x_i},$$

$$v_{xi} = \frac{\partial y}{\partial \ln x_i} = x_i \frac{\partial y}{\partial x_i} \approx \Delta y \bigg/ \frac{\Delta x_i}{x_i},$$

$$V_{xi} = \frac{\partial \ln y}{\partial \ln x_i} = \frac{x_i}{y}\frac{\partial y}{\partial x_i} \approx \frac{\Delta y}{y} \bigg/ \frac{\Delta x_i}{x_i}, \quad i = 1,\dots,n.$$

$$u_{pj} = \frac{\partial y}{\partial p_j} \approx \frac{\Delta y}{\Delta p_j},$$

$$v_{pj} = \frac{\partial y}{\partial \ln p_j} = p_j \frac{\partial y}{\partial p_j} \approx \Delta y \bigg/ \frac{\Delta p_j}{p_j},$$

$$V_{pj} = \frac{\partial \ln y}{\partial \ln x_i} = \frac{p_j}{y}\frac{\partial y}{\partial p_j} \approx \frac{\Delta y}{y} \bigg/ \frac{\Delta p_j}{p_j}, \quad j = 1,\dots,k.$$

The simplest sensitivity coefficients u_{xi} and u_{pj} show the effects caused by small changes of x_i and p_j. The coefficients v_{xi} and v_{pj} are computed with respect to the relative change of x_i and p_j, and the logarithmic coefficients V_{xi} and V_{pj} show the relative change of y caused be the relative changes of x_i and p_j. For example, in the case of WPM we have $y^r = W_1 x_1^r + \dots + W_n x_n^r$ and consequently

$$u_{xi} = \frac{\partial y}{\partial x_i} = W_i \left(\frac{x_i}{y}\right)^{r-1},$$

$$V_{xi} = \frac{\partial \ln y}{\partial \ln x_i} = \frac{x_i}{y}\frac{\partial y}{\partial x_i} = W_i \left(\frac{x_i}{y}\right)^{r} \approx \frac{\Delta y}{y} \bigg/ \frac{\Delta x_i}{x_i}, \quad i = 1,...,n,$$

Consequently, the multiplicative weight directly affects the logarithmic sensitivity and in cases where $r = 0$, or for inputs close to the mean value $(x_i = y)$, we have

$$\frac{\Delta y}{y} \approx W_i \frac{\Delta x_i}{x_i}.$$

3.7.1.1 Sensitivity with Respect to Input Suitability Scores

The sensitivity coefficients u_{xi}, u_{pj}, v_{xi}, v_{pj}, V_{xi} and V_{pj} are functions of inputs $x_1, ..., x_n$ and parameters $p_1, ..., p_k$. Consequently, these are local indicators that are different in each point of the space $[0,1]^n \prod_{j=1}^{k} \left[p_j^{(max)} - p_j^{(min)}\right]$. From the practical point of view, however, it is more convenient to define sensitivity metrics that are overall indicators based on selected values of inputs and parameters.

In a general case, suppose that an evaluation model uses the values of parameters $\mathbf{p}^{(0)} = \left(p_1^{(0)},...,p_k^{(0)}\right)$. If the input suitability scores for a specific system are $\mathbf{x}^{(0)} = \left(x_1^{(0)},...,x_n^{(0)}\right)$, then the resulting suitability score is $y^{(0)} = F\left(\mathbf{x}^{(0)};\mathbf{p}^{(0)}\right)$. Typical effects of changing a selected input suitability score x_i in the full range from 0 to 1 are exemplified for conjunctive criteria[1] in Fig. 3.7.2, where we show the sensitivity function $y_i = f_i(x_i) = F\left(x_1^{(0)},...,x_{i-1}^{(0)},x_i,x_{i+1}^{(0)},...,x_n^{(0)};\mathbf{p}^{(0)}\right)$, $0 \le x_i \le 1$. If the aggregator is conjunctively polarized, then small values of x_i limit the value of the output. Consequently, in the interval $0 \le x_i \le x_i^{(0)}$ the output can be strongly affected by the value of x_i. Similarly, the saturation of function $f_i(x_i)$ in the range $x_i^{(0)} \le x_i \le 1$ is caused by strong limiting effects of multiple inputs $x_1^{(0)},...,x_{i-1}^{(0)},x_{i+1}^{(0)},...,x_n^{(0)}$. The limiting effects of multiple inputs regularly cannot be compensated by the single value of x_i, yielding the concave form of the sensitivity function $f_i(x_i)$ (a continuous function whose value at the midpoint of every interval in its domain exceeds the arithmetic mean of its values at the ends of the interval).

---

1 According to Definitions 2.4.5 and 2.4.6 conjunctive criteria are concave and disjunctive criteria are convex

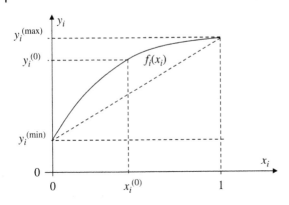

Figure 3.7.2 A typical concave form of the conjunctive sensitivity curve $f_i(x_i)$.

The overall effects of changing the input suitability score x_i are characterized using the limit values $f_i(0) = y_i^{(min)}$, $0 \le y_i^{(min)} \le y_i^{(0)}$ and $f_i(1) = y_i^{(max)}$, $y_i^{(0)} \le y_i^{(max)} \le 1$. We express sensitivity properties using the following seven indicators that are all expressed as percentages:

- Preference increment:

$$\delta_i^+ = 100\left(y_i^{(max)} - y_i^{(0)}\right) \ [\%].$$

- Preference decrement:

$$\delta_i^- = 100\left(y_i^{(0)} - y_i^{(min)}\right) \ [\%].$$

- Absolute influence range:

$$\rho_i = 100\left(y_i^{(max)} - y_i^{(min)}\right) \ [\%].$$

- Relative position of output:

$$\pi_i = 100\frac{y_i^{(0)} - y_i^{(min)}}{y_i^{(max)} - y_i^{(min)}} \ [\%].$$

- Relative influence range:

$$\rho_{ri} = 100\frac{y_i^{(max)} - y_i^{(min)}}{y_i^{(max)}} \ [\%].$$

- Conjunctive coefficient of impact:

$$\gamma_i = 200\frac{y_i^{(max)} - \int_0^1 f_i(x_i)dx_i}{y_i^{(max)}} \ [\%].$$

- Coefficient of balance:

$$\beta_i = 100 x_i/C_i \ [\%], \quad C_i = f_i(C_i).$$

These indicators express various aspects of the overall importance of input or subsystem preferences. The preference increment δ_i^+ shows what maximum improvement can be attained by the maximum satisfaction of the i-th input. If δ_i^+ is sufficiently large, then it is reasonable to make efforts to improve the i-th input. Similarly, the preference decrement δ_i^- shows the total individual contribution of the i-th input to the output suitability score. The absolute influence range is the sum of preference increment and the preference decrement: $\rho_i = \delta_i^+ + \delta_i^-$. The relative position π_i shows the location of $y_i^{(0)}$ within the interval $\left[y_i^{(min)}, y_i^{(max)}\right]$. It can be computed from the preference decrement and increment: $\pi_i = 100\delta_i^- / (\delta_i^+ + \delta_i^-) = 100\delta_i^- /\rho_i$.

The absolute influence range ρ_i can be used for ranking of inputs according to their overall significance in the evaluation process. The overall significance depends on combined effects of weights and aggregation logic.

The first four indicators (increment, decrement, range, and position) are general and can be used for all types of LSP criteria. Taking into account that the majority of evaluation criteria are conjunctive, there is practical interest in sensitivity indicators that are specialized for conjunctive criteria. The indicators of relative influence and impact are suitable only for conjunctive criteria (of course, symmetric specialized indicators can also be defined for disjunctive criteria).

The relative influence range ρ_{ri} is a normalized indicator that in the case of inputs that are mandatory requirements yields $\rho_{ri} = 100\%$, caused by $y_i^{(min)} = f_i(0) = 0$.

The conjunctive coefficient of impact γ_i is an indicator similar to the relative influence range, but it takes into account the shape of the function $f_i(x_i)$. If x_i is mandatory but not very significant, then it must be satisfied, but its value insignificantly contributes to the overall suitability. In such a case, $f_i(x_i)$ would quickly increase for small values of x_i and then quickly reach saturation $df_i(x_i)/dx_i \rightarrow 0$, yielding $\int_0^1 f_i(x_i)dx_i \approx y_i^{(max)}$ and a very small value of γ_i. On the other hand, if x_i is mandatory and extremely significant, then the overall suitability would critically depend on x_i, yielding $f_i(x_i) \approx y_i^{(max)} x_i$, $\int_0^1 f_i(x_i)dx_i \approx y_i^{(max)}/2$, and $\gamma_i \rightarrow 100\%$. If x_i is not mandatory, then $y_i^{(max)}/2 < \int_0^1 f_i(x_i)dx_i < y_i^{(max)}$ and the impact of x_i is a decreasing function of the value of the integral.

The coefficient of balance shows whether x_i is superior ($\beta_i > 100\%$) or inferior ($\beta_i < 100\%$) compared to other input attributes. According to Fig. 2.2.23 and related analysis (**P$_{33}$**), the concordance value $x_i = C_i = f_i(C_i)$ is the suitability of the ith attribute, which is in perfect balance with suitability scores of other attributes ($\beta_i = 100\%$). In other words, C_i is the aggregated suitability achieved by attributes different from x_i, without the contribution from x_i. Due to nondecreasing monotonicity of logic aggregators, we have $df_i(x_i)/dx_i \geq 0$, and if $x_i > C_i$ then $f_i(x_i) \geq f_i(C_i)$ and x_i is above the average of other attributes. Similarly, if $x_i < C_i$ then $f_i(x_i) \leq f_i(C_i)$ and x_i is below the average of other attributes. Therefore, in each evaluation project, we can identify the subset of attributes that are above the average and the subset of attributes that are below the average. Improvement efforts should be focused on attributes that are below the average.

The value of derivative $df_i(x_i)/dx_i$, for the concordance suitability $x_i = C_i$, can be used as an indicator of the importance of attribute x_i. The most important attribute, and the highest contributor to the aggregated suitability, has the highest value of $df_i(x_i)/dx_i$ in the concordance point $x_i = C_i$. The attribute suitability x_i is a function of the value of attribute: $x_i = g_i(a_i)$. In many cases, for example if a_i is the size of computer memory, the value of attribute a_i is a function of the cost of attribute: $a_i = h_i(c_i)$. Consequently, $x_i = g_i(h_i(c_i))$, and the sensitivity and tradeoff analyses can be performed with respect to the cost of attributes. In such cases, from equation $C_i = g_i(h_i(c_i^{con}))$ we can find the concordance cost $c_i^{con} = h_i^{-1}(g_i^{-1}(C_i))$. Then, the attributes can be compared from the standpoint of sensitivity to the increase of cost. If $c_i < c_i^{con}$, then the ith attribute is insufficiently supported. Of course, the optimum investment policy is to invest in improvement of those attributes where an increase of cost causes the highest increment of overall suitability.

Fig. 3.7.3 illustrates the concept of overall impact of x_1 in the case of a hard conjunctive WPM aggregator: $y = f_1(x_1) = \left(Wx_1^r + (1-W)x_2^r\right)^{1/r}$, $r \leq 0$. The impact of x_1 depends on weight W and increases as the weight increases. In the extreme case, if $W \to 1$ we have $y = x_1$. For $x_1 = 1$ we get the highest value of the sensitivity curve $y^{(max)} = f_1(1) = \left(W + (1-W)x_2^r\right)^{1/r}$. So, the impact of x_1 can be expressed as the proximity of sensitivity curve $f_1(x_1)$ and the line $y = x_1 y^{(max)}$. The proximity can be expressed using areas A, B, C shown in Fig. 3.7.3: the low impact gives small area A and the high impact gives a large area A. In all cases $\gamma_i[\%] = 100A/C$, where $A + B = C = y^{(max)}/2$.

The γ_i indicator can be used to justify the use of input attributes. Those attributes that have exceedingly small overall impact (e.g., $\gamma < 2\%$) can be considered

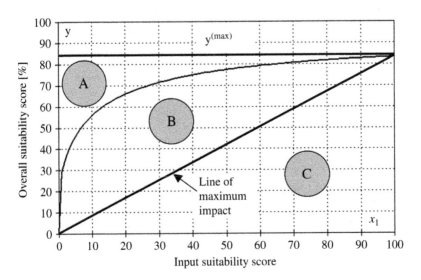

Figure 3.7.3 The concept of overall impact.

unnecessary and candidates for exclusion (see the analysis related to Fig. 2.2.30). A typical such situation is exemplified in Section 4.4.4.

The conjunctive coefficient of overall impact γ_i is defined having in mind hard aggregators like one shown in Fig. 3.7.3. Obviously, for soft aggregators, like one shown in Fig. 3.7.2, the values of γ_i are significantly smaller, reflecting their lower impact.

3.7.1.2 Sensitivity Properties of Basic Aggregators

Sample sensitivity curves for the very strong partial conjunction aggregator WPM.17/C++ and for the weighted geometric mean in the case of three average inputs $(x = y = z = 0.5)$ are presented in Fig. 3.7.4. In both cases, we use rather nonuniform weights (0.7, 0.25, and 0.05). In the case of high andness $(\alpha = 15/16$ for C++) and mandatory requirements, all inputs strongly affect the output preference in the range of low preferences $([0,0.5])$, yielding high preference decrement $\delta_i^- = 50\%$. In the range of high preferences, the preference increments δ_i^+ are rather small, because the output is limited by relatively low values (50%) of preferences of the remaining two inputs.

In the case of geometric mean, the situation is different. The most important input x has high overall impact and the curve $GCD(x, 0.5, 0.5)$ has low curvature causing high value of overall impact γ. On the opposite side, the sensitivity curve $GCD(0.5, 0.5, z)$ for the low weight input z illustrates a dramatic case of hypersensitivity. The geometric mean is a hard aggregator with the lowest andness (approximately $^2/_3$), and now the performance increments for higher weights can be rather significant. For low weights, the sensitivity curves are very nonlinear, with very high initial values of the first derivative. In the general case of geometric mean, we have

$$y = \prod_{i=1}^{n} x_i^{W_i}, \quad \ln y = \sum_{i=1}^{n} W_i \ln x_i, \quad \frac{\partial \ln y}{\partial \ln x_i} = W_i = const., \quad i = 1,\dots,n;$$

$$\frac{\partial y}{\partial x_i} = W_i \frac{y}{x_i} = x_1^{W_1} \cdots \left(W_i \frac{x_i^{W_i}}{x_i} \right) \cdots x_n^{W_n},$$

$$\lim_{x_i \to 0} \partial y / \partial x_i = +\infty.$$

In the case of the geometric mean shown in Fig. 3.7.4, we have the output suitability $S = x^{0.7} y^{0.25} z^{0.05}$ and $\partial S / \partial z$ is very high for small values of z. Assuming $x = y = 0.5$, we have $S|_{z=0} = 0$ and $S|_{z=0.005} = 0.4$ (an unjustifiable amplification of 80 times!). As we discussed in Section 2.2.6 ($\mathbf{P_{32}}$), it is easy to see that such spiky jumps of output suitability are not among observable properties of human reasoning. Humans do not use extremely fast continuous transitions of preference, but they do use values outside the narrow area of fast transition.

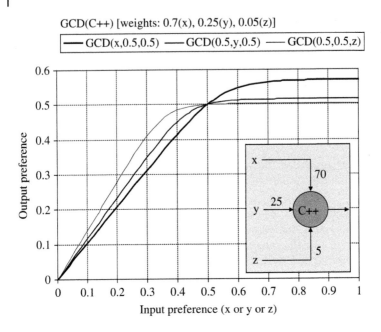

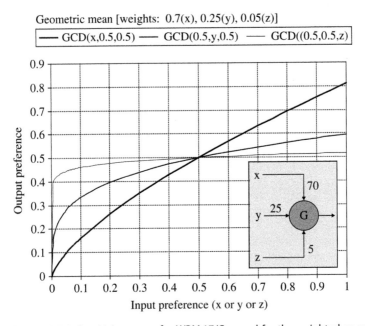

Figure 3.7.4 Sensitivity curves for WPM.17/C++ and for the weighted geometric mean.

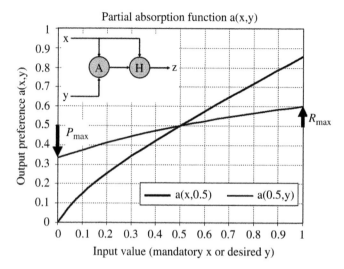

Figure 3.7.5 Sensitivity curves for the AH version of partial absorption.

A similar sensitivity analysis can be performed in the case of partial absorption. A simple AH version of partial absorption function is shown in Fig. 3.7.5. This model uses equal weights (0.5) and inputs $x = y = 0.5$. Consequently, we have

$$z = x \trianglerighteq y = a(x,y) = \frac{2x(x+y)}{3x+y} = \begin{cases} 2x/3, & y = 0 \\ \dfrac{2x(x+1)}{3x+1}, & y = 1 \end{cases}.$$

max penalty $P_{max} = a(x,y) - a(x,0) = 1/2 - 1/3 = 1/6$;
max reward $R_{max} = a(x,1) - a(x,y) = 3/5 - 1/2 = 1/10$.

The maximum penalty and reward are shown in sensitivity curves in Fig. 3.7.5 (see also similar examples in Figs. 3.4.14 and 3.4.15).

In the case of complex criteria, we can analyze the sensitivity of selected output with respect to selected inputs, weights, and andness. Such analyses help to validate the criterion before it is applied for evaluation and comparison of systems. An example of the sensitivity analysis of an LSP criterion for software evaluation can be found in [SU87].

3.7.1.3 Sensitivity with Respect to Input Attributes

Sensitivity analysis can also be performed directly with respect to input attributes. In such cases, the sensitivity functions also depend on elementary attribute criteria, and need not be monotonic functions as in the case of sensitivity with respect to input suitability. Fig. 3.7.6 shows the elementary criteria, the aggregation structure, and the default values of input parameters for a WPM.17 version of the home location problem introduced in Chapter 3.1.

The sensitivity analysis with respect to input attributes is most useful if performed for specific actual object (in our example, the location shown in Fig. 3.7.6). Then we explicitly see the impact of each specific attribute, as well as the capability to compensate the deficiencies of specific attribute by improving other attributes. The following sensitivity analysis is performed using the LSP.NT software tool.

The analyzed location has the overall suitability 89.17% and for nominal values of attributes shown in Fig. 3.7.6 all sensitivity curves must go through this point. The input attribute #112 (distance from food stores) is a mandatory requirement. Consequently, its sensitivity function shown in Fig. 3.7.7 includes the zero value. The output aggregator (#1) is a CPA, and its input #11 is mandatory, making mandatory both inputs #111 and #112. However, #111 is a disjunctive aggregate of #1111 and #1112, and if one of these two inputs is satisfied, the other is not mandatory. The idea behind this kind of aggregation is that the user is satisfied if there is good access to public transportation regardless of the type of transportation (either train or bus). However, if one type of public transport is missing, then the other one becomes the mandatory requirement. This is an example of conditionally mandatory inputs. Consequently, the sensitivity with respect to conditionally mandatory input can be rather low as shown in Fig. 3.7.8. As opposed to that, the sensitivity to nonmandatory inputs can be significant, as illustrated in Fig. 3.7.9: the distance from park is 0 and initial suitability is 89.17%, but as we move further from parks, the suitability decreases, eventually reaching 55%. This shows a significant sensitivity of the vicinity to parks, which can reduce the overall suitability for 35%.

An example of the nonmonotonic sensitivity function is shown in Fig. 3.7.10. It is easy to note that in the case of nonmonotonic sensitivity functions, the sensitivity indicators defined for input preferences must be cautiously interpreted. In particular, the overall impact of inputs cannot be evaluated using the coefficients γ_i and γ_{ri}. However, the absolute influence range $\rho_i = 100\left(y_i^{(\max)} - y_i^{(\min)}\right)$ and the relative influence range can be used as substitutes.

3.7.2 Tradeoff Analysis

Tradeoff analysis investigates compensatory properties of inputs of complex criteria. In many cases a higher satisfaction of a requirement can compensate for a lower satisfaction of another requirement. For example, a homebuyer

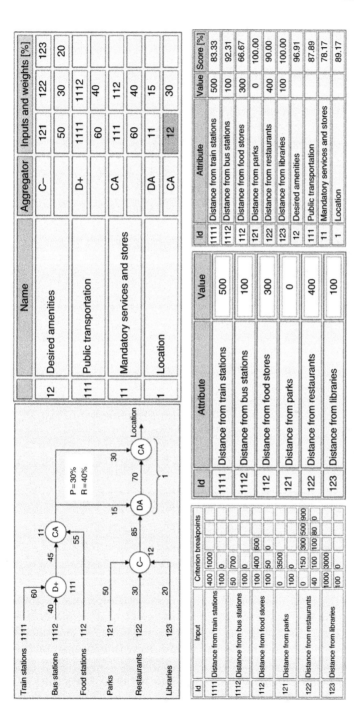

Figure 3.7.6 Top row: aggregation structure; bottom row: elementary criteria, the attributes of a home location, and the results of evaluation (generated using the LSP.web tool).

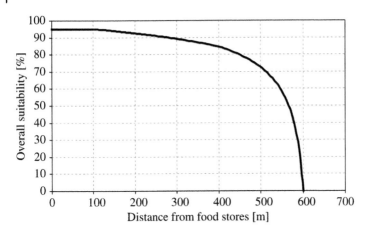

Figure 3.7.7 Sensitivity curve in the case of mandatory input #112.

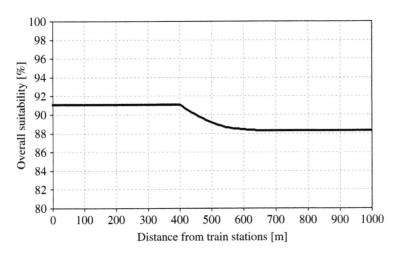

Figure 3.7.8 Sensitivity with respect to conditionally mandatory input #1111.

might consider that a better location of a home can fully compensate its lower area. If the compensation between requirements is not consistent with the evaluator's expectations, then the criterion must be modified and tuned to provide the expected compensatory properties. Similar to sensitivity analysis, tradeoff analysis is used for justification of complex criteria, and proper compensatory properties can significantly contribute to the confidence in evaluation results.

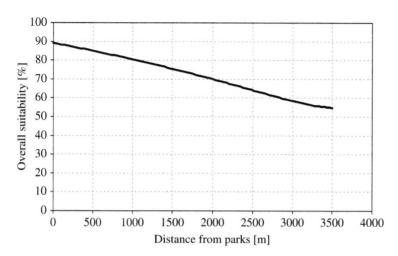

Figure 3.7.9 Sensitivity with respect to nonmandatory input #121.

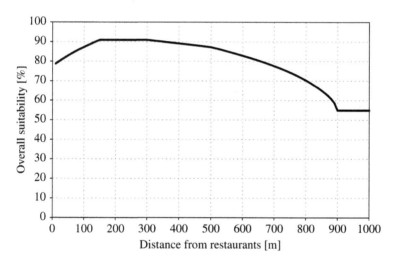

Figure 3.7.10 Nonmonotonic sensitivity function of input #122.

3.7.2.1 Compensatory Properties of LSP Criteria and Graded Logic Aggregators

Let $A : [0,1]^n \rightarrow [0,1]$ be an LSP suitability aggregation function. We assume that

$$\frac{\partial A(x_1,...,x_n)}{\partial x_i} \geq 0, \quad i = 1,...,n.$$

Consequently, there is a possibility of compensating a decrement of preference x_i using an appropriate increment of preference x_j:

$$A(x_1,...,x_n) = A\left(x_1,...,x_i - \Delta x_i,...,x_j + \Delta x_j,...,x_n\right), \quad i \in \{1,...,n\},$$
$$j \in \{1,...,n\}, \quad i \neq j.$$

The goal of the tradeoff analysis is to study relationships between Δx_i and Δx_j, or between multiple simultaneous increments and decrements. The fundamental practical problem is to find the conditions when the compensation is possible.

Suitability degrees $x_1,...,x_n$ are functions of attributes $a_1,...,a_n$. Unfortunately, functions $x_i = g_i(a_i)$, $i = 1,...,n$ are not always monotonic. Without monotonicity of $A(g_1(a_1),...,g_n(a_n))$, the compensation of unsuitable values of attributes can only be done empirically using sensitivity functions.

The sensitivity analysis presented in Figs. 3.7.7 to 3.7.10 can be used to exemplify the compensatory properties of location suitability criterion. The distance from food stores is 300 m and the overall suitability is 89.17%. According to Fig. 3.7.9, if we increase the distance to parks to 700 m, then the overall suitability drops from 89.17% to 83.24%, i.e., we are losing approximately 6% because of the increased distance from parks. On the other hand, according to Fig. 3.7.7, if the distance from food stores is reduced to 0 the overall suitability would increase from 89.17% to 95.09%. So, the proximity to food stores has *compensation power* to add close to 6% to the overall score. Therefore, there is the obvious possibility for tradeoff and compensation. Indeed, if we simultaneously have 0 distance from food stores and 700 m of distance from parks the overall suitability is 89.03%, which is practically completely successful compensation. In other words, according to this criterion, a distance of 300 m from food stores is approximately equivalent to 700 m from parks. Of course, we can easily compensate a deficiency in one attribute with a surplus created by a selected group of attributes. On the other hand, all compensations have limits. In our example, if the distance from park is greater than 700 m, that cannot be compensated by increasing the proximity to food stores. This example shows that sensitivity curves are suitable tools for verification of properties of LSP criteria. They can be used for the study of impact to attributes, as well as for compensatory tradeoff analysis. Such analysis consists of expressing for each attribute the *compensation power* as the preference increment δ_i^+, which is a limit of suitability improvement that can be contributed by the attribute a_i. Then, we can combine attributes with sufficient compensation power to compensate deficiency of some other attributes, or simply to increase the overall suitability in a cost-effective way.

All idempotent graded logic functions are monotonic, and therefore, their compensatory properties can be analyzed using contour lines of selected aggregation functions. In the case of two selected variables, x_i and x_j, we can first select a desired level of output preference $z_0 \in {]}0,1{[}$, and then use

$A(x_1,...,x_i,...,x_j,...,x_n) = z_0$ to analyze the relationship of x_i and x_j. For example, in the case of simple arithmetic and geometric means of two variables, the corresponding tradeoff (contour) lines for $z_0 = 0.1, 0.2,...,0.9$ are presented in Fig. 3.7.11. The contour lines for the quadratic means and a stronger disjunctive aggregator are shown in Fig. 3.7.12. It is easy to note that the contour lines for partial conjunction are convex and for partial disjunction are concave, as illustrated in two typical aggregators shown in Fig. 3.7.13. Contour lines of partial absorption aggregators are exemplified in Fig. 3.7.14. There are visible similarities between PC and CPA, as well as between PD and DPA.

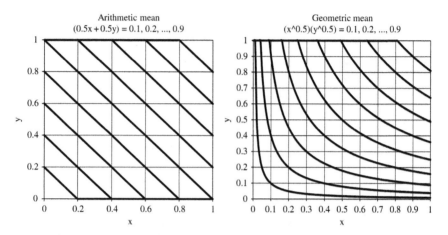

Figure 3.7.11 Tradeoff curves for the simple arithmetic and geometric means.

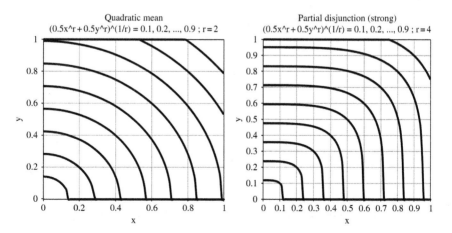

Figure 3.7.12 The effects of increasing orness for tradeoff curves of partial disjunction.

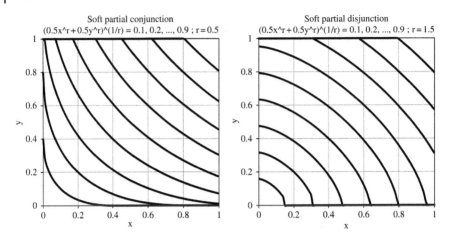

Figure **3.7.13** Tradeoff curves of two typical soft aggregators.

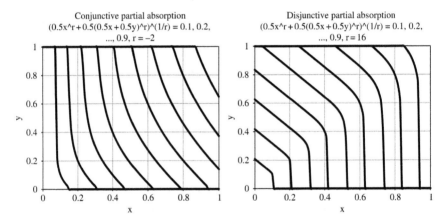

Figure **3.7.14** Tradeoff analysis for conjunctive and disjunctive partial absorption function.

Tradeoff properties of presented aggregators can be summarized as follows:

- All contour lines go through points $z = y = x$ (idempotency).
- All contour lines are strictly decreasing within the compensatory range.
- Conjunctive aggregators have convex contour lines.
- Disjunctive aggregators have concave contour lines.
- Contour lines of hard aggregators never touch coordinate axes.
- Some contour lines of soft aggregators touch coordinate axes.
- Similarly to PC, conjunctive PA has convex contour lines.
- Similarly to PD, disjunctive PA has concave contour lines.

- In the case of CPA, y cannot compensate $x = 0$ and x can compensate $y = 0$.
- Disjunctive partial absorption based on A and soft PD gives similar effects as PD.

3.7.2.2 The Concept of Compensation Ratio

Let $f : [0,1]^2 \rightarrow [0,1]$ be a nondecreasing preference aggregator:

$$z = f(x,y), \quad \frac{\partial z}{\partial x} \geq 0, \quad \frac{\partial z}{\partial y} \geq 0.$$

Let us select the value $z = z_0$, $0 < z_0 < 1$ and let $y = H_y(x, z_0)$ or $x = H_x(y, z_0)$ be the corresponding tradeoff line at the level z_0. Obviously, H_y is a decreasing function of x, because it shows how a decrement of y can be compensated by an increment of x: $dH_y(x, z_0)/dx \leq 0$. Similarly, $dH_x(y, z_0)/dy \leq 0$. Let X_{min} and X_{max} (or Y_{min} and Y_{max}) be respectively the smallest and the largest values of x (or y) inside $[0, 1]^2$ that satisfy $z_0 = f(x,y)$:

$$z_0 = f(X_{min}, Y_{max}) = f(X_{max}, Y_{min}),$$
$$X_{min} = H_x(Y_{max}, z_0), \quad X_{max} = H_x(Y_{min}, z_0),$$
$$Y_{min} = H_y(X_{max}, z_0), \quad Y_{max} = H_y(X_{min}, z_0).$$

These equations can be solved as follows:

$$X_{min} = \max(0, H_x(1, z_0)), \quad X_{max} = \min(1, H_x(0, z_0)),$$
$$Y_{min} = \max(0, H_y(1, z_0)), \quad Y_{max} = \min(1, H_y(0, z_0)).$$

The *compensation ratio* at the level z_0 can now be defined as follows:

$$C_{xy}(z_0) = \frac{Y_{max} - Y_{min}}{X_{max} - X_{min}} = \frac{\min(1, H_y(0, z_0)) - \max(0, H_y(1, z_0))}{\min(1, H_x(0, z_0)) - \max(0, H_x(1, z_0))},$$
$$C_{yx}(z_0) = 1/C_{xy}(z_0).$$

If $C_{xy}(z_0) > 1$, then the compensation power of x is greater than the compensation power of y. Conversely, if $C_{xy}(z_0) < 1$, then the compensation power of y is greater than the compensation power of x.

Example 1. Geometric mean at the level $z_0 = 0.5$:

$$z = \sqrt{xy} = 0.5, \quad x = 0.25/y, \quad y = 0.25/x,$$
$$X_{min} = \max(0, 0.25) = 0.25, \quad X_{max} = \min(1, +\infty) = 1,$$
$$Y_{min} = \max(0, 0.25) = 0.25, \quad Y_{max} = \min(1, +\infty) = 1,$$
$$C_{xy} = C_{yx} = 0.75/0.75 = 1.$$

For all symmetrical aggregators, the compensation ratio is 1.

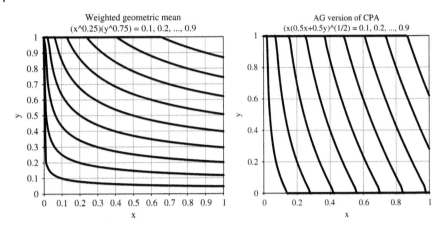

Figure 3.7.15 Two conjunctive aggregators used for computing the compensation ratio.

Example 2. Weighted geometric mean shown in Fig. 3.7.15 at the level $z_0 = 0.5$:

$$z = x^{0.25}y^{0.75} = 0.5, \quad x = 0.0625/y^3, \quad y = 0.397/x^{1/3},$$
$$X_{min} = \max(0,0.0625) = 0.0625, \quad X_{max} = \min(1, +\infty) = 1,$$
$$Y_{min} = \max(0,0.397) = 0.397, \quad Y_{max} = \min(1, +\infty) = 1,$$
$$C_{xy} = 0.6031/0.9375 = 0.643, \quad C_{yx} = 1/0.643 = 1.555.$$

At the level of 0.5, the compensation power of x is 64.3% of the compensation power of y.

Example 3. AG version of the partial absorption (Fig. 3.7.15) at the level $z_0 = 0.5$:

$$z = \sqrt{x(0.5x + 0.5y)} = 0.5, \quad x = -0.5y + \sqrt{0.25y^2 + 0.5}, \quad y = (0.5 - x^2)/x,$$
$$X_{min} = \max(0,0.366) = 0.366, \quad X_{max} = \min(1,0.707) = 0.707,$$
$$Y_{min} = \max(0, -0.5) = 0, \quad Y_{max} = \min(1, +\infty) = 1,$$
$$C_{xy} = 1/(0.707 - 0.366) = 2.93, \quad C_{yx} = 0.341.$$

Not surprisingly, (at $z_0 = 0.5$) the compensation power of the mandatory input x is almost three times bigger than the compensatory power of the desired input y.

Example 4. Weighted arithmetic mean at the level $z_0 = 0.5$:

$$z = W_x x + W_y y = 0.5, \quad W_x > W_y,$$

$$x = 0.5/W_x - y W_y/W_x, \quad y = 0.5/W_y - x W_x/W_y,$$

$$X_{\min} = \max(0, 0.5/W_x - W_y/W_x) = 0.5/W_x - W_y/W_x,$$

$$X_{\max} = \min(1, 0.5/W_x) = 0.5/W_x, \quad X_{\max} - X_{\min} = W_y/W_x,$$

$$Y_{\min} = \max(0, 0.5/W_y - W_x/W_y) = 0,$$

$$Y_{\max} = \min(1, 0.5/W_y) = 1,$$

$$C_{xy} = W_x/W_y, \quad C_{yx} = W_y/W_x.$$

Due to the symmetry between x and y, the same result is obtained if $W_x \leq W_y$. Only in the linear case of weighted power mean is the compensation ratio equal to the ratio of weights.

In the frequent case of monotonic elementary criteria (like preferred large values and preferred small values, Fig. 3.3.5), the compensatory properties of attributes are monotonic and similar to Figs. 3.7.11 to 3.7.15. In such cases, let p and q denote two compensative attributes and let the overall suitability S be a function of n aggregators: $S = f(..., p, ..., q, ...)$. Similarly to the case of GL aggregators, we can now determine $P_{\min}, P_{\max}, Q_{\min}, Q_{\max}$ which, for a given overall suitability S_0, satisfies the condition

$$S_0 = f(..., P_{\min}, ..., Q_{\max}, ...) = f(..., P_{\max}, ..., Q_{\min}, ...).$$

Then, the *attribute compensation ratio* can be computed as follows:

$$C_{pq}(S_0) = \frac{Q_{\max} - Q_{\min}}{P_{\max} - P_{\min}} = 1/C_{qp}.$$

3.8 Reliability Analysis

> *Risk comes from not knowing what you're doing.*
> —Warren Buffett

LSP criteria generate overall suitability degrees that are used to compare competitive systems. If the overall suitability degrees (X_a and X_b) of two competitive systems (*A* and *B*) differ for a value $\Delta = X_a - X_b$ we always face the question whether Δ is sufficiently big, so that we can be confident that the resulting ranking is correct. The errors in ranking are the consequence of various errors discussed in Section 2.2.6, primarily errors in parameter estimation. In the case of graded logic models, the main parameters are weights and andness of selected GCD aggregators. The first naïve reaction to this problem could be that if Δ is big, the ranking is reliable and if Δ is small, the ranking is not reliable. To show that this reasoning can be wrong, let us suppose that system A is in each and every attribute a smidgen better than system B. Then Δ would be tiny but the ranking would be 100% reliable because the ranking remains unchanged regardless the selected values of parameters and regardless the size of parameter estimation errors. On the other hand, if A is better than B in one group of attributes and worse in another group, then a wrong distribution of weights could result in significant values of Δ, but the ranking could still be wrong. Therefore, if we want to be confident in evaluation results, we need a reliability analysis. That is the topic for this chapter.

3.8.1 Sources of Errors in LSP Criteria and Their Empirical Analysis

Human perceptions are never perfectly accurate. These problems were analyzed in Section 2.2.6 and we found that sources of errors in LSP criteria include the following:

Soft Computing Evaluation Logic: The LSP Decision Method and Its Applications, First Edition. Jozo Dujmović.
© 2018 John Wiley & Sons, Inc. Published 2018 by John Wiley & Sons, Inc.
Companion website: www.wiley.com/go/Dujmovic/Soft_Computing_Evaluation_Logic

- Omission of attributes
- Uncontrolled redundancy of attributes
- Elementary criteria breakpoint parameter errors
- Errors in weights of preference aggregation functions
- Errors in the selected level of andness/orness
- Errors in the structure of suitability aggregation functions

In the case of system evaluation with professionally prepared evaluators, errors in the area of selection of attributes (either omission of excessive redundancy) and structuring aggregation function should not be a source of serious concern. Other errors are caused by human perceptual imperfection, and they can be reduced by professional training but cannot be avoided.

The selection of weights and andness/orness can be interpreted as Miller's absolute judgments of unidimensional stimuli [MIL56]. According to Miller, for this kind of judgment, the values of weights and andness should be reliably selected in 10 to 15 distinct positions along the unit interval. We found this result to be a lower bound of accuracy that can be expected from unmotivated or unprepared evaluators (for detailed analysis see [FAN04] and [DUJ04a]). Professionally prepared evaluators can attain substantially higher precision, and the andness/orness rating scales of medium and high precision are fully justified. This can be demonstrated in the case of weight assessment.

Weights are indicators of relative importance. They are selected by evaluators, and it is interesting to know what accuracy we can expect in that process. To investigate this problem we performed two experiments in absolute judgment. The experiments used geometrical patterns (segmented lines or pie charts). The first experiment included four lines divided into 2, 3, 4, and 5 unequal segments respectively. This experiment is similar to one of experiments reported in [MIL56], and verifies Miller's observation that in this area it is possible to achieve high accuracy of results. The second experiment was similar, but included four pie charts dividing 100% into 2, 3, 4, and 5 unequal parts. Participants were asked to assess the values of each of 14 linear and 14 circular segments as accurately as possible, using only observation (perception). In these experiments, we can assume that evaluators (computer science students) have sufficient expertise for the given evaluation. Segments that divide a line that has the assumed length of 100% are equivalent to weights that have the total sum of 100%, and our goal is to investigate the accuracy of perceptual instrument performing the assessment of individual components.

It is useful to classify all experimental results of weight assessment into four groups:

1) Outliers, that contain values that are far off the exact values
2) Data that violate the ranking of exact values
3) Data that have correct ranking but may contain outliers
4) Correct data that are without outliers and are consistent with exact ranking.

Table 3.8.1 Summary of weight assessment experiments for a group of evaluators.

Measured indicator [%] (L = Line segments, P = Pie charts)	Input	All data unfiltered	Correct data
Percent of modulo 5 rounded weights	L	72.26	68.23
Mean abs error of group estimates	L	0.52	0.66
Mean abs error of individual evaluator	L	2.71	2.37
Percent of modulo 5 rounded weights	P	63.50	55.12
Mean abs error of group estimates	P	0.64	0.69
Mean abs error of individual evaluator	P	2.56	2.18

Since the exact values in our experiments were selected to be sufficiently different from each other, we did not expect the ranking errors. However, 32% of evaluators made ranking errors in the linear pattern case, and 28% made ranking errors in the circular pattern case. These errors can be attributed to insufficient motivation, no preparation, and insufficient effort caused by short assessment time. Table 3.8.1 summarizes results obtained for two groups: all evaluators, and evaluators who generate correct data. It is reasonable to expect that professional evaluators put sufficient effort in their assessments and that they belong to the group with exact ranking and without outliers (correct data group).

In both experiments, the group assessment (based on mean values) is remarkably accurate. The absolute difference (the group estimate minus the exact value) is convincingly below 1%. Individual evaluators never achieve the accuracy of group estimates, but the mean absolute errors of individuals in the whole population that provides correct ranking is always below 2.5%. The linear results and the pie chart results are consistent, showing that errors are primarily related to the percept of size, and not to visual phenomena.

The quality of an individual evaluator is analyzed in Fig. 3.8.1. The points represent cumulative probability distribution of average absolute errors for linear and pie-chart segments for the population of rank-qualified evaluators (all evaluators except those who make obvious ranking errors). Minor differences in distributions between the linear and circular case can be attributed to visual effects and further justify that both approaches can be used for assessment of weight perception accuracy. Professional evaluators might be selected as the best 10% of this population. For them, the average absolute error is below 1.5%. In addition to average absolute errors, Fig. 3.8.1 also shows the number of distinct positions (denoted DP) that can be recognized by individual evaluators. Distinct positions are defined as reciprocals of the double average absolute error. For example, if the average absolute error is 2.5%, it follows that the evaluator perceives a segment of size 5% as a distinct unit. Thus, such an evaluator is capable of recognizing 20 such units. More than 60% of the population can

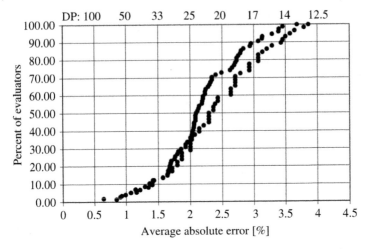

Figure 3.8.1 The distribution of evaluation errors (correct ranking, without outliers).

recognize 20 distinct positions and almost 40% of population can recognize 25 distinct values. Professional evaluators (top 10%) can recognize more than 33.

According to these results, it follows that UGCD.15 and GGCD.17 can be comfortably used by 80–90% of general population and UGCD.23 and GGCD.25 can be used by more than 40% of the general population. Taking into account effects of training and stepwise refinement algorithms for selecting the andness of GCD aggregators, we can confidently expect the correct selection of the most appropriate degree of andness defined in a selected rating scale.

The average absolute error of individual rank-qualified evaluators is almost independent of the value of weight, as shown in Fig. 3.8.2. The average error is between 2.2% and 2.4%, which is below the quality we attribute to professional evaluators. Unsurprisingly, constant absolute errors cause increasing relative errors of weights as the number of segments increases (Fig. 3.8.3).

If a GCD aggregator includes n inputs, it is necessary to simultaneously determine n weights. Evaluators must consider relationships between each pair of inputs. For 2, 3, 4, 5, 6, 7, ..., n inputs, there are 1, 3, 6, 10, 15, 21, ..., $n(n-1)/2$ pairs. Obviously, the complexity of selecting weights quickly increases with a growing number of inputs. To keep the number of pairs close to the "magical number seven plus or minus two" [MIL56], we suggest using up to five inputs (in the case of more inputs, we keep them in smaller groups, and then aggregate group suitability degrees). This conclusion is supported by the growth of the average relative error shown in Fig. 3.8.3.

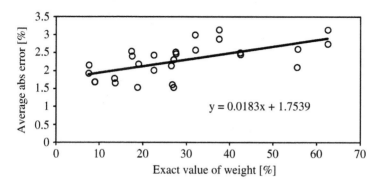

Figure 3.8.2 Average absolute error of individual evaluator as a function of weight.

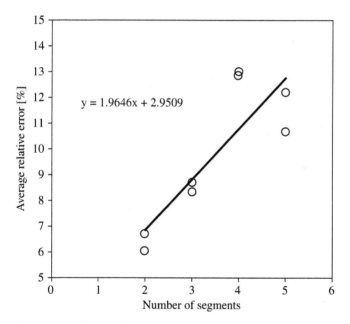

Figure 3.8.3 The growth of relative errors for experiments with line and pie-chart segments (2 to 5 segments).

The errors in weights are not negligible. Some of them are caused by the modulo 5 rounding problem (selecting weights from the sequence of 5%, 10%, ..., 95%, i.e., from the sequence that satisfies $w \mod 5 = 0$). We found that in all cases of parameter estimation evaluators can easily differentiate 20 levels of relative importance. This seems to be the average value for the majority of evaluators working at an average effort level. In situations characterized by insufficient expertise and/or insufficient motivation, the number of levels may be reduced to 10 (selecting weights from the sequence 10%, 20%, ..., 90%). If professional evaluators are defined as 10% of the best in general population, then their accuracy in weight assessment is expected to be in the range of 30 levels or more. Such accuracy can also be attained using specialized weight computation techniques and tools (Section 2.5.4 and Chapter 3.4).

3.8.2 The Problem of Confidence in Evaluation Results

Suppose that we evaluate and compare two competitive systems, A and B. Fig. 3.8.4 shows a general LSP logic aggregation structure for their comparison. This criterion contains two arrays of parameters: $\mathbf{W}$ (weights) and $\mathbf{P}$ (andness of GCD aggregators). Input values $x_1, x_2, ..., x_n$ are the attribute suitability degrees, but our analysis equally applies to cases where the input values are the suitability attributes.

In the case of system A, the inputs $x_{a1}, x_{a2}, ..., x_{an}$ generate the overall suitability X_a, and for the system B the inputs $x_{b1}, x_{b2}, ..., x_{bn}$ generate the overall suitability X_b, also shown in Fig. 3.8.4. If $X_a > X_b$, then our problem is to find whether the difference $X_a - X_b$ is sufficiently large to confidently claim that the system A is better than the system B.

Evaluators estimate the values of parameters $\mathbf{W}$ and $\mathbf{P}$. Unfortunately, the estimated values differ from the unknown optimum values $\mathbf{W}^*$ and $\mathbf{P}^*$.

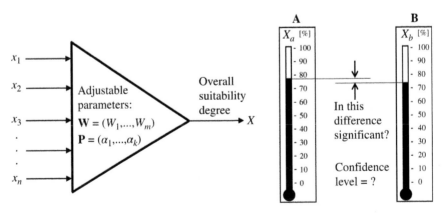

Figure 3.8.4 An LSP criterion with parameters **W** and **P**, and the corresponding reliability problem.

Consequently, the resulting overall suitability degrees X_a and X_b also differ from the unknown optimum values X_a^* and X_b^*:

$$|X_a - X_a^*| = \varepsilon_a \,, \quad 0 \le \varepsilon_a < 1$$

$$|X_b - X_b^*| = \varepsilon_b \,, \quad 0 \le \varepsilon_b < 1$$

The reliability problem can be defined as follows: if $X_a^* > X_b^*$ (system A is actually better than system B, denoted $A \succ B$), what is the probability that our model generates a correct ranking $(X_a > X_b)$? Conversely, if we computed $X_a > X_b$, at what level of confidence can we claim that $X_a^* > X_b^*$ and $A \succ B$?

We can assume that each individual evaluator gives his/her values of all parameters, and a population of evaluators generates a distribution of values for each component of the parameter arrays **W** and **P**. Two typical such distributions for a weight parameter w are shown in Fig. 3.8.5. A realistic distribution is a truncated normal distribution. If we want to generate upper bounds of error, we can use a pessimistic case of the uniform distribution. Assuming a large number of qualified evaluators, the mean value $\bar{w}$ can be interpreted as the optimum value.

Fig. 3.8.5 shows the process of estimation of the value of a selected weight. Theoretically, the correct value is the mean value of estimates given by the hypothetical population that includes all existing qualified evaluators. In Fig. 3.8.5, this unknown best value is denoted $\bar{w}$, $\bar{w} \in \mathbf{W}^*$. Our assessment of this weight is $w = (w_{\min} + w_{\max})/2$, and we can select the values $w_{\min}$ and $w_{\max}$ so that we are fully confident that $\bar{w} \in [w_{\min}, w_{\max}]$. The confidence in the selected size of the range $\rho = w_{\max} - w_{\min}$ comes from experimental analysis of errors expected in expert estimation of objective values shown in the previous section. Therefore, the only information that we have about each weight is reduced to w, $w_{\min}$, $w_{\max}$. We have similar information for all parameters (weights, andness, or parameters of attribute criteria). If we are fully confident that the correct weight

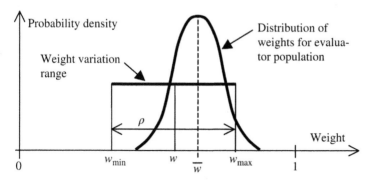

Figure 3.8.5 Characteristic distributions of an estimated weight.

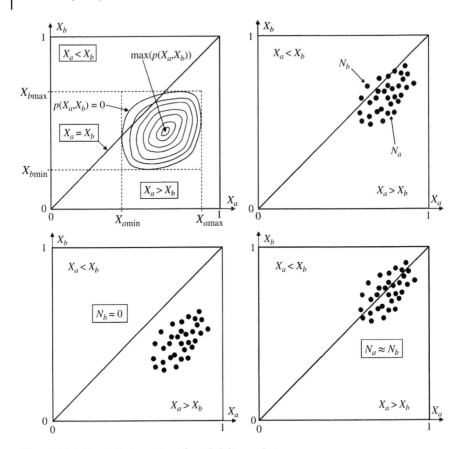

Figure 3.8.6 Monte Carlo method for reliability analysis.

is inside the interval [w_{min}, w_{max}], then its location can be everywhere inside the interval and, in the worst case, with equal probability.

If we assume that every parameter of the LSP criterion function is a random value, then we can use the LSP criterion and generate a large number of random (X_a, X_b) pairs (points) that create the probability density function $p(X_a, X_b)$ shown in Fig. 3.8.6, top-left. One of these points (with equal probability) is the correct result of evaluation $\left(X_a^*, X_b^*\right)$ where by assumption $X_a^* > X_b^*$.

Assuming that $X_{a\,min} \leq X_a \leq X_{a\,max}$ and $X_{b\,min} \leq X_b \leq X_{b\,max}$, the probability that $A \succ B$ can be computed as the fraction of the probability density surface located below the line $X_a = X_b$, as follows:

$$\Psi = \Pr(A \succ B) = \int\limits_0^1 dX_a \int\limits_0^{X_a} p(X_a, X_b) dX_b = \int\limits_{X_{a\,min}}^{X_{a\,max}} dX_a \int\limits_{X_{b\,min}}^{X_a} p(X_a, X_b) dX_b \in [0, 1].$$

Obviously, Ψ can be interpreted as the degree of confidence that $A \succ B$. For complex LSP criteria, the above integral cannot be analytically solved, but numerical Monte Carlo solution exemplified in Fig. 3.8.6 is rather simple. Let us generate N random sets of parameters, generating N random points in the (X_a, X_b)-plane. These points can be decomposed in two groups:

$N_a(N)$ = number of points where $X_a > X_b$,

$N_b(N)$ = number of points where $X_a \le X_b$,

$N_a(N) + N_b(N) = N$.

Then the confidence can be computed as follows:

$$\Psi = \int_0^1 dX_a \int_0^{X_a} p(X_a, X_b) dX_b = \lim_{N \to +\infty} \frac{N_a(N)}{N_a(N) + N_b(N)} \approx \frac{N_a(N)}{N} \bigg|_{N \gg 1}.$$

Therefore, we have to write a Monte Carlo simulator that creates N random points in the (X_a, X_b)-plane and counts N_a points below the $X_a = X_b$ line and $N_b = N - N_a$ points that are not below the $X_a = X_b$ line. Then, the confidence is computed simply as follows:

$$\Psi = \frac{N_a}{N_a + N_b}, \quad 0 \le \Psi \le 1.$$

Interesting programming details (how to generate uniformly distributed random weights that have the sum 1, and how to select the random andness, either continuously, or in discrete steps) can be found in [DUJ04b]. In a typical case $N = 10^6$, we can expect that the computed value of Ψ has three correct significant decimal digits.

Three characteristic values of Ψ are illustrated in Fig. 3.8.6. In the top-right case we have $N_a > N_b$, and consequently $\Psi > \frac{1}{2}$. Generally, we can claim that $A \succ B$ with the risk $1 - \Psi$. The bottom-left case has $N_b = 0$, and consequently $\Psi = 1$ (we can claim that $A \succ B$ with 100% of confidence). Finally, the bottom-right case shows the situation where $N_a \approx N_b$, and consequently $\Psi \approx \frac{1}{2}$; in this case, we have insufficient confidence for the claim $A \succ B$. However, in this case we can claim that systems A and B are equivalent and each of them can satisfy approximately $(X_a + X_b)/2$ of the specified stakeholder's requirements.

Both the probability density function $p(X_a, X_b)$ and the confidence Ψ depend on the variability of parameter vectors $\mathbf{W}$ and $\mathbf{P}$. This variability can be expressed as the range ρ (shown in Fig. 3.8.5) or similarly, using the standard deviation σ and the coefficient of variation v of components of the parameter vectors. Then the confidence can be computed as a function of these variability indicators. If the confidence Ψ is a function of the range ρ, then the function $\Psi(\rho)$ has the characteristic shape shown in Fig. 3.8.7.

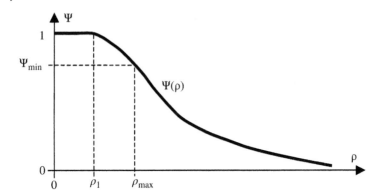

Figure 3.8.7 Confidence Ψ as a function of the range of variation of parameters.

The $\Psi(\rho)$ curve is important for reliability analysis, based on the following characteristic values:

ρ_1 = the safe range, defined as the largest variation range that still produces the maximum confidence $\Psi = 1$.

Ψ_{min} = the minimum acceptable confidence level (e.g., 90%) corresponding to the maximum acceptable range of variation of parameters.

ρ_{max} = the maximum acceptable range (the upper limit of the parameter estimation error)

If ρ_1 and ρ_{max} are larger than the expected errors of the evaluation team, then the ranking of competitors is reliable. The following section illustrates the use of these parameters.

3.8.3   Case Study of Reliability Analysis for a Computer Evaluation Project

The presented reliability analysis was applied to a real mainframe computer selection project performed for a steel industry company. In this study the LSP criterion was based on WPM.17 aggregators and had 94 attributes, 56 aggregation operators, with 60 andness parameters (WPM exponents) and 150 weights. There were 6 competitive systems (A, B, C, D, E, F) that attained the following overall suitability degrees:

$$A: X_a = 74.7\%; B: X_b = 71.7\%; C: 67.6\%; D: 67.0\%; E: 29.2\%; F: 27.1\%$$

If we focus on the leading two systems (A and B), then $\Delta = X_a - X_b = 3\%$. Therefore, the main question is whether the small difference of 3% is significant to claim that $A \succ B$.

According to the analysis of errors of weights and andness presented in the previous section, in the case of professional evaluation we can expect variations of weights to be in the range $2\sigma = 5\%$, and the variations of andness/orness to be in the range of 12.5%.

The first step in reliability analysis is to select the parameter variation ranges. In the case of uniform distribution of weights in the interval $[w_{min}, w_{max}]$, the corresponding standard deviation is $\sigma = (w_{max} - w_{min})/2\sqrt{3}$. The weight range is $\rho_w = w_{max} - w_{min} = 2\sigma\sqrt{3}$. We expected variations of weights to be in the range $2\sigma = 5\%$, giving the weight variation range $\rho_w = 8.66\%$. We also decided to vary the andness of each GCD aggregators for one level $(1/16 = 0.0625)$ above and below the selected WPM.17 aggregator giving the andness range $\rho_\alpha = 1/8 = 0.125$. This andness range means that if, e.g., we use the aggregator CA (where $\alpha = 0.75$), our simulator will randomly uniformly select between three adjacent aggregators: C-+, CA, and C + -. This is a discrete andness approach. We also used a continuous andness variation model where $\alpha \in [0.6875, 0.8125]$ (andness is selected uniformly from this interval, converted to the WPM exponent, and applied in corresponding GCD aggregator).

Using a uniform distribution of weights in the range of 8.66% and andness/orness in the range of 12.5%, we generated results that are summarized in Figs. 3.8.8 to 3.8.13. Figs. 3.8.8 to 3.8.10 correspond to continuous model of variation of andness/orness. Figs. 3.8.11 to 3.8.13 correspond to cases where the variation of andness/orness follows a discrete pattern of variation.

The independent distributions of overall suitability degrees of two leading systems in the case of simultaneous continuous variation of weights and andness/orness are shown in Fig. 3.8.8. The distributions of systems A and B clearly overlap, but the ranking remains stable, as shown in Fig. 3.8.9 where we computed

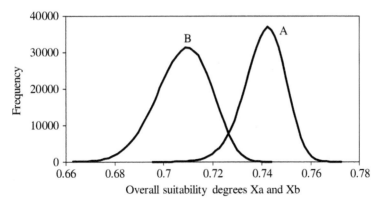

Figure 3.8.8 Distribution of overall suitability of two competitive mainframe computers (continuous andness).

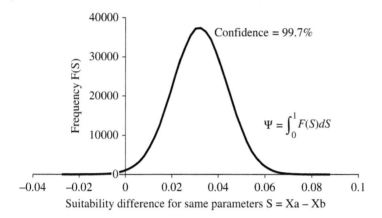

Figure 3.8.9 Distribution of difference of overall suitability of two mainframe computers (continuous andness).

frequency of differences $S = X_a - X_b$ where X_a and X_b are computed for same values of parameters. So, the confidence level Ψ, which is the probability that $S > 0$ can be computed as $\Psi = \int_0^1 F(S)dS$ giving the high confidence of 99.7%. This indicates that system A rather uniformly dominates system B. Fig. 3.8.10 shows the confidence level as a decreasing function of the range of variation of andness/orness. The presented curve corresponds to two cases: (1) variations only in andness/orness and (2) the variation in both andness/orness and weights. In this analysis, the difference between these two cases was negligible. The safe range is 12% (and even if the range comes to 25%, the confidence of

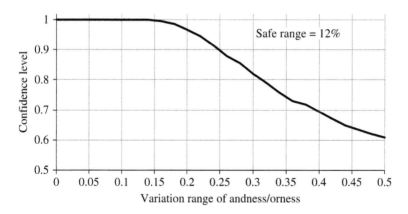

Figure 3.8.10 Degree of confidence (continuous andness).

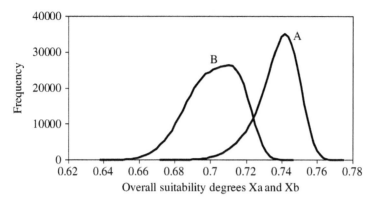

Figure 3.8.11 Distributions of overall suitability (discrete andness).

ranking remains at the level of 90%. This shows the robustness of ranking of two leading systems.

The results for discrete andness shown in Figs. 3.8.11 and 3.8.12 are similar to the case of continuous variation (Figs. 3.8.8 and 3.8.9). In the discrete case, the level of confidence is insignificantly reduced to 98.4%. As an alternative to confidence Ψ, we can define risk of wrong ranking $1 - \Psi = \int_{-1}^{0} F(S)dS$, and in this case, at the risk of 1.6%, we can claim that $A \succ B$.

Results in Figs. 3.8.8 to 3.8.12 correspond to the sample containing 500,000 simulated cases. In the case of a smaller sample containing 2000 simulated points, the points in the overall suitability plane are shown in Fig. 3.8.13. All the presented results convincingly prove that regardless of the small advantage

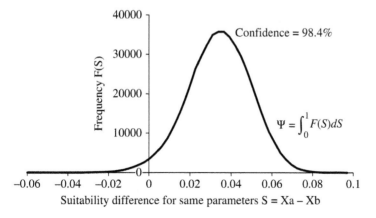

Figure 3.8.12 Distribution of difference of overall suitability degrees (discrete andness).

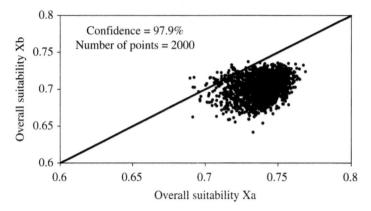

Figure 3.8.13 Reliability of ranking for two mainframe computer systems (discrete andness).

of only 3%, the system A outperforms system B at the high level of confidence. Thus, the difference of 3% is significant for selecting system A as the best alternative.

From this case study, we can conclude that the difference of overall suitability between competitive systems is not a direct indicator of the reliability of evaluation. Small differences do not automatically imply low reliability of ranking. In all system evaluation and selection projects, it is necessary to compute the confidence in ranking of competitive systems, and Monte Carlo simulation is an effective approach to solve this problem.

If one system consistently dominates another system in the most important inputs, then the ranking remains stable regardless of parameter errors. In such a case, the sensitivity of ranking with respect to parameter variations is low, and the confidence in ranking is high. In an opposite case, competitive systems can more significantly differ, and still provide a modest confidence in ranking.

The discrete models of andness variation give less confidence than continuous models because continuous models generate smaller deviations from the mean value and discrete models generate only the extreme cases. Indeed, in discrete case, if $\alpha \in \{\alpha_0 - \delta, \alpha_0, \alpha_0 - \delta\}$ with equal probability 1/3, the variance is $\mu = 2\delta^2/3$ and the corresponding standard deviation is $\sigma_{dis} = \sqrt{\mu} = \delta\sqrt{2/3}$. In the continuous case, $\sigma_{con} = \delta/\sqrt{3}$ and consequently $\sigma_{dis} > \sigma_{con}$.

In practice, the reliability analysis can be reduced to a simple three-step procedure. First, we determine for each parameter a realistic range of variation that can be heterogeneous, with different standard deviation, and with different discrete/continuous type. Then we use a simulator, which for each random set of parameters computes the difference $S = X_a - X_b$ and the probability density function $S \mapsto F(S)$. Finally, the confidence level is computed as

$\Psi = \Pr(A \succ B) = \int_0^1 F(S)dS$. All decisions are based on results of LSP evaluation and comparison can be facilitated and justified using the confidence degree Ψ, or the risk degree $1 - \Psi$.

Our approach to the computation of confidence degree using uniform distributions of weights and andness (instead of perhaps more realistic truncated normal distributions) adds an extra safety margin to our results. The presented application of the Monte Carlo confidence analysis method to a real-life computer selection project generated a high degree of confidence that convincingly supported the resulting LSP ranking. Therefore, the reliability analysis should be a standard part of the majority of evaluation projects. In addition, a confidence analyzer should be a part of professional system evaluation tools.

3.9 System Optimization

System optimization can be defined as a problem of finding the best configuration of an evaluated system, according to some optimization criterion. The optimization criterion is usually an appropriate combination of low cost and high suitability of the analyzed system. In an ideal case of system comparison and selection, we should optimize the configuration of each of competitive systems before the cost/suitability analysis and system selection.

3.9.1 Three Fundamental Constrained Optimization Problems

In a general case, a complex system has the total cost C and satisfies user requirements at the level of overall suitability S. In some cases, there are many possible configurations defined using various values of attributes. Typical examples of such decision problems are encountered in the area of computer evaluation and selection. While decision problems are human problems and they don't change over time, both computer hardware and software change rapidly every year, and the latest shiny computer becomes obsolete before a book is printed. So, if we want to study computer optimization problems (because of their complexity), then we can only use obsolete machines. For example, Table 3.9.1 shows the decision problem facing a buyer of a typical 2004 legacy model of a desktop PC. By combining various independent components of hardware and software it is possible to make $K = 2.92°10^{16}$ different configurations; one of them is the most suitable, and we want to find it. Today the number of options is equally big and can be easily calculated using configuration customization tools available on almost all computer manufacturer websites. Obviously, the method of searching for optimum configurations must deal with a large number of options.

Soft Computing Evaluation Logic: The LSP Decision Method and Its Applications,
First Edition. Jozo Dujmović.
© 2018 John Wiley & Sons, Inc. Published 2018 by John Wiley & Sons, Inc.
Companion website: www.wiley.com/go/Dujmovic/Soft_Computing_Evaluation_Logic

Table 3.9.1 Configuration options for a legacy desktop PC.

No.	Hardware Component	Options		No.	Software Component	Options
1	Processor chip	3		1	Operating system	2
2	Memory	4		2	Operating system enhancements	4
3	Video card	3		3	Software for CD or DVD burner	4
4	Sound card	1		4	Game controllers and specialized I/O	8
5	Hard drive	12		5	Productivity software	7
6	2nd hard drive	5		6	Gaming software	9
7	External hard drive	3		7	Digital music	4
8	CD or DVD drive	7		8	Digital photography	5
9	Removable storage devices	3		9	Video editing	2
10	Modem	3		10	Software bundles	2
11	Network interface	1				
12	Printers	3				
13	LCD TV	7				
14	Monitors	11				
15	Optional second monitor	2				
16	Speakers	6				
17	Keyboards	4				
18	Mouse	5				
Total hardware configurations		$2.26 \cdot 10^{10}$		**Total software configurations**		$1.29 \cdot 10^{6}$
TOTAL NUMBER OF PC CONFIGURATIONS = $2.92 \cdot 10^{16}$						

All possible configurations can be presented as K points in the cost-suitability plane, shown in Fig. 3.9.1. Obviously, some configurations are more desirable and others are less desirable. In this context, optimization is the problem of finding the most desirable configuration. Most frequently, we try to simultaneously satisfy two opposite criteria: minimization of cost and maximization of suitability. This type of search is indicated as moving in the direction of the big diagonal arrow shown in Fig. 3.9.1. Another direction, indicated with the vertical arrow, is the direction of maximizing suitability. There is also the direction of minimizing cost, i.e., movement in the direction of horizontal arrow.

In the context of the LSP method, the existing configurations are identified using the arrays of their overall cost/suitability coordinates: $(C_1, ..., C_K)$ and $(S_1, ..., S_K)$. Now, we can identify three characteristic optimization problems illustrated with three characteristic optimum configurations shown as black points in Fig. 3.9.1:

- *The maximum suitability system* (the most suitable configuration below a given maximum affordable cost limit C_{max}):

$$S_{max} = \max_{C \leq C_{max}} (S_1, ..., S_K).$$

- *The minimum cost system* (the cheapest configuration that attains a given minimum acceptable suitability S_{min}):

$$C_{min} = \min_{S \geq S_{min}} (C_1, ..., C_K).$$

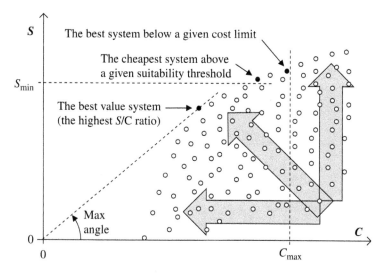

Figure 3.9.1 Three characteristic optimum configurations.

- *The best value system* (the configuration that attains the highest S/C ratio):

$$V_{opt} = S_{opt}/C_{opt} = \max(S_1/C_1,...,S_K/C_K).$$

Therefore, we defined three characteristic optimization problems: *the maximum suitability optimization, the minimum cost optimization, and the maximum value optimization.* A trivial solution of any of these optimization problems is to generate all possible configurations and select one that best satisfies the optimization criterion. This is possible only if the number of existing configurations is not too big. Unfortunately, in many cases the number of possible configurations can be very big. So, most optimization methods are focused on reducing the search time. Our optimization methodology is based on techniques developed in [DUJ98b, KAO04, DUJ05a].

3.9.2 The Cloud Diagram and the Set of Optimum Configurations

Each combination of attributes $a_1, ..., a_n$ represents a specific system configuration, and each configuration can be represented as a point in the cost-suitability plane. All K possible configurations create a "cloud diagram" illustrated in Fig. 3.9.2. The black points at the upper edge of the cloud are the optimum configurations. Note that these optimum points include the three characteristic optimum configurations introduced in Fig. 3.9.1. Each optimum configuration

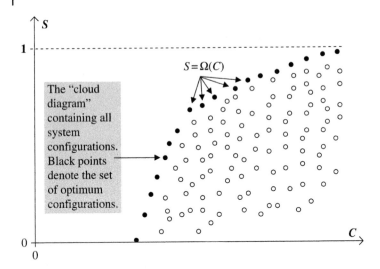

Figure 3.9.2 Cloud diagram and optimum system configurations (Pareto frontier).

$\{a_1^*,...,a_n^*\}$, which has the total cost $C^* = H(a_1^*,...,a_n^*)$ and the overall suitability $S^* = G(a_1^*,...,a_n^*)$, satisfies the condition $S^* = \max_{C \leq C^*}(S_1,...,S_K)$. In other words, for each optimum configuration there is no configuration that would be better and cheaper (the concept equivalent to Pareto optimum). Each optimum configuration can be costlier than another configuration only if it is better (more suitable). Optimum configurations relate the total cost and the maximum suitability as a mapping $S = \Omega(C)$, which includes solutions of all optimization problems.

A basic technique for selecting optimum configurations is illustrated in Fig. 3.9.3. Suppose that A, B, C, D, and E (black points) represent optimum configurations, sorted or linked according to increasing cost and suitability: A → B → C → D → E. Now, we create a new configuration (white point), which is located by cost between B and C and can have suitability that corresponds to points P or Q or R. If it is in location P, the new configuration is ignored and the set of optimum configurations remains unchanged. The configuration P is ignored also in cases where it has the same cost as B.

If the new configuration is in location Q, then it satisfies the condition that it is more suitable and more expensive than B and less suitable and less expensive than C. Consequently, it must be inserted in the set of optimum configurations, which now becomes A → B → Q → C → D → E.

If the new configuration is in location R, then it is more suitable and more expensive than B and it should be inserted in the set of optimum configurations.

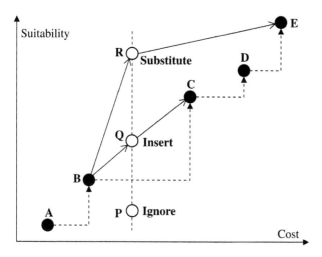

Figure 3.9.3 Insert-substitute-ignore technique for selecting optimum configurations.

However, it should be linked only with the next configuration, which is more suitable, and that is E. In this way, R substitutes C and D, which are now removed from the set of optimum configurations. The new set of optimum configurations is A → B → R → E. By repeating this filtering procedure systematically for all configurations, we eventually create the set of optimum configurations.

The set of optimum configurations includes the solutions of three standard optimization problems: the most suitable configuration under a given cost, the least expensive configuration that attains a given suitability, and the most valuable configuration. The solutions of these problems are exemplified in the next section.

In cases of computer evaluation, there can be millions of possible configurations, but there are much less possible total costs. Consequently, we can frequently generate (and filter) configurations that have the same cost. This is illustrated in Fig. 3.9.4.

3.9.3   A Case Study of Computer Configuration Optimization

Computer systems regularly have a large number of individually priced components, yielding a large number of possible configurations and complex optimization problems. In this section, we illustrate the LSP optimization methodology using a legacy desktop computer, which has 442,368 possible configurations based on 14 attributes presented in Table 3.9.2. The price range of

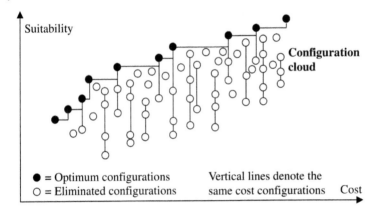

Figure 3.9.4 Elimination of configurations with equal cost.

Table 3.9.2 List of PC attributes and configuration options.

No.	Hardware component	Options
1	Processor speed	2
2	Memory size	2
3	Monitor	4
4	Video card	3
5	Hard drive	4
6	Modem	2
7	Optical drive	2
8	Keyboard	2
9	Network card	3
10	Tape drive	2
11	Sound card	2
12	Speakers	4
13	Floppy/Zip drive	2
14	Printer	3
Total hardware configurations		442,368

this machine was from \$2,022 to \$4,867. Our problem is to answer the following practical optimization questions:

a) What is the minimum cost necessary to satisfy 90% of requirements specified in the LSP criterion?
b) What is the highest satisfaction of requirements that can be achieved with funding that is limited to \$3000 per computer?
c) What is the best configuration under \$2500?
d) What is the most cost-effective system (the highest S/C value)?
e) In what cost range are configurations that achieve 90% of the highest S/C value?

Table 3.9.3 List of legacy PC attributes, attribute criteria, and cost/preference pairs.

Configuration Options and Elementary Criteria		Option				
		0	1	2	3	4
Processor	Speed		200 MHz	233MHz		
	Cost		2022	2100		
	Preference		85	100		
Main Memory	Capacity		32MB	64MB		
	Cost		0	239		
	Preference		75	100		
Monitor	Type		8HS 13.7"T	10LS 15.9"	10HS 15.9"T	20TD 19"T
	Cost		0	119	340	939
	Preference		40	60	85	100
Video Board	Type		Virge 2MB	Virge 4MB	Maxtor 4MB	
	Cost		0	40	139	
	Preference		30	60	100	
Hard Disk Drive EIDE	Capacity		2.1 GB	3.2 GB	4.3 GB	6.4 GB
	Cost		0	49	109	184
	Preference		20	50	80	100
Modem	Speed	0	33.6Kbd			
	Cost	0	129			
	Preference	0	100			
CD-ROM Drive	Speed		12-16X	12 / 24X		
	Cost		0	25		
	Preference		80	100		
Keyboard	Type		Spacesaver	Performance		
	Cost		0	29		
	Preference		50	100		
Network Card	Type	0	3C900 PCI	3C905-TX		
	Cost	0	99	109		
	Preference	0	85	100		
Tape Drive	Capacity	0	4GB			
	Cost	0	199			
	Preference	0	100			
Sound Card	Type		WaveSyn SW	WaveTbl 32		
	Cost		0	39		
	Preference		70	100		
Speakers	Type	0	ACS 90	ACS 290	ACS 490	
	Cost	0	49	124	189	
	Preference	0	70	90	100	
Floppy Disk	Capacity		1.44MB	1.44+100MB		
	Cost		0	138		
	Preference		75	100		
Printer	Type	0	HP DJ 820	HP LJ 6L		
	Cost	0	309	409		
	Preference	0	65	100		

The first step in solving this problem is to define the LSP criterion, which is presented in Table 3.9.3 and Fig. 3.9.5. The elementary criteria that contain legacy components and legacy costs show the solution of the problem of coding individual options using integers from 0 to 4. For example, printers are optional parts of this configuration. So, the corresponding criterion is $Crit(printer) = \{(0,0), (1,65), (2,100)\}$. Here 0 denotes the configuration without printer, 1 denotes HP DJ 820, and 2 denotes HP LJ 6 L. All attribute criteria that have 0 in the column denoted as option 0 describe independent optional

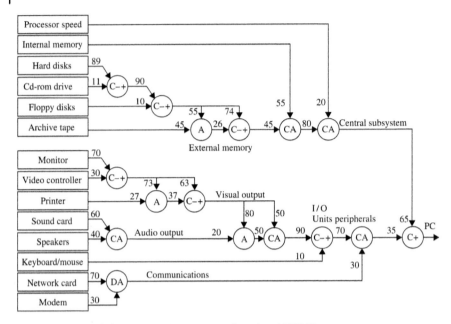

Figure 3.9.5 Suitability aggregation structure based on WPM.17 aggregators.

components that can be omitted. All attributes that have empty column 0 are mandatory components that are always included, and their cost in column 1 is 0, because it is included in the cost of the basic computer configuration, which is $2,022; this cost is listed in the processor criterion. For example, there are two keyboards, and the first is included in the basic configuration without extra cost. For an additional $29, it can be replaced by a second (better) keyboard. The corresponding criterion is $Crit(keyboard) = \{(1,50), (2,100)\}$. This method codes all discrete inputs using the integer option numbers that identify and quantify various devices, and serve as input attributes. That should not be used for components that are expected to continuously change between individual vertices (e.g., the size of memory).

The aggregation structure shown in Fig. 3.9.5 is organized as a binary tree. This permits a simple optimization procedure, performed separately for each node, described in [DUJ98b]. All attributes except tape, printer, audio components, and communication components are mandatory. This is the reason why the cloud diagram shown in Fig. 3.9.6 also includes many configurations that have the overall suitability zero (note the horizontal black line at level 0, which is the bottom of the cloud).

The cloud has 442,368 points, but only 130 configurations are parts of the optimum set. Since the cost range is [$2,022, $4,867], it is clear that there are

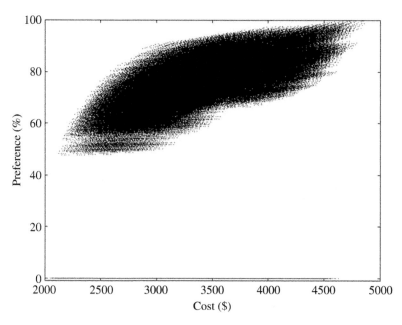

Figure 3.9.6 A cost/suitability cloud diagram for 442,368 configurations of a desktop PC.

many configurations that have the same cost and suboptimum suitability (as in Fig. 3.9.4). They are located in the black central region of the cloud.

The optimum configurations $S = \Omega(C)$ are shown in Fig. 3.9.7. They provide answers to all optimization questions. In addition, this function can also be used to compute the overall value $V = \Omega(C)/C$ as a function of cost, as shown in Fig. 3.9.8. Optimization results also include all optimum attributes as functions of total cost: $\{a_1^*(C),...,a_n^*(C)\}$. Three important optimum configurations are shown in Table 3.9.4.

From the optimization algorithm standpoint, we used the following two approaches to solving optimization problems;

1) If the number of possible configurations is not prohibitively high, it is possible to make an exhaustive search of all configurations, create the configuration cloud (Fig. 3.9.6), and filter optimum configurations using the method outlined in Figs. 3.9.3 and 3.9.4. More detail can be found in [KAO04, DUJ05a].
2) If the number of possible configurations is too big for the brute force approach, then the LSP aggregation structure should be organized as a binary tree. This is always possible using (exact or approximate) associativity of aggregation structures. If the number of input attributes is n, then the number of nodes in the binary aggregation tree is $n-1$ (in Fig. 3.9.5, there are 14 inputs and 13 GCD and PA nodes). The optimization can be

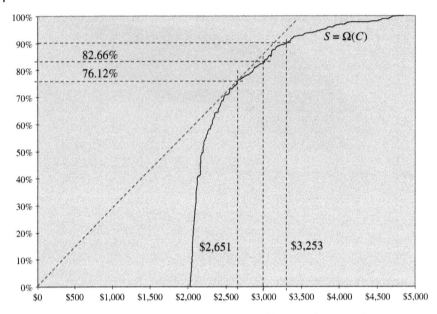

Figure 3.9.7 Optimum configurations: maximum suitability as a function of cost.

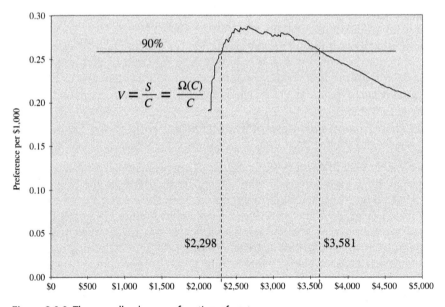

Figure 3.9.8 The overall value as a function of cost.

organized node by node, giving essentially a linear algorithm with time complexity $O(n)$. This method was introduced in [DUJ74c], implemented in the SEL language [DUJ76a], applied in [DUJ76c, DUJ76d], and refined in [DUJ98b, DUJ03a].

The presented results provide the following answers to the optimization questions:

1) What is the minimum cost necessary to satisfy 90% of requirements specified in the LSP criterion? According to Fig. 3.9.7, the least expensive way to satisfy 90% of stakeholder's requirements is to buy the configuration shown in Table 3.9.4. The minimum cost is $3,253 and the overall suitability is very close to the desired 90%.

2) What is the highest satisfaction of requirements that can be achieved with funding that is limited to $3,000 per computer? According to optimum configurations shown in Fig. 3.9.7, the optimum configuration that costs $3,000 satisfies 82.66% of stakeholder's requirements.

3) What is the best configuration under $2,500? The best configuration under $2,500 is shown in Table 3.9.4. It costs $2,477 and satisfies 70.51% of requirements.

4) What is the most cost-effective system (the highest S/C value)? The highest value configuration determined using the tangent to the optimum configuration curve in Fig. 3.9.7 (the max angle system in Fig. 3.9.1) costs $2,651 and satisfies 76.12% of user requirements. The components of that most valuable configuration are shown in Table 3.9.4.

5) In what cost range are configurations that achieve 90% of the highest S/C value? The value $V = S/C$ as a function of cost is presented in Fig. 3.9.8. The maximum of this curve is the maximum value configuration. All

Table 3.9.4 Three optimum configurations.

Configuration Parameter	Best configuration under $2,500	Best value configuration (maximum Preference/Cost)	Least expensive system satisfying 90% of requirements
Processor speed	200 MHz	200 MHz	233 MHz
Memory capacity	32 MB	32 MB	64 MB
Disk Capacity	4.3 GB	6.4 GB	6.4 GB
CD-ROM Speed	12-16X	12-16X	12/24X
Floppy Disks	1.44 MB	1.44 MB	1.44 MB
Tape Drive	None	None	None
Monitor	1000LS 15.9"	1000LS 15.9"	1000HS 15.9" Trinitron
Video Card	Virge 4MB	Maxtor 4MB	Maxtor 4MB
Printer	None	None	None
Sound Card	WaveSynth SW	WaveSynth SW	Wavetable AWE32
Speakers	ASC90	ASC90	ASC90
Keyboard	Performance	Performance	Performance
Network Card	3C905-TX	3C905-TX	3C905-TX
Modem	None	None	None
Total Cost	$2,477	$2,651	$3,253
Global Preference	70.51%	76.12%	89.64%

optimum configurations in the cost range [\$2,298, \$3,581] are in the 10% vicinity of the maximum value configuration. That includes all optimum configurations from the previous questions.

It is easy to note the practical value of answers to the above questions in the process of generating justifiable purchasing decisions. Inexpensive desktop computers deserve to be carefully optimized if the stakeholder is one of many organizations that buy such computers in large quantities. In such cases, it is very reasonable to perform careful optimization of each competitive computer, to find configurations that achieve the highest preference, and then use the suitability-affordability analysis (Chapter 3.6) to compare all competitive best configurations. Such a process generates strongly justified decisions. Obviously, the manufacturer's personnel cannot determine the best configurations. The stakeholder and professional evaluators must do that.

Computer systems consist of many individually priced hardware and software components. That creates a huge number of possible configurations. From the optimization point of view, the optimization of computer configurations is a rather difficult problem. Therefore, the presented optimization of a legacy PC is not selected to show what should be done when people buy cheap personal computers, but to show what the LSP method can do with complex optimization problems. Some complex industrial systems can cost several orders of magnitude more than a PC, but if the number of adjustable individually priced components is not too large, the optimization process can be significantly simpler than in the case of a simple PC. In addition, computer evaluation and selection in the case of mainframe computers, advanced servers, and computer networks generate situations where configuration optimization is very appropriate. Evaluation of advanced computer systems has been so far a frequent area of industrial applications of the LSP method.

3.10 LSP Software Technology

A scientist studies what is, whereas an engineer creates what never was.
—Theodore von Karman

Professional system evaluation is based on using a variety of software tools. In this chapter we present a short summary of existing software and related publications. The LSP software technology is designed to support three categories of users:

- Professional evaluators
- LSP end users
- LSP administrators

Professional evaluators are decision engineers who prepare and use complex criteria that support acquisition decisions of institutional (corporate, military, governmental, and other) users. Professional evaluators also include students (i.e., those who want to learn evaluation decision methods). LSP end users are those who use already prepared LSP criteria to evaluate, compare and select specific systems. In many cases the end users may be interested in customizing LSP criteria (changing default values of criterion function parameters to better express user's needs). LSP administrators are software and decision support personnel in charge of maintenance of the LSP project database and LSP software tools. LSP administrators can use all LSP software components as standalone tools. Other users can use the same tools as components (servers) in an integrated system evaluation environment. Most users access LSP evaluation software as a service over the Internet.

The LSP software architecture is summarized in Fig 3.10.1. It consists of core LSP technology, LSP evaluation frameworks, and three groups of supporting tools.

The core technology consists of two LSP engines (LSPcalc and MyLSP) that perform all numerical processing related to GL aggregators and LSP criteria.

Soft Computing Evaluation Logic: The LSP Decision Method and Its Applications, First Edition. Jozo Dujmović.
© 2018 John Wiley & Sons, Inc. Published 2018 by John Wiley & Sons, Inc.
Companion website: www.wiley.com/go/Dujmovic/Soft_Computing_Evaluation_Logic

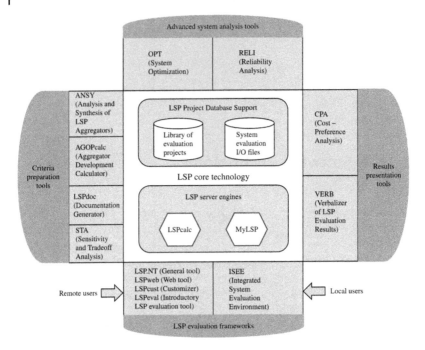

Figure 3.10.1 LSP software architecture.

LSPcalc is a fundamental engine used directly or indirectly by most other LSP tools. It is primarily responsible for fast calculation of all suitability scores and for numerical correctness of evaluation results. It can also be used as an interactive stand-alone tool. In such a case, it includes help and tutorial components, as well as a complete support for creating and editing LSP criteria, and system evaluation. It supports WPM, GCD, and UGCD aggregation. MyLSP is a numeric processor used by a web server based on canonical mandatory/optional model of LSP criterion.

The core technology uses an extensive database support that includes a library of LSP projects developed by the whole LSP user community. In addition, all projects include input system files, as well as output documentation files with numeric results and their verbalization.

LSP evaluation frameworks include three LSP frameworks for remote users (LSP.NT, LSPweb, and LSPeval) and one standalone framework for local users (ISEE). All of them have GUI for easy communication with users and support the basic LSP functionality.

Supporting tools include four criteria preparation tools (ANSY, AGOPcalc, LSPdoc, and STA), two result presentation tools (CPA and VERB), and two advanced system analysis tools: system optimizer (OPT), and reliability analyzer (RELI). Below we provide a short description of the functionality of all major LSP software tools.

- **ISEE** is a Java-based standalone tool that evaluators use on their local computers for building LSP criteria and evaluating competitive systems. It supports creating a system attribute and requirement tree, elementary criteria, and criterion aggregation structure. In addition, it provides comfortable GUI-based support for editing LSP criteria, and producing basic LSP documentation. ISEE also provides access to other LSP tools [KAD02, DUJ02, SEA16].
- **LSPdoc** is a specialized tool for design and editing of LSP criteria and production of professional LSP documentation. The documentation includes the system attribute tree, scalable elementary criteria (up to 10 per page), and rectangular preference aggregation diagrams [KAC07].
- **LSPcust** is a user interface tool that end users apply to modify LSP criteria according to their individual needs and specifications. The modified criteria can be immediately used for evaluation and comparison of competitive systems. Thus, LSPcust can also be used for experimental study of effects of modifying parameters of LSP criteria [PAT05].
- **ANSY** is a tool for analysis and synthesis of LSP aggregators (partial conjunction, partial disjunction, and partial absorption). ANSY uses LSP aggregators as preferential neurons and implements a neural network training process to compute optimum values of aggregator parameters. The optimum parameters are those values that minimize the difference between the attained input-output mapping of an aggregator, and a desired input-output mapping specified by the user-supplied training set. ANSY computes the optimum values of andness/orness and weights of aggregation operators according to user requirements [DUJ91, SEA10].
- **STA** is a tool for sensitivity and tradeoff analysis. The sensitivity analysis investigates the effects of changes of inputs or parameters on the value of selected preferences. The tradeoff analysis investigates compensatory features of LSP criteria, i.e., the possibility to compensate deficiencies in some inputs by improving selected other inputs.
- **AGOPcalc** is a tool for development of logic aggregators. In includes weight calculators, verbalizers, penalty/reward calculator, and andness/orness analyzers [SEA11a].
- **CPA** is a tool that combines the results of cost analysis with the results of preference evaluation. CPA uses various mathematical models that combine the global cost and the global suitability/preference of each evaluated systems in a single overall value indicator. Such overall indicators are necessary for system ranking.
- **VERB** is a presentation tool, an automatic generator of evaluation documentation that presents the evaluation results in verbalized and understandable

form at three different levels of detail: an executive summary, a detailed evaluation report, and a full documentation of all numerical results.

- **OPT** is a tool that solves three fundamental optimization problems: (1) finding an optimum system that attains the highest preference for constrained cost, (2) finding an optimum system that attains a given level of preference at a minimum cost, and (3) finding an optimum system that offers maximum quality per unit of cost. OPT also solves the optimum cost allocation problem, giving parameters of optimum system configurations for any available total cost [KAO04, DUJ05a, DUJ03a].

- **RELI** is a tool for the analysis of reliability of evaluation results. Any evaluation project includes a number of parameters that are assessed by evaluators and may contain errors with respect to unknown optimum values. The goal of reliability analysis is to compute the confidence levels for ranking of each pair of competitive systems. RELI enables evaluators to select the best system knowing the level of confidence that corresponds to the proposed decision [FAN04, DUJ04b].

- **VISAG** is a standalone tool for visualization and animation of aggregation operators. It is used for the development of new forms of aggregation operators and for visual presentations of their properties [ZHE07].

- **LSPNP** is a tool for using LSP method by nonprofessional users. It enables nonprofessional users to edit and customize LSP criteria and to interface them with LSPcalc without having the LSP theoretical background [DIS07].

- **LSPmed** is a tool for LSP-based evaluation of medical conditions. It enables successive evaluations of a patient's condition in order to track and control the development of the patient's disability over an arbitrary time period [DUJ08a].

- **LSPweb** is a web application for multiuser cooperative evaluation based on criteria developed using ISEE. LSPweb and ISEE support WPM.17 aggregators. LSPweb serves three categories of users (administrators, analysts, and evaluators), where each category has a specific role (definition, customization, and use of LSP projects and their criteria).

- **LSP.NT** is a web framework that enables work on evaluation projects to multiple users. LSP.NT is the most advanced LSP evaluation tool that supports WPM.17, as well as all UGCD and GGCD aggregators with adjustable threshold andness [SEA17]. LSP.NT also provides free access to demo users (offering full functionality for projects with limited size of criteria).

- **LSPeval** is an introductory web-based LSP evaluator tool based on canonical mandatory/optional aggregation structure with multiple mandatory inputs and multiple optional inputs [KAP17]. LSPeval is a free tool suitable for students and for general users interested in an easy first contact with the LSP method, without need to have mathematical background and know GL aggregators.

- **LSPhome** is a home selection system applied in online real estate [DUJ13] (see Chapter 4.2).

The presented software support is a second generation of LSP software tools. The first generation consisted of the Criterion Data Base System (CDBS) [DUJ76b] and the System Evaluation Language (SEL) [DUJ76a]. CDBS and SEL were primarily designed for professional system evaluators. The second-generation tools are more diversified and are designed to serve a wider spectrum of users. Some software tools were developed for applications in specific areas, such as real estate [DUJ13] and suitability maps [PIT10, YOK12, ZHU14, SEA11].

PART FOUR

APPLICATIONS

An ounce of application is worth a ton of abstraction.
—Booker T. Washington

Reduction to practice is desirable and necessary test of any theory.
—James E. Thornton

The purpose of Part Four is to show the applicability of the LSP method. LSP literature includes models for evaluation, optimization, comparison and selection of various systems: data management systems [SU82,DUJ82,SU87], web browsers [FUN00], search engines [BAI07, DUJ07b], windowed environments [BAY96, DUJ97a, DUJ97b], mainframe computers [DUJ73c, DUJ80, DUJ98b], analog computers [DUJ74d, DUJ76c], hybrid computers [DUJ76c, DUJ76d], websites [OLS99, OLS01], jobs [DUJ91], e-commerce sites [OLS00, BUC07, BUC08], medical disability [DUJ08a], homes [DUJ13], ecological systems [ALL11, DUJ11, MES18], space management [HAT14, DRA18, MON16c], suitability maps [TRE11, DUJ08, DUJ09, TRE10, DUJ10a, DUJ11a, YOK12, ZHU14], integrated development environments for Java [DUJ03, DUJ06a], agriculture [MON15a, MON15b, MON16a, MON16b], nitrate contamination of groundwater [REB14, REB16], cybersecurity [KAC08, DAS16], and others.

Some of analyzed systems are physical systems (e.g., computers and homes) and some are conceptual systems (e.g., jobs and software systems). Each LSP project assumes specific stakeholders and needs appropriate domain expertise. Evaluation projects can vary in a wide range, but the common core of all of them is decision making. LSP method is motivated by human reasoning, and consequently, it belongs to the wide area of computational intelligence [KAC15]. In

Soft Computing Evaluation Logic: The LSP Decision Method and Its Applications,
First Edition. Jozo Dujmović.
© 2018 John Wiley & Sons, Inc. Published 2018 by John Wiley & Sons, Inc.
Companion website: www.wiley.com/go/Dujmovic/Soft_Computing_Evaluation_Logic

all applications, our goal is to develop evaluation criteria that help decision makers to go far beyond limitations of intuitive reasoning.

Some evaluation criteria are time-sensitive and can quickly become obsolete from the standpoints of both performance and price. For example, according to Moore's law, computer performance for a long time showed exponential growth: $q(t) = q_0 2^{t/T}$, where q_0 denotes an initial performance at time $t = 0$, and T is the performance doubling time. The most frequent parameter was $T \approx 18$ months for computer memory capacity, and $T \approx 12$ months for performance/price. Therefore, most numbers related to the memory capacity may become useless after approximately two years.

It is normal that technologies evolve, and existing technologies become obsolete. Unfortunately, Moore's law seems also to hold for money. This book is written in the period when all economies have quasi-exponential inflation [WIK08b]. Inflation is sometimes associated with excessive money supply, an activity that is to some extent controlled by governments. For them, T denotes the number of years that is necessary to double the prices of everything and hopefully also to double the average salaries. For example, the job selection model presented in [MIL70] shows an MBA graduate student at the MIT Sloan School of Management who, after graduation in June 1966, got and accepted a job offer with the annual salary of $8,250. If 50 years later the same student can get the annual salary of $200,000 or more, then for the US dollar we have $T = (50 \log 2)/\log(200000/8250) = 10.87$ years.

A more precise analysis of the money supply in the United States can be based on [WIK08a, FR08]. According to [FR08], if the money supply is measured using the total physical currency plus checking and savings accounts and non-institutional money-market funds (money form M2), then, starting in January 1959, M2 doubled as follows: Feb 1969 ($T = 10.08$ years), Dec 1976 ($T = 7.8$ years), Dec 1984 ($T = 8$ years), Oct 1999 ($T = 14.83$ years). Therefore, T shows variations, but the growth of M2 is stable and quasi-exponential. This analysis shows that the values of cost in the LSP cost/preference analysis of real life systems must also rather quickly become obsolete, affecting the usability of some case studies.

Fortunately, there are also many attributes and criteria that remain constant (or change very little) over time. For example, in the job selection criterion, the acceptable time to commute to work is always evaluated as a fraction of the 24-hour day. So, the total daily commute time between 10 minutes and 1–2 hours might denote an acceptable home location as long as the economic situation remains without dramatic changes. The location of home can also be evaluated using the time children spend commuting to school and such criteria are also rather stable. The sufficient number of bedrooms for a young family with n members is usually $n - 1$. In the area of computing, the desired web application response time is stable, and it should be below 6–8 seconds. The quality of software documentation, help and tutorial systems is always evaluated in the same or similar way. In the case of medical criteria, physical abilities of humans remain unchanged, and disability criteria can stand the test of time. However, the number of such examples is smaller than the number of examples that are affected by fast changes. Not surprisingly, stability is found mostly in requirements that are directly or indirectly related to physical or perceptual abilities of humans. Instability is found in industrial products and technologies, as well as in economy.

Each LSP criterion is a mix of time-insensitive and time-sensitive elementary attribute criteria. Some criteria might need periodical adjustments to adapt to changing structure, performance and/or price of evaluated systems. In subsequent chapters we selected LSP applications that are predominantly time insensitive. A wider spectrum of applications is available in the literature as well as in the LSP application repository that is expected to grow on the website of this book

4.1 Job Selection

He who has a choice has trouble.
—Danish proverb

Most adults work. Therefore, the job selection problem is one of the most frequent nontrivial evaluation problems. This is also a problem that the majority of people usually solve intuitively, without quantitative methodology. Since everybody is familiar with the problem, it is reasonable to use it as the first application of the LSP method.

The job selection problem (based on linear scoring) was analyzed by J. R. Miller as the key example of his assessment of worth procedure [MIL66]. It is also an example for the professional decision-making methodology presented in [MIL70]. The first 12-attribute LSP version of the job selection criterion was presented in [DUJ91]. These examples are used as a starting point for developing the model presented in this chapter.

In the case of job selection, we have an atypical evaluation problem where we cannot define the "overall cost" and the "overall suitability" of the system, and perform the standard LSP cost/suitability analysis. Indeed, the goal of evaluation is to simultaneously maximize the overall monetary compensation and the overall positive characteristics of the job.

The job selection problem depends very much on political, social, and economic environment in which it is defined. All governments have laws and regulations on the variety of labor topics. For example, US Department of Labor [DOL16] offers many web pages that specify legal aspects of full-time and part-time employment, flexible schedules, holidays, family and medical leave, night work, shift work, overtime, breaks and meal periods, sick leave, seasonal employment, weekend work, and vacation leave. So, a very detailed criterion that would take into account all legal and social aspects of employment could easily become too complex for an average decision maker.

Soft Computing Evaluation Logic: The LSP Decision Method and Its Applications,
First Edition. Jozo Dujmović.
© 2018 John Wiley & Sons, Inc. Published 2018 by John Wiley & Sons, Inc.
Companion website: www.wiley.com/go/Dujmovic/Soft_Computing_Evaluation_Logic

The criterion for job evaluation and selection also very much depends on the specific requirements of each profession. Job scheduling for firefighters and obstetricians is very different from the job scheduling for teachers or priests. In addition, the attributes and parameters of job selection criteria also depend on the age and gender of workers: mothers of small children have different job criteria than older men. Consequently, the variability of job selection criteria is huge and each stakeholder has specific requirements. Since we expect that firefighters, obstetricians and priests will not read this book, our criterion will not be developed for them. Therefore, we assume that our criterion should be developed for the stakeholder who is a typical reader of this book, e.g., a scientist or a manager or an engineer, who works in an urban environment, in a stable company and in regular economic conditions. Our goal is to develop a moderate-size criterion and to show logic relationships that are used in making job selection decision.

4.1.1 Job Selection Attribute Tree

The structure of monetary compensation depends on economic and political system and differs from country to country, as well as between private and non–private sector in a country. An example of the total compensation package typical for some categories of employees in the United States is shown in Fig. 4.1.1. For some state employees, the employer's contributions include three components of retirement benefits: a particular retirement plan, social security (intergeneration transfer plan), and Medicare (health insurance coverage for people who are age 65 and over). The employee is also required to contribute to all these plans with appropriate retirement deductions.

In the case of health care (medical, dental, and vision protection) the situation is slightly different: the employee may select among various health protection plans, and if the employee selects plans that cost more than employer's limited contribution then the employee must contribute whatever is above the employer's limit. The same method is applied for some forms of insurance. In addition, the employee has paid vacations, sick leave (paid leave that can be taken during periods of sickness), and the possibility to take nonpaid vacations. Some employers may also contribute a variety of other benefits (typically relocation assistance, funding for education, etc.)

Assuming that retirement, health protection and paid vacations are the principal components of employee benefits, we can develop the attribute tree shown in Fig. 4.1.2. The tree includes the following 20 input attributes:

1) Starting salary
2) Retirement benefits
3) Health protection
4) Vacations
5) Anticipated salary in three years

Total compensation
1. Gross pay
    1.1. Net pay
    1.2. Deductions
        1.2.1. Taxes
            1.2.1.1. Federal tax
            1.2.1.2. State tax
        1.2.2. Retirement deductions
            1.2.2.1. Retirement plan deduction
            1.2.2.2. Social security deduction
            1.2.2.3. Medicare deduction
        1.2.3. Health care deductions
            1.2.3.1. Medical protection deduction
            1.2.3.2. Dental protection deduction
            1.2.3.3. Vision protection deduction
        1.2.4. Insurance deductions
            1.2.4.1. Life insurance
            1.2.4.2. Other forms of insurance
        1.2.5. Other deductions
            1.2.5.1. Membership dues
            1.2.5.2. Parking/recreation at work
2. Employee benefits (employer contributions)
    2.1. Retirement
        2.1.1. Retirement plan
        2.1.2. Social security
        2.1.3. Medicare
    2.2. Health care
        2.2.1. Medical protection
        2.2.2. Dental protection
        2.2.3. Vision protection
    2.3. Insurance
        2.3.1. Life insurance
        2.3.2. Other forms of insurance
    2.4. Vacations
        2.4.1. Paid vacations
        2.4.2. Non-paid vacations
        2.4.3. Sick leave
        2.4.4. Parental leave
    2.5. Other benefits
        2.5.1. Child care benefits
        2.5.2. Transportation benefits (e.g. company car)
        2.5.3. Allowances for lunch /cafeteria plans
        2.5.4. Relocation assistance
        2.5.5. Employee discounts
        2.5.6. Tuition reimbursement

Figure 4.1.1 Sample total compensation package (USA).

1 JOB
  11 Monetary compensation
    111 Starting salary and employee benefits
      1111 Starting salary
      1112 Employee benefits
        11121 Retirement benefits
        11122 Health protection
        11123 Vacations
    112 Anticipated future salary
      1121 Anticipated salary in three years
      1122 Anticipated salary in five years
  12 Job characteristics
    121 Nature of work
      1211 Attractiveness of job
        12111 Technical content of the job
        12112 Variety of job assignments
        12113 Obtained professional skills and experience
        12114 Obtained management skills
      1212 Required job training
    122 Time spent at work and working schedule
      1221 Total number of hours at work per week
      1222 Flexible working schedule
    123 Total travel requirements
      1231 Daily commuting requirements
      1232 Business travel
        12321 Maximum business trip length
        12322 Annual percentage of time away from home
    124 Location of job
      1241 Job location climate and environment
      1242 Degree of urbanity in the job location area
      1243 Proximity to relatives
    125 Job security

Figure 4.1.2 A job selection attribute tree.

  6) Anticipated salary in five years
  7) Technical content of the job
  8) Variety of job assignments
  9) Obtained professional skills and experience
10) Obtained management skills
11) Required job training
12) Total number of hours at work per week
13) Flexible working schedule
14) Daily commuting requirements
15) Maximum business trip length

16) Annual percentage of time away from home
17) Job location climate and environment
18) Degree of urbanity in the job location area
19) Proximity to relatives
20) Job security

The attribute tree is structured in two fundamental groups of attributes: the monetary compensation and the job characteristics. We assume that the employee/stakeholder wants an attractive and rewarding professional experience, the growth of professional skills, and simultaneously a significant monetary compensation. Since the structure of monetary compensation significantly differs for governmental employees and the employees in the private sector, we reduced the monetary compensation to starting salary, employee benefits, and the anticipated future salary. The starting salary and the basic fringe benefits are in the primary focus of each future employee. However, most people are also interested in jobs that offer growth and advancing. The anticipated future salary includes indicators for evaluating the expected advancing if the offered job is accepted. If needed, the monetary compensation list can be expanded using components presented in Fig. 4.1.1.

The second significant group of attributes is devoted to job characteristics. This group obviously very much depends on the type of stakeholder's profession. Our criterion includes attributes that are common for variety of professions. The job is expected to be attractive, with moderate required job training, and offering opportunities for development of professional skills. Time spent at work is a common concern for all jobs, as well as the working schedule and the daily commuting. In addition, many jobs require business travel and most stakeholders evaluate travel requirements in order to avoid excessive traveling. In a general case, a new job may require relocation and the location of the new job should also be evaluated. Last but not least, job security is also an important decision component that must be included in evaluation criterion.

4.1.2 Elementary Attribute Criteria for Job Selection

Elementary attribute criteria are presented in Table 4.1.1. The first three attributes (#1111, #11121, and #11122) are evaluated using relative criteria. We assume that the stakeholder has multiple competitive job offers and the relative criteria are suitable to compare the offered monetary compensation without specifying the actual amount and currency. The offered monetary compensations are expected to be balanced and the factor of 2 between offered compensations is considered unacceptable. Of course, in many cases the stakeholder may decide to replace the relative criteria with the absolute criteria that specify desired amounts. In particular, that is necessary if evaluating only one job offer.

Table 4.1.1 Elementary attribute criteria for job selection.

1111		Starting salary
Value	%	Evaluated as the following relative after-tax annual salary:
50	0	$\quad$ Srel = 100*S/Smax
100	100	Inputs:
		S $\;$ = offered annual salary decreased by taxes, social security, Medicare, and other
		$\quad$ mandatory deductions and locally adjusted to account for different living costs
		$\quad$ at various geographic locations
		Smax = the maximum offered S

11121		Retirement benefits
Value	%	Evaluated as the following relative annual retirement benefits:
50	0	$\quad$ Rrel = 100*R/Rmax
100	100	Inputs:
		R = total annual employer retirement contributions plus mandatory employee
		$\quad$ retirement contributions (retirement funds and social security)
		Rmax = the maximum offered R

11122		Health protection
Value	%	Evaluated as the following relative health protection benefits:
50	0	$\quad$ Mrel = 100*M/Mmax
100	100	Inputs:
		M $\;$ = total employer monthly contributions for medical, dental and vision protection
		$\quad$ plans plus mandatory employee contributions
		Mmax = the maximum offered M

11123		Vacations
Value	%	Vacations are evaluated using the total number of paid workdays of vacation per year,
0	0	including the paid vacation days and the paid public holidays. We assume employees
35	100	with 10 or more years of service.

1121		Anticipated salary in three years
Value	%	Evaluated as a percent increase with the respect to the starting salary. The anticipated
0	0	increase of 20% or more would completely satisfy the stakeholder.
20	100	

1122		Anticipated salary in five years
Value	%	
0	0	Evaluated as a percent increase with the respect to the starting salary. The anticipated
20	80	increase of 30% or more would completely satisfy the stakeholder.
30	100	

12111		Technical content of the job
Value	%	Evaluated using the following rating scale:
1	0	1 = not satisfactory, 2 = acceptable, 3 = average, 4 = good, 5 = excellent
5	100	

12112		Variety of job assignments
Value	%	Evaluated using the following rating scale:
1	0	1 = not satisfactory
2	60	2 = acceptable
3	100	3 = appropriate
4	80	4 = high
5	50	5 = excessive

12113		Obtained professional skills and experience
Value	%	Professional skills and experience realizable from the offered job:
1	0	1 = insufficient
2	20	2 = low
3	50	3 = medium
4	85	4 = high
5	100	5 = very high

Table 4.1.1 (Continued)

12114		Obtained management skills
Value	%	Evaluated using the following rating scale:
1	0	
4	100	1 = none, 2 = modest, 3 = good, 4 = excellent

1212		Required job training
Value	%	Necessary initial training as a prerequisite for the offered job
0	100	(expressed in months).
12	0	

1221		Total number of hours at work per week
Value	%	Number of hours spent at work is expected to be standardized to 40 for full time
40	100	employees.
65	0	

1222		Flexible working schedule
Value	%	Evaluated according to the following rating scale:
0	40	0 = unpredictable working schedule determined according to available work
2	80	assignments
4	100	1 = fixed 9-5, 40-hour work week
		2 = flexible arrival and/or departure times and presence during a daily "core time"
		3 = a combination of the work from office and the work from home
		4 = full flexibility (predominant work from home)

1231		Daily commuting requirements
Value	%	Total time spent daily in commuting (two-way travel time), expressed in hours.
0.5	100	
3	0	

12321		Maximum business trip length
Value	%	Maximum duration of an extended business trip expressed in days.
0	100	
30	0	

12322		Annual percentage of time away from home
Value	%	The percentage of total time spent yearly on business trips.
0	100	
40	0	

1241		Job location climate and environment
Value	%	Evaluated using the following rating scale:
1	0	1 = very poor, 2 = poor, 3 = average, 4 = good, 5 = excellent
5	100	

1242		Degree of urbanity in the job location area
Value	%	Evaluated as a standard metropolitan area population expressed in millions.
0	0	
1	75	
2	100	

1243		Proximity to relatives
Value	%	One-way air travel time for visiting relatives expressed in hours.
0	100	
6	0	

125		Job security
Value	%	Evaluated using the following rating scale:
1	0	1 = very low, 2 = low, 3 = medium, 4 = high, 5 = very high
5	100	

The starting salary is computed as after-tax locally adjusted amount decreased by mandatory deductions. In this way the deductions that are subtracted from starting salary are not neglected, because they subsequently appear in criteria for retirement benefits and health protection.

In the case of paid vacations (#11123) the situation is rather complex, as shown in [AA16b]. The total paid leave consists of paid vacation days plus the paid public holidays. The vacation days are normalized assuming the five-day workweek. The highest normalized value reported in [AA16b] is in Iran (26 + 26 = 52 days) and the lowest is in Japan (10 + 0 = 10 days). The most frequent values (depending on country) are between 25 and 35 days. Most countries have laws that specify the minimum mandatory paid vacation days. Some countries have vacation defined in calendar days (including Saturdays and Sundays). In many countries, the vacation days depend on the years of service and increase at a given rate (e.g., one day per three years of service). In addition, some countries have public holidays strictly bound to the calendar dates, while others move holidays that fall on a Saturday or Sunday to the nearest Monday. As an exception, the United States does not have a statutory minimum paid vacation or paid public holidays, but it is left to the employers to offer paid vacation. So, 77% of private employers offer paid vacation. Since the average reported number of paid vacation days after 1, 5, 10, and 20 years of service is respectively 10, 14, 17, and 20, our criterion #11123 is adjusted linearly to the maximum of 35 days of total paid leave (including public holidays), and assumes employees with 10 or more years of service.

Some of the presented criteria must be adjusted according to statistics for the assumed work environment. For example, according to Gallup [SAA16], adults employed full time in the United States work an average of 47 hours per week. Only 42% employees work 40 hours and 39% work more than 50 hours per week, which includes 18% of the full time employees who work more than 60 hours per week. In our criterion #1221 we expressed opinion that 40 hours is normal and 65 hours is fully abnormal and deserves the zero suitability. Criteria #11123 and #1221 are examples of absolute criteria.

According to the United States Census Bureau, the average travel time to work in the United States is 25.4 minutes. In criterion #1231, we propose that the two-way commute times of 0.5, 1, 1.5, 2, 2.5, and 3 hours are respectively assigned suitability of 100%, 80%, 60%, 40%, 20%, and 0.

The anticipated future salary after 3 and 5 years of service are predictable in some professions (e.g., military) and difficult or impossible to predict in others (e.g., Silicon Valley startups). We selected the default values of up to 20% and 30%. Of course, these values should be adjusted for each profession and for each economic situation.

Seven elementary attribute criteria are based on direct suitability assessment using rating scales. In most cases, we use standard verbalized five-level scales and the strictly increasing degrees of suitability. An exception is #12112, where we illustrate the situation where the variety of job assignment can be less then or greater than the stakeholder's desired mean value.

The stakeholder is assumed to be interested to hold in the future some managing positions and therefore our criterion includes evaluation of management skills obtained during the current job (#12114).

Some jobs require an initial training, and our criterion #1212 assumes stakeholder who is primarily interested in jobs where the initial training is not necessary. Of course, there are stakeholders who can have a different opinion about the desirability of training. A similar situation is encountered when evaluating the flexibility of working schedule. Our criterion #1222 reflects the type of stakeholder who is interested in full flexibility where the work can be done entirely from home. This is frequent standpoint of parents of small children. It is certainly possible to find stakeholders who would prefer a fixed 9 to 5 routine and in such cases the criterion #1222 should be readjusted.

The criteria for business travel (#12321 and #12322) reflect the stakeholder who is not interested in dynamic jobs that require frequent business trips. On the other hand, it is not difficult to find stakeholders who might have opposite interests, particularly among young single people at the beginning of career.

Some people look for a new job in the same city where they live and already have a job. However, in the case of young people looking for the first job directly following graduation, the situation is different: the jobs can be offered in various locations. So, in a general case, it is necessary to include the evaluation of climate, environment, and degree of urbanity of the new job location. The criterion #1242 reflects the stakeholder who is interested in higher degree of urbanity and is not interested to live in small communities. There are also stakeholders who would be interested in small communities, as well as those who do not think "more is better" but would decrease the suitability in locations where the standard metropolitan area population exceeds 1 or 2 million. The criterion #1242 can be easily adjusted to reflect such requirements. The criterion #1243 assumes the stakeholder who has relatives and prefers to work close to them.

The criterion #125 for job security uses a linear rating scale. Such as scale obviously reflects good economic times and standard/good job availability. In bad economic times, it might be more appropriate to use the criterion $\{(2,0), (5,100)\}$, focusing only on jobs that offer high or very high job security.

4.1.3 Logic Aggregation of Suitability for the Job Selection Criterion

The final step in the creation of an LSP criterion is the development of the suitability aggregation structure. In this step we use GL to build a criterion that reflects all stakeholder's logic conditions. At the beginning of this process we must select one of seven logic aggregation systems offered by the LSP method: WPM.17, UGCD.7, UGCD.15, UGCD.23, GGCD.9, GGCD.17, and GGCD25 (see rating scales in Tables 3.1.3–3.1.5). In this project it is sufficient to use the medium precision aggregators, and we will select the general-purpose group GGCD.17, which offers the possibility to select the threshold andness aggregator within the group C--, C-, C-+, CA, C +-, C+, and C++. To have sufficient number of both soft and hard aggregators, we will select CA as the threshold andness aggregator. This gives us the following distribution of aggregators (in the increasing sequence of orness, or decreasing sequence of andness with the step 1/16):

- Pure conjunction: C   (mandatory inputs)
- Hard partial conjunction: C++, C+, C +-, CA   (mandatory inputs)
- Soft partial conjunction: C-+, C-, C--   (optional inputs)
- Neutrality: A   (optional inputs)
- Soft partial disjunction: D--, D-, D-+   (optional inputs)
- Hard partial disjunction: DA, D +-, D+, D++   (sufficient inputs)
- Pure disjunction: D   (sufficient inputs)

Using these aggregators and the partial absorption aggregators specified using desired penalty and reward, we can develop the logic aggregation structure presented in Fig. 4.1.3.

The most important single input is obviously the starting salary. The salary requirement must be satisfied, and the salary is the mandatory input. Fringe benefits are very desirable, but they can always be compensated by a sufficiently large salary. On the other hand, the unacceptably low salary cannot be compensated by the fringe benefits. Therefore, the logic aggregation of the starting salary (#1111) and the fringe benefits (#1112) must be the conjunctive partial absorption (#111).

Among fringe benefits, we selected that the most important is health protection, while the retirement and vacations are less important. All fringe benefits are desirable but not mandatory, and we use the medium soft aggregator C-. In partial absorption #111, the penalty for having no fringe benefits, is P = 25%. The average reward for perfect fringe benefits is selected to be 15%. The reason for selecting these moderate values of penalty and reward is to adapt the criterion for interests of young employees who predominantly need the good starting salary, while the good health protection and good retirement plans are something that usually becomes visible and significant later in career and life.

For anticipated future salary (#112) we used the strongest soft aggregator and assume that the three-year increase is significantly more important than the five-year salary increase. The monetary compensation aggregator (#11) must be a conjunctive partial absorption because the starting salary and benefits are mandatory and cannot be fully compensated by the anticipated improvements in the insecure future. The penalty and reward are selected to be 20%, neither very significant nor negligible. Of course, all parameters that are selected in Fig. 4.1.3 can be modified to reflect different needs of different stakeholders.

In the group of aggregators for job characteristics, a critical decision is the selection of aggregator #1211 for attractiveness of the job. If we decide to use a hard conjunctive aggregator, then all inputs become mandatory. In such a case, jobs that do not develop management skills will be rejected, regardless of the attractiveness of remaining three components. On the other hand, if we select a soft conjunctive aggregator, the jobs that miss some of attractiveness components will be acceptable. We decided to use the weakest hard conjunctive aggregator and to make the attractiveness of the job a mandatory requirement with respect to required job training, which is considered optional. The need for job training is considered undesirable, and it is punished with a significant penalty of 30%. Jobs that need no training are expected in most cases, and consequently, we give them only the modest reward of 10%.

Business trips are assumed to be acceptable, and therefore they are aggregated with a medium soft conjunctive aggregator. However, daily commuting requirements are considered mandatory, and jobs with unacceptable commuting conditions will be rejected (#123). It the case of location (#124), we assume that the inputs are not mandatory and that the stakeholder is most interested in jobs that are in the proximity to relatives.

The job characteristics aggregator (#12) has five inputs. That is the largest number of inputs that we suggest to use in the LSP method. In this aggregator, we assigned the linear sequence of weights: 10%, 15%, 20%, 25%, 30%. The reason for this scale is that we first sorted inputs according to decreasing importance: (1) hours at work per week and the work schedule, (2) nature of work, (3) job location, (4) travel requirements, and (5) job security. Then, we assigned a linear scale of weights. If needed, in the next step we might perform fine tuning, by reassigning weights (subtracting a few weight points form some input and giving them to another, more deserving input). Job security is considered the least important because the criterion is assumed to be used in good economic times and professions that are in demand; so, the average job security is good and this input is used mostly for fine tuning and not as a significant source of discriminatory effects; in bad economic times and in different professions the situation would certainly change. The aggregator #12 is selected slightly below the strong hard partial conjunction: all its inputs are important mandatory requirements.

The final aggregator (#1) is the most influential (and consequently the most important) in the whole aggregation structure and has to be carefully selected. It is very important to simultaneously have the high monetary compensation and the attractive job characteristics. Therefore, the appropriate aggregator is a strong version of the hard partial conjunction, C+. The aggregator shown in Fig. 4.1.3 is prepared for the stakeholder who thinks that the monetary compensation is two times more important than the job characteristics.

Let us also note that the suitability aggregation structure shown in Fig. 4.1.3 follows a canonic pattern where the strongest aggregators are in the root area of

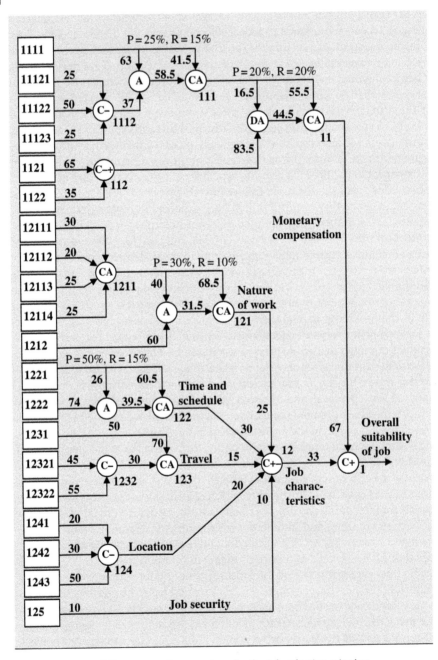

Figure 4.1.3 Suitability aggregation structure for the job selection criterion.

the aggregation tree. That is natural because each aggregator has its "shade," defined as the set of input attributes that contribute to its output value. As we approach the end of aggregation process, the shade increases, and so does the hardness and the strength of aggregators because it is generally not acceptable that any big group of input requirements is insufficiently satisfied.

At the end of development of the LSP criterion for job selection, it is useful to summarize the main characteristics of the process we just completed. The main property of LSP criteria is that they can be complex and sophisticated and have many degrees of freedom that the evaluator can use, but the development process is performed stepwise, in small and simple steps. In each step, we either focus on the evaluation of a single attribute or on the selection of a single aggregator type, or on the selection of a few weights. Each of these steps is justified by rational arguments that relate the selected parameters to stakeholder's goals and requirements. In each step, we provide a reasoning that proves why the selected parameters are the most appropriate. In such a way, we can build complex criteria that, in each component, precisely reflect the stakeholder's needs. At the end of development process, we have a criterion that is justifiable in each of its components. Of course, if the conditions change, the criterion can be easily adjusted to reflect different conditions and/or different stakeholder.

The process of selecting elementary attribute criteria and aggregation operators can be used as a proof that the absolute and relative criteria, as well as hard and soft, conjunctive and disjunctive, symmetric and asymmetric aggregators are absolutely indispensable if we want to express normal and justifiable stakeholder's requirements. All methods that fail to provide this necessary logic infrastructure are inconsistent with human reasoning and must be qualified as oversimplifications.

4.1.4 A Job Selection Example

Let us now use the job selection criterion (Table 4.1.1 and Fig. 4.1.3) to evaluate four job offers. All calculations will be performed using the web-based tool LSP. NT, [SEA16, SEA17]. The competitive jobs, denoted Alpha, Beta, Gamma, and Delta are presented in the input attribute table, Fig. 4.1.4. Alpha and Delta are essentially jobs that can be performed online from home with the flexible schedule and with low business travel, but require more hours of work per week. Beta is a traditional 9 to 5 job that needs low level of business traveling and offers highest job security. Gamma is a job that offers the best retirement benefits and has the same 40-hour week as Alpha.

The results of applying elementary criteria on input attributes are presented in the attribute suitability table, Fig. 4.1.5. This table compares input suitability degrees for the aggregation process and is suitable for comparison of individual good and bad properties of individual job offers. This table shows only one zero suitability degree—in the case of Gamma, attribute #12114.

The attribute suitability degrees are aggregated using the aggregation structure shown in Fig. 4.1.3. The results are presented in Fig.4.1.6 that includes all suitability degrees, from attributes to the overall suitability that is shown in the first row of the suitability aggregation table. This table shows an example of rejecting a job offer Gamma because Gamma does not provide the development of any management skills, and these skills are selected to be a mandatory requirement when developing the aggregator #1211. The suitability aggregation table shows the path 12114-1211-121-12-1 where the attribute zero suitability propagates from the leaf #12114 to the root #1 of the suitability aggregation tree (bottom-up through the sequence of shaded cells) and eventually generates the overall zero suitability and rejection of the Gamma offer.

The results in Fig. 4.1.6 yield the final ranking where the best offer is Beta (88.7% of satisfied requirements) followed by Delta (84.42%) and Alpha (78.69%). This ranking is sufficient to reach decision that it is the best to accept the job offer Beta because it is the best in monetary compensation (#11) and offers the most attractive job characteristics (#12). Fig. 4.1.6 provides data that can be used to verbally justify the final decision.

The results of LSP evaluation can be used to achieve other goals. If the stakeholder is a parent of a small child and prefers to work from home, s/he could be interested to work on improving the Delta offer that is closest to relatives, has good vacations, offers full flexibility of work from home, without any business trips and without the need for undesirable initial training; it even provides reasonable management skills that might be useful in the future. So, regardless the imperfect job security of Delta, the stakeholder could now investigate what should be improved in the Delta offer to match the Beta suitability. The first option would be to increase the salary from 94 to 100 and to match the salary of Beta; this option is denoted Delta$. The second option would be to reduce the working hours from 50 to 40; this option is denoted DeltaT. The third option would be DeltaT$, which obviously means to get simultaneously the salary of 100 and 40 work hours. These three options are also presented in Fig. 4.1.6 and show that both Delta$ and DeltaT options almost match the Beta offer, while the DeltaT$ option outperforms the Beta offer. The stakeholder can now use this information to negotiate better offer from Delta by providing justified conditions that if satisfied would yield the acceptance of the improved Delta offer. Of course, there are various additional "what if" questions that could also be answered using the LSP model (e.g., what if, in response to the improved Delta offer, Beta also decides to offer a significantly higher salary?).

The job selection example illustrates a general philosophy of development of LSP criteria, where the requirements are specified in a realistic way, yielding degrees of satisfaction above 75%, as well as the possibilities to improve the offers and increase the final overall suitability close to 90%. This creates an

Id	Attribute	Alpha	Beta	Delta	Gamma
1111	Starting salary	90	100	94	91
11121	Retirement benefits	89	98	96	100
11122	Health protection	100	79	76	88
11123	Vacations	25	20	28	30
1121	Anticipated salary in three years	14	18	22	15
1122	Anticipated salary in five years	22	25	30	28
12111	Technical content of the job	4	4	4	4
12112	Variety of job assignments	3	5	3	2
12113	Obtained professional skills and experience	3	5	4	4
12114	Obtained management skills	4	3	3.5	1
1212	Required job training	2	1	0	0
1221	Total number of hours at work per week	47	40	50	40
1222	Flexible working schedule	4	1	4	3
1231	Daily commuting requirements	0	0.75	0	1.2
12321	Maximum business trip length	3	5	0	0
12322	Annual percentage of time away from home	2	5	0	0
1241	Job location climate and environment	3	4	5	3
1242	Degree of urbanity in the job location area	1.2	3.5	1.4	0.65
1243	Proximity to relatives	0	1	0	1
125	Job security	3.5	5	3	4

Figure 4.1.4 Input attributes for the job selection project (LSP.NT).

opportunity for stakeholder to "synchronize" the numeric results of the LSP criterion and his/her intuitive percept of the value of each job offer. The intuitive validation of the final numeric results is necessary before the results can be accepted and used with confidence.

It is very important to always be aware that the results of LSP method are not meaningless numbers; these results have a clearly defined meaning, and in laymen interpretation that is the overall percentage of satisfied requirements. Inexperienced evaluators frequently make mistakes of specifying excessive and unrealistic requirements, which subsequently yield very low suitability scores. Obviously, nobody should accept a job that satisfies 17% of reasonable requirements. Similarly, a criterion function should be questionable if all competitors satisfy 95% of requirements or more.

When the first set of evaluation results of an evaluation project becomes available, it is necessary to validate both the LSP criterion model and the values of input attributes. In many cases, evaluators may discover the need for minor

Id	Attribute	Alpha	Beta	Delta	Gamma
1111	Starting salary	80.00	100.00	88.00	82.00
11121	Retirement benefits	78.00	96.00	92.00	100.00
11122	Health protection	100.00	58.00	52.00	76.00
11123	Vacations	71.43	57.14	80.00	85.71
1121	Anticipated salary in three years	70.00	90.00	100.00	75.00
1122	Anticipated salary in five years	84.00	90.00	100.00	96.00
12111	Technical content of the job	75.00	75.00	75.00	75.00
12112	Variety of job assignments	100.00	50.00	100.00	60.00
12113	Obtained professional skills and experience	50.00	100.00	85.00	85.00
12114	Obtained management skills	100.00	66.67	83.33	0.00
1212	Required job training	83.33	91.67	100.00	100.00
1221	Total number of hours at work per week	72.00	100.00	60.00	100.00
1222	Flexible working schedule	100.00	60.00	100.00	90.00
1231	Daily commuting requirements	100.00	90.00	100.00	72.00
12321	Maximum business trip length	90.00	83.33	100.00	100.00
12322	Annual percentage of time away from home	95.00	87.50	100.00	100.00
1241	Job location climate and environment	50.00	75.00	100.00	50.00
1242	Degree of urbanity in the job location area	80.00	100.00	85.00	48.75
1243	Proximity to relatives	100.00	83.33	100.00	83.33
125	Job security	62.50	100.00	50.00	75.00

Figure 4.1.5 Attribute suitability degrees for the job selection project (LSP.NT).

corrections of the criterion function that yield more realistic results. While this practice is fully acceptable, it can be abused and ultimately yield the "reverse evaluation problem," which is defined as the adjustment of criterion function so that a selected candidate satisfies a desired high degree of requirements and/or wins a competition. This situation is avoidable if the evaluation is verified by a team of unbiased stakeholder(s), evaluator(s), and domain expert(s).

The presented job selection criterion has 20 input attributes. If we compare this criterion with complex software evaluation projects, which can include from 300 to more than 500 inputs, it follows that the job selection is a small evaluation problem. However, it is certainly not a toy problem, and it properly illustrates that the need for logic sophistication is equally present in both small and large evaluation problems. The nature of job selection problem is that 20 inputs are sufficient to include the fundamental job characteristics and main components of monetary compensation, yielding a useful and trustworthy criterion. Using inappropriate number of inputs (either too big or too small) is a

Id	Attribute	Alpha	Beta	Delta	Delta$	DeltaT	DeltaT$	Gamma
1	JOB	78.69	88.70	84.42	87.34	88.17	91.77	0.00
11	Monetary compensation	78.82	91.42	89.28	95.28	89.28	95.28	82.12
12	Job characteristics	78.43	84.12	77.30	77.30	86.10	86.10	0.00
111	Starting salary and employee benefits	81.40	92.26	83.33	92.56	83.33	92.56	82.42
112	Anticipated future salary	74.53	90.00	100.00	100.00	100.00	100.00	81.61
121	Nature of work	76.45	74.30	86.71	86.71	86.71	86.71	0.00
122	Time spent at work and working schedule	79.13	86.12	69.35	69.35	100.00	100.00	96.96
123	Total travel requirements	97.72	88.64	100.00	100.00	100.00	100.00	78.83
124	Location of job	79.25	85.84	95.04	95.04	95.04	95.04	62.46
1112	Employee benefits	86.52	65.87	67.11	67.11	67.11	67.11	83.96
1211	Attractiveness of job	74.92	70.71	83.85	83.85	83.85	83.85	0.00
1232	Business travel	92.72	85.60	100.00	100.00	100.00	100.00	100.00
125	Job security	62.50	100.00	50.00	50.00	50.00	50.00	75.00
1243	Proximity to relatives	100.00	83.33	100.00	100.00	100.00	100.00	83.33
1242	Degree of urbanity in the job location area	80.00	100.00	85.00	85.00	85.00	85.00	48.75
1241	Job location climate and environment	50.00	75.00	100.00	100.00	100.00	100.00	50.00
12322	Annual percentage of time away from home	95.00	87.50	100.00	100.00	100.00	100.00	100.00
12321	Maximum business trip length	90.00	83.33	100.00	100.00	100.00	100.00	100.00
1231	Daily commuting requirements	100.00	90.00	100.00	100.00	100.00	100.00	72.00
1222	Flexible working schedule	100.00	60.00	100.00	100.00	100.00	100.00	90.00
1221	Total number of hours at work per week	72.00	100.00	60.00	60.00	100.00	100.00	100.00
1212	Required job training	83.33	91.67	100.00	100.00	100.00	100.00	100.00
12114	Obtained management skills	100.00	66.67	83.33	83.33	83.33	83.33	0.00
12113	Obtained professional skills and experience	50.00	100.00	85.00	85.00	85.00	85.00	85.00
12112	Variety of job assignments	100.00	50.00	100.00	100.00	100.00	100.00	60.00
12111	Technical content of the job	75.00	75.00	75.00	75.00	75.00	75.00	75.00
1122	Anticipated salary in five years	84.00	90.00	100.00	100.00	100.00	100.00	96.00
1121	Anticipated salary in three years	70.00	90.00	100.00	100.00	100.00	100.00	75.00
11123	Vacations	71.43	57.14	80.00	80.00	80.00	80.00	85.71
11122	Health protection	100.00	58.00	52.00	52.00	52.00	52.00	76.00
11121	Retirement benefits	78.00	96.00	92.00	92.00	92.00	92.00	100.00
1111	Starting salary	80.00	100.00	88.00	100.00	88.00	100.00	82.00

Figure 4.1.6 Suitability aggregation results for the job selection project (LSP.NT).

frequent mistake. Each evaluation problem has the most appropriate number of inputs. For the job selection problem, the reasonable number of inputs is between 15 and 30.

The job selection problem also illustrates that, in algorithmic notation, LSP criteria are $O(n)$ algorithms: the effort is linearly proportional to the number of attributes n. The development of an LSP criterion with 40 inputs takes very approximately two times more effort than the development of a criterion with 20 inputs. This is very good news for all decision makers.

4.2 Home Selection

Home selection is one of the most important evaluation and selection problems for all families. In this chapter we study this problem from two standpoints: (1) home selection using data provided by *online real estate* (ORE) websites, and (2) home evaluation using personalized evaluation criteria. The difference between these two problems is that in the case of personalized evaluation criteria, the user can create an arbitrary home attribute tree and use it to build a unique (personalized) evaluation criterion, while in the case of ORE websites the set of available attributes is predefined (fixed) and the user must adapt his/her criterion to the available data set.

In this context homes are defined as residential units of different types: single family house, duplex (a residential unit in house containing two residential units), townhouse (owned housing unit in a row of identical attached units), condo (an owned apartment in a residential building), and apartment (rented residential unit in a residential building). We will develop a criterion for home selection that is primarily focused on selecting single family houses, but can also be applied to other residential units.

4.2.1 Home Selection Using ORE Websites and LSPhome

ORE websites (e.g., [ZIL11]), based on MLS data [NAR06], provide access to all homes offered for sale in an area specified by a zip code. The search can be customized using a flexible query based on a few additional conditions like price range, home area, age, the number of bedrooms, and the number of bathrooms. The homebuyer is regularly interested in both the quality of home and the quality of home location. The quality of location primarily depends on positive and negative points of interest that exist in the vicinity of evaluated home. However, the ORE data are typically incomplete because they reflect only the selected

Soft Computing Evaluation Logic: The LSP Decision Method and Its Applications,
First Edition. Jozo Dujmović.
© 2018 John Wiley & Sons, Inc. Published 2018 by John Wiley & Sons, Inc.
Companion website: www.wiley.com/go/Dujmovic/Soft_Computing_Evaluation_Logic

basic properties of home, but not the properties of location. Therefore, the information about the quality of location must be collected from other websites.

A general organization of an LSP-based query answering system is shown in Fig. 4.2.1 (the LSP criterion is denoted as elementary attribute criteria EC1,..., ECn and the suitability aggregation structure, SAS). We assume that input attributes are distributed in m databases that are accessible using the Internet. For each database we have a data retriever application that provides an application programming interface (API) that remote client programs can use to access desired subset of data. So, at client's request, the remote data retrievers first perform the selection of appropriate objects (homes, points of interest, etc.).

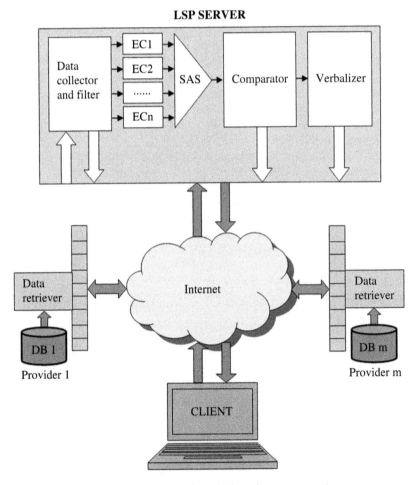

Figure 4.2.1 A general organization of an LSP-based query answering system.

The next step is marshalling, and the requested data (in the form of XSD, XML and JSON files) are usually delivered directly to the LSP server. The central component of the server is an LSP engine that processes n attribute values using elementary criteria (EC1,…,ECn) and the suitability aggregation structure (SAS). The LSP server includes an input subsystem and an output subsystem for the LSP engine.

In the case of home evaluation and selection, the LSP server initially retrieves home properties from a selected ORE website. The LSP server has a data collector that performs unmarshalling and collects n input attributes for each home. In dense urban areas the number of homes that are obtained from the ORE website can be rather large (e.g., more than 50). Detailed processing of all those homes is time consuming, and it is desirable to perform filtering that eliminates those homes that are not of interest for specific user.

The first attempt to use the LSP method in ORE was reported in [DUJ13]. Using these concepts, we developed a software tool called LSPhome that we describe and use in this chapter. The goals of LSPhome are visible in the first screen of that system, shown in Fig. 4.2.2. The idea is to use the LSP method for both buying and selling homes.

Figure 4.2.2 Three basic options offered by LSPhome.

The buying decisions are based on two groups of attributes: those that evaluate the suitability of home, and those that evaluate the suitability of home location. Of course, these two groups of data come from different providers and in some cases the time to collect all data is not negligible. In particular, the quality of home location is evaluated by processing large number of points of interest, i.e., locations of all relevant businesses, services, and institutions in the vicinity of each and every of competitive homes. This is the reason why the homebuyers can use the buy option in a fast mode (when evaluation includes only homes, without their locations), and in the detailed search mode (when the evaluation includes the attributes of homes and the attributes of locations). We assume that in many cases LSPhome can be accessed from mobile devices by people who are visiting open houses, and in such cases the response time should be low (typically below 8 seconds). In dense urban areas, the number of available homes can be large and the number of location attributes can also be large. In such cases, detailed searches can be significantly longer (e.g., up to 30 seconds). The home comparison process includes three fundamental components: home, location, and cost.

The process of selling a home is complementary to the process of buying a home. The role of LSPhome is to simulate the process of sale by comparing a given home with those homes that are currently offered for sale. The goal is to inform the potential seller about the value of his/her home compared with homes that are offered for sale. So, we can evaluate and compare the homes that are currently on the market and could compete with the analyzed home. Then we add the analyzed home to this group and perform a cost-suitability analysis. Assuming that the quality of home cannot be changed, the only adjustable variable is the asking price. If possible, we adjust the asking price so that the analyzed home wins the competition. That asking price is the maximum value the seller can ask in the current situation, if s/he wants to be the most competitive. This information is critical for the seller to decide whether to offer his/her home for sale or to wait for better opportunities.

Let us now investigate the process of buying a home. We assume that the user initially specifies the *basic mandatory requirements* that are used to reject inappropriate homes. The basic mandatory requirements (as well as user-specified degrees of importance) are collected using the interface exemplified in Fig. 4.2.3 and include the following five requirements:

1) Maximum distance from a desired ideal location
2) Maximum acceptable price
3) Minimum acceptable house area
4) Minimum acceptable number of bedrooms
5) Minimum acceptable number of bathrooms

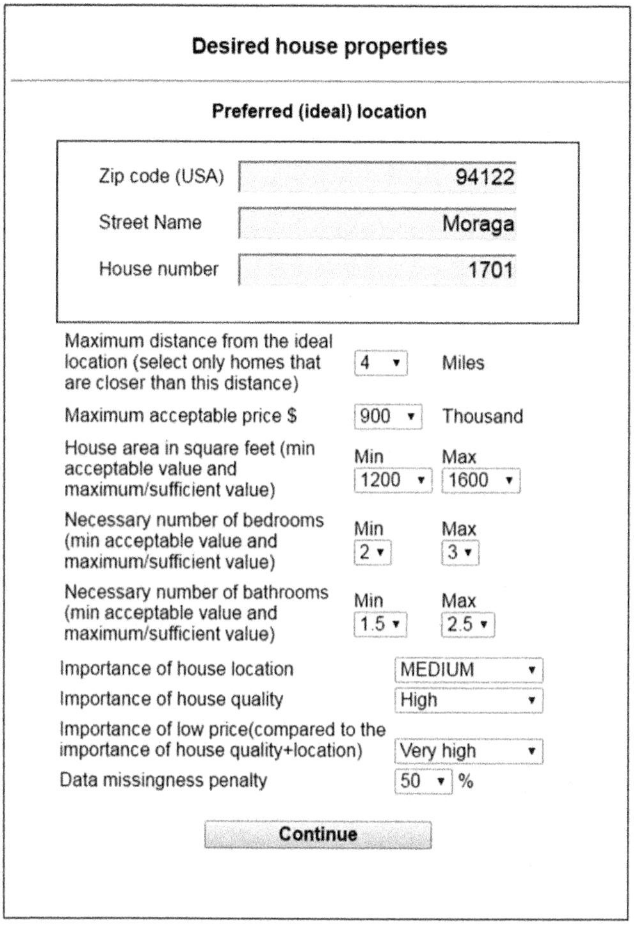

Figure 4.2.3 The LSPhome interface for specification of basic user requirements.

In order to optimize performance, the LSP server activates the home filtering and evaluation process that is based on the following steps:

1) Get the desired home location and basic mandatory requirements from the user.
2) Use basic mandatory requirements to adjust parameters of the evaluation criterion.
3) Collect data for homes on sale in the area defined by the desired zip code.
4) Reject homes that do not satisfy the basic mandatory requirements of price, area, the number of bedrooms, and the number of bathrooms (filtering step #1).

5) Reject homes that include invalid data, i.e., data that do not pass a logic control (filtering step #2).
6) Reject homes that are too far from the desired ideal location (filtering step #3).
7) Perform preliminary evaluation of the quality of homes that are selected after the first three filtering steps. The evaluation is based on home features and price, but not on the evaluation of the quality of home location. Selected up to N best homes, where N is selected according to the desired response time of the LSP server (filtering step #4).
8) For each of N best homes, collect data about adjacent *points of interest* (POI) that are used to evaluate the quality of home location. This can be a time-consuming process because the information about approximately 100 POI categories is available on the Internet, and each category in developed urban areas can contain a number of POIs.
9) Use the LSP criterion and the cost-suitability analysis to perform the overall evaluation and create the final ranking of N best homes. This is done by the comparator module of the LSPhome server. Use the verbalizer module to present results in user-friendly verbalized form (the verbalizer explains in a natural language all fundamental reasons why a specific home attains its ranking and outperforms some of remaining $N-1$ competitive homes).
10) Interface the LSP home server with other useful tools, such as location maps, property pictures, suitability maps, and driving directions. Using these tools the homebuyer can perform next steps toward deciding to visit some of N best homes.

4.2.2   Home Attribute Tree and Elementary Criteria

Real estate websites provide only limited information about features of available homes in the desired area (defined as a circle of specific radius whose center is in the user-specified ideal location). Of course, the overall suitability of home depends on the quality of home, but also on the quality of home location. The root structure of the criterion for home evaluation is shown in Fig 4.2.4, and the corresponding LSP suitability attribute tree is presented in Fig. 4.2.5. It includes only those data that can be *automatically retrieved* from various providers over the Internet.

The information about the quality of home location is based on the knowledge of POI distribution in the area close to the home location. The POI information comes from other sources (e.g., a city government or Google). So, the inputs for home evaluation using the LSP method are composed from components that are collected from multiple websites. As shown in Fig. 4.2.1, the

HOME SUITABILITY		
	QUALITY OF LOCATION	Suitability of neighborhood
		Walking distance from the ideal location
	QUALITY OF HOME	Available space
		Home features

Figure 4.2.4 A root structure of the home evaluation criterion.

processing is done by an LSP server and the final results are delivered over the Internet to the client machine.

In the case of home evaluation, it is obvious that each home evaluation criterion must reflect social, economic, geographic, and cultural conditions of the country and the region where the home is located. The specific standpoint used to develop the home evaluation criterion presented in this section reflects the conditions of so-called middle class, living in urban areas of California. This selection is based on convenience and does not diminish our awareness and respect for diversity of social and economic conditions of more than seven billion people living after October 31, 2011, on this fine planet.

Furthermore, it is important to emphasize that our home selection system cannot be based on arbitrary user requirements, and corresponding unique criteria. Our criterion is restricted to using only data that can be *automatically collected* over the Internet. This approach yields the fixed set of 36 attributes (6 for location and 30 for home features) shown in Fig. 4.2.6. Using these attributes, we developed elementary criteria shown in Table 4.2.1. The attribute criteria in the range from #112 to #121212 are adjustable by the user. All other attribute criteria are predefined and same for all users. This method offers a modest customization and reduces user's effort to almost zero.

4.2.3 Home Suitability Aggregation Structure as a Shade Diagram

After the development of the attribute tree and the set of elementary criteria, the next step is the development of the suitability aggregation structure. The resulting shade diagram based on WPM.17 aggregators is shown in Fig. 4.2.7. The sign + in the first column denotes mandatory inputs, and the sign − denotes nonmandatory inputs. The asymmetric aggregators include the conjunctive partial absorption (CPA) and the disjunctive partial absorption (DPA). CPA

```
1 HOME SUITABILITY

   11 QUALITY OF LOCATION
      111 Suitability of neighborhood
         1111 Walkability
         1112 Shopping and dining
         1113 Health support
         1114 Suitability for children
         1115 Suitability for seniors
      112 Walking distance from the ideal location

   12 QUALITY OF HOME
      121 Available space
         1211 Area belonging to home
            12111 Total internal living area of home
            12112 Outer usable area belonging to home
         1212 Rooms and other designated areas
            12121 Primary rooms
               121211 Number of bedrooms
               121212 Number of bathrooms
               121213 Kitchen
               121214 Dining room/area
               121215 Living/family room
            12122 Additional space and storage
               121221 Additional space
                  1212211 Breakfast room/area
                  1212212 Home office
                  1212213 Laundry
               121222 Storage and auxiliary areas
                  1212221 Walk-in closets
                  1212222 Pantry
                  1212223 Auxiliary utility areas
         1213 Parking space
            12131 Reserved parking
               121311 Garage
                  1213111 Private garage
                  1213112 Shared garage
               121312 Reserved uncovered parking space
            12132 Public parking (first-come, first-served)
               121321 Free public parking
                  1213211 Street parking next to home
                  1213212 Street parking close to home
               121322 Paid public parking
      122 Home features
         1221 Home organization/layout
            12211 Type of home
            12212 Number of floors
         1222 Home construction features
            12221 External wall material
            12222 Type of floor
            12223 Type of roof
         1223 Home energy supply
         1224 Home temperature regulation
            12241 Source of energy for heating
            12242 Type of heating system
            12243 Type of cooling system
         1225 Home age and maintenance
            12251 Home age
            12252 Last modification/improvement
```

Figure 4.2.5 The home attribute tree containing data available on the Internet.

```
 1 Walkability
 2 Shopping and dining
 3 Health support
 4 Suitability for children
 5 Suitability for seniors
 6 Walking distance from the ideal location
 7 Total internal living area of home
 8 Outer usable area belonging to home
 9 Number of bedrooms
10 Number of bathrooms
11 Kitchen
12 Dining room/area
13 Living/family room
14 Breakfast room/area
15 Home office
16 Laundry
17 Walk-in closets
18 Pantry
19 Auxiliary utility areas
20 Private garage
21 Shared garage
22 Reserved uncovered parking space
23 Street parking next to home
24 Street parking close to home
25 Paid public parking
26 Type of home
27 Number of floors
28 External wall material
29 Type of floor
30 Type of roof
31 Home energy supply
32 Source of energy for heating
33 Type of heating system
34 Type of cooling system
35 Home age
36 Last modification/improvement
```

Figure 4.2.6 The list of input attributes processed by LSPhome.

has two inputs: mandatory and optional. In the case of DPA, the two inputs are sufficient and optional. In both cases mandatory and sufficient inputs are explicitly denoted in the shade diagram. The negative value denotes the percent average penalty in the case where the optional input is not satisfied, and the positive value denotes the percent average reward in the case where the optional input is completely satisfied. By definition, the percent penalty/reward values are computed with respect to the value of the mandatory or sufficient input.

The most influential root aggregator #1 is not fixed. The user can adjust its properties by providing independently the percepts of overall importance of house location and the importance of house quality as shown in Fig. 4.2.3.

Table 4.2.1 Elementary criteria based on data available on the Internet (LSPhome).

1111		**Walkability**
Value	%	Walkability is a compound criterion that takes into account walking
0	0	accessibility of the following points of interest: (1) Bank, (2)
100	100	Barber shop, (3) Beauty salon, (4) Church (5) Dry Cleaner (6) Gym (7) Laundromat (8) Park, (9) Pharmacy, (10) Post office, (11) Restaurant, (12) Supermarket

1112		**Shopping and dining**
Value	%	Proximity to shopping areas and dining is a compound criterion that
0	0	takes into account distances from the following points of interest:
100	100	(1) Postal and mail services, (2) Book store, (3) Clothing store, (4) Electronics store, (5) Drug store, (6) Office supplies, (7) Hardware store, (8) Shoe store, (9) Shopping mall, (10) Food store, (11) Coffee shop / tea house, (12) Restaurant

1113		**Health support**
Value	%	Support for healthy living is a compound criterion that takes into
0	0	account distances from the following points of interest:
100	100	(1) Acupuncture clinic, (2) Beach, (3) Dentist, (4) Eye Care / Optometrist, (5) Gym (6) Hospital, (7) Medical center, (8) Organic restaurant, (9) Park, (10) Pharmacy, (11) Swimming pool, (12) Tennis court

1114		**Suitability for children**
Value	%	Suitability for children (age < 19) is a compound criterion that
0	0	takes into account distances from the following points of
100	100	interest: (1) Day care, (2) Kindergarten, (3) Elementary school, (4) Middle/high school, (5) Playground and amusement, (6) Gym, (7) Park, (8) Public library, (9) Public transportation (e.g., bus), (10) Swimming pool, (11) Zoo, (12) Restaurant (suitable for children)

1115		**Suitability for seniors**
Value	%	Suitability for seniors is a compound criterion that takes into
0	0	account distances from the following points of interest: (1) Public
100	100	transportation (bus/train/taxi), (2) Church, (3) Farmers market, (4) Gardening center, (5) Grocery store, (6) Library, (7) Medical center / hospital, (8) Pharmacy, (9) Optometrist, (10) Dentist, (11) Park, (12) Restaurant / coffee shop / tea house

112		**Walking distance from the ideal location**
Value	%	The ideal location is a user-specified location selected as a point
0	100	that completely satisfies all user requirements. The distance can be
40	86	expressed as (1) walking, (2) car, (3) public transport, or (4)
70	70	bicycle distance. We use the normalized relative walking distance
90	50.6	x=100D/Dmax, where
100	0	D = walking distance between an evaluated home and the ideal location (miles or km) Dmax = The maximum acceptable walking distance from the ideal location (miles or km) NOTE: Dmax must be selected by each user. <<<<<<<<<<<<<<<<<

12111		**Total internal living area of home**
Value	%	The total available space inside the home (or apartment) that can be
0	0	used for living, storage, and household purposes. Defined as the
100	100	following normalized value: a = 100*A/Amax. A = available area (square ft. or square m) Amax = maximum necessary area (square ft. or square m) NOTE: Amax must be adjusted by each user. <<<<<<<<<<<<<<<<<

12112		**Outer usable area belonging to home**
Value	%	The total available space outside the home/apartment that can be used
0	0	for gardening, recreation, storage, parking, etc. If it is shared by
100	100	several homes/apartments, then we take into account the share that belongs to a single home/apartment. Defined as the following normalized value: a = 100*A/Amax. A = available area (square ft. or square m) Amax = maximum necessary area (square ft. or square m) NOTE: Amax must be adjusted by each user <<<<<<<<<<<<<<<<<

121211		**Number of bedrooms**
Value	%	Defined as the following normalized value: b = 100*B/Bmax.
0	0	B = available number of bedrooms
100	100	Bmax = maximum necessary number of bedrooms NOTE: Bmax must be adjusted by each user. <<<<<<<<<<<<<<<<<

Table 4.2.1 (Continued)

121212		Number of bathrooms
Value	%	This criterion assumes full bathrooms. Both the bath/shower area and
0	0	the toilet area count as 1/2 of the full bathroom. Defined as the
100	100	following normalized value: b = 100*B/Bmax.
		B = available number of bathrooms
		Bmax = maximum necessary number of bathrooms
		NOTE: Bmax must be adjusted by each user. <<<<<<<<<<<<<<<<<<<<<

121213		Kitchen
Value	%	Kitchen is evaluated using a kitchen score based on available
0	0	appliances. Assign points as follows:
100	100	Range/oven: 20 Dish washer: 20 Refrigerator: 20
		Freezer: 20 Microwave: 10 Garbage disposal: 10
		Evaluation is based on the sum of assigned points.

121214		Dining room/area
Value	%	Defined as a separate room/area that is used only for dining.
0	0	0 = not available
1	100	1 = available

121215		Living/family room
Value	%	Defined as a separate room/area that is used only for social/family
0	0	life and events.
1	100	0 = not available 1 = available

1212211		Breakfast room/area
Value	%	Defined as a room or area used for consuming breakfast, snacks, or
0	0	light meals by the home residents.
1	100	0 = not available,
		1 = available

1212212		Home office
Value	%	Defined as a room equipped with appropriate facilities and used
0	0	exclusively for professional work (reading, writing, computing,
1	100	communicating, studying, music making, art studio work, etc.).
		0 = not available, 1 = available

1212213		Laundry
Value	%	Defined as a room or area equipped with appropriate appliances and
0	0	used exclusively for washing/drying/ironing of clothes.
100	100	Assign points as follows: Washer: 35, Dryer: 35, Laundry without
		appliances: 30 (Evaluation is based on the sum of assigned points)

1212221		Walk-in closets
Value	%	Defined as rooms large enough to walk inside or to walk
0	0	through and used exclusively to store clothes, shoes, etc.
1	100	0 = not available
		1 = available (one or more walk-in closets)

1212222		Pantry
Value	%	Defined as a small room used primarily as a storage for food.
0	0	0 = not available
1	100	1 = available

1212223		Auxiliary utility areas
Value	%	Defined as a multipurpose storage area, usually located in a
0	0	basement, attic, or ground floor, that can be used for general
1	100	storage and as a workshop. Utility areas may also hold home equipment
		(water heating, air heating/cooling, washing/drying machines, etc.).
		0 = not available
		1 = available

1213111		Private garage
Value	%	Defined as a vehicle storage area within the premises of the
0	0	evaluated home. The area of garage is not specified.
1	50	Evaluated as follows:
2	80	3 = attached garage (accessible from inside of home)
3	100	2 = detached garage (separate building close to home,
		typically in the back yard)
		1 = carport (covered structure used to offer limited
		protection for vehicles; typically roof without walls)
		0 = no garage

(Continued)

Table 4.2.1 (Continued)

1213112	Shared garage	
Value	%	Defined as a reserved (usually owned) parking space in a garage shared by all residents of a given community. Most frequent types are: - covered (e.g., underground) garage - shared carports 1 = available 0 = not available
0	0	
1	100	

121312	Reserved uncovered parking space	
Value	%	Defined as a private, designated and uncovered area within the premises of the home, where the home residents park their vehicles. Typical options are: - driveway - back yard - roof parking (for homes located below the access road) - reserved space in an outdoor parking lot (1 = available, 0 = not available)
0	0	
1	100	

1213211	Street parking next to home	
Value	%	Free public parking available on the street right in front of the evaluated home (or a street along any other side of the home), or a free outdoor parking lot next to the home. (1 = available, 0 = not available)
0	0	
1	100	

1213212	Street parking close to home	
Value	%	Free street parking or an outdoor parking lot in an acceptable vicinity of the evaluated home. (1 = available, 0 = not available)
0	0	
1	100	

121322	Paid public parking	
Value	%	Paid public parking of any type located in acceptable vicinity of the evaluated home. (1 = available, 0 = not available)
0	0	
1	100	

12211	Type of home	
Value	%	Defined as follows: 0 = apartment, assuming that this option denotes only rented apartments (not owned by the residents) 1 = condo, which is defined as an owned apartment in a residential building. 2 = townhouse, which is defined as an owned housing unit in a row of identical attached units. 3 = duplex, which is one residential unit with a separate entrance and parking in a house containing two residential units. 4 = single family house (separated from the neighboring houses in the sense that there are no shared walls).
0	0	
1	50	
2	70	
3	80	
4	100	

12212	Number of floors	
Value	%	Total number of vertical levels in the evaluated home accessible through stairs, excluding the basement and the attic. Two floors are more desirable for large families because they offer various options of use and more privacy.
1	70	
2	100	

12221	External wall material	

Value	%	Options include the following:
		B = brick C = cement/concrete S = stone
		SH = shingle W = wood ST = stucco
		V = Vinyl X = composite materials, metal, etc.
		
		Evaluation method:
		  1 = W/SH
		  2 = ST
		  3 = V/B/X
		  4 = S/C

1	60	
2	85	
3	90	
4	100	

12222	Type of floor	
Value	%	The type or material of the walking surface of the primary living areas of the home. Main options are: ST = stone HW = hardwood SW = softwood L = laminate floor V = vinyl/linoleum P = parquet SL = slate T = tile (ceramic) C = carpet Evaluation method: 1 = ST/SL/T, 2 = V, 3 = SW/C, 4 = L, 5 = HW, 6 = P
1	35	
2	50	
3	70	
4	75	
5	85	
6	100	

Table 4.2.1 (Continued)

12223		Type of roof
Value	%	Available types are:
1	70	T = clay tiles S = shake-shingle B = glued modified
4	100	G = tar and gravel P = plastic bitumen sheet
		A = asphalt shingle L = slate membrane
		C = composite or ceramic shingle
		Evaluated from the standpoint of durability and the need for
		maintenance in areas that use flat roofs as follows:
		1 = S/A/G/C 2 = P 3 = T/L 4 = B

1223		Home energy supply
Value	%	Sources of energy include the following options:
0	0	E = electric G = gas W = publicly supplied hot water
1	50	L = oil S = solar WD = wind
2	60	Evaluated as follows:
3	80	0 = no supply of energy
4	90	1 = E only
5	100	2 = E+L (L for heating water and home)
		3 = E+W (W for heating home)
		4 = E+G (G for cooking and water and home heating)
		5 = E++ (any combination of 2 or more other sources)

12241		Source of energy for heating
Value	%	Heating can be based on the following external sources of energy:
0	0	E = electric heating G = gas heating
1	50	W = hot water from a public supply L = oil heating
2	60	X = other forms of heating (carbon, wood, etc.)
3	90	Evaluated as follows:
4	100	0 = X 1 = L 2 = E 3 = G 4 = W

12242		Type of heating system
Value	%	Available options are:
0	0	A = forced air B = baseboard W = wall heating
1	50	F = floor heating R = radiant heaters
2	60	
3	70	Evaluation method:
4	100	0 = none 1 = R 2 = W or F 3 = B 4 = A

12243		Type of cooling system
Value	%	Availability of devices for air cooling and controlling the
0	0	temperature of home. Typical solutions include central A/C,
1	60	independent electric cooling units, fans, and gas units.
2	75	
3	100	0 = not available, 1 = fans, 2 = wall cooling,
		3 = cool air units

12251		Home age
Value	%	Age of home since its construction measured in years. Regardless of
0	100	material and maintenance, new homes are generally considered more
120	0	convenient than old homes.

12252		Time since last modification/improvement
Value	%	Time, measured in years, since the last major maintenance work or
0	100	upgrade/modification of the home. Upgrading and good maintenance are
10	70	assumed to partially compensate the age of home.
50	0	

The necessary andness and weights are computed from the desired overall percepts of importance of inputs (Chapter 2.5).

The presented criterion reflects a mandatory need for parking, where a private garage is the preferred solution. Taking into account that in many urban environments parking conditions can be difficult, all versions of parking are to some extent acceptable. Consequently, a private garage is considered a sufficient condition and its missingness can be significantly

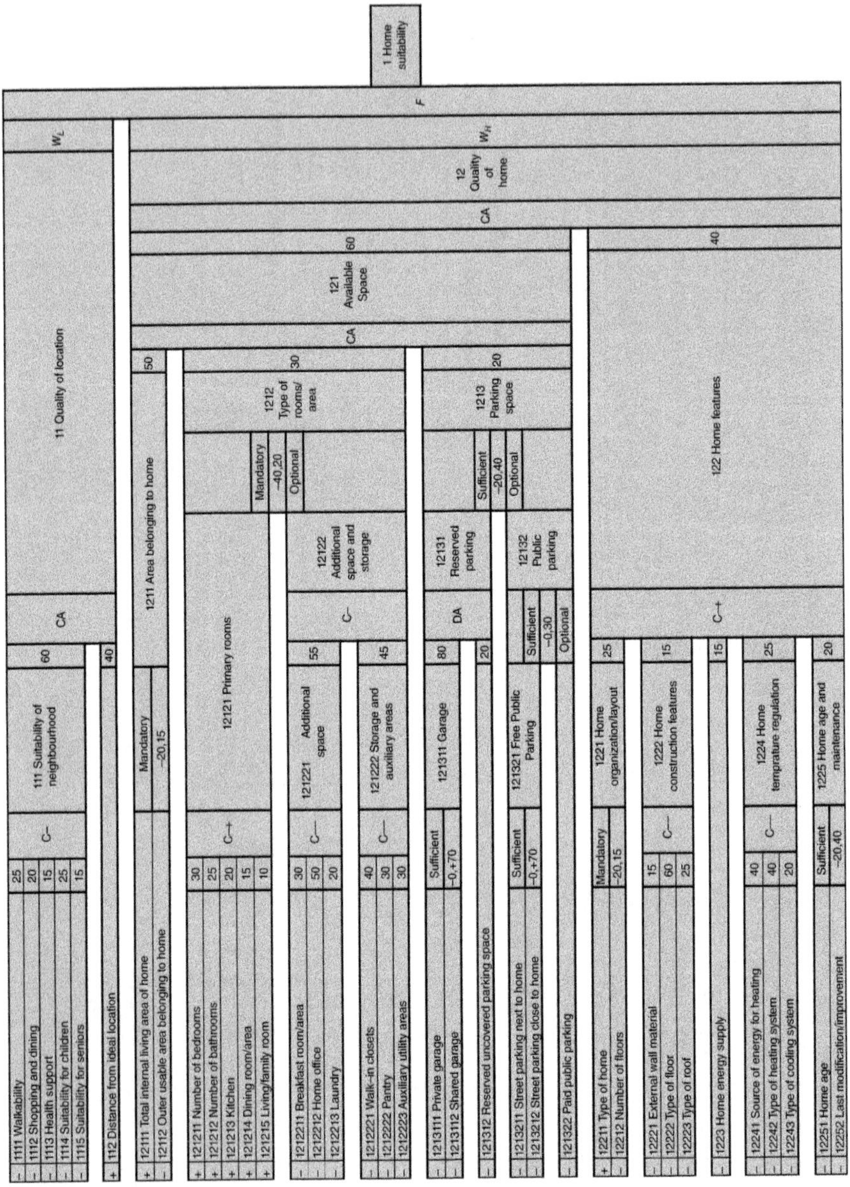

1 Home suitability

11 Quality of location W_L

12 Quality of home W_H

111 Suitability of neighbourhood

1111 Walkability
1112 Shopping and dining
1113 Health support
1114 Suitability for children
1115 Suitability for seniors

25
20
15
25
15

112 Distance from ideal location

121 Available Space

1211 Area belonging to home

12111 Total internal living area of home
12112 Outer usable area belonging to home

Mandatory −20,15

12121 Primary rooms

121211 Number of bedrooms
121212 Number of bathrooms
121213 Kitchen
121214 Dining room/area
121215 Living/family room

30
25
20
15
10

12122 Additional space and storage

121221 Additional space

1212211 Breakfast room/area
1212212 Home office
1212213 Laundry

30
50
20

121222 Storage and auxiliary areas

1212221 Walk-in closets
1212222 Pantry
1212223 Auxiliary utility areas

40
30
30

1212 Type of rooms/area Mandatory −40,20 Optional

55
45

1213 Parking space

12131 Reserved parking

121311 Garage

1213111 Private garage
1213112 Shared garage

30
30

1213121 Reserved uncovered parking space

Sufficient −0,+70

12132 Public parking

121321 Free Public Parking

1213211 Street parking next to home
1213212 Street parking close to home

Sufficient −0,+70

121322 Paid public parking

Sufficient −0,30 Optional

80
20

Sufficient −20,40 Optional

122 Home features

1221 Home organization/layout

12211 Type of home
12212 Number of floors

Mandatory −20,15

1222 Home construction features

12221 External wall material
12222 Type of floor
12223 Type of roof

15
60
25

1223 Home energy supply

1224 Home temperature regulation

12241 Source of energy for heating
12242 Type of heating system
12243 Type of cooling system

40
40
20

1225 Home age and maintenance

12251 Home age
12252 Last modification/improvement

Sufficient −20,40

25
15
15
25
20

50

60

40

40

121 Available Space 60

1212 Type of rooms/area 30

1213 Parking space 20

Figure 4.2.7 The suitability aggregation structure for the home selection criterion.

compensated using a shared garage. The absence of any garage can be partially compensated using a reserved uncovered parking space. So, any form of reserved parking is acceptable and in cases where reserved parking is not available it is acceptable to use some form of optional public parking. We use disjunctive partial absorption to aggregate reserved and public parking; if some form of reserved parking is available, then the overall quality of parking can be increased or decreased depending on the availability of an optional (free or paid) public parking. Due to the absence of input data, our criterion does not take into account the size of garage and the number of cars that can be kept in the parking.

The presented criterion is a typical case where the structure of criterion is mandated by the availability and the absence of input data that can be automatically retrieved from the Internet. Desirable attributes that are not included in this criterion include, e.g., the aesthetic value of home, the suitability of neighbors, the social reputation and the safety record of the neighborhood, the quality of public transportation system serving the home area, the role of home neighborhood in expected future developments and improvements, the distance from home to job locations for employed family members, and other similar attributes.

4.2.4 Using Missingness-Tolerant LSP Criteria

Typical evaluation results generated by LSPhome are exemplified in Fig. 4.2.8. The overall suitability is denoted as "score" and the results of cost-suitability analysis, normalized so that the best value is 100%, are shown in the column denoted "Value." The presented results include a short search report and the response time. The selected five best homes were selected from the group of 14 competitors.

One characteristic of real estate data available on the Internet is incompleteness. The majority of homes have incomplete attributes, and in the example shown in Fig. 4.2.8, the column "Data" shows the percent of available data about each house. In that example, on the average, 20% of attribute values were missing. Therefore, the fundamental requirement for LSP criteria that are used in ORE is the support for penalty-controlled missingness-tolerant aggregation. The incompleteness of attribute data is clearly illustrated in Fig. 4.2.9, where we present the available data for 12 homes on sale in San Francisco, CA 94122, in spring 2013 (missing data are denoted as shaded fields with asterisks). It is not unusual to find 50% or more missing data provided through the API of ORE websites. This is the reason why we must use a missingness-tolerant aggregation engine, as well as the data missingness penalty specified by the homebuyer using the LSPhome interface shown in Fig. 4.2.3.

LSPhome has found the following houses for you:

Rank	Score [%]	Price	Value	Address	Data [%]
1	56.99	649999	100.00	A: 1350 41st Ave, San Francisco, CA 94122	80.56
2	67.22	900000	92.99	S: 1770 35th Ave, San Francisco, CA 94122	80.56
3	68.49	988888	90.46	A: 1314 36th Ave, San Francisco, CA 94122	88.89
4	63.80	915000	89.61	S: 1686 47th Ave, San Francisco, CA 94122	69.44
5	64.19	930000	89.30	S: 44 Hugo St, San Francisco, CA 94122	80.56

Detailed search
The number of analyzed houses = 14
Average input data availability = 80.00%
Relative importance of low price = 50.00%
Missinggness penalty = 0.00%

Response time:8.331 seconds

Show all competitive systems	Show all evaluation results
Make LSP suitability maps	Analyze the quality of urban location
Reset	Exit

Figure 4.2.8 Sample results of home evaluation and comparison generated by LSPhome.

The missingness-tolerant aggregation is explained in Chapter 2.8. The missing data are frequent phenomenon in many areas of data processing. In the particular case of home evaluation and selection, there are two extreme possibilities: (1) data are missing because they are inconvenient for the seller, or (2) the value of an attribute is simply unknown. For example, the time since the last major roof maintenance might be intentionally not available, because it is inconvenient to disclose that an old roof is approaching the time when a major repair or replacement is necessary. Another example might be that the homebuyer is interested in the proximity of home to very special points of interest, which can be unknown to the seller and ORE data provider. In any case, it is reasonable to discourage hiding inconvenient data, and homebuyer might decide to penalize missing data. The simple idea is to use a normalized range of penalty (from 0 to 100%) where the consequence of maximum penalty is the zero suitability of missing attribute. The consequence of minimum penalty is that the aggregated suitability is computed using only the available data. As a trivial example, suppose that we have three suitability degrees x, y, and z and that we compute the suitability using the simple arithmetic mean $s = (x + y + z)/3$. Let $x = 50\%$, $y = 70\%$ and z is unknown. The maximum penalty considers that unknown is the same as unsatisfied, and the resulting suitability is

Code	Attribute												
1111	Walkability	49.0	42.0	52.0	50.0	25.0	27.0	23.0	30.0	27.0	43.0	73.0	34.0
1112	Shopping and dining	78.0	64.0	73.0	75.0	59.0	69.0	74.0	67.0	63.0	82.0	83.0	71.0
1113	Health support	72.0	48.0	55.0	68.0	56.0	47.0	50.0	49.0	50.0	58.0	55.0	64.0
1114	Suitability for children	60.0	52.0	36.0	67.0	75.0	43.0	55.0	73.0	41.0	55.0	79.0	64.0
1115	Suitability for seniors	55.0	57.0	45.0	58.0	40.0	30.0	43.0	36.0	28.0	52.0	60.0	50.0
112	Walking distance from the ideal location	0.34	2.12	1.58	0.82	1.5	1.12	0.41	1.27	1.24	0.23	0.5	1.31
12111	Total internal living area of home	1700.0	2167.0	982.0	1460.0	1750.0	1491.0	1024.0	1150.0	1460.0	1660.0	1585.0	1300.0
12112	Outer usable area belonging to home	1700.0	829.0	2014.0	1035.0	1214.0	2109.0	2147.0	1899.0	1536.0	518.0	1585.0	760.0
121211	Number of bedrooms	3.0	5.0	2.0	3.0	3.0	3.0	2.0	2.0	2.0	2.0	1.0	2.0
121212	Number of bathrooms	2.0	3.0	1.0	2.0	2.0	1.0	1.0	1.0	2.0	2.0	3.0	1.0
121213	Kitchen	60.0			80.0		0.0						
121214	Dining room/area	0.0			1.0		0.0						
121215	Living/family room	1.0			1.0		0.0						
1212211	Breakfast room/area	1.0			0.0		0.0						
1212212	Home office	0.0			1.0		0.0						
1212213	Laundry	100.0			70.0								
1212221	Walk-in closets	1.0			0.0		0.0						
1212222	Pantry	0.0			0.0		0.0						
1212223	Auxiliary utility areas	0.0			0.0		0.0						
1213111	Private garage	3.0		3.0	3.0						3.0		
1213112	Shared garage	0.0		0.0	0.0						0.0		
121312	Reserved uncovered parking space	0.0		0.0	0.0						0.0		
1213211	Street parking next to home	0.0		0.0	0.0						0.0		
1213212	Street parking close to home	0.0		0.0	0.0						0.0		
121322	Paid public parking	0.0		0.0	0.0						0.0		
12211	Type of home	1.0	0.0	4.0	4.0	4.0	4.0	4.0	4.0	4.0	4.0	1.0	4.0
12212	Number of floors	2.0	2.0	1.0	1.0	2.0	1.0						
12221	External wall material				2.0		2.0						
12222	Type of floor	2.0	5.0		2.0								
12223	Type of roof				1.0					0.0			
1223	Home energy supply	1.0	1.0	1.0	0.0	1.0	1.0	1.0	1.0	1.0	1.0	1.0	1.0
12241	Source of energy for heating				3.0								
12242	Type of heating system				4.0								
12243	Type of cooling system				0.0					0.0			
12251	Home age	12.0	69.0	109.0	73.0	72.0	90.0	62.0	74.0	86.0	82.0	12.0	73.0
12252	Last modification/improvement		9.0				20.0						

Figure 4.2.9 Incomplete attribute data for 12 homes on sale in San Francisco, CA 94122 (output of LSPhome).

$s = (50 + 70 + 0)/3 = 40\%$. If we want to avoid any penalty, then we can evaluate only the existing inputs yielding $s = (50 + 70)/2 = 60\%$. If we now assume that the suitability z is similar to x and y then we can assume $z = 60\%$, yielding $s = (50 + 70 + 60)/3 = 60\%$. The neutral value $z = 60\%$ is called the *concordance value* (see Section 2.2.6 and Chapter 2.8), Obviously, if the missing suitability is replaced by the mean value of remaining suitability degrees, the aggregated suitability will not be affected. So the aggregated suitability in the presented example will be between 60% (without penalty) and 40% (with the maximum penalty of 100%). Of course, the decision maker may find justification for selecting the most appropriate penalty inside the interval [0,100%], expecting that for penalty of 50% the aggregated suitability should be in the middle of the interval [40%, 60%], yielding the value of 50%. A high penalty is selected if the homebuyer suspects that missing data are intentionally not available because they are inconvenient. A low penalty is selected if the homebuyer believes that data are convenient but simply unknown. The mathematical method for penalty-controlled missingness-tolerant aggregation is presented in Chapter 2.8. This method is built in the evaluation engine used by the LSPhome decision support system.

4.2.5 The Optimum Home Pricing Problem

The home seller goal is to sell the property for the highest possible price. If the price is too high the home will not be competitive, or will spend too long time on the market. If the price is too low, the home will be sold very fast, but the seller may lose significant fraction of possible earning. Obviously, between these extremes there is an optimum point: the price that is high enough to satisfy the seller and reasonable enough to satisfy the buyer. That price can be found using the LSP method.

Suppose that S denotes the overall home suitability score (based on home location and home quality) and C denotes the home cost. The relative importance of home suitability is W_s and the relative importance of home cost is W_c. In a group of n competitive homes the cheapest home cost is $C_{min} = \min(C_1,...,C_n)$ and the highest suitability score is $S_{max} = \max(S_1,...,S_n)$. For simplicity, let us suppose that the overall value of each home is computed using the simple geometric mean as a representative of hard partial conjunction:

$$ V = \left(\frac{S}{S_{max}}\right)^{W_s} \left(\frac{C_{min}}{C}\right)^{W_c}, \quad W_s > 0, \quad W_c > 0, \quad W_s + W_c = 1 . $$

The best home is the home that attains the maximum value V_{max}.

Suppose now that we want to sell a home. We want to solve the following problem: Find the maximum price of our home C^*, so that the home is the most attractive in a selected area. Following is the algorithm for solving this problem:

1) Use LSPhome and enter as desired location the address of the home we want to sell.
2) Select the radius of the circle where we want to outperform the competition.
3) Specify the parameters of the home that we want to sell: number of bedrooms, bathrooms, area, etc.
4) Perform the evaluation of n existing homes on the market and find the best home, i.e., the home that attains the maximum value V_{max}. That is our main competitor.
5) Now, we add our home that has the score S_{n+1}, the cost C_{n+1} and the value $V_{n+1} = \left(\frac{S_{n+1}}{\max(S_1,...,S_{n+1})}\right)^{W_s} \left(\frac{\min(C_1,...,C_{n+1})}{C_{n+1}}\right)^{W_c}, \quad W_s + W_c = 1 .$
6) If we use a very low value of C_{n+1}, our home will have the highest value $V_{n+1} > V_i, \quad i = 1,...,n$. If we increase C_{n+1}, there will be a limit price

$C_{n+1} = C^*$ such that $V_{n+1} = \max(V_1,..., V_n)$. More precisely, the maximum price C^* is determined as the highest price that can still keep the leading position of our home:

$$V_{n+1} = \left(\frac{S_{n+1}}{\max(S_1,...,S_{n+1})}\right)^{W_s} \left(\frac{\min(C_1,..., C_n, C^*)}{C^*}\right)^{W_c}$$

$$\geq \left(\frac{S_i}{\max(S_1,...,S_{n+1})}\right)^{W_s} \left(\frac{\min(C_1,..., C_n, C^*)}{C_i}\right)^{W_c}, \quad i = 1,...,n .$$

7) If the seller is satisfied with the limit price C^*, s/he can select the price $C_{n+1} \leq C^*$ and offer the home for sale. If C^* is too low then the seller should wait until the market changes so that C^* becomes an acceptable value.

Example
The application of the presented algorithm is shown in Figs. 4.2.10 to 4.2.12. The home seller initially specifies the location of home and the desired selling price $C_{n+1} = 160000$ as shown in Fig. 4.2.10. The next step is to specify all home features by entering data in the home attribute form shown in Fig. 4.2.11. After the evaluation of the home considered for sale and the group of four competitive homes that are already offered for sale in the analyzed area, the obtained results are summarized in Fig. 4.2.12. The home considered for sale has the first position because of the minor advantage in the suitability score and the moderate price.

According to the optimum home pricing algorithm, the home seller might now consider the possibility to correct the initial price. Indeed, the winning price condition is now $C_{n+1} \leq C^* = 183072$. So, it is possible to increase the initial price for 23072 and still keep the leading position in this competition. For

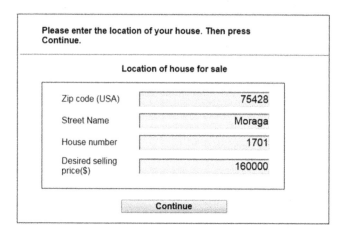

Figure 4.2.10 Specification of a home for sale.

Id	Attribute	Value	
12111	Total internal living area of home	1400	square ft.
12112	Outer usable area belonging to home	600	square ft.
121211	Number of bedrooms	2 ▾	
121212	Number of bathrooms	2 ▾	
121213	Kitchen: range/oven	available ▾	
121213	Kitchen: dishwasher	available ▾	
121213	Kitchen: refrigerator	available ▾	
121213	Kitchen: freezer	available ▾	
121213	Kitchen: microwave	available ▾	
121213	Kitchen: garbage disposal	available ▾	
121214	Dining room/area	available ▾	
121215	Living/family room	available ▾	
1212211	Breakfast room/area	not available ▾	
1212212	Home office	available ▾	
1212213	Laundry	laundry with washer∧dryer ▾	
1212221	Walk-in closets	available ▾	
1212222	Pantry	not available ▾	
1212223	Auxiliary utility areas	not available ▾	
1213111	Private garage	attached garage ▾	
1213112	Shared garage	not available ▾	
121312	Reserved ucovered parking space	not available ▾	
1213211	Street parking next to home	available ▾	
1213212	Street parking close to home	available ▾	
121322	Public paid parking	not available ▾	
12211	Type of home	single family ▾	
12212	Number of floors	2 ▾	
12221	External wall material	stucco ▾	
12222	Type of floor	parquet ▾	
12223	Type of roof	modified bitumen sheet ▾	
1223	Home energy supply	electric + gas ▾	
12241	Source of energy for heating	gas ▾	
12242	Type of heating system	forced air ▾	
12243	Type of cooling system	not available ▾	
12251	Home age	78	years
12252	Time since last modification/improvement	4	years

Figure 4.2.11 Specification of properties (input attributes) of the home for sale.

Rank	Relative value [%]	Suitability score [%]	Price	
			Actual price	Winning price
1	100.00	60.55	160000	183072
2	93.48	57.88	175000	152944
3	85.96	57.33	205000	151491
4	63.27	25.00	165000	66061 ?
5	63.16	19.63	130000	51871 ?

Figure 4.2.12 Sample results of a winning price calculation.

example, the seller could now decide to set the asking price at $C_{n+1} = 180000$ and still have a minor advantage over the other competitors. Another strategy might be to set the asking price $C_{n+1} = 185000$ and be ready to offer discount of 5000 during the financial negotiations with the potential buyer.

In each competition, the competitor in the leading position can increase the price up to C^*, but all other competitors can win only by reducing their asking prices. That is shown in Fig. 4.2.12. Let us consider the competitor having the rank 2 and the price 175000. If the leading competitor offers the home at the initial price 160000 then the second may win by decreasing the price from 175000 to 152944. Of course, the competitor with rank 2 might also decide to wait until the competitor with rank 1 leaves the competition, because in such a case it might be possible to significantly increase the price (approximately 30000) and still be better than the overpriced competitor with rank 3.

Competitors with very low suitability scores (last two competitors in Fig. 4.2.12) obviously have to make difficult decisions because they are too weak and should offer unrealistic discounts. They should correct the price or leave the market, or wait for a buyer who has a more convenient criterion, different from one that is used in this analysis. In any case, the LSP suitability scores and the cost/preference analysis offer clearly justified options that help all decision makers to understand their positions and make right decisions.

4.2.6 A Personalized Home Selection Criterion

The LSPhome online real estate model is restricted to using predefined LSP criteria that have low degree of customization. Of course, each homebuyer can make his or her specific criterion that fully reflects the specific need of the homebuyer. An example of such a criterion, based on 24 input attributes, is presented in this section. The proposed family house attribute tree is show in

```
9999 House
    1999 Location of house
        100 Average distance from job
        110 Average distance from school
        120 Distance from local shopping area
        130 Distance from important locations
    2999 Functional properties of house
        2222 The interior part of house
            2000 Total area
                300 The main area of house
                310 Auxiliary areas
            2110 Rooms and their arrangements
                2100 The number of rooms
                    400 The number of bedrooms
                    410 The number of other rooms
                    420 The number of bathrooms
                430 Quality of internal arrangement
            2200 House equipment
                500 Air conditioning
                510 Permanent household appliances
        2500 The auxiliary part of the house
            2300 Garage
                600 The size of garage
                610 Garage facilities
            2400 Laundry and storerooms
                710 Laundry
                710 Storerooms and closets
    3999 Exterior
        3000 Environment
                800 Environment and neighborhood
                810 Facing street
            820 The total size of lot
            830 Yard, porch and terrace(s)
    4999 General characteristics of house
            900 Expected remaining lifetime of house
            910 The number of floors
            920 The possibility of resale
            930 Aesthetics
```

Figure 4.2.13 A family house attribute tree with leaves to root numbering of nodes.

Fig. 4.2.13. It uses the leaves-to-root node numbering system (Section 3.4.7, Fig. 3.4.19) with four major groups of attributes (denoted 1xxx, 2xxx, 3xxx, and 4xxx). We evaluate the suitability of location, functional properties of house, exterior, and general characteristics of the house. The criterion is developed using the CDBS (a Criterion Data Base System) introduced in [DUJ76b].

The elementary criteria are presented in Fig. 4.2.14. The quality of house location is evaluated using the average distances from job, schools, local shopping, and other locations that are important for the homebuyer family. Of course, numeric rating scales can easily be adjusted according to different requirements. We also use point-additive elementary criteria as well as criteria based on direct preference assessment that can use standard rating scales.

The preference aggregation structure based on WPM.17 is presented in Fig. 4.2.15. CDBS uses connectors to connect aggregators that are distributed on different pages of the aggregation documentation. Partial absorption

System	LSP
Evaluation	ELC
Method	FORM

Project	FAMILY HOUSE
Date	
Author	Dr. Jozo Dujmovic
PAGE	1

E L E M E N T A R Y   C R I T E R I A

100 AVERAGE DISTANCE FROM JOB

Weighted average distance from job for all working members of the family.

(Expressed in minutes)

100-5
90-
80-
70-
60-
50-
40-
30-
20-
10-
0-60

110 AVERAGE DISTANCE FROM SCHOOL

Weighted average distance from school for all students in the family.

(Expressed in minutes)

100-5
90-
80-
70-
60-
50-
40-
30-
20-
10-
0-30

120 AVERAGE DISTANCE FROM LOCAL SHOPPING AREA

Average distance from local groceries, drugstores, etc.

(Expressed in minutes)

100-0
90-
80-
70-
60-
50-
40-
30-
20-
10-
0-15

130 AVERAGE DISTANCE FROM IMPORTANT LOCATIONS

Average distance from relatives, friends, main shopping areas, medical centers, libraries, churches, theaters, restaurants, parks, sport centers, etc.

(Expressed in minutes)

100-5
90-
80-
70-
60-
50-
40-
30-
20-
10-
0-50

300 THE MAIN AREA OF HOUSE

The total area of all main parts of the house including all rooms, kitchen, bathrooms, etc. and excluding auxiliary areas (garage, attic, etc.)

(Expressed in square meters)

100-220
90-
80-
70-
60-
50-
40-
30-
20-
10-
0-100

310 AUXILIARY AREAS

The total area of garage, laundry, auxiliary storerooms, attic, basement, etc.

(Expressed in square meters)

100-80
90-
80-
70-
60-
50-
40-
30-
20-
10-
0-40

400 THE NUMBER OF BEDROOMS

(The bedroom is defined by its function, according to user's needs.)

100-4
90-
80-
70-
60-
50-
40-
30-
20-
10-
0-3

410 THE NUMBER OF OTHER ROOMS

"Other rooms" include family rooms, a dining room, study rooms, etc.

100-3
90-
80-
70-
60-
50-
40-
30-
20-
10-
0-1

420 THE NUMBER OF BATHROOMS

100-3
90-
80-2
70-
60-
50-
40-
30-
20-
10-
0-1

430 QUALITY OF INTERNAL ARRANGEMENT

Direct preference assessment of the goodness of organization of all main house areas including rooms, kitchen, etc.

100-100
90-
80-
70-
60-
50-
40-
30-
20-
10-
0-0

500 AIR CONDITIONING

Assign 1 point for each of the following features:
a. Heating of a part of house
b. Heating of all house area
c. Complete heating (all house area and auxiliary areas)
d. Cooling of a part of house
e. Cooling of all house area
f. Complete cooling (all house area and auxiliary areas).

100-6
90-
80-
70-
60-
50-
40-
30-
20-
10-
0-0

510 PERMANENT HOUSEHOLD APPLIANCES

Assign 1 point for each of major household appliances belonging to house (various washing and drying machines, stoves, refrigerators, pavement cleaning machines, etc.)

100-5
90-
80-
70-
60-
50-
40-
30-
20-
10-
0-0

Figure 4.2.14 Elementary criteria for house selection created using CDBS.

System	LSP
Evaluation	ELC
Method	FORM

ELEMENTARY CRITERIA

Project FAMILY HOUSE
Date
Author Dr. Jozo Dujmovic
PAGE 2

---

600 | THE SIZE OF GARAGE

The number of cars that can be kept in the garage.

```
100-2
 90-
 80-
 70-1
 60-
 50-
 40-
 30-
 20-
 10-
  0-1
```

610 | GARAGE FACILITIES

Assign points as follows:

Direct connection with house 4
Heating 2
Cooling 1
Remote control of garage door 2

```
100-9
 90-
 80-
 70-
 60-
 50-
 40-
 30-
 20-
 10-
  0-0
```

700 | LAUNDRY

2 = Separate laundry with sufficient space
1 = Laundry as a part of garage or some other room
0 = A good laundry is not available

```
100-2
 90-
 80-
 70-1
 60-
 50-
 40-
 30-
 20-
 10-
  0-0
```

---

710 | STOREROOMS AND CLOSETS

Direct preference assessment of the quality of all space for clothes, supplies, tools, etc.

```
100-100
 90-
 80-
 70-
 60-
 50-
 40-
 30-
 20-
 10-
  0-0
```

800 | ENVIRONMENT AND NEIGHBORHOOD

Direct preference assessment of the quality of surroundings of the house (general impression, quiet, safety, neighbors, etc.)

```
100-100
 90-
 80-
 70-
 60-
 50-
 40-
 30-
 20-
 10-
  0-0
```

810 | FACING STREET

Direct preference assessment of the amount of traffic on facing street, the ease of access, cleanness, sidewalks, sewers, etc.

```
100-100
 90-
 80-
 70-
 60-
 50-
 40-
 30-
 20-
 10-
  0-0
```

---

820 | THE TOTAL SIZE OF LOT

The total area of lot expressed in square meters.

```
100-750
 90-
 80-
 70-
 60-
 50-
 40-
150-
 30-
 20-
  0-300
```

830 | YARD, PORCH, AND TERRACE(S)

Direct preference assessment of the suitability of yard (privacy, plants, swimming pool and other sport facilities, etc.), porch, and terrace(s).

```
100-100
 90-
 80-
 70-
 60-
 50-
 40-
 30-
 20-
 10-
  0-0
```

900 | EXPECTED REMAINING LIFETIME OF HOUSE

Estimated remaining lifetime of house taking into account its age, outside materials, inside materials, etc.

(Expressed in years)

```
100-80
 90-
 80-
 70-
 60-
 50-
 40-
 30-
 20-
 10-
  0-40
```

---

910 | THE NUMBER OF FLOORS

2 = Two floors
1 = One floor

```
100-2
 90-
 80-
 70-1
 60-
 50-
 40-
 30-
 20-
 10-
  0-0
```

920 | THE POSSIBILITY OF RESALE

Direct preference assessment of the possibility of selling again the property.

```
100-100
 90-
 80-
 70-
 60-
 50-
 40-
 30-
 20-
 10-
  0-0
```

930 | AESTHETICS

Global aesthetic impression of the evaluated house with yard and its surroundings.

(Direct preference assessment)

```
100-100
 90-
 80-
 70-
 60-
 50-
 40-
 30-
 20-
 10-
  0-0
```

Figure 4.2.14 (Continued)

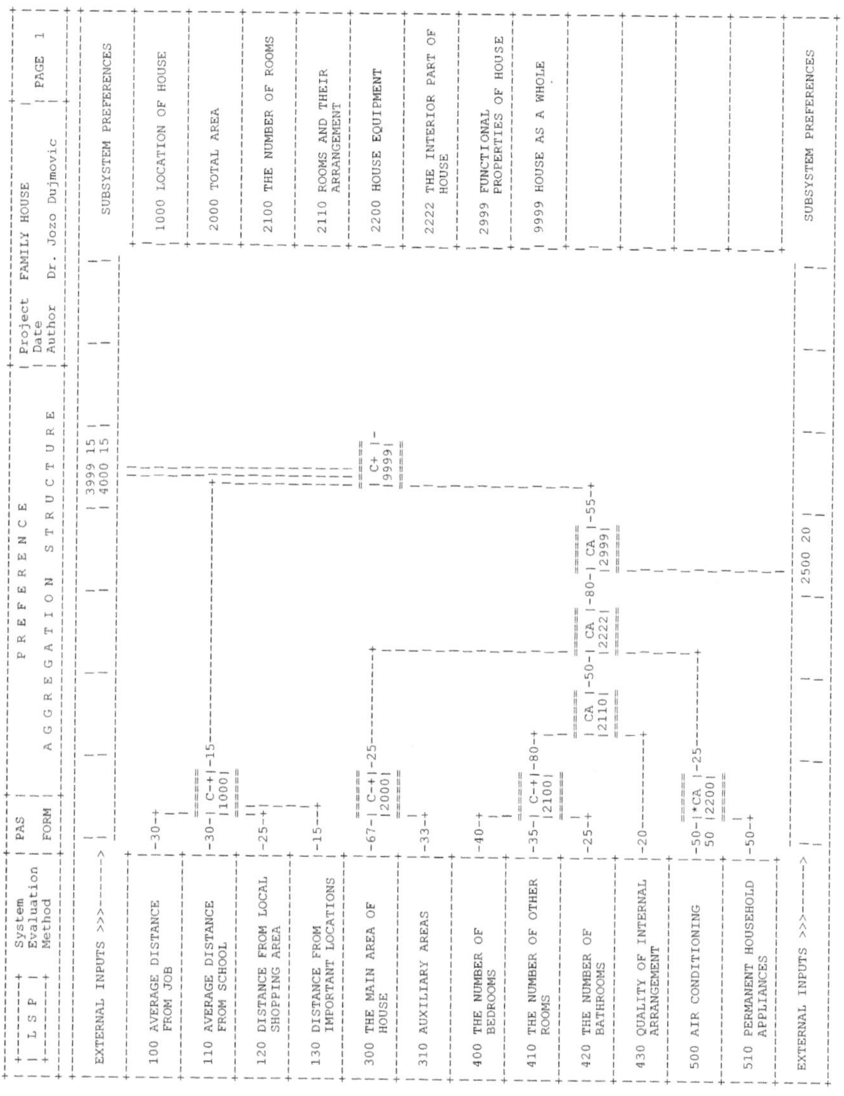

Figure 4.2.15 Suitability aggregation structure for house selection created using CDBS.

Project FAMILY HOUSE | PAGE 2
Date
Author Dr. Jozo Dujmovic

PREFERENCE AGGREGATION STRUCTURE

System Evaluation Method | PAS FORM | LSP

EXTERNAL INPUTS >>>

2222 80 | 1000 15

SUBSYSTEM PREFERENCES

2300 GARAGE
2400 LAUNDRY AND STOREROOMS
2500 THE AUXILIARY PART OF HOUSE
2999 FUNCTIONAL PROPERTIES OF HOUSE
3000 ENVIRONMENT
3999 EXTERIOR
4000 GENERAL CHARACTERISTICS OF HOUSE
9999 HOUSE AS A WHOLE

SUBSYSTEM PREFERENCES

600 THE SIZE OF GARAGE
610 GARAGE FACILITIES
700 LAUNDRY
710 STOREROOMS AND CLOSETS
800 ENVIRONMENT AND NEIGHBORHOOD
810 FACING STREET
820 THE TOTAL SIZE OF LOT
830 YARD, PORCH, AND TERRACE(S)
900 EXPECTED REMAINING LIFETIME OF HOUSE
910 THE NUMBER OF FLOORS
920 THE POSSIBILITY OF RESALE
930 AESTHETICS

EXTERNAL INPUTS >>>

-70-|*CA |-50-+ 10 |2300|
-30-+
|C+|-20-| CA |-55-+ |2500| |2999|
-40-| C- |-50-+ |2400|
-60-+
-60-|*CA |-30-+ 30 |3000|
-40-+
|CA |-55-+ |2999|
-40---
|C+|-15--- |3999|
-30---
|C+ |-9999|
-20-+
-15-| C+|-15- |4000|
-20-+
-45-+

Figure 4.2.15 (Continued)

aggregators (#2200, #2300 and #3000) use the CPA/A:CA aggregators and show the weights W_1 and W_2. For example, in the case of #3000 we have $W_1 = 60\%$, $W_2 = 30\%$ and according to the mean penalty/reward tables, in this case the mean penalty is selected to be 31.4% and the mean reward is 20.6%. The aggregation structure is a rather standard canonic increasing andness form that terminates with the strong C+ aggregator.

4.3   Evaluation of Medical Conditions[1]

In this chapter we present quantitative models for evaluation of disease severity and patient disability using the LSP method. The basic idea is that the LSP method can be used to evaluate medical conditions using general medical criteria, and to customize them according to needs of a specific patient. Such LSP criteria (first introduced in [DUJ08a]) can be implemented using software tools available over the Internet and used by both patients and doctors. Such tools are suitable for analyzing changes of patient condition over a period of time and making decisions related to selection of therapy.

The goal of this chapter is to discuss the following topics:

- Quantification of disease severity and patient disability
- Benefits of replacing medical rating scales with LSP criteria
- Development of LSP criteria for patient disability evaluation
- The decision problem of the best time to start a risky therapy
- Development of the LSPmed software tool for medical applications
- Case study of using LSP method in a real case of peripheral neuropathy

LSP models can incorporate both subjective symptoms and objectively measured impairments, can be used by both doctors and patients to quantitatively evaluate the current level of severity or disability, and can be serially applied to analyze the progression of disease over time and the response to therapy. The presented method is generally applicable to all medical evaluations where it is important to create precise quantitative severity or disability models based on sophisticated logic conditions.

---

1 Domain expertise for evaluation of peripheral neuropathy was provided by **Leslie J. Dorfman, M.D.**, Department of Neurology & Neurological Sciences, Stanford University School of Medicine, and **Jeffrey W. Ralph, M.D.**, Department of Neurology, University of California San Francisco School of Medicine.

Soft Computing Evaluation Logic: The LSP Decision Method and Its Applications,
First Edition. Jozo Dujmović.
© 2018 John Wiley & Sons, Inc. Published 2018 by John Wiley & Sons, Inc.
Companion website: www.wiley.com/go/Dujmovic/Soft_Computing_Evaluation_Logic

4.3.1 Evaluation of Disease Severity and Patient Disability

One of the main goals of soft computing is to develop mathematical models that describe phenomena based on variables that are a matter of degree [KOS93]. Many medical conditions cause symptoms and impairments that are also matters of degree, and which manifest the severity of the condition [FEI87, STE92, STR89, HER06]. In this section we focus on evaluating the disease severity and patient disability. We use peripheral neuropathy to exemplify the proposed method.

In the area of evaluation of medical conditions we differentiate three types of evaluation models, and three types of users. The basic types of disease evaluation models are:

- Medical criterion of disease severity
- Models of patient disability
  - Medical disability model
  - Patient disability model

Three main users of evaluation models are:

- Physicians
- Patients
- Social and/or health organizations

Our classification of three fundamental medical evaluation problems and corresponding severity and disability indicators is shown in Fig. 4.3.1. We assume that each medical condition can be characterized by a comprehensive

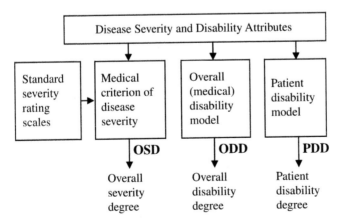

Figure 4.3.1 Types of disease evaluation models.

set of disease severity and disability attributes (S/D attributes). Appropriate subsets of S/D attributes are then used as inputs for each of the three basic models.

Disease severity is the focal point of medical interest. It reflects all symptoms and impairments (loss of anatomic structure or function) caused by the analyzed disease. The goal of severity evaluation is to generate highly standardized indicators that are suitable for comparison of patients and unified assessment of their condition. Disease severity is evaluated by medical examiners based on objective measurements of selected impairment degrees, and quantification of symptoms by patients (e.g., as scores on symptom questionnaires). The end result of evaluation is an *overall severity degree* (OSD). In our models, OSD∈[0,100%] where 0% corresponds to normal conditions and 100% corresponds to the maximum severity. OSD aggregates all relevant medical inputs and can also incorporate elements from existing severity rating scales [HER06, DYC93, DYC05, GRA06a, GRA06b]. A standardized OSD can be used by physicians as a reliable indicator whose threshold values support difficult decisions, particularly those that involve treatments that carry risk of serious adverse effects.

As opposed to the standardized evaluation of disease severity, patient disability refers to the degree of restriction in patient activities. Consequently, the level of disability depends on specific characteristics of each patient, such as his/her age, gender, profession, and hobbies. Some patients may be very disabled at a relatively low level of severity. Others may reach a high level of severity without significant disability. Disease severity and patient disability are positively correlated, but are different indicators [DYC93].

Regarding the level of standardization of disability indicators, we distinguish between the patient disability evaluation model and the overall medical disability model. The patient disability evaluation model is designed to be used by patients for self-evaluation and the disability trend estimation. The self-evaluation results can help patients make decisions about accepting or declining proposed treatments. Consequently, inputs to such models consist of S/D attributes that are easily understandable and easily assessed by the patient without technical assistance. The resulting *patient disability degree* (PDD∈[0,100%]) reflects the patient's view of his/her own disability.

Precise quantification of a standardized *overall (medical) disability degree* (ODD∈[0,100%]) is of interest both to physicians and to organizations that provide health and social services to patients. Such indicators should be designed by medical experts in order to provide support for administrative decisions, such as disability benefits or retirement conditions. In addition, ODD provides a standardized way to communicate the patient status between medical practitioners.

The three severity and disability indicators, OSD, ODD, and PDD, reflect various criteria, but they can be designed using the same LSP methodology.

In order to minimize medical prerequisites for understanding the proposed methodology, in this chapter we present a model for computing a PDD for peripheral neuropathy.

The disability and severity rating scales used in clinical practice are regularly based on simplistic additive scoring. These scales enjoy wide acceptance because they are easy to administer. The additive scoring approach yields indicators of low granularity and insufficient precision. Its validity is investigated in [FEI87, KIA94, STR89].

Current medical rating scales do not use graded logic functions and other useful features of soft computing decision models. The main goal of this chapter is to demonstrate how soft computing methods and corresponding software tools can increase the precision of medical evaluations.

4.3.2 Limitations of Medical Rating Scales

Since this approach is so simple, there must be something wrong with it.

—David L. Streiner and Geoffrey R. Norman
in Health Measurement Scales [STR89]

The primary goal of medical rating scales is to serve as standardized instruments for measuring disease severity or patient disability. Such scales usually score several attributes and add individual points to generate an overall score. The score can be used by medical personnel both to rate disease severity and to support treatment decisions. An impressive number of different rating scales are used in the neurological field [HER06].

In the area of peripheral neuropathy [BRO05], popular rating scales include the Neuropathy Symptom Score (NSS) and the Neurologic Disability Score (NDS) [DYC93, DYC05], the Overall Disability Sum Score (ODSS) [MER06] and its modified version the Overall Neuropathy Limitation Scale (ONLS) [GRA06a], Walk-12 [GRA06b] (same as the Multiple Sclerosis Walking Scale (MSWS) [HOB03]), and others.

The concept of medical rating scales is shown in Table 4.3.1. There are K evaluated S/D attributes, and each is scored according to the patient's degree of limitation. The patient is asked to select in each row one of N scores that best describes his/her degree of limitation. The value of N is typically small. For example, in the case of ONLS $N = 3$ (1 = not affected, 2 = affected but not prevented, and 3 = prevented); in the case of Walk-12 $N = 5$ (1 = not at all, 2 = a little, 3 = moderately, 4 = quite a bit, 5 = extremely).

Theoretically, individual scores in each row could belong to different ranges, to reflect different levels of importance of the investigated abilities. Unfortunately, this is not the case in many popular scales (including Walk-12); it is

Table 4.3.1 Scoring of the limitation of abilities.

S_{ij} = ability limitation score $S_{i1} < S_{i2} < ... < S_{iN}, \quad 1 \le i \le K$		Limitation Level		
		Min	...	Max
Limitations	Ability #1	S_{11}	...	S_{1N}
of K abilities	...	...	...	...
(S/D attributes)	Ability #K	S_{K1}	...	S_{KN}

Minimum score = $S_{11} + S_{21} + ... + S_{K1} = S_{min}$.

Maximum score = $S_{1N} + S_{2N} + ... + S_{KN} = S_{max}$.

Total score = $S = \sum_{i=1}^{K} S_{ij_i}$; $\quad j_i \in \{1,...,N\}$.

Normalized score:

$$S_{norm} = 100\frac{(S - S_{min})}{(S_{max} - S_{min})} \in [0,100\%].$$

assumed that all items have equal importance. The total score satisfies the condition $S_{min} \le S \le S_{max}$, and therefore it is useful to apply the normalized score that directly reflects the overall limitation of abilities. The corresponding calculations are shown in Table 4.3.1.

In the case of Walk-12 we use 12 S/D attributes shown in Table 4.3.2. Consequently, the calculation of the total normalized score is performed as follows:

$$K = 12, \quad N = 5, \quad S_{ij} = j, \quad j = 1,...,5;$$

$$S_{11} = \cdots = S_{K1} = 1, \quad S_{min} = K = 12;$$

$$S_{1N} = \cdots = S_{KN} = 5, \quad S_{max} = NK = 60;$$

$$S_{max} - S_{min} = NK - K = K(N-1) = 48;$$

$$S_{norm} = 100(S - 12)/48.$$

Table 4.3.2 Walk-12 S/D attributes.

1 Ability to walk	7 Effort needed to walk
2 Ability to run	8 Support for walking indoors
3 Climbing up/down stairs	9 Support for walking outdoors
4 Difficulties in standing	10 Slowed down walking
5 Balance problems	11 Smoothness of walk
6 Length of walk	12 Need to concentrate on walking

Each of the 12 Walk-12 S/D attributes has equal weight. The granularity of this scale (the increment of S_{norm} caused by a single increment of one of the attributes) is $\gamma = 100[1/S_{max} - S_{min})] = 100/(NK - K) = 100/48 = 2.08\%$. The maximum effect of any attribute (the difference between the case without limitations and the case with extreme limitations) is $N - 1 = 4$ such increments: $\delta = (N-1)\gamma = 100/K = 100/12 = 8.3\%$. So, according to Walk-12, the difference between a patient who is almost unable to climb up or down stairs and a patient who performs this activity without any problem is only 8.3%. Furthermore, the ability to run is initially weighted equally as the ability to walk, even though walking is much more important for most daily activities. The importance of standing in Walk-12 is only 1/12, even though standing is indispensable for a number of professions. Such properties, considered isolated, are highly questionable. The main reason why the results of such rating scales are not meaningless is that all the analyzed abilities are highly correlated (e.g., patients who have reduced ability to walk also have reduced ability to run, length of walk, smoothness of walk, etc.), and the positive correlation significantly compensates for errors in weights of additive scoring models [DUJ72b].

Now is the time to distrust simplicity. The presented properties of Walk-12 are typical for all simple additive scoring scales (see Chapter 1.3 for a detailed analysis of drawbacks of simple scoring models). The main disadvantages of the simple additive scoring approach used in medical rating scales are the following:

- All S/D attributes are equally important.
- Addition of points prevents the use of more appropriate logic aggregators of inputs.
- Increasing the number of inputs decreases their relative importance.
- Redundant questions artificially increase the relative importance of correlated inputs.

It is interesting to note that regardless the criticism of simple additive scoring models in health-related literature (e.g., [STR89]) and the use of advanced fuzzy evaluation and aggregation models in medical applications (e.g., [NET99a, NET99b]) the area of standardized medical rating scales remains unchanged and strictly committed to oversimplified additive scoring models.

Walk-12 is an example of a standardized medical rating scale. Patients of different gender and age are evaluated using the same criteria and Walk-12 requests patients to "answer all questions even if some seem irrelevant to you." This approach clearly reflects the standpoint of medical examiners, with the intention that all examiners use the same instrument and generate consistent scores. It also reflects the dangerous standpoint that simplicity is more important than accuracy.

This approach is not appropriate for evaluating the overall patient disability, but it has advantages based on automatic adjustment of rating scales. The five-level scale of S/D degree can be interpreted (verbalized) as the following percent degrees of limitation: "not at all" = 0%, "a little" = 25%, "moderately" = 50%, "quite a bit" = 75%, and "extremely" = 100%. Obviously, the meaning of the limit level of 100% is left undefined, and consequently, it is subjectively determined by each patient. This is a mechanism that can equalize the age and gender differences, and in some cases generate consistent and comparable results. For example, if a 40-year-old patient F and the 70-year-old patient S claim a "moderate limitation of the ability to walk," then it is reasonable to assume that the patient F has much higher expectations than the patient S. In this case, each patient feels that his/her ability is just 50% of the ability that should be expected in his/her age and gender group. Consequently, the reported limitations of ability may reflect the same severity of disease. This may yield comparable degrees of the limitation of ability, regardless of the obvious differences in expectations.

On the other hand, it is necessary to have a consistency in expectations. If the expectations are sufficiently different because of professional or any other specific demands, then the resulting scales yield inconsistent/incomparable results. For example, a patient whose profession demands long standing during work is expected to have very different expectations compared to the patient of the same age and gender who has no need to stand while working. Consequently, the standard medical rating scales have a problem to distinguish whether patient's answers reflect the severity of disease or the disability of the patient. In all medical evaluation problems, it is necessary to clearly distinguish the evaluation of disease severity and the evaluation of patient disability. It is reasonable to expect that the majority of patients without guidance could be more concerned about their disability than about the objective severity of their disease.

4.3.3 LSP Models for Computing OSD, ODD, and PDD

In the area of medical evaluation the LSP method can be used for building complex criteria for the evaluation of the disease severity and patient disability based on a set of S/D attributes. The structure of medical LSP criteria is summarized in Fig. 4.3.2. A general database of S/D attributes is used for selecting a subset of n attributes $(a_1, ..., a_n)$ that are appropriate inputs for one of the three fundamental evaluation models that generate OSD, or ODD, or PDD. Some inputs are provided by the doctor, and others are provided by the patient. Inputs include objective measurements, expert assessments, and subjective ratings of symptoms.

For each S/D attribute we create an individual attribute criterion that determines the individual degree of severity/disability (S/D degree). For example, a typical elementary attribute criterion for the patient's length of walk L is shown in Fig. 4.3.3.

If the patient can walk only some very small distance $L_1 \geq 0$, then we consider that the corresponding S/D degree is $D_L = 100\%$. If $L = L_2$ then $D_L = d_2 < 100\%$. Finally, if $L \geq L_3$ then there is no impairment and $D_L = 0$. The elementary

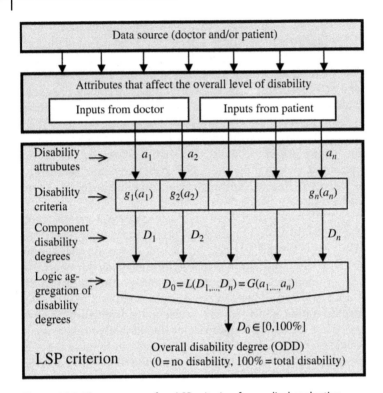

Figure 4.3.2 The structure of an LSP criterion for medical evaluation.

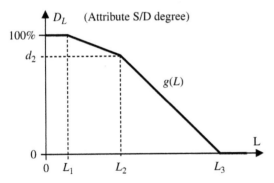

Figure 4.3.3 A disability attribute criterion $D_L = g(L)$ for the length of walk L.

disability criterion function $D_L = g(L)$ is usually defined as a piecewise linear approximation. In such cases, the elementary attribute criterion can be symbolically denoted as a set of breakpoints (vertex notation):

$$Crit(L) = \{(L_1, 100), (L_2, d_2), (L_3, 0)\}; \quad L_1 < L_2 < L_3.$$

It is important to note that all elementary attribute criteria generate S/D degrees that are continuous functions of the values of S/D attributes. This process yields better accuracy than the discrete rating scales.

After defining n individual S/D degrees, we are ready to aggregate them and generate the desired overall patient's S/D degree (OSD or ODD or PDD). The result of logic aggregation of individual S/D degrees is an overall S/D degree that quantitatively evaluates the severity or disability associated with the analyzed medical condition. The overall S/D degree is formally equivalent to the overall suitability in traditional evaluation models. However, while the desired value of the overall suitability should be as high as possible, the desired values of the overall S/D degree should be as low as possible. In addition, traditional evaluation models use predominantly conjunctive aggregators because evaluators generally want to have all good things simultaneously present and sufficiently satisfied. As opposed to that, the severity/disability models use predominantly disjunctive aggregators because in many cases any high component of severity/disability may significantly affect the overall S/D degree. The objective of most treatments is to simultaneously keep all component S/D degrees sufficiently low.

In medical applications the LSP method can be interpreted as a generalization of medical rating scales. It combines sophisticated scoring with complex and flexible logic conditions based on soft computing models, and consequently it is suitable for precise evaluation of medical conditions. The advantages of LSP criteria can be summarized as follows:

- Computation of a single OSD/ODD/PDD from any number of heterogeneous inputs.
- Flexibility to develop sophisticated quantitative severity criteria that have adjustable logic conditions between symptoms (or impairments) and adjustable degrees of their importance.
- Ability to customize severity and disability criteria according to opinions and needs of physicians and/or patients.
- Ability to efficiently track the development of severity and disability over any time interval.
- Use of software tools to reduce the cost of evaluation.

4.3.4 Evaluation of PDD for Peripheral Neuropathy

The first step in the PDD evaluation process is the development of the PDD attribute tree. A typical PDD tree presented in Fig. 4.3.4 contains 39 PDD attributes (in lay terminology) that can be adjusted according to the needs of the majority of patients. There are two groups of symptoms: sensory symptoms and motor symptoms. The sensory symptoms include main forms of sensory discomfort: numbness, pain, and tingling/itching. The motor symptoms are

PERIPHERAL NEUROPATHY
1 SENSORY SYMPTOMS
  11 Numbness
    111 Numbness of feet
      1111 Numbness of toes
        11111 Numbness of toes tips
        11112 Numbness of entire toes
      1112 Numbness of sole (nonuniform distribution)
        11121 Minimum numbness of sole
        11122 Maximum numbness of sole
      1113 Numbness of the upper surface of feet
    112 Numbness of hands
      1121 Numbness of fingertips
      1122 Numbness of fingers and hands
  12 Pain
    121 Pain in feet
      1211 Pain in toes
      1212 Pain in soles
    122 Pain in hands
      1221 Pain in fingertips
      1222 Pain in fingers and hands
  13 Tingling/Itching
    131 Tingling/itching in feet
    132 Tingling/itching in hands
2 MOTOR SYMPTOMS
  21 MUSCLE WEAKNESS
    211 Muscle weakness in legs
      2111 Muscle weakness in feet
      2112 Muscle weakness in calves
      2113 Muscle weakness in thighs
    212 Muscle weakness in arms
      2121 Muscle weakness in hands
      2122 Muscle weakness in arms/shoulders
  22 MOBILITY IMPAIRMENTS (PATIENT TESTS)
    221 Impaired standing
      2211 Short standing (<1h; e.g., teaching)
      2212 Medium standing (1 to 2h)
      2213 Long standing (more than 2h)
    222 Impaired walk
      2221 Fast (short) run
      2222 Slow run
      2223 Fast walk
      2224 Slow walk
    223 Impaired climbing
      2231 Impaired rising on toes
      2232 Impaired toe walk
      2233 Impaired jumping
      2234 Impaired stair-climbing
      2235 Impaired slopes (10% or more)
    224 Impaired (fast) transitions
      2241 Impaired arising from chair
      2242 Impaired arising from squat
      2243 Impaired arising from floor
  23 INCOORDINATION
    231 Imbalance
      2311 Imbalance with closed eyes
      2312 Imbalance with open eyes
    232 Tremor
      2321 Tremor in legs
      2322 Tremor in arms
    233 Clumsiness
      2331 Clumsiness in legs
      2332 Clumsiness in arms

Figure 4.3.4 The PDD attribute tree for peripheral neuropathy.

related to motor impairments and include the muscle weakness, mobility problems, and incoordination. The leaves of the decomposition tree are PDD attributes that can be directly evaluated to generate the attribute disability degrees.

The elementary criteria can be completely based on rating scales, either traditional multilevel scales (e.g., in the case of five levels of impairment $Crit(a) = \{(0,0),(4,100)\}$), or continuous direct disability assessment (DDA) scales (e.g., $Crit(a[\%]) = \{(0,0),(100,100)\}$). For multilevel scales the patient selects the most appropriate of the available discrete levels. For DDA scales the patient answers questions about the percent levels of sensory and motor symptoms.

In the case of mobility impairments, we use a set of tests that a patient can adjust, measure, and evaluate according to his/her age and the needs of his/her activities. Three sample criteria from the impaired climbing group (223) are shown in Fig. 4.3.5.

The criterion for rising on toes (#2231) can be based on the maximum number of seconds a patient can stand still on toes of both legs (with some arm support to avoid problems of balancing): $Crit_{2231}(Toes[Sec]) = \{(0,100),(60,40),(120,20),(240,0)\}$. This criterion reflects the strength of calf muscles.

For the elementary criterion #2232 (toe walk) we can define the disability attribute as the maximum number of steps a patient can make in toe walk. Suppose that for a given age/gender group 40 steps corresponds to the disability degree of 60%, 60 steps corresponds to the disability degree of 20%, and 80 or more steps denotes no disability. The corresponding criterion $EC_{2232}(Steps) = \{(0,100),(40,60),(80,0)\}$ is more demanding than the criterion 2231 because now the calf muscles of a single leg must be able to alternatively support the weight of the body.

The criterion for stair-climbing (#2234) is based on the maximum number of stairs a patient can climb without having to stop and rest, For example, the criterion $Crit_{2234}(Stairs) = \{(0,100),(50,0)\}$ reflects a patient in the age/gender group where climbing 50 stairs denotes normal ability.

The basic idea of elementary criteria exemplified in Fig. 4.3.5 is that every patient without assistance can easily perform all requested measurements and provide inputs for self-evaluation. If measurements and evaluations are performed in equal time intervals then it is possible to track the development of disability and use the results to make treatment decisions. In the majority of cases the initial tuning of the elementary criteria for each patient should be done by trained medical personnel. This process can be facilitated by using specialized software tools for customizing standard LSP criteria [PAT05, DIS07].

Presented sample elementary criteria show differences between absolute criteria that specify fixed quantitative requirements and relative criteria based on rating scales that evaluate difficulties using several levels, such as "none < low < medium < high < extreme." Obviously, absolute criteria evaluate the objective

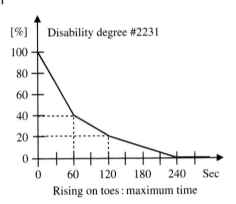

Rising on toes : maximum time

Figure 4.3.5 Three sample elementary criteria for impaired climbing.

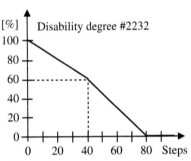

Toe walk : maximum number of steps

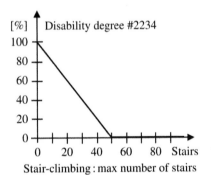

Stair-climbing : max number of stairs

patient ability, while relative criteria evaluate patient's subjective percept of disability. Absolute criteria must be adapted for each patient to take into account age, gender, and other conditions. Relative criteria are automatically adapted to specific patient, but on the other hand introduce imprecision and untrustworthiness caused by different and unknown interpretation of relative rating scales by individual patients. LSP method can combine absolute and relative criteria.

The logic aggregation of sensory and motor attribute disability degrees is shown in Fig. 4.3.6. The majority of aggregators are partial disjunctions or arithmetic means. The reason for predominantly disjunctive aggregators is clearly apparent in the case of pain: any of several sources of pain is sufficient

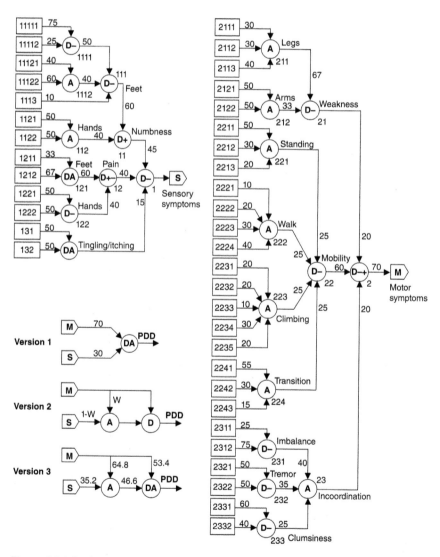

Figure 4.3.6 Logic aggregation of patient disability indicators using WPM.17 aggregators.

to create discomfort and need for medications. Similarly, any of motor symptoms can be sufficient to contribute to patient disability.

The aggregation of motor (M) and sensory (S) symptoms can be based on three versions of the final aggregator presented in Fig. 4.3.6. In the first version, the final aggregator is a medium partial disjunction of sensory and motor symptoms. In other words, either sensory or motor symptoms affect the overall PDD, but their relative importance is quite different. The motor impairments are considered substantially more important than the sensory impairments (70% vs. 30%). This criterion assumes that sensory problems can be tolerated and/or compensated more easily than motor impairments that cause overt disabilities and can substantially reduce the quality of life.

The second and third versions of the final aggregator use the disjunctive partial absorption (DPA) aggregators. The DPA aggregator in version 2 is used when we need asymmetric logic relationships of motor and sensory symptoms. If motor symptoms M are considered *sufficient* to cause the overall disability, and sensory symptoms S are considered an *auxiliary (undesired) component* that partially affects the resulting PDD, then DPA is an appropriate aggregator of M and S:

$$PDD = M \vee [WM + (1-W)S], \quad 0 < W < 1$$

$$= \begin{cases} M, & M > S \geq 0 \\ WM + (1-W)S, & S > M \geq 0 \end{cases}$$

$$= \begin{cases} M, & S = 0 \\ (1-W)S, & M = 0. \end{cases}$$

So, if motor symptoms are greater than sensory symptoms then the PDD is fully determined by M, and S does not affect PDD (it is totally absorbed). In some cases this can be considered an extreme approach that is insufficiently exposing the impact of noteworthy sensory symptoms.

If the total absorption of S is not desirable, then we can define a DPA that supports a partial absorption of S, shown as version 3 in Fig. 4.3.6. Requested asymmetric properties of M and S can be defined using a table of desired $\{M, S, PDD\}$ triplets. Such a table is shown in Fig. 4.3.7. If $M = 50\%$ (significantly high) and S is low (10%) we want a PDD that is 45% (close to M).

M	S	PDD
0.5	0.1	0.45
0.1	0.5	0.2

$PDD = [0.534M^{3.929} + 0.466(0.648M + 0.352S)^{3.929}]^{1/3.929}$

Figure 4.3.7 The training set table and the final form of the DPA aggregator.

Figure 4.3.8 DPA sensitivity curves.

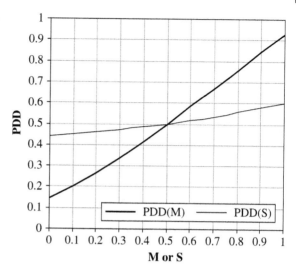

In the reverse case, where M is low (10%) and S is significant (50%), we want a moderate impact yielding PDD = 20%. To compute the parameters of the DPA aggregator (shown in Fig. 4.3.6 Version 3, and in Fig. 4.3.7), we can use ANSY (a training tool for preferential neurons [DUJ91]). The asymmetric and slightly nonlinear properties of this aggregator are illustrated in Fig. 4.3.8 where we show two sensitivity curves: PDD(M) for $S = 0.5$ and PDD(S) for $M = 0.5$. These curves include points defined in the table shown in Fig. 4.3.7.

The presented methodology includes all the main steps in the design of criteria for the evaluation of patient disability or disease severity, and the computation of the overall indicators OSD, ODD, and PDD. The practical use of the LSP method in medical applications is supported by the LSPmed software tool that was initialized in [DIS07] and further expanded for Internet use as shown in Section 4.3.7.

The medical condition evaluation process can be used both by physicians and by patients. Physicians can use the LSP evaluation methodology to precisely analyze the development and severity of disorders over long periods of time. Patients can use similar methodology and corresponding decision support tools to decide when it is reasonable to accept therapies that can cause adverse effects. In all cases the user (either a doctor or a patient) interacts with LSPmed by answering a list of questions, which are then used to compute an overall quantitative severity/disability indicator in the range [0, 100%]. By repeating this process at regular time intervals, it is possible to quantitatively analyze the level of severity (and/or disability) as a function of time. That is also necessary to evaluate patient's response to therapy.

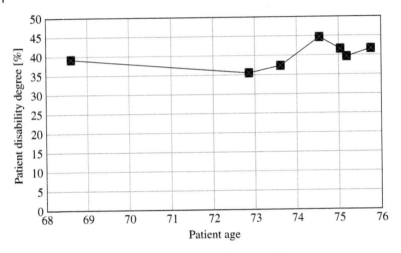

Figure 4.3.9 A patient disability degree as a function of time.

An example of applying the criterion shown in Fig. 4.3.6 to analyze the status of peripheral neuropathy in the case of a real patient over the period of seven years is presented in Fig. 4.3.9. After the diagnosis of an anti-MAG neuropathy, the doctor suggested an off-label chemotherapy that sometimes helps in cases of autoimmune neuropathies. This therapy can be considered risky and created a delicate decision problem: at what time to start the risky therapy to maximize patient's quality of life? If the risky therapy is taken too early, it can create consequences that can shorten the patient's life. On the other hand, if it is taken too late or not taken at all, then the neuropathy can make progress that significantly decreases patient's quality of life. Consequently, there is an optimum point in time where taking the risky chemotherapy maximizes patient's quality of life. This problem is analyzed in the next section.

4.3.5 The Risky Therapy Decision Problem

There are many diseases that are very difficult to treat, and most treatments yield inadequate response. In medical literature there are treatments that are reported to sometimes cause positive effects, sometimes negative effects, and sometimes no effect. Such treatments are risky, and decision makers (both physicians and patients) are faced with a delicate problem to determine the level of disability that justifies accepting risks and adverse effects associated with such treatments.

This problem is addressed in the conclusion of a general study of immune therapies for the anti-MAG neuropathy reported in [NOB00]: the authors found

(1) frequently observed considerable adverse effects and (2) unclear efficacy for the long-term outcome. They suggest that "until more effective or safer therapies become available, current immune therapies should probably be reserved for patients impaired in their daily life or in a progressive phase of the disease." Obviously, if we can reliably track the growth of PDD (or OSD), then it should be possible to find an optimum PDD threshold that justifies the decision to use a risky therapy. In this section we analyze this problem for the simplest possible growth model, a linear growth.

A simplified linear disability development model is shown in Fig. 4.3.10. It consists of two liner segments. We assume that the disability $D(t)$ grows linearly, and at the time t_1 a decision is made to start a therapy that improves the condition but causes adverse effects and an expected survival time of h years. After starting the risky therapy, we assume a linear improvement of patient's condition, and the end of life at the age t_2. The model includes the following parameters:

t_0, D_0 = patient's age and disability degree at the time the condition is diagnosed
t_1, D_1 = patient's age and disability degree at the time of the start of risky therapy (point S in Fig. 4.3.10)
t_2, D_2 = expected patient's age and disability degree at the time of death after the therapy (point C in Fig. 4.3.10)
t_3, D_3 = expected patient's age and disability degree at the time of death without the therapy (point E in Fig. 4.3.10)
h = average expected survival time after the therapy
g_0 = annual disability growth rate without the therapy ($g_0 > 0$)
g_1 = annual disability growth rate during the therapy ($-g_{max} \leq g_1 < g_0$)

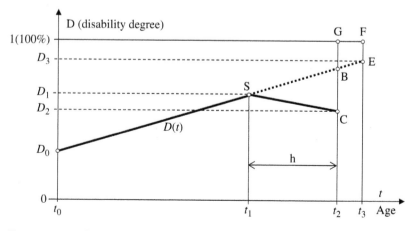

Figure 4.3.10 A linear disability development model.

The simple linear disability model is

$$D(t) = \begin{cases} D_0 + g_0(t - t_0), & t \le t_1 \\ D_1 + g_1(t - t_1), & t_1 \le t \le t_2; \end{cases}$$

$$t_2 = \min(t_1 + h, \ t_3), \quad t_1 < t_3;$$

$$D_1 = D_0 + g_0(t_1 - t_0);$$

$$D_2 = D_1 + g_1(t_2 - t_1);$$

$$D_3 = D_0 + g_0(t_3 - t_0).$$

We assume that all parameters are selected so that $0 < D_0 < D_1 < D_3 \le 1$ and $0 \le D_2 \le 1$. The average disability without therapy is $D_{03} = (D_0 + D_3)/2$. The average disability with risky therapy is a function of the beginning of treatment time t_1:

$$D_{02}(t_1) = \frac{1}{t_2 - t_0} \int_{t_0}^{t_2} D(t) dt = \frac{(t_1 - t_0)(D_0 + D_1) + (t_2 - t_1)(D_1 + D_2)}{2(t_2 - t_0)}.$$

The average ability of a patient can be defined as a complement of disability:

$$A_{03} = 1 - D_{03}, \quad A_{02}(t_1) = 1 - D_{02}.$$

We assume that patient's goal is a long life and the absence of disability. Thus, the average quality of patient life can be defined as a conjunctively polarized weighted aggregation of the average ability (A) and the average length of life (L): $Q = [wA^r + (1-w)L^r]^{1/r}$, $0 < w < 1$. The weight w denotes the relative importance of high ability and $1 - w$ is the relative importance of long life.

The elementary criterion for the length of life can be expressed as the ratio of remaining life and the maximum remaining life $L = (t_{death} - t_0)/(t_3 - t_0)$; if $t_{death} = t_3$ (expected natural end of life) then $L = 1$, and in all other cases $L < 1$. Therefore, the quality of life without therapy is

$$Q_{03} = \left[wA_{03}^r + (1-w) \right]^{1/r}, \quad 0 < w < 1, \ r < 1, \ (L = 1).$$

Similarly, the quality of patient life with risky therapy is

$$Q_{02}(t_1) = \left[wA_{02}^r(t_1) + (1-w)[(t_2 - t_0)/(t_3 - t_0)]^r \right]^{1/r}, \quad 0 < w < 1, \ r < 1.$$

The relative effects of therapy (therapy-related improvement of the quality of life) can now be expressed as the ratio of the qualities of life with and without therapy:

$$E(t_1) = Q_{02}(t_1)/Q_{03}$$

Of course, we are interested only in positive effects, i.e., a treatment that causes the improvement of the quality of life: $E(t_1) > 1$. In addition, the maximum of

$E(t_1)$ can be used for determining the optimum time for the beginning of treatment t_{1opt}:

$$E_{opt} = E(t_{1opt}) \geq E(t_1), \quad t_0 \leq t_1 \leq t_3.$$

4.3.6 A Case Study of Anti-MAG Neuropathy

Let us now illustrate the use of our models in the case of a patient who, at the age $t_0 = 60$ years, is diagnosed with the anti-MAG neuropathy. Patient's initial disability level is $D_0 = 20\%$. The neuropathy-related disability is slowly increasing at an average rate of 2.6% per year ($g_0 = 0.026$). The patient life expectancy is $t_3 = 88$ years. If a risky off-label chemotherapy can reverse the disability rate to be -1% per year ($g_1 = -0.01$) and yields the average survivability $h = 10$ years, the important questions are to find the maximum improvement caused by the risky chemotherapy and the optimum age for the beginning of the therapy. We will assume that the global andness of quality of life aggregator is 77%, yielding the exponent $r = -1$.

The analysis of various options in the range $w \in [0.1, 0.9]$ yields results shown in Figs. 4.3.11 and 4.3.12. For example, if the length of life is equally important as the low disability level ($w = 0.5$), then the optimum age for the start of therapy is

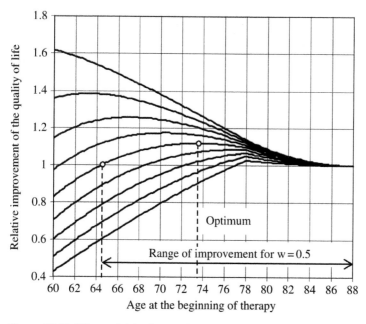

Figure 4.3.11 Effects of risky therapy for $w = 0.1, 0.2, \ldots, 0.9$ (top curve).

$t_{1opt} = 73.64$ years (a flat maximum between 72 and 76 years) and the average improvement of the quality of life attains the maximum value $E_{opt} = 1.12$ (i.e., only 12% above the situation without therapy). In this case, the expected length of life would be reduced from $t_3 = 88$ years to $t_2 = 83.64$ years, and the maximum disability level would be reduced from $D_3 = 92.8\%$ (at the natural end of life) to $D_1 = 55\%$ (at the beginning of therapy). Figs. 4.3.11 and 4.3.12 illustrate the role

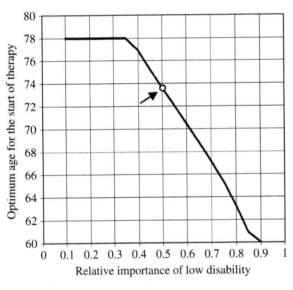

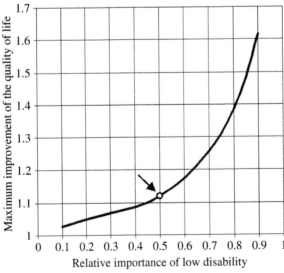

Figure 4.3.12 Optimum values t_{1opt} and E_{opt} for $w \in [0.1, 0.9]$.

of adjustable semantic components (e.g., degrees of importance) in medical decision models and the possibility to customize decision models according to specific priorities of each individual patient.

The presented criterion for the quality of life depends on two inputs only: the mean disability and the expected length of life. It is not difficult to expand that criterion with additional inputs. The candidates might be the maximum disability level and the cost of alternative approaches. Indeed, some patients would limit the maximum disability level they are ready to tolerate. Let the threshold disability level be $D_\theta = D_0 + g_0(t_\theta - t_0)$; that level is reached at the age $t_\theta = t_0 + (D_\theta - D_0)/g_0$. In this case the start time for therapy would be $t_1 = \min(t_\theta, t_{1opt})$. Furthermore, the cost of therapy should not be neglected. This cost should be compared with the cost of life without therapy, but at a high disability level $(D > D_\theta)$. The decision whether to pay for a risky therapy or for assistance necessary at high disability levels can be based on standard cost/preference analysis.

The presented models (or their improved versions) can be used for all cases of risky therapy decisions (including the treatment of neuropathy, arthritis, and many other conditions). Of course, the piecewise linearization is a simplification, but this model clearly shows that the evaluation and tracking of the overall disability or disease severity level is a prerequisite for making justified decisions. The point of this case study is that the acceptance or rejection of a risky therapy is a decision problem and that this problem can be quantified using a soft computing evaluation logic model.

Let us now look at the presented case study from the standpoint of opponents of the quantitative approach. The first problem that is easily visible is that we have to provide input parameters that are not very reliable: life expectancy, survivability of risky therapy, and the disability growth rate are parameters that are inherently imprecise. Furthermore, the presented model could be modified to include nonlinearities, because the peripheral neuropathy can be a nonlinear phenomenon. In addition, the growth of disability is also a function of age and the evaluated overall PDD is both the function of age and the progress of disease; the separation of these two impacts is not trivial.

Looking at this problem from various sides we are faced with the question whether it is reasonable to develop these kinds of evaluation and decision models. Our answer to this question is the same as the joke "growing old is tough, but beats the alternative." So, making quantitative decision models is hard, but beats the alternative. Indeed, millions of patients are every day left to make very difficult medical decisions about risky therapies without much help except the "second opinion," which is frequently opposite to the "first opinion." Therefore, every help is very welcome, and patients can benefit from taking a more active role in solving their medical problems. For example, the patient who knows his/her PDD shown in Fig. 4.3.9 can make easier and more educated decision about the progress of the measured medical condition, and find justification for rejecting a risky therapy for a condition that reached a stable state, or accepting the risky therapy if the disability degree increases.

We used the linear model in Fig. 4.3.10 in order to expose the essence of the risky therapy decision problems without the overhead of technicalities of non-linear models. Of course, we could easily introduce nonlinear models, using the same basic reasoning pattern.

If patients want to participate in periodical evaluation of their medical condition in the style illustrated in Fig. 4.3.9, then it is necessary to have appropriate software tools. Fortunately, such tools can be available on the Internet and accessible using any networked device, starting with a smartphone. So, it is appropriate to spend some time thinking about the properties of such software tools. This topic is addressed in the next section.

4.3.7 LSPmed—An Internet Tool for Medical Evaluation[2]

LSPmed is an Internet tool for evaluation of disease severity and patient disability using the LSP soft computing evaluation method. LSPmed is designed to be used by anonymous guests, or by interested patients, or by medical professionals interested in the area of quantitative evaluation of medical conditions. LSPmed can be easily customized and installed for medical practice in medical institutions. In such cases, the Internet version of LSPmed can be used as a demo version of the customized LSPmed.

LSPmed can be used in all situations where it is necessary to use evaluation criteria that include sophisticated logic conditions. Such criteria are an extension and refinement of additive scoring techniques that are used for traditional medical rating scales. The initial demo version of LSPmed includes a criterion for evaluation of patient disability degree caused by peripheral neuropathy (Section 4.3.4). By changing the criterion function, LSPmed can be used for evaluation of other medical conditions.

4.3.7.1 LSPmed User Types and Their Functions

LSPmed supports five user types shown in Table 4.3.3. *Patient* and *Guest* are the only user types that may evaluate their condition using LSPmed. *Doctor* and *Nurse* are serving *Patient*. *Admin* is serving all other types of users.

Admin and *Guest* are generic names: they are not identified by username. All other user types use their usernames and passwords. *Doctor*, *Nurse*, and *Patient* have a status flag that can be either enabled or disabled (En/Dis in Table 4.3.3). Only enabled users can use LSPmed. The status control is necessary to provide security and prepare for removing users who are no longer using LSPmed.

---

2 LSPmed was developed in cooperation with Mr. **Daniel Tomasevich**

Table 4.3.3 LSPmed user types.

User type	Username	Password	Status
Admin	No	Yes	Enabled
Doctor	Yes	Yes	En/Dis
Nurse	Yes	Yes	En/Dis
Patient	Yes	Yes	En/Dis
Guest	No	No	Enabled

Patient is the only user type that can save the results of previous evaluations, in order to monitor the development of his/her medical condition. The access to *Patient* records is controlled by the access authorization mechanism. Only authorized *Doctors/Nurses* (and *Admin*) can access *Patient* data. *Doctor* authorization can be established by assignment of *Patient* to a *Doctor* at the time of creation of Patient account. Subsequently, other *Doctors* and/or *Nurses* can be authorized to access *Patient* records, as illustrated in Fig. 4.3.13. In addition, some *Patients* can use the Internet demo version of LSPmed independently, without *Doctor* supervision. In such cases, as shown in Fig. 4.3.13, independent *Patients* are created by *Admin* and only *Admin* can see their records.

Patient can perform the following functions:

- Enter data for evaluation of current medical condition.
- Review and compare the results of all previous evaluations.
- View/edit/delete selected data sets.
- View/edit (i.e., customize) the LSP evaluation criterion file.
- Change his/her password.

Admin is the LSPmed system administrator. Following are the functions that can be performed by *Admin*:

- Create/Delete accounts for *Doctor, Nurse,* and *Patient.*
- Enable/Disable accounts for *Doctor, Nurse,* and *Patient.*
- Change passwords of *Doctors, Nurses,* and *Patients* (as well as his/her own password).

Figure 4.3.13 Assignment of *Patients* to *Doctors* and *Nurses.*

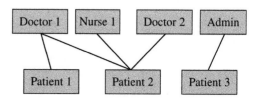

- Add/remove access authorization of specific *Doctors/Nurses* to *Patients.*
- View/edit LSP evaluation criterion files of all *Patients.*
- Access all *Patient* evaluation records.

Guest can use LSPmed without username and password to enter one data set and evaluate his/her condition. Guest cannot save the results of evaluation for further use. After logout, all *Guest* data are deleted. We assume that *Guest* who is interested to permanently use LSPmed will request a *Patient* account. *Doctor* has access to his/her *Patients* only. Following are the functions available to *Doctor:*

- Create/Delete *Patient* accounts.
- Create *Nurse* accounts.
- Enable/Disable *Patient* accounts.
- Change his/her own password.
- Access records of his/her *Patients.*
- Add/remove access authorization of other *Doctors/Nurses* to his/her *Patients.*
- View/edit/customize the LSP evaluation criterion file for each of his/her *Patients.*

Nurse is an account created either by *Doctor* or by *Admin. Nurse* can perform the following functions:

- Create *Patient* accounts.
- Access evaluation records of his/her *Patients.*
- Change his/her own password.

4.3.7.2   The Use of LSPmed

LSPmed includes a default version of evaluation criterion that is installed by *Admin* as a part of the LSPmed installation process. When an evaluation user (either *Guest* or *Patient*) logs in LSPmed, the user is assigned a criterion for evaluation, and that criterion is stored in user's area on the LSPmed server. In the case of *Guest*, the default criterion is copied each time when a *Guest* logs in. *Guest's* criterion cannot be customized (edited and modified), and the results of evaluation cannot be saved after the *Guest* logs out.

In the case of a registered *Patient*, the default criterion is copied in *Patient's* area only the first time when a *Patient* uses LSPmed. That is denoted as "initialize" procedure in Fig. 4.3.14. The user criterion of *Patient* can be edited and customized at any time. The goal of customizing is to adjust the criterion according to specific *Patient's* needs. Customization can be done by an independent *Patient* (*Patient* without *Doctor*) or by a *Doctor* (for any of his *Patients* and normally with *Patient's* assistance). The customized criterion is then saved, together with evaluation results and reused in all subsequent evaluations.

Figure 4.3.14 Patient evaluation process.

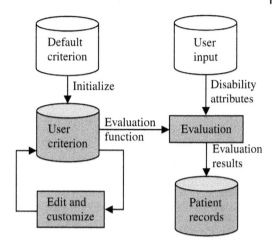

The default (demo) version of LSPmed can be used in the following two modes:

1) Unsupervised mode
   a) *Guest* mode
   b) Independent *Patient* mode (*Patient* without *Doctor*)
2) Supervised mode (*Patient* of a *Doctor*)

The expected use of LSPmed demo version is that an interested user first accesses LSPmed as *Guest*. If there is further interest, then such user can open an account either as an independent *Patient* or as a *Doctor*. *Patients* and *Guests* can use LSPmed to monitor development of their condition and to use evaluation results to help making difficult decisions (e.g., decisions about starting risky therapies). *Doctors* can use LSPmed demo version to evaluate the possibility of its use in medical practice. They can open accounts for their *Nurses* and *Patients*. Groups of *Patients*, *Doctors*, and *Nurses* are connected using the mechanism of *Patient* access authorization. Such a group is called a *Medical Group* (MG). Fig. 4.3.15 illustrates two independent (disjoint) MG's and four independent *Patients*.

Figure 4.3.15 Medical groups including patients (P), doctors (D) and nurses (N).

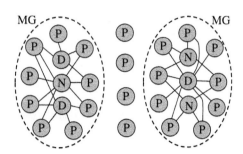

LSPmed can serve any number of independent MG's and independent *Patients* that are fully separated and protected from each other. LSPmed provides no mechanism that would enable any MG to be aware of the existence of other MG's. Similarly, *Patients* are aware only of *Doctors* and *Nurses* that serve them, and independent *Patients* communicate only with LSPmed without seeing other users.

4.3.7.3 Serving a Patient

Serving a *Patient* is the most important LSPmed function. A typical scenario of service includes the following steps:

1) A *Patient* visits a *Doctor* and *Doctor* or *Nurse* opens an LSPmed account for Patient and orders evaluation of *Patient*'s condition according to a given criterion (criterion may be standard or customized for each specific *Patient*).
2) *Patient* logs in LSPmed and is offered a menu of operations shown in Fig. 4.3.16. The *Patient* must first decide whether to use the word (verbalized) input or the numeric input to provide degrees of difficulty that characterize his/her condition. The word input is recommended to patients who are not comfortable with precise numeric assessment of their conditions. In the case of word input we use a rating scale with nine discrete levels of difficulty (from none to extreme) that are shown in Fig. 4.3.17. After selecting the corresponding level of difficulty for each of input attributes, *Patient* generates the table of word input data exemplified in the input data segment shown in Fig. 4.3.18. This example covers the period from 2009 to 2016 (shown in Fig. 4.3.9, and in Tables 4.3.21 and 4.3.22). Fig. 4.3.16 reflects the beginning of the experiment.

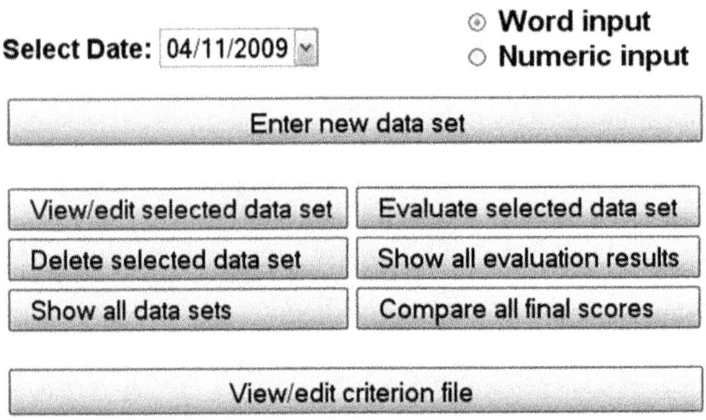

Figure 4.3.16 The main menu of *Patient* activities.

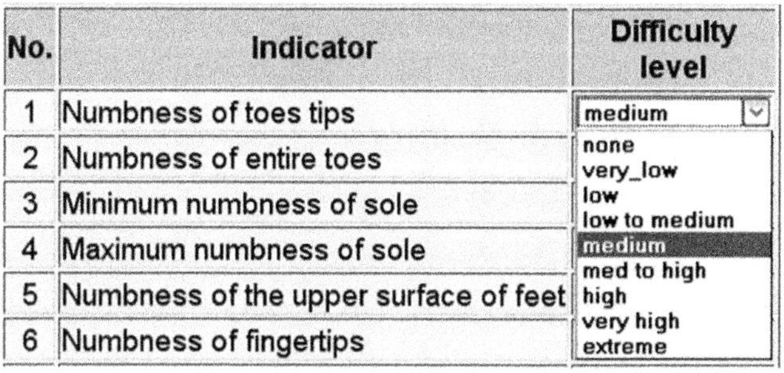

No.	Indicator	Difficulty level
1	Numbness of toes tips	medium ⌄
2	Numbness of entire toes	none very_low
3	Minimum numbness of sole	low low to medium
4	Maximum numbness of sole	medium
5	Numbness of the upper surface of feet	med to high high
6	Numbness of fingertips	very high extreme

Figure 4.3.17 Nine levels of difficulty (word input).

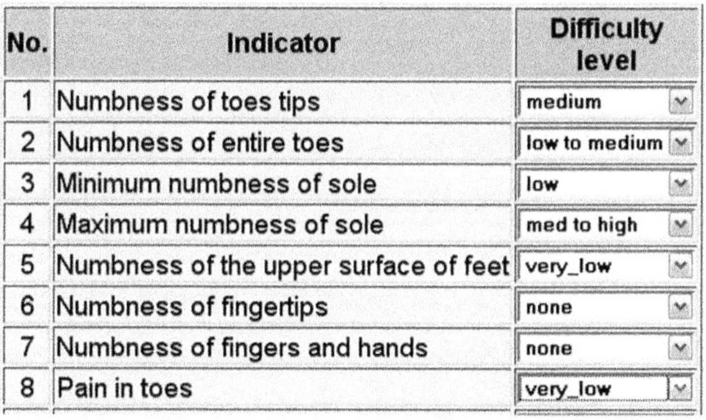

No.	Indicator	Difficulty level
1	Numbness of toes tips	medium ⌄
2	Numbness of entire toes	low to medium ⌄
3	Minimum numbness of sole	low ⌄
4	Maximum numbness of sole	med to high ⌄
5	Numbness of the upper surface of feet	very_low ⌄
6	Numbness of fingertips	none ⌄
7	Numbness of fingers and hands	none ⌄
8	Pain in toes	very_low ⌄

Figure 4.3.18 Sample input data based on word input.

The accuracy of the nine-level scale is limited because the difference between adjacent levels is 12.5%. Some *Patients* can provide more accurate inputs, and for them it is more appropriate to use the numeric input where the level of difficulty is expressed as a percentage in a way exemplified in Fig. 4.3.19.

Each LSP criterion file can be displayed as exemplified in Fig. 4.3.20. *Doctors* and individual *Patients* can edit parameters of the criterion function, and save new criterion files for experimental purposes or for customizing the default criterion according to *Patient*'s needs. Numeric data in Fig. 4.3.20 show elementary criteria of the direct preference assessment type, {(0,0), (100,100)}, followed by the aggregation structure that corresponds to the version 1 aggregation tree presented in Fig. 4.3.6. All these data are directly editable text.

LSPmed is designed to support clinical practice in medical organizations where *Patients* come for regular periodic control. So, each incoming *Patient* is assumed to enter data in the LSPmed attribute questionnaire either before or while waiting to see a *Doctor*. *Doctor* is supposed to read the results of evaluation before talking to *Patient*. In such a way *Doctor* and *Patient* can discuss

No.	Indicator	Difficulty level [%]
1	Numbness of toes tips	25
2	Numbness of entire toes	18
3	Minimum numbness of sole	20
4	Maximum numbness of sole	45
5	Numbness of the upper surface of feet	5
6	Numbness of fingertips	0
7	Numbness of fingers and hands	0
8	Pain in toes	8

Figure 4.3.19 Sample input data based on numeric input.

Save .cri file   Restore default .cri file   Back

No	Criterion component
1	111111 1 2 0 0 100 100 Numbness of toes tips
2	111112 1 2 0 0 100 100 Numbness of entire toes
3	111121 1 2 0 0 100 100 Minimum numbness of sole
4	111122 1 2 0 0 100 100 Maximum numbness of sole
5	11113 1 2 0 0 100 100 Numbness of the upper surface of feet
6	11121 1 2 0 0 100 100 Numbness of fingertips
7	11122 1 2 0 0 100 100 Numbness of fingers and hands

56	121 2 2.018 2 1211 67 1212 33 MUSCLE WEAKNESS
57	122 2 2.302 4 1221 25 1222 25 1223 25 1224 25 MOBILITY IMPAIRMENTS (PATIENT TESTS)
58	1231 2 2.018 2 12311 25 12312 75 Imbalance
59	1232 2 2.018 2 12321 50 12322 50 Tremor
60	1233 2 2.018 2 12331 60 12332 40 Clumsiness
61	123 2 1.0 3 1231 40 1232 35 1233 25 INCOORDINATION
62	12 2 2.018 3 121 20 122 60 123 20 MOTOR SYMPTOMS
63	1 2 3.929 2 11 30 12 70 PATIENT DISABILITY DEGREE (PDD)

Figure 4.3.20 An initial segment and a final segment of an editable LSP criterion.

the progress of disability, or the effects of a treatment, and make justifiable decisions about next steps that are needed to improve *Patient*'s condition.

Patients can enter data about their conditions either in the numerical form or in the verbal form. Numerical form is more precise, as illustrated in Fig. 4.3.21 and 4.3.22, which contain the same data sets. The evaluation results are

No.	Indicator	06/11/2016	04/19/2016	10/20/2015	11/06/2014	02/05/2014	11/11/2009
1	Numbness of toes tips	85	85	90	85	80	90
2	Numbness of entire toes	85	85	85	80	80	70
3	Minimum numbness of sole	60	70	70	30	40	60
4	Maximum numbness of sole	80	95	99	90	85	95
5	Numbness of the upper surface of feet	15	15	45	10	10	0
6	Numbness of fingertips	0	0	0	0	0	0
7	Numbness of fingers and hands	0	0	0	0	0	0
8	Pain in toes	3	2	0	0	2	0
9	Pain in soles	0	2	0	0	0	5
10	Pain in fingertips	0	0	0	0	0	0
11	Pain in fingers and hands	0	0	0	0	0	0
12	Tingling/itching in feet	3	0	3	0	0	0
13	Tingling/itching in hands	0	0	0	0	0	0
14	Muscle weakness in feet	60	50	50	75	20	40
15	Muscle weakness in calves	70	60	70	75	60	35
16	Muscle weakness in thighs	12	5	30	10	0	5
17	Muscle weakness in hands	0	0	0	0	0	0
18	Muscle weakness in arms/shoulders	0	0	0	0	0	0
19	Short standing (<1h; e.g. teaching)	3	0	0	5	5	0
20	Medium standing (1 to 2h)	5	5	5	5	5	0
21	Long standing (more than 2h)	10	15	10	5	15	10
22	Fast (short) run	88	90	90	60	90	70
23	Slow run	80	75	90	60	75	60
24	Fast walk	67	65	80	20	30	50
25	Slow walk	3	5	5	0	2	5
26	Impaired rising on toes	77	75	75	66	50	0
27	Impaired toe walk	66	75	75	66	50	40
28	Impaired jumping	88	75	80	88	80	0
29	Impaired stair-climbing	0	10	15	5	0	20
30	Slopes (10% or more)	0	10	15	5	5	0
31	Impaired arising from chair	0	2	5	10	0	0
32	Impaired arising from squat	5	40	20	33	4	0
33	Impaired arising from floor	5	40	25	25	2	0
34	Imbalance with closed eyes	67	75	80	80	80	65
35	Imbalance with open eyes	0	0	0	5	10	0
36	Tremor in legs	0	0	0	0	0	0
37	Tremor in arms	0	2	0	0	0	0
38	Clumsiness in legs	22	20	15	10	15	20
39	Clumsiness in arms	0	0	0	0	0	0

Figure 4.3.21 An example of six numeric data sets for evaluation of peripheral neuropathy.

No.	Indicator	06/11/2016	04/19/2016	10/20/2015	11/06/2014	02/05/2014	11/11/2009
1	Numbness of toes tips	very high	very high	very high	very high	high	very high
2	Numbness of entire toes	very high	very high	very high	high	high	high
3	Minimum numbness of sole	med to high	High	high	low	low to medium	med to high
4	Maximum numbness of sole	high	Extreme	extreme	very high	very high	extreme
5	Numbness of the upper surface of feet	very low	very low	medium	very low	very low	none
6	Numbness of fingertips	none	None	none	none	none	none
7	Numbness of fingers a nd hands	none	None	none	none	none	none
8	Pain in toes	none	None	none	none	none	none
9	Pain in soles	none	None	none	none	none	none
10	Pain in fingertips	none	None	none	none	none	none
11	Pain in fingers and hands	none	None	none	none	none	none
12	Tinglin g/itching in feet	none	None	none	none	none	none
13	Tingling/itching in hands	none	None	none	none	none	none
14	Muscle weakness in feet	med to high	Medium	medium	high	low	low to medium
15	Muscle weakness in calves	high	med to high	high	high	med to high	low to medium
16	Muscle weakness in thighs	very low	None	low	very low	none	none
17	Muscle weakness in hands	none	None	none	none	none	none
18	Muscle weakness in arms/shoulders	none	None	none	none	none	none
19	Short standing (<1h; e.g. teaching)	none	none	none	none	none	none
20	Medium standing (1 to 2h)	none	none	none	none	none	none
21	Long standing (more than 2h)	very low	very low	very low	none	very low	very low
22	Fast (short) run	very high	very high	very high	med to high	very high	high
23	Slow run	high	high	very high	med to high	high	med to high
24	Fast walk	med to high	med to high	high	low	low	medium
25	Slow walk	none	none	none	none	none	none
26	Impaired rising on toes	high	high	high	med to high	medium	none
27	Impaired toe walk	med to high	high	high	med to high	medium	low to medium
28	Impaired jumping	very high	high	high	very high	high	none
29	Impaired stair -climbing	none	very low	very low	none	none	low
30	Slopes (10% or more)	none	very low	very low	none	none	none
31	Impaired arising from chair	none	none	none	very low	none	none
32	Impaired arising from squat	none	low to medium	low	low to medium	none	none
33	Impaired arising from floor	none	low to medium	low	low	none	none
34	Imbalance with closed eyes	med to high	high	high	high	high	med to hi gh
35	Imbalance with open eyes	none	none	none	none	very low	none
36	Tremor in legs	none	none	none	none	none	none
37	Tremor in arms	none	none	none	none	none	none
38	Clumsiness in legs	low	low	very low	very low	very low	low
39	Clumsiness in arms	none	none	none	none	none	none

Figure 4.3.22 An example of six verbalized data sets for evaluation of peripheral neuropathy.

No.	Indicator	06/11/2016	04/19/2016	10/20/2015	11/06/2014	02/05/2014	11/11/2009
63	PATIENT DISABILITY DEGREE (PDD)	39.4374	41.5981	44.4804	37.5338	35.4374	39.0589
62	MOTOR SYMPTOMS	30.0764	30.3286	34.3616	27.7261	21.9889	19.8646
61	INCOORDINATION	17.7531	19.4714	19.010 6	18.1288	19.3668	16.9624
60	Clumsiness	17.08	15.5273	11.6455	7.76363	11.6455	15.5273
59	Tremor	0	1.41859	0	0	0	0
58	Imbalance	33.7078	37.7326	40.2481	40.4698	41.1386	32.7016
57	MOBILITY IMPAIRMENTS (PATIENT TESTS)	31.1704	33.6343	36.9332	25.1372	23.48 66	20.6681
56	MUSCLE WEAKNESS	35.9159	28.6999	39.3599	40.1799	19.68	20.09
55	Muscle weakness in hands	0	0	0	0	0	0
54	Muscle weakness in legs	43.8	35	48	49	24	24.5
53	Impaired (fast) transitions	2.25	19.1	12.5	19.15	1.5	0
52	Impaired standing	5	4.5	3.5	5	7	2
51	Impaired walk	46.1	45.5	53	24	33.8	36
50	Impaired climbing	37.4	42.5	45.5	37.7	29	14
49	SENSORY SYMPTOMS	49.9405	53.3548	55.9189	47.9771	46.7726	52.3881
48	Tingling/Itching	2.5148	0	2.5148	0	0	0
47	Pain	2.07175	1.83144	0	0	1.38117	4.13491
46	Pain in hands	0	0	0	0	0	0
45	Numbness	71.9286	76.8584	80.555	69.1196	67.3788	75.421
44	Numbness of feet	75.8931	81.0947	84.9951	72.9293	71.0926	79.578
43	Pain in feet	2.26243	2	0	0	1.50828	4.51547
42	Numbness of hands	0	0	0	0	0	0
41	Numbness of sole (nonuniform distribution)	72	85	87.4	66	67	81
40	Numbness of toes	85	85	88.7769	83.7785	80	85.4476

Figure 4.3.23 Numeric results in all aggregation blocks of the criterion for evaluation of peripheral neuropathy (the overall PDD is presented in the first row).

presented in numeric form, and the disability degrees for all nodes of the disability aggregation tree are shown in Fig 4.3.23.

At the end of this chapter, let us summarize basic results and discuss possible future work in the area of LSP models for medical decision making. Point-additive rating scales are used in medical practice as popular tools for quantitative evaluation of medical conditions [HER06, DYC93, DYC05, GRA06a, GRA06b, MER06, HOB03]. The primary goal of such medical scales is the ultimate simplicity, resulting in a small number of inputs, strictly additive aggregation, and the absence of patient-oriented and/or semantic customization; the result is the "one size fits all" approach. As the authors of *Health Measurement Scales* rightfully noticed [STR89], "Since *this approach is so simple, there must be something wrong with it.*"

Unsurprisingly, simplified point-additive rating scales have twofold impact on applicability. On one hand, the simplicity of point-additive models is appealing for medical practitioners because the use of such scales is very easy. On the other hand, the additive oversimplification reduces the expressive power, precision, and reliability of such quantitative models, limiting their applicability and the number of satisfied users. The consequence of imprecision is that for each value of ODD, medical personnel encounter a relatively wide variation of specific patient conditions. The simplicity is obviously not a proof of quality of ODD models. Point-additive rating scales provide the minimum of logic sophistication and customization of decision models, offering a number of opportunities to distrust simplicity. More precisely, excessive simplicity is equally as detrimental as excessive complexity. The best decision strategy is predictably located inside the interval bounded by the ultimate simplicity and the high complexity.

From the standpoint of evaluation decision models, it is possible to offer much more detailed, sophisticated, and customized quantifying of medical conditions. This chapter illustrates some areas where LSP models can be useful in medical decision making. LSP models can offer high precision based on an appropriate number of input attributes, logic relationships, semantic relationships, and customization of criteria to fit the needs of an individual patient or a specific category of patients.

There are many medical areas where LSP models can be useful. Patient disability degrees caused by peripheral neuropathy, multiple sclerosis, arthritis, or a spectrum of physical injuries can be computed in a way we exemplified in this chapter. It is also possible to develop a variety of disease severity models. One possible application area for LSP models is the evaluation of physical conditions based on the movement continuum theory of physical therapy [COT95]. Using six groups of measurable attributes (flexibility, strength, accuracy, speed, adaptability, and endurance, proposed in [ALL07]), it is possible to create a family of LSP criteria for evaluation of physical conditions, and quantitative assessment of effects of physical therapy applied in clinical practice.

All medical LSP applications must be supported by software tools, and such tools should be available over the Internet and accessible by simple mobile devices. Using such tools it is possible to create the practice of patient self-evaluation based on personalized criteria. Thus, the wide area of medical evaluation and decision models seems to offer plenty of space for new research, development, and applications.

4.4   LSP Criteria in Ecology: Selecting Multi-Species Habitat Mitigation Projects[1]

Ecology is an area where evaluation decision problems are frequent, visible, and have wide social impact because they directly or indirectly affect all population. Many human agricultural, industrial, and service activities create different forms of waste and then use environment as a waste sink. Natural systems recycle their waste. Economies are not natural recyclers; when forced, they try to recycle a fraction of waste, but environments are the final repositories of remaining waste products. In addition, even if waste is sufficiently recycled and/or assimilated by environment, the growing human presence creates development and transport activities that cause environmental problems, reducing the natural habitat for fish, wildlife, and plants. That creates a number of delicate decision problems, as well as increasing interest in soft computing techniques for solving such problems [MUN94, VAN04, PAS12, REB14]. LSP is one soft computing decision method that has been successfully used in that context [ALL11, REB16, MES18]. In this chapter, we show the use of LSP criteria for evaluation, comparison, and selection of multispecies habitat mitigation projects.

4.4.1   Multi-Species Compensatory Mitigation Projects

The first step in the development of LSP criteria is to define a stakeholder. In the case of criteria related to clean air, clean water, global warming, and preserving other species that exist on this planet, it might be possible to claim that the stakeholder is everybody. This is the reason why ecological problems are under governmental regulation: the Endangered Species Act of 1973 [ESA73, WIK16] is used in the United States to protect endangered species from extinction as a consequence of population growth, economic growth, and development. The goal to

---

1 Domain expertise for this chapter was provided by **Mr. Will L. Allen III**, Vice President, Sustainable Programs, The Conservation Fund.

Soft Computing Evaluation Logic: The LSP Decision Method and Its Applications, First Edition. Jozo Dujmović.
© 2018 John Wiley & Sons, Inc. Published 2018 by John Wiley & Sons, Inc.
Companion website: www.wiley.com/go/Dujmovic/Soft_Computing_Evaluation_Logic

"halt and reverse the trend towards species extinction" is regularly supported by environmental laws, international treaties [ESA73], and governmental agencies like the United States Fish and Wildlife Service (FWS) and the National Oceanic and Atmospheric Administration (NOAA). In addition, there are nongovernmental organizations devoted to many forms of conservation and environmental protection, such as The Conservation Fund (TCF) [TCF16a].

In this chapter, we describe methodology developed in the context of the TCF strategic conservation planning activity and strategic mitigation for pipelines [TCF16b]. More precisely, we present a family of soft computing decision models used in strategic multispecies habitat mitigation projects [TCF10, DUJ11, ALL11, MES18]. The goal of such projects is to reduce harmful effects on wildlife caused by major energy and/or infrastructure development projects. We present the multispecies habitat mitigation goals and related evaluation decision problems, the selection of soft computing decision models, and the development of the necessary decision support software. Our LSP approach is applicable in all compensatory mitigation projects that are undertaken to compensate wildlife-related negative effects of various development projects. We present a case study of soft computing decision models for selecting compensatory mitigation projects related to the 15,500-mile-long natural gas pipeline network going through 14 states from the Gulf of Mexico to the New York state, operated by NiSource [FWS16c] (before the Columbia Pipeline Group separation and Trans Canada acquisition of the Columbia Pipeline Group).

All major energy and infrastructure development projects cause harmful effects on wildlife habitat and the need for compensatory mitigation projects. That holds for fuel pipelines, wind turbine farms, traditional power plants, and transmission lines, road and rail networks, and others. Such projects may critically impact various threatened species or their habitat.

According to the Endangered Species Act and its amendments [WIK16], lawful development activities require an *incidental take permit* [FWS16b] issued by the FWS [FWS16a]. The incidental take permit holders provide a *Habitat Conservation Plan* [TCF16, FWS16c] and secure funding for a plan that minimizes and mitigates harm to the impacted species. In the case of the analyzed natural gas transmission and storage operation, the mitigation projects are related to the 15,500-mile-long network of natural gas pipelines that affect the following species: Indiana Bat, Madison Cave Isopod, Nashville Crayfish, Bog Turtle, Clubshell, Fanshell, Northern Riffleshell, Sheepnose, and James Spinymussel [FWS16c]. The implementation of the NiSource Multi-Species Habitat Conservation Plan (MSHCP) [COL15] is based on the ecological expertise of TCF [TCF16a, TCF16b, MES18], and uses the LSP decision support methodology and corresponding software [TCF16].

Each MSHCP mitigation project includes evaluation of alternatives (candidate species habitat areas), and selection of the most suitable alternative that satisfies the take species habitat mitigation requirements and provides other conservation benefits. Each mitigation project evaluates competitive areas that can be acquired and used primarily or exclusively for conservation of endangered species. Consequently, stakeholders and decision makers (NiSource, TCF, FWS, and state and local governments) must develop criteria that evaluate the overall level of satisfaction of MSHCP conservation requirements, taking simultaneously into account ecological benefits and financial constraints. The ultimate goal of the decision process is to develop solutions that offset the gas pipeline impacts, and offer maximum ecosystem benefits per habitat mitigation dollar.

The criteria for evaluation, comparison, and selection of competitive species habitats consist of a number of requirements that are considered mandatory and a number of requirements that are desired or optional. Such relationships can be modeled using the partial absorption function. Some of requirements must be simultaneously satisfied and need modeling with hard or soft partial conjunction. Other requirements may replace each other, and in such cases we need soft or hard partial disjunction.

Financial aspects of evaluated projects are very important and must be properly aggregated with ecological (nonfinancial) suitability scores to create an overall ranking of competitive mitigation solutions. This chapter exemplifies all major steps of LSP decision methodology in a way that is applicable in a variety of ecological mitigation decision problems. We also use this chapter to exemplify the role of sensitivity analysis in the process of creating LSP criteria.

4.4.2   A Generic LSP Attribute Tree for Evaluation of Habitat Mitigation Projects

The first step in the development of an LSP criterion consists of specifying the attribute tree. The tree must include all attributes that affect the ability of an evaluated area to satisfy MSHCP mitigation requirements for specific species. Some attributes represent mandatory requirements, and in such cases the logic properties of the evaluation criterion must be adjusted so that an MSHCP project is rejected if any of mandatory requirements is not satisfied. Other attributes represent nonmandatory requirements that are desirable and contribute to the suitability of the evaluated MSHCP project. However, if nonmandatory requirements are not satisfied, that will not automatically disqualify the evaluated project.

Our approach is based on a generic evaluation criterion that defines the structure of all MSHCP decision criteria and the corresponding aggregation logic. The generic criterion holds for the whole family of MSHCP projects and can be easily customized for each individual species taking into account specific ecologic requirements that a suitable species habitat must satisfy.

The proposed generic attribute tree, adapted for freshwater mussels, is shown in Fig. 4.4.1. The four top levels of decomposition are generic, i.e., they can be used in almost all mitigation projects. Further decomposition is specific for selected species.

The generic tree consists of two main attribute groups: the take species habitat mitigation requirements (#11) and other conservation goals and benefits (#12). The group #11 should be subsequently adjusted for each specific species. The group #12 includes requirements that are common for the majority of mitigation projects.

The most important subgroup of attributes includes 14 mandatory requirements inside the group #111. These attributes are grouped in five subgroups (denoted #1111 to #1115). Most of the attributes are composite inputs that need a domain expert evaluation. The habitat mitigation requirements also include seven desired and optional requirements that form the group #112. They evaluate the likelihood of protection in perpetuity and the protection of other listed species. These components are not mandatory, but they are certainly very desirable, and their absence should cause significant penalty for evaluated MSHCP projects.

In developing the attribute tree, it is also important to consider general strategic goals and benefits that form the group #12. This group includes six attributes that are used to evaluate whether the analyzed MSHCP projects provide other benefits, such as support for green infrastructure, support for other plans, and human benefits. The requirements in this group are not mandatory. Thus, the proposed generic tree is used to develop 27 elementary input attributes: 14 of them are mandatory and 13 of them are nonmandatory. These attributes should reflect the requirements that are nonredundant (independent of each other) and complete (no missing relevant attributes).

The presented generic tree creates the need for 27 elementary criteria. Some of these attribute criteria are compound and depend on multiple elementary input components. In such cases, there are two options. The first option is to continue decomposing the attribute tree until we reach all elementary inputs and further decomposition becomes impossible (in such cases, the elementary criteria are very simple). The second option is to create scoring attribute criteria where we assign scores to existing elementary inputs and then create the elementary criterion that evaluates the resulting total score. This technique is exemplified in the next section.

4.4.3 Attribute Criteria and the Logic Aggregation Structure

For each elementary input attribute we have to develop a justifiable elementary criterion. The criteria are different for various species and a small sample of typical elementary attribute criteria is shown in Table 4.4.1. The criterion

1 Freshwater mussel mitigation projects

11 Take species habitat mitigation requirements
  111 Mandatory habitat requirements
    1111 Habitat size / mitigation units
    1112 Project site assessment
      11121 Buffer size & shape
      11122 Intact buffer sites
      11123 Mussel distribution
    1113 Project physical conditions
      11131 Site substratum conditions
      11132 Water quality indicators
      11133 Bed stability
      11134 Barriers to fish passage
    1114 Project species occurrence
      11141 Known & potential host fish
      11142 Mussel population viability
      11143 Mussel diversity
      11144 Mussel density
      11145 Detrimental invasive species
    1115 Project location
  112 Desired and optional habitat requirements
    1121 Likely protection in perpetuity
      11211 Point & nonpoint pollution risk
      11212 Sedimentation & substrate removal risk
      11213 Stream impoundment risk
      11214 Stream buffer clearing potential
      11215 Project monitoring program
    1122 Protection of other listed species
      11221 Nisource mshcp take species
      11222 Other federal and state listed species

12 Other conservation goals and benefits
  121 Support for green infrastructure goals
  122 Planning goals and leverage opportunities
    1221 State wildlife action plans
    1222 Other state and regional plans
    1223 Collaboration and other ecosystem benefits
  123 Human benefits
    1231 State trail, greenway, and bikeway plan support
    1232 Stimulation of nature-based economic development

Figure 4.4.1 Generic multi-species habitat conservation plan attributes in the case of evaluation of freshwater mussel habitat mitigation projects [TCF10].

Table 4.4.1 Sample attribute criteria [TCF10] generated using LSP.web [SEA16]

1111		Habitat size / species mitigation units provided
Value	%	Evaluated as the following relative satisfaction ratio:
0	0	U = 100 * S / Smax [%]
100	100	where
		S = area (or the number of individuals) provided by project
		Smax = required area (or the number of individuals)
		(S and Smax are measured in same units)
		Smax is defined by the mitigation panel in one of the following ways:
		(a) As a total mitigation required in the MSHCP
		(b) As an annual mitigation requirement

11131		Site Substratum Conditions
Value	%	Assign one point for each of the following stream site characteristics:
0	0	(1) width from 10 to 75 feet
1	10	(2) depth of 1/2 to 3 feet
2	30	(3) slow to moderate water current
3	60	(4) clean sand and cobble bottom sediments
4	80	(5) optimal degree of embeddedness
5	90	(6) No barriers to mussel bed expansion
6	100	Evaluated as the sum of points:
		6 = Stream site contains ALL of these characteristics
		0 = Stream site contains none of these characteristics

11132		Water Quality Indicators
Value	%	Potential metrics include: ammonia, metals, dissolved oxygen, daily mean
0	0	temperature, conductivity, etc. In the case of insufficient data for water
4	100	quality, use benthic IBI scores. Evaluated using the five-level rating scale:
		4 = Excellent
		3 = Very Good
		2 = Good
		1 = Fair
		0 = Poor

11133		Bed Stability
Value	%	Assessment of mussel bed stability:
0	0	2 = Stable
1	40	1 = Somewhat stable
2	100	0 = Not stable

11134		Barriers to Fish Passage
Value	%	Assessment of barriers to fish passage:
0	0	2 = Absent
1	75	1 = Minor
2	100	0 = Major

#1111 is classified as the normalized-variable continuous absolute criterion. The criterion #11131 is an example of the point-additive criterion, which uses a simple scoring and then evaluates the total score. The criterion #11132 uses direct preference assessment based on a simple five-level rating scale, and the last two elementary attribute criteria are discrete.

The next step is to develop a generic multi-species logic aggregation structure. The basic idea is shown in Fig. 4.4.2 and then refined in Fig. 4.4.3. In Fig. 4.4.2 we show the concept of aggregation of the three basic groups of attributes: #111, #112, and #12. The Take Species Habitat Mitigation Requirements (#11) consist of two groups of attributes: mandatory (#111) and non-mandatory/optional (#112). In that way it is easy to assign each attribute to one of these groups. The aggregation is then performed using a conjunctive partial absorption aggregator. The result of this aggregation (the suitability degree denoted #11) has the mandatory status with respect to the non-mandatory #12 (Other Conservation Goals and Benefits). Therefore, we aggregate #11 and

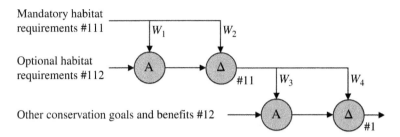

Mandatory habitat requirements #111

Optional habitat requirements #112

Other conservation goals and benefits #12

Figure 4.4.2 Basic concept of suitability aggregation for evaluation of MSHCP projects.

#12 using another conjunctive partial absorption. The resulting compound aggregator is a nested partial absorption with one mandatory and two optional inputs that should approximately have the same impact on the overall suitability #1 (this is verified in the next section).

The adjustment of CPA parameters is based on selection of desired penalty (average decrease of output suitability caused by the zero optional input) and reward (average increase of output suitability caused by the maximum optional input). The desired penalty and reward values are shown in Fig. 4.4.3 (P25/R20 denotes an average penalty of 25% and an average reward of 20%).

All other aggregators in Fig. 4.4.6 are various forms of GCD, i.e., either a partial conjunction or a partial disjunction. In the case of #1112, #1113, and #1114 we use the hard partial conjunction aggregator C-+, which is similar to the geometric mean. According to the canonical increasing partial conjunction form the aggregator #111 is also a hard partial conjunction but significantly stronger.

The aggregator #1121 is also hard, regardless its belonging to the group of optional aggregators. This is based on opinion that #1121 (protection in perpetuity) cannot be achieved if any of the five necessary inputs is missing. On the other hand, the aggregator #1122 is disjunctive because the protection of other species can be achieved by any of the two alternative inputs. Similarly, the aggregator #122 is also disjunctive because any of the three alternative plans can sufficiently contribute to the planning goals.

The logic aggregation structure shown in Fig. 4.4.3 is an initial generic solution. We assume that in practical use of the LSP method the criterion will be tuned and altered to generate results that are conformant with stakeholder's expectations. LSP criteria are expected to model human perceptions, and therefore the results of evaluation must not be significantly different from evaluator expectations. To occurrence of significant differences is sufficient to justify modification of the criterion function.

One of methods to test and verify the behavior of an aggregation structure before it is actually used in practice is to perform a sensitivity analysis. A typical sensitivity analysis is presented in the next section.

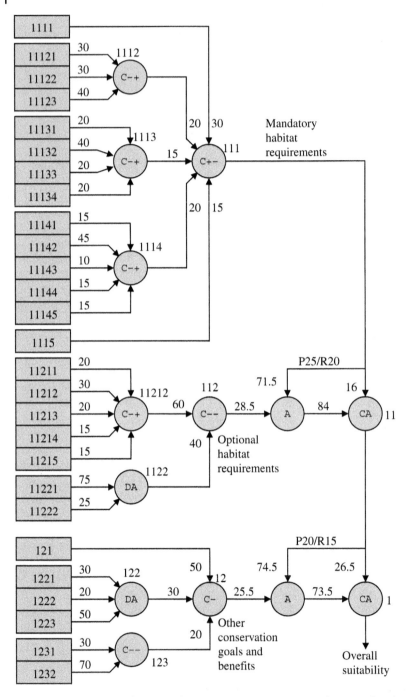

Figure 4.4.3 Generic multi-species logic aggregation structure in the case of evaluation of freshwater mussel habitat.

4.4.4 Sensitivity Analysis

A detailed suitability aggregation structure shown in Fig. 4.4.3 includes weights (the relative importance of all inputs), aggregation operators, and penalty/reward pairs (denoted P < percent penalty>/R < percent reward>). The weights and aggregation operators are selected to reflect the needs of MSHCP projects. To verify quantitative properties of the aggregation structure we use a sensitivity analysis, where we adjust all input suitability scores to have the same default value s, and then investigate the variations of output suitability caused by changing a single input or subsystem suitability in the range from 0 to 1 (or 0 to 100%). Assuming the default suitability $s = 75\%$, the effects of changing subsystem suitability scores are shown in Fig. 4.4.4. The lowest curve shows the component that causes the highest impact, and that is the subsystems

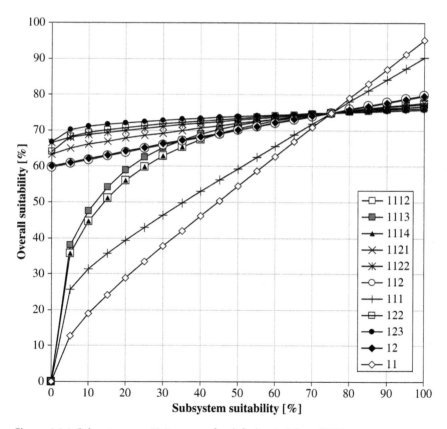

Figure 4.4.4 Subsystem sensitivity curves for default suitability of 75%.

#11 (take species habitat mitigation requirements). The second highest impact is caused by the mandatory habitat requirements subsystem (#111), followed by its components. The optional inputs (#112 and #12) have almost identical impact. All mandatory component curves start from the origin, and all non-mandatory component curves show lower impact and start from positive values. If the default suitability is positive the sensitivity curves are always strictly increasing.

In addition to sensitivity curves it is useful to define sensitivity coefficients that define the properties of sensitivity curves. Suppose that we use the default suitability $s \in]0,1[$. So, all inputs are s and due to idempotency the output is also s. The overall effects of changing an input (or subsystem) suitability x_i that affects an output suitability $f(x_i)$ can be characterized using the limit values $f_i(0) = y_i^{(\min)}$, $0 \le y_i^{(\min)} \le y_i^{(s)} = f(s) = s$, and $f_i(1) = y_i^{(\max)}$, $y_i^{(s)} \le y_i^{(\max)} \le 1$. We express sensitivity properties using the following basic indicators that are all expressed as percentages:

- Suitability increment: $\delta_i^+ = 100\left(y_i^{(\max)} - y_i^{(s)}\right)$ $[\%]$

- Suitability decrement: $\delta_i^- = 100\left(y_i^{(s)} - y_i^{(\min)}\right)$ $[\%]$

- Absolute influence range: $\rho_i = 100\left(y_i^{(\max)} - y_i^{(\min)}\right)$ $[\%]$

- Conjunctive coefficient of impact: $\gamma_i = 200\dfrac{y_i^{(\max)} - \int_0^1 f_i(x_i)dx_i}{y_i^{(\max)}}$ $[\%]$

Sensitivity coefficients reflect various aspects of the overall importance of input attributes and their subsystems. The suitability increment shows what improvement of the output suitability can be obtained if the input suitability increases from s to the maximum value (1 or 100%). The suitability decrement shows what worsening of the output suitability would occur if the input suitability decreases from s to the minimum value 0. For all mandatory requirements, $\delta_i^- = s$. The absolute influence range is the sum of the suitability increment and the suitability decrement. The criterion shown in Fig. 4.4.3 is predominantly conjunctive and the sensitivity curves in Fig. 4.4.4 are concave. For concave sensitivity curves the impact of analyzed input x_i is high if the mean value of the output suitability function $f(x_i)$ is low (no hypersensitivity). This property is characterized using the conjunctive coefficient of impact defined in Section 3.7.1. The use of sensitivity coefficients for ranking of all subsystems of the MSHCP criterion according to the decreasing influence range is shown in Table 4.4.2. In this case, the ranking by decreasing range gives similar results as the ranking according to the decreasing impact. Not surprisingly, the impact of subsystems varies in a wide range and the highest impact comes from subsystems in the group #111. As expected, the impacts of optional subsystems #112 and #12 are almost the same.

Table 4.4.2 Sorted sensitivity coefficients of MSHCP subsystems.

Rank	Subsystem	Increment	Decrement	Range	Impact
1	11	20.24	75.00	95.24	87.30
2	111	15.36	75.00	90.36	70.92
3	1112	2.33	75.00	77.33	31.36
4	1114	2.33	75.00	77.33	31.36
5	1113	1.72	75.00	76.72	27.02
6	112	4.80	15.27	20.06	24.64
7	12	4.60	14.95	19.54	23.88
8	1121	2.83	11.67	14.50	15.84
9	122	1.30	10.95	12.25	8.76
10	1122	1.87	8.40	10.27	10.88
11	123	0.86	8.36	9.22	6.04

A complete sensitivity analysis is usually performed also for all elementary input attributes. The goal is to verify that the ranking of sensitivity coefficients is consistent with evaluator's expectations. This analysis of MSHCP input attributes is presented in Fig. 4.4.5 and Table 4.4.3. Of course, the impacts of individual inputs are generally less than the impacts of subsystems. The most important mandatory inputs are #1111, #1115, and #11142, and the most important non-mandatory inputs are #121 and #11212. The ranking of input attributes according to sensitivity coefficients is a simple technique for verification of suitability aggregation properties, and it can be performed for various values of default suitability, including those that may be different for each input.

The sensitivity Table 4.4.3 also shows inputs that have a very small impact. This is a frequent in cases where the number of inputs is large. There are three possible actions in response to inputs that have very small impact: (1) to keep them expecting that they contribute to the completeness and precision of the criterion function, and in some cases to force vendors to take them seriously into account, regardless of their low impact; (2) to remove them from evaluation as insignificant, because they increase the cost of evaluation and have low contribution to the evaluation results; and (3) to consider the low impact as a reason to modify the criterion function in order to increase the impact of selected inputs.

4.4.5 Logic Refining of the Aggregation Structure

Elementary criteria for ecological problems are regularly rather complex and include composite indicators. For example, the criterion #11141 (Known & Potential Host Fish) is evaluated as $Crit(\#11141) = \{(0,0), (4,100)\}$ where the values 0–4 are interpreted as follows:

4 = Abundant population of multiple known host fish + high fish IBI score
3 = Abundant population of at least two known host fish + high fish IBI score

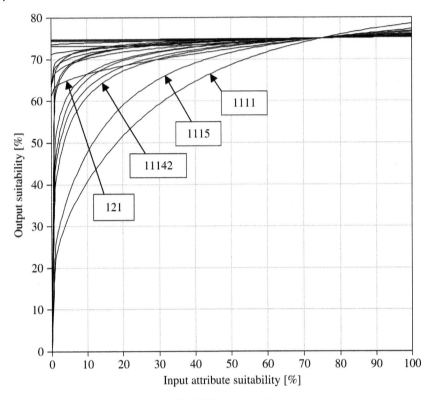

Figure 4.4.5 Sensitivity curves for 27 MSHCP input attributes.

2 = No known host fish + high IBI score
1 = No known host fish + medium IBI score
0 = No known host fish + low IBI score

Host fish are necessary for reproductive process of mussels, and if known host fish are present, that is a sufficient prerequisite for the suitability of evaluated site. However, for some mussel species, the host fish are not known. In such cases, it is possible to use the IBI score (Index of Biotic Integrity [KAR81], a composite index based on biological attributes of an aquatic community) as a proxy for the likely presence of host fish, both known and unknown. Therefore, the abundance of known host fish is a sufficient requirement, the high IBI score is a desired attribute, and the criterion #11141 can be composed as a disjunctive partial absorption of two subcriteria: #111411 Number of Known Host Fish, and #111412 The IBI Score. Assuming $12 \leq IBI \leq 60$, the appropriate elementary criteria are:

Table 4.4.3 Sorted sensitivity coefficients of MSHCP attributes.

Rank	Attribute	Increment	Decrement	Range	Impact
1	1111	3.60	75.00	78.60	38.52
2	1115	1.72	75.00	76.72	27.02
3	11142	1.11	75.00	76.11	15.62
4	11123	0.99	75.00	75.99	13.70
5	11122	0.75	75.00	75.75	10.32
6	11121	0.75	75.00	75.75	10.32
7	11132	0.74	75.00	75.74	11.34
8	11144	0.38	75.00	75.38	5.44
9	11145	0.38	75.00	75.38	5.44
10	11141	0.38	75.00	75.38	5.44
11	11134	0.38	75.00	75.38	5.66
12	11131	0.38	75.00	75.38	5.66
13	11133	0.38	75.00	75.38	5.66
14	11143	0.25	75.00	75.25	3.78
15	121	2.20	13.83	16.03	13.74
16	11212	0.76	11.67	12.43	6.44
17	11213	0.50	11.67	12.17	4.64
18	11211	0.50	11.67	12.17	4.64
19	11215	0.37	11.67	12.04	3.64
20	11214	0.37	11.67	12.04	3.64
21	1232	0.60	3.89	4.49	4.04
22	11221	1.54	1.81	3.35	6.16
23	1231	0.26	1.45	1.72	1.68
24	1223	0.82	0.63	1.46	2.90
25	11222	0.65	0.42	1.07	2.18
26	1221	0.56	0.33	0.89	1.84
27	1222	0.40	0.21	0.61	1.28

$Crit(\#111411) = \{(0, 0), (1, 40), (3, 100)\}$
  0 = No known host fish
  1 = Abundant population of one known host fish
  2 = Abundant population of two known host fish
  3 = Abundant population of more than two known host fish;
$Crit(\#111412) = \{(15, 0), (55, 100)\}$.

If we want to attain a penalty of 25% and a reward of 50% then the corresponding DPA aggregator and its sensitivity functions are shown in Fig. 4.4.6.

4.4.6 Cost/Suitability Analysis

The cost/suitability analysis provides final results of evaluation and comparison of competitive projects. It combines the analysis of relative suitability (a given competitor suitability score divided by the best competitor suitability score) and

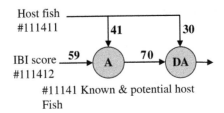

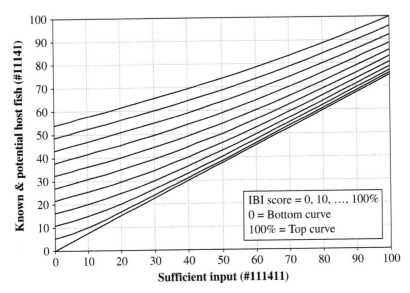

Figure 4.4.6 Refined known and potential host fish criterion.

affordability (lowest cost divided by a given competitor cost). The goal is to find projects that simultaneously offer high suitability and high affordability.

For M competitive MSHCP projects the LSP criterion function generates the overall suitability scores $X^{(m)}$, $m = 1,...,M$. The overall suitability scores are computed from strictly nonfinancial input attributes. All competitive projects must provide the overall suitability above the minimum suitability threshold value, which is usually selected from 67% to 75%. All projects that offer the overall suitability below the accepted threshold value are rejected. For projects that are above the minimum suitability threshold we compute the following relative overall suitability:

$$S_m = X^{(m)}/\max\left(X^{(1)},...,X^{(M)}\right), \quad 0 < S_m \leq 1, \quad m = 1,...,M .$$

For each competitive MSHCP project, it is necessary to perform a detailed financial analysis that generates the net present value of all cash flows (both expenses and earnings). This strictly financial analysis generates the overall cost indicators $C^{(m)}$, $m = 1,...,M$. We assume that the overall cost indicators must be below a selected maximum cost threshold value, and that projects that are above the maximum cost must be rejected. For projects that are below the maximum cost threshold we compute the following relative affordability indicator:

$$A_m = \min\left(C^{(1)},...,C^{(M)}\right)/C_0^{(m)}, \quad 0 < A_m \le 1, \quad m = 1,...,M .$$

In the majority of practical cases the decision makers are interested to simultaneously attain a high suitability and a high affordability. In a general case, the relative importance of high suitability ($W_s \in\,]0,1[$) is not the same as the relative importance of high affordability ($W_a \in\,]0,1[$). In some cases it is more important to find an affordable solution, while in other cases it might be more important to attain high suitability. In all cases, $W_s + W_a = 1$.

Now, we are ready to compute the overall values of all MSHCP projects as a logic aggregate L of relative suitability and relative affordability: $V_m = L(S_m, A_m)$, $m = 1,...,M$. The logic aggregator L can be selected either as a generalized conjunction/disjunction or a partial absorption. The most frequently used aggregator is the partial conjunction which can be implemented as a weighted power mean:

$$V_m = W_s S_m \Delta W_a A_m = \left(W_s S_m^r + W_a A_m^r\right)^{1/r}, \quad r < 1, \quad m = 1,...,M .$$

The highest value denotes the winning competitor. Consequently, the winning competitor offers simultaneously high suitability and high affordability. In a frequent special case, we can be satisfied with the andness of 67%, and compute the overall value simply as a weighted geometric mean ($r = 0$):

$$V_m = S_m^{W_s} A_m^{W_a}, \quad m = 1,...,M .$$

The overall values $V_1, ..., V_M$ are usually computed for all combinations of the weights of suitability and affordability. Then we can see in what range of relative importance of suitability/affordability the winner dominates other competitors. If the dominance is shown for a wide range of weight combinations, then the winner can be selected with high confidence.

4.4.7 MSHCP Software Support

The MSHCP projects are distributed in 14 states, and several evaluation teams may perform the evaluation process simultaneously. To provide centralized support over the Internet and simultaneous access to LSP criteria, the necessary software is developed as a web application called the LSPweb [SEA16]. The overall structure and functionality of the LSPweb system are shown in Fig. 4.4.7.

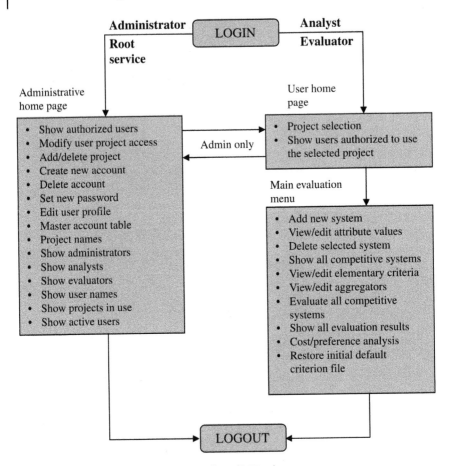

Figure 4.4.7 The structure and functionality of LSPweb.

LSPweb supports five types of users: *evaluator, analyst, administrator,* and two system users: *root* and *service*. Evaluators can define competitive systems and evaluate those using available LSP criteria. Analysts can customize existing LSP criteria (change all parameters) and use modified criteria for evaluation and comparison of competitive systems. Administrators and system accounts (root and service) are authorized to develop evaluation criteria: they can upload new criteria, open and close user accounts, and perform evaluation. Analysts and evaluators are primarily engaged in providing input for the evaluation process and in interpreting and distributing evaluation results.

4.5   Space Management Decision Problems

This chapter is dedicated to the memory of Dr. Goran Božović, architect,
urbanist, and contributor to space management methods.

Evaluation problems are very frequent in the area of city planning and space
management. Typical problems include decisions about optimum location of
city objects (schools, hospitals, theaters, sports centers, shopping centers, recreation areas, etc.), and the evaluation of suitability of geographic locations for
specific use. In this chapter we present two samples of typical space management problems. First, we present a model for selecting the best location for
building a new elementary school. This problem is similar to many other public
object location problems (e.g., see [KAH03, KUO99, CHO08]). The second
problem is the evaluation of the suitability of urban locations for specific use
(residential development).

4.5.1   A Decision Model for School Location

4.5.1.1   Statement of the Problem

Suppose that a city has existing schools that are used by a growing student population. The city has decided to build a new school. There are four possible locations that could be used for the new school. It is necessary to decide which
location is the most suitable, taking into account a variety of requirements.
The new school must have good accessibility and the location must have sufficient area and convenient shape. The construction should be completed in a
reasonable time, satisfying urbanistic and safety conditions. The available funding for the whole new school project is C_{max}, and it cannot be exceeded. Our
goal is to develop methodology for justifiable solution of this problem, following
all major steps of the LSP method.

Soft Computing Evaluation Logic: The LSP Decision Method and Its Applications,
First Edition. Jozo Dujmović.
© 2018 John Wiley & Sons, Inc. Published 2018 by John Wiley & Sons, Inc.
Companion website: www.wiley.com/go/Dujmovic/Soft_Computing_Evaluation_Logic

4.5.1.2 School Locations Attribute Tree

The first step in all evaluation problems is to identify attributes that affect the ability of school location to satisfy requirements. According to the statement of the problem, the main groups of attributes are the accessibility of the new school location (that includes the access time distribution and the student transport options), the area and shape of the location, the organization of project, and the site features (including urbanistic conditions, safety, and interaction with environment). Based on these main groups of attributes we can develop a tree with 21 elementary attributes presented in Fig 4.5.1 (note an alternative node numbering where the root node is denoted 0). Of course, there are many possible expansions or modifications of the presented tree. We selected the tree that has a typical size and contents; with minor modifications, the tree could be reused in cases of other public objects.

4.5.1.3 Elementary Criteria

Let the access time denote the time a student needs to come from home to the school. The access times for all students in the school form the distribution of access time. A typical distribution of access time is presented in Fig. 4.5.2. For this distribution we can compute the average access time T and the standard deviation of the access time σ. These parameters can be used to organize elementary criteria. The complete set of 21 elementary criteria for evaluating competitive school locations is presented below.

(111) Average Access Time

This indicator is computed for all students with respect to each of the alternative new school locations. For the majority of elementary schools we expect a predominantly walking access and a relatively short average access time T. The evaluation of T is based on the following elementary criterion:

$$Crit(T \, [\text{minute}]) = \{(5,100), (30, 0)\}; \quad g(T) = \min(100, \max(0, \, 4(30 - T))) \, [\%].$$

If the average access time is 5 minutes or less than 5 minutes, we would be perfectly satisfied (100%). The average access time of 30 minutes or more is considered completely unsatisfactory. For other values, we use the linear interpolation; e.g., the average access time of 15 minutes satisfies $g(15) = \min(100, \max(0, 4(30 - 15))) = 60\%$ of our requirements.

(112) Access Improvement Ratio

A new school is expected to reduce the average access time for students. Let the average access time for the new location be T_{new}. The same student population going to the closest old schools has the existing average access time T_{old}. So, we can define the access improvement ratio $R = T_{old} / T_{new}$. Of course, we expect

SCHOOL LOCATION

1 Accessibility
    11 Access time distribution
        111 Average access time
        112 Access improvement ratio
        113 Percent of very far students
    12 Student transport
        121 Walking access
        122 Public transportation
        123 Other transport modes
2 Area and shape of school location
    21 Total area of property
    22 The shape of property
3 Project organization
    31 Legal status of location
    32 School conditions fulfillment
    33 Project completion time
4 Site features
    41 Urbanistic conditions
        411 Integration into urban tissue
        412 Compatibility with urban development strategy
        413 Urbanistic constraints
    42 Safety hazards
        421 Air pollution
        422 Acoustic pollution
        423 Traffic intensity in the school area
        424 Walking access hazards
    43 Interaction with environment
        431 Adjacent public parking areas
        432 Proximity to compatible institutions
        433 Distance from incompatible institutions

Figure 4.5.1 School location attribute tree.

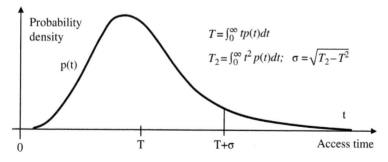

$$T = \int_0^\infty t p(t) dt$$

$$T_2 = \int_0^\infty t^2 p(t) dt; \quad \sigma = \sqrt{T_2 - T^2}$$

Figure 4.5.2 A typical probability density function for access time.

$T_{new} < T_{old}$, and $R > 1$. Therefore, we can evaluate R using the following elementary criterion:

$$Crit(R) = \{(0,0), (2, 100)\}; \quad g(R) = \min(100, 50R) \; [\%].$$

This preference scale reflects the case where a new school could be realized as an upgrade of one of existing schools. If the access time remains unchanged our satisfaction is only 50%; to achieve the total satisfaction the existing average access time must be reduced two times or more. However, we also consider that cases where $R < 1$ are inconvenient, but not unacceptable.

(113) Percent of Very Far Students
The standard deviation of the access time distribution should be small. We want to reduce the number of students who live very far and must travel excessively long to reach the school. An indicator of the number of such students is the percentage of students P who travel more than $T+\sigma$, where T is the average access time, and σ is the corresponding standard deviation. Therefore, $P = 100 \int_{T+\sigma}^{\infty} p(t)dt$. We would like to have the distribution where the percent of students who travel more than $T+\sigma$ is less than 25%; if $P \leq 5\%$ that would completely satisfy our requirements. The corresponding criterion is the following:

$$Crit(P\,[\%]) = \{(5,100), (25, 0)\}, \quad g(P) = \min(100, \max(0, 5(25-P))) \; [\%].$$

(121) Walking Access
We would prefer that the majority of students have the walking access to the new school location. If WA denotes the percentage of students who walk to school, and if a realistic expectation is that from 20% to 50% of students could have walking access, then the corresponding criterion is the following:

$$Crit(WA\,[\%]) = \{(20, 0), (50, 100)\},$$
$$g(WA) = \min(100, \max(0, 3.33(WA-20))) \; [\%].$$

(122) Public Transportation Access
We would prefer that students who don't have the walking access to the new school location can use the existing public transportation system. If PT denotes the percentage of students who can use public transportation, then the suggested criterion can be similar to the criterion for the walking access, as follows:

$$Crit(PT\,[\%]) = \{(20, 0), (50, 100)\};$$
$$g(PT) = \min(100, \max(0, 3.33(PT-20))) \; [\%].$$

(123) Other Transport Modes

Students who cannot use public transportation, or walk to the school, must use other transport modes: car pools, bicycle, of a dedicated school bus. In the case were these transport modes are not desirable, and OTM denotes the percentage of such students, the corresponding criterion might be the following:

$$Crit(OTM\,[\%]) = \{(0,\ 100),\ (60, 0)\};$$
$$g(OTM) = \min(100,\ \max(0,\ 100 - 10(OTM)/6))\ [\%].$$

(21) Total Area of Property

The necessary area depends on the number of students and the selected school program. Let Q denote the area that is considered standard for this type and size of school and let A denote the actual area of the analyzed location. The relative area $RA = A/Q$ will be used for evaluation as follows:.

$$Crit(RA) = \{(0.6,0),(1,80),(1.2,100)\}.$$

(22) The Shape of Property

Regular shapes are usually more suitable than irregular shapes. In this case we will assume that the ideal shape is a square. In the ideal case of the square having the side s, the ratio of the circumference $C = 4s$ and the area $A = s^2$ is $C/A = 4/s = 4/\sqrt{A}$. For irregular shapes the ratio C/A will be greater than $4/\sqrt{A}$. The shape irregularity ratio for arbitrary shapes is $I = (C/A)/(4/\sqrt{A}) = C/(4\sqrt{A})$. This ratio can be used to realize the following elementary criterion:

$$Crit(I) = \{(1,\ 100),\ (2, 0)\}; \quad g(I) = \min(100,\ \max(0,\ 100(2-I)))\ [\%].$$

(31) Legal Status of Location

The legal status (LS) of the analyzed property can be evaluated using the following evaluation scale:

0 = unknown or currently not available   1 = questionable marketability

2 = marketable private property   3 = public property

The corresponding criterion is the following:

$$Crit(LS) = \{(0,\ 0),\ (3,\ 100)\}; \quad g(LS) = \min(100,\ \max(0,\ 100(LS)/3))\ [\%].$$

(32) School Conditions Fulfillment

Schools must satisfy a variety of conditions (necessary area, type of buildings, classrooms, faculty offices, sport areas, laboratories, library, restaurant, medical, and/or dental services, etc.). We evaluate each location from the standpoint of its support to the fulfillment of school conditions. If the evaluation of school conditions (SC) is based on the five-level scale (4 = very good, 3 = good, 2 = average, 1 = poor, 0 = very poor), then the corresponding criterion can be defined as follows:

$$Crit(SC) = \{(0, 0), (4, 100)\}; \quad g(SC) = \min(100, \max(0, \ 100(SC)/4)) \ [\%].$$

(33) Project Completion Time

We assume that the deadline for project completion is fixed and it is specified in relation to the beginning of the school year. Various locations may have different completion times, and the location having the shortest completion time is generally preferred. The criterion for the completion time (CT) can be based on the following scale:

0 = cannot be completed before the deadline,
1 = possible (but not guaranteed) completion on time,
2 = completed 2 months before the deadline,
3 = completed 4 months before the deadline.

We use the following criterion: $Crit(CT) = \{(0, 0), (1, 60), (2, 90), (3, 100)\}$.

(411) Integration Into Urban Tissue

The school must well integrate in the environment and should not disturb the existing urban contents. The degree of compatibility (UT) with the urban area can be directly assessed by domain experts. The corresponding criterion is the following:

$$Crit(UT\,[\%]) = \{(0, 0), (100, 100)\}.$$

(412) Compatibility with Urban Development Strategy

The evaluation can be based on two subcriteria: (a) the contents compatibility, and (b) the access compatibility. The contents compatibility relates to future urban areas in the environment of the school location, and the access compatibility is based on the expected average access time to the future residential areas that the school might serve. Each subcriterion can be evaluated on the scale from 0 to 4: 4 = excellent, 3 = good, 2 = average, 1 = fair, 0 = poor. The sum of points (DS) can be from 0 to 8 and the corresponding criterion is defined as follows:

$$Crit(DS) = \{(0, 0), (8, 100)\}; \quad g(DS) = \min(100, \max(0, \ 100(DS)/8)) \ [\%].$$

(413) Urbanistic Constraints

This criterion is based on direct preference assessment by domain experts who investigate all relevant urbanistic factors, such as the type of architecture, the maximum allowed height of buildings, the floor space ratio (the ratio between the total gross floor areas of a building, and the site area of the land upon which such building is to be erected). The corresponding criterion is

$$Crit(UC[\%]) = \{(0, 0), (100, 100)\}.$$

(421) Air Pollution

According to standards for the analyzed area the following scale can be used: 0 = very high pollution (very low air quality), 1 = high pollution (low air quality), 2 = low (standard level) pollution, 3 = very low pollution (high air quality), 4 = no pollution (very high air quality). The corresponding criterion for the air pollution/quality (AIR) is the following:

$$Crit(AIR) = \{(1, 0), (4, 100)\}; \quad g(AIR) = \min(100, \max(0, 100(AIR-1)/3)) \ [\%].$$

(422) Acoustic Pollution

The evaluation of acoustic pollution (AP) can be based on the same scale as the evaluation of the air pollution. The corresponding criterion can be slightly less demanding, as follows:

$$Crit(AP) = \{(0, 0), (4, 100)\}; g(AP) = \min(100, \max(0, \ 25(AP))) \ [\%].$$

(423) Traffic Intensity in the School Area

The traffic intensity (TI) in the school area is evaluated as a risk factor for students, regardless the transport mode. The evaluation scale is: 0 = very high traffic intensity, 1 = high traffic intensity, 2 = medium (normal) traffic intensity, 3 = low traffic intensity, 4 = no traffic in the school area. The corresponding criterion function is

$$Crit(TI) = \{(0, 0), (4, 100)\}; g(TI) = \min(100, \max(0, \ 25(TI))) \ [\%].$$

(424) Walking Access Hazards

The walking access hazards can be evaluated as the average number of traffic street crossings (TSC) during a student's approach to the new school location. Following is the corresponding criterion:

$$Crit(TSC) = \{(0, 100), (10, 0)\}; \ g(TSC) = \min(100, \max(0, \ 10(10-TSC))) \ [\%].$$

(431) Adjacent Public Parking Areas

For graduation and similar events a large number of visitors is expected to simultaneously visit the school. It is desirable to have adjacent public parking areas that can fully satisfy these needs. We consider only those public parking areas that are within a 300 meter distance from the school and define PP as the percentage of satisfied needs, taking into account only those students who do not normally walk to the school. The corresponding criterion function is defined as follows:

$$Crit(PP) = \{(50, 0), (100, 100)\}; \quad g(PP) = \min(100, \max(0, \ 2(PP-50))) \ [\%].$$

(432) Proximity to Compatible Institutions

A number of institutions can be considered compatible with schools. They include: (1) museums, (2) food shopping centers, (3) public libraries, (4) bookstores, (5) theaters, (6) movie theaters, (7) concert halls, (8) nursery schools, (9) sport stadiums, (10) parks and recreation areas, (11) universities, and (12) industrial or other sponsor institutions. The total number of compatible institutions (*CI*) can be used to create the following criterion:

$$Crit(CI) = \{(0, 0), (6, 100)\}; g(CI) = \min(100, \max(0, \ 100(CI)/6)) \ [\%].$$

(433) Distance from Incompatible Institutions

The incompatible institutions and areas include (1) drug intensive areas, (2) adult contents areas, (3) cemeteries, (4) main bus terminals, (5) main railway station, (6) major airport, (7) polluted industrial centers and areas, and (8) major hospitals. These areas and institutions are taken into account only in cases of excessive proximity, where they interfere with the students attending the school at the analyzed location. The total number of incompatible institutions (*II*) can be used to create the following criterion:

$$Crit(II) = \{(0, 100), (4, 0)\}; \quad g(II) = \min(100, \max(0, \ 25(4-(II)))) \ [\%].$$

4.5.1.4   Aggregation of Suitability Degrees

The suitability aggregation structure (WPM.17 aggregators) is presented in Fig. 4.5.3. The main aggregators are hard and soft partial conjunctions (HPC, and SPC) and conjunctive partial absorptions (CPA). The logic properties of this criterion can be summarized as follows:

1) Individual mandatory attributes that are modeled using HPC are 111, 112, 21, 31, 32, 33, 421, 422, 423, and 424. Therefore, it is necessary to have a good access time, a sufficient area of school property, and all components of the project organization and safety hazards.
2) Group mandatory attributes are 41, 43, and the (121,122)-group. For them it is not acceptable that all components of the group are not satisfied.
3) Nonmandatory desired attributes, aggregated using CPA, include 113, 123, and 22. We would like to minimize the number of very far students, no

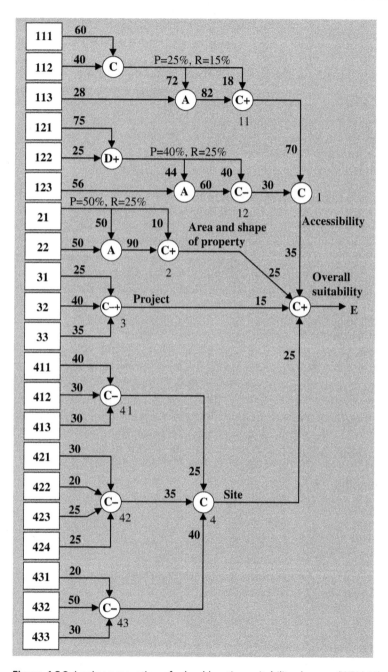

Figure 4.5.3 Logic aggregation of school location suitability degrees (WPM.17).

students with access inconveniences, and a good shape of school property, but even if these attributes are not satisfied, this is not considered the reason for rejecting a proposed location.

4) The walking access and the public transportation (121 and 122) are disjunctively aggregated. These are two alternative school access methods. The walking access is substantially more important, reflecting the objective to select the location where children can freely walk to school.

5) All the four main groups of attributes (1,2,3,4) are mandatory and must be strongly simultaneously satisfied; the accessibility is considered the most important of all main decision components.

The presented logic properties illustrate a specific evaluation philosophy. Of course, other approaches could also be possible. For example, instead of the use of partial disjunction for aggregating the transport modes, some evaluators might consider that locations which do not offer walking access are not acceptable. In such cases, we could define a criterion function where walking access is a mandatory requirement. Obviously, the presented approach provides a high flexibility in expressing any type of logic relationships that evaluators may need.

Asymmetric logic relationships, such as CPA, have adjustable penalty and reward features (P and R in Fig 4.5.3). For example, the total area of the evaluated property is considered a mandatory requirement: all locations having insufficient area will be rejected. However, a suitable shape of the property is considered desirable, but not mandatory. The output suitability is predominantly determined by the suitability of the mandatory input (the area), while the desired input (the shape) can moderately increase or decrease this value. For example, an inconvenient shape should decrease the total suitability of the area and shape by up to 50%, but not to the extent to produce the zero output suitability even if the shape is rather poor but the total area is sufficiently large. If the shape is regular and close to square, this should to some extent (up to 25%) increase the total suitability of the area and shape subsystem.

4.5.1.5   Cost Analysis

The cost of the whole project must be carefully computed. Basic cost items are identified during the cost analysis, and in our case, they can be itemized as follows:

$C1$ = cost of the property
$C2$ = cost of the site preparation
$C3$ = cost of the access preparation
$C4$ = cost of the school conditions fulfillment
$C5$ = operational costs

In the case of public property C1 is assumed to be 0. C2 reflects only the cost of preparing the location, and can vary substantially depending on the land quality, geologic conditions, slope, height, shape irregularities, and so on. In cases where the school access preparation needs additional costs for access roads and areas, traffic regulation, parking improvement, and security of students, these costs contribute to C3. The cost of school conditions fulfillment (C4) is not the same for all locations. The shape and area of each available property affect architectural solutions, the cost of buildings and other related costs. Finally, all locations will not have the same operational costs (C5). The costs of heating, student transport, equipment and building maintenance, and salaries of additional workers will not be the same for all locations. Therefore, it is reasonable to consider these costs for an extended period of time (10 to 20 years), and take them into account as a part of the location decision process.

The total cost of the project is $C = C1 + C2 + C3 + C4 + C5$. After a careful assessment of all possible cost items and available resources the stakeholders determine the maximum total cost of the project C_{max}. We assume that C_{max} is a hard limit, and that all locations must satisfy the condition $C \leq C_{max}$. For convenience we will consider that the costs are normalized, and $C_{max} = 1$ (or equivalently, we define cost as $(C1 + C2 + C3 + C4 + C5)/C_{max}$).

4.5.1.6 Competitive Locations

We will evaluate four competitive locations, denoted U, L, R, and S. Their shapes and basic parameters are presented in Fig. 4.5.4 and Table 4.5.1.

The location U is the most expensive, and the most irregular. It has the second largest area and it best integrates in the urban tissue. It has no incompatible institutions in its proximity.

The location L has the largest area. It is the second least expensive, and the second most irregular. The property is public domain and it has the best school program fulfillment. The integration with urban tissue is the least convenient of all locations.

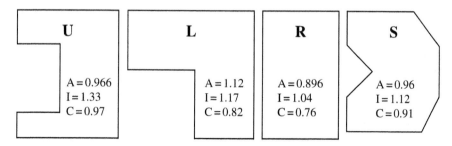

Figure 4.5.4 The shapes, areas, irregularity ratios, and total costs of four competitive locations.

Table 4.5.1 Values of attributes for locations U, L, R, and S.

School Location Attributes	Location U	Location L	Location R	Location S
1. Average Access Time [minutes]	14	10	15	7
2. Access Improvement Ratio	1.2	1.75	1.1	1.8
3. Percent of Very Far Students	11	9	8	9
4. Walking Access	45	55	15	60
5. Public Transportation	45	40	60	35
6. Other Transport Modes	10	5	25	5
7. Total Area of Property	0.966	1.12	0.896	0.96
8. The Shape of Property	1.33	1.17	1.04	1.12
9. Legal Status of Location	2	3	3	1
10. School Conditions Fulfillment	3	4	2	3
11. Project Completion Time	2	2	1	3
12. Integration with Urban Tissue	100	75	80	90
13. Compatibility with Urban Development	6	6	8	5
14. Urbanistic Constraints	80	95	95	70
15. Air Pollution	4	3	3	4
16. Acoustic Pollution	4	4	3	3
17. Traffic Intensity in the School Area	2	4	3	2
18. Walking Access Hazards	4	2	2	3
19. Adjacent Public Parking Areas	60	85	70	65
20. Proximity to Compatible Institutions	2	5	5	4
21. Distance from Incompatible Institutions	0	1	2	1

The location R is rectangular, public domain, and it has the best shape. It is also the least expensive, and the smallest of the four competitors. It has the worst completion time and access improvement ratio. It has an excellent compatibility with future urban developments.

The location S has a sufficient area and a reasonable shape and cost. It is the closest location to students with the largest percentage of walking students, and a very fast completion time. However, it has some legal status problems.

4.5.1.7 Cost/Suitability Analysis

The main results of the evaluation process are the overall suitability E and the total cost C for each of competitive locations. The final comparison and ranking of the locations is based on the cost/suitability analysis, which combines E and C to create a unique location value indicator V. There are various mathematical models for computing V, and for simplicity we are going to use the indicator $V = E/C$, which shows the level of satisfaction of total requirements per unit of total cost. In addition to condition $C \leq C_{max}$, we are also going to assume the satisfaction of the condition $E \geq E_{min}$, where E_{min} denotes the minimum acceptable level of satisfaction of overall requirements. Competitive locations having the overall suitability less than the threshold value E_{min} will not be considered. We will use $E_{min} = 67\%$ (all locations must satisfy at least two-thirds of the total requirements).

Table 4.5.2 Summary of the location evaluation and comparison results.

Indicator (suitability, cost, value, rank)	Location U	Location L	Location R	Location S
Accessibility	68.98	85.77	66.93	90.48
Area and Shape of Location	70.38	87.91	74.51	79.01
Project Organization	77.93	96.45	64.83	71.09
Site Features	62.09	81.97	73.16	69.02
Overall suitability (E)	**68.52**	**86.68**	**69.79**	**78.12**
Total cost (C)	0.97	0.82	0.76	0.91
Overall value (V = E/C)	70.64	105.71	91.82	85.85
Normalized value (Vnorm=100V/Vmax)	66.83	100.00	86.86	81.21
Rank	4	1	2	3

The final results of the evaluation and comparison of locations U, L, R, and S are summarized in Table 4.5.2 and Fig. 4.5.5. In Table 4.5.2 we first present the subsystem preferences for four main subsystems: (1) accessibility, (2) area and shape of location, (3) project organization, and (4) site features. For accessibility, the best location is S and the worst is R. For the area and shape, the best is L and the worst is U. The best project organization is obtained for the location

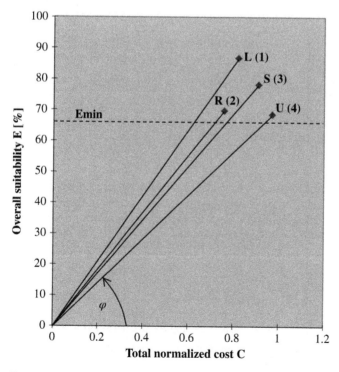

Figure 4.5.5 Cost/suitability analysis.

L, and the worst is location R. Location L has the best site features, and the worst is the location U.

Subsystem preferences are used to compute the overall suitability degrees of the analyzed locations. The best overall suitability (86.68% of satisfied requirements) is obtained for location L. The second is the location S (78.12% of satisfied requirements). The locations U and R satisfied respectively 68.52% and 69.79% of requirements. The difference between U and R is not significant if we only consider suitability scores. However, the comparison of competitive locations is based on both suitability and cost, and a simple example of the cost/suitability analysis is presented in Fig. 4.5.5. Assuming that the region of acceptable solutions includes all suitability scores that are greater than 66.7% and costs that are less than 1, it follows that all four analyzed locations belong to the region of acceptable solutions. Such locations can be compared using the overall value indicator $V = E/C$. Thus, the best location can be identified in Fig. 4.5.5 as the location having the steepest line connecting the origin and the location's (C,E) point (the largest angle φ). The resulting ranking is (1) L, (2) R, (3) S, and (4) U. The best location is the location L. This location satisfies more than 80% of requirements in each of the four main groups of criteria. It outperforms other locations in three out of four groups of criteria. The very good performance of location L is combined with a reasonable cost. Thus, the reasons for selecting the location L can be clearly identified and justified. In addition, the presented method can be similarly used for finding optimum locations of many other public objects.

4.5.2 Suitability of Locations for Residential Development

One of frequent urban planning problems is the evaluation of suitability of locations for residential development and urban expansion. Before deciding to expand a city in a specific area it is necessary to have terrain with suitable properties, good natural environment, accessibility using ground and air transportation, convenient density of population, and employment opportunities. In this section, we present LSP criteria for evaluation and comparison of localities for residential development.

In some cases of simple LSP criteria, it is possible to combine the attribute tree and elementary criteria in a single table. That gives an expanded attribute tree exemplified in Fig. 4.5.6. For each attribute we specify whether the attribute is mandatory (+) or optional (−). If a mandatory attribute is not satisfied then the overall suitability for residential development is considered unacceptable and rated zero. On the other hand, there are attributes that are in our example

SUITABILITY FOR RESIDENTIAL DEVELOPMENT
1 Terrain and environment (+)
  11 Terrain properties (+)
      111 Slope (+)   [%] {(20, 100), (80, 0)}
      112 Altitude (+)   [m] {(600, 100), (2000, 0)}
      113 Aspect (180° = south) (−)   [°] {(45, 0), (135,100), (225, 100), (315,0)}
  12 Environment (−)
      121 Proximity of major green areas (−)   [m] {(200, 100), (2000, 0)}
      122 Proximity of a lake/river (−)   [m] {(200, 100), (2000, 0)}
2 Location and accessibility (+)
  21 Ground transportation (+)
      211 Proximity of an interstate highway (+)   [m] {(25,0), (100,100), (1000,100), (10000, 0)}
      212 Proximity of a regional highway (+)   [m] {(25, 0), (100, 100), (200, 100), (2000, 0)}
      213 Proximity of an intercity railroad station (+) [min] {(15, 100), (30, 0)}
  22 Proximity of an international airport (−)   [min] {(15, 100), (120, 0)}
3 Population and employment opportunities (+)
  31 Density of population (+)   [hab/km^2] {(20,0), (500,100), (1000,100), (5000, 0)}
  32 Proximity to employment opportunities (+)   [min] {(15, 100), (90, 0)}

Figure 4.5.6 Expanded attribute tree for residential development with mandatory (+) and optional (−) components, units of measurements, and elementary attribute criteria.

considered nonmandatory (optional) and denoted by (−). If a nonmandatory requirement is not satisfied, that will not cause rejection of the proposed location. For example, while appropriate slope and altitude are considered mandatory requirements, a good aspect (direction in which a slope faces) of the new urban complex is considered desirable, but it is not mandatory. Similarly, good environment is highly desirable but not necessary: If other conditions are satisfied, new urban areas can be built in cases where green areas and lakes are missing. Finally, the proximity to an airport is also considered nonmandatory. However, good ground transportation is considered mandatory. Of course, such requirements depend on other circumstances (climate, country, etc.) and can be changed.

The next step in the LSP method is to specify requirements for all attributes. The elementary attribute criteria in vertex notation are also shown in the expanded attribute tree in Fig. 4.5.6. For example, the criterion #212 specifies that it is desired that an urban complex is located in proximity to a regional highway. The proximity is measured in meters and the unit of measurement is denoted [m]. The proposed elementary criterion considers that an ideal distance from the regional highway is from 100 to 200 meters. If the distance is greater than 2000 meters (causing excessive local traffic) or less than 25 meters (causing both the air pollution and the acoustic pollution), such a location is considered unacceptable.

The logic aggregation of attribute preferences is based on WPM.17 aggregators and presented in Fig. 4.5.7. The aggregation structure includes mostly conjunctive aggregators that reflect the need for simultaneous satisfaction of

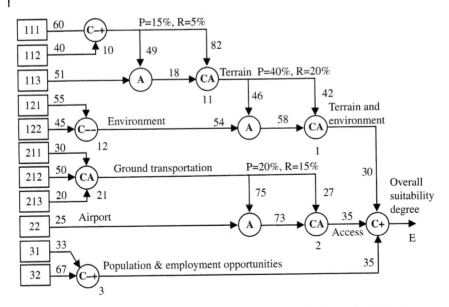

Figure 4.5.7 The aggregation structure for computing the suitability for residential development.

requirements. The aggregators identified in Fig. 4.5.7 by (arbitrarily selected) block numbers #11, #1, and #2 are conjunctive partial absorptions that aggregate mandatory and optional inputs. If the optional input is 0, this causes a penalty (the average decrement of the output value) P, and if the optional input is 1, this causes a reward (the average increment of the output value) R. Desired values of P and R are expressed as percentages.

For simplicity, let us compare three locations: $L_1 = (X_1, Y_1)$, $L_2 = (X_2, Y_2)$, and $L_3 = (X_3, Y_3)$. These locations are selected as typical representatives for three areas that are candidates for urban expansion. Their attributes are shown in Table 4.5.3. Because of differences in the available infrastructure, the cost of building in location L_2 is 30% more expensive than building in location L_1, and building in location L_3 is 20% more expensive than building in location L_1. The problem is to find which location is the most suitable for the urban expansion, and the basic results are shown in Table 4.5.4.

Table 4.5.3 Input attributes and costs for three competitive locations (L_1, L_2, L_3).

Loc	111	112	113	121	122	211	212	213	22	31	32	C
L_1	40	1200	180	3000	250	1500	50	20	100	555	30	1
L_2	18	400	90	150	500	1100	300	20	20	800	20	1.3
L_3	35	700	0	1600	700	1700	400	15	35	1500	35	1.2

Table 4.5.4 Resulting suitability degrees [%] and cost/suitability indicators.

Loc	10	11	12	21	1	2	3	$E[\%]$	$V = E / C$
L_1	62.7	65.5	26.8	48.5	51.7	42.9	86	**51.75**	51.75 [72.5%]
L_2	100	94.5	92.4	88.6	93.8	89.8	95.5	**92.83**	71.41 [100%]
L_3	81.6	69.7	42	92	60.3	89.9	77.7	**72.63**	60.52 [84.8%]

The most suitable location is L_2 because it satisfies 92.83% of the suitability requirements. The location L_3 is second; it satisfies 72.63% of the requirements. The least suitable location is L_1; it satisfies only 51.75% of the suitability requirements for residential development. If the importance of high suitability is the same as the importance of low cost, then we can compare the locations using the overall value expressed as the simple E/C ratio, and in such a case the location L_2 is still the most convenient regardless the highest cost; the overall value of L_3 is approximately 15% lower than the value of L_2.

The presented 11-attribute example of suitability for urban residential land development can easily be modified and expanded taking into account the needs of specific geographic region. Such an expanded 20-attribute criterion (Fig. 4.6.16) was proposed in [HAT14] and used for development of suitability maps of Vancouver metropolitan area.

An expanded 26-attribute version of the residential development criterion is shown in Fig. 4.5.8. The aggregation structure is presented in the form of rectangular diagram. In the case of CPA, mandatory inputs are denoted M and optional (desired) inputs are denoted O. Pairs of negative and positive values denote the average penalty and reward expressed as percentages.

The aggregation structures shown in Figs. 4.5.7 and 4.5.8 show two fundamental groups of attributes: mandatory and optional. Mandatory attributes must be satisfied, because in the opposite case the analyzed location must be rejected. Suppose now that this example is analyzed using simple additive scoring (in the GIS area also called weighted linear combination, WLC [MAL99, MAL00, MAL06, MAL11]). This approach (which is the most frequently used in the GIS area) makes all input attributes nonmandatory, i.e., optional. Consequently, all locations that have at least one nonzero suitability attribute would be reported as more or less acceptable. For example, in our criterion for residential development (as well as the criterion for agriculture, Fig. 4.6.17) we claim that low slope is mandatory for residential development (or agriculture) and that good aspect is optional. In other words, it is obvious that nobody can build houses on excessive slopes regardless whether they face south or north. However, on the northern hemisphere, a WLC criterion would qualify all locations that face south as partially suitable regardless their slopes that could

ATTRIBUTES OF THE SUITABILITY OF LOCATION FOR RESIDENTIAL DEVELOPMENT	
1. Terrain orientation (azimuth/aspect)	14. Distance from medical services (composite travel t.)
2. Vegetation cover (affecting solar access)	15. Distance from parks (weighted composite travel time)
3. Slope (building suitability)	16. Distance from trails (weighted composite travel time)
4. Relative buildable area (% of total area)	17. Distance from recreation (composite travel time)
5. Soils and wetlands (soil suitability for building)	18. Availability of road access (suitability for building)
6. Drainage (# of cells draining to the analyzed cell)	19. Availability of water supply (suitability for building)
7. Stormwater: the probability of water emergencies	20. Availability of sewage system (suit. for building)
8. Climate (component of environment evaluation)	21. Views (aesthetic values)
9. Vegetation (environment evaluation)	22. Buffers (protection of privacy)
10. Wildlife habitat (environment evaluation)	23. Distance from amenities and beneficial surrounding
11. Distance from shopping : mean travel time to POIs	24. Zoning district (lot size/water/landscape regulations)
12. Distance from schools (composite travel time)	25. Restricted lands (national parks, land trust, etc.)
13. Distance from urban entertainment (composite)	26. State and federal restrictions/regulations (probability)

#	Attribute													
1	Terrain orientation						M	CPA	Solar access	O				
2	Vegetation cover						O	−10+5						
3	Slope (building suitability)	60	CA	Slope and rel. area	M	CPA −80 +25	Suitability for construction	77	CA	Suitability for construction and hydrologic cond.	M	CPA −30 +30	Terrain
4	Relative buildable area(% of area)	40												
5	Soils and wetlands				O									
6	Drainage				70	C−	Hydro. cond.	23						
7	Stormwater				30									
8	Climate										30			
9	Vegetation										40	A	Environment
10	Wildlife habitat										30			
11	Distance from shopping	40					Degree of urbanity	65		Accessibility (Distance from points of interest)	25			
12	Distance from schools	10												
13	Distance from urban entertainment	30	C−						C−+				Location and accessibility
14	Distance from medical services	20												
15	Distance from parks	20					Access to natural resources	35						
16	Distance from trails	50	C−											
17	Distance from recreation	30										CA		
18	Availability of road access							M	CPA −40 +30	Suitability for building	50			
19	Availability of water supply							O						
20	Availability of sewage system							O						
21	Views							70		Aesthetic values	25			
22	Buffers (protection of privacy)							15	C−−					
23	Distance from amenities and beneficial surrounding							15						
24	Zoning district (min lot size/water/sewer/stormwater/landscape)										60		Potential restrictions
25	Restricted lands (national parks, land trust, etc.)										20	CA	
26	State and federal restrictions/regulations										20		

Terrain (suitability for building)	80	CA	LAND PROPERTIES	45	C+	**OVERALL SUITABILITY OF LOCATION**
Environment	20					
Location and accessibility				40		
Potential restrictions of use (probability of problems in this area)				15		

Figure 4.5.8 An expanded version of the residential development criterion.

provably prevent any residential development. Such obviously wrong results are sufficient to disqualify WLC as a decision method, particularly in the area of suitability maps (see Chapter 4.6). As discussed in Chapter 1.3, WLC is not acceptable as a general decision method because it is a special case, incompatible with all logic forms of human evaluation reasoning.

4.6   LSP Suitability Maps

For each geographic location we can compute its suitability for particular use (e.g., agriculture, urban development, etc.). The LSP suitability map is defined as a spatial distribution of the degree of suitability of geographic locations for a specific use. LSP suitability maps are usually presented as transparent overlay of suitability on top of geographic maps (e.g., Google maps, or GIS maps such as TerrSet/Idrisi or ArcGIS).

   The most frequent decision problems that need suitability maps are problems of planning and development, and problems of environmental protection [CHA07, GOO97, JOE01, RIG02, TOM90, WAC95]. The most common types of development include commercial, industrial, residential, and military development, as well as the use of selected regions as the farmland (agriculture) or the forestland. In the protection area we are interested in the use of selected regions as natural areas that may be ecologically important (for wildlife habitat and biodiversity), or important as natural heritage areas. More specific examples of suitability for development include the suitability for construction of industrial objects, homes, hospitals, schools, recreation areas, entertainment centers, sport facilities, shopping centers, airports, etc. The LSP method for computing suitability in suitability maps was first proposed in [DUJ08]. Various refinements, expansions, and applications of this basic concept can be found in [DUJ09, TRE09, TRE10, DUJ10a, DUJ10b, TRE11, DUJ11, HAT14].

4.6.1   The Concept of Map Logic and LSP Suitability Maps

The proposed technique for creating LSP raster suitability maps is summarized in Fig. 4.6.1. The investigated area is divided in an orthogonal grid of square cells of size h where X, Y denote the coordinates of the center of a specific cell. Each analyzed cell is characterized by an array of n cell attributes $(a_1(X, Y), a_2(X, Y), ..., a_n(X, Y))$. The attribute suitability maps are $e_i(X, Y) = g_i(a_i(X, Y)) \in [0,1]$,

Soft Computing Evaluation Logic: The LSP Decision Method and Its Applications,
First Edition. Jozo Dujmović.
© 2018 John Wiley & Sons, Inc. Published 2018 by John Wiley & Sons, Inc.
Companion website: www.wiley.com/go/Dujmovic/Soft_Computing_Evaluation_Logic

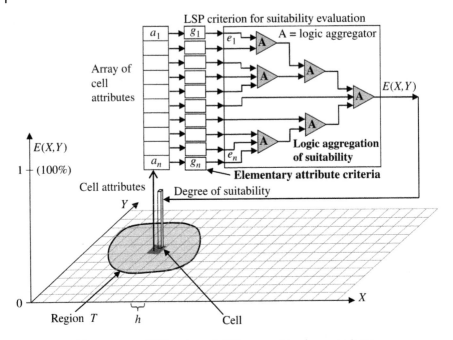

Figure 4.6.1 The concept of LSP raster suitability maps, based on map logic.

$i = 1,...,n$. Logic aggregation of attribute suitability maps generates the overall LSP suitability map $E(X,Y) = \lambda(e_1,...,e_n) = \lambda(g_1(a_1),...,g_n(a_n)) \in [0,1]$, $X_{min} \leq X \leq X_{max}$, $Y_{min} \leq Y \leq Y_{max}$. The process of logic aggregation of maps is called *map logic* and it represents a generalization of traditional map algebra. Of course, our goal is to identify areas of high suitability and to use them for rational and justifiable decision making.

The precision of LSP suitability maps depends on the cell size h. In GIS databases the size of cell (or pixel) can be rather small; e.g.: 16 ft × 16 ft = 256 ft^2 = 4.88 m × 4.88 m = 23.8 m^2. Theoretically, suitability maps can be created by computing suitability value for each pixel. That approach has two main disadvantages:

1) The number of pixels (cells) is typically very large and the consumption of resources (both memory space and processor time) can be substantial.
2) The adjacent pixels have frequently identical or slow changing characteristics and the suitability can change slowly or have areas of equal value.

Therefore, it can be reasonable to compute suitability in selected points (e.g., using a grid) and then to interpolate the suitability values in all other points. A simple interpolation method is shown in Fig. 4.6.2.

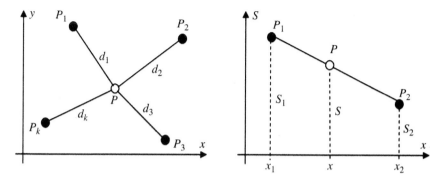

Figure 4.6.2 Point P surrounded by k adjacent points $P_1, ..., P_k$ and a special linear case $k = 2$.

Assuming that we have $k \geq 2$ points $P_1, ..., P_k$ with known suitability scores $S_1, ..., S_k$, let us compute the suitability S in point P. The distance between point P_i and P is d_i, $i = 1,...,k$. In this case, it is reasonable to use the following interpolation formula:

$$S = \frac{S_1 d_1^{-1} + S_2 d_2^{-1} + ... + S_k d_k^{-1}}{d_1^{-1} + d_2^{-1} + ... + d_k^{-1}}$$

$$= \frac{S_1/\sqrt{(x-x_1)^2 + (y-y_1)^2} + ... + S_k/\sqrt{(x-x_k)^2 + (y-y_k)^2}}{1/\sqrt{(x-x_1)^2 + (y-y_1)^2} + ... + 1/\sqrt{(x-x_k)^2 + (y-y_k)^2}}.$$

So, as P approaches to P_i, the suitability S approaches to S_i, $i = 1,...,k$. In the special linear case ($k = 2$, Fig. 4.6.2) this formula, as expected, yields the following linear interpolation:

$$S = \frac{S_1 d_1^{-1} + S_2 d_2^{-1}}{d_1^{-1} + d_2^{-1}} = \frac{S_1/(x-x_1) + S_2/(x_2-x)}{1/(x-x_1) + 1/(x_2-x)} = \frac{S_1(x_2-x) + S_2(x-x_1)}{x_2-x_1}.$$

Therefore, we can reduce the resource consumption by using lower density of cells and then computing the suitability using simple interpolation instead of more complex aggregation. The distance between points P and P_i can be defined as $d_i = \sqrt{(x-x_i)^2 + (y-y_i)^2}$ (the minimum Euclid walking distance), or as $d_i = |x-x_i| + |y-y_i|$ (the city block driving distance), or a weighted linear combination of these two distances.

The overall suitability can be computed in various situations, as illustrated in Fig. 4.6.3. The most frequent application is the comparison of suitability of several discrete locations (e.g., the suitability of selected locations A, B, and C for building an airport). The suitability can be computed along a line or a curve (e.g., a pipeline path suitability, or the suitability of building a rest area along the

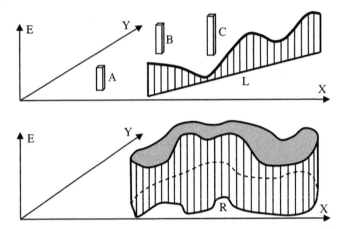

Figure 4.6.3 Suitability in discrete points A, B, C, along a path L, and in a closed region R.

highway L). Finally, the suitability can also be computed inside a closed region R or along its contour line (e.g., the suitability of a coastal line of an island for building new hotels, or the suitability of the area of the island for food production or for urban development).

The average suitability along the line/path/contour $Y = L(X)$ consisting of line segments $\ell_1, \ell_2, \ldots$ and inside the region R consisting of cells with areas $A_1, A_2, \ldots$ can be computed by averaging $E(X, Y)$ as follows:

$$\bar{E} = \frac{\displaystyle\int_L E(X,Y)\,d\ell}{\displaystyle\int_L d\ell} \approx \frac{\displaystyle\sum_i E(X_i, L(X_i))\ell_i}{\displaystyle\sum_i \ell_i} \quad, \quad \bar{E} = \frac{\displaystyle\iint_R E(X,Y)\,dXdY}{\displaystyle\iint_R dXdY} \approx \frac{\displaystyle\sum_{A_i \in R} E(X_i, Y_i)A_i}{\displaystyle\sum_{A_i \in R} A_i}$$

The mean suitability $\bar{E}$ is a useful indicator only if the distribution $E(X, Y)$ satisfies some basic acceptability criteria, primarily a sufficient smoothness and a low variability.

4.6.2 Suitability Maps Based on Points of Interest[1]

The majority of modern online maps (e.g., Google maps, GPS maps, and others) include a variety of points of interest (POIs). Typical POIs are the locations of services, stores, restaurants, public transportation stations, schools, and so on.

---

1 This section, based on [DUJ10b], benefited from contributions of **Mr. David Scheer**.

A sample distribution of bus stations, train stations, food stores, park entry points, restaurants, and public libraries in an urban square having the area of $4\,km^2$ is shown in Fig. 4.6.4. Our problem is to analyze the suitability of each point inside the square as a residence of a senior citizen who needs access to these POIs.

This problem was studied in Chapter 3.1 (Figs. 3.1.11, 3.1.12, and 3.1.14). We are now going to reuse the same attribute tree and elementary criteria. However, the logic aggregation structure shown in Fig. 4.6.4 is systematically relaxed (with respect to those used in Chapter 3.1) to reflect a less-demanding stakeholder who is ready to accept amenities aggregated using a weak substitutability, as well as transport options aggregated using a strong substitutability taken from WPM.17. In addition, the CPA aggregator is selected to provide a significant mean penalty of 30% for having no amenities and a relatively large reward of 40% for having all amenities.

Using the presented POIs, the balanced combined Euclid and city block distance metric applied to the closest POI, and the LSP criterion showed in Fig. 4.6.4, we get the LSP suitability maps for intermediate results presented in Figs. 4.6.5, 4.6.6, and 4.6.7, as well as the overall suitability map shown in Fig. 4.6.8. These maps are obtained using the pixel-wise LSP suitability evaluation and directly reflect the logic conditions specified in Fig. 4.6.4. In the black and white presentation, the dark areas denote high suitability.

It is important to note large white areas in Fig. 4.6.8 that correspond to zero overall suitability. In those areas, all locations fail to satisfy the stakeholder's mandatory criteria. Consequently, such areas are unacceptable from the stakeholder's standpoint. The dark areas of high suitability include the regions where the overall suitability is above 75%; these areas can be considered sufficiently suitable for stakeholder's home.

An alternative suitability map, based on standard additive aggregation functions [MAL99, MAL00], is shown in Fig. 4.6.9. This map uses the same primary attributes (access distances) and elementary criteria as the LSP map shown in Fig. 4.6.8 except that all logic aggregators are replaced by the weighted arithmetic mean. According to this map, all locations inside the analyzed square are to some extent suitable, even in areas where mandatory criteria are not met. The highest errors of the additive aggregation method can be seen in all regions where the 75% contour line of the additive model includes the areas that are in Fig. 4.6.8 proved to be fully unsuitable. Furthermore, if the disjunctive aggregators are replaced by the arithmetic mean, then the overall suitability may be improperly reduced, creating regions where the additive models unjustifiably suggest lower suitability than the LSP models (in this case, up to 6%). This is also inconsistent with the initially specified logic conditions. Obviously, additive models can easily generate wrong and unacceptable results.

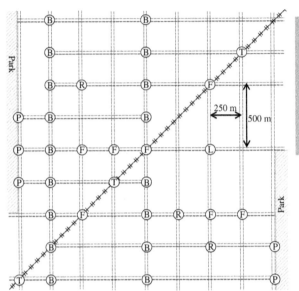

Analyzed urban area:
2 km × 2 km = 4 km²

B = bus station
T = train station
F = food store
P = park entrance
R = restaurant
L = public library

Suitability attribute tree	Logic conditions
Location of apartment/house	Must satisfy 75% of requirements
Services and stores	Mandatory (must be satisfied)
Public and transportation	Mandatory (must be satisfied)
Train stations	Substitutable by bus stations
Bus stations	Substitutable by train stations
Food stores	Mandatory (must be satisfied)
Amenities	Nonmandatory/partially substitutable
Parks	Most desired in the amenities group
Restaurants	More desired than libraries
Libraries	Desired

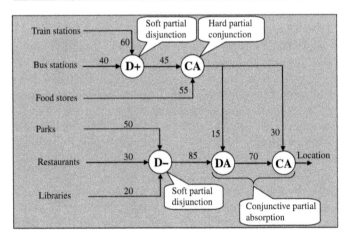

Figure 4.6.4 The distribution of points of interest in an urban area of 4 km², and the LSP criterion for development of suitability maps (WPM.17).

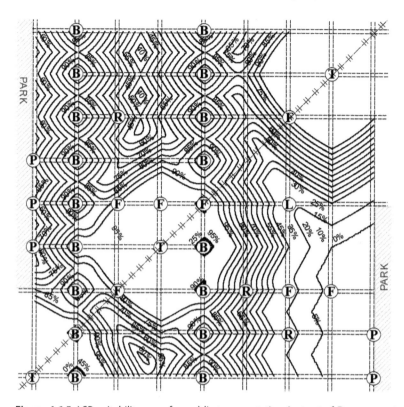

Figure 4.6.5 LSP suitability map for public transportation (output of D+ aggregator).

The differences between the LSP model and the additive weighted scoring model can also be expressed as a map, shown in Fig. 4.6.10. White areas denote regions where the LSP model and the additive model create similar (and correct) results. That happens primarily in the areas of highest suitability. The differences become significant in the areas that are not white in Fig. 4.6.10. These are mostly the areas of low (or zero) LSP suitability due to stakeholder's mandatory requirements, which cannot be expressed using additive models. In these areas additive models generate positive errors (denoted with "+" symbols in Fig. 4.6.10), suggesting much higher suitability than is actually derived from the stakeholder criteria. In addition, additive models also ignore stakeholder's disjunctive requirements, yielding the areas of negative errors (denoted with "−" symbols in Fig. 4.6.10). In these areas, additive models generate lower suitability than the LSP models.

The similarities between additive models and LSP models are an indirect consequence of the idempotency of averaging aggregators. Indeed, all averaging operators generate similar results if input values are close to the region of idempotency (similar values of inputs), and this is encountered whenever all input

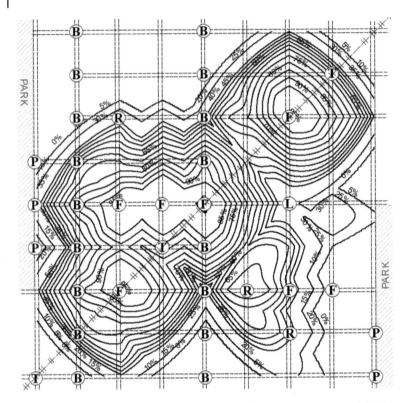

Figure 4.6.6 LSP suitability map for mandatory public transportation and food supply.

suitability values are rather high. Unfortunately, the fact that additive models can generate useful results causes illusion that additive models can generate useful results in all regions of the parameter space, which is not true. Even if the majority of the additive model errors are ignored (say, the lower 60% of suitability), a very significant error is still included. In order to generate correct (justifiable) suitability results in all regions of the parameter space, it is necessary to use nonlinear models of logic aggregation of suitability that precisely reflect the stakeholder's requirements. This fact is the main reason for the use of the LSP method in suitability maps and in other areas of evaluation.

4.6.3 The Problem of Optimum Location of City Objects

The primary use of LSP suitability maps is to compute the distribution of suitability score in a given region and in making decisions based on these results.

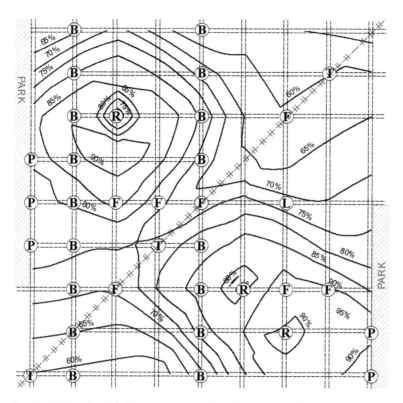

Figure 4.6.7 LSP suitability map for amenities (the output of D- aggregator).

Another area of application is the analysis of the optimum location of city objects (insertion of new POIs). Let $E_m(x, y)$ be the overall suitability in point (x,y) of region R caused by m POIs. Let us now add one more POI, and compute $E_{m+1}(x,y)$. We differentiate two cases: positive POI and negative POI. The positive POI is each POI where $E_{m+1}(x,y) \geq E_m(x,y)$, $(x,y) \in R$. Examples of positive POIs are all desirable services and amenities. The negative POI is each POI where $E_{m+1}(x,y) \leq E_m(x,y)$, $(x,y) \in R$. Examples of negative POIs are all POIs that cause pollution (chemical or acoustic), or bring undesirable activities, or reduce the safety of the region R. The introduction of a new POI in the location (x_{POI}, y_{POI}) causes the following *average suitability increment* in the analyzed region R:

$$D(x_{POI}, y_{POI}) = \frac{\iint\limits_R E_{m+1}(x,y)\,dxdy - \iint\limits_R E_m(x,y)\,dxdy}{\iint\limits_R dxdy}$$

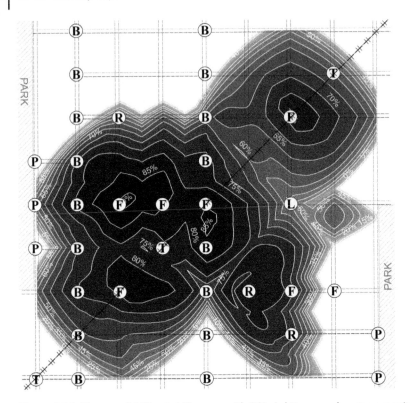

Figure 4.6.8 The overall LSP suitability map with POIs (white areas denote zero suitability).

We can present $D(x_{POI}, y_{POI})$ as a map. For example, Fig. 4.6.11 shows the map of suitability increment when adding a new food store in all cells of the previously analyzed square region that has the area of $4\,km^2$. The new food store should be located in the areas of high suitability increment. Therefore, if the new food store is located in the upper-left quadrant of the analyzed quadrangle, it is possible to attain the average value of performance increment that is above 8%. The addition of a new food store in other regions has insignificant or negligible effect on the improvement of suitability because the existing food stores already satisfy the food store requirements.

The addition of the food store is an example of a positive POI. In the case of a negative POI, $D(x_{POI}, y_{POI}) < 0$, and the location (x_{POI}, y_{POI}) should be selected so to minimize the negative impact (and this is again the point of the maximum value of $D(x_{POI}, y_{POI})$).

LSP suitability maps can be evaluated from the following two standpoints: (1) the degree of expressive power of used mathematical models and (2) satisfaction of the explicit logic requirements specified by the stakeholder.

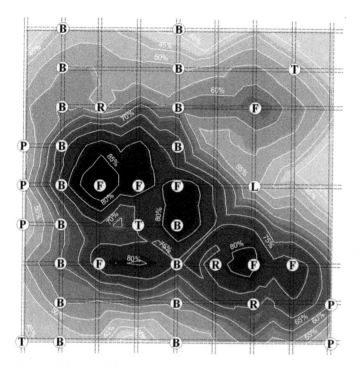

Figure 4.6.9 A suitability map based on strictly additive aggregation functions.

Let us first discuss the issue of expressive power. In human reasoning, some criteria include components that are mandatory and some include components that are nonmandatory (optional). Once we know that this is an indispensable component of human evaluation reasoning, it is unacceptable to ignore this fact and behave as if all attributes are optional or all are mandatory. However, published suitability studies are still dominated by the use of a fixed aggregator, most frequently the arithmetic mean (e.g., [PAL02]) or the geometric mean (e.g., [VAN04]). Such models make all attributes strictly optional (the arithmetic mean) or strictly mandatory (the geometric mean). Obviously, that is unacceptable because it is inconsistent with observable properties of human evaluation reasoning (see Chapter 2.2). Similarly, it is easy to find many examples where human evaluators combine mandatory (or sufficient) and optional requirements. This immediately creates the need for the partial absorption function and delimitation of hard and soft partial conjunction/disjunction.

These conditions and others discussed in *Part Two* show that LSP models satisfy all necessary logic conditions, whereas other multiattribute models satisfy only a subset of necessary conditions. LSP models use flexible aggregators that can express any level of andness and orness, as well as compound asymmetric

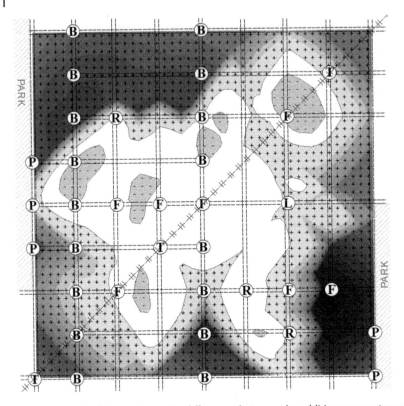

Figure 4.6.10 Positive and negative differences between the additive aggregators map and the LSP map.

aggregators. In particular, the presented LSP model is capable of satisfying all of the explicit logic requirements of the decision maker exemplified in Fig. 4.6.4. In the verification process of LSP maps, we first investigate areas where mandatory requirements are not satisfied. These areas must have zero suitability. The next step is to verify the suitability in areas known to the evaluator. During these *spot checks,* evaluators may discover through sensitivity analysis that some requirements are too severe or too soft and will then fine-tune LSP criteria to bring results into compliance with expectations of the stakeholder.

Decision methods that are used in space management and land-use evaluation problems cannot be selected randomly or without appropriate justification. The justification for using a specific evaluation method in a GIS environment should be based on investigating the capability of the method to support features that are proved to characterize human decision making. Many oversimplifications that are frequent in GIS literature (particularly those based on simple additive models) originate from the fact that they are "easy-to-understand

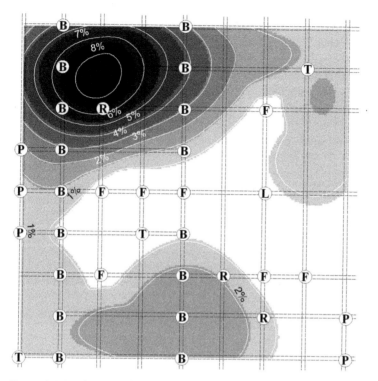

Figure 4.6.11 The map of food store suitability increment $D(x_{POI}, y_{POI})$.

and intuitively appealing to decision-makers" [MAL06]. Unfortunately, that is provably not enough. Before using mathematical models, it is first necessary to prove that they are capable of generating meaningful results in all desired application domains and under all conditions.

Prerequisites for correct modeling of decision maker's requirements are the availability of flexible GCD aggregators that can model conjunction, hard partial conjunction, soft partial conjunction, neutrality, soft partial disjunction, hard partial disjunction, and disjunction. All other aggregators that do not support the above seven fundamental logic aggregation properties frequently generate wrong results that are inconsistent with requirements and justifiable expectations of decision makers.

The LSP map logic is a highly expressive generalization of the map algebra, aggregating through a sequence of intermediate maps. Consequently, the LSP method can provide highly accurate and justifiable models for GIS applications, such as suitability maps, land-use evaluation, and natural resources planning. Indeed, the land-use evaluation and suitability maps are primarily logic decision problems solvable using GL aggregators and LSP criteria.

4.6.4 Suitability Analysis of Urban Locations Using the LSPmap Tool

In this section we present LSP suitability maps created by the LSPmap web application [SEA11]. Our goal is to present LSP maps that can be developed and used by nonprofessional users to evaluate the suitability of a location of home or apartment in urban areas. The decision about the suitability of a given location depends on the easy access to points of interest (POIs) that are important for a specific decision maker. Typical POIs that are taken into account include stores, restaurants, schools, parks, and public transportation stations, selected among almost 100 different types of POIs that are available in online maps. In each point, the decision maker can determine the overall suitability based on proximity to selected POIs. The distribution of such suitability values is the POIs suitability map.

The majority of modern online maps (e.g., Google maps [GGL16b], GPS maps, and others) include a variety of points of interest. In particular, Google offers several APIs for accessing the database containing a wide variety of POIs [GGL16a]. We use Google maps and Google API to develop LSP/POI suitability maps that are displayed as a (transparent, semitransparent, or nontransparent) layer on top of Google maps.

Selecting Elementary Attributes
The first step in building an LSP criterion function consists of selecting elementary input attributes. In the case of POI-based suitability maps, the attributes are distances from specific categories of POIs. There are various ways to evaluate categories of POIs (e.g., restaurants, schools, stores, etc.). For simplicity, in this presentation we use attributes that are defined as distances from the closest POI of specific type, and select their groups based on the desired type of suitability map. A menu for selecting one among eleven editable (adjustable) types of LSP/POI maps is shown in Fig. 4.6.12.

Each type of LSP/POI map is defined using a set of representative POIs that describe the needs of specific category of users. For example, the "Students" category is described using the following 12 POIs: bookstore, bus station, coffee shop, college, deli, fast-food restaurant, grocery store, gym, library, swimming pool, tennis court, and train station. The "Retirement" category is characterized by 16 POIs: bus station, church, coffee shop, farmers market, garden center, grocery store, hospital, library, medical center, park, pharmacy, restaurant, taxi service, tea house, train station, and travel agency. For the first 10 types we use predefined but editable representative sets of POIs. In the last category, denoted as "make your own map," the user is offered a list of 94 types of POIs to select appropriate subset and use it in creating a desires specific LSP/POI map.

Figure 4.6.12 A menu for selecting the type of LSP/POI suitability map.

Young Family Home

Arts
Business
Children
Entertainment
Healthy Living
Retirement
Shopping and Dining
Students
Walkability
Young Family Home
MAKE YOUR OWN MAP

Canonical Forms of Elementary Criteria

The second step in building an LSP criterion function consists of building elementary criteria for evaluation of input attributes. Since our attributes are distances from an evaluated location to selected POIs, it is convenient to differentiate three canonical forms introduced in Section 3.1.3: (1) preferred large distances, (2) preferred small distances, and (3) preferred range of distances. The first case occurs in situations where the decision maker wants to avoid vicinity of undesirable objects. Indeed, some decision makers would not like to live next door to a funeral home, cemetery, airport, hospital, or a very popular restaurant. The second case corresponds to situations where proximity to selected POIs is desirable. That might be the case of proximity to parks, grocery stores, or children day care centers. In the third case, the decision maker wants to avoid both the excessive proximity and the excessive distance. Such criteria are frequently used for restaurants and schools: excessive proximity is generally inconvenient (noise, too much traffic, etc.), but a walking distance is highly desirable, yielding a preferred range of distances.

The presented three canonical forms of elementary criteria are implemented in the LSPmap system using the interface shown in Fig. 4.6.13. These forms are convenient for nonprofessional decision makers, because of simplicity in selecting parameters A, B, C, D. The users can select three types of inputs: A, B only (A < B), or C, D only (C < D), or all four parameters A, B, C, D (A < B < C < D). This interface also specifies the logic aggregation.

Canonical Logic Aggregation Structure

The suitability aggregation process is based on the canonical aggregation structure (CAS) presented in Fig. 4.6.14. The design of this CAS is presented in Section 3.5.4. This structure is selected taking into account that the maps must be produced and used by nonprofessional decision makers, the

CUSTOMIZING THE ATTRIBUTE CRITERION [Show Suitability Map]

The values A,B,C,D are used for defining the attribute criterion. There are three available types of attribute criteria.
1. Select C and D only (C<D) if you prefer small values of the attribute (e.g. a small distance from a grocery store)
2. Select A and B only (A<B) if you prefer large values of the attribute (e.g. a large distance from a cemetery)
3. Select A,B,C,D (A<B<C<D) if you prefer a range of values (e.g. neither too close nor too far from a restaurant)

Attribute (POI)	Type of Attribute	Relative importance level 1-9	A — I will not be satisfied at all if the distance, in yards, is less than or equal to:	B — I will be perfectly satisfied if the distance, in yards, is greater than or equal to:	C — I will be perfectly satisfied if the distance, in yards, is less than or equal to:	D — I will not be satisfied at all if the distance, in yards, is greater than or equal to:
Barber Shop	Optional ▼	5 = medium ▼	Not Used ▼	Not Used ▼	200 ▼	800 ▼
Beauty Salon	Optional ▼	Select / 1 = lowest / 2 = very low	Not Used ▼	Not Used ▼	200 ▼	800 ▼
Church	Not Included ▼	3 = low / 4 = medium-low	Not Used ▼	Not Used ▼	200 ▼	800 ▼
Dry Cleaner	Optional ▼	5 = medium	Not Used ▼	Not Used ▼	200 ▼	1000 ▼
Gym	Mandatory ▼	6 = medium-high / 7 = high	Not Used ▼	Not Used ▼	200 ▼	800 ▼
Laundromat	Optional ▼	8 = very high / 9 = highest	Not Used ▼	Not Used ▼	200 ▼	600 ▼
Park	Optional ▼	6 = medium-high ▼	Not Used ▼	Not Used ▼	500 ▼	2500 ▼
Parking Garage	Mandatory ▼	7 = high ▼	Not Used ▼	Not Used ▼	200 ▼	800 ▼
Pharmacy	Optional ▼	6 = medium-high ▼	Not Used ▼	Not Used ▼	200 ▼	800 ▼
Post Office	Optional ▼	5 = medium ▼	Not Used ▼	Not Used ▼	200 ▼	800 ▼
Restaurant	Optional ▼	5 = medium ▼	Not Used ▼	Not Used ▼	200 ▼	800 ▼
Supermarket	Mandatory ▼	7 = high ▼	Not Used ▼	Not Used ▼	100 ▼	600 ▼

REQUIREMENTS: [Standard ▼] MAP DISPLAY OPTIONS: [Show Scores ▼] [Selected POIs ▼] [Color Overlay ▼] [50% transparent ▼] [Hide Home Marker ▼]

Show Suitability Map

Figure 4.6.13 LSPmap interface for customizing the criterion for POI-based suitability.

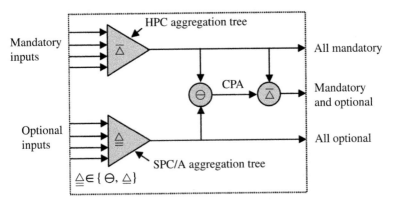

Figure 4.6.14 The map logic aggregation structure for LSP/POI suitability maps.

aggregation structure should not be too complex, the number of input attributes in LSP/POI maps is usually small (e.g., less than 20), and the high precision of results is not critical. So, the users should specify POIs that are mandatory and POIs that are optional, and for each selected attribute they should select the degree of importance as shown in Fig. 4.6.13. In addition to regular (mandatory and optional) output, this aggregation structure also provides two special cases where all inputs are mandatory or all inputs are optional.

In the first step of the adjustment of aggregation structure in Fig. 4.6.13 users are requested to select the type of attributes: each attribute can be mandatory, or optional, or not included in the LSP/POI map. Mandatory attributes are aggregated using a HPC aggregation tree, and optional attributes are aggregated using a SPC tree. The results of the two preliminary aggregations are then combined using the CPA aggregator.

Each input in the LSP/POI model can have nine verbalized levels of relative importance (from 1 = lowest to 9 = highest), as illustrated in Fig. 4.6.13. The selected levels are then used to compute relative weights of attributes. For example, if we use three attributes that have the importance levels 8, 7, 5, they will be aggregated using normalized weights $8/20 = 0.4$, $7/20 = 0.35$, and $5/20 = 0.25$.

Nonprofessional users cannot perform fine-tuning of properties of the CPA, HPC, and SPC aggregator. However, it is convenient to offer users to select between three levels of severity of requirements (*relaxed, standard,* and *strict*), shown in Fig. 4.6.13 and in Table 4.6.1 (for more detail, see Section 3.5.4). As the requirements move from *relaxed* to *strict*, the penalty of CPA increases, the reward decreases, and the andness of HPC and SPC aggregators increase.

Implementing LSP/POI Suitability Maps

Our implementation of LSP/POI suitability maps (LSPmap [SEA11]) is based on Google maps and the suitability map is presented as either gray or color-coded layer with adjustable transparency on top of a Google map of specific area.

Table 4.6.1 Three selectable levels of requirements.

Aggregated Mandatory/ Optional CAS Parameters	Requirements		
	Relaxed	**Standard**	**Strict**
Mean CPA penalty [%]	15	30	45
Mean CPA reward [%]	30	25	20
HPC andness [%]	67	77	87
SPC andness [%]	38	50	62

The default area is a 2-mile square divided into $35 \times 35 = 1225$ cells, where in each cell we compute suitability according to a selected LSP/POI criterion (e.g., young family home requirements, suitability for children, healthy living, retirement, etc.).

A typical black-and-white transparent LSP suitability map with POIs and visible cell structure and cell suitability scores, on top of a Google map of Sunset area in San Francisco, is shown in Fig. 4.6.15. Of course, black-and-white maps are less convenient than color maps where we use the "traffic light" color coding: areas of high suitability are green, areas of low suitability are red, and the average suitability is yellow.

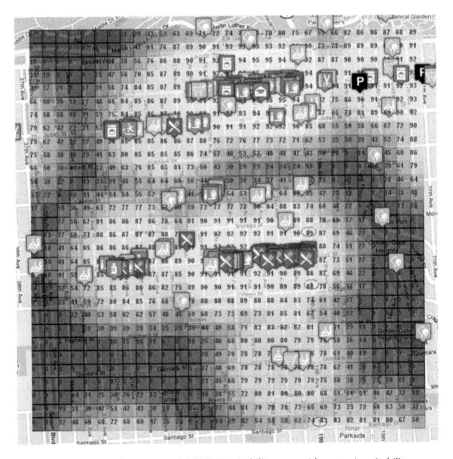

Figure 4.6.15 A sample transparent LSP/POI suitability map with numeric suitability scores [%].

4.6.5 GIS-LSP Suitability Maps Based on TerrSet/Idrisi

The integration of LSP method with raster-GIS and geospatial data has been made to generate LSP maps. Idrisi GIS software is a geographic information system developed by Clark Labs in the mid-1980s [CLA16] to facilitate GIS and remote sensing analysis as well as multicriteria evaluation methods [MAL99]. LSP method was implemented with IDRISI GIS software related to series of projects with geographical context, as reported in [DRA18, HAT14, MON15a, MON15b, MON16a, MON16b, MON16c].

Residential Development

The first such project was a residential development suitability analysis for Bowen Island Municipality, Canada [DRA18]. A more detailed criterion for urban residential land development and use was presented in [HAT14]. This criterion (based on 20 attributes) is suitable for urban planners and developers.

The version outlined in Fig. 4.6.16 (a refinement of the model shown in Fig. 4.5.6) was prepared for the Vancouver metropolitan area. It used three different stakeholder scenarios that resulted in three different suitability aggregation structures. Different scenarios are implemented using different

```
1 Urban residential land use
  11 Terrain and environment
    111 Slope [degrees] {(30,100), (40,0)}
    112 Aspect [degrees] {(45,0), (135,100), (225,100), (315,0)}
    113 Elevation [meters] {(50,100), (1000,0)}
  12 Accessibility
    121 Distance to major roads [meters] {(0,0), (100,100), (500,100), (2000,0)}
    122 Distance to public transportation / bus lines [meters] {(0,0), (100,100), (250,100), (1000,0)}
    123 Distance to light rail transit [meters] {(0,100), (1500,75), (3000,0)}
    124 Distance to airport [km] {(0,0), (2,100), (20,100), (50,0)}
    125 % of population using sustainable transportation [%] {(0,0), (40,100)}
  13 Amenities
    131 Distance to beach [km] {(5,100), (15,0)}
    132 Distance to coast [meters] {(0,0), (100,100), (200,100), (2000,0)}
    133 Distance to parks [meters] {(200,100), (2000,0)}
    134 Distance to shopping centers [km] {(5,100), (15,0)}
    135 Distance to healthcare facilities [km] {(5,100), (20,0)
    136 Distance to schools [meters] {(0,0), (200,100), (1500,100), (10000,0)}
  14 Population
    141 Distance to residential housing areas [meters] {(100,100), (1000,0)}
    142 Population density (distance to low density areas) [pop/km²] {(min,100), (max,0)}
    143 Family areas (% of population with children) [%] {(0,0), (15,100)}
    144 Population growth in the analyzed area [%] {(0,0), (max,100)}
    145 Median income in the analyzed area [monetary units] {(min, 100), (max,0)}
    146 Average housing prices [monetary units] {(min, 100), (max,0)}
```

Figure 4.6.16 An attribute tree and elementary criteria for urban residential land use analysis of the Vancouver metropolitan area.

distributions of weights and appropriate selection of aggregation operators, producing different suitability maps and illustrating the use of LSP maps as flexible decision support tools.

A more condensed 15-attribute LSP model for urban land use suitability analysis is proposed in [MON16c]. That paper also discusses software details for modeling LSP aggregation functions in Idrisi. In addition, it includes a comparison of suitability maps generated by the GIS-based AHP, OWA, AHP-OWA, and LSP methods.

LSP Applications in Agriculture

LSP maps are convenient tools for the analysis of land capability and suitability for agriculture [MON15a, MON15b, MON16a, MON16b, PAS12, REB14, REB16]. Two related criteria proposed in [MON16b] are the land capability criterion and the suitability for agriculture criterion. The land capability criterion plays the fundamental role and includes terrain (slope, evaluation, and aspect), fertility (soil texture, and organic matter), depth (depth to restrictive layer, and available water), and density (drainage class, and bulk density).

In order to develop a criterion for suitability for agriculture the land capability criterion is expanded with four more groups of attributes: climate, economics, accessibility, and management. The climate is evaluated using precipitation, temperature, frost-free days, water retention, and flooding. Economic effects are evaluated using cash crops demand, and economic hazards. The accessibility depends on location of highly capable soils, the distance of water for irrigation, the distance to open space, and the distances to local roads and major roads. The attributes related to management include the crop type, farm product consumption, designated land use (urban/forest/wetlands/grassland/open space), and zoning (forest/commercial/residential/rural/agriculture).

A sample aggregation structure (map logic) for evaluating suitability for agriculture is shown in Fig. 4.6.17. It includes the land capability criterion expanded with other attributes (total 31) for climate, accessibility, management, and economics. The analyzed area was Boulder County, Colorado, USA, where careful land-use planning is necessary to balance agricultural and urban development. The corresponding suitability map is shown in Fig. 4.6.18, where darkest areas denote missing data and/or the lowest suitability. More detail and the results of using multiple scenarios can be found in [MON15a, MON16b].

Suitability maps show the spatial distribution of suitability in selected region. Similarly to all other distributions, LSP suitability maps can be summarized in various statistical ways. One such summary is presented in Fig. 4.6.19. It shows that 33.8% of the analyzed area has the suitability for agriculture that is above the average. Taking into account that in the 39.6% of the analyzed area input data were not available, we can estimate that approximately 56% of the analyzed area is convincingly suitable for agriculture.

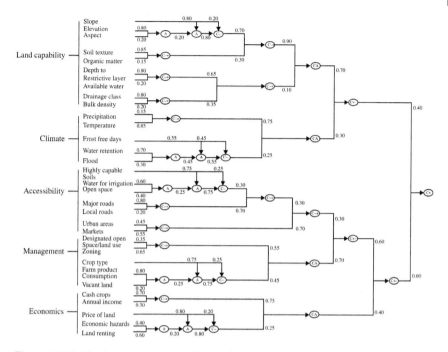

Figure 4.6.17 Map logic structure used for evaluation of suitability for agriculture [MON15a].

4.6.6 GIS-LSP Suitability Maps Based on ArcGIS

In this section, we present LSP suitability maps based on ArcGIS [ESR16]. LSP criteria and ArcGIS system are combined in the work of Yufei Zhuang [ZHU14]. The goal of Zhuang's work was to provide logic aggregation of suitability on top of basic ArcGIS functionality [WAY03, ESR09, ESR10] and to develop a graphical user interface capable of accepting and editing user requirements in order to create customized LSP suitability maps.

Let us first illustrate the LSP map logic using a simple example of creating a suitability map, layer by layer. An attribute map of the vicinity to parks in San Francisco is shown in Fig. 4.6.20. The corresponding attribute criterion is expressed as distance in feet: $Crit(P \, [\text{ft}]) = \{(200, 100), (3000, 0)\}$. The usual color coding of suitability (red = unsuitable, yellow = average suitability, green = maximum suitability) is transformed in Fig. 4.6.20 in black and white as follows: dark regions represent parks or green areas, or areas that are not considered; yellow is transformed to the light gray areas; green is shown as darker circular gray areas around parks. So, this map shows a typical distribution of circular suitable areas

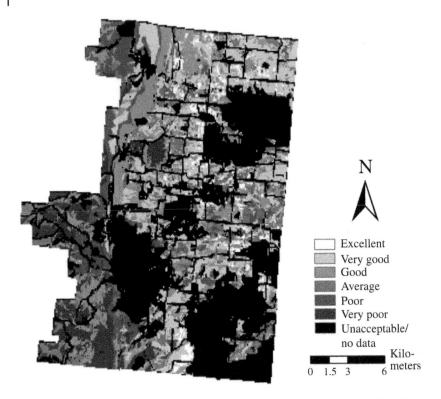

Figure 4.6.18 Suitability map of the overall suitability for agriculture for Boulder County, Colorado, USA [MON15a].

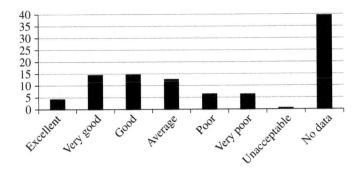

Figure 4.6.19 Agricultural suitability distribution in the analyzed area [%].

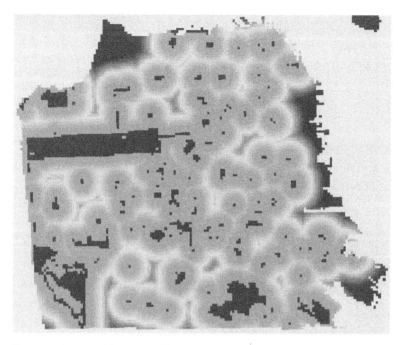

Figure 4.6.20 Suitability map of San Francisco for distance from parks *Crit(P)*.

around big and small parks (the biggest is the Golden Gate Park, shown as a large rectangular dark area close to Pacific Ocean in the left part of the map).

The next attribute map is the distance from public schools, shown in Fig. 4.6.21. Public schools are denoted as points of interest and show relatively uniform distribution in most areas of the city. The attribute criterion used for this map is *Crit(S* [ft]) = {(200, 100), (9000, 0)}, where *S* denotes the distance from the nearest school. This criterion permits rather large distances because of the availability of public transportation. The darkest areas in this map are those that don't have suitable access to public schools and the lightest areas are those that show modest (average) suitability because they are located equally far from the available public schools.

The last attribute map in this example is the distance from health care facilities shown in Fig. 4.6.22. Health care facilities are denoted *H* and the elementary attribute criterion used for this map is *Crit(H* [ft]) = {(300, 100), (10000, 0)}, where *H* denotes the distance from the nearest healthcare facility. This criterion assumes that the health care facilities are reachable by car or public transport. In other words, the health care facilities are not required to be in the immediate proximity of residential areas.

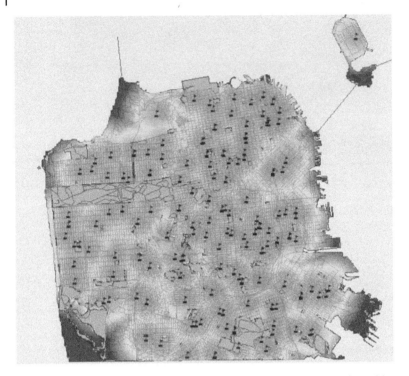

Figure 4.6.21 Suitability map of San Francisco for distance from schools *Crit(S)*.

The attribute suitability maps can be logically aggregated to create an overall suitability map. In this example, a simple CPA aggregation structure is shown in Fig 4.6.23. The aggregation structure reflects the standpoint of young people interested in mandatory schools and parks for children, and very little in hospitals. The aggregator G denotes the geometric mean (HPC). So, the overall suitability is $X(P,S,H) = \sqrt{(0.8\sqrt{PS} + 0.2H)\sqrt{PS}}$. If $P = S = 0.5$ then from $X(0.5, 0.5, 1) = \sqrt{0.3} = 0.55$ and $X(0.5, 0.5, 0) = \sqrt{0.2} = 0.45$ it follows that in this case the penalty and reward for proximity to hospitals are small (the order of 10%). The resulting aggregated LSP suitability map based on ArcGIS with contour lines for the overall suitability is shown in Fig. 4.6.24.

The presented example shows that LSP aggregation structures can be interpreted as a logic form of map algebra. Inputs are suitability maps of attributes. In each node of the aggregation tree, we get a new suitability map. Eventually, in the root of the aggregation tree we generate the map of overall suitability. In

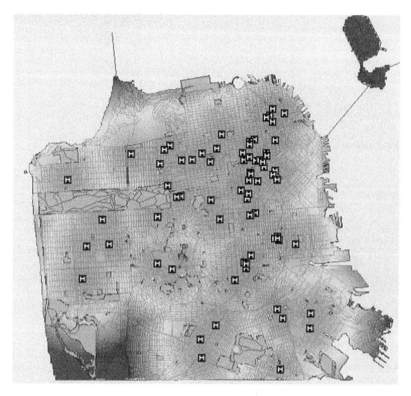

Figure 4.6.22 Suitability map of San Francisco for distance from health care facilities *Crit(H)*.

Figure 4.6.23 A simple map logic based on arithmetic and geometric means.

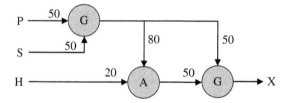

cases where the analysis includes the distribution of cost, we can use a traditional suitability/affordability analysis to combine a cost map and the overall suitability map to generate the overall value map.

In all cases of suitability maps, it is useful to compute the distribution of suitability in selected area. Six characteristic forms of suitability distribution (from very low to very high) are shown in Fig. 4.6.25. Medium distributions can be

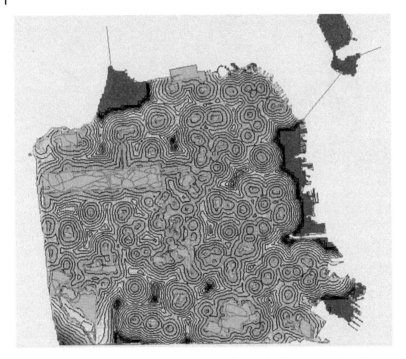

Figure 4.6.24 Overall (aggregated) LSP suitability map of San Francisco with contour lines.

homogeneous (if suitability scores are similar) and heterogeneous (if the distribution of suitability scores are close to uniform). For uniform distribution in [0,1], the mean value is 0.5 and the standard deviation is $1/\sqrt{12}$; the corresponding coefficient of variation is $1/\sqrt{3}$ or 57.7%. Using the suitability distribution analysis technique introduced in [YOK12], and a tool developed in [ZHU14], we made sample suitability distributions for the Sunset district in San Francisco, shown in Fig. 4.6.26.

The most important suitability distribution is the dstribution of overall suitability. A comprehensive criterion for quality of urban locations in San Francisco produced the result for a selected downtown area shown in Fig. 4.6.27. The resulting distribution can be classified as good (mean overall suitability of 61% and coefficient of variation of 29%). This distribution is based on 26 attributes grouped as follows: *physical environment* (elevation, air pollution, park/green areas), *social environment* (population density, house density, community centers), *accessibility and transport* (bus/train stations, parking), *safety* (crime rate, fire stations, police stations), *food supplies* (food vendors, grocery stores, farmers market), *general supplies* (pharmacies, liquor stores, shopping centers), *health services* (medical offices, recreation centers), *children services* (childcare

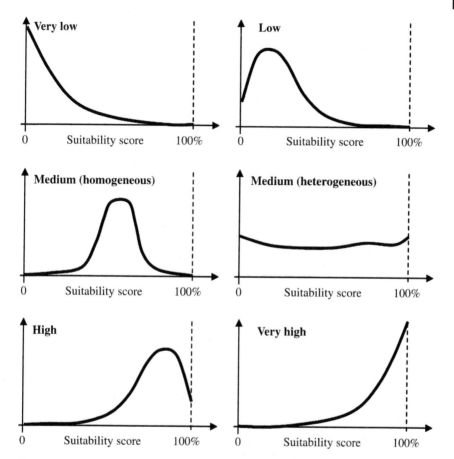

Figure 4.6.25 Six characteristic forms of suitability distribution.

centers, schools), *general services* (banks, post offices), *amenities* (restaurants, theaters, public libraries).

Some of these attributes are classified as mandatory (e.g., low crime rate, food vendors, grocery stores, medical offices, etc.) and others are optional, i.e., desired but not mandatory (e.g., farmers markets, fire station proximity, public libraries, etc.). Of course, the main problem in the evaluation of the quality of urban locations is the availability of reliable input attribute data. If the data for specific attributes are not available, then such attributes must be omitted and LSP criteria must be developed using only those attributes that are available in the analyzed city. Incompleteness of input data is a frequent problem in the area of suitability maps. It can reduce the applicability of any quantitative evaluation method.

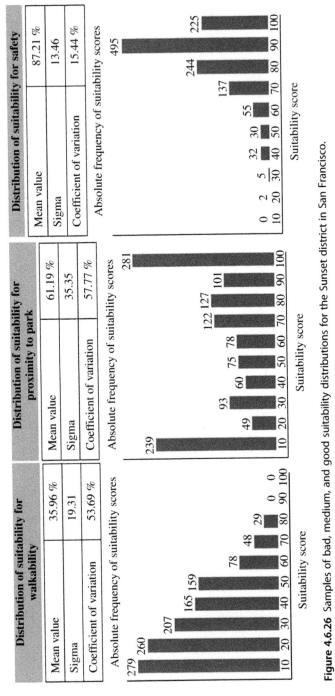

Distribution of suitability for walkability	
Mean value	35.96 %
Sigma	19.31
Coefficient of variation	53.69 %

Distribution of suitability for proximity to park	
Mean value	61.19 %
Sigma	35.35
Coefficient of variation	57.77 %

Distribution of suitability for safety	
Mean value	87.21 %
Sigma	13.46
Coefficient of variation	15.44 %

Figure 4.6.26 Samples of bad, medium, and good suitability distributions for the Sunset district in San Francisco.

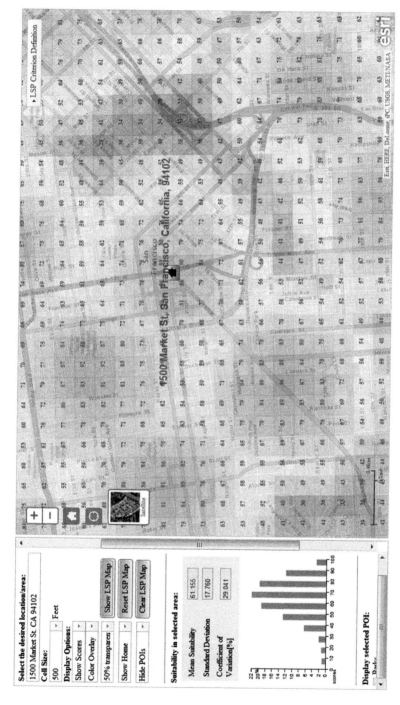

Figure 4.6.27 Suitability analysis of selected area in downtown San Francisco [ZHU14].

The conclusion of our study of LSP suitability maps is that each suitability map is primarily a logic problem that should be solved using the map logic approach. A complete LSP infrastructure for creating and using logic suitability maps is available and can be used to replace the oversimplified additive aggregation models, traditionally used in GIS practice in the context of WLC, AHP, OWA or fuzzy additive weighting [MAL99, MAL14]. Graphic interpretation of GIS results provides an easy way to detect wrong and unacceptable results and to justify rejection of strictly additive scoring models, as shown in previous chapters and in [DUJ10b, DRA18].

4.7 Evaluation and Comparison of Search Engines

Search engines (SE) were introduced in 1993, and the first attempts to develop techniques for their evaluation were published in 1996 [CHU96]. During the period from 1996 to 2006, search technology made a significant progress [BRI98, BAE99, SPA97, CHA03, HAW06] and search engines became the most influential web tools. Table 4.7.1 presents a survey of major search engines available in 2006 [DUJ06c, BAI07] and 10 years later, in 2016. Some of the presented engines use proprietary search technology (PST), some of them are meta search engines that distill and aggregate results of multiple PST search engines, and some of them offer specialized search services using a selected PST provider.

General search services are accessible through all web browsers (e.g., Chrome, IE, etc.) and are also offered by various Internet service providers (e.g., AOL). According to survey reported by searchenginewatch.com in July 2006, out of the 5.6 billion searches placed in that month, the leading GYM trio (Google, Yahoo, Microsoft) handled more than 80% of the total traffic, with Google taking a leading 49.2% (see [BAE99] for a very different distribution in 1998, and [RAT16] where the worldwide market share in 2016 is Google 72.48%, Bing 10.39%, Yahoo 7.78% and Ask 0.22%). A ranking of search engines based on Estimated Unique Monthly Visitors (EUMV), provided by [EBI16], is also shown in Table 4.7.1. Shaded search engines those that appear in both 2006 and 2016 ranking.

General industrial ranking of popular search engines is usually based on the recorded traffic intensity or market share, and research papers in the area of information retrieval are primarily focused on selected aspects of search technology. Consequently, in most cases search engines are not quantitatively evaluated as complex industrial products that are designed to satisfy specific user requirements.

There are two basic problems related to decision aspects of SE evaluation: (1) the area of search engines is very dynamic, characterized by permanent developments and improvements, so that specific requirements can quickly become

Soft Computing Evaluation Logic: The LSP Decision Method and Its Applications,
First Edition. Jozo Dujmović.
© 2018 John Wiley & Sons, Inc. Published 2018 by John Wiley & Sons, Inc.
Companion website: www.wiley.com/go/Dujmovic/Soft_Computing_Evaluation_Logic

Table 4.7.1 A survey of search engines 2006–2016.

English Domain SE Introduced before 2006				SE Ranking in August 2016		
Search Engine	Begin [year]	Traffic July'06	Type May'06	Rank	Search Engine	EUMV [million]
Aliweb	1993	-	PST	1	Google	1600
WebCrawler	1994	-	Meta	2	Bing	400
Infoseek/Go	1994	-	Provider	3	Yahoo! Search	300
Lycos	1994	-	PST	4	Ask	245
Altavista	1995	-	Provider	5	AOL Search	125
Excite	1995	-	Meta	6	WOW	100
Mamma	1996	-	Meta	7	WebCrawler	65
Dogpile	1996	-	Meta	8	MyWebSearch	60
Ask	1996	2.6%	PST	9	Infospace	24
Google	1998	49.2%	PST	10	Info	13.5
AlltheWeb	1999	-	Provider	11	DuckDuckGo	13
Teoma	2000	-	Provider	12	Contenko	11
Vivisimo	2000	-	PST	13	Dogpile	10.5
Kartoo	2001	-	Meta	14	Alhea	7.5
AOL Search	2003	6.3%	Provider	15	ixQuick	4
Yahoo! Search	2004	23.8%	PST			
MSN Search	2004	9.6%	PST			
A9	2004	-	PST			
Snap	2004	-	PST			
Quaero	2006	-	PST			

obsolete, and (2) stakeholders can vary in the wide spectrum from recreational to highly professional users, generating very different workloads and different requirements that search engines must satisfy. Taking into account the nature of SE evaluation problems, our goal in this chapter is to present the methodology for building comprehensive LSP decision models for evaluation and comparison of general PST search engines. We are not going to evaluate a particular SE for a particular stakeholder in a specific point in time, but to show how to develop criteria that aggregate functionality, usability and measured performance of search engines to generate a compound indicator of the overall SE suitability taking into account the needs of both nonprofessional and professional searches. Our goal is to develop a criterion that is fully consistent with the ISO and IEEE standards for software product evaluation [ISO91, IEE93].

4.7.1 Search Engine User and Workload Models

All parameters of SE evaluation models, as well as the SE benchmark workloads, reflect a specific model of the SE user. We characterize users by two primary attributes: (1) volume, and (2) significance of search. The volume is measured in searches per day of a specific topic. In Table 4.7.2 the significance is

Table 4.7.2 Characteristic search engine users.

Symbol	Type of search engine user	Volume of search	Significance of search
GP	General population	High	Low
SU	Specialized user	Low	High

Table 4.7.3 Top 10 Google queries in years 2002, 2003, and 2004.

Rank	2002	2003	2004
1	BBC	Prince Charles	BBC News
2	Big Brother	Eastenders	Big Brother
3	Easyjet	Winnie the Pooh	CBBC
4	Britney Spears	Jonny Wilkinson	Autotrader
5	Ryanair	Easyjet	Dictionary
6	Gareth Gates	David Beckham	Tesco
7	Weather	Michael Jackson	Eastenders
8	Kylie Mingue	2 fast 2 furious	Weather
9	World Cup	Paris Hilton	British Airways
10	Holly Valance	Simpsons	National Lottery

characterized as "low" if the search is purely recreational (as the majority of searches in Table 4.7.3). The significance is "high" if the results of search significantly affect professional work, health, security, and family activities. That yields two characteristic extreme types of users shown in Table 4.7.2.

Short-term high-intensity search traffic is generated by special events that cause high level of public interest. Such events are illustrated by the search frequency distribution shown in Fig. 4.7.1 [GGL06, GGL16]. After important events (e.g., natural disasters, war events, global-scale diseases, terrorist attacks, events related to celebrities, sport events, etc.) the frequency of searches related to such events rapidly increases, reaches the maximum, followed by an almost exponential decrease. In many cases, the interest in special events fades out rather quickly and does not affect the top 10 yearly queries that characterize the GP user.

The GP user is defined using the statistics of most frequent requests obtained from search engine traffic monitors. The GP traffic is dominated by large public interest in special (sometimes accidental) events and popular public personalities. Table 4.7.3 shows an example of the top 10 Google queries reported in Google zeitgeist (and subsequently Google trend) archives [GGL16] that illustrate the worldwide activity of the GP user. The overlap of each pair of consecutive sets is only 10%, showing the shift of public interest.

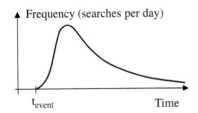

Figure 4.7.1 A typical event search frequency.

The SU search load is generated by many categories of special interest user groups, where the most important are professional searches. The SU group reflects the fact that Internet is today a critical component of the majority of professional activities, education, business, research, health protection, politics, social work, entertainment, and many others. A significant fraction of SU search activities is related to search of literature.

Performance and quality of information retrieval are important components of our search engine evaluation model. In the case of GP workload, the performance and retrieval quality attributes can be measured using a specialized benchmarking tool. In this case, the drive workload must reflect the interest of general public, and we used the statistics of most frequent requests obtained from traffic monitors of major search engines. Table 4.7.4 shows examples of GP workload that we used in performance measurements [BAI07].

The SU workload has strong semantic component and the quality of information retrieval can be fully analyzed only by experts in a specific area. For example, the recall of a query about "andness" should be evaluated by decision analysts, and the recall of a query about "Rituximab" should be evaluated by medical experts. A complete analysis of performance and quality of search engines for SU workload cannot be done automatically using a benchmark tool. Therefore, an automatic analysis of performance and quality of search is reasonable for GP workload, and this is done by our SEben tool. In the case of SU workload, a benchmarking tool has limited applicability.

Table 4.7.4 Samples of GP workload.

Workload	Queries	Retrieved URLs
Top 10 Google Queries 2003	10	8000
Top 20 Yahoo Queries 2006/May	20	12816
Top 200 MSN Queries 2005/Aug/19	200	112183
Top 10 Google Queries 2002/Apr	10	6922
Top 10 Ask Queries 2006/Nov/3	10	6803

4.7.2   SEben—A Search Engine Benchmarking Tool

SEben is a tool for search engine benchmarking and for measurement of information retrieval (IR) quality [DUJ06c, BAI07]. Following are the main SEben design goals:

- Measurement of IR quality (precision, recall, and coverage of search)
- Measurement of response time
- Comparison of competitive search engines
- Continuous measurement of distributions of performance indicators
- Extensibility to support more search engines

The global organization of SEben is outlined in Fig. 4.7.2. The performance measurement consists of C cycles, where each cycle selects one of b information retrieval benchmark queries (Q_1, ..., Q_b), and applies this query to all n analyzed search engines. Measured performance values (quality of search, response time,

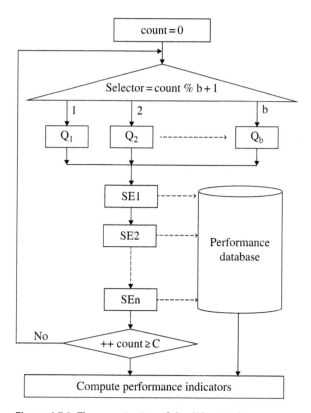

Figure 4.7.2 The organization of the SEben tool.

etc.) are stored in a performance database, and the accumulated data are processed at the end of measurement to compute global performance indicators for each search engine.

The goal of selecting the benchmark queries is to have a representative workload that primarily includes those queries that have high frequency. Our benchmark queries (initially $b > 300$) reflect the activities of the general public and include most popular search topics reported by Yahoo! Search, MSN, Google, and Ask over a period of six years.

SEben operates as follows. It first submits selected queries to analyzed search engines and measures response times. Then, the returned pages are analyzed to collect URLs for later analysis. Coverage, recall, and precision are calculated at a later time based on the collected URLs in the database. Detailed presentation of this process can be found in [BAI07] and a summary in [DUJ06c].

4.7.3   LSP Criterion for Evaluation of Search Engines

General models for software quality evaluation have been analyzed by many authors [BOE78, FEN97] and standardized by ISO [ISO91] and IEEE [IEE93]. Fig. 4.7.3 shows the basic idea of evaluating software from the standpoint of its operation and upgrading.

In the case of search engines, the general software quality model must be modified to reflect specific features of search engines. First, from the end user standpoint, it is only interesting to evaluate the operation of the software product (i.e., no need to evaluate upgrading). In addition, the performance evaluation

1. **Operation of software product**
    1.1 Functionality (suitability, accuracy, security, interoperability, compliance)
    1.2 Usability (understandability, learnability, operability)
    1.3 Performance (processing time, throughput, resource consumption)
    1.4 Reliability (maturity, fault tolerance, recoverability)
2. **Upgrading of software product**
    2.1 Maintainability (analyzability, changeability, stability, testability)
    2.2 Portability (adaptability, installability, conformance, replaceability)
    2.3 Reusability (structuredness, conciseness, self-descriptiveness, device independence)

Figure 4.7.3 General attributes of software quality.

area must be expanded with the evaluation of information retrieval quality. At the same time, the reliability group is found not to be critical and can be omitted. This approach yields the attributes shown in Fig 4.7.4. Each of the search engine evaluation attributes contributes to the engine ability to satisfy user requirements. The attributes are individually evaluated, and the results of the evaluation are aggregated to get a compound performance indicator for each search engine as a whole. This process takes into account desired logic relationships of inputs, as well as their relative importance.

1 Functionality
11 General search methods
 111 Basic search
  1111 Single keyword
  1112 Multiple keyword
  1113 Phrase
 112 Advanced search
  1121 Boolean expression
  1122 Number range search
  1123 Negative terms
 113 Non-English search
 114 Multimedia search
  1141 Images
  1142 Video clips
   11421 Categorization of material
   11422 Popularity rating
   11423 Search criterion
  1143 Audio clips
 115 Extended search
  1151 Case-sensitive search
  1152 Common words exclusion
  1153 Word variations (plural etc.)
  1154 Use of synonyms
12 Data filters
 121 Adult content
 122 Time filters
  1221 Last update time
  1222 Time interval
 123 Domain/page/link filtering
  1231 Domain or site
  1232 Location in page
  1233 Linked pages
  1234 Keyword frequency in page
  1235 Pages from same site
 124 Miscellaneous filters
  1241 Access rights
  1242 Countries
  1243 File types
  1244 RSS file format support
  1245 Similar pages

13 Topic-specific search
 131 Technologies
 132 Academic
 133 Local life
 134 Maps
 135 Blog

2 Usability
21 Operability
 211 Visibility of functionality
 212 Ease of customization
 213 User interface quality
 214 Direct display of best match
22 Result presentation
 221 Customizable page size
 222 Customizable ranking of results
 223 Availability of cached results
23 Learnability
 231 Online help (short references)
 232 User manual (book quality)
 233 Independent literature
 234 Tutorial (learning by example)
 235 Frequently asked questions

3 Performance of information retrieval
31 Measured response time
 311 Time to return first page
 312 Time to return first 100 records
32 Resource consumption

4 Quality of information retrieval
41 Coverage
42 Recall
43 Precision

Figure 4.7.4 The attribute tree for SE evaluation.

Some attributes are single scalar values and some are compound, including several components. Consequently, our LSP criterion consists of 52 elementary criteria, which include 83 individual quality attributes, collected using various measurements and analyses. Following are two examples of typical compound elementary criteria.

The criterion #134 is used to evaluate maps as a topic-specific special search. Of course, maps can have many features, and in the case of extreme precision, maps can be evaluated using a separate LSP criterion. In the case of minimum precision, maps can be evaluated using direct suitability assessment based on rating scales. In the case of medium precision, we can use simple point-additive criteria. For example, we can use the scoring criterion that assigns points to selected properties as follows:

Driving directions 10

Fly-over map 5

Information overlays 8

3D map 5

Printable map.......................... 8

In this case, the maximum total score (the sum of assigned points) is 36 and the corresponding map elementary criterion can be defined as $Crit(map) = \{(0,0),(36,100)\}$.

As the second example, let us consider the adult content filter attribute (#121). Let K be the availability of children-specific user interface and let F be the adjustable level of filtering. Assuming $K \in \{0,1\}$ and $F \in \{0,1,2\}$, we can evaluate the adult content filter using Table 4.7.5.

The adult filter score $S[\%]$ can be expressed as the following function of K and F:

$$S = 70F(2-F)(1-K) + 80F(2-F)K + 45F(F-1)(1-K) + 50F(F-1)K$$

$$= F(95 + 15K - 25F - 5FK).$$

Table 4.7.5 Adult content filter score.

F	K	$S[\%]$
0	0	0
0	1	0
1	0	70
1	1	80
2	0	90
2	1	100

Since $0 \leq S \leq 100\%$, the corresponding attribute criterion is $Crit(S) = \{(0,0),(100,100)\}$.

Performance-related SE attributes require sophisticated measurement and analysis. Such attributes are *coverage, recall, precision* [BAE99], *response time*, and *resource consumption*. The coverage is a user-oriented indicator determined as the number of relevant documents returned by the SE, normalized by the total number of relevant documents known to the user [BAE99, BRA16]. Let R be the set of all relevant documents that can be returned by the search process. The number of documents in the set is denoted $|R|$. The search engine returns the set of answers A which includes both relevant documents $R \cap A$ and irrelevant documents $A \setminus (R \cap A)$. The precision of answers is defined as the fraction of correct answers: $P = |R \cap A|/|A|$. Similarly, recall is defined as the fraction of all relevant documents returned by the SE: $recall = |R \cap A|/|R|$.

The response time (the time between the request send time, and the HTML response stream reception time) includes the server response time plus the network routing and transportation overhead. Our measurements are based on an empty search request (the search without any keyword) immediately followed by the actual search request. Then, the server response time is obtained by subtracting these two times. In this way, we approximately eliminate the network routing and transportation overhead and compare only the SE server response times.

All elementary criteria that evaluate performance and quality of information retrieval can be organized as combination of GP and SU workload. In the case of coverage, recall, and precision, the results of SU workload are generated by expert evaluators. These results can be aggregated with results for GP workload collected by SEben. The GP and SU results can be aggregated using complementary weights (w and $1 - w$, $0 < w < 1$) that can shift the emphasis of evaluation continuously from GP to SU type of user. The default approach characterized by $w = \frac{1}{2}$ reflects the standpoint that high volume deserves equal attention as the high significance of search.

Elementary criteria are used to compute normalized suitability degrees (from 0 to 100%) for all 52 inputs. The next step is to organize the logic aggregation of suitability structure shown in Fig. 4.7.5. The overall suitability score E_0 corresponds to the evaluated system as a whole. The aggregation of suitability degrees is a process of averaging that reflects desired formal logic and semantic relationships between aggregated values and follows the pattern of the attribute tree shown in Fig. 4.7.4.

The presented logic aggregation structure is based on WPM.17 aggregators and the most frequent canonic aggregation form that implements a monotonic increase of andness. In the area of general search methods, the number range search and the negative terms search are considered optional. Similarly, the components of multimedia search and extended search are defined as

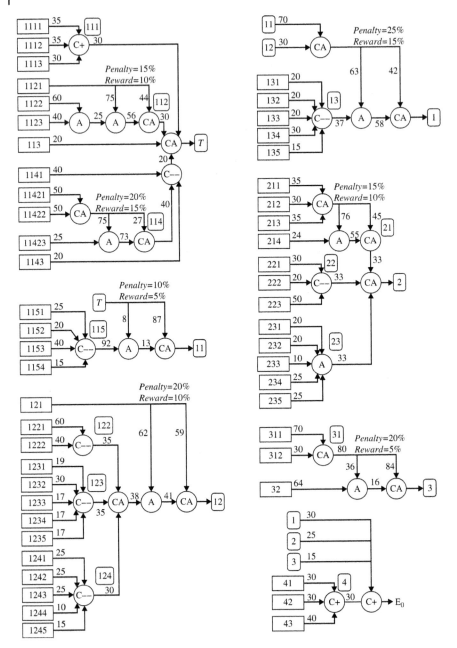

Figure 4.7.5 SE suitability aggregation structure (segmented and linked using connectors).

desirable but not mandatory. In the area of data filters, the adult filter is mandatory and all other components are nonmandatory inside their respective groups, but the absence of each group (#122, #123, #124) is penalized using the hard CA aggregator. Then, the functionality is evaluated using mandatory general search methods and data filters, and optional topic-specific search. In the logic structure of usability aggregation, the only mandatory attributes are #211, #212, and #213, while all others are optional inside softly aggregated groups, but the complete absence of any group (#21, #22, or #23) is not tolerated. The performance criterion has a standard form where good response times are mandatory and the low resource consumption is optional. The overall suitability is computed using a strong version of hard partial conjunction.

4.7.4 Search Engine Evaluation Results

In this section, we use the presented LSP criterion for search engine evaluation to compare four major PST search engines: Yahoo! Search, Ask, Google, and MSN. The final results of evaluation are presented in Table 4.7.6. Google has a leading position by satisfying 86.67% of requirements. MSN (currently Bing), and Yahoo! are in a close match, with only 2% of difference in overall suitability score. Ask ranks last with a rather low overall score (54.72%). It is interesting to note that these results, based on the status of evaluated search engines in June 2006, represent a very good prediction of the ranking of the same engines in 2016.

A very high information retrieval quality (92.57%) and rich functionality help *Google* to establish the dominating position. In addition, *Google* has the best balance of quality—all major groups of *Google* features satisfy more than 80% of evaluation requirements. On the other hand, *Google* could improve some usability components. For example, one of the negative aspects in *Google*'s UI is the "I'm Feeling Lucky" button. Regardless its long history, this label makes no sense

Table 4.7.6 Evaluation results.

Suitability degrees [%]	Search engine			
	Google	MSN	Yahoo!	Ask
Functionality	**83.10**	63.38	62.98	39.44
Usability	82.84	**86.44**	77.35	73.38
Performance	87.94	81.84	**91.45**	76.98
Quality of information retrieval	**92.57**	82.80	80.27	56.04
Overall suitability	**86.67**	**77.85**	**75.74**	**54.72**

and the button creates confusion to new users. There is also enough space for further development of functionality.

MSN Search has the best usability and ranks second because it dominates the third-placed *Yahoo! Search* in all areas except performance. In particular, *MSN* attains a higher coverage of page indexes, and gets a high usability score due to its easy-to-use customized ranking feature. On the other hand, *MSN* has usability areas that can be improved. For instance, in the case of function visibility, *MSN* gets a low score due to its strange design of putting some search categories on top of the page, while putting some other categories in a drop-down list besides the "Search" button. *MSN* offers a good balance of usability, performance, and information retrieval quality. However, its functionality is insufficient and could be significantly improved.

Yahoo! Search dominates the performance area. It ranks third, close to *MSN Search*. It has good results in the average server response time. In addition, *Yahoo!* result pages show a good balance of information richness and efficiency. Compared to *Google, Yahoo! Search* provides less topic-specific search options and less advanced search options such as word variations and word synonyms. *Yahoo! Search* functionality could be significantly improved and main groups of features are insufficiently balanced.

Ask got the lowest scores in all subsystems, resulting in the last position. Its weakest subsystems are functionality and information retrieval quality. In the area of information retrieval quality, *Ask*'s low index coverage significantly hurts its global preference score. In addition, *Ask* provides fewer search options and filters comparing with other three search engines. In the performance area, *Ask*'s resulting HTML source documents are badly organized, with lots of spaces and empty lines. The average length of *Ask*'s result pages is four times longer than the length of *MSN*'s result pages. Ask is competitive in the area of usability and performance, but needs improvements in the areas of functionality and information retrieval quality. Its poor balance of features indicates an imbalanced development strategy. As we mentioned earlier, all these results reflect the status as of June 2006.

Evaluation of search engines is a typical nontrivial software evaluation problem. It includes a spectrum of functionality, usability, and two types of performance inputs, including more than 80 individual quality attributes. In the case of performance, it was necessary to develop a specialized tool for measurement of response times, resource consumption, and the quality of information retrieval. The presented numeric results indicate strength and weaknesses of evaluated products, and show where to focus new development and improvement efforts. So, LSP evaluation models can be used by both software users and software manufacturers.

The area of search engines is characterized by fast changes in offered services, the scope of search, functionality, usability, performance, and business relationships between competitors. In such an environment, we cannot expect that evaluation criteria or evaluation results can last very long. Consequently, the presented criterion needs periodic updating, according to functionality of new search engines and other developments. However, the presented case study shows that the proposed approach, the structure of the evaluation criterion, and the way of logic aggregation of functionality attributes with usability, quality, and performance of IR can stand the test of time. Therefore, the future work should be focused on expanding and improving the performance measurement tool, refinement and evolutionary adjustment of the LSP criterion, development of specialized criteria for specific areas of search, and the coverage of all currently operational search engines.

References

AA15   Anonymous Author, Borda count. Wikipedia, https://en.wikipedia.org/wiki/Borda_count, 2015.

AA16a   Anonymous Author, Present value. Wikipedia, https://en.wikipedia.org/wiki/Present_value, 2016.

AA16b   Anonymous Author, List of minimum annual leave by country. Wikipedia, https://en.wikipedia.org/wiki/List_of_minimum_annual_leave_by_country, 2016.

AAK97   Aaaker, J. L. Dimensions of brand personality. Journal of Marketing Research 1997;34(3)(August):347–356.

ACZ48   Aczél, J. On mean values. Bull. Am. Math. Soc. 1948;54:392–400.

ALL01   Allison. P. D. Missing data. Thousand Oaks, CA: Sage Publications; 2001.

ALL07   Allen D. D. Proposing 6 dimensions within the construct of movement in the movement continuum theory. Phys. Ther. 2007;87:888–898.

ALL11   Allen, W. L., O. M. Amundsen, J. Dujmović, and K. D. Messer. Identifying and selecting strategic mitigation opportunities: Criteria design and project evaluation using Logic Scoring of Preference and optimization. Journal of Conservation Planning 2011;7:61–68.

ARI10   Ariely, D. Predictably Irrational. Revised and expanded edition. New York: Harper Perrenial; 2010.

BAC07   Baczynski, M. and B. Jayaram, 2007. Yager's classes of fuzzy implications: some properties and intersections. Kybernetika 2007;43(2):157–182.

BAC08   Baczynski, M., and B. Jayaram. Fuzzy implications. Studies in Fuzziness and Soft Computing. New York: Springer; 2008, 231.

BAE99   Baeza-Yates, R., and B. Ribeiro-Neto. Modern information retrieval. Reading, MA: Addison-Wesley; 1999.

BAI07   Bai, H. Evaluation and comparison of search engines using the LSP Method. San Francisco State University, Computer Science Dept., Report SFSU-CS-CE-07.12, 2007.

BAY96   Bayucan, A. R. Quantitative evaluation of windowed environments. M.S. Thesis, San Francisco State University, Department of Computer Science, 1996.

BEL02   Belton, V., and T. J. Stewart. Multiple criteria decision analysis: an integrated approach. The Netherlands: Kluwer Academic Publishers; 2002.

BEL07   Beliakov, G., A. Pradera, and T. Calvo. Aggregation functions: a guide for practitioners. New York: Springer; 2007.

BEL07a Beliakov, G., T. Calvo, and A. Pradera. Absorbent tuples of aggregation operators. Fuzzy Sets and Systems 2007;158:1675–1691.

BEL16   Beliakov, G., H. Bustince Sola, and T. Calvo Sanchez. A practical guide to averaging functions. Studies in Fuzziness and Soft Computing 329. New York: Springer; 2016.

BEL16a Beliakov, G., and J. Dujmović. Extension of bivariate means to weighted means of several arguments by using binary trees. Information Sciences 331, pp. 137–147.

BEN75   Benwell, N. (Ed.). Benchmarking. New York: John Wiley & Sons; 1975.

BOE78   Boehm, B. W., et al. Characteristics of software quality. Amsterdam: North Holland Publishing Co.; 1978.

BOO47   Boole, G. The mathematical analysis of logic. Cambridge: MacMillan, Barclay & MacMillan; 1847.

BOO54   Boole, G. An investigation of the laws of thought, on which are founded the mathematical theories of logic and probabilities. Cambridge: Macmillan; 1854, and Dover, New York: 1958.

BOS12   Bosc, P., and O. Pivert. On four noncommutative fuzzy connectives and their axiomatization. Fuzzy Sets and Systems 2012;202:42–60.

BOU00   Bouyssou, D., T. Merchant, M. Pirlot, P. Perny, A. Tsoukias, and P. Vincke. Evaluation and decision models: a critical perspective. The Netherlands: Kluwer; 2000.

BRA16   Bramer, W., D. Giustini, and B. M. R. Kramer. Comparing the coverage, recall, and precision of searches for 120 systematic reviews in Embase, MEDLINE, and Google Scholar: a prospective study. BioMed Central Systematic Reviews 2016;(5):39, https://systematicreviewsjournal.biomedcentral.com/articles/10.1186/s13643-016-0215-7.

BRI22   Bridgman, P. W. Dimensional Analysis. New Haven, CT: Yale University Press; 1922.

BRI98   Brin, S., and L. Page. The anatomy of a large-scale hypertextual web search engine. http://www-db.stanford.edu/~backrub/google.html.

BRO05   Bromberg, M. B. An approach to the evaluation of peripheral neuropathies. Seminars in Neurology 2005;25(2):153–159.

BUC07   Buckley, G. Interfacing the LSP method with e-commerce web sites. San Francisco State University, Computer Science Dept., Report SFSU-CS-CE-07.16, 2007.

BUC08   Buckley, G., and J. Dujmović. Interfacing the system evaluation method LSP with e-commerce web sites. ComSIS 2008;5.

BUL03   Bullen, P. S. Handbook of means and their inequalities. The Netherlands: Kluwer; 2003 (and 2010).

BUL88   Bullen, P. S., D. S. Mitrinović, and P. M. Vasić. Means and their inequalities. Dordrecht: D. Reidel; 1988.

CAL02   Calvo, T., A. Kolesarova, M. Komornikova, and R. Mesiar. Aggregation operators: properties, classes, and construction methods. In: T. Calvo, G. Mayor, and R. Mesiar, editors, Aggregation operators. New trends and applications. Heidelberg: Physica-Verlag; 2002, pp. 3–104.

CAL03   Calvo, T., and R. Mesiar. Fusion with Quantitative Weights. EUSFLAT 2003 Proceedings, edited by M. Wagenknecht and R. Hampel. http://www.eusflat.org/publications_proceedings_EUSFLAT_2003.php, pp. 312–317.

CAL04   Calvo, T., R. Mesiar, and R. Yager. Quantitative weights and aggregation. IEEE Trans. on Fuzzy Systems 2004;12(1)(February):62–69.

CAR02   Carlsson, C., and R. Fullér. Fuzzy reasoning in decision making and optimization. Heidelberg: Physica-Verlag; 2002.

CAS08   Castillo, O., and P. Melin. Type-2 fuzzy logic: theory and applications. Berlin: Springer-Verlag; 2008.

CHA01   Chang, Y-H, and C-H Yeh. Evaluating airline competitiveness using multiattribute decision making. Omega 29 (2001):405–415.

CHA03   Chakrabarti, S., Mining the web: analysis of hypertext and semi structured data. Amsterdam: Elsevier, 2003.

CHA07   Chakhar S., and V. Mousseaua. An algebra for multicriteria spatial modeling. Computers, Environment and Urban Systems 2007;31 (5):572–596.

CHE72   Chernousko, F. L. O vesovih koeficientah v ekspertnih ocenkah. Kibernetika 1972;6:128–130.

CHE92   Chen, S-J., and C-L Hwang. Fuzzy multiple attribute decision making: methods and applications. Springer, 1992.

CHI29   Chisini, O. Sul concetto di media. Periodico di Matematiche 1929;4:106–116.

CHO08   Chou, S-Y., Y-H. Chang, C-Y Shen. A fuzzy simple additive weighting system under group decision-making for facility location selection with objective/subjective attributes. European Journal of Operational Research 2008;189:132–145.

CHU96   Chu H., and M. Rosenthal. Search engines for the World Web Web: a comparative study and evaluation methodology, ASIS 1996 Annual Conference Proceedings October 19–24, 1996.

CLA16   Clark Labs. TerrSet geospatial monitoring and modeling software. https:// clarklabs.org/terrset, 2016.

COD86   Codd, E. F. Missing Information (Applicable and Inapplicable) in Relational Databases. ACM SIGMOD Record 1986;15(4): 53–78.

COL15   Columbia Pipeline Group. Multi-species habitat conservation plan, 2014 Annual Report, https://www.fws.gov/Midwest/endangered/permits/hcp/ nisource/pdf/NisourceHCP2014AnnualReport.pdf, 2015.

COT95   Cott C. A., E. Finch, D. Gasner, et al. The movement continuum theory of physical therapy. Physiother. Can. 1995;47:87–95.

COX80   Cox III, E. P. The optimal number of response alternatives for a scale—a review. J. of Marketing Research 1980;17(4):407–422.

CUR84   Curram, J., and C.H.C. Leung. Measurement and modelling of an interactive distributed system using operational analysis. Computer Performance September 1984;5(3):178–181.

DAS16   Dasso, A., A. Funes, G. Montejano, D. Riesco, R. Uzal, N. Debnath. Model based evaluation of cybersecurity implementations. In: S. Latifi (ed.), Information technology: new generations. advances in intelligent systems and computing 448, Springer, 2016, pp. 303–313.

DEE10   Deemeter, Kees van. Not exactly—In praise of vagueness. Oxford: Oxford University Press; 2010.

DEF31   De Finetti, B., Sul Concetto di Media. Giornale dell'Istituto Italiano degli Attuari, Anno II 3 (Roma 1931): 369–396.

DEM47   De Morgan, A. Formal logic or the calculus of inference necessary and probable. London: Taylor and Walton; 1847.

DET00   Detyniecki, M. Mathematical aggregation operators and their application to video querying. Doctoral Thesis, Universite Pierre & Marie Curie, 2000.

DIS07   Disyawongs, T. Customizer of LSP method for nonprofessional users. San Francisco State University, Computer Science Department, Report SFSU-CS-CE-07.15, 2007.

DOL16   United States Department of Labor, Flexible Schedules. https://www.dol. gov/general/topic/workhours/flexibleschedules, 2016.

DOM82   Dombi, J., and P. Zysno. Comments on the Gamma-Model. In R. Trappl (Ed.) Cybernetics and Systems Research. North-Holland: Springer; 1982, pp. 711–714.

DRA18   Dragićević, S., J. Dujmović, R. Minardi. Modeling urban land-use suitability with soft computing: the GIS-LSP method. In: Thill, J-C, Dragićević, S. (Eds.) GeoComputational analysis of regional systems. Springer, 2018, pp. 257–275.

DUJ02   Dujmović, J., and M. Kadaster. A technique and tool for software evaluation. Proceedings of the Sixth IASTED International Conference Software Engineering and Applications (Editor: M. M. Hamza). Calgary, Canada: ACTA Press; 2002, pp. 743–748.

DUJ03   Dujmović, J., and H. Nagashima. Evaluation of IDE's for Java Enterprise Applications. Proceeding of the Seventh IASTED International Conference Software Engineering and Applications (Editor: M.M. Hamza). Calgary, Canada: ACTA Press; 2003, pp. 703–708.

DUJ03a   Dujmović, J. Optimizing computer system configurations. Journal of Automatic Control 2003:13(2): 22–33.

DUJ04a   Dujmović, J., and W. Y. Fang. An empirical analysis of assessment errors for weights and andness in LSP criteria. In: V. Torra and Y. Narukawa (Ed.). Modeling Decisions for Artificial Intelligence. Springer LNAI 3131; 2004, pp. 139–150.

DUJ04b   Dujmović, J., and W. Y. Fang. Reliability of LSP Criteria. In: V. Torra and Y. Narukawa (Ed.). Modeling Decisions for Artificial Intelligence. Springer LNAI 3131; 2004, pp. 151–162.

DUJ05a   Dujmović, J., and M. K. Kao. Stepwise filtering method for system optimization. Proceedings of Eurofuse 2005, edited by B. De Baets, J. Fodor, and D. Radojević. Belgrade: Mihajlo Pupin Institute; 2005, pp. 46–55.

DUJ05b   Dujmović, J. Continuous Preference Logic for System Evaluation. Proceedings of Eurofuse 2005, edited by B. De Baets, J. Fodor, and D. Radojević. Belgrade: Mihajlo Pupin Institute; 2005, pp. 56–80.

DUJ05c   Dujmović, J. Seven Flavors of Andness/Orness. Proceedings of Eurofuse 2005, edited by B. De Baets, J. Fodor, and D. Radojević. Belgrade: Mihajlo Pupin Institute; 2005, pp. 81–92.

DUJ06a   Dujmović, J., and H. Nagashima. LSP Method and its use for evaluation of Java IDE's. International Journal of Approximate Reasoning 2006;41 (1):3–22.

DUJ06b   Dujmović, J., Nine forms of andness/orness. Proceedings of the Second IASTED International Conference on Computational Intelligence, edited by B. Kovalerchuk. ISBN Hardcopy: 0-88986-602-3 / CD: 0-88986-603-1, 2006, pp. 276–281.

DUJ06c   Dujmović, J., and H. Bai. Evaluation and comparison of search engines using the LSP method. ComSIS, December 2006;3(2):31–56.

DUJ07a   Dujmović, J., and H. L. Larsen. Generalized conjunction/disjunction. International Journal of Approximate Reasoning 2007;46: 423–446.

DUJ07b   Dujmović, J. Properties of local andness/orness. In O. Castillo et al. (Eds.). Theoretical advances and applications of fuzzy logic and soft computing. Advances in Soft Computing 2007;42:54–63.

DUJ07c   Dujmović, J. Preference logic for system evaluation. IEEE Transactions on Fuzzy Systems 2007;15(6)(December):1082–1099.

DUJ08   Dujmović, J., G. De Tré, and N. Van de Weghe. Suitability maps based on the LSP method. Proceedings of the 5th MDAI conference (Modeling Decisions for Artificial Intelligence), Sabadell (Barcelona), Catalonia, Spain, October 30–31, 2008. Lecture Notes in Computer Science, Vol. 5285, pp. 15–25, Springer-Verlag, Heidelberg, Germany, 2009.

DUJ08a   Dujmović, J., J. W. Ralph, and L. J. Dorfman. Evaluation of disease severity and patient disability using the LSP method. In L. Magdalena, M. Ojeda-Aciego, J. L. Verdegay (Eds.), Proceedings of the 12th Information Processing and Management of Uncertainty international conference (IPMU 2008), pp. 1398–1405, Torremolinos (Malaga), June 2008.

DUJ09   Dujmović, J., G. De Tré, and S. Dragićević. Comparison of multicriteria methods for land-use suitability assessment. Proceeding of the 13th IFSA World Congress and the 6th EUSFLAT Conference, July 20–24, 2009, in Lisbon, Portugal, pp. 1404–1409, ISBN: 978-989-95079-6-8, 2009.

DUJ10a   Dujmović, J., G. De Tré, and N. Van de Weghe, LSP Suitability Maps. Published online June 5, 2009, ISSN 1433–7479, by Springer Verlag. Soft Computing 2010;14(5),(March): 421–434.

DUJ10b   Dujmović, J., and D. Scheer, Logic Aggregation of Suitability Maps. Proceedings of the 2010 IEEE World Congress on Computational Intelligence, pp. 2222–2229, ISBN 978-1-4244-6920-8. Barcelona, Spain, July 18–23, 2010.

DUJ11   Dujmović, J., and W. L. Allen, III. A family of soft computing decision models for selecting multi-species habitat mitigation projects. Proceedings of the World Conference on Soft Computing, edited by R. R. Yager, M. Z. Reformat, S. N. Shahbazova, and S. Ovchinnikov, paper 101, May 2011.

DUJ11a   Dujmović, J., and G. De Tré. Multicriteria methods and logic aggregation in suitability maps. International Journal of Intelligent Systems 2011;26 (10),(October): 971–1001.

DUJ12   Dujmović, J. Andness and orness as a mean of overall importance. Proceedings of the IEEE World Congress on Computational Intelligence, June 10–15, 2012, Brisbane, Australia, pp. 83–88, 2012.

DUJ12a   Dujmović, J. The problem of missing data in LSP aggregation. Proceeding of the 14th International Conference on Information Processing and Management of Uncertainty in Knowledge-Based Systems, IPMU, 2012. In S. Greco et al. (Eds.): Advances in Computational Intelligence, IPMU 2012, Part III, CCIS 299, pp. 336–346, Springer 2012.

DUJ13   Dujmović, J., G. De Tré, N. Singh, D. Tomasevich, and R. Yokoohji. Soft computing models in online real estate. In: M. Jamshidi, V. Kreinovich, and J. Kacprzyk (Eds.). Advance trends in soft computing, WCSC 2013. Studies in Fuzziness and Soft Computing 2013;312:77–91.

DUJ14 Dujmović, J. Interpolative GCD Aggregators. Proceedings of the 2014 IEEE World Congress on Computational Intelligence, Beijing, China July 6–11, 2014, DOI: 10.1109/FUZZ-IEEE.2014.6891841, pp. 1778–1785.

DUJ14a Dujmović, J. An analysis of penalty and reward for partial absorption aggregators. Proceeding of the 2014 World Conference on Soft Computing, pp. 126–133, Berkeley, CA, May 25–27, 2014.

DUJ15a Dujmović, J. Weighted compensative logic with adjustable threshold andness and orness. IEEE Transactions on Fuzzy Systems 2015;23(2), (April):270–290.

DUJ15b Dujmović, J. GCD Aggregators: Scales and Implementations. Proceedings of the IEEE International Conference on Fuzzy Systems, August 2–5, 2015, Istanbul Turkey, Paper No. 15128, 2015.

DUJ15c Dujmović, J. An Efficient Algorithm for General Weighted Aggregation. Proceedings of the 8th International Summer School on Aggregation Operators (AGOP 2015), edited by M. Baczynski, B. De Baets and R. Mesiar. Katowice, Poland: University of Silesia; 2015, pp. 115–120.

DUJ16a Dujmović, J. Gamma Aggregators and Extended Generalized Conjunction/Disjunction. Proceedings of the 6th World Conference on Soft Computing, pp. 155–160, Berkeley, CA, May 22–25, 2016.

DUJ17 Dujmović, J. Relationships between fuzziness, partial truth and probability in the case of repetitive events. In: V. Kreinovich (Ed.), Uncertainty modeling, Springer International; 2017, pp. 61–69.

DUJ17a Dujmović, J., and G. Beliakov, Idempotent Weighted Aggregation Based on Binary Aggregation Trees. International Journal of Intelligent Systems, 2017;32(1),(January):31–50.

DUJ69 Dujmović, J., and Pjević, N. An Algorithm for Comparison and Selection of Digital Computers (in Serbo-Croatian). Proceedings of the First Yugoslav International ADP Conference, Zagreb, Croatia, 1969.

DUJ72a Dujmović, J. Some Aspects of Error Analysis When Selecting Computers by Weighted Scoring Techniques (in Serbo-Croatian). Proceedings of the 7th Informatica Congress, Bled, Yugoslavia, October 1972.

DUJ72b Dujmović, J., Correlational aspects of error compensation in the weighted scoring method for selection of data processing systems (in Serbo-Croatian). Proceedings of the 7th Informatica Conference, Bled, 1972.

DUJ73a Dujmović, J. Two integrals related to means. Journal of the University of Belgrade EE Dept., Series Mathematics and Physics, No. 412 to No. 460, 1973, pp. 231–232.

DUJ73b Dujmović, J. A generalization of some functions in continuous mathematical logic—evaluation function and its applications (in Serbo-

Croatian). Proceedings of the Informatica Conference, paper d27, Bled, Yugoslavia (1973).

DUJ73c Dujmović, J. Mixed averaging by levels (MAL)—a system and computer evaluation method (in Serbo-Croatian). Proceedings of the Informatica Conference, paper d28, Bled, Yugoslavia, 1973.

DUJ74a Dujmović, J. Weighted conjunctive and disjunctive means and their application in system evaluation. Journal of the University of Belgrade, EE Dept., Series Mathematics and Physics, 1974;483:147–158.

DUJ74b Dujmović, J. New Results in the Development of the "Mixed Averaging by Levels" Method for System Evaluation (in Serbo-Croatian). Proceedings of the Informatica Conference 1974, paper 4.36, Bled, Yugoslavia, 1974.

DUJ74c Dujmović, J. Optimization of complex systems using the MAL method (in Serbo-Croatian). Proceedings of the Informatica Conference 1974, paper 4.38, Bled, Yugoslavia, 1974.

DUJ74d Dujmović, J. and Džigurski, O.D. Evaluation and comparison of analog computers (in Serbo-Croatian). Proceedings of the Informatica Conference 1974, paper 4.37, Bled, Yugoslavia, 1974.

DUJ74e Dujmović, J. Components for evaluation and selection of data processing systems (in Serbo-Croatian). Praksa, No. 10, 1974.

DUJ75a Dujmović, J. Extended continuous logic and the theory of complex criteria. Journal of the University of Belgrade, EE Dept., Series Mathematics and Physics, 1975;537:197–216.

DUJ75b Dujmović, J. A graphic approach to weighted conjunctive and disjunctive means calculation. Journal of the University of Belgrade. EE Dept., Series Mathematics and Physics, 1975; 536:191–196.

DUJ75c Dujmović, J. Evaluation of digital computers Using the System Evaluation Method MAL (in Serbo-Croatian). Proceedings of the Informatica Conference 1975, paper 6.9, Bled, Yugoslavia, 1975.

DUJ76a Dujmović, J. System evaluation language (SEL)—Programming language for evaluation, comparison and optimization of complex systems (in Serbo-Croatian). Proceedings of the Informatica Conference, Bled, Yugoslavia, 1976, Paper 1/121.

DUJ76b Dujmović, J., and Tomašević, I. A criterion data base system (CDBS) (in Serbo-Croatian). Proceedings of the Informatica Conference, paper 1/122 Bled, Yugoslavia, 1976.

DUJ76c Dujmović, J. A technique for determining optimum configurations of the computing units of analog and hybrd computers (in Serbo-Croatian). Proceedings of the ETAN Conference, 1976, pp. 1181–1188.

DUJ76d Dujmović, J. Evaluation, comparison and optimization of hybrid computers using the theory of complex criteria. Simulation of Systems. Dekker L. (Ed.). Amsterdam: North-Holland; 1976, pp. 553–566.

DUJ76e   Dujmović, J. Criterion aggregation technique for evaluation, optimization and selection of computer systems. Paper presented at the OECD Ankara Meeting, March 1976 (Published also in Greek in the Bulletin of the General Directorate of Public Administration, No. 3, Athens, 1976, pp. 51–70).

DUJ77a   Dujmović, J. The preference scoring method for decision making—survey, classification, and an annotated bibliography. Informatica 1977 (2):26–34.

DUJ77b   Dujmović, J. Professional Evaluation and Selection of Computer Systems. Proceedings of the Informatica Conference 1977, paper 4.1, 1977.

DUJ78a   Dujmović, J. Criteria for computer reliability evaluation (in Serbo-Croatian). Proceedings of the Informatica Conference 1978, paper 3.208, 1978.

DUJ78b   Dujmović, J. An indicator of quality of the configuration of channels and controllers of computer system peripheral devices (in Serbo-Croatian). Proceedings of the Informatica Conference, 1978, Paper 2.109.

DUJ79a   Dujmović, J. Partial absorption function. Journal of the University of Belgrade, EE Dept., Series Mathematics and Physics 1979;659:156–163.

DUJ79b   Dujmović, J. Criteria for computer performance evaluation. Performance Evaluation Review 1979;8(3): 259–267.

DUJ80   Dujmović, J. Computer selection and criteria for computer performance evaluation. International Journal of Computer and Information Sciences December 1980;9(6):435–458.

DUJ82   Dujmović, J., and R. A. Elnicki. DMS Cost/benefit decision model: Mathematical models for data management system evaluation, comparison, and selection. National Bureau of Standards, Washington D.C., No. GCR 82–374. NTIS No. PB 82-170150 (150 pages), 1982.

DUJ87   Dujmović, J. The LSP method for evaluation and selection of computer and communication equipment. Proceedings of MELECON'87, Mediterranean Electrotechnical Conference and 34th Congress on Electronics (Joint Conference), IEEE/RIENA, Rome, Italy, 1987, pp. 251–254.

DUJ91   Dujmović, J. Preferential neural networks. Chapter 7. In: P. Antognetti and V. Milutinović (Eds.). Neural networks—concepts, applications, and implementations, Vol. II. Prentice-Hall Advanced Reference Series. Englewood Cliffs, NJ: Prentice-Hall; 1991, pp. 155–206.

DUJ97a   Dujmović, J., and A. R. Bayucan. Evaluation and comparison of windowed environments proceedings of the IASTED International Conference on Software Engineering, edited by M. H. Hamza, pp. 102–105. Katowice, Poland: IASTED/Acta Press; 1997.

DUJ97b Dujmović, J. Quantitative Evaluation of Software. Proceedings of the IASTED International Conference on Software Engineering, edited by M.H. Hamza, pp. 3–7. Katowice, Poland: IASTED/Acta Press; 1997.

DUJ98a Dujmović, J., and I. Dujmović. Evolution and evaluation of SPEC benchmarks. Performance Evaluation Review 1998;26(3), (December):2–9.

DUJ98b Dujmović, J. Optimizing computer system configurations. The 24th International Conference for the Resource Management and Performance Evaluation of Enterprise Computing Systems. CMG 98 Proceedings, 1998.

DYC05 Dyck, P. J., R. A. C. Hughes, P. C. O'Brien. Quantitating overall neuropathic symptoms, impairments, and outcomes. In: P. J. Dyck and P. K. Thomas (Eds.). Peripheral neuropathy. 4th ed. Philadelphia: Elsevier; 2005, pp. 1031–52.

DYC93 Dyck, P. J. Quantitating severity of neuropathy. In: P. J. Dyck, P. K. Thomas, J. W. Griffin, and J. F. Podeslo (Eds.). Peripheral Neuropathy, 3rd ed. Philadelphia: Saunders; 1993, pp. 686–697.

EBI16 eBizMBA. Top 15 most popular search engines. August 2016. http://www.ebizmba.com/articles/search-engines.

EDW82 Edwards, W., and J. R. Newman with the collaboration of K. Snapper and D. Seaver. Multiattribute Evaluation. SAGE Publications, 1982.

ERD96 Erdeljan A., and J. Dujmović. A comparison of training methods for preferential neural networks. Proceedings of the IASTED International Conference on Artificial Intelligence, Expert Systems and Neural Networks. Katowice, Poland: IASTED / Acta Press; 1996, pp. 86–89.

ESA73 Endangered Species Act of 1973. Public law 93-205. US Government Publishing Office, https://www.gpo.gov/fdsys/pkg/STATUTE-87/pdf/STATUTE-87-Pg884.pdf.

ESR09 ESRI. Using the conceptual model to create a suitability map. ArcGIS Desktop 9.3 Help, http://webhelp.esri.com/arcgisdesktop/9.3/index.cfm?TopicName=Using%20the%20conceptual%20model%20to%20create%20a%20suitability%20map, April 24, 2009.

ESR10 ESRI. ArcGIS spatial analyst tutorial. http://help.arcgis.com/en/arcgisdesktop/10.0/pdf/spatial-analyst-tutorial.pdf, 2010.

ESR16 ESRI. ArcGIS—Apply geography to every decision. http://www.esri.com/software/arcgis, 2016.

FAN04 Fang, W-Y. Analysis of Reliability of LSP Models. San Francisco State University, Computer Science Dept., Report SFSU-CS-TR-04.06, 2004.

FEI87 Feinstein, A. R. Clinimetrics. New Haven: Yale University Press, 1987.

FEN97   Fenton, N. E., and S. L. Pfleeger. Software Metrics. ITP, 1997.

FER78a   Ferrari, D. Computer systems performance evaluation. Englewood Cliffs, NJ: Prentice-Hall, 1978.

FER78b   Ferrari, D., G. Serazzi, and A. Zeigner, Computer system performance (in Italian). Published by Franco Angeli, Milano, Italy, 1978.

FIS64   Fishburn, P. C. Decision and value theory. New York: John Wiley & Sons, 1964.

FIS70   Fishburn, P. C. Utility theory for decision making. New York: John Wiley & Sons, 1970.

FOD94   Fodor, J., and M. Roubens, Fuzzy preference modelling and multicriteria decision support. Dordrecht, The Netherlands: Kluwer Academic Publishers, 1994.

FR08   Federal Reserve. Money stock measures. 2008, www.federalreserve.gov/releases/h6/hist.

FRI99   Friedman, H. H., and T. Amoo. Rating the rating scales. The Journal of Marketing Management 1999;9(3):114–123.

FUL10   Fülop, J., W. W. Koczkodaj, and S. J. Szarek. A different perspective on a scale for pairwise comparisons. In: N.T. Nguyen and R. Kowalczyk (Ed.). Transactions on CCI I LNCS 6220. Berlin: Springer-Verlag 2010, pp. 71–84.

FUN00   Funes, A., A. Dasso, J. Dujmović, G. Montejano, D. Riesco, R. Uzal. Web browsers performance analysis using LSP method. Proceedings of the International Conference on Software Engineering Applied to Networking and Parallel/Distributed Computing. Reims, France, 2000.

FWS16a   U.S. Fish & Wildlife Service, Endangered Species Program. http://www.fws.gov/endangered/, 2010.

FWS16b   U.S. Fish & Wildlife Service, Permits for Native Species under the Endangered Species Act. http://www.fws.gov/endangered/esa-library/pdf/permits.pdf, 2010.

FWS16c   U.S. Fish & Wildlife Service. Endangered species permits, NiSource Habitat Conservation Plan. https://www.fws.gov/Midwest/endangered/permits/hcp/nisource/index.html, 2016.

GGL06   Google. https://www.google.com/press/zeitgeist2003/graph_sars.gif.

GGL16   Google trends. https://www.google.com/trends/.

GGL16a   Google Inc., Google maps APIs. https://developers.google.com/maps/, 2016.

GGL16b   Google Inc., Google maps. http://maps.google.com/, 2016.

GIL76   Gilb, T. Software metrics. Studentlitteratur, Lund, Sweden, 1976 and Winthrop Publishers, 1977.

GIN58   Gini, C. et al. Le Medie (Means) Unione Tipografico-Editorice Torinese, Milano 1958. (Russian translation: Srednie Velichiny, Statistika, Moskva, 1970).

GOO97   Goovaerts, P. Geostatistics for natural resources evaluation. New York: Oxford University Press, 1997.

GRA06a   Graham, R. C., and R. A. C. Hughes. A modified peripheral neuropathy scale: the Overall Neuropathy Limitations Scale. J Neurol Neurosurg Psychiatry 77 (2006): 973–976.

GRA06b   Graham, R. C., and R. A. C. Hughes. Clinimetric properties of a walking scale in peripheral neuropathy. J Neurol Neurosurg Psychiatry 77 (2006): 977–979.

GRA09   Grabisch, M., J-L. Marichal, R. Mesiar, and E. Pap. Aggregation functions. Cambridge: Cambridge University Press, 2009.

GRI06   Global Reporting Initiative. Sustainability Reporting Guidelines. GRI, 2006.

HAO16   Hao, M., and J. M. Mendel. Encoding words into normal interval type-2 fuzzy sets: HM approach. IEEE Transactions on Fuzzy Systems 2016;24(4) (August): 865–879.

HAT14   Hatch, K., S. Dragićević, and J. Dujmović. Logic Scoring of Preference and spatial multicriteria evaluation for urban residential land use analysis. In: M. Duckham et al. (Eds.): Geographic Information Science, Springer LNCS 8728 (2014):64–80.

HAW06   Hawking, D. Web search engines. Computer 2006:39(6)(Part 1) and 39(8) (Part 2).

HEN06   Henning, J. L. (Ed.), SPEC CPU2006 Benchmark Description. https://www.spec.org/cpu2006/publications/CPU2006benchmarks.pdf.

HEN15   Hensher, D. A., J. M. Rose, and W. H. Greene. Applied choice analysis. Cambridge: Cambridge University Press; 2015.

HER06   Herndon, R. M. Handbook of neurologic rating scales. Second edition. Demos Medical Publishing; 2006.

HIL69   Hillegass, J. R. Systematic techniques for computer evaluation and selection. Management Sci. (July–August 1969):36–40.

HOB03   Hobart, J. C., A. Riazi, D. L. Lamping, et al. Measuring the impact of MS on walking ability: the 12 item multiple sclerosis walking scale (MSWS-12). Neurology 2003;60:31–36.

HOW07   Howell, D. C. The analysis of missing data. In: W. Outhwaite and S. Turner (Eds.). Handbook of social science methodology. London: Sage Publications, 2007.

HOW09   Howell, D.C. Treatment of missing data. http://www.uvm.edu/~dhowell/StatPages/More_Stuff/Missing_Data/Missing.html, 2009.

IEE93   IEEE Standard for a Software Quality Metrics Methodology. IEEE Std 1061-1992, ISBN 1-55937-277-X. Published 1993.

INT10   Interbrand, Best Global Brands 2010. http://www.interbrand.com/en/best-global-brands/best-global-brands-2008/best-global-brands-2010.aspx, 2010.

ISH13   Ishizaka, A., and P. Nemery. Multi-Criteria Decision Analysis. Hoboken, NJ: John Wiley, 2013.

ISO91   ISO/IEC, International Standard ISO/IEC 9126 (E). Information technology—Software product evaluation—Quality characteristics and guidelines for their use. International Organization for Standardization, First edition, 1991.

IVA63   Ivanović, B., Discriminant analysis (in Serbo-Croatian). Scientific Book Publishers, Belgrade, 1963.

JOE01   Joerin, F., M. Thériault, and A. Musy. Using GIS and outranking multicriteria analysis for land-use suitability assessment. International Journal of Geographical Information Science (IJGIS) 2001;15(2): 153–174.

JOS64   Joslin, E. O., and M. J. Mullin. Cost-value technique for evaluation of computer system proposals. Proceedings–Spring Joint Computer Conference, 1964, pp. 367–381.

JOS68   Joslin, E. O. Computer selection. Reading, MA: Addison-Wesley, 1968. (An augmented edition was published in 1977 by The Technology Press Inc., Box 125, Fairfax Station, Virginia 22039.)

KAC07   Kacherginsky, P. System security evaluation using LSP method. San Francisco State University, Computer Science Dept., Report SFSU-CS-CE-07.13, 2007.

KAC15   Kacprzyk, J., and W. Pedrycz (Eds.). Springer Handbook of Computational Intelligence. Heidelberg: Springer; 2015.

KAD02   Kadaster, M. A Java-based system evaluation tool. San Francisco State University, Computer Science Dept., Report SFSU-CS-TR-02.08, 2002.

KAH03   Kahraman, C., D. Ruan, I. Dogan. Fuzzy group decision-making for facility location selection. Information Sciences 157 (2003): 135–153.

KAH08   Kahraman, C. (Ed.). Fuzzy multi-criteria decision making. Heidelberg: Springer; 2008.

KAH11   Kahneman, D. Thinking, fast and slow. New York: Farrar, Strauss and Giroux; 2011.

KAH79   Kahneman, D., and A. Tversky. Prospect theory: An analysis of decisions under risk. Econometrika (1979)47: 263–291.

KAH84   Kahneman, D., and A. Tversky. Choices, values, and frames. American Psychologist 1984;39:341–350.

KAH99   Kahneman, D. Objective happiness. In: D. Kahneman, E. Diener, & N. Schwarz (Eds.), Well-being: The foundations of hedonic psychology (pp. 3–25). New York: Russell Sage Foundation; 1999.

KAO04   Kao, M-K. A tool for optimizing computer configurations. San Francisco State University, Computer Science Dept., Report SFSU-CS-TR-04.36, 2004.

KAP17   Kapre, K. LSP evaluator—A suitability evaluation tool based on the LSP method. San Francisco State University, Computer Science Dept., Report SFSU-CS-CE-17.18, 2017.

KAR81 Karr, J. R. Assessment of biotic integrity using fish communities. Fisheries 1981;6:21–27.

KEE76 Keeney, R. L., and H. Raiffa. Decisions with multiple objectives/ preferences and value tradeoffs. New York: John Wiley & Sons, 1976.

KEE92 Keeney, R. L. Value-focused thinking. Cambridge, MA: Harvard University Press, 1992.

KEE97 Keefe, R., and Smith, P. (Eds.) Vagueness: a reader. Cambridge: MIT Press; 1997.

KIA94 Kianifard, F. Evaluation of clinimetric scales: basic principles and methods. The Statistician 1994;43(4):475–482.

KIR97 Kirkwood, C. W. Strategic decision making. Belmont, CA: Duxbury Press, 1997.

KLE78 Kleijnen, J. P. C. Scoring methods, multiple criteria, and utility analysis. Research Memorandum, Tilburg University, Holland, Department of Economics, October 1978. (Published also in Sigmetrics Performance Evaluation Review.)

KLE80 Kleijnen, J. P. C. Computers and profits. Reading, MA: Addison-Wesley, 1980.

KLI95 Klir, G. J., and B. Yuan. Fuzzy sets and fuzzy logic. Englewood Cliffs, NJ: Prentice-Hall, 1995.

KOC14 Koczkodaj W. W., K. Kulakowski, and A. Ligeza. On the quality evaluation of scientific entities in Poland supported by consistency-driven pairwise comparison method. Scientometrics 2014;99:911–926.

KOC16 Koczkodaj W. W., L. Mikhailov, G. Redlarski, M. Soltys, J. Szybowski, G. Tamazian, E. Wajch, K. K. F. Yuen. Important facts and observations about pairwise comparisons, Fundamenta Informaticae, January 2016.

KOL09 Kolesarova, A., and R. Mesiar. Parametric characterization of aggregation functions. Fuzzy Sets and Systems 2009;160(March):816–831.

KOL30 Kolmogoroff, A. N. Sur la notion de la moyenne, Accad. Naz. Lincei Mem. Cl. Sci. Fis. Mat. Natur. Sez. 1930;12:388–391.

KOS93 Kosko, B. Fuzzy Thinking. New York: Hyperion; 1993.

KOV92 Kovalerchuk, B., and V. Talinsky. Comparison of empirical and computed values of fuzzy conjunction. Fuzzy Sets and Systems 1992;46:49–53.

KRI92 Krishnapuram, R., and J. Lee. Fuzzy-connective-based hierarchical aggregation networks for decision making. Fuzzy Sets and Systems 1992;46:11–27.

KRO10 Krosnick, J. A., and S. Presser. Question and Questionnaire Design, chapter 9 of Handbook of Survey Research, Emerald Group Publishing (2nd ed.) 2010.

KUO99 Kuo, R. J., S. C. Chi, & S. S. Kao. A decision support system for locating convenience store through fuzzy AHP. Computers & Industrial Engineering 1999;37:323–326.

LAR03   Larsen, H. L. Efficient andness-directed importance weighted averaging operators. International Journal of Uncertainty. Fuzziness and Knowledge-Based Systems 2003;12(Suppl.):67–82.

LAR09   Larsen, H. L. Multiplicative and implicative importance weighted averaging aggregation operators with accurate andness direction. In: J. P. Carvalho, D. Dubois, U. Kaymak, J. M. da Costa Sousa (Eds.): Proceedings of the Joint 2009 International Fuzzy Systems Association World Congress and 2009 European Society of Fuzzy Logic and Technology Conference, Lisbon, Portugal, July 20–24, 2009, pp. 402–407.

LAR12   Larsen, H. L. Importance weighting and andness control in De Morgan dual power means and OWA operators. Fuzzy Sets and Systems 2012;196:17–32.

LAW94   Lawrence, J. Introduction to neural networks design, theory, and applications. California Scientific Software Press; 1994.

LEE05   Lee, K. H. First course on fuzzy theory and applications. Heidelberg; Springer Verlag; 2005.

LIA99   Liao, S. Y., Wang, H. Q., and Liu, W. Y. Functional dependencies with null values, fuzzy values, and crisp values. IEEE TFS 1999;7(1):97–103.

LIT87   Little, R. J. A., and Rubin, D. B. Statistical analysis with missing data. New York: John Wiley & Sons, 1987.

LIU08   Liu, F., and J. M. Mendel. Encoding words into interval type-2 fuzzy sets using an interval approach. IEEE Trans. On Fuzzy Systems 2008;16 (6):1503–1521.

MAC77   Mackie, J. L. Ethics: Inventing Right and Wrong. New York: Penguin Books, 1977.

MAL00   Malczewski, J. On the Use of Weighted Linear Combination Method in GIS: Common and Best Practice Approaches. Transactions in GIS 2000;4 (1):5–22.

MAL06   Malczewski, J. GIS-based multicriteria analysis: a survey of the literature. International Journal of Geographic Information Science2006;20 (7):703–726.

MAL11   Malczewski, J. Local weighted linear combination. Transactions in GIS 2011;15(4):439–455.

MAL14   Malczewski J., and X. Liu. Local ordered weighted averaging in GIS-based multicriteria analysis. Annals of GIS 2014;20(2):117–129.

MAL99   Malczewski, J. GIS and multicriteria decision analysis. New York: John Wiley & Sons; 1999.

MAR08   Marichal, J.-L. Multivariate integration of functions depending explicitly on the minimum and the maximum of the variables. Journal of Mathematical Analysis and Applications 2008;341(1),(May):200–210.

MAR99   Marichal, J.-L. Aggregation operators for multicriteria decision aid. Doctoral Thesis, Universite de Liege, 1998–1999.

MCQ78   McQuaker, R. J. Computer choice. Amsterdam: North-Holland; 1978.

MEN01   Mendel, J. M. Uncertain rule-based fuzzy logic systems: introduction and new directions. Englewood Cliffs, NJ: Prentice-Hall; 2001.

MEN01a   Mendel, J. M. The perceptual computer: an architecture for computing with words. Proceedings of Modeling with Words Workshop in the Proceedings of FUZZ-IEEE 2001, pp. 35–38, Melbourne, Australia, 2001.

MEN02   Mendel, J. M. An architecture for making judgments using computing with words. Int. J. Appl. Math. Comp. Sci. 2002;12(3):325–335.

MEN08   Mendel J. M., and D. Wu. Perceptual reasoning for perceptual computing. IEEE Trans. On Fuzzy Systems 2008;16(6):1550–1564.

MEN10   Mendel, J. M., and D. Wu. Perceptual computing. Hoboken, NJ: IEEE Press and John Wiley & Sons; 2010.

MER06   Merkies, I. S. J., and P. I. M. Schmitz, Getting closer to patients: the INCAT Overall Disability Sum Score relates better to patients' own clinical judgement in immune-mediated polyneuropathies. J Neurol Neurosurg Psychiatry 2006;77:970–972.

MES15   Mesiar, R., A. Kolesarova, and M. Komornikova. Aggregation functions on [0,1]. In Springer Handbook of Computational Intelligence, edited by J. Kacprzyk and W. Pedrycz, pp. 61–74. Springer, 2015.

MES18   Messer, K. D. and W. L. Allen, III. The science of strategic conservation: protecting more with less. Cambridge: Cambridge University Press; 2018.

MIL56   Miller, G. A. The magical number seven, plus or minus two: some limits on our capacity for processing information. The Psychological Review 1956;63:81–97.

MIL66   Miller, J. R., III. The assessment of worth: a systematic procedure and its experimental validation. Ph.D. Dissertation, M.I.T., 1966.

MIL70   Miller, J. R., III. Professional decision-making. New York: Praeger; 1970.

MIT69   Mitrinović, D. S., and P. M. Vasić. Means (in Serbo-Croatian). Mathematical Library, Vol. 40, Belgrade, 1969.

MIT70   Mitrinović, D. S., and P. M. Vasić. Analytic inequalities. Berlin: Springer-Verlag; 1977.

MIT77   Mitrinović, D. S., P. S. Bullen, and P. M. Vasić. Means and related inequalities (in Serbo-Croatian), Publications of the University of Belgrade EE Dept., No. 600, Belgrade, 1977.

MIT89   Mitrinović, D. S., and J. E. Pečarić. Mean values in mathematics. Scientific Book Publishers, Belgrade, 1989 (in Serbo-Croatian: Srednje vrednosti u matematici, Naučna knjiga, Beograd, 1989).

MOL97   Mollaghasemi, M., and J. Pet-Edwards. Making multiple-objective decisions. IEEE Computer Society Technical Briefing, IEEE, 1997.

MON15a   Montgomery, B. Expanding and comparing GIS-based multi-criteria decision making methods: a soft computing logic for agricultural land suitability evaluation. Unpublished MSc thesis, Department of Geography, Simon Fraser University, 2015.

MON15b   Montgomery, B, S. Dragićević, and J. Dujmović, A soft computing logic method for agricultural land suitability evaluation. Proceedings of GeoComputation 2015 Conference. Dallas, USA, 20–23 May 2015, pp. 298–304, 2015.

MON16a   Montgomery, B., S. Dragićević, J. Dujmović, Using soft computing logic and the logic scoring of preference method for agricultural land suitability evaluation. In: Griffith, D., Chun, Y., Dean D. (eds) Advances in GeoComputation. Springer; 2017 pp. 217–227.

MON16b   Montgomery, B., S. Dragićević, J. Dujmović, M. Schmidt, A GIS-based Logic Scoring of Preference method for evaluation of land capability and suitability for agriculture. Computers and Electronics in Agriculture 2016;124:340–353.

MON16c   Montgomery, B., and S. Dragićević. Comparison of GIS-based Logic Scoring of Preference and multicriteria evaluation methods: Urban land use suitability, geographical analysis, 2016.

MUN94   Munda, G. Fuzzy information in multicriteria environmental evaluation models. Joint Research Centre, European Commission, Institute for Systems Engineering and Informatics. Catalogue number: CL-NA-15602-EN-C, ECSC-EEC-EAEC Brussels—Luxembourg, 1994.

NAG30   Nagumo, M. Über eine Klasse der Mittelwerte, Japanesse. Journal of Mathematics 7 (1930) pp. 71–79.

NAR06   National Association of Realtors. 2006 MLS Technology Survey. Center for REALTOR(r) Technology, 2006.

NBS77   National Bureau of Standards. Guidelines for benchmarking ADP systems in the competitive procurement environment. Federal Information Processing Standards Publication 42–1. May 15, 1977.

NEL64   Nelder, J. A., and R. Mead. A simplex method for function minimization. Computer Journal 1964;7(4): 308–313.

NET99a   Nettleton, D., and L. Hernandez. Questionnaire screening of sleep apnea cases using fuzzy knowledge representation and intelligent aggregation techniques. Intelligent Data Analysis in Medicine and Pharmacology, IDAMAP '99, Washington, United States, pp. 91–102, 1999.

NET99b   Nettleton, D. F. Attribute fusion using a heterogeneous representation of crisp and fuzzy data. IFSA '99. Eight International Fuzzy Systems Association World Congress, Tapei, Taiwan, Vol. II, pages 618–623, 1999.

NIH13   NIH. Scoring System and Procedure. Last reviewed on March 25, 2013. http://grants.nih.gov/grants/peer/guidelines_general/scoring_system_and_procedure.pdf

NOB00   E. Nobile-Orazio et al. Long-term prognosis of neuropathy associated with anti-MAG IgM M-proteins and its relationship to immune therapies. Brain 2000;123:710–717.

NUN67   Nunnally, J. C. Psychometric theory. New York: McGraw-Hill; 1967.

OLS00   Olsina, L., D. Godoy, G. Lafuente, and G. Rossi. E-commerce site evaluation: a case study. EC-Web 2000, 239–252 (2000).

OLS01   Olsina, L., G. Lafuente, and G. Rossi. Specifying quality characteristics and attributes for websites. Web Engineering, Software Engineering and Web Application Development. London: Springer-Verlag; 2001.

OLS96   Olson, D. L. Decision aids for selection problems. London: Springer-Verlag; 1996.

OLS99   Olsina, L., D. Godoy, G. Lafuente, and G. Rossi. Assessing the quality of academic web sites: a case study. The New Review of Hypermedia and Multimedia 1999;5:81–103.

PAL02   L. Palmeri, L., and M. Trepel. A GIS-based score system for siting and sizing of created or restored wetlands: two case studies. Water Resources Management 2002;16:307–328.

PAS12   Passuello, A., O. Cadiach, Y. Perez, and M. Schuhmacher. A spatial multicriteria decision making tool to define the best agricultural areas for sewage sludge amendment. Environment International 2012;38:1–9.

PAT05   Patsute, M. A customizer system for LSP criteria. San Francisco State University, Computer Science Dept., Report SFSU-CS-TR-05.13, 2005.

PAU78   Paunović, D. S. Acceleration of the Nelder-Mead algorithm in the case of the time consuming complex function optimization (in Serbo-Croatian). Proceedings of the Informatica Congress 78, Bled, Yugoslavia, paper 3–116, 1978.

PED13   Pedrycz, W. Granular computing. Boca Raton, FL: CRC Press; 2013.

PIT10   Pittas, M. A. Location suitability maps based on the LSP method. San Francisco State University, Department of Computer Science, Report SFSU-CS-CE-10.08, 2010.

PIT85   Pittenger, A. O. The logarithmic mean in n variables. The American Mathematical Monthly 1985;9(22), (February):99–104.

POW64   Powell, M. An efficient method for finding the minimum of a function of several variables without calculating derivatives. Computer Journal 1964;7:155–162.

PRE00   Preston, C. C., and A. M. Colman. Optimal number of response categories in rating scales: reliability, validity, discriminating power, and respondent preferences. Acta Psychologica 2000;104:1–15.

RAT16   Ratcliff, C. What are the top 10 most popular search engines? Search Engine Watch, https://searchenginewatch.com/2016/08/08/what-are-the-top-10-most-popular-search-engines/, August 9, 2016.

REB14   Rebolledo, B. Spatial vulnerability to nitrate contamination from agricultural origin: development and application of parametric model IVNA-LSP (in Spanish). Doctoral Thesis, University of Zaragoza, Instituto Universitario de Investigaci n Mixto CIRCE, http://zaguan. unizar.es, 2014.

REB16   Rebolledo, B., A. Gil, X. Flotats, and J. A. Sanchez. Assessment of groundwater vulnerability to nitrates from agricultural sources using a GIS-compatible logic multicriteria model. Journal of Environmental Management 2016;171:70–80.

REI34   Reichenbach, H. Wahrscheinlichtkeitslogic, Erkenntnis 1934;5 (1–3):37–43.

REI86   Reiter, R. A sound and sometimes complete query evaluation algorithm for relational databases with null values. J. Assoc. Comput. Mach. (ACM) 1986;33(2):349–370.

RIG02   Rigaux, P., M. Scholl, and A. Voisard. Spatial databases with applications to GIS. Morgan Kaufman Publishers; 2002.

ROH07   Rohrmann, B. Verbal qualifiers for rating scales: Sociolinguistic and psychometric data. Project report, University of Melbourne, Australia. http://rohrmannresearch.net/pdfs/rohrmann-vqs-report.pdf, 2007.

ROS10   Ross, T. Fuzzy logic with engineering applications. Third edition. Hoboken, NJ: John Wiley & Sons; 2010.

SAA01   Saaty, T. L. Fundamentals of decision making and priority theory. Second edition. Pittsburgh: RWS Publications; 2001.

SAA06   Saaty, T. L., and L. G. Vargas. Decision making with the analytic network process. Springer 2006.

SAA10   Saaty, T. L. Principia Mathematica Decernendi. Pittsburgh: RWS Publications; 2010.

SAA16   Saad, L. The "40-hour" workweek is actually longer—by seven hours. Gallup, http://www.gallup.com/poll/175286/hour-workweek-actually-longer-seven-hours.aspx, 2016.

SAA77   Saaty, T. L. A scaling method of priorities in hierarchical structures. Journal of Mathematical Psychology 1977;15:234–281.

SAA80   Saaty, T. L. The analytic hierarchy process. New York: McGraw-Hill; 1980.

SAA90   Saaty, T. L. Decision making for leaders. Pittsburgh: RWS Publications; 1990.

SCH02   Schwartz B., A. Ward, J. Monterosso, S. Lyubomirsky, K. White, and D. R. Lehman. Maximizing versus satisficing: happiness is a matter of choice. Journal of Personality and Social Psychology 2002;83(5): 1178–1197.

SCH69   Scharf, T. Weighted ranking by levels. IAG Journal 1969;2(2):7–18.

SCH70   Scharf, T. Weighted ranking by levels computer evaluation method—one year of experience. IAG Journal 1979;3(3):71–91.

SEA10   SEAS Co. Analysis and synthesis of aggregation operators. AnSy User Manual V.3.2. SEAS, 2010.

SEA11   SEAS, Co. LSP suitability maps, http://seas.com/LSPmap/index2.php, 2011

SEA11a   SEAS, Co. AGOPcalc—Calculator for analysis and design of aggregation operators. AGOPcalc User Manual, SEAS, 2011.

SEA16   SEAS Co. LSP software products. www.seas.com, 2016.

SEA17   SEAS Co. LSP.NT—LSP method for evaluation over the Internet. LSP.NT User Manual. SEAS, 2017.

SEI69   Seiler III, K. Introduction to systems cost-effectiveness. New York: Wiley-Interscience, 1969.

SHA69   Sharpe, W. F. The Economics of Computers. A RAND Corporation Research Study, Columbia University Press, New York, 1969.

SIM08   Simić, S. An extension of Stolarsky means. Novi Sad J. Math. 2008;38 (3):81–89.

SIM55   Simon, H. A. A behavioral model of rational choice. Quarterly Journal of Economics 1955;59:99–118.

SIM56   Simon, H. A. Rational choice and the structure of the environment. Psychological Review 1956;63(2):129–138.

SIM57   Simon, H. A. Models of man, social and rational: Mathematical essays on rational human behavior. New York: John Wiley & Sons; 1957.

SIM79   Simon, H.A. Rational decision making in business organizations. The American Economic Review 1979;69(4):493–513.

SLA74   Slavić, D. V., and Dujmović, J. Numerical computation of weighted power means. Journal of the University of Belgrade, EE Dept., Series Mathematics and Physics, 1974;485:167–171.

SMI08   Smith, N. J. J. Vagueness and degrees of truth. Oxford: Oxford University Press, 2008.

SMI13   Smith, W. D. Rating Scale Research relevant to score voting. http://rangevoting.org/RateScaleResearch.html, 2013.

SPA97   Sparck Jones, K. et al. Readings in information retrieval. Morgan Kaufmann Series in Multimedia Information and Systems. Amsterdam: Elsevier, 1997.

SPE06   Standard Performance Evaluation Corporation, SPEC CPU 2006. https://www.spec.org/cpu2006/

STE92   Stewart, A. L., and J. E. Ware, Jr., Editors. Measuring functioning and well-being. Durham, NC: Duke University Press; 1992.

STR89   Streiner, D. L., and G. R. Norman. Health measurement scales: a practical guide to their development and use. Oxford: Oxford University Press; 1989.

SU82   Su, S.Y.W., D. S. Batory, J. Dujmović, et al. A DMS cost/benefit decision model: cost and preference parameters. National Bureau of Standards, Washington D.C., No. GCR 82–373. NTIS No. PB 82-169566 (393 pages), 1982.

SU87   S.Y.W. Su, J. Dujmović, D. S. Batory, S. B. Navathe, and R. Elnicki. A cost-benefit decision model: analysis, comparison, and selection of data management systems. ACM Transactions on Database Systems 1987;12 (3):472–520.

TCF10   The Conservation Fund, Mitigation Site Report—Freshwater Mussels. Section 6 Cooperative Endangered Species Conservation Fund Grant. https://www.fws.gov/Midwest/endangered/permits/hcp/nisource/ 2011NOA/pdf/NiSourceMitigationMusselsSiteReportDec2010.pdf, December 2010.

TCF16   The Conservation Fund. Implementing the NiSource Multi-Species Habitat Conservation Plan. http://www.conservationfund.org/images/ projects/files/The-Conservation-Fund-NiSource-Summary-2011. pdf, 2016.

TCF16a   Strategic Conservation Planning. http://www.conservationfund.org/ what-we-do/strategic-conservation- planning, 2016.

TCF16b   The Conservation Fund, Strategic Mitigation for Pipelines: NiSource Gas. http://www.conservationfund.org/projects/using-strategic-conservation- to-address-pipeline-impacts, 2016.

THO79   Thole, U., H.-J. Zimmermann, and P. Zysno. On the suitability of minimum and product operators for the intersection of fuzzy sets. Fuzzy Sets and Systems 1979;2:167–180.

TIM73   Timreck, E. M. Computer selection methodology. Computing Surveys 1973;5(4):199–222.

TOM63   Tomović, R. Sensitivity analysis of dynamic systems. New York: McGraw-Hill, 1963.

TOM90   Tomlin, C. Geographical information systems and cartographic modelling. Englewood Cliffs, NJ: Prentice Hall; 1990.

TOR07   Torra, V. and Y. Narukawa. Modeling decisions. Berlin: Springer; 2007.

TRE08   De Tré, G., R. De Caluwe, and H. Prade. Null values in fuzzy databases. Journal of Intelligent Information Systems 2008;30(2):93–114.

TRE09   De Tré, G., J. Dujmović, N. Van de Weghe, T. Matthé, and N. Charlier. Bipolar criteria satisfaction handling in geographic decision support systems. Proceedings of the 24th Annual ACM Symposium on Applied Computing, pp. 1704–1708, 2009.

TRE10   De Tré, G., J. Dujmović, and N. Van de Weghe. Supporting spatial decision making by means of suitability maps. In J. Kacprzyk, F. E. Petry, and A. Yazici (Eds.). Uncertainty Approaches for Spatial Data Modeling and Processing. Berlin: Springer-Verlag; 2010, pp. 9–28.

TRE11 De Tré, G., J. Dujmović, A. Bronselaer, and T. Matthé. Quantifier based aggregation in LSP suitability map construction. Proceedings of the World Conference on Soft Computing, edited by R. R. Yager, M. Z. Reformat, S. N. Shahbazova, and S. Ovchinnikov, paper 111, May 2011.

TRE14 De Tré, G., J. Dujmović, and S. Zadrozni. Bipolarity and multipolarity in aggregation structures. Proceeding of the 2014 World Conference on Soft Computing, pp. 118–125, Berkeley, CA, May 25–27, 2014.

TRE16 De Tré, G., J. Dujmović, and S. Zadrozni. Bipolarity and multipolarity in aggregation structures. In: L. Zadeh, A. M. Abasov, R. R. Yager, S. Shabazova, and M. Reformat (Eds.). Recent Developments and New Direction in Soft-Computing Foundations and Applications, Studies in Fuzziness and Soft Computing 2016;342:49–70.

TRI00 Triantaphyllou, E. Multi-criteria decision making methods: a comparative study. The Netherlands: Kluwer Academic Publishers; 2000.

TZE11 Tzeng, G-H., and J-J. Huang. Multiple attribute decision making. Methods and applications. Boca Raton, FL: CRC Press; 2011.

VAN04 Van Lonkhuyzen, R. A., K. E. Lagory, and J. A. Kuiper, Modeling suitability of potential wetland mitigation sites with a geographic information system. Environmental Management 2004;33(3):368–375.

VON44 von Neumann, J., and O. Morgenstern. Theory of games and economic behavior. Princeton University Press, 1944.

WAC95 Wackernagel, H. Multivariate Geostatistics—An Introduction with Applications. Berlin: Springer; 1995.

WAY03 Wayne, C. Suitability analysis with raster data. ArcUser 2003(April–June):54–57.

WHI63 White, D. R. J., D. L. Scott, and R. N. Schulz, POED—A method of evaluating system performance. IEEE Transactions on Engineering Management 1963;EM-10(4),(December):177–181.

WIK08a Wikipedia. Money supply. http://en.wikipedia.org/wiki/Money_supply, 2008.

WIK08b Wikipedia. Inflation. http://en.wikipedia.org/wiki/Inflation_%28economics%29, 2008.

WIK11b Wikipedia. Fuzzy logic. http://en.wikipedia.org/wiki/Fuzzy_logic#cite_ref-3, 2011.

WIK16 Wikipedia. Endangered Species Act. http://en.wikipedia.org/wiki/Endangered_Species_Act. 2010.

WIL94 Williamson, T. Vagueness. London: Routledge; 1994.

WOL03 Wolfram, S. The Mathematica Book, 5th ed. Champaign, IL: Wolfram Media; 2003.

WRI73 Wright, M. G. Discounted cash flow. Second edition. London: McGraw-Hill Book Co. (UK) Ltd.; 1973.

WU11 Wu, D. A brief tutorial on interval type-2 fuzzy sets and systems. http://www-scf.usc.edu/~dongruiw/files/A%20Brief%20Tutorial%20on%20Interval%20Type-2%20Fuzzy%20Sets%20and%20Systems.pdf, 2011.

WU12 Wu, D., J. M. Mendel, and S. Coupland. Enhanced interval approach for encoding words into interval type-2 fuzzy sets and its convergence analysis. IEEE Transactions of Fuzzy Systems 2012;20(3), (June).

YAG04 Yager, R. R. Weighted triangular norms using generating functions. International Journal of Intelligent Systems 2004;19:217–231.

YAG04a Yager, R. R. On some new classes of implication operators and their role in approximate reasoning. Inform. Sci. 2004;167:193–216.

YAG80 Yager, R. R. An approach to inference in approximate reasoning. Internat. J. Man-Machine Studies 1980; 12:323–338.

YAG87 Yager, R. A note on weighted queries in information retrieval systems. J. of the American Society for Information Science 1987;38(1):23–24.

YAG88 Yager, R. R. On ordered weighted averaging aggregation operators in multi-criteria decision making. IEEE Trans. SMC 1988;18:183–190.

YAG97 Yager, R. R., and J. Kacprzyk (Editors). The ordered weighted averaging operators—theory and applications. The Netherlands: Kluwer Academic Publishers; 1997.

YOK12 Yokoohji, R. LSP suitability maps for the quality of urban locations. MS thesis SFSU-CS-CE-12.09. Department of Computer Science, San Francisco State University, 2012.

YOO95 Yoon, K. P., and C-L Hwang. Multiple attribute decision making. Thousand Oaks, CA: Sage Publications, 1995.

ZAD08 Zadeh, L. A. Toward human level machine intelligence—is it achievable? The Need for a Paradigm Shift. IEEE Computational Intelligence Magazine 2008;3(3) (August):11–22.

ZAD15 Zadeh, L. A. Letter about the semantics of natural languages sent 11/28/2015 to the BISC group.

ZAD16 Zadeh, L. A. Letter to BISC community sent 7/9/2016.

ZAD65 Zadeh, L. A. Fuzzy Sets. Information and control 1965;8(3):338–353.

ZAD73 Zadeh, L. A. Outline of a new approach to the analysis of complex systems and decision processes. IEEE Transactions on Systems, Man and Cybernetics 1973;SMC–3:28–44.

ZAD74 Zadeh, L. A. On the analysis of large-scale systems. In: Gottinger, H., Ed., Systems Approaches and Environment Problems. Gottingen: Vandenhoeck and Ruprecht; 1974, pp. 23–37.

ZAD76 Zadeh, L. A. A fuzzy-algorithmic approach to the definition of complex or imprecise concepts, Int, J, Man-Machine Studies 1976;8:249–291.

ZAD89   Zadeh, L. A. Knowledge representation in fuzzy logic. IEEE Transactions on Knowledge and Data Engineering 1989;1(1)(March):89–100.

ZAD94   Zadeh, L. A. Fuzzy logic, neural networks, and soft computing. Communications of the ACM. 1994;37 (3),(March):77–84.

ZAD96   Zadeh, L. A. Fuzzy logic = computing with words. IEEE TFS 1996;4: 103–111.

ZHE07   Zhen, J.-H. A tool for visualization and animation of aggregation operators. San Francisco State University, Computer Science Dept., Report SFSU-CS-CE-07.14, 2007.

ZHU14   Zhuang, Y. LSP suitability maps based on ArcGIS. MS Thesis, Department of Computer Science, SFSU-CS-CE-14.13, San Francisco State University, 2014.

ZIL11   Zillow, Inc. Real estate and mortgage data for your site, http://zillow.com/howto/api/APIOverview.htm, 2011.

ZIM79   Zimmermann, H.-J., and P. Zysno. Decisions and evaluations by hierarchical aggregation of information. Fuzzy Sets and Systems 1979;10:243–266.

ZIM80   Zimmermann, H.-J., and P. Zysno. Latent connectives in human decision making. Fuzzy Sets and Systems 1980;4:37–51.

ZIM84   Zimmermann, H.-J., L. A. Zadeh, B. R. Gaines (Ed.), Fuzzy sets and decision analysis. North-Holland, 1984.

ZIM87   Zimmermann, H.-J. Fuzzy sets, decision making, and expert systems. The Netherlands: Kluwer Academic Publishers; 1987.

ZIM96   Zimmermann, H.-J. Fuzzy set theory and its applications. New York: Springer Science + Business Media; 1996.

ZYS79   Zysno, P. One class of operators for the aggregation of fuzzy sets. EURO III Congress, Amsterdam, 1979.

Index

Soft Computing Evaluation Logic: The LSP Decision Method and Its Applications,
First Edition. Jozo Dujmović.
© 2018 John Wiley & Sons, Inc. Published 2018 by John Wiley & Sons, Inc.
Companion website: www.wiley.com/go/Dujmovic/Soft_Computing_Evaluation_Logic